HISTORICAL HANDBOOK OF MAJOR BIBLICAL INTERPRETERS

EDITOR
DONALD K. McKIM

InterVarsity Press
Downers Grove, Illinois
Leicester, England

InterVarsity Press, USA
P.O. Box 1400, Downers Grove, IL 60515, USA
World Wide Web: www.ivpress.com
E-mail: mail@ivpress.com

Inter-Varsity Press, England
38 De Montfort Street, Leicester LE1 7GP, England

InterVarsity Press®, U.S.A., is the book-publishing division of InterVarsity Christian Fellowship/USA®, a student movement active on campus at hundreds of universities, colleges and schools of nursing in the United States of America, and a member movement of the International Fellowship of Evangelical Students. For information about local and regional activities, write Public Relations Dept., InterVarsity Christian Fellowship/USA, 6400 Schroeder Rd., P.O. Box 7895, Madison, WI 53707-7895.

Inter-Varsity Press, England, is the book-publishing division of the Universities and Colleges Christian Fellowship (formerly the Inter-Varsity Fellowship), a student movement linking Christian Unions in universities and colleges throughout the United Kingdom and the Republic of Ireland, and a member movement of the International Fellowship of Evangelical Students. For information about local and national activities write to UCCF, 38 De Montfort Street, Leicester LE1 7GP.

Cover illustration: background image by Siede Preis Photography/Cowgirl; Author Dictating to a Scribe. Moralized Bible, France., c. 1230 by The Pierpont Morgan Library/Art Resource, NY.

USA ISBN 0-8308-1452-3
UK ISBN 0-85111-752-X

Printed in the United States of America ∞

Library of Congress Cataloging-in-Publication Data

Historical handbook of major biblical interpreters/editor, Donald K. McKim.
   p. cm.
   Includes bibliographical references and index.
   ISBN 0-8308-1452-3 (cloth: alk. paper)
   1. Biblical scholars.   2. Bible—Criticism, interpretation, etc.—
History.   I. McKim, Donald K.
   BS501.A1H57   1998
   220.6'092'2—dc21   98-13824
                                CIP

British Library Cataloguing in Publication Data

A catalogue record for this book is available from the British Library.

23	22	21	20	19	18	17	16	15	14	13	12	11	10	9	8	7	6	5	4	3	2	1
17	16	15	14	13	12	11	10	09	08	07	06	05	04	03	02	01	00	99	98			

PART 4: BIBLICAL INTERPRETATION IN THE 18TH & 19TH CENTURIES

PART 5: BIBLICAL INTERPRETATION IN EUROPE IN THE 20TH CENTURY

Preface

The Christian church has been interpreting its Scriptures since its earliest days. Within the pages of the New Testament we find Jesus interpreting Moses and the prophets, and opening the Scriptures to the travelers on the road to Emmaus (Lk 24:27, 32). In Philip's encounter with the Ethiopian eunuch, who was reading from the prophet Isaiah, he posed a basic question: Do you understand what you are reading? (Acts 8:30). As the New Testament church grew and Christianity expanded into different lands, the task of interpreting sacred texts was constantly present and pressing.

Gradually, the canons of the Old and New Testaments were formed. The church began to look to a collection of biblical books as its source for gaining a knowledge of God. So the work of interpreting the Scriptures took on major importance. For the church to grow in its theological understandings as well as in its mission and ministries, its canonical Scriptures must be understood. The biblical materials needed to be comprehended by contemporary persons and by successive generations. While the church believed it was being led by the Holy Spirit, it is the Spirit acting in conjunction with the Word of God in the Scriptures that brings new knowledge and wisdom for the people of God.

Through the centuries the church's biblical scholars and theologians have interpreted the Scriptures of the Old and New Testaments. This work has been carried out in formal ways by those who have been trained for this task. Yet the Christian Scriptures are also interpreted by persons who read the Bible and comprehend its meaning without having formal training and within the contexts of their own lives and circumstances. The practice of biblical exegesis takes place at a host of levels by a wide array of people. Indeed, whenever anyone reads the Bible and explicates its meaning, biblical interpretation is taking place.

The present volume focuses on the work of many of the most significant biblical interpreters through the last two thousand years. It brings together scholarly essays that show the methods, practices and interpretive stances adopted by a number of the church's most important biblical scholars. These writers, from the early church to the present, are leading biblical interpreters by virtue of their particular approaches; the importance of their insights or their development of theological perspectives is rooted in their interpretations of Scripture. Some who are included have pioneered distinctive viewpoints. Others have engaged in thorough expositions of Scripture over a long period of time. Still others have made particular advances in some aspect that shapes the interpretive process. While their contributions have varied, all who are included have made important advances to our overall understandings of the Old and New Testament Scriptures.

The biblical interpreters in this volume have been significant. But they are not the only interpreters who could or should be included in a book of this kind. The size limits of this work have made it impossible to include a longer list of interpreters. Perhaps a companion volume can some day be produced. It is also fair to ask whether or not many other important biblical interpreters have been omitted or whether some who are left out could replace some who are included. To this the only reply is that those included are there by virtue of my own considered judgment, in consultation with others. But I bear responsibility for the list. I would not claim that it is exhaustive or by any standard to be a full list of the very most important biblical scholars. I would simply suggest that those studied here are important; I recognize that a strong case can be made that others, who are not surveyed here, could or should be included. This is an attempt to produce a work that will give a unique perspective on biblical interpretation during the last two millennia by studying approximately one hundred major biblical interpreters.

A number of other limitations to this work also appear. Studies of women interpreters are underrepresented, as are studies of those who are not Western, white males. This volume is clearly oriented toward those who have produced significant work in the Western branch of the Christian church and whose writings have, on the whole, emerged from Europe or North America. This is where predominant writings have been produced since the Middle Ages. Further books should one day be created to highlight the contributions of those not represented in this volume. The work of non-Western and nonmale persons must also be examined. The present work is only a first step. It is a resource from which others should follow and which tries to help us understand major elements in the history of biblical interpretation through biographical studies of major biblical interpreters. I invite others to supplement this volume by producing additionally needed resources.

The overview pieces that introduce each section help synthesize and supplement the materials that follow in the biographical studies. These essays bring coherence to the study of the period by focusing on major trends, contributions and movements that helped shape the exegetical history of the particular epoch. The writers of these pieces have had to be selective and orient their work to a focus on major elements, without the luxury of being exhaustive or even to approach such a goal for each period. These overviews can be particularly helpful as introductions to each age, as well as by collectively providing a descriptive narrative of the ebb and flow of biblical interpretation through major identifiable eras. The essays on biblical interpretation in twentieth-century Europe and in North America are oriented to these particular times and places.

A work of this nature benefits from the help of many people. I commend the essay writers for their outstanding abilities to bring the salient points about each biblical interpreter into the short compass of a single article. These articles vary in length, according to the editor's requests. But none of the pieces is long enough in itself to present the fullest exposition of an interpreter's views. I wish to thank the writers for accepting these assignments, for working within or in close proximity to my requested size limits and for doing such a splendid job in producing these marvelous pieces. Their labors are the heart of this volume, and I am grateful to all the participants. I selected the writers on the basis of their special knowledge of the interpreter or their expertise. None have disappointed me!

Two friends have served as consultants who gave valuable insights and suggestions in the early stages of the project. Richard A. Muller of Calvin Theological Seminary and

Gerald Sheppard of Emmanuel College of the University of Toronto generously shared their expert knowledge and perspectives to help shape the way this work was put together. I am grateful to them both. Their own respective overview essays are written from their vast reservoirs of knowledge and are eminent contributions in their own right.

My gratitude is also deep to Daniel G. Reid, Academic and Reference Book editor of InterVarsity Press. Dan willingly listened to early ideas about this volume, made important suggestions and helped conceptualize the work so it could be what it has become. He advocated for it and guided it through the publishing process. He has been a marvelously cooperative, supportive and insightful editor whose careful work as well as friendship has enhanced the book and meant much to me.

Others too deserve thanks. My work with the late Ford Lewis Battles, while I was a student at Pittsburgh Theological Seminary, was certainly formative in leading me to a love for the history of biblical interpretation. My teacher and colleague Jack B. Rogers has always been before me as a scholar who is vitally concerned with Scripture and its interpretation.

This volume is dedicated to four of my professors at Westminster College, New Wilmington, Pennsylvania: J. William Carpenter, Robert A. Coughenour, Thomas M. Gregory and Peter W. Macky. During my student days each helped deepen and strengthen my interest in biblical studies and interpreting the Scriptures. I am thankful for each of them. It is especially gratifying that Robert Coughenour has contributed an essay.

I would also like to acknowledge the wonderful friends in the community at Memphis Theological Seminary, where I serve. Special care, love and hope are marvelous blessings that we share together.

Finally, my family, Linda Jo, Stephen and Karl, blesses my life in countless ways. For their ongoing love and the joys of life together, I am most grateful of all.

Donald K. McKim
Epiphany 1998

How to Use this Handbook

Abbreviations
A comprehensive table of abbreviations used in this work may be found on pages xv-xvii.

Arrangement of Articles
The articles in this *Handbook* are arranged by historical periods. Each period begins with an overview essay, which is followed by alphabetically arranged articles on major interpreters of the period.

Contributors
The authors of articles are indicated by their first initials and last name at the end of each article. A full list of contributors and their articles may be found on pages xix-xxiii, in alphabetical order of their last names.

Bibliographies
A bibliography has been appended to each article. The bibliographies are divided into the "Works" of the interpreter and "Studies" which focus on or otherwise illuminate the work of the interpreter.

Cross-references
The articles have been cross-referenced by asterisks in order to aid readers in utilizing this *Handbook*. An asterisk has been placed in front of the name (on its first occurrence) of each interpreter for whom a separate article exists in the *Handbook*. Thus, for example, "*Chrysostom" in the article on Augustine indicates that an article on John Chrysostom may be found in the *Handbook*.

Indexes
In addition to the table of contents, which presents the articles by period, an alphabetical index of essays and articles, an index of subjects and an index of persons (including significant figures not assigned a separate article) may be found at the end of the *Handbook*.

Abbreviations

AAR	American Academy of Religion	CE	*Christenlijke Encyclopedie*
AB	Anchor Bible	CF	Church Fathers
ABD	*Anchor Bible Dictionary*	CFr	Collectanea Franciscana
ABR	*Australian Biblical Review*	*CH*	*Church History*
ABRL	Anchor Bible Research Library	*CHB*	*Cambridge History of the Bible*
AC	*Analecta Cisterciensia*	*CJT*	*Canadian Journal of Theology*
ACW	Ancient Christian Writers	*Coll*	*Colloquium*
AEAT	*Archiv für wissenschaftliche Erforschung des Alten Testamentes*	*CQ*	*Classical Quarterly*
		CR	*Contemporary Review*
AFH	*Archivum Franciscanum Historicum*	*Crit*	*Criterion*
		CRS	Classics in Religious Studies
AHR	*American Historical Review*	CSCO	Corpus Scriptorum Christianorum Orientalium
ANQ	*Andover Newton Quarterly*		
ANB	*American National Biography*	CSEL	Corpus scriptorum ecclesiasticorum latinorum
ANF	Ante-Nicene Fathers		
ANL	Ante-Nicene Christian Library	*CT*	*Christianity Today*
Ant	Anton	*CTM*	*Concordia Theological Monthly*
ARG	*Archiv für Reformationsgeschichte*	*CTJ*	*Calvin Theological Journal*
ARW	*Archiv für Religionswissenschaft*	*DAB*	*Dictionary of American Biography*
ASTI	*Annual of the Swedish Theological Institute*	*DBI*	*Dictionary of Biblical Interpretation*
ATANT	Abhandlungen zur Theologie des Alten und Neuen Testaments	DCA	*Dictionary of Christianity in America*
ATR	*Anglican Theological Review*	DCT	*Dictionary of Christian Theology*, ed. Alan Richardson
Aug	*Augustiniana*		
BB	The Books of the Bible	*Dial*	*Dialogue*
BGBE	Beiträge zur Geschichte der biblischen Exegese	DLNTD	*Dictionary of the Later New Testament & Its Developments*
Bib	*Biblica*	DNB	Dictionary of National Biography
BibO	Biblia e Oriente	*DPL*	*Dictionary of Paul and His Letters*
Bijdragen	*Bijdragen, tijdschrift voor filosofie en theologie*	*DR*	*Downside Review*
		DTC	*Dictionnaire de théologie catholique*
BJRL	*Bulletin of the John Rylands University Library of Manchester*	*DUJ*	*Durham University Journal*
		EA	Encyclopedia Americana
BRep	*Biblical Repository*	EB	Encyclopedia Britannica
BRev	*Bible Review*	EF	*Études franciscaines*
BRMT	Blackwell Readings in Modern Theology	ELTG	*Evangelisches Lexikon für Theologie und Gemeinde*
BSHPF	*Bulletin de la Société de l' histoire du Protestantisme Français*	ENCPT	*École Nationale des Chartres: Positions des Thèses*
BW	*Biblical World*	ER	*Epworth Review*
BZ	*Biblische Zeitschrift*	ETE	*Expository Times*
BZAW	Beihefte zur Zeitschrift für die alttestamentliche Wissenschaft	*EvQ*	*Evangelical Quarterly*
		EvTheol	*Evangelische Theologie*
BQ	*The Baptist Quarterly*	FC	Fathers of the Church
CBQ	*Catholic Biblical Quarterly*	*FN*	*Filologia Neotestamentaria*
CC	*Christian Century*	FRLANT	Forschungen zur Religion und Literatur des Alten und Neuen Testament
CCSL	Corpus Christianorum, Series Latina		
CD	*Church Dogmatics*, Karl Barth	*FS*	*Franciscan Studies*

HQ	*Hartford Quarterly*	ODCC	*Oxford Dictionary of the Christian*
HLF	*Histoire littéraire de la France*		*Church*
HR	*Historical Research*	OER	*Oxford Encyclopedia of the Refor-*
HTR	*Harvard Theological Review*		*mation*
HiTR	*Historical Theological Review*	OTL	Old Testament Library
IB	*Interpreter's Bible*	PBA	*Proceedings of the British Academy*
ICC	International Critical Commen-	PBR	*Patristic and Byzantine Review*
	tary	Per	*Perspective*
IDB	*Interpreter's Dictionary of the Bible*	PG	Patrologia Graeca
Int	*Interpretation*	PGL	*Patristic Greek Lexicon*
JBL	*Journal of Biblical Literature*	PIBA	*Proceedings of the Irish Biblical*
JCBRF	*Journal of the Christian Brethren*		*Association*
	Research Fellowship	PL	Patrologia Latina
JE	*Jewish Encyclopedia*	PR	*Presbyterian Review*
JEH	*Journal of Ecclesiastical History*	PRR	*Princeton Repertory and Review*
JSJ	*Journal of Jewish Studies*	PTR	*Princeton Theological Review*
JMRS	*Journal of Medieval and Renais-*	RB	*Revue Bénedéctine*
	sance Studies	RPTK	*Realencyklopädie für protestant-*
JPH	*Journal of Presbyterian History*		*ische Theologie und Kirche*
JR	*Journal of Religion*	RGG	*Die Religion in Geschichte und*
JSOT	*Journal for the Study of the Old*		*Gegenwart*
	Testament	Recherches	*Recherches de théologie ancienne et*
JSOTSup	Journal for the Study of the Old		*médiévale*
	Testament Supplemental Series	REJ	*Revue de études juives*
JSS	*Journal of Semitic Studies*	RHPR	*Revue d' histoire et de philosophie*
JTS	*Journal of Theological Studies*		*religieuses*
LCC	Library of Christian Classics	RivB	*Rivista biblica*
LTK	*Lexikon für Theologie und Kirche*	RSR	*Religious Studies Review*
LTPM	Louvain Theological and Pastoral	RBML	*Repertorium für biblische und*
	Monographs		*morgenländische Litteratur*
LU	*Lutherthum*	RT	*Revue Thomiste*
Luc	*Lucas*	SABH	Studies in American Biblical
LXX	Septuagint		Hermeneutics
M&W	*Man and World*	SBEC	Studies in the Bible and Early
MCM	*Mansfield College Magazine*		Christianity
ME	*Mennonite Encyclopedia*	SBET	*Studia Biblica et Theologica*
MER	*Macmillan Encyclopedia of Religion*	SBF	*Studii Biblici Franciscani*
Mon	*The Monist*	SBT	Studies in Biblical Theology
MQ	*McCormick Quarterly*	SC	Sources chrétiennes
MQR	*Mennonite Quarterly Review*	ScanJT	*Scandanavian Journal of Theology*
MR	*Methodist Review*	SCJ	*Sixteenth Century Journal*
MSR	*Mélanges de Science Religieuse*	SE	*Sacris Erudiri*
NCB	New Century Bible	Sem	*Semeia*
NCE	*New Catholic Encyclopedia*	SJT	*Scottish Journal of Theology*
NDT	*New Dictionary of Theology*	SMR	*Saint Mark's Review*
NICNT	New International Commentary	SP	*Studia Patristica*
	on the New Testament	Spec	*Speculum*
NIGTC	New International Greek Testa-	SR	*Studies in the Renaissance*
	ment Commentary	ST	Stemmen des Tijds
NPNF	Nicene and Post-Nicene Fathers	STC	*Short-Title Catalogue*
NRT	*La nouvelle revue théologique*	StT	*Studia Theologica*
NSHERK	*New Schaff-Herzog Encyclopedia*	TB	*Theologische Beiträge*
	of Religious Knowledge	TBT	*The Bible Today*
NT	*Novum Testamentum*	TCBS	*Transactions of the Cambridge*
NTS	*New Testament Studies*		*Bibliographical Society*

TD	*Theology Digest*	*USR*	*Union Seminary Review* (Richmond)
TDNT	*Theological Dictionary of the New Testament*	WBC	Word Biblical Commentary
TGIT	*The Great Ideas Today*	*W&W*	*Word and World*
Th	*Thomist*	*WTJ*	*Westminster Theological Journal*
Them	*Themelios*	*VC*	*Vetera Christianorum*
ThZ	*Theologische Zeitung*	*Viator*	*Viator*
TL	*Theologische Literaturzeitung*	*Wor*	*Worship*
TNTC	Tyndale New Testament Commentary	*ZAW*	*Zeitschrift für die Alttestamentliche Wissencschaft*
Tr	*Traditio*	*ZK*	*Zeitschrift für Kirchengeschichte*
TRE	*Theologische Realenzyklopaedie*	*ZNW*	*Zeitschrift für die neutestamentlische Wissenschaft*
TS	*Theological Studies*		
TSK	*Theologische Studien und Kritiken*	*ZPT*	*Zeitschrift für Praktische Theologie*
TT	*Theology Today*	*ZST*	*Zeitschrift für die systematische Theologie*
TTs	*Teologisk Tidsskrift*		
TU	Texte und Untersuchungen	*ZTK*	*Zeschrift für Theologie und Kirche*
TZ	*Theologische Zeitschrift*		
USQR	*Union Seminary Quarterly Review* (New York)		

Contributors

Bandstra, Andrew J., Ph.D. Professor of New Testament, Emeritus, Calvin Theological Seminary, Grand Rapids, Michigan, USA: **Zahn, Theodor.**

Bock, Darrell L., Ph.D. Research Professor of New Testament Studies, Dallas Theological Seminary, Dallas, Texas, USA: **Meyer, Heinrich August Wilhelm.**

Brogan, John J., Ph.D. Assistant Professor of Religion, Northwestern College, Orange City, Iowa, USA: **Athanasius.**

Brown, Colin, D.D. Professor of Systematic Theology, Fuller Theological Seminary, Pasadena, California, USA: **Reimarus, H. S.; Weiss, Johannes.**

Brown, Dennis, M. Litt. Head of Religion and Philosophy, Manchester Grammar School, Manchester, UK: **Jerome.**

Burrows, Mark S., Ph.D. Associate Professor of the History of Christianity, Andover Newton Theological School, Newton Centre, Massachusetts, USA: **Gerson, Jean.**

Buss, Martin J., Ph.D. Professor of Religion, Emory University, Atlanta, Georgia, USA: **Gunkel, Hermann.**

Church, Christopher, Ph.D. Assistant Professor of Philosophy and Religion, Baptist College of Health Sciences, Memphis Tennessee, USA: **Westcott, B. F., and F. J. A. Hort.**

Clements, Ronald E., D.D. Emeritus Professor of Old Testament Studies, King's College, University of London, London, UK: **Mowinckel, Sigmund; Wellhausen, Julius.**

Cook, James I., Th.D. Anton Biemolt Professor of New Testament Emeritus, Western Theological Seminary, Holland, Michigan, USA: **Goodspeed, Edgar J.**

Coughenour, Robert A., Ph.D. Professor of Old Testament Emeritus, Western Theological Seminary, Holland, Michigan, USA: **Robinson, H. Wheeler.**

Crenshaw, James L., Ph.D. Robert L. Flowers Professor of Old Testament, Duke University, Durham, North Carolina, USA: **Von Rad, Gerhard.**

Dearman, J. Andrew, Ph.D. Professor of Old Testament, Austin Presbyterian Theological Seminary, Austin, Texas, USA: **Smith, W. Robertson.**

De Vries, Dawn, Ph.D. Professor of Theology, Union Theological Seminary and the Presbyterian School of Christian Education, Richmond, Virginia, USA: **Schleiermacher, Friedrich Daniel Ernst.**

Dorman, Ted M., Ph.D. Professor of Religion, Taylor University, Upland, Indiana, USA: **Cullmann, Oscar.**

Dunn, James D. G., D.D. Lightfoot Professor of Divinity, University of Durham, Durham, UK: **Lightfoot, J. B.**

Farthing, John L., Ph.D. Professor of Religion and Classical Languages, Hendrix College, Conway, Arkansas, USA: **Beza, Theodore; Zanchi, Jerome.**

Feldmeth, Nathan P., Ph.D. Assistant Professor of Church History, Fuller Theological Seminary, Pasadena, California, USA: **Tyndale, William.**

Fergusson, David A. S., D.Phil. Professor of Systematic Theology, University of Aberdeen, Aberdeen, UK: **Bultmann, Rudolf.**

Froehlich, Karlfried, Dr. Theol. Benjamin B. Warfield Professor of Ecclesiastical History Emeritus, Princeton Theological Seminary, Princeton, New Jersey, USA: **Aquinas, Thomas.**

Gasque, W. Ward, Ph.D. President, Pacific Association for Theological Studies, Seattle, Washington, USA: **Bruce, F. F.**

Hafemann, Scott J., Dr. Theol. Gerald F. Hawthorne Professor of New Testament Greek and Exegesis, Wheaton College, Wheaton, Illinois, USA: **Baur, F. C.**

Hagen, Kenneth, Th.D. Professor of Theology, Marquette University, Milwaukee, Wisconsin, USA: **Luther, Martin.**

Hagner, Donald A., Ph.D. George Eldon Ladd Professor of New Testament, Fuller Theological Seminary, Pasadena, California, USA: **Dodd, C. H.**

Hare, Douglas R. A., Th.D. William F. Orr Professor of New Testament Emeritus, Pittsburgh Theological Seminary, Pittsburgh, Pennsylvania, USA: **Davies, W. D.**

Harrisville, Roy A., Th.D. Professor of New Testament Emeritus, Luther Theological Seminary, St. Paul, Minnesota, USA: **Von Hofmann, Johann Christian Konrad.**

Hart, D. G., Ph.D. Associate Professor of Church History and Theological Bibliography, Westminster Theological Seminary, Philadelphia, Pennsylvania, USA: **Machen, J. Gresham.**

Haugaard, William P., Th.D. Professor Emeritus, Diocese of Chicago Chair of Church History, Seabury-Western Theological Seminary, Evanston, Illinois, USA: **Coverdale, Miles; Hooker, Richard.**

Hicks, R. Lansing, Th.D. Professor Emeritus of Old Testament, Yale University Divinity School, New Haven, Connecticut, USA: **Wright, George Ernest.**

Hurst, Lincoln D., D.Phil. Associate Professor of Religious Studies, University of California, Davis, California, USA: **Caird, G. B.**

Jackson, Jared Judd, Th.D. Professor of Old Testament Emeritus, Pittsburgh Theological Seminary, Pittsburgh, Pennsylvania, USA: **Muilenburg, James.**

James, Frank A., III, D.Phil. Associate Professor of Historical Theology, Reformed Theological Seminary, Orlando, Florida, USA: **Vermigli, Peter Martyr.**

Johnson, William Stacy, Ph.D. W. C. Brown Chair of Theology, Austin Presbyterian Theological Seminary, Austin, Texas, USA: **Barth, Karl.**

Jones, Scott Jameson, Ph.D. McCreless Assistant Professor of Evangelism, Perkins School of Theology, Southern Methodist University, Dallas, Texas, USA: **Wesley, John.**

Kannengiesser, Charles, Ph.D. Professor Emeritus of Theology, University of Notre Dame, Notre Dame, Indiana, USA: **Augustine of Hippo; Biblical Interpretation in the Early Church.**

Kearsley, Roy, Ph.D. Lecturer, Glasgow Bible College, Glasgow, Scotland, UK: **Tertullian.**

Kolb, Robert, Ph.D. Director, Institute for Mission Studies and Professor of Systematic Theology, Concordia Seminary, Saint Louis, Missouri, USA: **Flacius Illyricus, Matthias.**

Krey, Philip D. W., Ph.D. Dean of the Faculty and Professor of Church History, The Lutheran Theological Seminary at Philadelphia, Philadelphia, Pennsylvania, USA: **Lefèvre d'Étaples, Jacques.**

Limburg, James, Ph.D. Professor of Old Testament, Luther Seminary, St. Paul, Minnesota, USA: **Westermann, Claus.**

McCollough, C. Thomas, Ph.D. Professor of Religion, Centre College, Danville, Kentucky, USA: **Theodoret of Cyrus.**

McCreery, David W., Ph.D. Professor, Willamette University, Salem, Oregon, USA: **Noth, Martin.**

McDonald, Bruce A., Ph.D. Adjunct Professor of Religion, Texas Wesleyan University, Fort Worth, Texas, USA: **Theodore of Mopsuestia.**

McDonald, Lee M., Ph.D. Senior Pastor, First Baptist Church, Alhambra, California, and Adjunct Professor of New Testament Studies, Fuller Theological Seminary, Pasadena, California, USA: **Ladd, George Eldon.**

McKim, Donald K., Ph.D. Academic Dean and Professor of Theology, Memphis Theological Seminary, Memphis, Tennessee, USA: **Perkins, William.**

Martens, Elmer A., Ph.D. Professor Emeritus of Old Testament, Mennonite Brethren Biblical Seminary, Fresno, California, USA: **Eichrodt, Walther.**

Martin, Ralph P., Ph.D. Distinguished Scholar in Residence, Fuller Theological Seminary, Pasadena, California, Azusa Pacific University, Azusa, California, Evangelical Seminary, El Monte, California, USA: **Käsemann, Ernst.**

Mercer, Calvin R., Ph.D. Associate Professor of Religion and Director, Religious Studies Program, East Carolina University, Greenville, North Carolina, USA: **Perrin, Norman; Schweitzer, Albert.**

Minor, Mitzi L., Ph.D. Associate Professor of New Testament, Memphis Theological Seminary, Memphis, Tennessee, USA: **Schüssler Fiorenza, Elisabeth.**

Mitchell, Margaret M., Ph.D. Associate Professor of New Testament, McCormick Theological Seminary, Chicago, Illinois, USA: **Chrysostom, John.**

Morgan, Robert C., M.A. Reader, University of Oxford, Oxford, UK: **Bornkamm, Günther; Strauss, David Friedrich.**

Muller, Richard A., Ph.D. P. J. Zondervan Professor of Historical Theology, Calvin Theological Seminary, Grand Rapids, Michigan, USA: **Biblical Interpretation in the 16th & 17th Centuries; Lightfoot, John.**

Nassif, Bradley, Ph.D. Director of Academic Programs, Fuller Theological Seminary, Southern California Extension, Irvine, California, USA; Visiting Professor of Eastern Orthodox and Evangelical Theology, Antiochian House of Studies, Ligonier, Pennsylvania, USA: **Origen.**

Noll, Mark A., Ph.D. Professor of History, Wheaton College, Wheaton, Illinois, USA: **Hodge, Charles.**

Norris, Richard A., Jr., D.Phil. Emeritus Professor of Church History, Union Theological Seminary, New York, New York, USA: **Irenaeus.**

Ocker, Christopher, Ph.D. Associate Professor of History, San Francisco Theological Seminary, San Anselmo, California; Member of Core Doctoral Faculty, Graduate Theological Union, Berkeley, California, USA: **Biblical Interpretation in the Middle Ages.**

Olbricht, Thomas H., Ph.D. Distinguished Professor of Religion Emeritus, Pepperdine University, Malibu, California, USA: **Barnes, Albert; Biblical Interpretation in North America in the 20th**

Century; Briggs, Charles Augustus; Tholuck, Friedrich August Gottreu.

Old, Hughes Oliphant, D.Theol. Member, Center of Theological Inquiry, Princeton, New Jersey, USA: **Henry, Matthew.**

Painter, John, Ph.D. Professor of Theology, Charles Sturt University, Canberra, Australian Capital Territory, Australia: **Barrett, C. K.**

Parrish, V. Steven, Ph.D. Associate Professor of Old Testament, Memphis Theological Seminary, Memphis, Tennessee, USA: **Brueggemann, Walter.**

Patton, Corrine, L., Ph.D. Assistant Professor, University of St. Thomas, St. Paul, Minnesota, USA: **Hugh and Andrew of St. Victor; Nicholas of Lyra.**

Paulsell, Stephanie, A., Ph.D. Director of Ministry Studies and Senior Lecturer in Religion and Literature, University of Chicago Divinity School, Chicago, Illinois, USA: **Hugh of St. Cher.**

Payne, John B., Ph.D. Diefenderfer Professor of Mercersburg and Ecumenical Theology and Professor of Church History, Lancaster Theological Seminary, Lancaster, Pennsylvania, USA: **Erasmus, Desiderius.**

Peabody, David B., Ph.D. Professor of Religion and Chair, Department of Religion and Philosophy, Nebraska Wesleyan University, Lincoln, Nebraska, USA: **Griesbach, Johann Jakob.**

Penchansky, David, Ph.D. Associate Professor, University of St. Thomas, St. Paul, Minnesota, USA: **Barr, James.**

Petersen, Rodney L., Ph.D. Executive Director, Boston Theological Institute, Newton Centre, Massachusetts, USA: **Bullinger, Heinrich.**

Puckett, David L., Ph.D. Professor of Church History, Southeastern Baptist Theological Seminary, Wake Forest, North Carolina, USA: **Calvin, John.**

Rempel, John D., Th.D. Minister, Manhattan Mennonite Fellowship and Mennonite Central Committee Liaison to the United Nations, New York, New York, USA: **Marpeck, Pilgram.**

Rogerson, John W., D.D. Emeritus Professor of Biblical Studies, University of Sheffield, Sheffield, UK: **De Wette, Wilhelm Martin Leberecht; Michaelis, Johann David.**

Rollmann, Hans, Ph.D. Professor, Department of Religious Studies, Memorial University of Newfoundland, St. John's, Newfoundland, Canada: **Semler, Johann Salomo; Wrede, William.**

Rosas, L. Joseph, III, Ph.D. Pastor, Union Avenue Baptist Church, Memphis, Tennessee, USA: **Kierkegaard, Søren Aabe.**

Rumscheidt, H.-Martin, Ph.D. Professor, Atlantic School of Theology, Halifax, Nova Scotia, Canada: **Harnack, Adolf von.**

Running, Leona Glidden, Ph.D. Professor Emerita of Biblical (and Semitic) Languages, Andrews University, Berrien Springs, Michigan, USA: **Albright, William Foxwell.**

Sandys-Wunsch, John, D.Phil. Professor, Thorneloe University, Sudbury, Ontario, Canada: **Eichorn, J. G.; Ernesti, Johann August.**

Schneider, John Q., Ph.D. Professor of Religion and Theology, Calvin College, Grand Rapids, Michigan, USA: **Melanchthon, Philipp.**

Sheppard, Gerald, Ph.D. Professor of Old Testament Literature and Exegesis, Emmanuel College of Victoria University and the Toronto School of Theology in the University of Toronto, Toronto,

Canada: **Biblical Interpretation in the 18th and 19th Centuries; Biblical Interpretation in Europe in the 20th Century; Childs, Brevard.**

Shoemaker, Lorna A., M.Div., Ph.D. Candidate, Graduate Theological Union, Berkeley, California, USA: **Denys the Carthusian.**

Shotwell, Willis A., Ph.D. Assistant Director, Student Advising, Retired, University of California, Berkeley, California, USA: **Justin Martyr.**

Snavely, Iren L., Jr., Ph.D. Reference Department Manager, Samuel Paley Library, Temple University, Philadelphia, Pennsylvania, USA: **Zwingli, Ulrich.**

Soards, Marion L., Ph.D. Professor of New Testament Studies, Louisville Presbyterian Theological Seminary, Louisville, Kentucky, USA: **Brown, Raymond E.**

Spencer, Stephen R., Ph.D. Professor of Systematic Theology, Dallas Theological Seminary, Dallas, Texas, USA: **Scofield, C. I.**

Sweeney, Douglas A., Ph.D. Assistant Professor of Church History and the History of Christian Thought, Trinity Evangelical Divinity School, Deerfield, Illinois, USA: **Edwards, Jonathan.**

Talbert, Charles H., Ph.D. Distinguished Professor of Religion, Baylor University, Waco, Texas, USA: **Conzelmann, Hans.**

Tamburello, Dennis E., Ph.D. Professor of Religious Studies, Siena College, Loudonville, New York, USA: **Bernard of Clairvaux.**

Taylor, Marion A., Ph.D. Associate Professor of Old Testament, Wycliffe College, University of Toronto, Toronto, Ontario, Canada: **Driver, Samuel Rolles.**

Vander Broek, Lyle D., Ph.D. Professor of New Testament, The University of Dubuque Theological Seminary, Dubuque, Iowa, USA: **Jeremias, Joachim.**

Weborg, C. John, Ph.D. Professor of Theology and Coordinator of Spiritual Formation, North Park Theological Seminary, Chicago, Illinois, USA: **Bengel, J. A.**

Willey, Patricia Tull, Ph.D. Associate Professor of Old Testament, Louisville Presbyterian Theological Seminary, Louisville, Kentucky, USA: **Trible, Phyllis.**

Wright, David F., D.D. Senior Lecturer in Ecclesiastical History, University of Edinburgh, Scotland, UK: **Bucer, Martin.**

Wylie, Amanda Berry, Ph.D. Adjunct Instructor, Drew University, Madison, New Jersey, USA: **Clement of Alexandria.**

Yarbrough, Robert W., Ph.D. Associate Professor of New Testament Studies, Trinity Evangelical Divinity School, Deerfield, Illinois, USA: **Schlatter, Adolf; Stuart, Moses.**

PART ONE

Biblical Interpretation
in the Early Church

The earliest Christian groups were galvanized by the power of the ancestral Scriptures. They found in the Law, the Prophets and the Writings constant vindication of their experience of a religious conversion. The gospel event was a call to a new understanding of their ancestral tradition of faith, the risen Jesus drawing them, like the disciples on the road to Emmaus, to a new reading of the Torah. It was in "searching the Scriptures" that they reached to the ground of their inner transformation as disciples of Jesus. It was in a hermeneutical context, that is, in interpreting the Scriptures, that their encounter with Jesus was producing an unpredictable renewal of their identity as believers.

The venerable Scriptures read anew by Christ's first witnesses exercised such a power that when they began to articulate the Scripture's personal implication in the Jesus event, all became gospel for them. Paradoxically, while the Scriptures seemed old in the immediate context of the Christ event, these same Scriptures were vehicles of a new message. In nascent Christianity the founding self-identification of true discipleship proceeded through a coherent rewriting of the whole salvation history of Israel. Thus among the proto-Christians old Scripture generated a sacred literature of a new kind, centered on the figure of Jesus as the messianic culmination of all times, the Son of God whose mission was to inaugurate the events of the end. The narratives and testimonies that were to fill the future writings collected as the New Testament are founded upon a hermeneutical conversion within their ancestral tradition. In the broader cultural and religious background of the first two centuries of Christianity, the production of what became the New Testament is forever linked with the reading of the old Scriptures in the life and thought of the tenuous string of Christian communities around the Mediterranean world.

The First Two Centuries

During the first two centuries no attempt was made to present a proper exegesis of the Bible, nor was the Bible as such seen by the earliest Christians as a classic calling for its own commentary. The contrast between the learned and rich Jew of Alexandria, Philo, a contemporary of Jesus, who wrote one treatise after another on the Torah as a monument of cultivated exegesis, and the many illiterate minorities among earliest Christians could not be more stark. For Jesus' disciples of the first two centuries, the appeal of the Scriptures was a more immediate call to conversion rather than to an intellectual analysis. The Bible remained for them what it was expressly for Paul and the Gospel writers, a power of the Spirit, capable of transforming their minds in giving them a new sense for their own religious past, a divine authority of revelation legitimizing their claim of faith in Jesus.

Rather than scholarly exegesis, the earliest literary activity of the Christian churches, apart from the New Testament itself, was the so-called apocryphals of the New Testament and similar writings, all of which espoused literary forms of a biblical type. That productivity witnessed the persistent centrality of the Old Testament in the earliest circles of Christian converts. One of these writings is the *Ascension of Isaiah,* a Jewish apocryphal interpolated by Christians before the end of the first century. In it the vision of the gospel event is filled with apocalyptic motifs, in the description of the transcosmic descent and ascent of the Savior, which was supposed to have been contemplated by the prophet of old.

In the Jewish-Christian community of Rome, also before the end of the first century, the Roman elder Clement tried his skills in the style of ancient wisdom literature when he wrote a *Letter to the Corinthians.* There is little doctrinal overtone from Paul's letter, but the author cites exclusively from the Old Testament. One or two generations later, also in the Jewish-Christian community of Rome, a layman called Hermas fused traditional wisdom literature and apocalyptic elements when he composed his ambitious synthesis, *The Shepherd of Hermas,* on the debated question of the forgiveness of sinners in the church.

The call on the Old Testament was not without ambiguity in these works. While Christian leaders, vocal in the name of their communities of recent converts, remained eager to keep the literary standards of the ancient Scriptures, their true focus was the Christian experiment. However, whether in Corinth, Rome, or elsewhere, their public testimony was still pervaded by the symbols and the authoritative power of the Old Testament. Even in the case of Pseudo-Barnabas, a Christian zealot of the later second century whose work is often disfigured by anti-Jewish bigotry, the same is true: he denounces in such "biblical" terms the practical implications of the old covenant that his work, like that of Hermas, could be considered as belonging to Scripture. Hermas's *Shepherd* and the *Letter of Barnabas* enjoyed a special status in liturgical use until the fourth century.

Apologists

From the middle of the second century a new category of writers emerged, the so-called apologists. J. Quasten enumerates twelve of these Greek-speaking intellectuals from pagan backgrounds. Most significant is Justin of Rome, martyred in 165 after having served in his community as a teacher of philosophy, or religious truth.

*Justin Martyr (c. 100-165) announces a decisive shift in the Christian use of the Old Testament during the second century. Having found Christ as the most valid response to his longing for absolute truth, Justin elaborated a rational demonstration of that validity. Therefore he inaugurated a methodical use of Scripture. Against the pagan unbelief and the hostility of the rabbis, he wrote two *Apologies* and later a *Dialogue with Trypho,* which may well be more than a literary fiction. Each time Justin explained Christian faith in constant reference to Scripture. Acknowledged as the first of the Christian authors, he calls explicitly on the written text of the Gospels of Matthew, Mark and Luke, citing them from memory (*1 Apology* 15—17, 62, 66).

In *1 Apology* 31 Justin offers historical information about the making of the Septuagint, the Greek translation realized in Alexandria. In *1 Apology* 33—53 he follows closely the Gospel narratives. In his *Dialogue with Trypho* he quotes Matthew abundantly and Luke more occasionally, always with the purpose of citing the literal content of written sources. In *Dialogue with Trypho* 29, he indulges in an abrupt reply to his rabbinic counterpart: "They [the controverted words in the Old Testament] are contained in your Scriptures, or rather not yours, but ours."

Another important apologist is Theophilus of Antioch (late second century), whose homeland was in eastern Syria. Deeply versed in Hellenistic learning, Theophilus had undertaken a careful study of the Prophets and other biblical texts before taking over episcopal ministry in the imperial city of Antioch. Shortly after 180 he wrote the *Apology to Autolycus,* in which he is the first Christian leader to quote primarily from the New Testament, including the Pauline letters, which like the Gospels are cited as "divine word."

In the context of Gnostic debate, Theophilus succeeded in formulating the principle of a creation of the world out of nothing, a novel definition characteristic of the way in which the rationality of Greek thought was interacting with biblical beliefs in Christian circles. With a stringent display of logic the bishop elaborated on the philosophical evidence in complete assumption of what he understood to be the deepest biblical intent of Genesis. In a culture very different from the culture of the biblical author, this Christian bishop concentrated all the intellectual tools at his disposal to argue that all things depend radically on God.

Melito (late second century), bishop of Sardis in what is modern Turkey, is another distinguished author among the apologists. In his *Homily on Passion* and its recital of the gospel message we hear the tones of a sophisticated culture dominated by literature and rhetoric. While its real significance is doctrinal, the *Homily* demonstrates how the christological focus of the canonical gospel narratives perdured intact throughout this Hellenizing shift of the Christian movement into the high culture of late antiquity. In Melito's poetic homily, delivered from the pulpit as a psalmodic song, the passion and death on the cross of the Messiah are rendered with passionate emphasis.

With his anti-Gnostic bias Melito also illustrates how the literary celebration of the central evangelical message reached the congregations of his time, strongly framed by a theological system: God as such, the Father, one with the Son and Holy Spirit, operates our salvation in Jesus Christ. Naming God as Trinity, Melito still understood deity according to the Yahwism of biblical faith, as Unique Principle, in Greek Mon-archy. Thus his use of Scripture complies with monarchian theology. As was the case in Semitic thought, principally in the New Testament itself, the shift of the gospel into Hellenism opened a new space for the metaphysical imagination. Once again Scripture, and only Scripture, was able to secure the appropriate resources for the Christian creativity in that cultural odyssey leading from the milieu of the gospel to Melito and from Melito to *Origen of Alexandria.

Gnostic Crisis

The Gnostic crisis of the first two centuries after Christ produced profound changes in all major churches during the third century. Scripture was the strategic issue in that crisis, one of the distinctive features of all leading Gnostic teachers being to reject the Old Testament as received in the churches. Hence the need to reformulate the relevance of Scripture for a Christian doctrine of faith was all the more urgent as most Gnostic teachers were spreading their views inside Christian communities. At the grassroots level it was sometimes difficult, even impossible, to distinguish between Gnostic and non-Gnostic trends. A sure criterion for the needed discernment was provided by Scripture. For instance, insofar as the *Odes of Solomon,* a superb piece of poetry from the second half of the second century, present a psalmic analogy with old Scripture free from polemical overtones against Israelite faith, the odes should not be labeled Gnostic, even if their mystic enthusiasm and symbolic imagery are akin to Gnostic spirituality.

The Gnostics' rejection of the creation story in Genesis and their declared war against all forms of biblical faith were motivated by a pessimistic prejudice about the human condition on earth and about the very fact of a material cosmos. While church leaders denounced the arbitrary and abusive appropriation of scriptural verses in Gnostic circles, the Valentinian school of Gnosticism, originating in Alexandria, challenged traditional interpreters of Scripture in laying down the first elements of a proper method for systematic exegesis, as can be seen in Heracleon's *Commentary on John,* known only through its refutation by Origen.

The clarification resulting from the Gnostic crisis inside the main churches was a new foundation for the appropriation of Scripture. Against Marcion's attempt to compose a canon of Scripture in conformity with his anti-Jewish bias, the churches consolidated and almost completed the building up of a collection of Old and New Testament writings unanimously accepted. Against the Gnostic claim of a religious faith based on the mostly secret teaching of individual masters, the churches maintained a strict distinction between what they called the apostolic tradition of faith and any kind of exegetical initiative launched by individuals. Tradition as such became normative as an institutional vehicle for transmitting the legacy of the first disciples of Jesus and for entertaining a public unanimity among highly diversified churches. In short, in reaction to Gnosticism the Christian churches established their oldest form of catholicism, based on their mutual agreement to be linked by the rule of faith, by a common possession and interpretation of old Scripture, and by a shared willingness to celebrate the gospel event in symbiosis with high culture.

*Irenaeus (fl. c. 180) was born in Smyrna (modern Turkey) and emigrated to Rome and then to Gaul, in what may have been a missionary impulse. He always kept ties with friends in his native province. At their request he brought together documentary data concerning Gnostic teaching, data that were processed in a synthesis entitled *Against the Heresies.* Irenaeus handled the polemical dossier with a deeply biblical focus in mind, crystallized in the following formula: One God, one Scripture, one salvation, one rule of faith in all churches. A man of the Bible, the bishop of Lyons moved through the Prophets and other sacred writings in hammering and chiseling all his arguments in accordance with Scripture. He was also the first Christian theologian who integrated Pauline doctrine systematically in the biblical texture of his own thought. Traces of Paul's dialectics may be detectable in other second-century sources, such as the *Letter to Diognetus,* which is probably contemporary with Irenaeus; but it is the merit of Irenaeus to have first addressed Paul as a true theologian. Again there is proof of a creative response against Gnostic precedents, by which Paul's teaching had been compromised. That Pauline theology began to flourish in the intellectual history of the Christian churches is in no small measure due to Irenaeus.

The Alexandrian Tradition

By the beginning of the third century, Alexandria, the intellectual capital of the Roman Empire in late antiquity, also took the lead in the history of biblical exegesis. There the Greek version of Hebrew Scripture, called the Septuagint, had been elaborated under King Ptolemy II Philadelphius three centuries before Christ. That translation, completed with additional texts directly composed in

Greek, served as literary matrix for the writing of the New Testament.

Once it was couched in written form, the gospel found an access to universal culture. One of the highly developed elements of the Alexandrian legacy to this universal culture was the exegesis of the classic texts held in veneration in the ancient world. To speak of Alexandrian exegesis immediately evokes the term *allegorism,* and rightly so, since the foundation of its library, the learned contribution of Alexandria to classical culture, had been a methodical exploration of ancient poets, philosophers, and even nonwritten myths with a purpose of allegory. Allegory by definition means saying something different from what one reads in the written source, allowing a legitimate appropriation of the cultural tradition. Even in artificial word games and comparisons, foreign to our modern sensibilities, allegories nurtured the Alexandrian imagination. The task meant interpreting the sources not by paraphrase and imitation but by transposing mythical contents and obscure sentences into the rational discourse of contemporary Alexandrian culture. Gods and goddesses, including their sometimes scandalous behavior, offered to the Alexandrian interpreters symbols, best understood in reference to actual standards of ethics and society. Greek classics started a new life thanks to Alexandrian scholarship. Allegorism became part of the international success of Alexandria in the Hellenistic world, a world in which Christian exegesis was searching for its own proper cultural expression.

Generally labeled as the allegorical method of exegesis, biblical interpretation in Christian Alexandria went through many phases that militate against simplistic qualification. What may be properly called Christian exegesis started in Alexandria in response to Heracleon, the disciple of Valentinus, in the late second century. The response to Heracleon in the name of Alexandrian church was formulated by *Clement of Alexandria (c. 160-215) and his pupil *Origen (c. 185-253/4), who combined allegorical methodology with far-reaching theological intuitions and with a passionate scrutiny of the text of Scripture. Origen is still acclaimed as the founder of biblical criticism in the church, the most influential Christian interpreter of Scripture, and the founder of systematic theology.

Origen's basic distinction between the literal and spiritual sense of biblical statements fused christological typology, as inspired by Paul, with the presuppositions of Alexandrian allegorism. The sacred text, said Origen, even when otherwise making no sense, appeals to the inner self of the readers and teaches them something about their soul and destiny.

Backed by a Platonic anthropology and urged toward intellectual synthesis, Origen set out on his lifelong mission as a Christian interpreter of Scripture. He worked for more than fifteen years on the Hexapla ("Six Columns"), trying to establish a corrected text of the Septuagint by comparing the Hebrew original and its transcription in Greek with three other Greek versions. Inspired by Philo's treatises on Torah, he wrote innumerable commentaries on both Testaments.

When in his forties he was ordained a priest, he preached countless exegetical sermons, of which a few are preserved in the original Greek and more are saved thanks to Latin translations.

From the mid-third century on, Origen's accomplishment radiated over all provinces of the empire. After him, disciples and admirers produced a whole exegetical literature in the Origenian style: Eusebius of Caesarea, the founder of church history, who became a biblical scholar in his own right; Ambrose of Milan and Hilary of Poitiers, who introduced him to the Latin West; the Cappadocian bishops, Gregory of Nazianzus and Gregory of Nyssa, who glorified his method of exegesis in their own commentaries, even when repudiating some of his philosophical premises; and many others.

Origen's admirers did not always content themselves with emulating his allegorical explanations but were moved to produce biblical interpretations of their own in response to the challenges of their time. Such a response is clear in the writings of *Athanasius of Alexandria (c. 296-373), who held the most powerful episcopal office of Alexandria from 328 to 373. Political circumstances and personal commitment trapped Athanasius in the heat of an ecclesiasti-cal turmoil, chastening the greater part of his forty-five years in office. Between five exiles, and even when he was banished, he became a writer by duty and necessity. A first essay, *On the Incarnation of the Divine Word* (c. 335), was soon followed by more lengthy *Orations Against the Arians* and other polemical essays, linked with the crisis around Arius and in defense of the synod of Nicea in 325. Each year, whenever possible, Athanasius sent a circular letter to the churches under his leadership. After 356 he wrote the *Life of Antony,* the earliest Christian biography. Athanasius's use of the Bible is atypical for an Alexandrian in that he did not compose a biblical commentary as such. Rightly acclaimed as someone steeped in Scripture, he abstained from exegesis proper and ignored the Alexandrian orchestration of allegorism. His reading of the Bible was less conditioned by a preconceived system of philosophical ideas about the human self, as in Origen, than linked with his practical experience of faith and church.

Following conventional directions of school rhetorics, Athanasius draws upon Scripture in order to highlight the issues at stake, all the time couching his thoughts in a vivid narrative style. He makes no formal distinction between a literal and a spiritual sense of Scripture. The *Letter to Marcellinus on the Psalms* demonstrates the inner dynamic of his biblical hermeneutics: he does not analyze semantic levels and multiple senses in the Psalter verses; he rather wants the psalms to speak for themselves in the context of Marcellinus's experience of life and faith. He encourages his friend to contemplate the different circumstances in which psalmic verses could be most appropriate. In the kind of advice he offers his sick friend, we can glimpse some autobiographical accents of the bishop's own experience, which underlines the fact that the pastoral ministry of the church was for Athanasius the proper arena of biblical experience. Experiencing the active presence of Christ's salvation all around him meant for Athanasius the constant verification of God's action described in both Testaments. Hence his comments upon the events in which he was involved read as a realized analogy of what one reads in Scripture. The great biblical saving actions are to be celebrated constantly in the now of the church.

In contrast to Athanasius, Cyril of Alexandria (c. 375-444), bishop from 412 to 444, expressed his own relationship to Scripture essentially in writing commentaries. In this fifth-century bishop, biblical exegesis and episcopal ministry neatly coincided. Prior to Cyril, the learned exercise of biblical interpretation by Didymus the Blind had attracted much attention in Alexandria. Didymus, who had been appointed a private teacher under the ruling of Athanasius, reiterated Origen's project in a more systematic way. In addition to public teaching, he distributed more esoteric lessons to the inner circle of his disciples in conformity with strict Origenism. He died in 398, while Cyril was eagerly studying theology in the city under the supervision of his uncle Theophilus, the local patriarch, whom he would succeed. When he was installed as a powerful pontiff of the Alexandrian hierarchy in a position of wealth and comfort, Cyril produced a biblical exegesis presenting all the marks of a magisterial teaching: solemn diction, a display of vast knowledge and rhetorical skills, a constant affirmation of doctrinal correctness. Verse by verse, Isaiah, the Psalms, the Gospels of John and of Matthew, and other books were commented on, the mass of Cyril's prose filling thousands of pages in a modern edition. In his doctrinal works Cyril discussed scriptural passages with much scholarly pathos, but one may suspect that ordinary church people were no longer the primary addressees, as they had been in Athanasius's similar writing. School procedures determine Cyril's exposition of well-organized exegetical works in which the author grasps readers by the hand and, with eloquence and erudition, leads them to the spiritual sense. Christological typology is applied in full confidence: the whole Scripture leads straight to the Christ the Pantocrator of Byzantine mosaics. A substantial content of doctrine inside the exegetical frame assured Cyril's works an afterlife of many centuries in Eastern and Western traditions.

After Cyril, the exegetical tradition of Alexandria lost its impetus. In the anti-Chalcedonian camp, Severus of Antioch, a leading Monophysite who found refuge in Alexandria under the emperors Justin and Justinian, wrote 125 *Cathedral Homilies*. They are filled with traditional Alexandrian allegorism, balanced with a careful attention given to the letter of Scripture, as had been the case with Cyril.

The Latin West
There is a reference to the earliest Latin translation of Scripture in the *Acts of the*

Martyrs of Scilli (modern Algeria): "Books and Letters of Paul" were in the hands of the accused in July 180, when they stood in front of the proconsul Saturninus before their condemnation to capital punishment. Christian proselytes coming from Greek-speaking churches, some of them with Jewish backgrounds, sooner or later rendered their message in Latin. Early translations of Scripture from the second and early third century can still be identified by a careful scrutiny of biblical quotations in the works of Tertullian or Cyprian. In particular, Tertullian felt free to quote Scripture at his convenience on the basis of different translations, when he did not translate directly himself. While Cyprian adopted a more consistent line of quoting, suggesting that an old Latin version of the Bible was then emerging with some distinctive authority, Augustine would later feel free to quote different translations. The status of biblical exegesis in the West would be marked forever by its Eastern provenance. Rendered in Latin, the principles and methods of interpreting Scripture would keep their original profile, mainly determined by the initiatives of the Alexandrian interpreters.

Roman Africa retained its pioneering role during the second and third centuries, the well-established rhetorical traditions of Carthage favoring among Christians a special interest in the way of handling sacred Scripture. In response to liturgical and polemical needs, there were collections of *Testimonia*, quotations from the Old Testament organized around specific issues.

The rhetor and advocate *Tertullian (fl. 200), born in Carthage of pagan parents and known as a jurist in Rome, converted to Christianity about 193. A critic of society with a sharp tongue and a passionate eye, the new convert turned against his pagan compatriots in two major essays, *To the Heathen* and *Apology*. Soon followed *The Testimony of the Soul, The Prescription of Heretics* (namely, Gnostics), the monumental *Against Marcion,* the treatise *Against the Valentinians,* another *On Baptism,* one on *The Flesh of Christ,* and finally the more metaphysical *Against Praxeas* when Tertullian had joined the Montanists. In his interpretation of Scripture, he essentially followed Irenaeus's anti-Gnostic stance. More explicitly than Irenaeus, Tertullian opposed the attempt made by Marcion to impose a scriptural canon of his own. He held divine inspiration in high esteem. Except for a few traces of allegorism (e.g., Tertullian *Against Marcion* 2.25; 3.16; 5.1), he read biblical narratives in a realistic way and always applied the juridical bias of his professional past. In letting Scripture explain itself his basic rule was to proceed from clear passages to the more obscure. He argued that a sound explanation of difficult passages was always secured by Christ and the apostles. The ancient prophets announced parables and allegories (Tertullian *Against Marcion* 3.5) and contemplated past events as future.

Bishop Cyprian of Carthage (c. 200/210-258), a famous and rich master of eloquence in Carthage before he converted, was promptly chosen as priest and elected bishop by the local community in 248/49. His literary legacy includes a commentary *On the Lord's Prayer,* the first exegetical essay in Latin produced as a separate work, each verse of the Gospel text being applied to different aspects of the Christian experience. *To Quirinus: Three Books of Testimonies* provided riches of biblical quotations for Latin authors of later times.

While *Augustine of Hippo ranks above all intellectual leaders in the Latin West, two great bishops played a decisive role in shaping Latin exegesis before the ascendancy of Augustine: Hilary of Poitiers, bishop from 350 to 367, and Ambrose of Milan, bishop from 373 to 397. Both men succeeded in their careers as biblical interpreters thanks to what they learned in reading Origen's works.

Hilary spent five years in banishment among Eastern bishops, which gave him an opportunity to become fluent in Greek. First, in *On the Trinity,* he produced a massive scriptural argument against Arianism. Then he imitated a lost commentary of Origen in his own *Commentary on the Psalms.* Written in a style remarkably dense and consonant with classical sources, that vast explanation of all the Psalms remains a masterpiece of ancient Christian literature. It illustrates the status of biblical hermeneutics in the Western churches: while the mystical and thematic inspiration comes from Origen, the inculturation of the sacred text is based on major Latin classics.

Before his exile Hilary wrote a short *Commentary on Matthew,* the first of that sort preserved in Latin. In search of the deeper meaning of main episodes into the gospel narrative, he found it by stressing their symbolic significance: how they were announcing salvation, the church or the hostility of the Jews. Close to Tertullian and other Latin predecessors, Hilary revealed himself at once as a gifted writer, a strong leader and a man of solid convictions, rooted in the classical tradition.

After his return from exile Hilary composed a *Book of Mysteries,* in which he explained figures and names of the Old Testament as prefigurations of God's incarnation in Christ, a thoroughly Origenian exercise.

Ambrose of Milan (c. 339-397) found his first model of biblical exegesis in Philo, who had originally served as a role model for Origen as well. A former rhetor and governor of the province of Liguria in his early thirties, Ambrose was baptized in the same week as he was consecrated a bishop. He was equally at home in both cultures, Greek and Latin, being one of the last Christian leaders in the West to be bilingual. A man of intense learning and immense reading, he appropriated Scripture with ascetic fervor. He introduced the best of Origen's legacy into Western culture and enjoyed the philosophical circles of Milan.

Ambrose's contribution to biblical exegesis, mainly based on preached homilies, witnesses a special interest on Genesis: *On the Six Days (Hexameron); On Paradise, On Cain and Abel, On Noah, On Abraham, On Isaac and the Soul, On Jacob and the Happy Life, On Joseph, On the Patriarchs.* He found in Genesis essential foundations for a Christian way of life, and he communicated them in a brilliant synthesis of allegorical styles inherited from Philo and Origen, fused with the ethical wisdom of Cicero, Virgil, Seneca, Livius and other classical sources.

The three levels of spiritual meaning, taken over from Origen, are called moral, mystical (focusing on the mystery of Christ and church), and anagogical (leading to "upper," *ana-*, transcendent, reality). Ambrose combines them according to pastoral needs and concerns in recreating the symbolic universe of Origenian allegorism, with a genuine focus on ethical issues proper to the genius of his Latin heritage. He also preached on a certain number of psalms, stressing their relevance in the social and political situation of his time. His only known work on the New Testament is an *Explanation of the Gospel According to Luke*, also based on preached homilies.

With *Jerome (c. 340-420), an older contemporary of Augustine, biblical exegesis became a professional business, detached from episcopal ministry. Born in the late 340s at Stridon, on the border of Dalmatia and Pannonia, Jerome studied grammar and rhetoric in Rome, where Donatus was his teacher. With his friend Rufinus he went to the East, where he learned Greek and Hebrew. Ordained a priest by the pro-Nicene and ultraconservative Paulinus of Antioch, he enjoyed some lessons by Apollinarius of Laodicea. Although he was in Rome for a short time after the council of Constantinople (381), he returned to the East and traveled through Jerusalem and Palestine to Egypt, where he enrolled among the students of Didymus the Blind (313-398). Finally he settled in a Latin monastery at Bethlehem until his death.

In Rome, Pope Damasus had encouraged Jerome to revise an older Latin version of the Psalter in comparing it with the Septuagint. But in Caesarea of Palestine he had discovered the unique copy of Origen's Hexapla, which convinced him to produce a Latin text of the Old Testament directly from the Hebrew. This task took him almost fifteen years. The occasional help of some rabbis, but mainly Jerome's talent, made possible his reconstitution of the "Hebraic truth" *(veritas hebraica)*, as he called it, in the freshness and clarity of classical Latin prose. He also created the reference books needed: a biblical *Chronicle*, a *Book of Hebrew Names* and a *Book of Place Names (Onomasticon)* in Palestine with their etymological significance, *Hebraic Questions on Genesis* about old Jewish traditions, and finally a handbook of patrology, *On the Lives of Illustrious Men (De Viribus Illustribus)*, a catalogue of Christian writers until 393, which allowed him to advertise his own work. Jerome also wrote commentaries on Matthew, the Pauline letters, Ecclesiastes, Psalms, the Prophets, and other hagiographic or polemical essays. He took the care to edit 150 of his letters.

Jerome's significance in the history of Christian exegesis remains tied to the fact that he radically changed direction from Origen. The latter focused on the Bible born in his native Alexandria in trying to establish a correct text of the Septuagint; Jerome turned his back on the Septuagint and decided to grasp the meaning of the Hebrew original. Thereby he not only produced the Vulgate, the Latin translation soon to become standard in the Latin churches, but also established a basic presupposition for modern exegesis—the focus on the original setting and the Semitic thinking behind the sacred texts.

A contemporary of Ambrose and Jerome, Tyconius (fl. 370-390), a lay scholar in Carthage, composed a Christian treatise of biblical hermeneutics, the first of its kind, entitled *Book of Rules:* "There are certain mystic rules which obtain in regard to the inner recesses of the entire Law and keep the treasures of the truth invisible for some people," he wrote. The rules are mystic because they are inner structures of divine Scripture. Tyconius hopes "to fabricate something like keys and lamps," to help to understand the mystic rules. His treatise offers a dense and systematic analysis of seven such rules in focusing on their ecclesiological relevance. Tyconius was a Donatist who refused to be sectarian. The rules show that a pure church is a myth, antichrist is in our midst as long as we struggle for salvation. Augustine would be deeply impressed by that lesson.

Augustine of Hippo (354-430), one of the greatest interpreters of Scripture in the Latin West, comparable only with Origen, was a man of intense spirituality, vibrant with all the trends of contemporary culture, literary and philosophical. In reading Paul and discovering Isaiah he overcame the decisive crisis of his conversion in August 386. He spent his first five years as a convert in reading Scripture and learning the Psalms by heart. Even when he was ordained a priest, he still felt himself inadequately prepared to articulate in biblical terms his innate longing for divine transcendency. As soon as he found himself invested with episcopal duty (396), his first major project consisted in planning an essay on biblical interpretation, the treatise *On Christian Doctrine*. It witnesses the fervent commitment of the educated pastor eager to harmonize the values of his personal philosophy with the pastoral need of a methodical explanation of Scripture. After a few months Augustine interrupted his writing, aware of his lack of a proper method for handling the peculiar obscurities of the biblical text. The *Confessions*, which he decided to compose thereafter, gave him a chance to use Scripture in his own way, as a vehicle for passionate prayer and self-awareness.

Augustine had hardly finished gathering and editing the final part of the *Confessions* (itself an attempt to practice exegesis in the frame of an intense subjectivity) when he engaged in a crucial experiment, trying to exercise his skills in strict conformity with the objective content of Scripture. *The Literal Interpretation of Genesis* would become Augustine's hermeneutical laboratory for a lifetime. He termed such a methodology literal because he dared this time to take the letter of the biblical statements as the starting point of his inquiries. Rarely did a rational genius exhaust its own resources as Augustine did in this enterprise. The still inexperienced interpreter of Scripture discovered thereby the priceless value of accepted ignorance. A renewed future opened for him as he plunged once more into a relentless preaching on sacred texts: the *Commentary on John* delivered in 124 sermons, the *Commentary on the First Letter of John* in ten sermons, the lifelong *Exposition of the Psalms*. In addition, five hundred other sermons testify to Augustine's constant immersion in the Scriptures, whether exhorting to the Christian way of life, castigating heretics or celebrating the mysteries of faith.

Augustine had limited access to Greek but absorbed much of Origen, Athanasius, Basil and other Eastern predecessors through reading Ambrose and translations. Thus he keeps a traditional profile in his exegesis, with a basic distinction between spiritual and literal sense of the Bible, christological typology, occasional allegorism and some attention given to the historical context in which Scripture originated. His originality in the hermeneutical task was to communicate a personalized language of biblical discourse and a doctrinal substance as a foundational legacy for the centuries to come in Western Christianity.

Antiochene and Syrian Traditions

The priest Lucian, martyred in 312, is considered the founder of the exegetical tradition of Antioch. Like Origen, he revised the Septuagint text, but he was more familiar with the Hebrew language. His revision was broadly adopted in the Eastern churches. He is said to have favored a literal interpretation of the sacred texts. One of his contemporary fellow Christians in Antioch, Dorotheus, was also a studious reader of the Hebrew Bible.

In 323 or 324, Eustathius became bishop of Antioch. He wrote a tract, *On the Witch of Endor Against Origen* (1 Kings 28), still preserved, in which he denounced allegorical exegesis as depriving Scripture of its historical character. He also wrote a letter to Alexander of Alexandria with an exegesis reducing the figure of Melchizedek to that of an ordinary man, in close connection with the letter to the Hebrews. Some anti-Arian comments of Eustathius on Psalm 15, Psalm 92 and Proverbs 8:22 were published soon after Nicea.

Apollinarius of Laodicea (c. 310-c. 390), condemned for heresy in the last decade of his life, was the most celebrated interpreter of Scripture at Antioch when Jerome enrolled among his students in 374. Well-trained in classical rhetorics, he was imbued with Alexandrian theology, but his "countless volumes on the Holy Scriptures" (Jerome *On Illustrious Men [De Viris Illustribus]* 104) showed an independence of interpretation. Fragments survive on the Psalms, Ecclesiastes, Isaiah, Hosea, Malachi, Matthew, 1 Corinthians, Galatians, Ephesians and Romans. Apollinarius did not perpetuate Origenian allegorism, nor did he formally adhere to the philological method of Antiochene exegetes, though his sharp remarks on the letter and the logic of the text were filled with moral applications and christological overtones.

On the island of Cyprus, Epiphanius of Salamis (c. 315-403) wrote a biblical dictionary, *On Weights and Measures,* in which he discusses the canon of Scripture, the translations of the Old Testament, biblical measurements, and the geography of Palestine. Another treatise, *On the Twelve Precious Stones,* offers allegorical comments on the breastplate of the high priest. This was composed by Epiphanius (394) at the request of Diodore of Tarsus. A *Commentary on the Canticle of Canticles,* attributed to Epiphanius, belongs to a Cypriot contemporary, Bishop Philo of Carpasia.

Diodore of Tarsus (d. 390) was the most distinctive theoretician of the Antiochene school of exegesis. He studied in Athens, presided for a while over a monastery, and became bishop of Tarsus (378). He started teaching at a young age and among his pupils were John *Chrysostom and *Theodore of Mopsuestia. He is said to have written sixty treatises, with commentaries on all the books of the Old Testament, all four Gospels, Acts, Romans, 1 Corinthians, 1 Thessalonians and 1 John. Only fragments survive. A theoretical presentation of his method stressed the need for philological and grammatical analysis in strong opposition to Alexandrian allegorism.

Diodore's closest pupil, Theodore of Mopsuestia (350-428), was born in Antioch and was trained in his hometown by the famous rhetor Libanius. Theodore was consecrated bishop in 392 and was widely celebrated for his learning and orthodoxy. Long after his death, he, like Diodore, was labeled a heretic, a fact that entailed the destruction of his literary legacy. Fragments exist of his commentaries on Genesis, Psalms, the Minor Prophets, Matthew, Luke, John and Acts. A *Commentary on the Ten Minor Epistles of Paul* survives in a Latin translation. Theodore also wrote on all the Pauline letters. Before becoming a bishop he also composed the treatise *On the Incarnation,* in which his thoughtful interpretation ignores Alexandrian allegorism but rests on sound theological judgment. Likewise his brother, Polychronius of Apamea, privileged historical and archaeological data proper to confirm the literal meaning in his biblical commentaries. He refused any allegorical explanation.

John Chrysostom (c. 347-407), first attracted by eremitism and ascetic excesses, was ordained a priest (386) by Bishop Flavian. For twelve years he demonstrated his exceptional gift for oratory from the pulpit. Chosen to replace Nectarius, the patriarch of Constantinople (397), his reformatory zeal caused him much trouble—as much as did the animosity against him of Theophilus, the patriarch of Alexandria. His exegetical homilies on both Testaments, most delivered at Antioch, are among the best Christian literature of antiquity. Chrysostom is concerned about the literal meaning and the practical applications of the sacred text. He analyzes human behavior, with a constant emphasis of Christian ethics. In the year 400 he delivered fifty-five sermons on Acts, the only complete commentary on Acts dating from the patristic era. A deep admiration for the apostle Paul vibrates throughout his homilies. In the ancient church

Chrysostom is the most eloquent commentator on Paul.

Severian of Gabala in Syria, hostile to Chrysostom at the court of Empress Eudoxia and a pedestrian and sectarian representative of the Antiochene school of exegesis, used the Old Testament mainly as a textbook for natural science. Fragments of a *Commentary to the Epistles of Paul* witness his dependence on Diodore of Tarsus.

Niles of Ancyra (modern Ankara), abbot of a monastery in the early fifth century considered John Chrysostom as his teacher, but his *Commentary on the Song of Songs* positions him more closely with Origen. His allegorical interpretation identifies the bride with the church and the human soul.

Mark the Hermit, a contemporary of Niles and another disciple of Chrysostom, picked up the "law of the spirit" in Romans 7:14 and presented sayings entitled *On Spiritual Law,* a complete code for monastic duties (201).

In the second half of the fifth century, Gennadius, the patriarch of Constantinople, wrote commentaries on Genesis, Exodus, the Psalms, Daniel and all the Pauline letters, attesting that he belonged to the exegetical school of Antioch. Fragments survive.

*Theodoret of Cyrus (393-458), born in Antioch, educated in its monasteries and a bishop for thirty-five years, wrote some of the best-known essays in line with Antiochene exegesis. He was a man of great integrity, moderate in his judgment. In a continuous *Interpretation of the Psalms* and a commentary *On the Song of Songs* he combined Origen's exegesis with the historical analysis privileged at Antioch. A strongly anti-Jewish *Commentary on Daniel,* a *Commentary on Ezekiel* and another *On the Twelve Minor Prophets* followed. Theodoret's *Commentary on Isaiah,* rediscovered in its entirety and published for the first time in 1932, clearly displays his exegetical method, which avoids the one-sidedness of some of Theodore of Mopsuestia's views and admits allegorical or typological interpretations, in addition to a lucid philological analysis. Theodoret also wrote commentaries on Jeremiah and on the Pauline letters.

Final Stage of Patristic Exegesis

In the West, Gregory the Great and Isidore of Seville (d. 636) are the last fathers of the church. Gregory (d. 604) was an enthusiastic expositor of Scripture who interiorized the legacy of Ambrose, Jerome and Augustine concerning the spiritual sense of Scripture. His monastic piety reflected the medieval hunger for supernatural data in daily life, but his popular narratives continued to diffuse the distinctive principles of Christian ethics proper to the Latin tradition. Isidore of Seville (d. 636) wrote introductions to different biblical books that constituted an encyclopedic collection of data from earlier exegetes and that were popular among medieval scholars. He also wrote a set of homilies on Gospel quotations, limited in their use of allegories and attractive in their simplicity.

In the East, patristic exegesis ended with the creation of a new genre, the catenae, or collections of exegetical excerpts. Procopius of Gaza in Palestine (died c. 526) was the first to produce such a compilation. From one biblical book to another he added, verse by verse, short citations from Philo, Origen, Basil, Theodoret, Cyril and others. Symphonic commentaries of that sort were written in Palestine during the sixth century. The same compilatory technique prospered in Constantinople from the year 700 on. By quoting numerous sources lost in the meantime, the authors of catenae preserved substantial traces of interpretations otherwise unknown, due to Origen, Eusebius, Athanasius, Apollinarius, Didymus, Cyril of Alexandria, Evagrius, Hesychius and Theodore of Mopsuestia. The genre proliferated in the Byzantine world until the twelfth century. Near the end of the eleventh century, Nicetas of Heraclea still fabricated a valuable catena on the Psalms. The last church father in the East, John of Damascus (c. 650-750), a Christian Arab who served under the caliphs before retiring to the monastery of St. Sabbas near Jerusalem, produced a similar compilation *(Sacra Parallela)* of scriptural and patristic quotations. At least thirty-five such catenae survived. But during the Arab conquest in 638 the library of Caesarea was destroyed, and with it the main center of patristic compilations.

In Old Slavonic translation, the legacy of ancient Christian exegetes soon reached new cultural areas north of the Black Sea, and Chrysostom's works would be copied diligently in the monasteries of what would come to be Russia. A similar northerly migration of the traditional interpretation of Scripture occurred in the West, where the Venerable Bede (672-735) engineered almost single-handedly the Northumbrian renaissance of classical and patristic traditions. His commentaries on the Apocalypse, Acts, Luke, Mark and, sometime later, Genesis offer an intricate lacework of patristic quotations comparable only to the illuminated capitals on the front pages of the contemporary manuscripts.

BIBLIOGRAPHY

Works. Standard sources include ACW, ANF, CF, FC, NPNF, PG, PL. T. C. Oden, ed., Ancient Christian Commentary on Scripture (27 vols; Downers Grove, IL: InterVarsity Press, 1998-).

Studies. B. Altaner and A. Stuiber, *Patrologie* (Freiburg: Herder, 1960); A. Di Berardino, ed., *Encyclopedia of the Early Church* (2 vols.; New York: Oxford University Press; Cambridge: James Clarke, 1992); *CHB* 1, 2; F. W. Farrar, *History of Interpretation* (London: Macmillan, 1886); E. Ferguson, ed., *Encyclopedia of Early Christianity* (New York: Garland, 1990); R. M. Grant and D. Tracy, *A Short History of the Interpretation of the Bible* (2d ed.; Minneapolis: Fortress, 1989); C. Kannengiesser, "The Spiritual Message of the Great Fathers" in *Christian Spirituality: Origins to Twelfth Century,* ed. B. McGinn (New York: Crossroad, 1985); J. Quasten, *Patrology* (vols.1-3; Utrecht and Antwerp: Spectrum, 1960), A. Di Berardino, ed., *Patrology* (vol. 4; Westminster, MD: Christian Classics, 1986); M. Simonetti, *Biblical Interpretation in the Early Church: An Historical Introduction to Patristic Exegesis* (Edinburgh: T & T Clark, 1994).

C. KANNENGIESSER

Athanasius *(c. 296-373)*

Athanasius was one of the key ecclesiastical and theological leaders of the fourth century A.D. He played a central role in the fight against the Arians, who held that the Son was different in essence from the Father and that the Son was a created being who had a time of origin. Athanasius consistently defended the Nicene doctrine of *homoousios,* that the Father and Son shared the same essence. This doctrine eventually became the orthodox view of the Trinity. But the question concerning the essence of the Son was not easily settled. It involved intense polemical battles, theological debates and political maneuvers. The Arian controversy was both a hermeneutical battle that focused on the interpretation of several key biblical passages and a political battle embroiled in the machinations of the emperors who followed Constantine. At the center of Athanasius's polemical and theological argumentation was his use and interpretation of Scripture.

Life. Athanasius was born between A.D. 296 and 298. Little is known of his familial or educational background. He was trained in the catechetical school in Alexandria. Gregory of Nazianzus claimed that Athanasius received a brief study of literature and philosophy so that he might not appear unskilled (Gregory of Nazianzus *Oration* 21.5). Athanasius's writings reveal only a cursory knowledge of the Greek classical authors, though he does display a familiarity with rhetorical devices. It does not appear that he received the same type of philological training in text-critical matters that *Origen did. Instead his training included a thorough grounding in Scripture and biblical exegesis. Gregory praises him: "From meditating on every book of the Old and New Testament, with a depth such as none else has applied even to one of them, he grew rich in contemplation, rich in splendor of life" (Gregory of Nazianzus

Oration 21.6). Although this assessment is overly adulatory, there is some truth in it. Athanasius's writings are closely tied to Scripture. He frequently cited and adapted biblical passages, and his own prose is filled with biblical language and imagery.

Athanasius was ordained a deacon by the bishop Alexander around 319. He attended the Council of Nicea in 325 and three years later succeeded Alexander as bishop of Alexandria. His bishopric was opposed from the beginning by both the Arians and the Meletians. As his support from political leaders waxed and waned, Athanasius was forced into exile on five occasions: Trier (July 335 to November 337), Rome (April 339 to October 346), Upper Egypt (twice: February 356 to February 362; October 362 to February 363) and outside Alexandria (October 365 to February 366). Arian leaders such as Eusebius of Nicomedia continued to fight against Athanasius, raising such charges as desecration of holy objects, political treason and even murder. But Athanasius had many supporters both within Alexandria and in the Roman West. He regained his office for the last time in 366 and remained there until his death May 2, 373.

Writings. Athanasius produced some exegetical writings. *Jerome mentions a commentary on the Psalms (Jerome *On Illustrious Men [De Viris Illustribus]* 87), and Photius mentions commentaries on Ecclesiastes and Song of Solomon (*Photius Bibliotheca cod.* 139). Fragments of these commentaries, as well as other exegetical fragments from Genesis, Exodus, Job, Matthew, Luke and 1 Corinthians, have been preserved in catenae, medieval collections of commentaries made by earlier church fathers. Unfortunately the authenticity of most of these fragments is difficult to establish. Athanasius also wrote a letter to Marcellinus on the *Interpretation of the Psalms* in which he speaks of the beauty of the

Psalms and their liturgical use. The surviving evidence from Athanasius's exegetical writings is too superficial and in many cases too suspect to reconstruct his interpretive approach by using this material alone.

Most of Athanasius's writings can be categorized as apologetical, dogmatic, historico-polemical, ascetic or letters. Most were written in the heat of battle with his opponents. In these writings he defends his own actions and beliefs as well as those of other pro-Nicene fathers. He attacks his enemies' actions and false doctrines and expounds correct doctrine. Through it all Athanasius supported his own positions and refuted his opponents by using Scripture. It is these writings that provide the clearest evidence of Athanasius's method of interpretation.

Interpretive Framework. Most of Athanasius's biblical interpretation took place within polemical contexts. The polemical nature of his writings influenced his selection of biblical material and how he cited that material. He used Scripture to serve his larger goal of arguing for his own positions and against those of his opponents. Athanasius rarely cited or interpreted longer passages of Scripture. Most of his citations are single verses or partial verses, and much of his use of Scripture could be described as proof-texting. He cited a passage with little or no interpretation and used it to support his apologetical or theological point as if the relevance of the text were self-evident. Athanasius had a group of passages that he frequently cited in support of his christology. These included passages that indicated unity between the Father and the Son (e.g., Mt 10:40; 11:27; 28:19; Jn 5:17, 23; 10:30, 38; 14:6, 9-10; 1 Cor 8:6), the divinity or unique status of the Son (Mt 16:16; Jn 1:1, 14, 18; 8:58; 10:33; 1 Cor 1:24; 2:8; Phil 2:6-7; Heb 1:2-3; 13:8), or the Son's unique position in comparison with the created order (Jn 1:3; 3:35; 16:15; 17:10; Rom 8:29; Col 1:16-17; Heb 1:4). Often he would list groups of passages in succession without explanation, implying that their application to his

point were obvious (e.g., Athanasius *De Decretis* 13; *Orationes Contra Arianos* 1.12, 59).

The polemical nature of Athanasius's writings also affected the way in which he cited Scripture. He did not appear to be concerned that anyone would compare his citations with biblical manuscripts for accuracy. Added to this is the likelihood that Athanasius cited much of his biblical material from memory, especially when writing during periods of flight or exile when biblical manuscripts might not have been readily available. Since his focus was argumentation rather than exegesis, his writings display great freedom in his citation techniques. He was not tied to a verbatim transmission of the biblical text. He freely adapts his biblical citations through omissions (e.g., Jn 5:39 in *Thirty-Ninth Easter Letter* 6), grammatical changes (e.g., Mt 7:6 in *Apol. Contra Arianos* 11.2), word substitutions (e.g., Mt 22:29 in *Thirty-Ninth Easter Letter* 6), conflations (Lk 21:8 plus Mt 24:4-5; Mk 13:5-6 in *De Decretis* 35), additions (e.g., Mt 12:30 in *Orationes Contra Arianos* 1.1) and in a few cases, even outright inventions of biblical texts (see *Orationes Contra Arianos* 2.16, where he invents a speech of Peter). Athanasius makes no distinctions between instances in which he cites the biblical text "word for word" and those places in which he has made changes. He seldom makes a point from one wording over against another. His writings indicate none of the text-critical concern or acumen of his forebear Origen.

Exegetical Goals and Methods. The polemical contexts of Athanasius's writings also determined his exegetical goals and methods. Athanasius rarely indulged in allegorical interpretation to the excess found in Origen's works. Instead Athanasius sought what he described as the "correct," "right," "true," "religious" or "orthodox" meaning of the passage. On several occasions Athanasius stated that certain biblical passages have a right "meaning" or "sense" (*dianoia;* Athanasius *De Decretis* 13; *Ora-*

tiones Contra Arianos 1.44, 53; 2.1, 44, 77; 3.1, 18, 19, 21, 35). He contrasted this "true sense" of the passage to the Arians' misinterpretation, which was due their heretical "private sense" (see Athanasius *Orationes Contra Arianos* 1.37). Athanasius did not claim that the true meaning of a passage was easily obtained. When he was speaking about the interpretation of Proverbs 8:22, Athanasius said that

since, however, these are proverbs, and it is expressed in the way of proverbs, we must not expound them nakedly in their first sense, but we must inquire into the person, and thus religiously put the sense on it. For what is said in proverbs is not said plainly, but is put forth latently. . . . Therefore it is necessary to unfold the sense of what is said and to seek it as something hidden, and not nakedly to expound as if the meaning were spoken "plainly," lest by a false interpretation we wander from the truth. (Athanasius *Orationes Contra Arianos* 2.44 [NPNF 2 4:372])

For this reason Athanasius emphasized that one must "genuinely apply one's mind to" (Athanasius *De Incarnatione* 56), "study and ponder" (Athanasius *De Decretis* 14) and "scrutinize" (Athanasius *Orationes Contra Arianos* 77) the Scriptures.

Though he did not explicate an exact exegetical methodology, throughout his writings Athanasius did identify at least three requirements for proper interpretation. First, the interpreter must live a pure and virtuous life. He stated:

But for the searching of the Scriptures and true knowledge of them, an honourable life is needed, and a pure soul, and that virtue which is according to Christ; so that the intellect guiding its path by it, may be able to attain what it desires and to comprehend it, in so far as it is accessible to human nature to learn concerning the Word of God. (Athanasius *De Incarnatione* 57 [NPNF 2 4:67])

Using this argument, Athanasius could dismiss the Arians' interpretations because they are ungodly and irreligious people (Athanasius *De Decretis* 17).

Second, the interpreter must consider the context of the passage that is being interpreted (Athanasius *Orationes Contra Arianos* 1.11; 2.7). For Athanasius the true sense of a passage can be found by examining the time, the person(s) and the point or purpose that the biblical author is addressing. He stated that "anyone may find this sense duly given in the divine oracles, who instead of accounting their study a secondary matter, investigates the time and persons and the object, and thus studies and ponders what he reads" (Athanasius *De Decretis* 14 [NPNF 2 4:159]). Elsewhere he explained:

Now it is right and necessary, as in all divine Scripture, so here, faithfully to expound the time which the Apostle wrote, and the person, and the point; lest the reader, from ignorance missing either these or any similar particular, may be wide of the true sense. (Athanasius *Contra Arianos* 1.54 [NPNF 2 4:338])

Thus, according to Athanasius, the right sense of the passage is determined by its context and the intentions of the biblical author. The context includes consideration of such things as the time, person(s) and purpose the biblical author intended in the passage (Athanasius *Orationes Contra Arianos* 2.8).

Third, the interpreter must interpret the biblical passage in light of the entire "scope of Scripture." In his argument against the Arians' interpretation of Proverbs 8:22 he remarked:

we must show from the passage too how greatly they err, not realizing the scope of divine Scripture. . . . But what is well written is ill understood by heretics. If they had understood and grasped the terms in which Christianity is expressed, they would not have called the Lord of glory a creature nor stumbled over what is well written. (Athanasius *Epistula ad Serapionem* 2.7 [Shapland 162-63])

Athanasius spoke of the "scope of faith"

(*Orationes Contra Arianos* 3.28, 35) and the "ecclesiastical scope" (*Orationes Contra Arianos* 3.58) as synonymous with the "scope of Scripture" (*Orationes Contra Arianos* 3.29). In his view the "scope of Scripture" has been faithfully passed down in the teaching of the Fathers and has become the church's rule of faith. The Arians' problem is that they do not understand this "scope of faith," and thus they misinterpret the Scriptures. Athanasius said:

> [The passages] that they now allege from the Gospels, they certainly give an unsound interpretation, we may easily see if we now consider the scope of that faith which we Christians hold, and using it as a rule, apply ourselves, as the Apostle teaches, to the reading of inspired Scripture. For Christ's enemies, being ignorant of this scope, have wandered away from the way of truth . . . (Athanasius *Orationes Contra Arianos* 28 [NPNF 2 4:409])

Thus the Arians misinterpreted Scripture because they do not hold to the church's true teaching.

In describing the "scope of Scripture," Athanasius provided further insight into what he meant by the time, person and purpose of the context.

> Now the scope and character of Holy Scripture, as we have often said, is this—it contains a double account of the Saviour; that he was ever God, and is the Son, being the Father's Word and Radiance and Wisdom; and that afterwards for us He took flesh of a Virgin, Mary Bearer of God, and was made man. And this scope is to be found throughout inspired Scripture . . . (Athanasius *Oratones Contra Arianos* 3.29 [NPNF 2 4:409])

Athanasius's notion of the "double account of the Savior" is further clarified in *Epistula ad Serapionem* 2.7:

> These then are the terms in which we express our faith in Christ: the Son of God, being the Word of God, . . . being the Wisdom and Power of the Father . . . at the end of the ages became man for

our salvation. . . . Being made man, and having fulfilled his human economy, having overthrown and abolished death, the penalty we had incurred, he now sits at the right hand of the Father, being in the Father and the Father in him, as always was and forever is.

Athanasius used the expression "scope of Scripture" and "terms of the Christian faith" synonymously to refer to the theological unity of the entire Bible. He construed this unity christologically, describing it as the Son's preexistence with the Father, the incarnation of the Son for the purpose of the salvation of humanity, and the Son's present glory and union with the Father. When he was interpreting a biblical passage, Athanasius argued that it is imperative that the interpreter consider the "time" (pre-incarnation, incarnation or present glorification), the "person" (the pre-incarnate Son, the incarnate Word or the glorified Son), and the purpose (salvation) to which the biblical author is referring. Thus the interpreter must interpret the passage in light of the entire scriptural, ecclesiastical scope of faith.

Several biblical passages were problematic for the Nicene christology of *homoousios*. The Arians used these passages to support their claims that the Son was a "creature" who had a time of origin. Athanasius felt compelled to provide the correct, true, religious meaning of these passages. The bulk of his three *Orations Against the Arians* disputes the Arians' interpretation of Psalm 45:7-8 (*Orationes Contra Arianos* 1.46-52), Proverbs 8:22 (in *Orationes Contra Arianos* 2.18-82), Acts 2:36 (in *Orationes Contra Arianos* 2.11-18), Philippians 2:9-10 (in *Orationes Contra Arianos* 1.37-45), Hebrews 1:4 (in *Orationes Contra Arianos* 1.53-63) and Hebrews 3:2 (in *Orationes Contra Arianos* 2.1-11). Athanasius's primary argument is that the Arians have not considered the correct time, person and purpose of the passage. For example, the Arians interpreted the clause "who was faithful to him who made him" in Hebrews 3:2 as proof that the Word of God was created. Athanasius argued that this verse is not speaking about the time before creation or the Word's essence but rather is speaking about the incarnation (Athanasius *Orationes Contra Arianos* 2.7). Similarly the Arians interpreted the clause "The Lord created me at the beginning of his work" in Proverbs 8:22 as stating that the Son, the Wisdom of God, was a creature and had a time of origin. Once again Athanasius claimed that a correct interpretation of this verse would acknowledge that it is speaking about the Incarnation, not the essence of the Word or the eternal generation of the Word by the Father (Athanasius *Orationes Contra Arianos* 2.45; cf. *De Decretis* 13—14).

Significance. Athanasius's interpretation of Scripture reflected his desire to examine the context of a passage, to consider authorial intent and to permit Scripture to interpret Scripture. Yet it would be incorrect to characterize him as a modern grammatical-historical exegete. Athanasius construed context and authorial intent much more broadly than do modern interpreters. For example, a modern critic would recognize that the author of Proverbs 8:22 had no knowledge of or interest in christology. Nor was Athanasius encumbered by the actual wording of Scripture to the extent that modern interpreters are. The umbrella concept of the "scope of Scripture" permitted him to castigate the Arians for their use of nonscriptural terms (Athanasius *De Decretis* 18) and to warn his readers of the Arians' misuse of scriptural language (Athanasius *Epistula Encyclica ad Episcopos Aegypti et Libyae* 8—9, 11; *Orationes Contra Arianos* 1.8) and at the same time defend the Nicene Council's use of the nonscriptural phrases "from the essence" *(ek tou ousios)* and "of the same essence" *(homoousios)* because they "contain the sense of the Scriptures" (Athanasius *De Decretis* 21; cf. 19, 31—32). Athanasius's insistence that the Scripture cannot contradict itself (Athanasius *Nineteenth Easter Letter* 3) and that correct interpretation

demands consideration of all Scripture remain important guidelines for interpreters.

BIBLIOGRAPHY

Works. Athanasius NPNF 2d series, vol. 4; *Athanasius: The Life of Antony and the Letter to Marcellinus,* trans. R. Gregg (New York: Paulist, 1980); idem, *"Athanasius Contra Gentes": Introduction, Translation and Commentary,* ed. E. Meijering (Philosophia Patrum 7; Leiden: E. J. Brill, 1984); idem, *Select Treatises of St. Athanasius in Controversy with the Arians,* trans. J. Newman (London: Pickering, 1881); idem, *The Letters of Athanasius Concerning the Holy Spirit,* trans. C. Shapland (London: Epworth, 1951); idem, *The Resurrection Letters, St. Athanasius, Bishop of Alexandria from A.D. 328-373,* trans. J. Sparks (Nashville: Thomas Nelson, 1979); idem, *Athanasius: "Contra Gentes" and "De Incarnatione,"* ed. and trans. R. Thomson (Oxford: Clarendon, 1971).

Studies. D. Arnold, *The Early Episcopal Career of Athanasius of Alexandria* (Notre Dame, IN: University of Notre Dame Press, 1991); M. Barnes and D. Williams, eds., *Arianism after Arius: Essays on the Development of the Fourth-Century Trinitarian Conflicts* (Edinburgh: T & T Clark, 1993); T. Barnes, *Athanasius and Constantius: Theology and Politics in the Constantinian Empire* (Cambridge, MA: Harvard University Press, 1993); D. Brakke, *Athanasius and the Politics of Asceticism* (Oxford: Oxford University Press, 1995); J. J. Brogan, "The Text of the Gospels in the Writings of Athanasius" (Ph.D. diss., Duke University, 1997); A. Clayton, "The Orthodox Recovery of a Heretical Proof-Text: Athanasius of Alexandria's Interpretation of Proverbs 8:22-30 in Conflict with the Arians"(Ph.D. diss., Southern Methodist University, 1988); J. Ernest, "Athanasius of Alexandria: The Scope of Scripture in Polemical and Pastoral Context," *VC* 47 (1993) 341-62; R. Gregg and R. Groh, *Early Arianism: A View of Salvation* (Philadelphia: Fortress, 1981); M. Handspicker, "Athanasius on Tradition and Scripture," *ANQ* 3 (1962) 13-29; R. P. C. Hanson, *The Search for the Christian Doctrine of God: The Arian Controversy, 318-391 C.E.* (Edinburgh: T & T Clark, 1988); C. Kannengiesser, *Arius and Athanasius: Two Alexandrian Theologians* (Hampshire: Variorum, 1991); idem, "La bible et la crise arienne" in *Le Monde grec ancien et la Bible,* ed. C. Mondesert (Paris: Beauchesne, 1984); idem, *Holy Scripture and Hellenistic Her-*

meneutics in Alexandrian Christology: The Arian Crisis (Berkeley: Center for Hermeneutical Studies, 1982); T. Kopacek, *A History of Neo-Arianism* (Cambridge, MA: Philadelphia Patristic Foundation, 1979); A. Pettersen, *Athanasius* (Harrisburg, PA: Morehouse, 1995); T. Pollard, "Exegesis of the Scripture and the Arian Controversy," *BJRL* 41 (1959) 414-29; J. Quasten, *Patrology*, 3: *The Golden Age of Greek Patristic Literature* (Utrecht: Spectrum, 1966); H.-J. Sieben, "Hermeneutique de l'exegese dogmatique d'Athanase" in *Politique et theologie chez Athanase d'Alexandrie,* ed. C. Kannegiesser (Paris: Beauchesne, 1974); G. C. Stead, "Rhetorical Method in Athanasius," *VC* 30 (1976) 121-37.

J. J. Brogan

Augustine of Hippo *(354-430)*

In analyzing Augustine's place in the long line of biblical interpreters, it must be noted that the Bible helped Augustine to interpret himself as much as he became an interpreter of the Bible. Therefore a biographical outline is an indispensable starting point for understanding how Augustine's inner journey became interwoven with his personal appropriation of Scripture.

From Birth to Baptism. In *Confessions* 3.4.8 Augustine observes that he had the Gospels at hand since childhood under the religious influence of his Christian mother, Monica. He lost his father when he was fifteen years of age, a circumstance that perhaps explains the way in which he would later welcome the authority of Scripture, warranted for him by the church. At nineteen his reading of a lost Ciceronian pamphlet entitled *Hortensius* induced an inner contest between Cicero and the Bible. His enthusiastic response to the Ciceronian text was an indication of his need for spiritual values, but when he turned to the Bible (missing any reference to Christ, as he notes in *Confessions* 3.8.9), he quickly gave up in disgust because it so lacked the Ciceronian quality of style.

As a result of that failure, Augustine committed himself for the next nine years to the sect of the Manicheans, who introduced him to the study of the book of Genesis, albeit with their own mythological bias. They also introduced him to their peculiar use of Pauline letters (Augustine *Confessions* 3.7.2). When he freed himself from Manichean influence after 383, one is not surprised to see the newly baptized Augustine focus again on Genesis and Paul, while adding a personal predilection for the Psalms.

Fascinated by the sermons of Bishop Ambrose in Milan, Augustine entered upon a religious crisis that would decide his destiny (Augustine *Confessions* 6.11.8, 30). After his baptism by Ambrose during the Easter vigil of 384, Augustine was advised by the bishop to read Isaiah and the Psalms. Again the unfamiliar style of the prophet proved a stumbling block. Augustine would never recover from that initial reluctance, whereas the book of Psalms was to become the marrow of his Christian identity. It is noteworthy that his friend Possidius, writing the biographical outline of Augustine's career immediately after the latter's death in 430, would mention large inscriptions of verses from the Psalms fixed on the walls of the bedroom where the bishop of Hippo was dying.

At the time of his baptism Augustine had taken leave from his official position as a teacher in Milan. The influence of the Platonic school of thought, flourishing in a local circle befriended by Bishop Ambrose, remained strong in him. He would spend much time and intellectual energy during the three years following his baptism in clarifying the philosophical principles emanating from that circle, such as the spiritual and immortal nature of the soul, the vital need for a transcendent fulfillment of human life, the negative reality of evil, and the ethical requirements for overcoming it. Even more so, from his contacts with Platonic thought Augustine assimilated the alphabet of his spiritual discourse about the human longing for God. That Christianized form of mystical Platonism would haunt his creative mind ten years later, when he would try to compose his first theoretical essay on the interpretation of Scripture, *On Christian Doctrine.*

Early Exegetical Writings. In the meantime, first in the retreat of Thagaste, where he settled with his son and some friends after his return to Africa, and later in Hippo, where he found himself obliged to accept a priestly ordination in 391, Augustine had written his first essays on Genesis (*De Genesi Adversus Manichaeos Libri II* [389]; *De Genesi ad Litteram Liber Imperfectus* [393], also against the Manicheans). He also preached on Genesis (Augustine *Sermons* 1 and 2) between 391 and 393. He exercised his skills in a first exegetical essay of modest proportions, the *De Sermone Domini in Monte Libri II* (392), as well as in a series of extended notes on Pauline letters not initially destined for publication, in 394, the *Expositio Quorundam Propositionum ex Epistola Pauli ad Romanos,* the *Epistolae ad Romanos Inchoata Expositio,* and the *Epistolae ad Galatas Expositionis Liber Unus,* of which he proudly notes at the end of his life that it was his first attempt to produce a commentary "not by isolated quotations, in omitting some parts, but continuous and complete" (Augustine *Revisions [Retractationes]* 1.23.1).

To the senior priest Simplicianus, who had been instrumental in Milan as his spiritual mentor, he addressed similar notes, *De Diuersis Quaestionibus ad Simplicianum Libri II,* after Simplicianus had been installed as replacement for Ambrose, who died on April 4, 397. In all these early biblical writings the original genius of Augustinian exegesis makes a powerful statement. Augustine assumes the task of interpreting Scripture with questions and reactions of such a density in his mind that his whole explanation of Genesis or Paul was focused exclusively on these questions. He never indulged in the technicalities of academic exegesis. His exegesis was born out of his innermost commitment as a believer and would continue to be driven by his passionate involvement in the service of the church community.

The real difficulty faced by the newly appointed (395 or 396) bishop in the first years of his ministry was the discovery of the inadequacy of his rhetorical culture for a proper explanation of the sacred text. He became aware of being called upon to exercise leadership in the African church without having yet acquired the facility to give a full account of the divine revelation hidden in the biblical writings. He knew that his grasp of hermeneutical method, while fairly sophisticated on the level of high culture in Italy, was as yet inadequate to treat properly the intricacies of obscure passages in the Bible. Buoyed up with idealistic dedication, Augustine, now in his early forties, began *On Christian Doctrine* in the spring of 397 with the expectation that his educated self-awareness would enable him to face the challenge of articulating the methodological problems linked with a coherent interpretation of Scripture. After an intense burst of creative energy Augustine gave up in the middle of a sentence in book 3 (Augustine *On Christian Doctrine* 3.25.36). This writing was to be continued thirty years later, in 427, when the elderly Augustine wrote some *Revisions* of his works. The fact that the hermeneutical treatise *On Christian Doctrine* was the only one then completed, among several unfinished essays, may well underline the special challenge imposed by it on Augustine.

Three Masterpieces. As yet unable to articulate at length an interpretative theory about the Bible, Augustine decided to appropriate the Scriptures more intimately in focusing on his inner self. He decided to promote that self as the theme of a literary project that would allow him to try a practical exercise of biblical hermeneutics. Written between 397 and 400, the *Confessions* recounts Augustine's story through a lacework of explicit or implicit quotations (biblical experts have noted seventeen hundred), mainly from his favorite sacred books, the Psalms and the letters of Paul. In books 11-13 the work ends with a remarkable exegesis of Genesis 1, full of the same intensely subjective concentration that informed the earlier books. The author cannot hide his satisfaction in overcoming the deficiencies of his earlier anti-Manichean attempts to comment on Genesis.

A much more ambitious step was taken by Augustine as interpreter of Scripture in the episcopal office of Hippo when he conceived his first and only theological synthesis, *The Trinity (De Trinitate)*. In this enormous project, culminating in as many as fifteen books when the work was edited around 420, Augustine started (399-400) by composing books 1-4, which develop the biblical foundations of trinitarian faith.

At the same time Augustine wrote a more apologetic and more circumstantial essay in four books on the concordance of the four canonical Gospels, the *De Consensu Evangelistarum Libri IV*. Soon he felt ready to face once again the challenge of theoretical hermeneutics, the reason for his interrupting *On Christian Doctrine* in 397. With a stubborn determination he engaged in the most difficult piece of exegetical writing he could imagine, *A Literal Commentary on Genesis (De Genesi ad Litteram)*, which would include twelve books and keep him busy until 415. At least from 401 to 402, he composed the first nine books, commenting on the biblical text verse by verse until Genesis 3:24. This was initially a private enterprise, as he invented step by step a new way of exposing the relevance of sacred Scripture. He progressed slowly, taking all the time needed for submitting, to the literal content of each biblical phrase, the various questions that phrase brought to his mind. His commentary was literal because it was to the letter of the sacred text that he devoted himself with his learned background and inquisitive passion, with existential hopes and anxieties, increasingly with an acknowledged ignorance of which he became more and more aware as he persevered in that experiment. Even in turning the work into a well-written book for an inner circle of educated friends, Augustine persisted in composing that unusual commentary on Genesis for himself. The multivoiced debate that he conducted in a frenzy of questioning throughout the commentary reflected the main philosophical trends of his time. The author gave himself a clear proof that he had overcome his intellectual paralysis in front of scriptural obscurities. He emerged from his hermeneutical experiment matured by "learned ignorance," *docta ignorantia*, as he would call it in 411 (Augustine *Letter* 130).

Preached Interpretations. On a different level of activity, from 396 on Augustine preached at least twice a week, sometimes more often. Therefore it is not surprising that his major exegetical contribution would be channeled through his preaching. His *Commentary on John (Tractatus in Euangelium Ioannis)* derived from a series of 124 sermons *(tractatus)*, some preached, others only written, dating from different periods in his episcopal career. The *Commentary on the First Epistle of John (Tractatus in Epistolam Ioannis ad Parthos)* was initially a set of ten sermons delivered at Eastertime, sometime around 415. *The Exposition of the Psalms (Enarrationes super Psalmos)* started when Augustine was a priest in 392. He completed it thirty years later and produced the only interpretation of the whole Psalter dating from ancient Christianity. In it he offered a perfect expression of his biblical spirituality. Approximately five hundred sermons survive of the thousands left behind by Augustine at his death. Most of them were only drafted and unedited, and they perished. The old bishop himself selected a collection of 50 sermons on the Old Testament and secured copies of at least 133 sermons on the New Testament (all of them being now made available in the vivid translation of E. Hill, published by the Augustinian Heritage Institute).

Other Interpretative Writings. Among Augustine's *Letters*, amounting to approximately three hundred (the latest were discovered in the 1970s), those addressed to *Jerome are of special interest, as is *Letter* 140 from the year 412 or so, addressed to Honoratus and edited with the title "On the Grace of the New Testament." In his apologetic works such as the monumental *City of God,* many biblical themes are quoted and interpreted according to the issues at stake. The *City of God (De Civitate Dei)* was written between 413, when Augustine was fifty-nine years old, and 426, when he was seventy-two, as the first Latin Christian attempt to produce a global philosophy of history. Many pages of the work are saturated with biblical quotations, most often from Pauline letters. In this respect one of Augustine's passing remarks has a particular significance: "I see that I must omit many of the statements of the gospels and epistles . . . but I can on no account omit what the Apostle Paul says" (Augustine *City of God* 20.19). The emblematic figures of the biblical salvation stories from Abraham to antichrist are seen as decisive for humanity as such. The optimistic apologist retraces the biblical narratives with the sole purpose of introducing a coherent logic into an incoherent history. If scriptural obscurity puts him to the test, he does not blink, keeping in mind the hard lesson of his hermeneutical experiment in *De Genesi ad Litteram:* "Though the obscurity of the divine word has certainly this advantage, that it causes many opinions about the truth to be started and discussed, each reader seeing some fresh meaning in it, yet what ever is said to be meant by an obscure passage should be either confirmed by the testimony of obvious facts, or should be asserted in other and less ambiguous texts. This obscurity is beneficial" (Augustine *De Genesi* 21.19).

At an unknown date the bishop wrote a short *Pamphlet Against the Jews (Tractatus Aduersus Iudaeos),* in which he discusses Romans 11:22. From around 419 date the two impressive collections of working "Notes on the Heptateuch" (*Quaestionum in Heptateuchum Libri VII* and *Locutionum in Heptateuchum Libri VII).* In the volume of *Questions,* the first chapter of the first book, dedicated to Genesis, discusses no fewer than 173 points for investigation. Some marginal notes collected by others

are handed down under the title *Adnotationes in Iob Liber I.*.

Around 420, informed about a tract circulating in Carthage, the aging bishop found it necessary to publish a treatise in two books against Marcionite ideas, *Contra Aduersarium Legis et Prophetarum Libri II.* He ended his publications as a biblical and pastoral interpreter around 427 in producing a *Mirror of Sacred Scripture (Speculum de Scriptura Sacra),* in which he presented an assortment of moral precepts selected from the Old and New Testaments, a last initiative that seems to anticipate the genre of catenae, typical of the final stage in the history of Greek patristic literature.

Basic Paradigms and Principles of Interpretation. Augustine's interpretation of Scripture was too deeply part of his personal journey for resting on a paradigmatic basis other than the one provided by his inner quest. First, as witnessed by the *Confessions* in their conception and central themes, he was a self-centered intellectual whose theoretical interests could not detach themselves from subjective concerns. His lifelong journey was a lonely one, despite his constant need to be surrounded by friends. From the moment when he publicly identified himself as a Christian convert, his spontaneous use of Scripture was determined by his individual odyssey. Unlike *Origen of Alexandria and other leading exegetes in the Greek-speaking churches of antiquity, Augustine had not been immersed in the Bible from childhood within a traditional Christian community. He had to endure crisis after crisis before finding peace at the feet of Ambrose, who from the pulpit of Milan opened to Augustine a first personal access to Scripture. Even after his baptism Augustine deliberately chose an individualistic path in the quasi-solitude of Thagaste in order to enter more personally into the universe of the Bible, so foreign to his education and his taste. His exegesis would become influential for that reason: the task of interpreting Scripture meant for Augustine a total investment of his educated self with all its resources and individual limitations. In short, the first paradigm of Augustine's exegesis is personal passion.

Another difference between Augustine and his Greek predecessors or his contemporaries in the office of interpreter of Scripture has to deal with their respective attitudes toward secular culture. More than his Eastern counterparts, Augustine, all too soon invested as a bishop with the duty of delivering authorized comments on Scripture, found it normal to engage in that commentary with the mental habits, the methodology and the rich memory of his secular culture. Ambrose's influence on him had been decisive because the bishop of Milan had brilliantly demonstrated the possibility of a rational exegesis of the Old Testament embedded in contemporary culture.

One major characteristic of the Ambrosian approach to Scripture was similar to the treatment imposed by non-Christian interpreters on Homer's legacy. Ambrose considered the whole body of biblical writings as a consistent message, best understood by letting one assertion of the sacred authors explain another. Thus the indisputable authority of divine Scripture as received in the church opened for Ambrose, and then for Augustine, an immense space for allegorical intertextuality, in direct parallel with the literary criticism on ancient sources practiced among their pagan contemporaries. A second paradigm regulating Augustine's interpretation of Scripture is that the expositor of God's message in the Bible is consistently challenged to rewrite the whole of the cultural discourse to which he or she belongs.

Third, it was of fundamental importance for Augustine that, in the rhetorical culture of late antiquity, the written revelation of God in the Bible called for an equally written commentary. To become a biblical interpreter needed the full strength and endurance of a born writer. With that imperative in mind Augustine stole hours from the night to add to the few hours spared from his pastoral schedule in pro-

ducing the ninety-three literary works, embracing 232 books enumerated in chronological order in his *Revisions*. Thus in the act of interpreting God's word, Augustine created a new quality of Ciceronian style and became one of the founders of Christian literature for the Latin Middle Ages to come. The quality of style was new in the sense that style itself was taken out of the courtrooms and the academic circles of ancient Rome where Cicero had experienced the end of the Republic half a century before Christ, and it was introduced into the new worldwide community of faith. For the bishop, a church calling itself "catholic," "in principle universal," replaced a locally determined forensic space and a private circle of students.

With the teaching mandate and the moral leadership of his episcopal office, his speech was freely directed to fellow citizens of all ages and social conditions and could thus focus on their existential needs in the name of God's written commandments. Augustine would never miss an opportunity to give his oral injunctions the revised, written form proper to secure their broader circulation and stable reception. The limits of space and time no longer inhibited the religious imagination of the church leader. A feeling of God's universal relevance in scriptural terms pervaded his exegesis. The destiny of humanity as such, the beginning and end of the world, the ultimate questions of human consciousness, as well as universal history, became familiar themes of his biblical interpretation. In sharing with church audiences the meaning of innumerable passages in Scripture, Augustine's vision embraced the whole mystery of salvation. Beyond the limits of the city or of the local church, that vision reached out to the transcendent realm of divine realities.

Principles of Interpretation. A first principle of Augustinian exegesis is to limit the textual basis of biblical studies to the Latin translations of the Septuagint and to the Septuagint itself. It is a linguistic principle biased by cultural provincialism. Augustine would remain allergic to

Jerome's enthusiasm for the "Hebraic truth" of Scripture. As a believer Augustine needed to identify himself within a cultural continuity. He experienced receiving God's biblical revelation through the channels of his own civilization. Ambrose had convinced him of the overwhelming richness of meaning deriving from the Septuagint as understood by Philo and Origen. As much as Cyprian of Carthage and Hilary of Poitiers in an earlier generation, Ambrose was a living proof that the Latin genius adequately translated the interpretive tradition of the Greek-speaking churches. Proof of his adherence to this principle is the copy of the Septuagint that Augustine regularly consulted in order to correct or to evaluate its Latin versions.

A second principle of Augustine's exegesis was to read the Scripture as it was received in the church. *"Tolle, lege"* ("take up and read," Augustine *Confessions* 8.29), the mysterious voice in the garden urged, immediately to be followed by the visitor from Trier ordering Augustine, in his confused anguish, to encounter the sacred text directly. At Augustine's baptism Ambrose and Simplicianus encouraged him to familiarize himself with the Psalms, to venture if possible into Isaiah, and to deepen further his knowledge of Paul. A decade later Augustine was persevering in the task undertaken before he was a priest, which consisted in systematically learning from older interpreters how to handle the sacred writings. For Augustine the hermeneutical problem was never to invent his own rules of interpretation; it was to assimilate personally all the traditional rules in the church.

Thus one finds frequently in his works the kind of christocentric typology popularized in the churches by the admirers and disciples of Origen, who had himself been inspired by Paul's example (Gal 4:24; Rom 4—6). Old Testament narratives and oracles found a new life for Augustine in being referred to Jesus and the Gospels. The letter of the sacred text, with its immediate sense mentioning a date, a person or a circumstance carries on God's message; at the same time it has a spiritual sense. One has only to read the opening paragraph of the first *Tractatus in Euangelium Ioannis:* the vibrant preacher rests his whole case on the distinction between the carnal, or literal, and the spiritual sense of John 1:1 on which he focuses. For Augustine, interpreting Scripture in the persona of a church leader, "spiritual" meant essentially ecclesial. Interpretation was exercised in conformity with the rule of faith and in view of promoting the distinctive values of church experience. Always prompt to perceive a spiritual reality suggested by the sacred words, Augustine was inspired by his rich notion of the church.

His personal culture makes an obvious mark when speculation on numbers is at stake, and his polemical inclination as a formidable controversialist explains his obsession with given verses of Scripture, but as a whole Augustine's interpretation of the Bible harmonizes well with the most traditional patristic exegesis, though one cannot classify him in a specific school of exegesis like those of Alexandria or Antioch. Similarly, one hardly can compare him with other Latin interpreters, the closest being Ambrose of Milan, as he transcends their ranks by his unique creativity.

A final word is in order about *On Christian Doctrine,* the writing that frames Augustine's career as an independent interpreter of Scripture, from its first part (Augustine *On Christian Doctrine* 1—2.25.35) dating from 397 to its final section (Augustine *On Christian Doctrine* 3.36—4) approximately three years before his death. It offers a vivid spectrum of his hermeneutics. With the idealistic vision that had guided the auditor of Ambrose's exegetical homilies, book 1 directs the interpretive task toward the secret recesses of Scripture. Book 2 builds up a general theory of the symbolic language proper to Scripture, a theory in which Augustine combines his newly assimilated Christian doctrine with traditional rules of rhetorical scholarship. Book 3 aims at specifying the rules to be applied in cases of Scripture's unsolved ambiguities, but it halts in failure for thirty years, until the author finally integrates Tyconius's *Book of Rules* into his own exposition. The old bishop's critical awareness still remained sharp as he carefully adjusted the Tyconian citations to his own interpretive concerns. In particular one notices how he changed most of the scriptural proofs invoked by Tyconius for each of the seven rules. The notion of these *regulae* becomes Augustinian in *On Christian Doctrine*, in line with the rhetorical teaching in secular academia, whereas Tyconius had insisted on rules as *regulae mysticae*, that is, mystic structures of the sacred text itself, calling for their own proper initiation. Hence the short prologue of the *Book of Rules* announces "keys" and "windows" for opening the mind of the Christian readers in readiness to perceive the hidden mysteries of Scripture.

Tyconius's essay, written shortly before Augustine's return to Africa, was the first systematic treatise ever written by a Christian on biblical hermeneutics. However, Augustine persistently ignored the sacral character of the hermeneutics that had been developed in the African church—for him a provincial tradition tainted by Donatism. In a letter to Bishop Aurelius of Carthage (397), Augustine admitted to being at a loss with regard to that treatise, and Tyconius's work was powerful enough soon to force him to interrupt *On Christian Doctrine*. By 427 the bishop had enough pastoral authority and exegetical experience for giving the Tyconian citation the needed correctness when summarizing it for the benefit of his readers. He assimilated Tyconius's rules to the Ciceronian precepts familiar to him, as if his African predecessor had claimed to invent the regulae by himself, when the earlier writer had explicitly taken the more humble role of only introducing the reader to these rules. At all events, Augustine's rectified application of the Tyconian rules, inspired by his own hermeneutical attitude, was consistent with book 4, which brings the treatise *On Chris-*

tian Doctrine to a conclusion. In book 4 he gives practical and doctrinal directions for preaching on sacred Scripture. The significance of such an ending should not be underestimated. It was fitting that from his decades-long exercise of pastoral care and biblical preaching Augustine found the inspiration for completing an essay that he had started in the more abstract enthusiasm of his early dedication to the ideals of biblical exegesis.

BIBLIOGRAPHY

Works. The Works of Saint Augustine: A Translation for the Twenty-First Century: 3.1-4, Sermons; 1.5, The Trinity, Augustine, trans. E. Hill, and ed. J. E. Rotella (Augustinian Heritage Institute; Brooklyn, NY: New City Press, 1990). *Studies.* D. W. A. Arnold and P. Bright, eds., *"De Doctrina Christiana": A Classic of Western Culture* (Notre Dame, IN: University of Notre Dame Press, 1995); W. S. Babcock, *Tyconius: The Book of Rules* (SBL Texts and Translations 31, Early Christian Literature Series 7; Atlanta: Scholars Press, 1989); G. Bonner, "Augustine as Biblical Scholar" in *CHB* 1:541-62; P. Bright, *The Book of Rules of Tyconius: Its Purpose and Inner Logic* (Notre Dame, IN: University of Notre Dame Press, 1988); C. Kannengiesser, "Local Setting and Motivation of De doctrina christiana" in *Augustine: Presbyter Sum*, ed. J. T. Lienhard, E. C. Muller and R. J. Teske (Collectanea Augustiniana; New York: Peter Lang, 1993) 331-40; C. Kannengiesser and P. Bright, *A Conflict of Christian Hermeneutics in Roman Africa: Tyconius and Augustine* (58th Colloquy, Center for Hermeneutical Studies in Hellenistic and Modern Culture; Berkeley, 1989); M. R. Miles, "Augustine" in *Encyclopedia of Early Christianity*, ed. E. Ferguson (New York: Garland, 1990) 121-26; J. Quasten, *Patrology* (4 vols.; Westminster, MD: Christian Classics, 1986) 4:342-462; A. Trapè, "Augustine of Hippo" in *Encyclopedia of the Early Church*, ed. A. Di Berardino (Cambridge: James Clarke, 1992) 97-101.   C. Kannengiesser

Chrysostom, John *(c. 347-407)*

John, deacon and priest at Antioch and later patriarch of Constantinople, bears the surname Chrysostom, "golden mouth," in tribute to his great oratorical powers. An impassioned preacher and pastor, Chrysostom was one of the most prolific, important and influential exegetes in the early church.

Context. Reared in Antioch, John received a classical education that was to lead him to the profession of law. Though the question has been debated, there is some strong evidence to suggest that he was a pupil of the orator Libanius, a judgment that the rhetorical character of Chrysostom's writings does nothing to diminish. Legend has it that when on his deathbed Libanius was asked who should be his successor, he replied: "John, if only the Christians hadn't stolen him from us."

John's other teacher, whose influence had proved ultimately decisive upon him, was the theologian Diodore of Tarsus, who also taught such notables as Chrysostom's contemporary and friend, *Theodore, later bishop of Mopsuestia. From Diodore Chrysostom learned an intense focus on Scripture and the orientation toward exegesis of the Antiochene school.

Already as a young man John had been drawn to the monastic disciplines, though in deference to the wishes of his mother, Anthusa, he practiced them at home until her death. Subsequently he trained in the solitary life as a hermit. According to one of his biographers, Palladius, during two years spent living in a cave Chrysostom memorized the entire New Testament, thus laying the groundwork for his later vocation as a biblical commentator and preacher. His health severely compromised by the physical hardships of those years, Chrysostom returned to Antioch, where he served as deacon (381-386) and then priest (from 386). During this Antiochene period (386-398) he wrote and delivered a large bulk of the corpus of his exegetical homilies. In 398, with great reluctance, Chrysostom was forced to accept the post of patriarch of Constantinople. During the last nine years of his life, at Constantinople and in banishments and the exile that led to his death in 407, Chrysostom was involved in fierce controversies with ecclesiastical and imperial powers, particularly the empress Eudoxia, for his attempts to reform that city and its leadership.

Work. To understand Chrysostom as a biblical interpreter one must always keep in mind his primary role as a preacher. As a priest in Antioch and later bishop in Constantinople, Chrysostom preached on Sundays and on the many feast days that already dotted the liturgical calendar in the fourth century. During Lent and other seasons he sometimes preached daily. His expositions of Scripture always have in mind and specifically address a congregation of the faithful, whom he seeks to confront with the meaning of the written word and spur to action. Though we do not know the precise mechanics of the composition and publication of Chrysostom's homilies (What was the role of stenographers? How much did Chrysostom edit his homilies after delivery?), their occasional references to incidental events that occurred during the delivery of the homily, such as the lighting of the candles, the applause of the congregation, or a rejoinder to those who complained that his previous day's sermon was too long or too offensive, bring vividly to mind their real pastoral setting. We see this also in the frequent and pointed references sprinkled throughout the homilies to life in Antioch and Constantinople and to the behavior of his congregation. Though not all the homilies contain such situation-specific comments, and some may have been written primarily for publication (see Baur, 1:222-23), all have the edification of a church audience as their chief purpose.

Chrysostom's corpus of exegetical writings contains both homily sets, which treat a particular biblical book seriatim and were delivered over an extended period of time (which in many cases can be specifically dated; see Bonsdorff; Quasten, 3:433-51), and occasional homilies on single passages. The homily sets are sometimes called commentaries, although the manuscript tradition applies the two terms somewhat indiscriminately. Extant are homily series on the Gospels of Matthew and John, the

Acts of the Apostles, and on all of the fourteen New Testament letters that claim Pauline authorship (including Hebrews). Only fragments remain of Chrysostom's homilies on the Catholic Epistles (James, 1-2 Peter and 1 John).

While among Old Testament books only Genesis is covered in full (and there is a second set of homilies on Gen 1—3), we possess his homilies on more than a third of the Psalms (Ps 4—12; 43—49; 108—17; 119—50), on Kings (five treating Hannah and three on David and Saul), on Isaiah 6 and Isaiah 1—8, and fragments on Jeremiah, Daniel, Proverbs and Job preserved in the catenae (anthologies of selected portions of patristic exegesis collected and handed down in the medieval church). Occasional homilies by Chrysostom on individual passages from both Testaments have also been preserved (Ps 48:17; 115:1-3; 145:2; Is 6:1; 45:7; Jer 10:23; Mt 7:14; 18:23; 26:39; Jn 5:19; Acts 9:1; Rom 5:3; 8:28; 12:20; 16:3; 1 Cor 7:2; 7:39; 10:1; 11:19; 15:28; 2 Cor 4:13; 11:1; Gal 2:11; Phil 1:18; 1 Tim 5:9; 2 Tim 3:1).

Chrysostom's homilies tend to follow a common structure. The homily sets treating a whole biblical book usually begin with a homily entitled *Hypothesis* (Latin *Argumentum*), in which Chrysostom sets forth the historical setting of the book, including discussion of the author, the addressees (especially in the case of the Pauline letters), salient features of the context, and the major themes and plan of the book. In the rest of the homilies on a given book Chrysostom will begin with a reading and detailed exposition of the next passage in the sequence of the work, often with comments linking the present homily with previous ones to establish both the literary and homiletical contexts. His exegetical treatments focus in detail on the flow and logic of the passage, on key terms, and on the historical meaning of central concepts at the time of the work's composition (though also sometimes with an eye to their role in current theological controversies). After the exegetical portion, most of

Chrysostom's homilies turn to an exhortatory or moralistic section, in which he directly addresses his audience and engages in paraenesis that prods them to certain behaviors mandated by the gospel (especially almsgiving and greater devotion to things spiritual) and away from aspects of their life and urban culture that he considers reprehensible (such as the theater and the racetrack). Sometimes these moral exhortations emerge naturally from the exegetical first half of the homily; at other times the connection is oblique at best.

Texts and Editions. All of Chrysostom's homilies were written in Greek. The Greek texts are most readily available in J. P. Migne, *Patrologiae Cursus Completus: Series Graeca* (see the exact references to individual works in *PGL* [xvii-xviii] or the standard reference work *Clavis Patrum Graecorum* [Geerard, 2:491-672]). Critical editions of the Greek text of the homilies on portions of Job and Isaiah (two sets) can be found, along with French translations, in the series Sources chrétiennes (SC). A superior critical edition of the Greek text of the homilies on the Pauline letters can be found in the nineteenth-century edition of F. Field.

The sixty-seven homilies on Genesis have been translated in the Fathers of the Church series (FC) by R. C. Hill. One of the sets of homilies on Isaiah has been rendered into English by D. A. Garrett. All of Chrysostom's homily sets on the New Testament books are translated into English in the standard Nicene and Post-Nicene Fathers (NPNF) series, which revises the Oxford Fathers of the Church translations. A more contemporary English translation of the eighty-eight homilies on the Gospel According to John by Sister Thomas Aquinas Goggin may be found in the Fathers of the Church (FC) series. The other works, which are chiefly occasional homilies on individual passages and fragments, have not yet been translated into English.

Although the homiletical texts are of primary importance, Chrysostom also engaged in biblical interpretation in all the other writings that comprise his voluminous corpus, particularly the treatises and letters. This is so because the Bible, which he cited readily and richly, is the main source of Chrysostom's theological and pastoral reflections. Those seeking Chrysostom's treatment of a particular passage may be assisted in accessing his full corpus of writings by R. A. Krupp.

Because of Chrysostom's great popularity and the subsequent wide dissemination of his writings, many works were falsely attributed to him in an effort to attain broad readership. These texts, identified by critical scholarship as *spuria*, include a large number of exegetical homilies treating single verses (see *PGL* [xix]; de Aldama).

Analysis. Chrysostom's exegesis of the Bible, in line with the Antiochene school of which his writings are the best representative, has been characterized as logical, literal, sober, restrained, commonsensical, grammatical, detailed and historical. This "matter-of-fact exposition of the text" (Pelikan, 19) is the hallmark of the Antiochene school, in distinction from its rival, the Alexandrian school, which emphasized the allegorical, the symbolic, the spiritual meaning of the text. Though the split was not absolute, and one can see each school as inheriting a side of the single legacy of *Origen (Chase, 5), still the major prevailing emphasis of the Antiochenes on the plain sense of the text in its literary and historical contexts (understood within certain prescribed cultural and theological parameters) is evident in Chrysostom's writings.

For example, in one of his homilies on the opening of the Acts of the Apostles, Chrysostom sets forth the major historical assumptions of his exegesis: in order to understand a text we need to know who wrote it, when he wrote it, why he wrote it and why it has this title and addressee (Chrysostom *Hom. in Princ. Ac.* 1.3 [PG 51:71-72]). Elsewhere, in dealing with the Pauline epistles, Chrysostom maintains a principle that contemporary historical critics unanimously employ (though with simi-

lar limits of historical knowledge as Chrysostom had): that in order to understand Paul's letters one must be attentive to their relative chronology and their place in the context of Paul's life and mission (Chrysostom *Hom. in Rom.* Argumentum 1 [PG 60:392]). He invokes the same rule for the teachings of Jesus (Chrysostom *Hom. in Rom.* 16:3 2.2 [PG 51:197]).

Two hermeneutical principles, which make up a theology of Scripture, provide the conceptual background from which Chrysostom proceeds in his interpretation. *Synkatabasis,* traditionally translated "condescension" (though more recently the translation "considerateness" has been proposed [R. C. Hill, 74:17-18]), summarizes Chrysostom's theology of biblical inspiration. In the biblical writings God chose to speak to human beings through human language and to tailor that speech to the level of comprehension of which human beings were capable at the time. God inspired the human authors of the Bible, but in God's considerateness of human limitations God's revelation was "conditioned by the instruments through which it came . . . [and] by the powers of those to whom it was given" (Chase, 42). The locus of this revelation was the biblical writers, who were inspired by God or by the Holy Spirit (see, for example, Chrysostom *Hom. in Rom.* 16:3 1.1 [PG 51:187], of Paul, and Chrysostom *Hom. in 1 Cor.* 7:39 2 [PG 51:220], of the prophet Malachi). Though the principle of *synkatabasis* is applicable to both Testaments, it has a particular role in regard to the Old Testament, for it supports a doctrine of progressive revelation that makes sense of God's total plan in history. This progressive revelation in history extends also to the act of reading, in which the God who exactly inspired the sacred author also inspires the interpreter to pay reverent attention to all aspects of the text. The inspiration that the reader receives is mediated by the author of the text, who, as the words are read, is actually present, speaking with the reader (see R. C. Hill, 74:17, on Moses, and Mitchell, 18-28, on

Paul). Chrysostom's hermeneutical approach places a high emphasis upon the human author of the text in cooperation with divine inspiration, for he regards all Scripture as a "relic" of the saints of old, which mediates their presence and gives access to their example of virtuous, godly living. This hermeneutic is well entrenched in the conceptions of the emergent cult of the saints in the fourth century (see Brown).

The consequence of Chrysostom's doctrine of inspiration as divine "considerateness" is a high estimate of the success of this divine initiative. Thus the Bible may be relied upon for its *akribeia,* its "accuracy," or "precision," in all its details. Because it is God who stands behind Scripture, every comment, every word, every syllable of the Bible is intended and has pointed meaning. Thus Chrysostom repeatedly counsels his hearers against "running past" any single detail in the text, for in his estimation all the Bible's words reflect the precision of the God who stands behind them. This assessment of the origin and nature of Scripture entails a correlative mandate for all biblical interpretation: "[one must] respond to the *akribeia* of the Scriptural accounts with a like *akribeia* in our study of them; precision and care must mark the approach of any interpreter of what God has deigned to speak to us" (R. Hill, 35). Chrysostom's patient, detailed and literal exegesis is rooted in these two principles of *synkatabasis* and *akribeia,* for, as he frequently insists, "there is nothing superfluous, nothing added at random in the Scriptures" (Chrysostom *Hom. in Rom.* 31.1 [PG 60:667]).

In addition to these principles, Chrysostom expressed his hermeneutical approach to Scripture by means of some powerful, recurrent metaphors. The Bible is a treasure hidden in a field that is waiting to be dug up (Chrysostom *Hom. in Ac.* 9:1 4.3 [PG 51:148]); a well with no bottom (Chrysostom *Hom. in Ac.* 19.5 [PG 60:156]); a sea upon which the experienced sailor may sail from earth to heaven (Chrysostom *Hom.*

in Ac. 55.3 [PG 60:383- 84]); a meadow of flowers that upon attendance can release the fragrance of the Spirit that nourishes the soul (*De Statuis* 1.1 [PG 49:18]). The Pauline letters are an ark, even greater than Noah's, that carries all humanity to salvation (Chrysostom *Hom. De Laudibus S. Pauli* 1.5 [SC 300:118-20]). Elsewhere the Pauline corpus and all of Scripture are described as a medicine chest containing the requisite prescriptions for all diseases of the human soul, which must be carefully and selectively applied (Chrysostom *De Sacerdotio* 4.7 [PG 48:670]; *Hom. in Gen.* 29.1-2 [PG 53:261-62]; *Hom. in Jo.* 37.1; 83.3 [PG 59:207, 459]).

The hallmark of his homilies is Chrysostom's unabashed devotion to Scripture: "It is a great thing, this reading of the Scriptures!" (Chrysostom *Hom. in Ac.* 19.4 [PG 60:155]). Above all he sought by his example to inspire in his hearers a like enthusiasm. Thus he was furious at those who ignored the Bible or who did not apply themselves rigorously to its comprehension. At times his frustration boils over into castigation, as when he complained that though people can tell you every detail about horse racing and choral dances, "they do not even know the number of Paul's letters, or, if they do know the number, cannot answer if you ask them the names of the cities which received them" (Chrysostom *Hom. in Rom* 16:3 1.1 [PG 51:188]). Chrysostom's love for the Bible extended also to its authors and central characters, about whom he wrote with genuine admiration and affection as living characters ("saints") who inhabited his life. This was particularly true of the apostle Paul, who was the object of special devotion on Chrysostom's part, which he urged his congregation to share (see Mitchell). Thus we see in Chrysostom not only the biblical expositor but also the pastor, the teacher of Scripture and of the necessary virtues for faithful reading and appropriation by all believers.

Chrysostom's historical and literal approach to the Bible does not, however, make him a modern historical critic. For example, Chrysostom's interpretation of the Old Testament suffers the severe limitation that he did not know Hebrew. Though he at times quoted "those who know the Hebrew tongue" to explain a phrase or to debunk an interpretation he deemed faulty, his exegesis was of the Greek text, and he found its significance and built lofty castles of meaning upon the words and letters of the Greek. Chrysostom's interpretation of the Old Testament is also, like that of most early church commentators, vividly christological in its interest and typological in its approach. More valuable exegetically are Chrysostom's New Testament homilies, especially those on the Pauline letters, which combine a careful attention to the historical context in which each letter was written with a judicious appreciation for the logical and rhetorical progression of Paul's arguments. His homilies on the Gospels somewhat uneasily combine his acute and honest attention to the divergences among the four accounts (which he takes to be sure proof of their independent testimony, and consequent historical reliability) and his need to assert over and over that despite those differences the four Gospels proclaim a unified message. (Chrysostom *Hom. in Mt.* 1.2 [PG 57.16]

His exegesis, though not predominantly apologetic, at times is much influenced by contemporary dogmatic and ecclesiastical struggles. Chrysostom does not shy away from rebuking and refuting heretical interpretations (e.g., Marcionite, Arian, Manichean) along the way. He is supremely confident that because "the Scriptures . . . are simple and true, it is easy to judge. If someone agrees with the Scriptures, she or he is a Christian. If someone conflicts with the Scriptures, that person is far away from the standard of faith" (Chrysostom *Hom. in Ac.* 34.4 [PG 60:244]).

The major theme of Chrysostom's homilies, which emerges abundantly, even redundantly, in their exhortative conclusions, is the pursuit of genuine Christian living, which for him in his historical context meant striving for social justice for the poor through almsgiving and turning one's back on material goods to strive for spiritual virtues. He advocated the widespread cultivation of monastic virtues for all Christians, pointedly including his lay audience. For Chrysostom biblical interpretation was at the service of his catechetical ministry and was a tool to inspire changed behavior.

Significance. Because he was spared the later accusations of heresy that befell other prominent members of the Antiochene school and led to the suppression of their writings (such as his teacher, Diodore, and his contemporary, Theodore of Mopsuestia), John Chrysostom's well-preserved and extensive corpus constitutes the best example we have of Antiochene exegesis, a key movement in early church biblical scholarship. In particular Chrysostom's homilies contain the most complete exposition of the Pauline epistles that we have from the early church. Chrysostom's writings are of fundamental importance for the history of biblical interpretation, both for what they tell us of patristic exegesis and because of their pervasive influence on subsequent interpreters. Since his preaching was loved and admired during his own lifetime and immediately thereafter, the bulk of his writings gained immediate circulation. Within decades of his death the task of translating selected works into Latin had begun. Through Latin translations and Greek anthologies of patristic exegesis (the catenae, or chains of exegetical passages), Chrysostom's biblical interpretations became one of the main sources for medieval exegesis. Thomas *Aquinas is said to have exclaimed that he preferred Chrysostom's homilies on the Gospel According to Matthew, in the Latin translation of Burgundio of Pisa, to the entire city of Paris (Smalley, 337).

Chrysostom's homilies were also a major influence on exegesis in the Reformation era. Martin *Luther often quoted Chrysostom with approval, especially in his lectures on Hebrews and Romans, though according to an anecdote preserved in *Ta-*

ble Talk (*Tischreden* no. 252), he complained that Chrysostom was "only a gossip!" John *Calvin quite frequently referred to Chrysostom as a major exegetical authority, especially in his commentaries on the Pauline corpus. Calvin's appreciation of Chrysostom can be traced directly, since his own copies of Chrysostom's writings, along with his marginal notes and underlining, are extant and have been published (Ganoczy and Müller).

Even modern scholars give Chrysostom's homilies on the New Testament writings high marks, as his major biographer C. Baur noted in 1929: "Chrysostom's commentaries on the New Testament are considered, even in our own day, from a literary and exegetical point of view, the best and most useful that the patristic age has bequeathed to us" (Baur, 1:322). That judgment is no less true at the end of the twentieth century, when contemporary critical scholarship, especially of the New Testament, can find in Chrysostom a rich exegetical resource for his attention to Greek terms, styles, rhetorical and literary forms, and historical matters. Though at times in the history of biblical interpretation Chrysostom was deemed faulty for his focus on the literal meaning of the text and concomitant lack of philosophical or metaphysical interest, in our day his historical and literary approach, together with his prevailing interest in social justice, seems again at home.

BIBLIOGRAPHY

Works. J. Chrysostom, PG vols. 47-63; NPNF vols. 10-14; J. A. de Aldama, *Repertorium Pseudo-Chrysostomicum* (Documents, études et répertoires 10; Paris: Éditions du centre national de la recherche scientifique, 1965); J. Chrysostom, *Jean Chrysostome: Homélies sur Ozias,* trans. J. Dumortier (SC 277; Paris: Éditions du Cerf, 1981); idem, *Jean Chrysostome: Commentaire sur Isaïe,* trans. J. Dumortier and A. Liefooghe (SC 304; Paris: Éditions du Cerf, 1983); idem, *Sancti Patri Nostri Joannis Chrysostomi Interpretatio Omnium Epistolarum Paulinarum per Homilas Facta,* ed., F. Field (7 vols.; Oxford: Parker, 1845-1862); idem, *Clavis Patrum Graecorum,* ed., M. Geerard (5 vols.; Corpus Christianorum; Turnhout: Brepols, 1974-1987) 2:491-672; idem, *Saint John Chrysostom: Commentary on Saint John the Apostle and Evangelist,* trans. T. A. Goggin (FC; New York: Fathers of the Church, 1957-1960) vols. 33, 41; idem, *St. John Chrysostom: Homilies on Genesis,* trans. R. C. Hill (FC; Washington, DC: Catholic University of America Press, 1986-1992) vols. 74, 82, 87; idem, *Jean Chrysostome: Commentaire sur Job,* trans. H. Sorlin and L. Neyrand, (2 vols.; SC 346, 348; Paris: Éditions du Cerf, 1988).

Studies. C. Baur, *John Chrysostom and His Time* (2 vols.; Westminster, MD: Newman, 1959); M. von Bonsdorff, *Zur Predigttätigkeit des Johannes Chrysostomus: Biographisch-chronologische Studien über seine Homilienserien zu neutestamentlichen Büchern* (Dissertation, Universität Helsingfors, 1922); P. Brown, *The Cult of the Saints: Its Rise and Function in Latin Christianity* (Haskell Lectures on History of Religions, n.s. 2; Chicago: University of Chicago, 1981); F. H. Chase, *Chrysostom: A Study in the History of Biblical Interpretation* (Cambridge: Deighton, Bell, & Co., 1887); A. Ganoczy and K. Müller, *Calvins handschriftliche Annotationen zu Chrysostomus: Ein Beitrag zur Hermeneutik Calvins* (Veröffentlichungen des Instituts für Europäische Geschichte Mainz 102; Wiesbaden: Steiner, 1982); D. A. Garrett, *An Analysis of the Hermeneutics of John Chrysostom's Commentary on Isaiah 1—8 with an English Translation* (SBEC 12; Lewiston, NY: Edwin Mellen, 1992); P. Gorday, *Principles of Patristic Exegesis: Romans 9—11 in Origen, John Chrysostom and Augustine* (New York: Edwin Mellen, 1983); R. Greer, *The Captain of Our Salvation: A Study in the Patristic Exegesis of Hebrews* (BGBE 15; Tübingen: J. C. B. Mohr/Paul Siebeck, 1973); R. Hill, "*Akribeia:* A Principle of Chrysostom's Exegesis," *Coll* 14 (1981) 32-36; J. N. D. Kelly, *Golden Mouth: The Story of John Chrysostom—Ascetic, Preacher, Bishop* (Ithaca, NY: Cornell University Press, 1995); R. A. Krupp, *Saint John Chrysostom: A Scripture Index* (New York: University Press of America, 1984); M. M. Mitchell, "The Archetypal Image: John Chrysostom's Portraits of Paul," *JR* 75 (1995) 15-43; J. Pelikan, *The Preaching of Chrysostom: Homilies on the Sermon on the Mount* (Philadelphia: Fortress, 1967); J. Quasten, *Patrology* (4 vols.; Westminster, MD: Newman, 1960) 3:424-82; B. Smalley, *The Study of the Bible in the Middle Ages* (2d ed.; Oxford: Blackwell, 1952).

M. M. Mitchell

Clement of Alexandria
(c. 150-c. 215)

Clement of Alexandria, or Titus Flavius Clemens, was born around 150, but little is known about the details of his life. He probably studied first in Athens and then traveled in Italy, Syria and Palestine to seek further instruction. Eventually he came to Alexandria in Egypt, where, Eusebius reports, he succeeded Pantaenus as teacher in the school for catechumens around 200. Clement died shortly before 215 in Cappadocia in Asia Minor, where he went to avoid persecution in Egypt under the emperor Septimius Severus.

Little is known about the so-called catechetical school of Alexandria where *Origen later gained renown. Clement may have been responsible for training new Christians in the rudiments of the faith in preparation for baptism, a process that could often take as many as three years to complete. It is also likely that with his erudition and philosophical training, Clement served as a teacher for those Christians who wished to pursue advanced study in Christian teachings. Whatever form the school in Alexandria took, those associated with Christian education in that urban center followed in the tradition of Philo, a Jewish scholar who was known for his allegorical interpretation.

Alexandria was a large port city and a hub of intellectual life where the study of philosophy, history and literature flourished. It was the location of a famous library and a center of manuscript production where many copies of biblical and other books were made. There was a large Jewish population in the city, and several Egyptian and Greek gods remained popular in Clement's day. In the context of this diverse metropolis Clement developed a system of thought that sought to resolve the meaning of Christian truth in light of other philosophical ideas.

Writings. The bulk of Clement's writing that we have consists of three major works, the first two of which were intended to be part of a trilogy. The first is called the *Protrepticus,* or *Exhortation to the Greeks,* in which Clement portrays Christianity as the true philosophy. In the second work, the *Paedagogus,* or *Tutor,* Christ the Logos is portrayed as a teacher who instructs converts on how to live as Christians. The text gives specific directions for the Christian life, including treatments of clothing, morality, and even table etiquette. Scholars question whether the third major extant work is what Clement intended as the continuation of the first two works. It seems that he had intended to write a volume called the *Teacher,* which would have given instruction to more advanced Christians. Instead we have a work called the *Stromata,* or *Miscellanies* (literally "carpets," perhaps better understood as "patchwork"), which is an assortment of notes compiled into eight books.

In addition to these three major works, there are other, smaller texts. In *Who Is the Rich Man That Is Saved?* Clement gives an exposition of Mark 10:17-31, in which he avoids a strictly literal interpretation in order to make applications for Christians of his day. Other exegetical works on the Old and New Testaments that demonstrate his allegorical approach to Scripture are described by the early Christian historian Eusebius, but the work itself has been lost. Some traces of other lost works exist only in fragments, which can only hint at the full body of Clement's writing.

It is notable that a figure who is regarded as significant in the development of an Alexandrian style of interpretation of the Bible has left us no complete biblical commentaries. What we know about Clement's methods of interpretation arise from comments he makes about Scripture and the kinds of examples of interpretation that he gives in his works. These examples, however, are representative of the kind of interpretation that was done in the Alexandrian context.

Scripture. Although most of Clement's writing does not set out to provide a running commentary on the biblical text, it is nonetheless steeped in the biblical text. He cites often from both the Old and New Testaments and has a high estimation of the authority of Scripture. This derives from his understanding that Scripture conveys a direct message from God—that the voice of God speaks through the biblical text. Clement calls the Scriptures inspired and holy, citing 1 Timothy 3:16-17. Scripture demonstrates its divine source by its ability to effect change on the hearer: "For truly holy are those letters that sanctify and deify" (Clement *Protrepticus* 9 [ANF 2:196]). At all times the voice of the Lord is speaking through Scripture for our benefit, providing guidance, illumination and exhortation. While Clement has a clear notion of the text as inspired, the individual words are seen as sacred not in themselves through their specific phrasing or diction but because they reflect God's teaching. The voice of God is present in all of Scripture, but not through dictation. The meaning behind the words, which is delivered through human language, is how Clement comprehends the voice of God.

God's voice speaks consistently through all of Scripture, but the voice finds different forms of expression in various parts of Scripture. The Bible is not a monologue, for Clement recognizes that the voice of God speaks through different human writers. God teaches in the Scriptures in different ways at different times. Thus, when a writer such as the apostle Paul expresses his inspired message in the writing of an epistle, he "becomes the interpreter of the divine voice" (Clement *Protrepticus* 9 [ANF 2:196]).

Biblical Interpretation. A correct understanding of the inspired nature of the text will allow one to interpret the text with discernment. The interpreter must look beyond the letters themselves to hear the voice behind the literal text. Clement compares the simple reading according to the letter with a more sophisticated approach to the meaning of the text, which he describes as reading according to the syllables. This means that a more accurate interpretation of Scripture comes from seeing each text in its place within God's full message.

The differences in how the voice communicates are most notable in the comparison of the Old and New Testaments. While God's voice in the Old Testament differs from the explicit proclamation of Christ in the New Testament, the same voice speaks in both. Unlike writers such as Marcion, who sought to divorce the personalities of the deities of the two Testaments as irreconcilable, Clement maintained that there is a unified message from one divine source. Clement defined this unity through his theology of the Logos, which brings together the philosophical concept of universal reason and the biblical notion of Christ as the divine Word. The Gospel of John tells of the incarnation of the Word, who was with God from the beginning of creation and whose voice is one with the creator God. Clement identifies the Logos as the same one who gave the law through Moses and spoke through the prophets. Thus the Logos may be found throughout the Old Testament writings.

Since the voice speaks through different times and experiences before and after the Incarnation, the Old and New Testaments need to be read with different interpretative strategies. What is plainly revealed in the New Testament may appear in symbolic language in the Old. The law, says Clement, is the shadow of the truth. Thus an allegorical reading, in which things are seen to stand for something else, is a way of leading from the shadowy language to the truth behind it. In its use of figurative language or forms of speech that are not to be taken literally in order to express an idea, Scripture is like other works of literature. Clement points out that the books of other cultures have also spoken of divine things in "veiled" language and "delivered the truth in enigmas, and symbols, and allegories, and metaphors, and such like tropes" (Clement *Stromata* 5.4 [ANF 2:449]). Clement's reliance on allegory comes from the belief that the same Logos gives order to the universe and meaning to biblical language.

All Scripture bears God's full meaning, yet it may be read in different senses by those with different levels of understanding. For example, Clement mentions four senses in which the law is taken. The law gives a literal precept for right conduct, exhibits a type or symbol or utters a prophecy (Clement *Stromata* 1.28 [FC 85:153]). The Christian who knows the revelation of the incarnate Christ has the insight to find the deeper meanings of the law. The voice of Christ can then be found in words that may not be easily recognized as speaking about Christ.

An example is found in the writings of Paul. Paul's theology depends upon the foundation of the Old Testament, but at the same time, says Clement, its full meaning can be known through Paul's christological reading of the law. "For faith in Christ and the knowledge of the Gospel are the explanation and fulfillment of the law" (Clement *Stromata* 4.21 [ANF 2:434]). By Christ's appearance is the Old Testament expounded. The apostle himself demonstrates the kind of interpretation that Clement describes.

The way that the meaning of the text is expressed in language is not always to be apprehended clearly by all. Just as the parables spoken by Jesus were not clear to his followers without further explanation, so the teachings of the Old Testament are also parabolic, according to Clement. Clement defines a parable as "a narration based on some subject which is not the principal subject, but similar to the principal subject, and leading one who understands to what is the true and principal thing" (Clement *Stromata* 6.15 [ANF 2:509]). Such teachings are not meant to be clear to the multitudes.

The Scripture is not written merely for the sake of beautiful language, and Clement gives reasons why the meaning of Scripture is hidden to some people. The first reason is that the unclear figurative language will encourage those who read it to ask questions. More central to Clement's

view of the text is his point that the truth is not open to all but is for those who have been initiated into knowledge and seek the truth through love. He adds a third reason: that if the text were plain for all to see, those who took in another sense what is necessary for salvation might be harmed by it.

Like the meaning of Scripture, which is a message from God, the ability to interpret that meaning is a gift from God. The "unwritten rendering of the written" text has been handed down, inscribed by God on the hearts of some people (Clement *Stromata* 6.15 [ANF 2:511]; see also *Stromata* 6.7 [ANF 2:494]). In describing this separate gift of knowledge about the meaning of Scripture, Clement uses the word *gnostic* to identify the one who has received this knowledge. By so doing he rejects those commonly known as Gnostics (specifically the followers of Basilides and Valentinus) who claim to have a secret gnosis or knowledge that will save them. For Clement the true gnostic is a spiritual Christian.

Only the gnostic (an advanced disciple of the Spirit), having received wisdom from the Holy Spirit, is able to understand the obscure and enigmatic parts of Scripture. God's teachings are intelligible to the gnostics, for whom they appear as clear as icy hail, while they remain as opaque as coal to most people (Clement *Stromata* 6.15 [ANF 2:507]). While other believers may see the foundation of faith in the Scripture when it is clearly expressed, the gnostic understands the elaboration and adornment of a symbolic structure built upon this foundation. The ability to advance further in expounding the truth of the difficult parts of Scripture is like a craft practiced by these disciples. This ability to understand parables and enigmas is advanced training beyond what the common Christian learns about the faith.

From his own advanced education Clement gained an appreciation for the benefit that such study can bring to the biblical interpreter's task. Unlike some early Christian writers who were suspicious of secular learning or competing philosophies, Clement found in various fields of study a wealth of knowledge to aid the gnostic's reading of the Scriptures. Figurative language may be more easily understood with the information gathered from geometry, music and other sciences (Clement *Stromata* 6.10-11 [ANF 2:498-502]). Those who have studied these subjects will be able to know the meaning of the texts that refer more obscurely to things such as stars and numbers. In a discussion of the Ten Commandments the number symbolism is treated at length. For example, the two tables of law signify creation, that is, heaven and earth, or the two covenants. The commandment to rest on the seventh day leads to an exposition of the prevalence of the number seven in heavenly bodies, such as the phases of the moon, and in the seven stages in a human life.

While some persons may object that the sciences are human teaching and not the source of divine truth, Clement responds that one who is holy will be able to use such knowledge rightly. Clement gives an allegorical illustration of the usefulness of education from Scripture. Sarah, who represents wisdom, had not produced a child. She entrusted her husband, Abraham, who represents faith, to her maidservant Hagar, who was from Egypt and as an outsider stood for secular education. Therefore, explains Clement, it is possible to go through a secular education before coming to wisdom with the fruits of that knowledge (Clement *Stromata* 1.5 [FC 85:44]).

Although gnosis unlocks the enigmas of the text, Clement warns that this does not give license to the reader to assign arbitrary meanings to difficult passages. Ambiguous meanings are problems that must be solved by listening for the true voice in Scripture. He is concerned about those who manipulate ambiguous expressions in order to force their own wrong ideas. He complains that heretics quote from Scripture by selecting only those parts that suit them or by quoting out of context. They are, according to Clement, using only the words and not the sense of the text. One way to ensure that the true sense of the text has been found is to compare what is read with what is stated plainly elsewhere in Scripture.

Clement recognizes that there are limits to the utility of human knowledge. To learning and study must be added wisdom. The enigmatic passages of the text are there not only to test the linguistic knowledge of the reader but also to obscure a meaning that can be heard only by those with spiritual ears to hear. The kind of learning that comes from the Spirit begins with catechetical instruction, faith and baptism. Those who have been initiated and baptized into the faith become disciples who are schooled in both knowledge and discipline. The gnostic has learned to find in Scripture both the demonstration of truth and training in discipline. Thus the two sources of sin, ignorance and inability to act rightly, are remedied by Scripture.

Clement demonstrates his method of interpretation in the short treatise entitled *Who Is the Rich Man That Is Saved?* in which he finds a practical message in the story of Mark 10:17-31 for the Christians of Alexandria. At the beginning of the third century, the church was experiencing growth and diversity, incorporating more Christians from wealthier segments of society. People were questioning what it meant to be faithful adherents to the teachings of Jesus in a thriving metropolitan center. Jesus' words recorded to the rich young ruler made some people wonder whether their wealth would hinder them from receiving salvation.

Clement's exposition of the text hinges on his view of the text as divine teaching. Jesus' specific words to one person can reveal a more general message for all Christians, but they must not be too tied to the literal text. Clement acknowledges that the parallel passages in the other Gospels do vary in detail, but in what is most important—the essence of Christ's teaching—the Gospel accounts are in agreement. Jesus "teaches nothing in a merely human way, but teaches all things to His own with divine and mystic wisdom, we must not listen to His utterances carnally; but with due investigation and intelligence must search out and learn the meaning hidden in them" (Clement *Who Is the Rich Man That Is Saved?* 5 [ANF 2:592]). Even though the words in the passage may seem to be plain in their meaning, Clement says, the abundance of wisdom in them requires more careful interpretation to get at the fullness of the message. More attention must be applied to discern Christ's intent and the hidden, unspoken meaning of his words.

The story is to be taken figuratively. The talk of wealth should not distract us from seeing that the passage is really about the condition of the soul. The young man had progressed only so far as to obey the law and needed further change. According to Clement, Jesus did not ask the man to sell his material possessions but to rid his soul of his desires for wealth. Clement points out that true wealth of the soul comes from obedience to God and a pure heart. With such spiritual wealth, one will be able to handle material matters appropriately. Giving practical advice to his own audience, Clement explains that Christians should not dispose of their wealth totally, but they should use it to serve God and benefit those in need.

Significance. Clement remains one of the major representatives of the Alexandrian style of exegesis in the early church. In his efforts to unlock the symbolic language of Scripture he was less systematic but also less rigid than was his follower Origen. He recognized the danger in isolating words or phrases from their context and using them as biblical evidence against those who held contradictory theological views. It must be conceded that Clement himself seems guilty at times of this selectivity. Nevertheless he strongly upheld the unity of Scripture, and his work was the product of careful and thorough investigation, even leading him to secular branches of study to inform his theology. He was able to reconcile a conviction of the truth of Christianity with a willingness to recognize

truth in other philosophies. From his Alexandrian milieu, he demonstrates for us an appreciation of both the power and the limitations of language.

BIBLIOGRAPHY
Works. Clement, *Christ the Educator,* FC 23; idem, *Protrepticus,* ANF 2; idem, *Stromata: 1-8,* ANF 2; *Stromata* 1-8, FC 85; idem, *Who Is the Rich Man That Is Saved?* ANF 2; *Fathers of the Second Century* ANF 2.
  Studies. H. Chadwick, *Early Christian Thought and the Classical Tradition* (Oxford: Clarendon, 1966); J. Daniélou, "Typologie et allégorie chez Clément d'Alexandrie" in *Studia Patristica* IV (Berlin: Akademie Verlag, 1961) 50-57; D. Dawson, *Allegorical Readers and Cultural Revision in Ancient Alexandria* (Berkeley: University of California Press, 1992); J. Ferguson, *Clement of Alexandria* (New York: Twayne, 1974); A. Méhat, "Clement d'Alexandrie et les sens de l'Écriture" in *Epektasis, Mélanges J. Daniélou* (Paris: Beauchesne, 1972) 355-65; M. Simonetti, *Biblical Interpretation in the Early Church* (Edinburgh: T & T Clark, 1994).   A. B. Wylie

Irenaeus *(fl. c. 180)*

Irenaeus was an ecclesiastical writer of the late second century and the bishop of Lyons (Lugdunum), a Roman colony located at the confluence of the Rhone and Saône rivers that was the governmental and transport center of the three Gauls. The Christian community there, with an outpost at Vienne, may have been the first church to be established in these territories conquered by Julius Caesar.

One of the two fairly certain dates in the life of Irenaeus is the year 177, when the church at Lyons was subjected to a bitter persecution (reported in a letter that was sent to fellow Christians in Asia Minor; for the text, see Eusebius *Ecclesiastical History* 5.1-2). In the course of the persecution, the bishop, Pothinus, was martyred, and the presbyter Irenaeus, who was on an official visit to the Roman church, eventually succeeded him.

Like most of the members of the church

at Lyons, however, Irenaeus was not a native of the city, which was founded in 43 B.C., but an immigrant from Asia Minor who counted Latin a barbarian tongue. He reports (Irenaeus *Against Heresies* 3.3.4) that in his youth he had caught sight of Polycarp, the bishop of Smyrna, whose martyrdom is dated around 156. Irenaeus was probably a native of Smyrna, perhaps born in 140 or a bit later. He wrote a letter to Victor, the bishop of Rome, in 190, on behalf of Quartodecimans (Christians who observed the Christian Passover on the same day as the Jewish Passover). He probably died sometime in the next decade.

Writings. Eusebius gives a careful if rambling account of Irenaeus's writings. Of those he names, however, only two can be read today. The first, and the one Irenaeus would have regarded as his magnum opus, was titled *Exposure and Overthrow of the Pseudo-Knowledge (tou pseudōnymou gnōseōs;* cf. 1 Tim 6:20) but is more commonly referred to as his treatise *Against Heresies.* It is an attack on Christian Gnosticism, primarily of the Valentinian brand, and on Marcion, whom Irenaeus associated with such Gnostics. Written in five books, the last three of which are formally devoted to argumentative scriptural exegesis, this work has come down to us in a complete Latin translation, which was made not too long after *Against Heresies* was first circulated. The original Greek text is known only in part, that is, as it is quoted in later authors. There are also fairly extensive Syriac and Armenian fragments, the existence of which suggests that the work was widely read in the course of the first four or five centuries.

The second work is one whose title has long been known from a reference made to it by Eusebius (*Ecclesiastical History* 5.26.1): *Proof of the Apostolic Preaching.* The work itself, however, first became available when an Armenian manuscript containing it was edited in 1907 (*Texte und Untersuchungen* 31.1). This has the form of a catechetical instruction expounding the tradition—what Irenaeus elsewhere

calls "the rule of truth"—that the church passed on to new believers in their instruction for baptism. There is no doubt, however, that this book too, which traces the history of salvation from creation through the work of Christ, is written with the problem of heresy in mind and hence with a view to establishing the credentials of the church's contemporary message.

In the *Proof* Irenaeus expounds the sense of both the Christian and the Mosaic dispensations by reference to texts of the "prophets," of the Jewish Scriptures as represented by the Septuagint. These for him were and remained the Scriptures par excellence, and much of the argument of *Against Heresies,* in particular of books 3 and 4, is devoted to controverting the Valentinian thesis that the God of Moses, David and the other prophets, the fashioner and ruler of this cosmos, is other than and inferior to the God and Father of Jesus Christ. In order to establish this thesis persuasively, however, Irenaeus appealed to the testimony of the apostles and of the words of the Lord, in order to show that they acknowledged only one God and identified God with the Creator figure named in Genesis 1.

Canon. Irenaeus belonged to the Asian tradition that emphatically counted Paul among the apostles and, like the church of Rome, declined to see any inconsistency between the Pauline tradition and that associated with the name of Peter. His list of apostolic writings, therefore, included not only four Gospels (Mark's conveying the testimony of Peter; Luke's, that of Paul; cf. Irenaeus *Against Heresies* 3.3.1-2) but also the Pauline corpus (including the Pastoral Epistles but not Hebrews), as well as the Apocalypse, the Acts of the Apostles, and in all probability 1 John and 1 Peter. His opponents would surely have taken exception to some of the writings in this list: Acts and the Apocalypse almost certainly. It is doubtful, however, whether the Valentinians, as distinct from followers of Marcion, would have taken offense at the works named in his list of Gospels, and they would have applauded his loyalty to Paul, even if they had little use for the Pastoral Epistles (which had little use for them). Irenaeus would not have thought of himself as an innovator in the matter of the proper list of apostolic books, nor did his Valentinian opponents deny the authority of those to which he principally appealed. Nevertheless his use of them in *Against Heresies* to establish and defend the true sense of the older Scriptures is something of an innovation; and it helps to explain why it is he who first begins to quote the apostolic writings with formulas customarily employed to cite Scripture ("It is written" or "the Spirit says").

Exegesis. It is sometimes asserted that Irenaeus repudiated the allegorical exegesis typical of his Valentinian opponents. It is certain that he derided and repudiated their "inverse exemplarism" (F. Sagnard) that made the events recorded in the Gospels secondary reflections of goings-on in the realm of Light, the Fullness. Furthermore, it was his view that the prophets—a category that for him included Abraham, Moses and David as well as the usual list of major and minor prophets—saw, though in the form of visions, "the dispensations and the mysteries through which humanity should afterwards see God" (Irenaeus *Against Heresies* 4.20.10). Nevertheless Irenaeus himself employed typology regularly and enthusiastically (as when he argues that in the events of the exodus "our affairs were being rehearsed, the Word of God at that time prefiguring what was to be," *Proof* 77) and even a sort of allegory (as when in the same place he insists that the "twelve springs" of Numbers 33:9 represent the twelve apostles), so that events and phenomena of the Old Covenant as he portrays them seem to have those of the New as their originals (not just their fulfillments), even as Christ was for him the original of Adam.

Irenaeus's difficulty with his opponents' exegesis, then, was not that it was figural or spiritual but that the correspondences they discerned were false because they assumed the reality of a supreme Deity and an over-world that were unknown to the Scriptures and contrary to them. For example, they assumed that the Scriptures were talking—obscurely, to be sure—about "the mystery of the Fullness," when in fact it was clear to anyone who could read that the Scriptures never intimate that alleged mystery. Irenaeus agrees that the books of the Bible can be and often are obscure and that there are many passages whose interpretation is uncertain. He thinks, however, that in dealing with such passages one must always read them in the light of the plot or (Greek) *hypothesis* that is evident in the many passages whose meaning is plain—the *hypothesis* that is also stated in the church's "rule of truth" (i.e., its elementary catechesis, which asserts that there is one God, who sent his Son and Word to become incarnate and to originate a new life for humanity by pouring out the divine Spirit on all flesh). It is his opponents' worldview and not their exegetical method that Irenaeus systematically repudiates.

The source of Irenaeus's understanding of the church's rule or norm of faith is, therefore, those passages in the Jewish and Christian Scriptures that seemed to him straightforward and plain, of which some spoke to him with special persuasiveness: the Genesis narrative of creation, for example, or the opening verses of John's Gospel, not to mention certain passages in Galatians (Gal 4:4-7), Romans (Rom 5:12-14; 8:11-17, 23), 1 Corinthians (1 Cor 8:6; 15:35-58) and 2 Corinthians (2 Cor 12:9). It was the economy set forth in such texts that Irenaeus believed the prophets had seen ahead of time, for they were under the tutelage of the very Word who later became incarnate in order to exhibit humanity to itself and to elevate men and women to that immortality and incorruptibility that God alone possesses by right but that God had created the *anthrōpos* (Gen 1:26-27 LXX) to share in.

BIBLIOGRAPHY

Works. Irenaeus, *Irenaeus: Proof of the Apostolic Preaching,* trans. J. P. Smith, ACW 16; idem,

Demonstration of the Apostolic Preaching, trans. J. A. Robinson (London: SPCK, 1920); idem, *Against Heresies,* trans. A. Roberts and J. Donaldson, ANF 1 (both the translation and the text on which it is based leave much to be desired; the first volume of a new English version has been published in the ACW series).

Studies. G. T. Armstrong, *Die Genesis in der alten Kirche* (Tübingen: J. C. B. Mohr, 1962); A. Benoît, *Saint Irénée: Introduction à l'etude de sa théologie* (Paris: Presses universitaires, 1960); H. von Campenhausen, *The Formation of the Christian Bible* (Philadelphia: Fortress, 1972); O. Cullmann, "The Plurality of the Gospels as a Theological Problem in Antiquity" [1945] in *The Early Church* (Philadelphia: Westminster, 1956) 40-56; D. Farkasfalvy, "Theology of Scripture in Irenaeus," *RB* 78 (1968); P. Ferlay, "Irénée de Lyon exégète du quatrième évangile," *NRT* 106 (1984); S. Herrera, *Saint Irénée de Lyon exégète* (Paris, 1920); J. Hoh, *Die Lehre des heiligen Irenaeus über das Neue Testament* (Münster: Aschendorff, 1919); M. Jourjon, "Saint Irénée lit la Bible" in *Le monde grec ancien et la Bible,* ed. C. Mondesert (Paris: Beauchesne, 1984); R. A. Norris, "Irenaeus' Use of Paul in His Polemic Against the Gnostics" in *Paul and the Legacies of Paul,* ed. W. A. Babcock (Dallas: Southern Methodist University Press, 1990); M. Simonetti, *Biblical Interpretation in the Early Church: A Historical Introduction to Patristic Exegesis,* ed. A. Bergquist and M. Bockmuehl (Edinburgh: T & T Clark, 1994); idem, " 'Per typica ad vera.' Note sull'esegesi di Ireneo," [Bari] 18 (1981).

R. A. Norris Jr.

Jerome *(c. 340-420)*

Eusebius Sophronius Hieronymus is better known as Jerome, doctor of the church, and one of the most important interpreters of the Bible in the early centuries of Christianity. Jerome was born in the town of Stridon, in what was until recently northwestern Yugoslavia. He died in 420, having acquired an international reputation for biblical scholarship, for extensive literary activity and for living a holy and ascetic life.

Context. The Roman Empire into which Jerome was born had been changing rapidly. The Christian emperor Constantine the Great had pushed through policies that favored Christianity, and many churches were built throughout the empire. Constantine's benevolent actions, and those of his successors, had a dramatic effect on the church. Instead of being persecuted, the church now enjoyed many privileges, and it was increasingly to have an influential role in society. Christianity was becoming more and more popular and respectable, and consequently people were streaming into the church. One result of this was that the church population wanted to learn more about the Scriptures, and scholars like Jerome had an important function to fulfill by writing commentaries to explain the biblical books.

Jerome inherited a long tradition of biblical interpretation, both Jewish and Christian. In Judaism rabbinic scholars had developed a system of interpretative rules and techniques for studying biblical texts. These may be broadly classified under two headings: haggadah and halakah. Haggadah ("information" or "anecdote") is seen largely in collections of midrash (a kind of commentary on Scripture) and often takes the form of moralizing exegesis. Various techniques were used to achieve this, including juxtaposing originally discrete biblical texts, creative elaboration of the biblical narrative, and the use of parable. This midrashic method could provide profound theological insights. Jerome used a great deal of haggadic material in his works, and he was the main source through which echoes of the haggadah reached some of the Western church fathers. Halakah ("procedure") was concerned with the implementation of the Torah into practical matters and with ensuring that the Torah could be successfully adapted to the changing conditions in the life of Jews. Jerome also used this halakic principle in his own exegesis of Scripture.

One Jewish scholar who found favor with Jerome was Philo of Alexandria. Jerome calls Philo an "ecclesiastical" writer, on the grounds that Philo praises Christians at Alexandria and mentions that Christianity is present in other provinces (Jerome *On Illustrious Men [De Viris Illustribus]* 11).

Philo had been aware of the haggadic and halakic traditions but found that the "impossibilities" and "absurdities" produced by a literal reading of Scripture could be unravelled by using an allegorical method based on Stoic ethics and Platonic cosmology. By searching carefully in Scripture for clues like contradictions, strange expressions, word derivations and mysterious numbers, the interpreter could discover the real message that God intended to convey.

This allegorical interpretation of biblical texts spread from Philo to Christianity and became widely used by the catechetical school at Alexandria, particularly by its two greatest scholars, *Clement and *Origen. Jerome spoke approvingly of Clement but was much more deeply influenced by Origen.

Not all Christian scholars were convinced, however, that allegorical exegesis was the best method of discovering the truth of Scripture. The school of Antioch developed in reaction against the allegorizing tendencies of Alexandria. The school's early history is associated with Lucian, the teacher of Arius. But the most influential Antiochenes were Diodore of Tarsus, *Theodore of Mopsuestia and John *Chrysostom. The Antiochenes insisted on the historical basis of the text of Scripture and that, wherever possible, it should be interpreted literally. Only where this could not be done was the typological or allegorical sense to be explored. The Antiochene approach on the literal or historical sense is seen in Lucian's emphasis on the details of the text of Scripture. He knew Hebrew and corrected the Septuagint from the original Hebrew. Jerome praised this recension and used it widely in his own work on the biblical text. Against this general background of schools of interpretation in Judaism and Christianity Jerome's own contribution may be seen.

Biblical Languages. Before it was possible to interpret the text properly, it was necessary to have the best text available. This meant that Jerome had to learn the original languages of the Bible. As far as the New Testament was concerned, Jerome encountered no problems, for he had learned Greek at school and had attended the lectures of Gregory of Nazianzus in Constantinople. But for the text of the Old Testament, Jerome was faced with a considerable hurdle for, apart from Origen, few other Christian scholars had any knowledge of Hebrew. Jerome took lessons in Hebrew from a Jewish convert to Christianity, and it is clear that he found it a difficult language to master. It must be remembered that no grammars or concordances were available, so he had to learn the language orally, memorizing the sounds of the consonants and vocabulary. Presumably he practiced writing the Hebrew characters by copying out manuscripts. When Jerome's knowledge and use of Hebrew is compared with that of other ancient scholars, such as Philo and Origen, it is clear that Jerome had a much more extensive and profound knowledge. Jerome has the same quantitative use of Hebrew as does Origen, but he added to it a qualitative use of Hebrew as a guide to the right meanings. This extensive knowledge of Hebrew helped Jerome in his major task of translating the Bible from its original languages.

Jerome was, as he himself says, a *vir trilinguis,* one who knew Hebrew, Greek and Latin. One of the greatest achievements for which Jerome is remembered is the translation of the Bible known as the Vulgate. Jerome is generally thought to have been responsible for much of this version, though it is not exclusively his own work. In the Old Testament he did not translate the books of Wisdom, Ecclesiasticus, 1 and 2 Maccabees or Baruch, as he believed these to be noncanonical. In the Vulgate these survive in an earlier, Old Latin version. Similarly, most of the New Testament, with the exception of the Gospels, was translated by a number of unknown persons and exists in a revised Old Latin version. The Gospels and most of the Old Testament are attributable to Jerome to a greater or lesser extent. Some books are new translations (though there is considerable variation in the care and thoroughness with which they were prepared), and some are revisions of the Old Latin text.

Biblical Translations. Jerome's initial motivation for translating biblical books came from his patron, Pope Damasus, who commissioned him to revise the New Testament in the light of the original Greek text. Damasus was concerned about the vast number of differing Latin translations that were circulating at the time and wished to impose some order on them by introducing an accurate, standard translation. Jerome completed his revision of the Gospels in 384 and proceeded to revise the Psalter on the basis of the Septuagint. This was the first of three attempts at translating the Psalms, twice from the Greek text and once from the Hebrew.

Around 390 Jerome became convinced that if he was to interpret the biblical text properly, his translations of biblical books must be based on the original languages rather than on the Septuagint. It was particularly important, in arguing points of Scripture against Jews, to have as accurate a text as possible. During the following fifteen years, Jerome produced a new translation of the Hebrew books of the Old Testament, which had never before been translated directly into Latin. In addition, at the request of two friends, Heliodorus and Chromatius, Jerome translated the books of Tobit and Judith from the Aramaic, even though they were not part of the canon of Scripture.

Theological Translations. Jerome did not restrict his translation activities solely to Scripture. He is also responsible for translating into Latin a considerable number of Greek theological works. The first of these translations was made in 380, when he rendered Eusebius of Caesarea's *Chronicle* into Latin. Presumably, having spent several years studying the works of Greek theologians, Jerome was eager that the Latin-speaking world should have the opportunity of benefiting from the scholarship of Greek Christians. Jerome was not

content simply to translate this particular work. He omitted sections he thought unnecessary and added a new section, bringing the *Chronicle* up to date and thereby providing the Western world with a history of the world from Abraham to 379.

Jerome then turned to translating into Latin the works of Origen, the great third-century Greek theologian and exegete. Jerome was interested in translating most if not all of Origen's works but was prevented from doing so by a painful eye irritation caused by constant reading and by a lack of copyists, owing to a shortage of money. Jerome did succeed, however, in translating quite a number of Origen's homilies. He also translated a work of Didymus the Blind, *On the Holy Spirit,* from Greek into Latin. This work, along with some of Origen's homilies, is now lost in Greek, and Jerome's translation is the only way we can know these important works.

Biblical Interpretation. The major part of Jerome's literary output is in commentary form. He states that the purpose of a commentary is "to discuss what is obscure, to touch on the obvious, to dwell at length on what is doubtful" (Jerome *Commentary on Galatians* 4.6). For Jerome Scripture was full of obscurities, and a reliable guide is needed. A commentary ought to "repeat the opinions of the many . . . so that the judicious reader, when he has perused the different explanations . . . may judge which is the best and, like a good banker, reject the money from a spurious mint" (Jerome *Apology Against Rufinus* 1.16). In most of his commentaries, Jerome acknowledged the previous authors from whom he has borrowed, and they are valuable because they transmit a great wealth of comments from other scholars, some of which would otherwise have been lost.

Jerome gave a great value to the literal sense of Scripture. Even in his first piece of exegesis on the call of Isaiah, Jerome begins with a strictly literal historical exposition of "who this Uzziah was, how many years he had reigned and who among the other kings were his contemporaries" (Jerome

Epistle 18A, 1). Only after this does he move on to the spiritual interpretation of the passage.

Again, in the *Commentary on Ephesians* (5.14), composed in 388, Jerome interprets "Therefore it is said, 'Awake, O sleeper, and arise from the dead, and Christ shall give you light' " by explaining that the words were spoken to Adam, who was buried at Calvary where Christ was crucified. The place was called Calvary because the head of some ancient man had been buried there and because, when Christ was crucified, he was hanging directly above the place where it was buried. It is likely, though Jerome does not acknowledge it, that he was mainly dependent here on a work by Apollinarius of Laodicea.

While Jerome followed the Antiochene school's emphasis on the priority of the historical sense, he nevertheless believed that Christians must go beyond this to discover the fuller, deeper meaning of a passage. It was possible to understand this deeper meaning only with the aid of the allegorical or spiritual method.

A study of Jerome's allegorical exegesis shows that he takes many of the specific interpretations directly from Origen, even to the extent of verbal borrowing. This is the case both before the Origenist controversy, in which Jerome played a leading part (393-402), and later, when Jerome had renounced Origen's theology as heretical. The influence of Origen, whom Jerome had once proudly called "my master," can be seen on almost every page of Jerome's writings.

One example of this influence is in the *Commentary on Matthew.* This is an interesting example because Origen's comments on this passage are also extant. Jerome wrote his *Commentary on Matthew* in fourteen days, in order to provide a friend with some reading matter on a long sea voyage. In his interpretation of the parable of the hidden treasure (Mt 13:44) Jerome has clearly followed Origen. The main points of their respective interpretations are set out:

The treasure is the word of God which appears to be hidden in the body of Christ, or the Holy Scriptures in which rests the knowledge of the Savior. When the treasure is discovered, one must give up all the *emolumenta* in order to possess it. (Jerome *Commentary on Matthew*)

This is not a parable but a similitude. The field equals the scripture. The treasure equals the mysteries lying within the Scripture, and finding the treasure a man hides it, thinking it dangerous to reveal to all and sundry the secrets of Scripture. He goes, sells all his possessions, and works until he can buy the field, in order that he may possess the great treasure. (Origen *Commentary on Matthew*)

Jerome's interpretation appears to have links with that of Origen, in addition to the similarities one would expect in the interpretation of this parable. Yet Jerome's interpretation is simpler and more direct than that of Origen in its application of the meaning of the parable. Jerome is not interested in Origen's distinction between a parable and a similitude, the latter being a generic term, the former a particular form of similitude. It should be noted that Jerome sets down two different interpretations of the treasure: either it is the word of God hidden in the body of Christ, or it is the knowledge of the Savior hidden in Scripture. His first interpretation does not stem from Origen but comes rather from Jerome's characteristic ascetic interests.

It is not only specific passages of spiritual interpretation that Jerome borrows from Origen in the *Commentary on Matthew* but also certain themes. One of these, very important for Origen, was the goodness of God, which he used to combat the Gnosticism of the day. This theme runs through Jerome's own *Commentary on Matthew.*

Toward the end of his life, after the trauma of the Origenist controversy, Jerome was more critical of some of Origen's contentious exegetical interpretations. This trend appears most clearly in his *Commentary on Jeremiah,* where Origen is denounced as "that allegorist!" and his unorthodox views are fiercely attacked, and where Jerome relies less than in any other commentary on Origen's allegorical interpretations.

Use of Jewish Sources. Jerome, then, used to his own advantage specific interpretations from representatives of both the Alexandrian and Antiochene schools. He was also the only church father in the fourth century to learn Hebrew, having taken lessons from leading Jewish scholars. Jerome also used many Jewish interpretations of scriptural passages. Jerome believed that Jewish traditions of exegesis were of great importance for Christians in their interpretation of the Old Testament, so long as they were consistent with the teaching of the Bible.

In his *Commentary on Daniel* (5.2) Jerome records the following Jewish tradition concerning Belshazzar:

> The Hebrews hand down a story of this sort: Belshazzar, thinking that God's promise had remained without effect until the seventieth year, by which Jeremiah had said that the captivity of the Jewish people would have to be ended [cf. Jer 25:12; 29:10-14]—a matter of which Zechariah also speaks in the first part of his book [cf. Zech 1:12-17]— and turning the occasion of the failed promise into a celebration, gave a great banquet by way of mocking the expectation of the Jews and the vessels of the Temple of God.

Jeremiah had promised Israel that their exile would be temporary. After seventy years they would return to their own land and glory in the destruction of their oppressors, the Babylonians. The chronological problem is to determine which year begins the seventy-year period. In *Megillah* 11b it is explained that Belshazzar began his count with the first year of Nebuchadnezzar's reign (605 B.C.). This rabbinic source explicitly says that Belshazzar was mistaken in his calculations, a point that is implicit in Jerome's statement. The seventy-year period should have begun from the second year of Nebuchadnezzar's reign, not the first (cf. 2 Kings 24:1). Jerome is the only church father to mention this tradition.

Scholars studying Jerome's use of rabbinic traditions have usually assumed that Jerome had taken those traditions directly from Jewish sources. There are, however, a few instances in which it is clear that he has copied out the Jewish material from the writings of Origen, who also made some use of Jewish traditions. One example is given below.

In one of his early letters (Jerome *Epistle* 18A, 15) dealing with the topic of the two seraphim in Isaiah 6:6-9, Jerome makes a comparison between Isaiah and Moses. He says that he had discussed this with some Jews and assures his reader that this tradition comes from an excellent (Jewish) source and should be accepted. Jerome gives the impression that he has gleaned this tradition from direct conversation and study with Jews. In fact, however, he borrowed it from Origen, who had reported it in his sixth *Homily on Isaiah,* saying that both Isaiah and Moses had refused God's command at first, on the basis of their unworthiness, but had subsequently accepted.

Biblical Commentator. Jerome was essentially an eclectic scholar. He searched diligently in the works of others and drew the best points from each while avoiding the errors of each. This holds true also of the different schools of interpretation accessible to Jerome: Alexandrian, Antiochene and Jewish.

From the Antiochene school Jerome learned that an interpreter of the Bible must first study and explain the literal, plain sense, and only after this has been accomplished should he venture beyond this to the deeper, spiritual interpretation. From the Alexandrian school, especially from Origen, Jerome borrowed many specific allegorical interpretations. Jerome cites Alexandrian authors much more frequently than he does Antiochenes. The reason for this is not that he was more dependent on the former but rather that the works of

Alexandrian exegetes were more readily accessible to Jerome. Also the Antiochene school was still in its youth when Jerome was writing and had produced a relatively small collection of commentaries from which he could borrow. From Jewish exegesis Jerome learned the primary importance of the original text of the Old Testament, so that he was unique among the early fathers of the church in his use of the Hebrew text as the basis of his exegesis of the Old Testament.

Even during his lifetime, Jerome was held to be a great authority on the interpretation of the Bible. Jerome's contemporary, Sulpicius Severus, wrote in 405: "I would be surprised if he [Jerome] were not already known to you through his writings since he is read throughout the world" (Sulpicius Severus *Dialogues* 1.8).

In the centuries following Jerome's death he was universally acknowledged as the prince of Christian biblical scholars, and his works became a fertile ground for the labors of subsequent exegetes. The reasons for this fame were twofold. First, Jerome's translation of the Bible became accepted everywhere as the standard biblical text in the Western church; second, for centuries Jerome's immense and intimate knowledge and understanding of the Bible surpassed that of any other Christian scholar.

Although Jerome wrote commentaries on several of the Pauline letters and on Matthew's Gospel, he is chiefly remembered for his Old Testament commentaries. He is the only ancient author who commented on all the books of the major and minor prophets. Jerome saw it as his special task to explain these Old Testament books, because they are more difficult to understand than are the books of the New Testament. Jerome's erudition is exhibited on every page of his writings. He quotes frequently from classical authors, as well as from the Bible and other Christian writers. In addition, Jerome, with his highly developed powers of observation, makes many suggestive and original contributions to the understanding of the biblical text.

Significance. The writings of Jerome are of lasting value to Christians because they offer us a splendid example of the state of biblical interpretation in the West in the fourth century, because they give us an interesting insight into relations between Christians and Jews in the generations after Christianity became the religion of the state, and also because they paint for us, in vivid colors, a picture of the "irascible monk" who devoted his life to the study of the sacred Scriptures. In his own words: "What other life can there be without the knowledge of the Scriptures, for through these Christ himself, who is the life of the faithful, becomes known?" (Jerome *Epistle* 30.7).

BIBLIOGRAPHY

Works. Jerome, CCSL 72-80; PL 22-30; NPNF Series 2 Vols. 3, 6; *Commentary on Galatians and Ephesians*, PL 26; *Commentary on Matthew*, PL 26; *Dogmatic and Polemical Works*, FC 53; *Letters and Select Works*, NPNF Series 2 Vol. 6; *Lives of Illustrious Men*, NPNF Series 2 Vol. 3:359-84.

Studies. J. Braverman, *Jerome's "Commentary on Daniel": A Study of Comparative Jewish and Christian Interpretations of the Hebrew Bible* (CBQMS 7; Washington, D.C.: Catholic Biblical Association of America, 1978); D. Brown, *Vir Trilinguis: A Study in the Biblical Exegesis of Saint Jerome* (Kampen: Kok Pharos, 1993); P. Jay, *L'Exegese de Saint Jerome d'apres son "Commentaire sur Isaie"* (Paris: Etudes Augustiniennes, 1985); A. Kamesar, *Jerome, Greek Scholarship and the Hebrew Bible* (Oxford: Clarendon, 1993); J. N. D. Kelly, *Jerome: His Life and Controversies* (London: Duckworth, 1976); P. Rousseau, *Ascetics, Authority and the Church in the Age of Jerome and Cassian* (Oxford: Oxford University Press, 1978); J. H. D. Scourfield, *Consoling Heliodorus: A Commentary on Jerome Letter 60* (Oxford: Clarendon, 1993). D. Brown

Justin Martyr *(c. 100-c. 165)*

Justin, who was the first great apologist of the church, wrote for both the pagan and the Jewish world. Because of this fact and the influence he seems to have had on those who followed him, the way he thought about and used Scripture is important.

Little is known of Justin apart from what he tells us in his writings. In *1 Apology* 1 he states that was born in the city of Flavia Neapolis in Samaria and was the son of Priscus, the son of Baccheius. He also states that he was brought up a heathen (Justin *Dialogue with Trypho* 29.1, 3), and according to *Dialogue with Trypho* 2.3-6 he searched after truth among the Stoics, Peripatetics, Pythagoreans and Platonists. He tells how he became a Christian by meeting an old man who showed him the futility of philosophy and led him to the study of the Scriptures (Justin *Dialogue with Trypho* 3—8). Justin was martyred sometime between 163 and 167, traditionally under the prefect Rusticus, hence his name. (For the traditions concerning Justin, see Grant 1948b, 105-12).

Work. Of the three books that we accept as genuine, *1 Apology* and *2 Apology* (which appears to be only an appendix), were written to the emperor Antoninus Pius between 150 and 155. Justin argued that Christians should be condemned and punished only for proven crimes, not for their mere name. They were atheists only in that they did not count the popular gods to be worthy of worship in respect to the only true God. They were anarchists only to those who did not understand the true nature of the spiritual kingdom for which they sought. He then argued the truth of Christianity from the fulfillment of Old Testament prophecy and briefly explained the Christian sacraments and worship.

The third book, the *Dialogue with Trypho,* supposedly records a two-day discussion between Justin and a learned rabbi. Each tried to convert the other, and they finally agreed to disagree. Trypho advised Justin to be circumcised, to keep the sabbath and to do all the things commanded in the law. Then he might find mercy with God. Moreover, if the Messiah had ever been or did then exist, he had no power until Elijah came, anointed him and made him known (Justin *Dialogue with Trypho* 7.4). To answer, Justin had to provide an analysis of the relevance of the law for Christians. He did not deny the historical relation of God to Israel, but he insisted that the earlier covenant itself declared that it would be superseded. He showed from the writings of the prophets that they looked forward to a new and different covenant with God. Then he argued that the patriarchs were saved without circumcision or keeping the sabbath or the law. Hence Christians did not need to observe any of them. About the Messiah he argued that the Old Testament, interpreted in many ways, proved that Jesus was the Messiah, the Lord, Son of God and the one to be worshiped.

Concept of Scripture. Justin wrote to the emperor and his court as a philosopher addressing other philosophers. Thus he used an idea that was common to many philosophers of the day to explain his idea of Scripture. The Logos, or reason of God, had been granted to every man, and this had led them to those things they had discovered and explained well (Justin *2 Apology* 10). However, philosophy could not lead a person to God because it was dependent on human reason, which is incomplete. The way to God is through the whole Logos, incarnate in Christ (Justin *2 Apology* 10). In this way he turned from reason to revelation as the source of authority for his faith. This revelation was twofold in nature. It was the Logos, the first begotten of God who had become the man called Jesus Christ (Justin *1 Apology* 5). It was also a book that had pointed to and foretold the Logos to come because God, through the Logos, had inspired the Old Testament prophets to speak (Justin *1 Apology* 33, 36). Moreover, for Justin the Scripture was the Old Testament translated into Greek, and it was true in every point (Justin *Dialogue with Trypho* 68.7).

Not only had God inspired the prophets to speak, but also the words they spoke were of inestimable value because they were from God. Every word and phrase was to be looked at carefully, and Scripture obviously was such that it could not contradict itself (Justin *Dialogue with Trypho* 65.2). It took faith to understand the Scriptures, and true understanding was the gift of God to Christians (Justin *Dialogue with Trypho* 92.1; 119.1). As a result there was only one true key to understanding the Scriptures, Christ. To him all Scripture looked, for he it was who had inspired all the writers of the Old Testament, and all the writers were prophets.

Justin was primarily concerned not with the message the biblical writers gave for the people of their day but with the predictive element in Scripture. This predictive element was divided into two portions: those commands that were spoken because of the hardness of Jewish hearts and those writings that spoke of the mystery of Christ, which contained any material that was explicitly predictive of the Messiah or any material that could be construed to be so (Justin *Dialogue with Trypho* 44.2). In the *Dialogue with Trypho,* Justin used the predictive element about the hardness of Jewish hearts to help dispose of the law, but it was with the material about the mystery of Christ that he was primarily concerned.

Methods of Interpretation. One of Justin's most common methods of interpreting Scripture was that of pointing to prophecies that he considered to have been literally fulfilled. Since the Bible was a predictive book, the original context and meaning of the words were unimportant. He cited a passage and then pointed to a historical event that he claimed fulfilled the prophecy. Or he listed a historical event and stated that this was prophesied in a certain passage. He used the Old Testament as one great mass of proof-texts (Shotwell, 29-31).

Although Justin quoted Scripture apart from any context when he used the method of literal fulfillment of prophecy, he did use the argument from the context of a passage or connection when it fit his purposes. For example, he insisted that the context of Isaiah 42:8 must be considered for proper understanding (Justin *Dialogue with Trypho* 65.1). Then he quoted Isaiah 42:5-13 as the means to explain it. By using the close connection of the "one who is the light to the Gentiles" in Isaiah 42:7 to Isaiah 42:8, he pointed out that God had not reserved his glory for himself but for the one who was to be the light of the Gentiles.

In the type of argument called general and particular, the former refers to a class of objects or things while the latter refers to an individual object in the group of things. Thus the general is defined by the particular; by reversing the argument, the particular is more precisely defined by the general. In the *Dialogue with Trypho* 119.4 Justin called Abraham the father of many nations. Then he said that Abraham became the father of Ishmael, a great nation. Thus he has defined the general term *nations* by particular descendants of Abraham. He used the reverse in an argument that circumcision was not needed: Enoch, Noah, Lot and Melchizedek were all uncircumcised, but they all found favor with God (Justin *Dialogue with Trypho* 19.3). Thus the particular instances prove the general statement that circumcision is not needed to find favor with God.

Another method of interpretation used by Justin was that of the lesser to the greater, or an inference from a minor to the major. In *Dialogue with Trypho* 95.1 Justin quoted Deuteronomy 27:26, which states that everyone who does not follow all the commands of the law is cursed. Then he argued that if this were true of those who had the law and did not keep it, how much more it must be true that Gentiles who worshiped idols would be cursed.

Analogy was the favorite method of interpretation that Justin used, and he used four types. One was an inference from two objects or words in the same verse. In *Dialogue with Trypho* 1.6.12 he quoted Genesis 19:24-25. Since two Lords are mentioned, the Lord who rained down fire and brimstone and the Lord in heaven, there must be two Lords. Justin was then able to state that there were two who were called Lord and divine. The one in heaven is God; the other is Christ. In *Dialogue with Trypho* 56.14, Justin used the same method to prove from Psalm 110:1 that the words "The LORD said to my Lord" referred to God and Christ. These instances are typical of Justin's inferences from two objects or words in the same verse.

A second type of analogy was that of an inference from similar ideas. After quoting from Psalm 110, "You are a priest forever, after the order of Melchizedek," Justin reasoned that Melchizedek was both a priest of God and a priest to those in uncircumcision (Justin *Dialogue with Trypho* 33.2). Therefore the one to whom the spirit of God spoke was both a priest forever and a priest to those in uncircumcision. This, of course, referred to Christ.

A third type of analogy was the inference from two objects in two verses. In *Dialogue with Trypho* 58.6-7 Justin quoted Genesis 32:22-30, the story of Jacob's wrestling match. In this passage there appear the words "a man wrestling with him" and the words "I saw God face to face." Here were two objects, the man and the one called God. Hence the man is called God. However, the man called God could not be the God in heaven. Therefore there were two in the Old Testament who were called God. In *Dialogue with Trypho* 62.4-5 he used Joshua 5:13—6:2. In this passage there appeared to Joshua one who called himself the chief commander of the hosts of the Lord. Later in the same passage, the Scripture states that "the LORD said to Joshua . . ." Although the Scripture spoke of only one personage appearing to Joshua, two are mentioned. From the analogy of two objects in two verses, the one called "chief commander" is also called "LORD" and yet is under the Lord. There must then be two who are called Lord mentioned in the Old Testament.

The last type is the analogy from one passage by the similar in another. In *Dialogue with Trypho* 9.4-5, Justin stated that there appeared to Moses an angel of the Lord in a flame of fire from a bush. Later the Scripture stated that "the LORD called

to him out of the bush." Since the bush was found in both verses, the same person must be in the bush. Thus it must be concluded that the "angel of the LORD" was also called "LORD." Therefore there is one called "LORD" who is second to God and ministers to him.

Allegorical Method. From Justin's acquaintance with philosophy, he knew that many of the philosophers claimed that their ideas went back to Homer and Hesiod. These were the two great writers before the philosophers, and it was only natural for philosophers to find their thought in these poets. However, the poets wrote poetry rather than philosophy, and to find their thoughts in poetry the philosophers had to find them in hidden or obscure language. Thus the poets were read as saying one thing but meaning another. Allegory became the means of restating poetry in terms of philosophy.

However, Justin did not use philosophical allegory. Perhaps that was because Justin's idea of philosophy was distinctively his own. In the story of his conversion, the old man led Justin to the place where he could turn from philosophy to the Old Testament prophets. They, rather than philosophy, were the source of knowledge of the truth. Hence for Justin philosophy consisted of the study and explication of the prophets.

That allegory was also in use in the Jewish world is evident. In the *Testament of Judah* 241 "the star of Jacob" (Num 24:17) is used to refer to the coming of the Messiah. Among the Damascus Covenanters there was the same type of interpretation. There, however, the star of Jacob referred to the leader of the group who left Jerusalem and went to Damascus. The same group interpreted the phrase "the priest and the Levites and the sons of Zadok" (Ezek 44:15) to refer to themselves. The priests were the penitents of Israel who went out of Judah, and the Levites were those who joined them. In the *Manual of Discipline* 5.2 and 5.9, which is from the Qumran community, a similar group of people, the sons of Zadok are the priests who keep the covenant. This can be called predictive allegory.

In Galatians 4:21-31 Paul used an extended allegory about Sarah and Hagar to prove that the Galatians and all Christians are children of freedom and not the children of slavery. Likewise the author of the letter to the Hebrews used allegory at length, although, unlike Paul, he did not call it allegory. Melchizedek pointed to the eternal Christ who became a priest of his order, and the vessels of the tabernacle were copies of the heavenly originals.

Whether he found it in philosophy, in others or in his Christian predecessors, allegory was another favorite method of interpretation used by Justin. Since the Old Testament was a predictive book, it was full of predictive allegories. A typical example of Justin's use of the allegorical method is found in *1 Apology* 27, in which he quoted Genesis 49:10. After interpreting the first part of this verse in terms of literal fulfillment, Justin stated that the phrase "washing his robe in the blood of the grape" was a forewarning of what Christ would suffer for those who believed in him. "His robe" are those who believe in Christ. The words "blood of the grape" mean that Christ would have blood that came from the power of God and not from the seed of humans. For just as the blood of grapes comes from God and not from humans, so also the blood of Christ comes from God and not from humans. Justin made extensive usage of such allegories; he found at least ninety-eight of them to use in the *Dialogue with Trypho* (Shotwell, 43). Ninety-four of these instances were noted to have a hidden meaning, to be an obscure saying, or to be a mystery, a sign, an announcement, a symbol, a parable or a type.

Justin and Jewish Interpreters. One of the unexpected things about Justin's exegesis was his knowledge of Jewish rabbinical teaching. In the *Dialogue with Trypho* there are at least forty instances in which he made reference to Jewish teachings that can be fairly well confirmed as similar or exact.

Five of those that are nearly exact are from contemporary or near-contemporary rabbis (Shotwell, 71-90).

In addition, when Justin's nonallegorical methods of exegesis are compared with the great Jewish traditional methods ascribed to Hillel, who was active during the reign of Herod the Great (37-4 B.C.), they are found to be so similar that one could conclude that Justin had used the rules of Hillel as his basic guides to interpretation of Scripture, although it is possible that three of the so-called seven rules of Hillel could have been learned from his Christian predecessors (Shotwell, 93).

Since Justin had a rather large knowledge of rabbinical lore, some of which was contemporary, and since he seems to have used the rules of Hillel as the basic guides to his biblical interpretation, it should be no surprise that his methods of allegorical interpretation were in line with those of the rabbis and of the writers of the Qumran material. He seems to have taken the allegorical methods of the rabbis as his own. All of this points to a closer relationship and a greater exchange of ideas between Jews and Christians than would have seemed possible at this point in history.

Summary. Although Justin furthered the use of Jewish interpretation in Christianity, he was first of all a Christian who aligned himself with the tradition of the church. He sought to present his faith to those around him in the way most acceptable to them. He approached the Greek world with the concept of the Logos and the Jewish world with rabbinical interpretation. The main weapon he used in his apologetic was the interpretation he presented of the Old Testament, a book that had been written by men who were possessed of God. Every word of it was from God, extremely valuable and unable to contradict itself. It was written in Greek and all might read, but it could be understood only by those to whom God had given a special grace. Justin had this grace, and the key to understanding the Scriptures was Christ-centered interpretation.

This book contained moral and ethical guides, but most of all it was a book full of predictions about the one whom God had sent into the world: Jesus Christ, the Son of God. Many of these predictions were spoken in veiled language and various mysterious ways. The best way to understand these veiled references was to interpret them allegorically with the help of analogy. Besides the method of allegory, there were other methods of interpreting the Scripture. One of these methods was the method of proof-texts to show the literal fulfillment of prophecy, and the other seven were similar to the rules of Rabbi Hillel. The rabbis were to be used as sources of knowledge about the interpretations of the Jews, but even more, their interpretations were to be used in one's own argument from Scripture. When they were used with the key of christocentric interpretation, the methods of the rabbis were the best methods of interpreting Scripture. This then was true philosophy—the love and explication of the prophets and all the Scriptures were prophetic.

Justin knew how to relate his Christianity to the world around him, and his methods must have been fairly effective. That this was true is evident from the fact that *Irenaeus, *Tertullian, *Origen and even Eusebius adopted his apologetic material for their own apologies.

BIBLIOGRAPHY

Works. Justin Martyr, *1 & 2 Apology,* FC; ANF 1; idem, *Dialogue with Trypho,* FC; ANF 1.
Studies. L. Ginzberg, "Allegorical Interpretation," *JE* 1 (1921); R. M. Grant, *The Bible in the Church* (New York: Macmillan, 1948a); idem, *Second-Century Christianity* (London: SPCK, 1948b); W. A. Shotwell, *The Biblical Exegesis of Justin Martyr* (London: SPCK, 1965); O. Skarsaune, *The Proof from Prophecy* (Leiden: E. J. Brill, 1987); J. D. Smart, *The Interpretation of Scripture* (Philadelphia: Westminster, 1961); J. Tate, "On the History of Allegorism," *CQ* 28 (April 1934) 142-54; A. L. Williams, *Justyn Martyr: The Dialogue with Trypho* (London: SPCK, 1930).   W. A. Shotwell

Origen *(c. 185-253/4)*

Origen of Alexandria was the most significant biblical scholar in the first three centuries of Christian history. Other early Christian thinkers reflected seriously on the Scriptures but did not write biblical commentaries, formulate a developed theory of hermeneutics, or do extensive work on the text of the Bible. In the history of biblical interpretation Origen deserves to be recognized as the father of biblical criticism. Some eight hundred of Origen's writings have survived, and at least seventy-five percent are devoted to the exposition of Scripture. The ancient church historian Eusebius indicated that Ambrosius, a wealthy friend, provided him with a trained staff of stenographers, copyists and calligraphers. Eusebius offers a colorful account: "For as Origen dictated there were ready at hand more than seven shorthand writers who relieved each other at fixed times, and as many copyists, as well as girls skilled in penmanship" (Eusebius *Ecclesiastical History* 6.23.2).

What compelled Origen to be so prolific a writer? Clearly it was a combination of his worldview and impassioned love for the Bible. Origen's cosmology, shaped by a mixture of Christian doctrine with the Greek literary and philosophical tradition, formed his hermeneutical theory and exegetical method. In everything he wrote, he was simultaneously an exegete, theologian and mystic. Origen's labors on the text of the Bible are among the most outstanding of any age, not just of the early church. His influence on the history of biblical interpretation has been exceeded perhaps by no one except the apostle Paul himself.

Backgrounds. Origen's historical context needs to be established in order to understand his contributions to the history of biblical interpretation. The cultural, religious and philosophical milieu of Alexandria played a decisive role in shaping his perspectives on the Bible.

Alexandria was the greatest intellectual, cultural and commercial center of the Roman Empire. Alexander the Great founded the city (331 B.C.) and Hellenized it, making Greek language, philosophy, art and literature dominant features of its cultural life. Several harbors were built for commercial trade. Businessmen and sailors traveled back and forth, making Alexandria the chief seaport of Egypt. Dating from the mid-third century B.C., an advanced institute of research known as the Museum was still in existence in Origen's day. The library was reputed to have six hundred thousand volumes. It contained a repository of scholarship on the classics of Greek antiquity, philosophy, literature, philology, mathematics, astronomy, algebra and geometry. The great algebraist Diophantius and Hero, author of famed textbooks on geometry and ballistics and inventor of a functioning steam engine, may have been Origen's contemporaries. The second-century grammarian Apollonius Dyscolus authored the Canon of Apollonius, which is still cited by exegetes of the Greek New Testament.

Like other Christians living in Alexandria, Origen was educated in the classical curriculum. Much of his work is characterized by the same concerns of those disciplines. Classical learning was viewed as a prerequisite for the study of philosophy, and subsequently, for Christians, scriptural interpretation. Origen probably started to study the elementary principles of reading, writing, counting and doing sums at age seven. After that, he went on to study general education and grammar. General education included arithmetic, musical theory, astronomy and geometry. Grammar focused on Homer, Hesiod, Euripides and other Greek authors from the literary tradition. In the grammar curriculum, pupils went through four stages of learning. In the first phase the class engaged in criticism of the text. Students went over their manuscripts together with the teacher, line upon line, to make sure all had the same text. Next came oral reading, in which they spoke the text aloud. In the third stage students engaged in exposition (or exegesis, as it was called), in which the linguistic

and historical background of the texts was discussed. Fourth came judgment, in which the instructor assisted students with the drawing out of moral lessons from their reading. After Origen completed his literary education he became a teacher of grammar.

From the philosopher Ammonius Saccas (c. 175-242) Origen learned Platonic doctrines. He acquired from Ammonius a sympathetic yet critical attitude toward classical antiquity and even appropriated Ammonius's language and style of writing. The technical vocabulary of Platonism, such as "the incorporeal" *(asomaton)*, "the mind" *(nous)* and "the governing faculty" *(hegemonikon)*, appears on virtually every page of Origen's writings. Consequently Middle Platonism (first century B.C. to second century A.D.) and Neo-Platonism (developed by Plotinus from A.D. 205-270) provided the philosophical framework for much of his work. Platonism was put in the service of Christian apologetics against the Gnostics.

Jewish religion in Alexandria also influenced Origen's biblical scholarship. Until around 115, Alexandria had a flourishing Hellenistic Jewish population. The Jewish community produced the Septuagint translation of the Old Testament from Hebrew to Greek, the book of Wisdom and the works of the great Jewish philosopher Philo (c. 20 B.C.-A.D. 50). By Origen's day the influence of the Jewish community had diminished, but it still posed a significant challenge to the Christian community there. Origen's contact with the Jews is not entirely clear, but it is beyond doubt that they induced him to produce his most important work on the text of the Old Testament, the Hexapla.

Finally, Origen's theological work was developed in the face of heretical Christian groups such as the Gnostics. The forms of Gnosticism that Origen fought against were those by Basilides, Valentinus and Marcion. Their most serious attacks were aimed at the church's belief that Jesus' Father is identical with the Creator God of the Old Testament, the applicability of messianic prophecies to Christ, the reality of his humanity and the validity of the entire Old and New Testament books of the Bible. Origen sought to refute Gnostic objections rationally and to preserve the whole biblical canon and the church's rule of faith. Yet despite his valiant attempts to speak meaningfully to his own generation, vital issues within his theological system were judged negatively by his successors. Those issues were spelled out in detail in the posthumous condemnation of Origen(ism) by the Fifth Ecumenical Council (553). But the condemnations may not have always been fair to Origen due to certain distortions of his thought by overenthusiastic followers, especially Evagrius Ponticus. The anathemas should not diminish the value of his immense contributions to the history of biblical interpretation.

Literature. A large number of Origen's writings have been lost due to his condemnation by Justinian in 553 and the subsequent confiscation and burning of his books. Nevertheless, modern scholarship has been able to reconstruct some of those writings, many of which focused on biblical interpretation. There remains a vast legacy of materials to evaluate from Origen's work on the Bible. *Jerome classified Origen's biblical writings into three types of literature: *scholia,* biblical commentaries and homilies (Jerome [PL 25.585-86]).

1. He composed a number of brief explanatory notes on the biblical text called *scholia.* Following the literary methods of the classical curriculum, Origen made marginal notes on manuscripts, notes that could include textual, grammatical or interpretive comments. No *scholia* on individual books of the Bible, however, have come down to us in their entirety.

2. Origen wrote extensive biblical commentaries on most books of the Old and New Testaments. From all that we know, it appears that Origen was the first exegete in Christian history to form a systematic commentary on an entire book of the Old or New Testaments. These commentaries are longer and less numerous than the homilies. None of them has survived in complete form. J. Quasten estimates that "out of 291 commentaries 275 have been lost in Greek and very little is preserved in Latin" (Quasten, 2:51; see this source for information on the specific titles of *scholia,* exegetical works, homilies and commentaries with critical editions). Of all his writings, the insights recorded in the commentaries come closest to the historical-critical method of modern exegesis. Yet they are written in a style that is unlike that of modern commentaries in that Origen used Scripture to elaborate on philosophical concepts while also providing philological, grammatical, historical and literary observations on the text. This hybrid of philosophical theology and critical exegesis was the result of Origen's overarching interest in finding an inner unity of Scripture through allegorical exegesis.

3. There are homilies, or expository sermons, on select chapters or passages from the Bible. These Origen preached almost every day during the later part of his ministry, when he lived at Caesarea. Toward the end of his life, when he was more than sixty years old, he allowed these sermons to be taken down in shorthand by stenographers as they were delivered. That is why they seem to read more like conversational lectures than like modern sermons. The devotional emphasis of the homilies shows them to be more valuable for tracing the history of Christian spirituality than for understanding Origen's biblical scholarship.

4. We should add to Jerome's threefold classification of Origen's exegetical works a systematic treatise entitled *On First Principles* (Latin *De Principiis;* Greek *Peri Archon*). This is the first systematic exposition on Christian hermeneutical theory.

Old Testament. Origen's study of the Old Testament involved two problems: the text and the boundaries of the canon. A major catalyst for addressing these issues arose out of the need to find common ground for dialogue with the Jews. Any meaningful arguments that could be used to persuade the Jews had to be based upon a common Bible. But the Jewish Bible and the Christian Old Testament differed in the books they contained and the original text used (Hebrew versus the Greek Septuagint [LXX]).

Origen used both the shorter Hebrew canon and the longer Septuagint, which included apocryphal books like Judith, Tobit and the Wisdom of Solomon. He was content to conduct his apologetics against the Jews within the framework of their own shorter canon but freely referred to the Septuagint as needed. The reason for this was that the church itself accepted the Septuagint as authoritative Scripture. Against Jews who protested that the Septuagint was an illegitimate Bible, Christians had come to believe the legend that the Septuagint was a divinely inspired translation and therefore a definitive replacement of the Hebrew text. When Origen encountered differences between the Hebrew and Greek Bibles he occasionally preferred the original Hebrew; but most often he accepted the Septuagint readings because he considered them to be divinely appointed advances over the original (e.g., by contributing christological nuances to the Hebrew by addition or alteration). Ecclesiastical usage served as the criterion for Origen's acceptance and defense of the Septuagint.

Having been trained as a grammarian, Origen realized that the first requirement for understanding the Bible was to establish its correct wording. This led to his creation of the Hexapla, one of his most important contributions to biblical interpretation. The Hexapla, or Sixfold Bible, was an ongoing edition of the text of the Old Testament. Through painstaking labors, Origen produced it in Alexandria and Caesarea over a period of thirty-one years (c. 212-243). It was a manuscript of approximately sixty-five hundred pages. Because of its length, it was probably never copied in its entirety. Only parts of the Hexapla have survived. The church historian Eusebius apparently had the column which con-

tained the revised Septuagint copied for public use, and Jerome states that he used the original in the library of Pamphilus at Caesarea. The original was destroyed there in the seventh century during the Muslim conquest of Palestine.

Although the number of columns was not consistently six, as the title suggests, the main work was set out in six parallel columns: (1) the original Hebrew text, (2) a transliteration of that Hebrew text into Greek letters, presumably to assist in the vocalization of the unpointed Hebrew text, (3) a translation by Aquila (a second-century Jew whose rendering was the most literal of the group, being closest to the Hebrew; the translation preserved Hebrew word order and idiomatic turns of phrase), (4) a translation by Symmachus (another Jewish translator, but his was a more readable Greek rendering of the Hebrew), (5) a revised Septuagint, presumably the text current in Alexandria, and (6) a translation by Theodotion (a person who may have been a Jewish Christian). Prior to its inclusion in the Hexapla, the last four columns existed in a separate form known as the Tetrapla, or "Fourfold Bible." The Tetrapla was available to Origen through its current use in Jewish synagogues in Alexandria.

The most important column of the Hexapla was the Septuagint. Since Origen did not have a full mastery of the Hebrew language, he consulted Jewish scholars and compared the Septuagint to the other Greek translations of the Old Testament to understand the Hebrew original. Following the symbols of classical grammarians, Origen added to the Septuagint words that were in the Hebrew but not in the Greek by using an asterisk (*) to mark the spot. Words that were in the Greek but not in the Hebrew were marked by an obelus (_ or â). To mark the conclusion of a passage to which the asterisk or obelus referred, a metobelus was used (: or /). These signs are still used by textual critics. Minor disagreements between the Hebrew and Greek were silently corrected by Origen. The evidence indicates that in all his changes, Origen did not rely on a direct translation from the Hebrew but on one or another of the adjacent columns that contained the three versions by Aquila, Symmachus and Theodotion. Origen wrongly assumed that the Hebrew text current in his day was identical to that from which the Septuagint translation was originally made. This resulted in a recension (edition) of the Greek Old Testament rather than a restoration of the Septuagint. In the early church this recension was regarded as having great authority.

Modern textual critics of the Septuagint have often been unfair to Origen in their assessment of his work on the Hexapla. The claim made is that Origen's lack of knowledge of Hebrew caused him to rely on the Jewish Greek editions rather than to make a fresh Greek translation. But Origen's goal for the Hexapla was not the same as that of the modern critic who seeks to recover the original text. The primary goal of the Hexapla was immediately apologetic. Origen sought to obtain a revised text of the Septuagint that would be acceptable in Greek-speaking Jewish circles of his day so as to provide a sound basis for dialogue. To be sure, he recognized the priority of the Hebrew text and its authoritative use in his controversies with the Jews. But this did not mean that Origen wanted to substitute the Hebrew for the Septuagint, for he considered both to be inspired by God. But whether the Septuagint or the Hebrew was regarded as the final court of appeal in theological matters remains a disputed question. Origen appears to have adopted an unsettled conviction about which was the authoritative text of the Old Testament canon. S. Brock puts the matter in perspective: "It is this apologetic purpose of the Hexapla that one must always keep in mind when considering Origen's practice as a textual critic. He was not interested in constructing any 'original text' of the LXX, in the way that modern scholars are, but simply in providing the Christian controversialist with a text that would be acceptable in the authoritative eyes of contemporary

Jewish scholars" (Brock, 216).

New Testament. Origen's textual criticism of the New Testament is less substantial than that of the Old Testament. But his chief contributions to the New Testament focused on two problems: the text and boundaries of the New Testament canon. Within those areas Origen illuminates the number of books, original wording and history of the New Testament text (i.e., the dating of different text types and establishment of their geographical locations). As with the Old Testament, Origen made wide use of the New Testament Scriptures in commentaries, homilies, doctrinal discussions or controversies with his contemporaries. His apologetics were directed against the Jews, various pagan authors, Marcionites, Gnostics, modalists, adoptionists, docetists and various chiliasts. As a necessary defense against Judaism and Gnosticism, Origen developed a well-conceived system of allegorical hermeneutics.

An exceptionally valuable contribution was made to the history of the canon when Origen refers to all twenty-seven books of the New Testament. He divides them and others into three categories: those that were universally accepted, those that were disputed and those that were rejected. The accepted books included the four Gospels, Acts, thirteen letters of Paul, Hebrews (apparently because he accepted its apostolic content but doubted its Pauline authorship), 1 John, 1 Peter and Revelation. The disputed books were 2 Peter, 2 John, 3 John, James, Jude, the *Shepherd of Hermas,* the *Didache,* the *Epistle of Barnabas* and the *Gospel of the Hebrews.* Other writings were put in the false category. The primary criterion that guides his selection is general usage by the church (see Eusebius *Ecclesiastical History* 6.25.8-14). Sometimes, however, Origen quotes or makes reference to a gospel beyond the four canonical Gospels with qualifying phrases such as "which the church approves" or "if any one receives it" (e.g., the *Gospel of Peter, Gospel According to the Hebrews*). He also frequently makes use of unwritten sayings of

Jesus. However, in an important passing comment in the *Homilies on Joshua* 7.1 (c. 240), we find Origen making a list of all the authors of the New Testament. The list implies an acceptance of the same twenty-seven books that are contained in our New Testament canon. But the sermon was likely given for the purposes of edification, not technical analysis, so it is difficult to ascertain his certainty about which books belong in the canon. All this points to the fact that while the canon was far down the path toward the church's final definition of a list of authoritative books, the question was still open in Origen's day.

Origen probably never attempted to edit a critical edition of the New Testament, although some modern scholars think otherwise (for a summary of opinions, see Metzger 1963, 78-95). Furthermore, no definitive answer has been given to solve the great riddle of what New Testament text type Origen used. Yet, in all his writings, especially his exegetical treatises, one finds comments about the sometimes poor condition of a manuscript or variant readings of a given text. When deciding between which variant to accept, his choice is often based on theological considerations more than on objective textual evidence. For example, when Origen rejects the reading "Jesus Barabbas" in favor of "Barabbas" (Mt 27:16-17), he does so because he believes that the name *Jesus* was never applied to evildoers. Again, Origen's well-known preference for the reading "Bethabara" instead of "Bethany" as the place where John baptized (Jn 1:28) was based on geographical and etymological grounds rather than on textual evidence. In other instances Origen withholds choosing between two variant readings since, because of his allegorical hermeneutics, he is able to find spiritual truths in both texts. Origen provides invaluable information to the modern textual critic who is concerned with the history of the transmission, corruption and restoration of the text of the New Testament.

Hermeneutics. Origen was not interested in biblical criticism for its own sake.

The issues he grappled with concerning the texts and boundaries of the Old and New Testaments were essential prerequisites for a higher task. That task was the interpretation of the Scriptures themselves. Origen's theory of biblical inspiration, eschatology, anthropology and the unity of the Old and New Testaments had a profound effect upon his theory of biblical interpretation.

Origen was persuaded that all truth necessary to humankind is contained in the inspired Scriptures. Holy Scripture is ultimately authoritative and divine because it has God himself as its author. Origen compares the harmonious nature of Scripture to "one perfect and attuned instrument of God, producing from its various notes a single sound of salvation for those who are willing to learn" (Origen *Commentary on Matthew,* homily 2). The terminology that Origen used resembles that of Philo or Josephus. Yet Origen is more careful than they were to emphasize the self-consciousness and free will of the prophets. He did not eliminate human agency. The biblical authors put the teachings of the Spirit in writing but knew their allegorical meanings. He rejects the ecstatic, irrational idea of inspiration applied by the Greeks to their poets, as well as that of the Montanists.

In every book, chapter, verse and letter of the Bible, Origen traces the breath of the Holy Spirit at work. The text, not the author, is the locus of inspiration. "The wisdom of God has penetrated to all the inspired Scripture even as far as the slight-est letter" (Origen *Philocalia* 2.4 [PG 12:1081]). From beginning to end the Bible is entirely truthful in all its assertions. Yet from a historical or literal perspective, the Spirit "wove into" the text a great many inconsistencies, contradictions, inaccuracies or impossibilities. So truth for Origen is not always factual information but saving knowledge. The trustworthiness of Scripture is sometimes to be found on strictly literal grounds but always on the level of its spiritual or allegorical meaning (Origen *De Principiis* 4.2.9; 4.3.1-5). In many cases, for the allegorical to be true, the literal should be as well. Where the literal sense could not be true the so-called error was a signal put there by God to move the reader beyond the literal level to a higher spiritual plane. How does one know when to move beyond the literal to the allegorical meaning? When the historical or literal meaning seems to be impossible, unworthy or in some other way fraught with difficulty, such as when the different Gospels do not seem to harmonize completely (see Daly, 137, and Trigg 1988). On this point Origen contrasts sharply with *Augustine, *Chrysostom and other early church fathers who upheld the Bible's complete truthfulness even in factual matters.

Origen views both Testaments as sharing two parts of one complete covenant record. The Old Testament was a "shadow" (skia), the New an "image" (eikōn). The Old Testament has been fulfilled through the incarnate presence of the divine Logos and must therefore be interpreted christologically (Homily on Joshua 2.1 in Tollington, 51-52). All of Origen's commentaries and homilies on the Old Testament endeavor to find Christ in the law and the prophets. The divine Logos is everywhere present, if not literally then at least in a concealed manner, that is, metaphorically, typologically or allegorically. The New Testament fulfills the foreshadowings of the Old but also is seen as a prefiguration of the kingdom that is to come. This kingdom Origen refers to as the "eternal gospel" (euangelion aiōnion; taken from Rev 14:6 in Origen De Principiis 4.3.13). Consequently the Old Testament is a shadow that points to the New Testament and even reaches beyond it to the eternal state. That "eternal gospel" is as far greater to the New Testament as the New Testament is to the Old.

Origen does not conceive this eschatology in terms of "this age" and "the age to come." Rather there are an infinite number of ages preceding and following this world in which we live. Beyond the horizon of history, when all ages have passed away, time will cease and eternity will reign

wherein life will reach its perfect end and God will be "all in all" (apokatastasis tōn pantōn): "But after the present age, there will yet be further ages to come . . . when all things are no longer in an age, but 'God is all in all' " (Origen De Principiis 2.3.5). For this reason Origen continually insisted that the Old and New Testaments had as their goal the mystical union of the soul with the Logos. But if that union is mediated through a knowledge of the Scriptures, what is the content of that knowledge and how is it to be grasped? Origen answered by developing a method of exegesis that conformed to the goal of mystical union and which presupposed a Platonic cosmology and its views concerning the nature of humanity and its relation to God.

Methods of Exegesis. Origen did not invent his interpretive techniques but borrowed them from a complex hermeneutical environment that was already present in his day. These included both Christian and non-Christian elements. Christian influences on his approach to Scripture came from the Bible itself and the precedents set by early Christian interpreters (such as *Justin Martyr, Melito and the apostolic fathers, who bequeathed to Origen certain terms and symbols that he adapted and used in his own homilies).

Non-Christian influences on Origen's exegesis came from Greek, Jewish and heretical sources. Allegorical interpretation was first developed in the Hellenism of ancient Greece. It attempted to bring ancient mythology and poetry into line with prevailing philosophical and moral opinions. The mythologies of Homer and other Greek gods included immoral stories that needed to be allegorized so as to move readers beyond the offensive historical account to a higher spiritual meaning that would improve the gods' moral standing. The object of Greek allegory was to present absolute, eternal, ahistorical or at least transhistorical truth. The historical was unimportant. If a religious document was divine it required an allegorical interpretation, and if such a document was interpreted allegorically it must be divine. For a religious document to have more than a temporary value in the Hellenic world, it had to contain mysteries and obscurities that demanded allegorical interpretation. That method was adopted by Origen and applied to the Bible. Moreover, Alexandrian Jews such as Philo employed a Platonic philosophy that Philo believed was allegorically contained in the Scriptures. In Origen's debates with the Marcionites and pagans such as Celsus, Origen forged literary techniques that answered charges that the Bible contained impossible literalisms. Finally, one cannot understand Origen's exegetical goals without relating them to the underlying structure of his worldview. The chief philosophical presupposition that guided Origen's exegesis was the metaphysics of Platonism. Since Platonism is the true metaphysic, Scripture must yield Platonic truth and reflect its vision of reality. Platonic cosomology corresponds to the nature and purpose of the Bible.

The controlling hermeneutic that dominated Origen's approach to Scripture was the interconnectedness of God, his Logos and humanity. In both Platonism and Christianity there is a similar belief in a direct link between the image *(eikōn)* and the "model" or "original" *(pros ti)*. The Logos is the direct Image of God who reveals the paternal Archetype. Humans are an image of the Image of God in the Logos. Everything concerned with the destiny of humanity must be related to the divine Image. The image of God in humans is therefore both a self-manifestation of God and the foundation of their relationship with God. Within this worldview Scripture serves as a vital link that unites the human image with the divine Image. Insofar as humans contemplate the Bible's spiritual message, they fulfill their own human nature as spiritual creatures made in the image of God.

Origen explains his hermeneutical theory in book 4 of *On First Principles,* which was written in Alexandria between 220 and 230. Basing himself squarely in the tradition of allegorical exegesis as exemplified by Aristobulus, Philo, Pantaenus and *Clement, Origen claims that Scripture itself reveals how we should understand the Bible. A Platonic trichotomony, supported by Proverbs 22:20-21 (LXX) and 1 Thessalonians 5:23, instructs the faithful to interpret Scripture in a threefold manner. Just as human beings consist of body, soul and spirit, so also do the Scriptures. The bodily sense of a text was either the historical or literal meaning. The literal was defined in a nonmetaphorical sense (e.g., the expression "hand of God" means that God really has flesh and bones; this level is for the simple, fleshly Christian). The soul revealed a nonmystical level of allegory (possibly the moral or ethical significance of a text, but this is doubtful and debated; it is known to those growing in perfection). The spirit contained the allegorical sense, the most profound level appropriate to God and humanity (known only to the mature elite; see Simonetti 1994, 39-48, for important distinctions between the literal and spiritual senses and the impact of Origen's christology on his doctrine of Scripture). Origen's threefold theory of ascending exegesis, however, was not consistently practiced. The criteria by which he discovered the various levels of meaning remains an understudied topic in Origenian studies. In addition, his anthropological model of exegesis unites biblical ideas with Neo-Platonic dualistic presuppositions that create an unresolved ambiguity between Scripture and Platonism.

In the fourth century, representatives from the Antiochene school of exegesis, such as John Chrysostom and *Theodore of Mopsuestia, attacked Origen's allegorical method for its dehistoricizing, philosophizing, arbitrary and elitist characteristics. The Antiochene exegetes proposed an alternate form of mystical exegesis *(theōria)* that attempted to be consistent with the literal meaning of the text (for a survey of the issues and current state of scholarship on this neglected and misunderstood principle of Antiochene exegesis, see Nassif).

Despite their efforts to restrain the tide of Alexandrian exegesis, Origen, more than anyone else, became famous for making allegory the dominant approach to biblical interpretation down through the Middle Ages. It prevailed as the foremost method of exegesis in both theological and monastic literature, even though Origen's theology was often opposed.

BIBLIOGRAPHY

Works. Origen, *Commentary on Matthew:* ANF 4:409-512; idem, *The Commentary of Origen on St. John's Gospel: The Text Revised with a Critical Introduction,* ed. A. E. Brooke (2 vols.; Cambridge: Cambridge University Press, 1896); ANF 9:297-408; FC 80; idem, *On First Principles* (New York: Harper & Row, 1966); idem, *Homilies on Leviticus: 1-16,* FC 83; idem, *Homilies on Luke and Fragments on Luke* FC 94; idem, *The Philocalia of Origen: A Compilation of Selected Passages from Origen's Works Made by St. Gregory of Nazianzus and St. Basil of Caesarea* (Edinburgh: T & T Clark, 1911); idem, *Der Römerbrieftext des Origenes,* ed. O. Bauernfeind (TU 44.3; Leipzig, 1923); *Selections from the Commentaries and Homilies of Origen,* ed. R. B. Tollinton (London: SPCK, 1929); idem, *Song of Songs: Commentary and Homilies,* ACW 26.

Studies. K. Aland and B. Aland, *The Text of the New Testament* (Grand Rapids: Eerdmans, 1987); S. Brock, "Origen's Aims as a Textual Critic of the Old Testament," SP 10 (1970) 215-18; H. Crouzel, *Origen* (San Francisco: Harper & Row, 1989); R. Daly, "The Hermeneutics of Origen" in *The Word in the World: Essays in Honor of Frederick L. Moriarty,* ed. R. J. Clifford and G. W. MacRae (Weston, MA: Weston College Press, 1973); J. Daniélou, *Origen* (New York: Sheed & Ward, 1955); D. Dawson, *Allegorical Readers and Cultural Revision in Ancient Alexandria* (Berkeley, CA: University of California Press, 1992); K. A. Ecklebarger, "Authorial Intention as a Guiding Principle in Origen's Matthew Commentary" (unpublished Ph.d. dissertation, University of Chicago, 1987); B. Ehrmann et al., *The Text of the Fourth Gospel in the Writings of Origen* (Atlanta: Scholars Press, 1992); R. M. Grant, *The Letter and the Spirit* (London: SPCK, 1957); idem, *Heresy and Criticism: The Search for Authenticity in Early Christian Literature* (Louisville, KY: Westminster John Knox, 1993); R. P. C. Hanson, *Allegory and Event* (Richmond, VA: John Knox, 1959); B. de Margerie, *Introduction to the History of Exegesis* (Petersham, MA: St. Bedes, 1993); B. M. Metzger, *The Canon of the New Testament: Its Origin, Development and Significance* (Oxford: Clarendon, 1987); idem, "Explicit References in the Works of Origen to Variant Readings in New Testament Manuscripts" in *Biblical and Patristic Studies in Memory of Robert Pierce Casey,* ed. J. N. Birdsall and R. W. Thomson (Freiburg: Herder, 1963) 78-95; idem, *The Text of the New Testament: Its Transmission, Corruption and Restoration* (3d ed.; New York: Oxford University Press, 1992); B. Nassif, " 'Spiritual Exegesis' in the School of Antioch" in *New Perspectives on Historical Theology: Essays in Memory of John Meyendorff,* ed., B. Nassif (Grand Rapids: Eerdmans, 1996); B. Neuschafer, *Origenes als Philologe* (Basel: Friedrich Reinhardt, 1987) 1:263-76; E. A. Parsons, *The Alexandrian Library, Glory of the Hellenic World: Its Rise, Antiquities and Destructions* (Amsterdam: Denmark Publishing, 1952); J. Quasten, *Patrology* (Westminster, MD: Newman, 1953) 2:37-101; M. Simonetti, *Biblical Interpretation in the Early Church: A Historical Introduction to Patristic Exegesis* (Edinburgh: T & T Clark, 1994); idem, *Lettera e/o allegoria: un contributo alla storia dell'esegesi patristica* (Rome: Oriental Institute Press, 1985); K. J. Torjeson, *Hermeneutical Procedure and Theological Method in Origen's Exegesis* (Berlin: Walter de Gruyter, 1986); J. Trigg, "Divine Deception and the Truthfulness of Scripture" in *Origen of Alexandria: His World and His Legacy,* ed. C. Kannengiesser and W. L. Petersen (Notre Dame, IN: University of Notre Dame Press, 1988) 147-65 (see other essays in this important volume); idem, *Origen: The Bible and Philosophy in the Third-Century Church* (Atlanta: John Knox, 1983); M. F. Wiles, "Origen as Biblical Scholar" in *CHB,* 1:454-89.   B. Nassif

Tertullian *(fl. 200)*

Tertullian appears in Christian history more as a vigorous defender of the Christian faith than as a systematic scholar and exegete. He enjoyed an impressive scholarly training in classical knowledge and rhetoric and wrote in both Latin and Greek, though nothing of his work has survived in Greek.

Born in North Africa in the second half

of the second century, Tertullian gave the Latin-speaking church its first significant library of theological works. He did not adopt the prevailing view of philosophy as an endless noble trek toward knowledge of the infinite. He plundered the methods of the philosophers but did not share their vision, and he condemned some Christian mutations of philosophy, though not all philosophical activity. Unlike the philosophers, he wrote not to explore grand ideas but to protect what he called orthodox Christianity. Almost everything he wrote was reactive, though often creative. Hence he mainly used the Bible to sponsor "orthodoxy" or rigorous forms of Christian living. He battled against anti-Christian propaganda, corruptions of the faith and tendencies to relax church discipline or spiritual vigor. For Tertullian faith and practice, doctrine and ethics, heresy and idolatry all hung together (Merrill, 154-55).

To the end of his life Tertullian remained in sympathy with the primary beliefs of catholic orthodoxy. However, in later life he embraced the "new prophecy" of the Montanists with their stress on life in the Holy Spirit. During this period he was critical of the actions and disciplinary standards of the bishops but showed no weakening in his main doctrinal convictions. His work on the Trinity, *Against Praxeas,* came to completion during this phase, and it laid the foundation for mainline, Western trinitarian thought and terminology.

Context. The second century proved stormy for the church. Sporadic waves of persecution devastated it in some localities and created tensions between those who maintained a costly profession and those who managed to evade edicts. At the same time Christians were beginning to pit the Christian faith against classical learning and religion, with varying degrees of adaptation as a result. This engagement provoked attack from pagan philosophers and political authorities, who all had a vested interested in the religious status quo. In addition, experiments in hybrid forms of the faith spawned theories more indebted to Greek non-Christian ideas than to the distinctives of Christian thinking.

Major Writings. Approximately thirty of Tertullian's writings survive, but these vary greatly in length, quality and weight. Although almost all his works fall under the heading *polemical,* they are commonly placed in three major groups: apologetic, theological and ecclesiastical or moral.

Tertullian's writing almost certainly began with works addressed to outsiders. Although he wrote other defenses of the Christian faith, Tertullian's *Apology* is easily his most impressive literary tract promoting the church in a pagan empire. It is full of incisive rhetoric, merciless irony and entertaining debate. It is a fine distinctive response to philosophical and political criticism of the Christians, but it does not show to best advantage Tertullian's skills as a biblical interpreter. For that we must look to his duels with writers influenced by Christianity.

The bulk of Tertullian's work falls into the category of theological writings. His early work *On the Prescription of Heretics (De Praescriptione Haereticorum)* lays the foundation for a series of searing attacks on what Tertullian saw as deviant versions of the faith. The targets of these varied in their agendas. However, in Tertullian's view, they all enslaved the biblical text to some philosophical vagary in the varied menu of Greek thought. The Valentinians dumped history and christology in favor of myth and endless speculation. Marcion endorsed a gulf between divine and physical natures and between Old and New Testaments. Hermogenes taught the eternity of matter, so veering dangerously off into dualism. "Praxeas" (whose real identity is now uncertain) so hiked up the simple oneness of God that the Trinity, now an inconvenience, disappeared.

Tertullian saw his work as rescuing the text from such ill-treatment, and this often entailed substantial discussion of the heretics' proof-texts. His withering onslaughts on the ideas of the long-dead Marcion and

Valentinus would each stretch to a substantial hardback book today.

Marcion's low view of the physical creation, a feature of much Greek philosophy, struck out also at Christian belief in the Incarnation and the resurrection of the body. Having set about Marcion's view of the creation, Tertullian went on to defend these central beliefs as well.

Tertullian united doctrine and ethics but also virtually invented Christian legalism. For him all Christian belief nurtured a rigorous life of obedience to the law of Christ. It was as important to defend the moral life of Christianity as it was to protect its foundation beliefs. Ironically, however, he could defend with the same confidence biblical moral standards (as in his work on patient suffering) and his own dubious new laws (as in his personal edict against remarriage). Although he had a clear picture of salvation through God's grace and condescension, he also overplayed confession and penance and began the fateful Western fascination with them that cracked only with Martin *Luther's protest in the sixteenth century. As Tertullian's rigor increased, so did his powers of exaggeration in defending his own quirks. These features have a bearing on his handling of biblical texts.

Boosted by his uncompromising and rigorous approach to Christian life and faith, Tertullian's practical and ethical approach to the Bible has passed into the tradition of Western theology.

Biblical Interpretation. Only rarely did Tertullian work simply as a biblical scholar in search of knowledge. He was invariably driven by apologetic and theological considerations. Exegesis for its own sake gave way to the need for "more effective forms of apology and the refutation not so much of interpretations regarded as faulty as of erratic doctrines in their entirety" (Waszink, 18). Tertullian's interpretation was not carried out in an objective, leisurely way. He worked from pressure rather than pleasure, responding to threats to the church's central convictions. This had both advantages and disadvantages. Negatively, he

sometimes succumbed to the temptation to massage the text to prove his case and was therefore not always consistent in applying declared principles. Positively, it meant that to create a watertight case he had to be critical and thorough. Fighting for faith also focused the interpreter's mind and sidelined the trivial.

Tertullian preferred unadorned simplicity to the freewheeling allegory popular in his time. According to J. H. Waszink (19-20) Tertullian wanted to use Scripture as a powerful witness or testimony against the growth of speculative, even bizarre, doctrines and to do so with an impression of "certitude." The key qualities to this impression were brevity, or conciseness, and simplicity. Tertullian championed these principles against his opponents' tendency to "curiosity," a constant searching for knowledge without arriving at any particular truth. Tertullian approached the Bible on the understanding that it set questions and answered them rather than simply broached matters in a mysterious way for the curious to pursue inconclusively. We could arrive at a high degree of certainty through the least complicated or convoluted reading of texts. This was the way he used Paul's writings, for instance, drawing on quotations powerfully to drive home an argument. He also reinforced his prooftexts with other arguments from nature, moral discipline and the traditional teachings of the churches.

It is most probable that Tertullian's rhetorical training supplied the drive for certainty. It required the debater to start with the clear and obvious and move on from there (Tertullian *De Resurrectione Carnis* 19; *Scorpiace* 11). It also put a premium on frequency. What cropped up frequently carried more weight than a clear but solitary instance. Tertullian probably thought here of the cumulative value of several witnesses in a court (Waszink, 28).

Tertullian's approach excluded the open-ended and disputable results of allegorizing. He recognized allegory as a quality of Scripture alongside prophecy, but he made limited use of it. His Latin training preferred serviceable clarity, simplicity and directness in the handling of Scripture rather than philosophical speculation (cf. Tertullian *De Carne Christi* 13). The starting point should always be the clear and unambiguous (Tertullian *De Resurrectione Carnis* 19; *Scorpiace* 11).

However, he could venture beyond the simple himself. This chiefly happened in two situations. First, he resorted to going beyond the plain meaning of the biblical text when upholding ethical standards not easy to impose. For instance, he did not believe in second marriages. Never mind that Paul had no problems with it. An interpreter with the Spirit could see a more rigorous intent beneath Paul's concessions (Tertullian *De Monogamia* 3).

This startling approach sprang from Tertullian's later Montanist stress on the Spirit's activity in prophetic gifts. It also belonged to a polemic against the official church leaders, questioning their competence to pronounce absolution and to interpret texts. In the striving for clarity, definition and simplicity he drove paradoxically toward "a non-rational source of certitude" (O'Malley, 133) in the "new prophecy." Second and more important, Tertullian sometimes resorted to allegory when defending the unity of the Old and New Testaments. However, even here his use of figurative interpretation is quite restrained for its day.

Tertullian's use of imagery frequently aimed at explanation and exposition rather than interpretation. It was a way of developing texts for polemical purposes. He was far more at home with the word *figura* than *allegoria,* though he defends them both specifically in *Adversus Marcionem* 3.5.3 (O'Malley, 129). Normally when he did use allegory, it was only by the classical rule found in Philo: an interpreter had first to recognize the literal sense and then show its inadequacy (cf. Tertullian *Adversus Marcionem* 3.5.3, 4).

A major area of Tertullian's exegetical work is the Latin rendering he gave to Greek texts. He frequently paraphrased and interpreted, or glossed, as he translated (O'Malley, 14-17). Occasions of translation, with or without glossing, nearly always arose from controversy. He did not lack confidence to depart from existing Latin translations (which were piecemeal) in order better to underscore his case.

The Two Testaments. For Tertullian the underlying issue in exegesis was one that haunts biblical discussion today: the relationship of the Old Testament to the New. How Jewish should Christianity be? Marcion's answer was dismissive and anti-Jewish. He branded the creating God of the Old Testament as unlikable, wrathful and unloving. The "good" God of Jesus in the New Testament, however, soared above squalid earthly affairs. Marcion had bowed to the pressure of Platonism and given Christianity a God of the static realm above history. In this way he had also made the interpretation of the Bible as historical reality irrelevant. Marcion's method bore fruit in a docetic Christ, one who only seemed to be humanly real and physical.

Tertullian responded, or rather exploded, by uniting the Creator of the Old Testament and the Redeemer of the New Testament. Along with *Irenaeus he laid the foundation for a tradition of biblical interpretation that assumed the substantial unity of the Jewish and Christian Scriptures. More important, it drilled into readers the historical nature of the Bible and its interpretation. For interpreters then as now, this produced a clutch of events and themes in the Old Testament difficult to assimilate to the New Testament picture. Tertullian was even prepared on occasion to bear the flaws of figurative interpretation rather than tolerate Marcion's wedge between the Testaments. So Christ, for example, inhabits the Old Testament in the person of Moses (Tertullian *Adversus Marcionem* 2.26.4), learns in the Old Testament to converse with the human world (Tertullian *Adversus Marcionem* 3.9.6; *De Carne Christi* 6.8; *Adversus Praxeas* 16) and accompanies the young men in the furnace (*Adversus Marcionem* 4.21.8).

The decision to unite the Testaments profoundly influenced all Tertullian's interpretation and theology. It made him view Jesus in the proper historical, Jewish context as narrated in the Gospels. Inadvertently, however, it also strengthened his legalism.

Tertullian nagged at the heretics' habit of wresting texts from their context. The whole Scripture came from the Spirit, and texts should take their meaning from the context. This includes the style, tone or argument of a passage (Tertullian *De Pudicitia* 17; *De Resurrectione Carnis* 10, 18, 21; *Adversus Praxeas* 20, 26; *De Praescriptione Haereticorum* 14). Although Tertullian did not outline a hard rule of interpretation based on the whole Bible (collection into a single book was still to come), he did have more controls than his opponents. An interpretation stood or fell by its faithfulness to the central agreed doctrines of the orthodox churches (the rule of faith). Consistency ran through the New Testament: Paul must not contradict himself (Tertullian *De Anima* 21; *De Monogamia* 11), and apostles did not contradict each other (Tertullian *De Pudicitia* 19).

Tertullian's most famous maxim for interpretation was his limitation upon the search for truth and understanding in biblical texts. His chosen boundaries confront us in the *regula fidei*, the rule of faith. The regula was a summary of the essential beliefs of apostolic Christian faith handed down, possibly through the catechizing of new converts. Wording and order varied, but the main points centered on confession of God the Creator and Father of Jesus, the Incarnation, ministry and resurrection of Jesus and the work of the Holy Spirit. According to Tertullian, where the regula gave answers curiosity must end.

With this weapon he slew the heretics. *On the Prescription of Heretics* argued that because his opponents wheeled away from the regula they forfeited access to the New Testament texts. The Bible was not a legiti-

mate source for argument by them. In doing this, did Tertullian place tradition (teaching handed down in the church) on the same level as Scripture itself, or even make it identical to Scripture? Probably not. Almost certainly he saw the *regula* as the best interpretation of Scripture and so a benchmark for other interpretations. He also wanted all exegesis to take place in the community that was loyal to Christ and the apostles. The actual New Testament writings remained for him God's revelation.

Significance. The impact of Tertullian's writings on Western Christianity remains problematical, but since he was much admired by Cyprian and *Jerome it must have been considerable. Several areas now emerge.

Tertullian could use philosophy when he wished, though not with a philosopher's flair. He took a practical line in handling Scripture. It was all either live application or live ammunition. Texts functioned to regulate belief and practice, not gently to expand the borders of speculative knowledge. Western Christianity accepted this legacy with its strengths and weaknesses. On the whole the approach was fruitful, but it could also bend the text away from its original intention, so deserting Tertullian's usual devotion to historical context.

Tertullian's commonsense approach to the text fed into traditional Western method up to the modern period. Some of his more typical principles especially gained prominence in the work of the Protestant Reformers: primary attention to the literal sense of a text; regard for the natural sense of the word or text; initial focus on the clear and unambiguous; interpretation of a text within the encircling situation or flow of argument; concern for coherence with the biblical writer's general thought.

Most important, an interpretation had to be Christian. It had to remain true to the doctrinal legacy of the apostolic or orthodox churches. The revelation was not abstract but was rooted in historical events supported and expressed in the rule of faith. This argument, as Tertullian himself observed, had little effect on his opponents. His exclusiveness here foreshadowed the sometimes restricting weight of tradition and magisterium (church teaching authority) in biblical work.

Tertullian would not tolerate an interpretation that disdained the historical, incarnational nature of Christian faith in favor of an ahistorical philosophy. God was the God of nature and history, and his revelation arose in human history. The interpreter had no room to massage the message into a more palatable myth.

Unrestrained by the discipline of Tertullian's strongly historical and literal approach, the more speculative writers felt free, with the aid of allegory, to find what they wished in the text. Tertullian attacked this with gusto. The approach of his opponents has a curiously similar ring to postmodernism, which is reluctant to attach a single, clear meaning to any text. Tertullian had a confidence in the capacity of the text to yield conclusions with some certainty. Undoubtedly his rhetorical training sometimes exaggerated his expectations, but this approach has fueled constructive biblical research in a way the Gnostics could never have done.

The combined weight of Marcion and the gnostic writers might easily have severed Christianity from its roots in Jewish history. The work of Irenaeus and Tertullian strengthened Christian recognition of the Jewish sacred books. Modern attention to the Jewish context of Jesus is just one late fruit of this. Through work such as theirs the Old Testament remained a major tool in the interpretation of the New Testament, and the collection of New Testament writings did not itself suffer emasculation.

Conclusions. Tertullian is full of examples both to follow and to avoid. His stress on historicity, simplicity, clarity and brevity, though an oversimplification, is preferable to ultimately meaningless typology. However, he was sometimes too confident about certainty of meaning. Moreover his denial of access to the text for all except the truly

Christian sounds unduly defensive. Ultimately, however, his work has not undermined sound exploration of the biblical text for the health of the church but advanced it. By reinforcing a commonsense and historical approach to biblical interpretation Tertullian has justly earned a place among major interpreters.

BIBLIOGRAPHY

Works. Tertullian, ANF 3-4; ANL 7, 11, 15, 18; CSEL 20, 47, 69, 70; FC 10, 40; PL 1-2.

Studies. T. D. Barnes, *Tertullian: A Historical and Literary Study* (Oxford: Clarendon Press, 1971); P. I. Kaufman, "Tertullian on Heresy, History and the Reappropriation of Revelation," *CH* (1991) 167-79; T. F. Merrill, "Tertullian: The Hermeneutical Vision of *De Praescriptione Haereticorum,* and Pentateuchal Exegesis," *PBR* (1987) 153-67; T. P. O'Malley, *Tertullian and the Bible: Language—Imagery—Exegesis* (Nijmigen: Van de Vegt, 1967); E. F. Osborn, "Reason and the Rule of Faith in the Second Century A.D." in *The Making of Orthodoxy: Essays in Honor of Henry Chadwick,* ed. R. Williams (Cambridge: Cambridge University Press, 1989) 40-61; D. Rankin, *Tertullian and the Church* (Cambridge: Cambridge University Press, 1995); idem, "Tertullian's Use of the Pastoral Epistles in his Doctrine of Ministry," *ABR* (1984) 18-37; R. D. Sider, *Ancient Rhetoric and the Art of Tertullian* (Oxford: Oxford University Press, 1971); idem, "Literary Artifice and the Figure of Paul in the Writings of Tertullian," in *Paul and the Legacies of Paul,* ed. W. S. Babcock (Dallas: Southern Methodist University Press, 1990) 99-120; T. F. Torrance, *Divine Meaning: Studies in Patristic Hermeneutics* (Edinburgh: T & T Clark, 1995); J. H. Waszink, "Tertullian's Principles and Methods of Exegesis" in *Early Christian Literature and the Classical Intellectual Tradition,* ed. W. R. Schoedel and R. L. Wilken (Paris: Beauchesne, 1979) 17-31. R. Kearsley

Theodore of Mopsuestia (350-428)

Theodore was born to wealthy parents in Antioch (Syria) about 350. He trained in rhetoric under the Sophist Libanius, who also taught John *Chrysostom. It was during this time that Theodore and John began their lifelong friendship. Like Chrysostom, Theodore joined a monastic community but left it for a time, contemplating marriage and a career in law. His departure prompted Chrysostom's two fervent letters, *Ad Theodorum Lapsum,* which brought Theodore back to clerical life. In 392 he was appointed to the see of Mopsuestia, a town in Cilicia (in modern Turkey) about halfway between Antioch and Tarsus. Here he remained until his death in 428.

Theodore was fortunate in that he did not fall from ecclesiastical favor until after his death. The trouble began at the Council of Ephesus (431), which was dominated by the archenemy of the Antiochenes, Cyril of Alexandria. Theodore was viewed as the spiritual father of Nestorianism. In spite of his contribution to the later Chalcedonian christology, his writings were condemned by Justinian (in the Three Chapters edict, 543-544) in the latter's attempt to gain the support of the Monophysites, who hated Theodore's christology. The Nestorian Syrian church still reveres him as the greatest of biblical exegetes, and the discovery in this century of some of his works preserved in Syriac manuscripts has greatly expanded the number of his extant writings.

Inspiration. Theodore began his literary work with a high traditional doctrine of the inspiration of Scripture, stressing the divine factor almost to the obliteration of the human in the writing of revelation. However, there is evidence that during his exegetical career he modified this position so as to view inspiration as a collaboration between the Holy Spirit and the writers. Yet "this . . . can only be discovered in his later writings; in all of his earlier works he adheres to the doctrine of plenary and verbal inspiration" (Zaharopoulos 1964, 110).

Theodore's emphasis on the importance of the human vessel led him to take grammatical and linguistic questions seriously. In connection with this, he also insisted on treating the biblical narratives as history. He refused to take isolated verses out of context to prove a theological point and was strongly opposed to the spiritualizing allegory that characterized the church of Alexandria. Inspiration, according to Theodore, occurred in a specific historic context from which it could not be separated, even in the interest of theology.

Old Testament. The only complete Old Testament commentary to survive in the original Greek is Theodore's work on the Minor Prophets. Additionally, we have a large portion of his early commentary on the Psalms, plus a few fragments on Genesis 1—3 and four passages in Exodus. Some details of his lost works are known from other writers, notably the fourteenth-century Nestorian writer Ebedjesu. The surviving works reveal a sharply defined approach to the Scriptures in reference both to the Old Testament canon and to exegesis.

Canon. Theodore seems to have been the first of the Fathers consistently to reject the Apocrypha. As Zaharopoulos comments, "owing to a rigid conception of canonicity, [he] was the only one among the early Christian commentators who restricted his Old Testament to the limits of the Bible of Palestinian Judaism, not only in theory but also in practice" (Zaharopoulos 1989, 55). He also rejected much of the book of Job, saying that the author of the verse portions was a learned Edomite (and hence a pagan) who inserted his creation into the story of the historical Job. Theodore also rejected the Song of Songs, which he viewed merely as a wedding poem composed by Solomon for his marriage to the daughter of Pharaoh.

It is still debated whether Theodore knew Hebrew; if so, his knowledge of it seems to have been very limited. Although he believed the Hebrew Old Testament to be authoritative, he regularly quoted from the Septuagint, rationalizing this by saying that the Seventy followed the Hebrew text more closely than did the other translators. Although he consulted other Greek translations and the Peshitta, he rejected them as nonauthoritative. In matters of textual criticism he was far weaker than *Jerome.

Interpretation. In both Theodore's

commentary on the Psalms and his work on the Minor Prophets, the reader becomes quickly aware of Theodore's doctrine of the two ages, which is essential for understanding his exegesis. He posited a radical split between the time of Christ and all that went before and was thus cautious about referring any Old Testament prophecy unequivocally to Christ. For Theodore the prophets, speaking from a specific historical setting, were far more likely to refer to events within Israel's contemporary situation or at least no further in the future than the era of the Maccabees. To cite isolated verses from either the Psalms or the prophets as proof-texts for the time of Christ was to blur the distinction between the Testaments, to minimize the progressive nature of revelation and to lessen the newness of the Christ event. Thus Theodore allowed that only three of the psalms had a primary reference to Christ: Psalms 2, 8 and 45 (on the basis of his extant works, many scholars think that he also included 110, but that part of his commentary has not survived). At times Theodore did refer to the two ages as the current age (still suffering from the curse of sin) and the future age (in which the reign of Christ will triumph), but the former approach is foundational to his Old Testament exegesis.

Closely related to this concept was Theodore's insistence upon the unity of the passage that he was interpreting. He was contemptuous of those exegetes who referred "successive verses to Zerubbabel, to Christ, and back to Zerubbabel again in expounding Zech. 9:8-10" (Wiles, 502). He held that the Old Testament passages should have "a consistent, connected interpretation" (Wiles, 502). This idea is perhaps the most evident in Theodore's treatment of the Psalms, particularly when his work is seen against the backdrop of much contemporary exegesis, especially that of Alexandria, which viewed Scripture as a treasure box from which any verse could be taken to verify or amplify the meaning of any other. Against this, Theodore insisted that each psalm was and must

be treated as a single unit. Consequently there must be only one speaker in each psalm. Theodore rejected the theory of some Jewish expositors that some psalms were dialogues between the speaker and God or between different speakers.

Coupled with this belief in the unity of each psalm was Theodore's belief that the entire book of Psalms was the work of David. But on the basis of internal evidence, he realized that the historical setting of some of them belonged to a later date than the time of David. For instance, Psalm 51, in spite of the reference in the superscription to David and Bathsheba, belongs to the time of the exile, since mention is made in its closing verses to the rebuilding of the walls of Jerusalem—something that had no application in David's day. To resolve this quandary of his belief in Davidic authorship and his insistence upon inner unity, Theodore said that David was speaking not in his own person but as a prophet. Coupled with Theodore's doctrine of the two ages, the prophecy would normally not go beyond the Maccabean period. In the psalms that Theodore admitted to have a christological focus, David was speaking in the "prophetic person" of Christ. Psalm 22 was rejected as referring to Christ, since the ending of the Septuagint version of it refers to "the account of my sins," and since Christ had none, the psalm could not apply to him.

Theodore did believe that there could be a secondary application to the Christian era in certain passages, but he was cautious about applying this; he lists only five such instances in the Minor Prophets: Joel 2:28, Amos 9:11-12, Micah 5:2, Zechariah 9:9 and Malachi 3:1 (Wiles, 502-3).

New Testament. During the nineteenth century, scholars discovered and published (1897) a complete Syriac version of Theodore's commentary on John. Before this, only fragments of it were known, many of them spurious. In 1940 the Syriac version was published with a Latin translation. Theodore's commentary on the Pauline epistles from Galatians through Philemon survived in a complete Latin translation included among the works of Ambrose. Greek fragments of this work have survived, as have fragments of Theodore's commentary on the four major Pauline epistles (Romans, 1 Corinthians, 2 Corinthians and Hebrews, which Theodore regarded as Pauline).

Typology. In light of Theodore's drastic separation of the Christ event from all that went before, one might well ask how he dealt with the New Testament passages that claim to be the fulfillment of events or statements in the Old Testament. To the Alexandrian exegetes, with their view of Scripture as a repository from which any verse could be cited with no reference to its historical setting, this posed no problem. But it did to Theodore, due to his distinctive understanding of the two ages.

Theodore's answer was to resort to typology, by which he meant that certain events in the Old Testament prefigured some in the New. He did not do this at random. Rather, when Paul cited Old Testament passages, it was because the circumstances that Paul was addressing in the Christian era were not without resemblance to those that had occurred when the Old Testament citation under discussion had occurred. With Theodore's strong awareness of history, he also insisted that both the Old Testament and New Testament passages had to be factual; otherwise the New Testament reference would make no sense. By the proper use of typology, one could appreciate both the historicity of the Old Testament passage and its application to the Christian era.

Commentary on the Gospel of John. It is not surprising to see that Theodore paid close attention to history and chronological development in his commentary on the Fourth Gospel. This made him ascribe Nathanael's reference to Christ as "Son of God" (Jn 1:49) to current Jewish messianic hopes rather than to a fully developed christology. Likewise Thomas's cry of "My Lord and my God" (Jn 20:28) was, according to Theodore, an ascription of praise to God, not an anticipation of the Nicene christol-

ogy. However, Theodore's exegesis of the Gospel definitely set forth a Christ in accord with Nicene orthodoxy, with the strong Antiochene emphasis on two natures in one Christ. Although Theodore attributed certain of the sayings of Jesus to either his human or his divine nature, he never divided the unity of the person of Christ. In spite of this, it is easy to see how Theodore's commentary would raise questions in Alexandrian and particularly Mon-ophysite circles.

Commentary on the Pauline Epistles. Theodore seems to have been much more at home with the writings of Paul. Certainly the apostle's emphasis on the limitations of the pre-Christian era, the impotence of the law, and the greater glory of the Christ event and what has flowed from it gave strong support to Theodore's understanding of the two ages. His careful attention to the meaning of words and phrases and even to punctuation is everywhere evident, although he was guilty "of here and there overlooking or even misrepresenting the force of a preposition" (Swete, 1:lxv) and of blurring the distinction between various verbal tenses. He was primarily interested in the thoughts behind the words and in clarifying the course of Paul's logical progressions. His approach was not only critical but also practical. Yet his basic theological interest was more intellectual than devotional. Like many other exegetes, he also revealed a tendency unconsciously to read his own theology into the text.

Assessment. Theodore's ideas are of considerable interest in themselves, but when they are viewed against the backdrop of current and preceding exegetical procedures, they seem particularly startling. His refusal to treat the Scriptures as a timeless given from which any passage may be quoted in support of the interpretation of another, with no reference to its historical setting, has been noted. One of Theodore's strongest points is his emphatic insistence on history. His awareness that the biblical texts were produced in particular times and settings is everywhere evident, and it provides a healthy corrective to the exegesis that viewed the Old Testament merely as a prophecy of the events of the Christian era.

The emphasis on the human and earthly characteristics of the Bible was a characteristic of Antiochene theology, and Theodore's writings are a case in point. His focus on history also led him to castigate the allegorizing of difficult Old Testament passages, a custom that had become accepted in the church, particularly since the time of *Origen. Theodore found typology to be a far safer method for understanding the relationship between the two Testaments, inasmuch as it guarded the historicity of the Old Testament. The strong difference of his exegetical approach from that of Alexandria was illustrative of the differences between the two great churches, and the later condemnation of Theodore's writings is part of the same warfare that had earlier led to the condemnation of John Chrysostom at the Synod of the Oak, under the leadership of Theophilus of Alexandria.

Theodore's insistence on history but also his careful attention to words, grammar and structure set him further apart from much contemporary exegesis. Even when he made mistakes in these areas, one can still sense that he was a scholar passionately eager to understand a text accurately, in order to allow it its full force. In comparison with the sermons of Chrysostom, "Theodore's interest in theology is intellectual rather than spiritual or devotional" (Swete, 1:lxx), and his textual criticism suffers by comparison with that of *Jerome. In style, his terse, difficult Greek lacks the elegance characteristic of Chrysostom and *Theodoret, but the force of his ideas still communicates, and the brilliance and freshness of his approach are impressive.

In spite of disagreement with Alexandria in both christology and exegesis, Theodore was no radical when it came to the accepted traditions of the church. Although the Nicene Creed had left open some christological questions that needed further definition in the fifth century, Theodore held firmly to its authority. Likewise, his insistence upon the Davidic authorship of all the psalms has been noted. In the same way, recently discovered catechetical lectures reveal his allegiance to current sacramental tradition. Where he differed was in his refusal to accept some of the current exegetical practices as normative for the church.

Many of Theodore's writings have been lost. This was often the case with writers judged to be heretical. Yet even in its surviving fragmentary form, his work shows the marks of a powerful intellect imbued with a great respect for the textual material and with a desire to express its truths carefully and accurately for the benefit of the church and its theology.

BIBLIOGRAPHY

Works. Theodore of Mopsuestia, CPG 2.3827-3873; CSCO 115-16; PG 33:633-46 (Frag. Genesis); 56.9-1020 (texts); 66:124-632 (Minor Prophets); 66:703-14 (Frag. Matthew); 66:713-16 (Frag. Mark); 66:716 (Frag. Luke); 66:728-85 (Frag. John); idem, *Le Commentaire de Theodore de Mopsueste sur les Psaumes (1-80),* ed. R. Devreese (*Studi e Testi* 93; Vatican City: Biblioteca Apostolica Vaticana, 1939); idem, "The Commentary of Theodore of Mopsuestia on the Lord's Prayer and on the Sacraments of Baptism and the Eucharist," vol. 6, and "The Commentary of Theodore of Mopsuestia on the Nicene Creed," vol. 5, *Woodbrook Studies,* ed. A. Mingana (Cambridge: Cambridge University Press, 1933, 1932); idem et al., *Pauluskommentare aus der griechischen Kirche,* ed. K. Staab (Münster: Aschendorff, 1933) 113-212; idem, *Theodori Episcopi Mopsuesteni in Epistolas B. Pauli Commentarii,* ed. H. B. Swete (2 vols.; Cambridge: Cambridge University Press, 1880-1882).

Studies. R. Devreese, *Essai sur Theodore de Mopsueste (Studi e Testi* 141; Vatican City: Biblioteca Apostolica Vaticana, 1948); R. A. Greer, *The Captain of Our Salvation* (Tübingen: J. C. B. Mohr, 1973); idem, *Theodore of Mopsuestia: Exegete and Theologian* (Philadelphia: Westminster, 1961); L. Pirot, *L'oeuvre exégétique de Théodore de Mopsueste* (Rome: 1913); M. Wiles, "Theodore of Mopsuestia as Representative of the Antiochene School" in *CHB* 1:489-510; D. Z. Zaharopoulos, *Theodore of Mopsuestia on the Bible* (New York: Paulist, 1989); idem, *Theodore of Mopsuestia's Critical Methods in Old Testament Study* (Ph.D. diss., Boston University, 1964).

B. A. McDonald

Theodoret of Cyrus *(393-458)*

Theodoret of Cyrus was born to moderately wealthy parents in Antioch. He spent his first twenty-three years in Antioch, where he was exposed to the secular education offered by rhetors, as well as Christian teachings from the monks living in the mountains surrounding Antioch and possibly the writings and sermons of John *Chrysostom, *Theodore of Mopsuestia and Diodore of Tarsus. Theodoret refers at one point to Theodore and Diodore as his teachers, but this should not be read literally, as we lack evidence of an organized school of Antiochene theology as might has been found in Caesarea or Alexandria.

Upon the death of his parents, Theodoret says, he distributed all of his inherited wealth and, taking the advice of his monk mentors, left Antioch (416/417) to enter the monastery at Nicerte. Theodoret recalls the life at Nicerte with great fondness, as it offered not only quiet retreat from the world but also an opportunity to continue his education in secular and religious thought. At Nicerte Theodoret composed his celebrated apology *Graecarum Affectionum Curatio (The Cure of Pagan Maladies)*, which in comparing Christian and pagan answers on questions of philosophy and religion displays a remarkable level of erudition. It was also at Nicerte that Theodoret likely encountered the bishop of Apamea, Polychronius, brother of Theodore of Mopsuestia. Theodoret is one of our few witnesses for the life and work of Polychronius, and in the fragments we have left of Polychronius's work there are several points of similarity of exegetical interests and tendencies.

After seven years in the monastery, Theodoret was called to assume the duties of the bishop of the diocese of Cyrus. The diocese was named after the town of Cyrus, which was the chief town of Cyrrhestica, a territory of the province of Euphatensis in eastern Syria. The diocese covered some sixteen hundred square miles and, according to Theodoret, was home to eight hundred parishes, each with its own church as well as a large population of monks. Theodoret served the diocese as bishop until his death in 458.

Work. Theodoret was a conscientious and vigorous bishop who not only attended to the concerns of the faithful in the diocese but also became deeply enmeshed in the christological debates and councils culminating with the Council of Chalcedon. This range of demands and the vigor of response is mirrored in the corpus of writings left by Theodoret. Aside from the apology mentioned above, Theodoret composed a history of the monks of Syria, a history of the church, theological tracts on christology and providence, and a corpus of exegetical works covering most of the books in the Septuagint (the exceptions being Job, Ezra/Nehemiah, Proverbs and Ecclesiastes) as well as the letters of Paul.

The form of the exegesis varies from a series of questions and responses on the Octateuch and the so-called historical books (Kings and Chronicles) to verse-by-verse commentary. Theodoret's earliest commentary is that on Canticles (431), and his most extensive is his *Commentary on Psalms*. He makes few references to a Hebrew or Syriac variant from the Greek text. However, Theodoret frequently compares "his text" with other Greek recensions (most often that of Symmachus). While it is not certain what text Theodoret is using as the standard text, it appears he uses a Lucianic recension in conjunction with Origen's *Hexapla*.

With the exception of the *Questions on the Octateuch,* the principal text for the commentaries remains that found in J. P. Migne's *Patrologia Graeca*. Very little of this work has been translated into modern languages. In the case of the verse-by-verse commentaries, certain formal traits along with comments by Theodoret suggest that most of the commentaries were initially given as expository lectures. These lectures were then transcribed (at Theodoret's direction) for circulation to other bishops, abbots and perhaps patrons among the laity. A telling remark in this regard occurs in the *Commentary on Daniel,* where he concludes his interpretation of the fourth chapter with an apology that he is unable to describe at length all the prophecies concerning the pride and cruelty of Nebuchadnezzar "neither for the present listeners nor for those who read these things later." Unlike *Jerome, however, Theodoret never makes explicit the occasion or the patron for the lectures or commentaries. It may be that he was invited by other clerics who knew of his talents, as he says was the case for the *Discourses on Providence.*

At the same time Theodoret acknowledges with some regularity that the interpretive task was taken on either as a response to concerns or questions brought to him from the diocese or as a result of his own perception of a problem that needed a biblical answer. In other words, the right interpretation of the Bible was for Theodoret no mere retelling of the story or an exercise in the display of methodological finesse. The exegesis is linked to a setting (late Roman Syria) and to a commitment to the pastoral tasks. Theodoret conveys this exegetical posture most clearly in a letter written to monks in Constantinople (449) in which he comments on his life's work in these terms:

> My task has been to contend on behalf of the apostolic decrees, to bring this pasture of instruction to the Lord's flock, and to this end I have written thirty-five books interpreting the divine Scriptures and proving the falsehood of the heresies . . . not on behalf of a duality of sons, but of the only begotten Son of God, against the heathen, against the Jew . . . I have never ceased to struggle, trying the convince the heathen that the Eternal Son of the living God is creator of the universe and the Jew that about him the prophets uttered their predictions.

This quote shows not only the centrality of pastoral and apologetic concerns but also a convergence of these factors with theological convictions. Especially in the commentaries on the Old Testament, Theodoret

drives the interpretation in the direction of displaying God's providential design in the events and persons of the biblical history and making clear the prophetic foundation for the claim that Jesus of Nazareth is the Christ. These convictions are brought out by way of a methodology that is influenced by his Antiochene mentors, Theodore of Mopsuestia and Diodore of Tarsus, but Theodoret is no slave to their approach.

Interpretive Approach. Theodoret's approach defies easy alignment with either of the two prominent methodological camps, the Antiochenes or the Alexandrians. Theodoret utilizes an array of interpretative strategies from a simple historical reading, to typology, to direct prophecy. Like Theodore, but even more frequently, Theodoret finds in the Old Testament a typological connection to the New Testament. For example, Theodoret comments at one point in the commentary on Psalms: "Because in truth the ancient events are a type of the things of the New Testament, so as the body has alongside of it the shadow, we must set forth this affinity. There the pious King Hezekiah, and here Christ, the helmsman of piety" (Theodoret *Commentary on Psalms* 28:1 [PG 80:1063]).

Theodoret's use of typology is, however, no simple parroting of Theodore. It finds its place in the exegesis as support for Theodoret's deeply held convictions about providence and the integrity of the two natures of Christ. The biblical text is a witness to the "untiring philanthropy of God" (Theodoret *Commentary on Hosea* 1:4 [PG 81:1556]) as it also demonstrates that "He [Christ] was sent not as God but as man. For as God he is equal to the Father. . . . Yet he was sent as man, carrying out the plan of God, and not diminishing the divine nature. . . . The prophet shows us therefore the duality of the nature but also the equal worth of the natures" (Theodoret *Commentary on Zechariah* 2:8-9 [PG 81:1888]).

In sharp contrast to Theodore, Theodoret also finds ample texts that serve as a direct prophecy of the coming and work of

Christ, the apostles and the spread of the church. In several instances Theodoret chides not only the Jews but also the "teachers of the faith" for failing to recognize a text as a direct prophecy of some aspect of the Christian dispensation. The prophecies of the Old Testament make plain that "the Christian religion was announced from the beginning" (Theodoret *Orations on Providence* [PG 83:772]), and they provide the "pasture" that nourishes the flock. The Psalms are, for example, replete with direct prophecies of events related to Christ and the church. He comments in the preface to the commentary on Pslams:

> I have consulted various commentaries of which some fell into allegory, while others adapted the prophecies themselves to past history, so that their interpretation applied more to Jews than to Christians. All that is relevant to ancient history ought to be acknowledged, but predictions concerning Christ our savior, the Church of the nations, the spread of the gospel, the preaching of the apostles ought not be diverted from their proper sense and applied to other things. . . . It may seem to some that there is little significance in recalling these divine oracles; but those spiritual melodies from holy David have been recalled many times in many houses, on the streets, and on the roads . . . and through this gratifying activity there are many who gain benefit. (Theodoret *Commentary on Psalms, Prefatio* [PG 80:860-61])

Theodoret's sole work on the New Testament, the *Commentary on the Letters of St. Paul,* composed around 436-438, draws deeply from the well of the commentaries of John Chrysostom and Theodore of Mopsuestia. At the same time, as P. Parvis has observed, "Theodoret is not slavishly dependent on his sources, and he does reshape their theology in the struggle to understand the Pauline foundations of his own thought" (Parvis, 6). While Theodoret uses the commentary to offer devo-

tional and moral exhortations, the heart of the exegesis is given over to christology. The commentary written after the christological battles at the Council of Ephesus (431), during which Theodoret was attacked as being Nestorian, spends much energy in affirming the unity of the person of Christ, the primacy of the Word and a soteriology emphasizing ransom and sacrifice.

Significance. The biblical commentaries of Theodoret have been characterized as being unoriginal and given over primarily to charting a methodology somewhere between the charybdis of allegory and the scylla of a historical reading. Theodoret does utilize the work of earlier commentators, and his approach does often move between Antioch and Alexandria. The real value of the work is the way in which Theodoret uses the insights and methods of his exegetical forebears to address the various dimensions of the world of a bishop in late Roman Syria. Theodoret brings to the interpretive moment the resources and convictions of a well-educated citizen (turned monk) of the Greek East, a committed theologian, a rigorous defender of the truth of the Christian religion and a conscientious bishop of a frontier diocese. The result is an exegesis that is a marvelous window into a bishop at work using biblical interpretation to solve crises and create a worldview.

BIBLIOGRAPHY

Works. Theodoret of Cyrus, *Théodoret de Cyr: Commentaire sur Isaie,* ed. J.-N. Guinot (3 vols.; Paris: Le Editions du Cerf, 1981, 1982, 1984);idem, *The Ecclesiastical History, Dialogues and Letters of Theodoret,* ed. B. Jackson, NPNF 3; PG 80-84; SC 276, 295, 315.

Studies. G. W. Ashby, *Theodoret of Cyrus as Exegete of the Old Testament* (Grahamstown, South Africa: Rhodes University Publications, 1972); J.-N. Guinot, *L'Exégèse de Thédoret de Cyr* (Paris: Editions Beauchesne, 1995); idem, "Theodoret of Cyrus: Bishop and Exegete" in *The Bible in Greek Christian Antiquity,* ed. and trans. P. M. Blowers (Notre Dame, IN: University of Notre Dame Press, 1997) 163-93; C. T.

McCollough, "A Christianity for an Age of Crisis: Theodoret of Cyrus' Commentary on Daniel" in *Religious Writings and Religious Systems*, ed. J. Neusner, E. Frerichs and A. Levine (Atlanta: Scholars Press, 1989) 157-74; idem, "Theodoret of Cyrus as Biblical Interpreter and the Presence of Jews in the Late Roman Empire" in *Studia Patristica*, ed. E. Livingston (Kalamazoo, MI: Cistercian Press, 1983) 18:327-34; P. Parvis, "Theodoret's Commentary on the Epistles of St. Paul: Historical Setting and Exegetical Practice" (unpublished Ph.D. dissertation, Oxford University, 1975); R. Sellers, *Two Ancient Christologies* (London: SPCK, 1940).

C. T. McCollough

PART TWO

Biblical Interpretation
in the Middle Ages

TWO GENERATIONS OF INTENSE SCHOLARSHIP HAVE OVERTHROWN THE OLD
Protestant opinion that medieval Europe was a civilization with no ear for the
Bible. The Bible informed religious beliefs, popular piety, the academic study of
theology, literature and literary attitudes, monasticism and art. Moreover, its
interpretation was consistent with fundamental attitudes toward nature, science,
history and politics. The Bible not only fed theology but also was at the center
of much cultivated human imagination in the Middle Ages. To study the history
of its interpretation during those centuries, when the societies of Europe and
much of their common religion first took definite shape, is to seek origins of what
later became a culture of global influence—modern Western Christianity.

Books and Commentaries
The Christian Bible was a book of distinct form, and this form had something to
do with its genre and the way it was seen alongside other kinds of literature.
Whereas the Jewish Scriptures retained the shape they had enjoyed in late
antiquity, Christians, beginning in the second century, abandoned scrolls for
another structure, the codex, a book of leaves of papyrus, then parchment (and
beginning in the fourteenth century in Europe, paper), folded into sections and
sewn together between two boards. By the end of the fourth century in Western
Christianity, sixty-six books with an additional eight books of less certain authenticity were accepted as canonical Scripture, yet the border distinguishing these
books from other kinds of sacred literature was neither frozen nor fluid but
somewhere in between, and this can be seen in the codices themselves.

*Jerome's translation of the Bible, the Vulgate, which became the Bible primarily used in the medieval West, was usually copied with prologues, brief texts that served to introduce the sections and books of Scripture. Though Jerome's authorship was presumed for many of these prologues, he was responsible for only some of them, and they incorporate material of surprising authorship, such as the Pelagian prologue to the Pauline epistles that circulated with most Vulgate manuscripts, and the Monarchian material that hid awkwardly beneath a first sentence taken from a letter of Jerome in the prologue to the Catholic Epistles, the book of Acts and the Apocalypse, the last section of the medieval New Testament (see Schild, 69-102, for a discussion of the prologues).

Medieval scholars knew that these texts were not Scripture, even if they did not know the unorthodox origins of some of them, and they took this material critically. But the physical form of the Bibles they used nevertheless displays well the intimate connection of Scripture and interpretation that they made. The Bible itself was a library of documents that gave the record of salvation from the past to the future, and reflection upon the same was expected to be taken up into its world of thought. Even the monastic library, according to *Hugh of St. Victor (d. 1141), ought to be organized according to biblical categories: the Old Testament section should include pseudipigrapha, together with law, prophets and hagiography, and the New Testament section should include decrees, or the authoritative pronouncements of popes, bishops, councils and church fathers in the canon law, and the writings of the "fathers and doctors of the church" (Petitmengen, 42).

The codices included noncanonical prologues; in addition, those Bibles designed for study often combined Scripture and exegesis by adding glosses to the page (see Petitmengen, 35). Glosses in what are known as glossed Bibles were brief explanatory notes added between the lines (interlinear glosses) and longer explanations mostly culled from patristic literature and placed in the margins (marginal glosses, a technique also found in Jewish commentaries on the Talmud; see Lobrichon, 98; Waxman, 1:250-80; Graboïs, 234-35). The earliest biblical glosses known in the West were probably written in Northumbria and Ireland by the turn of the eighth to ninth centuries (Lobrichon, 98-99), but the technique did not catch on until the third quarter of the eleventh century, in the monastic and cathedral schools that spawned the beginnings of scholasticism in the north of France (see Landgraf, 39-47; de Ghellinck 1948; Châtillon; De Hamel; Lobrichon, 99-110; Smalley 1964, 46-52).

This form of commentary was first applied to single books that were interpreted by a school's master. Glosses gradually assumed a more uniform design, while striving, especially under the influence of Anselm of Laon (d. 1117), to encompass patristic exegetical opinion for the whole Bible. They finally enjoyed good distribution after the mid-twelfth century, apparently from a center of production at Paris, whose famous schools attracted book-buying students and teachers from throughout Christendom. Around 1220 the first complete glossed Bibles were produced, and about the same time what was by then a more or less standard text came to be called the *Glossa Ordinaria,* the Ordinary Gloss to Scripture, its status propagated if not at first achieved in connection with the theology faculty of the new university of Paris (Lobrichon, 101, 103, 112-14; Froehlich and Gibson provide a facsimile reprint of the edition that best preserves the format and content of the final form of the *Glossa Ordinaria*).

The Ordinary Gloss exercised tremendous influence within scholastic exegesis, even though its production in western Europe seems to have been on the wane by 1300 (Lobrichon, 101 n. 18, 110), but it was not the only form of exegetical literature. In the Middle Ages, these books were not called commentaries (see Froehlich 1987). A somewhat indistinct nomenclature reveals the slippery character of the emerging genres. While glosses multiplied in the twelfth century, scholars also collected topical opinions in books of sentences (the school of Laon again playing an important role), and they explored contradicting authorities and problems of interpretation in books of questions (Landgraf, 35-39, 40-42; de Ghellinck 1948, 133-48). Some of these were taken from the exegesis of masters like Anselm of Laon. Other works, like the commentary on the Psalms of Bruno the Carthusian, founder of the Carthusian order (d. 1101), integrated the treatment of questions into exegetical work, while the commentary on the Pauline epistles also posed questions and tried to get the apostle to answer by evoking arguments proved by Paul, proofs discovered by considering the circumstances, subject matter and intention of the author (Châtillon, 172-75).

In connection with the school of St. Victor in the second and third quarters of the twelfth century, a variety of works on theology and on the Old Testament clarified the distinctions between "historical" and "spiritual" meanings, according to principles adapted from Augustine's *On Christian Doctrine (De Doctrina Christiana)* and explained in the *Didascalicon* of Hugh of St. Victor), principles that could serve either literal exegesis (at the hands of *Andrew of St. Victor [1110-1175]) or the spiritual senses (at the hands of Richard of St. Victor [d. 1173]). The clarity achieved at St. Victor allowed Peter Comestor, a master at Paris and chancellor of the school of Notre Dame, to succumb to the pleas of his friends and compile, by 1175, the knowledge scattered throughout the Bible and its glosses within a coherent and continuous narrative. The result came to be known as the *Historia Scholastica,* the first comprehensive and fairly coherent treatment of the Bible in Europe and one of the most widely used exegetical works of the later Middle Ages (Smalley 1964, 179; Châtillon, 195). But this compellingly sensible form of exegetical writing did not immediately provoke imitators. Rather it took its place beside the Ordinary Gloss.

A consistent and coherent kind of literature employed widely by professional interpreters (that is, theologians) did not arise until the second quarter of the thirteenth century. That kind of commentary was developed at the Dominican school at the university of Paris under the leadership of a master there, *Hugh of St. Cher (1195-1263), and it was given the inexplicable name *postilla (post illa,* "after that" or "after those things," though no one knows to what "that" refers). The postilla was a running commentary, ordinarily composed at school, especially the schools of the mendicant orders in the thirteenth century. (The four principal mendicant orders were the Franciscans, the Dominicans, the Augustinian Hermits and the Carmelites, whose theologians played an important role in the development of scholastic exegesis.) Originally the postilla was supposed to complement the Ordinary Gloss, which compiled patristic opinion, by adding interpretations from the principal exegetes of the twelfth and early thirteenth centuries.

Although this new form of exegetical literature came to dominate biblical interpretation, it never did so exclusively. Scholars could still compose questions on a book of the Bible as late the 1360s, as a master at the university of Oxford, Johannes Klenkok, did. And by the mid-fourteenth century the name *postilla* was used in central Europe not only for running commentaries but also for sermon collections. The classic postilla is represented in some of the greatest achievements of scholastic interpretation: the commentaries of Bonaventure and Thomas *Aquinas (1224/25-1274) in the mid-thirteenth century and of the Dominican Nicholas of Gorran in the fourth quarter of that century, the postilla of the Franciscan *Nicholas of Lyra (c. 1270-1349) in the second quarter of the fourteenth century, the commentaries of John Wyclif in the third and fourth quarters of that century, and the commentaries of *Denys the Carthusian (also known as Denys van Leeuwen [1402/4-1471]) in the second and third quarters of the fifteenth century. One early fourteenth-century interpreter, the Franciscan Pierre Aureol, made a handy *Compendium* to rival the old *Historia Scholastica.* But the form of these achievements was not exclusive.

In addition to the erratic appearance of questions on a book of the Bible, some interpreters continued to gloss Bibles (a Dominican, Johann Müntzinger, in the second quarter of the fourteenth century, and an Augustinian Hermit, Martin *Luther, in a commentary on Psalms [1513-1515]). Others, like Meister Eckhart, wrote commentaries with a strong mystical and theological bent that defy easy classification. Still others, like the Dominican Robert Holcot and the Augustinian Hermit Heinrich of Friemar, wrote commentaries with a pronounced moral or homiletical bias. Even at its later stage of development, the medieval commentary remained a book with loose ends, a living if sometimes evasive genre.

The requirements of universities encouraged the production of exegetical literature. Both the Bible and Peter Lombard's *Four Books of Sentences* were the standard texts of theology there, and the university's curriculum, at times in a less regular form, also trickled into the widely distributed schools of the mendicant orders (Asztalos, 417-20; Verger, 175-203). Scholastic interpreters drew from twelfth-century accomplishments: the *Glossa Ordinaria* and the *Historia Scholastica*. They also devised new tools of study, beginning with an edition of the Bible itself, which Stephen Langton divided into chapters shortly before 1203, a task completed by another scholar, Thomas Gallus, who divided the chapters into paragraphs.

Langton's work became the standard edition of the Bible at Paris, and from there it moved to all universities. At the Parisian Dominican cloister of St. Jacques, friars made an alphabetical concordance of Latin terms that covered the Old and New Testaments (the new chapter divisions providing an efficient means of referencing), probably between 1230 and 1235. It was succeeded by a deluxe bookstore edition put together by 1275, which enjoyed wide distribution. Interpreters also used concordances to canon law as a source of authoritative opinions to apply in their exegesis, and two concordances composed in the fourteenth century harmonized canon law and Scripture. One of these concordances was composed by an abbot, Jean of Nivelles, and another by a Bolognese law professor, Johannes Calderinus.

The Ordinary Gloss, the *Historia Scholastica,* postillae and concordances, together with a Bible divided into chapters, became the chief tools of scholastic exegesis. They were not the only means of biblical interpretation, however. Interpretation also occurred in sermons, in art, in devotional literature and derivatively even in saints' legends, which quote Scripture, especially the narratives of the passion of Christ, the way a movie might quote a classic film—by alluding to older stories and images. But the tools of exegesis made up a technology of exposition that navigated the realms of authoritative, reliable thought within the Bible and outside of it. What did that technology produce?

Ways to Understand
In the twelfth century, scholars who began to collect questions and sentences were introducing a separation of logically disciplined theology from exegesis (de Ghellinck 1947; Smalley 1964, 271; De Vooght, 27-28). The difference between exegesis and reflection was thought to be complementary, not adversarial, and consistent with the nature of language and with the composition of the universe. The Victorines were the great theorists of this complementary difference, and it was best expressed in a brief sentence by one of them: "not only words, but also things are representational" (Richard of St. Victor *Excerptiones* 2.3 [PL 177:205]; Ohly, 1-31). The Victorines believed that this theory of signification explained how the Bible, a literary product, was like all literature and better than all literature at the same time. Words mediate knowledge of the subject matter of a piece of writing; pagan (that is, classical) writing does only that: it tells a story. But "in divine literature not only do meanings signify things, those things signify other

things. Whence it is clear how greatly useful knowledge of the [liberal] arts is for understanding the divine scriptures" (Richard of St. Victor *Speculum Ecclesiae* [PL 177:375]). In other words, the Bible not only tells stories, but also the minute elements of a story—rocks, trees, virtually any objects—in turn function as signs that indicate meanings that may have nothing to do with the biblical passage. But those meanings were believed to be closer to spiritual truth. They were called the spiritual senses or allegory.

Belief in creation buttressed the theory of allegory. Creation was a divine work, and the qualities of created things, their properties, betrayed the character of their maker. "All nature bespeaks God. All nature teaches human beings. All nature imparts reason, and there is nothing barren in the universe" (Hugh of St. Victor *Didascalion* 6.5 [PL 176:805]). The visible world was the necessary starting point of knowledge of God, and in the same way so was sacred literature. What distinguished the Bible from other literature was not magical language but accurate representation of the real connection between visible and invisible reality, between a microscopic perspective on particular objects and a macroscopic, abstract perspective on the universe. Therefore it was necessary to start with the most tangible things, the books, their histories and their manner of speaking, and to move very gradually and scientifically, girded with the liberal arts, from sign to thing to divine matters.

The progressive movement from biblical texts to abstract religious knowledge began with literal, historical meaning. Scholars who played a key role in the consolidation of gloss technique—Lanfranc, abbot of Bec (d. 1089), Berengar of Tours (d. 1088), Drogon of Paris (late eleventh century) and Bruno the Carthusian—promoted the use of grammar, rhetoric and dialectic in literal interpretation, techniques that were especially evident in the exegesis of the school of Laon at the turn of the eleventh to twelfth centuries and in the work of its most important teacher, Anselm of Laon (Lobrichon, 105). The Victorines built on those foundations and demonstrated how the labor was prerequisite to spiritual knowledge. The result was a new sophistication in literal exegesis, represented in Andrew of St. Victor's Hebrew scholarship and in his recourse to rabbinical commentary for historical information (Smalley 1964, 112-95). His accomplishment was only superseded nearly two hundred years later by the Old Testament sections of Nicholas of Lyra's postilla.

The difference between literal and spiritual senses seemed clear. The fourfold division of meanings laid out by John Cassian in the early fifth century now was taken to describe the standard alternatives. It was expressed in a rhyme repeated at the beginning of Nicholas of Lyra's postilla:

The letter teaches events
allegory what you should believe
tropology what you should do

anagogy where you should aim.

The typical example is Jerusalem, which comes straight from Cassian (*Collationes* 19.8). According to history, Jerusalem is a city of the Jews. According to allegory, it is the church. According to tropology, it is the human soul. According to anagogy, it is the heavenly city of God. This was a cliché, and like most clichés it exaggerated the obvious: that biblical texts and nouns yielded historical meanings more remote from the reader or the reader's world and other meanings that touched on a present religious life—the church, the moral condition of the soul, the future. The fourfold sense indicated a process of abstraction and the possibility of lithe movement, seldom if ever a procedure for chopping Bible passages into quarters.

But theologians had difficulty assuming that the literal sense of the Bible was indeed remote from contemporary readers. In the thirteenth century some theologians—Aquinas perhaps was the most famous—constructed their discipline as a unique human science about divine things, and in this science the literal sense of Scripture was to exercise a definitive role (Lang, Chenu). Nevertheless scholars did not always restrict themselves to literal meanings when they argued. Moreover, the elaborate use of the spiritual senses in preaching suggests that people generally took allegory as persuasive interpretation (Smalley 1985; Winkler, 65-69).

In some books of the Bible the language seemed literally spiritual. Bonaventure and Aquinas recognized a multiple literal sense and a "parabolic" meaning of texts (Lubac, 2/2:283; Winkler, 7-8). According to Nicholas of Lyra, some psalms refer to Christ according to their historical meaning, not according to allegory as the classical fourfold division of senses would imply. Late medieval interpreters like Lyra, Paul of Burgos, Matthew Döring and Jean *Gerson (1363-1429) argued that prophets wrote with a view to their own circumstances and with the intention of predicting the coming of Christ—a double literal sense in the prophets (Werbeck, 120-21, 130). How could the difference of literal from spiritual senses be absolute?

In late antiquity, Christians had argued that some Old Testament texts required allegorical interpretation; they would otherwise appear absurd or obscene. That point was not forgotten in the late Middle Ages. But it had lost some of its force. Denys the Carthusian once criticized theologians who say that "the literal meaning is that which is first signified by the literal words" while claiming that there are places in Scripture, "especially the Prophets," impossible to interpret literally. He offers an alternative directly opposite the Victorine theory of biblical signification, built on the idea of authorial intention. The literal sense is the meaning first intended by the author; therefore "every passage of holy Scripture has a literal meaning, which is not always what is first signified by the literal words, but is often what is designated through the thing that is signified by the literal words" (Denys the Carthusian [Dionysius Carthusianus] *Ennaratio in Job* art. 13, 4:362-63). What the Victorines called spiritual meaning, Denys calls literal. Even Nicholas of Lyra was too allegorical, by occasionally appealing to a sense "rather mystical and spiritual than literal," for example, in his exegesis of Jacob's deathbed speech to his son. Jacob, Denys argued, "speaks metaphorically . . . namely through similies of corporal things. In such language, the literal sense is not what is immediately signified through terms but what is signified through those things, according to their properties and the similarities to that which is principally designated." He rehearses examples: a lion is David, "or rather Christ"; a vine "literally designates the synagogue, Christ, and even the church" (Denys the Carthusian *Ennaratio in Genesis* art. 100, 1:444).

These theologians needed the help of Desiderius *Erasmus. Exegetes began to recognize that what in the twelfth century was described as a quality of thought *beyond* speech in fact was a quality *of* speech (Brinkmann, 214-26; Winkler, 85-89). In the late Middle Ages interpreters still talked about progressively abstract knowledge and literal meaning as analogous to knowledge of the natural world. For example, the Carmelite John Baconthorpe described cognition according to the "fourfold sense" of natural knowledge. The first is literal, in which one proceeds from ideas in one's mind to ideas of nature itself, much the way one moves from the letter of the Bible to a thing indicated by it. This begins an abstract movement that can go in three directions, to God (spiritual knowledge), to the forms of natural things (figurative knowledge), or to human society (moral knowledge).

The Franciscan Pierre Aureol had a more poetic way of expressing similar convictions. He encouraged his reader to ascend from the corporeal to the spiritual: to take "the brisk flight of meditation," "like birds," by seeking profound meaning in the sacred letter, by going from term to meaning, from meaning to matter, from matter to reason, and from reason to the truth. Truth is derived from the "literal understanding, the superficial meaning, the plain discourse of the narrative" (*Compendium Litteralis Sensus Totius Divinae Scripturae*, ff. 2vb-3ra). But a gradual, rhetorical turn in the way scholars understood literal meaning reduced the difference between literal and spiritual interpretations: it looked like a fine distinction, but it was not quite so relevant any more (see Froehlich 1977, 42-43). For their convictions about ascending knowledge could rest upon a literal understanding of figurative speech.

Why? All exegetes agreed that the subject of the Bible is theology. In the words of Nicholas of Gorran, it is a simple form of theological narrative; its subject is God, according to Lyra, or Christ, according to Johann Michael. In the prefaces to their commentaries (often expounding the letter of Jerome that served as a preface to the Bible), theologians adapted Aristotle's theory of causation to describe Scripture as literature, and this helped them clarify the importance of human, historical authors with circumstantial intentions that determined meanings (Minnis 1988a, 1988b). But the causes were multiple, and they always included divine authorship. The actual exegesis of people as scholastic as Aquinas, a champion of authorial intention, or as mystical as Meister Eckhart was extremely doctrinal, and this characteristic reflects their conviction that biblical language informed their intellectual enterprise. It was also reflected in the survival of old habits, especially the addition of questions and digressions within carefully executed works, like John Baconthorpe's commentary on the Gospel according to Matthew with its discussions of political theory or Jacques Fournier's commentary on the same Gospel with its refutation of textbook heresies, and in hasty expositions, like Johann Müntzinger's gloss to the Lord's Prayer. This was consistent with common opinions about the authority of Scripture and with the desire, even among interpreters critical of the church, like Wyclif, to find interpretations consistent with church tradition.

The language of Scripture embraced a realm of thought that invited abstraction and argument and debate. Before the twelfth century, the Bible had been a monastic text; now it became a professional text for clergy and their teachers. Exegesis likewise became a workshop of ideas, and one's knowledge of medieval intellectual life is incomplete without it. The study of commentaries has revealed the categories, terms and motivations within medieval civilization that mobilized the shift from egalitarian to hierarchical notions of power, the transition from allegorical to scientific approaches to nature and the innovations of papalist theory. But much work remains to be done along the technical lines of the history of exegesis and intellectual history, but also in the study of the convergence of exegetical techniques, the fashions of thought at play in them, and popular culture.

BIBLIOGRAPHY

Works. P. Aureol, *Compendium Litteralis Sensus Totius Divinae Scripturae* (Barcelona: Biblioteca de Universidad) Ms. 121; *Biblia Latina cum Glossa Ordinaria,* introductions by K. Froehlich and M. T. Gibson (4 vols.; Turnhout: Brepols, 1992); J. Cassian, *Collationes,* ed. E. Pichery (SC 42, 54, 64; Paris: Éditions du Cerf, 1955-1959); P. Comestor, *Historia Scholastica;* Denys the Carthusian [Dionysius Carthusianus], *Ennaratio in Genesis* in *Opera Omnia,* vol. 1 (42 vols.; Tournai: S. M. de Pratis, 1896-1935); idem, *Ennaratio in Job* in *Opera Omnia,* vol. 4 (42 vols.; Tournai: S. M. de Pratis, 1896-1935); Hugh of St. Victor, *Didascalicon,* PL 176; Nicholas of Lyra, *Postillae in Bibliam, cum Additionibus Pauli Burgensis, ac Replicis Matthiae Dorinck* (Venice, 1482); Richard of St. Victor, *Excerptiones,* PL 177; idem, *Speculum Ecclesiae,* PL 177.

Studies. M. Aszlatos, "The Faculty of Theology" in *Universities in the Middle Ages,* 1: *A History of the University in Europe,* ed. H. De Ridder-Symoens (Cambridge: Cambridge University Press, 1992) 409-41; H. Brinkmann, *Mittelalterliche Hermeneutik* (Tübingen: Max Niemeyer, 1980); M. S. Burrows and P. Rorem, eds., *Biblical Hermeneutics in Historical Perspective* (Grand Rapids: Eerdmans, 1991); J. Châtillon, "La Bible dans les Ecoles du xiie siècle" in *Bible de tous les temps,* 4: *Le Moyen Age et la Bible,* ed. P. Riché and G. Lobrichon (Paris: Beauchesne, 1984) 163-97; *CHB* 2; M.-D. Chenu, *La theologie comme sciene au xiie siècle* (3d ed.; Paris: J. Vrin, 1957); J. de Ghellinck, *Le mouvement thèologique du xiie siécle* (Bruges: Éditions de Tempel, 1948); idem, " 'Pagina' et 'sacra pagina':

Histoire d'un mot et transformation de l'objet primitivement designe" in *Melanges Auguste Pelzer* (Louvain: Bibliotheque de l'Université, 1947) 23-59; C. De Hamel, *Glossed Books of the Bible and the Origins of the Paris Booktrade* (Woodbridge, England: D. S. Brewer, 1984); P. De Vooght, *Les sources de la doctrine chrétienne* (Bourges: Descleé De Brouwer, 1954); K. Froehlich, " 'Always to Keep to the Literal Sense Means to Kill One's Soul': The State of Biblical Hermeneutics at the Beginning of the Fifteenth Century" in *Literary Uses of Typology from the Late Middle Ages to the Present,* ed. E. Miner (Princeton, NJ: Princeton University Press, 1977) 20-48; idem, "Bibelkommentare—Zur Krise einer Gattung," *ZTK* 84 (1987) 465-92; A. Graboïs, "L'exégèse rabbinique" in *Le Moyen Age et la Bible,* ed. P. Riché and G. Lobrichon (Paris: Beauchesne, 1984) 233-60; A. M. Landgraf, *Einführung in die Geschichte der theologischen Literatur der Frühscholastik* (Regensburg: Gregorius-Verlag, 1948) 39-47; A. Lang, *Die theologische Prinzipienlehre in der mittelalterlichen Scholastik* (Frieburg: Herder, 1964); G. Lobrichon, "Une nouveauté: les gloses de la Bible" in *Bible de tous les temps,* 4: *Le Moyen Age et la Bible,* ed. P. Riché and G. Lobrichon (Paris: Beauchesne, 1984) 31-53; H. de Lubac, *L'Exégèse médiévale: Les quatre sens de l'Ecriture* (4 vols.; Paris: Aubier, 1959-1964); A. J. Minnis, *Medieval Literary Theory and Criticism, c. 1100-1375* (Oxford: Clarendon, 1988a); idem, *Medieval Theory of Authorship* (2d ed.; Philadelphia: University of Pennsylvania Press, 1988b); F. Ohly, *Schriften zur mittelalterlichen Bedeutungsforschung* (Darmstadt: Wissenschaftliche Buchgesellschaft, 1977); P. Petitmengen, "La Bible à travers les inventaires de biliothèques médiévales" in *Bible de tous le temps,* 4: *Le Moyen Age et la Bible,* ed. P. Riché and G. Lobrichon (Paris: Beauchesne, 1984) 95-114; C. H. Roberts, "Books in the Greco-Roman World and in the New Testament" in *CHB* 1:48-66; M. Schild, *Abendländische Bibelvorreden bis zur Lutherbibel* (Gütersloh: Gerd Mohn, 1970); H. Schüssler, *Der Primat der Heiligen Schrift als theologisches und kanonistisches Problem im Spätmittelalter* (Wiesbaden: Franz Steiner, 1977); B. Smalley, *The Study of the Bible in the Middle Ages* (Notre Dame, IN: University of Notre Dame Press, 1964); idem, "Use of the 'Spiritual' Sense of Scripture in Persuasion and Argument by Scholars in the Middle Ages," *Recherches* 52 (1985) 44-63; F. Stegmüller, *Repertorium Biblicum Medii Aevi* (11 vols.; Madrid: Consejo Superior de Investigaciones Científicas, 1940-80); J. Verger, "Studia et universités" in *Convegni del Centro di Studi sulla spiritualità medievale,* 17: *Le scuole degli ordini mendicanti (secoli xii-xiv)* (Rimini: Maggioli Editore, 1978); M. Waxman, *A History of Jewish Literature* (4 vols.; New York: T. Yoseloff, 1960); E. Winkler, *Exegetische Methoden bei Meister Eckhart* (Tübingen: J. C. B. Mohr, 1965); W. Werbeck, *Beiträge zur historischen Theologie,* 28: *Jacobus Perez von Valencia: Untersuchungen zu seinem Psalmenkommentar* (Tübingen: J. C. B. Mohr, 1959).

C. OCKER

Aquinas, Thomas *(1224/25-1274)*

Canonized as a saint by Pope John XXII (1323), this most brilliant and respected theologian of the Latin church in the Middle Ages and his works were declared normative for the teaching of theology in Catholic schools by Pope Leo XIII (1879) and the old code of canon law (CIC canon 589:1).

Life. Born into the noble family of the counts of Aquino near Naples in central Italy, Thomas was destined for a clerical career. He received his first instruction at the Benedictine abbey of Monte Cassino and afterward at Naples, where he studied the liberal arts (1239-1244). Against the wishes of his family, he joined the Dominican Friars at Naples, whose leaders sent him for further theological studies to Paris and Cologne, his main teacher there being Albert the Great.

In 1256 Thomas began his formal teaching career at Paris, where he acquired the license to teach and the degree of master of theology. It took papal intervention for him and his Franciscan contemporary, Bonaventure, to be fully accepted as regent masters into the university, the corporation of masters whose opposition to the Friars had earlier led to strikes and riots in the city. Thomas occupied the second Dominican chair, reserved for foreigners. The Dominican priory of St. Jacques in the university quarter was his residence and regular place of teaching. From 1259 to 1268 he was assigned to teach at Dominican houses of study *(studia)* in his native Italy in places such as Orvieto and Viterbo, where popes and their curia were residing at that time.

From 1265 to 1267 Aquinas was in Rome, charged with organizing theological and philosophical studies at the Dominican priory of Santa Sabina. Late in 1268 he was ordered to go back to Paris for a second regency in his former chair during a time of renewed tensions in the university, but returned to the university of his youth, Naples, as the regent master of theology in 1272. Having ceased to write and dictate on December 6, 1273, reportedly in reaction to a visionary experience, he died at the Cistercian abbey of Fossanova near Priverno on March 7, 1274, on his way to the Council of Lyon, which Pope Gregory X had asked him to attend.

Work. Aquinas is best known as the systematic theologian whose synthesis of Aristotelianism and the Christian faith marked the high point of medieval scholastic theology. His *Summa Theologiae,* originally designed as a textbook for his students at Santa Sabina, and his *Summa contra Gentiles,* disputed questions, expert opinions and miscellaneous treatises were eagerly copied and widely studied throughout the later Middle Ages and beyond. All of his writings grew out of his assignments as an academic teacher and theological expert.

The definitive edition of his works is the so-called Leonine edition, named after Pope Leo XIII, who appointed the Leonine Commission for this purpose in 1880. It is still in progress; about twenty-five volumes, half of the projected total, have been published to date. Two complete vulgate editions from the nineteenth century are still in use: The Parma *Opera Omnia* and the Paris *Opera Omnia.* We will refer to individual writings by the catalogue numbers in J. A. Weisheipl (355-405). Weisheipl also lists English translations where they are available.

Biblical Lectures. It needs to be stressed that at the universities of the twelfth and thirteenth centuries, the teaching of theology served a curriculum that revolved around the Bible and its interpretation. The usual designation of a master of theology was Master of the Sacred Page *(magister sacrae paginae).* The young teacher would begin as *cursor biblicus,* a graduate student *(baccalaureus)* who, under the supervision of a master, taught surveys of the biblical literature to beginners with a minimum of interpretation. Thomas probably discharged this duty as a *lector* under Albert at the Dominican house of studies in Cologne; the commentary on Isaiah was most likely a product of that period.

In Paris, where he lived at St. Jacques, Aquinas advanced to the next stage, lecturing for four years (1252-1256) as *baccalaureus sententiarum* on Peter Lombard's *Sentences,* a required textbook organizing biblical teaching and Catholic doctrine by topics. The *Sentences Commentary* was the first major work from Thomas's pen; much of it is preserved in the autograph. The Lombard lectures were a prerequisite for his inception as a master, which he achieved at the unusually young age of thirty-one.

Two of Aquinas's inaugural speeches connected with this solemn event *(principia)* are extant (Weisheipl 35). Both expound a Bible verse ("From your lofty abode you water the mountains" [Ps 104:13]; "It is the book of the commandments of God" [Bar 4:1]). The thematic assignment is the praise of Holy Scripture *(commendatio sacrae scripturae).* It also seems likely that two disputed questions preserved as questions 6 and 7 (art. 14-18) of Quodlibet VII (Weisheipl 12) belong in the context of Thomas's inception in April or May 1256. The first of these questions explores the various senses of Scripture and, together with *Summa Theologiae* I q.1:8-10, is a basic text for Thomas's hermeneutics.

As Thomas himself reports, a master's duties included three basic activities: lecturing, disputing and preaching (*Principium* "Rigans montes," Weisheipl 35, with a reference to Tit 1:9). Magisterial lectures invariably had as their subject the explanation of the biblical text. Parisian masters lectured in the morning from 6 to 8:30, by medieval standards the best hours of the day. The choice of books in a given academic year was their own; Thomas seems to have endeavored to alternate between Old and New Testament books. During the class period the text was first read aloud, then analyzed ("divided") according to its rhetorical structure. After this, a running interpretation was given, paying attention to scriptural parallels, the patristic tradition and rational arguments that often required skillful harmonization or the recognition of multiple perspectives. The procedure involved much dictation as well as note taking by the students. It also presupposed the use of a glossed Bible.

Commentaries and Exegetical Writings. Contemporary witnesses indicate that Thomas lectured on Job, the Psalter, the Song of Songs, Isaiah, Jeremiah, Lamentations, the Gospels of Matthew and John, and the Pauline epistles. But neither the full extent of his biblical lectures nor their exact chronology can be reconstructed. Written expositions under his name exist on eight biblical books or groups of books; the interpretation of the Song of Songs has left no trace.

Furthermore, Thomas's scriptural commentaries come in two forms, *reportatio* and *ordinatio.* A reportatio presents the content of lectures written down by a student or a secretary. An ordinatio may be based on such notes but is a finished literary product *(expositio)* written or dictated by the author himself and carefully edited for publication. Authentic expositions are extant for the book of Job (Weisheipl 25); Isaiah (Weisheipl 28 and pp. 479-81; chaps. 1-11 are fully treated, the remainder very briefly); Jeremiah (Weisheipl 29 and p. 481; chaps. 1-42, brief annotations only); Lamentations (Weisheipl 30); and two Pauline epistles (Weisheipl 34; Rom—1 Cor 7:9). The reportationes include interpretations of Psalms 1—55:16 (Weisheipl 26); Matthew (Weisheipl 32; missing: Mt 5:11—6:8; 6:14-19); John (Weisheipl 33 and p. 481; reported by Thomas's assistant, Reginald of Piperno, and corrected by the author); the Pauline epistles (Weisheipl 34 and p. 481; 1 Cor 11—Hebrews); and a separate commentary on Hebrews in two parts (Weisheipl 34).

One modern attempt to fit these writings into the framework of Thomas's career (Mandonnet) assigns the commentaries on Isaiah and Matthew to the first Parisian regency; Lamentations, Jeremiah and the reportatio on the Pauline epistles to his teaching in the Dominican studia in Italy; Job and John to the second Parisian regency; Psalms and Romans to the final years at Naples. At the suggestion of Pope Urban IV, Thomas also compiled a continuous gloss on the four Gospels, later called the Golden Chain (Aquinas Catena Aurea; Weisheipl 31; Orvieto and Rome, c. 1262-67). Following the text verse by verse, Thomas here wove excerpts from patristic and medieval exegetes into a continuous commentary, identifying his sources and adding scores of quotations from Eastern fathers to those known in the Western tradition. The collection, an astonishing scholarly achievement for its time, enjoyed a considerable success. An English translation was prepared by Oxford scholars in the nineteenth century and edited by J. H. Newman.

Extending his textual work beyond the Bible, Thomas also wrote substantial commentaries on numerous works of Aristotle as well as on two theological treatises by Boethius, the Pseudo-Dionysian treatise "On Divine Names" and the anonymous Liber de Causis (Weisheipl 36-51). These were not necessarily connected with his teaching activity but belong in the Italian period, when new Latin translations of the Greek originals became available to him through his association with the papal court.

Disputations and Sermons. The central role of the Bible for Thomas's teaching is not restricted to his lectures and commentaries, however. In the several series of disputed questions of which written records survive (Weisheipl 4-24), biblical texts and issues of interpretation frequently provide the topic for discussion, and the magisterial solution of a problem *(determinatio)* sel-

dom fails to include exegetical considerations. In the *Summa Theologiae*, whose articles follow the formal structure of a disputation—question *(quaestio)*, first argument *(videtur quod)*, counterargument *(sed contra)*, solution *(determinatio)*, and response to first argument *(responsiones ad obiecta)*—biblical texts play a prominent role. Frequently they express a counterargument from authority that is taken with utmost seriousness in the otherwise strictly rational discussion.

There can be no question that the theology Thomas develops is biblical theology. His term for theology is sacred doctrine *(sacra doctrina)*, a synonym for sacred page *(sacra pagina)*, scriptural truth unfolded by the doctors of the church. The outline of the three parts of the *Summa* presents the understanding of salvation in terms of the basic Pseudo-Dionysian dynamics (from God—to God—through God) that Thomas regarded as the sum total of biblical revelation.

There is ample evidence that Thomas preached regularly. Out of the large number of sermons ascribed to him in manuscripts and early editions, however, only nineteen have so far been recognized as undoubtedly genuine (Weisheipl 90; Bataillon). They expound biblical texts but follow the rhetorical style of the age, organizing major themes culled from individual verses into three to five sections and moralizing freely. Three brief expositions, of the Ten Commandments (Weisheipl 89), the Lord's Prayer (Weisheipl 87) and the angelic greeting (Lk 1:28 in the expanded form of the *Ave Maria;* Weisheipl 88) seem to belong in this context. They were probably delivered as sermons before lay audiences in Naples or Paris and then edited in the form of *reportationes.* Thomas followed the text closely but applied the key concepts unpolemically to the contemporary spiritual situation.

Hermeneutics. Thomas has been hailed as the creator of a scientific biblical hermeneutics. Sacred doctrine for him was a science, indeed the queen of sciences, which found its subject matter, admittedly by derivation, through participation in the highest *scientia,* God's own knowledge (Aquinas *Summa Theologiae* Ia q.1:1-3). In his earliest writings Thomas assigned to theology a threefold task: destruction of errors, instruction of morals and the contemplation of truth (Aquinas I *Sentences Commentary* prol. q.1 a.5). Much truth, even ethical truth, can be found by reason alone, but everywhere reason's search for truth encounters limits beyond which it must depend on revelation that God is providing through Scripture, the church's teaching and the special grace of personal inspiration.

Thomas did not hesitate to analyze the phenomenon of the Bible with the help of the Aristotelian notion of causality. The distinction between principal and auxiliary causes in efficient causality allowed him to affirm both its divine authorship and human composition. God is the primary cause, the biblical writers the instrumental causes of the books of the Bible; both aspects must be considered together. Thomas could speak emphatically of God or the Holy Spirit as the author of the Bible; he could with equal enthusiasm probe the literary intentions of authors such as Isaiah and Jeremiah, Matthew and John, or admire the rhetorical skill of the apostle Paul. What fascinated him was the linguistic nature of the biblical revelation and the relation of language to truth. Different from the nominalists of the later Middle Ages, Thomas still trusted words. Human language about God, though never adequate to encompass its subject, does speak the truth analogically (Aquinas *Summa Theologiae* Ia q.13:10), certainly in the Bible. Plato's and Aristotle's dialectic already assumed that truth is to be sought through dialogue. Similarly, Thomas stated that the threefold task of theology, especially the apologetic effort of the destruction of error, requires argument. At this point he drew on the traditional hermeneutical system of the four senses of Scripture.

Fourfold Sense. Following *Origen, the

Augustinian tradition in the West had expanded the hermeneutical ascent, the dynamic progression from literal to spiritual sense by subdividing the spiritual sense into three. A devout, expectant consideration of the letter of the biblical text will yield all the doctrinal (allegorical), ethical (tropological) and eschatological-mystical (anagogical) instruction needed for the Christian life. Obviously the spiritual senses enjoyed pride of place in this process.

In theology, however, Thomas assigned primacy to the literal sense; from it alone can an argument be constructed: "No sense except the literal has the power of confirming anything" (Aquinas Quodl. VII.6 a.14:3). Precisely because of their multivalence, the spiritual senses are disqualified for the task. Thomas's emphasis on the literal sense continued a trend inaugurated by the school of St. Victor in the twelfth century. Of course, his exegesis did not end in literalism. But the careful investigation of the literal meaning of a passage, Thomas was convinced, must remain the foundation for any spiritual reading. Figurative expressions, poetic images, rhetorical tropes and metaphors belong to the literal sense, according to Thomas. Yet, while in human language only words can signify, God in his providence also uses the things signified as signs of invisible realities and thus of further levels of truth.

The narratives, prophecies and commandments of the Bible contain additional meanings beyond the literal sense that the spiritual senses must unlock. No merely human book can have these multiple senses if the intention of the author determines the meaning of the words and thus the literal sense (Aquinas Quodl. VI.6 a.16): one word, one meaning—the Aristotelian univocity of language. Not so in the Bible. "Since the literal sense is that which the author intends, and the author of Holy Scripture is God who comprehends everything all at once in his understanding, it comes not amiss, as St. Augustine observes, if many meanings are present even in the literal sense of one passage of Scripture"

(Aquinas *Summa Theologiae* I q.1:10). This statement does not argue for a multiple literal sense but for the theological necessity of spiritual senses that allow the deployment of the literal or historical sense (Thomas uses both terms) in its universal dimension as history of salvation, ordained by God and extending from the creation to the apocalypse, with its center in Jesus Christ, the one true "Word of God" in Thomas's understanding (Corbin).

A discussion of Genesis 1:2 in one of the disputed questions articulates the other consequence of this conviction: One must not force an interpretation on Scripture that would exclude any other interpretations that are actually or possibly true. "Every truth that can be adapted to the sacred text without prejudice to the literal sense is the sense of Holy Scripture" (Aquinas *On the Power of God* q.4 a.1:8; Weisheipl 5).

Exegetical Sources and Practices. Thomas's actual exegesis, informed by his scientific hermeneutics, benefited greatly by the new tools of biblical scholarship provided by members of his own order and others: A corrected text of the Vulgate, a verbal concordance of the Latin Bible that *Hugh of St. Cher assembled at St. Jacques, and improved access to the exegetical tradition.

It is recognized today that philosophically Thomas was deeply indebted not only to the Aristotelian tradition rediscovered in its wider scope during his lifetime but also to the Platonic tradition mediated through Neo-Platonic sources such as Proclus and, on the Christian side, Pseudo-Dionysius. He used the Christian exegetical tradition as it was presented by standard collections such as the *Glossa Ordinaria,* Peter Lombard's revised gloss on the Psalms and the Pauline epistles, and Hugh of St. Cher's postilla on the entire Bible. But he tried to correct their deficiencies, the lack of context and the virtually exclusive reliance on Latin fathers, by going back to the full texts and including a large number of Eastern sources, fathers and councils, in his reading.

Thomas did not know Greek or Hebrew, but he used the best of contemporary scholarship to procure, for example, translations of Greek patristic writings. John *Chrysostom and Cyril of Alexandria were special favorites of his among Eastern exegetes. For the knowledge of Jewish interpretation he not only drew on *Jerome but also on contemporary resources. He read Moses Maimonides's "Guide of the Perplexed" and appears to have been familiar with the fruits of a renewed interest in Hebrew studies on the part of Victorine scholars such as *Hugh, Richard and *Andrew of St. Victor in the twelfth century.

Among the Victorines these studies were part of an insistence on the literal sense as the necessary foundation of the doctrinal edifice that was constituted by the totality of all revealed, teachable truth. Hugh did not yet call his exposition a *Summa* but gave it the title "On the Sacraments of the Christian Faith," treating the whole sweep of the salvation history told in the Bible as God's work of foundation and of restoration. Occasionally Thomas did give some room to a consideration of the literal-historical sense of the Jewish Scriptures in their own right. With the entire Christian tradition, however, he appropriated them as the Christian Old Testament, which he read primarily as a figure *(figura)* of the New, as speaking of Christ and the church in a prophetic mode that could even include knowledge of these future implications on the part of prophets and inspired prophetic writers (Aquinas *Summa Theologiae* II-II q.173-74; Synave and Benoit).

In his biblical hermeneutics and his exegetical writings, Thomas undoubtedly represented the best of contemporary biblical scholarship. He was not, however, an innovator on this turf. His originality and creativity as a biblical exegete is perhaps best revealed in those sections of his major syntheses where, for whatever reason, he discusses biblical materials at some depth. Examples are the sections on the Word of God, the Holy Spirit, the Incarnation, the

Cross, and the individual sacraments in *Summa contra Gentiles* IV; in the *Summa Theologiae* one could mention the treatise on the work of the six days (I q.65-74), the questions on the Old law and the New in the treatise on law (I-II q.94-108), the question on Paul's rapture (II-II q.175), and especially the treatise on the life of Christ, his passion and resurrection (III q.35-45, 46-59).

Significance. The influence of Thomas's thought on the subsequent history of theology in East and West has been enormous. Several of his works, including the two *Summae*, were translated into Greek by D. Kydones as early as the fourteenth century. Armenian theologians developed a deep affinity to Thomas's systematic thought, a fact that contributed to attempts at union with Rome by parts of the Armenian church in the fifteenth century.

In the West, soon after the master's death, a Thomistic school tradition began to emerge. It had its own history as one of the abiding options in Catholic theology, especially in the inner-Catholic controversies of the sixteenth and seventeenth centuries. Neo-Thomism still has a considerable influence in Catholic intellectual circles.

The interest of Thomistic scholars over the centuries, however, has concentrated almost exclusively on Thomas the philosopher, systematician and apologist. Thomas the exegete has not attracted much attention until quite recently. Among his biblical commentaries, the *Literal Exposition of Job* had an impact in the later Middle Ages because of its novel analysis of the speeches in the book as thematic disputations on God's providence.

The most influential exegetical work, however, judging by the number of extant manuscripts and editions, has been the *Catena Aurea*. It is still being consulted by Catholic and Protestant exegetes and will remain as a monument to the value of even the most humble efforts of an exceptional medieval scholar.

BIBLIOGRAPHY

Works. T. Aquinas, *Aquinas Scripture Series,* ed. F. A. Larcher et al. (vols. 1-4 [Gal, Eph, 1 Thess, Phil, Jn 1—7]; Albany, NY: Magi Books, 1966-1980); idem, *Opera Omnia* (25 vols.; Parma: Fiaccadori, 1852-1873; New York: Musurgia, 1948-1950); idem, *Opera Omnia,* ed. P. Fretté and E. Maré (34 vols.; Paris: Louis Vivès, 1871-1882); idem, *Sermon Matter from St. Thomas Aquinas on the Epistles and Gospels of the Sundays and Feast Days (Advent to Easter),* ed. C. J. Callan (St. Louis: Herder, 1950); idem, *Saint Thomas Aquinas: On the Truth of the Catholic Faith,* trans. A. Pegis et al. (4 vols. in 5; Garden City, NY: Hanover House, 1955-1957; reprinted as *Saint Thomas Aquinas: The Summa contra Gentiles* [Notre Dame, IN: Notre Dame University Press, 1975); idem, *Sancti Thomae Aquinatis Opera Omnia, jussu impensaque Leonis XIII, P.M., edita* (Rome: Commissio Leonina, 1882- [Leonine Edition]; idem, *St. Thomas Aquinas, Summa Theologiae: Latin Text and English Translation,* ed. T. Gilby et al. (61 vols.; New York: McGraw Hill, 1964-1981 [Blackfriars Edition]); idem, *Thomas Aquinas: Catena aurea. Commentary on the Four Gospels,* ed. J. H. Newman (4 vols.; Oxford: J. H. Parker, 1841-1845); idem, *Thomas Aquinas. The Literal Exposition of Job: A Scriptural Commentary Concerning Providence,* trans. A. Damico, essay and notes by M. D. Jaffe (CRS 7; Atlanta: Scholars Press, 1989).

Studies. M. Arias Reyero, *Thomas von Aquin als Exeget* (Einsiedeln: Johannes-Verlag, 1971); L. J. Bataillon, "Les sermons attribués à Saint Thomas: Questions d'authenticité" in *Miscellanea Mediaevalia* 19, ed. H. Zimmermann (Berlin: Walter de Gruyter, 1988) 325-41; C. C. Black, "St. Thomas' Commentary on the Johannine Prologue: Some Reflections on Its Character and Implications," *CBQ* 48 (1986) 681-98; M.-D. Chenu, *Toward Understanding St. Thomas* (Chicago: Henry Regnery, 1964); M. Corbin, *Le chemin de la théologie chez Thomas d'Aquin* (Paris: Beauchesne, 1974); T. Domanyi, *Der Römerbriefkommentar des Thomas von Aquin* (Basler und Berner Studien zur historischen und systematischen Theologie 39; Frankfurt and Bern: Peter Lang, 1979); M. D. Jaffe and A. Damico, *Thomas Aquinas: The Literal Exposition on Job: A Scriptural Commentary Concerning Providence* (Classics in Religious Studies 7; Atlanta: Scholars Press, 1989); R. G. Kennedy, *Thomas Aquinas and the Literal Sense of Sacred Scripture* (Ph.D. diss., University of Notre Dame, 1985); P. Mandonnet, "Chronologie des écrits scripturaires de saint Thomas d'Aquin," *RT* 33 (1928) 27-45, 116-55; 34 (1929) 53-69, 132-45, 489-519; P. E. Persson, *Sacra Doctrina: Reason and Revelation in Aquinas* (Philadelphia: Fortress, 1970); B. Smalley, *The Study of the Bible in the Middle Ages* (3d ed.; Oxford: Blackwell, 1983); P. Synave and P. Benoit, *Prophecy and Inspiration: A Commentary on the Summa Theologica II-II Questions 171-178* (New York: Desclée, 1961); T. F. Torrance, "Scientific Hermeneutics According to St. Thomas Aquinas," *JTS* 13 (1962) 259-89; S. Tugwell, ed., *Albert and Thomas: Selected Writings* (Classics of Western Spirituality; New York: Paulist, 1988); J. Van der Ploeg, "The Place of Holy Scripture in the Theology of Saint Thomas," *Th* 10 (1947) 398-422; G. T. Vass, *Secundum Illud Apostoli: A Study of the Use of Biblical Authorities in the Systematic Theology of Thomas Aquinas* (Rome: Pontificia Università Gregoriana, 1963); J. A. Weisheipl, *Friar Thomas d'Aquino: His Life, Thought, and Work* (rev. ed.; Washington, DC: Catholic University Press, 1983); M. Wyschogrod, "A Jewish Reading of St. Thomas Aquinas on the Old Law" in *Understanding Scripture: Explorations of Jewish and Christian Traditions of Interpretation*, ed. C. Thoma and M. Wyschogrod (New York: Paulist, 1987) 125-38.   K. Froehlich

Bernard of Clairvaux (1090-1153)

Bernard of Clairvaux was a monk of the Cistercian order, a reformed branch of the Benedictines founded in 1098 by Robert of Molesme. One of the most famous people of his time, Bernard was known not only as a monk but also as a statesman, mystic and theologian. His use of the Bible, while not breaking any new exegetical ground, was characterized by a unique synthesis of patristic methodology combined with a highly personal spiritual reading of texts.

Context. Bernard was born of a noble family in a village near Dijon, France. He was the third of seven children, of whom six were sons. In 1111 he decided to enter the monastic life. His family was stunned when he opted to join not a well-established Benedictine monastery but a new, reformed monastic movement centered in Cîteaux in the region of Burgundy.

Robert of Molesme founded the order of Cîteaux with the purpose of returning to the strictest possible interpretation of the Rule of St. Benedict. Cistercian monasteries did not accept feudal revenues but supported themselves by the labor of the monks and some lay brothers. They also returned to a simplified form of the liturgy, rejecting contemporary liturgical practice as too elaborate and extravagant.

Bernard lived such an exemplary life as a Cistercian that he was made abbot of a new foundation at Clairvaux (1115) only a few years after he had entered the order. He later was responsible for the foundation of more than sixty additional houses, both in France and elsewhere. It has been suggested that Bernard's own fame was largely responsible for the rapid growth of the Cistercian order, which numbered more than five hundred houses by the end of the twelfth century.

For a person who believed that monks should never leave their monasteries, Bernard came to have an extensive public career in the twelfth-century church. He was involved in several ecclesiastical controversies, both political and theological. For example, he played a mediating role in a conflict between the Cistercians and the more traditional Cluniac Benedictines. He was also instrumental in ending a schism that started in 1130, when Anacletus claimed that he, and not Innocent II, was the legitimate pope. The success of these and other mediations led to Bernard being sought out frequently to intervene in church conflicts. One of the most famous of these was his attack on Peter Abelard, of which more will be said.

Writings. Bernard's writings are extensive and diverse, including both dogmatic and mystical treatises, numerous sermons (most of which, in the form that they have come down to us, are literary creations and not transcripts of preached texts), and a great number of letters. A key dogmatic treatise is *On Grace and Free Choice*, which expounds clearly and succinctly the medieval theology of justification. The mystical treatise *On Loving God* presents the essential elements of Bernard's mysticism. The *Sermons on the Song of Songs* are stunning literary sermons that reflect playfully on the image of a spiritual marriage between Christ and the soul.

Biblical Interpretation. Bernard's writings burst with references to the Scriptures. His use of the Bible was both traditional and novel. At the outset we must note that Bernard left no systematic work that describes his method of exegesis. J. Leclercq reminds us that "we are dealing here with a poet, rather than a professor, who freely casts his ideas in every direction, leaving his readers to organize them according to their needs and inclination" (Leclercq in *Selected Works* 1987, 30). What follows is an attempt to outline the methodology that is implicit in Bernard's works.

There are the traditional elements of Bernard's exegesis. As a monk, Bernard had constant contact with a rich liturgical tradition. The monastic liturgy included the weekly recitation of all 150 psalms as well as readings from the rest of Scripture. Bernard's "biblical memory" was largely formed by this experience of monastic prayer. It is hardly accidental, for example, that in his works he frequently quoted the psalms. The monastic life also exposed Bernard to the writings of the patristic period. This may explain his practice of frequently quoting the Pauline letters, in which he followed the example of major patristic writers like *Jerome and *Augustine. Thus Bernard's use of the Bible was "deeply embedded in patristic and liturgical tradition" (Farkasfalvy, 4).

It was his fidelity to tradition that sometimes led Bernard to quote Scripture inaccurately. Some of the passages that he knew from the liturgy were in fact variants from the canonical text. Bernard was not unaware of this; on the contrary, he defended the church's right to alter the wording or the context of a biblical passage when it was used in the liturgy (Farkasfalvy, 6).

The most famous example of this appears in Bernard's third sermon for the vigil of Christmas, in which Bernard recognized that a variant of Exodus 16:6, which was used in the liturgy that day, was being taken out of its original context. That text in the Vulgate can be translated, "In the evening you shall know that it was the LORD who brought you out of the land of Egypt." The variant text from the liturgy reads, "Today you shall know that the LORD will come." Bernard not only defended this usage; he even declared the adapted text to be "stronger" *(fortior)* than the original and to possess greater authority. As D. Farkasfalvy points out, for Bernard "the liturgical use of a text offers a sort of interpretation approved by the church" (Farkasfalvy, 6).

This conviction of a certain flexibility in interpreting the Scripture was not new. It was by this time considered a commonplace that a passage from Scripture could have several senses, for example, historical, moral and mystical. Bernard in fact adopted this distinction, as in sermon 23 on the Song of Songs 1:3 [Vulgate], "The king has brought me into his chambers" (Song 1:4 NRSV). Making reference to the garden and the bedroom that are mentioned later (Song 5:1, 4 in the Vulgate), Bernard suggests: "Let the garden . . . represent the plain, unadorned, historical sense of Scripture, the storeroom its moral sense, and the bedroom the mystery of divine contemplation" (*Sermon on the Canticles* 23.3; *On the Song of Songs II*, 28).

Bernard followed the church fathers in his basic understanding of biblical interpretation. He began with a study of the "plain, unadorned, historical sense of Scripture" noted above. But this kind of exegesis was only a prelude to spiritual understanding (Farkasfalvy, 7). Bernard never tired of stressing that this spiritual understanding was the work and gift of the Holy Spirit. Indeed, he spoke of the close connection between the Scriptures and the Holy Spirit in a way that would later characterize the Protestant Reformers.

On one level Bernard's spiritual interpretation was based on the common principle that God's word could not have an undignified or purely commonplace meaning. If a literal reading of a passage produced such an interpretation, it would have to be rejected. For example, in sermon 53 on the Song of Songs, Bernard reflected on the significance of the "mountains and hills" of Song 2:8. He suggested a physical image of a large man literally leaping over towering hills in search of his "absent girlfriend." Bernard commented: "Surely it will not do to fabricate physical images of this kind, especially when treating of this spiritual Song; and it is certainly not legitimate for us who recall reading in the Gospel that 'God is a spirit and those who worship him must worship in spirit'" (*Sermon on the Canticles* 53.3, *On the Song of Songs III*, 61).

However, Bernard's adoption of a spiritual mode of interpretation can also be read on another level. Leclercq has noted that "for Bernard everything begins and ends with experience and, in between, experience is the object of reflection" (Leclercq in *Selected Works* 1987, 31). In the case of his sermons on the Song of Songs, Leclercq has suggested that "the verses of the Song of Songs are little more than a pretext for the expression of a personal experience" (quoted in Lubac, 54). At times Bernard made this connection to his own experience explicit. For example, commenting on Song 3:1 ("Upon my bed at night I sought him whom my soul loves"), he remarked: "I am not ashamed to admit that very often I myself, especially in the early days of my conversion, experienced coldness and hardness of heart, while deep in my being I sought for him whom I longed to love" (*Sermons on the Canticles* 14.5, *On the Song of Songs I*, 102).

This is not to say that Bernard was a pure subjectivist. Bernard certainly thought that interpretation had to remain within the bounds of the text itself (its literary or historical sense) and of the tradition of the church (Farkasfalvy, 12). But within those parameters, Bernard saw a great deal of room for freedom to relate the Word to his own experience. A sustained reading of his works gives one the sense of a person who combined a profound reverence for the Word of God with an ability to approach that Word as a mirror that reflected his own life. It was the Holy Spirit who grounded and guided this process.

We have already noted Bernard's free use of Scripture in which he often does not cite it exactly or explicitly. While sometimes he is quoting the Bible from memory or through his recollection of the Fathers or the monastic liturgy, at other times the phenomenon can be attributed to Bernard's overall use of what we might call a biblical vocabulary—Bernard, like many of his forebears, writes in a way that constantly echoes the Bible (Leclercq 1960, 227).

Sometimes a statement seems close to a biblical text, but it is not clear whether the reference is conscious or intended. An example of this can be found in sermon 43 on the Song, in which Bernard speaks of people who always kept Christ in front of them (e.g., Mary, Simeon, Joseph). He states: "They are an example for you," a parallel to, but not an exact citation of, John 13:15 (*Sermons on the Canticles* 43.5; *On the Song of Songs II*, 224; see Leclercq 1960, 228). There may be more allusions to biblical texts in Bernard's writings than can be definitively counted.

Even when Bernard claims to be quoting Scripture exactly, he takes liberties with it. For example, in sermon 58 on the Song, he quotes 2 Timothy 4:2, "Convince, rebuke and exhort," as "Convince, exhort, and rebuke, indicating by the first and second of these pruning and eradicating, in the last planting" (*Sermons on the Canticles* 58.4, *On the Song of Songs III*, 110; Leclercq 1960, 232). Notice that Bernard changes the order because his explanation involves a pairing together of the first and the third terms of the text from Timothy.

Another manifestation of Bernard's freedom is that he will sometimes use a biblical formulation in a context that is clearly opposed to the one from which it came. Thus, for example, in sermon 71, Bernard makes an allusion to John 16:16, where Jesus says, "A little while, and you will no longer see me, and again a little while, and you will see me." But Bernard simply takes the word *little* and uses it in a different context, namely, that "little seems to remain" of the text that he has been considering (*Sermons on the Canticles* 71.14, *On the Song of Songs IV,* 61; Leclercq 1960, 229).

Bernard takes pleasure in "playing not only on the words of the sacred text, but on the ideas that they evoke" (Leclercq 1960, 231). Thus he will sometimes combine into one formula references from different biblical texts. A good example is his allusion to Jesus as healing oil in sermon 16 on the Song. He says that this oil "anoints the head of the man who fasts [a reference to Mt 6:17], causing him to ignore the oil of sinners [a reference to Ps 141:5; 140:5 in the Vulgate]" (*Sermons on the Canticles* 16.15, *On the Song of Songs I,* 125).

Similarly Bernard sometimes takes formulas from the patristic tradition that do not exist in the Bible per se but consist of different scriptural elements that had come to be combined. A striking example of this is found in sermon 9 on the Song. Here Bernard purports to be quoting Scripture when he says, "At whatever hour the sinner will repent, his sin will be forgiven him." This text as such does not exist in the Bible, but it is reminiscent of such texts as Ezekiel 33:12, 15, 16, 19 and Isaiah 30:15. The same formula is found in the patristic tradition, particularly in a letter of Gregory the Great (*Sermons on the Canticles* 9.5, *On the Song of Songs I,* 57; Leclercq 1960, 236).

The strong influence of patristic and monastic readings of biblical texts on Bernard has raised the question of how much he read the Bible apart from these contexts. It seems clear that Bernard knew at least some books of the Bible primarily through his personal reading. Leclercq suggests that the New Testament falls into this latter category, while Bernard probably knew much of the sapiential literature through the monastic liturgy (Leclercq 1960, 235). In any case, it should be apparent from many of the examples that Bernard often enough followed his own method of interpretation that was in continuity with but was not directly borrowed from that of his forebears.

Themes. Perhaps the most important theme in the works of Bernard is that of the love of God and neighbor. He wanted his readers to attain a level of love that would make them "one spirit with God" (see 1 Cor 6:17). This would only happen when believers adopted a spirit of humility, recognizing their own sinfulness and their absolute need for God's grace to be made righteous and to accomplish anything good. Bernard often conceived of the perfect love relationship in terms of a spiritual marriage (elucidated at great length in the sermons on the Song of Songs). While he was a great promoter of the contemplative life, he recognized that in practice most people, even monks, were called to lead an active life in service of God's people. For Bernard, Scripture was the living source that both revealed this path of love and humility and guided people along the way.

Significance. Bernard's contribution to biblical interpretation is perhaps best summarized by Leclercq: "He achieved the first great synthesis in the West between all of scriptural and patristic theology on the one hand, and the totality of human experience on the other" (Leclercq in *Selected Works* 1987, 14). Bernard was not so much an innovator as a synthesizer, one who had a deep sense of the biblical tradition, particularly in its patristic expression, as well as an extraordinary ability to integrate this with his own experience. His sermons on the Song of Songs are surely the most striking example of this.

References to Bernard in later medieval and Reformation literature are extensive. As early as the thirteenth century, he was being cited as one of the "fathers," illustrating how quickly he became an important figure in the history of theology. His ideas on mystical union influenced many later mystics, including those (e.g., Meister Eckhart) whose notion of mystical union was more one of identity (essential) rather than love (affective). Bernard also influenced the theology of the Protestant Reformers, especially Martin *Luther and John *Calvin, who were especially attracted to his theology of justification and his teachings on the saving work of Christ (Köpf). Although his later commentators did not generally reflect thematically on Bernard's hermeneutic as such, they regarded him as a sound and reliable interpreter of the biblical tradition.

It has been suggested that Bernard may have influenced the transmission of the Vulgate text through the introduction of his own variants. The extent to which this may be true can be discerned only through a thorough study of medieval versions of the Vulgate, which has yet to be conducted (see Leclercq 1960, 237-44).

Bernard's theology can be described above all as monastic. His attack on scholastic theology (particularly Abelard's) is legendary and was in some respects unduly harsh. However, Bernard has received an undeserved reputation as a despiser of scholarship. He was a genuine scholar, but one who insisted on "the unity of mysticism and scholarship, theology and spirituality, exegesis and mysticism" (Farkasfalvy, 10). Thus his theology was existential and biblical rather than speculative, which was yet another ground for his positive reception by the Reformers. For Bernard as for his monastic forebears, the purpose of all learning, and indeed all reading of the Bible, was to draw one closer to God. Thus Bernard characterized his own purpose in expounding the Scriptures as "not so much to explain words as to move hearts" (*Sermons on the Canticles* 16.1, *On the Song of Songs I*, 114).

BIBLIOGRAPHY

Works. Bernard of Clairvaux, *Selected Works*, introduction by J. Leclercq (The Classics of Western Spirituality; New York: Paulist, 1987); idem, *On the Song of Songs I* (Cistercian Fathers Series 4; Kalamazoo, MI: Cistercian Publications, 1971); idem, *On the Song of Songs II* (Cistercian Fathers Series 7; Kalamazoo, MI: Cistercian Publications, 1976); idem, *On the Song of Songs III* (Cistercian Fathers Series 31; Kalamazoo, MI: Cistercian Publications, 1979); idem, *On the Song of Songs IV* (Cistercian Fathers Series 40; Kalamazoo, MI: Cistercian Publications, 1980).

Studies. P. Dumontier, *Saint Bernard et la Bible* (Paris: Desclée de Brouwer, 1953); G. R. Evans, *The Mind of Bernard of Clairvaux* (Oxford: Clarendon, 1983); D. Farkasfalvy, "The Role of the Bible in St. Bernard's Spirituality," *AC* 25 (1969) 3-13; B. S. James, *St. Bernard of Clairvaux: An Essay in Biography* (New York: Harper & Brothers, 1957); U. Köpf, "Die Rezeptions und Wirkungsgeschiche Bernhards von Clairvaux" in *Bernhard von Clairvaux: Rezeption und Wirkung im Mittelalter und in der Neuzeit*, ed. K. Elm (Wiesbaden: Harrassowitz, 1994) 5-58; J. Leclercq, "S. Bernard et la tradition biblique d'après les Sermons sur les Cantiques," *SE* (1960) 225-48; L. J. Lekai, "Cistercians," *NCE* 3 (1967); H. de Lubac, *L'Exégèse médiévale: Les quatre sens de l'Ecriture* (4 vols.; Paris: Aubier, 1959-1964); B. McGinn, *The Presence of God: A History of Western Christian Mysticism*, 2: *The Growth of Mysticism: Gregory the Great Through the Twelfth Century* (New York: Crossroad, 1994); D. E. Tamburello, *Union with Christ: John Calvin and the Mysticism of St. Bernard* (Louisville, KY: Westminster John Knox, 1994).   D. E. Tamburello

Denys the Carthusian (1402/3-1471)

Cartusia sanctos facit, sed non patefacit ("The Chartreuse [or charterhouse] makes saints but does not make them known"). This epithet presents an insight into the world and social location of Denys the Carthusian and also illuminates a paradox. In desire, training, life and scholarly repertoire, Denys was a Carthusian hermit, an ascetic and contemplative mystic focused on the inner life of the spirit. All these characteristics were in accord with the foundational intentions and attitudes of the Carthusian order, which was established by Bruno of Cologne in 1084 within the context of the eleventh-century monastic reforming movement that also produced the Cistercians and Camaldolese.

Yet in his lifetime and in the remembrance of succeeding centuries, Denys has been variously known as a church administrator, a prolific and wide-ranging author, a political as well as spiritual counselor, a moral theologian, a preacher and, if only briefly, a peripatetic church reformer; and all of these characteristics are in direct and surprising contrast to the silence and solitude of his chosen Carthusian eremitic cell.

Historians know Denys by several names: Denys of Ryckel (Rijkel), Denys van Leeuwen, Denys the Carthusian or Dionysius Cartensiensis. The man thus named was born of unprepossessing parents in 1402 or 1403 in Ryckel (Limburg), Belgium. Early in life he demonstrated an aptitude and a disposition for education that eventually led to study at the University of Cologne, from which he received the master of arts degree (1424).

Denys also manifested an early and deep devotion to the Virgin Mary, perhaps the origin of his vocation as a contemplative monk. Denys's autobiographical comments indicate that while yet a boy of ten he was already eager to enter a Carthusian charterhouse; however, the order did not accept young men under age twenty. Perhaps for this reason Denys initially pursued an academic degree. It is certain that upon completing his basic studies at Cologne, or not later than the following year, he was allowed to take vows as a Carthusian brother in the Bethlehem Mariae Charterhouse at Roermond.

Like many of his contemporaries, Denys was vitally concerned with the reform of the Catholic church in head and members. He considered and wrote about the relationship between popes and councils. His desire for internal church reform caused him to compose numerous treatises on the various forms of Christian vocation and the appropriate exercise of ecclesiastical offices. During 1451 and 1452 he accompanied Bishop Nicholas of Cusa (1401-1464) on a series of reforming visitations to monasteries in the Rhine region of Germany. In 1465 Denys himself assumed monastic adminis-

trative authority when he was appointed prior of a newly-founded Charterhouse at Bois-le-Duc. Ill health forced him to resign that position in 1469, however, and he returned to Roermond, where he died in 1471.

Work. It appears that Denys began writing sometime before 1430 and continued until close to the end of his life, probably 1467. Judging from the variety of genres he employed, he wrote for a multifaceted audience that included Carthusian brothers, church prelates, civil rulers, students and scholars—and himself. During his lifetime and immediately after, his articles on many spiritual, ecclesiastical and theological topics and his biblical commentaries were in great demand, the latter particularly because they brought into one place the comments of many other, older scholars from whose work Denys made a synthesis. His comprehensive writings were first collected and put into print from existing autographs and copies under the supervision of another Carthusian, Dietrich Loer (Loher) with the assistance of Johan Host von Romberg, beginning in 1530. That numerous editions of his commentaries and treatises were subsequently made during the sixteenth century attests to the popularity of his thought and the stature he unintentionally gained during his life.

An essentially modern edition was begun by the Carthusians of Montreuil-sur-Mer in 1896 to 1901 (vols. 1-14, 17, 18), continued at Tournai (vols. 15-16; 19-42), and concluded at Parkminster (volume 25 completed in 1935). Commonly referred to as the *Opera Omnia,* this edition includes fourteen volumes of the comprehensive biblical commentaries *(Enarrationes),* a harmony of the letters attributed to Paul, commentaries on several works of Pseudo-Dionysius (*De Coelesti Seu Angelica Hierarchia* 5.15.3-283; *De Ecclesiastica Hierarchia* 5.15. 343-590; *De Divinis Nominibus* 5.16.1-346; *De Mystica Theologia* 5.16.443-95; *Commentaria in Epistolas S. Dionysii Areopagitae* 5.16.499-592; an explication of *The Sentences* of Peter

Lombard (5.19-25), commentaries on the books of Boethius (*Errationes in Quinque Libros Boetii: De Consolatione Philosophiae* 5.26.11-496), an exhaustive compendium of Thomas Aquinas's *Summa Theologiae* (*Summa Fidei Orthodoxae, Alias Enterione, Id Est Medulla Operum Sancti Thomae* 5.17.11-523), sermons, works on the spiritual life, letters offering pastoral care and spiritual direction, apocalyptic visions, political treatises, twenty-one articles on reform of the church and on ecclesiastical and civil governance, and general correspondence. A new edition of *Opera Selecta* is in progress for the collection *Corpus Christianorum, Continuatio Mediaevalis* under the editorial supervision of K. Emery Jr.

What is particularly noteworthy about Denys's collection of works, biblical and theological, political and pastoral, is that he accomplished it despite never finishing the expected university course of study. He completed his master's degree in the arts faculty of the University of Cologne but did not continue in a formal and systematic study of theology as might have been expected. Perhaps one benefit of not being licensed as a master of theology was his relative freedom from the constraint of ecclesiastical authority over the positions he expressed in his writing.

The scope and volume of Denys's outpouring has caused historians to wonder at his ability to produce so much work while living under the discipline of a Carthusian charterhouse. It does seem that Denys did not have the benefit of a secretary. He composed, corrected, wrote and illuminated his own articles, and, when necessary, copied his work for distribution to friends and petitioners. The bibliographical resources that he was able to consult are in part suggested by the authors and materials on which he chose to comment directly or that he cited in his biblical interpretations. An analysis of the books that might have been available to him for consultation at Roermond, either belonging to the charterhouse or on loan or presented to Denys himself is still in progress (see Emery 1982

and more recently his introduction to *Dionysii Cartusiensis Opera Selecta* 1991). Denys modestly attributes his prodigious capacity to the blessing of the Holy Spirit and a strong constitution.

Biblical Exegesis. Between 1434 and 1440 Denys completed the first series of his biblical commentaries, an exposition of the Psalms. When he initiated this work he composed an article separate from the commentary itself that functions as a methodological prologue to his lifelong exegetical work (*Omnia Opera* 5.30.398.B, art. 4). In it he describes his understanding of the fourfold meaning of Scripture. The four meanings, or senses, that he recognizes are *litteraliter*, the actual or literal sense of the text; *historice*, the historical meaning of the text; *spiritualiter*, the spiritual significance of the text; and *mystice*, the mystical import of the text. The mystical sense is understood in three subdistinctions: the allegorical; the tropological, or moral; and the anagogical.

Denys's delineations are neither unique nor surprising. They accord with those first articulated by John Cassian (360-435) and encapsulated in the school rhyme *Littera gesta docet, quid credas alligoria, quid agas moralis, quo tendas anagogia* ("The literal sense provides the historical data; the allegorical, that which one should believe by faith; the tropological or moral, how one should behave; the anagogical, where one is going in terms of spiritual progress" (Minnis, 34).

Denys maintained that the literal and historical senses of Scripture are the foundations upon which all other exegetical activity must rest. This is so because it is only when one first understands the literal or historical sense of a text that one can then begin to perceive the deeper meanings from which one constructs interpretive arguments for the proof of faith that can have validity and authority. Once one acknowledges the literal sense of a text, then it is possible to consider the allegorical meaning the text has to impart and to discern the way in which a word, a historical figure or an action demonstrates truth about the nature of Christ and the nature of his mystical body, the church.

Denys asserted that a right perception of the allegorical significance of a text was the necessary prologue to an appreciation of the tropological sense, which directs one's understanding through revelations about Christ, the saints and church toward a personal understanding of moral and ethical obligation in the light of the gospel. Having proceeded thus far through the exposition of a given text, Denys explained, it is then possible for one to enter into the most fruitful engagement with Scripture, the anagogical, in which one is conveyed through contemplation from the secular or earthly events recounted in a text toward the intended revelation of what is eternal.

Perhaps because of his early abandonment of an academic career and his call to an essentially eremitic, reflective life among the Carthusians, Denys displayed a certain freedom from doctrinal and ecclesiastical authoritarianism in his expository enterprises. His biblical commentaries make encyclopedic use of the thought of his predecessors, in style if not volume, for the exegetical works known to him. But his own works do not attempt to provide an analysis of the patristic and medieval sources upon which he drew, only a recapitulation. As Emery notes,

> [Denys also] rejected every simply positive notion of ecclesiastical authority. We do not believe the Scriptures because the Church tells us they are inspired by God. Rather, the Scriptures derive their authority *causaliter et exsistentialiter,* directly from uncreated wisdom. Thus, a reason of the Scriptures is always there to be discovered, difficult though it may be to discern. Ecclesiastical pronouncements, in turn, are the more binding the more they bear the marks of intrinsic authority, that is, the more evidently they relate to the analogies of faith and right thinking. (Emery 1992, 337)

Denys wrote his commentaries as a personal meditative exercise designed to lead him toward both faith and right thinking and secondarily to benefit those who might read what he wrote. Nonetheless his own approach to contemplation shows a pronounced strain of theological speculation that is in contrast to the anti-intellectual tendency in much late medieval spirituality. As he was eclectic in the collection of his commentary sources, so Denys was remarkably open to eclecticism in his own thought processes.

Over the course of his life Denys constructed commentaries on every book of the Scriptures. Having begun with the book of Psalms, he concluded with the book of Baruch, at the close of which he wrote an *explicit,* or closure to the textual unit. In this case it was his complete set of biblical commentaries. He neatly summarizes both his attitude to his labor and the focus of his life: "Herewith I make an end [to my commentary] of the entire Bible, to the praise, for the honor and glorification of the almighty and eternally praiseworthy God, in the year of our Lord 1457 on the feast of the Visitation of Mary the Blessed Virgin. Amen" (5.9.408.A).

Significance. Denys the Carthusian does not figure largely in historical works on biblical interpretation, though his commentaries were highly valued during the fifteenth and into the sixteenth centuries. He is rather remembered by subsequent centuries as a mystic and spiritual guide, the author of works on contemplation (especially *De Contemplatione* 5.41.133-289), prayer and Christian vocation. While he wrote only with reluctance about his lifelong, frequent revelatory visions, his sobriquet among his contemporaries and through centuries of Carthusian history as *Doctor Ecstaticus* ("ecstatic doctor") suggests how prominent this aspect of his own spiritual journey must have been and how influential it was in all his work. J. Huizinga has referred to Denys as "the perfect type of the powerful religious enthusiast produced by the waning Middle Ages" (Huizenga, 218). He was a mystic, an ascetic, a theologian, an author, a reformer, an administrator. "It is as if through him the entire stream of medieval theology flows once again. *Qui Dionysium legit nihil non legit* [whoever reads Denys reads everything], was said by the theologians of the sixteenth century" (Huizinga, 218).

BIBLIOGRAPHY.

Works. Dionysii Cartusiensis Opera Selecta, ed. K. Emery Jr. (Corpus Christianorum. Continuatio Mediaevalis 121; Turnhout: Brepols, 1991-); *Opera Omnia* (42 vols.; Montreuil-sur-Mer, Tournai, Parkminster: Carthusians, 1896-1935). *Studies.* M. Beer, *Dionysius des Kartäusers Lehre vom desiderium naturale des Menschen nach des Gott[es]chau* (Munich: Max Hueber, 1963); K. Emery Jr., *The Carthusians, Intermediaries for the Teaching of John Ruysbroeck During the Period of Early Reform in the Counter-Reformation* in *Miscellanea Catrusiensis 4,* 43: *Analecta Carthusiana* (Salzburg: Institut für Anglistik und Amerikanistik, 1979); idem, "Denys the Carthusian and the Doxology of Scholastic Theology" in *Ad Litteram*, ed. M. Jordan and K. Emery Jr. (Notre Dame, IN: University of Notre Dame Press, 1992); idem, *Dionysii Cartusiensis Bibliotheca et Manuscripta: Prologue and Queries* in *Analecta Cartusiana, Kartausermystik und-Mystiker* (Salzburg: Institut für Anglistik und Amerikanistik, 1982) vol. 4; idem, "Introduction" in *Corpus Christianorum, Continuatio Mediaevalis 121, Dionysii Cartusiensis Opera Selecta, vv. la and lb* (Turnholt: Brepols, 1991); H.-G. Gruber, *Christliches Eheverstandnis in 15n Jahrhundert: Eine moralgeschichtliche Untersuchung zur Ehelehre Dionysius' des Kartäusers* (Regensburg: Pustet, 1989); J. Huizinga, *The Autumn of the Middle Ages* (Chicago: University of Chicago Press, 1996); J. Leclercq, F. Vanderbroeck and L. Bouyer, *La Spiritualité du Moyen Age* (Paris: Aubier, 1961) vol. 2; H. de Lubac, *Exégèse médiévale: Les quatre sens de l'Écriture* (4 vols.; Paris: Aubier, 1954-64); N. Maginot, *Der Actus humanus moralis unter dem Einflus des Heiligen Geistes nach Dionysius Carthusianus* (Munich: Max Hueber, 1968); A. J. Minnis, *Medieval Theory of Authorship: Scholastic Literary Attitudes in the Later Middle Ages* (London: Scolar Press, 1984); M. Zadnikar and A. Wienand, *Die Kartäuser: Der Orden des schweigenden Mönchen* (Koin: Wienand, 1983).

L. A. Shoemaker

Gerson, Jean *(1363-1429)*

Jean Gerson was one of the leading university theologians of the late fourteenth and early fifteenth centuries. As a conciliarist and an active participant in the Council of Constance (1414-1418), Gerson worked for reform of the church "in head and members," devoting attention to the political crisis of the papal schism and seeking to renew the integrity of faith and life among clergy, monks and laity. An ardent advocate of the centrality of Scripture in this work, Gerson devoted himself to biblical exposition and wrote numerous treatises on the theory of interpretation (hermeneutics). His writings address a wide range of themes, both constructive and controversial, as these emerged in the complex arena of university theology during this period.

Born near Rethel in the Ardennes on December 14, 1363, as Jean le Charlier de Gerson, he entered the College of Navarre (Paris) in 1377 and attained there the licentiate in arts (1381) and in theology (1392). The following year he was appointed deacon at St. Donatien (Bruges), a benefice he held until 1411. In 1393 he was inaugurated as master in theology at Paris, and in 1395 succeeded his mentor, Pierre d'Ailly (d. 1420), as chancellor of the university.

His writings, which appeared in many early printings (incunabula include Cologne, 1483/84; Strasbourg, 1488, reprinted 1489 and 1494; Nürnberg and Basel, 1489) and numerous editions from the sixteenth and seventeenth centuries, fill five folio volumes in the edition of L. E. du Pin and ten volumes in the recent critical edition of P. Glorieux. (References to texts are cited from this edition and are noted as G [= Glorieux] followed by volume and page number.) The collected works represent many genres and explore a wide range of themes, including sermons in French and Latin; poems and hymns; educational treatises on university studies, adult catechism and the pedagogy of children; explorations of mystical theology; letters on topics related to official and pastoral matters; university lectures; biblical commentary; treatises on spirituality; ecclesiological writings devoted to matters of church reform, discipline and authority; speculative and practical discussions of mysticism; polemical treatments of disputed questions. His stature as theologian, churchman, preacher and spiritual guide won for him the posthumous appellation "the most Christian doctor" *(doctor christianissimus)*.

Gerson's contribution as a biblical interpreter must be appreciated within the peculiar horizon of late medieval European life. As a man of his times, his exegetical intentions and practices seem often far removed from modern critical canons. He must be understood as a theologian trained during a period of significant shifts in the philosophical and epistemological realms, a new way *(via moderna)* often referred to as nominalism or Ockhamism, after William of Ockham (d. 1347). Yet Gerson persisted in honoring an older tradition of scholarship, identifying himself in continuity with traditions of an older school *(via antiqua)* and often citing in his own writings citations from "spiritual" theologians who combined inquiry with devotion, intellectual rigor with pastoral commitment. Among these, his favored "ancient" authorities included Pseudo-Dionysius (c. sixth-century pseudonymous mystic), *Bernard of Clairvaux (d. 1153), the Victorines (*Hugh of St. Victor [d. 1141]; Richard [d. 1173]), Bonaventure and Thomas *Aquinas (both d. 1274); among the "modern" voices he followed were *Nicholas of Lyra (d. 1349) and his own teacher, Henry Totting of Oyta (d. 1396).

As university chancellor, Gerson found himself called upon to mediate in disputes of both a local and an international nature. In this capacity he became known as an advocate for a lay movement of new piety *(devotio moderna)*, defending the Brothers and Sisters of the Common Life against the attack of a Dominican named Matthew Grabow (see G 10, 70-72). He also championed the Carthusian order as an adamant supporter of their eremetical form of monastic life and wrote a celebrated defense of

their refusal to eat meat (see *On the Carthusian Rejection of Meat,* G 3, 77-95), which he based upon a careful exegesis of relevant biblical texts. The preface of his commentary on the Song of Songs opens with the words "You do I love, holy order of Carthusians" (see G 8, 565).

At the conclusion of the Council of Constance, he abandoned his university career and stayed with the Benedictine monastery of Melk before eventually associating himself with the Coelestine priory in Lyons. There he spent the last years of his life, devoting himself to various writing projects and teaching boys in the monastic grammar school. Gerson died on July 12, 1429, and was buried in the church of St. Lawrence (Lyons).

Writings. Gerson's importance as a leading voice in academic, ecclesial and pastoral affairs of this period can hardly be overestimated. He would not have understood himself as a biblical theologian in the modern sense, but he did bring to his passionate work as theologian and church reformer a profound appreciation of Scripture and its significance as the foundation for the church's faith and life. Biblical erudition, as he often called it (see, for example, G 3, 237), was a wisdom both necessary and sufficient for university theologians and unlettered laypeople alike. His writings are saturated with scriptural citations, allusions and echoes and include exegetical treatises devoted to the practice of interpretation alongside theoretical discussions of hermeneutics.

These works could be grouped into three categories. The first are the sermons, a large number of which are preserved in both their Latin and French forms; these receive a thorough discussion in D. C. Brown's study, which focuses on the vernacular sermons as the material basis for illumining the pastoral dimensions of Gerson's thought.

The second and third categories consist of academic lectures and writings commenting (sometimes rather loosely, by modern standards) on biblical texts on the one hand and treatises devoted to hermeneutical questions of a theoretical and methodological scope on the other. First we will consider selected university lectures, including Latin sermons, and writings.

Most of these writings come from Gerson's years in residence as teacher and subsequently university chancellor at Paris, until his departure for the Council of Constance (1415). During the early years of the fifteenth century he inaugurated a reform of the theology curriculum at the university and offered guidelines for the teaching approach to be utilized. The tradition of this period was for students of theology who aspired to become masters first to comment upon the *Sentences* of Peter Lombard (d. 1160) before turning to the interpretation of Scripture, a pattern later followed by the Protestant Reformer John *Calvin, who wrote his *Institutes of the Christian Religion* (final Latin edition, 1559) to prepare Reformed students for biblical study.

Gerson's concern was not with the formal structure of this curriculum but with what theologians had made of it. In his mind, they devoted too much attention to what he called the "subtle questions" of logic, to the neglect of more pressing pastoral concerns. He first outlined a program for university reform in a detailed memoir (see the letter of April 1, 1400; G 2, 27-28) addressed to his mentor, d'Ailly. Later he returned to this theme in a lengthier lecture series, published in the form of a programmatic treatise entitled "Against the Curiosity of Scholars" (G 3, 229-49), in which he advocated humility among theologians as a means of abiding by the Pauline admonition "not to think [of oneself] more highly than one should, but to think soberly" (Rom 12:3).

Throughout this treatise Gerson emphasized the central role of Scripture in the theological vocation and the need for theologians "to elucidate its truths humbly" but to also recognize the proper and pious limits of such investigation (see G 3, 234). Thus he insisted that the teaching of faith

(doctrina fidei), although it "surpassed philosophy, has its predetermined limits in the sacred writings [Scripture] revealed to us," adding the unambiguous warning that "beyond these limits no one should dare define or teach anything" whatsoever (see G 3, 233). The ascent to God always begins with the ladder of Scripture *(scripturarum scala)* and not with philosophical speculation, even if finally it gives way to another ladder of a higher mystical knowledge of God (*altera . . . scala ad ulteriorem de Deo cognitionem,* G 3, 233). Scripture remained sufficient for all matters of salvation, even if the mystical path led beyond it. For discerning the matters necessary to be believed for salvation, Scripture remained the sufficient basis in what it affirmed in its literal sense and in what could be "necessarily and formally inferred" from this (here he followed his teacher's lead; see Henry Totting of Oyta, *Quaestio de Sacra Scriptura et de Veritatibus Catholicis,* art. 3).

During the first decade of the fifteenth century, Gerson took up a sustained project of commentary on the Gospel of Mark. This took the form of academic sermons delivered in Latin and occasional treatises on a variety of subjects, all based at least formally on Gospel texts (through Mk 3:29). Many of these sermons offer straightforward scriptural exposition, while some utilize biblical texts as starting points for theological discussion of disputed questions, controversial practices, and pastoral or ecclesial matters; the latter follow a rather loose exegetical approach judged by modern standards. Among these, for example, we find a complex and lengthy treatise entitled *A Comparison of the Contemplative and Active Life,* which Gerson associates with the text from Mark 1:5, 6. Examples of the former state in their titles the substance of his message (e.g., "On John's Humility," a sermon on Mk 1:7).

Other writings associated directly with Scripture include Gerson's *Monotessaron* (1420; G 9, 245-373), a Gospel harmony made for student use, and several lengthy commentaries written late in his life, one on the Magnificat (Lk 1:46-55) entitled *Collectorium super Magnificat* (1427/28; G 8, 163-534) and one on the Song of Songs, *Super Cantica Canticorum* (1429; G 8, 565-639). The modern French edition of Gerson's writings does not designate a separate volume for exegetical writings, including such major commentaries instead in the volume of "spiritual and pastoral writings" *(L'oeuvre spirituelle et pastorale)*.

Of the second group of writings devoted to hermeneutical questions, several stand out with particular significance. These include an important treatise *On the Literal Sense of Sacred Scripture and the Causes of Error* written during his last years in Paris (1413/14; see G 3, 333-40), his *Response to the Consultation of Masters* (1415; see G 10, 232-53) of the same period, the methodological preface to his polemical treatise against the Hussites, *On the Necessity of Communion for the Laity under Both Kinds* (1417; see G 10, 55-59; the du Pin edition includes this treatise under a different title, *Against the Heresy of Communion for the Laity under Both Kinds;* see 1:457-67) written in the wake of Hus's trial at the council and subsequent execution, and sections of a dialogue-treatise written just after the council, *On the Consolation of Theology* (1418; G 9, 185-245 passim).

Biblical Interpretation. We now turn our attention to those texts in which Gerson explores hermeneutical questions and controversies of his day. These texts offer a penetrating insight into Gerson's exegetical strategies and hermeneutical convictions, since we here see Gerson as university chancellor at work, delineating the proper methods and right use of authority in response to ecclesial crises and political disputes.

In a treatise devoted entirely to this question (*On the Literal Interpretation of Sacred Scripture and the Causes of Error,* G 3, 333-40), we find Gerson turning his attention to what had become a fundamental controversy in his day: how one could delineate the so-called literal sense of Scrip-

ture. This matter had become particularly problematic in cases of textual ambiguity, when competing interpretations found evident support in various texts or, often, in different ways of reading the same text.

To address this question Gerson favored what he called a rhetorical interpretation of Scripture, following *Augustine's lead (see especially Augustine *On Christian Doctrine* books 2 and 3, where we find the conclusion that "hardly anything may be found in the obscure places [of Scripture] which is not found plainly said elsewhere" [2.6.8; see also 3.26.37]). But what was the peculiar rhetoric of Scripture, and how could one delineate what was said plainly in disputed cases? In such cases Gerson followed Aquinas, who instructed the interpreter of Scripture "to consider not the words alone but their [proper] sense" (*non considerare verba sed sensum;* see Aquinas *In Matthew* 27.1, n. 2321, ed. R. Cai [Turin and Rome: Marietti, 1951], 358). In order to implement this mandate, Gerson defended the role tradition played in biblical interpretation, arguing that the interpreter should be obedient not to the rules of logical argument but to the inspired sense of the text as this had been discerned and handed down by the Fathers (i.e., the *sensus a sanctis patribus traditus;* see G 9, 237). This traditioned sense revealed the proper meaning *(sensus)* of Scripture, particularly in such disputed cases where controversy surrounded the plain reading.

Because of this circumstance, Gerson suggested that it ought to be affirmed "in accordance with the manner in which the church, inspired and governed by the Holy Spirit, has determined it and not according to a capricious decision or interpretation" (G 3, 335). In other words, Gerson disallowed an individualistic reading (see thesis 12 in this treatise, where he argued against "those who prefer their own sense to the judgment of those who are more prudent and wise"; G 3, 335), just as he resisted identifying the interpretive authority solely with the current magisterium. The exegetical approach he favored, in contrast to such possibilities, was both ecclesial (residing in the church's memory) and spiritual (emphasizing the Spirit's past and present witness). "We believe," he concluded with abrupt emphasis, "on the basis of the church's tradition" (*credimus ex traditione ecclesiae*, G 3, 335; we also find this argument in the prologue to Henry Totting of Oyta's commentary on Lombard's *Sentences*).

This led Gerson to argue against not only "vain curiosity" but also rationalizing tendencies he detected among the arts faculty. Against such trends he insisted that faith "does not come naturally" (*fides non est naturalia*). The proper interpretation of Scripture always depended upon the divine gift of understanding, or what he called "the light of grace which God infuses" into us (G 3, 333). But Gerson understood that this normally occurred through the ordinary channels of the hierarchical church. He concluded this treatise with a warning against any who "corrupt" such order, in either the church or in the secular realm. Echoing a theme from Pseudo-Dionysius's *Ecclesiastical Hierarchy* often found in his writings, Gerson insisted that proper church order (ecclesiology) required that "the lower be led back to God through those above them" and that no one could appoint themselves "judges and supreme authorities" in interpreting Scripture or addressing theological questions (G 3, 340). If anyone disrupted this order and opposed what the church had "publicly decided and settled," punishment was not only permissible but also necessary in order to preserve the church's integrity (see thesis 7, G 3, 334; the argument derives from Augustine's anti-Donatist writings, also borrowing from Aquinas for the definition of correction as "a spiritual almsgiving"; see Aquinas *Summa Theologiae* IIaIIae, a.33, a.1).

Gerson's *Response to the Consultation of Masters* clarifies his approach to the Scripture's peculiar "rhetoric," identifying three rules that biblical interpreters must follow. First, they must honor the wider biblical context (echoing Augustine and anticipating Martin *Luther's familiar dictum that Scripture must interpret itself); second, they must heed the *modus loquendi*, the means of speaking, which requires an appreciation of "figures of speech, tropes, and rhetorical expressions"; and, finally, they must follow the *usus loquendi*, the established precedent by which the "holy doctors and expositors" had already interpreted Scripture.

Here Gerson distinguishes how tradition is to function as a safeguard against a rationalist interpretation: Scripture must not be read "according to a power of logic or dialectic applied in speculative sciences," since it has "its own proper logic and grammar" (*sed habet Scriptura Sacra suam propriam logicam et grammaticam, quemadmodum scientiae morales habent pro logica rhetoricam*, G 3, 241). His argument followed the nominalist tendency to elevate revealed texts over those of secular provenance (i.e., the arts and letters), but he went further by highlighting how the biblical text's proper sense came into being within the church's historical witness. Once again we find him emphasizing the most ancient readings, which he assumed represented a consensus that could settle controverted modern questions, an instance of his adherence to the Renaissance return "to the sources" (*ad fontes*, in this case, Scripture in tradition).

Finally, in Gerson's lengthy dialogue *On the Consolation of Theology*, we find him insisting that since "the tradition of theology is revealed through Scripture" (*theologiae traditio per scripturam revelatum*; see G 9, 204), the theologian is not one trained in the formal modes of scholastic disputation but one who is "a good man learned in sacred Scripture—not indeed the erudition of the intellect only, but much more of the heart" (G 9, 237). Gerson's emphasis thus falls upon the precondition in the reader, the moral integrity required for a faithful understanding of Scripture. Right interpretation depends upon, just as it also promotes, a virtuous life. He thus warned against those who "impudently forced the sacred Scriptures to serve their own corrupt habits and desires, distorting the sense [of the text] handed down by the holy fathers—if they are not indeed ignorant of it" (G 9, 237). Echoes to this warning in later indictments declared at the Council of Trent against presumed excesses of Protestant exegesis are probably not accidental (see in particular the decrees of the fourth session [April 1546], in H. J. Schroeder, ed., *The Canons and Decrees of Trent* [St. Louis and London: Herder, 1941], 18-19, 298).

Gerson's defense of tradition was intended to safeguard and not diminish the Bible's authority. But his approach held tenaciously to the necessity of an ecclesial exegesis, a reading of Scripture in obedient conversation with the church's tradition but one that always recognized that Scripture rather than tradition constituted the rule of faith (*regula fidei;* see G 10, 55). But Scripture could not be loosed from tradition; it must be received in its traditioned form. To borrow Aristotelian categories, as some modern Roman Catholic interpreters have done to clarify this approach, we might say that Scripture was the matter and tradition the form by which revelation reached us.

Significance. The significance of Gerson as a biblical interpreter in his own context is impressive, and his historical influence is also significant. Thus, for instance, his writings were widely circulated in various complete editions in the early years of printing, and many were translated into German and circulated under the patronage of John Geiler of Kaysersberg and others. Johannes Altenstaig, in his important encyclopedia of theology (the so-called *Vocabularius Theologiae,* 1517), referred to him as "the most learned Gerson" *(doctissimus Gerson),* and citations to his works appeared frequently in the publications of both Roman Catholic and Protestant theologians during the early decades of the Reformation. His influence upon late medieval theologians was immense and wide-

reaching, prompting one historian to describe this period as "the century of Gerson" (E. Delaruelle).

But his significance cannot be confined to historical influences, as important as these were in the centuries after his death. Gerson's exegetical approach, which could be described as tradition-oriented, theologically engaged and pastorally grounded, continues to have relevance to questions in the modern context. Three of these questions merit particular mention.

The first area in which Gerson's contribution might still yield fruit is his high valuation of the laity in their role as bearers of the church's life. This is not to say that he should be understood as a proto-Protestant. This would be not only anachronistic but also a gross distortion of his intentions as a stubbornly conservative theologian. Nor is it to suggest that Gerson was opposed to theology as a profession. But he refused to conclude that the substance of Christian faith is the result of either technical competence in theological argument or intellectual achievement alone. Gerson approached exegesis as a lived discipline, reminding us that those he called the simple (*idiotae* or *les simples*), in whom "simple faith, sure hope and sweet charity" are to be found, and not the professional per se, had a crucial role in conveying "the spirit of Catholic understanding" (*anima catholicae sententiae;* see, for example, G 9, 238). The character of one's life, and not simply the pedigree of one's formal academic training, determined whether one was capable of grasping Scripture's intent, which involved the formation of the whole person and of the church.

Second, his lifelong interest in mystical theology and the care with which he sought to understand its relation to Scripture, human experience and other scholastic modes of theological discourse offers a dimension of his thought responsive to the current cultural interest in spirituality. Gerson's commentary on the Song of Songs is on its own worthy of a wider reading than it has received, offering those who might venture to study it a provocative means of encountering the one biblical text that stood at the heart of medieval monastic culture. But this interest arose from a deeper conviction: that Scripture in its literal sense was meant to lead us toward God, to encourage us in what we might today refer to as our discipleship. It was not only a document of an ancient culture that we might interpret with dispassionate care; rather, it was a "living voice" meant to accompany us in our faith and life, engaging both mind and spirit in the quest for faithful living.

Third, his interest in an ecclesial exegesis that underscores the normative role of tradition reveals a thinker who understood that authoritative texts could not be read in isolation, that the text's posthistory also belongs to its meaning. He was not alone in this recognition. But his approach to tradition, or as suggested above, Scripture in tradition, moves us beyond an older polemical debate between Protestant and Roman Catholic theologians, anticipating what H.-G. Gadamer has called the "effective history" of texts as one vital dimension of a text's living "voice" (see, for example, Gadamer, *Truth and Method* [rev. ed.; New York: Crossroad, 1989] esp. 2.2.1). Gerson appreciated this dimension of the text's authority, thereby recognizing Scripture as the church's book. This interest in the text's influence as part of its meaning has guided B. *Childs's commitment to a canonical approach to Scripture (most recently, *Biblical Theology of the Old and New Testaments* [Minneapolis: Fortress, 1992], esp. chap. 2, 70-78). Gerson reminds us, in anticipation of Gadamer's philosophical defense of tradition and with certain affinities to Childs's canonical method of reading, that the context in which biblical texts have been read constitutes one of the horizons within which we should try to locate their meaning, particularly in the case of the church as a community of interpretation that is always both historical and modern. This might also be a way of understanding the history of interpretation as one expression of the Holy Spirit's activity, an extension of the divine witness in past space and time.

BIBLIOGRAPHY

Works. J. Gerson, *Oeuvres Complètes,* ed. P. Glorieux (10 vols.; Paris: Desclée & Cie, 1960-1973), in which an extensive list of manuscripts and printed editions is found (*Introduction Générale,* 1:71-103); idem, *Opera Omnia,* ed. L. E. du Pin (4 vols.; Antwerp: Sumptibus Societatis, 1706). English translations of Gerson's works are few; the several that are accessible include *On Leading Children to Christ* in *Basic Writings in Christian Education,* ed. K. B. Cully (Philadelphia: Westminster, 1960) 119-32, and miscellaneous excerpts in S. Ozment, ed., *Jean Gerson: Selections from 'A Deo exivit,' 'Contra curiositatem studentium,' and 'De mystica theologia speculativa* (Textus Minores 38; Leiden: E. J. Brill, 1969).

Studies. D. C. Brown, *Pastor and Laity in the Theology of Jean Gerson* (Cambridge: Cambridge University Press, 1986); C. Burger, *Aedificatio, Fructus, Utilitas: Johannes Gerson als Professor der Theologie und Kanzler der Universität Paris* (Tübingen: J. C. B. Mohr, 1986); M. S. Burrows, *Jean Gerson and 'De Consolatione Theologiae' (1418): The Consolation of a Biblical and Reforming Theology for a Disordered Age* (Tübingen: J. C. B. Mohr, 1991); idem, "Jean Gerson on the 'Traditioned Sense' of Scripture as an Argument for an Ecclesial Hermeneutic" in *Biblical Hermeneutics in Historical Perspective,* ed. M. S. Burrows and P. Rorem (Grand Rapids: Eerdmans, 1991) 152-72; A. Combes, *Essai sur la critique de Ruysbroeck par Gerson* (Paris: J. Vrin, 1945-1972); idem, *La théologie mystique de Gerson: Profil de son évolution* (2 vols.; Romae: Desclée, 1963-1964); W. Dress, *Die Theologie Gerson: Eine Untersuchung zur Verbindung von Nominalismus und Mystik im Spätmittelalter* (Gütersloh: Bertelsmann, 1931); K. Froehlich, " 'Always to Keep the Literal Sense in Holy Scripture Means to Kill One's Soul': The State of Biblical Hermeneutics at the Beginning of the Fifteenth Century" in *Literary Uses of Typology from the Late Middle Ages to the Present,* ed. E. Miner (Princeton: Princeton University Press, 1977) 20-48; F. Hahn, "Die Hermeneutik Gersons," *ZTK* 51 (1954) 34-50; M. Hurley, " 'Scriptura sola': Wyclif and His Critics," *Traditio* 16 (1960) 275-352; L. Mourin, *Jean Gerson, prédicateur francais* (Belgie: Brugge, 1952); H. Oberman, *The Harvest of Medieval Theology: Gabriel Biel* *and Late Medieval Nominalism* (Cambridge, MA: Harvard University Press, 1963); L. Pascoe, *Jean Gerson: Principles of Church Reform* (Leiden: Brill, 1973); G. H. M. Posthumus Meyjes, *Jean Gerson: Zijn Kerkpolitiek en Ecclesiologie* ('S-Gravenhage: Martinus Nijhoff, 1963); J. Schwab, *Johannes Gerson: Professor der Theologie und Kanzler der Universität Paris* (2 vols.; New York: B. Franklin, 1969 [1858]).

M. S. Burrows

Hugh *(1096-1141)* and Andrew *(1110-1175)* of St. Victor

As biblical scholars both Hugh and Andrew of St. Victor were noted for their insistence on the primacy of the literal sense of the Bible. Hugh, often termed the new Augustine, utilized biblical exegesis as the foundation for spiritual training, bridging the gap between mystical and dialectical approaches to the Bible. While he was not the first theologian of the Middle Ages to discuss the literal sense of the Bible, he was innovative in his insistence on the literal-historical interpretation as the basis of all other meanings.

Hugh's work was a crowning achievement of the first phase of scholastic theology exhibited by his ability and desire to integrate traditional patristic learning, Augustinian theology and burgeoning scholastic dialectic. Andrew, more noted as a biblical scholar than a theologian or mystic, was the first medieval commentator to use Jewish interpretation of the Old Testament systematically, becoming the source book for Jewish interpretation and biblical history within the Christian West for many years.

Lives. The biographical details of Hugh of St. Victor have been the subject of some debate. With few clues supplied in his own writings, a traditional reconstruction of Hugh's life maintains that he was born in Saxony or Flanders in 1096. After initial schooling near his home he joined the Canons Regular of St. Augustine at Hamersleven, arriving at the abbey of St. Victor around 1115. His renown earned

him the directorship of the school from 1120 to 1141 and a brief stint as prior in 1133. He died at an early age on February 11, 1141.

Somewhat more is known about the life of Andrew of St. Victor. He was born in England in 1110. He entered the monastery of St. Victor sometime around 1130, and he probably studied under Hugh. He became the first abbot of Wigmore Abbey, Herefordshire, England, about 1147, returning to academic life at St. Victor at a later date. He eventually returned to Wigmore Abbey at their request, serving again as abbot from 1161 to 1163, and there he stayed until his death on October 19, 1175.

Context. In the eleventh and twelfth centuries two opposing approaches to biblical interpretation arose. One, the dialectic method, best exemplified by Peter Abelard (d. 1142), stressed the primacy of reason over faith. While this method accepted the Bible as authoritative, it also recognized the necessity of its careful study. On the other side were mystics, such as *Bernard of Clairvaux (d. 1153) and William of Champeaux (d. 1121), who saw Scripture as a primary tool for spiritual experience. Their individualistic approach fostered allegorical interpretations. William of Champeaux, the former teacher of Abelard, had founded an Augustinian abbey at St. Victor in Paris in 1108, originally as a hermitage that fostered a life of prayer and contemplation. His reputation followed him, however, and he was soon pressed upon to teach. The curriculum of the school was influenced by the more prestigious school at Laon with its emphasis on Scripture and patristic exegesis. Throughout the twelfth and thirteenth centuries the school at St. Victor gained prominence because of the excellence of its scholars, among whom were Hugh and Andrew.

Hugh of St. Victor as Biblical Exegete. While contemporary scholars have long recognized the importance of Scripture to Hugh's thought, his commentaries on the Bible have received little attention. Yet Hugh's importance in the history of Christian biblical exegesis cannot be denied. Although he was not the first theologian of the Middle Ages to discuss the literal sense of the Bible, he was innovative in his insistence on the literal-historical interpretation as the basis of all other meanings. The major sources for understanding Hugh's literal exegesis are his *Adnotationes Elucidatoriae,* short notes on the literal meaning of selected biblical texts, the *Didascalicon de Studio Legendi,* probably written sometime before 1125 as a theoretical reworking of Augustine's *De Doctrina Christiana,* and the subsequent *De Scripturis et Scriptoribus Sacris.* Other works that incorporate Scripture, such as *De Noe Arche* and *De Sacramentis Christianae Fidei,* expressly utilize allegorical and/or tropological interpretations. Other biblical works attributed with some certainty to Hugh by the J. P. Migne edition (vols. 175-77) include *In Salomonis Ecclesiasten Homiliae 19, Expositio Moralis in Abdiam, Explicatio in Canticum Beatae Mariae, Quaestione et Decisiones in Epistolas D. Pauli,* and *De Filia Jephte.*

No part of Hugh's thought can be singled out for study in a vacuum. All of his works exhibit a systematic unity, epitomized by his famous statement, "Learn everything; afterwards you will see that nothing is superfluous" (*Didascalicon* 6.3 [PL 176:801]). The aim of reading Scriptures, like education in general, is for the student to gain knowledge and to develop proper morals. The moral purpose cannot be overstated for Hugh, who stressed that any study of Scripture that did not lead to an understanding of the way a person should live was not merely incomplete but also evil. As a mystic Hugh believed that the crowning point of all learning was the mystical experience, but he recognized the need for rational foundations evident in the criticisms of contemporary dialecticians.

The *Didascalicon* is written as a guide to learning in which the literal reading of Scripture forms the backbone of the student's education. Scripture provides the path to the two goals of Christian education: the development of a moral life and

knowledge of God. Hugh begins the section on Scriptures, as in *De Scripturis* and *De Sacramentis,* with an exposition of the order and number of books considered canonical. He upholds the threefold division of the Hebrew Bible: Law, Prophets and Hagiographa, to which the New Testament corresponds with its threefold division of Gospels, apostles and Fathers. He maintains the canonical order of the books in the Hebrew Bible, rather than that of the Vulgate, as well as the primacy of the Hebrew as a textual witness. In addition he separates out the apocryphal writings as being edifying but not canonical, here following *Jerome. He also increases the size of the New Testament by adding, in the section he calls the Fathers, the canons and rules of the church fathers, including Jerome, *Augustine, Gregory, Ambrose, Isidore, *Origen, Bede and others "too numerous to list," a clear indication of the role that tradition played in the medieval period.

Hugh holds to a threefold division of the senses or meanings of sacred Scripture: the literal, which he usually terms the historical; the allegorical, which includes both simple allegory and anagogy; and the tropological or moral sense. Hugh maintains the primacy of the literal sense at all times, illustrated in his theoretical debate with the allegorists found in *De Scripturis* 5 [PL 175:13]:

> Since, therefore, the mystical sense is not deduced except from those things which the letter proposed in the first place, I wonder by what effrontery some of the allegorists make a show of themselves as scholars who are still ignorant of that very first meaning of the letter. . . . Therefore, I do not want those to be honored about their knowledge of Scripture who are ignorant of the letter. On the contrary, to be ignorant of the letter is to be ignorant of what the letter signifies, as well as what is signified by the letter.

For Hugh words themselves did not hold symbolic or allegorical meaning, but rather the things the words signified pointed beyond themselves to other realities. Unless the words on the page signified something real, they could not act as meaningful symbols for a greater reality. Such reasoning depends on a conception of the unity of revelation in which God is revealed through the natural created order itself. For Hugh both revelation and the mystical experience are not outside of nature but embody nature in its fullest realization. The impact on biblical exegesis manifests itself in the insistence on the ultimate reality of biblical events as revelatory of a God who acts in and through history and nature.

The historical meaning can contain contradictions and impossibilities. The spiritual meaning, however, while it is able to show variation, cannot contradict itself. This leads to a dialectical reading of Scriptures. When the student is doing the fundamental historical work, the reading should proceed in chronological order with the historical books of the Bible: Genesis, Exodus, Joshua, Judges, Samuel, Kings, Chronicles, the Gospels and Acts. While a first reading should try to understand the literal sense, sometimes this remains obscure. When one pursues allegory, however, Hugh recommends a reverse order, starting with the New Testament and then working through much of the literary prophets and the wisdom literature. This follows the order of knowledge, starting first where the message is obvious, then back to where it is obscure. As the spiritual meaning of the text is explored, formerly obscure literal passages become clear.

While the literal sense does not negate the traditional allegorical interpretation, Hugh claims that neither does the allegorical interpretation negate the literal. However, it is the spiritual meaning that is essentially unified and correct, and it ultimately takes precedence over the literal sense. "Therefore it is necessary that we follow the letter in such a way that we do not prefer our sense to the divine authors; and that we do not follow it in such a way that we believe that the whole judgment of

truth depends on it. Not the 'literal,' but 'the spiritual judges all things' (1 Cor 2)" (*Didascalicon* 6.4 [PL 176:804-5]). The unity of the message of Scriptures is undeniable for Hugh, as for others of his time, but this unity of message is contained in the spiritual sense, which depends on the literal meaning.

M.-D. Chenu elucidated the connection between *historia* and *lectio* by highlighting Hugh's use of the phrase *series narrationis* (Chenu, 165-73). For Hugh, God's primary revelation is expressed in the whole series of events we call history. This history is a sequence that must be read and understood as a sequence, rather than as something immutable and unchanging. The unity of the message of sacred history, however, is provided by its divine source, which creates history on a grand scheme. This means that the interpretation of historical events, based on the literal sense, is limited by its connection to the meaning of the whole history (van Zwieten, 327-35).

Hugh's respect for history is exhibited throughout his works, including *De Sacramentis* and *De Noe Arche,* which demonstrate his conviction that history itself is sacramental. In *De Sacramentis* Hugh maintains that the sacraments cannot be understood apart from their place in redemptive history, forming the whole discussion of the sacraments as an exposition of this history. For instance, the six days of the creation are mirrored in history by the six ages of the restoration of humanity, an expressly allegorical treatment of the biblical text. However, this reading demonstrates the importance of the historical sequence for the understanding of all of theology. History is the best place to look for knowledge of God. The created world is the surest sign of God's work and power, and to ignore it is to willfully limit one's self.

The work that best shows Hugh's historical interpretations of the Bible is the *Adnotationes Elucidatoriae,* an often ignored work. Part of the difficulty in analyzing this work is its obviously incomplete condition. The commentary on Genesis probably retains most of the original structure, opening with a commentary on Jerome's prologue to the book, then moving on to a commentary that remarks only on difficult verses dealt with in the order in which they occur in the biblical text. This work is concluded with some additional notes on the Vulgate, based on the Hebrew text. However, in PL all the commentaries show obvious holes, while some of the works contained there may not be attributable to Hugh. In addition, quotes from Hugh's pupils, such as Andrew, show further evidence that the text is missing sections. Various theories have been offered for this: either that we have only lecture notes or that we have only the literal third of a three-part work.

Hugh's literal exposition is comprised of three things: the syntax and meaning of the words themselves, the surface meaning of the text itself, and the theological significance of the text. However, these meanings are not often clearly differentiated.

The first approach to the text is seen in the comments on Exodus 4:22, in which Hugh discusses the tense of the verbs, or Exodus 19:9, where Hugh suggests an incorrect ordering of the text. The surface meaning of the text lies behind his comment on Exodus 4:10, that Moses was reluctant to speak because he had resided in Midian too long, or his assertion at Exodus 2:17 that Moses had traveled with colleagues who aided him in his defense of Jethro's daughters.

The literal sense is never thoroughly divorced from theological issues, since theological principles are extensions of the meaning of the implications of the literal sense. This is most evident in passages whose surface meaning seems to contradict theological tenets. Thus creation poses a problem. Both Ecclesiastes 1:8, "The one who lives eternally created all things at once," and Genesis 2, "These are the generations of heaven and earth when they were created on the day when God made heaven and earth and every plant in the dirt," seem to contradict the six days of creation in Genesis 1. Some exegetes, such as Augustine and Abelard, had claimed that the six-day creation story was not to be understood literally, not only because it was contradicted but even more because it implied God's first acts were imperfect and "deformed." While Hugh maintains a simultaneous creation of pure matter, he upholds the necessity of the first account for full creation: "Against this reasoning also we can say that God, who was able to make everything in a moment, distinguished his works in six days, not because of his own impotence, which is absurd, but for the sake of instruction and imitation of the rationality of the creation."

Hugh not only avoids christological interpretations but often refutes them. Commenting on Genesis 22:4, "On the third day Abraham lifted up his eyes," he says, "Because it is not a three day journey from Beersheba to Jerusalem, some say that this mountain upon which Abraham sacrificed Isaac may be the same one where Christ was crucified. But, (we believe) those who say these things are mistaken. For Abraham could make so small a distance each day, since he was a man, who was so strongly distressed at one time about the death of his own son, at another about the command of the Lord, that he considered even less the speed of the trip" (*Adnotationes* on Gen 22 [PL 53]). Here, then, Hugh replaces a traditional interpretation that emphasizes Christ with a humanistic plain sense.

Perhaps one of the more intriguing elements of Hugh's work is his use of Jewish ideas throughout the *Adnotationes*. Andrew relates that Hugh tried to learn Hebrew. Hugh himself warned that one must not regard the Latin text as better than either the Septuagint or the Hebrew text; in fact, it should be just the opposite. Hugh at times tries to compare the Vulgate with a literal translation of the Hebrew (see the comment on Ex 28:30). Hugh's use of Jewish ideas and independent knowledge of Hebrew remains a matter of debate. Any examination of the sources of a medieval work is complicated because of the rare use of nominal citation and extensive use of nonverbatim quotation. The complication is furthered by the fact that many traditions were held in common among Christians and Jews. That there was contact between the intellectual centers of Jews and Christians, there is no doubt. Although much of the Hebrew in his work can be found in Jerome, H. Hailperin found sixty glosses in the *Notulae* from Hebrew sources, most of these from Rashi. M. Awerbuch asserts that Hugh must have had extensive, albeit primarily oral, contact with the Jewish community because of the breadth of his use of Jewish sources (Awerbuch, 197-230).

We have then a possibility of contact between Hugh and Jewish thinkers and the probability of the use of some of their ideas as evidenced in his commentaries. More importantly, however, the Victorines and the school of Rashi both exhibit a stress on the literal-historical meaning of Scripture, not in place of the allegorical but as a foundation and guide to it. Such similarity of purpose provided a context for Christian appropriation of Jewish exegesis as that which was most literal. Both Hugh and Rashi stand in the balance, synthesizers of earlier mystical and rationalistic debates, expounders of their own discovered meanings in the text and authors of new exegetical methods, albeit new primarily because of their emphases but thereby no less important and influential for those scholars who came after them.

Andrew of St. Victor as Biblical Exegete. Preeminent among Andrew's writings are his biblical commentaries. These include commentaries on the first seven books of the Bible (Genesis, Exodus, Leviticus, Numbers, Deuteronomy, Joshua and Judges) and all of the literary prophets, as well as the books of Proverbs and Ecclesiastes (Qoheleth). Andrew explored the literal meaning of the biblical text, without interest in either spiritual meanings or theological ramifications, leaving those pursuits to other scholars. Such purpose

explains some of the anomalies of his work.

Andrew is most noted for his extensive use of Jewish exegesis. Again, the source of this information is debated. But like Hugh, he probably did not have independent access to Jewish texts, rather learning of traditions through contact with the Jewish community. Again like Hugh, this community was heavily influenced by the school of Rashi, evidenced by the fact that those Jewish traditions Andrew reports reflect the plain sense of Rashi's exposition, rather than the allegorical meanings of Jewish mysticism. Because of such contact Andrew is able to use Jerome's opinion that Jewish exegesis represents the literal sense of the text, passed down in a living tradition. Therefore Andrew accepts the testimony of his witnesses as plainly literal.

When confronted with difficulties in interpretation Andrew prefers the more natural explanation; thus Joseph's dreams of greatness spring from his own internal desires to be great. Andrew also shows great sensitivity to historical sequence, as is evidenced by his chronological harmonization of the creation accounts in Genesis 1 and Genesis 2 (Smalley, 134-35). When confronted in tradition with less literal readings of the text, Andrew does not hesitate to point out the more obvious reading, even if that reading had been suggested by Jewish sources. He was criticized for his unwillingness to refute these interpretations, most notably by Richard of St. Victor. But his influence and following remained strong throughout the Middle Ages.

Hugh's influence on Andrew is evident in that Hugh himself had made clear that the literal sense is a subject worthy of study on its own. B. Smalley points out that Andrew does not represent a new method in biblical study; rather he carries out Hugh's principles in literal exegesis to their furthest end. As such his impact was both more immediate and limited. Yet his work embodies the acceptance of the revelation of God in the natural order and in human history. The details of history are not outside Andrew's Christian exegesis but form the soul and spirit of God's message. If Isaiah's virgin is his wife, it is still a sign for the believing community provided by God, just as surely as Joseph's dreams and Daniel's visions.

Significance. The influence of Hugh of St. Victor cannot be exaggerated. His rereading of Augustine's *De Doctrina Christiana* became the lens through which Augustine was read in subsequent generations. While his influence in systematic and sacramental theology were far more extensive than his conclusions as a biblical exegete, his biblical method remained in force, even if individual conclusions and interpretations were not reiterated. Foremost among these was his insistence on the reality of the things signified by the words in the text as the necessary prerequisite for any allegorical expansion (double significance), a principle refined by both Aquinas and *Nicholas of Lyra centuries after Hugh's formulation.

Andrew's influence as biblical exegete was far more obvious yet less sustained than that of his mentor. Andrew became the source book for the historical sense and as such was quoted more directly within biblical interpretation than was Hugh. His works were used by such scholars as Peter Comestor, Peter Cantor, Stephen Langton, *Hugh of St. Cher and *Nicholas of Lyra. However, unlike Hugh, Andrew's work did not provide a new paradigm for biblical interpretation but rather the best example of the principles set out by Hugh. Andrew's use of Jewish interpretation revitalized a precedent set by Jerome, encouraging expositions of biblical history by uncovering the literal sense. As Smalley summarizes, "Hugh of St. Victor seemed to his contemporaries like a 'second Augustine;' Andrew was their second Jerome" (Smalley, 185).

BIBLIOGRAPHY

Works. Hugh of St. Victor, *De Arrha Animae* (Muséum Lessianum; Section ascétique et mystique 12; Bruges: Beyaert, 1923); idem, *La contemplation et ses espèces*, ed. R. Baron (Monumenta Christiana selecta; dossiers et textes d'etude 2; Tournai: Descleé, 1958); idem, *The Didascalicon of Hugh of St. Victor: A Medieval Guide to the Arts* (Records of Civilization: Sources and Studies 64; New York: Columbia University Press, 1961); idem, *The Divine Love: The Two Treatises De Laude Caritatis and De Amore Sponsi ad Sponsam* (Fleur de Lys 9; London: Mowbray, 1956); idem, *Expositio in Regulam B. Augustini episcopi* (London: Sands, 1911); idem, *Hugh of Saint Victor: Selected Spiritual Writings* (Classics of the Contemplative Life; New York: Harper & Row, 1962); idem, *Hugonis de Sancto Victore Didascalicon de Studio Legendi*, ed. C. H. Buttimer (Washington, DC: The Catholic University Press, 1939); idem, *Hugues et Richard de Saint-Victor*, ed. R. Baron (Témoins de la foi; Tournai: Bloud & Gay, 1961); idem, *Les machines du sens: Fragments d'une sémiologie mediévale* (Archives du commentaire; Paris: Cendres, 1987); idem, *On the Sacraments of the Christian Faith (De sacramentis)* (Medieval Academy of America 58; Cambridge, MA: Medieval Academy of America, 1951); idem, *Practica Geometriae* (Medieval Philosophical Texts in Translation 29; Milwaukee: Marquette University Press, 1991); idem, *Selections* (University of Notre Dame Publications in Medieval Studies 20; Notre Dame, IN: University of Notre Dame Press, 1966); idem, *Six opuscules spirituels par Hugues de Saint-Victor* (SC 155; Serie des textes monastiques d'Occident 28; Paris: Éditions du Cerf, 1969); idem, *Soliloquium 'De arrha animae' und 'De vanitate mundi'* (Kleine Texte für Vorlesungen und Übungen 123; Bonn: A. Marcus & E. Weber, 1913); idem, *Soliloquy on the Earnest Money of the Soul* (Medieval Philosophical Texts in Translation 9; Milwaukee: Marquette University Press, 1956); idem, *Textes spirituels de Hugues de Saint-Victor* (Paris: Descleé, 1962); W. Schultz, ed., *Mittelalterliche Mystik unter dem Einfluss des Neuplationismus: Hugo von St. Viktor, Meister Eckhart, Johannes Tauler* (Quellen; ausgewahlte Texte aus der Geschichte der christlichen Kirche 24, 1; Berlin: Evangelische, 1967); P. Wolff, ed., *Mystische Schriften* (Trier: Paulinus, 1961); PL 175-77.

Works. Andrew of St. Victor, *Andreae de Sancto Victore Opera* (Corpus Christianorum; Continuatio Medievalis 53; Turnholt: Brepols, 1986-91); idem, *Expositio super Danielem*, ed. M. A. Zier, microform, 1983.

Studies. M. Awerbuch, *Christlich-jüdische Begegnung im Zeitalter der Frühscholastik* (Abhandlung zum christlich-jüdischen Dialog 8; Munich: Chr. Kaiser, 1980); R. Baron, *Etudes sur Hugues de Saint Victor* (Paris: Descleé de Brouwer, 1963); idem, *Science et Sagesse chez Hugues de Saint-Victor* (Paris: Lethielleux, 1957); R. Berndt, *Andre de Saint-Victor (1175): Exégète et théologien* (Bibliotheca Victorina 2; Paris: Brepols, 1992); M.-D. Chenu, *Nature, Man, and Society in the Twelfth Century: Essays on New Theological Perspectives in the Latin West* (Chicago: University of Chicago Press, 1968); S. Ernst, *Gewissheit des Glaubens: Der Glaubenstraktat Hugos von St. Viktor als Zugang zu seiner theologischen Systematik* (Beitrage zur Geschichte der Philosophie und Theologie des Mittelalters, n.f., Bd. 30; Münster: Aschendorff, 1987); R. Guy, *Die Überlieferung der Werke Hugos von St. Viktor: Ein Beitrag zur Kommunikationsgeschichte der Mittelalters* (Stuttgart: Hiersemann, 1976); H. Hailperin, *Rashi and the Christian Scholars* (Pittsburgh: University of Pittsburgh Press, 1963); J. P. Kleinz, *The Theory of Knowledge of Hugh of St. Victor* (Catholic University of America Philosophical Studies 87; Washington, DC: The Catholic University Press, 1945); H. de Lubac, *Exégèse médiévale les quarte sens de l'ecriture* Seconde partie, 1 (Aubier: Montaigne, 1961); H. J. Pollitt, "Some Considerations on the Structure and Sources of Hugh of St. Victor's Notes on the Octateuch," *Recherches* 33 (1966) 5-38; J. S. Preus, *From Shadow to Promise: Old Testament Interpretation from Augustine to the Young Luther* (Cambridge, MA: Belknap, 1969); P. Riché and L. Guy, *Bible de tous le temps,* 4: *Le Moyen Âge et la Bible* (Paris: Beauchesne, 1984); P. Sicard, *Hugues de Saint-Victor et son école* (Témoins de notre histoire; Turnhout: Brepols, 1991); B. Smalley, *The Study of the Bible in the Middle Ages* (Oxford: Clarendon, 1941); J. Taylor, *The Origin and Early Life of Hugh of St. Victor: An Evaluation of the Tradition* (Text and Studies in the History of Medieval Education; Notre Dame, IN: University of Notre Dame Press, 1956); G. A. Zinn, "*Historia fundamentum est:* The Role of History in the Contemplative Life according to Hugh of St. Victor" in *Contemporary Reflections on the Medieval Christian Tradition: Essays in Honor of Ray C. Petry,* ed. G. H. Shriver (Durham, NC: Duke University Press, 1974), 135-58; J. W. M. van Zwieten, "Jewish Exegesis within Christian Bounds: Richard of St. Victor's *De Emmanuele* and Victorine Hermeneutics," *Bijdragen* 48 (1987) 327-35.

C. L. Patton

Hugh of St. Cher *(c. 1195-1263)*

Born near the end of the twelfth century in Saint-Chef (which medieval patois transformed into Saint-Cher) on the outskirts of Vienne in the Dauphiné, Hugh of St. Cher became an important Dominican biblical scholar, theologian and church leader. As a biblical scholar he directed the production of three massive aids to interpretation: the *Postillae in Totam Bibliam,* a continuous gloss on every book of the Bible; the *Correctorium Bibliae,* which made available alternate readings of the Vulgate in an attempt to establish a reliable text; and an alphabetical concordance to the Bible, the first of its kind.

When Hugh joined the Dominican order (1225), he was already a doctor of canon law and a bachelor of theology. He was soon named provincial of the order in France, an office he served from 1227 until 1229. In 1230 Hugh succeeded his own teacher, Roland of Cremona, as a master in the faculty of theology at the University of Paris, becoming only the second Dominican to hold such a position. He taught there until 1236. During much of his teaching career, Hugh also served as prior of the Dominican house of St. Jacques, where he directed his ambitious scholarly projects, making St. Jacques "the most remarkable of all medieval research institutes" (Minnis, 66-67). In 1236 Hugh again became provincial of France, and his university teaching career came to an end, although he continued to work with his team at St. Jacques.

In 1244 Pope Innocent IV named Hugh the first Dominican cardinal. A reform-minded churchman, Hugh participated in the twelfth ecumenical council in Lyons (1245) and reformed the Carmelite rule and liturgy (1247). Hugh is also responsible for the feast of Corpus Christi, which he sanctioned in Liège (1251-1253) and encouraged the pope to extend to the whole church. In 1255 and 1256 Hugh helped to judge disputes regarding the works of Joachim of Fiore and William of St. Amour. As cardinal, Hugh was a valued adviser for several popes and so helped to strengthen the relationship between his order and the papacy. He died in 1263.

Context. Hugh became a Dominican around the time that the order was establishing its general house of studies at St. Jacques in Paris. Committed to intellectual work since its inception, the order sought at Paris to integrate study and preaching, contemplation and action, interpretation and reform. Hugh's work as a biblical scholar exemplifies these Dominican ideals. Working collaboratively with a team of Dominican students, Hugh sought to provide for other preachers and teachers the best of what the twelfth and early thirteenth century had to give to biblical interpretation. Hugh was a scholar's scholar, laboring on behalf of others to make available the richest resources of his age.

Hugh also began his life as a Dominican at a time when the landscape of biblical interpretation was beginning to change, in part due to the influence of the friars in the University of Paris. While much of Hugh's exegesis, especially his commentaries on the Old Testament, repeated twelfth-century themes and methodology, his prologues to his commentaries on Mark and Acts looked forward to later thirteenth-century use of Aristotelian categories and epistemology. As A. J. Minnis has shown, Hugh described the authorship of Mark and Acts in terms of Aristotle's four causes, thus inviting analysis of how the human author had constructed the text. Likewise his commentary on Peter Lombard's *Sentences* departs from the twelfth-century method of glossing individual words in order to address entire questions, thus opening a path that Thomas *Aquinas and others would follow.

In short, Hugh of St. Cher came into his vocation as a Dominican biblical scholar at an auspicious historical moment. Through the integration of his desire to understand and present the work of those who had preceded him and his participation in the new role of the friars in the university, he took some important steps

that made possible the great strides of others.

Work. Hugh wrote in many genres and for a variety of audiences. In addition to his sermons, a commentary on the Mass and other writings, he bequeathed to future generations three important works of biblical scholarship and a ground-breaking commentary on Peter Lombard's *Sentences*. These works were used by subsequent generations and helped to shape the scholarly work of the later thirteenth century.

Commentaria in Quatuor Libros Sententiarum, Hugh's sentence commentary, was written between 1230 and 1232, around the time he was lecturing on the *Sentences* in Paris. The only known sentence commentary of its kind from the years between 1226 and 1240, Hugh's text marks an important change in theological method in this genre.

From the death of Peter Lombard until the end of the twelfth century, commentaries on the *Sentences* took the form of marginal or interlinear glosses. From the end of the twelfth century until around 1225, catchword glosses of the *Sentences,* in which individual words were examined and glossed, were typical. From 1225 until the end of the thirteenth century, the "classical or true commentary" (Fisher, 58), like those of Thomas *Aquinas and Bonaventure, emerged. Each stage allowed more room for the original theological contribution of the commentator.

Hugh's sentence commentary marks the change from the second to the third stage. His commentary is one of the first to abandon the catchword gloss method of commenting on the *Sentences* in favor of addressing entire questions. This new, more intellectually spacious method allowed the commentator to "pursue as many new avenues of development as his diligence and speculative virtuosity [could] devise" (Fisher, 60-61). Hugh did not take full advantage of this freedom himself, but the new form that he helped to shape made it possible for others to break new ground in the content of theological commentary.

Like his sentence commentary, *Postillae in Totam Bibliam* began as lectures but grew to a continuous gloss on the entire Bible, book by book. Produced during the five years of Hugh's teaching career, the *Postillae* were a product of Hugh's close collaboration with his brothers at St. Jacques.

Hugh meant for his postillae to serve as a supplement to the *Glossa Ordinaria,* a twelfth-century biblical commentary that compiled interpretations from patristic and medieval sources, to provide in as complete a way as possible for his students and others the advances in biblical interpretation since the compilation of the *Glossa.* B. Smalley has described the postillae as "a mosaic of quotations, with occasional comments probably original to Hugh" (Smalley 1964, 120). His team of collaborators at St. Jacques compiled these quotations for him, culled from twelfth- and early thirteenth-century sources. The material is theologically diverse; as R. E. Lerner has argued, some of the material compiled so contradicts Hugh's own positions that "when the real Hugh of St. Cher 'signed his name' to a finished commentary he may not even have known all that was in it" (Lerner, 82).

Hugh's *Postillae* provided an invaluable aid to study both for teachers who had to comment on the whole Bible in their classes and for their students, who would leave the university to preach or continue on as teachers themselves. This massive scholarly project exemplifies Hugh's commitment, and the commitment of his order, to integrate study and preaching.

Under the direction of Hugh, the team of scholars at St. Jacques produced a *Correctorium Bibliae* that listed alternate readings for the Vulgate in an attempt to establish a reliable text. Not suprisingly, the genre of *Correctoria* originated with the Dominicans, for whom study was an important part of their apostolic vocation.

The *Correctorium* prepared by Hugh and his colleagues was widely used among university students and teachers. Later in the thirteenth century Roger Bacon criticized Hugh's methods as inadequate, arguing that Hugh had produced a new version of the Vulgate rather than a corrected one. Although it was not immune to such criticisms, Hugh's *Correctorium* encouraged others to seek scholarly ways of establishing reliable biblical texts from which to teach and study.

Hugh and his collaborators also produced the first verbal concordance to the Bible, *Concordantiae Bibliorum,* another invaluable aid for preachers, teachers and students. Lists of passages in which a particular word could be found in the Bible were given, without context, for words arranged alphabetically. Although it was rudimentary in form, the St. Jacques concordance became the model for all future concordances.

Interpreter. Hugh was a deeply Dominican biblical interpreter, fully committed to the Dominican ideals of integrating the life of prayer with the life of study and of giving equal weight to the study of the Bible and speculation, rather than valorizing one over the other. Hugh inaugurated the continuous lecturing on Scripture that so differed from the way the secular masters of Paris taught. Like his fellow Dominicans, Hugh wanted to bring biblical interpretation back to the center of study without dismissing speculative theology. Hugh believed moralities and questions to be of equal importance and refused to reject one in favor of the other. He eagerly embraced the scholarly methods that would allow biblical study to flourish: *correctoria,* concordances, postillae.

Although Hugh was an innovator in new forms and methods of biblical study, it is generally agreed that he broke little new ground in theological content. His approach to the biblical text relies heavily on earlier commentators, especially Stephen Langton. Like Langton, Hugh emphasized the spiritual sense of Scripture over the literal. Hugh was influenced by Aristotle, but in a formal way rather than a substantive way. By dividing up books and chapters in the manner of philosophical texts, Hugh began to treat substantial sections of the Bible as whole entities that might be commented upon, rather than focusing on words or paragraphs alone. It would remain for later Dominicans, such as Albert the Great and Aquinas, to bring Aristotle's categories to bear on biblical interpretation and theological reflection in a more substantial way.

The themes of Hugh's exegesis tend to be quite traditional. Unlike other friars, he showed little interest in the daring, eschatological readings of Joachim of Fiore; Hugh seems uneasy about such interpretation. Many of Hugh's readings of biblical narratives reflect his position as a teacher in the schools concerned with the formation of his students as preachers and reformers. For example, Hugh interpreted Isaiah 2:4 ("swords shall be turned into plowshares") to mean that the knowledge acquired through scholarship ought to be turned into preaching. Hugh advocated a fluid movement between contemplation and action in which each nourished the other, as shown in his reading of John 2:12, which describes Jesus withdrawing with his family and his disciples for a few days after the miracle at Cana. For

> those preachers conquer the devil who not only sally forth to preaching, but sometimes stay quiet in their order to care for their own souls and for discussion. Such a soul is Christ's bride truly, being both Rachel and Lia, Martha and Mary together. She has chosen the better part, since action is good, but contemplation better. The best part is that which includes them both, having a mother's fruitfulness in preaching without loss of a virgin's purity, which she keeps in contemplation. (quoted in Smalley 1964, 137)

Smalley has argued that Hugh does present "a new vision of poverty and the apostolate" (Smalley 1964, 141) in his exegesis. Hugh argues, through his readings of the Gospels, that preachers ought to be poor; preachers who preach poverty but retain riches themselves are liars. For Hugh poverty is like a moat that keeps out the devil. Those who are involuntarily poor, says Hugh, are in no danger of damnation. Hugh's embrace of poverty and its relationship to preaching extends, in his exegesis, to political commentary on contemporary church issues. Hugh's belief that holding a plurality of benefices was a mortal sin, for example, is reflected in his postillae, in which he links Jesus' cleansing of the temple in John 2 to the misuse of church appointments.

Thematically Hugh's commentaries are traditional, drawing on what he believed to be exemplary biblical interpretation from the Fathers and medieval commentators. Following closely the fourfold interpretation of Scripture, in which the commentator uncovered the literal, allegorical, moral and anagogical layers of meaning in a text, Hugh was able to continue in the footsteps of his ancestors while shaping their legacy in a way that undergirded Dominican ideals binding study to preaching and preaching to poverty.

Significance. In spite of his largely traditional readings of biblical texts, Hugh's contribution to biblical interpretation cannot be underestimated. The scholarly works he directed and completed bear witness, if not to breathtaking originality, then to the kind of patient, generous acts of scholarship that enliven the originality of others. The practices he embodied in his scholarly vocation—collaborative work, dedication to providing the next generation with the scholarly resources it needs, a commitment to relating contemplative study to active work in the world—still hold promise for contemporary biblical scholarship. It is Hugh's practices, as much as the content of his work, that beckon to us across the centuries.

BIBLIOGRAPHY

Works. Hugh of St. Cher, *Postillae in Totam Bibliam* (Basel: J. Amerbach, 1498-1502); idem, *Concordantiae Bibliorum* (Venice: N. Pezzana, 1687).

Studies. J. Fisher, "Hugh of St. Cher and the Development of Medieval Theology," *Spec* 31 (1956) 57-69; A. Hinnebusch, *The History of the Dominican Order* (New York: Alba House, 1973); R. E. Lerner, "Poverty, Preaching, and Eschatology in the Revelation Commentaries of 'Hugh of St. Cher'" in *The Bible in the Medieval World: Essays in Memory of Beryl Smalley* (Oxford: Blackwell, 1985) 157-89; A. J. Minnis, *Medieval Theories of Authorship: Scholastic Literary Attitudes in the Later Middle Ages* (2d ed.; Philadelphia: University of Pennsylvania Press, 1988); W. H. Principe, *Hugh of St. Cher's Theology of the Hypostatic Union* (Toronto: Pontifical Institute of Medieval Studies, 1970); B. Smalley, *The Gospels in the Schools, c. 1100-c. 1280* (London: Hambledon, 1985); idem, *The Study of the Bible in the Middle Ages* (Notre Dame, IN: University of Notre Dame Press, 1964).   S. Paulsell

Nicholas of Lyra *(c. 1270-1349)*

Nicholas of Lyra was one of the most influential biblical exegetes in the late Middle Ages. A French Franciscan, Lyra was most known for his literal approach to biblical exegesis and his extensive use of Jewish interpretation. While the approach itself was not new, Lyra's work provided later exegetes with a virtual encyclopedia of literal interpretation derived by the best scholarship of his day. Using every source available to him, Lyra's work was thorough, logical, balanced. He stood firmly within Christian interpretive traditions, showing obvious influence from *Jerome, *Augustine and *Andrew of St. Victor, among others. His knowledge of Hebrew allowed him to read both the Hebrew Bible and Jewish interpreters. His use of sources reveals a critical eye that balanced one opinion over against another in order to arrive at the one deemed most literal within the confines of Christian exegetical principles. Such an even approach led him to be used widely throughout Europe and guaranteed his lasting influence on such scholars as Martin *Luther and John *Calvin.

Context. Not much is known with certainty about Nicholas's life. He was born in Lyre, Normandy, around 1270. He joined the Friars Minor at Verneuile (c. 1300) and received his doctorate at the University of Paris (1309), where he was a noted lecturer at the university and a prominent member of the faculty. He became the Franciscan provincial of Burgundy twice, first in 1314 and again in 1325. His name appears on a few transactions in Paris, the latest of which (1349) provides an approximate date for his death. Lyra was a Christian by birth, although stories circulated after his death that he was a converted Jew. Such stories, however, are not substantiated by any public record of conversion or any mention in Lyra's writings (Langlois, 355-67).

Nicholas's writings reflect biblical interpretative methods characteristic within the universities. Although mystical and allegorical interpretations remained in force throughout the twelfth and thirteenth centuries, especially for preaching, the theological training of the universities shaped biblical exegesis for centuries to come. Since initial training on the Bible, viewed as the primary vehicle for knowledge about God, was the prerequisite for any further theological training, theological conclusions presumed a biblical basis. However, the increased use of pagan philosophers, such as Aristotle, within theological discussions initiated changes in the modes of argumentation and in the understanding of the nature of language (Evans). Scholastic metaphysics stressed philosophical reasoning, which proceeded from natural intelligence, as a second valuable source of knowledge about God. While natural reason remained subordinate to revelation, it was increasingly utilized to understand supernatural revelation. Scholastic approaches to the Bible, utilizing the dialectic method of Peter Abelard, first gained prominence in the school of St. Victor. Scholastic biblical exegesis, however, eventually served primarily to illuminate broader metaphysical issues, thereby subordinating the biblical text to speculative theology. Scholastic exegesis divided and subdivided the text into discrete units from which theological arguments could be made (Verger, 217-20). By atomizing the text, scholastic use of the Bible tended to dampen its original integrity and to overlook texts that did not serve a theological purpose. The biblical text was mined for proof-texts of philosophical conclusions or became the springboard for reasoned extensions of the biblical text. The legacy of scholastic inquiry into the Bible was the elaboration, extension and further development of literal interpretations of the Bible. Although historical awareness remained naive, an appreciation of the text's original or plain sense was further developed.

Scholastic inquiry used Augustine's principle that the literal meaning of the text alone could serve as the basis for argument and debate. This high esteem for the theological value of the literal meaning of the text triggered a rise in the development of methods and tools to arrive at the literal sense. First, it sparked a renewed interest in the meaning of the text in its original languages; Christian scholars, especially within the mendicant orders, studied Hebrew and Greek. Second, the interest in the original text provided impetus for the production of the earliest exegetical tools, including concordances and lexica (Verger, 214-17). Third, commentaries based on the lectures of the masters first began to appear. Fourth, Christian scholars increasingly began to use Jewish sources for access to the literal meaning. J. Cohen (1986) has shown that Christians tended to assume that Jewish interpretation was literal, even when to our eyes it is obviously mystical. On the one hand, this nascent acquaintance with Jewish sources led to questions about the limits of the use of non-Christian exegesis. On the other hand, even late medieval exegesis maintained that the literal sense served only to illuminate the real aim of the text, which was knowledge about God. The rise of emphasis on literal interpretation in the twelfth through fourteenth centuries did not place value on the literal sense as an end in itself but valued literal exegesis as a firm base for knowledge about God, whether attained by philosophical speculation, alle-gorical interpretation or mystical experience. Opposition to literal interpretation, seen in the charge of judaizing, was actually a critique of the failure to utilize the literal meaning of the text to illuminate its true theological message (Verger, 217).

The most effective objections to scholasticism came from the Franciscans, culminating in the development of nominalism in the fourteenth century. Speculative reasoning of scholastic dialectic failed to reach assured conclusions, while the proliferation of scholastic systems led to a distrust of metaphysical conclusions (Leff, 22). This in turn gave rise to a critique of Thomist causality. The "necessary conclusions" of scholastic metaphysics seemed to limit God to human constructs (Oberman 1986). Scotus and William of Ockham, while maintaining the integrity of both philosophy and revelation, insisted on the distinction between philosophical conclusions derived from pagan philosophers from the true basis of Christian theology: the revelation of God's will in history (Oberman 1978, 82-85). Franciscan theology replaced metaphysics, then, with a kind of meta-history, the conviction that human knowledge of God is limited to what is known in historical time, beyond which God retains "divine absolute power" (Kennedy, 339-40). History proceeds not out of necessity but from God's *promissio* freely given to humanity, which then drives Christian history. Such divine foreknowledge implies a metaphysical teleology for Christian history. Concomitantly, God is known only through the pursuit of concrete individual knowledge, not universal necessary conclusions. The supreme locus for this discrete knowledge was scriptural revelation.

Work. Nicholas of Lyra produced many texts utilizing biblical exegesis. Among the works of lesser importance are an official response to Pope John XXII's statement on the Beatific Vision *(De Visione Beatifica),* two anti-Jewish tractates, a piece entitled *De Differentia Nostrae Translationis ab Hebraica Littera,* and a meditation on the life of St. Francis (*Oratio seu contemplatio de* *vita Sancti Francisci* [Labrosse, 1908, 153]).

In addition, Lyra's second most important work is the *Postilla Moralis,* a running commentary on the spiritual meaning of biblical texts. Although this work uses a method quite different from the literal exegesis for which Lyra is known, its interpretations provide clearer insight into Nicholas's use of the text within Christian theology. In the prologue to this text Lyra states that spiritual interpretations are many, only a few of which are addressed by this commentary. Within the body of the work the moral concerns of this exegesis are fully evident. For instance, Lyra shows concern for the formation of novices, financial abuses by the church, and the pride and greed of some clergy. Here similar to *Hugh of St. Victor, Lyra assumes that learning is done not for its own sake but to further moral development.

Lyra's most important work by far was the *Postilla Litteralis super Totum Bibliam* (written between 1322 and 1332), a running commentary on the whole Bible, including the deuterocanonical books that he considered apocryphal. In the two prologues to the commentary, Lyra states that while Scripture provides complete knowledge of God, the literal sense serves as the base for this knowledge, either by directly revealing knowledge of God or by signifying things that themselves provide knowledge about God. Lyra does not consider literal interpretation to be an end in itself but sees it as a primary and necessary basis for theology. However, he continues that literal interpretation has been both underutilized and poorly executed. In the second prologue to the *Postilla Litteralis,* Lyra cites three abuses in biblical interpretation that he hopes to correct: the overuse of unfounded allegory, scholastic atomization of the text, and uncritical use of Jewish sources. All three of these approaches to the Bible had been prominent within mendicant exegesis of the thirteenth century.

Interpretive Methods. Nicholas's insistence on a literal interpretation was fully in line with scholastic methodology. Lyra objected to allegorical interpretations that ignored or devalued the literal meaning of the text; Hugh of St. Victor, Thomas *Aquinas and Abelard, to name a few, had all voiced similar objections. Lyra assumes that the literal sense was the one arrived at through natural reason and therefore was the one meaning of the text accessible to everyone, even non-Christians. Lyra's purpose was to determine the one literal sense of the text, without which no theological or spiritual interpretation could be drawn. Without the proper base in the literal sense, according to Lyra, the whole exegesis collapses like a building without a solid foundation (second prologue). Therefore, any theological or spiritual meaning of the text must work off of, and not contradict, the established literal sense.

Lyra produced his commentary to address a wide range of aspects of literal interpretation: textual, factual, semantic. Nicholas included in his literal exegesis text criticism, philology and semantics, as well as an examination of the plain sense of the text, whether that be the plot line *(res gestae),* the internal coherence of the story at hand, or the intention of the author. In order to arrive at a correct literal meaning, the text itself must be trustworthy. For this reason Nicholas used the Hebrew text of the Old Testament, except in those places in the Old Testament that referred to Christ, which, he believed, Jews had deliberately changed.

Nicholas utilized not only the Hebrew text itself but also the works of Jewish scholarship, in particular Rashi, whom he deemed the most literal of Jewish interpreters. Disputations with Jews in the thirteenth century as well as the production of Raymond Martin's *Pugio Fidei,* with which Lyra was familiar, sharpened Christian awareness of the complexity and integrity of Jewish interpretation. Lyra's critical use of Jewish scholarship demonstrates this awareness (Cohen 1986, 612). His appropriation of Jewish interpretation was governed by a critical eye that employed the same criteria for determining the literalness of each individual conclusion. Although Lyra was later criticized for judaizing, a charge that probably reflects his restraint from addressing theological issues in a work he claims is devoted exclusively to literal interpretation, Lyra himself did not automatically prefer conclusions by Jewish exegetes. In the second prologue he stated, "One should not adhere to the words of the Hebrew scholars, except in so far as they accord with reason, and with the truth of the literal sense." Only those Jewish interpretations that accorded to the same criteria for literal meaning as any Christian interpretation were accepted. In addition, since the literal meaning was accessible to any reader of the text, even Jewish interpretation could be used in the service of establishing a firmer base for Christian theology.

When Lyra used Jewish interpretations he merely replaced the traditional comment present in Christian sources, such as the gloss, or the commentaries of Jerome or Augustine, with those of Hebrew scholars. Only occasionally did he cite both viewpoints, and that occurred only when he wished to refute one or the other. The freedom to replace traditional interpretations in general is characteristic of Lyra. P. C. Spicq notes that Lyra is the first expressly to reject the authority of traditional interpretations not based on Scripture. In his comment to Matthew 1:3 he states, "The words of the saints are not of such great authority that one is not allowed to understand something that is contrary (to them) in those things which have not been determined by Sacred Scripture."

Finally, Lyra's attitude toward scholastic inquiry is complex. J. S. Preus (61) has noted his dependence on dialectic method and scholastic argumentation. Lyra tends to divide the text into discrete units; he draws philosophical conclusions as part of his literal interpretation; he applies metaphysical reasoning to biblical texts. Lyra also adheres to Thomistic causality, often stressing that his interpretation is based on either the efficient or the material cause.

His most important development of scholastic methods is his principle of the double literal sense, which honed the definition of the literal sense advanced by Aquinas (Preus, 68).

Thomas claimed that Old Testament texts that prefigure Christ have both a literal-historical sense and a prophetic-spiritual sense. Thus the woman with child in Isaiah 7:14 referred both to a literal, historical figure and prophetically to Christ at the same time. This fits well with his comprehensive view of the scope of the literal meaning. Aquinas states that the literal meaning is the one intended by the author. Since the author of the biblical text is God, and since God both creates the texts and the things the text signifies, the literal meaning, broadly understood, essentially encompasses every meaning of the text (Aquinas *Summa Theologiae* 1a.1.10). Therefore, when Isaiah refers to the virgin and child, God intends the meaning to contain both the historical figure, as well as Christ. Nicholas also states that the literal meaning is the one intended by the author, but, although he admits that this can include the divine author, he usually limits his discussion of authorship to the more proximate cause, the human author. As such, then, the author of the text of Isaiah intended to signify only the historical figure. When the author of the New Testament text uses the passage in Isaiah to refer to Christ, it creates a second literal interpretation of the verse in the context of the New Testament, since the New Testament author literally intends to refer to Christ in this context. Nicholas therefore avoids the imprecision of a literal sense that ultimately subsumes all others.

However, Nicholas complains about scholasticism in the second prologue. He writes:

It must also be known that the literal sense is obscured in many ways because of the method of interpretation commonly handed down by those who admittedly said many good things, but . . . divided (the text) into so many parts and brought in so many agreements to their own propositions that they partially confused the intellect and the memory by drawing the mind away from understanding the literal sense.

In addition Lyra shows evidence throughout his commentary of Franciscan ideals. First, his appreciation of the value of the literal meaning of the text demonstrates an awareness of God's revelation in history. Although Lyra would not maintain that literal interpretation alone is sufficient for a proper understanding of the biblical text, he derives more value for it than does almost any previous biblical scholar, except perhaps Andrew of St. Victor. Second, Lyra's evaluation of history as a further means of revelation is evident both in his commentary on Revelation, as well as many parts of the *Postilla Moralis*. Although these works display considerable restraint in comparison with similar work by either previous Franciscans or the Spiritualists, these commentaries reveal Lyra's fundamental belief in a meta-history and his willingness to identify theological ages of human history, the culmination of which is God's ultimate fulfillment of the *promissio* of history. Third, Lyra finds no need to baptize his non-Christian sources but instead accepts their views as evidence of what can be known using human reason (Oberman 1978, 84). Fourth, Lyra consistently looks for proximate causes to explain phenomenon in the biblical text as a basis of theology (Preus, 67). Such explanations also reveal a typical Franciscan respect for nature, defined in the broad sense as the whole created order, as an arena of God's revelation (Würzburg).

Significance. The influence of Lyra's work over the next two centuries cannot be exaggerated. His was the first commentary to be printed, and as such it enjoyed a wide distribution. There are more than seven hundred extant manuscripts of his biblical commentary dating between 1350 and 1450 in European libraries alone (Wood, 451), as well as more than one hundred editions of this commentary printed between 1471 and 1641 (Labrosse, 1906,

383; Gosselin). It became the standard commentary in the university, often printed with both the complete Vulgate text and the *Glossa Ordinaria* on the same page. R. Wood argues that the practical effect of Lyra's commentary on the biblical interpretation of Luther was to provide a literal sense of the text that Luther could assume would match that of his audience. In addition to his influence among biblical exegetes, evidence of his influence has been found on figures as diverse as Chaucer (Wurtele) and Michelangelo (Gutman).

Nicholas's work did not avoid criticism, however. Paul of Burgos found it necessary to defend Lyra's methodology against its critics, while at the same time publishing extensive addenda to correct comments he felt were not faithful to the "saints and scholars" (Lubac, 355-59). Jean *Gerson rejected such literal interpretation because it opposed the tradition (Preus, 79-84). Desiderius *Erasmus considered Lyra a theologian who "dares to tutor Jerome and to tear apart many things hallowed by the consent of so many centuries on the basis of Jewish books" (in Oberman 1966, 311-12). Luther felt Lyra was too literal and too reliant on Jewish interpretation.

Nicholas's popularity, however, stemmed from his ability to crystallize many of the things important within the universities: a rising sensitivity to history and philology, as well as a growing insistence on the literal meaning as the primary basis for theological argumentation. Lyra also demonstrated a successful independence of thought and method within biblical studies. By placing effective limits on both overjudaizing as well as overallegorization, he showed in practical terms that "new" or even non-Christian interpretations can be theologically fruitful. His care to remain solidly within Christian tradition and his consistent demonstration of the value of the literal meaning of the Bible effectively insured the success of his endeavor.

BIBLIOGRAPHY

Works. Biblia Latina cum Glossa Ordinaria, introductions by K. Froehlich and M. T. Gibson (4

vols.; Turnhout: Brepols, 1992);
Studies. P. M. Adinolfi, "Maria SS. nelle Postille de Nicola di Lyre, a Gen. 21.6, 28.12 e 2 Sam. 23.4," *RivB* 8 (1960) 337-50; idem, "De Mariologicis Lyrani Postillis in Prophetas Medii Aevi Exegeseos Lumine Perpensis," *SBF* 9 (1958) 199-237; idem, "De Mariologicis Lyrani Postillis in Pss 8, 5; 19, 5c-6; 22, 10-11; 67, 7a," *Ant* 34 (1959) 321-35; idem, "De protoevangelio (Gn 3, 15) penes Lyranum," *Ant* 35 (1960) 328-38; idem, "De quibusdam Lyrani Postillis Marianis (Pss 72, 6; 85, 12-13; 110, 3)," *CFr* 31 (1961) 80-89; J. Cohen, *The Friars and the Jews: The Evolution of Medieval Anti-Judaism* (Ithaca, NY: Cornell University Press, 1982); idem, "Scholarship and Intolerance in the Medieval Academy: The Study and Evaluation of Judaism in European Christendom," *AHR* 91 (1986) 592-613; Y. Delègue, *Les machines du sens: Fragments d'une sémiologie médiévale. Textes du Hugues de Saint-Victor, Thomas d'Aquin et Nicolas de Lyre* (Archives du commentaire; Paris: Cendres, 1987); G. R. Evans, *The Language of Logic and of the Bible: The Earlier Middle Ages* (Cambridge: Cambridge University Press, 1984); P. Glorieux, "Nicolas de Lyre (Lyr.)" in *La littérature quodlibétque* (Bibliothèque Thomiste XXI; Paris: J. Vrin, 1935) 2:200-201; idem, "Nicolas de Lyre" in *Répertoire des maitre en théologie de Paris au XIIIe Siècle* (Études de philosophie médiévale 18; Paris: J. Vrin, 1933) 215-31; E. A. Gosselin, "A Listing of the Printed Editions of Nicholaus de Lyra," *Tr* 26 (1970) 399-426; H. B. Gutman, "Nicholas of Lyra and Michelangelo's Ancestors of Christ," *FS* 4 (1944) 223-28; H. Hailperin, "Nicolas de Lyra and Rashi: The Minor Prophets" in *Rashi Anniversary Volume* (Texts and Studies 1; Philadelphia: Jewish Publication Society, 1941) 115-47; idem, *Rashi and the Christian Scholars* (Pittsburgh: University of Pittsburgh Press, 1963); idem, "De l'utilisation par les chrétiens de l'oeuvre de Rachi (1125-1300)," *Rachi,* ed. E. Manès Sperber (Paris: Service Technique pour l'Education, 1974) 163-200; L. A. Kennedy, "Martin Luther and Scholasticism," *Aug* 42 (1992) 339-49; D. C. Klepper, "The Dating of Nicholas of Lyra's *Quaestiò de adventu Christi,*" *AFH* 86 (1993) 297-312; P. D. Krey, "Nicholas of Lyra: Apocalypse Commentary as Historiography" (Ph.D. diss., University of Chicago, 1990); H. Labrosse, "Biographie de Nicolas de Lyre," *EF* 17 (1907) 189-505, 593-608; idem, "Oeuvres de Nicolas de Lyre," *EF* 19 (1908) 41-52, 153-75, 368-79; idem, "Oeuvres de Nicolas de Lyre

(suite)," *EF* 35 (1923) 171-87, 400-432; idem, "Recherches sur la vie et l'oeuvre de Nicolas de Lire de l'ordre des Frères mineurs," *ENCPT* 57 (1906) 129-39; idem, "Sources de la biographie de Nicolas de Lyra," *EF* 16 (1906) 383-404; C. V. Langlois, "Nicolas de Lyre, Frère Mineur," *HLF* 36 (1927) 355-400; G. Leff, *The Dissolution of the Medieval Outlook: An Essay on the Intellectual and Spiritual Change in the Fourteenth Century* (New York: New York University Press, 1976); H. de Lubac, *Exégèse médiévale: Les quatre sens de l'ecriture* (Paris: Aubier, 1959) 345-67; F. Maschkowski, "Rashi's Einfluss auf Nikolaus von Lyra in der Auslegung des Exodus: Ein Beitrag zur Geschichte der Exegese des Alten Testamentes," *ZAW* 11 (1891) 268-316; E. H. Merrill, "Rashi, Nicholas de Lyra and Christian Exegesis," *WTJ* 38 (1975) 66-79; A. J. Michalski, "Rashis Einfluss auf Nicolaus von Lyra in der Auslegung der Bücher Leviticus Numeri und Deuteronomium," *ZAW* 35 (1915) 218-45; 36 (1916) 29-63; idem, "Rashis Einfluss auf Nicolaus von Lyra in der Auslegung des Buches Josua," *ZAW* 39 (1921) 300-307; J. Neumann, "Influence de Rashi et d'autres commentateurs Juifs sur les *Postillae Perpetuae* de Nicolas de Lyre," *REJ* 26 (1893) 172-82; 27 (1893) 250-62; H. A. Oberman, *The Dawn of the Reformation: Essays in Late Medieval and Early Reformation Thought* (Edinburgh: T & T Clark, 1986); idem, *Forerunners of the Reformation: The Shape of Medieval Thought* (New York: Holt, Rinehart & Winston, 1966); idem, "Fourteenth-Century Religious Thought: A Premature Profile," *Spec* 53 (1978) 80-93; S. Ozment, *The Age of Reform 1250-1550: An Intellectual and Religious History of Late Medieval and Reformation Europe* (New Haven, CT: Yale University Press, 1980); C. Patton, "Selections from Nicholas of Lyra's Commentary on Exodus" in *The Theological Interpretation of Scripture: Classic and Contemporary Readings,* ed. S. E. Fowl (BRMT; Oxford: Blackwell, 1997) 114-28; J. S. Preus, *From Shadow to Promise: Old Testament Interpretation from Augustine to the Young Luther* (Cambridge, MA: Harvard University Press, 1969); K. Reinhardt, "Des Werk des Nikolaus von Lyra im mittelalterlichen Spanien," *Tr* 43 (1987) 321-58; H. Rosenau, "The Architecture of Nicolaus de Lyra's Temple Illustrations and the Jewish Tradition," *JJS* 25 (1974) 294-304; H. Rüthing, "Kritische Bemerkungen zu einer mittelalterlichen Biographie des Nikolaus von Lyra," *AFH* 60 (1967) 42-54; C. Siegfried, "Raschi's Einfluss auf Nicolaus von Lira und Luther in der

Auslegung der Genesis," *AEAT* 1 (1869) 428-56; R. W. Southern, "The Changing Role of Universities in Medieval Europe," *HR* 60 (1987) 133-46; P. C. Spicq, *Esquisse d'une histoire de l'exégèse Latine au Moyen Age* (Bibliothèque Thomiste 26; Paris: J. Vrin, 1944); J. Verger, "L'exégèse de l'Université" in *Bible de tous les temps*, 4: *Moyen Âge et la Bible,* ed. P. Riché and G. Lobrichon (Paris: Beauchesne, 1984) 199-230; J. Viard, "Date de la mort de Nicolas de Lire," *Bibliothèque de l'École des Chartres* 56 (1895) 141-43; A. S. Wood, "Nicolas of Lyra," *EvQ* 33 (1961) 196-206; R. Wood, "Nicholas of Lyra and Lutheran Views on Ecclesiastical Office," *JEH* 29 (1978) 451-62; D. Wurtele, "Chaucer's *Canterbury Tales* and Nicholas of Lyre's *Postillae litteralis et moralis super totem bibliam*" in *Chaucer and Scriptural Tradition,* ed. D. L. Jeffrey (Ottawa: University of Ottawa Press, 1984) 84-107; H. F. Würzburg, *Die Anfänge der modernen biblischen Hermeneutik in der spätmittelalterlichen Theologie* (Institut für europäische Geschichte Mainz Vorträge 66; Wiesbaden: Franz Steiner, 1977).

C. L. Patton

PART THREE

Biblical Interpretation in the 16th & 17th Centuries

BIBLICAL INTERPRETATION FROM THE EARLY SIXTEENTH THROUGH THE LATE seventeenth century is separated from medieval exegesis by the philological advances associated with the Renaissance and by the theological and ecclesiological developments associated with the Reformation. In relative contrast with patristic and medieval exegesis, the exegetical efforts of the sixteenth and seventeenth centuries rested on a profound recourse to the biblical text in its original languages and on an increased focus on the literal sense of the text. Still, the interpretive efforts of the Reformers (their successors) and their Roman Catholic contemporaries belong to the so-called precritical model. Medieval interest in the meaning of the text for faith, love and hope (the three spiritual directions of the *quadriga* or allegorical method) finds parallels in the sermons and commentaries of the Reformers, as does the traditional sense of the unity of the scriptural message as grounded in the inspiration of the prophets and apostles by the divine Author. Even so, the exegetical work of the Reformers cannot be easily detached from the work of their successors: there is a continuity of interpretive principles and of textual assumptions, just as there is continuity in exegetical result between the commentators of the sixteenth and those of the seventeenth century.

The Era of the Reformation

The era of the Reformation (c. 1500-1565) is one of the great eras of biblical interpretation in the history of the church. The biblical commentary received even greater emphasis than it had during the Middle Ages. This was particularly so given an increased emphasis on and mastery of classical languages and given the impetus toward exegesis created by the understanding of Scripture alone as the final norm for Christian doctrine. Nonetheless, the time is past when scholarship could ignore the significant continuities between the exegetical and hermeneutical patterns typical of the Reformation and the biblical interpretation of preceding eras. The time is also past when scholarship could identify Reformation-era biblical interpretation as the beginning of the modern, critical address to the text.

The exegetical mind of the sixteenth century was precritical, at least in the sense that it was pre-historical-critical. Biblical criticism in the sixteenth century was textual and theological. The historical sense of the text was identified with its literal, grammatical meaning. If a brief comparison with the higher critical method can be drawn, the Reformation (like the preceding centuries) was concerned to find the meaning of the Bible in the received, canonical text rather than behind or under it in hypothetical predecessor-documents or in hypothetically reconstructed life situations of individual pericopes. In its sense of the integrity of the text and of the relationship of individual portions of the text to the meaning of the whole of the canon, the Reformation and the post-Reformation period had more in common with medieval and patristic exegesis than with the modern higher-critical interpretation of the Bible.

The Reformers drew heavily on the textual and philological skills of Renaissance humanism and also on the exegetical tradition of the church reaching back through the Middle Ages to the patristic period. Nor is it possible to separate the efforts of sixteenth- and seventeenth-century commentators from the major effort of the age to establish a critical text of Scripture and to render the original languages into adequate translations, whether into the vernacular or into Latin. Many of the commentators understood it as an integral part of their task to offer either a critical examination of an extant translation, like the Vulgate or Erasmus's New Testament, or to provide a new translation in their commentaries. Both among the Lutherans and the Reformed we can now discern fairly intense programs designed to produce commentaries on the major portions of Scripture.

Nor were Roman Catholic exegetes negligent in applying the new philological skills of the Renaissance to the establishment of the text and to its interpretation. What separates exegesis in the Reformation and post-Reformation eras from their past is their union of renewed emphases on the ancient languages and rhetorical analysis with an increasing sense of the location of meaning in the literal sense of the text. Yet even in this emphasis the potential breadth of the literal sense, as guaranteed by the intention of its divine author and defined by scope of the canon, there is a degree of continuity with the older exegetical tradition.

The full history of biblical interpretation in the sixteenth and seventeenth centuries remains to be written. Whereas there are significant essays on the work of individual exegetes and major surveys and collections of essays on various themes and issues in sixteenth- and seventeenth-century biblical interpretation, there is no exhaustive study that surveys the exegetes, catalogues their works and assesses the content and impact of their exegesis. Until this detailed work has been done, it will be possible only to offer an outline of the method and import of early Protestant exegesis (not to mention the major Roman Catholic expositors) and an initial prospectus of the commentators and their writings. [Note that the dates of commentaries given in this essay identify the earliest editions found, not necessarily first editions in all cases.]

The text and versions of Scripture. Although it is customary to speak of the Renaissance as a distinct movement that began perhaps two centuries before the Reformation, it is nevertheless impossible to separate the Reformation of the sixteenth century from the development of Renaissance humanism, particularly when humanism is understood as the application of revised theories of logic and rhetoric and of vastly increased philological skills to the critical examination of ancient texts. Recognition that the text of the Vulgate (as well as its translation of the Hebrew and Greek originals) was imperfect had brought about massive editorial work, including detailed comparison of the Latin with Hebrew and Greek texts as early as the thirteenth-century Dominican correctories. But the two keys to establishment and the widespread accessibility of a critical text of Scripture, both in the original languages and in a revised translation, were the printing press and the broad revival of skills in ancient languages in the fifteenth century. Increased access to Hebrew was often made possible through recourse to the linguistic skills of Jewish converts to Christianity.

At the foundation of Reformation-era exegesis were the efforts of Renaissance editors of the biblical text in the last decades of the fifteenth and the first decades of the sixteenth century. These included editors of the Soncino and Bomberg Bibles, Lorenzo Valla (1405-1457), Jacques *Lefèvre d'Étaples (c. 1455-1536), Cardinal Ximenes de Cisneros (1436-1517), Desiderius *Erasmus, and later Robert Estienne or Stephanus (1503-1559), Sebastian Münster (1489-1552), and Sebastian Castellio (1515-1563). A Psalter in Hebrew was printed at Bologna in 1477, and the entire Hebrew Old Testament appeared at Soncino in 1488. Jean *Gerson (1363-1429) superintended an edition published at Brescia in 1494 that was subsequently used by Martin *Luther (1483-1546) in the preparation of his German translation.

Independent of these editions was the Hebrew text of the *Complutensian Polyglott* (printed 1513-1517; published 1520 with permission from Leo X), superintended by Ximenes, priest-confessor to Isabella of Aragon and founder of the University of Alcala, where he saw to the installation of four professors in Hebrew and Greek. The Complutensian text (so called from Complutum, the old Roman name of Alcala) included the Hebrew Old Testament (vocalized but not accented), the Targum of Onqelos to the Pentateuch, the Septuagint and the Vulgate, plus Latin translations of both the targum and the Septuagint. The

Hebrew text and the targum were edited by Alphonso of Alcala, Alphonso of Zamora and Paul Coronel, all converts from Judaism. This was the first publication of a printed Septuagint, made less significant by editorial work conforming the Greek text to the Vulgate. For all his interest in the establishment of the text in its ancient languages, Ximenes remained an adamant opponent of translation into the vernacular. The Hebrew-Chaldee (i.e., Hebrew-Aramaic) lexicon and grammar of Zamora, initially the sixth volume of the Polyglott, was frequently reprinted in the sixteenth century.

A great critical advance was made with the *Biblia Rabbinica* published by Bomberg (Venice, 1517-1518; 1525-1526). The second of these Bomberg Bibles marked a major textual advance: in it the vowel points and the Masora (Ben Asher) were included complete, the text was corrected from the Masora, and the Aramaic paraphrases and rabbinic commentaries were added. This second edition was frequently reissued during the sixteenth century.

The Greek text of the New Testament did not appear in print until several decades after the Soncino Hebrew Old Testament. Erasmus and his publisher, Froben of Basel, raced their Greek text of the New Testament to print in 1516 in order to precede the publication of the text in the final volume of Ximenes's *Complutensian Polyglott* (dated 1514 but printed in 1520). Subsequent editions of Erasmus's New Testament (1519, 1522, 1527 and 1535) improved the text by removing many typographical errors of the first edition—although the third edition is famous for its insertion, under pressure, of the disputed Johannine Comma (1 Jn 5:7). Valla did not produce an edition of the New Testament, but his *Adnotationes* (1505) remained significant in the first half of the sixteenth century for the examination and establishment of the New Testament text.

The great Stephanus Bibles (Paris, 1546, 1549, 1550; Geneva, 1551) are typographically superior and, albeit heavily reliant on Erasmus and Ximenes, rest on a better text-critical apparatus than do earlier editions of the New Testament. Stephanus, himself a linguist, used a series of codices in Paris that Erasmus had not consulted. He established the text for the sixteenth century in the basic form of the Textus Receptus, which was followed with minor emendations, until the nineteenth century. Stephanus also introduced a pattern of enumeration of verses in his 1551 New Testament and 1555 Old Testament that rapidly became standard and that remains virtually unchanged in the Bibles of the twentieth century. This versification passed over into English in Whittingham's New Testament (1557) and in the Geneva Bible (1560).

This pattern of versification also was taken over into the New Testament text prepared by Theodore *Beza (1519-1605) and published by Stephanus in 1556 and incorporated into the Stephanus Bible in 1557. Beza drew on several more codices than Stephanus had, including the so-called Codex Bezae and Codex Claromontanus, still cited in modern editions of the text. Beza's text became the basis for his most significant work, the *Annotationes in Novum Testamentum*. The text and the running commentary of the *Annotationes* in turn had a major impact on the Geneva Bible (1560), the marginalia of which are often summaries of Beza's running commentary, minus its text-critical remarks.

Throughout the era of the Reformation, Latin versions of Scripture, including the Vulgate, retained a significant place in scholarly (as distinct from popular) exegesis. The first Bibles to be printed in the fifteenth century were editions of the Vulgate. A revision of the Vulgate was made for the *Complutensian Polyglott*, and further corrections were introduced by Stephanus in his editions of 1528 and 1540. The Council of Trent also demanded revision of the text, culminating in the edition issued by Pope Sixtus V in 1590 and then revised by Clement VIII and published in 1592. Independent Latin translations of the New Testament were published by Erasmus (1516, reprinted many times), Cardinal Cajetan (1530), Beza (1556) and Castellio (1551); the Old Testament appeared in new Latin translations by Münster (1534-1535) and Leo Jud, the latter assisted by Theodor Bibliander, Petrus Cholinus and Robert Gwalther (1543). Various parts of the Bible were also rendered in to Latin by the major commentators; thus much of the Old Testament was retranslated in the commentaries of Oecolampadius and nearly the entire Bible in John *Calvin's commentaries. Conrad Pellican's commentary on the whole Bible (1523-1535) offered a corrected Vulgate.

Hermeneutical issues. The era of the Reformation produced, in addition to biblical texts and commentaries, a number of significant discussions of biblical interpretation, ranging from Luther's prefaces to all the books of the Bible and his *Open Letter on Translating* to Ulrich *Zwingli's (1484-1531) *On the Clarity and Certainty of the Word,* Martin *Bucer's (1491-1551) short treatise on the method of reading Scripture, and sections of Wolfgang Musculus's *Loci Communes* and Heinrich *Bullinger's (1504-1575) *Decades.* Bucer's treatise stresses the necessity of beginning with the Gospels and moving on to the Pauline epistles as the core of Scripture before the reading of the Old Testament. Bullinger's *Ratio Studiorum* (1527) details a course of biblical study, with heavy reliance on linguistic tools.

Reformation exegesis cannot be understood apart from a sense of the relative continuity of development of exegesis from the patristic period to the eighteenth century. There were several basic assumptions concerning the text of Scripture held in common by the Fathers, the medieval doctors, the Reformers and their seventeenth-century successors that unite all ages of precritical exegesis in their distinction from modern, so-called critical exegesis. These are that the historical import of the text was found in and not under its literal, grammatical meaning; that the primary intention of the text was to offer a divinely inspired message to the ongoing community of faith and not to recount the sentiments of the dead;

that the meaning of a passage is governed not by a hypothetically isolatable unit
of text that has its own *Sitz im Leben* distinct from surrounding texts or from the
biblical book in which it is lodged but by the scope and goal of the biblical book
in the context of the scope and goal of the canonical revelation of God; and that
the primary intention of the text demanded a churchly locus of interpretation
and a reading of the text in conversation with the exegetical tradition rather than
an isolated, scholarly encounter in the confines of an academic study.

As implied by this approach to the meaning of the text, Reformation-era
exegesis assumed the inspiration of the text and the divine illumination of its
human authors. Despite the intensity of Reformation debate over the relationship
between biblical and churchly authority, there was virtually no disagreement
between Protestants and Roman Catholics over the inspiration of the text and
the identification of God as the primary author and of the prophets and apostles
as the secondary authors of the text, on the analogy of dictation. Most theologians
and exegetes of the era assumed that the prophets and apostles spoke in their own
words and out of their own contexts in history but that their words and, more
importantly, the sense of their words was guaranteed by the Holy Spirit as the
Word of God. Protestant insistence on the authority of the original languages of
the text rested on the assumption that the words of the text in these languages
alone were finally and ultimately authoritative.

In addition to these shared assumptions that link its exegesis to the tradition,
a host of specific interpretive issues mark continuity as well as discontinuity
between the Reformation and the exegetical patterns of the Middle Ages. In
contrast to the major theological shifts that took place in the exegesis of individual
verses of Scripture, like Romans 3:20-27 and Romans 4:1-4 (on justification) or
Luke 22:19-20 (the Lord's Supper), the hermeneutical change had been gradual.
In the first place, the *quadriga* or fourfold exegetical model of the late patristic
and medieval eras was not at all inimical to a powerful interest in the literal
meaning of the text. Not only did the three spiritual senses (allegory, tropology
and anagogy, referring to doctrine, morals and Christian hope) presume a
foundation in the literal sense; there was, beginning in the twelfth and thirteenth
centuries, an increasing interest in the literal meaning as the primary meaning of
the text—an interest evidenced in the commentaries of Thomas *Aquinas (c.
1224-1274) and later in the work of *Nicholas of Lyra (c. 1270-1349). Lyra
departed from a fourfold sense and argued a twofold literal-spiritual sense of the
text founded on a model of promise and fulfillment. Second, both in the textual
efforts of thirteenth-century Dominicans and in the work of Lyra, there is an
interest in the establishment of an accurate text of Scripture, for the sake of
accurate interpretation.

The common ground between medieval exegesis, including the quadriga, and
the exegetical work of the Reformers can be seen in the constant movement, not

only in sermons but also in commentaries themselves, from the literal sense of the words of the text to doctrinal, moral and eschatological understandings of the implication of the text for the church. A tendency toward tropology is evident in Luther's exegesis, even in his last lectures on Genesis. Calvin's commentaries consistently raise doctrinal issues and, for example, when the topic of the kingdom of God is broached in the text of the Old Testament, point not only to the obvious christological and eschatological topics but also to the work of the kingdom in Calvin's own time.

The literal or historical sense of the text argued by the Reformation-era exegete was not therefore a bare literal understanding of the text but rather an understanding that took into consideration the larger theological context and specifically the meaning of the divine author as presented in the Bible as a whole. Thus the literal meaning of a prophetic text was understood as the fulfillment of the prophecy. So too was the literal sense understood as the thing signified by a figurative or metaphorical passage. The doctrinal, moral and eschatological dimensions of the quadriga were not lost but rather were found more precisely lodged in the literal sense. Thus a distinct allegorical and anagogical sense was often scorned by the Reformers at the same time that the immediate reference of the text for Christian doctrine or Christian hope was emphasized. So too a separate tropological sense was set aside, but the moral issues and demands raised in the text for Israel and the early Christian community were understood as directly raised for the ongoing community of belief.

Given the strong emphasis of the Renaissance on the study of formal rhetoric, sixteenth-century exegetes were attuned to the identification of forms of argument and figures of speech. They also emphasized identification of the scope or focus of the text, usually in extended discussions of the argument or disposition of a book or chapter in Scripture. Exegetes pointed to the scope of individual chapters and of entire biblical books or of the Scriptures as a whole as integral to the interpretive task. In the latter sense the scope or foundation of Scripture was often identified as Christ, the saving work of Christ or God's covenant with human beings.

Exegetes of the Reformation era differed considerably in their application of this understanding of the larger scope of Scripture. Whereas Luther and Johannes Brenz assumed a profound trinitarian and christological content throughout the Old Testament, particularly in the Psalter, Calvin is remembered for his restraint. Calvin's commentary on Psalms hesitates to find a type of Christ in every mention of David and tends to reserve christological readings for the most clearly messianic psalms. So too Calvin refused to argue a trinitarian reading of Genesis 1. Other Reformed exegetes, however, like Peter Martyr *Vermigli (1499-1562) and Musculus, retained the more trinitarian and christological patterns of interpretation.

If an increasing medieval emphasis on the letter and the text provided a context for the beginnings of Reformation exegesis, so did the textual, rhetorical and philological emphases of Renaissance humanism. The Reformation-era commentary was not only rooted in the Hebrew and Greek text, made available in increasingly finely edited editions; it was also directed toward the establishment of valid and serviceable translations of text, both in the vernacular and in Latin. Characteristic of the era is the gradual replacement, among Protestants, of the Vulgate by more accurate translations, notably those of Münster (Old Testament) and Beza (New Testament).

The gradual movement away from the forms and methods of medieval exegesis is nowhere more evident than in the style of commentaries. Whereas the medieval commentary had been largely theological, the Reformation-era commentary added to the theological dimension significant interests in rhetoric and philology. Thus the recasting of logic and rhetoric that occurred in the Renaissance led exegetes like Philipp *Melanchthon (1497-1560) and Bullinger to emphasize the rhetorical forms, such as the larger patterns of introduction, exposition and presentation of standard topics or *loci* in disputations or digressions throughout the text. In addition these exegetes brought a highly detailed sense of figures of speech and forms of argument, such as the syllogism and enthymeme, to their understanding of the flow of biblical discourse. So too do Oecolampadius, Calvin, and others well versed in the biblical languages offer detailed examination of problems of text and translation.

Among Protestants in particular, commentaries tended to move away from the medieval form of gloss and *scholion* to forms dictated more closely by the text itself or by the movement from text to theology. Thus the medieval pattern of interlinear gloss was set aside as commentaries moved away from the Vulgate text and the more extensive pattern of running commentary found in the *Glossa Ordinaria* was replaced by a more individualized and discursive comment. In some cases, notably Beza's *Annotationes,* the philological interest of the exegete nearly entirely governed the form of the commentary. The *scholia* were replaced by the identification of loci or *topoi,* either in the context of the running commentary, appended to the analysis of chapters of a book, or (in the case of Melanchthon) a rhetorically governed analysis of an entire book in terms of the loci found in it, without any attempt to offer a gloss or running comment on every verse.

Exegetes and their commentaries. G. Ebeling's famous remark that the history of theology is in fact the history of New Testament exegesis, when emended to remove its somewhat Marcionite tendency, well reflects the theological mind of the Reformation. The theology of the Reformation was profoundly exegetical, and the written efforts of the great Reformers took with greatest regularity the form of the biblical commentary. From the purely dogmatic perspective, the Reformation altered a precious few theological topics—notably the doctrines of justification, the Lord's

Supper and the church—but from an exegetical perspective it marked a renewed interest in the entire text of Scripture that resulted in a wealth of commentaries on every book of the Bible and a revision of the whole of theology in view of the exegetical result. Major commentators of the era, like Luther, Oecolampadius, Musculus, Brenz and Calvin, are notable for the balance of their interest in both Old Testament and New Testament.

Luther's work as a Reformer rested squarely on his primary vocation as a biblical exegete. His reformatory work assumed his calling to be a doctor or a teacher of the church in the specific role of professor of biblical interpretation. Although he is famous for his lectures on Romans (1515-1516) and Galatians (1516-1517/1531), it was also as an Old Testament exegete that Luther left his mark on his times. Luther's style changed considerably over the course of his life: his early commentaries, notably those on the Psalter, Hebrews and Romans, reflect precisely the medieval model of gloss or running comment followed by scholia or detailed notes on the more significant theological issues raised by the text. Later commentaries, beginning with the second lectures on Psalms, follow the more discursive style of *enarratio* or *lectio continua*. In addition to the lectures already noted, Luther also commented on the Catholic Epistles, the Gospel of John, Genesis, Deuteronomy, Judges, Ecclesiastes, Isaiah and the Minor Prophets.

Melanchthon's contribution to Reformation-era exegesis was primarily a rhetorical analysis of the biblical text designed to elucidate both the structure of a book and its main theological topics. Once he had offered a rhetorical analysis of an entire biblical book, Melanchthon moved on to examine only the major topics or loci found in the text rather than move through the text verse by verse. Inasmuch as Luther's lectures on Romans were not published until the twentieth century, it is the several versions of Melanchthon's commentary on Romans that represented the Lutheran exegesis of the early Reformation. Melanchthon also labored at length on Colossians and John. He also commented on portions of Genesis (1523), select psalms, Proverbs (1524), Daniel (1543) and Ecclesiastes (1550).

Johannes Brenz (1499-1570), the Lutheran Reformer of Swabia, also stands out as a major early Lutheran exegete who commented on the Pentateuch (1539-1551), Judges and Ruth (1535), the Psalter (1565-1571), Job (1527), Hosea (1530), Amos (1530), Isaiah (1550), Ezra and Nehemiah (1565), the Synoptic Gospels (1537-1560), the Gospel of John (1527), Acts (1530), Galatians (1527), Philippians (1548) and Romans (1565). Brenz understood the Psalter as a prayerful conversation between God and his people and Job as belonging to the genre of tragedy. His commentaries are characterized by both dogmatic and practical interests.

Johannes Bugenhagen (1485-1558), the Reformer of Brunswick, Lübeck and

Pomerania, collaborated in the publication of a Low German version of Luther's New Testament and wrote an exposition of the Psalter (1524), characterized by strong christological and typological emphases. He also wrote annotations on Deuteronomy and Samuel (1524) and on 1 Kings and 2 Kings (1525), a commentary on Job (1526) and annotations on the Pauline epistles (1525). Among the other early Lutherans, Erasmus Sarcerius (1501-1559), the Reformer of Nassau, remembered for his *Loci Communes,* commented on the Gospel of John (1540), and Andreas Osiander (1498-1552), an associate of Luther and one of the Reformers of Nürnberg, lectured on 1 John and produced an annotated harmony of the Gospels (1537). Georg Maior (d. 1574), the follower of Melanchthon and professor at Wittenberg, produced commentaries on the Pauline epistles that followed the Melanchthonian pattern of detailed structural and rhetorical analysis.

Numbered among the earlier Reformed commentators are Johann Oecolampadius (1482-1531), Ulrich Zwingli (1484-1531), Conrad Pellican (1478-1556), Sebastian Münster (1489-1552), Martin Bucer (1491-1551) and Wolfgang Capito (1478-1541). Oecolampadius, the Reformer of Basel, was trained both in theology and in languages and is remembered for his philologically and theologically detailed work on all the major and minor prophets (1525-1535) as well as 1 John (1524), Romans (1525), Job (1532), John (1533), Hebrews (1534), Matthew (1536), Genesis (1536) and Colossians (1546). Zwingli produced expositions of Genesis, Exodus (as far as chapter 24), Isaiah and Jeremiah, and annotations on the four Evangelists. His exegesis is characterized by rejection of allegory but also by frequent recourse to nominally allegorical readings of the text and a strong practical bent. Zwingli attempted to distinguish carefully between figures found in the text and figurative meanings imposed on it.

The humanistically trained Pellican served as professor of Hebrew and Greek in Zürich and was known in his day as the author of the first (1501) Christian textbook on Hebrew: Reuchlin's more famous textbook appeared in 1506. Pellican published a lucid running commentary on the entire text of Scripture (5 vols., 1532-1535), noted for its concise argument, absence of digression and attention to the grammatical sense of the text. The New Testament commentary is, unfortunately, highly derivative of the works of others. Münster was a student of Pellican who followed in the steps of his master by publishing the first Aramaic grammar (1527) written by a Protestant. Münster also published the grammatical works of the the Jewish scholar Elias Levita in Latin editions and edited the text of the Hebrew Bible with his own Latin translation (Basel, 1535). Münster's Hebrew Bible, notable for its annotations on the text and its continuous use of rabbinic materials, became the standard tool of Protestant Old Testament exegetes in the sixteenth century. Münster also echoed the ancient tradition of a

Hebrew original for the Gospel of Matthew by translating the Gospel into Hebrew (1537).

Bucer is remembered for his weighty, often digressive, theological examination of central books of the New Testament, notably the Synoptic Gospels (1527), Romans (1536), Ephesians (1527) and the Gospel of John (1528), and his translation of Bugenhagen's Psalter (1529). Bucer also commented on Psalms (1554) and Judges (1554). Bucer's associate Capito commented on Habakkuk (1526), Hosea (1528) and the first chapter of Genesis (1539).

On the English scene, William *Tyndale (c. 1494-1536), Miles *Coverdale (c. 1487-1569), William Whittingham (1524-1579), Anthony Gilby (d. c. 1584) and Christopher Goodman (1519-1602) were less notable as commentators and interpreters than they were as translators. Tyndale and Coverdale collaborated in the first two English Bibles, the Matthew (1535) and the Great Bible (1537). While they were exiled at Geneva, Whittingham, Gilby, Goodman, Coverdale and others prepared a translation of the New Testament (1557) and subsequently the Geneva Bible (1560). Gilby, an expert Hebraist, commented on Micah (1551). David Whitehead (d. 1571), chaplain to Anne Boleyn, published his homilies on the Pauline epistles. The tenure of such Continental exegetes as Bucer and Vermigli at Oxford, however, brought models of technical exegesis to Protestant England early in the Reformation. The Scottish theologian Alexander Alesius (1500-1565), briefly professor at Cambridge, later at Frankfurt-on-Oder and Leipzig, and a friend of Melanchthon, wrote a series of commentaries, notably on the Gospel of John (1553).

Calvin was surely the most eminent Reformed commentator of the sixteenth century. He took the work of exegesis as his central task and with incredible single-mindedness preached, lectured and commented through nearly the entire Bible, omitting only Revelation from his work on the New Testament and, if the sermons are considered as well as the commentaries, only Ruth, 1 Chronicles and 2 Chronicles, Ezra, Nehemiah, Esther, Proverbs, Ecclesiastes and the Song of Songs from his work on the Old Testament. In his preface to the posthumous lectures on Ezekiel, Beza indicated that had Calvin lived longer, he would have completed commentaries on the entire Bible. Calvin is significant not only for his own efforts but also for the influence he exerted on several trajectories of Reformed interpretation. He offered models for the running textual and theo-logical commentary and for the homiletical commentary. He also provided a precedent for highly literal reading of the Old Testament, according to which christological and trinitarian themes were invoked only in the context of clearly prophetic and messianic passages. His sermons on Job, for example, respect the Gentile location and characters of the book and are notable for the virtual absence of christological and trinitarian themes. It is true, however, that in general his Old Testament sermons tend to be more christological than do his commentaries.

Calvin also collaborated in the translation of the entire Bible into French and an independent translation of nearly the entire Bible into Latin can be culled from his commentaries.

Among Calvin's Reformed contemporaries, Bullinger, Musculus (1497-1563) and Vermigli also were eminent as commentators. Bullinger was particularly prolific, writing formal commentaries on all of the books of the New Testament except the Apocalypse (Matthew [1542], Mark [1545], Luke [1546], John [1543], Acts [1533], the Pauline Epistles [1537], 1-2 Peter [1534], 1 John [1532]), an exposition of Lamentations (1561), and massive collections of sermons on Daniel (1565), Jeremiah (1575), Isaiah (1567) and Revelation (1557). His commentaries typically offer both a running comment on the entire text and theological loci on specific problems. Nearly forgotten in the twentieth century, Musculus was one of the eminent theologians and exegetes of his time, known for his ability in Hebrew and also for his rather prolix style: his commentaries are massive and consistently examine textual and philological matters as well as theological issues. Musculus commented on Matthew (1548), John (1545), Psalms (2 vols., 1551), the Decalogue (1553), Genesis (1554), Romans (1555), Isaiah (1557), 1 Corinthians and 2 Corinthians (1559), Galatians and Ephesians (1561), and Ephesians, Colossians, 1 Thessalonians and 2 Thessalonians and 1 Timothy (1565). Calvin stated of Musculus's *Psalms* that, had he seen it before he began his work on the Psalter, he would not have needed to publish.

Among Calvin's contemporaries, Vermigli was probably the most erudite of the Hebraists. His commentaries on 1 Corinthians (1551), Romans (1558), Judges (1561), Jeremiah (1562), 1 Samuel and 2 Samuel (1564), Genesis (1569) and 1 Kings and 2 Kings (1571) all evidence profound study of not only the Christian but also the rabbinic tradition of biblical interpretation. Two of Vermigli's commentaries, Judges (1564) and Romans (1568) were translated into English in the sixteenth century. By way of contrast, Rudolph Gualther (1519-1586), pastor of St. Peter's in Zürich, assistant and eventually successor to Bullinger, produced a series of homiletical meditations: Acts (1557), Matthew (1583-1584), Mark (1561), John (1565), Luke (1570), Romans (1566), the Minor Prophets (1566), 1 Corinthians and 2 Corinthians (1572), Galatians (1576) and the Catholic Epistles (1588). Of these, the homilies on Old Testament books and on the Acts were all translated into English in the sixteenth century. His meditations are characterized by a formal, discursive eloquence and are sometimes contrasted with the more extemporaneous style of earlier works in the same genre.

Nor was it only the Protestant exegetes who stressed the need to return to the Hebrew and Greek texts: Thomas de Vio, Cardinal Cajetan (1469-1534), master general of the Dominican order, bishop of Gaeta and a major exponent of

Thomism, devoted the last decade of his life to exegesis, producing a new translation of Psalms from Hebrew and commentaries on the Gospels and Acts (1527-1528), the Epistles (1528-1529), the Pentateuch (1530-1531), the Old Testament histories (1531-1532), Job (1533) and Ecclesiastes (1534). Cajetan's exegetical method, although it did not oppose the quadriga, emphasized the literal sense. He shared with Luther and many others of the age a distinction between homologoumena (fully agreed upon books) and antilegomena (questioned books) in the New Testament, viewing Hebrews, James, 2 Peter, 2 John, 3 John and Jude as being of doubtful authorship, and he questioned the validity of such texts as Mark 16:9-20 and John 8:1-11 on the basis of collations of Greek codices.

Also eminent among the early sixteenth-century Roman Catholic commentators were Ambrosius Catharinus Politus (1483-1553); Jacopo Sadoleto (1477-1547), bishop of Carpentras, a noted humanist, reformer, and opponent of Calvin; Jean de Gagnée (d. 1549), rector of the University of Paris who wrote a significant commentary on the Pauline epistles (1539) and the four Gospels and Acts (1552); and Isidorus Clarius (d. 1555), who revised the Vulgate New Testament on the basis of the Greek text (1542). Catharinus produced major commentaries on the Pauline and Catholic epistles (1546), de Gagnée wrote a series of scholia on the text of the Gospels and Acts (1552), and Sadoleto commented on the Psalms and Romans (1536).

Among the Roman Catholic exegetes of the post-Tridentine era, Sixtus Senensis (1520-1569), a convert from Judaism, stands as the preeminent linguist and exegete. His *Bibliotheca Sancta* (1566), also published as *Ars Interpretandi Sacras Scripturas,* discusses the canon and authority of Scripture, the individual biblical authors and their writings, and the interpretation of the text in its various senses and offers comments on passages of theological and critical interest in both Testaments. Sixtus's work is noteworthy for its critical and hermeneutical dimensions, such as its argument for the multiple authorship of the Psalter, its assumption of a twofold literal sense much like that taught by Nicholas of Lyra, and its advocacy of the use of original texts and multilingual tools like the *Complutensian Polyglott.*

The Post-Reformation Era

When it is examined from the perpective of the history of exegesis, the era of Protestant orthodoxy (c. 1565-1700) must be regarded not only as a continuation of the philological and interpretive development of the Renaissance and Reformation but also as the great era of Protestant linguistic study, whether in the biblical or in the cognate languages. Since it has so often been implied that the Reformation was a time of exegesis, virtually without dogma, and the era of orthodoxy was a time of dogmatic system without exegesis, it must be added that at no time before or since the era of orthodoxy was systematic theology so closely wedded to the textual and linguistic work of the exegete. The loci of the theological system arose directly out of meditation on specific texts and issues in Scripture and continued, throughout the seventeenth century, to be understood in that relationship. Thus if the theological works of the late sixteenth and seventeenth centuries are characterized by a great deal of proof-texting, it is also the case that these citations of texts point the readers of theological works directly toward the work of exegesis being done in the era, often by the same writers. The post-Reformation era ought not, however, to be viewed as a time during which the intimate connection between exegesis and theology rendered exegesis an ancillary discipline. The flowering of hermeneutical, philological and text-critical work in the post-Reformation era argues the opposite case.

The text and versions of Scripture. If Beza is to be regarded as one of the founding fathers of Protestant orthodoxy, his prominence in that development was in no small measure due to the textual and theological achievement of his *Annotationes in Novum Testamentum* (1556; much augmented, 1582, 1589, 1598), which remained a touchstone of Protestant exegesis for more than a century. Beza collated the best codices available to him, two of which, the Codex Bezae and Codex Claromontanus, remain significant to the textual analysis of the New Testament; he examined previous translations, notably the Vulgate, Erasmus, Calvin and Castellio; he presented a philological analysis that justified his own version of the text; and he presented a running set of theological glosses on the meaning and import of the text. Beza also engaged in controversy with Castellio over the latter's highly literary translation of the New Testament into Latin (1561) on the ground that it distorted the theology of the text.

The era of orthodoxy also saw the production of a series of great polyglot Bibles. The first of these, the Antwerp Polyglot, funded by Philip II of Spain and therefore also called the *Biblia Regia,* represents the flowering of sixteenth-century Roman Catholic philology. It was published in eight folio volumes by Plantin between 1569 and 1572, under the editorial supervision of Benedictus Arias Montanus (1527-1598). Volumes 1 through 4 offer the Old Testament; volume 5, the New Testament. The Polyglot consists in the original texts in Hebrew and Greek, with the Vulgate, the Septuagint and the targums, each with a Latin translation, the Peshito or Syriac New Testament (in both Hebrew and Syriac characters, with a Latin translation). Volumes 6 and 7 contain the apparatus, including critical notes, a Hebrew lexicon by Paginus, a Syriac-Chaldee (i.e., Syriac-Aramaic) lexicon by Guy le Fèvre, a Syriac grammar by Masius and a Greek lexicon and grammar by Arias Montanus. The final volume offered the original texts of the Old Testament and New Testament with interlinear translation into Latin, Paginus's Latin of the Old Testament and the Vulgate of the New Testament.

The Paris Polyglot, published in ten volumes between 1629 and 1645, reprinted the Antwerp Old Testament without alteration and the Antwerp New Testament with texts of the Syriac antilegomena (2 Peter, 2 John, 3 John, Jude and the Apocalypse) lacking the in original Antwerp printing, and with an Arabic version and its Latin translation. The remaining volumes presented the text of the Samaritan Pentateuch and an Arabic Old Testament. Editorial work on the new sections of text was done by Jean Morin (1591-1659), priest of the Oratory and a student of the linguist Simeon de Muis, and Gabriel Sionita (1578-1648), a Maronite and professor of Arabic in the Collége de France.

Four polyglot Bibles appeared from Protestant editors: the *Polyglotta Sanctandreana* in Heidelberg (5 vols., 1586-99), based largely on the Antwerp Polyglot; the Hamburg Polyglot (6 vols. 1596); the Nürnberg Polyglot (5 vols., 1599-1602); and the great London Polyglot (8 vols., 1657-1669). The Hamburg Polyglot, edited by David Wolder, marks a significant departure from the Roman Catholic polyglot Bibles with its replacement of the Vulgate New Testament with Beza's Latin and its inclusion of Luther's German translation of both Testaments. Its Hebrew Old Testament is the 1587 text of Elias Hutter (1553-c. 1609). Hutter's own polyglot edition, published in Nürnberg, offered the Old Testament from Genesis to Ruth (in Hebrew, Chaldee, Greek, Latin and German, with some passages rendered into French, Italian and Slavic), plus the Psalter (in Hebrew, Greek, Latin and German). Hutter's New Testament included, in addition to the traditional texts and translations, versions in Italian, Spanish, French, English, German, Danish and Polish.

The London Polyglot, edited by Brian Walton, has the greatest critical and textual significance of the all the polyglot Bibles of the era. Walton gathered together such impressive philologists of the day as John *Lightfoot (1602-1675), Edmund Castell (1606-1685), Thomas Hyde (1636-1703), Dudley Loftus (1619-1695), Abraham Wheelocke (1593-1653), Thomas Greaves (1612-1670), Samuel Clarke (1625-1669) and Edward Pococke (1604-1691). Lightfoot was responsible for the critical edition of the Samaritan Pentateuch, while Pococke's contribution to the Polyglot was a critical edition of the Arabic version of the Pentateuch together with an appendix analyzing the variant Arabic readings.

In addition, the London Polyglot contained a pointed Hebrew text of the Old Testament, the Greek New Testament, a corrected Vulgate, the extant fragments of the Old Latin or Itala, the Septuagint with variant readings from the Codex Alexandrinus, the Peshitto, the targums, a Persian Pentateuch and Gospels, and Ethiopic versions of the Psalms, Song of Songs and the New Testament—each accompanied by an independent Latin translation. Castell is known for his *Lexicon Heptaglotton* (1669), a dictionary of Hebrew, Chaldee, Syriac, Samaritan, Ethiopic and Arabic, published as the final two volumes of the Polyglot's apparatus. Of the editors of the Polyglott, Lightfoot was also a major commentator in his own right, producing a commentary, based on Judaica, on the New Testament as far as 1 Corinthians (1658-1674), a harmony of the Gospels (1644-1650) and a commentary on the Acts (1645). Textual and philological expertise also characterize the work of Pococke, who served as professor of Hebrew, Arabic and cognate languages at Oxford. Pococke commented on Micah and Malachi (1677), Hosea (1685) and Joel (1691). His *Specimen Historiae Arabum* (1648) was one of the first books issued with Arabic font in England.

Hermeneutical issues. The era of orthodoxy also saw the production of such significant interpretive essays as Matthias Flacius *Illyricus's (1520-1575) *Clavis Scripturae* (1567), William Whitaker's (1548-1595) *Disputation on Holy Scripture* (1588), Andreas Rivetus's (1572-1651) *Isagoge in Novum Testamentum* (1616), Johannes Drusius's (1550-1616) *Ad Voces Ebreas N.T. Commentarius Duplex* (1606) and his critical annotations on the Old Testament, printed in *Critici Sacri* (1660), John Weemes's (1579-1636) *Christian Synagogue* (1623), Salomon Glassius's (1593-1656) *Philologia Sacra* (1626), and Benjamin Keach's (1640-1704) *Tropologia, a Key to Open Scripture Metaphors* (1682).

Separate notice needs also to be given to the great *Critici sacri . . . in Vetus ac Novum Testamentum* (9 vols., 1660; repr. 1695, 1698-1732), in which essays on biblical interpretation, antiquities, text criticism and exegesis gathered from the most significant theologians of the era were compiled under the direction of John Pearson (1612-1686), Anthony Scattergood (1611-1687) and Francis Gouldman (d. 1688). Illyricus's and Whittaker's guides to biblical interpretation are notable for their emphasis on the literal, historical sense of the text as the source of doctrinal, moral and eschatological meaning and for their careful examination of texts used by Roman Catholic polemicists to undermine the Protestant understanding of the literal sense. Illyricus ought also to be remembered for his commentary on the New Testament in the form of a gloss (1570). Drusius, who served as professor of Hebrew at Oxford, Leiden and Franecker, and Weemes, who served as minister in Berwickshire and afterward as prebend of Durham, were pioneers in the attempt to understand Bible in the light of Jewish sources.

The hermeneutic described in works of Whitaker, Rivetus and Glassius built on the Reformers' work by stressing use of the original languages and emphasizing the literal, historical sense of the text. Whitaker and Rivetus after him were concerned to argue the source of all theological conclusions in the literal sense of the text but also to recognize that the literal sense included the various figures and types in the text. Allegories, tropes and anagogy were understood as false readings, therefore, only when they were grafted onto the text rather than identified as integral to it. Glassius, professor of theology at Jena, continued this line of argument and provided both a critical and historical introduction to Scripture and a discussion of interpretive principles notable in particular for its ability to draw on the terminology of classical rhetoric to identify the wide variety of rhetorical figures present in the text. By building on his analysis of figures and types, Glassius was able to argue a double sense, literal and spiritual, of the text of Scripture and to insist that the spiritual sense be identified in terms of the New Testament fulfillment of Old Testament promise and prophecy. Keach, an English Particular Baptist minister, followed Glassius's work closely and offers an instance of the vitality of the orthodox Protestant hermeneutic in the late seventeenth century.

Rather than a turn away from Renaissance and Reformation developments, the post-Reformation era should be seen as a time of intensification of Protestant interest in the original languages of the text to the inclusion of cognate Semitic languages in the curriculum of major universities. It was typical of seventeenth-century exegesis to examine closely such ancient versions as the Samaritan Pentateuch and the targums both as aids to the critical establishment of the text and as guides to the nuances of Hebrew meaning. Thus the work of the Johannes Buxtorf Sr. and Johannes Buxtorf Jr. and Louis Cappel (1585-1658) contributed to a massive development of interest in Judaica.

The elder Buxtorf is remembered for his vast *Biblia Hebraica cum Paraphrasi Chaldaica et Commentariis Rabbinorum* (4 vols., 1618-1619), in which he made the resources of the Jewish interpretive tradition obvious and available to his Christian contemporaries, for his edition of the Masorah (1620) and for his various linguistic tools: a grammar (1602) and a lexicon (1607) of Hebrew and Aramaic, a study of Hebrew abbreviations (1613), and two posthumous works, both completed by his son, a concordance to the Hebrew and Chaldee Bible (1632) and a lexicon of Chaldean and of Talmudic and rabbinic Hebrew (1639). The younger Buxtorf, a superb scholar in his own right, published a lexicon of Aramaic and Syriac at the age of twenty-three (1622) and devoted much of his later energy to the defense of his father's view of the vowel points against the work of Cappel. Cappel's most significant exegetical and text-critical efforts are found in his *Critica Sacra* (1650) and his commentary with critical notes on the Old Testament (posthumous 1689), but he is most famous for his early work *Arcanum Punctationis Revelatum* (1623) on the origin of the vowel points in the Hebrew Bible, in which he disputed the findings of Johannes Buxtorf Sr.

Cappel's work on the vowel points advanced no new theories. A Masoretic origin of the punctuation marks (c. 500-600) had been argued by Elias Levita as early as 1538 and had been advocated by Roman Catholic exegetes like Gilbertus Genebrardus (1537-1597) at the end of the sixteenth century. What made Cappel appear revolutionary is that he was a Protestant biblical theologian who not only held forth in detail against the views of the revered elder Buxtorf but also espoused a position that was then used by Roman Catholic exegetes to argue a human element in the text of Scripture. Cappel's insight into the historical nature of the redaction of the Old Testament identifies him as a precursor of the historical criticism of the eighteenth century. His work unleashed one of the major debates of the seventeenth century and brought to the fore a question that was not resolved for nearly two hundred years.

Adumbrations of the historical-critical method also appear in the works of Grotius, Simon and others in the era—often either misinterpreted or rejected by more traditional exegetes. Thus, because of his highly critical stance on numerous texts, Hugo Grotius's (1583-1645) *Annotationes* on the Old Testament and New Testament (1645) frequently disagreed with the exegetical tradition and were often linked by the orthodox exegetes and theologians of the day with the Socinian efforts, notably in his identification of the servant songs in Isaiah as prophetic references to the sufferings of Jeremiah. His argument for Matthean priority and the use of Matthew's Gospel, perhaps a Hebrew version, by the other Synoptists, however, has its parallels in the orthodox exegetes of the day. The form of Grotius's annotations can be viewed as a descendant of the gloss, combining shorter running comment with longer scholia as needed. The *Histoire critique du Vieux Testament* (1678-1685), *Historie critique* of the New Testament text (1689), versions (1690) and commentators (1693) of Richard Simon mark a watershed in the critical reading of Scripture, particularly in the use of literary and historical analysis to establish the original forms of texts. Simon, a Roman Catholic associated with the Oratorians, could argue that the superscriptions of the Gospels and Hebrews and the ending of the Gospel of Mark were not original to the text. Elements of historical-critical method also appear in Baruch Spinoza's (1632-1677) *Theological-Political Treatise* (1670), in which Spinoza insisted that Scripture does not offer knowledge of God so much as religious devotion, and devotion, moreover, presented in the forms given it by an ancient people in which customary teachings were mingled with eternal truths.

The hermeneutics of Protestant orthodoxy, like that of the Reformation era, was bound to a high view of the inspiration of Scripture. Just as, moreover, there is a clear continuity between the Reformation and post-Reformation eras in their view of the literal sense of the text, their emphasis on linguistics and philology, and their location of the work of biblical interpretation in the believing community, so also is there a clear continuity in their approach to the inspiration of the text. The orthodox Protestant assumption of inspiration on the analogy of dictation in no way undercut but rather supported the text-critical efforts of the age, given the churchly and theological importance of the establishment of an authoritative text as the basis of exegesis.

Exegetes and their commentaries. The era of early orthodoxy (c. 1565-1640) perpetuated all of the various genres of Reformation-era exegesis. It also maintained the diversity of hermeneutical patterns found in the era of the Reformation, with the result that even among the Reformed, Calvin's christologically reserved approach to the Old Testament represented only one line of development. Reformed ancestors of the federal school, like Piscator, produced highly typological and christological readings of the Old Testament, whereas others, like Ainsworth, retained Calvin's reserve.

Augustine Marlorat, who provided the first Scripture index to Calvin's 1559 *Institutes,* perpetuated the medieval catena style in commentaries in a finely chosen gathering of the thoughts of major Reformers woven into a seamless web of theological comment. Marlorat commented on the entire New Testament (1561), several volumes of which appeared separately in English: Matthew (1570), Mark and Luke (1583), John (1575), 2 John and 3 John (1578) and Revelation (1574). He also produced a topical *Thesaurus* or concordance to the Bible. Marlorat's contemporary Pierre Merlin commented on Esther (1599). Among their Continental contemporaries, Jerome *Zanchi (1516-1590), Ursinus's successor in Heidelberg, wrote theological commentaries on Hosea and Ephesians in which he followed each chapter with a series of theological loci. Lambert Daneau (1530-1595), who studied in Geneva during Calvin's final years and subsequently served as professor of theology at Leiden, commented on Matthew (1583), Philemon (1577), 1 Timothy (1577), the Gospel of John (1585), the epistles of John and Jude (1585) and the Minor Prophets (1578). Daneau's *Methodus Sacrae Scripturae* (1570) proposed a method for moving from the text of Scripture to preaching, illustrated from the text of Philemon. Daneau, like Melanchthon, stressed the identification of rhetorical forms and of logical argumentation in the text, the elicitation of theological loci, and the careful delineation of the sections or units of the text in their interrelationships.

The prolific Louis Lavater (1527-1586), Bullinger's associate and successor in Zürich, produced commentaries on Genesis (1579), Proverbs (1562), 1 Chronicles and 2 Chronicles (1573), Ruth (1578), Job (1577), Esther (1585) and Ecclesiastes (1584), as well as homiletical expositions of Joshua (1565), Ezekiel (1571), Judges (1585), Ezra (1586) and Nehemiah (1586). Benedictus Aretius (1505-1574), professor of theology in Bern, a classical scholar who wrote a treatise on Pindar, was known for his set of theological loci and also for a series of major posthumous commentaries on the four Gospels (1580), the Gospel of John (1578), Acts (1590), Romans (1583), 1 Corinthians, Ephesians (1579), 1 Thessalonians and 2 Thessalonians (1580) and Philippians and Colossians (1580). David Paraeus (1548-1622), the pupil of Ursinus and editor of his theology, commented on Matthew (1631), Romans (1609) and Revelation (1618) and wrote series of loci on Mark and Luke. Paraeus was also known in his day as the editor of the Neustadt Bible (1587), a printing, for the German Reformed church, of Luther's translation, accompanied by Paraeus's own annotations—a point of considerable contention with the Lutherans and a strong indication of the need for a German Reformed Bible. Several Reformed exegetes of the era also translated the Bible into German, at least in part to offer the German Reformed an alternative to Luther's version: Amandus Polanus (1561-1610) produced a German Old Testament, and Johannes Piscator (1546-1626) translated the entire Bible into German.

Among the Reformed, several major running commentaries on the entire text of the Bible appeared in the early seventeenth century. Jean Diodati (1576-1649) and Daniel Tossanus (1541-1602) wrote annotations on the entire Bible. Tossanus's work is notable as following the pattern of the *Glossa Ordinaria,* offering a text with gloss and scholia. Piscator commented on the entire Old Testament (1612-1618) and New Testament (1595-1609) and also wrote a series of Ramistic logical analyses of the New Testament; Louis de Dieu (d. 1642) produced a commentary on the New Testament (1631) and a massive analysis of the critical problems of the New Testament text *Critica Sacra* (posthumous 1693). Johann Grynaeus, professor at Heidelberg, commented on Galatians (1583). Fransiscus Junius (1545-1602), professor of theology at Heidelberg and Leiden, commented on the Gospel of Mark; his work on Revelation was the basis of the revised annotations to the last book of the Geneva Bible of 1602. Associated also with the names of Beza and Junius was Johannes Immanuel Tremellius (1510-1580), who converted to Christianity from Judaism before 1540, converted to Protestantism, and served as professor of Old Testament at Heidelberg and Sedan. Tremellius's Latin New Testament (1569) never rivaled Beza's Latin translation, but his Latin Old Testament (1575-1579), based on Hebrew, Aramaic and Syriac texts, became the standard Reformed version. He also published an Aramaic and Syriac grammar (1569). Junius's more famous opponent in debate, Jacob Arminius (1559-1608), commented at length on Romans 7 and Romans 9, providing highly technical theological analyses of both texts.

Of the theologians who sat at the synod of Dort (1618-1619), there were several notable exegetes: Antonius Walaeus (1573-1639) wrote a commentary on the entire New Testament (1653); the English delegate, John Davenant (1570-1641), produced a theological commentary on Colossians (1627); Francis Gomarus (1563-1644), professor of theology at Leiden, published a series of topical loci on the four Gospels and Philippians, prefaced by an interpretive treatise on the covenants. He also commented on Hebrews (1644).

Meinardus Schotanus (d. 1644), professor of theology at Utrecht, commented on Philippians (1637). A commentary on the Gospel of John (1627) came from the pen of Daniel Heinsius (1580-1655). Heinsius, himself a major classical scholar of the age, also wrote a study of the language and meaning of the New Testament in the light of his study of patristic exegesis. Henry Airay (d. 1616), provost of Queens College, Oxford, lectured through Philippians; his commentary was published posthumously (1618). His contemporary, William Attersoll, commented on Numbers (1618) and Philemon (1612) and wrote a treatise on the conversion of Nineveh (1632). The London minister Thomas Taylor (d.

1632) commented on Philemon (1659). The Scottish covenant theologian Robert Rollock wrote notable commentaries on the Gospel of John (1599) and Galatians (1602); and Conrad Vorstius (d. 1629), a professor at the academy of Steinfurt, renowned in his day for his questioning of the doctrine of divine simplicity, wrote a *Commentary on all the Apostolic Epistles, Excepting 2 Timothy, Titus, Philemon, and Hebrews* (1631). The theological and homiletical commentary was represented by John Cameron's (d. 1625) three volumes of loci on the New Testament (1626-28).

Among the major Lutheran exegetical productions of the era are the commentaries of Nicolas Selneccer (1530-1592) on the Psalter (2 vols., 1564), Acts (1567), the Pauline epistles (1595) and Revelation (1567); David Chytraeus (d. 1600) on Matthew (1594), the Gospel of John (1588) and Galatians (1567). Chytraeus both carried forward the Melanchthonian emphasis on loci and mirrored the older tradition by identifying his topical comments as scholia. Aegidius Hunnius (1550-1603) wrote commentaries on Genesis (1589), the Evangelists, Acts, the epistles and Revelation. Hunnius's views on the trinitarian and christological content of Old Testament exegesis led to his famous polemic against Calvin, *Calvinus Judaisans*. The Danish Lutheran theologian Nicholas Hemmingsen (1513-1600), professor in Copenhagen, remembered for his soteriological synergism, commented on the Gospel of John (1591). Joachim Camerarius (1500-1574), professor of Greek at Leipzig, analyzed on the four Evangelists and the Pauline epistles (1572) in a philological commentary emphasizing the figures of speech found in the text. Another controversial Lutheran figure of the day, Georg Calixt (1586-1656), the syncretistic professor of theology at Helmstedt, followed out the Melanchthonian approach to the text in a harmony of the Gospels in which he worked through the difficult theological loci (1624).

A majority of the dogmatic theologians of the era were also accomplished exegetes. Thus the Reformed scholastic Amandus Polanus (1561-1610) began his career as a professor of Old Testament and was noted as a commentator on Malachi (1597), Daniel (1599), Hosea (1601) and Ezekiel (1608) and as translator of the Old Testament before he gained renown as author of the dogmatic *Syntagma Theologiae*. On the Lutheran side, the Melanchthonian synergist of Wittenberg, Victorin Strigel (d. 1569), wrote annotations on the entire New Testament (1565), and Johannes Tarnovius (d. 1629), professor at Rostock, wrote four books of loci on difficult texts throughout Scripture (1619) and a commentary on the Minor Prophets. Like other Lutheran exegetes of his day, he emphasized a christological reading of the Old Testament. Polycarp Leyser (1552-1610), the editor of Chemnitz's posthumous *Loci Theologici*, produced commentaries on Genesis (1604) and Galatians (1586). The great dogmatician Johann Gerhard (1582-1637) completed Chemnitz's commentary on the harmony of the Evangelists (3 vols., 1626-1627), commented on Genesis (1637), Amos and Jonah (1663) and Hebrews (1661), wrote annotations on Matthew (1663) and Revelation (1643), and wrote a significant study of theological method (1620) in which he emphasized the study of Scripture as the basis for all other theological efforts. His exegesis manifest an interest in the interpretive use of ancient versions, notably the targums and the Septuagint.

The English homiletical commentary was notably represented in this era by Thomas Cartwright (1535-1603) on the harmony of the Gospels and Colossians (1612), William *Perkins (1558-1602) on Hebrews 11, and Nicholas Byfield (1579-1622) on Colossians (1615) and 1 Peter (1637). All three commentators are notable for their practical emphasis and, in the cases of Cartwright and Perkins, were recognized by Reformed contemporaries on the Continent as significant theological commentators. Of considerable importance for the development of millennial theology are the analysis (1627) and commentary (1632) on Revelation by Joseph Mede (1586-1638), fellow of Christ College, Cambridge.

Among the more technical commentaries of the early seventeenth century, the works of Andrew Willet (1562-1621), fellow of Christ College, Oxford, offer evidence of the breadth of the method and scope of the older commentary. His *Hexapla* on Genesis (1605), Exodus (1608), Leviticus (1631), Daniel (1610) and Romans (1620) attempt to offer, as it were, full coverage of all issues confronting commentators of the day. The term *hexapla* refers not to the text but to the sixfold pattern of comment on each chapter: Willet offers an rhetorical analysis of each chapter, verse-by-verse technical discussion of the text and translations, exegetical analysis of difficulties in interpretation, a discussion of theological topics related to the text, a resolution of theological debates, and a final section of practical application. Willet thus not only summarizes the state of discussion of the texts on which he comments but also presents a synopsis of the various styles or genres of Protestant commentary in his day. Willet also commented in briefer form on Jude (1602).

An example of the marriage of technical annotation to more practical interests is seen in the work of Henry Ainsworth (1560-1623), whose *Annotations on the Psalms* provided an independent translation of the Psalter, a metrical version with musical settings, and a fairly technical series of comments on text and translation in which Ainsworth drew explicitly on ancient sources, notably the targums, in order to elucidate the text. Ainsworth continued his work with a series of annotations on the Pentateuch in which he continued to emphasize use of the targums. Throughout these works Ainsworth attempted to echo Hebrew syntax and even to create compound words, such as "earthy-man" and "mighty-man" to render *adam* and *geber* with reference to their connotation. Ainsworth's sense of the hermeneutical importance of the targums was echoed by Weemes and developed by Christopher Cartwright in his targumico-rabbinic commentaries on Genesis (1648) and Exodus (1658). A similar interest in rabbinics characterizes the work of Constantijn L'Empereur (1591-1648), professor of Hebrew and theology at Leiden.

Despite the intense doctrinal polemics, mutual respect between Protestant and Roman Catholic exegetes can be detected even in the era of orthodoxy. Among the major Roman Catholic exegetes were Alfonso Salmeron (1515-1585), whose massive homiletical commentary on the New Testament (16 vols., 1598-1601) cultivated a popular style and also defended the teachings of Trent, and Johannes Maldonatus, (1534-1583) known for his commentaries on the four Gospels (2 vols., 1596-1597) and on the Major Prophets (1609). Vast Hebraic learning coupled with a strong interest in rabbinic exegesis was characteristic of the work of Genebrardus, a Benedictine who wrote a treatise on the pronunciation of unpointed Hebrew (1563), a commentary on Joel that included the targum text and rabbinic exegesis (1563), a response to Beza's paraphrase of the Song of Songs (1585), a commentary on the Psalter (1577), and numerous treatises on philological matters. Also among the major Hebraists of the Age was Arias Montanus, who supervised the production of the Antwerp Polyglot (1571-1580), wrote the annotations on the Evangelists for the polyglott, and produced a significant treatise on Jewish antiquities (1593). François Lucas (d. 1619), dean of St. Omer, produced a two-volume commentary on the Evangelists (1606). Gulielmus Estius's (1542-1613) commentary on the Pauline epistles (1614-1613) offered both a masterful literal exegesis and an urbane response to Protestant interpretation of key texts. Juan de Mariana (1536-1604) adopted theological genre of the older exegesis in his *Scholia in Vetus et Novum Testamentum* (1613). Gaspar Sanchez (d. 1628), a Jesuit professor of Scripture at Alcala, published a commentary on Acts (1616). The Antwerp Jesuit Johannes Tirinus (d. 1636) wrote a two-volume commentary on the entire Bible (1645).

A vast theological commentary on the entire Bible, excepting only Job and Psalms, came from the pen of Cornelius à Lapide (1567-1637) between 1614 and 1645 (later editions of his works are augmented by commentaries on Job and Psalms by de Pineda and Bellarmine respectively). His work is notable for its grasp of patristic and medieval exegesis and its ability to sum up the tradition by offering not only literal but also allegorical, moral and anagogical meanings and by engaging more contemporary developments in the examination of the Hebrew and Greek texts. The Jesuit exegete Balthasar Corderius (d. 1650) translated the catena of Greek fathers on Matthew (1647) by Nicetas and published a similar catena on Luke (1628). His fellow Jesuit Giovanni Menochio (d. 1655) produced a three-volume commentary on the Bible emphasizing the literal sense of the text (1630) and an analysis of Acts (1634). Protestant exegetes of the seventeenth century were concerned to respond to Estius, and they often cited Maldonatus,

Arias Montanus and Sixtus Senensis with approval.

The era of high orthodoxy (c. 1640-1700) was also notably productive in the genre of commentary—so productive that discussion of its achievement must recognize a series of subgenres in the field of exegesis. First there was the running theological commentary on all of Scripture—Poole's *Annotations on the Holy Bible* (2 vols., 1683-1685), Calovius's *Biblia Illustrata*, the so-called Dutch and Westminster Commentaries—that received heavy use throughout the period as normative readings of the text for both laity and clergy. Second were numerous highly textual commentaries of a technical nature, in the tradition of Beza, notably Grotius's annotations on the Old Testament and New Testament and Poole's *Synopsis Criticorum* (5 vols., 1669-1674). Whereas Poole's work was highy revered among the Protestant orthodox, Grotius's annotations were used primarily by the Arminians and viewed with considerable suspicion by the orthodox. Third were technical theological commentaries on specific books, often produced first in the form of lectures, a form pioneered for the Reformed tradition by Calvin and carried forward in great detail by later Reformed theologians. Fourth were homiletical commentaries that carried the theological tradition to the pulpit and the pew.

Johannes Cocceius (1603-1669), who is remembered for his analysis of the covenantal history of the Bible, the *Summa Doctrinae de Foedere et Testamento Dei* (1648), was a linguist and philologist as well as a theologian. His works include a lexical study of Hebrew and Syriac and commentaries on Job, Psalms, Ecclesiastes, the Song of Songs, Jeremiah, Malachi, John, Romans, Galatians, Ephesians, Colossians, 1 Timothy and 2 Timothy, Titus, Hebrews, Jude and Revelation. Among the later Cocceians, Franz Burman (1628-1679) produced Dutch-language commentaries on the historical books of the Old Testament, and Campegius Vitringa (1659-1722) wrote on biblical chronology (1698) and geography (1723) and commented on Revelation (1705), Romans (posthumous 1729), the Song of Moses (posthumous 1734), the first four chapters of Zechariah (posthumous 1734) and Isaiah (2 vols., 1714-1720). Vitringa also wrote six volumes of critical-exegetical observations (1683-1708) and a posthumously published work on interpretive difficulties in 1 Corinthians. His importance as an exegete lay in his philological skills and his examination of historical and geographical background in the interpretation of texts. He stands in the tradition of seventeenth-century chronologists and chorographers, among whom Ussher and Lightfoot are also to be numbered.

Herman Witsius (1636-1708), a student of Gisbert Voetius (1589-1676) and sometime opponent of the Cocceians, wrote both an "economy of the covenants" from an orthodox perspective and a series of significant essays on textual and theological themes, primarily from the Old Testament. Johannes Suicerus, professor of Greek at Heidelberg, commented on Colossians (1699). Salomon Van

Til (d. 1713), professor at Leiden, wrote commentaries on Matthew (Dutch, 1683), Romans and Philippians (Dutch, 1721), and 1 Corinthians, Ephesians, Philippians and Colossians (Latin, 1726). The younger Francis Spanheim (d. 1707), professor of theology at Leiden, wrote three volumes of loci on disputed passages in the Gospels (1663-1685). Lambertus Bos (d. 1717), professor of Greek at Franecker, wrote two volumes of philological studies on the New Testament (1700, 1707), both of which are notable for their examination of non-Christian Greek literature for the sake of understanding the syntax and meaning of the New Testament. Their contemporary, the Arminian professor of theology at Amsterdam, Philip van Limborch (1633-1712), produced a commentary on Acts, Romans, and Hebrews (1711).

Among the Lutheran efforts of the late seventeenth century, Abraham Calovius's *Biblia Illustrata* stands out as a most influential example of the running commentary on the entire text of the Bible. It functioned both as a somewhat polemical textual response to Grotius's *Annotationes* and as a highly respected devotional Bible, treasured well into the next century by J. S. Bach, among others. Calovius also commented on Genesis. His opponent in the synergistic controversy, Georg Calixt (1586-1656), also wrote widely on both the Old Testament and New Testament. The vast posthumous biblical commentary of the Finnish Lutheran bishops, Johannes Gezelius Sr. (1615-1690) and Johannes Gezelius Jr. (1647-1718), published in 1711 to 1713 (New Testament) and 1724 to 1728 (Old Testament), also deserves mention as a pastoral and homiletical effort, despite the vehement anti-Pietist sentiments of both its authors.

Perhaps the greatest Lutheran commentator of the century, Sebastian Schmidt (1617-1696) is remembered for his *Collegium Biblicum* (1671), in which he attempted to gather significant theological loci from his efforts as a commentator and thereby make the transition between exegesis and dogmatics. Schmidt commented extensively on the text of Scripture: annotations on Genesis, Joshua 1—8, Ruth and 1 Kings and 2 Kings (1692); paraphrases of the prophetic Psalms, Titus and Jude; commentaries on Judges (1684), Ruth (1696), 1 Samuel and 2 Samuel (1687-1689), Job (1680), Ecclesiastes (1691), Isaiah (1693), Jeremiah (1685), Hosea (1687), the Gospel of John (1685), Romans 1—6, 1 Corinthians (1691), Galatians (1690), Ephesians (1684), Colossians (1691), 1 Thessalonians and 2 Thessalonians (1691), Philemon (1691), 1 Timothy (1691), Hebrews (1680) and 1 John (1687), with an emphasis on philological problems. He also translated the entire Bible into Latin (1696) in a rigorous word-equivalent version. His exegesis stressed the grammatical sense of the text but also evidenced profound interest in the work of the Fathers, notably *Jerome (c. 340-420), and of rabbinic exegetes like David Kimchi, Aben Ezra and Salomon ben Melekh. Like other exegetes of the age, Schmid stressed the use of ancient versions like the targums and the Septuagint.

Balthasar Stollberg (1640-1684), professor of Greek at Wittenberg, commented on Galatians (1667) and entered the fray of philological debate over the text of the New Testament in a treatise arguing against barbarisms or solecisms in the Greek. Michael Walther (1593-1662), professor of theology at Helmstedt, commented on Hebrews (1646), argued the theological harmony of the Old Testament and New Testament (1649), and wrote a homiletical commentary on select Psalms (1647) and a treatise on the tetragrammaton (1660). Johannes Kromayer (1610-1670), remembered primarily as a dogmatician, wrote on the importance of Arabic for the interpretation of Hebrew and produced commentaries on Galatians (1670) and Revelation (1662). Augustus Varen (d. 1684), professor of theology at Rostock, commented on the epistle to the Romans (1696).

Theologians of the so-called Dutch Second Reformation, a movement of piety and theology that drew on both the orthodox and federal schools, were also prolific commentators—and like the Lutheran Pietists, they were profoundly interested in biblical philology. Theodorus Akersloot (1645-1721) wrote a Dutch commentary on 1 Corinthians (1706). Hieronymus van Alphen (1665-1742) commented on Galatians (1695), Hebrews (1699), Colossians (1706), 1 Corinthians and 2 Corinthians (1708), 1 Peter (1734), select psalms (1745), 1 Thessalonians (1741) and Galatians (1742). His commentary on 1 Peter is significant in its attempt to explain the Petrine theology in terms of a detailed harmony of themes from the Pentateuch, Psalms and Prophets. A similar hermeneutical interest was evident in van Alphen's dissertation of the relationship between Moses and Christ (1715). Abraham Hellenbroeck (1658-1731), whose work is notable for its combination of philological, theological and devotional interests, commented on the Song of Songs (1718-1720) and Isaiah (1718-1721).

Although the focus of this essay is on the two traditions of the magisterial Reformation, no examination of seventeenth-century exegesis can omit mention of the commentaries by Johann Crell (d. 1633), a teacher in Cracow; Jonas Schlichting (d. 1664) and Johann Wolzogen (d. 1661), located in the Socinian *Bibliotheca Fratrum Polonorum* (1656). Crell wrote a critical commentary on the entire New Testament (posthumous 1656), and Wolzogen commented on the four Evangelists (posthumous 1668) and Acts. Schlichting completed Crell's commentary on Hebrews (1634). The Socinian exegetes were masters of New Testament philology and pressed hard on the question of textual variants such as the Johannine Comma and 1 Timothy 3:16.

The erudition of the precritical exegete, however, was generally directed toward text-critical, philological or theological ends. Thus Thomas Adams's (fl. 1614-1653) massive commentary on 2 Peter (1633) illustrates the closely argued homiletical-doctrinal commentary of the age. It begins and concludes the exposition of each chapter with summaries of contents and analyses of argument or scope and proceeds to a detailed examination of each verse, beginning with an identification of the topic of the verse in its several parts, followed by an exposition of each part, statements of problems, objections and observations—the latter usually of a hortatory nature. The hermeneutic employed by Adams rests on the analogy of Scripture and the use of juxtaposed texts as a basis for drawing doctrinal conclusions. A similar erudition both in the biblical languages and in the use of classical allusions is found throughout John Trapp's (1601-1669) five-volume commentary on the Old and New Testaments (1654-1662)—Trapp's eloquence, grasp of the text and often pithy style have identified him as one of the best of the Puritan commentators. Noteworthy too from this era is the *Annotations upon all the Books of the Old and New Testament, wherein the Text is Explained, Doubts Resolved, Scriptures Parallelled, and Various Readings observed,* by the Joynt-Labour of certain Learned Divines (1645), often called the *Westminster Annotations* because of the significant number of commentators enlisted for the project from the Westminster Assembly.

Edward Leigh (1602-1671), remembered primarily for his massive *System or Body of Divinity* (1654), evidenced strong philological interests in his *Annotations upon the New Testament* (1650) and his volume of *Critica Sacra* (1639). William Gouge (d. 1653) produced a homiletical commentary on Hebrews (2 vols., 1655). Thomas Gataker's (1574-1654) expositions of Isaiah, Jeremiah and Lamentations (1645) are found in the so-called *Westminster Annotations*. A volume of Gataker's critical works, including his essays on the tetragrammaton and the style of New Testament Greek, was published at Utrecht in 1698. In the latter he disputed a German philologist, Pfochenius, who had argued that Hebrew, Greek, Latin and German were original tongues not derived from earlier languages. Gataker argued against the easy identification of such languages, definitively denied such status to Latin on the basis of cognates to Greek and other ancient languages, and demonstrated that New Testament Greek was not only different from classical Greek but also contained numerous Hebraisms and Syriasms.

Several English commentators of the late seventeenth century should be noted as archtypical of the era. William Greenhill's (1581-1671) exposition of Ezekiel (5 vols., 1645-1667) illustrates the erudition of the seventeenth-century commentator in its consistent reference to the Hebrew text and its consultation of the Syriac, the Vulgate and the Septuagint, as well as its frequent citation of the views of Protestant translators and commentators (Calvin, Beza, Oecolampadius, Polanus, Junius, Castellio, Rivetus, Ainsworth, Diodati, Lavater, Weemes, Buxtorf, Grotius), rabbis (Rashi, David Kimchi), church fathers (*Tertullian, Cyprian, Lactantius, Leo, Jerome, *Theodoret of Cyrus, Gregory the Great) and eminent Roman Catholic scholars (Thomas Aquinas, Arias Montanus, à Lapide, Mariana, Maldonatus, Vatable), in arguing the meaning of words and phrases.

Similar erudition coupled with interest in the scope and structure of the text and its theological content is evident in Jeremiah Burrows's (1599-1646) exposition of Hosea (4 vols., 1643-1651). John Owen's (1616-1683) single commentary, a massive exposition of the epistle to the Hebrews (4 vols., 1668-1684), is a synthesis of the textual, philological style of the seventeenth century, with an interest in the interpretive use of Judaica and with a highly technical theological apparatus that evidences significant ties to the federal school and strong interest as well in the cultural background of temple ritual in both Old Testament and New Testament eras. Similar interest in the cultural life of ancient peoples as background for exegesis and theology is evident as well in Owen's *Theologoumena Pantodapa* (1661), or introduction to the history and character of theology.

The textual emphasis of Beza, the Buxtorfs and Cappel continued through the era of orthodoxy in the production of such tools as the London Polyglot Bible, the multivolume *Critica Sacra,* edited by John Pearson (1613-1686), and Matthew Poole's *Synopsis Criticorum*—paralleled among the Lutherans by the work of Sebastian Schmidt. John Mayer's (1583-1664) seven volumes of comment on the whole Bible—Pentateuch (1653), historical books (1647), Job, Psalms, Proverbs, Ecclesiastes and the Song of Songs (1653), the Prophets (1652), the Evangelists and Acts (1631), the Pauline epistles (1631), the Catholic Epistles and Revelation (1627)—are children of Melanchthon's locus method with strong philological overtones. Mayer avoids running commentary and examines only textual and theological problems. A similar technique is found in the work of Samuel Clarke (d. 1701), not to be confused with the orientalist of the same name who contributed to the London Polyglott. Clarke's paraphrase and annotations on the Bible (1690) attend primarily to the difficult passages.

Among the homiletical commentaries of the era, those of the English Puritans are most eminent. Thomas Manton (1620-1677) published a two-volume commentary on Psalm 119, as well as single volumes on James and Jude and the Lord's Prayer. The prolific David Dickson (1583-1662) commented on Hebrews (1631), Matthew (1651), the Psalter (1656) and the epistles (1645/59), all in a largely homiletical vein. Richard Baxter (1615-1691), noted for his works on practical piety, also published a paraphrase of the New Testament with annotations (1685). George Hutcheson (1626-1674) commented on the Minor Prophets (1654), John (1657) and Job (1669) and wrote an exposition in forty-five sermons of Psalm 130 (posthumous 1691). His work on John is stylistically notable for its perpetuation of a model like that used in the sixteenth century by Zanchi, namely, the inclusion of a series of doctrinal loci at the end of his exposition of each pericope. Matthew *Henry's (1662-1714) commentary on the entire Bible evidences the pastoral strength of the older exegesis in its ability to preach with relevance to the congregation on virtually every text of the Bible. This was accomplished in Henry's case through a consistent christological and covenantal interest throughout the Old Testament. The tenacity of the older or precritical exegesis is seen in John Gill's (1697-1771) massive commentary on the entire Bible. Here the traditional theological exegesis is supported by a continuation of the seventeenth-century emphasis on Judaica.

In sum, the Protestant exegetical tradition of the sixteenth and seventeenth centuries evidences a fairly continuous and highly variegated development. In theological content and in their use of textual, philological, homiletical and dogmatic styles, the commentaries of the seventeenth-century exegetes follow the models and the substance of their sixteenth-century predecessors. Notable developments in approach include the increasing Protestant interest in Judaica and in so-called oriental languages, namely, the cognate languages of the ancient Near East plus Ethiopic and Persian. Immersion in textual and philological study was characteristic of the era of orthodoxy. It also produced, in such authors as Cappel, Grotius and Simon, the first stirrings of what would become the historical-critical method.

BIBLIOGRAPHY

Biographical essays on most of the exegetes can be found in the *RPTK, NSHERK* and *DNB* (for Protestant exegetes) and *DTC, NCE* or *Biographie Universelle* (for Roman Catholic exegetes).

Studies. J.-R. Armogathe, ed., *Bible de tous les temps, 6: Le Grand Siècle de la Bible* (Paris: Beauchesne, 1989); I. D. Backus and F. M. Higman, *Théorie et pratique de l'exégèse: Actes du troisieme Colloque international sur l'histoire de l'exégèse biblique au XVIe siècle, Genève, 31 aôut-2 septembre 1988* (Geneva: Droz, 1990); G. Bedouelle and B. Roussel, eds., *Bible de tous le temps, 5: Le temps des Réformes et la Bible* (Paris: Beauchesne, 1989); J. H. Bentley, *Humanists and Holy Writ: New Testament Scholarship in the Renaissance* (Princeton, NJ: Princeton University Press, 1983); S. G. Burnett, "The Christian Hebraism of Johann Buxtorf (1564-1629)" (Ph.D. diss., University of Wisconsin, 1990); *CHB;* B. S. Childs, "The *Sensus Literalis* of Scripture: An Ancient and Modern Problem" in *Beiträge zur alttestamentlichen Theologie: Festshcrift für Walther Zimmerli zum 70. Geburtstag,* ed. H. Donner, R. Hanhart and R. Smend (Göttingen: Vandenhoeck & Ruprecht, 1977) 80-93; L. Diestel, *Geschichte des Alten Testamentes in der christlichen Kirche* (Jena: Mauke's Verlag, 1869); O. Fatio and P. Fraenkel, eds., *Histoire de l'exégèse an XVIe siècle: textes du colloqui international tenu á Genève en 1976* (Geneva: Droz, 1978); *The Geneva Bible (The Annotated New Testament, 1602 Edition),* ed. G. T. Sheppard with introductory essays by G. T. Sheppard, M. W. Anderson, J. H. Augustine, N. W. S. Cranfield (Pilgrim Classic Commentaries; New York: Pilgrim, 1989) vol. 1; F. Laplanche, *L'Écriture, le sacré et l'historie: Érudits politiques protestants devant la bible en France au XVIIe siècle* (Amsterdam and Maarssen: APA-Holland University Press/Lille: Presses Universitaires, 1986); E. Mangenot, "Correctoires de La Bible" in *Dictionnaire de la Bible,* 2, Pt. 1, cols. 1022-26; R. A. Muller, "The Debate Over the Vowel Points and the Crisis in Orthodox Hermeneutics" *JMRS* 10, 1 (1980) 53-72; idem, *Post-Reformation Reformed Dogmatics,* 2: *Holy Scripture: The Cognitive Foundation of Theology* (Grand Rapids: Baker, 1993); R. A. Muller and J. L. Thompson, eds., *Biblical Interpretation in the Era of the Reformation: Essays Presented to David C. Steinmetz* (Grand Rapids: Eerdmans, 1996); W. Perkins, *A Commentary on Galatians,* ed. G. T. Sheppard with introductory essays by B. S. Childs, G. T. Sheppard and J. H. Augustine (Pilgrim Classic Commentaries; New York: Pilgrim, 1989) vol. 2; idem, *A Commentary on Hebrews 11 (1609 Edition),* ed. J. H. Augustine with introductory essays by J. H. Augustine, D. K. McKim, G. T. Sheppard and R. A. Muller (Pilgrim Classic Commentaries; New York: Pilgrim, 1991) vol. 3; P. T. van Rooden, *Theology, Biblical Scholarship and Rabbinical Studies in the Seventeenth Century: Constantijn L'Empereur (1591-1648), Professor of Hebrew and Theology at Leiden* (Leiden: E. J. Brill, 1989); R. Stauffer, *Interprétes de la Bible: Études sur les réformateurs du XVIe siécle* (Paris: Beauchesne, 1980); D. C. Steinmetz, ed., *The*

Bible in the Sixteenth Century (Second International Colloquy on the History of Biblical Exegesis in the Sixteenth Century; Durham, NC: Duke University Press, 1990); idem, *Calvin in Context* (Oxford and New York: Oxford University Press, 1995); idem, "The Superiority of Pre-Critical Exegesis," *TTs* 37 (1980) 27-38 (repr. D. K. McKim, ed., *A Guide to Contemporary Hermeneutics* [Grand Rapids: Eerdmans, 1986] 65-77).

R. A. MULLER

Beza, Theodore *(1519-1605)*

John *Calvin's successor at Geneva, Théodore Beza (or de Bèze), played a vital role in the institutionalization of Reformed Protestantism on an international scale. In 1559, at Calvin's invitation, he became the first rector at the Geneva Academy, a position that he held until 1563. Following Calvin's death (1564), Beza was elected moderator of the powerful *Compagnie des Pasteurs*. Serving in that position until 1580, he helped shape and consolidate the Reformed tradition in Switzerland and beyond.

Beza took a special interest in the struggles of Reformed churches in his French homeland. In 1574, responding to the St. Bartholomew's Day massacre, he published *Du droit des Magistrats sur leurs sujets*, in which he revised his earlier position favoring passive civil disobedience and instead asserted the right of the people to take up arms, under the leadership of their elected magistrates, against any ruler who becomes a tyrant. Along with the *Vindiciae contra Tyrannos* (published in 1579 under the pseudonym Junius Brutus), Beza's tract became a locus classicus for the right of revolution in early modern political theory.

Beza was most influential, however, in his role as a theologian. Within his theological writings, materials bearing on the interpretation of Scripture occupy a central position. In addition to sermons and commentaries on Job, Ecclesiastes and the Song of Songs (not to mention his lectures on Romans and Hebrews), Beza made crucial contributions to establishing the Greek text from which Protestant Bibles in the vernacular were to be produced.

Translation and Textual Criticism. Embracing the Reformed vision in 1548, Beza, who had been trained as a humanist scholar at Bourges and Orléans under the tutelage of Melchior Wolmar, deployed his considerable linguistic and philological skills in the service of his new faith. Although his competence in Hebrew was somewhat limited, his mastery of Greek was without parallel. After serving as professor of Greek at the Lausanne Academy (1549-1558), he taught Greek and theology at the Academy of Geneva (1558-1599). In 1561 he completed a metrical version of the French Psalter that had been undertaken (1533-1543) by Clément Marot; within four years it had appeared in more than sixty editions. Complete with musical notations, the Marot-Beza Psalter became enormously influential in the French Reformed community; indeed, Beza's rendering of Psalm 68 became "the Huguenot battle song" (Sayce, CHB 3:121).

In 1556 Beza published an annotated Latin translation of the Greek New Testament, which appeared in numerous printings. In his *Annotationes* Beza implemented Desiderius *Erasmus's suggestions about critical and comparative approaches to variant textual readings. Although he was attacked for amending the text in support of his own dogmatic agenda, his textual instincts were quite conservative. (Reformed theological emphases do appear in his *Annotationes* and in his Latin translations, such as a Reformed doctrine of election in Beza's notes on *tous sōzōmenous* in Acts 2:47.) In 1565 Henri Estienne published Beza's celebrated edition of the Greek New Testament (including the Vulgate and Beza's annotated Latin translation), which established his reputation as the leading biblical critic of his generation. A later edition (1582) included the Codex Bezae Cantabrigiensis, a body of manuscripts dating from the fourth or fifth century, which are among the best specimens of the Western text of the four Gospels, the greater portion of Acts, and a fragment of 3 John. These manuscripts had been discovered by Beza (1562) at Lyons when the city fell to the Huguenots near the beginning of the wars of religion.

In addition to the Codex Bezae, Beza had before him the Codex Claromantanus, a sixth-century manuscript of the Pauline letters and Hebrews. Yet he made little use of these codices. Although the Codex Bezae was in his possession for nearly two decades (from 1562 until 1581, when he donated it to Cambridge University; Raitt, *OER* 1:150), Beza made little use of its variant readings, preferring to follow, with only slight emendations, Estienne's fourth edition and the Complutensian text.

Between 1565 and 1604 Beza was responsible for a total of nine printings of the Greek New Testament; a posthumous tenth edition was published in 1611. The effect of these editions was to standardize and popularize the Textus Receptus. Beza's work in textual criticism helped form the basis of the English Geneva Bible (1555-1560; revised under the leadership of Beza and the Hebraicist Corneille Bertram in 1588). The translators of the Authorized Version of 1611 consulted the Geneva Bible but relied especially on Beza's editions of 1588-1589 and 1598 (see B. M. Metzger, *A Textual Commentary on the Greek New Testament* [London: United Bible Societies, 1971], xxii. See the detailed account of Beza's place in the history of the English Bible in Backus 1980).

Exegesis, Homiletics and Polemics: Beza as Commentator and as Preacher. Scholars such as E. Bizer, J. Dantine and W. Kickel tended to portray Beza as a scholastic dogmatician par excellence, author of a rigidly deterministic metaphysical system (see Muller 1988, esp. chap. 4). Recent studies, however, have made it clear that this conventional wisdom involves a vast oversimplification that distorts the significance of Beza's career. Among his contemporaries, Beza's reputation rested primarily on his critical editions and the numerous printings of his *Annotationes,* which served as a landmark of Reformed exegesis well into the seventeenth century. It is important, therefore, to consider Beza's theological contributions not just in dogmatics

but also in exegesis and homiletics. (Raitt 1986 and Dukert show the piety in Beza's sermons is incompatible with viewing him as only a rigid metaphysician; cf. Delval and Bray, who show his sermons are not at all scholastic.)

By admitting that there are solecisms and barbarisms in the Greek text, Beza aroused the wrath of the Lutheran scholastics at Wittenberg. His cautious handling of the text, however, is seen throughout his commentaries and *Annotationes.* On the question of the authorship of the epistle to the Hebrews, for instance, he rejects Calvin's suggestion that Paul was not the author of the epistle to the Hebrews, along with his arguments against the Petrine authorship of 2 Peter (see Hagen, 91-96; Hall, 91). Such a position does not call into question the canonicity or apostolic authority of the texts, however. Indeed, Beza reveals a certain impatience with the question of human authorship, since the true author of Scripture is the Holy Spirit. (Beza wrote: *Sufficiat hoc nosse, vere esse dictatam a Spiritu sancto* ["Epistola Pauli ad Habraeos" (1556), f. 284[r]] as cited in Hagen, 92 n. 53.)

Such a high view of the origin of Scripture demands a careful, sober exegetical procedure. An arbitrary or fanciful treatment of the text, after all, amounts to an insult to its Author (see his dissatisfaction with exegetes who do not seek the truth of Scripture [*Annotationes,* 1589; 1.359 on Jn 5:39] as cited in Pelikan, 37). Beza approaches the text grammatically, philologically, historically. He insists that any biblical passage must be understood contextually, in terms of the internal structure of the larger setting in which it appears (cf. Beza's *Ratio Studii Theologici,* undated and unpublished in his own lifetime, for an expression of an exegetical method that is sensitive to the internal coherence of the text; Backus 1984). He is not given to flights of fancy. Although he follows tradition in treating the Song of Songs allegorically, even here historical and sociological context governs allegory. When the text speaks of "virgins" (Song 1:3), for instance, Beza hastens to rule out any use of this language as a basis for monastic celibacy, appealing instead to the sociological milieu from which the text emerged. This virginity, he argues, cannot be understood as something physical, since in Solomon's day celibacy was not regarded as a virtue; on the contrary, to leave one's children unmarried would have been viewed not as meritorious but as an act of negligence and injustice (Beza, *Canticles,* 54)!

The divine authorship of Scripture requires Beza to show harmony among all the canonical writings, lest the Holy Spirit seem guilty of self-contradiction. It also means that critical and expository work is never a matter of scholarship for its own sake; nor is it for the sake of satisfying human curiosity (see Perrottet, 91, 95). The point of exegetical work is to make it possible for believers to hear the truth of the Word of God.

Beza's exegesis is in service to a Reformed vision, which polishes the lenses through which he reads the text. An Augustinian/Calvinist perspective, for instance, finds expression in his treatment of soteriological issues posed by Song 1:2. The feminine party to the relationship, corresponding to the church, takes the initiative. Both literally and allegorically—culturally and theologically—Beza is troubled by the implications. He is quick to guard against a Pelagian use of the text; the virgin's apparent initiative, he insists, is no more than a response to an initiative already taken by her beloved. He writes: "we must take diligent heede how we thinke, that this desire of hers which opened the mouth, began from her. It is the Bridegrome which hath spoken first unto her & prepared her within to seeke and search after him" (Beza, *Canticles,* 15).

Similarly, a Reformed christology lies in the background of Beza's interpretation of the sense of longing expressed in the opening verses of the Song. He distinguishes two degrees in the special intimacy with Christ that is the theme of the Song. Here

and now—by faith in a promise, through the instrumentality of gospel and sacraments—the church experiences in a partial way her union with Christ; "the real and entire actual union," however, awaits the eschaton, since "the place of the true communion is not in earth but in heaven" (Beza, *Canticles,* 21).

At points Beza's exegesis takes on a sharply polemical tone; polemics are less evident in the 1565 *Annotationes,* however, than in his lectures at the Academy (Perrottet, 92). Exegesis and polemics come together in Beza's criticism of Castellio's tendency to sacrifice grammatical exactness for Ciceronian eloquence. In an excursus on Romans 9 (published in 1582 and based on his lectures from around 1580), Beza goes out of his way to deliver a devastating critique of the arguments by which Castellio's note on Romans 9 seeks to undermine the Reformed doctrine of election (see Fraenkel and Perrottet's introduction in Beza, *Cours sur les Épîtres aux Romans et aux Hébreux,* 7). Beza's lectures on Romans are often polemical, renewing ancient controversies over grace, free will and predestination: his sense of the centrality of Christ the mediator gives rise to a radically Augustinian exegesis of Romans.

Similarly, in Beza's thirtieth sermon on the Song (Song 3:11), the christocentrism of his soteriology motivates a thoroughgoing refutation of Roman notions concerning the merits of the saints and the treasury of the church: "And if the Saintes, as they call them, have hadde so manie and such plentie of *merites* that there is an infinite surplussage of them, what neede hadde they of those of Iesus Christ?" (Beza, *Canticles,* 408). In the thirty-first sermon he continues in the same vein. Commenting again on Song 3:11, Beza sees insults to Christ's glory not only in the practical expressions of unreformed piety (fasting, alms, paternosters, Ave Marias, pilgrimages, indulgences, requiems, holy water) but also in key theological underpinnings for the whole system of Roman Catholic devotion (including purgatory and limbus, along with the pivotal distinctions between mortal and venial sins and between guilt and penalty; Beza, *Canticles,* 421-23).

No less sharp than his exegetical polemic against those who are outside the Reformed community is Beza's indictment of the moral failings and tepid spirituality of his own flock in Geneva. Commenting on Song 1:3 ("Drawe me: we wil runne after thee"), Beza observes that it is mockery of God to say "Draw me" while at the same time neglecting the preaching of the Word, which is the means by which God is at work to draw us to himself (Beza, *Canticles,* 60). The promise to run after the beloved excludes all forms of spiritual negligence or half-heartedness; Beza, however, paints a sharp contrast between such spiritual intensity and the nominal religiosity of those to whom his sermons are addressed. Allegorically the "daughters of Jerusalem" (Song 1:5) are "those who are in such sort in the Church, that notwithstanding they care not greatly for it" (Beza, *Canticles,* 75). Beza senses that all too many in the church at Geneva fall into that category: "I dare not say that there are found any runners amongst us, but too many idle, too many deaffe, too many lame, too many cold, yea too many which draw back. I speak it to my great regret and grief" (Beza, *Canticles,* 62).

It would be a serious misreading of Beza's exegesis, however, to find the pastoral interests of his commentary only in such tones of rebuke and reproach. A warmly pastoral sensitivity is evident in his wrestling with the dilemmas posed by the sufferings of the pilgrim church (Beza, *Canticles,* 76-83 and passim). What Beza seeks to arouse in those who take his expository work seriously is a fervent, wholehearted spirituality that draws near to Christ "with a most full and lively affection of a most assured faith, and with so ardent a zeale and desire, as none can be greater" (Beza, *Canticles,* 23).

Scripture and Tragedy. While he was still a professor of Greek at Lausanne, Beza composed what is sometimes regarded as

the first tragedy written in French, *Abraham sacrifiant* (1550). Some have judged the work as merely didactic, with little literary merit (Greenslade, *CHB,* 3:497). Beza himself was keenly aware of its defects. Yet the play enjoyed considerable success; it was translated into Latin, Italian, German, Spanish and English, appearing in eleven editions between 1550 and 1598 (see Pelikan, 172).

In this work Beza makes no effort to conceal his doctrinal agenda. The title page includes as its epigraph the French text of Romans 4:3: *"Abraham a creu à Dieu, il luy a esté reputé a iustice."* But far more is at stake here than justification by faith. Beza finds in the story of Abraham and Isaac an occasion for articulating a voluntarist value theory that presupposes what D. K. Shuger terms "the radical heteronomy of the divine will" (Shuger, 161). Abraham responds to God's bizarre imperative by offering his unquestioning obedience to the inscrutable will of an incomprehensible God. (A. Golding's 1577 translation has Abraham saying to God, "For sith it is thy will, it is good right/It should be doone. Wherefore I will obey." See Shuger, 161.) In exile himself, sharing the life of a community that is subject to all the precariousness of exilic existence, Beza identifies with Abraham's anguish. He finds in Abraham's implicit obedience a compellingly relevant paradigm for those who are living out their faith under the conditions of the Reformed diaspora. Here again a deeply pastoral instinct shapes his appropriation of the sacred text.

Significance. In both textual criticism and biblical exegesis, Theodore Beza set the standard for Reformed scholarship in the sixteenth century. His dogmatic commitments are evident at various points in his use of Scripture; his exposition of the text is sometimes structured by polemical necessities. Yet pastoral and spiritual concerns permeate his exegesis in ways that can hardly be reconciled with the older view of Beza as little more than a Calvinist dogmatician. I. McPhee, among others, rightly notes that a shared involvement in the dynamics of French humanism provided a basis for continuity between Beza's vision and Calvin's (McPhee, 92; Beza's theological continuity with yet intellectual independence from his mentor Calvin's exegesis is indicated in Muller 1993, 139-70). It is hardly surprising, then, that Beza's exegesis bears witness to a religious sensitivity that is fully worthy of Calvin's legacy.

BIBLIOGRAPHY

Works. T. Beza, *Abraham sacrifiant* (Geneva, 1550; ET *A Tragedie of Abraham's Sacrifice* [London, 1577]); idem, *Canticum Canticorum Latinis Versibus Expressum* (Geneva, 1584); idem, *Cours sur les Épîtres aux Romans et aux Hébreux, 1564-66,* ed. P. Fraenkel and L. Perrottet (Geneva: Librairie Droz, 1988); idem, *Ecclesiastes Salomonis Paraphrasi Illustratus (Geneva, 1588); Eternal Predestination and Its Execution in Time: Beza's Tabula Praedestinationis (1555)* (Texts and Studies in Reformation and Post-Reformation Protestant Thought 6; Grand Rapids: Baker, 1997); idem, *Jesu Christi Domini Nostri Novum Testamentum Sive Novum Foedus Cujus Graeco Textui Respondent Interpretationes Duae, Una Vetus, Altera Nova Theodori Bezae Diligenter ab Eo Recognita* (Geneva, 1565); idem, *Jobus Commentario et Paraphrasi Illustratus* (Geneva, 1583); idem, *Lex Dei Moralis, Ceremonalis et Politica ex Libris Mosis Excerpta et in Certas Classes Distributa* (Basle, 1577); idem, *Master Bezae's Sermons upon the Three First Chapters of the Canticle of Canticles* (Oxford, 1587); idem, *Methodica Apostolicarum Epistolarum Brevis Explicatio* (Geneva, 1565); idem, *Psaumes mis en vers français* (Geneva: Droz, 1984); idem, *Ratio studii Theologicii* (n.d.).

Studies. M. W. Anderson, "Theodore Beza: Savant or Scholastic," *TZ* 43, 4 (1987) 330-32; I. D. Backus, *The Reformed Roots of the English New Testament: The Influence of Theodore Beza on the English New Testament* (Pittsburgh: Pickwick, 1980); idem, "Some Remarks on Robert Rollock's Illogical Analysis' of Hebrews 9," *JMRS* 14, 1 (1984) 113-19; E. Bizer, *Frühorthodoxie und Rationalismus* (Zurich: EVZ-Verlag, 1963); J. S. Bray, *Theodore Beza's Doctrine of Predestination* (Nieuwkoop: de Graaf, 1975); H. Clavier, *Théodore de Bèze: un aperçu de sa vie aventureuse, de ses traveaux, de sa personalité* (Cahors: A. Coueslant, 1960); J. Dantine, "Das christologische Problem in Rahmen der Prädestinationslehre von Theodor Beza," *ZK* 77 (1966) 81-96; M. Delval, "La prédication d'un réformateur au XVIᵉ siècle: l'activité homilétique de Théodore de Bèze" *MSR* 41 (1984) 61-86; A. Duckert, *Théodore de Bèze: Prédicateur* (Geneva: Romet, 1891); F. Gardy and A. Dufour, eds., *Bibliographie des oeuvres théologiques, littéraires, historiques et juridiques de Théodore de Bèze* (Geneva: E. Droz, 1960); P. F. Geizendorf, *Théodore de Bèze* (Geneva: Labor et fides, 1949); K. Hagen, *Hebrews Commenting from Erasmus to Beza, 1516-1598* (BGBE 23; Tübingen: J. C. B. Mohr, 1981); B. Hall, "Biblical Scholarship: Editions and Commentaries" in *CHB* 3:38-93; W. Kickel, *Vernunft und Offenbarung bei Theodor Beza* (Neukirchen: Neukirchener Verlag, 1967); R. Letham, "Theodore Beza: A Reassessment," *SJT* 40 (1987) 25-40; I. McPhee, "Beza, Theodore," *NDT* 91-92; T. Maruyama, *The Ecclesiology of Theodore Beza: The Reformation of the True Church* (Geneva: Droz, 1978); R. A. Muller, "Calvin, Beza, and the Exegetical History of Romans 13:1-7" in *Calvin and the State,* ed. P. de Klerk (Grand Rapids: n.p., 1993); idem, *Christ and the Decree* (Grand Rapids: Baker, 1988 [1986]); J. Pelikan, *The Reformation of the Bible—The Bible of the Reformation* (New Haven, CT: Yale University Press, 1996); L. Perrottet, "Chapter 9 of the Epistle to the Hebrews as Presented in an Unpublished Course of Lectures by Theodore Beza" *JMRS* 14, 1 (1984) 89-96; J. Raitt, "Beza, Guide for the Faithful Life," *SJT* 39, 1 (1986) 83-107; idem, *The Eucharistic Theology of Theodore Beza: Development of the Reformed Doctrine* (Chambersburg, PA: AAR, 1972); idem, "Theodore Beza" in *Shapers of Religious Tradition in Germany, Switzerland and Poland,* ed. J. Raitt (New Haven, CT: Yale University Press, 1981) 89-103; idem, "Théodore de Bèze," *OER* 1:149-51; D. K. Shuger *The Renaissance Bible: Scholarship, Sacrifice, and Subjectivity* (Berkeley, CA: University of California Press, 1994); D. C. Steinmetz, "Theodore Beza" in *Reformers in the Wings* (Philadelphia: Fortress, 1971) 162-71.   J. L. Farthing

Bucer, Martin *(1491-1551)*

A native of Sélestat in Alsace, Martin Bucer (Butzer) was educated at its famous grammar school and entered the Dominican order. Soon he encountered works of Desiderius *Erasmus, including the *Novum Instrumentum,* Erasmus's fresh Latin translation of the New Testament together with a Greek text to justify its divergence from the official Vulgate version. After being transferred to the Dominicans' house in Heidelberg, Bucer was present at Martin *Luther's disputation with fellow Augustinians in the city (1518). The ardent Erasmian now became also a Martinian, taking special delight in Luther's commentary on Galatians. Bucer's commitment to reform of theology and church was soon sealed. Early in 1521 he left the Heidelberg Dominicans, and at the end of April he was released from his monastic vows. In the summer of 1522, in the midst of much traveling and a series of short-lived engagements as chaplain and pastor, he married Elisabeth Silbereisen, a former nun. Forced to flee after preaching for six months at Wissembourg, he arrived at Strasbourg in mid-May 1523. Within three weeks he had secured the city council's permission to expound John's Gospel, but only in Latin. By mid-August he was preaching in the cathedral. Before long he had become the chief animating spirit of the Reformation of Strasbourg and then developed into a significant player on the wider stage of religious reform in Germany and beyond.

After a quarter of a century Bucer was expelled from Strasbourg (April 1549) for his unrelenting opposition to the Augsburg Interim, the settlement imposed by Emperor Charles V after defeating the Protestants in the Schmalkaldic War. The settlement, in Bucer's view, made only marginal concessions to the Protestants. In preference to other invitations, Bucer chose exile in the England of King Edward VI and Archbishop Thomas Cranmer. He spent the last two years of his life as Regius Professor of Divinity at Cambridge. There he contributed to the revision of the *Book of Common Prayer* (1552), produced for the young king a remarkably comprehensive blueprint for reform of church and society entitled *The Kingdom of Christ,* influenced some of the present and future leaders of the English church, especially John Bradford, Matthew Parker and Edmund Grin-

dal, and by his lectures on Ephesians stimulated a renewal of biblical exegesis in England.

Bucer's multifaceted achievements while based in Strasbourg are not easily summarized. The city had become a haven for the dissenting radicals of the reform movements, whose disorderliness provoked the pastors led by Bucer into constitutional definition of the church's doctrine and polity at synods in 1533 to 1534. Bucer emphasized discipline as a mark of the church (alongside service of the Word and the sacraments) and developed evangelical confirmation. From the later 1520s the goal of Protestant agreement on the Lord's Supper consumed his energies, with some success in the Wittenberg Concord (1536). His ecumenical zeal extended to Protestant-Catholic rapprochement in Germany, and he was a major participant in the series of colloquies that climaxed at Regensburg in 1541. John *Calvin, who accompanied Bucer from Strasbourg on this occasion, was not alone in judging his flexibility and verbal dexterity in quest of agreed statements dangerously unprincipled. Nevertheless, during his years of exile from Geneva spent at Strasbourg (1538-1541), Calvin observed and assimilated so much in so many different fields that he may with justice be termed a Buceran. Through Calvin and Geneva, Bucer left his formative mark on several salient features of the distinctively Reformed pattern of Protestantism.

No Buceran church or Buceran tradition emerged to perpetuate the memory of his services to the Reformation and in particular to ensure the availability of his writings in accessible editions. As a consequence Bucer's stature as a scholarly interpreter of the Bible remains largely unrecognized. Yet fulsome tribute to the merits of his work was paid by Calvin himself, whose own corpus of biblical commentaries continues to enjoy widespread use. In the preface to his commentary on Psalms (1557), Calvin explained that until a few years earlier he had held back from expounding the

Psalms "because that most faithful teacher of the church of God, Martin Bucer, had labored in this field with such outstanding learning, diligence and fidelity that, as a result, there was certainly not so much need for my efforts." Some two decades earlier, in the dedicatory epistle to his first published commentary, on Romans (1540), Calvin discussed the qualities of Bucer's commentaries at greater length:

Bucer has spoken the last word, as it were, by his published expositions. As you know, in addition to his profound learning, abundant knowledge of many subjects, sharpness of intellect, wide reading and many other diverse strengths, in which he is surpassed today by hardly anyone and matched by few and excels most, this scholar enjoys the special credit of devoting himself to the interpretation of Scripture with more dedicated exactitude than anyone in our time.

Yet there is a place, Calvin argues, for his own distinctive kind of commentary alongside the works of such as Bucer. For Bucer is

too verbose to be read quickly by people preoccupied with other responsibilities, and too sublime to be capable of being easily understood by unpretentious readers lacking concentration. For whatever the subject-matter he sets himself to expound, so many things are suggested to his pen by the incredible fertility of his powerful mind that he does not know how to stop writing.

With the exception of his commentary on John, published in a remarkable scholarly edition by I. D. Backus of Geneva in the Latin series (*Opera Latina* 2) of his collected works (1988), Bucer's commentaries can still be read only in their sixteenth-century editions. Although editions of the Psalms (by R. G. Hobbs of Vancouver) and Romans (by B. Roussel of Paris) should follow before long, translations will be needed to open up access for most modern readers. Any assessment, therefore, of Bucer as a biblical interpreter

can be only provisional until scholars with varying expertise are able to benefit from critical editions and translations.

Commentaries. Although throughout his other writings of diverse kinds Bucer dealt with Scripture extensively, pride of place in this article must go to his own commentaries on biblical books: on Matthew, Mark and Luke (1527; Stupperich no. 14; on Matthew, with a treatment of the other two Synoptics' divergent and additional contents); on John's Gospel (1528; Stupperich no. 20); on the four Gospels together, in a revised edition (1530; Stupperich no. 28), and in a further revision of 1536 (Stupperich no. 28a; Backus's edition of the commentary on John covers 1528, 1530 and 1536); on Ephesians (1527; Stupperich no. 17), and lectures on the same letter of Paul given in Cambridge (1550-1551) and published posthumously unrevised in 1562 (Stupperich no. 112); on Zephaniah (1528; Stupperich no. 22); on the Psalms (1529; Stupperich no. 25), partly revised and enlarged in 1532 (Stupperich no. 25b); on Paul's epistle to the Romans, projected as the first of a treatment of all his letters (1536; Stupperich no. 55); on Judges, probably composed in 1544 and somewhat selective in coverage (1554; Stupperich no. 101); and finally annotations on Matthew 1—8, done at Croydon in 1549, while Bucer was Cranmer's guest, and with contributions by Cranmer also (first edited by H. Vogt in 1972). Of this corpus, the most important are inevitably the works on Gospels, Romans and the Psalter.

Biblical Interpretation. Bucer wrote no treatise on interpreting the Bible, though he apparently envisaged it more than once. The memorandum he wrote for a friend in 1531, entitled *Instruction on How the Holy Scriptures Should Be Handled in Preaching*, is disappointing. After a discussion of the choice and sequence of the books of Scripture to be expounded, he comes to methods. After warning against exposing the discrepancies between the Gospels to an unlearned audience, Bucer scornfully rejects resort to allegorism: "For my part, although this abuse is ancient and although today it is enjoyed by learned and well-established people quite extravagantly, I have no doubt that it is the most blatant insult to the Holy Spirit and the cunning infliction of Satan to lure us away from the true and efficacious teachings and examples of Christ in the direction of fruitless human inventions" (Scherding and Wendel, 56). Since the Gospels were written for the common people and not for intellectuals, they should be interpreted as simply as possible. The primary factor, whether in a passage or a whole book, is to have regard to its aim or intention *(scopus);* the *scopus* of the Gospels is "so to explain the birth, life and teaching of Christ that believing in him we may have eternal life" (Scherding and Wendel, 58). This must shape any exposition to be given from the Gospels.

Having begun his guidance by stressing that God has endowed human beings with reason, Bucer now commends the value of dialectic (and Rudolph Agricola's work on it) in expounding Scripture, first with reference to the author. Since the author of a Gospel is an Evangelist and above all else proclaims Christ, the preacher must remember that the Lord everywhere wished to teach his hearers to believe in him as Savior and to follow his example in loving others. The expositor should also note the variety of persons Christ spoke with in the Gospels. And he must know that "no one will skilfully explain the nature of faith and love, even though it is beautifully and lucidly described everywhere in Scripture, without personal experience of it, at least to some degree" (Scherding and Wendel, 62).

The practical bent of Bucer's engagement with the Bible emerges clearly from this memorandum, but it does not take us very far. Much more revealing are Bucer's discussions of the task of interpreting Scripture in his commentaries of the late 1520s. In the preface to the commentary on the Gospels (1527, reprinted in the 1530 revision with only minor changes), Bucer explained the genesis of the published work in his oral expositions in Strasbourg. He had concluded that they would be of no little value to many in printed form. For all of the older commentators on the Gospels, with the one exception of John *Chrysostom, indulged in so-called allegories and mystical expositions to excess, while so many things in the narratives had been perversely distorted by more recent writers that "the holy mysteries of Christ" had to be freed of misinterpretation. Nothing more reliable and accomplished had been written on the Gospels by present-day writers than the *Paraphrases* of Erasmus, yet those unversed in Scripture needed a more extended explanation than the paraphrase form *(ratio paraphraseon)* allowed. In any case, at some points Bucer read the Gospels differently from Erasmus; he was confident that this "man of incomparable learning" would not take it amiss. Others had produced annotations, together with common places (*loci communes,* i.e., general discussions of theological topics), but the selectiveness of the annotations had exposed less educated readers to their own absurd concoctions on other verses or passages. Then again were those who commented only on the lections for the Mass, often inexpertly selected from the Gospels and epistles, which had left many in the churches ignorant of the rest of the Gospels. Bucer affirmed his own commitment to preaching through the whole of the Gospels in sequence (fol. 4a-b; Lang, 379-80).

Bucer sets out his chief purpose in his Gospel commentaries:

> to help inexperienced brethren [particularly in France and Italy] . . . to understand each of the words and actions of Christ, and in their proper order as far as possible, and to retain an explanation of them in their natural meaning, so that they will not distort God's Word through age-old aberrations or by inept interpretation, but rather, with a faithful comprehension of everything as written by the Spirit of God, they may expound all to the churches to their firm upbuild-

ing in faith and love. (fol. 5a; Lang, 380) His task is no easy one, for the true meaning of important words and names has been lost, such as "grace, law, satisfaction, prayers, fasts, ministers, church, marriage, keys of the kingdom of heaven"; they have been perverted into some other signification than the Holy Spirit used. In addition there is the curse of false allegory, on which Bucer expatiates at length. He is amazed at some contemporary writers who, amid the new unveiling of the Scriptures, still allow themselves "to play with those insecure and monstrous allegories rather than to teach, especially since they know full well the damage these have done to the faith." They appeal to Paul's use of the word *allegory* in Galatians 4:24 but fail to see that he is following the biblical narratives and the judgments of God in Scripture (fol. 5a-b; Lang, 380-81).

Bucer particularly attacks the speculative character of allegories. One could get the same out of Virgil and Homer with no less cleverness, he added in 1530: "In the churches none but the certain words of God should be spoken, on which the mind can rely free of all doubt." Allegories made Scripture a wax nose *(nasus caereus)*. He had rightly called them "monstrous" *(portentosas)*, because not only were they unknown to Scripture but also they had nothing to do with the allegory or "inversion" *(inversio)* of common speech, whereby one thing was said and another meant. When Christ warned against the "leaven" of the Pharisees, he meant their teaching. When he said, "If your eye offends you, cast it out," it was an allegory (fol. 6a-b, Lang, 382). In 1530 Bucer added: "Just as the sacred writers, like others, say many things figuratively *(translatis verbis)*, so they express only one meaning, not different ones at the same time, nor is it unclear when they are speaking literally *(simpliciter)* and when allegorically" (Lang, 382). The rule should be, as John Colet affirmed in a letter to Erasmus, "If you are teaching the sheep of Christ, you should offer them only what will feed their

minds, and that is the truth alone, God's truth of course, and none of your inventions" (fol. 6b-7a; Lang, 383).

So Bucer claims the right to dissent at times from those who likewise dare to disagree with *Jerome, *Augustine and other venerable Fathers. And his readers must be free to reject what he writes if, after consideration in the light of "the analogy of faith," they conclude it is merely human. Although he has included many common places in the commentary on the Gospels, he has sought to serve "the simple faith of the Scriptures" (fol. 7b; Lang, 384).

In an excursus in his 1527 commentary on Ephesians entitled "Rule *(canon)* to be followed in interpreting Scripture," evoked by the "mystery" of Ephesians 5:22-33, Bucer discussed Old Testament types. Their pedagogic purpose is identified: by means of types God teaches us not in words only but also in actions and events, giving prior intimation of "almost all the mysteries in Christ" and so revealing their significance beyond what was immediately apparent "so that godly minds were aroused to reflect on more hidden and divine realities, while the impure were debarred from the realm of the sacred" (101r). Bucer illustrates from God's promise to David in 2 Samuel 7 (and 1 Chron 17; Ps 87; 132). All are agreed that it relates to Christ, but it also fully fits *(quadrare)* Solomon, as 2 Samuel 7:14, "If he does anything wrong," proves. Other elements surpass the successes of Solomon, such as "I will establish the throne of his kingdom for ever" (2 Sam 7:13); to prevent this being perversely applied to Solomon, divine providence overthrew his kingdom. "So another, heavenly Solomon is to be discerned in this son of David, whose type Solomon was, and he is Christ whom the truly magnificent things here square with" (101v). We should do likewise with other predictions of Christ.

Bucer returns to Ephesians 5. Genesis 2:24 undeniably refers to marriage, so how can Paul interpret it of Christ and his church? It is

because marriage *(coniugium)* is a type
of the union *(coniunctio)* between
Christ and the church, and a husband's
fondness for his wife is a figure of
Christ's love for his church. Furthermore the wording [of Genesis] speaks
of a more exalted *(augustior)* union and
love than is evident between husband
and wife, for when between a married
couple is there such a union of mind and
heart that they become "one flesh" and
live wholly as one person? Hence a more
perfect marriage than mortals experience is indicated here by both type and
word. (102r)

On the journey to Emmaus Christ enabled
his disciples to understand the Old Testament (Lk 24:25-27):

But where in Moses can you read such-
like—that Christ the only-begotten of
God must be born as a human being,
and die, and then two days later rise
from the dead? . . . Yet there in Luke
Christ said that thus it was written. Not
without the veiling of types, therefore,
as I have said. Undoubtedly the story of
Jonah was one of these passages, but
where in the whole of Jonah is it written
that Christ, the Son of God, will die and
will be shut in a tomb for two whole days
and thereafter arise? Nevertheless Christ
himself derived that from it. (102v)

Bucer's first Johannine commentary in
1528 includes on John 3:14 a lengthy excursus "On expounding scriptural types
and on certain allegories or anagoges." His
starting point is remarkably fundamental:
because everything was made and will be
restored through the divine Word, "absolutely everything that exists and happens in
the world in its own way conveys *(refert)*
the Word and contains the potential for the
godly mind, stimulated by the Spirit, to be
able to rise to the knowledge of the Word."
The experiences of Israel portray "a much
more certain image of the Word," but it lies
"in the nature of humankind that in every
kind of thing the more mundane lead by
likeness and analogy to knowledge of the
more concealed. Thus the spiritual is un-

derstood from the physical, and from small,
visible works of God greater and invisible
are ascertained" (Backus, 142). Bucer sees
Scripture as full of such "metaphors":
"sun" and "day" are ready examples
(Backus, 143).

Bucer proceeds to review as types of
Christ, Adam, Noah, Melchizedek and
Abraham, and with him Sarah as a type of
the church: "In the blessings conferred on
the saints of old, we may see a certain
likeness and shadow of those assuredly bestowed on us in Christ, and so by transference *(per translationem* [Gal 4:24]) may
apply what is written about theirs to ours
analogically *(cum proportione)*, that is, read
it typologically and figuratively *(allegorein
kai tropologein)*." Bucer insists that the parallelism and analogy *(proportio)* must be
obvious and "strike the sense of faith as
certain" (Backus, 145). By this criterion
Bucer faults *Origen and Jerome and other
Fathers for their license in allegorization.
To avoid repeating their errors, we must
differentiate in Scripture among history,
prophecy and law. Each occupies Bucer's
attention in turn.

History embraces the Old Testament
persons who are types of Christ, as well as
events and other features. The rule is always
to move from like to like, from lesser to
greater, from external to internal, such as
from Canaan to the kingdom of heaven.
Transferences of this kind are *anagogies,*
that is, elevations *(subductiones)*, by which
the mind is elevated from the lower to the
higher. But nothing must be transferred to
Christ or his church that does not "certainly and obviously match" (Backus, 147-
49).

Some prophecies *(vaticinia)* are so direct that no transference is needed. Far
more numerous are those like 2 Samuel 7
(and here Bucer refers back to his treatment
in his Ephesians commentary), which relate
appropriately first to types of Christ and
then to Christ himself (Backus, 149-50).

Within the category of laws *(praecepta)*
also, some instill piety so directly that no
anagoge is required. Bucer concentrates on

laws that are "ancillary to piety," that is, the ceremonial and the civil or judicial. On the latter he comments only that, although true justice (*aequitas*, equity) is required of us and hence we are not bound to the precise terms of Israelite legislation, "yet few, I think, are the cases in which it would not be better to follow those laws of God than other ones" (Backus, 151).

On the laws of the sacrificial cultus, Bucer refers repeatedly and unremarkably to the epistle to the Hebrews. He emphasizes, however, that it would be folly to attempt to apply to Christ and the church very many of the Mosaic rites and ceremonies. The rawness (*ruditas*) of that ancient people made them necessary, just as in Bucer's day ceremonies proliferated in the "incredible inventiveness" of papal and monastic service books. In both alike Bucer recognized spiritual infancy. Neither the prophets nor the apostles transmitted the mystical meanings of each and every ritual. Indeed, Paul cited types sparingly, except in combat with false apostles who tried to make the ceremonial laws binding. Above all we should learn from the apostles, in a health-giving teaching ministry in the church, that in all the multifarious civil and ceremonial laws God required one thing: "that we fear and love him and depend wholly upon him, and live with our fellow men and women in full integrity and dutiful love" (Backus, 153).

Significance. Most of the characteristic features of Bucer's work as an interpreter of Scripture are recognizable in the above summaries. In many respects he is one with the best of Reformed exegetes, such as Calvin and Peter Martyr *Vermigli. B. Roussel and G. Hobbs have sought to situate Bucer in a Rhineland school of exegesis, alongside Ulrich *Zwingli, Johann Oecolampadius, Sebastian Münster, Conrad Pellican and others. The humanist foundations remain solid throughout. But Bucer built on them a familiarity with medieval Jewish commentators that made him one of the ablest Christian Hebraists of his day, as R. G. Hobbs's studies of the commentary on

Psalms have steadily revealed. But as a humanist committed to the natural sense of Scripture, he refuses to overdo the typological reading of passages such as Psalm 22, unafraid of the accusation of sticking to Jewish literalism.

As his discussions from the late 1520s reveal, he cannot be charged with leveling out the differences between the two Testaments. By the standards of modern liberal scholarship, which generally consigns the Old Testament, if not like Marcion to an alien god, at least to an alien past, Bucer and his contemporaries held a high estimate of it. He insisted that, if the Old Testament's sacraments signified a Savior still to come, this did not prevent them actually conferring the salvation to be accomplished by him, through faith in the coming one (Wright 1972, 293). Yet he retained a grasp of the historical distance between Old and New, and of the theological development from Old to New (Stephens, 109-21). Though Bucer tends to identify the New Testament Jesus with the Christ of the patristic creeds, he knows, for example, that infant baptism is found only in unwritten tradition.

Romans is the most elaborate of Bucer's commentaries (see Parker, 81-84). It provides not only an extensive set of prefaces, numerous common places and a paraphrase but also a running exposition of Paul's teaching, alongside the elucidations of words and sentences that are every commentator's bread and butter, and finally generalized application for the unlearned. For ultimately for Bucer, and for the Rhineland expositors, the interpretation of Scripture must feed the people of God. Godliness justifies exegesis, especially of the learned and massive kind practiced by Bucer.

BIBLIOGRAPHY

Works. M. Bucer, *Enarratio in Evangelion Iohannis (1528, 1530, 1536)* in *Opera Latina* 2, ed. I. D. Backus (Leiden: E. J. Brill, 1988); idem and T. Cranmer, *Annotationes in Octo priora capita Evangelii secundum Matthaeum*, ed. H. Vogt (Frankfurt a.M.: Athenäum Verlag, 1972);

P. Scherding and F. Wendel, eds., "'Un Traité d' exégèse pratique de Bucer," *RHPR* 26 (1946) 32-75 (*Quomodo S. Literae pro Concionibus Tractandae sint Instructio*, 1531 = Stupperich no. 33); H. Bornkamm, *Martin Bucers Bedutung für die europäische Reformationsgeschichte*, R. Stupperich, *Bibliographia Bucerana*, (Gütersloh: C. Bertelsmann, 1952); D. F. Wright, ed., *Common Places of Martin Bucer* (Appleford, England: Sutton Courtenay Press, 1972; largely translated extracts from commentaries).

Studies. G. Bedouelle and B. Roussel, eds., *Le Temps des Réformes et la Bible* (Paris: Beauchesne, 1989); H. Eells, *Martin Bucer* (New Haven, CT: Yale University Press, 1931); M. Greschat, *Martin Bucer: Ein Reformator und seine Zeit 1491-1551* (Munich: Beck, 1990); R. G. Hobbs, "How Firm a Foundation: Martin Bucer's Historical Exegesis of the Psalms," *CH* 53 (1984) 477-91; idem, "An Introduction to the Psalms Commentary of Martin Bucer" (unpublished doctoral dissertation, Strasbourg, 1971); idem, "Martin Bucer on Psalm 22: A Study in the Application of Rabbinic Exegesis by a Christian Hebraist" in *Histoire de l' exégèse au XVIe siècle*, ed. O. Fatio and P. Fraenkel (Geneva: Droz, 1978) 144-63; A. Lang, *Der Evangelienkommentar Martin Butzers und die Grundzüge seiner Theologie* (Leipzig: Dietrich, 1900); P. Lutz, "Le commentaire de Martin Bucer sur le livre des Juges" (unpublished doctoral dissertation, Strasbourg, 1953); J. Müller, *Martin Bucers Hermeneutik* (Gütersloh: Gutersloher Verlagshaus G. Mohr, 1965); T. H. L. Parker, *Calvin's New Testament Commentaries* (2d ed.; Edinburgh: T & T Clark; Louisville, KY: Westminster John Knox, 1993); B. Roussel, "Bucer Exégète" in *Martin Bucer and Sixteenth Century Europe: Actes du colloque de Strasbourg . . .* , ed. C. Krieger and M. Lienhard (2 vols.; Leiden: E. J. Brill, 1993) 1:39-54; idem, "Martin Bucer Exégète" in *Strasbourg au coeur religieux du XVIe siècle*, ed. G. Livet, F. Rapp and J. Rott (Strasbourg: Librairie Istra, 1977) 153-66; idem, "Martin Bucer, Lecteur de l' epître aux Romains" (unpublished doctoral dissertation, Strasbourg, 1970); idem, "De Strasbourg à Bâle et Zurich: Une 'école rhénane' d'exégèse (ca 1525-ca 1540)," *RHPR* 68 (1988) 19-39; B. Roussel and G. Hobbs, "Strasbourg et l'école rhénane d' exégèse," *BSHPF* 135 (1989) 36-53; W. P. Stephens, *The Holy Spirit in the Theology of Martin Bucer* (Cambridge: Cambridge University Press, 1970); D. F. Wright, ed., *Martin Bucer: Reforming Church and Community* (Cambridge:

Cambridge University Press, 1994).

D. F. Wright

Bullinger, Heinrich *(1504-1575)*

Heinrich Bullinger's importance for biblical interpretation lies in his exegesis of Scripture as well as in the social structures he worked to develop in the sixteenth century. Each relates to the other. His interpretation of the role of the prophet relates to his reconception of the ministry. His conception of the growth of idolatry and religious error led to a reworking of the monastic hours of prayer so as to focus on the study of Scripture in the original languages and in the vernacular. These innovations would make for a paradigm shift in ministry and theological education. His idea of the constancy of God in history led to an organization of theology around the fidelity of relationships, later to be called covenantal theology. Bullinger's belief in the sovereignty of God led him to propound the idea of a Christian commonwealth wherein the two offices of minister and magistrate were subject to the Christian ruler in ways identical with his conception of rule in old Israel; this belief made for a shift in millennial ideology and patterns of political legitimacy. Whether in sermons, theological treatises, Reformed confessions or his voluminous correspondence, Bullinger would become a pivotal figure in both Lutheran-Reformed relations and among the Reformed, the most prevailing form of international Protestantism.

Contributions. Bullinger was at heart a pastor. His formation began at home, where his father was dean of the chapter for the parish church of Bremgarten, Canton Aargau. Through both his father and mother, Anna Wiederkehr, he grew up as a member of the prevailing establishment and, like his siblings, was first educated at St. Martin's School in Emmerich, duchy of Cleves. Here he was introduced to the piety of the Brethren of the Common Life and to Italian humanism. The spiritual and philological debt that Bullinger owed to this early formation is without doubt.

In 1519 Bullinger entered the University of Cologne, citadel of the *via antiqua*—theology largely derivative of Thomas *Aquinas and Scotus, with some sense of becoming a Carthusian monk. At the university he became familiar with conceptions of natural law and the humanism of Jacques *Lefèvre d'Étaples and Desiderius *Erasmus. Although he would never follow the latter's idea of the freedom of the will, both helped to shape Bullinger's literary method and sense for the original languages of the Bible. Others, like Marsilio Ficino and Jean *Gerson, shaped his understanding of original sources and idea of the early church as norm.

Bullinger drew from Lorenzo Valla his understanding that through idolatry and ignorance the church fell after Gregory the Great (d. 604), an idea given further shape by the medieval Joachite tradition, which traced the course of that fall. Biblical symbolism that suggested moral regression in history was given an added historical dimension by way of Bullinger's understanding of the historicist exegesis of *Nicholas of Lyra. This was especially true of apocalyptic language that appears to sketch temporal conflict with idolatry through allusions to the prophetic literature of the Old Testament. For Bullinger the history of old Israel was a figure of the new, not merely in a symbolic way but filled with immediate historical significance in the era of the dispensation of Christ. Through reading Peter Lombard, Bullinger, like Martin *Luther, was led to the church fathers and the Bible. Philipp *Melanchthon's *Loci Communes* (1521), with its emphasis upon salvation by God's grace, left a lifelong stamp on Bullinger's understanding of religion and reform in relation to history. This interest, which developed in tandem with that of such contemporary exegetes as Theodor Bibliander, Luther, Francis Lambert and Sebastian Meyer, was deepened in symbolic value through his debt to the spiritual and allegorical emphases characteristic of the exegete Tyconius (died c. 400), whom Bullinger followed through *Augustine or by way of newly edited patristic commentaries.

Bullinger's theology shares in the larger Augustinian heritage with respect to the spiritual intent of the text. Together with Augustine and the more recent Gerson, Bullinger understood Scripture to be best interpreted by Scripture. He was led via this path to a trinitarian conception of God, sovereign with respect to providence and predestination, to an ecumenical conception of Christ as framed by the work of *Irenaeus, Cyril of Alexandria and *Athanasius, and to a pervasive sense of the Holy Spirit, particularly present in baptism and the Lord's Supper. To this orthodox doctrine was added the idea of doctrinal primacy over apostolic succession, a debt to *Tertullian (died c. 215/20) that separated Bullinger from medieval Catholicism.

Having earned his master of arts degree (1522), Bullinger returned to Switzerland. He became a teacher, hired by abbott Wolfgang Joner to teach Latin at the newly founded Kappel Cloister School. This evident break from medieval orders and sacramental understanding would later become central to his idea of religious error in such works as *The Old Faith (Der alte Glaube,* 1537) and *On the Origin of Error (De Origine Erroris,* 1528/1539). Bullinger was well on his way toward reconceiving the Christian ministry, which he saw as a restoration of the prophetic office in ancient Israel. While at Kappel he began the process of educational reform for this idea of the pastorate that would have far-reaching consequences. Such reform represented the living word of the gospel, rather than the sacramental altar, as the symbolic center of the Reformed ministry. The Zurich translation of the Bible, to be revised in every generation, was to be a continuing reminder of this exegetical revolution.

J. Staedtke has demonstrated that it was in his years at Kappel that Bullinger developed an enlivened interpretation of Scripture that would be important throughout his ministry (Staedtke 1962). As his reputation grew, so too did the responsibilities placed upon him. At Ulrich *Zwingli's request Bullinger took part in the Zurich delegation at the Berne Disputation (1528). This disputation over Anabaptism marked a continuing theme in Bullinger's work. Though he laid stress on a living and intuitive sense of God's voice, Bullinger did not mean something unfettered to doctrinal fidelity as revealed in Scripture. Anabaptism was of concern to Bullinger from at least 1525, and it was against the baker John Pfistermeyer, exiled in 1526, that Bullinger directed his first attacks on Anabaptism as contrary to God's order (Williams, 243-45, 310-13), a theme he would continue in several works when after 1529 he returned to his hometown to join Gervasius Schuler, the new pastor at Bremgarten, in ministry. Still in demand by Zwingli to help find reconciliation between the Swiss and Luther at the Colloquy of Marburg (1529), Bullinger was unable to go due to the protests of his parish. However, the process of reform in Bremgarten was soon subverted by the Second Kappel War (1531), compelling Bullinger and his young wife, Anna Adlischwyler, to leave the parish for her natal Zurich. There Bullinger was called to be Zwingli's successor following the latter's death.

Antistes and Author. As overseer of the church in Zurich, Bullinger performed the functions of a Reformed bishop, mediating among the churches, presiding over the cantonal synod, which he helped to reorganize, and intermediating between the Zurich council and the clergy. By insisting on the right to preach the gospel as it applied to all of life, not just about religious issues narrowly conceived, Bullinger was insisting upon the sovereignty of God and upholding the role of the minister as the prophet of God. He insisted that the city council enforce the Morality Ordinance of 1531 and guarantee the clergy's freedom to preach about civic matters. This was the church of the prophets, of which Zwingli was one. Bullinger found prophets among

many peoples—Greeks, Romans, Jews—and among early Christians. However, the office of prophecy was particularly evident in Hebrew history and was characterized by the interpretation of Scripture and its public application.

By 1531 Bullinger had begun his repetitive and massive literary activities, delineating the nature of the church and its ministry, theological doctrine and practice, and the church's role in the civic order. In addition to such works, Bullinger's correspondence is voluminous, with about twelve thousand letters recorded to his name, a number that far exceeds that of the other Reformers. These letters testify in their commentary on politics and church affairs to Bullinger's leadership across Europe and, in the *Zurich Letters* (2 vols., 1542, 1545), reveal the extent to which Bullinger was interested in reform in Great Britain from Henry VIII through the reign of Elizabeth I.

Church and State. Bullinger's interests in civic humanism, particularly through the work of Marsilio of Padua, came together with his conception of the sovereignty of God to shape his understanding of church and state. This Marsilian view of the relation of the two offices, minister and magistrate, functioning together under the one Christian ruler, was derived, as had been the case for Zwingli, from Erasmus's *Paraphrases of the New Testament* and his *Annotations.* It also reflects the way by which the new millennial ideology of this civic humanism drew upon the history of old Israel for contemporary ecclesial and political legitimacy and rejected papal juridical authority. It goes far to explain his insistence upon maintaining inherited patterns of infant baptism, as much a sign of the covenant as that of loyalty to the Christian commonwealth in Zurich, which faced Ottoman and Habsburg/Roman Catholic hostility and radical/Anabaptist unrest.

Bullinger's basic understanding of the function of the priest is made clear in his early exegesis of such formative texts as Matthew 16:13-18 and Matthew 18:15-

18. Christ Jesus, the head of the church, granted limited authority to his ministers so as to govern the church by laws discerned in Scripture. This church was the invisible kingdom of God, defined by way of Augustinian teaching on grace, moderate when compared to the more rigorous views of predestination advanced by John *Calvin yet more fully extensive into all areas of life. Together with Lutheran theorists, Bullinger traced the church through history by way of doctrinal unity, not apostolic succession, innovating on what he read in Melanchthon by connecting this to a perception of religious truth inherent in humanity back to Adam.

Interpretation of Scripture. Behind this concern for the church and its civic expression in the commonwealth lay Bullinger's conception of religious order, characterized by its theological simplicity and spiritual immediacy.

Bullinger believed that humanity knows of the existence of God and of the most basic religious principle, simply to follow God. Living prophets call God's people to live consciously before God through prophesying or preaching. They mediate the reality of Christ through the power of the Spirit in aural cultic practices rather than through a reenactment of God's sacrifice in Christ. As G. Locher has written: "The experience of the whole Reformation was that the real presence of the Lord of the church is to be found fundamentally in the *viva vox evangelii* instead of in the sacrament" (Locher, 61). This order is known through an inner illumination that reflects the importance of the natural law with its pedagogical function in the conscience of individuals and in the government of society, an idea perhaps derived by Bullinger from Aquinas.

Though God is free to choose any means of communication, Bullinger argued that because of the human tendency toward error or idolatry, "God cannot rightly be known but by his word." God normally uses the preaching of this word to instruct people about his will for them, though he

was free to do otherwise if he so chose (*II [Second] Helvetic Confession,* 2). The Holy Spirit guided the word's authors such as Moses and those who gave us the canon. Following Augustine *(On Lying [De Mendacio],* 8), Bullinger argued that the Scriptures share in the integrity of God. They are "true, just, without deceit and guile, without error or evil affection, holy, pure, good, immortal and everlasting" (Bullinger, *Decades* 1, sermon 1, 37-47). The *Decades* and the *Second Helvetic Confession* begin with the first four councils of the ecumenical church as a guide to our understanding of the word. God, as defined in the Nicene-Constantinopolitan Creed, revealed the plan of salvation for humanity in Christ as conceptualized by the Chalcedonian formula. This is the triune God who works by way of the Spirit in every aspect of life (Nullinger, *Decades* 4, sermon 8, 307-19).

The preaching of the Word is not made superfluous by Scripture or by inner illumination. God wills this proclamation by human agency as he did by sending Cornelius to minister to Peter (cf. Augustine *On Christian Doctrine* prologue). True religion is restored in times of crisis by prophets whose work is to restore, rebuild, replace or reinstate the covenant. This covenant, the symbol and center of religious order, is encapsulated in God's reliability and humanity's obligation to walk in God's ways. Locher indicates that this idea of the preaching of the word unites and makes visible different currents of reform in the sixteenth century: "Accordingly for Erasmus the key word is *Philosophia christiana;* for Luther, *Certitudo;* for Zwingli, *Evangelion,* God's Word, or Spirit; for Calvin, *Doctrine.*" The unity of this reforming thrust is caught up by Bullinger's prophets, who stress the relationship itself with God(Locher 1981, 283).

Bullinger writes that the sum of Scripture is the covenant, and Jesus Christ is its guarantor.

Covenantal thinking appears in Bullinger's work as early as 1528, while he was at Kappel, in the context of conflict with Anabaptists. Both Balthasar Hubmaier and Zwingli had each gravitated toward different metaphors for the Christian life, the symbolism of dying and rebirth in adult baptism for the former and of the newly covenanted Israel with civic implications for the latter. The use of equivalent terms for the covenant by Bullinger, such as *confederation* or *league,* remind us of the political context and patterns of alliances in the Swiss Confederacy in which both Bullinger and his mentor, Zwingli, moved. In his celebration of Zwingli as a prophet, Bullinger offers us an introduction to the office and function of a prophet as "one who restored the principle of the Testament and the eternal covenant and renewed what was worn out" (Bullinger, *De Prophetae Officio,* sig. Ei r-v). Luther was another such prophet. Reform came through Hebrew prophets before Christ. For Bullinger, Zwingli was a part of a contemporary outburst of prophetic zeal that stood in continuity with Moses, Isaiah, Paul and Athanasius. He sought to reinstate the covenant and establish a Christian commonwealth.

Adherence or departure from the terms of the covenant gave an inner structure and meaning to history. Bullinger points to parallels between the idolatry and errors of earlier ages and that which arose in Europe in the Middle Ages. He finds a repeating pattern in history whereby initial monotheism, when God is known by names that reflect his attributes, degenerates into idolatry through the confusion of those names with powers and heroes. Whether among the Jews in the Baal worship of the time of Ahab or in the growth of idolatry in medieval Europe, in each such instance people fall away from the terms of the covenant. The real danger to the welfare of church and state lay not in the ravages of the Turks, "God's whip," but in the hypocrisy and superstition of the "protectors" of the church (Bullinger, *De Origine Erroris,* fol. 2r). In these times God calls prophets to bring an erring people back to the terms of the covenant (Petersen, 121-24).

By tracing the origin of error and setting it within the perspective of the covenant, Bullinger develops a notion of evil that strains the Augustinian idea of its privative nature by appearing to give it a reality of its own. Religious regression, whether defined as the growth of antichrist in papal dominion or the humanist idea of the Dark Ages, gives definition to history by drawing out a moral lesson. Bullinger's idea of an intensification of evil undercuts an attempt to see history purely in terms of natural causes. The tropological use of the text takes on concrete historical features: as the papacy is more clearly labeled antichrist, Bullinger and his exegetical heirs will more fully identify with the adventual witnesses (Rev 11), prophets of consolation and restitution. In light of Joachite and humanist antecedents, there is a melding of the Tyconian and Joachite traditions in Bullinger's interpretation of Scripture. His use of Joachim of Fiore helped to promote this identification of evil, and the spiritual symbolism derivative of Tyconius deepened the moral lesson. This moral dimension that is given to historical causation stands in tension with developing humanist interests in history. This tension with the growth of error, or evil, also has an opposite tendency in Bullinger, that of finding a progressive trajectory to history. While he is dependent for this upon the same late medieval lines of biblical interpretation, Bullinger rejects the radical Franciscanism to which it sometimes led. However, his repudiation of medieval millenarian hopes stands in contrast to the history of the Word which, in Bullinger's works, lays a foundation for later Protestant millenarian thinking in seventeenth-century Continental and Anglo-American biblical exegesis.

Bullinger's God is a good rhetor. S. Hausammann demonstrates this but finds his use of humanist rhetoric grounded in theology and Scripture. The three classical tasks of the orator, *docere, delectare, movere,* are transformed into *docere, hortari, consolari* (Hausammann, 179, 161-82). Her argument represents Bullinger's understanding of God with respect to humanity: God teaches, preaches and consoles. The sum of Scripture, with Jesus Christ as its guarantor, is meant to show this divine intentionality. It is implicit in the covenant which teaches the constancy and reliability of God's commitment to humanity, reminds humanity of its obligation to God, and through baptism and the Lord's Supper consoles us by offering us the gifts of God's work on our behalf through Christ (Bullinger, *Decades* 3, sermon 6, 157-9).

Water, bread and wine signify invisible and heavenly things that can be seen with "the eye or mind of faith." Christ's body remains in heaven during the Supper, but it can be seen with the eye of faith as the believer eats Christ "mystically and sacramentally" in faith (Bullinger, *Decades* 5, sermon 6, 251). Fulfillment in time, rather than reenactment in space, becomes the primary metaphor of reality for Bullinger and the Reformed. At creation God promised his grace. God has kept his word in history as symbolized in the sacraments, signs and seals of the covenant. They are symbolic representations of the rhetoric of God. They do not confer or contain grace but are figural witnesses of grace. They keep God's people from idols insofar as they are allowed to speak clearly of God's work in history. Through the power of the Spirit the sacraments are efficacious through time. Bullinger's idea of church history is replicated in the life of the one marked by the sacraments, signs that reveal our adoption by God and, as such, provide consolation in times of suffering.

Nowhere is this clearer in Bullinger's works than in his sermons on the Apocalypse. We learn in the preface that this book is a revelation of Jesus Christ. The doctrine found there is a summary of that taught elsewhere in Scripture. The Apocalypse is a paraphrase of the prophets. It directs us to Christ and his work, "And I doubt, whether there exists in the canonical books after the prophecy of Isaiah, after the story of the Gospel, but especially after the Gospel of

blessed John . . . any other book which has more . . . elegant descriptions of Christ, than this book" (Bullinger, *In Apocalypsim*, sig. A6v., p. 6, 126). It tells the story of the church by summarizing the intent of the prophets for the new dispensation. It is visionary like Daniel, "a prophecy, that is, an exposition which opens up and illustrates the old prophets" (*In Apocalypsim*, 8). The affective nature of prophetic work and vision is appropriate to times of crisis and show us "that Jesus Christ our Lord will never fail his church on earth but will govern it with his spirit and word through the ecclesiastical ministry." The gifts given God's prophets, ministers by the Spirit, symbolize Protestant spirituality: power through the Word, grace through preaching, damnation through rejection and plagues for impenitence. It is with these weapons that the new temple, or reformed church, is to be constructed. Christ vows that in the latter days his church will be rebuilt through his ministers, though their number be small. They teach, admonish and console. Their work is that of Enoch and Elijah, Joshua and Zerubbabel, Moses and Jeremiah. In fulfilling their task "they imagine nothing out of their own minds, neither add to nor take away anything from God's word, but simply declare to the church of God the things they have seen in the story of the gospels and heard from prophets and apostles" (*In Apocalypsim*, sig. A2r, 105-12).

The *Second Helvetic Confession* is brought to a close with the practical affairs of the church and life in the world rather than with a chapter on eschatology or eternal life. This emphasis is indicative of Bullinger's civic humanism set within the narrative of Scripture. As Elijah called upon Israel to leave its baals and "Jezebelism," so contemporary prophets and preachers were calling upon Christendom to leave idolatry and superstition. Error with its civic implications in the medieval church is set next to Bullinger's treatise on the fall of the Jews, who had turned to the gods of Egypt and Canaan. Elijah had destroyed the prophets of Baal in his day; now Zwingli, the "idol-smasher and impious iconoclast," performed the work of Elijah (Bullinger, *De Origine Erroris,* fol. 94r, 46r). Bullinger's ethics assume that a knowledge of God is possible and that such knowledge calls for fidelity in relationships. The purpose of such is the restoration of humanity to the image of God. While God may use any agency as a means of grace toward this end, prophets are the goad toward that end and a sign of hope that it can be achieved.

While the covenant gave an inner structure and meaning to history, the outward signs of its observance made possible citizenship in the commonwealth as much as membership in the church, a logical view considering the prevailing concept of political legitimacy and accepted legality. The two tables of the Decalogue were foundational to all good works and a guide for life. As a reflection of the mind or will of God, judicial laws enacted by the magistrate were to reflect the substance of God's laws. The state stood in the same line of accountability as the church. The magistrate was "ordained of God and is God's minister," a theme Bullinger emphasized with the many rulers who sought his advice. He hailed both Edward VI and Elizabeth I of England as new Josiahs, advising them to submit to the "rule of God's holy word" so as to be guided by the Holy Spirit in the right ordering of church and state (Bullinger, *Decades* 3, sermons 7-8, 220, 280).

Bullinger applied covenantal thinking to changing patterns of economic life. His reinterpretation of the Deuteronomic prohibition of usury challenged prevailing scholastic-Aristotelian theories of money. This method of interpretation of Scripture by Scripture, informed by his theology of the covenant, was used to distinguish between fair interest and extortion. The problem was not in the use of money, or profit, but in failing to help one who is in need. Distinguishing between covetousness and theft, he related the Love Commandment (Lk 6:34-35) to his sense of Christian duty to one's neighbor, thereby avoiding the

proof-texting he associated with Rome or the radicals. Together with a careful Augustinian yet humanist-inspired reading of Scripture, Bullinger and his theology of covenantal relationships preceded Calvin with this conception of money. Bullinger's biblical argument was grounded in the message that God wished "well to mankind" both in divine as well as human affairs (Bullinger, *Decades* 1, sermon 1, 38-42).

Significance. Bullinger interpreted Scripture through the philological and historical lens of contemporary literary humanism. He drew upon early Christian and patristic sources to frame his exegetical interests and doctrine, while a number of medieval writers helped to shape his intuitive sense of God and of a fall from biblical faith and practice between the sixth century and his own day. These themes led to a deepened appropriation of the Hebrew Scriptures, the Christian Old Testament, for models of faith and practice in the context of a millennial ideology that highlighted the prophetic word as shaped by the concerns of contemporary civic humanism.

In Bullinger's work the array of types, or *figura,* found in the Bible were deepened in symbolic value so as to resonate with fresh prophetic significance. His work built on and paralleled that of Luther with respect to the priesthood of all believers yet, unlike Calvin, without casting that idea into a politics of evolving dissent. Bullinger provided for a new conception of the ministry and of theological education. He set this in the context of an integrated Christian commonwealth that redefined Hebrew models of ministry and magistracy in the contemporary vernacular of civic humanism.

BIBLIOGRAPHY

Works. H. Bullinger, *The Decades of Henry Bullinger, Minister of the Church of Zürich,* ed. T. Harding (5 vols.; Cambridge: Cambridge University Press, 1848); idem, *Heinrich Bullinger Werke,* ed. F. Büsser (Zurich: Theologischer Verlag, 1972-); idem, *Quellen zur schweizerischen Reformationsgeschichte* 2: *Diarium (Annales Vitae) der Jahre 1504-1574,* ed. E. Egli (Zurich:

Theologische Buchhandlung, 1985); idem, *Das Zweite Helvetische Bekenntnis Confessio Helvetica Posterior* (Zurich: Zwingli Verlag, 1966).

Studies. J. W. Baker, *Heinrich Bullinger and the Covenant: The Other Reformed Tradition* (Athens, OH: Ohio University Press, 1980); F. Blanke, *Der junge Bullinger, 1504-1531* (Zurich: Zwingli, 1942); A. Bouvier, *Henri Bullinger, Reformateur et Conseiller Oecumenique: le Successeur de Zwingli* (Neuchatel/Paris: Librairie E. Droz, 1940); G. W. Bromiley, ed., *Zwingli and Bullinger* (LCC 24; Philadelphia: Westminster, 1953); M. Burrows, " 'Christus intra nos Vivens': The Peculiar Genius of Bullinger's Doctrine of Sanctification," *ZK* 98 (1987) 48-69; H. Fast, *Heinrich Bullinger und die Täufer: Ein Beitrag zur Historiographie und Theologie im 16. Jahrhundert* (Weierhof [Pfalz]: Mennonitischen Geschichtsverein, 1959); U. Gäbler and E. Herkenrath, eds., *Zürcher Beiträge zur Reformationsgeschichte, 7, 8: Heinrich Bullinger 1504-1575 Gesammelte Aufsätze zum 400. Todestag* (2 vols.; Zürich: Theologischer Verlag, 1975); U. Gäbler and E. Zsindely, eds., *Bullinger-Tagung, 1975. Vorträge, gehalten aus Anlass von Heinrich Bullingers 400. Todestag* (Zurich: Theologischer Verlag, 1979); S. Hausammann, *Römerbriefauslegung zwischen Humanismus und Reformation: Eine Studie Heinrich Bullingers Römerbrief Vorlesung von 1525* (Zurich: Zwingli, 1970); W. Hollweg, *Beiträge zur Geschichte und Lehre der Reformierte Kirche, 8: Heinrich Bullingers Hausbuch* (Neukirchen: Verlag der Buchhandlung des Erziehungsvereins, 1956); E. Koch, *Beiträge zur Geschichte und Lehre der Reformierten Kirche, 27: Die Theologie der Confessio Helvetica Posterior* (Neukirchen: Neukirchener Verlag des Erziehungsvereins, 1968); G. Locher, " 'Praedicatio Verbi Dei Est Verbum Dei' " in *Zwingli's Thought: New Perspectives,* ed. G. Locher (Leiden: E. J. Brill, 1981) 277-87 (first published in *Zwingliana* 10, 1 [1954] 47-57); C. McCoy and J. W. Baker, *Fountainhead of Federalism: Heinrich Bullinger and the Covenantal Tradition with a Translation of* De Testamento seu Foedere Dei Unico et Aeterno *(1534)* (Louisville, KY: Westminster John Knox, 1991); C. Pestalozzi, *Heinrich Bullinger: Leben und ausgewählte Schriften* (Elberfeld: R. L. Friderichs, 1858); R. L. Petersen, *Preaching in the Last Days: The Theme of 'Two Witnesses' in the Sixteenth and Seventeenth Centuries* (New York: Oxford University Press, 1993); G. Schrenck, *Gottesreich und Bund im älteren Protestantismus* (Darmstadt: Wissenschaftliche Buchgesellschaft, 1967); J.

Staedtke, *Die Theologie des jungen Bullinger (Studien zur Dogmengeschichte und systematischen Theologie* 16; Zurich: Zwingli, 1962); J. Staedtke, ed., *Glauben und Bekennen: Vierhundert Jahre Confessio Helvetica Posterior. Beiträge zu ihrer Geschichte und Theologie* (Zurich: Zwingli, 1966); P. Walser, *Die Prädestination bei Heinrich Bullinger* (Zurich: Zwingli, 1957); R. C. Walton, "Heinrich Bullinger, 1504-1575" in *Shapers of Religious Traditions in Germany, Switzerland and Poland, 1560-1600,* ed. J. Raitt (New Haven, CT: Yale University Press, 1981) 69-87; G. H. Williams, *The Radical Reformation* (3d ed.; Kirksville, MO: Sixteenth Century Journal Publishers, 1992).   R. L. Petersen

Calvin, John *(1509-1564)*

John Calvin has long been recognized as one of the great theologians of the Christian tradition, largely because of the influence of his magisterial *Institutes of the Christian Religion.* In recent decades Calvin's other writings, especially his exegetical works, have received increased scholarly attention. As a result his reputation as a major figure in the history of biblical interpretation is well established.

Calvin's name will forever be associated with Geneva, his adopted Swiss home, where he spent most of the last half of his life and where he died in 1564. But he was French by birth and upbringing. He was born in Noyon and was educated in Paris, Orléans and Bourges. He studied at the Collége de Montaigu in Paris as a youth, receiving an education that was intended to prepare him to study theology and enter the service of the church. Around 1528 he terminated his preministerial studies and began the study of law. Through his study at Orléans and Bourges he encountered the new approach to ancient legal texts advocated by humanists. While traditional legal scholarship was interested in the layers of glosses of earlier generations of interpreters, the humanist approach was especially attentive to the historical context in which the text was produced and to the linguistic and literary features of the text. In 1531 Calvin received his *licencié ès lois* from Orléans and returned to Paris, but not to pursue a career in law. He directed his energies toward gaining a reputation as a humanist writer and soon published his first work, a commentary on Seneca's *De Clementia.*

The direction of Calvin's life changed dramatically in the early 1530s through what he describes as a "sudden conversion," which he says led him to reject papal superstitions. His only account of the transformation is a sketchy one found in the preface to his commentary on the Psalms, published a quarter of a century after the fact. He indicated that beginning with his conversion he had a zeal for the study of "true religion" and that his interest in other studies diminished. The early 1530s were a time of persecution of Protestants in France, and Calvin fled. In 1535 he arrived in Basel, where he hoped to find a peaceful life and devote himself to scholarly writing in the service of his newfound faith. He never experienced the quiet and leisure for which he longed, but in 1536 his aspiration to serve his new religious community as a scholar began to be realized when the first edition of his *Institutes of the Christian Religion* appeared.

Calvin's life took an unanticipated turn in 1536 when, while traveling from France to Strasbourg, he was forced to make a detour to the south through the city of Geneva. His presence was made known to William Farel, who had just led the city in its rejection of the papacy. Farel convinced a reluctant Calvin to remain in Geneva and help with the reform of the church. Except for a three-year exile (1538-1541), during which he pastored a congregation of French refugees in Strasbourg, the remainder of Calvin's life was spent in Geneva seeking to guide the church into a true reformation in accord with the Scriptures. In three decades of conflicts, accomplishments, disappointments and illnesses, he preached, lectured or wrote on almost every part of the Protestant Bible.

Context. In the Renaissance the study of Bible, along with the study of other ancient literature, was undergoing revolutionary change through the labor of humanist scholars. Generally it may be said that a more historically and philologically grounded approach to biblical study was being developed. The increasing popularity of the new historical approach represented a break with the dominant methods of the past. Although it would not be accurate to suggest that all Christian exegetes prior to the sixteenth century lacked interest in the historical meaning of the Bible, it is clear that many Christian thinkers were not seriously concerned with interpreting the text historically. The popularity of proof-texting and of allegorical exegesis bears eloquent witness to the perceived dispensability of historical exegesis.

Calvin's first published work, his commentary on Seneca's *De Clementia,* was very much what one might expect of a humanist interpreter. He corrected the Latin text; analyzed its structure, vocabulary and idioms; and sought to understand the text in its original historical and cultural context. In short, he studied the text historically. When he later took up the work of biblical interpretation, he retained this historical approach.

When Calvin's interests changed from the interpretation of Seneca to the exegesis of the Bible, he became part of a community of Protestant interpreters who in varying degrees were influenced by the humanism of the Renaissance. Philipp *Melanchthon and Martin *Bucer were among those who were most oriented toward humanism. Calvin explained in the preface to his commentary on Romans (the first of his biblical commentaries) that, while he saw some virtues in the exegetical methods of his two friends, there was room for improvement. He faulted neither for failing to arrive at the true meaning of the text, but he gently criticized Melanchthon for neglecting many points that deserve attention and Bucer for being too verbose. In his preface to the commentary on Romans he offered one of his few statements of exegetical principle: "The chief virtue of an interpreter lies in lucid brevity *[in per-spicua brevitate]*. Since it is almost his only task to unfold the mind of the writer whom he has undertaken to expound, he misses his mark, or at least strays outside his limits, by the extent to which he leads his readers away from the meaning of his author." This is a statement of both the goal of exegesis ("to unfold the mind of the writer") and of how to present the results of one's exegesis ("lucid brevity"). It does not explain how Calvin hoped to reach his goal.

Work. Calvin intended his *Institutes of the Christian Religion* for several purposes. It served a catechetical function for those who had rejected the papacy and turned to Protestantism. It served as a confession of the Protestant faith to the French king, Francis I, and thus functioned as an apologetic for many who were suffering persecution. In the final edition of the work (1560) Calvin indicated that he also intended the *Institutes* to serve as an interpretative key "to open a way for all children of God into a good and right understanding of Holy Scripture." While this function is in part fulfilled by the many brief exegetical sections and proof-texts in the *Institutes,* the work includes several extended sections that have an important bearing on the interpretation of Scripture. Book 1, chapters 6-9 discuss the authority of Scripture and the relation of the Word and Spirit. Book 2, chapters 7-11 discuss the law and the similarities and differences between the Old and New Testaments.

Most of Calvin's preaching was in keeping with the tradition Ulrich *Zwingli had introduced among the Swiss: verse-by-verse expositions of books of the Bible. He desired to accommodate his preaching to the understanding of his congregation, and his sermons were as a result generally free from references to the biblical languages and other technical matters and free from refutations of other interpreters. They thus reveal the substance of his beliefs but do not reveal a great deal about his method of interpretation.

Over the last fifteen years of his life

Calvin preached extensively on Hebrews, Psalms, Jeremiah, John, Acts, Lamentations, Micah, Zephaniah, Hosea, Joel, Amos, Obadiah, Jonah, Job, 1 Thessalonians and 2 Thessalonians, 1 Timothy and 2 Timothy, Deuteronomy, Titus, 1 Corinthians and 2 Corinthians, Isaiah, Galatians, Ephesians, the Synoptic Gospels, Genesis, Judges, 1 Samuel and 2 Samuel and 1 Kings. Most of his manuscripted sermons were lost in the early nineteenth century when they were sold, apparently in the belief that they were of little value. Some of the volumes were later recovered, but most were not.

In 1540 Calvin's first biblical commentary, a commentary on Romans, appeared. This was followed by an interval of six years in which no commentaries were issued, probably due to the urgency of other tasks. The remainder of his commentaries on the epistles (1 Corinthians and 2 Corinthians, Galatians, Ephesians, Philippians, Colossians, 1 Thessalonians and 2 Thessalonians, 1 Timothy and 2 Timothy, Titus, Philemon, Hebrews, 1 Peter and 2 Peter, James, 1 John and Jude) were published over a five-year period from 1546 to 1551. Calvin's commentary on Acts was issued in two parts (Acts 1—13 in 1552; Acts 14—28 in 1554). His commentary on John was published in 1553 and was followed by a commentary on a harmony of the Synoptic Gospels in 1555. Calvin's commentaries are extant for every portion of the New Testament except 2 John, 3 John and Revelation. T. H. L. Parker argues convincingly that Calvin produced no commentaries on these three writings.

Many of Calvin's Old Testament commentaries are edited transcripts of his lectures. In the late 1540s he began lecturing on the Old Testament, and all his known lectures are extant. In 1551 he allowed his lecture series on Isaiah to be published as his commentary on Isaiah. All his Old Testament commentaries were published over the next decade and a half: Genesis (1554); Psalms (1557); Hosea (1557); Isaiah (revision, 1559); Minor Prophets (1559);

Daniel (1561); Jeremiah and Lamentations (1563); harmony of the last four books of Moses (1563); Ezekiel 1—20 (1565); Joshua (1565).

Calvin produced only three expositions of Old Testament books that were intended from the first for the written medium. In 1557 he published his *Commentary on the Psalms;* in 1563, a *Harmony of the Last Four Books of Moses.* In 1565 his *Commentary on Joshua* was published posthumously. According to Parker, the three commentaries cover the same books as were discussed in the *Congrégations* (weekly meetings of ministers and other interested persons) after 1549. This suggests that the *Congrégations* served as the basis of the commentaries or vice versa.

Presuppositions. The *locus classicus* for Calvin's view of the divine inspiration of Scripture is his exposition of 2 Timothy 3:16. There he argued that Scripture is authoritative because it has its source in God. Scripture came from prophets who were instruments of the Holy Spirit; it was "dictated by the Holy Spirit"; it "has nothing of human origin mixed with it." He elsewhere insisted that the Holy Spirit's involvement in the production of Scripture extends to the selection of what material to include in the biblical text and to the choice of the wording of the text.

That Calvin did not hold to a mechanical dictation view of Scripture is also evident. The inspiration of Scripture did not occur at the expense of the personalities of the human writers. His comments on the literary style of the biblical text reflect his belief that the human authors' minds remained active in the production of Scripture. He attributed stylistic variations in the Bible to the human writers. He rejected Pauline authorship of the epistle to the Hebrews because he found significant stylistic differences between it and the epistles he believed to be genuinely Pauline. He expressed doubts about the apostle Peter's authorship of 2 Peter because he did not recognize in it "the genuine language of Peter."

Since Calvin viewed Scripture as having both a divine side and a human side, the question naturally arises: Is the meaning the interpreter is to seek that of the Holy Spirit or that of the human writer? Calvin's comments on Leviticus 11:13 point in one direction: The interpreter must always consider the intention of God. It was not uncommon for Calvin in his biblical commentaries to refer to the intention of the Holy Spirit as something that must be understood. A statement in his exposition of Psalm 8, however, points in a different direction: "I have now discharged the duty of a faithful interpreter in opening up the mind of the prophet." He frequently rejected interpretations he believed were foreign to the intention of the prophet. The most interesting examples of the intimate connections between the human and divine sides of Scripture are found in several instances in which Calvin attributed a statement to the human writer, then appears to have corrected himself and attributed it to the Holy Spirit. In his interpretation of Psalm 87 he wrote, "We must consider the intention of the prophet, or rather the object of the Spirit of God, speaking by the mouth of the prophet." For Calvin the intention, thoughts and words of the prophet and of the Holy Spirit in the production of Scripture were so closely related there was no practical way to distinguish them.

In the *Institutes* Calvin wrote: "The covenant made with all the patriarchs is so much like ours in substance and reality that the two are actually one and the same" (Calvin 1960, 2.10.2). He could hardly have chosen stronger words to describe how the dispensation of the patriarchs is related to the New Testament dispensation. The differences between the revelation under the old and new covenants pale when compared with that which remains the same.

Calvin viewed the Old and New Testaments as one in substance. They proclaimed the same message. Against the Jews and the Anabaptists Calvin insisted that

Christ is the true substance of the Old Testament. He did not, however, deny that Old and New Testament economies had their differences, and he believed that the New Testament is clearly superior to the Old Testament. While there is nothing contradictory in Calvin's twin affirmations of the unity and diversity of Scripture, the exegetical implications are potentially significant. If his emphasis on biblical unity dominated his exegesis, we might expect to find him embracing traditional christological interpretations of the Old Testament. If, however, his recognition of diversity played a major role in his exegesis, we might expect him to nuance or even reject a christocentric approach to the Old Testament. Some scholars have argued that Calvin's theology of the unity of Scripture as stated in the *Institutes* is betrayed by his historical exegetical practice as expressed in his commentaries.

Method. More than once Calvin stated in his commentaries that he was restrained in arguing against the interpretations of others. Some people have taken his words at face value and assumed that Calvin was reluctant to break with exegetical tradition. But in fact Calvin quite often found it necessary to oppose the views of others, including such heroes as *Augustine and Martin *Luther. He usually did not name commentators when he refuted their exegesis. In a letter defending himself against the charge that he had been overly critical of Luther's exegesis, he explained that he tried to protect the anonymity of those interpreters with whom he differed: "If others have gone wrong on something, I reprove it without mentioning names and without violence, and indeed I bury errors in silence unless necessity forces." Calvin's reticence to use names makes it difficult to identify with confidence the sources he may have used.

Calvin was quite at home with the Hebrew and Greek texts of Scripture. He was, according to Parker, confident enough of his knowledge of the biblical languages to preach from Greek and Hebrew texts of the

Bible without using notes. In his days in law school, Calvin had learned the rudiments of Greek under the tutelage of Melchior Wolmar, to whom he would later affectionately dedicate his commentary on 2 Corinthians. He continued his Greek studies in Paris for a brief period under Pierre Danès. He regarded the Greek text as authoritative, though he also made use of Latin translations.

Calvin's use of Hebrew fits the pattern of what Friedman calls "the Strasbourg-Basel-Zurich school of Hebraica." This school placed great value on the Old Testament exegete knowing the Hebrew language and favored a relatively restrained use of rabbinic sources to clarify the meaning of the Old Testament. Calvin probably began his Hebrew study under François Vatable during his second stay in Paris (1531–1533). He later lived in Basel for a little over a year (1535–1536) and in Strasbourg for three years (1538–1541), studying Hebrew in both cities, perhaps drawing upon the expertise of Sebastian Münster in Basel and Wolfgang Capito in Strasbourg. Calvin was competent enough in his use of Hebrew to attempt rather extensive word studies. He often based his interpretations on points of Hebrew grammar. He showed a sensitivity to peculiarities of Hebrew style, comparing or contrasting Hebrew idioms with Latin or Greek idioms.

Calvin did not believe that an understanding of the meaning of Greek or Hebrew words would lead the interpreter to a precise understanding of the text. Lexical and grammatical considerations were important in providing him with the interpretive "possibilities" of a text. Similarly the usage of a Hebrew or Greek term in different passages alerted the interpreter to the interpretative possibilities of the text being studied. But it was context that allowed one to move beyond the possibilities and settle on the "probable" meaning of a text.

Before the interpreter could apply the message of Bible to the person of the sixteenth century, Calvin believed, the meaning for the original writer and his contemporaries must be determined. The exegete should neither uproot a text from its immediate literary context nor neglect the historical environment in which the document was originally produced.

Though he sometimes chastised Jewish interpreters for failing to interpret the Bible contextually, it was far more likely that Calvin would criticize Christian exegetes for this fault. He frequently dissented from those christological interpretations of the Old Testament that he believed derive no support from the context of the passage. This insistence on the necessity and adequacy of contextual interpretation led Aegidius Hunnius, a prominent Lutheran theologian, to accuse Calvin of judaizing.

Calvin insisted that failure to interpret contextually may lead to the wrong application of Scripture. A proper contextual interpretation of Amos 6:5 ("who sing idle songs to the sound of the harp") recognizes that it was addressing the condition of evildoers who were living overindulgently. The reader who lifts the verse out of context may draw the improper generalization that the verse should be understood as a blanket condemnation of music.

While strong philological skills and careful attention to context were important, Calvin believed, it was essential for the interpreter to read Scripture with the proper goal: that of finding Christ. The true meaning of the Old Testament could not be known apart from Christ, and the knowledge of Christ came through the work of the Spirit. The problem with Jewish exegesis was at its core a spiritual one—spiritual blindness. If, as Calvin taught elsewhere, the remedy for spiritual blindness is the illuminating work of the Holy Spirit, then such illumination might be understood as a precondition of proper exegesis. If the Jews possessed the Spirit, they would understand that Christ is the substance of the Old Testament.

Illumination by the Holy Spirit and philological expertise were both needed by the biblical exegete. But they were not necessary in the same way. The exegete needed illumination in order to understand the meaning of the Old Testament in its true spiritual meaning, that is, as a witness to Jesus Christ. Apart from such illumination, any other understanding of the Old Testament was empty and useless. However, while spiritual illumination might guarantee that the interpreter would understand the message of the Old Testament as a whole, it in no way guaranteed that he would understand the meaning of any specific text. Augustine and Luther certainly understood the Old Testament's witness to Jesus Christ, yet in Calvin's view they often twisted the interpretation of individual texts away from their natural meaning. The best exegesis of the Old Testament combined piety (a product of the Holy Spirit) and scholarship.

Special Issues of Old Testament Interpretation. For the first millennium and a half of the church's history the scales of Christian biblical interpretation were often tipped away from a historical exegetical method as interpreters of the Bible grappled with the problem of how to understand the Old Testament in light of the reality that Jesus Christ had fulfilled what was promised or foreshadowed there. Historical interpretation did not consistently produce results that were doctrinally orthodox and spiritually edifying.

In three areas of Old Testament interpretation that often divided Jewish and Christian interpreters, Calvin's approach seems to reflect something of a middle way. In his treatment of allegory, typology and prophecy, he adopted a moderate position that he believed avoided the temptations that too often befell Jewish and Christian exegesis. He did not uproot the Old Testament from its historical soil, nor was he content to look only at the roots once the full flowering had taken place in Jesus Christ. He used the New Testament interpretation of the Old to establish the meaning of the Old Testament text. Yet he believed his Old Testament interpretations could be demonstrated to be correct through sound philological and historical reasoning as well.

Calvin called interpretations "allegorical" when they disregarded the historical context or when they interpreted the details of a biblical text apart from a consideration of the immediate literary context. Allegorical exegesis was the antithesis of historical exegesis. His severest criticism, apart from his criticism of Jewish interpreters, was reserved for those who allegorized Scripture excessively. He contrasted his own method (which was concerned only with what is useful) with the allegorical approach of other interpreters (which served simply as a display for their cleverness). Allegorical interpretation, he insisted, originates with the devil. It was a means by which Satan had attempted to undermine the certainty of biblical teaching.

In light of his harsh critique of allegorical interpretation, it is striking that Calvin sometimes approved of what he clearly regarded as an allegorical understanding of the text. He believes that many of the Old Testament promises of a future kingdom were meant to be taken allegorically. His principle for determining which Old Testament passages are allegories was this: If there has been no historical fulfillment of the promise, one should look for a fulfillment that is not literal. Since New Testament reality was often presented in an earthly, shadowy form in the Old Testament, it is reasonable to look for a spiritual interpretation of prophecies that were not literally fulfilled. Calvin's approach did not reflect a lack of concern for historical exegesis. On the contrary, he would argue that his view was necessitated by that concern—specifically by his failure to find an earthly, historical fulfillment of the promises of the text.

Typology for Calvin was true prophecy, albeit shadowy and somewhat obscure. God chose to accommodate his revelation to the weakness and ignorance of his people in Old Testament times by presenting spiritual truth under earthly symbols. The symbols did not set forth the full truth but directed the people toward the truth. The

symbols varied, but in almost every instance they were intended as pictures of the redeemer who was to come. Calvin believed an understanding of the symbolic nature of persons and institutions was indispensable if one was to profit from the study of the Old Testament.

Calvin depended on two basic arguments in his attempt to substantiate his typological exegesis: first, the New Testament writers provide sound guidance when they treat Old Testament texts as prophecies that are fulfilled in Jesus Christ; second, the language of the Old Testament sometimes does not suit the reign of David or any other Old Testament figure, yet it perfectly suits the reign of Christ. He believed that typological interpretation, as he practiced it, rested on a solid, defensible base. The Jews, he insisted, were able to cite no adequate Old Testament referent for the texts he interprets typologically; thus a christological interpretation was necessary. To fellow Christians he argued that one should not tear a text out of its historical context in order to apply it to Christ; it must have a historical referent nearer to the time of the original audience. The Jewish approach robbed Jesus Christ of his honor; the traditional Christian approach robbed the Old Testament of significance for its original audience.

Calvin opposed the exclusivity of the either/or mentality that he believed characterized much Jewish and Christian exegesis of Old Testament prophecies. He often advocated what he called the "extended" meaning of the text. His was an inclusive approach that found the beginning of the historical fulfillment of prophecy in Old Testament times, yet saw the complete fulfillment coming only in Jesus Christ or in the Christian church.

Calvin believed that his interpretations of Old Testament prophecies could be justified against the traditional approaches of Jews and Christians alike. He rejected Christian interpretations when they ignored the historical meaning of the text. He rejected Jewish interpretations because he believed the language of the text could not possibly be understood as having been completely fulfilled in Old Testament times.

Use of the New Testament as Exegetical Guide. Though Calvin charged that *Origen was the source of confusion and uncertainty in the handling of Scripture, he agreed with him on one point: the New Testament is a reliable guide in interpreting the Old Testament. This, Calvin argued, was true because the Holy Spirit was responsible for all of Scripture, and the Spirit was best able to interpret the Spirit's own words. The Holy Spirit's authorship of all Scripture did not yield for Calvin an unambiguous hermeneutic. But it did have great hermeneutical significance. Calvin could not imagine sober historical interpretation of the Old Testament operating apart from the context provided by the New Testament writings.

Calvin conceded that the New Testament writers sometimes appeared to twist the Old Testament to meanings that were foreign to the original writer's intention. In some places they appeared to be overly subtle and made apparent mistakes in quoting the Old Testament. Calvin sometimes solved the difficulty by arguing that it was not the intent of the New Testament writers to interpret the Old Testament texts they cited. Sometimes they simply used the Old Testament for illustrative purposes. Since it was not their intent to offer a historical interpretation, they should not be regarded as misconstruing its meaning. In other places he believed that the New Testament writers' seemingly forced use of the Old Testament was intended to be an interpretation. In such cases he allowed the New Testament to guide him in his view of what the Old Testament writer must have understood and intended.

The role of the New Testament in guiding Old Testament exegesis is nowhere more apparent than in Calvin's interpretation of the Decalogue. His treatment of the sixth commandment is representative of his general approach. The commandment

"Thou shalt not kill" included much more than a prohibition of murder. The word *kill* was a synecdoche for all violence and aggression. Calvin found confirmation in the teaching of Jesus for his belief that "negative precepts" or prohibitions in the Bible should be understood to include the opposite affirmations. While the sixth commandment may appear only to have prohibited murder, it also instructed us that we are to defend the lives of our neighbors. Jesus' teaching in Matthew 5:22 that hateful thoughts and words deserve judgment was intended to be an exposition of the genuine sense of this commandment. The apostle John confirmed this teaching in 1 John 3:15, where he wrote that whoever hates his brother is a murderer.

Significance. Philip Schaff designated Calvin the "founder of modern historical-grammatical exegesis." In Schaff's judgment Calvin's exegesis was more oriented to matters of language and history than was the exegesis of those who preceded him. But Calvin was probably not all that different from other interpreters of his day who were influenced by humanist concerns and methods. His contribution is probably best seen in the remarkable clarity and compactness with which he packaged the fruits of his labor and in the moderation and balance reflected in his exegesis.

In recent years many commentators have found Calvin's exegetical writings to be helpful. Brevard *Childs recommends Calvin's commentaries on Genesis and Psalms as sober, literal and even brilliant expositions. C. E. B. Cranfield praises Calvin for his solid exposition of Romans—for his faithful, simple and succinct effort to unfold the mind of the writer.

Some scholars have suggested that a tension exists in Calvin's approach to biblical interpretation between a traditional Christian approach that emphasizes the divine side of Scripture and its unity and a more modern approach that recognizes the human element and diversity to be found in Scripture. Ironically, it may be the fact that Calvin did not resolve the tensions that accounts for the current popularity of his commentaries with many Christian biblical interpreters. His affirmation of the human side of Scripture suggests that there is hope of interpreting Scripture through the use of familiar methods; his affirmation of the divine side of Scripture suggests that once interpreted, the message of Scripture is of eternal importance.

BIBLIOGRAPHY

Works. J. Calvin, *Calvin's Commentary on Seneca's "De Clementia,"* ed. and trans. F. L. Battles and A. M. Hugo (Leiden: E. J. Brill, 1969); idem, *Ioannis Calvini: Opera Omnia,* series 2: *Opera Exegetica, Veteris et Novi Testamenti* (Geneva: Librairie Droz, 1992); idem, *Ioannis Calvini Opera Quae Supersunt Omnia,* ed. G. Baum, E. Cunitz and E. Reuss (59 vols.; Brunswick, Germany: Brunsvigae 1863-1900); idem, *Johannis Calvini Opera Selecta,* ed. P. Barth and G. Niesel (5 vols.; Munich, 1926-1952); idem, *Supplementa Calviniana* (Sermons Indits; Neukirchen: Neukirchener Verlag, 1961); idem, *Calvin: Commentaries,* ed. J. Haroutunian (LCC 23; Philadelphia: Westminster, 1958); idem, *Calvin's Commentaries,* ed. D. W. Torrance and T. F. Torrance (12 vols.; Grand Rapids: Eerdmans, 1959-1972); idem, *Calvin's Old Testament Commentaries* (The Rutherford House Translation; Carlisle: Paternoster; Grand Rapids: Eerdmans 1993-); idem, *The Commentaries of John Calvin* (Calvin Translation Society; 22 vols.; Grand Rapids: Baker, 1979 [1843-55]); idem, *Institutes of the Christian Religion,* ed. J. T. McNeill (LCC 21-22; Philadelphia: Westminster, 1960).

Studies. F. L. Battles, "God Was Accommodating Himself to Human Capacity," *Int* 31 (January 1977) 19-38; A. J. Baumgartner, *Calvin Hébraïsant et interprète de l'Ancien Testament* (Paris: Librairie Fischbacher, 1889); Q. Breen, *John Calvin: A Study in French Humanism* (Hamden, CT: Archon, 1968 [1931]); W. J. Bouwsma, *John Calvin: A Sixteenth-Century Portrait* (New York: Oxford University Press, 1988); E. Doumergue, *Jean Calvin: Les hommes et les choses de son temps,* 4: *La pensée religieuse de Calvin* (Geneva: Slatkine, 1969 [1899-1927]); H. J. Forstman, *Word and Spirit: Calvin's Doctrine of Biblical Authority* (Stanford, CA: Stanford University Press, 1962); A. Ganoczy, *The Young Calvin* (Philadelphia: Westminster, 1987); A. Ganoczy and S. Scheld, *Die Herme-*

neutik Calvins: Geistesgeschichtliche Voraussetzungen und Grundzüge (Veröffentlichungen des Instituts für Europäische Geschichte Mainz Abteilung für Abendländische Religionsgeschichte 114; Wiesbaden: Franz Steiner Verlag, 1983); H-J. Kraus, "Calvin's Exegetical Principles," *Int* 31 (1977) 8-18; J. T. McNeill, "The Significance of the Word of God for Calvin," *CH* 28 (June 1959) 131-46; T. H. L. Parker, *Calvin's New Testament Commentaries* (2d ed.; Edinburgh: T & T Clark, 1993); idem, *Calvin's Old Testament Commentaries* (Edinburgh: T & T. Clark, 1986); idem, *Calvin's Preaching* (Louisville, KY: Westminster John Knox, 1992); idem, *John Calvin: A Biography* (Philadelphia: Westminster, 1975); D. L. Puckett, *John Calvin's Exegesis of the Old Testament* (Louisville, KY: Westminster John Knox, 1995); S. E. Schreiner, *Where Shall Wisdom Be Found? Calvin's Exegesis of Job from Medieval and Modern Perspectives* (Chicago: University of Chicago Press, 1994); T. F. Torrance, *The Hermeneutics of John Calvin* (Edinburgh: Scottish Academic Press, 1988); H. H. Wolf, *Die Einheit des Bundes: Das Verhältnis von Altem und Neuem Testament bei Calvin* (Beiträge zur Geschichte und Lehre der Reformierten Kirche 10; Neukirchen: Verlag der Buchhandlung des Erziehungsvereins, 1958); M. H. Woudstra, *Calvin's Dying Bequest to the Church: A Critical Evaluation of the Commentary on Joshua* (Calvin Theological Seminary Monograph Series 1; Grand Rapids: Calvin Theological Seminary, 1960).

D. L. Puckett

Coverdale, Miles *(c. 1487-1569)*

Miles Coverdale gave the English people both their first published Bible in the vernacular (1535) and the subsequent version that Henry VIII ordered to be placed in all parish churches. Coverdale's career spans and reflects the zigzag course of Reformation years in England. Born in York about 1487, this Augustinian friar in the early 1520s participated in the heady theological conversations in Cambridge; these conversations were stimulated by the Reformation writings that crossed the North Sea. Associated with the Continental Reformation more intimately and over more years than was any other major figure of the English Reformation, Coverdale's three periods of prudent exile from his native land (1528-1535, 1540-1548 and 1555-1559) included six years in which he ministered to a congregation and its school in the Rhenish Palatinate. After the first exile Coverdale made his major contributions, the biblical translations, while Henry's policies leaned toward the Reformers. After the second exile, while English reform flourished under the government of Edward VI, the crown named Coverdale Bishop of Exeter, but two years later he was ejected in the wake of Mary Tudor's accession to the throne. Coverdale returned home after Elizabeth I succeeded her sister. For his last ten years he ministered in London to those who shared his distaste for the terms of the Elizabethan settlement.

Context. Fellow Reformer and exile John Bale reported that Coverdale was "one of the first in the English Church's renaissance to profess Christ purely," being initially led to such "good teachings under Robert Barnes," Coverdale's Augustinian prior at Cambridge (Bale, sig. Ppp1). By 1528 Coverdale had left the friars, and the attention he had drawn from heresy hunters led to his first exile.

Coverdale emerged in Hamburg (1529) assisting William *Tyndale in the translation of the Pentateuch, Tyndale's initial foray into the Hebrew Scriptures. When John Rogers arrived in Antwerp (1534) to serve as chaplain to the company of English Merchant Adventurers, he found the two men occupied with scriptural translations.

Tyndale's translations from the Hebrew were progressing slowly, with only the book of Jonah added to the published Pentateuch. In the summer of 1534 a Protestant merchant in Antwerp, Jacob van Meteren, commissioned Coverdale to prepare an English Bible even though it was not directly translated from the original Hebrew and Greek. Within a year Coverdale had his manuscript in hand. Before the 1535 printing in Cologne was completed, a recently naturalized Flemish printer in Southwark, James Nicolson, was in touch with Thomas Cromwell. Nicolson sent the

king's chief minister a section of Coverdale's Bible and its dedication to Henry VIII with a request that "the pure word of God may once go forth under the king's privilege" (Mozley, 111). No such license was forthcoming, but copies of this Bible were circulating early in 1536.

In contrast with most Continental countries, in which printed vernacular Scriptures had already appeared, in England, as a legacy of John Wyclif and his Lollard followers, church authorities had firmly associated an English Bible with heresy. When Tyndale's New Testament appeared (1526), most church officials judged it Lutheran in vocabulary and notes. Henry VIII (1530) ordered all vernacular Scriptures turned in, suggesting, however, that he and the bishops might later appoint "learned and Catholic persons" to translate the Bible when it shall "seem to his grace convenient" (Pollard, 168). The clerical Convocation of Canterbury (1534) agreed that Archbishop Cranmer should request the king to appoint such translators. Henry made no response. Yet the English religious climate was changing under Cranmer's cautious leadership. A cluster of evidence cogently assembled by J. F. Mozley suggests that Henry had given tacit approval for Coverdale's Bible and came close to ordering it to be placed in every English parish church (Mozley, 36-40; 110-21).

After Tyndale was burned as a heretic, Rogers prepared the text of the Bible tabbed the Matthew Bible by reason of its pseudonymous "translator." The text was based on Tyndale's published translations, a set of his unpublished manuscripts, Coverdale's texts for the Old Testament books from Ezra to Malachi (except Jonah) and all the Apocrypha (except the Prayer of Manasseh), and a fresh translation of the Prayer of Manasseh.

Cranmer declared in a letter to Cromwell seeking a royal license for the Matthew Bible that he liked it "better than any other translation heretofore made" (Pollard, 215). Cromwell obtained the royal license, which incidentally provided Nicolson with the official authorization that appeared in the next edition of Coverdale's text. In 1538 Cromwell, in the king's name, ordered all clergy with pastoral cures to procure "one book of the whole Bible of the largest volume in English," to be set up in some convenient place in the church where "parishioners may . . . read it" (*Injunctions,* 2:35-36). Cranmer's preference for the Matthew Bible prevailed. The Bible's unedited promulgation with the Protestant flavor of its accessory materials would have been strategically unwise. Coverdale became its editor.

It was determined to print the new Bible at the press of Francis Regnault in Paris. For seven months Coverdale worked in Paris to edit and oversee the printing, but interference from the French Inquistion forced a hasty retreat to London, where the edition was completed. After the Great Bible appeared (1539), Coverdale continued revising the text. The second edition (1540), with a masterful preface by Cranmer, provided the norm, which was reproduced with only trifling changes in succeeding editions.

Coverdale's major contributions to biblical literacy in England were completed. Although his active ministry was henceforth to be channeled into less central streams of reforming endeavors, Coverdale made one further minor contribution to biblical translation. For the final ten months of his exile during Mary's reign, he lived in Geneva, where fellow exiles were preparing a new translation. Coverdale took a lively interest in the project, but the Genevan team's competence in the biblical languages and Coverdale's relatively short stay suggest that his role was that of a senior consulting advisor.

The 1535 Bible. Coverdale understood translation to be both the foundation of interpretation and, inevitably in human hands, an inexact science in which a comparison of varying texts provided an interpretive key. He wrote that "there cometh more knowledge and understanding of the scripture by their sundry translations than by all the glosses of our sophistical doctors" (prologue to the 1535 Bible, Coverdale 1844, 19), and that "one translation declareth, openeth, and illustrateth another, and . . . in many places one is a plain commentary unto another" (prologue to the 1538 Renault Diglot New Testament, Coverdale 1844, 36). To his readers he suggested an approach reflecting the principles of Renaissance literary criticism:

It shall greatly help thee to understand scripture, if thou mark not only what is spoken or written, but of whom, and unto whom, with what words, at what time, where, to what intent, with what circumstances, considering what goeth before, and what followeth after. (Coverdale 1846, 15)

Although where Scripture "is taught and known, it . . . leaveth no poor man unhelped," interpretation was a community, not an individual, enterprise. Sound scholarship was essential for passages of "strange manners of speaking and dark sentences." He advised readers to "commit them unto God, or to the gift of the Holy Spirit in them that are better learned than thou" (dedication and prologue, Coverdale 1846, 15, 10).

Coverdale himself depended on the "variety of translations," for he never claimed the trilingual mastery on which Renaissance biblical scholarship was based. In the preface to his first publication, a translation of a Latin paraphrase of the Psalms, he ventured the work even though "I durst not be so foolish hardy as to put forth any text, because I have not such understanding in the three tongues as is needful for him that should well and truly translate any text of scripture" (Mozley, 60).

In his dedication Coverdale reported that he had "translated this out of five sundry interpreters" (Coverdale 1846, 11). Studies have concluded that the five are in English, Tyndale; in German, Luther and the Zurich Bible; and in Latin, the traditional Vulgate and the Old Testament translation of the Italian Hebraist Sanctes Pagninus. In the Pentateuch, Jonah and the

New Testament, Tyndale's published translations provided the working text into which Coverdale introduced changes drawn from his other sources. The Germans and in particular the Zurich Bible played the largest part in these changes and in his fresh translations of the other books. As a consequence Coverdale's texts have a strong Germanic flavor, and they favor words with Anglo-Saxon roots more commonly than does Tyndale's text. In spite of increasing familiarity with Greek and Hebrew as he worked under Tyndale and on his own, Coverdale always took care to inform readers of his scholarly strictures in scriptural translation.

Fully sensitive to the political realities of the day, Coverdale, unlike Rogers, designed his ancillaries to avoid impediments to the Bible's distribution. Although for the most part he maintained the items of Tyndale's diction that had outraged conservatives, he carefully omitted polemical prologues, prefaces and notes. Except for anti-Roman rhetoric welcome to Henry in the dedication, the closest he approached to theological polemics is in the prologue to the reader, in which he defended his interchangeable use of "repentance" and "penance." Both, he argued, must be understood as "a very repentance, amendment, or conversion unto God," hardly a retreat from the principle that the word did not denote "auricular confession" (Coverdale 1846, 19-20). Coverdale's primary goal consistently shaped the book and the manner of its presentation: to make the vernacular text accessible to the English people.

The Great Bible. Coverdale's editing of the Great Bible provides solid evidence of the sincerity of his statement that "wherinsoever I can perceive by myself, or by the information of other, that I have failed [in a point of translation], . . . I shall now by the help of God . . . amend it" (prologue to 1535 Bible, Coverdale 1846, 14).

He looked with new eyes at the texts of the Matthew Bible. He went thoroughly through Tyndale's sections, introducing changes for stylistic as well as interpretive

reasons. For the New Testament Coverdale relied on Desiderius *Erasmus's Latin version, and for the Old he drew from the newly available Hebrew-Latin Old Testament of Sebastian Münster. Except for the Apocrypha, Coverdale also revised his own sections, primarily seeking to improve the critical accuracy of the texts. The changes from the new Latin sources reduced the Germanic flavor of Matthew's text.

Those accessory preliminaries and notes in Matthew's Bible that offended conservatives disappeared. As a further concession, Coverdale added in distinctive small type materials from the Vulgate that did not have a foundation in the Hebrew or the Greek. In this form the Great Bible served as the basic text for both the 1560 Geneva Bible and the 1566 Bishops' Bible, the two most important contributors to the 1611 King James Bible.

Concern for the Psalter. The Psalter of the Great Bible merits special attention. From 1552 it was regularly included in the *Book of Common Prayer,* and down to the twentieth century, successive editions of the prayer book retained Coverdale's Psalter with few changes. Coverdale's first publication (1534) was a translation of John Campensis's Latin paraphrase of the psalms. In 1537 Nicolson printed Coverdale's translation of Martin Luther's "very excellent and sweet exposition" of Psalm 23.

In 1540 Coverdale produced yet another text of the Psalms, this time with the Latin Vulgate in a column parallel to the English translated "out of the texte in Latyne which customably is red in the churche." Priests with limited Latin could deepen both their piety and learning when they read the psalms in their daily offices from the diglot edition.

Other Biblical Scholarship. Some of Coverdale's lesser contributions to biblical scholarship are easily overlooked. His 1535 *Concordance of the New Testament,* based on Tyndale's text, was the first biblical concordance in English. Two books from Coverdale's 1535 Old Testament joined three from the Apocrypha to form "The Bookes of Salomon" published in 1537. In 1538 Nicolson printed Coverdale's translation of Luther's expositions of the Magnificat (Lk 1:46-55) and of Solomon's prayer for wisdom (1 Kings 3:6-9).

When Coverdale took on the editing of the Great Bible, he was completing another project similar to the bilingual Psalter: a New Testament with its English translated from the accompanying Vulgate text. The diglot may also have been coordinated with attempts, such as that of Bishop Latimer of Worcester, to require clergy to own the Scriptures "both in Latin and English [to] read over and study every day one chapter" (*Injunctions*, 2:12-15). In 1540 Coverdale published a devotional work patterned after a work of Ulrich *Zwingli: *Fruitfull Lessons upon the Passion, Buriall, Resurrection, Ascension, and of the Sending of the Holy Ghost.* Biblical passages were followed by a commentary that interpreted the passage, applied it to the readers' lives, and often concluded with a prayer.

When Coverdale returned to England in the spring of 1548, he became associated with the translation of Erasmus's *Paraphrase upon the New Testament* with its biting allusions to current corruption in church life. The first volume had already been published. Coverdale oversaw the second volume, writing its dedication to Edward VI and translating the paraphrases on the first four Pauline letters. The prominent inclusion of Tyndale's prologue to Romans, based heavily on Luther's preface to the book, added a strong Protestant coloring to the moral landscape of Erasmus's Renaissance critique.

Significance. Coverdale's work was firmly based in Renaissance biblical scholarship and the Continental Reformation. Lutheranism, through Robert Barnes, initiated his new theological orientation. Coverdale served his apprenticeship as a translator under Tyndale who, in spite of a primary debt to Luther, tinged the gospel proclamation of Wittenberg with a stronger moralistic color which, if not legalistic, did,

in the words of Tyndale's recent biographer, move "towards a theme of sanctification, the need for believers to 'grow' in the Lord" (Daniell, 208; cf. Clebsch, passim). This shift, consistent with Renaissance humanism, was also one reflected in the Reformed churches of the Rhineland, Switzerland and Geneva. Coverdale shared this shift from Luther to the Reformed. The advice he gave his readers in the prologue to the 1535 Bible has a strong Reformed flavor:

Sit thee down at the Lord's feet, and read his words. . . . And above all things, fashion thy life and conversation according to the doctrine . . . therein, that thou mayest be partaker of the good promises of God in the Bible and be heir of his blessing in Christ: in whom if thou put thy trust, . . . thou shalt . . . spy wondrous things, to thy understanding, to the avoiding of all seditious sects, to the abhorring of thy old sinful life, and to the stablishing of thy godly conversation. (Coverdale 1846, 16-17)

Coverdale, like Luther, delivered the vernacular Scriptures to his people, although unlike Luther, he lacked mastery of the biblical languages and depended on the scholarship of those who provided translations into Latin, English and German. The King James Bible came almost a century later than Luther's, yet just as the German Bible provided the chief formative literary fountainhead for the cultural development of northern Germany, so the succession of English translations from 1535 to 1611 provided a similar source for English culture. Although many after Tyndale and Coverdale contributed to the King James Version, few would disagree with Mozley's judgment that in that line of scholars, "the name of Coverdale stands second only to Tyndale" (Mozley, 109).

Coverdale was committed to bring the English people to the understandings of the loving outreach of God in Jesus Christ that he had discovered anew in the Scriptures in the light of Reformation teachings. His translations and original writings, his reputation as a preacher, and his pastoral work testify to the importance he gave to instruction, prayer and corporate worship, and patient ministry. Yet above all he judged that the people's acquaintance with the text of the Bible was key to all the rest. To make that text available was the crowning achievement of his life. After the publication of the 1535 Bible, English church, English religion and English culture were never quite the same.

BIBLIOGRAPHY

Works. M. Coverdale, *Remains of Myles Coverdale, Bishop of Exeter,* ed. G. Pearson (Parker Society 14; Cambridge: Cambridge University Press, 1846); idem, *Writings and Translations of Myles Coverdale, Bishop of Exeter,* ed. G. Pearson (Parker Society 13; Cambridge: Cambridge University Press, 1844). Pearson's two volumes are incomplete and contain translations incorrectly attributed to Coverdale.

Studies. J. Bale, *Illustrium Maioris Britanniae Scriptorum . . . Summarium* (Wesel: D. van der Straten, 1548); W. A. Clebsch, *England's Earliest Protestants* (New Haven, CT: Yale University Press, 1964); D. Daniell, *William Tyndale: A Biography* (New Haven, CT: Yale University Press, 1994); J. Foxe, *The Acts and Monuments of John Foxe,* ed. J. Pratt (8 vols.; London: Religious Tract Society, 1877); S. L. Greenslade, *The Cambridge History of the Bible,* 3: *The West from the Reformation to the Present Day* (Cambridge: Cambridge University Press, 1963); W. P. Haugaard, "The Bible in the Anglican Reformation" in *Anglicanism and the Bible,* ed. F. H. Borsch (Wilton, CT: Morehouse Barlow, 1984) chap. 1; J. Hooker [or Vowel], *A Catalog of the Bishops of Excester* (London: Henry Denham, 1584); *Injunctions: Visitation Articles and Injunctions of the Period of the Reformation,* ed. W. H. Frere and W. M. Kennedy (Alcuin Club Collections 14-16; 3 vols.; London: Longmans, Green, 1910); L. Lupton, *Miles Coverdale,* 2 vols. *Endurance* and *Heaven* (History of the Geneva Bible 11, 12; London: The Olive Tree, 1979-1980); T. More, *Confutation of Tyndale's Answer* in *The Complete Works of Thomas More* (18 vols.; New Haven, CT: Yale University Press, 1963-) vol. 8; J. F. Mozley, *Coverdale and His Bibles* (London: Lutterworth, 1953); *Original Letters: Original Letters Relative to the English Reformation, Written During the Reigns of King Henry VIII, King Edward VI and Queen Mary: Chiefly from the Archives of Zurich* (Parker Society; Cambridge: Cambridge University Press, 1846-47); K. Parr, *The Lamentacion of a Synner* (2d ed.; *STC* 4828; London: Whitchurch, 1548); A. W. Pollard, *Records of the English Bible: The Documents Relating to the Translation and Publication of the Bible in English, 1525-1611* (Oxford: Oxford University Press, 1911); *Sectes Anonymous: The Original & Sprynge of All Sectes and Orders* (Southwark: J. Nicolson, 1537); *Zurich Letters: The Zurich Letters, comprising the Correspondence of Several English Bishops and Others with Some of the Helvetian Reformers During the Reign of Queen Elizabeth,* ed. H. Robinson (Parker Society 37-38; 2 vols.; Cambridge: Cambridge University Press, 1842-1855).

W. P. Haugaard

Erasmus, Desiderius (c. 1466-1536)

Desiderius Erasmus of Rotterdam was the prince of the Renaissance humanists north of the Alps. Renaissance humanism, which first emerged in fourteenth-century Italy, was an intellectual movement with the purpose of renewing study of the liberal arts (grammar, rhetoric, literature, history and moral philosophy) in order to bring about a more cultivated and morally complete humanity. The models for this program were the writings of classical antiquity, both Greek and Latin. Many of the humanists, especially those in northern Europe, sought a revival of not only classical but also Christian antiquity. They wished to bring about a fresh understanding of the Bible and the church fathers (*Origen, John *Chrysostom, *Jerome, *Augustine) in order to effect the reform of church and society. They are sometimes called Christian humanists or biblical humanists.

Erasmus was the generally acknowledged head of this movement of Christian humanism. On the one hand he was a great classical scholar who edited, translated and published Greek and Latin authors and who culled quotations from them for his ever-expanding editions of the *Adages.* On the other hand he was also a Christian theologian, a biblical and patristic scholar who edited, translated and interpreted the New Testament and the Greek and Latin fathers. Erasmus wanted both the classics and the New Testament to be known as widely as possible. Thus he writes in one of the introductions to his 1516 edition of the New Testament, the *Paraclesis (The Exhortation to the Study of Christian Philosophy):*

Christ wishes His mysteries published as openly as possible. I would that even the lowliest women read the Gospels and the Pauline Epistles. . . . I would that they were translated into all languages. . . . Would that . . . the farmer sing some portion of them at the plow, the weaver hum some parts of them to the movement of his shuttle, the traveler lighten the weariness of the journey with stories of this kind. (Erasmus 1987, 101)

Erasmus did not consider his double vocation to be in conflict. As he wrote also in the *Paraclesis,* the "philosophy of Christ" (this term he derived from the Fathers) has much in common with certain sentiments of the classical writings: "what else is the philosophy of Christ, which He Himself calls a rebirth, than the restoration of human nature well formed? By the same token, although no one has taught this more perfectly and effectively than Christ, nevertheless one may find in the books of the pagans very much which does agree with His teaching" (Erasmus 1987, 104).

Early in his career Erasmus was more enamored of the classics than he was of biblical studies. By 1500 he came under the spell of *Jerome, who showed him how an eloquent writer and outstanding classicist could also be a biblical scholar par excellence. He was perhaps also inspired to a certain extent to pursue biblical studies by John Colet, whose lectures on Romans he had heard at Oxford in 1499. He began a commentary on Romans himself and completed four volumes of it before eventually giving up the project. At the same time he set out to learn Greek, convinced that one could not seriously study Scripture without the requisite languages. Within a short time he had so mastered it that he was able to

translate Greek authors into Latin. He tried Hebrew but was repelled by the strangeness of the language and overcome by the realization of the limits of his capacity to take up at his age another difficult language.

Erasmus determined to devote himself principally to the study of the New Testament, no doubt because he perceived it as containing the pure philosophy of Christ, the knowledge of which was so much needed in the church of his time. He did not give up his studies of the classics, but more and more he saw these efforts as providing preparatory training for the most important task, that of mastering the New Testament in Greek and Latin. Erasmus received further stimulus for his New Testament studies from the annotations on the New Testament by the Italian humanist Lorenzo Valla, which he discovered in an abbey near Louvain in 1504 and which he had published in 1505. Erasmus's own annotations, which accompanied his New Testament edition, exceeded the work of Valla in quality and scope. Whereas Valla's were brief textual critical notes, Erasmus's annotations offered not only more extensive textual criticism but also literary and theological exegesis.

New Testament Editions. Erasmus's New Testament research—the seeking out of Greek and Latin manuscripts, collating them, reading commentaries by the Fathers and writing notes on the text—bore fruit in the publication of the first critical New Testament edition (1516). The publication took place in Basel with the printer John Froben, who, aware of the imminent publication of the Complutensian Polyglot New Testament at Alcala, Spain, wished to speed the process along so that Erasmus's edition would be the first published Greek New Testament text. The Complutensian edition had already been printed in 1514, but it did not receive formal approval for publication until 1520. The result of the haste in publishing the Erasmian edition was that there were many printing and editing errors, which Erasmus greatly regretted. He therefore set out immediately to prepare an emended edition.

The volume consisted of two columns of text—one the Greek and the other Erasmus's Latin translation—and annotations, which were placed at the back. In front stood considerable introductory material: the preface dedicated to Pope Leo X; the *Exhortation (Paraclesis);* the *Method (Methodus),* which Erasmus greatly expanded for the 1519 edition under the title *The Method of True Theology (Ratio Verae Theologiae);* and the *Apology (Apologia).*

For the Greek text of his first edition, Erasmus used five manuscripts he discovered in Basel, but he relied chiefly on two of them, dating from the twelfth century, which follow the Byzantine textual tradition. That these manuscripts served as copies for the printer can be discerned by corrections made on them. The only manuscript that contained the book of Revelation lacked the last six verses. Erasmus made up for this omission by translating the verses from the Latin Vulgate back into Greek and including them in his edition. It was not until the fourth edition (1527) of his New Testament that he replaced his translation with the Greek text from the Complutensian Polyglot. For comparison with the Greek text and for use in his Latin translation, Erasmus consulted a number of Latin manuscripts, some of which he had examined in England. He had likewise already looked at a few Greek manuscripts in England before coming to Basel. For the succeeding editions (1519, 1522, 1527 and 1535), Erasmus sought out additional Greek and Latin manuscripts for correcting the text.

Among his most controversial exercises in textual criticism was his rejection of the passage concerning the three witnesses in heaven at 1 John 5:7. In response to heated criticism for this omission, Erasmus reported that he did not find it in any Greek manuscript. A manuscript containing it was discovered in England, perhaps manufactured for the purpose, so that Erasmus restored the reading in his third edition (1522).

Erasmus's Latin translation for the first edition did not differ greatly from the Vulgate. Until recently scholars thought that Erasmus had begun his Latin translation when he was in England in 1505 and 1506 because manuscript copies of Erasmus's translation in the hand of Peter Meghen and dated 1506 and 1509 exist in British libraries. But A. Brown has proved conclusively that the dates on these manuscripts apply only to the Vulgate, not to Erasmus's translation. Erasmus's translation presented in these manuscripts originated in the early 1520s. By that time his translation had become bolder in its variance from the Vulgate, as is evident already in the 1519 edition.

Even if the idea of his own fresh Latin translation from the Greek was not in Erasmus's mind from the beginning, it came to assume great importance to him. Though to most modern scholars his Greek text, the first one to be published, has received the most attention, to Erasmus himself and his contemporaries his Latin translation loomed larger in significance (de Jonge). He considered the teachings of Jesus and the apostles to have been obscured by the Vulgate translation which, because of its many errors, he could not ascribe, at least in its present form, to the supreme Latinist Jerome.

As his introductions to his New Testament edition inform us, Erasmus sought to improve the Vulgate translation in several respects. He aimed at faithfulness to the Greek text, greater clarity of expression, the removal of solecisms and improvement of the Latin style. The humanist was intent on conveying the original Greek as accurately as possible, but he did not favor literal translations, of which the Vulgate was sometimes guilty, for they often obscured the sense. Intelligibilty and clarity were just as important to him. Throughout his translation Erasmus sought to remove as many grammatical errors and unidiomatic Latin expressions as possible. In addition he was concerned with style. Although he understood the New Testament as a whole not to have been written in the elevated style of classical Greek literature, he did recognize examples of splendid rhetoric in it. He thought that, as much as possible, the Latin should match the style of the Greek—indeed in some cases to improve upon it. But he did not regard style as important as accuracy and clarity.

Some of Erasmus's translations modified centuries-long theological understandings of important texts. For example, he changed the Vulgate's translation of Matthew 3:2 and Matthew 4:17 from *poenitentiam agite* ("do penance") to *poeniteat vos* or *respisicite* ("repent" or "come to one's senses") because the Greek word *metanoiete* signifies a change of mind. Under attack from his critics for seeming to undermine the foundation of the sacrament of penance, Erasmus restored the Vulgate's translation of Matthew 3:2 but kept *resipiscite* for Matthew 4:17. It is probable that Martin *Luther made use of this translation and the accompanying annotation for the first two of his 1517 Ninety-Five Theses.

Erasmus's *Annotations* were so expanded in succeeding editions that a second volume was required for them. They display the full range of his New Testament scholarship: his work as textual and literary critic and theological exegete. In the first edition the *Annotations* consisted of brief philological notes explaining his criticism of the Vulgate renderings on the basis of the Greek and Latin manuscripts and of his knowledge of Greek and Latin grammar and style. In later editions the *Annotations* greatly increased in number and length partly because he needed to answer critics of his translation but also because he introduced more textual-critical evidence as a result of his discovery of additional manuscripts and extended reading in the Greek and Latin fathers. Subsequent editions also contain much more literary and theological exegesis.

On the basis of his examination of the manuscripts themselves and of his wide reading in the Fathers, Erasmus showed himself a master of an embryonic textual criticism that anticipated in several respects its modern form. He was able to detect the probability of scribal errors and give reasons for them. He noted, for example, textual corruption due to homonyms, words that either sound or look alike, and assimilation, the introduction of a passage from one place into another because of similarity. Erasmus especially deplored textual corruption that resulted from a scribe's deliberate changes in the text because it offended the scribe's literary taste or his religious scruples, and he pointed out many cases of this kind. In addition he not only exploited the New Testament quotations and interpretations in the Greek Fathers but also inferred the Greek that lay behind the readings in the Latin fathers.

Furthermore, Erasmus determined the correct reading on the basis of the literary and theological context. For example, at Romans 5:1, Erasmus, noting that the witnesses are divided between ἔχομεν ("we have") and ἔχωμεν ("let us have"), argued that "the sense here does not allow the imperative mood. For the Apostle is speaking here about those who, justified through faith, now have peace with God" (Erasmus 1994, 127). Erasmus anticipated the modern textual critical principle of the harder reading, namely, that between two readings the more difficult one is probably the correct one because of the tendency of scribes to smooth out rough texts.

Even though the *Annotations* exhibit chiefly textual and literary criticism, some of them touch on matters of theological substance. His lengthy annotation on Romans 5:12 is based on his understanding of the Greek, which he thought the Vulgate had misconstrued. He was the first in the history of exegesis to argue that ἐπι with the dative has a causal meaning so that the translation should not be, as with the Vulgate, "in whom all sinned" but rather "because all men sinned." Erasmus argued in his annotation that this text cannot be used to support the doctrine of original sin as had been the case ever since Augustine.

Many other notes deal with important

theological topics, such as the note on John 1:1 defending his translation of *logos* (word) by *sermo* rather than the Vulgate's *verbum* and displaying Erasmus's rhetorical theology. In addition to philological and theological exegesis, there are also moral diatribes, often loosely related to the text, in which Erasmus expresses himself freely on some of his favorite topics: the immorality of war, the squabbling of monastic orders with each other, the hypocrisy of the mendicants, greedy bishops, bellicose popes, ceremonial legalism, the vanity and contentiousness of theologians.

Erasmus's translation and annotations came under attack from several Roman Catholic theologians such as the Spaniard Diego Lopez Zuniga and the Englishman Edward Lee. Both in his expanding annotations and in the *Apologies,* Erasmus answered his critics at great length.

Paraphrases on the New Testament. At the same time that Erasmus was revising his New Testament edition, he was also at work on another form of New Testament interpretation, the *Paraphrases.* Between 1517, when the *Paraphrase on Romans* appeared, and 1524, Erasmus published *Paraphrases* on the entire New Testament except for the book of Revelation. While the *Annotations* were intended for scholars and theologians, the *Paraphrases* were aimed at a wider audience, both clergy and laity. They were therefore written in a clear and free-flowing style with the intention not so much to display fancy rhetoric as to communicate the meaning of the text even if rhetorical devices were not avoided. The classical models for his rhetoric were Aristotle, Cicero and especially Quintilian, whose teaching on paraphrasing he had previously recommended to students.

In contrast to a translation that seeks to adhere as closely as possible to the language of the author, the paraphrase "must say things differently without saying different things." In difference from a commentary, a paraphrase is a continuous narrative rather than an interrupted one, and yet it is "a kind of commentary." It is in a sense a commentary, for the paraphraser puts the text into his own words and carries on interpretation under the voice of the evangelist and the apostle. Erasmus is able in the *Paraphrases* to give expression to his view of the "philosophy of Christ" as having to do not with theological dialectics or ceremonial religion but with true piety and transformed living according to the life and teachings of Jesus. Unlike the commentary, the paraphrase does not provide a critical analysis of issues in the text, nor does it refer explicitly to previous commentators. Nevertheless, even if Erasmus did not name his sources, the volumes of the *Paraphrases* so far published in the *Collected Works of Erasmus* have shown that for his interpretations he made abundant use not only of the ancient Fathers but also of several medieval authors.

Commentaries on the Psalms. In addition to his monumental work of exegesis on the New Testament, Erasmus published eleven commentaries on the Psalms (1515-1536). He carried on this work with less confidence and persistence than on his exegesis of the New Testament. His lack of Hebrew no doubt played a role here, as well as less enthusiasm for the Old than the New Testament. His writings on the Psalms take on a greater variety of forms than those on the New Testament: paraphrase, of which there is only one example (Ps 3), since he found that form inappropriate for the Psalms; sermons, of which there are two (Ps 4; 85); untitled commentaries (Ps 1; 4; 22 [23]; 33 [34] and 38 [39]); and three commentaries with an exact title (Ps 14 [15]; 28 [29] and 83 [84]). But even in the cases of those that were called commentaries, Erasmus did not adhere rigidly to the traditional form of commentary. The untitled commentaries are largely sermonic in style, and the titled ones are actual treatises: Psalm 14 *(A Deliberation Concerning War with the Turk);* Psalm 28 (29) *(Concerning the Purity of the Tabernacle, or the Christian Church);* and Psalm 83 (84) *(On Mending the Peace of the Church).*

Method of Interpretation. In the introductory writings to his 1516 New Testament edition, especially in the *Methodus,* which evolved into the *Ratio Verae Theologiae (The Method of True Theology,* 1519), and in his late work for preachers, the *Ecclesiastae* (1535), Erasmus set forth his method of biblical interpretation. He combined a philological with a spiritual (allegorical and tropological) approach to Scripture. The philological method is concerned with textual, literary and historical criticism. It has to do first of all with the restoration of the pure, original text as far as possible, an endeavor that Erasmus's New Testament exhibits. It attends also to the language and context of the scriptural passages. One should weigh "not only what is said but also by whom, to whom, with what words, at what time, on what occasion, what precedes and what follows" (Erasmus 1933, 196).

In order to carry out this method, it is necessary for the exegete to be trained in the biblical languages, grammar, rhetoric, history and other secular disciplines. Especially important to the humanist is the training in grammar and rhetoric in order better to understand the language of Scripture with its many figures. Even though most of the obscurities of Scripture are removed by the exercise of this philological method, some remain. These may be elucidated by collating them with other passages of Scripture. In addition an understanding of the doctrine of Christ summarized from the Gospels and the apostolic letters is necessary in order to illuminate the meaning of specific texts. This doctrine is in harmony with Christ's life and with nature. Finally the Fathers need to be consulted for help in determining the proper exegesis of texts both in their grammatical and spiritual meaning. Erasmus posited a dialectical relationship between Scripture and the patristic tradition. On the one hand the Fathers are useful for the task of exegesis; on the other hand they must be measured against the rule of Scripture. Erasmus was frequently critical of what he regarded as their forced interpretations.

Erasmus followed the tradition going back to Origen, a tradition that held that Scripture has not only a literal but also a spiritual sense. Medieval exegesis had set forth a fourfold sense: literal, allegorical (christological and ecclesiological), tropological (moral) and anagogical (eschatological). Like Origen, Erasmus tended to limit the senses to three: literal, allegorical and tropological.

Allegorical interpretation is necessary in Erasmus's view when the literal meaning of the text is clearly absurd or when it obviously conflicts with the doctrine of Christ or morality. The anthropomorphic language concerning God and the immoralities of the patriarchs, as well as some of Jesus' commands concerning cutting off the right hand or plucking out the eye, are examples of this category. On the other hand, when the literal sense exhibits no absurdities, allegorical interpretation is not so necessary as it is very desirable and useful. The commentator needs to penetrate beneath the husk to the kernel of spiritual truth. Whereas in the *Enchiridion* (1503) Erasmus, under the influence of Origen, veered toward a spiritualistic, allegorical exegesis, by the time of his 1515 preface to the New Testament he had come to insist that the lowest sense is not to be scorned, since it is the foundation upon which the mystical meaning is built. In the *Ratio Verae Theologiae* and in the *Annotations* he was quite critical of the allegorizing of Origen and other church fathers and set forth the principle of simplicity in exegesis: "in divine literature the simplest and least forced interpretations are more satisfactory" (Erasmus 1994, 6). In his last great work, the *Ecclesiastae* (1535), Erasmus set forth a middle way between literalism and wild allegorization.

In addition to the literal and allegorical sense, the tropological was especially important for Erasmus. Not all of Scripture can be interpreted allegorically, but all passages can be accommodated to the moral sense. In fact the moral sense was so significant to him that he permitted a departure from the literal sense of the passage, "provided it is of value for the good life" and "agrees with the remaining passages of Scripture" (Erasmus 1703-5, V 274D).

Because Scripture contains allegory and tropology as well as letter, the exegete must approach it not only with the tools of philology but also with a clean heart and a pure mind. Erasmus insisted upon a spiritual and an ethical as well as a philological understanding of Scripture. The mature biblical humanist combined in an uneasy balance the Jeromian philological, historical traditions and the Origenistic spiritualizing traditions of biblical exegesis. In the *Annotations* the philological, critical aspect predominates. In the *Paraphrases* Erasmus used the allegorical sense sparingly. In the expositions of the Psalms, however, it is prominently displayed. The moral sense is pervasive throughout his exegesis of the Psalms and the New Testament.

Significance. Through his New Testament editions and his *Paraphrases* Erasmus was the most widely influential New Testament scholar of his time. Luther made use of Erasmus's 1519 New Testament for his German translation in 1522, as did William *Tyndale for his 1525 English version. Erasmus's Greek text underlay Robert Estienne's Greek New Testament (1550) and the New Testament editions of Theodore *Beza, whose texts would in turn form the basis of the King James Version (1611) and the Elzevir Greek Testament (1633) that came to be known as the Textus Receptus ("the received text"). Erasmus's New Testament was used by many commentators well into the seventeenth century. His was the first truly fresh Latin translation since that of Jerome. His philological method broke new ground and anticipated in several respects modern New Testament criticism. The *Paraphrases* were especially highly regarded by the Swiss Reformers, one of whom, Leo Jud, translated them into German. The English translation, which began under the auspices of Henry VIII's last queen, Katherine Parr, was ordered (1547) to be placed in every parish church, and every clergyman under the degree of bachelor of divinity was to buy a copy.

BIBLIOGRAPHY

Works. D. Erasmus, *Collected Works of Erasmus,* 56: *Annotations on Romans,* ed. R. D. Sider, (Toronto: University of Toronto Press, 1994); idem, *Concio in Ps. 4, Desiderii Erasmi Roterodami Opera Omnia,* ed. J. Clericus (Leiden, 1703-1705); idem, *Paraclesis* in *Christian Humanism and the Reformation,* ed. J. C. Olin (New York: Fordham University Press, 1987); idem, *Ratio verae Theologiae* in *Desiderius Erasmus Roterodamus: Ausgewählte Werke,* ed. H. Holborn and A. Holborn (Munich: Beck, 1933).

Studies. J. H. Bentley, *Humanists and Holy Writ: New Testament Scholarship in the Renaissance* (Princeton, NJ: Princeton University Press, 1983); A. Brown, "The Date of Erasmus' Translation of the New Testament," *TCBS* 8, 4 (1984) 351-58; H. J. de Jonge, "*Novum Testamentum a nobis versum,* The Essence of Erasmus' Edition of the New Testament," *JTS* 35 (1984) 394-413; M. Hoffmann, *Rhetoric and Theology: The Hermeneutic of Erasmus* (Toronto: University of Toronto Press, 1994); J. B. Payne, "Toward the Hermeneutics of Erasmus" in *Scrinium Erasmianum,* ed. J. Coppens (2 vols.; Leiden: E. J. Brill, 1969), 2:14-49; J. B. Payne, A. Rabil Jr. and W. S. Smith, "The *Paraphrases* of Erasmus: Origin and Character" in *Paraphrases on Romans and Galatians: Collected Works of Erasmus,* ed. R. D. Sider (Toronto: University of Toronto Press, 1984), 42:xi-xix; E. Rummel, *Erasmus' "Annotations" on the New Testament* (Toronto: University of Toronto Press, 1986).   J. B. Payne

Flacius Illyricus, Matthias (1520-1575)

A theologian of Italian-Croatian birth, Flacius came to the University of Wittenberg (1541) after studying in the Erasmian circle at the University of Basel. There he absorbed the humanistic skills and attitudes of Desiderius *Erasmus and became acquainted with works of other contemporary exegetes, among them Guillaume Budé. Flacius's abilities in biblical studies led to his appointment as professor of Hebrew at Wittenberg (1544-1549), where he also lectured on Pauline epistles and Aristotle. Martin *Luther's theology met Flacius's deep spiritual concerns, and he dedicated his life to the propagation of his mentor's insights. His friendship with Philipp *Melanchthon, who exercised extensive and abiding influence upon the content and method of his theology, broke when Flacius strongly objected to his preceptor's positions regarding the Augsburg and Leipzig Interims (1548). In a series of intra-Lutheran controversies (especially the adiaphoristic, Majoristic, synergistic) Flacius established himself as the leading thinker in the Gnesio-Lutheran party (the more radical followers of Luther)..

Flacius's understanding of Scripture expressed itself particularly in his polemic against Roman Catholic views of authority in the church and the theology of the Word of God taught by the spiritualist Caspar Schwenckfeld. As professor at the University of Jena (1557-1561) and thereafter in fourteen years of exile, from havens in Regensburg and Strasbourg, Flacius immersed himself in biblical hermeneutics and exegesis. His contributions to Lutheran theology stem above all from these activities, from his carefully argued defense of his understanding of Luther's theology and from his marshaling of evidence from church history for his views, in his *Catalogus Testium Veritatis* (1556) and the *Magdeburg Centuries* (1559-1574; though he did not participate in writing this massive work of church history, he was highly influential in organizing and planning the enterprise).

Flacius placed himself and his Wittenberg contemporaries within an analytical scheme that defined the place of the Scriptures in the church's history through four epochs. The first, from the apostles to Pope Gregory I, witnessed the intrusion of alien philosophical conceptions into the church's biblical interpretation, particularly in ethics and the doctrines of the law and the human creature. In two succeeding epochs other authorities asserted themselves in the teaching of the biblical message; these included the Fathers, the tradition and the decrees of councils. A period of monks' quarrels, increasing sophism and the decay of ecclesiastical life followed, as the focus of public doctrine turned from Scripture to Peter Lombard's *Sentences*. "Our age" was producing a return to the biblical authority and to the proper study of the text. Flacius's assessment reflects the fact that Luther and Melanchthon began a new approach to biblical studies and bequeathed its methods and doctrinal orientation to their students.

Hermeneutical and Exegetical Works. As an instructor at Wittenberg, Flacius had begun to publish initial elements in his program of biblical interpretation. In his public promotion to the degree of master (1546), he entered the contemporary debate over Hebrew vowel points, insisting they were part of the original, inspired text because he believed this necessary to defend the certainty of biblical revelation.

Three years later Flacius began laying down principles of hermeneutics in his *De Vocabulo Fidei*, initiating work on the proper mode of understanding the Scriptures that he would continue in *Regulae et Tractatus Quidem de Sermone Sacrarum Literarum* (1551) and in the revision of the former work, *De Voce et re Fidei* (1555, 1563). The former attacked the allegorical method and defended the clarity of the literal meaning of the biblical text. The latter laid down rules for the study of the grammar and vocabulary of the Bible *(de voce)* and of its content, according to the analogy of faith *(de re)*. These efforts climaxed in his *Clavis Scripturae Sacrae* (1567), called by W. Dilthey "the origin of hermeneutics"; it shaped the science of textual exposition for centuries to come. New editions appeared until the second quarter of the eighteenth century.

The *Clavis* embraced two parts. The first part was a biblical dictionary that went beyond philological analysis to theological exposition of biblical concepts (not only in biblical vocabulary but also in the theological vocabulary of ecclesiastical tradition).

Flacius aimed at avoiding the intrusion of philosophical principles and even the opinions of the ancient Fathers into the definitions of these terms. Although he cited ancient pagan writers, including Aristotle, he sought definitions from within the biblical context and usage alone, exemplifying the principle that Scripture must interpret Scripture. Having begun his career as a Hebrew instructor, Flacius laid great weight upon the Hebraic nature of biblical revelation in both Testaments and thus frequently provided assistance to readers in interpreting Hebraisms.

The second part of the *Clavis* consisted of seven hermeneutical treatises. The first offered tools for definition and interpretation of the biblical text as well as extensive isagogical, or introductory, information for the study of various parts of Scripture. The second sought to establish the rules that governed proper understanding of the text of Scripture as set forth in the writings of the first three centuries. Tractates 3 and 4 treated grammar and tropes in Scripture. The fifth treatise has been called "the first approach to evaluating biblical styles," including a comparison of Pauline and Johannine usage. In Tractate 6 readers found academic addresses on the study of Scripture, along with a series of short reports on biblical geography, Hebrew vowels and other topics. The last treatise analyzed several issues under dispute with Roman Catholics.

Flacius's *Gloss on the New Testament* (1570) relied on Erasmus's Greek text and Latin translation, with his own improvements. In the *Gloss* annotations to the books and the chapters of the New Testament treated the author's purpose and goal for each Gospel or epistle, the situation in which the book was written, and the person and style of the individual author. He relied on *Jerome for much of the information on the authors, used the available content summaries ascribed in part to the sixth-century exegete Cosmas Indicopleustes, and also supplied the "Synopsis of Saint Athanasius" for most books.

Flacius composed outlines of the structure of the argument of each book, often in chart form, and compared texts with other relevant biblical material. God, according to Flacius, had caused the same theology to be uttered in different times and situations, and he wished to help the reader coordinate revelation in its several forms. The actual comment on texts was taken in part from the ancient Fathers, with Flacius's own guidance to proper interpretation set according to the analogy of faith.

Key to the Scriptures: Flacius's Hermeneutical Center. For Flacius the key to the Scriptures is Christ. His hermeneutic centered in Luther's understanding of justification through faith (Gadamer). Scripture has one goal; its entire message points above all, in its essence, to the Lamb of God, who takes away the sin of the world. Christ himself is presented in Scripture both in prophecy (both rectilinear and typological) and in its fulfillment. Only God's truthfulness and his confirmation that Jesus is the true Messiah makes the Bible trustworthy.

The analogy of faith guides all biblical exegesis. All interpretation must be congruent and consonant with the sum of faith and lead to trust in the Messiah. Flacius was convinced that this takes place only when the interpreter presumes the proper distinction of law (that which accuses and condemns the sinner) and gospel (that which forgives sin and bestows life through faith [Jn 20:31]). For only through the use of this distinction can the biblical text reach its proper goal of making wise unto salvation and equipping for every good work through a proper understanding of God's revelation of himself in Christ (2 Tim 3:15-17).

God's Word is one, but it was given in two testaments or three covenants, the covenants with Adam, Moses and Christ. Adam's covenant (reaffirmed with Abraham) was confirmed and completed by the covenant given in and through Christ. The Old Testament could be summarized in the affirmation that whatever God says is true, the New Testament with the statement that the true promise of the Messiah to God's people has been fulfilled in Christ. The gift of the law through Moses has become the sinners' enemy because of their hostility and rebellion against God. Therefore in the seed of the promised Messiah alone could life be found, restored anew. For that purpose God gave the biblical revelation. All study of the Scriptures has as its goal the knowledge of God, the justification of the sinner and the resulting praise of God.

The interpretation of Scripture cannot be, according to Flacius, a private matter, executed by human effort. The Holy Spirit, who had spoken through his holy instruments, the original writers, has to continue to guide the interpretation of his Scripture and guide its interpreters into its truth. The Spirit alone makes its message clear to its readers.

Method of Textual Study. Flacius's method for assessing biblical language and concepts owed much to the tools and approaches developed by contemporary biblical humanists, especially Melanchthon but also Andreas Hyperius. Flacius posited three methods of biblical interpretation: the synthetic, which begins with a consideration of the doctrine of God and continues to review scriptural teachings by topics; the analytical, which begins with the goal of eternal life and poses questions regarding the basis of salvation and the means and way of attaining it (a method valuable for postils and preaching on texts); and the definitive, which focuses on defining terms. Flacius preferred the synthetic method.

In the biblical writers Flacius found five styles: the historic, prophetic, poetic, sentential (which set forth truths in aphoristic or thetical form) and the epistolary. He rejected allegorical interpretations more decisively than did some of Luther's students, who continued to use allegory for homiletical embellishment. In his *Clavis* Flacius outlined a simple approach to interpreting a biblical text, gleaned from his Melanchthonian education, designed to establish both the *cognitio verbi* and the *cog-*

nitio rei (the former being the presuposition for and avenue to the latter).

This approach began with grammatical interpretation: the definition of individual words on the basis of the original languages and the understanding of these words in their literary context. Then, the intention of the author—not only the basis for the content of a passage but also the reason for the composition, goal or purpose of the entire book—must be determined. This is the task of theological interpretation. Finally the use to which the passage should be put in the church's life must be established by the interpreter. Interpretation moves from the whole of the individual biblical book and its argument, or its summary and scope, to its individual parts and then to the dark passages that defy initial interpretation, either on linguistic or theological grounds.

Flacius's humanistic orientation may also be seen in his eager use of other disciplines to illuminate the meaning of biblical texts. The entire array of disciplines might serve the interpreter: astronomy, meteorology, animal sciences, legal and political theory, geography, ethnography, mathematics or history, and the linguistic and philosophical disciplines—grammar, rhetoric and particularly logic—are servants of the revealed word.

For the inexperienced reader who might be confused by the difference in the language of individual authors or by differences in focus between Old and New Testaments, Flacius suggested a process of mining a text for meaning. This involves the following: (1) a general orientation that focuses on the triune God and God's work; (2) a broad knowledge of the fundamental topics and concerns of Scripture; (3) the use of linguistic helps; (4) perseverance in meditation and study of the text; (5) passionate prayer; (6) Christian experience in daily life; (7) a comparison of parallel passages in Scripture; and (8) the use of good translations and faithful exegetes. The study of individual authors must first establish their own word usage and specific concerns and then place them in the broader biblical context.

Canonical questions were not of great importance to Flacius. He placed the books of biblical times in four categories: canonical, those of doubtful canonicity (2 Peter, Hebrews, James, 2 John, 3 John, Jude, Revelation), apocryphal (Wisdom, Sirach, Judith, Tobit, Maccabees, 2 Ezra, 3 Ezra, Baruch, Bel, Susanna, Song of Three Men), and pseudepigraphal (the gospels of Nicodemus, Thomas, Bartholomaeus, *Shepherd of Hermas,* and others).

The Nature and Efficacious Use of the Scripture. Against Schwenckfeld, Flacius argued that the literal and the spiritual sense of the biblical text dare not be separated, for the nature of Scripture and its usage in the lives of God's people are inseparable (2 Tim 3:15-17; Rom 15:4; 2 Pet 1:19-21). Just as God had actually worked salvation through the incarnation of the second person of the Trinity as Jesus of Nazareth, so God's effective and powerful word took form in ordinary human language. God had revealed himself in human language in a manner that resembles God's placing his saving power in the word in its sacramental forms of baptism and the Lord's Supper. Christ continues his ministry in the preaching of his word as recorded in Scripture.

God effectively works through the biblical word because it is God's word, Flacius believed. God inspired the entire Scripture; through its words God addresses his people in all ages with his message of salvation. The Holy Spirit had bestowed the gift of the prophetic and apostolic office upon chosen instruments, human authors. The Spirit enlightened them with his saving message, which they proclaimed, and then they recorded these words, which the Spirit gave them, as individual human personalities, in their own styles and thought patterns.

Against Roman Catholic views of the Bible, Flacius insisted that because God had inspired the biblical text through the human writers who served as his writing tools,

its text is clear, sufficient and certain *(claritas, sufficientia, certitudo Scripturae sacrae),* and thus it alone determines the teaching of the church.

Significance. Flacius organized the principles that Luther, Melanchthon, and other evangelical theologians had been employing in the revolution in exegesis that accompanied the Reformation. At the same time he was codifying them, he was transforming them and depositing them in the system of his *Clavis,* a work that served as the anchor of much of Protestant exegesis for two centuries. His careful attention to grammatical, contextual and textual analysis and his formulations leading toward the classical Protestant theory of verbal inspiration helped shape Western Christian views of the Bible and its interpretation through the leading theologians of Protestant orthodoxy and even through figures such as the seventeenth-century Franciscan Richard Simon and the eighteenth-century critic Johann Salomo *Semler, who were retracing Flacius's steps, albeit unwillingly. Hermeneutical discussions of the last century (e.g., by Dilthey and Gadamer) have continued to take his work into consideration.

BIBLIOGRAPHY

Works. M. Flacius Illyricus, *Catalogus Testium Veritatis* (Basel: Johannes Oporinus, 1556); idem, *Clavis Scriptura Sacra* (Basel: Jo. Operinum & Euseb. Episcopium, 1567); *Novum Testamentum Jesu Christi filii Dei, ex Versione Erasmi Innumeris in Locis ad Graecam Veritatem, Genuinumque Sensum Emendata: Glossa Compendiaria* (Basel: Petrum Pernam et Theobaldum Dietrich, 1570); idem, *De Ratione Cognoscendi Sacras Literas* (Dusseldorf: Stern-Verlag Janssen, 1968); idem, *De Voce et Re Fidei* (Basel: Ioannem Oporinum, 1555).

Studies. H-G. Gadamer, *Rhetorik und Hermeneutik* (Göttingen: Vandenhoeck & Ruprecht, 1976); R. Keller, *Der Schlüssel zur Schrift: Die Lehre vom Wort Gottes bei Matthias Flacius Illyricus* (Hannover: Lutherisches Verlagshaus, 1984); G. Moldaenke, *Schriftverständnis und Schriftdeutung im Zeitalter der Reformation* (Stuttgart: Kohlhammer, 1936); K. A. von

Schwarz, "Die theologische Hermeneutik des Matthias Flacius Illyricus," *LutherJahrbuch* 15 (1933) 139-75.   R. Kolb

Henry, Matthew *(1662-1714)*

Matthew Henry was an English nonconformist minister famous for his six-volume commentary on the Bible. The work has enjoyed considerable popularity in the English-speaking world, having a reputation for giving a solidly Protestant interpretation of Scripture useful in nurturing the Christian life.

Although for almost three hundred years Henry's commentary has been regarded as a classic, there has been little in the way of critical evaluation of his great work. Before a completely accurate picture of Henry as an expositor can be drawn there need to be a number of historical studies that would allow us to put Henry in his proper historical and theological setting. Until such work has been done the following observations may be helpful in understanding this work.

Life. Matthew Henry was born a few months after his father, Philip, was forbidden to continue his ministry as pastor of Worthenbury. Under the Act of Uniformity some two thousand ministers of Presbyterian or Congregational persuasion were removed from their parishes. For the next twenty-five years these Puritans were to one degree or another deprived of both public worship and theological education. Matthew Henry was the child of a persecuted Christianity. No doubt this fact explains the spiritual depth and intensity of devotion found in his work.

Only those who conformed to the Anglican state church were allowed entrance to the universities of Oxford and Cambridge during that period. It was therefore that young Matthew received his theological education from his father, who had a superb education. Philip Henry was born and brought up in London, where in turn his father, John Henry, was in the service of the Earl of Pembroke. Philip had been prepared for the university at the famous Westminster School, where he mastered the Greek and Latin classics. No school in England did a better job of training students in the disciplines of Christian humanism. Every Sunday the Henry family listened to Stephen Marshall preach. To this day Marshall is remembered for his work on the Reformed doctrine of sanctification.

At Oxford Philip Henry studied at Christ's Church College. He was at Oxford in the days when such Puritan giants as John Owen and Thomas Goodwin were at the height of their influence, producing at that time some of the classics of Puritan theological literature. Philip Henry also eagerly profited from the work of a number of erudite Anglicans such as Dr. Henry Hammond, widely known for his *Paraphase and Annotations to the New Testament.* Philip Henry took his degree and accepted the church at Worthenbury, a village in Flintshire close to the Welsh border, not far from Chester.

Matthew Henry, having such a well educated father as his private tutor, lacked nothing that a more formal theological education might have brought him. Every day his father preached to his household at family prayers, and every day young Matthew translated for his father a passage from the Scriptures in the original languages. In addition his father guided him thorough the Latin classics, and Henry's mastery of this literature is evident throughout his literary legacy. He was assigned readings in his father's ample library. In 1685 he was sent to London to study law at Gray's Inn. It was not that either he or his father intended him to enter the legal profession but only that the law schools of London were open to nonconformists whereas the schools of philosophy and theology at Oxford and Cambridge were not. Being in London gave young Matthew an opportunity to hear the leading conformist preachers of the day such as Tillotson and Stillingfleet. What nonconformist preachers he may have heard we are not told. We do know, however, that he had the courage to visit Richard Baxter in prison.

As he finished his course of study it became more and more clear to Matthew Henry that he had been called to the ministry. He considered carefully the possibility of receiving episcopal ordination and conforming to the Church of England, but finally in 1687 he decided to accept a call to be pastor of the Presbyterian church in Chester. Twenty-five years had passed since his father and so many other Puritans had been ejected. After a generation of High Church liturgy and theology the average English churchgoer was weary of formal religion. The regular services of the state church were found by many to be a dreary routine. Charles II was converted to Roman Catholicism on his deathbed and was succeeded by James II, who openly professed his Catholicism. England was by this time much more open to a thoroughgoing Protestantism.

With the reign of William and Mary, England entered an age of moderation. The biblical interpretations of Matthew Henry are an expression of that age. Far from expressing a partisan backlash, his interpretation of Scripture sought a practical meaning, easily applicable to the Christian life as well as an informal worship expressing a simple and sincere inward devotion.

Matthew Henry's ministry in Chester was well received. In 1690 his congregation was able to build its own building. Henry frequently preached throughout the surrounding countryside, gathering nonconformist congregations. Baptists, Congregationalists and Presbyterians worked together in reestablishing a straightforward Protestant witness in the area. Because of his moderation he was listened to by conformist and nonconformist alike. His deep understanding of biblical teachings and his spiritual maturity were recognized by all. Several attempts were made to call him to London, but Henry was convinced that his ministry was needed in Chester. From time to time he was in London, and he became

a fast friend of John Howe, the city's leading Presbyterian preacher. Howe offered much the same sort of broad and generous interpretation of the Puritan heritage as did Henry. In 1712 Henry accepted the call to London extended by the congregation at Hackney. His ministry there was cut short by his sudden death scarcely two years later.

Work. The work of Matthew Henry is a good example of the sort of Christian piety that can develop from a serious attempt to form one's life according to Scripture. From earliest childhood Matthew Henry was brought up to live by the Word of God. Reading Henry's biography of his father, *The Life of the Reverend Philip Henry, A.M.*, it becomes clear that the ministry of the son was but a public manifestation of the piety of the father. After his ejection the father continued to be a minister of the Word in secret, or as Philip loved to put it, "He remained quiet in the land" (Prov 1:33; Ps 35:20). He submitted himself to a rigorous discipline of prayer and Bible study, the fruit of which was known only to his family and those who spent time in his household. This biography gives us an invaluable look at the spirituality of the Puritans. It gives us a practical example of how they understood what it meant to live from the Word of God.

Biblical Interpretation. When Henry interpreted Scripture, he did it with the understanding of one who had lived a profoundly Christian life. *A Church in the House, A Sermon Concerning Family Religion* (London, 1704) tells us much about the disciplines of prayer and Bible study maintained in the Puritan home. It was out of these that Henry's interpretations came. In 1712 he published *Directions for Daily Communion with God.* In this work we sense the intensity of Henry's devotional life. For Henry the study of Scripture was part of the life of prayer. The two always went together. One prayed that one might understand Scripture and studied Scripture that one might know how to pray.

One of the characteristics of Matthew Henry's interpretation of the Bible is its pastoral tendency. In *The Pleasantness of a*

Religious Life (London, 1714) the point he wants to make is essentially pastoral. He wants to show that the Scriptures teach that the Christian way of life is a good way of life. In the preface to the work he quotes the Cambridge Platonist Henry More. The concern of More was to establish the value of a moral life by means of a Christianized Platonic philosophy. Henry considered this all well and good, but for him the task was to work this out from Holy Scripture. This, for Matthew Henry, had authority.

In his *Communicant's Companion* (Chester, 1704) Henry used his art of exposition to develop a eucharistic piety that he has drawn from Scripture. Here we find a thorough elaboration of the meaning of the Lord's Supper in terms of covenant theology. The sacrament is explained by carefully unfolding the biblical imagery used in regard to it. Henry tries to avoid a polemical discussion of this theme, which ever since the Reformation had been hotly debated in England. He delineates the biblical imagery and leaves the debated questions aside. Most of all, for Henry the question is not the elements of the liturgy that must accompany the rite but rather the disposition of heart appropriate to those participating in the service.

The pastoral tendency of Henry's interpretation is above all found in his commentary on the whole Bible. The commentary represents his expositions which according to the *Westminster Directory for Worship* were to accompany the reading of the Scripture lesson. These readings followed the *lectio continua;* that is, they proceeded through the whole of the Bible beginning at each service where the lesson had left off the Sunday before. They were not considered sermons. The sermon came later in the service and was generally considerably longer. It was in those days common practice for a minister to give both an exposition and a sermon on Sunday morning and Sunday afternoon and then a lecture on some week day. These expositions have come down to us in Henry's *An Exposition of the Old and New Testament,* which began

to appear in 1708 but had not gotten past the Acts of the Apostles before he died. The work was brought to completion by a number of Henry's colleagues.

Looked at as a whole the biblical interpretations of Matthew Henry are remarkable for their high sense of the authority of Scripture. His doctrine of Scripture was no doubt shaped by the Westminster Confession. One place in which his understanding of Scripture comes to clarity is his discussion of the perfections of the Word of God in his commentary on Psalm 19. The Word of God has authority because it is God's word. It is necessary and sufficient for our salvation. It is eternally true and unfailing. It is clear and understandable; "it is perfectly free from all corruption, perfectly filled with all good, and perfectly fitted for the end for which it is designed."

There is a strong continuity between the Old Testament and the New for Henry. Jesus is the Messiah promised by the Old Testament prophets. The church is the new Israel. The gospel is the fulfillment of the law. All through the Old Testament there are types, intimations and foreshadows of the New Testament. The Lord's Day is the Christian sabbath, the Lord's Supper is the Christian Passover, and baptism is the Christian circumcision.

A favorite method of interpretation that we find often in Henry's work is what he calls the improving of the biblical imagery. By this he meant the drawing out and elaborating of the metaphors, similes and illustrative figures found in Scripture. Henry had a gift for grammatical and historical analysis. He applies it so subtly and so simply that those who lack his formal training are not bothered by his literary technology. He has a way of analyzing a sentence structure so that instead of sounding like a pedantic schoolmaster he sounds like a poet. Henry teaches us a great deal about the meaning of Scripture simply by a careful literary analysis of the text and a profound understanding of the literary forms of biblical language. He understood the biblical language because he lived it.

The interpretation of Scripture by Scripture was central to Henry's approach. He was particularly successful in illuminating passages of Scripture by bringing to them parallel passages. This is a classic principle of interpretation emphasized alike by the Protestant Reformers and the Fathers of the ancient church.

With Henry's solid education in the literature of classical antiquity, he was quite capable of grammatical-historical exegesis. Indeed, the study of the text in the original languages and in their historical context is assumed by Henry. He does not rely on allegorical interpretation, although he does follow traditional Christian interpretations, especially those already found in the New Testament. The Christian interpretation of the exodus, the worship of the tabernacle and the temple, the messianic psalms, the Song of Solomon, and the Suffering Servant, all clearly found in the New Testament, are amply treated by Henry.

Much of the value of Henry's commentary is due to his poetic imagination and his disciplined use of language. No doubt it was to a large extent due to his father's careful tutelage in the rudiments of literary form that on one hand Henry had such brilliant insights into the meaning of the sacred text and on the other such facility in expressing that insight. Almost three hundred years later the clarity and the beauty of his language is still to be admired.

When all is said, Henry provides a good example of what Christians have often called the *sensus spiritualis*. He is always concerned to understand what Scripture says about transcendent reality, about saving faith and about the way of life that leads to eternity. Critical concerns interested him little. Problems of the historical reliability of Scripture, the harmony of the different documents and the authors to which they were to be attributed were beyond his scope of interest. To borrow the words of the second question of the Westminster Catechism, what interested Henry was what Scripture has to say that will direct us in how we are to glorify God and enjoy him forever.

BIBLIOGRAPHY

Works. M. Henry, *The Complete Works of the Rev. Matthew Henry . . . (His Commentary Excepted)* . . . (2 vols.; Grand Rapids: Baker, 1979 [1855]); idem, *An Exposition of the Old and New Testament* (1708-posthumously reedited with additions and frequently reprinted); idem, *A Method for Prayer . . . and Directions for Daily Communion with God,* ed. J. L. Duncan III (Greenville, SC: Reformed Academic Press, 1994).

Studies. C. Chapman, *Matthew Henry, His Life and Times* (London, 1859); *DNB* 26 (1891); A. B. Grosart, *Representative Nonconformists* (London, 1879); H. O. Old, "Matthew Henry and the Puritan Discipline of Family Prayer" in *Calvin Studies* 7, ed. J. H. Leith (Davidson, NC: Davidson College, 1994) 69-91; H. D. Roberts, *Matthew Henry and His Chapel* (Liverpool, 1901); W. Tong, *An Account of the Life and Death of . . . M. Henry* (London, 1716); J. B. Williams, *Memoirs of the Life, Character and Writings of the Rev. Matthew Henry* (London, 1828; repr. with Henry's biography of his father [Edinburgh: Banner of Truth Trust, 1974]).   H. O. Old

Hooker, Richard *(1554-1600)*

During the two centuries after Richard Hooker's death, no sixteenth-century English theologian was more widely read in his native land. Though historians have usually concentrated on other aspects of his work, his skills as an interpreter of the Bible provided significant exegetical tools that enriched the English theological tradition.

Career and Writings. Richard Hooker was four years old when Elizabeth I ascended the English throne, and he died two and a half years before she did. Scholarship aid from Bishop John Jewel enabled Hooker, born to a penurious middle-class Exeter family, to matriculate in Corpus Christi College, Oxford, where he received bachelor's and master's degrees, served as deputy professor of Hebrew and was ordained to the ministry. In 1585 the queen named him master of the Temple Church in London, a post in a setting rife with the ecclesiastical debates and tensions of the reign. Hooker became pastor to two Inns of Court, the Middle and Inner Temples, communities of lawyers and law students. Subsequently the queen named Hooker to a parish along with cathedral responsibilities in the diocese of Salisbury and later to the parish of Bishopsbourne in Kent, where he served until his death.

Hooker's moderately successful clerical career would have passed into historical oblivion had it not been for one work, part of which remained unpublished at his death: *Of the Laws of Ecclesiastical Polity.* The preface and first four of seven books appeared in 1593; book 5, lengthier than the whole first volume, four years later; books 6 and 8 in 1648 and book 7 in 1662. These latter three constitute working drafts toward the author's perfected texts. If he had completed such texts, they were destroyed by accident or malice (Hooker, 3:xiii-lxxv; introduction, 6:37-51 [Haugaard], 233-47 [McGrade], 249-55 [Gibbs], 237-39 [McGrade]). In addition to *Laws,* eight sermons or tractates have survived along with a significant body of drafts and other manuscript material.

Church Context. The zigzag course of established religion in England reached a resting place with Elizabeth's accession. From 1530 to 1558 English people had successively experienced four different sets of praxes in their communal Christian faith, and Elizabeth intended the 1559 parliamentary acts and royal injunctions to settle the independence of the Church of England under royal supremacy and its worship according to the new *Book of Common Prayer.* Throughout Elizabeth's reign, two groups attempted to undo or modify the terms of the settlement: Roman Catholic recusants hoping to restore papal authority and militant Protestants seeking to complete the reformation that they judged barely half-done in 1559. The latter group, tagged Puritans, all looked to the Continental Reformed churches for models but differed among themselves on their goals. Some Puritans would have been satisfied with the elimination of a few ceremonies that they judged "popish"; others judged

that only Genevan presbyterian polity met the New Testament standard. All Puritans, however, were frustrated by their inability to modify Elizabeth's 1559 religious settlement. The president of Corpus Christi for most of Hooker's years there, William Cole, a moderate Puritan, wrote to a Zurich friend in 1579 complaining that the state of religion in England "is precisely the same as it has been from the beginning of the reign. . . . There is no change whatever" (*Zurich,* 2:308).

Works in Context. The London law communities to whom Hooker ministered, with their many ties to members of Parliament, included staunch Roman Catholic recusants and committed Puritans. When Hooker arrived in 1586 to take over his duties, he found he was to be assisted by Walter Travers, a cousin by marriage, firmly ensconced for four years in the post of reader. Travers had recently published a scholarly Latin treatise on the "aberrations" of the English church from New Testament polity and discipline (*Explicatio*). Finding "sour leaven" (unsound doctrine) in Hooker's sermons, Travers proceeded to correct the master in his afternoon preaching. In the seventeenth-century Thomas Fuller's words, from the Temple pulpit came "pure Canterbury" on Sunday mornings and "Geneva" in the afternoons until Archbishop John Whitgift put an end to the homiletic debate by forbidding Travers to preach.

Thus drawn into a defense of the Elizabethan religious settlement, Hooker envisioned the *Laws* as an articulation of the theological underpinnings of the church in which his faith had been nourished. The *Explicatio* and a polemical trilogy by its English translator, Thomas Cartwright, provided the weightiest arguments of disciplinarians, those more militant Puritans who looked for guidance to John *Calvin's Genevan church. Cartwright's trilogy comprised his learned responses to Whitgift's attacks on the 1572 Puritan *Admonition to the Parliament,* which urged a full reform of the Elizabethan church (Cartwright, 1573, 1575, 1577).

In responding to Travers and Cartwright, Hooker ignored the detailed specific Puritan complaints about English "papistry" until he reached book 5 of *Laws* (Booty [introduction], 6:183-231). He first completed books 1 through 4, in which he identified what he judged to be "the general grounds and foundations" of the Puritan case (Hooker, preface.7.5; 1:35.18). In book 1 he employed the concept of law as a basic theological category for describing creation and its relation with its Creator (Gibbs [introduction], 6:81-124). He proceeded in book 2 to consider what he judged to be "the very main pillar of [the whole Puritan] cause": a scriptural omnicompetence defined in the insistence "that scripture ought to be the only rule of all our actions." Book 3 discusses a second principle of the disciplinarians: that the New Testament prescribed a form of church government that no one "should ever presume in any wise to change and alter" (Hooker, preface 7.3-4; 1:35.4-6, 13-14; Haugaard [introduction], 6:125-81). These two books provided the occasion for Hooker to articulate his principles of biblical interpretation.

Interpretive Principles. Throughout the theological debates of the sixteenth century, Reformers protesting the papal magisterium firmly asserted scriptural authority against what they judged its errors. They did little, however, to describe the process by which they applied that authority. Following Desiderius *Erasmus and other humanists, Protestant theologians were on the whole careful to recover the original Hebrew and Greek of the Bible, to take account of linguistic and grammatical issues, to try to use lucid passages to clarify the difficult ones and to give priority to literal over allegorical interpretations. Hooker's handling of Scripture reflected all these humanist hermeneutics; his New Testament quotations are often direct translations from the Greek, and he expressly wrote, "I hold it for a most infallible rule in expositions of sacred scripture, that where a literal construction will stand, the

farthest from the letter is commonly the worst" (Hooker, 5.59.2; 2:252.5-7). Beyond these, the hermeneutical practices of Protestant exegetes were instinctive common sense; even those most dedicated to the principle of *sola scriptura* did not systematically discuss the processes by which they exegeted and applied the text. They quoted and cited the Bible and presumed the appropriateness of their methodology.

Martin *Luther, in his celebrated statement at Worms, added "clear reason" to the "testimony of the Scriptures" as the only grounds on which he would recant his writings. He and other Protestant theologians were generally content, however, to claim Scripture against an argument from human reason without discussing the circumstances under which reason might be accorded authority. The task Hooker assumed in the *Laws* led him to explore new ground in the reciprocal relationship of reason and Scripture and to develop explicit hermeneutical principles in response to the Puritan challenge. Hooker's hermeneutics evolved from two traditions that, along with patristic and Reformation writers, informed his theology: Thomistic scholasticism and Renaissance humanism.

Grace and Nature: Human Reason in the Bible. Hooker understood God's acts in creation and in redemption to be intimately intertwined. Like Thomas *Aquinas, Hooker insisted on the complementary character of nature and grace: "Nature hath need of grace ... grace hath use of nature" (Hooker, 3.8.6; 1:223.28-29). The human mind, in spite of its infection by sin, retained the capacity not only to interpret God's special revelations in Scripture but also to learn from creation something about God and about God's intentions for humankind: "Nature and scripture do serve in such full sort, that they both jointly and not [separately] either of them be so complete, that unto everlasting felicity we need not the knowledge of any thing more than these two" (Hooker, 1.14.5; 129.10-13).

Hooker repeatedly reached into the

Bible itself to illustrate the operation of reason as a natural, God-given human faculty. Examples of convictions "grounded upon other assurance than Scripture" are found in Jesus' own call to recognize the Father in his works and in Thomas's demand to see and feel the nail prints in Jesus' flesh (Hooker, 2.4.1; 152.5-12 [Jn 10:38; 20:25]). Hooker pointed to the apostles' reasoning on the text of the psalms, to Paul and Barnabas winning the unconverted through reason, to Peter arguing in the council of Jerusalem, to Peter insisting that Christians render a reason for their faith, and finally to "our Lord and Savior himself" reasoning in disputation with the crowd (Hooker, 3.8.16-17; 1:233.9-15 [Acts 13:32-37], 234.9-18 [Acts 14:15-17] and 18-25 [Acts 15:8-11]; 233.21-25 [1 Pet 3:15]; and 234.2-7 [Mt 22:41-45]).

Discerning the use of reason within the Bible, Hooker not unexpectedly grants reason the major role in its interpretation. Even to acknowledge the authority of Scripture, he insists, one must employ reason. In asserting this claim for reason, Hooker puts a distinctive twist to an understanding of "grave and learned" Reformed theologians. As Calvin had put it, not "proofs and reasoning" but "the testimony of the [Holy] Spirit" authenticates the Bible's authority (Hooker, 3.8.15; 1:232.16-17; Calvin, *Institutes*, 1.7.5). Hooker construed such assertions to mean that the "special grace of the holy ghost" must "concur" with whatever inducements *"consonant unto reason"* lead one to acknowledge "the authority of the books of God" (Hooker, 3.18.14-15; 1:232.1-6 and 20-25; italics added). Whatever may be the "secret and undiscernible" operations of the Spirit in the inner life of human beings, only its "enlightening of our minds," our rational faculty, provides the basis for discovery of truth:

Albeit the spirit lead us into all truth and direct us in all goodness, yet because these workings of the spirit in us are so privy and secret, we therefore stand on

a plainer ground, when we gather by reason from the quality of things believed or done that the spirit of God hath directed us in both; than if we settle ourselves to believe or to do any certain particular thing as being moved thereto by the spirit. (Hooker, 3.8.15; 1:232.20—233.7)

Just as reason leads us to acknowledge the authority of the scriptural text, so it provides us with ability to interpret it; since "misconstrued [text] breedeth error, between true and false construction, the difference reason must show" (Hooker, 3.8.16; 1:233.18-20).

Teleology and Historical Perspective. Hooker's understanding of the relation of grace and nature undergirds his recognition of the continuity of the sacred history of revelation with the larger human scene to which it belonged. He paired Paul and Tacitus as common witnesses of the world's "execrable" estimation of the name *Christian,* and Peter and Josephus's autobiography as symmetrical witnesses to Jewish fasting customs (Hooker, 3.1.4 and 6.1; 1:196i [1 Cor 1:23 and Tacitus *Annales* 15:44] and 216.8-11 [Acts 2:15 and Josephus *Life* 54.279]). Appropriating the greater sense of historical perspective provided by Renaissance thought, Hooker applied that perspective to his reading of Scripture.

In the course of rebutting arbitrary applications of God's commands from the Old Testament to sixteenth-century England, Hooker drew on Aristotelian Thomism to insist that "the words of [God's] mouth are absolute . . . for *performance of that thing whereunto they tend*" (Hooker, 2.6.1; 1:168.3-5; italics added). Teleology—purpose—provided a principle of historical analysis. God's purpose in any particular command to human beings could only be accurately determined by taking account of their era and their distinctive situation. Its appropriateness to another situation in another age depended upon a congruity of circumstances. Those human circumstances were, for Hooker, a given of God's creation. By discerning purpose within a historical perspective, exegetes might understand the scriptural text in its original context and more appropriately employ it in their own age.

Hooker applied this interpretative tool to the central and unique purpose of the Bible as a whole. He identified this purpose in accordance with the English Reformation standard that the Bible "containeth all things necessary to salvation" (*Articles of Religion*, 6):

> Although the scripture of God . . . be stored with infinite variety of matter in all kinds, although it abound with all sorts of laws, yet the principal intent of scripture is to deliver the laws of duties supernatural.
>
> The law of reason doth somewhat direct men how to honor God as their Creator, but how to glorify God . . . to the end that he may be an everlasting Savior, this we are taught by divine law [Scripture]. (Hooker, 1.14.1 and 16.5; 1:124.29-32 and 139.3-7; in C. Hardwick, *A History of the Articles of Religion* [London: George Bell, 1895], appendix 3)

"Supernatural laws"—the salvation story of God's redeeming love—is the unique property, the principal purpose of the Bible, but the "infinite variety" of its writings includes much else: permanently applicable God-given laws of reason—laws that can also be known through nature—and occasional laws that are framed for identifiable situations in a changing human society (Hooker, 1.12, 15; 1:119.26—122.5, 130.7—134.18). Hooker regarded all these laws to have come from God by revelation, but the conditions under which they operate are subject to the limitations of their human settings just as are natural laws derived through the processes of reason and positive laws determined by human decree or legislation.

Historical perspective provides Hooker with a primary hermeneutical tool in his attack on the insistence of Cartwright and Travers that the New Testament prescribed a presbyterian church polity for all ages.

Although Hooker judged that an episcopal polity was more compatible with his reading of Scripture, in book 3 he chose to attack the proposition that "in scripture there must be . . . a form of Church-polity . . . [that] may in no wise be altered" (Hooker, 3 [title]; 1:193.3-6; cf. 3.4.1; 1:213.16-25, 11.16; 1:264.3-15; Haugaard and McGrade [introduction], 6:177-78; 309-36). He insisted that for changes of "times, places, persons, and . . . like circumstances," Christ has not left his church without "liberty in making orders and laws for itself" (Hooker, 3.11.13; 1:261.10-11; 260.26-27).

In the conventional division of Old Testament laws into moral, ceremonial and judicial categories, Christian theologians generally agreed that the moral laws (Hooker's laws of nature) continued in force and ceremonial laws had been abrogated. But they did not always agree on the force of judicial laws (among Hooker's positive laws). The judicial laws provided Hooker with key test cases for identifying issues of biblical omnicompetence. A law ought to be maintained only if "the end for which it was made and . . . the aptness of things therein prescribed unto the same end" continued in the present historical circumstances (Hooker, 3.10.1; 1:239.32-240.2). In laws for ancient Israel, "Almighty God in framing their laws had an eye unto the nature of that people and to [their] country," respecting "these peculiar and proper considerations . . . in the making of their laws" (Hooker, 3.11.6; 1:251.2-5). Hooker could write that scriptural texts literally contained "manifest testimony cited from the mouth of God himself"; yet at the same time he developed tools that made it possible to take full account of human limitations inherent in that testimony (Hooker, 2.7.5; 180.25-26). Since God took account of the human situation in framing the law, the exegete could hardly ignore it!

Hooker's interrelated analyses of "end" and "aptness" provided him with a flexibility that freed his exegesis from a literal biblicism that often marked English Protestant writing of his day. For example, in considering the severity of God's order to Moses to execute a man caught gathering sticks on the sabbath (Num 15:32-36), Hooker proposed that such severity was

perhaps the more requisite at that instant both because the Jews by reason of their long abode in a place of continual servile toil could not suddenly be weaned and drawn unto contrary offices without some strong impression of terror, and also . . . there is nothing more needful than to punish with extremity the first transgressions of those laws that require a more exact observation for many ages to come.

This penalty for sabbath breaking in the book of Numbers was "apt" in its day, but the same "end," namely, "rest from labor wherewith publicly God is served," is better promoted in later ages by recognizing "occasions" when people may "with very good conscience" be drawn "from the ordinary rule" (Hooker, 5.71.8; 2:380.10-16; cf. 3.11.8; 1:252.20-26).

When Cartwright argued that all human actions ought to be based on a scriptural command, he cited Isaiah's condemnation of the Jews who had not sought "counsel at the mouth of the Lord" when they made an alliance with Egypt (Cartwright 1573, 26 [Is 30:1-2]). In refuting Cartwright, both Whitgift and Hooker agreed that Isaiah was not laying down a general principle for all human actions, but they differed in their exegetical reasonings. Whitgift pointed to a verse of Deuteronomy in which God had said that the Jews must not return to Egypt (Whitgift, *Defense*, 78; Whitgift, *Works*, 1:177, 179-80 [Deut 17:16]). Ignoring Whitgift's citation, Hooker expressly stated that the Jews merited Isaiah's rebuke even though they had received "no charge precisely given them that they should always take heed of Egypt." The Deuteronomic command was appropriate to the human context when God gave it, but it could not be literally applied, as Whitgift had done, to the later

times of Isaiah. Hooker roots his reason for the validity of the prophet's argument in the historical situation of Israel at the time: they "had prophets to have resolved them from the mouth of God himself" (Hooker, 2.6 [initial note] and 3; 1:167.2-3; 169.9-14; 170.7-13). The notion of a telephone line to God for the determination of foreign policy may not appeal to many modern readers, but it was for Hooker a given historical "fact" of Old Testament times. Rather than borrow Whitgift's biblical literalism to confound Cartwright, Hooker turns to historical contextualization within the terms of his understanding of Israel's situation in Isaiah's day.

Divine revelation was itself subject to the limitations of the creaturely circumstances in which it was embedded, and accordingly the exegete must take these into account in delineating God's purposes and in applying scriptural texts to situations that might differ from those in the particular biblical passage in which they occur. Hooker's quiet dissent from his archbishop's exegesis suggests that his hermeneutics distanced his biblical interpretations not only from disciplinarians and more moderate Puritans but also from the broad sweep of other Elizabethan Protestants as well. Hooker never undervalued the Bible; it was consistently his primary text throughout the *Laws*. His efforts to relate the divine law of Scripture to the natural law perceived by reason and to take account of the human elements in Scripture did not, in his understanding, disparage biblical authority; on the contrary, they established it. He warned that we must "take great heed, lest in attributing unto scripture more than it can have, the incredibility of that do cause even those things which indeed it hath most abundantly to be less reverently esteemed" (Hooker, 2.8.7; 191.29—192.1).

BIBLIOGRAPHY

Works. R. Hooker, *The Folger Library Edition of the Works of Richard Hooker*, ed. W. Speed Hill

(Cambridge, MA: Harvard University Press [vols. 1-5]; Binghamton, NY: Medieval and Renaissance Texts and Studies [vol. 6]), 1977-1993; *Of the Lawes of Ecclesiasticall Politie*, vols. 1-3 (the form of the reference is first to book, chapter and section, then to volume and page of the Folger edition; sixteenth-century spelling preserved in this edition has been normalized in the quotations); introductions to the *Laws* in vol. 6: preface and books 2, 3 and 4 (pp. 1-80, 125-82), W. P. Haugaard; books 1 and 6 (pp. 81-124, 249-308), L. W. Gibbs; book 5 (pp. 183-231), J. E. Booty; autograph notes and books 7 and 8 (pp. 233-48, 309-83), A. S. McGrade; T. Cartwright, *A Replye to an Answere Made of M. Doctor Whitgifte . . . Agaynste the Admonition* By T. C. Hemel (Hemptstead: J. Stroud, 1573); idem, *The Second Replie of Thomas Cartwright: Agaynst Maister Whitgiftes Second Answer* (Heidelberg: M. Schirat, 1575); idem, *The Rest of the Second Replie Agaynst Master Whitgiftes Second Answer* (Basle: Thomas Guarin, 1577); W. Travers, *Ecclesiasticae Disciplinae, et Anglicanae Ecclesiae ab Illa Aberrationis, Plena è Verbo Dei, & Dilucida Explicatio* (Heidelberg: M. Schirat, 1574; ET: A *Full and Plaine Declaration* [Heidelberg: M. Schirat]); J. Whitgift, *The Works of John Whitgift*, ed. John Ayre (Parker Society 46-48; 3 vols.; Cambridge: Cambridge University Press, 1851-1853). In these volumes nearly all the texts of the *Admonition*, Whitgift's *Answere*, Cartwright's *Replye*, Whitgift's *Defense of the Aunswere* appear in the text of the *Defense*. Ayre includes some passages of Cartwright's *Second Replie* and his *Rest of the Second Replie* in notes to the *Defense; The Zurich Letters, Comprising the Correspondence of Several English bishops and Others with Some of the Helvetian Reformers During the Reign of Queen Elizabeth*, ed. Hastings Robinson (Parker Society 37-38; 2 vols.; Cambridge: Cambridge University Press, 1842-1855).

Studies. D. H. Compier, "Hooker on the Authority of Scripture in Matters of Morality" in *Richard Hooker and the Construction of Christian Community*, ed., A. S. McGrade (Tempe, AZ: Medieval and Renaissance Texts and Studies, 1997) 251-59; J. S. Coolidge, *The Pauline Renaissance in England* (Oxford: Clarendon, 1970); A. B. Ferguson, "The Historical Perspective of Richard Hooker: Renaissance Paradox," *JMRS* 3 (1973) 17-49; E. Grislis, "The Hermeneutical Problem in Hooker" in *Studies in Richard Hooker*, ed. W. S. Hill (Cleveland: Case Western Reserve University Press, 1972) 159-206; W. P. Haugaard,

"The Scriptural Hermeneutics of Richard Hooker: Historical Contextualization and Teleology" in *This Sacred History: Anglican Reflections for John Booty* (Cambridge, MA: Cowley, 1990); P. Lake, *Anglicans and Puritans: Presbyterianism and English Conformist Thought from Whitgift to Hooker* (London: Unwin Hyman, 1988); W. S. Hill, ed., *Studies in Richard Hooker* (Cleveland: Case Western Reserve University Press, 1972).   W. P. Haugaard

Lefèvre d'Étaples, Jacques (c. 1455-1536)

A renowned French humanist and Neo-Platonist, Jacques Lefèvre d'Étaples (Latin, Faber Stapulensis; frequently called Lefèvre d'Étaples or Faber) was born between 1455 and 1460 in d'Étaples, a seaport in Picardy in northern France. An admirer of Ulrich *Zwingli and familiar with William Farel and the young John *Calvin, who both came from Picardy, Lefèvre never identified himself openly with the cause of the Reformation but corresponded with and dialogued with some of the major Reformers of the sixteenth century. He is known for his moderating views on Reformation issues. He died in the same year as did Desiderius *Erasmus; the two had shared friendship, respect and sharp academic disagreements over the duration of their careers.

Not much is known of Lefèvre's early years; he studied and taught at the Collège de Lemoine in Paris. He graduated as master of the arts and became an ordained priest but never a doctor in theology, for which he was later criticized by his adversaries. In 1492 he went to Italy and associated with the Renaissance humanists Ficino and Pico della Mirandola. Influenced by the late medieval spirituality of the Modern Devotion *(Devotio Moderna)*, Lefèvre decided to enter the monastic life but was unable to do so for reasons of health. A movement within the Modern Devotion called the Brethren of the Common Life, founded by Gerhard de Groote (1340-1384), was influential for the education and formation of many of the early Reformers of the sixteenth century.

Work. A prolific editor, translator and scholar of classical and early church sources (as a humanist he returned to the sources— *ad fontes*), he committed himself to the study of the Platonic tradition, including the works of Dionysius the Areopagite, the fifth-century scholar whom Lefévre thought was a genuine convert of Paul on the Areopagus (Acts 17:34) in spite of Lorenzo Valla's fifteenth-century discovery to the contrary. He studied and published the contemplative and anti-Muslim works of the Spanish monk and mystic Raymond Lull (c. 1235-1315); he studied astrology and published works in the Hermetic tradition, an eclectic collection of Greek and Latin religious and philosophical writings in the Platonic tradition from the first to the third centuries ascribed to Hermes Trismegistus (Hermes the Thrice-Greatest). In addition he and his associates published editions from the patristic era: for example, the *Shepherd of Hermas,* the medieval mystical theologians Richard of St. Victor, Hildegard of Bingen and John Ruysbroek, and a major edition of the works of Nicholas of Cusa, whose philosophical and mystical theology influenced his ideas. In this phase of his life he cultivated his interests in the sources of the early church, medieval spirituality and philosophy. He was celebrated by his humanist contemporaries, however, as one who for his time rediscovered Aristotle, whose works he edited, translated or retranslated and commented upon for students.

Bibles, Translations and Commentaries. In 1509 Lefèvre's focus shifted dramatically from philosophy, mystical theology and especially scholastic theology to the Bible and the gospel. At the invitation of his friend Guillaume Briconnet he had moved from the Collège de Lemoine to the abbey of Saint-Germain-des Prés, where Briconnet had become abbot. In this year he published the *Fivefold Psalter* (the *Quincuplex Psalterium*), five parallel Latin versions of the Psalter in which he tried to emend the Latin version by comparing it with the Hebrew text. As an indication of the shift in his thinking he wrote in the preface to this work:

Indeed for a long time I pursued human concerns and paid only "lip service," as the expression goes, to theological studies (which are exalted and ought not to be approached casually). But even after a haphazard sampling of divine things I saw so much light shine forth that, by comparison, the human disciplines seemed like darkness. . . . For our spirits live "by every Word that proceeds from the mouth of God," and what are these words but Holy Scripture itself? (Oberman, 297)

In 1512 he produced a major (530 folio pages) commentary on Paul's epistles in which he emended the Latin Vulgate with references to the Greek original. This homiletical commentary was an exercise in biblical theology that sought not Paul's instrumental intention but that of the Holy Spirit. In the introduction he writes, "Therefore, one ought not give attention to the mind itself, to the human agent (or whoever might finally be commissioned by God as His instrument), but one ought to attend above all to the heavenly gift and to the Divine giver himself" (Oberman, 303). The structure of the commentary itself included a summary of the contents of each epistle, a list of the articles of faith and a comparison between the Latin Vulgate and the Greek original (see Hughes, 71).

Lefèvre's career was not without controversy. Throughout his life he had regular conflicts with the faculty of the Sorbonne and other theologians and bishops. From 1518 to 1519 he was engaged in continuous controversy over three treatises he wrote on whether the Mary Magdalene celebrated in the church's calendar was one or three different persons in the Gospels, how many days Jesus lay in the tomb, and on the immaculate conception of Mary. His interpretations did not always demonstrate the best exegesis on these matters, as Erasmus noted in opposition to his position on the three days in the grave, but he did argue for the authority of the Bible over legend and extrabiblical tradition (Hughes, 118-28).

In 1521 Lefèvre's Latin commentary on the Gospels was published in Meaux, a town twenty miles east of Paris where he had been preaching, translating and commenting on the Bible for reform at the request of his friend Briconnet, who had become bishop there (Hughes, 154). In the preface he wrote,

> For the Word of Christ is the Word of God, the Gospel of peace, liberty, and joy, the Gospel of salvation, redemption, and life; the Gospel of peace after continuous warfare, of liberty after the most harsh servitude, of joy after constant sadness, of salvation after complete perdition, of redemption after the most dreadful captivity, and finally of life itself as an escape from eternal death. If this word is called the Gospel, "the good news," it is because, for us, it is the herald of all good things, and of infinite blessings which are prepared for us in heaven. (Lefèvre 1953, 84)

In this preface he also shows that he is aware of the spread of the gospel to the New World. The publication of this prompted his enemies at the Sorbonne to launch an investigation against him, but the king interceded on his behalf.

To make the grace of the gospel accessible to everyone, Lefèvre translated the four Gospels into French and began to translate the whole New Testament (1523). After the publication of the New Testament, a translation of the Psalms was published (1524), and it was followed by a publication of a Latin edition of the New Testament. Though he knew little Hebrew, in 1530 his influential translation of the whole Bible appeared. His last commentary was a Latin work on the Catholic Epistles (1527). At Meaux Lefèvre and his disciples collected the epistles and Gospels in French for fifty-two Sundays, together with some feast days, and included evangelical sermons for them. Lefèvre was attacked by the faculty of the University of Paris for his translations and commentaries but especially for the collection on the epistles and Gospels. Forty-eight propositions extracted from the sermons that had been supervised by him were condemned (Hughes, 164).

Hermeneutics. Lefèvre's hermeneutics follow in part the tradition of the late medieval period in emphasizing the literal sense epitomized by *Nicholas of Lyra (c. 1270-1349). More than most of his predecessors, Nicholas attempted to utilize the rabbinic tradition of exegesis in his exposition of the Old Testament. He found a double literal sense in the Old Testament: one concerned with the historical context of the human author and the other with the literal-prophetic sense providing a christological or theological significance. Nicholas expanded the meaning of the literal to include spiritual meanings, but he insisted upon the validity of the literal historical sense. Nevertheless, in the preface to the *Fivefold Psalter* Lefèvre takes issue with Nicholas's historical and literal interpretation of the psalms. He writes,

> It is impossible for us to believe this one to be the literal sense which they call the literal sense, that which makes David a historian rather than a prophet. Instead let us call that the literal sense which is in accord with the Spirit and is pointed out by the Spirit. . . . This true sense is not what is called the allegorical or tropological sense, but rather the sense the Holy Spirit intends, as he speaks through the prophet. (Oberman, 300)

Lefèvre thus clearly insists upon Nicholas of Lyra's second literal sense, the christological sense, as the primary literal sense. Nicholas would have agreed that the second sense is primary, but he limited its application in the Old Testament such that in many psalms, in Lefèvre's words, "[He] did not regard David as a prophet but rather as a chronicler of what he had seen and done, as if he were writing his own history" (Oberman, 298). For Lefèvre, Christ is therefore the key to the understanding of David and about whom David spoke. As he develops his argument in this preface, he grants a twofold literal sense but calls the first distorted, fleshly, based on human understanding alone, and false. At this point he breaks with Nicholas's proposals. As he notes, this second literal sense is not the traditional allegorical or tropological sense, though he does not reject the usefulness of the fourfold method when a genre in the Bible calls for it. He is moving toward one literal, albeit hidden, sense intended both by the writer of Scripture and the Holy Spirit. The spiritual senses in their totality were subsumed under one principal sense and appeared under the designation of the true literal.

In the New Testament this christocentric interpretive method is easier to come by, and he argues against trying to discover Paul's intention in the epistles over that of the Holy Spirit. The true literal-spiritual sense is thus "the sense the Holy Spirit intends as he speaks through the prophet" (Oberman, 300). For Lefèvre it is impossible for the sense intended by the Spirit not be the spiritual sense. "Let Christ, the author of divine gifts, be present to give grace to all, to preserve and increase it in order that no one should presume to interpret by his own sense" (Oberman, 304).

Significance. Lefèvre's edition of the Psalms became an important aid to Luther from 1513 to 1516. Luther insisted, as did Lefèvre, on the historical-prophetic sense of the Psalms and criticized Lyra time and again in his first commentary on Psalms for having allowed himself to be misled by "rabbinic" literal exegesis. The young Luther found in Lefèvre that letter and spirit were not simply synonymous with literal and spiritual exegesis but rather that, regardless of the technical sense aimed for by the interpreter, the interpreted text always functioned either as killing letter or as vivifying spirit in the mind of the reader (Bedouelle 1976, 182; Oberman, 290).

Although Lefèvre's commentaries were used and commented upon by some of the Reformers (the notes on his psalm com-

mentary of the early Luther and Zwingli have been preserved), his theological views did not completely break with late medieval Roman Catholic theology, especially in Pauline interpretation on congruous merits (works prepare one for justification), faith and works as necessary for justification, free will, the imitation of Christ *(Christoformitas),* and the mystical union of Christ and the believer. However, he differed with Erasmus in his understanding of original sin, seeing it as the individual curved in oneself *(incurvatus se;* a concept also found in Luther). Contrary to Erasmus, he understood the law that the gospel abrogates to be not only the ceremonial law but also the moral law. He also disagreed with Erasmus in christology by stressing the divinity of Christ more than the humanity, especially in regard to their argument over Psalm 8:5 and its New Testament commentary, Hebrews 2:5-9. He regularly emphasized the priority of Scripture, grace and faith in an evangelical manner and articulated a commemorative understanding of the Eucharist that makes him representative of the state of the Reformation in France at that time (Bedouelle 1976, 234).

BIBLIOGRAPHY

Works. J. Lefèvre d'Étaples, *S. Pauli Epistolae XIV ex Vulgata . . . cum Commentariis* (Stuttgart: Frommann Holzboog, 1978 [1512]); idem, *Quincuplex Psalterium* (Geneva: Droz, 1979 [1513]); idem, *Epistres et Evangelis pour les cinquante et deux dimanches de l'an,* ed. G. Bedouelle and F. Giacone (Leiden: E. J. Brill, 1976); idem, *Le Nouveau Testament,* Fac-similé de la première édition Simon de Colines, ed. M. A. Screech (2 vols.; New York: Johnson Reprint, 1970 [1523]); idem, "Preface to the Commentaries of the Four Gospels," a partial translation in *The Portable Renaissance Reader,* ed. J. B. Ross and M. M. McLaughlin (New York: Viking, 1953); J. Lefèvre et ses disciples, *Epistres et Evangelis pour les cinquante et deux sepmaines de l'an,* ed. M. A. Screech (Geneva: Droz, 1965 [1525]); E. F. Rice Jr., *The Prefatory Epistles of Jacques Lefèvre d'Étaples and Related Texts* (New York: Columbia University Press, 1972).

Studies. G. Bedouelle, *Lefèvre d'Étaples et l'intelligence des écritures* (Geneva: Droz, 1976);

idem, *Le Quincuplex Psalterium de Lefèvre d'Étaples: Un guide de lecture* (Geneva: Droz, 1979); J. W. Brush, "Lefèvre d'Étaples, Three Phases in His Life and Work" in *Reformation Studies in Honor of Roland H. Bainton*, ed. F. H. Littell (Richmond, VA: John Knox, 1962); R. Cameron, "The Attack on the Biblical Work of Lefèvre D'Étaples, 1514-1521," *CH* 38 (1969) 9-24; idem, "The Charges of Lutheranism Brought Against Jacques Lefèvre d'Étaples (1520-1529)," *HiTR* 63 (1970) 119-49; P. E. Hughes, *Lefèvre: Pioneer of Ecclesiastical Renewal in France* (Grand Rapids: Eerdmans, 1984); H. A. Oberman, *Forerunners of the Reformation: The Shape of Late Medieval Thought Illustrated by Key Documents* (Philadelphia: Fortress, 1981); J. B. Payne, "Erasmus and Lefèvre d'Étaples as Interpreters of Paul," *ARG* 65 (1974) 54-83; E. F. Rice Jr., "The Humanist Idea of Antiquity," *SR* 9 (1962) 126-60; R. Stauffer, "Lefèvre d'Étaples, artisan ou spectateur de la Reforme?" in *Interprètes de la Bible* (Paris: Beauchesne, 1980).

P. D. W. Krey

Lightfoot, John *(1602-1675)*

John Lightfoot was born at Stoke-upon-Trent in Staffordshire on March 29, 1602, the second of five sons born to Thomas Lightfoot, then curate of Stoke and later rector of Uttoxeter, Staffordshire, and his wife, Elizabeth Bagnall Lightfoot. At an early age John was sent to study with a Mr. Whitehead, a schoolmaster at Morton Green, Chester. Under Whitehead, Lightfoot learned Latin and Greek and may have gotten an initial acquaintance with Hebrew. In June 1617 he left Morton Green for Christ's College, Cambridge, where his tutor was the eminent William Chappel, then fellow of Christ's College and later professor of divinity at Trinity College, Dublin, and eventually bishop of Cork. At Cambridge Lightfoot rapidly distinguished himself, particularly as an orator and classical scholar. He did not pursue the study of Hebrew while he was at Cambridge.

After completing his bachelor of arts, Lightfoot became the assistant to his former teacher, Mr. Whitehead, at Repton in Derbyshire. There Lightfoot honed his knowledge of classical Greek. After some two years at Repton, Lightfoot entered the ministry and took a parish at Norton in Shropshire. While he was at Norton, his preaching came to the attention of the noted Hebraist Sir Rowland Cotton, who engaged him as chaplain to his family. Cotton, who had studied privately with Hugh Broughton, one of the translators of the King James Version, not only was capable of reading biblical Hebrew but also could converse in the language. He urged Lightfoot to study oriental languages, not only Hebrew but also its cognates, particularly, Aramaic. Lightfoot rapidly became adept at Hebrew, including the rabbinic Hebrew of the Mishnah and Talmud. There is no indication that Lightfoot ever studied under any teacher other than Cotton. His further expertise was probably gained from continuous personal study.

In 1628, on his marriage to Joice Crompton, Lightfoot moved from Norton to Hornsley, near London, in order to avail himself of the famous library of Hebraica at Sion College. These resources led to the publication in 1629 of his first work, *Erubhim, or Miscellanies, Christian and Judaical, and Others.* The book was a collection of short essays on diverse themes in which Lightfoot effectively charted out his life's work: many of his later works are expansions of these essays. After spending the early part of 1630 at Uttoexeter, Lightfoot was appointed by Sir Rowland Cotton to the rectory at Ashley in Stafforshire, where he remained for more than a decade.

In 1642 Lightfoot took up residence in London, most probably at the call of the Westminster Assembly, of which he became an influential and vocal member. In a series of eloquent sermons before the House of Commons, he argued for an Erastian view of church-state relations and a Presbyterian theory of church government. His journal of the Assembly (Lightfoot, vol. 13) remains a significant documentation for historians. Shortly after his arrival in London, Lightfoot was called to be the minister of St. Bartholomews-Behind-the-Exchange, where he preached regularly during the time of the assembly. In addition he was given the rectory of Much-Munden in Hertfordshire on the death of Samuel Ward in 1643, assuring Lightfoot an income. Munden became Lightfoot's favorite home and place of study. He also pursued his ministry in the parish diligently and is remembered both for his regular preaching and his conscientious visitation of the sick. Two volumes of the collected works are devoted to his sermons.

Work. The period of the Puritan Revolution was also one of the most productive eras in Lightfoot's literary career: he produced his *Harmony of the Four Evangelists, among Themselves and with the Old Testament* (1644-50), *A Commentary Upon the Acts of the Apostles, Chronical and Critical* (1645), *A Chronical of the Times and Order of the Text of the Old Testament* (1647), *The Temple Service as it Stood in the Days of Our Saviour* (1649), *The Harmony, Chronical and Order of the New Testament* (1655) and *Collatio Hebraici Pentateucho cum Samaritico* (1660). Lightfoot was also the editor of the works of Hugh Broughton (1662).

Lightfoot was appointed master of St. Catherine Hall, Cambridge, most probably before 1650. The award of his doctor of divinity followed in 1652, and in 1655 he became vice chancellor of Cambridge University, an appointment that remained his even after the Restoration in 1660. An apparent decrease in publication following 1650 can be explained by Lightfoot's role in the production, under the general editorship of Brian Walton, of the great London Polyglot Bible (1657) and by the assistance that he gave both to Edmund Castell in the production of the latter's *Lexicon Heptaglotton* (1669) of Hebrew and cognate languages and to Matthew Poole in the production of Poole's *Synopsis Criticorum* (1669-76). Lightfoot was responsible for the edition of the Samaritan Pentateuch found in the Polyglot. He also engaged in an extensive correspondence with Johannes Buxtorf Jr. and other biblical

scholars of the day (Lightfoot, vol. 13). The correspondence offers significant illumination of the issues encountered by exegetes in his time and insights into Lightfoot's own habits of study.

Methods. Although Lightfoot was preceded in his interest in Judaica as a means to the understanding of the linguistic, cultural and religious background of the New Testament by such important seventeenth-century exegetes as Henry Ainsworth, Johannes Buxtorf Sr., John Weemes and Christopher Goodwin, he was the exegete who most clearly and convincingly applied the knowledge of Judaica, and specifically of the Talmud, to the text of the New Testament. He was also one of the first to argue the profound significance of the rabbinic Judaism as a context for understanding the life and ministry of Jesus.

Lightfoot's genius for languages was supplemented by tireless discipline in study. He took copious notes on his readings and divided his written work neatly into categories, examining first the chronology of Scripture, then the "chorography" or places mentioned, next the original texts and versions, and finally the collateral evidence offered by the Talmud and other Judaica. It was also Lightfoot's custom to examine individual texts chronologically, as evidenced by his efforts to develop a harmony of the Gospels; to argue the case for his arrangement, noting at the same time textual difficulties; and then to examine all textual variants, translations and commentators at his disposal in order to come to a conclusion concerning the text. His attention to detail is also evident from the unpublished manuscripts noted by J. Strype, three of which are devoted to the text of Septuagint and discrepancies between it and the Hebrew text.

These interests in chronology, geographical data and collation of texts also place Lightfoot's methods squarely into the context of seventeenth-century hermeneutics. Many of the other exegetes and scholars of the day manifest profound interest in biblical chronology—notably James Usher and Isaac Newton—particularly in problems created by the juxtaposition of Kings and Chronicles and of the Hebrew Old Testament with the Septuagint, or by the comparison of the Synoptic Gospels with the Gospel of John. Nor was the primary issue addressed the date of creation or the age of the world, but rather the literal historical meaning of the text. Thus biblical chronology, together with the intense examination of geography or of the architectural features of famous buildings (like the temple), belongs to the same hermeneutic as the detailed collation and critical establishment of the text. Lightfoot's interest in Judaica, largely for the identification of customs and for cultural information, belongs to the same emphasis on the literal, historical sense of Scripture.

Despite his learning in Judaica and his expertise in Hebrew and cognate languages (and unlike his learned contemporary, Edward Pococke, professor of Hebrew, Arabic and cognate languages at Oxford), Lightfoot had little or no interest in establishing positive relationships with Jews. He had no hope for their national conversion and therefore saw dialogue as fruitless. He held rabbinic theology in rather low esteem, commenting often on what he viewed as absurd legends, excessive legalism, superstitions and childish theology. His expertise in these materials, like his interest in biblical chronology and geography, was intended to aid in the creation of a text-critical apparatus for understanding the canonical Scriptures and linked to a program intended to support the Reformed theological orthodoxy of the day.

Lightfoot was also given to polemic against Rome, the Anabaptists, Jesuits, Antinomians, Arians and Socinians, all in the support of a strict theological orthodoxy. Characteristic of his approach was his debate with Jewish opinion over the identification of Jesus as Messiah in which he used rabbinic exegesis of messianic texts to prove the rectitude of Christian doctrine. His only known contact with a Jewish scholar occurred in 1671, when Cambridge University appointed him to supervise the translation of the Mishnah then being undertaken by Isaac Abendana (1650-1710). All that is known of their encounter appears from the positive reports offered by Lightfoot on the progress of the translation.

Canon of Scripture. Lightfoot had pronounced views on the canon of Scripture, views that are of particular importance in light of his approach to Judaica. As is clear from his Fast Sermon, *Elias Redivivus* (1643), on Luke 1:17, he opposed the continuance of the Apocrypha in printed Protestant Bibles. He recognized the chronological placement of the Apocrypha between the Testaments and held their importance both for Hellenized Jews and for converted Gentiles before the time of Christ. He also assumed the importance of the materials in the Apocrypha for establishing the cultural and linguistic background for Old and New Testament exegesis. He nonetheless viewed the Apocrypha as presenting a popular and superstitious form of religion unworthy even of association with the canon of the Old and New Testaments. He recommended that the Reformed churches apply to the Apocrypha "the counsel of Sarah concerning Ishmael" that they "cast out the bond woman and her son" and remove this "wretched . . . patchery of human invention" from the Bible.

Lightfoot also ought to be remembered as one of the exegetes who contributed to seventeenth-century Protestant orthodoxy. Although his expertise in and use of Judaica placed him on the forefront of critical scholarship in his day, he also consistently upheld traditional Christian doctrine and, in the controversy over the origin of the vowel points, argued the origin of the points in the time of Moses, largely on the ground that, however the text of the Old Testament had been transmitted, the form of the Hebrew language presupposed the vocalization necessary for speech and reading. This latter conclusion belonged very much to the scholarship of his time, which was with few exceptions textual rather than historical in nature. Even so, Lightfoot's text-critical use of Judaica tended away from considerations of Judaism as a developing, historical religion and simply drew on Jewish sources for linguistic and cultural materials.

Use of Judaica. Lightfoot's interest in Judaica was primarily for the sake of elucidating the New Testament. In the dedicatory epistle to his commentary on Matthew in the *Horae Hebraicae et Talmudicae,* Lightfoot stated categorically and quite bluntly for the seventeenth century that the entire New Testament had been written by Jews and that, albeit in Greek, it retained the "style, idiom, form, and rule of speaking" of first-century Judaism. The difficult portions of the New Testament could, he argued, be clarified only with reference to the "ordinary sense and speech" of the Jews, which was nowhere more available for study than in the Talmud.

For example, Lightfoot disputed the standard assumption that John the Baptist had been a solitary hermit who lived in the wilderness. He argued that "desert" indicated only a non-urban setting, noting the identification of the hill country of Judah as "desert" in Psalm 75:6 and a fairly consistent rabbinic usage of "desert" or "wilderness" as a reference to rural areas. Even more interesting theologically is the extensive list of rabbinic references to the "kingdom of heaven" offered by Lightfoot. The phrase refers, he notes, both to the "manifestation of the Messiah" and to the "inward love and fear of God" characteristic of a spiritual kingdom. Lightfoot also offers an interpretation of John's baptism in the context of Jewish baptismal practices, comparing and contrasting it with proselyte baptism and with ritual cleansings. Lightfoot saw here also an argument for infant baptism: his rabbinic sources indicated to him that baptism accompanied the circumcision of the infant children of converts to Judaism.

Lightfoot similarly drew on the Talmud to dispute the Roman Catholic reading of Matthew 16:19. "Binding" and "loosing,"

Lightfoot argued, should be understood rabbinically as forbidding and permitting observance of commandments in the ceremonial law, particularly for the sake of drawing Gentile converts in to the Christian community, and not as a basis for papal or priestly power to forgive sin or to excommunicate sinners. His discussion of the preparation for Passover (Mt 26:19-30) also provides significant evidence of his use of Judaica, with its detailed discussion of the first cup of wine, the bitter herbs and the unleavened bread. Lightfoot draws on the historical reflection of exodus in the Jewish Passover celebration, moreover, to interpret the Lord's Supper. Against various doctrines of a local eucharistic presence he paraphrases: "This is now my body, in that sense, in which the paschal lamb hath been my body hitherto."

Toward the end of his life Lightfoot was offered the prebendary at Ely. In late 1675, as he journeyed from Cambridge to Ely, Lightfoot caught cold and fever. He died at Ely on December 6, 1675, and was interred at Munden. Lightfoot's final major work, the *Horae Hebraicae et Talmudicae,* a commentary on the New Testament extending as far as 1 Corinthians, appeared in six volumes between 1658 and 1678. The fame of the work, which comments on the text of the New Testament from the perspective of Judaica, led to its republication at Leipzig (1675; the four Gospels only) and, together with his other Latin works, at Rotterdam (1686) and Franecker (1699). The translation appeared first in Lightfoot's collected works in 1684 and has been reissued numerous times, including several modernized printings in the nineteenth and twentieth centuries.

On his death Lightfoot left a collection of Judaica to the library of Harvard University and his personal papers to his son-in-law. The latter bequest proved the most profitable inasmuch as his books perished in a fire at Harvard in 1769, whereas his papers passed into the hands of the archivist and historian J. Strype, who edited the second volume of the seventeenth-century edition of Lightfoot's collected works (1684) and provided that edition with a memoir and a review of Lightfoot's papers. It was in Strype's publication (1700) of Lightfoot's "remains" that Lightfoot's correspondence and several posthumous treatises were finally made available. The standard edition, gathering all these materials, is the complete *Works,* edited by J. R. Pitman (Oxford, 1822-1825). The most detailed discussions of Lightfoot's life remain the essays of Pitman and Strype.

BIBLIOGRAPHY

Works. J. Lightfoot, *The Whole Works of John Lightfoot, Master of Catharine Hall, Cambridge,* ed. J. R. Pitman (Oxford, 1822-1825).

Studies. I. Abrahams, "Isaac Abendana's Cambridge *Mishnah* and Oxford Calendars" in *Transactions of the Jewish Historical Society of England* 8 (1915-1918) 98-122; R. A. Muller, "The Debate Over the 'Vowel Points' and the Crisis in Orthodox Hermeneutics," *JMRS* 10, 1 (spring 1980) 53-72; J. R. Pitman, "Preface to the Octavo Edition of Dr. Lightfoot's Works" in *The Whole Works of John Lightfoot,* ed. J. R. Pitman (Oxford, 1822-1825), 1:v-cvi (contains a biography and a series of essays on Lightfoot's works and views); C. E. Schertz, "Christian Hebraism in 17th Century England as Reflected in the Works of John Lightfoot" (Ph.D. diss., New York University, 1977); J. Strype, "Some Account of the Life of the Reverend and Most Learned John Lightfoot, D.D." and "An Appendix, or Collection of Some More Memorials of the Life of the Excellent Dr. John Lightfoot" in *The Whole Works of John Lightfoot,* ed. J. R. Pitman (Oxford, 1822-1825) 1:43-125; D. M. Welton, *John Lightfoot: The English Hebraist* (Leipzig, 1878).   R. A. Muller

Luther, Martin *(1483-1546)*

Martin Luther, son of Hans Luther, a miner, and Margrete Lindermann, was born November 10, 1483, in Eisleben, Saxony. After early schooling he attended Erfurt University (1501-1505), earning his bachelor's and master's degrees. While he was returning to Erfurt in July 1505, Luther was thrown to the ground during a thunderstorm; frightened, he declared "I will become a monk," a promise he honored by entering the Black Cloister of the Augustinian Hermits in Erfurt (July 7, 1505). Ordained February 27, 1507, he was assigned to study theology and was transferred to Wittenberg to study and lecture on moral philosophy in the arts faculty. He received the degree of bachelor of biblical studies in March 1509 from the theological faculty of Wittenberg; he also became a lecturer on Peter Lombard's *Sentences* that year (his notes from 1509 to 1511 on the *Sentences* are extant). In 1512 Luther received his doctorate in theology and was appointed professor of Bible. In 1513 Luther began lecturing in Wittenberg on the Bible and did so for more than thirty years.

Context. Luther's reformation was theological and pastoral. A basic presupposition of his reform program is the conviction that external behavior reflects internal attitude. A favorite image for Luther is that a good tree bears good fruit and, conversely, a bad tree, bad fruit. The bad fruits in Christendom could be reformed only by rooting out the bad tree that produced them. Too many reformers had come no further than attacking the bad fruit. A good tree can grow only in the soil of the one, holy, catholic and apostolic faith expressed in the Scriptures, and therefore a reform of the church's life (fruit) could effectively come about only through a reformation of the church's faith (tree).

Luther's theological effort for reformation could be described as his effort to catholicize the church, feeling as he did that the church had ceased to be that one, holy, catholic and apostolic church it confessed to be. The church that Luther sought to bring about by his theological efforts was a church unified by the universal faith of the forebears, rooted in the holy gospel of Jesus Christ.

Luther's self-understanding revolved around his being a doctor of the church, a theologian responsible for the church's faith. Throughout his life, his professorial, pastoral and personal activities reflected his training as a doctor of sacred Scripture and the effort on his part to allow the Word of God to interact with faith and life. Theology must be biblical and vernacular.

The historical context for Luther's thought included his reaction to late medieval currents of thought. His response was both negative and positive.

First, Luther was negative toward nominalism, the philosophy that reality (universals) exists in name only. He had experience with nominalist currents of thought through his education. Because he was antagonistic toward nominalism does not mean that he favored scholasticism (academic theology), nominalism's opponent. Luther rejected scholasticism in general because of its speculative bent (theology of glory), seeking to penetrate into the nature and necessity of divine essence; for the same reason nominalism also rejected scholasticism. Luther was negative toward nominalism because of its optimistic and nonbiblical view of human, natural powers—that one is able and responsible to initiate and build up good works for salvation. The covenantal model of nominalism placed responsibility on both parties to carry out the obligations of their pact.

Luther later accused humanism of the same anthropological optimism. Humanism and nominalism held to the dignity and freedom of human will and reason. By opposing these two movements Luther was being critical of human, natural abilities to initiate and cooperate with God. In his response to these movements Luther emphasized that human will and reason are in bondage until they are liberated by God's grace.

Second, Luther was positive toward certain late medieval movements. For example, he was impressed with the genuine piety of various mystical treatises, so much so that he edited and published some of them. Luther was a part of the movement of spiritual renewal. He was also inclined to mysticism because of its strong emphasis on the personal (noninstitutional, nonacademic) relationship with God. Like many mystics, Luther felt that pilgrims had been beset with too many roadblocks on their way up the mountain, whereas Christ had come to clear away the many roadblocks of legalism and speculation.

Luther also favored Augustinianism, the revival of Augustinian thought, because he held to the authority of that doctor of the church, *Augustine. Luther often appealed to the great doctor in his quarrels with scholasticism and nominalism and in his opposition to late medieval Pelagianism (works righteousness). What attracted Luther in Augustine was the theology of grace that made humans incapable of earning it and God totally able to give it. Luther was impressed with Augustine's christological interpretation of Scripture: the unity of Scripture in Jesus Christ expressed in one testament of justification. Humans are concupiscent; God is grace.

Luther inclined toward conciliarism, at least through the 1520s, because like other (pre-)reformers he felt that Christendom was encumbered with corrupted and corrupting power that would not bring about the necessary reformation. Politically and ecclesiastically Luther felt the best chances for the reform of Christendom lay with a council; but as his and other calls for a council were aborted, he became disillusioned with conciliar possibilities as the 1520s wore on.

The historical context of Luther's thought was to carry on in the doctoral tradition of Augustine and the Fathers, monasticism and mysticism (Benedictinism to *Bernard), seeking theological renewal of his one, holy, catholic and apostolic church based on Scripture.

Major Writings. Early exegetical writings were *Lectures on the Psalms* (1513-1515), preceded by the Preface of Jesus Christ, and lectures on Romans (1515-1516), Galatians (1516-1517) and Hebrews (1517-1518). The first writing in German was *The Seven Penitential Psalms* (1517). Here the major Augustinian themes are present throughout as in all of his work: grace, faith, Christ, the testament of Christ, Scripture interpreting itself and the centrality of the Word.

The *Heidelberg Disputation* (1518) is the major source for Luther's theology of the Cross. He issued several polemics on indulgences (1517-1518), including the Ninety-Five Theses (October 31, 1517). Important instructional treatises appeared in 1519 and 1520: penance, baptism, Lord's Supper, death, good works and the Lord's Prayer. Famous reformation treatises were issued in 1520: *To the Christian Nobility* (on social reform), *Babylonian Captivity* (on sacraments) and *Freedom of the Christian* (Christian life). *The Magnificat* (1521) shows Luther as a medieval theologian whose Mariology, typical of the age, was lost in later Lutheranism.

Luther's *Bondage of the Will* (1525), which along with his commentary on Galatians he regarded as his two most important works, is a fierce appeal for the freedom of God to save without any interference from will, reason or good intent. His sharp rhetoric sought to establish that before God we come with nothing; if we were to come with something, then God would not be totally free to save and totally Savior. It is a positive treatise on the power of the electing will of God to save.

Beginning in 1519 Luther published more commentaries on Galatians and the Psalms. He had a lifelong attachment to the Psalms, Paul and John. The prefaces to the Old Testament (1523) and New Testament (1522), continuing into the 1530s and 1540s, provide excellent entry into Luther's view of individual books of the Bible. An excellent overview of Luther's theology for church and home are his Small and Large Catechisms of 1529. Luther's major writing on the history of the church and the marks of the church is his 1539 treatise *On the Councils and the Churches*. Luther's last major exegetical course was on Genesis (1535-45).

Approaches and Methods of Biblical Interpretation. From early times through the Reformation, theology was practiced as the discipline of the sacred page *(sacra pagina)*.

The monastery became the place and the monks' daily liturgy was the context for the practice of theology. Holy Writ was the sacred page; the canon of Scripture was the rule of faith. The goal of life for the medieval pilgrim *(viator)* as well as the final goal of theology was to go home, home to God, home to the Trinity (in Augustine's words).

The sacred page was seen as coming directly from God, about God and for the pilgrim's journey to God. Theology, whether expressed in doctrine, liturgy or catechesis, was the discipline of the sacred page. The sacred page was the record of God's creation and redemption. Theology, Scripture, commentary and God were bound up in one world and were focused on the sacred page.

The rise of scholastic theology in the twelfth century was linked to the discipline of dialectic and its use of the question. The discipline of scholastic theology practiced in the schools (universities) was the discipline of faith seeking understanding. In the universities in the twelfth century, theology shifted to sacred doctrine *(sacra doctrina)*. The schoolmen wrote Bible commentaries, and they also wrote sacred theology.

Scholastic theology was based on the method of *quaestio* (question) and dialectic. By the later Middle Ages, a caricature of the scholastic question was, How many angels can dance on the head of a pin? Such a question cannot be found in scholastic sources themselves, although scholasticism, described as decadent by sixteenth-century Reformers, may have become too abstract by the eve of the Reformation. In the twelfth and thirteenth centuries the final goal of theology was still the Beatific Vision. The shift from sacred page to sacred doctrine was the shift from locating the substance of theology in Scripture to locating the substance in doctrine.

The scholarship of Christian humanists and the invention of the printing press in the latter part of the fifteenth century contributed to a shift within theology: the sacred letter as literature. Theology was seen not as the monk's work of prayer and praise or as the professor's academic questions and propositions but as the educative task of reviving the pagan and Christian classics. The study of the sacred letter of Scripture was intended to lead men and women not so much to God as to a better society, church, education and government. Theology as the study of the philosophy of Christ (Desiderius *Erasmus) was to lead to piety, morality and justice.

The goal of the historical-critical method beginning with the sixteenth century is to understand the letter of the original text. The goal of sacred doctrine is to understand the faith of the church. The goal of the sacred page is to understand and reach God (the Trinity).

These approaches to the sacred page (monastery), sacred doctrine (university) and sacred letter (printing press) continued in the early and late Reformation. Luther continued the monastic discipline of the sacred page minus monastic rules. The Council of Trent and Lutheran orthodoxy continued the discipline of sacred doctrine. Philipp *Melanchthon approached Scripture as sacred letter (literature).

It is often assumed that Luther ended the medieval approach to the Bible and started the modern methods, but Luther approached Scripture in a manner appropriate to what the document is *(sacra pagina)*. Luther did not superimpose his agenda onto Scripture; he took out and applied the message of Scripture as he claimed to do and thus was consistent with the grammar and vocabulary of Scripture.

Major Themes. Several major themes emerge in Luther's works.

Bible and theology. Luther was concerned to place the Bible in the center of everything: church, theology and especially preaching. The main point of the Reformation was that the gospel must be proclaimed. Along with the important pamphlets, the pulpits of the evangelical cities (Wittenberg, Zurich, Geneva) were the media for information. The Reformation was a movement of the Word: Christ, Scripture and preaching—in that order.

They all are the Word of God. The Reformers used the printed Word, studied the Word, prayed the Word; but their concern was to bring preaching back into the Mass, preaching in the vernacular and preaching on the text of Scripture. When Luther said that the church is not a pen-house but a mouth-house, he meant that the good news cannot properly be put in (dead) letters but is to be proclaimed loudly (in German).

What the scholastics separated—theology and commentary on Scripture—Luther sought to bring together again along the lines of *sacra pagina*. Scripture alone is the sole authority for the church, the discipline of theology and the life of faith. Luther continued the call for the reform of the church on the basis of Scripture. Every office and activity in the church falls under the judgment of Scripture. All of theology is contained in Scripture. God has revealed all that we need to know about God in Christ. Theology must be biblical theology; any other kind is human invention.

Scripture is its own authority because it is clear. No other authority is needed to see through its meaning. Luther was not concerned about a theory of inspiration. That came later. In his view the Bible is the Word. The Reformers were aware of the critical discussions among the humanists about the text, authorship and language, and Luther engaged in some of this. The point of the Word is the presence of the Word in Scripture, church and preaching. The humanist sense of the distance of Scripture from the present was not accepted. The scholastic separation of theology from Scripture was attacked. The purpose of theology is to serve preaching, the main task of the church.

Interpretation of the Bible. Luther was premodern; he continued the general medieval understanding of interpretation as commentary, annotation and exposition. The modern interpreter continues to develop the humanist perspective of the historical past; thus interpretation in modern time is bridging the gulf between ancient literature and modern thinking. The early Reformers continued the monastic approach of total immersion into the thinking and language of Scripture so that there is only one language, one biblical theology.

Luther emphasized that Scripture is its own interpreter. He argued that the papacy had built a wall of authoritative interpretation around itself so that Scripture could be read only as the papacy interpreted it. One late medieval synthesis maintained that Scripture is to tradition as foundation is to interpretation (Ockham). Strong in the sixteenth century was the question of an authoritative interpretation of Scripture. Summarizing the Roman position, the Council of Trent decreed later in the century: No one, relying on his own skill in matters of faith and morals, "wresting" the sacred Scriptures to his own senses, should presume to interpret the said sacred Scripture contrary to the sense that holy mother church, whose it is to judge of the true sense and interpretation of the Holy Scripture, has held and does hold.

For Luther Scripture itself attests to its message and meaning. Christ and the Spirit are at work in the Word. The Reformers insisted that postapostolic claims of authoritative interpretation were precisely the reason the Word of God lost its central place in the life of the church.

The Reformation interpretation of Scripture was engaged in theological polemics. The humanists used Scripture to attack the church, but they were not so much interested in the pure doctrines of Scripture as they were in exposing the corruption and folly of the present situation in the light of the piety of Scripture. The early Reformers fought for pure doctrine on the basis of Scripture and the Fathers. The doctrine of justification by faith alone, by grace alone, by Christ alone was seen as the central doctrine of Scripture. The doctrine of justification by faith is the criterion by which all other doctrines, offices and practices in the church are judged. The criteriological priority of justification by faith is

established in Scripture. The church stands or falls, said Luther, on the scriptural teaching of justification. There were other issues, other polemics, but the procedure was the same. Doctrinal reform was forged and pleaded on the basis of Scripture.

Law and gospel. Basic for Luther's understanding of Scripture was his distinction between law and gospel. The gospel of Jesus Christ is the fulfillment and end of the Mosaic law. Law and gospel are in all books of the Bible. The gospel is the good news that salvation is in Christ alone. Abraham and others saw that gospel in the promises; they believed and were justified. Luther transposes Augustine's distinction between Old Testament and New Testament as ways of salvation to law and gospel. The way of the law is do this, and do not do that. The way of the gospel is believe, and it has already been done for a person in Christ. The law is command; the gospel is gift, the gift of forgiveness. When the law commands, failure results because one cannot fulfill the law on one's own power ("The good I would, I do not"). The law humbles; the gospel picks up. One cannot be picked up unless one is put down to size. Being brought low (law) and being raised up (gospel) are the downs and ups of the Christian life, the experience of sin (brought by the law) and the experience of forgiveness (brought by Christ). The distinction between law and gospel, the doctrine of justification by faith apart from works, and the understanding of the core of Scripture are all the same for Luther.

Christ the center of Scripture. The center of Scripture for Luther is Christ, present in both the Old and New Testaments. Christ is the eternal Word of God, present in Old Testament times in the form of promise, present in New Testament times in the person of Jesus, and present in the church through Word and sacrament. In all cases Christ the Word is the effective means of grace. The center or core of Scripture is "what drives Christ" *(was Christum treibet)*, that is, what preaches Christ, what promotes or points to Christ. Christ is at the core of God's plan of salvation. God promises through prophets; God delivers in person. All of Scripture leads to Christ, and Christ leads to salvation.

The simple sense. Luther's response to the various senses of meaning in the Middle Ages (fourfold, double-literal) was that Scripture has one simple sense (most often, Christ). Or Luther will talk about the grammatical sense as the meaning of the text, that the grammatical meaning and theological meaning are the same. Luther availed himself of humanist scholarship and was a part of a late medieval trend to highlight (once again) the christological meaning of a text. Luther also used allegory, not to establish a doctrine but to embellish it. He also used the other spiritual senses. Luther on Scripture is often presented as a total break from the medieval world. That came later. In the area of the senses of meaning, Luther is a part of the medieval trend to call for a return to the letter of the text and then in practice to go on and find other senses of meaning. After all, and all the medieval scholars knew this, the New Testament itself uses allegory.

Theology of testament. Luther's distinction is his construction of Scripture as containing a single testament (will, promise) of Christ. God's last and only will and testament is that he would die for our salvation. The promise is the declaration of the will and testament. The death of the God-man validates his testament. The inheritance is the forgiveness of sins and eternal life. The (new) testament of Christ is eternal. It is played out in time, but there is no development in the eternal. Augustine and medieval theologians generally saw a development and transformation within and between the Old and New Testament. Luther held that the New Testament is older than the Old because it is the oldest (eternal). The Old Testament begins and ends in time.

Luther's response to his contemporary situation was the response of a theology of testament. Testament or will is the model that accounts for most of the pieces in

Luther's supposedly nonsystematic theology. The word *testament* is a short summary of all God's grace fulfilled in Christ. Testament or will is the testament of God promised throughout the Old Testament era and books that he would send a testator (Christ) to bring the inheritance of forgiveness of sins and eternal life, which is received in faith. The death and resurrection of the testator, God in flesh, validates the testament.

Promise, one ingredient in the category of testament, is God's announcement of redemption. Redemption as well as creation is ex nihilo. The totality of the testament from promise through inheritance is a reality present from the beginning to the end of time. The New Testament is the eternal testament of Christ.

The second ingredient in testament is Luther's theology of Word. The Word is the dynamic manifestation of the person of God. Important for Luther is the passage in Isaiah that God's Word will not return void, which means that the Word will accomplish that which it sets out to do. The Word accomplishes a faithful response that brings about the forgiveness of sins and eternal life. The promise is God's Word that he will one day die and rise and validate his testament.

The third part of Luther's testament theology is a theology of the cross. The theology of the cross has an antispeculative force to it which is directed against a theology of glory. The theology of the cross is contextual, working within what God did in Christ on the cross. Rather than using philosophical terms, Luther talks about the wounds of Christ on the cross and Christ as a worm on the cross, thus emphasizing the total humiliation of the God-man. The humiliation of the cross is God's total identification with the human situation in order to redeem that situation so that we can live by faith.

The fourth aspect of Luther's theology of testament is grace. Grace for Luther is a unilateral gift. One of the primary functions of testament is that the testator makes out his will without the recipient having done anything to deserve the inheritance. Testament, at least God's way, is gratuitous. The heir in no way merits the inheritance. Testament for Luther stands in contrast with covenant. Often Luther will use covenant as a synonym for testament and understand it as unilateral gift. In late medieval covenant theologies, the covenant is a bilateral, two-way pact, bond or agreement. These various covenant theologians were at least semi-Pelagian because they called for some human action as a necessary part of the pact. The grace of the unilateral testament, however, is the cross and resurrection. A covenant does not require death. The unilateral act of grace proves that God's promise is true. The cross is final proof that God's testament is valid. The resurrection completes God's action. For Luther, then, grace is God's self-actualizing Word that accomplishes its purpose without requiring any act on our part.

The fifth aspect of testament is faith or trust in the inheritance. One receives faith through the Word accomplishing its purpose. Faith is a gift of grace. Trust is confidence that Christ not only died for the sins of humankind but also he died for me. Trust is intimately bound up with Luther's notion of the certitude of salvation. Christians are certain of their salvation because their salvation is in Christ, and Christ is for me and for us. If salvation were dependent on something that we were to do, free will, free reason, then Luther in no way could have any confidence. Confidence rests in Christ alone.

Principles of Biblical Interpretation. Technically Luther did not have a hermeneutic because hermeneutics is a nineteenth-century discipline that presupposes the distance of the biblical text and the need for the interpreter to bridge the gap and make any interpretative moves necessary to bring the text into modern linguistic jargon understandable in post-Enlightenment philosophy.

To be a theologian, the three rules (1539), prayer *(oratio)*, meditation *(medi-*

tatio) and temptation or experience *(tentatio)*, need to be practiced every day. These show Luther indebted to the sacred reading *(lectio divina)* of Scripture deep in the theological tradition of the church.

The core of Scripture is what drives, teaches and pronounces Christ *(was Christum treibet)*. *Treiben* has to do with transportation; so that in Scripture, the important thing is to see that the sacred page drives us and brings us to Christ.

Canon within the canon is a principle often associated with Luther. The danger of this dictum for Luther would be that some subjective principle of selectivity would choose the inner canon and force everything into that mold. And yet several scholars feel that Luther did exactly that with his insistence that the first article, justification by faith, interprets the whole. Christ, not a doctrine or principle, is at the center of Scripture; Luther consistently maintains that Christ is the babe in the manger and Scripture is the manger that supports him.

Scripture alone means Scripture as the sole authority as opposed to the human traditions of the papacy. Scripture alone means Christ alone.

Scripture has a single, christological meaning. Luther recognized and used the biblical and medieval fourfold sense (literal, allegorical, tropological, anagogical) where it embellished the single simplest, that is, the grammatical sense.

Scripture is the living voice of the gospel *(viva vox evangelii);* it can never be contained in a writing, much less a law; nor can an interpretation take the place of the text itself (himself).

Scripture is it own interpreter *(scriptura sacra sui ipsius interpres)* means Scripture is to be used to interpret itself based on the echo of Scripture within Scripture. The Old Testament is ruminating over the Psalter, exodus, covenant and law, as the New Testament interprets the Old Testament and its own articles of faith.

Scripture confirms (authenticates) itself *(Die Schrift verbügt sich selbst)* means no outside authority is needed to bring credibility to Scripture. Scripture attests to its own veracity.

Scripture is clear because the message of salvation delivered by the Holy Spirit is overwhelmingly clear and persuasive.

Significance. Luther's understanding of his discipline of theology was that it was the discipline of the sacred page *(sacra pagina)*. The linkage of Luther with the tradition of *sacra pagina* goes counter to much of modern effort to see Luther as the first Enlightenment figure, the first rationalist, nationalist, romantic, liberal, historical critic and/or hermeneutician. The distinctive feature of this discipline is that it sees sacred matters as a page, which is a more logical approach to Holy Writ than are the efforts of the eighteenth- and nineteenth-century Enlightenment to interpret the Bible as ancient literature because it is consistent with the text of Scripture. The sacred page is the work of God directly and immediately; it bears the imprint of God, God's will, God's action, God's Word.

The discipline of the sacred page, not new to Luther, assumes the unity of God's Word. The view of God is thoroughly trinitarian. The Christian confession of faith is based on the sacred page. The form that the confession or creed or rule of faith takes is trinitarian. The unity of Scripture thus is trinitarian. The action of God as recorded from beginning to end is the action of Three-in-One.

Scripture has a unique grammar. Luther was concerned to promote that grammar, that faith. Faith is the shape or form that the words take. It is true that Luther clung only to the grammatical meaning *(sensus)* of the words. He did so to preserve the single and simple sense, which most often is Christ. But Christ is not a meaning or sense. Christ is the *res,* the very thing itself of God.

Luther frequently urged the reader to pay special attention to the peculiar phrase, idiom, example or expression that Scripture employed. The grammatical sense points to Christ. The vocabulary of the sacred page takes the form of the creed. The faith of the church based on the grammar of faith is trinitarian. Thus the unity of the grammar of faith is the unity of God the Father, God the Son, and God the Holy Spirit. Luther was the doctor of faith.

When Luther used the word *interpret,* he attacked the idea and argued instead that Scripture is to be promoted and applied to the present age but not interpreted. Luther's work of commenting on Scripture continued the medieval genre of *enarratio,* which means to narrate and apply the message of Scripture in public. The use of Scripture is not to provide evidence or proof for an interpretation. Rather, Scripture is used to promote God.

To work with Scripture as Luther did is to employ the discipline of the sacred page. Theology for Luther employs the discipline of prayer, meditation and temptation. Such a discipline comes from the Psalter. Luther was consistent to follow Scripture's lead for the discipline of theology. The goal of this discipline is God.

Medieval commentators have been described as walking concordances. The same must be said for Luther. For Luther it was necessary that God's Word be consistent in its grammar, rhetoric and theology. The importance of Luther for our time is his clear perception and practice of theology in the tradition of *enarratio* and *sacra pagina.*

BIBLIOGRAPHY

Works. *Kritische Gesamtausgabe.* (104 vols.; Weimar: Herman Bohlau, 1883-); *Luther's Works,* ed. J. Pelikan and H. Lehmann (55 vols.; St. Louis: Concordia; Philadelphia: Muhlenberg, 1955-).

Studies. H. Bornkamm, *Luther and the Old Testament* (Philadelphia: Fortress, 1969); K. Hagen, *Luther's Approach to Scripture as Seen in His 'Commentaries' on Galatians* (Tübingen: J. C. B. Mohr [Paul Siebeck], 1993); B. Hall, "Biblical Scholarship: Editions and Commentaries" in *CHB* 3:38-93; W. J. Kooiman, *Luther and the Bible* (Philadelphia: Muhlenberg, 1961); B. Lohse, *Martin Luther: An Introduction to His Life and Work* (Philadelphia: Fortress, 1986); H. de Lubac, *The Sources of Revelation* (New York:

Herder & Herder, 1968); J. Pelikan, *Luther the Expositor* (St. Louis: Concordia, 1959); J. Reumann, ed., in collaboration with S. H. Nafzger and H. H. Ditmanson, *Studies in Lutheran Hermeneutics* (Philadelphia: Fortress, 1979); J. W. Zophy, "Martin Luther. 1483-1546" in *Research Guide to European Historical Biography*, ed. J. Moncure (Washington, DC: Beacham Publishing, 1993) 8:3705-19.   K. Hagen

Marpeck, Pilgram
(c. 1495-1556)

Pilgram Marpeck was born in Tyrol of devout Catholic parents. When and under what circumstances he was drawn to the cause of reform is unknown. It is known, however, that radical, theological influences were abroad in the Tyrol during the time of Marpeck's theological awakening in the 1520s (see Boyd, Klassen 1984). Marpeck's baptism as an adult into the Anabaptist church was the result of a deeply personal profession of faith but was neither significantly anti-Catholic nor anticlerical. There is no evidence that Marpeck had formally studied theology, even though he critically engaged Lutheran and Reformed theological influences before and after embracing Anabaptism. The originality and even eccentricity of his theological formulations suggest he was an autodidact.

Like most of his fellow Anabaptists, Marpeck thought and wrote for a dissident, persecuted minority. He was an engineer by profession, which provided him with a socially protected position, less immediately threatened than most of his fellow believers. This allowed him the freedom to think more of his thoughts through to the end and to muster tact and charity toward his detractors. Even so, his writing (including his eight-hundred-page concordance of the Bible) can best be described as occasional pieces emerging from the challenge of controversy. During his crucial years in Strasbourg, Marpeck was among the most important disputants with fellow Anabaptists, who represented the entire spectrum of that movement, and with leaders of the magisterial Reformation, who were more tolerant than were those in most places.

Context. Before looking at Marpeck's work as an interpreter of the Bible, the context of his ministry needs to be identified. Protestantism as a whole reacted against Roman Catholic sacramentalism, in which sacraments worked *ex opere operato* (the ability of an external rite to bring about what it signifies). Anabaptism asserted that sacraments, which it preferred to call ceremonies, were sacred actions only when they were received by faith (Marpeck, *Admonition*, 186-87 et passim). It drew this conclusion from the New Testament descriptions of conversion and baptism. The consequence of this conclusion was that the church was made up only of people who had come to faith. Since such members were all people who had received the Spirit and promised to live in the Spirit, they were a hermeneutical community; that is, they possessed the resources to interpret the Bible together (Marpeck, *Admonition*, 166-67).

For Marpeck there was a dynamic quality to the Bible. On the one hand it was the word of God: everything the church holds to must be grounded in this written revelation of truth. In the Bible, as in sacraments, God uses outward means to draw us to God. The Bible is not just for immature believers or those of past ages, as various schools of spiritualism taught; it is the repository of truth in history, the way God reaches us as long as we are creatures of flesh and blood (Marpeck, *Instruction*, 94). On the other hand this revelation comes to life through the Spirit's work in the praying individual and the gathered congregation. It is not a dead letter but a living encounter because the Spirit who inspired its writing now indwells every believer and inspires their reading of it.

With the Reformation came a spiritualistic impulse, a locating of the Spirit's presence in the individual believer rather than in clergy, sacraments and even the Bible. Most Protestants resisted the complete individualizing and internalizing of religion, but thoroughgoing spiritualists saw their road to reform as the logical outcome of the Reformation. Anabaptism and spiritualism occupied common ground in the early Reformation because both of them sought to supersede hierarchy and reconceptualize sacraments consistent with an existential relationship of believers to Christ and to one another (Marpeck, *Refutation*, 55). When spiritualism began to present itself not as a corrective to medieval religion but as an understanding of the gospel in its own right, Marpeck was among the first and most perceptive of the Anabaptists in seeing its dangers.

Marpeck's interpretive key in responding to spiritualism was the Incarnation. In his view the Incarnation was the golden thread that wove its way through the New Testament. In it he saw the greatness of God's compassion. Because we are creatures of flesh and blood, God came to us on those terms (Marpeck, *Instruction*, 85; *Response*, 298). God did not despise our creatureliness. Here we have the basis of Marpeck's defense of the Bible as God's written Word and of the sacraments as God's prototypical way of uniting us with Christ. To summarize his teaching, it may be said that the church and the Bible are the prolongation of the Incarnation. The Bible preserves God's commandments; it testifies to the finality of God's revelation in Christ; it speaks authoritatively for Christ until his return (Marpeck, *Refutation*, 52-56 et passim).

The church is the "humanity of Christ" (by which Marpeck means the extension of his earthly life). It lives in lowliness and surrender as its Master did. It is this lowliness, this outward frailty through which God chooses to be revealed (1 Cor 1:18-31). Marpeck places supreme weight on the humanity of Christ as the mode of Christ's presence in history, even after the ascension. Just as the church prolongs the Incarnation, so too the ceremonies prolong the church: if the church is the body of Christ, the ceremonies are his hands and feet.

Marpeck's christology, more than any-

thing else, accounts for his distinctiveness within the radical Reformation. For many of its thinkers, the Incarnation was inseparable from Roman Catholic interpretations of it. Many Protestants, especially Anabaptists, concluded that they had to reject Roman Catholic incarnational thought in its entirety when they rejected priestly office and sacraments as realities that exist independent of a faith response. Marpeck's teaching on the Holy Spirit and, springing from it, his understanding of the old and new covenants, allow him to marry pneumatology and christology; that is, the Spirit works inwardly what the Son works outwardly (Marpeck, *Admonition*, 195, 228-33). Marpeck argues that God continues to draw people to himself through the humanity, the visible, outward participation in our flesh and blood, of his Son.

Because of his lofty conception of the atonement, Marpeck emphasized the novelty of the new covenant, the basis for the New Testament. In his saving work Christ descended to the dead to reach past generations with the gospel. In so doing he undid the fall and inaugurated the restoration of all things. The power of Adam's sin has been broken and is no longer held against us. Christ alone is the source of this salvation. Therefore baptism cannot be the mere prolongation of circumcision, as the Reformed taught. The new covenant can be received only in an existential act of faith; hence believer's baptism. Marpeck sees the decisive novelty of Christ more fully expressed in John and Paul (particularly Galatians and Corinthians) than in the Synoptics. Yet in his doctrine of the covenants, Marpeck sought an alternative to Anabaptists, like those in Münster, who focused on the literal fulfillment of the promises and way of life in the Hebrew Bible, and to spiritualists, who sometimes reduced the Old Testament to a carnal prologue to religion of the heart. Marpeck's incarnationism wears well here: he taught that God is always revealed in history, through flesh and blood.

Work. A selection of Marpeck's writings shows how his use of the Bible led him to this novel synthesis of the outwardness of the church and the inwardness of faith, the humanity of Christ as God's final revelation of himself yet received only through the Spirit. Marpeck's works consist of a few tracts, more than a score of pastoral letters, a confession of faith, the revision of Bernard Rodlmann's treatise on baptism and the Lord's Supper, and a massive concordance of the Bible. But the apex of Marpeck's creativity is an extended, sophisticated written debate with his chief opponent, the spiritualist Caspar Schwenkfeld.

A look at two tracts, *A Clear Refutation* and *A Clear and Useful Instruction*, two pastoral letters, *Judgment and Decision* and *To Helene Streicher*, his revision of a sacramental treatise called *The Admonition*, and his debate on the Incarnation, *The Response*, show how Marpeck worked with the Bible. Let us begin with the tracts, which set the tone for the rest of his work.

A Clear Refutation is Marpeck's first extant defense of ceremonies, the term he preferred for sacraments. The center of Marpeck's treatise is his teaching on the Holy Spirit. Marpeck develops a profile of Old and New Testament references to the work of the Spirit to show that spirit and matter, inner and outer, are not at variance with one another. His goal is to show that outward practice and inward reality cannot be separated from one another. In both Testaments God calls his people to keep the commandments he has given: an inward call was given to the prophets, as it was to Jesus, to observe the signs God has given. Marpeck mines the epistles for warnings not to quench the Spirit, by which he means to heed the authority of Scripture because it physically preserves the voice of Jesus (Marpeck, *Refutation*, 57).

Without a hint of self-consciousness, Marpeck writes as if there is no distance between the world of the Bible and his own; he writes of the apostolic church as if he is contemporary with it. One senses that the Bible is believable for Marpeck because the Spirit who came to stay at Pentecost is as

powerfully at work now as then. Though Roman Catholics and Protestants in the sixteenth century at large followed the urge to "return to the sources," Anabaptist primitivism (holding that the church in the sixteenth century could be just like that of the first century) gave it a particularly intense affinity with the Acts of the Apostles and the epistles. It therefore saw less need than other movements did for the mediating structures of sacraments and dogma: the Bible did not have to be interpreted and explained; it could be grasped and lived out directly.

The role of the true church in the sixteenth century is the same as that of the prophets: "the restoration of the pure order of Christ" (Marpeck, *Refutation*, 51; *Letter*, 379). Though in a scattered fashion, Marpeck engages in enough exegesis of Jesus' teaching, especially references to his return, to show that all his teaching is binding until "the close of the age" (Mt 28:18; Marpeck, *Refutation*, 56). He scours the whole Bible—remarkably, because of his careful distinction between the covenants—to make his case. God's instruction to Moses to teach his statutes (Deut 4) is placed side by side with Paul's claim that he speaks as someone who stands in the presence of God (2 Cor 2; Marpeck, *Refutation*, 48-52). In short, the Bible is the record of God's dealings with humanity: "without the Scriptures, no one knows how, why, and in what form Christ died, was buried and was raised" (Marpeck, *Refutation*, 59).

Yet the outwardness of God's revelation (in the Bible, the Incarnation and ceremonies) can be grasped only through the outpouring of the Spirit (Marpeck, *Refutation*, 60). Here Marpeck is defending his interpretation first against spiritualists, who reduce God's presence to the human heart, and then against literalists—some of them fellow Anabaptists—who reduce Scripture to an accumulation of rational laws. Here we have the scaffolding within which the task of interpretation will be carried out. Its elements are the following. The Bible is the faithful and binding revelation of God's will; the Incarnation is the revelation of God's heart, of the mystery long hidden (Eph 3); the Spirit keeps this revelation in history alive in believers in every age.

A *Clear Instruction* continues the defense of ceremonies but grounds their reality more explicitly in Christ's human nature. Here we see for the first time Marpeck's indebtedness to the Gospel of John. His most important borrowing concerns the nature of God's self-revelation. The Father works inwardly through the Spirit while the Son works outwardly through his incarnation. One cannot believe in the Son's "human voice and speech" without being drawn by the Father (Jn 6:44); at the same time God's Spirit would have remained a secret without the human voice of Christ (Marpeck, *Instruction*, 76ff.; 99-102; *Response*, 298). From the time of his earthly ministry, people who sought salvation in esoteric knowledge and "sublime things concerning the deity of Christ" "have despised the humanity of Christ" (Marpeck, *Instruction*, 81, 79). The prologue of the Fourth Gospel stands in the shadow of these thoughts. Likewise we hear echoes of Jesus' conversation with Nicodemus (Jn 3, especially Jn 3:12) in the arguments advanced. Though the author seems unaware of it, his language gradually changes and becomes a doctrinal commentary on the passage rather than a simple expositional restatement of it as was the case in the *Refutation* and elsewhere. Here and much more so in parts of the *Response* the language of "deity" and "essence" moves closer to the world of the Fathers than to that of the apostles.

Marpeck is not always successful in carrying with him the exquisite subtleties in which the Fourth Gospel abounds, but he clearly sets forth the Johannine synchronicity among the work of Father, Son and Spirit. There is no antagonism between inward and outward because they are grounded in God's actions in both realms. Out of this theologizing comes a concept of the church as a spiritual body entered only by faith yet a visible, historical community.

The Admonition of 1542 is a surprising document in several ways. For one thing, it was written by the Münsterite Bernard Rothmann before he became an apocalypticist. Like the non-Lutheran Reformers as a whole before John *Calvin's ascendancy, Rothmann is indebted to Ulrich *Zwingli for his literal and rational exegesis of the narratives of the institution of the Lord's Supper. In his revision of the received text Marpeck adds his Johannine description of the Trinity's workings, and this leads to a higher sacramentology than Zwinglian exegesis is capable of (*Admonition* 228-33, 267, 283). As the section on baptism moves closer to the text of Scripture, it becomes an exposition of broad biblical notions rather than the exegesis of particular texts. Clearly they are in the mind of the writer— Mark 8 (*Admonition* 184), Romans 6 (*Admonition* 188), 1 Peter 3 (*Admonition* 187 et passim)—yet what we get is not detailed exegesis but a composite picture of how the New Testament understands baptism. Baptism is like the signs that John's Gospel records: they show outwardly what the Father does inwardly (*Admonition* 195).

The apology against infant baptism similarly takes New Testament concepts and builds them into a larger argument. "True baptism is a burial of the old being and the resurrection of the new" (*Admonition* 205). It can happen only in one who confesses that he has died to sin. Illustrations follow from the Acts of the Apostles. To the claim of the magisterial Reformers that the covenant inaugurated by circumcision is now sealed by baptism, Marpeck responds with the Johannine claim that the Holy Spirit has indwelled us only since the glorification of Christ. This refined distinction between the Old and New Testaments is one of Marpeck's hermeneutical keys. The ceremonies of the new covenant need to be novel to express that fact (Jn 7:39; 16:7; Marpeck, *Admonition* 225-28). After this point Marpeck shifts from particular pieces of thought steeped in biblical sources to a more general dogmatic argument against infant baptism based on the claim that infants are not sinners (Marpeck, *Admonition* 241-46). This approach, moving from proof- texting to exegesis to dogmatic generalization, is typical of Marpeck and many of his contemporaries. It reminds us that biblical exposition is seldom separated from an urge to generalize on the basis of favorite texts.

The Response is Marpeck's theological magnum opus. It is a polemical counterattack to Schwenkfeld's treatise *The Judgment*. In its essence their debate concerns the true meaning of the Gospel of John (481-559 of the *Response,* which plays off of quotations from the *Judgment).* Marpeck believes that John is talking about the inward working of the Father through the Spirit and the outward working of the Son through the flesh; hence the place for outward signs as means of grace. Schwenkfeld's argument is that the presence of Christ in the world is profaned by associating him in any way with fallen matter.

The centerpiece of Schwenkfeld's argument is a "celestial flesh" christology in which only for the duration of his earthly life Christ partakes in an unfallen human nature. This is precisely the point at which Marpeck attacks him with his much more positive view of the Incarnation and its prolongation in the church and its ceremonies. Both of them exegete a range of biblical passages intended to prove how God works in the world. In the end so much weight is placed by both of them on the Lord's Supper that it becomes in opposite ways the paradigm for both men's mature theology. Their argument becomes so fierce because they both claim the Fourth Gospel as their authority and because they both interpret John 6 as teaching the real eating of Christ's flesh and blood but in mutually exclusive ways (Marpeck, *Response,* 483- 86 et passim).

In his pastoral letters Marpeck is concrete and specific. *Judgment and Decision,* written around 1541 to overcome the schism between the rigorous Swiss Breth- ren and Marpeck's congregations, is a fine illustration of Marpeck's use of the Bible. He is writing to fellow Anabaptists whose interpretive key for the life of the church, according to Marpeck, is the law of Christ rather than the Spirit of Christ. Marpeck's approach does not lack for moral rigor, but he bases the living of a sanctified life clearly in the work of grace. He accuses his fellow believers of so emphasizing the law that they leave scant room for forgiveness and growth. Whereas the goal of church discipline among strict Anabaptists seems to be punishment, in Paul, for whom Marpeck proposes to speak, it is forgiveness and guidance.

At times the letter is almost an extended paraphrase of Galatians 5. Love is presented as the end of the law (Marpeck, *Judgment and Decision,* 312, 316, 327 et passim). The Song of Songs is then quoted to underscore the primacy of love in all of Scripture (327). Through the "law of grace" Christ indwells the believer (320). There are warnings against human commandments and quarrels that undermine the freedom Christ offers believers to make moral decisions (Marpeck, *Judgment and Decision,* 313, 320 et passim). John 3 and Romans 7 are invoked to underscore the freedom of the Spirit in contrast to the bondage of the flesh (321). Scripture interprets Scripture: perfect love casts out fear, the sabbath was made for people. These and many similar allusions testify to the truth of Paul's message to the Galatians.

At the end of *Judgment and Decision* Marpeck summarizes his "understanding of divine Scripture." It has three uses: to teach one who knows nothing of the gospel, to admonish the one who is already taught, and to announce punishment in the hope of repentance. Each of these uses depends entirely on "the Holy Spirit, the true teacher" (358).

Significance. The significance of Marpeck for biblical interpretation in the sixteenth century is not so much his erudition in exegeting specific texts as his ability to turn to the Bible as his contemporary, with a freshness and receptivity that transcended the positions various schools of the magisterial and radical Reformation had mapped out. Among the Anabaptists, for example, Marpeck resisted the legalism of his Swiss and Dutch siblings on the basis of the New Testament itself. His canon within the canon consisted of the Gospel of John and the epistle to the Galatians. From their vantage point he interpreted the rest of the New and Old Testaments and saw love and grace writ large. A study of Marpeck shows that the biblicism for which Anabaptism was renowned was not only a matter of proof-texting and exegesis. Anabaptism of the sort Marpeck represented was capable of a synthesis of biblical themes and methodically reflected on them.

Within the Continental Reformation as a whole, Marpeck's approach to biblical interpretation is noteworthy because he refused to cede the Bible to either sacramentalists or spiritualists. On the basis of John's rendering of the doctrine of the Trinity and of a consequent theology of the Incarnation, Marpeck held in a perpetual tension the inward and the outward, spirit and sacrament. This gives him an unusual relevance to the theological and liturgical agenda of the ecumenical movement today.

BIBLIOGRAPHY

Works. P. Marpeck, *The Writings of Pilgram Marpeck,* ed. W. Klassen and W. Klaassen (Scottdale, PA: Herald, 1978); idem, *Pilgram Marbecks Antwort auf Kaspar Schwenkfelds Beurteilung Des Buches Der Bundesbezeugung von 1542,* ed. J. Loserth (Vienna: Carl Fromme, 1929); idem, *Testamenterleütterung* (Augsburg: Phillip Ulhart, 1550).

Studies. There is an extensive literature on Marpeck in German. A. Beachy, *The Concept of Grace in the Radical Reformation* (Nieuwkopp: B. de Graaf, 1977); H. S. Bender, "Pilgram Marpeck" in *ME* 3C; idem, "Pilgram Marpeck, Anabaptist Theologian and Civil Engineer," *MQR* 38 (July 1964) 231-65; S. Boyd, *Pilgram Marpeck, His Life and Social Theology* (Durham, NC: Duke University Press, 1992); J. Kiewit, *Pilgram Marpeck* (Kassel: J. G. Oncken, 1958); W. Klassen, *Covenant and Community* (Grand Rapids: Eerdmans, 1968); idem, "Pilgram Mar-

peck" in *Profiles of Radical Reformers,* ed. H.-J. Goertz (Scottdale, PA: Herald, 1984); R. Emmet McLaughlin, *Caspar Schwenkfeld, Reluctant Radical* (New Haven, CT: Yale University Press, 1986); H. Quiring, "The Anthropology of Pilgram Marpeck," *MQR* 9 (October 1935) 155-64; J. Rempel, *The Lord's Supper in Anabaptism* (Scottdale, PA: Herald, 1993); A. Snyder, *Anabaptist History and Theology, An Introduction* (Kitchener, ON: Pandora, 1995); G. Williams, *The Radical Reformation* (Philadelphia: Westminster, 1962).   J. Rempel

Melanchthon, Philipp (1497-1560)

Philipp Melanchthon was born in 1497 and spent his childhood as Philipp Schwarzerd, son of an armsmaker, in the little Black Forest town of Bretten. He died in 1560, at age 63, as Philipp Melanchthon, the ablest classical scholar his nation had ever known. But his greater fame was as Martin *Luther's right arm (and sometimes left) during the early years of the Reformation. Any one of his major feats in those forty years would have been enough to put his name in history books. He invented Protestant dogmatics and wrote the first Lutheran confession; he was officer-in-chief over an army of Protestant educators who brought fresh vision and reform to schools and universities all over Europe; he labored beside Luther to reshape the churches of Saxony in the new way of reform; and he more than Luther navigated the Lutheran ship of state through the deadly dangerous waters of negotiation between Roman Catholic and Protestant doctrinal factions during the first three fateful decades of the Reformation.

It has gradually come to light that Melanchthon's work as a reformer of school, church and society was about the interpretation and use of texts, especially the writings of the Bible. No mere secretary to Luther, as is commonly believed, he performed pathbreaking service in forging a uniquely Protestant (Lutheran) method of reading Scripture. This was a masterly fusion of others' ideas, especially those of

Rudolf Agricola, Luther and (in limited senses) Desiderius *Erasmus into an important and useful system of interpretation that was very much his own.

Life and Work. Melanchthon's journey began with a meteoric rise to fame as a classical linguist. When his father and maternal grandfather died in 1507, Philipp went with his widowed grandmother to live in Pforzheim, so that he might attend the celebrated Latin school there and be near to his granduncle, John Reuchlin, the greatest Hebrew scholar of his time. Before graduating from Latin school, the boy had also progressed in the Greek language to such an extent that Reuchlin publicly gave him the name Melanchthon. The Greek renaming ritually signified his baptism into that elite society of humanists that was just beginning to form north of the Alps.

At twelve Melanchthon entered the University of Heidelberg (1509). By the time he graduated with the B.A. degree (1512), his mastery of Greek was renowned among the teachers and students. In autumn 1512 he enrolled at Tübingen, where he remained, first as an M.A. student, then as master and tutor, until the summer of 1518. By then he had managed to gain recognition on an international scale mainly by publishing, among other things, a Greek grammar that quickly became a standard in its field.

In spring 1518 Elector Frederick of Saxony conducted a search for the best classical scholar available to teach at his university in Wittenberg. The post was offered to Reuchlin, who turned it down. Instead the old man recommended his grandnephew, whom he candidly ranked ahead of everyone in Europe, save Erasmus. In August of that year Philipp made the journey to the (for him) strange new land of the Saxons. There, in Luther, as one writer put it, he would meet "not so much a colleague as a destiny" (H. Bornkamm in Rupp, 375).

Early on Melanchthon fell naturally into the part of Luther's advocate among the learned of Europe. He wrote bravely in Luther's defense during the critical period

(1519-1521) of excommunication and then imperial banishment. When Luther went into hiding at the Wartburg Castle in 1521, a young Melanchthon stepped into very large shoes as first-in-command in Wittenberg. He faltered somewhat under the pressures of unrest that year in the city and thus, deservedly or not, began a lifelong downward trend in his credibility among the most uncompromising followers of Luther. But in 1529 and 1530, when it came time for the Lutherans to put their position clearly into writing and to defend it in public, no one was better suited for the job of composing the Augsburg Confession than was Melanchthon. For the next nearly twenty years he was the point man and go-between in the tense negotiations with both Protestants (especially on disagreements over the Eucharist) and Roman Catholics (until the Leipzig Interim of 1547, when Saxony was occupied by enemy forces and it seemed that all might be lost, Melanchthon to blame).

In these middle and later years Melanchthon agonized over what he judged were unjustified divisions between Christians, and for his worry he suffered through a series of bitter brush wars with purists in his own camp. Accusations of his having compromised the true gospel of faith (in various ways) with the devil human reason (in various forms) persist to this day and are the subject of debate.

Meanwhile, through it all, as professor of Greek he faithfully taught his courses, performed his administrative work, and led his special home seminars (without pay). Somehow he managed a steady flow of publications, both secular and sacred, that is impressive in any age. His magnum opus was the *Loci Communes Theologicae*, the first Protestant dogmatics, which was first published in 1521 and then grew and evolved through five editions, the last in 1555.

Although he lacked a formal degree in theology until 1519 (and even then attained only to the barely minimal baccalaureate, and unlike Luther, never to the status of doctor), the authorities at Wittenberg approved his lecturing on biblical texts in both Latin and Greek. These lectures, wildly popular, usually grew into sizable commentaries that became published, sometimes against his wishes. The list of titles is very long; it includes commentaries on parts of Genesis, on Proverbs, several Psalms, Daniel and Jeremiah in the Old Testament (he could also handle teaching Hebrew in a pinch). A glance, however, reveals his preference for the writings of the New Testament: huge commentaries emerged on John and Matthew, as parts of a larger reformist series by a welter of mainly young authors who had joined themselves to the evangelical cause. But his main passion was for the writings of Paul, particularly the epistle to the Romans, which (with Luther) he deemed the pass key into the treasure room of Scripture. His lifelong preoccupation with Romans came to harvest in the massive and (to Melanch-. thon scholarship) crucial commentary of 1532, and his systematic theology, while broadly biblical, was obviously shaped in the main by this epistle as he construed and interpreted it.

Dialectic and Rhetoric as Interpretive Philosophy. Only recently have scholars come to see how important Melanchthon's work in the field of rhetoric was to his entire life and teaching, and that he really had a theory of interpretation that guided his practice. Unlike Erasmus, he showed almost no interest in textual criticism; nor was he greatly concerned, as other humanists were, to work with the purest possible manuscripts in original languages. He was above all an interpreter of the received text, concerned mainly with getting the purest possible grasp of the text's rhetorical structure and argument. In brief, as a humanist Melanchthon viewed rhetoric as a kind of practical philosophy, not as mere speech making. Going back to the ancients, humanists discovered a new world of enlightened public discourse wherein truth *(res)* took shape as word *(verbum)* and thus became a power for good *(virtus)* in all

things. The unity of substance and style, *res et verbum*, was the root of all that was right and true.

Melanchthon thus put his own stamp upon this broadly humanistic intuition. In the likes of Rudolf Agricola, Boethius and Aristotle, he believed he had discovered a rhetoric that was controlled, guided and sharpened by dialectic, which was itself grounded in the deepest elemental truths of reality. Early on he announced plans to produce a renewed text of Aristotle's rhetoric. Instead he produced his own.

The textbook on rhetoric, *De Rhetorica Libri Tres (Three Books on Rhetoric),* was near completion already when he traveled to Wittenberg in 1518. In the preface Philipp explained that dialectic and rhetoric must be fused in such a way that the one is never rightly separate from the other. Attacking regnant approaches in each discipline, he argued that they were in essence the same, different only in that rhetoric is a looser method of persuasion than dialectic. But the dialectical techniques (definition, division and argument) underlay all great public discourse. Likewise, in a circular manner, the profound human questions and answers of rhetoricians must always underlay great dialectic. Hence, when rhetoric is rightly crafted, there could be no mere flourish for the orator, as was common in the courts, and no pointless hair-splitting for the logician, as was common in the schools.

This meant that all great texts handled humanly momentous topics, basic *loci communes,* and they made use of already-proven wisdom to form arguments and present truths (*loci communes* in a secondary sense) to inspire action. It also meant that every great text had a main point, idea, theme or thesis (*argumentum, status* or *scopos dicendi)* to which everything was logically related and toward which everything moved. Rhetoric could come packaged as straightforward, no-nonsense demonstration or in other forms, such as historical narrative *(narratio).* When written rightly, rhetoric secured the complete certainty and truth of the thesis, so that the honest hearer or reader could not but be moved to the sort of assent that breeds action. Human beings did not manufacture the world and values, as postmoderns think of it. This was the very power of nature *(vis naturae)*, not to be abstracted from the creative word of God who made it for us and us for it. In this way Melanchthon's classical textual theory was at once deeply Christian.

Scripture as Sacred Rhetoric. Perhaps most remarkable thing about how Melanchthon applied his textual theory to the text of Scripture is that even before going to Wittenberg he believed the Scriptures really were texts of rhetoric. He did not just use rhetoric (as did almost all interpreters, including Luther) as a method of reading Scripture and writing Christian literature. He rather believed that the writers of Scripture had themselves knowingly written according to fixed, classical rhetorical rules. The authors had selected ("invented") primary topics or *loci communes,* arranged ("disposed") them in the manner prescribed for standard species of writings, and thus offered arguments in the technical rhetorical senses of that term to prove ("confirm") their points. In that way Scripture was a library of sacred *loci communes,* put forth in the clearest, most convincing and inspiring way possible for human beings. To the end of his career Melanchthon construed the Bible as sacred rhetoric, its authors, especially Moses and Paul, as inspired rhetoricians. Giving his own slant to Erasmus's comparable description of Christ as the *sermo dei,* he even imagined Jesus, the Word of God made flesh, as God's *oratio,* his human vocation that of a wandering orator. The Word of God was the "oration of God," Christ the primary orator.

Luther and the Sense of Scripture as Rhetoric. It is difficult to know what the state of Melanchthon's theology was before the fateful encounter with Luther in 1518. Studies have shown that he was not a rank beginner, as was previously thought. There is strong case for placing him in the camp of Tübingen nominalism as it had descended from Gabriel Biel and somewhat aligned itself with the principles of humanism. In his inaugural speech at Wittenberg Melanchthon laid out a program for pedagogical reform that included use of Scripture as an original rhetorical text and as very much a part of his classical outlook on education.

Within a year or so the influence of Luther on Melanchthon had become profound. By his own testimony, Luther had opened to him the clear and true sense of Scripture through his rendering of law and gospel, sin and grace. There was not exactly a break with his past, as has commonly been believed. It is perhaps best to think of it as rapid movement forward—in the same direction but in new theological and spiritual light. To Melanchthon these doctrines became God's *loci communes,* together a divinely given status and scopos of all Scripture.

The ground of this insight, he now believed, was in the writings of Paul, especially Romans but also Galatians and the epistles to the Corinthians. He lectured, commented and eventually published on them all. Briefly, Romans was a work of rhetoric in the "demonstrative genus" (*genus demonstrativum;* later he viewed it as legal rhetoric, *genus iudicale,* but without substantial difference), complete with all the required loci of that class of writing. The status was the doctrine of justification by grace through faith alone; the main seats of argument were the *loci communes* of law, sin and grace; the methods used were definition, inference and especially syllogism to confirm the conclusion beyond doubt. Paul was to the rest of Scripture what Demothsenes was to antiquity—an orator whose ingenious invention uncovered the meaning of the whole and thus of every part. Scripture was now more than sacred rhetoric in a broadly Christian sense; it was specifically "Lutheran," which meant that Luther's reading was indisputably the true reading of Scripture. Melanchthon's hermeneutic was thus also a polemical device and means of (optimistically) making his case in negotiations with Rome and to assist Christians to complete certainty of their faith.

Genesis, the Psalms, Proverbs, historical writings, Gospels and non-Pauline epistles all came more or less into conformity with both the structures of rhetoric and the theology of justification by grace through faith. All Scripture, and every Scripture, was either law, or promise of grace, or both together. Unlike Luther, Melanchthon pressed for conceptual harmony among all the voices, even between James and Paul. For instance, he sought to show how the birth narratives of Matthew and Luke might be viewed as consistent with each other. Moreover, he believed it was obvious that Matthew had written his Gospel as rhetorical narrative *(narratio)*, building it around the didactic framework of law and gospel, selecting and using examples *(exempla)* to illustrate and confirm these truths. Unlike Erasmus, Melanchthon was led to place allegorical interpretation, which he did not entirely spurn, under strict evangelical rhetorical supervision— allegory must always come to express the *loci communes* that come naturally to mind in the context of law, sin, grace and other majestic biblical themes. Cain, for instance was not just Cain, brother and murderer of Abel, but also a sinner and thus a living locus, example or type of what that doctrine of sin is about. In that way Cain's story is logically interconnected with all the biblical stories and with that story as a whole. Scripture was God's special *oratio*, which never wavered from its main theme.

Melanchthon's approach to biblical interpretation belied a deeper system of concepts (not explicitly worked out) related to the inspiration, authority, unity, clarity and efficacy of Scripture. His rhetorical vision of the text shaped this entire cluster of concepts with an almost pure inner logic. On inspiration and authority, what gave Scripture authority was not that God had inspired it by dictation or intervention into human processes of composition. Rather, the authors of the Bible, by God's special favor (the analogy here is not specified), uncovered ("invented"), put forth and confirmed the truths (loci) of what God had done and especially spoken in sacred history. With respect to unity, his rhetorical vision thus required that Scripture was true, clearly and powerfully so, in all its propositions as a function of successful albeit divinely aided human rhetoric. The whole oration was sacred and divine.

On the so-called perspicuity of Scripture as God's unified and sacred oration, Melanchthon made what might seem conflicting claims. He repeatedly asserted that interpreting Scripture was more a job simply of indicating than of proving what its literal sense was.

However, to sustain this "clarity-awareness" required all the methodological sophistication in Melanchthon's power. The simple sense (Luther's sense) of Scripture was obvious so long as readers used Melanchthon's rhetorical method of reading, rather than Erasmus's *Method* or Peter Lombard's *Sentences*. In later years, however, his rhetorical intuitions were in part what drove Melanchthon to negotiate terms of logical peace between biblical traditions of grace and texts of nature. His terms for a doctrinal peace were as controversial as those by which he sought to reconcile factions on the brink of religious war. But whatever the matter, this was not timidity on his part. His respect for the dialectical coherence of all of Scripture would not permit even loyalty to Luther to obscure clear assertions in the text and the need to integrate even troubling arguments into a coherent whole.

On the efficacy of Scripture, it is inadequate to describe Melanchthon's position as intellectualistic and propositional, as is often done. It is more accurate to describe it as rhetorically propositional. The essence of Scripture was in its propositions *(doctrinae)*, but its propositions were invariably *loci communes* and therefore more like events for the whole person than mere ideas. Through the mind, biblical truths worked into the heart and inspired outward actions in the world. So far, the efficacy of Scripture was quite human. However, Melanchthon was quick to add that our efforts to put the truth into the desired responses would come to nothing but for the Holy Spirit.

Significance. In weighing Melanchthon's contribution to biblical interpretation, it must be stressed that he was consciously and deliberately a theoretician of texts. In that way he was a creative and innovative force in the history of the Reformation and Protestantism. His method of arranging theology as loci became the paradigm for generations of Protestant theologians. Shortcomings, it is true, were apparent even to admirers. The likes of Heinrich *Bullinger, Ulrich *Zwingli, Johannes Brenz, John *Calvin, and countless others used his exegetical and theological writings. But it seems that none quite replicated his identification of the biblical text with Aristotle's and Cicero's sort of rhetoric. Likewise none was so single-minded as he about proving the single (Lutheran) sense of Scripture as evident in every nook and corner of the Bible.

Still, while his categories of rhetoric were sometimes deficient, Melanchthon's acute sensitivity to the thematic structure and polemical character of biblical texts adumbrated that long path toward modern critical biblical scholarship and narrative theory. Today all scholars agree that the chronicles of the Bible are structured theological narratives and that the writings everywhere show evidence of rhetorical (if not exactly in Cicero's sense) influence. Melanchthon's literary nose had put him on the trail of something important and challenging for his day. Furthermore, his proposal that law and gospel, or law and promise, form the theological core of the canon need not lead to an intolerably parochial reading of Scripture. With adjustments, a serious biblical hermeneutic can well be constructed with use of this sort of framework (see Thiemann).

Finally, although his positivistic dialecti-

cal approach to the literal sense of Scripture will seem impossibly naive to scholars of today, as it sometimes did to scholars of his own, self-declared postmodern thinkers ironically find the rhetorical tradition of philosophy more convincing than the Cartesian one (Grassi, Kimball). Melanchthon's stress on the rhetorical truth of doctrine in the heart *(doctrina efficax)* sounds quite contemporary to scholars seeking to build bridges between doctrines past and present (Aune).

In biblical interpretation as in letters, Melanchthon was, as his contemporaries called him, the Preceptor of Germany. It seems we can still learn from encounters with him.

BIBLIOGRAPHY

Works. P. Melanchthon, *A Melanchthon Reader* (New York: Peter Lang, 1988); idem, *Melanchthon on Christian Doctrine: Loci Communes 1555,* ed. C. L. Manschreck (Grand Rapids: Baker, 1982 [1965]); idem, *Loci communes theologici* in *Melanchthon and Bucer,* ed. W. Pauck (LCC 19; Philadelphia: Westminster, 1969); idem, *Melanchthons Werke in Auswahl: Studienausgabe,* ed. R. Stupperich (Gütersloh: Verlagshaus Gerd Mohn, 1978-) Bd. 1-7;

Studies. M. B. Aune, *To Move the Heart: Philip Melanchthon's Rhetorical View of Rite and Its Implications for Contemporary Ritual Theory* (San Francisco: International Scholars Publications, 1994); P. Fraenkel, *Testimonia Patrum: The Function of the Patristic Argument in the Theology of Philipp Melanchthon* (Geneva: Libraire E. Droz, 1961); E. Grassi, *Rhetoric as Philosophy* (University Park, PA: Penn State University Press, 1980); L. C. Green, *How Melanchthon Helped Luther Discover the Gospel* (Fallbrook, CA: Verdict Publications, 1980); K. Hartfelder, *Melanchthon als Praeceptor Germaniae* (Nieuwkoop: B. de Graaf, 1964 [1889]); G. Kennedy, *Classical Rhetoric and Its Christian and Secular Tradition from Ancient to Modern Times* (Chapel Hill, NC: University of North Carolina Press, 1980); B. A. Kimball, *Orators and Philosophers: A History of the Idea of Liberal Education* (New York: Teachers College, Columbia University, 1986); J. Knape, *Philip Melanchtons Rhetorik* (Tübingen: Niemeyer, 1993); P. Mack, *Renaissance Argument: Valla and Agricola in the Traditions of Rhetoric and Dialectic*

(Leiden: E. J. Brill, 1993); W. Maurer, *Der junge Melanchthon* (Göttingen: Vandenhoek & Ruprecht, 1967-1969) Bd. 1, 2; E. P. Meijering, *Melanchthon and Patristic Thought: The Doctrines of Christ and Grace, the Trinity and the Creation* (Leiden: E. J. Brill, 1983); E. G. Rupp, "Philip Melanchthon and Martin Bucer" in *A History of Christian Doctrine*, ed. H. Cunliffe-Jones (Philadelphia: Fortress, 1980); A. Schirmer, *Das Paulusverständnis Melanchthons 1518-1532* (Wiesbaden: Steiner, 1967); H. Sick, *Melanchthon als Ausleger des Alten Testaments* (Tübingen: J. C. B. Mohr, 1959); J. R. Schneider, *Melanchthon's Rhetorical Construal of Biblical Authority: Oratio Sacra* (Lewiston, NY: Edwin Mellen, 1990); R. Stupperich, *Melanchthon* (Philadelphia: Westminster, 1965); R. F. Thiemann, *Revelation and Theology: The Gospel of Narrated Promise* (Notre Dame, IN: University of Notre Dame Press, 1985); T. J. Wengert, *Philipp Melanchthon's Annotationes in Johannem in Relation to Its Predecessors and Contemporaries* (Geneva: Librairie Droz, 1987); T. J. Wengert and M. P. Graham, ed., *Philipp Melanchthon and the Commentary* (Sheffield: Sheffield Academic Press, 1997); S. Widenhofer, *Formalstrukturen humanistischer und reformatorischer Theologie bei Philipp Melanchthon* (Bern, Frankfurt and Munich: Herbert Lang; Peter Lang, 1976) Bd. 1, 2.

J. R. Schneider

Perkins, William *(1558-1602)*

William Perkins was a leading English theologian who had great influence on both English and American Puritanism. He wrote widely over the range of polemics, theology, biblical commentaries and ethics. His hermeneutical principles, as conveyed in his *Arte of Prophecying* (Latin *Prophetica*, 1592; ET 1606) are a crystallization of Puritan thought and provide a basis for his and others' interpretations of biblical passages.

Context. Perkins was born in Marston Jabbet, Warwickshire, and entered Christ's College as a pensioner (1577). There he studied under Laurence Chaderton (1536?-1640), a leading figure who was called the pope of Cambridge Puritanism. Perkins completed his B.A. (1581) and M.A. (1584) and underwent a religious conversion while he was at the college. His new faith led him to preach at the Cambridge jail, where he gained a reputation as an effective preacher. He was appointed lecturer (preacher) at Great St. Andrew's Church parish, Cambridge, and also was elected a fellow of Christ's College (1584). Perkins continued at Christ's until his marriage (1595). He continued preaching until his death on October 22, 1602.

Perkins was a leader of the Elizabethan Puritan movement but did not identify himself with either the Presbyterian or Separatist parties. He represented a non-separating Puritanism and focused more directly on spiritual and theological issues than on church reform or polity. Perkins and others such as Richard Rogers, Henry Smith, Chaderton and Richard Greenham sought church reform through their writings, teaching, preaching and personal examples. Perkins's theological formation was shaped by John *Calvin's *Institutes* and commentaries. Other influential writers were Peter Martyr *Vermigli, Theodore *Beza, Jerome *Zanchi, Caspar Olevianus and Franciscus Junius.

Perkins's influence was substantial, and he became the first English theologian of the reformed church to gain an international reputation. His works were collected and published by 1603 and went through many English editions as well as translations. His pupils during his period at Christ College included a number of future leaders, including Daniel Rogers, Thomas Taylor and William Ames, an important seventeenth-century Puritan theologian.

Perkins's theological writings were significant in conveying Reformed theology to wider arenas, and his collected *Works* were found on the bookshelves of most American Puritan preachers in early New England. Among his works were a number of biblical commentaries and expositions of Scripture. As an biblical interpreter, Perkins's influence was also substantial.

Ramist Backgrounds. Study has shown that Perkins's biblical commentaries and exposition of Scripture followed the pattern and method advocated by the French logician and philosopher Pierre de la Ramée (Peter Ramus [1515-1572]). Ramus sought to reform the arts and to simplify Aristotelian logic. He developed a system of logic that could be quickly taught and grasped. This Ramism was applied by his followers to the catalog of liberal arts. Ramus was converted to Protestantism, which gave a special impetus toward applying his system to theology.

The Puritans of Cambridge University used Ramism as a framework for biblical exegesis. It is possible to trace a line of Cambridge Ramists from Chaderton through Perkins and others such as George Downame (1565?-1634), Paul Baynes (d. 1617), Arthur Hildersham (1563-1632) and William Ames (1576-1633). These scholars used Ramism to present their systematic theological works. They also found it a highly useful tool by which to approach and exegete Scripture. Ramism provided a theoretical framework for Puritan use in interpreting the Bible. It functioned to show how a text should be "logically analyzed," "resolved" or "unfolded" in ways that Ramus prescribed.

A main aspect of Ramus's system was "method." Ramus believed all subjects could be understood by using a method that proceeded by way of definition and division. This had the effect of enabling a Ramist treatise to be graphically represented as a schematized chart. For Ramists an "analysis" is an "unweaving" or disentangling of the various strands that make up a discourse. Analysis reduced the discourse to its simplest components and showed how these related to each other. This showed what the discourse means.

The result of Ramist methods was a bracketed outline that spread horizontally on a page. Most often an "axiom" was divided into two parts or into dichotomies. One division could continually be subdivided down to its smallest unit. Often these bifurcations consisted of one part that was more "theoretical" in orientation, and the other was more "practical." The logician's

task was classification and arrangement of the elements of discourse in their proper places.

Some Ramist charts are included at the beginning or in the midst of Perkins's works. Study shows that virtually all his works can be diagrammed in this way, indicating that Perkins was self-consciously using Ramist method in his theological and exegetical writings. Earlier Continental biblical commentators such as Johannes Piscator (1546-1625), Franciscus Junius (1545-1602) and Lambert Daneau (1530-1595) also used Ramist methods for biblical interpretation. Their approach was frequently called grammatical exegesis.

Some of Perkins's Ramist charts treat an entire biblical book; others, several chapters or a single passage. Perkins believed the exegete needed to use the arts of logic and rhetoric and that the Bible itself contained the natural divisions that the exegete needed to uncover by using logical and rhetorical tools.

Perkins produced a considerable number of biblical expositions. He wrote commentaries on the complete books of Galatians and Jude, parts of books such as Revelation 1—3 or Hebrews 11, and interpretations of individual texts of Scripture. His theological treatises often took their starting point from verses of Scripture. Examples are treatises on witchcraft (Ex 22:18), idolatry (1 Jn 5:21) and Christian equity (Phil 4:5).

Interpretive Principles. Perkins's *Arte of Prophecying* turned out to be a manual for preachers, advising them on the preparation and promulgation (Ramist dichotomy) of sermons.

The preparation of sermons consisted of two parts: interpretation and "right diuision or cutting." Interpretation meant the "opening of the words and sentences of Scripture, that one entire and naturall sense may appeare." The "supreme and absolute meane of interpretation, is the Scripture it selfe," according to Perkins (Perkins 1616-18, 2:652). The three subordinate means were "the analogie of faith, the circumstances of the place propounded, and the comparing of places together." Each was explained in turn: "The analogie of faith, is a certaine abridgement or summe of the Scriptures, collected out of most manifest & familiar places." It has two parts, the Apostles' Creed and the Ten Commandments. The "circumstances of the place propounded" are "who? to whom? upon what occasion? at what time? in what place? for what ende? what goeth before? what followeth?" (Perkins 1616-18, 2:652).

When Perkins wrote of the Scripture interpreting itself, he meant the use of one part of Scripture as a "testimony" to illuminate or elucidate another part. This was a key tenet of Protestant hermeneutics: that Scripture is the best interpreter of itself. As Perkins wrote in his commentary on Galatians to answer the question of whether it is the church that must convey the interpretation of Scripture: "Scripture it selfe is both *the glosse*, and *the text*. Scripture is the best interpreter of it selfe. And the sense which is agreeable to the words of the text, to the scope of the place, to other circumstances, and to the analogie of faith, in the plainer places of Scripture, is the proper and infallible sense of Scripture" (Perkins 1616-18, 2:334).

Perkins repeatedly made the claim that "there is one onely sense, and the same is the literall" sense of Scripture (Perkins 1616-1618, 2:651, 298). He opposed the fourfold senses of literal, allegorical, tropological and anagogical, which he associated with the church of Rome. For Perkins "the principall Interpreter of the Scripture, is the holy Ghost" (Perkins 1616-1618, 2:651), and the Spirit works to interpret the literal sense.

Perkins divided the "places" of Scripture into "Analogicall and plaine, or Crypticall and darke." His primary rule was that when the natural sense of the scriptural words coincided with the circumstances of the same place and where there was no conflict with the analogy of faith or other parts of Scripture, then the literal sense should be adopted. But if this natural meaning of the words disagreed with the context, the analogy of faith or other places in Scripture where the meaning was much clearer were to be consulted. The sense of a passage should be recognized as agreeing with the rest of the Scriptures. Thus the sense of the whole biblical record should be considered when interpreting particular passages.

Perkins illustrated this principle with Jesus' saying: "This is my body which is broken for you" (1 Cor 11:24). He rejected a completely literal reading because it violated the phrase in the Apostles' Creed that Jesus "ascended into heaven." Also, Perkins said, a completely literal reading violated the nature of a sacrament, which "ought to be a Memoriall of the body of Christ absent." Therefore "a new exposition is to bee sought for" (Perkins 1616-1618, 2:654).

Perkins's solution was to interpret this verse in another sense. He wrote: "In this place the bread is a signe of my body: by a Metonymy of the subiect for the adiunct" (Perkins 1616-1618, 2:654). He offered justification of "the fitness of this exposition" since it does agree with the analogy of faith and the phrase that Christ "ascended into heaven." For Jesus was "taken vp out of the earth into heauen locally and visibly. Therefore his body is not to be receiued with the mouth at the Communion, but by faith apprehending it in the heauen" (Perkins 1616-1618, 2:655). Perkins said his view "consenteth with the circumstances of the place propounded," accords with "the nature of a sacrament," "agrees with like places," "agreeth the lawes of Logicke," and is "agreeable to the common custome of speaking."

Perkins went on then to indicate other helps for scriptural interpretation. These included adding words for clarification; distinguishing in great detail the various kinds of rhetorical figures of speech used in the Bible, how to reconcile contrary places, and how to determine meanings that are vague (Perkins 1616-1618, 2:665-72).

The second part of Perkins's dichotomy of the parts of preparation was the "right cutting" or "right diuiding" of Scripture. "Right cutting" is that "whereby the word is made fitte to edifie the people of God" (2 Tim 5:15; Perkins 1616-18, 2:662). This was further bifurcated into "Resolution or partition, and Application." Resolution (in the tradition of Ramus) meant "analysis." Perkins used Ramist imagery to define resolution as "the place propounded is, as a weauers web, resolued (or vntwisted and vnloosed) into sundry doctrines" (Perkins 1616-1618, 2:662). It was Perkins's standard procedure throughout his biblical commentaries to "draw doctrines" from the biblical texts. Doctrines may be drawn from "the place propounded" ("notation") or by "collection" when the doctrine is "not expressed" but must be gathered out of the text. Nine arguments help here: of the "causes, effects, subiects, adiuncts, dissentanies, comparatives, names, distribution, and definition" (Perkins 1616-1618, 2:663). Drawing scriptural doctrines was a key goal of biblical interpretation.

Some places in Scripture were clearly congruent with the analogy of faith—the summaries of faith found in the Ten Commandments or Apostles' Creed ("analogicall"). Other places were "hidden" ("cryptical") in that further exegetical procedures must be used to ascertain the Scripture's true meaning. Often these further procedures were to subject texts to the rules of the syllogism as understood by Ramus. Yet Perkins varied from Ramus in that Perkins issued the theological proviso that "Scripture alone" was the supreme authority, rather than logic itself. Reason was useful as a tool; but it was always to be subject to Scripture itself.

It is significant that Perkins turned next to the "waies how to use and apply doctrines" (Perkins 1616-1618, 2:664). When doctrines have been rightly "collected," they must be properly "applied" so that the lives of readers (or hearers in the case of preaching) could be edified. The "foundation of application" is "to know whether the place propounded be a sentence of the Law, or of the Gospell." The law declares the "disease of sinne"; the gospel "teacheth what is to be done." Perkins indicated how the interpreter could decide on application, based on his description of seven conditions of people. This was particularly for the work of preachers.

Yet Perkins's emphasis on the application and usefulness of doctrines was a distinguishing feature of his work and was a mark of the biblical interpretation and preaching of Puritanism in general. The Ramist method gave impetus to the close relationship of "theory" and "practice" or "doctrine" and "life." Puritan interpreters wanted to understand what doctrines were being presented in the texts of Scripture as well as what the implications of those doctrines were for Christian living. In this concern Perkins was a model and an example.

Perkins indicated that application itself was "either Mentall or Practicall" (Perkins 1616-18, 2:668). Mental related to the mind and was either "doctrine" or "redargution" (improving, confuting). Doctrine informed the mind of right belief; redargution is the teaching used "for the reformation of the mind from error." Practical application was that which "respecteth the life and behauior." It also was dichotomized by Perkins into "instruction" (Greek *paideia*) and "correction" (Greek *epanorthsis*). Instruction shows how to live well in family, commonwealth and church. Correction was that "whereby the doctrine is applied to reforme the life from vngodlinesse and vnrighteous dealing" (Perkins 1616-1618, 2:668-69).

Significance. Perkins was a major Puritan biblical interpreter as well as being early English Puritanism's premier theologian. His biblical commentaries, as well as his other types of writings, convey a bipolar thrust: theory/practice; word/deed; theology/ethics. Right belief should lead to right living; right living is grounded in right belief. The biblical interpreter's task is to make clear both the "doctrine" and the "application to life" of the biblical texts. For Perkins the goal of hermeneutics, with all its rules and divisions, was to ascertain a Scripture text's meaning so that "the word is made fitte to edifie the people of God" (Perkins 1616-1618, 2:662). This goal was consistent with Perkins's description of the whole of Scripture as a "doctrine sufficient to liue well" and theology as "the science of liuing blessedly for euer" (Perkins 1616-1618, 1:11). The Ramist philosophy gave Perkins and the Puritans tools for approaching biblical interpretation that enabled them to maintain and practice these theological emphases.

Perkins made good use of the tools of logic and rhetoric as he interpreted Scripture. His *Arte of Prophecying* displays a high level of sophistication in using and applying these tools to the biblical texts. His biblical commentaries, constructed along Ramist lines, convey his concern for the Protestant tradition of the literal sense of the text and for its application to practical Christian living. The exegete's task is to lay open the text of Scripture since there, Perkins and the Puritans believed, one could encounter the very mind of God.

BIBLIOGRAPHY

Works. W. Perkins, *A Commentary on Galatians* with introductory essays, ed. G. T. Sheppard (New York: Pilgrim, 1989); idem, *A Commentary on Hebrews 11 [1609 Edition]* with introductory essays, ed. J. H. Augustine (New York: Pilgrim, 1991); idem, *The Work of William Perkins,* ed. I. Breward (The Courtenay Library of Reformation Classics; Appleford, England: Sutton Courtney, 1970); idem, *The Workes of the Famovs and Worthy Minister of Christ in the Vniuersitie of Cambridge, Mr. William Perkins* (3 vols.; Cambridge, 1616-1618).

Studies. I. Breward, "The Life and Theology of William Perkins" (Ph.D. diss., University of Manchester, 1963); D. K. McKim, "The Functions of Ramism in William Perkins' Theology," *SCJ* 16, 4 (Winter 1985) 503-17; idem, "Ramism in William Perkins" (unpublished Ph.D. dissertation, University of Pittsburgh, 1980); idem, *Ramism in William Perkins' Theology* (New York: Peter Lang, 1987); W. J. Ong, *Ramus, Method and the Decay of Dialogue* (New York: Octagon, 1974 [1958]); J. G. Rechtien, "The Visual Memory of William Perkins and the End of Theological Dialogue," *JAAR* 44, 1, supplement (March 1977) 69-99.   D. K. McKim

Tyndale, William *(c. 1494-1536)*

William Tyndale was a man at the leading edge of a new and rapidly developing approach to biblical studies. He was the first English writer of significance who can clearly be called a Protestant. His was a bold spirit, which when denied royal and ecclesiastical sanction to translate the Bible into English chose to break the law and go into exile. Tyndale visited Martin *Luther in Wittenberg; he lived in various Rhineland cities and finally settled in the Netherlands. He completed the New Testament in English and was turning to the Hebrew texts when he was arrested, imprisoned, strangled to death and burned. His translation survived despite repeated attempts to eradicate it, and through its profound impact upon the King James Version of 1611 it lives today in beauty and power.

Biblical Expositor. Tyndale's monumental success as a translator has tended to eclipse his contributions in biblical exposition. His early biographers were prone to ignore or minimize Tyndale's exegetical work. Most felt that he merely translated and edited Luther for the English-speaking world. P. Hughes argued that "Tyndale can hardly be reckoned a religious thinker of any real importance. The ideas he puts forth are none of them his own, nor does he add anything of importance to their content" (Hughes, 1:138; cf. Rupp, 48-56). Recent work has focused on Tyndale's theological contributions (Clebsch, 137-204), but no systematic analysis of his expository method has yet been done. A closer look at Tyndale the expositor reveals a man who grew beyond a dependence upon Luther to find his own voice.

Tyndale's work as an exegete rested upon the very skills that made him an exceptional translator, namely, his capacity for language. He earned his first degree from Oxford in 1512, and three years later received his master's degree. As a student at

Oxford his linguistic abilities were recognized (Foxe, 5:115). There is evidence that Tyndale continued his studies at Cambridge University. By the time he was beginning to work as a translator he was known to speak seven languages like a native. These included the modern European languages of English, French, German and Italian, as well as the biblical languages, Greek and Hebrew, and Latin. Tyndale's works are liberally sprinkled with evidence of keen etymological interest and investigation. He regularly compares word meanings in Greek and Hebrew. He also uses cognate terms to clarify a word or phrase in question. This key of linguistic analysis allowed Tyndale to enter the labyrinth of medieval exegesis and find his way to the one sense of a text.

The Literal Sense. Since the days of the early church the Bible was seen as consisting of several senses, or layers of meaning. The literal sense was considered by most as merely a vehicle by which the other senses were expressed. These "spiritual" meanings expressed truths metaphorically or allegorically and were considered far more meaningful than was the base literal sense. It was as if the Holy Spirit had hidden veins and nuggets of truth in the strata of Holy Scripture. For Tyndale, however, as for other Christian humanists like John Colet, Desiderius *Erasmus, Luther and John *Calvin, the literal sense was the primary path to truth. In Tyndale's words, "Thou shalt understand . . . that the Scripture hath but one sense, which is the literal sense. And that the literal sense is the root and ground of all, and the anchor that never faileth" (Tyndale, *Obedience of the Christian Man,* 1:310). By following the side trails of allegory one can "not but go out of the way" (Tyndale, *Obedience* 1:310).

Just what was meant by the literal sense? A linguist and biblical scholar of Tyndale's stature was well aware of the perils of wooden literalism, taking the words at face value instead of seeking the author's meaning. The Bible, he argued, contained various genres of speech like "proverbs,

similitudes, riddles or allegories, as all other speeches do; but that which the proverb, similitude, riddle or allegory signifieth, is even the literal sense, which thou must seek out diligently" (Tyndale, *Obedience* 1:310). This literal sense could better be called the normal sense, that which the author intended. Figures of speech, metaphors and allegories are merely meant to enhance and illustrate this basic sense.

This general rubric of interpretation, to search for the one primary meaning of the text, was applied by Tyndale to the interpretation of parables. Look for the one primary message of the parable, he instructed. Avoid the temptation of "pushing" a parable beyond its intended purpose: "They that will interpret parables word by word, fall into straits ofttimes whence they cannot rid themselves; and preach lies instead of truth" (Tyndale, *Parable of the Wicked Mammon* 1:86). The parable of the good Samaritan (Lk 10:30-35) furnished a good example. Some interpreters, he warned, see great significance in the two coins the Samaritan gave the innkeeper as pointing allegorically to the Old and New Testaments, or on another level of meaning this generous provision was seen to signify the doctrine of supererogation. Tyndale cautioned:

> Remember, this is a parable, and a parable may not be expounded word by word; but the intent of the similitude must be sought out only in the whole parable. The intent of the similitude is to show to whom a man is a neighbour . . . and what it is to love a man's neighbour as himself. (Tyndale, *Parable* 85).

Tyndale's most systematic application of this principle came in *The Parable of the Wicked Mammon.* Christ's story contained one simple truth: "thou shouldest do good; and so it will follow . . . that thou shall find friends and treasure in heaven, and receive a reward" (Tyndale, *Parable* 65). The interpreter need not relate extraneous elements of the narrative to the Christian life. The "unrighteous steward" was praised for his wisdom alone in providing for himself. His action was not to be condoned merely because it was a part of Christ's story. His dealings simply illustrate that we should be as diligent in providing for our souls as he was in providing for his body (Tyndale, *Parable* 70).

In the same way the parable of the prosperous farmer who planned to build larger barns, only to die that night (Lk 12:16-21), was not meant to teach that God forbids acquiring wealth. The central meaning of the text is that we must not love or put trust in earthly securities (Tyndale 1849, *Exposition of Scripture* 2:101).

Tyndale was in the first wave of Reformers who broke from allegorical model of interpretation. Such an approach, he felt, led to the decay of faith. The misuse of allegory led to false teachings that held the church in thrall: prayers to saints, purgatory, auricular confession, the preference of fish over meat, the belief that widowhood was better than matrimony and that the Virgin Mary was without original sin (Tyndale, *Obedience* 1:313).

Tyndale, following Luther's lead, saw the Alexandrian father *Origen as most responsible for the popularity of allegorical interpretation (Tyndale, *Obedience*, 1:307). As this spiritualized interpretation dominated in the medieval era, the literal sense of the Old Testament began to sink into obscurity. Interpreters found it superfluous to preach the "plain text" but "got them into allegories, feigning them every man after his own brain, without rule" (Tyndale 1849, *Exposition of Scripture* 2:75). Laypeople were the ones to suffer. With no clear teaching of the central themes of the Bible, they "lost the meaning of ceremonies."

Speaking of his own generation of expositors, Tyndale viewed the scene as moving from bad to worse. They were as apt to cite a fable from Ovid or some other poet, as John's Gospel or Paul's epistles: "Yea, they are come unto such blindness, that they not only say the literal sense profiteth not, but also that it is hurtful, and noisome,

and killeth the soul" (Tyndale, *Obedience* 1:307-8).

What was the proper use of allegories and metaphors? Tyndale limited their use to that of illustration, especially in preaching. There is not a mightier thing, as an aid to understanding, he taught, than an allegory: "Allegories make a man quick-witted, and print wisdom in him, and make it abide, where bare words go but in at the one ear, and out the other" (Tyndale, *Leviticus* 1:428). They are tools to make the text clear, to make the message stick, but they are not building blocks of biblical truth. Allegories prove nothing, he urged. In preaching and biblical exposition, unless the point or issue that the allegory illustrates is openly taught in a clear passage of Scripture, then such an allegory becomes "a thing to be jested at, and of no greater value than a tale of Robin Hood" (Tyndale, *Obedience* 1:307).

Tyndale had much more use for biblical typology, in which an event or a personality from the Hebrew Scripture (the type) is a precursor of a corresponding event from the life of Christ (the antitype). In writing about the levitical ceremonies and sacrifices, he saw in them "a star light of Christ, yet some there be that have . . . the light of broad day . . . and express him, and the circumstances and virtue of his death so plainly, as if we should play his passion on a scaffold, or in a stage play" (Tyndale, *Prologue to Leviticus* 1:422). Tyndale was convinced that God showed Moses "the secrets of Christ" and "the very manner of his death" and that the scapegoat, the brazen serpent, the ox burned outside the gate, and the passover lamb were clear historical types (Tyndale, *Leviticus* 1:422).

Clearly Tyndale's exegesis has a christocentric focus. The Scriptures, he argued, "spring out of God" and "flow unto Christ, and were given to lead us to Christ" (Tyndale, *Obedience* 1:317). "Thou must go along by the Scripture as by a line," he continued, "until thou come at Christ, which is the way's end and resting place" (Tyndale, *Obedience* 1:218).

A major part of sound exposition is the use a writer makes of authorities, great teachers of the past. An analysis of authorities is a great aid in tracking the development of exegetical method. Tyndale cites authorities sparingly, and this is partly explained by the fact that most of his writings were targeted toward lay readers who would have little knowledge of or access to the ancient and medieval Fathers. *Augustine of Hippo was his favorite among the early church expositors, perhaps followed by *Jerome. Origen was the most dangerous (Tyndale, *Answer to Sir Thomas More* 3:154). Among the medieval writers, the Venerable Bede was his favorite. Bede's treatment of the problematic pronouncement, "Thou art Peter, and upon this rock I will build my church," for example, Tyndale found to be "a faithful exposition" (Tyndale, *Obedience* 1:218). The schoolmen of the scholastic era were seen as being responsible for the corruption of biblical exegesis that still held sway in sixteenth-century Europe and are mentioned only with biting criticism (Tyndale, *Practice of the Prelates* 2:291).

Tyndale and His Contemporaries. When it came to his contemporaries, Tyndale was silent about everyone except Erasmus and Luther. Tyndale had translated Erasmus's influential *Enchiridion Militis Christiani* into English. He saw Erasmus's paraphrases of the New Testament to be useful, and he occasionally pointed to references in the annotations that were a part of the first printed Greek New Testament (1516). With Luther, however, it is clear Tyndale liberally borrowed and often expanded upon whole passages. In Tyndale's first attempt at printing the New Testament, generally referred to as the Cologne fragment, almost two-thirds of the marginal notes were direct translations of Luther's notes in *Das Neue Testament Deutsch* (Gruber, 73). The same pattern is followed in Tyndale's *The Parable of the Wicked Mammon,* which is an expansion on Luther's published sermon on the same text (Luther, *Werke,* [Weimar] Bd. 10, Pt.

3:283-93). These were among his earliest works. In writings after 1530, Tyndale clearly sets off on his own. He began his translation of the Old Testament by writing prologues to the Penteteuch. Although he was aware of Luther's corresponding German prologues, the English introductions were original compositions. The same cannot be said for his New Testament prologues, but Tyndale's marginal notes in the 1534 edition of the New Testament were for the most part original.

The Hermeneutical Key. In 1533 Tyndale wrote a treatise on Matthew 5—7, which chapters he felt were the "key to the door of the Scripture, and the restoring again of Moses' law corrupted by the scribes and pharisees" (Tyndale, *Matthew* 2:1). In this text and in subsequent writings he developed a unique theological interpretation that in turn influenced his hermeneutic. The true key to Scripture was the proper understanding of the law. With true salvation, Tyndale argued, comes a God-given love for the law and the power to follow the law (Tyndale, *A Pathway into Holy Scripture* 1:11). Such a love was a natural, spontaneous outgrowth of justification. This leads Tyndale to the conclusion that all promises made throughout the Scriptures are "all made us upon this condition and covenant on our party, that we henceforth love the law of God, to walk therein, and to do it, and fashion our lives thereafter" (Tyndale, *Pathway* 1:11). The crucial words are "upon this condition and covenant." This idea is amplified further in his prologue to the Pentateuch, where Tyndale wrote that "all the promises throughout the whole Scripture do include a covenant: that is, God bindeth himself to fulfil that mercy unto thee *only if thou wilt endeavor thyself to keep his laws*" (Tyndale, *Prologue Upon the Five Books of Moses* 1:403, emphasis added). The conditional covenant is expanded here to include all the promises of Scripture. It has become Tyndale's organizing principle for biblical interpretation. Even when one finds a promise with no conditions mentioned, "there must thou understood a covenant" (Tyndale 1938 *New Testament*, 5). Is this teaching salvation by works? Tyndale answered no! Salvation, and with it the rest of God's promises, is initially received as a free gift of God's grace. However, that salvation is sustained only if the Christian continues to love and do the law. In his words, "none of us can be received to grace but upon a condition to keep the law, neither yet continue any longer in grace that purpose lasteth" (Tyndale, *Matthew V-VII 2:7*).

BIBLIOGRAPHY

Works. W. Tyndale, *Doctrinal Treatises and Introductions to Different Portions of Holy Scripture* (Parker Society; Cambridge: Cambridge University Press, 1848); idem, *Expositions of Scripture and Practice of the Prelates* (Parker Society; Cambridge: Cambridge University Press, 1849); idem, *The New Testament*, ed. N. H. Wallis (Cambridge: University Press, 1938 [1534]). Individual Works in Parker Society Series: W. Tyndale, *Answer to Sir Thomas More* (1530); idem, *Exposition of Matthew V-VII* (1533); idem, *The Obedience of the Christian Man* (1528); idem, *Parable of the Wicked Mammon* (1528); idem, *A Pathway into Holy Scripture* (1531); idem, *The Practice of the Prelates* (1530); idem, *Prologue to Leviticus* (1530); idem, *Prologue Upon the Five Books of Moses* (1530).

Studies. W. Clebsch, *England's Earliest Protestants* (New Haven, CT: Yale University Press, 1964); D. Daniell, *William Tyndale* (New Haven, CT: Yale University Press, 1994); J. Foxe, *Acts and Monuments of These Latter and Perilous Dayes, Touching Matters of the Church* (London: R. B. Seeley and W. Burnside, 1838); L. F. Gruber, *The First English New Testament and Luther* (Burlington, IA: The Lutheran Literature Board, 1928); P. Hughes, *The Reformation in England* (London: Hollis, 1956); E. G. Rupp, *The English Protestant Tradition* (Cambridge: Cambridge University Press, 1964).

N. P. Feldmeth

Vermigli, Peter Martyr (1499-1562)

Pietro Martire Vermigli was born in Florence on September 8, 1499. Little is known of his early years except that he had an abiding affection for the Bible. Reflecting on his youth in his inaugural speech at Zurich in 1556, Vermigli revealed: "For even from my youth, when I yet lived in Italy, this one thing I minded to follow above all arts and ordinances of men: even chiefly to learn and teach the Holy Scriptures, neither had I other success than I purposed." Following this conviction, even though it went against the wishes of his father, Vermigli joined the Lateran Congregation of Canons Regular of St. Augustine in 1514. Academically precocious, Vermigli was sent to study at the University of Padua, at that time one of the most famous universities in the world.

At Padua he lived a dual intellectual existence. On the one hand he was inundated with the study of Aristotle in the faculty of theology at the university; on the other hand he imbibed Renaissance humanism at his monastery, S. Giovanni di Verdara. His years of study at Padua culminated in priestly ordination and a doctorate in theology (1526). During the Italian phase of his career he was well known as a distinguished theologian, eloquent preacher and moral reformer. He was the colleague of powerful prelates under Pope Paul III and probably a consultant to the *Consilium de emendanda ecclesia* of 1537; he also was appointed by Cardinal Contarini to the first delegation to represent the Roman Catholic cause at the Colloquy of Worms in 1540.

Vermigli's theological transformation was initiated during his Neapolitan abbacy (1537-1540) by the Spanish reformist Juan de Valdés. In the Valdesian circle in Naples Vermigli encountered the Italian reform movement, first read the works of Protestant Reformers Martin *Bucer and Ulrich *Zwingli, and embraced the pivotal doctrine of justification by faith alone. Evidence of his theological reorientation manifested itself during his priorate in Lucca, where he established "the first and last reformed theological college in pre-Tridentine Italy" (McNair 1967, 221). However, the papal bull *Licet ab initio* of July 1542 changed everything. With the reinstitution of the Roman Inquisition under Carafa, Vermigli fled north of the Alps to nascent Protestantism.

Almost immediately after his apostasy in the summer of 1542, Vermigli was catapulted into prominence as a biblical scholar and Reformed theologian. In his new Protestant capacity, his sphere of influence extended to the major centers of the reformation movement: Bucer's Strasbourg, Archbishop Cranmer's Oxford (where he was Regius Professor of Divinity from 1547 to 1553), Bullinger's Zurich and indirectly Zacharias Ursinus's Heidelberg. His reputation in the Reformed church was such that one Protestant contemporary could say, "The two most excellent theologians of our times are John Calvin and Peter Martyr" (Huelin, 178). Although he was widely acknowledged as one of the leading theologians of his day, Vermigli fell into obscurity until he was rediscovered in the 1950s by doctoral students at British universities.

Major Works. The most impressive indication of Vermigli's importance as a theologian is the repeated publication of his books. His works went through 110 separate printings in the century following his death. Vermigli made his mark primarily as a biblical commentator but also as an important theologian of the Reformed branch of Protestantism. The only commentaries published during his lifetime were on 1 Corinthians, Romans and Judges. However, a number of his lectures on biblical books were published posthumously as commentaries on Genesis, Lamentations, 1 Samuel and 2 Samuel, and 1 Kings and 2 Kings. Vermigli also wrote theological treatises, most notably on the Eucharist. His *Defensio* against Stephen Gardiner on the Eucharist is a massive tome of impressive erudition. It was, as P. M. McNair states, "incontestably the weightiest single treatise on the eucharist of the entire Reformation" ("Biographical Introduction" in Vermigli 1994, 12).

Vermigli also wrote two smaller eucharistic treatises on the famous Oxford debate of 1549, in which he represented the Protestant cause. While eucharistic concerns tended to predominate, Vermigli's theological interests were wide-ranging. His theological attentions extended to such matters as clerical celibacy and the two natures of Christ; his writings on both were published as treatises. Some of the *loci* (theological essays) in his biblical commentaries were substantial theological treatises. One need only examine the two loci on justification and predestination in his commentary on Romans for verification.

Easily the most influential of Vermigli's writings was the *Loci Communes (Common Places),* a posthumous compilation of various loci from his biblical commentaries arranged according to key theological topics. The *Loci Communes* was not the work of Vermigli but of Robert Masson (a French pastor in London) and was deliberately calibrated to coincide with the organizational structure of John *Calvin's *Institutes.* Reciprocally, the first Latin edition of the *Institutes* to appear in England, the Vautrollier edition of 1576, was keyed to the *Loci Communes* of Vermigli. This pattern of coordination between Calvin and Vermigli reflected the prevailing conviction that two of the most important Reformed theologians of this period were in significant theological agreement. This arrangement is splendidly maintained in the modern English edition of the *Institutes* (LCC 20-21; ed. J. T. McNeill [Philadelphia: Westminster, 1960]).

Biblical Interpretation. Though no full-length monograph has been published on Vermigli's theory and method of biblical interpretation, it is apparent that he, along with Calvin, Philipp *Melanchthon, Bucer and Heinrich *Bullinger, was among the leading representatives of a distinctive literary tradition of Protestant commentators on the Bible. Just as early Reformed theology emerged from a group of reform-minded scholars with shared convictions and outlooks, so also there was a kind of cross-fertilization regarding the manner and method of writing a biblical commentary that tended to follow the same general pattern. Vermigli's own method of biblical commentary shares with his fellow Protestants the commitment to the Renaissance notion of *ad fontes* (to the source), that is, going back to the original sources, as well as the conviction that is summed up in the Latin phrase *Scriptura Scripturae interpres* ("Scripture is the interpreter of Scripture"). Within this general hermeneutical framework the peculiar aims, methodological traits and intellectual influences on Vermigli manifest themselves.

Vermigli states that his aim as biblical commentator is to "make plain the words" of the biblical writer. He sought to elucidate what he described in the preface to his commentary on 1 Corinthians as the *verum genuinumque sensum Scripturae* ("the true and natural sense of Scripture"). He lays particular stress on the "verbal sense" *(verborum sensus)* of the text, which is nothing other than the grammatical-historical method.

A corollary to his goal of determining the plain meaning of the text is that Vermigli, like most Protestant exegetes, explicitly rejects the allegorical method of interpretation. As a biblical interpreter he sought not the "mysterious deeper meaning," as did *Origen and interpreters in the Alexandrian tradition, but the plain meaning that is based on the verbal sense. This orientation places Vermigli well within the boundaries of mainstream Protestants biblical exegetes.

In his desire to present the plain meaning of the text, Vermigli was recognized for the unusual clarity of his biblical commentaries. In his own day Theodore *Beza contrasted Vermigli's clarity to Bucer's prolixity (Aubert et al., 6:115). Josiah Simler, Vermigli's successor in Zurich, made the same observation (McLelland and Duffield, 52-53). Even Vermigli's opponents noted the clarity in his writings. Cornelius Schulting, a Roman Catholic controversialist, declared that Vermigli's *Loci Communes*

displayed a "greater perspicuity" than did Calvin's *Institutes* (Schulting, vol. 1, sig. Ai). Modern scholars have also observed Vermigli's "unusual precision" and his "tidy-mindedness."

But Vermigli's goal as a biblical commentator was not completely satisfied by achieving clarity and explicating the plain meaning of the text. Both are linked to a christological focus. Vermigli declared that "the Spirit of Christ" must be the centerpiece of biblical interpretation. J. C. McLelland echoes the same sentiment when he states that for Vermigli "the argument and scope of any passage includes two things, the historical events and the pointing to Christ" (McClelland 1957, 91).

Methodology. Like most other Protestant scholars, Vermigli followed a standard methodology in his biblical commentaries. He supplied his own translation of the biblical text, which usually tended toward the literal. Having established the biblical text, he provided general introductory remarks to orient his reader to the content of the biblical book. For example, in his commentary on Lamentations Vermigli explains the etymology of the Hebrew name for Lamentations, considers the authorship of the book, acquaints his hearers with the Hebrew canon, and then sets forth the general theme of this "mournful poem." Turning to the text itself, Vermigli's normal procedure was to divide each verse into key words or clauses and then explain the meaning within the immediate context. Often he will paraphrase to make the meaning clearer. One observes his frequent employment of the Protestant principle of *analogia fidei*, or the analogy of faith, whereby clearer passages of Scripture are brought forward to clarify the passage under consideration.

Also characteristic of Vermigli's commentary style are the many classical literary allusions. When it comes to exegesis he is fairly detailed and exhibits considerable grammatical and historical sensitivity. At points Vermigli indulges in esoteric points of grammar, yet he also periodically takes time to make spiritual applications for the individual believer. He was obviously a first-rate Greek scholar and, in the judgment of D. Shute, among "the top ten Gentile Hebraists of his time" (Shute, 39). When he judges it appropriate, he will also draw out the doctrinal implications. However, Vermigli believed that the interpreter's primary responsibility is to explicate the sense of each verse. If the biblical commentator has fulfilled his responsibility, the Christian reader, under the inspiration of the Holy Spirit, will be able to understand the meaning of the biblical text and draw personal applications.

Vermigli was renowned for his knowledge of the church fathers, both Greek and Latin. Although he is unheralded today, he may have been one of the greatest patristic scholars among his sixteenth-century contemporaries. Vermigli's patristic orientation profoundly informed his grammatical-historical method of exegesis. He is clear that Scripture is the final source for theology. However, the church fathers may provide vital guidance for the right and proper interpretation of the biblical text. Among the galaxy of church fathers cited in his writings, none is more luminous than *Augustine. Although Vermigli can disagree with Augustine, he more often defers to him. In his commentary on Romans, Vermigli explicitly identifies his doctrine of predestination with Augustine. Theologically Augustine is Vermigli's guiding light.

Vermigli does not confine himself exclusively to Christian church fathers. In his Old Testament commentaries, Vermigli frequently interacts with the opinions of the rabbinic commentators. In his commentary on Lamentations he availed himself of the 1525 Bomberg Bible and was especially attracted to the *peshat* tradition of rabbinic commentators (those inclined toward a simple and straightforward grammatical exegesis). Shute concludes: "I have not been able to discover any Christian commentator on the Old Testament who has made such great and such positive use of the Rabbinic Bible's commentators"

(Shute, 29-30).

Perhaps the most notable characteristic of Vermigli's biblical methodology is his use of *loci communes,* or common places. These loci were mostly systematic theological expositions of the biblical text. In his more extensive loci, after having completed the grammatical-historical exegesis and having consulted with the patristic and Jewish commentators, Vermigli brings the main exegetical and patristic considerations together in a theological essay. For him it is vital to appreciate that theological formulation is preceded by and grounded upon biblical exegesis. This biblical-theological interaction can be seen in his commentary on Romans, where Vermigli places his extensive locus on predestination at end of his comments on Romans 9. Only after having completed his exegesis of Romans 8—9 does Vermigli draw out the theological significance of the doctrine of predestination (James 1996b, 82).

The various loci differ in detail and depth of analysis. Some loci are brief and to the point. Others are extensive and amount to a treatise in their own right. In a typical developed locus he provides a general introduction to orient his reader, often displaying pastoral concerns, before turning to linguistic analysis of key theological terms and consideration of their Latin, Greek and Hebrew etymology. After offering a working definition, he then explicates each word or phrase of the definition, incorporating passages from other parts of Scripture. He also consults various church fathers, especially Augustine, and only then does he engage in thorough theological analysis. Vermigli's loci contain theological analysis that is informed by church fathers and grounded upon the biblical text.

Influences. The major debate among Vermigli scholars centers on the degree to which Vermigli's biblical hermeneutic was influenced by medieval scholasticism. All agree that he employed scholastic distinctions, such as Aristotle's fourfold system of causation. J. P. Donnelly typifies those scholars who point to the influence of

Thomas *Aquinas and Aristotle. M. W. Anderson agrees that Vermigli displays certain scholastic tendencies but argues that he is fundamentally indebted to a humanistic methodology that is joined to a Protestant theological motive. These concerns, says Anderson, dominated Vermigli's biblical hermeneutic.

Part of the problem in deciding who is a scholastic depends on how one defines the term *scholastic*. Historians of the sixteenth century must bear in mind that scholastic categories, terminology and distinctions were the common inheritance of all sixteenth-century theologians. This did not necessarily mean one was a scholastic in any philosophical sense. It meant that one was using the intellectual tools at his disposal. Even Calvin, who was deeply indebted to French humanism, at times employed Aristotelian causal categories in his commentaries. But the use of Aristotelian causality does not necessarily make one a scholastic.

How then can one explain the fact that Vermigli shows traces of both scholastic and humanistic methodology? Two considerations are helpful. First, one can begin to gain insight by considering the historical context. Before Vermigli's era, the hermeneutical tradition centered on the fourfold sense of Scripture (literal, topological, allegorical and anagogical). From Augustine to the Middle Ages the fourfold sense was normative, with a decided tendency toward the allegorical sense. What is interesting is that Vermigli does not follow Augustine or the scholastic hermeneutic. Rather, he allied himself especially with John *Chrysostom and a more literal-historical hermeneutic. This suggests that Vermigli had already broken with the main principles of scholastic biblical interpretation by the time he arrived in Bucer's Strasbourg in 1542 and thus that Vermigli drank deeply from the well of "Catholic humanism."

A second part of the answer is found in the fact that both the medieval scholastic and Renaissance humanist hermeneutical traditions trace their origins to Aristotle. Vermigli's loci methodology was not new.

Melanchthon had already employed a version of this approach in his *Loci Communes* of 1521. Melanchthon had borrowed the essence of the loci method from Rudolf Agricola, who took it from Cicero, who adapted it from the *topoi* ("places") of Aristotle. Even the humanist tradition ultimately traces its ancestry to Aristotle's topoi methodology. This goes a long way in explaining why many humanist-trained Protestant Reformers retained traces of Aristotelianism. It would appear that the reformation movement in part continued the trends of medieval Aristotelianism and in part received new direction under the influence of Renaissance humanism. One sees in Vermigli's hermeneutic this new combination of elements of the old methodology joined with new philological orientation and infused with a new theological motive. Thus Vermigli's method of biblical interpretation was not so much a rejection of scholastic methodology as a reconfiguration of scholastic and humanist approaches in the service of new theological convictions.

Significance. Vermigli's significance as a biblical interpreter is threefold. He is significant because he demonstrated, perhaps more vividly than any other major Reformer, that Aristotelianism and humanism are not necessarily antithetical. Having trained in the bastion of Aristotelianism at University of Padua but having also inhaled the rarefied air of Renaissance humanism, Vermigli displayed the new synthetic exegetical approach of emerging Reformed theology.

Vermigli's hermeneutical methodology is distinguished by a particularly vibrant Augustinianism. The most recent research suggests that Vermigli's hermeneutical approach was informed by a particular medieval intensification of Augustine, the so-called *schola Augustiniana moderna,* or modern Augustinian school, which can be traced back to the fourteenth-century Augustinian Gregory of Rimini (James 1996b, 335-42). So far as is known, no other sixteenth-century Reformed theologian was directly influenced by the *schola Augustiniana moderna*. By infusing the new humanist methodology with an intensive Augustinian theology, Vermigli added an important third ingredient to the Reformed hermeneutic mixture. Part of his significance as a biblical interpreter is found in this convergence of medieval scholasticism, Renaissance humanism and a revived Augustianism.

The Reformed hermeneutical tradition was not born of a single individual. It has been increasingly recognized that the hermeneutical origins of Reformed theology do not derive exclusively or even primarily from Calvin but rather from a coterie of theologians who tended to be associated with Swiss reform, including Bullinger, Vermigli, Bucer and Wolfgang Musculus in addition to Calvin. Together these theologians gave shape not only to Reformed theology but also to the Reformed interpretation of the Bible.

BIBLIOGRAPHY

Works. J. P. Donnelly, ed. and trans., *Dialogue on the Two Natures of Christ* (Peter Martyr Library 2; Kirksville, MO: Thomas Jefferson University Press, 1995); idem, ed. and trans., *Sacred Prayers: Drawn from the Psalms of David* (Peter Martyr Library 3; Kirksville, MO: Thomas Jefferson University Press, 1996); idem, ed. and trans., *Sermons and Letters* (Peter Martyr Library 5; Kirksville, MO: Thomas Jefferson University Press, 1998); J. P. Donnelly with R. M. Kingdon and M. W. Anderson, *A Bibliography of the Works of Peter Martyr Vermigli* (Kirksville, MO: Sixteenth Century Journal Publishers, 1990); J. C. McLelland, ed., *Early Writings: Creed, Scripture and Church* (Peter Martyr Library 1; Kirksville, MO: Thomas Jefferson University Press, 1994); idem, ed. and trans., *Philosophical Works: On the Relation of Philosophy to Theology* (Peter Martyr Library 4; Kirksville, MO: Thomas Jefferson University Press, 1996); J. C. McLelland and G. E. Duffield, eds., *The Life, Early Letters and Eucharistic Writings of Peter Martyr* (Abingdon, Oxford: Sutton Courtenay Press, 1989).

Studies. M. W. Anderson, "Biblical Humanism and Roman Catholic Reform 1444-1563: A Study of Renaissance Philology and New Testament Criticism from Laurentius Valla to Pietro Martyre Vermigli" (unpublished Ph.D. dissertation, Kings College, University of Aberdeen, 1964); idem, *Peter Martyr Vermigli, A Reformer in Exile (1542-1562): A Chronology of Biblical Writings in England and Europe* (Nieuwkoop: B. de Graaf, 1975); idem, "Pietro Maritre Vermigli on the Scope and Clarity of Scripture," *TZ* 30 (1974) 86-94; idem, "Word and Spirit in Exile (1541-1561): The Biblical Writings of Peter Martyr Vermigli," *JEH* 21 (1970) 193-201; F. Aubert et al., eds., *Correspondance de Theodore de Beze* (Geneva: Droz, 1960-) vol. 6; S. Corda, *Veritas Sacramenti: A Study in Vermigli's Doctrine of the Lord's Supper* (Zurich: Theologischer Verlag Zurich, 1975); M. Di Gangi, *Peter Martyr Vermigli, 1499-1562: Renaissance Man, Reformation Master* (New York: University Press of America, 1993); J. P. Donnelly, *Calvinism and Scholasticism in Vermigli's Doctrine of Man and Grace* (Leiden: E. J. Brill, 1976); idem, "Calvinist Thomism," *Viator* 7 (1976) 441-55; G. Huelin, "Peter Martyr in England" (Ph.D. diss., University of London, 1955); F. A. James III, "Juan de Valdes Before and After Peter Martyr Vermigli: The Reception of *Gemina Praedestinatio* in Valdes' Later Thought," *ARG* 83 (1992) 180-208; idem, "A Late Medieval Parallel in Reformation Thought: *Gemina Praedestinatio* in Gregory of Rimini and Peter Martyr Vermigli" in *Via Augustini: Augustine in Later Middle Ages, Renaissance and Reformation*, ed. H. A. Oberman and F. A. James III (Leiden: E. J. Brill, 1991) 157-88; idem, "Peter Martyr Vermigli" in *Blackwell's Encyclopedia of Medieval, Renaissance and Reformation Christian Thought*, ed. A. McGrath (Oxford: Blackwell, 1996); idem, *Peter Martyr Vermigli and Predestination: The Augustinian Heritage of an Italian Reformer* (Oxford: Oxford University Press, 1998); idem, "*Praedestinatio Dei:* The Intellectual Origins of Peter Martyr Vermigli's Doctrine of Double Predestination" (D.Phil. diss., Oxford University, 1993); J. C. McLelland, "Calvinism Perfecting Thomism?" *SJT* 31 (1978) 571-78; J. C. McLelland, ed., *Peter Martyr Vermigli and Italian Reform* (Waterloo, ON: Wilfrid Laurier University Press, 1980); idem, ed., *The Visible Words of God: An Exposition of the Sacramental Theology of Peter Martyr Vermigli, A.D. 1500-1562* (Edinburgh: Oliver & Boyd, 1957); P. M. McNair, *Peter Martyr in Italy: An Anatomy of Apostasy* (Oxford: Clarendon, 1967); idem, "Vermigli" in *New Dictionary of Theology*, ed. S. Ferguson and D. F. Wright (Downers Grove, IL: InterVarsity Press, 1988); R. A. Muller, *Christ and the Decree:*

Christology and Predestination in Reformed Theology from Calvin to Perkins (Durham, NC: Labyrinth Press; Grand Rapids: Baker, 1986); C. Schulting, *Bibliotheca Catholica contra . . . Loci Communibus Petri Martyris* (Cologne, 1602); D. Shute, "Peter Martyr and the Rabbinic Bible in the Interpretation of Lamentations" (Ph.D. diss., McGill University, 1995); D. Steinmetz, "Peter Martyr Vermigli (1499-1562): The Eucharistic Sacrifice" in *Reformers in the Wings* (Philadelphia: Fortress, 1971), 151-61; K. Sturm, *Die Theologie Peter Martyr Vermiglis während seines ersten Aufenthalts in Strassburg 1542-1547* (Neukirchen: Neukirchener Verlag, 1971).

F. A. James III

Zanchi, Jerome *(1516-1590)*

Along with Peter Martyr *Vermigli (1499-1562), Jerome Zanchi was a leading voice among the Italian refugees who, under pressure from the Inquisition, fled to Switzerland, where they came under the influence of Reformed theology. Zanchi himself spent nine months in Geneva, where he was exposed to the sermons and lectures of John *Calvin. Embracing Reformed perspectives on a wide range of issues, including predestination, perseverance, christology and the Eucharist, Zanchi articulated a theology designed to synthesize the best elements of the patristic and medieval heritage with a Reformed religious vision. In this way Zanchi made a distinctive contribution to the development of what J. P. Donnelly has called Calvinist Thomism.

Zanchi's training in Thomist theology greatly enriched his later work as pastor to the Reformed Italian congregation at Chiavenna (1563-1567) and as a teacher in the Protestant academies at Strasbourg (1553-1563), Heidelberg (1568-1577) and Neustadt an der Haardt (1578-1583). His responsibilities at Heidelberg included lectures on the common place theology; at Strasbourg and Neustadt, however, he was a professor of biblical interpretation. At Strasbourg Zanchi was a lecturer on the Old Testament; at Neustadt he was a professor of New Testament theology. This implies that Zanchi was both a systematic

theologian and a biblical scholar; reflecting that bifurcation in Zanchi's professional interests is a corpus of writings that includes both dogmatic treatises and biblical commentaries. Zanchi's image among historians has been shaped largely by his doctrinal and polemical works, such as *De Tribus Elohim* (1572) and *De Natura Dei* (1577). Zanchi's commentaries, which account for almost a fourth of his literary output, have been largely ignored.

Biblical Interpretation. Until recently it would have been remarkable to find Zanchi's name or that of virtually any other Reformed orthodox theologian in a list of major biblical interpreters. Prior to the publication of R. A. Muller's *Christ and the Decree* (1986), the conventional wisdom regarding Reformed orthodoxy was disdainful and dismissive. A major element in the case against Reformed orthodoxy was the claim that theologians such as Zanchi lost the biblical center of the original Protestant vision; sometimes the Reformed scholastics were accused of betraying the Protestant principle of *sola Scriptura* ("by Scripture alone") in favor of an approach that emphasized logic and metaphysics rather than an earnest encounter with the inspired text.

If that claim were well-founded, the story of Reformed exegesis could be written in a few paragraphs. If it were true that Zanchi substitutes logical analysis and a rigid metaphysical determinism for the Protestant principle, there would be little reason to investigate the exegetical and hermeneutical dimensions of his work. In fact, however, biblical exegesis is prominent, indeed pervasive, in Zanchi's project. A substantial proportion of his writings takes the form of biblical commentary, and even when he is working in some other genre Zanchi lives and breathes in dialogue with Scripture. Zanchi's knowledge of the Bible in its original languages combines with a deep immersion in the patristic and medieval traditions to give his work a depth and a solidity that can hardly be reconciled with the older assessment of Reformed orthodoxy as sterile and decadent.

Although Zanchi's work in polemics and dogmatics has largely shaped his image among historians, a survey of his collected works makes it clear that biblical interpretation held a central position on his agenda. His academic career began with his lectures on the Old Testament at Strasbourg; it ended with his lectures on the New Testament at Neustadt. C. J. Burchill has claimed that Zanchi's basically dogmatic interests can be seen in the development of thematic loci that take him away from exposition of the text itself. This suggests that Zanchi was a frustrated dogmatician who cared little about exegesis; required to teach the courses on biblical interpretation, he used the text as a pretext for elaborating the dogmatic themes that formed the real center of his theological interests. Whether Burchill's assessment of Zanchi's exegetical work will survive a close examination of the commentaries remains to be seen. What cannot be denied is that systematic biblical exegesis forms a substantial proportion of Zanchi's literary production. In the 1605 edition of his writings, two of the eight volumes are devoted to commentaries on the books of Hosea (Zanchi, 5), Ephesians (Zanchi, 6:1-262), Philippians (Zanchi, 6:1-242), Colossians (Zanchi, 6:241-360), 1 Thessalonians and 2 Thessalonians (Zanchi, 6:359-521) and 1 John (Zanchi, 6:1-136). A number of patterns emerge from a close reading of these samples of Zanchi's exegesis.

Christology. Zanchi was not alienated from the Jewish roots of Christianity or apologetic about his christocentric reading of the Hebrew Bible. A profound sense of the continuity between Israel and the church enabled him to speak of the Hebrew nation during the pre-Christian era as the *Ecclesia Israelitica.* Wherever Zanchi looks in the Bible, in the Old Testament no less than in the New, he sees Christ. In Hosea's prophecy, for example, Zanchi finds the renewal of God's covenant with Abraham's heirs, which he understands as a promise straining toward fulfillment in Christ. In

the epistle to the Ephesians, he sees the spousal relationship between Christ and the church as the highest fulfillment of what is implied in God's institution of marriage in the Garden of Eden.

Typology. One device that enables Zanchi to see Christ everywhere in Scripture is typology: he is convinced that persons and events in the Old Testament often bear a prophetic significance that reaches beyond their original historical context. At least since the defeat of Gnosticism and Marcionism in the second century, the orthodox tradition has affirmed that the Hebrew Bible is the church's book. Zanchi is orthodox at that point, and typology is the method that makes it possible for him to find evangelical themes in texts written long before the birth of Christ. Typological exegesis makes it possible for Zanchi to read the Old Testament as a prefiguring of the New and the New Testament as a fulfillment of what is promised in the Old. Thus prior to their fall into sin, Adam points toward ("typifies") the new Adam, Christ, while Eve prefigures the bride of Christ, the church. Zanchi's clearest use of the typological method is in his treatment of the spiritual union between Christ and the church (Zanchi, 6:234-39; cf. Farthing 1993, 624-27).

Linguistic and Traditional Resources. Since the Hebrew Bible plays a pivotal role in Zanchi's thought, it is not surprising that he shows a thorough grasp of Hebrew grammar and syntax or that he takes seriously the insights of the rabbinic commentators. He works comfortably not only with the Koine Greek but also with the Hebrew text *(phrasis Hebraeica)* of the Old Testament, the targums and rabbinic commentaries.

By the same token, Zanchi does not do his interpretive work in isolation from the traditions of the Fathers and the Middle Ages; he has access to the treasures summarized in *Nicholas of Lyra's *Glossa Ordinaria,* and he maintains an intense dialogue with a variety of Christian exegetical traditions. Zanchi's commentary on Hosea reveals the breadth of his dialogue with other interpreters, both Christian and Jewish. Prominent among his rabbinic sources are David Kimchi and Jonathan ben Uzziel (the Targum Jonathan). Among his patristic and medieval sources are *Augustine, John *Chrysostom, Gregory the Great, *Jerome, *Irenaeus, *Justin Martyr, *Bernard, Thomas *Aquinas and Nicholas of Lyra. In his commentary on Hosea Zanchi makes explicit references to Martin *Luther, John *Calvin and Wolfgang Musculus. In his commentaries on Pauline epistles he cites (in addition to many of the same sources to whom he appeals in commenting on Hosea) Philo, *Origen, *Tertullian, *Theodoret, Ambrose, Cyprian, Cyril, Eusebius, Lactantius, Leo I, John of Damascus, Bede, Photius, Theophylact, Peter Lombard and Gratian. In his New Testament commentaries Zanchi draws extensively on the critical work of Desiderius *Erasmus and Theodore *Beza. He also displays a wide-ranging familiarity with numerous figures from classical antiquity, including Socrates, Plato, Aristotle, Pythagoras, Virgil, Cicero and Seneca, and he does not hesitate to place these resources in the service of his exegetical enterprise.

Among Zanchi's extrabiblical sources Aquinas holds a special place. He does not hesitate to cite Thomas by name, often with bibliographical references to the *Summa Theologiae*. Thomas's influence is also apparent in Zanchi's tendency to structure his presentation in a systematic way that has a scholastic shape and tone: often Zanchi arranges his expositions of Scripture in terms of theses and distinctions, questions and answers, objections and responses. This scholastic style, however, is more evident in his New Testament commentaries than in his earlier work on Hosea. An example is his discussion of theft and usury in his commentary on Ephesians 4 (Zanchi, 6:169-73).

Zanchi's use of traditional and classical materials is not in tension with his commitment to the primacy of Scripture. The priority of the biblical revelation is apparent in

virtually all of Zanchi's theological and exegetical works. It is far more likely that his interpretation of Aristotle or Aquinas will be shaped by his reading of the biblical text than that his reading of Scripture will be unduly influenced by his extrabiblical sources. Even when he is at his most Thomistic, there is no real conflict between the scholastic style and the evangelical content of Zanchi's exegesis. His dogmatic treatises are grounded in biblical perspectives and supported by abundant references to Scripture. His commentaries exhibit a wide-ranging intertextuality. Even when his style and organization are reminiscent of the *Summa Theologiae,* scriptural citations are far more numerous and pervasive than are references to classical or medieval writers.

In keeping with the hermeneutical principle that obscure passages in Scripture must be interpreted in light of other passages that are clearer, Zanchi appeals to the Bible as a resource for its own interpretation. A sense of the organic unity of the entire canon enables him to find in Scripture itself illuminating parallels and hints to the meaning of the texts with which he is dealing. To say that he offers a plethora of proof-texts in support of his exegesis may not fully convey the depth and rigor with which he puts various biblical voices in dialogue with one another. It is not just that Zanchi's commentaries are filled with biblical citations; Zanchi knows that heretics and even the devil himself can quote Scripture when it suits their purposes. But Zanchi does not marshal proof-texts in a way that seems mechanical or arbitrary or artificial. Working within an interpretive tradition that assumes the unity of the biblical message, Zanchi views each text in the larger context of the entire canon; he looks for connections between and among various passages of Scripture in ways that suggest a serious attempt to treat the canonical text fairly and soberly.

Texts and Loci. The intertwining of Zanchi's dogmatic interests with his exegesis can be seen in the *loci theologici* that are often attached to his New Testament commentaries. After dealing with a chapter in a verse-by-verse way, Zanchi often spends several pages in a more systematic treatment of doctrinal topics *(loci)* suggested by the preceding exposition. It would be unfair, however, to accuse Zanchi of neglecting exegesis for the sake of dogmatics. His discussion of the *loci* never becomes a substitute for a serious grappling with the biblical text; his systematic treatments of the *loci* are less massive than are his expositions of the text itself. And it is important to note that when Zanchi is discussing doctrinal *loci*, his procedure does not diverge substantially from what is found elsewhere in his commentaries: in the *loci* no less than in his preceding comments on the text, Zanchi orchestrates a wealth of biblical, classical, patristic, medieval and contemporary resources to illuminate the question at hand. Zanchi's *loci* are neither more nor less "biblical" than the rest of his exegetical work.

Polemics and Piety. For the most part Zanchi is generous and ecumenical in his treatment of those with whom he disagrees. In his commentary on Hosea, for instance, he speaks of Luther in positive terms. Even when he disagrees with Luther, he does not go out of his way to call attention to Luther's error. He even grants that there are some within the Roman church who are among the elect. It is nonetheless true that Zanchi is the child of a polemical age. Convinced of the truth of the Reformed position, he finds in his exegetical program opportunities to articulate his criticisms of both Roman Catholicism and Lutheranism. Thus, for instance, Zanchi sees in some of the sexual imagery of Hosea 1—3 an allegorical description of Rome, seducing her own children into spiritual fornication. In Hosea's description of the harlot Gomer, Zanchi finds a picture of the Roman Catholic church, which he calls, with considerable irony, "our holy Mother the pimp" *(nostra sancta Mater lena),* who is now revealed to be "the Roman whore" *(meretrix Romana;* Zanchi, 5:35, 39).

A polemical note is also found in Zanchi's New Testament commentaries. During his tenure as professor of New Testament at Neustadt an der Haardt, Zanchi was actively involved in the christological and eucharistic controversies that were raging between Lutherans and the Reformed. Perhaps that is why he focused his exegetical work on texts that speak to the question of the nature of Christ. Ephesians 3, for instance, speaks of the spiritual union between Christ and the church in terms of marital intimacy. Zanchi finds in this marital metaphor a basis for protesting against the Lutheran doctrine of the ubiquity of the body of the risen Christ. Marital imagery implies that the believer's connection to Christ is like that of a wife to her husband. But Zanchi argues that the Lutheran notion of ubiquity would leave us with a Christ whose body is so unlike ours that he is no longer of the same species as his bride, which clearly would make the union impossible (Zanchi, 6:245; cf. Farthing 1993, 627-34). Here Zanchi's polemical thrust is sharp and uncompromising.

It would be misleading, however, to call Zanchi's exegetical work polemical without going on to take note of the generous, warmhearted spirituality that comes to expression in his exegesis. He treats eschatological texts, for instance, not in a spirit of idle speculation or curiosity but with the goal of nourishing a vigilant piety (Zanchi, 7:89-90; cf. Farthing 1994, 346-50). The tone of Zanchi's commentaries is anything but dry or cold or pedantic. His exegesis both reflects and reinforces an earnest piety that celebrates a growing, deepening union of believers, with Christ and with one another, in faith, hope, and love.

Significance. Zanchi was a pivotal figure in the consolidation of the Reformed tradition during the last half of the sixteenth century. His training in Thomism put him in touch with the richness of patristic and medieval theology, thus enabling him to nourish the catholic roots of a nascent Reformed tradition. Zanchi played a crucial role in making available to early

Reformed theology the treasures of medieval scholasticism. His biblical interpretation set a high standard of exacting scholarship, which was combined with a sensitive, creative responsiveness to the theological agenda of Reformed Christianity during the later decades of the sixteenth century.

BIBLIOGRAPHY
Works. J. Zanchi, *Opera Theologicorum D. Hieronymi Zanchii I-VIII* (Stephanus Gamonetus, 1605).
    Studies. C. J. Burchill, "Girolamo Zanchi: Portrait of a Reformed Theologian and His Work," *SCJ* 15, 2 (1984) 185-207; J. P. Donnelly, "Calvinist Thomism," *Viator* 7 (1976) 441-55; idem, "Italian Influences on the Development of Calvinist Scholasticism," *SCJ* 7 (April, 1976) 81-101; J. L. Farthing, "Christ and the Eschaton: The Reformed Eschatology of Jerome Zanchi" in *Later Calvinism: International Perspectives*, ed. W. F. Graham (Kirksville, MO: Sixteenth Century Journal Publishers, 1994) 333-54; idem, *"De coniugio spirituali,"* *SCJ* 24, 3 (1993) 621-52; idem, *"Foedus Evangelicum:* Jerome Zanchi on the Covenant," *CTJ* 29 (1994) 147-67; idem, "Holy Harlotry: Jerome Zanchi and the Exegetical History of Gomer (Hosea 1—3)" in *Biblical Interpretation in the Era of the Reformation: Essays Presented to David C. Steinmetz in Honor of His Sixtieth Birthday,* ed. R. A. Muller and J. C. Thompson (Grand Rapids: Eerdmans, 1996) 292-312; O. Gründler, *Die Gotteslehre Girolami Zanchis und ihre Bedeutung für sein Lehre von der Prädestination* (Neukirchen-Vluyn: Neukirchener Verlag, 1965); J. M. Kittelson, "Marbach vs. Zanchi: The Resolution of a Controversy in Late Reformation Strasbourg," *SCJ* 8, 3 (1977) 31-44; R. A. Muller, *Christ and the Decree: Christology and Predestination in Reformed Theology from Calvin to Perkins* (Durham, NC: Labyrinth Press, 1986) 115-21; D. Schmidt, "Girolamo Zanchi," *TSK* 32 (1859) 625-708; N. Shepherd, "Zanchius on Saving Faith," *WTJ* 36 (1973) 31-47; D. Sinnema, "Aristotle and Early Reformed Orthodoxy: Moments of Accomodation and Antithesis" in *Christianity and the Classics: The Acceptance of a Heritage* (Lanham, MD: University Press of America, 1990) 119-48; W. van't Spijker, "Bucer als Zeuge Zanchis in Strassburger der Prädestinationsstreit" in *Reformiertes Erbe: Festschrift für Gottfried W. Locher zu seinem 80. Geburtstag,* ed. H. A. Oberman et al. (Zurich: Theologischer Verlag, 1992) 2:327-42; J. N. Tylenda, "Girolamo Zanchi and John Calvin: A Study in Discipleship as Seen Through Their Correspondence," *CTJ* 10, 2 (1975) 101-41.

J. L. Farthing

Zwingli, Ulrich *(1484-1531)*
Ulrich Zwingli, the father of the Reformation in German Switzerland, is best known for his early theological statements of the Reformed faith, his eucharistic differences with Martin *Luther and the establishment of the Zurich synod. Fewer people know him as the founder of the influential Zurich school of Bible exposition known as the Prophecy. The Zurich Prophecy, however, most clearly demonstrates Zwingli's calling as steward of God's Word and guardian of its purity.

Like many of his contemporaries, Zwingli viewed the first decades of the sixteenth century as a period of rebirth and renewal for the church and society. But he also possessed an eschatological vision of his era. In 1522 he remarked that "Christ shows our age special favor, since he more clearly reveals himself [today] than in some centuries past" (*Sämtliche Werke,* 1:293). Zwingli was convinced that a divine breakthrough of the gospel had occurred in his day; consequently he considered his task to be a prophetic one. For Zwingli the prophet's duties were prescriptive rather than predictive. Using the sword of the Spirit, the Word of God, Zwingli taught that "it is the primary task of a prophet that he pluck up, tear down and destroy whatever is set up against God and that he build and plant . . . what God desires" (Zwingli 1984, 2:158).

Life and Work. The son of a village administrator in the Toggenburg community of Wildhaus, Canton Glarus, Zwingli matriculated at the University of Vienna in 1498 but finished his education at the University of Basel, where he earned a master of arts degree (1506). For ten years he served as parish priest of Glarus before transferring to the Benedictine shrine of

Einsiedeln as people's priest and preacher to its pilgrims.

In 1519 this popular shrine preacher was called to serve as people's priest of the Great Minster Church in Zurich. There Zwingli embarked on what was considered an unconventional sermon series: the continuous exposition of Matthew's Gospel. But his intentions were by no means subversive. He merely wished to tell the story of Jesus and the early church from the original sources, uninterrupted by the order of the traditional church lectionary.

Sometime between 1519 and 1522 Zwingli moved beyond his humanistic educational goals to espouse a reformation involving rejection of the authority and teachings of the medieval church. Ever since 1516 he had questioned the traditional sources of religious truth: the church fathers, councils and papal decrees. In a 1522 apologetic entitled the *Archeteles*, he concluded that he could trust in "no words so much as . . . those which proceeded from the mouth of the Lord [i.e., the Scriptures]." Furthermore, he resolved to test every doctrine to see whether it concurred with an understanding of Jesus Christ that reflected his glory. This christological touchstone came to play an important role in Zwinglian exegesis (Zwingli 1912-29, 1:204). By autumn 1520, Zwingli's popular preaching moved the Zurich city council to mandate that all preachers base their sermons solely on Scripture.

The result of the Word carefully "sown" by Zwingli's simple but popular preaching was a harvest of turmoil in Zurich. Matters came to a head as a result of a fast-breaking incident in March 1522 and a petition by Zwingli and his supporters to end priestly celibacy. The opposition of the Bishop of Constance and local friars to Zwinglian preaching led the Zurich city council to call for a public inquiry. The council asserted that all issues raised by Zwingli's preaching should be debated publicly in German and resolved on the basis of Holy Scripture.

By the opening of the First Zurich Disputation (January 29, 1523), the question of religious authority was largely settled. In the *Archeteles* Zwingli had rejected an episcopal admonition to retain traditional church ordinances. These he found contradictory and confusing. By contrast he considered the words of Scripture clear and certain to all who approached humbly with a desire to be taught by God. Although the perspicuity of Scripture was not evident to everyone at the First Zurich Disputation, it was a public triumph for Zwingli. The results of the First Disputation were the vindication of Zwingli's preaching and the affirmation of his *67 Articles* by the city council. More important for the Reformed exegetical tradition was Zwingli's articulation of a key expository principle that "the Scriptures interpreted the Scriptures, not the fathers the Scriptures" (Zwingli 1912-29, 105).

A second disputation, held in October 1523 to advise the city council on worship and the sacraments, proved less productive. Although the council studied the recommendations of the October assembly, no immediate worship reforms were enacted. One important outcome was Zwinglian support for the city council's executive authority over the Zurich church. Zwingli's radical followers, who later founded an Anabaptist movement known as the Swiss Brethren, rejected such a role for the magistrate and broke ranks with the Zurich Reformer shortly thereafter.

Extensive sampling of delegates' opinions at the second disputation exposed the theological ignorance of many cantonal clergymen and pointed to needed reforms in clerical education. Zwingli insisted upon the importance of philological training for preachers. In a June 1525 treatise, *On the Preaching Office*, Zwingli asserted that "there is no better way" to understand the Bible "than through languages" (Zwingli 1984, 2:173). This humanist conviction culminated in the Zurich Prophecy.

The theological school known as the Prophecy opened its doors on June 19, 1525. On the basis of 1 Corinthians 14:6-11, the city council envisioned the Prophecy as a group of scholars who would spend their days publicly reading and teaching the Scriptures, devoting "an hour to the Hebrew text, one hour to the Greek, and another to the Latin [translation]" until the correct meaning could be grasped (E. Egli 1879, no. 426) The Prophecy instructed schoolboys, ministerial students and cantonal ministers through daily, trilingual exegetical lectures on biblical books. In the process the Prophecy retrained cantonal clergy, educated a new generation of ministers and produced a fresh translations of biblical books.

During Zwingli's lifetime, Old Testament exegesis took place each morning in the choir of the Great Minster. The Hebrew instructor, first Jacob Ceporin (d. 1527) and later Conrad Pellican (1478-1556), began by analyzing the original text, after which Zwingli rendered a translation into Latin from the Septuagint. Then Leo Jud (1482-1542), pastor of St. Peter's church, preached a popular sermon in German. New Testament expositions, conducted at the Mary Minster each afternoon under the direction of Oswald Myconius (1488-1552), followed the same procedure.

The Zurich prophets were generally accorded greater authority than were ordinary ministers, because of their superior linguistic talents. The congregation, however, remained the final judge of any inspired interpretations of the Bible.

Out of the mass of exegesis emerging from Zwingli's sermons and his work in the Prophecy, interpretations and commentaries on the following biblical books have been preserved: Genesis, Exodus, Psalms, Job, Isaiah, Jeremiah, Ezekiel, the Minor Prophets, Matthew, Mark, Luke, John, Romans, 1 Corinthians and 2 Corinthians, 1 Thessalonians and 2 Thessalonians, Colossians, Philippians, Hebrews, 1 John and James.

Most of Zwingli's Old Testament commentaries were based upon student notes edited by Jud and Kaspar Megander (1495-1545). Zwingli personally arranged for the publication of only his commentaries on

Isaiah and Jeremiah. Many key hermeneutical principles, rhetorical terms and examples appear in Zwingli's Old Testament commentaries and the prefaces to them. In Genesis and Exodus he identified seventy rhetorical forms, and in Isaiah he discovered two hundred. Jud also published Zwingli's New Testament expositions in 1539. Like the Zwinglian commentaries, the 1531 Zurich Bible was a cooperative endeavor of the Prophecy. This new version was based upon Luther's Wittenberg Bible, though the Old Testament was wholly revised by the Zurich prophets.

In March 1525 Zwingli marked the consolidation of the Zurich Reformation with a systematic theological treatise dedicated to Francis I of France. In the *Commentary on True and False Religion* he described true religion as "that which clings to the one and only God." From this premise he infers that "true piety demands . . . that one should hang upon the lips of the Lord and not hear or accept the word of any but the bridegroom." Consequently, "it is false religion and piety when trust is put in any other than God" (Heller in Zwingli 1912-1929, 3:92, 97). Starting from this foundation, Zwingli offered a commentary of Christian doctrine and practice.

The appearance of the *Commentary* suggested a redirection of Zwingli's reforming energies into an offensive, extending outside Canton Zurich and even beyond the Swiss Confederation. Such a shift was prudent, given the gathering storm of Roman Catholic opposition within the Confederation and the Holy Roman Empire. Luther's nemesis, Johann Eck (1486-1543), challenged Zwingli to a public debate at Baden in 1526. However, the threat of personal danger and the prohibition of the Zurich council kept Zwingli from attending.

Although the Baden Disputation was a setback for Swiss evangelicals, the Berne Disputation (January 1528) clearly reversed the momentum. At Berne the Zwinglians constructed sophisticated theological arguments composed of carefully chosen, closely integrated chains of biblical passages. When they were confronted with arguments drawn from tradition, they demanded biblical proof.

Following the Berne Disputation, Zwingli further institutionalized his reformation in April 1528 by establishing a cantonal synod to examine the life, learning and doctrine of ministerial candidates and clergy. He and his ally, Prince Philip of Hesse, tried to heal the growing breach between Lutherans and Zwinglians over their understanding of the Lord's Supper.

A eucharistic split between Luther and Zwingli was probably inevitable given their fundamental difference over the manner in which God imparts salvation. Both Reformers affirmed the sufficiency of faith alone. Nevertheless Luther fixed upon the visible word (of Scripture) and sacrament of the Supper as the objects of faith. He also identified them as the means God uses to impart salvation and the external "bridge" of the Spirit into the human heart. Zwingli denied that God the Holy Spirit requires any vehicle or means to impart grace, since the Spirit is the bearer of salvation and the divine power behind all things. The shape of Zwingli's eucharistic teaching emerged clearly only in late 1524 and 1525. In contrast to Luther, who never doubted the real presence of Christ's body and blood in the Lord's Supper, Zwingli considered the Eucharist a memorial of Christ's sacrifice on the cross and a warranty of forgiveness for believers. The key element of the Supper, as Zwingli explained in a *Letter to Thomas Wyttenbach,* is faith. Drawing on *Augustine's interpretation of John 6, Zwingli later asserted that Christ's body is "eaten" by the faithful when they have "believed" that he died for them.

The words of institution presented a more serious problem for Zwingli since they seemed to promise Christ's bodily presence in the eucharistic bread and to attribute grace to it. Zwingli's solution to this problem was to interpret Christ's consecration metaphorically, using a rhetorical device known as metonymy. Zwingli's explanation hinged on the verb *is* (Latin *est),* which, he demonstrates, sometimes means "signifies" or "represents" in Scripture. Zwingli's most thorough analysis and significant response to Luther's eucharistic teaching was the *Friendly Exegesis of the Matter of the Eucharist* (February 1527). Zwingli judged that Luther "put the most important part of salvation in physically eating the body of Christ" (Zwingli 1984, 2:244). He warned that this superstition was the final prop of the pope's authority and expressed concern that it might lead to a restoration of papal power.

With this concern in mind, Zwingli argued from faith and Scripture. The former became his principal criterion for interpreting the latter. He struggled to show that faith cannot accept a literal interpretation of the words of institution because material bread can in no way strengthen believers, much less save them. For Zwingli faith derives solely from the Spirit of God. "The flesh is useless" (Jn 6:63). Likewise Zwingli argued that a literal understanding of Matthew 26:26 would be inconsistent with the reality of Christ's human nature, which must remain in one place.

A year and a half later, in early October 1529, Philip of Hesse brought Luther and Zwingli face to face to work out their differences at the Marburg Colloquy. Philip organized the conference as the first step toward a Protestant alliance. The colloquy, however, was doomed from the start. After erecting their respective scriptural bulwarks, each side blasted the other in proceedings that resembled a skirmish more than a theological discussion.

The following year, at the request of the Margrave Philip, Zwingli published the *Sermon on the Providence of God* that he had preached immediately prior to the colloquy. In the *Sermon* Zwingli offered a philosophical rationale for his figurative interpretation of biblical testimony on the sacraments. The colloquy had done little to cement Protestant confessional unity, and Zwingli's dreams of a grand alliance quickly unraveled after the 1530 Diet of Augsburg. By the end of 1530 Zwingli was abandoned by all of his German allies, who instead endorsed the Augsburg Confession and joined the Lutheran Smalcald League. Diplomatic isolation of the Swiss Protestant cities was followed in 1531 by a disagreement among them over strategies to force the Roman Catholic ("Forest") cantons to allow evangelical preaching. At Berne's insistence, an economic blockade of the Forest cantons was attempted, but it failed to move them. Instead, on October 9 the Roman Catholic cantons surprised Zurich with a declaration of war. An ill-led and ill-equipped Zurich army hurried to meet a Catholic force nearly twice its size at Kappel. In the rout that ensued, five hundred Zurichers lost their lives. Among the dead was the Zurich prophet Ulrich Zwingli.

Interpretation of Scripture. The doctrine of God lay at the core of Zwingli's prophetic ministry. Zwingli's whole purpose was to return believers to this divine focus. His concern is reflected in the predominant hermeneutical conviction that individuals must be "taught by God" *(theodidacti)*, not humans, in order to understand the truth of Scripture.

Zwingli considered the Bible God's word in a unique sense and supremely authoritative. He called Scripture the judge and teacher of all believers. The greatest danger arose when readers tried to confirm their own opinions from Scripture instead of humbly receiving its teaching in faith. He charged that the haughty, who followed their own spirits or preferred human teachings to God's Word, would never grasp the Bible's true meaning. True understanding of the Word arose from the inward teaching of the Holy Spirit in the human heart.

For Zwingli faith became the primary modality for understanding Scripture. Trusting in the illuminating power of the Holy Spirit and encountering a wide variety of biblical interpretations, Zwingli's hermeneutical convictions resonated with the "rule of faith" laid down by the prophet Isaiah: "If you do not believe, you will not understand" (Is 7:9; here Zwingli followed *Jerome's rendering in the Vulgate, *Si non credideritis, non permanebitis*). Even though faith was the dominant principle of Zwingli's exegesis, he frequently associated it with love and the principle of God's glory. These two principles in Zwingli's mind naturally impinged upon the interpretation of Scripture, since the former was the only law that bound Christians, and the latter was the central focus of true religion.

Hermeneutical Principles. Despite an emphasis on faith and the Spirit, Zwingli employed a number of traditional and humanistic hermeneutical principles in biblical exegesis. His training in classical philology and literature made him recognize the necessity of studying the languages, genres and literary forms of the Bible. Moreover, he realized the importance of setting a biblical passage in its literary and historical context to grasp its meaning. Zwingli's favorite hermeneutical method was to compare passages of Scripture on a given topic. This practice presupposed the inherent consistency of Scripture, penned by many human hands but divinely inspired by one Spirit. Comparison effectively placed passages in a broader context and illuminated obscure texts with clear ones. One of the most important forms of comparison for Zwingli was the analogy of faith used to validate or disprove an interpretation based upon its similarity or dissimilarity with other clear texts. Unlike the radicals, who followed the Spirit, or the Lutherans, who clung to the letter of Scripture, Zwingli stressed the importance of Word and Spirit. Scripture, he explained, is like the yoke of an ox, while the Holy Spirit is like the beast without whose strength the burden cannot be moved.

Perhaps in response to Anabaptist attitudes, Zwingli increasingly valued the Old Testament and emphasized the unity of the Testaments. He was convinced of Paul's teaching that "these things happened to them [i.e., Old Testament saints] to serve as an example, and they were written down to instruct us" (1 Cor 10:11). For Zwingli,

Old Testament events and characters were pregnant with symbolic meaning.

Thus Zwingli employed the traditional fourfold method of biblical exegesis, albeit in modified form. He followed the great Alexandrian exegete *Origen, who distinguished three levels of meaning or senses in Scripture. These were the literal, or natural, sense, the moral sense and the mystical sense.

Zwingli's primary concern was to understand the natural sense of Scripture. According to E. Kunzli, Zwingli defined the natural sense as the literal meaning of a text after consideration of its idioms, schemas and figures of speech. He was keenly aware of the dangers of biblical literalism and thought a firm grasp of common biblical metaphors might guard against it. Consequently he expounded at length on the figures such as alloisis, catachresis, synecdoche and metonymy.

Zwingli's esteem for the Old Testament led him to reevaluate the moral sense of Scripture. Certainly he found moral examples among the Old Testament saints. Nevertheless he considered the moral sense little more than an application of the natural sense of the message to the reader's existential situation.

Although Zwingli followed his patristic and medieval forebearers by embracing the mystical sense of Scripture, he exercised greater discipline in its interpretation. He included allegories, literal mysteries and typologies under this hermeneutical rubric. He made limited use of allegory even though he asserted Pauline precedent for the practice in Galatians 4:21-30. He feared that allegory endangered the Bible's authority and allowed only allegorical interpretations confirmed elsewhere by the literal sense. Also rare were attempts to interpret mysteries such as Abraham's three visitors, who for Zwingli represented the Trinity.

Typology, by contrast, played a key role in Zwinglian hermeneutics. It corresponded to the traditional anagogic or eschatological sense of medieval exegesis. In Zwingli's view typological exegesis transcended two moments, as well as two levels of meaning. The Old Testament type represented a historical fact in the natural sense but also pointed to a future antitype with a New Testament fulfillment. Examples of types in Zwingli's Old Testament exegesis are manifold. Abraham is a personal type whose willingness to sacrifice his son Isaac points to God the Father, who offered his son. Enoch, Sarah, Isaac, Rachel and Jacob represent types of the spiritual Israel, while Cain, Hagar, Ishmael and Esau all represent fleshly Israel. Most numerous, however, are the biblical types referring to Jesus Christ. They include people such as Melchizedek, Isaac, Moses, Joshua and Cyrus, but also things such as the rock that provided water to the Israelites in the wilderness or Moses's bronze serpent that saved the Israelites who gazed upon it.

In general, Zwingli's exegesis of the Old Testament was historical and christological, not merely allegorical. He stressed the historicity of Old Testament events but also insisted that they served as examples and symbols recorded for the instruction of believers. In Zwingli's eyes the characters and events of the Old Testament often transcended their own temporal significance. What they prefigured reached fulfillment in Jesus Christ.

Significance. Zwingli, the Zurich prophet, passed on a rich exegetical legacy that benefitted preachers and expositors far beyond the confines of his Swiss homeland. Impelled by a zeal for God and God's Word, Zwingli redirected Christian faith and practice by a new Scripture principle that excluded religious authorities outside the Bible. In public sermons and debates he denied the authority of the Fathers and church councils to judge the Scriptures, arguing instead that Scripture is self-interpreting. Simple comparison of the Scriptures in the light of faith, he claimed, would show that clear passages illumine obscure ones. Despite a humble reliance on the Holy Spirit to guide his exposition, Zwingli recognized that a firm grasp of the Bible's languages, idioms, metaphors and genres was also needed. In order to impart this knowledge to a new generation of Reformed ministers, Zwingli established the Zurich Prophecy. The Prophecy school was so successful that it was imitated in England, the Palatinate and the Netherlands. Some scholars have called Zwingli a rationalist for his reliance on humanist philology and classical philosophy. Others have rightly charged that he merely replaced a Roman Catholic magisterium with a Protestant one. Ultimately Zwingli put his confidence in the power of the Word. He never doubted its power and once predicted that "the word of God will take its course as surely as the Rhine; you can dam it up for a while, but you cannot stop its flow" (*Sämtliche Werke*, 3:488).

BIBLIOGRAPHY

Works. U. Zwingli, *Huldrych Zwingli Writings,* ed. E. J. Furcha and H. W. Pipkin (2 vols.; Allison Park, PA: Pickwick, 1984); idem, *The Latin* Works and Correspondence of Huldreich Zwingli, ed. S. M. Jackson (3 vols.; New York: Putnam's 1912, 1922, 1929); idem, *Huldrych Zwinglis Sämtliche Werke,* ed. E. Egli (Corpus Reformatorum; Leipzig: Heinsius, 1905-); idem, *Selected works of Huldreich Zwingli, 1484-1531,* ed. S. M. Jackson (Philadelphia: University of Pennsylvania, 1901); idem, *Zwingli and Bullinger,* ed. G. W. Bromiley (LCC 24; Philadelphia: Westminster, 1953).

Studies. R. E. Davies, *The Problem of Authority in the Continental Reformers: A Study in Luther, Zwingli and Calvin* (London: Epworth, 1946); E. J. Furcha, "In Defense of the Spirit: Zwingli Authenticates His Reforms" in *Prophet, Pastor, Protestant,* ed. E. J. Furcha and H. W. Pipkin (Allison Park, PA: Pickwick, 1984); E. Künzli, "Zwingli als Ausleger des Alten Testamentes" in *Huldrych Zwinglis Sämtliche Werke,* ed. E. Egli (Corpus Reformatorum; Leipzig: Heinsius, 1905-) 14:869-99; G. R. Potter, *Zwingli* (Cambridge: Cambridge University Press, 1976); W. P. Stephens, *The Theology of Huldrych Zwingli* (Oxford: Clarendon, 1986).

I. L. Snavely Jr.

PART FOUR

Biblical Interpretation in the 18th & 19th Centuries

Any brief sketch of the history of biblical interpretation over two centuries in Europe must make bold decisions about what is most important. Even the definition of "Europe" itself deserves debate. But here only a few seminal patterns in biblical interpretation can be treated, and many contributions and historical factors must be left undiscussed.

My first priority will be to call attention to some distinctive modes of perceiving texts and interpretation in different epochs pertaining to the eighteenth and nineteenth centuries. Second, I will emphasize major developments and alternatives in the ongoing Christian search for "the literal sense" of Scripture. Perhaps today we have almost forgotten how in the middle of the second century A.D., coinciding with the first official publications of Christian Scripture, Irenaeus and other church leaders recognized the "literal" or "plain sense" of the Bible as the primary basis for arguments about faith and doctrine. This assumption, persisting over the centuries, was not greatly affected by the Reformation; *Aquinas and *Luther both concurred on it. A few essential elements of the literal sense were that (a) it could be publicly discerned by the community of faith, (b) the rule of faith accompanied interpretation, and (c) the literal sense became evident only when the grammar of the human witness of the Scripture could be heard together with the subject matter of God's revelation. For Irenaeus the rule of faith was an oral, unfixed confession that Christians expressed in common at baptism. Later it sometimes became identified with ecumenical creeds and confessions, or even with the teaching magisterium in Roman Catholic theology.

One problem is that interpreters over the centuries see this same "literal sense" through a different set of spectacles (an outdated term I prefer here over *glasses*).

The lens of these spectacles, before which the spectacle of the world passes by, must be ground with the technology of an interpreter's own time, and any text the interpreter can see will be illuminated by light refracted through them as well. For that reason alone, an agreement in theory on the ancient Christian ideal may, in the practices of interpreters from different epochs, seem contradicted by radical differences in their techniques of exposition and in the results.

With this awareness, the following overview will describe some key aspects of the historical and intellectual landscape of the eighteenth and nineteenth centuries in Europe, followed by a consideration of the consequences for the classical Christian consensus on the priority of the literal sense of Scripture. Treatment of major individuals will be kept to a minimum, with the assumption that more complete portraits of many of these key figures appear elsewhere in this book.

Labeling the Epochs of Biblical Interpretation

While centuries measure time in hundreds of years, an "epoch," "age" or "era" denotes a less exact period of time when certain ways of perceiving reality—the forms or modes of knowing the world—seem dominant and distinctive in contrast to preceding or following epochs. This general feature in human history has important consequences for biblical interpretation, because it often explains why the most obvious question to ask of any text, including Scripture, in one epoch may become irrelevant or almost unthinkable in another. These changes can be evident even on a physical level. Handwritten literature published as books or codices instead of scrolls did not become commonplace before the second and third centuries A.D. The way readers handled and read a scroll or a codex also changed over the different epochs. Not long after the medieval period, people started to assume that texts should normally be read individually and in silence, while in earlier times almost everyone would at least sound out the text when reading it alone, and commonly the text was meant to be read out loud so it could be heard by a larger public. In one sense, even when a book was printed, its text was oral.

By the late seventeenth century most European languages had standardized spelling, a sign that the text had become more than a record of sounds to be reverberated for the sake of those hearing, including the reader. In this respect, readers in the eighteenth century knew the "words" of a "text" differently from before, including words that since the Reformation and Renaissance belonged to numbered "verses" of the Bible. Thus biblical interpretation participates in the changing climate of perception from one epoch to another, no matter how similar the goals of reading a Scripture passage may be.

So in order to describe a history of interpretation of a given text—here, specifically, Christian Scripture—we need to have critical insight into how the interpreters in previous centuries knew and envisioned the text that we today see before us. Otherwise we fall prey to the delusion that we must be smarter than past interpreters whenever they miss what is obvious to us, and we will be unable to grasp their own genius and insight. Many critics today make the error of judging the acuity of earlier interpreters by how well they seem to anticipate our own predominantly modern or postmodern ways of viewing texts. If we focus on the interpretation of the literal sense of Christian Scripture by interpreters over the centuries, then our awareness of important differences in what interpreters can and did do with texts in various eras ought not to preclude the possibility that they also often pursued the same goals. Yet some of our judgments about how well interpreters in any era found and articulated the literal sense will require us to admit openly certain convictions we hold regarding the gospel itself, which is the subject matter of the literal sense. Here we admit that no one can write a proper history of a similitude over time without some subjective beliefs regarding the thing itself.

Therefore when we interpret past interpretations of the Bible, we will inevitably reveal our perspectives on what is this text that we share with the past and, for Christian interpretation of Scripture, what we consider pertinent to the nature of the literal sense over the centuries. We will inevitably make some theological decisions, or at least decisions about theology, beyond merely hermeneutical choices.

A Comparative Look at the Eighteenth and Nineteenth Centuries
The French philosopher, historian and literary critic Michel Foucault (1926-1984) considers these two centuries in Europe to belong to two fairly distinct epochs that follow the Renaissance. He detects the rise of the Classical Age from the second half of the seventeenth century, with its full development in the eighteenth, until it began to lose dominance near the end of that century. The Modern Age began to gain wide public acceptance toward the end of the eighteenth century and held sway through the nineteenth and twentieth centuries until its decline in the 1960s. This analysis assumes that the coherency of perception that defines an epoch, and consequently the prevailing mode of being for things in that period, can undergo a radical change, a transition that might become self-evident to public consciousness within the span of a few decades. Today many scholars debate whether we have experienced a major adjustment within the Modern Age or if our situation today is, as Foucault suggests, emergently postmodern, with the exact terms of a new consensus about perception as yet ill-defined.

In his *The Order of Things* Foucault sought to describe dimensions of the Classical Age and the Modern Age without trying to draft an comprehensive "picture" or to circumscribe "the spirit" of each period. He prefers to offer various "regional" studies of important topics: madness, economy, grammar, sexuality, criminology, medical care and so forth. Foucault relies on comparisons with earlier and later periods to score his points and highlight differences. For each epoch he also searches for signs of "a positive unconscious" drive to improve on past knowledge (Foucault, xi). This positive sense of discovery accompanies the form of knowing that prevails simultaneously and persistently among scientists, doctors, artists, historians, jurists and economists of the period. On a less sophisticated level, the present overview of biblical interpretation in the Classical Age and the early Modern Period is itself another "regional" study, like those Foucault attempted.

The Classical Age

Though summarizing the essence of this epoch is not my intent here, we do need some generalizations that point to its coherency in thinking, or what might be seen as regularities amid the dispersion of perspectives. The Classical Age may be characterized by its tendency to understand language as *representing* knowledge of the world, in contrast to the earlier Renaissance assumption that in its depictions language actually *resembles* what is real. Foucault argues that Cervantes makes this contrast explicit in his seminal novel *Don Quixote*. In the first half of the book Don Quixote appears as an exemplary failure of the Renaissance perspective. He presupposes that his language—both his internal thoughts and his spoken words—resemble, even reduplicate linguistically, reality itself. When Don Quixote defeats a windmill which he knows as a dangerous enemy, he feels the same sense of triumph as did any victor of ages previous. Only in the second half of the novel does he suspect that his own language may not correspond exactly to the world, but he realizes that his thoughts and spoken words do represent reality in the only way he can know it.

His life, then, belongs to this particular, richly textured story unfolding before him. The story itself locates him in time and space and specifies the options he can play out while accepting an adventurous leading role toward an unforeseen conclusion. He discovers a new way that language gives him knowledge of his life and existence, a reality that persists in the realm of language regardless of how well it relates to an external world separate from his linguistic encounter with it. On the basis of Cervantes's critique of the Renaissance, Foucault calls *Don Quixote* "the first work of modern literature," even though it was published as early as 1605 (Foucault, 48).

The positive insights of the Classical Age, a period identified by many scholars with "the Enlightenment," can be seen in unparalleled endeavors to organize the language we use to represent and know things into comprehensive tables, classifications, systems, taxonomies, concordances and encyclopedias. Fueled by this enthusiasm, Denis Diderot (1713-1784) and Jean le Rond d'Alembert (1717-1783) launched their monumental *Encyclopédie* project in 1751. A fresh sense of the whole panorama of human history, the powers and limits of reason, and the possibility of grand revisions in our view of literature, art and culture summoned the imagination of Europe's most gifted thinkers. Coinciding with these developments, Samuel Johnson (1709-1784) published his now-famous *Dictionary of the English Language* in 1755.

By the beginning of the eighteenth century the foundations had been laid for a new empiricism in the work of scientific pioneers such as Isaac Newton (1642-1727) and, above all, by John Locke's (1632-1704) affirmation that everything in the intellect is a response to some prior impingement on the senses. This view of ideas as elicited by physical or mechanistic reactions to external stimuli affirmed an empirical basis for ideas; they could be seen as truly representative of the world rather than products of mental fantasies or gifts of divine revelation transcending tangible everyday experiences. In philosophy, the quest for a systematic analysis of human thought and reality led to grand idealistic schemes such as George Berkeley's (1685-1753) proposal (at the beginning of the eighteenth century) that reality consists essentially of ideas and ordered sense impressions which God alone orchestrates with regularity, in concert with a divine purpose for all humanity. Ironically, this "empirical" theory denies the necessity of any physical existence of the things that our sense impressions might suggest. We and everyone else around us can have the same sense of sitting in a chair, thanks to God's persistent design for our experience, without the need for an actual chair. Gottfried Wilhelm von Leibniz's (1646-1716) *Monalogy,* published in 1714, advocated a theory no less grandiose and optimistic in aiming to show that reality tends toward an equilibrium of the best of all possible worlds.

Scholars in the Classical Age saw the need for a more scientific view of "history," grounded now in confidence that ideas must correspond properly to the particularity of past events that gave rise to them. Therefore the truth of a historical account depends on how accurately a historian can document the events that were the catalysts of human response, so that later readers can understand empathically, reexperience imaginatively and evaluate critically the same sense impressions that elicited the past wise and foolish ideas. When educated historians put into words the empirical reality of events that impinged on a certain people at a particular time, they sought to represent as objectively as possible this stimulus and response, free of the extraneous ideas or dogmas that plagued attempts at historical writing in earlier epochs.

So Johann Joachim Winckelmann's (1717-1768) *History of the Art of Antiquity* (1762) evoked a fresh post-Renaissance interest in classical Greek art and culture throughout Europe. But perhaps more important for purposes of our overview, Edward Gibbon's (1737-1794) *The History of the Decline and Fall of the Roman Empire* (1776-1788) illustrates an ideal wedding of the new empiricism to ideas based on the consequences engendered by specific casual conditions and human error in response. Gibbon's vast accumulation of empirical historical knowledge gave credibility to his ambition to make profound historical judgments about what in fact undermines a strong civilized society, whether ancient or contemporary. What now seemed obvious was that original historical events and the tangible sensations experienced by human beings must underlie any insight into ideas, language or texts from antiquity. Biblical interpreters naturally joined full voice in this chorus.

The Classical Age itself came to a close in the late eighteenth century, when scholars began to doubt how adequately the prevailing historical empiricism could name the stimuli behind all major ideas and choices of a given era. David Hume (1711-1776) helped precipitate this skepticism by taking up Berkeley's observations and developing them in a nontheistic direction. Hume argued that not all ideas derive from sense impressions, because, as just one example, we never really experience "causation," nor can we empirically observe it. What we can see is at most a constant conjunction between two events. The habitual tendency of our minds to organize, to associate and hence to make further sense, beyond what we can actually experience about these constant conjunctions, explains the idea of causation. As useful as the notion of "causation" may be, we cannot prove it empirically, nor is it directly accessible to us by means of a sense impression.

Immanuel Kant (1724-1804) brilliantly proposed a nonmetaphysical argument that could reconcile his deep respect for the precise, mathematically ordered advances in science associated with Newton and the unsettling perception of Hume that the idea of causation, an essential feature of the sciences, did not derive from direct experience nor could it be empirically verified. Kant argued that the human mind did not encounter a neutral external reality, but operated as an active agent upon sense impressions, employing habits for organizing and structuring data into a sensible reality. Ideas like space and time belonged a priori to the nature of the human mind as part of the framework through which it filtered stimuli. Hence even scientific knowledge was not a description of reality but a construction of the human mind. External reality in and of itself lay beyond our capacity to know. Scientific ideas belonged to "pure reason" in the sense that they responded directly to external stimuli and could be disconfirmed by experimentation. Metaphysical and many moral and religious ideas could not meet this criteria and, therefore, could never be true only according to "practical reason" without the same type of verifiability as expected of the sciences. The negative conclusion of his *Critique of Pure Reason* (1781) found compensation in his *Critique of Practical Reason* (1788), with the proposal that different kinds of reason validly have access to different types of knowledge. Practical reason may lay claim, unlike pure reason, to the logical necessity of "divine imperatives," required of moral reasoning. By putting the knowledge of transcendental ideas at the disposal of a separate mode of reasoning, Kant seemed, to many scholars, to weaken his case for the validity of transcendental ideas.

In the place of premodern theories of "wisdom" as a multilayered discourse created as one self-consciously bracketed out one's own religious ideas in order to discuss topics shared with anyone else in the world, a new option became possible—"secularity," with its beliefs based on events and ideas that earn empirical verification and consensus in modern historical and scientific terms. An affirmation of secularity, like the classical affirmation of wisdom, does not necessarily preclude anyone's assuming a bolder stance of faith dependent on other modes of verification or personal trust. For its own good reasons, modern secularity showed less tolerance for many terms that had been widely accepted and used generically in earlier wisdom discourse from various traditions—terms such as *God, prayer, fasts* and *prophets.* For example, in the 1850s George Jacob Holyoake (1817-1906) advocated "secularism" as a social movement that founded morality on evidence of the human pursuit of well-being, without any need for beliefs in God or the afterlife. The ancient distinction between international wisdom and local idiosyncratic beliefs had been replaced by a modern distinction between "secular" claims approximating Kant's "pure reason" and dogmatic or metaphysical claims which could not meet that criteria.

Biblical Interpretation in the Classical Age
Hans Frei (1922-1988) states emphatically, "Modern theology began in England at the turn of the seventeenth to the eighteenth century" (Frei, 51). The decisive issue seems to have been a shift in the perception of "revelation" in relation to both "history" and the testimony of Scriptures, Jewish and Christian. In earlier centuries Christians had expressed in various ways their confidence that the literal sense could be heard only when an interpreter could hold together the grammar of the human testimony and its true subject matter, which is God's revelation. Revelation for all of Christian Scripture, including both the "Old" and "New Testament," could be expressed as "the gospel of Jesus Christ," which incorporated into itself, in one way or another, the former revelation of the Torah (law/teaching) through Jewish Scripture. During the eighteenth century, critics began to view the testimony of Scripture as an effort, inspired or not, to *represent* ancient history and God's revelation within it, instead of the earlier conception that in the literal sense the human words of Scripture may actually *resemble* God's own revealed Word within history, offering a revelation about the nature of history itself.

Consequently, the search for the literal sense in the eighteenth century required efforts to recognize the various representational dimensions of a biblical text, including its antecedents in what scholars identified as older written "sources." In line with this perception of the biblical text, "history" became an extrabiblical norm discovered by the Enlightenment, which logically assigned the greatest value to the "original" text of the Bible over the *textus receptus* of Bibles published in the intervening centuries, the earlier over the later "sources" that scholars could reconstruct from the Bible, and "the [human] author's original intent" over evidence of "nongenuine" additions, called "glosses," "supplements," secondary "interpolations," or other omissions and manipulations of the older sources by ancient editors and copyists. In turn, reconstructions of the original texts or sources, of the original history and of the original revelation could complement, check, confirm or rival the capacities of Scripture to represent the same.

This awareness of representational levels in a text of Scripture was made less threatening by an assumption, maintained until late modernity, that a scholar might validly call all the reconstructions of "original" texts and history "biblical tradition." So the original words of any prophet included in the Old Testament, words attributed to the historical Jesus, or the authentic letters of the apostle Paul were "biblical," and "biblical history" included whatever actually happened in ancient time implicit from the representations, even if accessible only by an enlightened reconstruction of the events. In other words, the idea that reconstructed texts and traditions taken *from* the Bible were usually "prebiblical" and became biblical only when they attained a different canonical context in Judaism or Christianity did not gain wide recognition before the late twentieth century.

Christians had traditionally expressed confidence that Jesus as the Messiah fulfilled Old Testament prophecies according to their literal sense. Now this long-held position had to be reexamined through the lens of a new historical and empirical acuity. While defending the old confessional position, William Whiston (1667-1752) had to admit that most citations of the Old Testament in the New go well beyond the literal sense when they appeal to prophecies fulfilled by Jesus Christ. He dubiously tried to solve the problem by blaming these discrepancies on Jews who, he speculated, had emended the "original" texts of the Old Testament for the purpose of discrediting what had been an earlier, successful Christian literal sense interpretation. Whiston proposed that the newer techniques of text criticism could recover the original text of the Old Testament on which the New Testament writers literally relied.

As anti-Semitic as Whiston's effort now appears, he illustrates well a confidence that new historical perceptions of his day might introduce anomalies that equally new technology might explain away. His solution thus is entirely up to date, since it depended on recent techniques of textual criticism, pioneered by Johannes Albrecht *Bengel (1687-1752) in the opening decades of the eighteenth century. Textual critics could try to ameliorate the results of newer historical criticisms, precisely because most historical and textual critics agreed that the earliest textual evidence found in Scripture is always better, a position that, again, would not be seriously questioned until late in the Modern Age.

In 1724 Anthony Collins (1676-1729), a deist and friend of John Locke, published a widely read treatise, *A Discourse of the Grounds and Reasons of the Christian Religion*, using Whiston's proposal as a foil. While Collins could easily make mockery of Whiston's suggestion that Jews emended the text, he seized upon Whiston's concession that the New Testament consistently depends on nonliteral interpretations of the Old Testament in appeals to messianic fulfillment. In a later publication (1727), Collins concluded that the New Testament writers used the same nonliteral midrashic rules of interpretation as did Jewish rabbis of their period.

Now a new problem presented itself in relation to the literal sense of Scripture. If New Testament writers depended on nonliteral interpretations, then their interpretive techniques contradicted the classical Christian norm of "the literal sense" as the only basis for arguments about doctrine and failed to make any compelling historical case for prophetic fulfillment. Hence the literal sense as the norm of theological interpretation seemed ignored within Scripture itself, by its own earliest Christian interpreters of the Old Testament.

The use of typology seemed to Collins an even easier target to dismiss as nonliteral interpretation, despite a long tradition of Christian interpreters who argued for its place, distinct from allegory or spiritual interpretations, within the literal sense. In the second half of the seventeenth century, when interpreters first began to view the Bible primarily in terms of its capacity to represent a past history, typology itself had to be reevaluated according to the perspective that the depictions in the biblical text represent past persons, events and things. Typology gave attention to the plastic *form* or *type* of certain past persons, events and things indicative of an archetype which according to phenomenal prophecy could be fully satisfied, made complete or fulfilled in later persons, events and things. David was thus a type of Christ, and Israel a type of the church. The avalanche of typological interpretation near the end of the seventeenth century exploited this possible strategy to its outer limits, causing its collapse under the weight of conspicuous abuse. If in fact the biblical text primarily *represents* past events, whether accurately or not, then few scholars could see room for the older logic of typology, which had looked to the Bible as inspired testimony to make known literally the prophetic potential and hope associated with the forms of past persons, events and things.

My point is that the evidence supporting typology within the literal sense did not look the same in the eighteenth century as it had looked to earlier interpreters. Any justification for typology's role within the literal sense seemed more difficult than ever, especially after the excesses in its use toward the end of the seventeenth century.

From a variety of other directions, additional questions could be raised about the rationality and likelihood of revelation itself. These questions were heightened by a new perception of intractable historical contradictions within the Bible, alongside extraordinary depictions of some events (e.g., the flood) and quasi-scientific statements at odds with the now-dominant Newtonian physics and an astronomy widely accepted since Copernicus, Galileo and Kepler. Christians who appealed to Scripture to assert that God had repeatedly intervened in the affairs of human history to reveal ideas and to work "miracles" now confronted scholars who sought plausible, nonmiraculous explanations for whatever appeared extraordinary in the past. Even when this disposition conjoined with a Romanticist sensitivity toward God's imminent presence in nature and history, scholars would still challenge the classical Jewish and Christian understanding of God's special revelation in history to one group of people over others. Hence Kant's practical reason made room for all religions on one level but cast doubt on the historical peculiarities of Jewish and Christian faith.

In Germany, Gotthold Ephraim Lessing (1729-1781) edited and published from 1774 to 1778 the *Wolfenbüttel Fragments,* posthumously making public the reflections of Hermann Samuel *Reimarus (1694-1768), a respected professor of Hebrew and oriental languages at Hamburg from 1744 to 1767. Reimarus appeared to prove by historical criticism that the biblical writers were frauds who did not hesitate to fabricate historical details. Reimarus identified the literal sense of the Bible negatively with "the letter" rather than "the spirit." He insisted that Christian faith rests on the "inner truth" of the Bible, not the surpluses of its external representations. The rule of faith in earlier centuries assumed a preunderstanding of the gospel that each reader brings to the reading of Scripture; this now began to be replaced by an "inner" truth discerned either by the spirit or by reason alone.

Lessing's publication of Reimarus helped him play a major role in the Aufklarüng (Enlightenment) in central Europe, a movement similar to that of the deists in England. He rejected miracles and advocated a humanitarian morality based on reason rather than claims of special revelation. Lessing himself also made some contributions to New Testament criticism and laid the groundwork for positions later held by Protestant liberalism, which dominated in the universities of Germany throughout the nineteenth century.

Other scholars such as Johann Salomo *Semler (1725-1791) openly encouraged the use of historical criticism in spite of the unorthodox views of history it inspired, yet they expected scholars to maintain classical Christian confessions, especially as they disclosed universal religious and moral truths. Semler presupposed a development in moral consciousness culminating in later Christian ideas. He invited scholars to reassess the inspiration, content and value of each biblical book according to "their [the scholars'] own representation of much better truths" (Frei, 331 n. 6). Luther's criticisms of the book of James on the basis of the rule of faith now warranted the right of these modern "neologians," as they

were called in the eighteenth century, to evaluate all biblical books in terms of
fidelity to a Christian consensus on universal ideas. Semler, by his reliance on an
external truth, was also a harbinger of scholars who bifurcated their loyalties,
practicing historical skepticism in academic commentaries while endorsing pious,
conventional confessional positions in their theology and preaching.

Noting the obscurity of Semler's statements on inspiration and revelation in
Scripture, Johann Gottfried *Eichhorn (1752-1827) made a more precise assessment of how biblical traditions gradually improved in their revelatory capacity
over time. The New Testament must be affirmed as the essential norm and guide
to those truths by which we might judge biblical traditions. Eichhorn's detailed
treatment of the first three chapters of Genesis, published in 1779, was elaborately
expanded by Johannes Gabler's (1753-1826) extensive introductions to other
parts of the Bible in 1790-1793. For his comments on the New Testament,
Gabler relied heavily on the impressive synthesis of Johann David *Michaelis
(1717-1791), published in 1788. The resulting five-volume work of Eichhorn-
Gabler was used as a reliable guide to the best of historical criticism and even
served as a resource during the rise of historical criticism in institutions of the
United States in the middle of the nineteenth century. While supernaturalists
might be offended by this work's tolerance for historical discrepancies in the
Bible, pietists felt just as threatened by the evidence of unresolved disagreements
in the teachings of the Bible, especially in the Synoptic Gospels.

A few scholars responded much more aggressively by taking various modified
supernaturalist positions. Sigmund Jacob Baumgarten (1686-1760) became a
professor at Halle, where he defended Scripture, as a confessional Lutheran, in a
sophisticated manner. He affirmed the inspiration of Scripture, with confidence
that the revealed Word of God cannot logically be separated from its true
representation of salvation history. While the Bible discloses a revelation beyond
that accessible in nature and history, Baumgarten regarded biblical revelation as
never in conflict with either reason or insights from physics, the natural sciences
or astronomy. He defended a variation of the older position on the literal sense
without denying alternative historical senses perceived by the newer historical
criticisms. His position included room for "biblical theology" as the endeavor of
technical biblical scholars to examine from various angles the key biblical texts
that provided the basis in revelation for church doctrine.

Baumgarten depended heavily on the hermeneutical ideas of Christian Wolff
(1679-1754), who in the new climate of the eighteenth century defended the
older idea that a concept or a text is a "representation of a subject matter." By
insisting on the reality of the subject matter ontologically rather than simply
historically, Wolff advocated a "meaning-as-reference" theory in support of a
possible reality, instead of treating reference as merely a middle term between the
words of a text and their meaning in the form of textually external ideas, persons

or events found elsewhere in the world. Wolff suggested a distinction between the clarification of words *(Worderklärung)* and clarification of subject matter *(Sacherklärung)*, while endeavoring not to sever the necessary relationship between the two. This proposal became a common feature of many later hermeneutical efforts.

Johann August *Ernesti (1707-1781) perhaps deserves recognition as the foremost contributor to the reformulation of classical hermeneutical rules for the clarification of texts, setting explicative practices of interpretation apart from efforts to apply biblical texts to contemporary life. Similarly, Gottlob Wilhelm Meyer (1768-1816) published a five-volume review of the history of biblical interpretation, focusing on the rules that best apply to the analysis of biblical texts. He concurred with Ernesti's effort to distinguish between the clarification of a text and its theological application. By reexamining the proper rules that might govern the literal sense of Scripture, and by distinguishing explication from application, Meyer and Ernesti helped define the role of biblical scholars as participating in a more neutral investigation than that expected from earlier expositions of church theologians and preachers.

Johannes Gabler, a new professor in Altdorf, gave his inaugural address in 1787 that picked up these major trends at the end of the eighteenth century and brought them together in an attractive synthesis. He identified "biblical theology" as not just an analysis of key texts used by theologians but its own unified, objectively attainable synthesis of the universal ideas embedded within the particular ideas of the Bible. He proposed a discipline of "biblical theology" on analogy to the efforts of scholars in the philosophy department of the university to describe systematically the views, for example, of the Sophists. The subject matter of the biblical text became for Gabler the enduring "Religious Content of the Hebrews," as the subtitle of his famous *oratio* states explicitly. The resulting synopsis of religion could subsequently be handed over to dogmatic theologians as an essential resource in the deliberation over contemporary theology.

Georg Lorenz Bauer (1755-1806) published one of the first attempts at Old Testament theology in 1796, with the subtitle *A Summary of the Religious Concepts of the Hebrews.* Christoph Friederich von Ammon's (1766-1849) biblical theology (circulated in 1792 and published as a revised edition in 1801-1802) tried to refine "Kantian hermeneutics" to allow for a critical assessment of the moral development of religion in ancient Israel. Like most biblical scholars, he found Kant's own meager efforts at biblical interpretation historically naive and too open to a similarly positive literary evaluation of scriptures from other religions.

In sum, "biblical theology," as an activity of biblical specialists distinct from dogmatic or church theologians, became an attractive possibility in the eighteenth century that was enthusiastically pursued in the following centuries, despite many serious disagreements over its strategies, goals and relation to Christian theology in general.

The Modern Age: The Nineteenth Century

We may in very general terms argue that the move from the Classical to the Modern Age entailed a shift from viewing language, literature and texts as representative of reality to a perception of language primarily as symbols or signs *referring* to a reality external to the text and accessible also by nontextual means of inquiry, often with a greater claim to scientific objectivity. In the Modern Age of nineteenth-century Europe, beyond the imagination of the Classical Age, the substance of persons, events, ideas and things became further grounded in the specificity of their time and place and a deeper assessment of circumstance. Regarding these radical changes from the Classical to Modern Age, Foucault summarizes:

The theory of representation [in the Classical Age] disappears as the universal foundation of all possible order; . . . Language . . . as the indispensable link between representation and things, is eclipsed in its turn; a profound historicity penetrates into the heart of things, isolates and defines them in their own coherence, imposes upon them the form of order implied by the continuity of time. (Foucault, xxiii)

Within this prevailing historicism, a tension became evident between two unharmonized sensitivities among nineteenth-century humanists. On the one hand, rationalist historians, building on Giovanni Battista Vico's (1668-1744) *Scienza nuova* (1725) sought to find greater precision in knowing how any text might mediate accurate information about actual historical events. These approaches often combined aesthetic criticism with social-scientific approaches to refine the understanding of specific genres of literature—for example, myth, fairy tale, legend and proverb—so that scholars could empathetically interpret the original, usually oral, form and social function of an ancient tradition. Since the modern genre of "history" lacked an exact precedent in antiquity, even the most historylike texts from premodern centuries now required a fresh critical analysis to determine when and how they can be trusted to report accurately past events and ideas. Likewise, rationalist historians could agree, as in the title of Leopold von Ranke's (1795-1886) publication in 1881, in the need for *Universal History*, which sought to extrapolate from particular historical events the persistent principles of historical reality. Ranke stressed the importance of using original sources and objective strategies. His own work on a history of the popes pursued these principles and stood apart from earlier studies that openly defended a denominational bias.

On the other hand, a nineteenth-century romanticist emphasis on a poetic pursuit of the depth of historical life can be associated with German scholars such as Johann Gottfried Herder (1744-1803) and Friederich *Schleiermacher (1768-1834). Both brought a profound aesthetic sensitivity, a poetically trained ear, to hear the inner resonances of ancient texts. Herder introduced the German term *Einfuhlung*, which we might best understand as an empathetic imagination, alert to the "spirit" of an age to which a text belongs. In general, German romanticists sought an inwardness or depth below the surface of narrative realism, as much as their historicist counterparts sought an idealistic height above.

A new option in "realistic," or "naturalistic," literature gained sway in the late nineteenth century almost everywhere in Europe outside Germany. Novels, short stories and plays endeavored to describe reality objectively on the basis of close observation, induction and a careful presentation of the details of character and manners, including the depiction of persons from the middle and lower classes. for them, "universal history" belonged to this accessible realism even when the characters and circumstances were fictional. Due to the high value placed on human feelings, impressions and moral outrage, these writers stood within the tradition of eighteenth-century romanticism, as argued in Jean-Jacques Rousseau's (1712-1778) *Discours sur les sciences et les arts* (1750) and as illustrated profoundly by Johann Wolfgang von Goethe (1749-1832). However, nineteenth-century realists rejected the romantic idealization of the hero, one-sidedly rhapsodic accounts of nature, and any assumption of innocence or immediacy of perception among the lower classes or primitive people. The sordid, low and trivial might be a clearer window into the soul of human life than the gestures of high culture. Although the term *realism* dates back to the turn of the century, to Johann Christoph Frederich von Schiller (1759-1805) and August Wilhelm von Schlegel (1767-1845), it became identified with a movement in art in France by the 1850s and was used as a literary slogan by Émile Zola (1840-1902) around 1880. Soon after, George Augustus Moore (1852-1933) and George Robert Gissing (1857-1903) brought new of this approach from France to England. This important literary movement included Honorè Balzac (1799-1850) and Gustave Flaubert (1821-1880) in France, Fyodor Dostoevsky (1821-1881) and Leo Tolstoy (1828-1910) in Russia, Charles Dickens (1812-1870) and Charlotte Brontë (1816-1855) in England, and Henrik Ibsen (1828-1906) in Norway. A well written narrative could figuratively render reality and illuminate the tangibly real stuff of life; that is to say, it fully corresponded to the selfsame reality that permeates the warp and woof of human history—yesterday, today and tomorrow. Some literary and theological scholars tried to apply such theory to the interpretation of the Bible, though most scholars of that era seemed more enamored by the debates over the results of modern historical criticisms.

Near the end of the nineteenth century, the realism of literary efforts associated with Romanticism began to be called into question, notably by the fathers of suspicion—Sigmund Freud (1856-1939), Friedrich Nietzsche (1844-1900) and

Karl Marx (1818-1883). The determinants of reality seemed to lie somewhere beneath the surface of historylike narratives. This shift in perspective may have been partly evoked by the revolutions that erupted throughout Europe around 1848. Literary scholars began to discover the hidden nodes of power and decisive factors that lurk in places accessible only to specialists—in the deep structures of language itself, in a materialist analysis of the modes of production that determine social order, in repressed psychological desires, or in the amoral egoistic drives hidden behind the superficial human language of virtues and vices (e.g., Nietzsche's *Beyond Good and Evil,* 1886). Many literary critics at the end of the nineteenth century bemoaned the decline of serious realistic novels as they were replaced by ponderous socioeconomic, ideological and psychological studies.

Shifts in these humanistic perspectives and the growing sophistication of literary-historical "methodologies" became especially significant for biblical interpretation in Europe. In the eighteenth century from Vico to Voltaire, Gibbon and Herder, and in the nineteenth century from Georg Wilhelm Friedrich Hegel (1770-1831) to Alexis de Tocqueville (1805-1859), Leo Tolstoy (1828-1910) and Leopold von Ranke, the effort to evaluate the historical references of texts to past events steadily became more refined, technical and double-checked by extratextual evidence. For the ancient classics, scholars sought to recover the oldest parts retained despite an alien editorial *Tendenz.* The reconstructed traditions were alone considered historically "genuine" and a true "primary source." Similarly, scholars distinguished "original authors" sharply from the later hands of editors, redactors or collators of texts.

Especially in England, critics became preoccupied with understanding "the historical author's original intent." This approach required one to move from the text, aided by extratextual information about the time when the text was written, to the mind of its supposed author. Once a critic entered the author's mind, he or she would need to nuance further the concept of "intention" to distinguish it from other psychic features, including secondary intentions and cultural conditioning. Continental critics in line with the legacy of Herder often applied an aesthetic criticism and spiritual sensitivity to the social function of specific genres, including myths. An empathic reimagining of the ancient form and function of a "living" tradition, usually oral, could allow the critic to describe its historical enactment and then find typical elements that were unconsciously retained in the tradition. These typical elements provided the critic with inadvertent and therefore historical vestiges of what an ancient people at a particular time believed to be true of their world.

To a degree, James Frazer's (1854-1941) *The Golden Bough* represented the British version of this effort to find some real historical significance in the recapitulation of the typical within nonhistorical genres of literature. At the same time, Romanticist approaches like those of Goethe, Hegel, Søren *Kierkegaard

(1813-1855), Nietzsche (in his own way) and William James (1842-1910) exerted great influence. However, by the end of the nineteenth century such articulate defenders of a refined sensitivity of the human spirit struggled against a tide of academic confidence in the secular search for greater scientific objectivity in literary, historical and social studies.

What the older empiricism of the Classical Age gained in the Modern Age was an effort to find a general theory of interpretation, perhaps analogous to the new unified theories in the sciences. The work of Friedrich *Schleiermacher (1768-1834), associated with the founding ideals of Berlin University, stands as a paragon in the triumph of a Modern form of knowing over its predecessors. He is arguably the most important transitional figure from the eighteenth to the nineteenth century. While Schleiermacher celebrated the new scientific impulse, he also encouraged a sensitivity akin to Romanticism, especially in his concern to grasp the decisive inner subjectivity of an author rather than merely the author's superficial intent. On this basis he conjoined the Romanticist cause to modern scientific investigations in his treatise *On Religion: Speeches to Its Cultured Despisers* (1799).

Another major contribution by Schleiermacher was his sharp distinction between the art of formulating speech, or even the rules and principles for explaining texts—which Schleiermacher called "the external side of understanding"—and the act of understanding itself. Hermeneutics should not focus primarily on "rules" as it had in the past but should seek an answer to prior and formerly neglected questions: What does it mean to understand text in general or how text? How do texts contribute to meaningful discourse? Wilhelm Dilthey (1833-1911) further developed these insights in his *Introduction to the Human Sciences* in 1883 by suggesting an interpreter of a text should try empathetically to "re-live" the experience of the other who has written it. The relation of biblical interpretation to such "general hermeneutics" for all literature became a major issue throughout the nineteenth and twentieth centuries.

Biblical Interpretation in the Modern Age

Alongside the challenges confronted in the eighteenth century, the Christian search for the literal sense of Scripture in the nineteenth century faced an intensification of historical-critical methods, accompanied by a whole array of newer scientific, sociological, economic and psychological means of analysis. Equally significant, Schleiermacher paved the way for the theory of a general hermeneutics applicable to all texts and dependent on current knowledge of the arts and human sciences. At several places in his work, Schleiermacher proposed that a "special hermeneutics" was needed to supplement the general hermeneutics whenever it is applied to Scripture, because of the peculiar relation of the biblical witness to inspiration and revelation. This suggestion never achieved an adequate development in his work. His later interpreters usually ignored it. In his own writings, it encompassed little more than attention to idiosyncrasies such as Aramaisms in the Greek of the New Testament. Still, his definition of revelation at the beginning of *Christian Faith* would seem to require far more than what one could expect from his theory of general hermeneutics. Schleiermacher's own piety and veneration of Scripture may have allowed him to leave many of these issues unaddressed.

In Germany, throughout Europe and in England, Schleiermacher's insights helped to make commonplace the assumption that one should read Scripture like any other book. The literal sense of Scripture, more often than not, would simply be identified with a fair-minded application to the Bible of the most promising general hermeneutics. Whether fair-mindedness required, in fact, a piety worthy of the authors of Scripture remained a debatable issue. In my view, Schleiermacher's reservations about letting a modern theory of general hermeneutics define the literal sense of Scripture will prove to be one of the greatest signs of his genius when we consider the end of the Modern Age in Europe, in the last decades of the twentieth century.

Frederic W. Farrar (1831-1903) was a worthy counterpart to Schleiermacher in England. In his brilliant *History of Interpretation,* delivered as the Bampton Lectures at Oxford in 1895 and published a year later, he states his "one object" to be an assertion of "the divine authority of the Holy Scriptures" (Farrar, 5). Farrar finds proof of the divine authority of the Bible "in its simple meaning, in its native majesty . . . as a manifold record of a progressive revelation" (Farrar, 6). He links this "simple meaning" with confidence in the Reformation that Christian faith depends on "the literal sense alone" (Farrar, 325-32). He quotes favorably Luther's observation that heresies arise "from *neglecting* the simple words of Scripture" (Farrar, 327). But the real key to Farrar's modern understanding of the literal sense can be seen in his comments on Schleiermacher. Farrar says, "He gave greater impulse to exegesis than any one since Calvin," and declares flatly, "The more constructive movement of the new epoch began with Schleiermacher" (Farrar, 410 n. 1, 409). Farrar also finds Schleiermacher's piety to be an important element that protected him from falling prey to a naive modern rationalism. The same proves true in Farrar's own proposals.

For Farrar, the aim of the interpreter is "to ascertain the specific meaning of the inspired teacher, and to clothe it in the forms which will best convey the meaning to the minds of his contemporaries." For support he quotes in a footnote lines from Augustine, Ernesti, Goethe and Kuenen. Also, a "perfect exegete" would possess "a genius cognate with that of the sacred writer," so that the interpreter would be thoroughly honest and devoid of any "misleading influences" due to "his own *a priori* convictions" (Farrar, 4-5). Under such analysis, the authority of the Bible rests solely on "the simplest statement of plain facts"

(Farrar, 6). Because "secular History" itself participates in a progressive revelation of the Holy Spirit, and because Christians have "inherited [from Jews] the fatal legacy of Palestinian and Alexandrian methods," Farrar does not flinch from showing that "past methods of interpretation were erroneous" (Farrar, 10-11). In brief, he identifies the development of modern views, like those of Schleier-macher, as themselves a revelation by the Holy Spirit within "secular History." With pious sensitivity Farrar seeks direct access to the "plain facts" confirming the divine authority of Scripture as superior to that of other books.

As an exponent of modern apologetics, Farrar employed historicism to refute both secularism and rationalism. While his own theory of a modern general hermeneutics applies to all literature, he hoped that same logic would help to prove the special nature of Scripture. He openly expressed his disappointment with the more radical historical conclusions of biblical critics in Germany after Schleiermacher.

When biblical scholars tried to apply a general hermeneutics to Scripture, most found in that strategy support for viewing the biblical text as essentially *referring* to an ancient world that invited explication in terms of historical, psychological, economic, sociological, idealistic or philosophical forces. Ironically, when biblical scholars relied on general hermeneutics to justify historical criticisms, comparative literary critics who taught in the same universities often looked to representational realism, as mentioned above. This situation in Europe commonly drove a wedge between interpretation by biblical scholars, conservative or liberal, and how the Bible was interpreted by scholars associated with literary departments. The historical bias of biblical scholars coincided with the birth of modern archaeology and discoveries of a plethora of inscriptions from the ancient Near East.

Much of modern biblical interpretation might be described as two types of translation. On the most simple level, fresh knowledge of cognate languages and the discovery of inscriptions spanning the entire biblical period justified a need for new translations of the Bible for public use. On a more complex level, if the words of the Bible were thought to have meaning primarily in terms of the ancient intentions and events to which they referred, then their mythic, edited and "secondary" features required a biblical specialist to translate into modern referential language the real world to which ancient texts referred. For most scholars the subject matter of the biblical text therefore could no longer be immediately a revelation from God to Jews and Christians; instead revelation had to be related in more explicitly historical manner to the flesh and blood of persons, things, ideas and events of an ancient world. The biblical text existed primarily as a tarnished surviving artifact.

Emphasis on the esoteric characteristics of the ancient world gained popular support in the discovery of dinosaurs and paleolithic remains, and especially Charles Darwin's (1809-1882) groundbreaking *On the Origin of Species* (1859).

The perceived distance between the present and the past seemed to increase. Language, particularly antiquarian mythic and ritual-related words in the Bible, now sounded more foreign than before to a modern audience who wished to know its true historical significance. While in premodern centuries Christians considered the subject matter of the literal sense to be the same as God's revelation of the gospel, the modern problem became how actual historical events reconstructed from the Bible could themselves disclose revelation, especially in the Old Testament.

This modern referential reading of the Bible gained enough consensus among biblical scholars that they could publicly agree to disagree about their differing conclusions. In the United States near the end of the nineteenth century, biblical scholars often seemed to be divided into two parties, "conservative" (or "orthodox") and "liberal." Both could claim to be "evangelical" in the marketplace of denominations constituting Protestantism. In Europe, "evangelical" usually meant the national Protestant church distinguished from Roman Catholics. A scholar's theological stance might be complicated by the inclusive nature of a national church and a confessional piety that often cut across the lines of difference between historical critics. Moreover, biblical scholars often sought their own sophisticated philosophical ways to reconcile the conflicts between the results of historical criticism and Christian faith. An emphasis on progressive revelation allowed many to make a moderately pejorative assessment of the Old Testament while preserving most of the New Testament as the primary basis for the gospel.

As an example, Wilhelm Vatke (1806-1882) sought to abandon the sterile rationalism of Kant for the Romanticist possibilities of Hegel's dialectical system. Vatke thought any epoch could find at most a relative objectivity, due to the limits of its own historical consciousness and mode of comprehending reality. In Hegel he found a grand scheme for moving beyond conflicting historical impulses toward a distant horizon of universal history. Only from the theoretical perspective of that universal history could a scholar's judgments about the value of religious ideas transcend the subjectivity inherent in both the ancient world to which a text referred and the contemporary scholar's own historical time and place.

Both Vatke and his friend David Friedrich *Strauss (1808-1874) faced strong criticisms, especially for their abandonment of conventional dogmatic categories in favor of more novel Hegelian constructions based on their historical estimate of the ancient religious ideas preserved in biblical texts. Strauss similarly had hoped to employ Hegel to move beyond the largely negative results of his historical reconstruction of the life of Jesus (*Life of Jesus*, 1835-1836). Unlike deists and naturalists, he sought to expose within the Gospels the mythological and contradictory elements that stood in the way of a positive reevaluation of the incarnation and other New Testament traditions. He was shocked by the reaction and condemnation his book evoked.

In Germany, Eduard Reuss (1804-1891), Karl Heinrich Graf (1815-1869), Abraham Kuenen (1828-1891) and especially Julius *Wellhausen (1844-1918) reordered the historical sequence of the various "sources" of the Pentateuch into what became a widely accepted theory of JEDP. The Priestly source (P) was viewed as a postexilic document composed when Jews abandoned the ethical dynamism of prophecy to accept the authority of priests, who molded Judaism into a religion of legalistic and ritualized behavior. Aside from the blatantly anti-Jewish tone of this view, it is predicated on a reappraisal of both what was "prophecy" and, ultimately, what was God's revelation in ancient Israel. "Prophecy" became a topic in its own right, defined by theories about the social role and nature of prophetic speech. By restricting the perception of prophecy to a particular kind of historical phenomenon, Christians could easily question the traditional Jewish belief that the writers of Scripture were "prophets" rather than priests. This historical interpretation of the prophets in the Old Testament, however, found its counterpart in similar questions that could be raised about the activity of "apostles" in the New. Although Christians had traditionally claimed all the writers of the New Testament were "apostles," modern historical definitions precluded such an historical appellation for Mark or Luke, for example. Hence the new studies could seem to threaten premodern Christian ideas about the "inspiration" of Scripture insofar as they depended on the assurance that Scripture was written by "the holy prophets" and the "apostles" (2 Pet 3:1-2; cf. 2 Tim 3:16; Heb 1:1-2). Most scholars granted that not all the writers of the Bible were "prophets" or "apostles" according to modern historical criteria.

Just as JEDP became an attractive reconstruction of "sources" in the Pentateuch, so similar studies found in the Gospels and letters of Paul earlier and later sources of tradition. In the last half of the nineteenth century, Schleiermacher, Karl Lachmann (1793-1851), Christian Gottlob Wilke (1786-1854) and Christian Hermann Weisse (1801-1866) had already made a convincing case for the dependence of Matthew and Luke on Mark, as well as on a lost, possibly oral tradition of sayings, later called Q (for German *Quelle,* "source"). This new position became a strong rival to the earlier critical position of J. J. *Griesbach (1745-1812), who argued that Matthew had been used as a primary source for Luke.

In the debate over the literal sense of Scripture, these historical proposals raised questions never before considered. Commonly scholars spoke of Q as a "biblical" tradition. If Q is an older, more historically reliable source than either Matthew or Luke, then is its literal sense superior biblically to that of the later Gospels? If the strength of a biblical tradition lies in the ability of its writers to refer to God's revelation in history, then is Q a more reliable witness to the gospel? With a modern awareness that Luke was not historically an apostle, what would prevent the author of Q from being as "inspired" as Luke, especially when much of Q claims to quote original words of Jesus?

Besides these developments, the opening decades of the nineteenth century included a large number of "biblical theologies." in Europe along the lines of Gabler's exciting proposal or in reaction to it. Wilhelm Martin Leberecht *De Wette (1780-1849) in 1813, Gottlieb Philip Christian Kaiser (1781-1847) in 1813, Ludwig Friedrich Otto Baumgarten-Crusius (1788-1843) in 1828, Carl Peter Wilhelm Gramberg (1797-1830) in 1829-1830, Wilhelm Vatke in 1835 and others explored this new terrain. Often their proposals concurred with Gabler's emphasis on the synthesis of ancient religious ideas, while others tried to write a history of religion or to describe the emergence of seminal theological positions (e.g., monotheism) in ancient Israel or in the time of Jesus and the apostle Paul. Some sought to present ideas objectively as modern historians of ancient ideas, while others asserted positive theological appraisals in anticipation of the classical Christian confessions.

The problem remained how a "biblical theology" might circumscribe a theological task designed for biblical specialists, distinct from the use of the Bible by dogmatic or church theologians in the same universities or seminaries. If Christian theology depends on the literal sense, one could ask how this distinction can avoid implying two literal senses, one for biblical specialists and one for church theologians. A similar problem had been seen much earlier when Luther initially accepted the idea of a double literal sense suggested by *Nicholas of Lyra (c. 1270-1349)—with one literal sense pertaining to grammatical and historical elements, similar to the Jewish plain sense *(peshat)*, and with a second literal sense in the hearing of the same words as a testimony to Jesus Christ. In any case, "biblical theology" itself, whether conservative or liberal, had become a modern preoccupation that moved in directions unprecedented in the premodern period and raised its own questions about the literal sense of Scripture.

Finally, we need to examine the conception of an "author," which seemed among most biblical scholars to be an almost self-evident idea and one even supported by the older formulation of the literal sense of Scripture. In earlier centuries, biblical interpreters presupposed that when interpreters found the literal sense of Scripture, they had concurrently grasped the human writer's intent. Matthias Flacius *Illyricus (1520-1575), often cited as an early pioneer who anticipated modern hermeneutical theory, advised interpreters in pursuit of the literal sense of Scripture that they ought to "keep in mind, first of all, the scope, purpose, or intention of the whole book/work which is, as it were, its head or face." But in Flacius's words, the "intent" is only one of several dimensions related more immediately to the context of a whole book than to the reconstruction of historical "authors" and exactly what they alone may have written or intended.

Schleiermacher himself carefully avoided the naive idea of an author's original "intent" as the goal of interpretation, but most biblical scholars simply employed the term *intent* as a natural adjunct to their modern focus on the text as a set of verbal references to the reality of an ancient past. In the Modern Age it became commonplace to try to reconstruct individual historical authors, and their original intents, by removing the intrusions of editors or atomizing the biblical context into its older "sources" without ever reading a biblical book as a whole. Of course the original historical authors might not have in mind any direct reference to God's revelation, or like the apostle Paul they might distinguish between moments of revelation and their own opinions. Therefore biblical scholars, even when they wrote "biblical theology," usually did not try to sustain the older Christian assumption that an interpreter finds the literal sense only when the words testify to the subject matter of God's revelation. Though premodern interpreters had needed to develop strategies for occasions when they could not find "the literal sense" of a biblical text, modern interpreters seemed to have trouble finding the literal sense only if they lacked philological resources in cognate languages or if they lacked adequately detailed knowledge of the historical circumstances addressed by a biblical author.

A related issue concerns what modern scholars thought the term *author* signified. In the so-called King James Version of the Bible from the seventeenth century, the three times the translators use the term *author* it denotes God rather than a human writer (1 Cor 14:33; Heb 5:9, 12:2). They undoubtedly thought that only God was the author of faith or could authorize a Scripture. While the Bible frequently identifies persons we might describe as "designated writers" of whole biblical books, the same biblical books may include overt statements by editors, such as those found in the last chapters of Deuteronomy, in the so-called superscriptions of Old Testament books, including individual psalms, in the epilogue of Ecclesiastes (Eccles 12:9-14), in the titles to the four Gospels, and in the lengthy editorial note in John 21, where the editors even address the readers in the first person plural ("we know his testimony is true") in reference to the writer of the Gospel. The modern idea of an "author" often required the exhuming of the mind of a particular historical person whose primary "intent," then, needed to be distinguished from secondary intentions and cultural "accommodations" typical of an ancient time. Again, this approach, whether conservative or liberal, introduced entirely new categories into the older conception of the literal sense of Scripture. How that conception could be maintained in the Modern Age became a major, largely unresolved, issue for biblical interpretation.

A prime illustration of this modern debate in the late nineteenth century can be seen in the arguments over whether Isaiah is "the author" of the entire book of Isaiah. Dual authorship of the book of Isaiah had been firmly argued earlier in publications in Germany by Johann Christoph Döderlein (1746-1792) in 1775 and especially Eichhorn in 1780-1783. However, near the end of the nineteenth century in England, highly confessional scholars such as Andrew Bruce Davidson (1831-1902) in 1883, George Adam Smith (1856-1942) in 1890 and Samuel Rolles *Driver (1846-1914) in his *Introduction to the Literature of the Old Testament* (1891) felt compelled to mount a detailed case against the authorship of the eighth-century prophet Isaiah, especially for Isaiah 40—66. Smith reminds us that most scholars had arrived at this conclusion only a few decades before.

Franz Julius Delitzsch (1813-1890), who was appointed professor at Erlangen in 1850 and at Leipzig in 1867, had resisted the modern critical position in his own commentary on Isaiah until he was persuaded, partly by the erudition of his confessional counterparts in England. In the fourth edition of his commentary on Isaiah (1892) he grants that the historical Isaiah probably did not write chapters 40—66. Delitzsch avers that the case against Isaianic authorship had not been raised "to the eminence of a science" until Heinrich Friedrich Wilhelm Gesenius (1786-1842), Ferdinand Hitzig (1807-1875) and Heinrich Georg August Ewald (1803-1875), all nineteenth-century German scholars. Furthermore, he speculates about those who actually wrote Isaiah 40—66: "These later prophets so closely resembled Isaiah in prophetic vision, that posterity might on that account well identify them with him" (Delitzsch, 38). Finally, Delitzsch assures readers of the new edition of his commentary, in which he revised his earlier historical views, that "the influence of criticism on exegesis in the Book of Isaiah amounts to nothing" (Delitzsch, 40). In his revised commentary he insists on an interpretation of the parts of the book within the whole, in preference to an emphasis on isolated traditions which he concedes to derive from authors other than the historical Isaiah. However, Delitzsch offers no elaborated justification for why the exegesis of his commentary could remain so unaffected after he conceded that Isaiah did not write large parts of the biblical book in his name.

By contrast, George Adam Smith, who was no less confessionally orthodox than Delitzsch, rearranged the chapters of the book of Isaiah in his own commentary in order to treat each passage according to its original historical circumstances and authorship. Still, Smith highlights what the historical Isaiah actually did predict about the fall of Jerusalem, the appearance of the Messiah and the Christian hope in the resurrection. On the traditional assumption of a promise of the Messiah in Isaiah 7:14, Smith speculates that the name Immanuel for a child who portends the doom of Judah would explain why Hezekiah himself might have at least "the dimmest presage" of messianic hope attached to the prophecy. Smith allows also for "a vaguer theory" that the child is "a representation of the coming generation of God's people, or a type." For Smith the historical fact that the child is given a "Divine name" confirms at least "the moral effect of the sign," which would allow us to view King Ahaz as "the Judas of the

Old Testament" who betrays such a promising infant. Whether the overtones of the child's name, Immanuel, signified "an individual, or a generation, or an age," Smith thinks we can still find in it support for Christian messianic hope (Smith, 115-18).

Obviously, Smith feels compelled to struggle in novel ways in order to justify to any degree the traditional view of the literal sense of this verse. Such impressive struggling shows us how seriously the modern perspective had reopened some of the most elementary questions for confessional Christian scholars. The classical assumption that the literal sense is the same as the intent, purpose and scope of human testimony within a biblical book (to paraphrase Flacius's words) became highly complicated by a modern appraisal of historical "authorship" unaddressed by preceding centuries.

My aim in this overview has been to show the sort of questions raised in both the Classical and the Modern age regarding the literal sense of Scripture. This book's consideration of twentieth-century biblical interpretation in Europe will presuppose this account and begin to show what alternative responses arose near the end of the Modern Age and its aftermath.

BIBLIOGRAPHY

F. J. Delitzsch, *Biblical Commentary on the Prophecies of Isaiah* (Edinburgh: T & T Clark, 1892); P. C. Erb, ed., *Pietists: Selected Writings* (New York: Paulist, 1983); F. W. Farrar, *History of Interpretation* (Grand Rapids: Baker, 1961 [1886]); M. Foucault, *The Order of Things: An Archaeology of the Human Sciences* (New York: Vintage, 1973); H. Frei, *The Eclipse of Biblical Narrative: A Study in Eighteenth and Nineteenth Century Hermeneutics* (New Haven, CT: Yale University Press, 1974); P. Hazard, *European Thought in the Eighteenth Century: From Montesquieu to Lessing* (New York City: Meridian, 1963 [1946]); D. E. Klemm, ed., *Hermeneutical Inquiry,* 1: *The Interpretation of Texts;* 2: *The Interpretation of Existence* (Atlanta: Scholars Press, 1986); H.- J. Kraus, *Die Biblische Theologie: Ihre Geschichte und Problematik* (Neukirchen-Vluyn: Neukirchener, 1970); W. G. Kümmel, *The New Testament: The History of the Investigation of Its Problems* (Nashville: Abingdon, 1972); O. Merk, *Biblische Theologie des Neuen Testaments im ihrer Anfangszeit* (Marburg: Elwert, 1972); S. Neill and T. Wright, *The Interpretation of the New Testament, 1861-1986* (2d ed.; New York: Oxford University Press, 1988); R. E. Palmer, *Hermeneutics. Interpretation Theory in Schleiermacher, Dilthey, Heidegger, and Gadamer* (Evanston, IL: Northwestern University Press, 1969); Daniel L. Pals, *The Victorian 'Lives' of Jesus* (San Antonio: Trinity University Press, 1982); H. G. Reventlow, *The Authority of the Bible and the Rise of the Modern World* (Philadelphia: Fortress, 1985 [1980]); J. Rogerson, *Old Testament Criticism in the Nineteenth Century: England and Germany* (London: SPCK, 1984); J. Rogerson, C. Rowland and B. Lindars, *The Study and Use of the Bible* (Grand Rapids: Eerdmans, 1988); J. Sandys-Wunsch and L. Eldredge, "J. P. Gabler and the Distinction between Biblical and Dogmatic Theology: Translation, Commentary, and Discussion of His Originality," *SJT* 33 (1980) 133-58; N. Schneider, *The Art of the Still Life: Still Life Painting in the Early Modern Period* (Köln: Benedikt Taschen, 1990); G. T. Sheppard, "Between Reformation and Modernity: The Perception of the Scope of Biblical Books" in *A Commentary on Galatians by William Perkins,* ed. G. T. Sheppard (New York: Pilgrim, 1989) xlviii-lxxvii; G. A. Smith, *The Book of Isaiah* (London: Hazell, Watson & Viney, 1880-1890); R. Tarnas, *The Passion of the Western Mind: Understanding Ideas That Have Shaped Our World View* (New York: Ballantine, 1991).

G. T. SHEPPARD

Barnes, Albert *(1798-1870)*

Albert Barnes, along with Charles *Hodge, was among the earliest American Presbyterian biblical commentators. The early Puritans had published commentaries on British presses, but the new commentary impulse in America, of which Barnes was one of the pioneers, occurred after a lacuna of two hundred years

Life. Albert Barnes was born December 1, 1798, at Rome, New York, to Methodist parents. He entered an academy in Fairfield, Connecticut, to prepare for a career in law and graduated from Hamilton College (1820). A conversion experience changed his life's goal. He became a Presbyterian and determined to enter the ministry. He enrolled at Princeton Theological Seminary in 1820 and graduated in 1824. Barnes's first pastorate was at Morristown, New Jersey, where he remained until 1830, at which time he was called to be minister of the First Presbyterian Church of Philadelphia. He remained with this church for forty years, until his death on December 24, 1870. During much of his career he spoke out and acted in behalf of the poor, disfranchised and oppressed, especially slaves. More than once he became embroiled in theological controversy and was criticized, especially by those who held to a strict Calvinist orthodoxy. But Barnes was exonerated by both his church and presbytery.

Work. Barnes's publications were principally commentaries, first *Notes Explanatory and Practical on the Gospels* (Philadelphia, 1832) designed for Sunday school teachers and Bible classes. This volume was followed by *Notes on the New Testament* (11 vols.), completing the New Testament, except for Revelation. On the Old Testament he published commentaries on Job (2 vols.), Isaiah (2 vols.), Daniel and the book of Psalms (3 vols., 1870). He was

the most prolific commentator of his generation. It was reported that by the 1920s more than a million copies of his commentaries had been sold. Conservative presses have kept his commentaries in print to the present.

Barnes characterized his approach in the introduction to his commentary on Romans:

The design has not been to make a *learned* commentary; nor to enter into theological discussions; nor to introduce, at length, practical reflections; nor to enter minutely into critical investigations. All these can be found in books professedly on these subjects. The design has been to state, with as much brevity and simplicity as possible, the real meaning of the sacred writer; rather the *results* of critical inquiry, as far as the author has had ability and time to pursue it, than the *process* by which those results were reached. (Barnes 1852, iii)

Despite his disclaimer, it is impressive that Barnes, who was engaged in an active ministry, nevertheless explored the resources available to him:

In particular, aid has been sought and obtained from the following works: The *Critici Sacri,* Calvin's *Commentary on Romans,* Doddridge, MacKnight, and Rosenmuller; and the commentaries of Tholuck and Flatt—so far as an imperfect knowledge of the German language could render their aid available. (Barnes 1852, iv)

Barnes especially commended the new commentary of Moses Stuart, which had recently appeared, declaring that "important aid has been freely derived from that work." He also cited numerous Greco-Roman sources, for example, in discussing the activities of the Gentiles in Romans 1. He often advanced philological arguments and cited Greek, Hebrew and Syriac. About the commentary, Stuart wrote in the "Preface to the Second Edition" (Stuart 1835, 35):

> in our own country, the Rev. A. Barnes of Philadelphia has also published a brief but very comprehensive and valuable work on the same epistle . . . From Mr. Barnes' work I have also derived aid; and especially have I been often cheered on my way, by finding the result of his investigations to tally so well with my own.

In the commentary on Romans Barnes argued that Romans was unquestionably written by Paul from Corinth about A.D. 57. Those addressed were both Jews and Gentiles. Barnes interestingly depicted the letter as directed to a specific historical situation, as does the consensus perspective of current scholarship. Barnes did not connect these developments with the eviction of the Jews from Rome by Claudius, though his knowledge of this history is obvious from his comments on the founding of the church in Rome (Barnes 1852, vi-vii). Paul's focus he perceived as the righteousness of God and justification by faith.

Old School members of the presbytery had previously registered charges against Barnes because of a sermon, "The Way of Salvation." He was acquitted, however, by the general assembly. When the commentary on Romans appeared, new complaints charged that he departed from the dictates of the Westminster Confession, especially in regard to the doctrines of original sin, justification by faith, the imputation of the guilt of Adam and the righteousness of Christ. Barnes was acquitted again, but such disputes in 1837 brought about a division of the Presbyterian church into Old and New School denominations.

In regard to imputed righteousness, Barnes and Stuart were allied against Charles Hodge. Hodge, who was Old School, held the view that Adam's sin was the juridical ground for Adam's condemnation but not of the rest of humankind. Adam's sin in turn was declared the sin of the whole race,

though actually not, since he was the first, and therefore his action was designated as identical with that of all persons. His sin therefore cast a long shadow across all of humankind.

Hodge's position was called nonparticipationalist or representationalist. Stuart and Barnes belonged to the New School, influenced by the New England theology of Samuel Hopkins, Nathaniel Taylor and Timothy Dwight, centered at Yale. They were seminalists, or sometimes designated participationalists or realists. They believed that humans by participating in Adam have a propensity to sin, but they do not share in Adam's guilt. Each person is guilty according to their own sin and not because of God's condemnation of the race as the result of Adam's sin. They "rejected the ideas of imputed guilt and derived depravity, attempting to escape any implication that God was responsible for sin" (Hannah, 1089).

The section of Romans particularly pertinent is Romans 5:12-21. The point of the passage, according to Barnes, is to *"show one of the benefits of the doctrine of justification by faith."* He was certain that the statement had in mind the

> fact that they sin in *their own person, sin themselves*—as, indeed, how can they sin in any other way?—and that *therefore* they die. If men maintain that it refers to any metaphysical properties of the nature of man, or to infants, they should not *infer* or *suppose* this, but should show distinctly that it is in the text. (Barnes 1852, 117)

The point Paul made therefore was not an explanation of how sin was introduced but that Christ came to provide its remedy. Barnes ended with an impassioned declaration against Calvinistic explanations:

> The difference contemplated is not that Adam was an *actual* sinner, and that *they* had sinned only by *imputation*. For, (1) The expression 'to sin by imputation' is unintelligible, and conveys no idea. (2) The apostle makes no such distinction, and conveys no such idea. (3) His very

object is different. It is to show that they
were actual sinners; that they trans-
gressed law; and the proof of this is that
they died. (4) It is utterly absurd to
suppose that men from the time of
Adam to Moses were sinners *only by
imputation*. All history is against it; nor
is there the slightest ground of plausibil-
ity in such a supposition. (Barnes 1852,
119)

Thereupon Barnes discussed the views of
Jonathan *Edwards, John *Calvin, and
others.

Barnes also published four commentaries on the Old Testament, including one on
Isaiah. It was prepared to meet the needs
of "the pastors of the churches, for whose
use more especially this work is intended"
(Barnes 1847, vii). Barnes's was the first
commentary on Isaiah to be published by
an American, though the work of Joseph
Addison Alexander appeared a few years
later. Barnes drew on a wide range of
sources:

The books from which I have derived
most assistance are Walton's *Polyglott;*
the *Critici Sacri;* Pool's *Synopsis;* Cal-
ment's *Dictionary;* Virtringa; Rosen-
müller; Calvin; Gesenius; Jerome;
Bochart's *Hierozoicon;* Taylor's Heb.
Con.; Lowth's and Noyes' Versions;
Keith on the Prophecies; Newton on the
Prophecies; Hengstenberg's *Christology;* and the writings of oriental travellers to which I have had access. I have
also derived considerable aid from the
Biblical Repository, and from Prof.
Bush's *Scripture Illustrations.* (Barnes
1847, vi)

Obvious materials Barnes bypassed were
introductions by Johann Gottfried *Eichhorn and Wilhelm Martin Leberecht *de
Wette. Barnes affirmed the unity of the
composition of Isaiah in the introductory
remarks but recognized that the settings
were different:

It is admitted, on all hands, that the
second part of Isaiah, comprising the
prophecies which commence at the for-
tieth chapter, and which continue to the

end of the book is to be regarded as the
most sublime, and to us the most important part of the Old Testament. In
the previous portions of his prophecies,
there was much that was local and temporary. (Barnes 1847, 2:50)

Following the chronology of Augustin Cal-
met (1672-1757), Barnes offered 754 B.C.
as the year of Uzziah's death. He believed
that Isaiah lived into the 600s having had
about sixty-two years of ministry. His chronology likewise depended on Johann Jahn
(1750-1816) and offered dates about fifty
years earlier than those later proposed by
the William Foxwell *Albright school. Barnes believed that Hebrews 11:37, which he
attributed to Paul, was about Isaiah and his
death by being sawed in half. He argued
that Cyrus read about himself in Isaiah 45
and that was the reason he permitted the
Jews to return to Jerusalem and rebuild it
(Barnes 1847, xvii). He asserted that Hugo
Grotius was the most quoted commentator
and that Wilhelm Gesenius was the most
helpful on philological matters.

The commentary on Isaiah is sometimes
very good and sometimes engaged in peripheral matters such as details about various natural phenomena. Sometimes
Barnes's best contribution is to quote at
length from some other work; for example,
in discussing Isaiah 40:3, he quoted George
Paxton (1762-1838), who had an excellent
collection of materials in regard to magistrates who set out on a journey and dis-
patched servants to clear the way of
obstacles and obstructions. In regard to
Barnes as a commentator on Isaiah, Joseph
Addison Alexander wrote:

Particular and even disproportionate attention has been paid to archaeological
illustration, especially as furnished by
the modern travellers. Practical observations are admitted, but without sufficient uniformity or any settled method.
The author's view of inspiration in general, and of the inspiration of Isaiah in
particular, are sound, but not entirely
consistent with the deference occasionally paid to neological interpreters, in

cases where their judgments are, in fact though not in form, determined by a false assumption, which no one more decidedly rejects than Mr. Barnes. (Alexander, 42)

Barnes's comments on Isaiah 7 reflect the continuing interests of commentators in the late twentieth century. On the word *virgin*, since he followed the King James Version, he wrote:

> The etymology of the word requires us to suppose that it means one who is growing up to a marriageable state, or to the age of puberty. The word maiden, or virgin, expresses the correct idea. Hengstenberg contends that it means one *in the unmarried state*; Gesenius, that it means simply the being of marriageable age, the age of puberty. (Barnes 1847, 171)

Though he had the benefit of Gesenius's superior knowledge of Semitic languages, Barnes chose to argue that the word in the context meant an unmarried woman.

Barnes was exhaustive in exploring the possibilities as to whom the child might be. In the first edition he limited the sign to Ahaz's time, but in the second edition he proposed that the sign also looked ahead to the Messiah (Barnes 1847, 176). In declaring that the child was both one born in the time of Ahaz and the Messiah, he wrote, "nothing is more common in Isaiah than for him to *commence* a prophecy with reference to some remarkable deliverance which was soon to occur, and to *terminate* it by a statement of events connected with a higher deliverance under the Messiah" (Barnes 1847, 177-78). He argued that evidence that the prophecy referred to an event that was soon to occur resided in the obvious interpretation, and no one would think otherwise were the passage not mentioned in the New Testament; that a contemporary child is demanded by the circumstances, in that it is about an immediate threat; Isaiah indicated his conviction that the birth of children was a sign for this time by declaring the same in the case of his own children; the sign was to be a public

assurance in this specific context (Barnes 1847, 176-77).

As to whom the child might be, Barnes apparently preferred the view that the child was a son expected by the prophet's wife. As to other positions he stated, some suppose it is the wife of Ahaz, as is held by most modern Jewish commentators. *Jerome, he asserted, showed this to be false. Other scholars designated a virgin then present (Johann Lorenz Isenbiehl, Bruno Bauer, Johann David Cube and Johann Christian Friedrich Steudel). Another interpretation was that the virgin was not actual but ideal (Johann David *Michaelis, Johann Gottfried Eichhorn, Heinrich Eberhard Gottlob Paulus, Christian Gotthilf Hensler and Christoph Friedrich von Ammon). The information Barnes cited in most cases was attributed to Ernst Hengstenberg (175).

Barnes was industrious in employing the materials available to him. He tended to ignore more radical views, for example, those of Eichhorn, and the more moderate views of de Wette on Isaiah. Hengstenberg was especially respected in Barnes's circle of commentators, but on occasion Barnes as freely rejected the views of Hengstenberg as of anyone. He was by no means wed to conclusions of his own theological tradition, as for example the interpretation of Romans 5, or the sign in Isaiah 7. It is clear that he attempted to explain the text, as he was able, in light of its grammatico-historical meaning.

Significance. Barnes represented an early stage in the publishing of commentaries in the United States. He broke little new ground, but he raised perceptive questions of the sort with which scholars continue to struggle. Because of the solidarity of his work and because that work continues to be circulated among ministers and church members, Barnes deserves a niche in the catalog of important biblical scholars.

BIBLIOGRAPHY

Works. A. Barnes, *Life at Three-Score and Ten* (New York: American Tract Society, 1871); idem, *Notes, Explanatory and Practical on the*

Epistle to the Romans Designed for Bible-Classes and Sunday-Schools (9th ed.; New York: Harper & Brothers, 1852 [1834]); idem, *Notes, Critical, Explanatory, and Practical, on the Book of the Prophet Isaiah* (New York: Leavitt, Trow & Co., 1st 1838, 2d 1845, 1847); idem, *A Popular Family Commentary on the New Testament, being notes practical and explanatory* (11 vols.; London: Gresham, 1868).

Studies. J. A. Alexander, *The Prophecies of Isaiah Translated and Explained* (New York: Charles Scribner, 1870); A. H. Freundt Jr., "Albert Barnes," *DCA*, 117; J. D. Hannah, "Sin," *DCA* 1088- 90; G. M. Marsden, *The Evangelical Mind and the New School Presbyterian Experience* (New Haven, CT: Yale University Press, 1970); M. Stuart, *A Commentary on the Epistle to the Romans with a Translation and Various Excursus* (Andover, MA: Gould & Newman, 1835).

T. H. Olbricht

Baur, F(erdinand) C(hristian) (1792-1860)

Born June 21, 1792, in Schmiden (now a suburb of Stuttgart), Germany, Ferdinand Christian Baur was professor of New Testament at the University of Tübingen from 1826 until his death in 1860. He is buried in the town cemetery, directly across from the building that today houses the theological faculty and library. Baur was reared in a pastor's home, sent to a theological preparatory school at thirteen, and entered the seminary at the University of Tübingen in 1809. Suited to a life of scholarship by temperament and intellectual ability, Baur excelled in his studies under the Old Tübingen School of theology, which was known for its orthodoxy.

By Baur's day, however, the school's earlier goal of substantiating the authority of the Bible through historical study and reason had led to a rationalistic approach in which Jesus' deity and authority were derived from his greatness as an ethical teacher and not from his uniqueness as the Son of God. Baur's earliest writings as a student reflect this same rationalism. During his school years Baur still held to some orthodox Christian doctrines, such as the

historicity of the resurrection, but he eventually denied the idea of a special, divine revelation given in the Christian Scriptures. Revelation was instead seen to be a general and universal disclosure of truth to all people, so that theology became the search for an ideal religious truth or principles that could be found in all religions. Hence, with his basic rationalism already in place, Baur graduated from the university in 1814.

From 1814 to 1826 Baur served as a pastor for a brief time, taught classics and ancient history in theological preparatory schools, and served as a tutor in the Tübingen seminary from 1816 to 1817. During this period he encountered Friedrich Daniel Ernst *Schleiermacher's *The Christian Faith,* which impressed Baur as the first full-scale attempt to write a systematic theology from a nonsupernatural viewpoint. As Baur put it in a letter to his brother on July 26, 1823, shortly after he read Schleiermacher's work for the first time, "The distinction between this new viewpoint and the old customary one consists, to put it briefly, in the fact that while the old view accepts the external revelation or the writings of the New Testament as the sole source of knowledge of Christianity, according to Schleiermacher, the primary source of Christianity lies in the religious self-consciousness, out of whose development the principle doctrines of Christianity are to be obtained" (quoted in Harris, 148). Though Baur did not accept Schleiermacher's positions uncritically, in his first major work (1824/1825) Baur argued for Schleiermacher's view that the essence of religion was to be found in the "'consciousness (or feeling) of dependence upon God." Furthermore, this universal religious experience manifested itself in various religions and myths as a result of a divine process of education within history itself (Harris, 19-20).

In the years following his university studies, Baur broke completely from the more moderate Old Tübingen School of thought. By the time that Baur was considered for a position at the University of

Tübingen, it was apparent that although his language had the ring of piety, he had left the orthodox fold, having adopted "the new ideas of a mystic-pantheistic rationalism" (Harris, 21, quoting Professors Süskind's and Schmid's evaluations of Baur in 1826). Baur was impressed with Schleiermacher's ability to develop a system in which all of the central doctrines of Christianity could be interpreted from a nonsupernatural basis (Harris, 151). For this same reason, in his later lectures on 19th-century theology, Baur was also highly critical of the content of Schleiermacher's theology, since Schleiermacher failed to apply his own nonsupernatural and pantheistic view of religion to the miracles of the New Testament (Harris, 152). Baur accused Schleiermacher of "duplicity," since

> Schleiermacher cannot hold all those events in Jesus' life to be actual miracles, because for him, from his standpoint, there are no miracles at all. But why does he not say this openly? Why does he try to give the impression that he does not set in doubt the actual reality of these miraculous events, as if it were not a question of the events, but only of their significance . . . this can have its ground only in the fact that he wants his *Christian Faith* to appear more orthodox than it really is. No other Dogmatics has . . . so methodically loosened and undermined the basis of the orthodox view as Schleiermacher's, and none will so little admit it and allow it to come to an open break with the traditional doctrines of the Church. (Harris, 153-54, quoting Baur's lecture [1877, 5:185-88])

In contrast, Baur's own work was marked by his willingness to acknowledge the implications of his antisupernatural presuppositions and his rejection of divine revelation in the New Testament.

Despite some initial opposition by the more conservative faculty and church leaders, Baur was called to the University of Tübingen in 1826. At that time Tübingen was not considered a top-rung university.

But because of his skeptical views, Baur was subsequently passed over for other appointments at what were then the more prestigious universities of Berlin (in 1834, as Schleiermacher's successor) and of Halle (in 1836). As he moved through the middle of his career (1832-1847), Baur became increasingly convinced that the new speculative philosophy of Hegel offered the best explanation of history and of the nature of reality (Harris, 156-63). Moreover, due to the explanatory power of Hegel's paradigm as used by Baur, Baur's influence grew exponentially. As a result, in spite of his eventual rejection of Hegel's abstract view of God as an infinite Spirit or eternal Idea that works itself out in the evolving process of history, Hegel's influence on Baur's understanding of early Christianity became determinative for later scholarship (Harris, 163-67, 172). By the time of his death, the University of Tübingen, previously of only second-rate importance, had become the center of an intense international controversy due to what became known as the new Tübingen school under the leadership of Baur. Indeed, though Baur wrote multivolume histories of the church and its theology from the earliest years to his own time, not to mention his works on Christian gnosticism and Manicheanism, it is Baur's paradigm for reading the New Testament that has had the most significant impact on modern biblical interpretation, an impact unrivaled by any other person or school of thought. The central problems and questions concerning the history of the apostolic age identified by Baur remain unresolved.

Work. Baur laid out the foundation for his understanding of the development of the early church in his seminal essay (1831) on the conflicts within the Corinthian church and early Christianity in general. Beginning with this essay, Baur attempted to provide a comprehensive understanding of the development of early Christianity from a historical, nonsupernatural perspective. Applying the conflict, evolutionary approach of Hegel's philosophy to the New

Testament, the key to Baur's systematic explanation was the positing of a fundamental opposition between a Gentile Christianity on the one hand and a Jewish Christianity on the other. The former was represented by Paul, with his universal, law-free, Hellenistically determined gospel; the latter was formed around Cephas, who maintained a particular, law-orientated, Jewish-bound interpretation of the significance of Jesus. According to Baur, this bitter conflict and its eventual resolution within the emerging unity of the hierarchical Catholic church not only dominated the writings of the New Testament but also drove the historical development of the early church itself until the end of the second century (Hafemann, 667).

Baur found support for his thesis in 1 Corinthians 1:11-12, which he interpreted with J. E. C. Schmidt to refer to two distinct factions within the Corinthian church, a Pauline and a Petrine party, rather than four rival groups of jealous and boastful believers. The Apollos faction was seen to side with the Pauline party, while the Christ-party was a Jewish Christian faction that gained its name from its emphasis on their direct relationship to Christ via the apostles like Peter, whom Christ himself had appointed. Threatened by the emergence of a law-free, Gentile Christianity led by the outsider Paul, the original apostles opposed Paul's ministry and sought to undermine his influence. To do so, Peter, James and the rest of the Jerusalem apostles stressed Jesus as the Jewish Messiah and the necessity of obedience to the law of Moses. It was against these attacks by his Jewish-Christian opponents that Paul developed his doctrine of justification by faith as the center of his theology and developed his law/gospel contrast as a polemic response to those whom he considered "judaizers."

In his 1836 work on the purpose of Paul's letter to the Romans, Baur further confirmed his thesis by arguing that Romans was an apologetic defense of Paul's gospel written to a predominantly Jewish-Christian church in Rome rather than a doctrinal treatise written to Gentile Christians for the purpose of further instruction. As such, Romans gave evidence of the same conflicts seen in 1 Corinthians. The key to Baur's analysis was his conviction that rather than being a parenthesis in Paul's argument, the relationship between Israel and the Gentiles in Romans 9—11 provides the center and main theme of Paul's letter, since Romans 13—14 indicate that the problem in the Roman church was the relationship between Jewish and Gentile Christians. But the strongest support for Baur's thesis was Paul's letter to the Galatians, in which Peter and the "judaizers" were both named explicitly and countered directly with Paul's doctrine of justification by faith apart from works of the Law (Gal 2:11-21).

The climax of the Tübingen school was the publication of Baur's *Paulus, der Apostel Jesu Christi. Sein Leben und Wirken, seine Briefe und seine Lehre* (1845), in which he raised the crucial question of the relationship between Paul's own letters and the accounts in the book of Acts. He concluded that the two accounts could not be harmonized. Furthermore, due to the failure of Acts to mention the dispute between Peter and Paul at Antioch, together with Paul's own silence concerning the Jerusalem council in Galatians, Acts must be rejected as historical and interpreted as a mediating and conciliatory document from the mid-second century. Conversely, the authentic Paul could be found only where both the conflict between Jewish (Petrine) and Gentile (Pauline) Christianity and Paul's own doctrine of a law-free justification by faith can be clearly seen. Those writings that evidence an attempt to mediate this conflict by finding a middle ground are to be regarded as a second stage in the development of the early church. Any document that reflected an authoritarian, ecclesiological attempt to resolve this conflict, such as the Pastoral Epistles, was considered evidence of the third stage in the history of early Christianity, the subsequent Catholic resolution of the Jewish/Gentile Christian conflict around A.D. 200 that came about in response to the common threat of Gnosticism.

Based on this historical reconstruction, Baur concluded that only Romans, Galatians and the Corinthian epistles could be considered authentic. The Pastoral Epistles were late second-century documents written against Gnostics and Marcionites; the Prison Epistles and Philemon were written against Gnostic opponents between 120 and 140 as late expressions of the Pauline school. The epistles to the Thessalonians were written in the generation after Paul (A.D. 70-75) but were of inferior quality theologically since they had no trace of either the Pauline doctrine of justification by faith or the Paul/Peter conflict, and their eschatology conflicted with that of 1 Corinthians 15. Within this framework Baur's students and followers (E. Zeller, A. Schwegler, K. Planck, K. Köstlin, G. Volkmar, A. Hilgenfeld, the early A. Ritschl) attempted to apply this basic scheme to the rest of the New Testament writings by interpreting and categorizing them as either Pauline (e.g., Hebrews, 1 Peter), Petrine-judaizing (e.g., James, Matthew, Revelation), mediating and conciliatory (e.g., Luke-Acts; Mark) or catholicizing (2 Peter, Jude; Gospel of John; see Harris, 55-133).

Significance. The work of Baur and the Tübingen school under him was characterized by his commitment to provide a consistently historical, nonsupernatural interpretation of the rise of early Christianity in the first two centuries. At the heart of this attempt was an evaluation of the origin, date and character of the writings of the New Testament according to their theological tendency (German *Tendenz*) as it was understood within the context of Baur's historical reconstruction. As a result of its systematic nature, comprehensive scope and theological compatibility with the traditional Lutheran and Reformed paradigms, Baur's conviction that a Peter/Paul, law/gospel, judaizing/antilegalistic conflict was the generating force

during the first two Christian centuries set the agenda for the next century of biblical scholarship.

Yet within Baur's own lifetime, some of his own students and members of the Tübingen School began to question whether the conflict between Pauline and Jewish Christianity had not been overdrawn and exaggerated at key points. In 1857 Albrecht Ritschl officially broke with the Tübingen School by rejecting the idea of a long-lasting conflict between Paul and the other apostles, the inauthenticity of the other Pauline epistles and the pitting of Acts against Galatians that were such a part of the Tübingen perspective. This marked the beginning of the end of the Tübingen School's direct influence, and the school itself ended with Baur's death.

Today, Baur's evaluation of the late date and origin of the majority of the Pauline epistles has been rejected. It became increasingly clear that Baur had forced the New Testament and the early church theologians into a framework that he had not derived from the documents themselves but that he had brought to them. Thus, in order to make his system work, Baur had to reject all but four of Paul's letters as authentic. Most New Testament scholars have also rejected Baur's radical historical skepticism and philosophical rationalism, which excluded the supernatural as impossible a priori and led to the radical skepticism of David Friedrich *Strauss's *Life of Jesus* (1835) as the beginning of the critical reevaluation of the Gospels. Nor has the Tübingen school's analysis of the second century as a continuation of the conflict between a Pauline and Jewish Christianity, based on Baur's groundless identification of Simon the magician in the Clementine Homilies with Paul himself, proved convincing.

Despite the weaknesses of his historical and theological judgments, Baur's work nevertheless propelled biblical studies into the modern world by its consistent attempt to provide a comprehensive and coherent understanding of the history of the early church on the basis of historical reasoning alone, with no room for supernatural interventions or explanations based on the miraculous. With the rise of Baur, a purely historical and critical investigation of the Bible established itself as orthodoxy within the world of scholarship. Ever since Baur all interpretations of the New Testament have had to pass the test of historical probability in a way not enforced prior to the nineteenth century, even for those who accept the reality of divine intervention and the authority of Scripture. Because of this, H. Harris rightly argues that "no single event ever changed the course of Biblical scholarship as much as the appearance of the Tübingen School. All New Testament criticism and, derivatively, much Old Testament criticism from the mid-nineteenth century onwards finds its origin, consciously or unconsciously, in this School" (Harris, 1).

Moreover, Baur's conflict theory of the development of the early church and the New Testament is still widely accepted among scholars, as is his fundamentally Lutheran view of the contrast between law and gospel. His work has therefore raised the five central and interrelated issues with which all subsequent interpreters have had to wrestle in attempting to work out their own comprehensive picture of the New Testament writings: the identity of Jesus and his relationship to the church created in his name; the identity and theology of Jewish and Gentile Christianity and their interrelationship; the meaning of the old covenant and Sinai law in relationship to the gospel of the new covenant; the nature and identity of the opposition faced by Paul, John and the Catholic Epistles; and the question of the theological center and corresponding unity of the New Testament and the early church that it represents. These five questions have determined the course of biblical interpretation for the last 150 years.

BIBLIOGRAPHY
Works. F. C. Baur, "Die Christuspartei in der

korinthischen Gemeinde, der Gegensatz des petrinischen und paulinischen Christenthums in der ältesten Kirche, der Apostel Petrus in Rom," *Tübinger Zeitschrift für Theologie* 4 (1831) 61-206; idem, *Geschichte der christlichen Kirche* (5 vols.; Tübingen: Fues, 1863-1877) vol. 5; idem, *Kritische Untersuchungen uber die kanonischen Evangelien* (Tübingen: Fues, 1847); idem, *Paulus, der Apostel Jesu Christi. Sein Leben und Wirken, seine Briefe und seine Lehre* (2 vols.; Tübingen: Fues, 1845; ET: *Paul, the Apostle of Jesus Christ, His Life and Work, His Epistles and His Doctrine* [2 vols.; London, Edinburgh: Williams and Norgate, 1873-1875); idem, *Symbolik und Mythologie oder die Naturreligion des Alterthums* (2 vols.; Stuttgart: Metzler, 1824-1825; repr. Aalen: Scientia-Verlag, 1979); idem, *Vorlesungen uber neutestamentliche Theologie* (Leipzig: Fues, 1864).

Studies. W. Baird, *History of New Testament Research*, 1: *From Deism to Tübingen* (Minneapolis: Augsburg Fortress, 1992); S. J. Hafemann, "Paul and His Interpreters," *DPL*, 666-79; H. Harris, *The Tübingen School, A Historical and Theological Investigation of the School of F. C. Baur* (Grand Rapids: Baker, 1990), which includes a complete bibliography of Baur's writings and a listing of the most significant secondary literature; P. C. Hodgson, *The Formation of Historical Theology: A Study of Ferdinand Christian Baur* (New York: Harper & Row, 1966); W. G. Kümmel, *The New Testament: The History of the Investigation of Its Problems* (Nashville: Abingdon, 1972); R. Morgan with J. Barton, *Biblical Interpretation* (Oxford: Oxford University Press, 1988); J. Munck, *Paul and the Salvation of Mankind* (Atlanta: John Knox, 1959); P. Stuhlmacher, *Historical Criticism and Theological Interpretation of Scripture* (Philadelphia: Fortress, 1977).   S. J. Hafemann

Bengel, J(ohann) A(lbrecht) (1687-1752)

Johann Albrecht Bengel is known as the exegete of Pietism. Yet, as one of his biographers says, his major contribution was the *Schreibtisch*, or writing table. But his designation as the exegete of Pietism is well-deserved (*Kirche und Welt*, 674).

Life. Bengel was born June 24, 1687, in Winnenden, Württemberg, Germany. His childhood was marked by physical weakness, the death of his father (a pastor) at age forty-three, and refugee status when the troops of Louis XIV plundered the area. Bengel was reared in the home of David Spindler, who opened a Latin school in Marbach and later moved to Stuttgart, where Bengel enrolled in the gymnasium. Spindler hosted conventicles in his home and came under suspicion of being a radical Pietist with sympathies toward the views of Gottfried Arnold and Jakob Böhme and of embracing chiliasm. It was at Stuttgart that Bengel achieved proficiency in languages, both ancient and modern. He entered the University of Tübingen in 1703 and completed his theological studies there.

From 1708 to 1713 Bengel served as a vicar in various congregations and as a tutor at Tübingen. After having been named to the faculty of the revived cloister school at Denkendorf, Bengel served in leadership of the school for twenty-eight years as it prepared young men to enter the University of Tübingen to be educated for ordination to the Lutheran ministry. In 1741 he entered pastoral ministry again and later assumed responsibilities of ecclesiastical governance in the consistory at Stuttgart. The University of Tübingen awarded him an honorary doctorate in 1751. Having enjoyed great favor among students, congregations and family—he was survived by six of twelve children—he died in 1752.

Context. Johannes Brenz, one of the major Lutheran Reformers in Württemberg, was also an advocate of church discipline and reforms in personal piety and the great-grandfather of Bengel's mother. The major impetus to the growth of Pietism came from a visit of Philip Spener to Württemberg in 1662. He established a close relation with one of Bengel's major teachers, Johann Andreas Hochstetter, and helped to foster an already indigenous conventicle life.

Two professors at Tübingen stand out for their influence on Bengel. Hochstetter was a strong supporter of conventicles and the concern for a deepened spiritual life. He took a particular interest in younger schol-

ars and enabled them to pursue their own research interests. In the case of Bengel, Hochstetter asked him to superintend the corrections being made to a new edition of the German Bible with special reference to the problem of punctuation. No doubt this assignment fostered Bengel's later interest in problems of textual criticism.

Wolfgang Jäger tended to be oppositional to the conventicle movement and more aligned with Lutheran orthodoxy. Yet his major work, *Corpus Doctrinae Federalis,* published in 1725, shows Reformed influence. Jäger had been influenced by Johannes Cocceius, who shifted the focus of Reformed theology from eternity into time, from decrees to covenantal theology, and whose theology took the shape of a salvation history, expressing itself in a succession of covenants. Thus Jäger had a deepened understanding of the historical character of God's work, including church history. Bengel was given the role of primary researcher for Jäger's church history and for the preparation of a document on Baruch Spinoza, from whom especially he may have received the initial appreciation for the role of the emotions in life and reflection.

In preparation for his teaching vocation at Denkendorf, Bengel took a trip from March to September 1713. He visited eighteen cities to study a variety of educational institutions. During this trip he met Johann May and Johann Lange, both of whom had been influenced by Cocceius. May had rejected covenant, or federal, theology and proposed instead the notion of a divine economy, an idea stressed by Pierre Poiret. Successive covenants gave the appearance of closed-off periods; the divine economy stretched from eternity to eternity, inclusive of parts working in harmony all under the stewardship of God. From Poiret, Bengel received the idea of a systematic totality, not a succession of the times. What joined Cocceius and Poiret together for Bengel was the notion of salvation history. Economy theology became a decisive concept for Bengel (Gerdes, 30-

32; in Bengel's preface [1978] see nos. 14, 24 and 27).

Bengel's trip included a visit to Halle, the home base of August Hermann Francke's educational and charitable endeavors. Bengel knew of Francke's work, some of which had produced a spiritual and theological crisis for Bengel. Francke had written a preface to the 1702 Leipzig edition of the Greek New Testament, an edition noting the plethora of textual variants. For Bengel it meant working through the issues of the divine inspiration of the Scriptures and their course through human history. But perhaps this planted the seed of his vocation, to become, as K. Aland says, "the father of textual criticism" (Aland, 136).

Francke had also written a work on the interpretation of Scripture. It conveyed themes prominent in Bengel: context, the setting of texts in the whole context of Scripture, grammar, geography and other themes. But Francke also gave an extended treatment of the relation between the affections and language and argued that a true understanding of the apostles' words is enabled not only by linguistic accuracy but also by having the same affections as the apostle one is reading (Francke). In the preface to the *Gnomon* (the Greek word means "pointer"), Bengel's best-known work, he explores the role of the feelings in interpretation (Bengel 1978, see nos. 12, 15).

While he was at Halle Bengel also explored pedagogical practices in preparation for assuming his duties at the Denkendorf school. His visit convinced him that it was not sufficient for students to have committed facts to memory. It was the teacher's role to elicit meaning and reflection. This theme appeared in the address he gave at the opening of the school at Denkendorf, when he told the teachers they were more than lecturers and that excessive authoritarianism may only harden the temper of a student. They were educators whose presence as such either enabled or disabled students.

Literary Contributions. The major areas of Christian life and thought to which he made copious and lasting contributions are biblical interpretation and literature about edification. An assessment of the scope of Bengel's contributions includes six areas of scholarly and literary work: pedagogical, commentaries, text-critical materials, apocalyptic, edification and controversial.

Bengel prepared critical editions of texts in Latin and Greek that ranged from Cicero to John *Chrysostom to Macarius. He taught these languages by having students translate from one to the other. His trip to Halle had convinced him that languages were not taught there with enough precision, a matter that Bengel desired to remedy.

Bengel's commentaries have received worldwide recognition; in particular the *Gnomon,* published in 1742, which was more than twenty years in the making. It began simply enough with Bengel making marginal notes and comments on the biblical text as he lectured or returned to his study. These notes were exegetical, text-critical or edificatory as the case may be. Although such a publication may appear to be informal, impulsive and unreflective, the *Gnomon* draws deeply from tradition, both classical and Christian, and in pithy aphorisms captures both the letter and spirit of the Scriptures.

Until recently, J. Pelikan says, the *Gnomon* was commonplace in the libraries of evangelical pastors, and its ubiquity was pervasive enough to exert influence on biblical scholarship comparable to that of Martin *Luther in the sixteenth century (Pelikan, 785). Such a judgment may be grounded in part on the extent to which the *Gnomon* continued to be published. E. Gerdes numbers nine German editions, numerous reprints (1970 being the latest), and excerpts in other books and abridgements. The original was published in Latin. English-speaking people came into contact with Bengel via John *Wesley, who used his works copiously, particularly in his *Ex-*

planatory Notes on the New Testament (1715), and thus Bengel became part of the confessional corpus of the Methodist church. Several other editions appeared in English, notably Kregel's 1971 publication of C. T. Lewis's and M. R. Vincent's translation (1860-1862). Primarily through this book Bengel continues to be what Wesley called him: "That great light of the Christian World" (Gerdes, xx-xxvii).

Bengel's work in textual criticism has won him a lasting place in that discipline. B. M. Metzger reports that Bengel was the first to distinguish two families of New Testament manuscripts: the Asiatic, originating in Constantinople and environs, including the more recent manuscripts, and the African, which he subdivided into the two subfamilies of Codex Alexandrinus and Old Latin (Metzger, 112-13). Bengel's foreword to the *Gnomon* provides some access to the principles of his work. Among those principles still used by critics one may note the following: scribes are more likely to make a difficult reading easier; the difficult is to be preferred to the easy reading; where the Greek manuscripts differ from each other the greatest authority lies with those agreeing with versions and the Fathers; more witnesses are to be preferred then fewer, but the more important consideration lies with witnesses from differing countries, ages and languages who agree than with witnesses who come forth closely connected; and high value was placed on the role of the Vulgate and the most ancient of texts (Fritsch, 206-7).

Between 1725 and 1753, a year following Bengel's death, no fewer than seven publications dealt with text-critical questions. He sought the best *Grundtext* that could be found (1734, two editions) and defended it (1734), following later with a German translation that sought to make appropriate changes in the Luther Bible, an effort that engendered much criticism. The translation of the copious title of the 1736 publication of the harmony of the four Evangelists is an indication of Bengel's aims in this very technical work: *True Harmony*

of the Four Evangelists Where the Stories, Works and Speeches of Jesus Christ Our Lord Are Presented in Their Proper Rational Order Toward the Establishing of the Truth As Also Toward Practice and Edification in Godliness.* The economy theology seeks to establish the natural order of these things, not just in the case of the Gospels but in the entire biblical story, and the aim is piety and edification.

Bengel is noted for his apocalyptic interests. He calculated a date for the end: 1836. He wrote two major works on the book of Revelation and two works specifically coordinating time, nature and astronomy with the prophetic material. His *Ordo Temporum* (1741) attempted to be a history of the divine economy and a proper accounting of prophecy and how parts and whole form one story. The *Cyclus* (1745) especially tried to link astronomy with prophetic material, and the *Explained Revelation* (1740), a massive commentary on the text, concludes with six excurses detailing the history of the exegesis of Revelation.

From all accounts Bengel was an irenic person, but he did engage in polemics on three fronts. One was the controversy engendered by his text-critical work and publication of both his foundational Greek text and his translation of the text into German. Another focus of literary work was directed against the critics of his eschatological and apocalyptic views. Basing their criticisms on Article 17 of the Augsburg Confession, many Lutheran scholars accused him of being either judaistic or Anabaptistic because of his defense of an earthly millennium and literal fulfillment of prophecy. Would the kingdom be established by human means (i.e., by law instead of gospel) or worse, by force of arms (in recollection of the Peasants' Revolt)? Bengel argued that just as God worked justification monergistically, so eschatology did not need to succumb to synergism.

Finally, his controversy with Count von Zinzendorf was threefold. First was the reference to the motherhood of the Holy

Spirit. A second was christomonism, that Jesus Christ virtually replaces God the Father, and, with an overemphasis on the wounds of Jesus, suffering and death eclipse the resurrection. The third issue was the alleged remarks of Zinzendorf that the Lutheran church was beyond spiritual recovery and that in effect his own community functioned as the ideal.

Bengel wrote *Sixty Edifying Speeches on the Revelation of John or Much More, of Jesus Together with Gleanings of Similar Content* (1747). This major work of edification literature was initially given as evening lectures during his ministry at Herbrechtigen. It was written down by listeners and later edited by Bengel. Among the features that characterized this literature should be noted primarily its theocentric character. God's will was central to Jesus' will. Along with this feature one should note the emphasis on God's glory and holiness. God's glory extended itself into life so that circumstances, ordinary or extraordinary, could signal the divine presence. At points Bengel's exploration of the mystery and glory of God anticipates Rudolph Otto's notion of the *mysterium tremendum et fascinans*. Human beings have the capacity to think back over life and in this work of recollection be led either to praise or to penitence. Given Bengel's eschatological views and sense of the whole of God's economy working toward its providential end, life was lived in certain hope of God's vindication of God's word and God's Christ. The fidelity and fruitfulness of Scripture are the foundation of his piety, and the church is the vehicle of its expression, both in the exposition of the text and in the exhibition of its life lived for the glory of God.

Significance. Bengel's legacy of text-critical principles gave New Testament scholarship standards of discernment among texts based on grounds other than dogmatics or subjectivity. Shifting the fulcrum of piety to theocentricity enabled him to explore issues of creation, redemption and history not available via christomonism

or an exclusive pneumatology. By using the attribute of God's glory and holiness Bengel was able to do justice both to God's transcendence and immanence and of retaining the whole Bible of Old and New Testaments. This led Bengel to embrace a theology of God's economy expressed in salvation history, both as narrative and prophecy. When the older categories of Aristotelian, scholastic theology and the orders of creation gave way to salvation history, God's ongoing relation with the world could more easily be expressed in the way history moved toward its goal. This contribution of Bengel found later expression in Johann Christian Konrad *von Hoffmann, Adolf *Schlatter and Jürgen Moltmann.

Bengel's apocalypticism, especially the fixing of dates, has been a source of much critique. It might be said that the failure in making two distinctions led to this dubious emphasis in his work.

The first distinction is between eschatology and apocalypticism. While the former has confidence in God's final vindication of Christian hope and faith, the latter ends up as a program for God to follow, despite all protests to the contrary. In addition, cosmic and historical events and persons are absolutized as parts of this program, which in its most perverse form amounts to human beings playing God.

The second distinction is between biblicism and being biblical. The former presumes that interpreters can uncover every literal meaning and presses to do so, whereas the latter allows the Bible the freedom not to answer every question put to it and does not suppose that it ought to. Being biblical means to live in the story and to let the story live out its plot in human life. To do so one needs to practice Bengel's famous line: Apply the text wholly to yourself; apply yourself wholly to the text.

BIBLIOGRAPHY

Works. J. A. Bengel, *New Testament Word Studies (The Gnomon)* (2 vols.; Grand Rapids: Kregel, 1978 repr.); J. C. F. Burk, comp., *A Memoir of*

the *Life and Writings of Johann Albrecht Bengel*
(London: R. Gladding, 1842).

Studies. K. Aland, "Bibel und Bibeltext bei
August Hermann Francke und Johann Albrecht
Bengel" in *Pietismus und Bibel Herausgegeben
von Kurt Aland* (Arbeiten Zur Gershichte der
Pietismus 9; Witten: Luther Verlag, 1970); C.
Fritsch, "Bengel, the Student of Scripture," *Int*
5 (1951) 203-15; E. Gerdes, "Vorwort" in *Gnomon*, Deutsch von C. F. Werner, mit Vorwort von
Egon W. Gerdes and Johann Albrecht Bengel (2
vols.; Stuttgart: J. F. Steinkopf Verlag, 1970); A.
H. Francke, *A Guide to the Reading and Study of
the Holy Scriptures* (Philadelphia: David Hogan,
1823); *Kirche und Welt* 10 Jahrgang (November
6, 1977); G. Mälzer, *Johann Albrecht Bengel:
Leben und Werk* (Stuttgart: Calwer Verlag,
1970); B. M. Metzger, *The Text of the New
Testament: Its Transmission, Corruption and Restoration* (3d ed.; New York and Oxford: Oxford
University Press, 1992); J. Pelikan, "In Memoriam: Joh. Albrecht Bengel June 24, 1687 to
November 2, 1752," *CTM* 33 (November 1952)
785-96; J. Weborg, "The Eschatological Ethics
of Johann Albrecht Bengel: Personal and Ecclesial Piety and the Literature of Edification in the
Letters to the Seven Churches in Revelation 2
and 3" (Ph.D. diss., Northwestern University,
1983).   J. Weborg

Briggs, Charles Augustus
(1841-1913)

Charles Augustus Briggs was born in New
York City on January 15, 1841, to a successful businessman and his wife, Alanson
and Sarah Mead (Berrian) Briggs. He studied at the University of Virginia from 1857
to 1860. While he was at Virginia (November 30, 1858) he experienced a conversion
and decided to enter the ministry rather
than his father's barrel-making enterprise.
In 1861 Briggs spent a few months in the
Civil War and then attended Union Theological Seminary (1861-1863). At Union
he studied under Edward Robinson, who
encouraged him to go to Germany. Robinson was the first of many Americans to
study at Halle with Wilhelm Gesenius and
Friedrich August Gottreu *Tholuck.

The most influential person in Briggs's
decision to study abroad, however, was

another Union professor, Henry Boynton
Smith. It is important to understand
Smith's contribution because, although
Briggs was a biblical scholar all his life, his
interests were much wider, especially regarding the Presbyterian church and its
doctrinal development, along with international ecumenics.

Briggs brought his skills as a biblical
scholar to bear upon these larger concerns,
and these in turn were the contexts that
informed his biblical studies. Smith had
studied at Berlin and was convinced by
Neander to take up a scientifically oriented
historical approach in the teaching of theology. In regard to biblical studies Smith
was especially influenced by Ernst Hengstenberg. It is not surprising, then, that
Briggs went to Berlin in 1866 in order to
attend Hengstenberg's lectures. But reflecting on studies with Hengstenberg
thirty years later, Briggs wrote:

> In 1866 it was the author's privilege to
> study with Hengstenberg in the Univer-
> sity of Berlin. His studies were at first
> chiefly on the traditional side. He can
> say that he worked over the chief
> authorities on that side, and they had all
> the advantages of his predilections in
> their favor. But Hengstenberg himself
> convinced him in his own lecture room
> that he was defending a lost cause.
> (Briggs 1893, 62)

In Berlin the professors who most impressed Briggs were Isaac August Dorner
in theology and Emil Roediger in biblical
languages. Dorner was a foremost scholar
in the new discipline of the history of doctrine. He was an evangelical by commitment and believed that not only the
exterior facts of history but also the inner
realities of religious life can be chronicled
in doctrinal development. In this manner
Briggs was able to embrace the newer historical-critical approach without turning
his back on earlier Pietist commitments.
Briggs described Dorner's approach in a
letter to Smith, an approach that was to
become his own:

> he gives us 1) the scriptural ground, or

biblical theology, and 2) ascends to the historical or confessional ground in the doctrinal development of the church, especially in the comparison of the confessions or symbols, and on these bases he gives us 3) his systematic statement. (quoted in Massa, 40)

In 1870 Briggs returned to the United States and became pastor of the Presbyterian church in Roselle, New Jersey. In 1874 he was appointed to a professorship in Hebrew and cognate languages at Union Theological Seminary. In these years Briggs was active with publishing articles in various Presbyterian journals, including a response to recent premillennialism, in which he disputed its pessimistic perspective on Christian history.

Work. All efforts to assess the Christian faith in the present, Briggs argued, required historical scrutiny and perspective. Critical historical exploration of both Scripture and church contributed helpful strategies for addressing challenges facing Christendom.

In 1879, at the suggestion of Briggs, William Adams, president of Union Theological Seminary, wrote A. A. Hodge of Princeton proposing that Union and Princeton launch a new journal as a unifying effort among Presbyterians. Upon Hodge's agreement, *Presbyterian Review* appeared on January 11, 1880, identifying Briggs and Hodge as editors. Briggs was interested not only in biblical criticism but also in a new historical analysis of mileposts in Reformed theology.

Briggs's contribution in the first journal was "The Documentary History of the Westminster Assembly." *Presbyterian Review* soon became controversial as the result of publishing the proceedings of the William Robertson *Smith libel trial in the Church of Scotland. In his *Lectures on the Religion of the Semites,* Smith approached the Old Testament in its religion from an anthropological perspective. He also wrote a favorable introduction to the translation of Julius *Wellhausen's *Prolegomena to the History of Ancient Israel.*

Following this report, eight articles ap-peared in the *Review* by persons from both schools. Hodge and B. B. Warfield published their opening articles on inspiration. Warfield argued that the original autographs of the Scripture were without error and that charges of inaccuracy contradicted not only the Scriptures but also Presbyterian doctrine. Briggs responded with "The Critical Theories of the Sacred Scriptures" (April 1881). He argued that the Reformation itself advanced the principle that critical assessment is appropriate for new developments, the category in which he situated the Princetonian declaration on inspiration. Briggs made the same point in an article on Pentateuchal criticism, declaring that critical investigations helped realize the ancient hope that the Scripture would shine forth, uninhibited by wooden, traditional interpretation. Because of growing rancor over Briggs's views on inspiration, the revision of the Westminster Confession, and biblical criticism, the *Presbyterian Review* dissolved in 1889.

In 1890 Briggs was appointed to the Edward Robinson Chair of Biblical Theology at Union. Because of the charged atmosphere, Briggs proposed an innocuous inaugural address on biblical geography, Robinson's specialty. But the donor, who was also the chairman of Union's board of trustees, convinced him that the occasion called for a defense of the school, the donor and Briggs himself. Briggs therefore popularized his lecture, "The Authority of the Holy Scripture," and spoke so pointedly that when it was over his friends felt compelled to apologize.

Briggs commenced by observing that Christianity rested upon a threefold authority, the church, reason and the Holy Scripture. Protestants, he observed, recognized only the authority of the Scriptures, while the authority of the church seemed Romish and the authority of reason, deistic. Though Briggs gave primacy to the Scripture, he argued that in Protestant circles neither the church nor reason had been given their due. It was especially in biblical theology, however, that God's authority is located. "We are now face to face with Biblical Theology. Here, if anywhere, the Divine authority will be found" (Briggs 1891, 65).

Even so, potential dangers accrue in locating ultimate authority in Scripture. These take the form of superstition, the doctrine of verbal inspiration, authenticity of authors, inerrancy, natural law and one-to-one prophetic prediction. Biblical theology consists of the religion, faith and ethics of the Scriptures. Biblical theology differs from conservative dogmatic theology in that the sanctification of many persons continues after their death. For Briggs the theology of the Scriptures is to be identified with the faith and the ideas, not the facts in regard to history and geography. The theology of the Scripture remains, and hence its authority, even if factual errors are uncovered. Briggs ended by expressing the hope that in the future all three types of authority would achieve their appropriate role and a correct understanding of the Bible emerge.

Briggs's lecture was widely discussed, even in the public media. In May 1891 the New York presbytery appointed a committee to formulate a case against Briggs's unorthodoxy. The charges were dismissed in October. In May 1892, in an unusual move, the general assembly meeting in Portland, Oregon, charged the New York presbytery to proceed with the case. The alleged heresies were that Briggs taught that reason and the church are also sources of divine authority, that Scripture contains error, that Moses did not write the Pentateuch, and that Isaiah wrote only half of the work attributed to him. In December 1892 the presbytery acquitted Briggs, but an appeal was made to the general assembly in Washington, D.C., which reversed the decision and suspended Briggs's ordination.

In future years Union Theological Seminary withdrew from the Presbyterian church and became nondenominational. In 1899 Briggs was ordained an Episcopalian. In the 1890s and until the end of his life Briggs spent much time in Protestant ecu-menical efforts. He also maintained numerous contacts with Roman Catholic modernists and anticipated rapprochements between Roman Catholics and Protestants. In 1906 he strategized with Baron von Huegel in an effort to discourage Pope Pius X from making a pronouncement against biblical criticism, but unsuccessfully. He died on June 8, 1913.

Significance. According to Briggs himself, his contributions to biblical studies resided in his work in Hebrew lexicography and biblical theology (Briggs 1916, 2:189, 192). But we may also add his exegetical studies in the Psalms.

The name of Briggs still remains in Hebrew lexicography as the result of his work on *A Hebrew and English Lexicon of the Old Testament* along with Francis Brown and Samuel Rolles *Driver. The project spanned twenty-three years. The contributions of Briggs were the entries on "Old Testament Religion, Theology, and Psychology" (Brown, Driver and Briggs, ix). Though two major efforts are currently underway to revise the *Lexicon,* the work is still perceived as foundational.

Briggs claimed to be the first American to set forth a perspective of his own on biblical theology in his essay "Biblical Theology" (*American Presbyterian Review,* 1870). He saw this as a programmatic statement in the manner of the classic statement by J. P. Gabler. Briggs's daughter, Emilie Grace Briggs, claimed for him the distinction of offering the first complete course of lectures on biblical theology (Briggs 1916, 2:192). At about the same time, however, if not earlier, Lutheran seminaries offered courses based on the work of Gottlob Christian Storr, *An Elementary Course of Biblical Theology* (Andover, MA: Flagg & Gould, 1826). Briggs, however, ignored this work on the grounds it did not qualify as biblical theology. He argued that biblical theology could serve as a guard against mysticism, scholasticism and speculation, creating instead a genuine biblical, evangelical perspective (Briggs 1883, 367-73).

Briggs believed that the proper course

has been established for biblical theology in stages, Gabler establishing the historical principle; J. Neander, the variety in different biblical materials; S. Schmidt, that it was a type of exegetical theology (Briggs 1883, 389). Later Briggs declared it the highest level of exegesis and brought exegesis to its proper conclusion. Briggs charged biblical theology to focus on the canon, though as situated against the backdrop of surrounding religions. It included ethics, religion, doctrines and morals. Biblical theology must not take a step beyond the Bible itself since going beyond is the task of systematic theology (392). Biblical theology differs from biblical dogmatics in that it is not an effort to systematize biblical topics. The possible organization is provided by "supernatural divine revelation and communication of redemption in the successive covenants of grace" (396). The various covenants focus on God, humanity and redemption (402).

Much like Gabler, Briggs set forth a prospectus of biblical theology but did not write one. His daughter, however, listed *Messianic Prophecy* (1886), *The Messiah of the Gospels* (1894), *The Messiah of the Apostles* (1895), *The Incarnation of the Lord* (1902) and *The Ethical Teaching of Jesus* (1904) as works in biblical theology. Briggs's prospectus is by and large accepted by biblical theologians, the main current disputes pertaining to the limits. Since Briggs set his purpose and method in a historical context, his insights are still valuable.

The first major work of Briggs on the Psalms was his translation and additions to Moll's commentary *The Psalms* in the Lange series, the translated set being edited by Philip Schaff. Briggs translated the sections on Psalms 1—41 and Psalms 51—72. In the preface to his commentary on Psalms (ICC), he wrote that the Lange volume contained "twenty-five per cent additional matter." His additions cited supplementary commentaries and studies in philology as well as clarifications and organization of materials. It is clear that he had an excellent command of the bibliography, especially German works.

Briggs was founding editor of The International Critical Commentary, along with Driver for the Old Testament commentaries and Alfred Plummer for the New. He worked on his two-volume commentary on the Psalms for forty years and finally finished it with the help of his daughter. He focused upon lexicographical matters along with poetical features. With Briggs's interest in theology, one might suppose that reflections on theology would be a strong suit in this commentary. Though he prepared a discourse on the theological aspects, he left it out of the commentary. His evangelical presuppositions are clearly expressed in the preface:

> The Psalter expresses the religious experience of a devout people through centuries of communion with God. I cannot explain either Gospels or Psalms except as Books of God, as products of human religious experience, inspired and guided by the Divine Spirit. (Briggs 1872, ix)

Briggs's work is solid in philology and in comments on poetic structure and is still worth consulting for these reasons.

A. C. McGiffert viewed Briggs as "thoroughly conservative except in the field of Biblical criticism" (*DAB* 2). Briggs, however, challenged many orthodox doctrinal positions through critical historical investigation and departed from the consensus Baconian common sense epistemology. In his last years he became critical of younger scholars, especially in their christology and rejection of the virgin birth. In 1904 he resigned his chair of biblical theology in order to teach symbolics and irenics. He was a crucial leader among the founders of the Society of Biblical Literature in 1880 and served as the fourth president (1890-1891).

BIBLIOGRAPHY

Works. C. A. Briggs, *American Presbyterianism: Its Origin and Early History* (New York: Scribner's, 1885); idem, "The Ante-Nicene Church and Premillenarianism," *New York Evangelist* (January 2, 1879); idem, *The Bible, the Church and the Reason* (New York: Scribner's, 1892); idem, *Biblical History* (New York: Scribner's, 1889); idem, *Biblical Study: Its Principles, Methods and History* (New York: Scribner's, 1883); idem, *Church Unity* (New York: Scribner's, 1909); idem, *Critical and Exegetical Commentary on the Book of Psalms* (2 vols.; ICC; New York: Scribner's, 1906-1907); idem, "The Critical Theories of the Sacred Scriptures in Relation to Their Inspiration," *Presbyterian Review* 2 (1881); idem, *The Ethical Teaching of Jesus* (New York: Scribner's, 1904); idem, *The Fundamental Christian Faith* (New York: Scribner's, 1913); idem, *General Introduction to the Study of the Holy Scripture* (New York: Scribner's, 1899); idem, *The Higher Criticism of the Hexateuch* (New York: Scribner's, 1893); idem, *History of the Study of Theology* (2 vols.; London: Duckworth, 1916); idem, "The Authority of Holy Scripture" in *Inspiration and Inerrancy* (London: James Clarke & Co., 1891); idem, *The Incarnation of the Lord* (New York: Scribner's, 1902); idem, *The Messiah of the Gospels* (New York: Scribner's, 1894); idem, *The Messiah of the Apostles* (New York: Scribner's, 1895); idem, *Messianic Prophecy* (New York: Scribner's, 1886); idem, trans. *Psalms and Ezra* (Lange Bible Commentary; New York: Scribner's 1872); idem, *Whither? A Theological Question for the Times* (New York: Scribner's, 1889); F. Brown, S. R. Driver and C. A. Briggs, *A Hebrew and English Lexicon of the Old Testament with an Appendix Containing the Biblical Aramaic* (Oxford: Clarendon Press, 1906); Lange Bible Commentary, translated *Psalms and Ezra* (New York: Scribner's, 1872).

Studies. C. E. Hatch, *The Charles A. Briggs Heresy Trial* (New York: Exposition Press, 1969); W. J. Hynes, "A Hidden Nexus Between Catholic and Protestant Modernism: C. A. Briggs in Correspondence with A. Loisy, von Huegel and Genocchi," *DR* 105 (July 1987) 193-223; L. A. Loetscher, *The Broadening Church* (Philadelphia: University of Pennsylvania Press, 1954); idem, "C. A. Briggs In the Retrospect of Half a Century," *TT* (1955) 31-39; M. S. Massa, *Charles Augustus Briggs and the Crisis of Historical Criticism* (Minneapolis: Fortress, 1990); E. Robinson, *Biblical Researches in Palestine* (3 vols.; Boston: Crocker & Brewster, 1841); J. B. Rogers and D. K. McKim, *The Authority and Interpretation of the Bible: An Historical Approach* (San Francisco: Harper &

Row, 1979); H. Rollmann, "Holtzmann, von Huegel and Modernism—II," *DR* 97 (July 1979) 221-44; M. J. Sawyer, *Charles Augustus Briggs and Tensions in Nineteenth-Century American Theology* (New York: Peter Lang, 1994).
                                    T. H. Olbricht

De Wette, Wilhelm Martin Leberecht *(1780-1849)*

Wilhelm Martin Leberecht de Wette was born on January 12, 1780, in the village of Ulla, near Weimar in the independent state of Saxony-Weimar. He attended the gymnasium in Weimar and was taught by the general superintendant, J. G. Herder. In 1799 he entered the University of Jena, where he remained until 1807. Here he completed his doctorate and wrote the two-volume work that made a major impact on Old Testament scholarship, the *Beiträge zur Einleitung in das Alte Testament* (1806-1807).

In 1807 de Wette was appointed to a professorship in Heidelberg but stayed there for only three years. In 1810 he became a professor at the newly opened University of Berlin, with colleagues such as Friedrich Daniel Ernst *Schleiermacher. What promised to be an outstanding career in Prussia's most prestigious university was cut short when de Wette was dismissed in 1819. He had written a letter of sympathy to the mother of a theological student, Karl Ludwig Sand, who had assassinated the well-known playwright August Kotzebue in 1817. Kotzebue's death was the signal to restrict all democratic movements in the German states, including student movements. The investigations reached de Wette, whose democratic and radical theological views were well known, and his letter to Frau Sand gave the Prussian authorities the opportunity to make an example of him.

Without work and with a family to support, de Wette spent 1819 to 1822 in Weimar. His election in 1821 to the prestigious position of Lutheran pastor of the St. Katherine Church in Braunschweig was blocked by George IV of Britain (then ruler of Brauschweig), and in desperation de Wette reluctantly accepted a professorship in Basel, Switzerland. He remained there until his death on June 16, 1849. He had become a Swiss citizen and had been ordained as a Reformed clergyman.

Background. De Wette lived at a time when the two main theological parties in Germany were the rationalists and the supernaturalists. He belonged to neither and tried to be a mediating theologian. Inevitably supernaturalists labeled him a rationalist, while the rationalists felt that he made too many concessions to the supernaturalists. Also, as he grew older, de Wette became increasingly sensitive to the way in which biblical criticism affected the faith of ordinary churchgoers, so that he moderated some of his earlier critical views. Because de Wette's biblical interpretation cannot be divorced from it, his theological and philosophical development must be outlined.

Temperamentally de Wette was both a mystic and a scrupulously honest and radical thinker. As a student in Jena he lost his childhood Christian faith under the impact of the philosophy of Immanuel Kant and the rationalism of his biblical teachers. But his mystical side was dissatisfied and helped by the lectures of F. W. J. Schelling in Jena on the philosophy of art, De Wette came to believe that religion, like art, enables us to experience the eternal values of truth and beauty in a world where suffering and misfortune abound. He thus became concerned to interpret the Bible symbolically and aesthetically rather than historically. While he was at Heidelberg he became friendly with and made a close study of the neo-Kantian philosophy of J. F. Fries, thus enabling him to express his position in terms of a coherent philosophical system. There was, however, a void at the center of this position that was to be filled in 1817 in a sort of conversion experience that affected his subsequent work. Prior to de Wette's "discovery" he believed that artistic forms such as literature, art, music and architecture were attempts to express human intuitions of eternal values without, however, it being possible to know exactly what these values were like. The life of Christ as presented in the Gospels were similarly an expression of values whose true nature could be glimpsed but not fully apprehended.

De Wette's discovery was that the life of Christ was a visible embodiment of the eternal values and not merely an expression of them, so that in Christ it was possible to see and apprehend the eternal values of truth and beauty. This discovery transformed de Wette's commitment to Christ. Although his view of the divinity of Christ remained far from orthodox, he was able to convince leading Pietists such as C. F. Spittler of the sincerity of his devotion to Christ, even though Spittler was repelled by de Wette's critical attitude to the Bible.

Work. In 1804 de Wette presented a doctoral dissertation to the University of Jena on the date and composition of Deuteronomy. It argued that Deuteronomy could not have been written before the seventh century B.C. and that it was most likely the law book found in the temple in the reign of Josiah (2 Kings 22:8). The connection between Deuteronomy and the law book came in a lengthy footnote, which also provided the rationale for the identification and anticipated both de Wette's *Beiträge* (1806-1807) and Julius *Well-hausen's classical *Geschichte Israels* (1878) and *Prolegomena* (1883). It pointed out that in the books of Samuel and Kings, Samuel, Saul, David and Solomon offer sacrifices at various sanctuaries without incurring divine displeasure, whereas if the Deuteronomic command of the single sanctuary was really Mosaic, they were acting illegally. De Wette therefore concluded that Deuteronomy could not be Mosaic and was most likely to be connected with Josiah's reform.

This view was spelled out in greater detail in volume 1 of the *Beiträge*. But two other epoch-making features of the *Beiträge* must be mentioned: the treatment of Chronicles and the attempt to show that much of the Pentateuch was mythical.

Prior to de Wette, the standard critical view was that the material common to Samuel and Kings on the one hand and the books of Chronicles on the other was to be attributed to a common source. In volume 1 of the *Beiträge* de Wette argued that Chronicles were dependent on Samuel and Kings and were guilty of exaggeration and of bias in favor of Judah. De Wette thus attempted to discredit Chronicles as a reliable source for reconstructing the history of Israel.

Volume 2 discussed the composition of the Pentateuch and Joshua. Here de Wette occupied a mediating position between the older documentary hypothesis (he accepted that an *Elohim* document was the framework of Genesis—Numbers) and the fragmentary hypothesis that identified parts of the narrative as independent fragments. However, a main theme was that much of the material was mythical in the sense that it consisted of originally isolated stories whose aim was to express Israelite religious intuitions. At first sight this part of de Wette's work was destructively negative, but seen in the light of his beliefs at the time, as well as the discussions about the nature of myth that were going on in literary and philosophical circles, de Wette's mythical interpretation was an attempt to rescue and vindicate the religious content of the Old Testament.

This attempt was continued in de Wette's next important work, the "Beytrag zur Charakteristik des Hebraismus" (1807). In this work de Wette noted that more that half of the Psalms are concerned with suffering and misfortune, that the book of Job wrestles with the problem of suffering and that Ecclesiastes contains much pessimism. No doubt his sensitivity to these matters was heightened by his own personal misfortunes, chief of which was the death of his wife, Eberhardine, in childbirth in February 1806. De Wette attributed this preoccupation with suffering to the particular religious genius of the He-brew people and their awareness of the contradiction between suffering and religious intuitions of the ultimate goodness of reality. In their different ways Psalms, Job and Ecclesiastes were attempts to grapple with and to overcome the realities of a harsh world. Thus de Wette was trying to interpret Hebrew religion aesthetically and existentially.

The treatment of the Psalms in the "Beytrag" was expanded into de Wette's forward-looking *Commentar über die Psalmen* (1811; 4th ed., 1836), which proved to be the first and only volume in a projected commentary on the whole Bible by de Wette and J. C. W. Augusti. De Wette classified the Psalms into various types, such as laments, hymns, royal psalms and national psalms, thus anticipating the form criticism of the Psalms by a century, although his classification, like much form criticism, was based on content and on the aesthetic character of the Psalms. De Wette dated the majority of the Psalms to the postexilic period.

The commentary on Psalms (1811) brought to an end de Wette's first and main period as a biblical interpreter. It is true that while in Berlin he wrote an introduction to the Old Testament that went through six editions in his lifetime (1817 to 1844), as well as a basic student textbook on Old Testament history and archaeology and a biblical dogmatics of the Old Testament and New Testaments (1813). But these were works of synthesis of the prevailing scholarship, albeit from de Wette's particular standpoint. De Wette's interest and thus his writings turned more to theology and ethics after 1815, and during his period of unemployment in Weimar he wrote a two-volume semi-autobiographical novel and collected material for the first scholarly edition of the letters of Martin *Luther (eventually published in 5 vols., 1825-1828). His second period as a biblical interpreter began in the 1830s, when he produced a series of commentaries on all the books of the New Testament (1836-1848).

De Wette's *Kurzgefasstes exegetisches*

Handbuch zum Neuen Testament was a partial fulfillment of the abortive plan to write a commentary on the whole Bible. It ran to eleven volumes, of which nine enjoyed second editions and five, third editions. The commentaries condensed an enormous amount of scholarly material into a format that made it accessible to readers such as clergy, and they were characterized by scrupulous fairness. For example, although David Friedrich *Strauss's *Life of Jesus* had caused an uproar in 1835, de Wette treated it fairly in his commentaries on the Gospels, and in the first edition of the commentary on Matthew (1836) he offered a measured critique that accepted some of Strauss's arguments while de Wette maintained a positive view of what could be known of the life of Christ as a basis for faith. Again, if he gave measured attention to the work of an extreme radical critic such as Strauss, he was equally attentive to orthodox commentators such as Friedrich August Gottreu *Tholuck. The New Testament commentaries were typical of his life's work. They were radical and critically honest, yet they never ignored the primary function of the New Testament, which was to uphold Christ as the source of true religious life.

Significance. De Wette occupies a key position in the history of Old Testament criticism because he was the first scholar to use certain parts of the Old Testament against other parts in order to produce an account of the history of Israelite religion that was radically at variance with the account given in the Old Testament itself. By attempting to discredit the books of Chronicles and by contrasting the legitimate multiple use of holy places in Samuel and Kings with the Deuteronomic command that there should only be one legitimate place of sacrifice, de Wette laid the groundwork for the position classically expounded by Wellhausen in 1878. De Wette's work was initially taken up and expanded by scholars such as C. P. W. Gramberg and J. F. L. George and with important modifications by W. Vatke

(1835). It then lost favor in the face of criticism from orthodox scholars such as Ernst W. Hengstenberg and from critical scholars with a much more positive view of the biblical picture of Israel's history, such as Heinrich Ewald. De Wette's dismissal from Berlin and his banishment to Switzerland, where he had few students, also contributed to his loss of influence, except that his Old Testament introduction and his New Testament commentaries were valued for the shrewd and concise way in which they represented the various strands of contemporary scholarship. It was not until the late 1860s that the position worked out by the *Beiträge* was taken up by other scholars and which in a refined form led to the so-called Graf-Wellhausen hypothesis.

Of all de Wette's work, that which has best stood the test of time is his argument that Samuel and Kings was the source used by the writer of Chronicles. This has become a standard view, although it has recently been challenged by A. G. Auld. His observations about the apparent contradiction between the Mosaic Deuteronomic command of a central sanctuary and the legitimate use of multiple sanctuaries by figures such as Samuel remain observations that call for explanation, however this is done.

De Wette was a man of the future not so much in the solutions that he proposed but in the questions that he raised and the way he tried to answer them. He believed that the study of the Bible could not be divorced from the study of literature and aesthetics. He was also convinced of the contribution to be made by philosophy, by which he understood the study of what and how we have knowledge of the world, including our moral and aesthetic knowledge. De Wette's opposition to rationalism came from his conviction that it concentrated on empirical knowledge at the expense of moral and aesthetic experience. He was unusual in being a radical critic who was at the same time sensitive to the damage that biblical criticism could do to the faith of ordinary believers. He was truly a mediating theologian.

BIBLIOGRAPHY

Works. W. M. L. De Wette, *Beiträge zur Einleitung in das Alte Testament* (Halle: Schmimmel-pfennig und Compagnia, 1806-1807); idem, "Beytrag zur Charakteristik des Hebraismus" in *Studien,* ed. C. Daub and F. Creuzer 3.2 (Frankfurt: J. C. B. Mohr, 1807) 241-312; idem, *Christliche Sittenlehre* (Berlin: G. Reimer, 1819-1923); idem, *Commentar über die Psalmen* (Heidelberg: Mohr & Zimmer, 1811); idem, *A Critical and Historical Introduction to the Canonical Scriptures of the Old Testament* (Boston: Crosby, Nichols, 1858); idem, *Kurzgefasstes exegetisches Handbuch zum Neuen Testament* (11 vols.; Leipzig: Weidmannsche Buchhandlung, 1836-1848); idem, *Lehrbuch der historisch-kritischen Einleitung in die kanonischen und apokryphischen Bücher des Alten Testaments* (Berlin: G. Reimer, 1817); idem, *Das Wesen des christlichen Glaubens* (Basel: Schweighauser'sche Buchhandlung, 1846).
Studies. J. W. Rogerson, *W. M. L. de Wette, Founder of Modern Biblical Criticism: An Intellectual Biography* (JSOTSup 126; Sheffield: Sheffield Academic Press, 1992); R. Smend, *Wilhelm Martin Leberecht de Wettes Arbeit am Alten und am Neuen Testament* (Basel: Helbing & Lichtenhahn, 1958).   J. W. Rogerson

Driver, Samuel Rolles
(1846-1914)

Samuel Rolles Driver was born into a Quaker family in Southampton, England, where his father was a successful merchant. He studied at Winchester and New College, Oxford, where he received an education in the arts, humanities and mathematics before specializing in Hebrew, Arabic, Syriac and other Semitic languages. Although Driver distinguished himself in languages, his interests in mathematics and natural sciences surfaced often throughout his career in his engagements with issues relating to science and the Bible and in his commentaries, which are replete with detailed information about plants, insects, animals, geography and geology, as well as history and archaeology.

Driver was made a fellow of New College in 1870 and a tutor in 1875. In 1874 he published his *Treatise on the Use of the Tenses in Hebrew,* which earned him a position on the committee that produced the Revised Version of the Old Testament (1875-84). In 1881 he was ordained deacon in the Church of England. Following E. B. Pusey's death in September 1882, Driver was nominated as Regius Professor of Hebrew at Oxford and canon of Christ Church. He took up his duties in January 1883 after his ordination to the priesthood, which was a requirement for the position. Five years later Driver made his first visit to Palestine. Nearer the end of his career (1910), he spent four months visiting Egypt and Palestine.

During his career Driver held many responsible positions in the university. His administrative and academic achievements brought him a number of honors. He was elected fellow of the British Academy (1902); he presented the first of the series of Schweich Lectures (1908); he was made corresponding member of the Royal Prussian Academy of Sciences (1910); and he received honorary degrees from Trinity College, Dublin, and from the universities of Glasgow, Cambridge and Aberdeen. He was married in 1891 and had five children.

Driver was a modest, sincere, steadfast, generous and kind person. He was also a very private person. His life centered around his academic work, to which he devoted great energy, and his family, with whom he had deep and loving relationships. His religious life was similarly private and quiet, and yet it was also steadfast and profound. He had a great distaste for church politics and for what one friend called "religious conversation in the ordinary sense," since for Driver "things of religious import were very sacred, hardly to be approached with words" (Brown, 294). Two of his favorite hymns, "Just As I Am" and "Jesus, Lover of My Soul," both sung at his funeral, testify to his Christian faith, which was wed to his scholarship in a way that commanded the respect of many and the disdain of those who thought that "believing criticism" was a contradiction in terms.

Context. Driver's academic career blossomed during a time of great transition in England. In 1880 his contemporary Alfred Cave believed that 99 percent of biblical scholars in England, Scotland and the United States held to traditional views on such critical issues as the Mosaic authorship of the Pentateuch, but that percentage was significantly lower ten years later (Glover, 36). The publication of *Essays and Reviews* (1860), the controversial writings and trials of William Robertson *Smith, the writings of Old Testament scholars like A. B. Davidson and T. K. Cheyne, and the availability of German critical works in English made many people aware of the new ideas emanating from Germany.

Aware of challenges that scientific research and the new literary and historical critical analyses of the Old Testament were presenting, Driver cautiously and systematically broadened the base of his scholarly expertise and moved gradually and yet determinedly during the decade of the 1880s toward an acceptance of the main lines of Julius *Wellhausen's critical position (Cheyne, 248-50). Driver then felt constrained to make the critical views known to English clergy and laity in a way that was amenable to Anglican theology and philosophy. He did this through sermons, addresses, articles, popular commentaries and most effectively through *An Introduction to the Literature of the Old Testament* (1891).

Because Driver was so esteemed personally and academically both in the church and in the academy, he was able to convince many of the legitimacy of the higher-critical approach to the study of the Scriptures. The decision of the committee appointed by the Conference of Bishops of the Anglican Communion, held at Lambeth in July 1897, to affirm both the right and the duty of qualified Christian teachers and theologians to undertake the critical study of every part of the Bible and their expectation that such study would lead to "an increased

and more vivid sense of the Divine revelation" shows how quickly the critical approach was accepted by the church in England (Driver 1891, xvii). Driver's influence on this decision and on the history of the reception of higher criticism in England in general was decisive.

Work. Driver was a prolific writer. Moreover, he was both an outstanding scholar and a popularizer. His writings included technical treatises, articles and dictionary entries on the Hebrew language, commentaries on almost half of the books in the Old Testament, and published sermons, addresses, articles and books that dealt with issues related to modern literary and historical criticism of the Old Testament.

A Treatise on the Use of the Tenses in Hebrew (1874) was Driver's first and probably most original contribution. G. A. Cooke accurately assessed the book's importance as marking "an epoch in the modern study of Hebrew; . . . quite the most interesting book ever written on the subject, intellectually satisfying to a rare degree by its inductive method and combination of breadth with exactness in detail" (Cooke 1916, 250). Driver's systematic discussion of the various Hebrew verb forms and their usage made the work a classic.

Driver's *An Introduction to the Literature of the Old Testament* has as its stated aim "to furnish an account, at once descriptive and historical, of the Literature of the Old Testament" (Driver 1891, xii). Accordingly Driver introduces his discussion of each particular book with a bibliography, an account of the contents, structure and aim of each book and a discussion of problematic features of the text that a critical approach attempts to explain (i.e., date, historical veracity or authorship). Driver's treatment of Genesis, for example, begins with a discussion of the title of the book and a summary of its contents, structure and unity of plan, which leads into a detailed and remarkably dispassionate presentation of phenomena "which show incontrovertibly that it [Genesis] is composed of distinct documents or sources, which have been welded together by a later compiler or redactor into a continuous whole" (Driver 1891, 8). Driver then discusses the P and JE sources and finally suggests the process by which the book "probably" received its present form. Only following an analysis of all the books of the Hexateuch does Driver discuss the question of the dates of the sources at length. But again on this controversial subject Driver exhibits great candor and caution that have the effect of disarming the skeptic. Thus he writes:

> Have we done rightly, it will perhaps be asked, in distinguishing J and E? . . . is it probable that there should have been two narratives of the patriarchal and Mosaic ages? . . . The writer has often considered these questions; but, while readily admitting the liability to error . . . he must own that he has always risen from the study of "JE" with the conviction that it *is* composite. . . . The grounds alleged may seem to be slight in themselves, but in the absence of stronger grounds on the opposite side, they make it at least *relatively* probable that E and J belonged to the Northern and Southern kingdoms respectively . . . [and] both J and E may be assigned with the greatest probability to the early centuries of the monarchy. (Driver 1891, 116, 123, 125)

Thus with erudition and skill Driver introduced and defended the legitimacy and usefulness of higher criticism to a reader who, like himself, had to be personally satisfied that the grounds alleged in support of the notion that the Pentateuch was composed of four sources were adequate.

Driver's *Introduction* was immensely popular and was soon regarded as the most scholarly and authoritative exposition of the principles of higher criticism in the English language. Though it contained little that had not been published elsewhere—Driver himself acknowledged that the book was "founded largely on the labors of previous scholars"—its power lay in

its lucid and persuasive exposition of both the methods and conclusions used by critical scholars, especially Wellhausen, and carefully verified by Driver, who "satisfied himself, by personal study, that the grounds alleged in their support are adequate" (Driver 1891, xvi). Moreover, the devout and reverent spirit with which Driver approached his task did much to persuade many people that criticism and faith were compatible. Even those who did not accept Driver's conclusions recognized that his *Introduction* was the most accurate and reliable presentation of the higher-critical approach to the study of the Old Testament.

In 1892 Driver published his *Sermons on Subjects Connected with the Old Testament* as a kind of supplement to his *Introduction*. Driver intended this collection of sermons to show that he was not indifferent to either the theological aspects of the Old Testament or the permanent value of its moral and religious teaching. The collection begins with a paper entitled "On the Permanent Moral and Devotional Value of the Old Testament for the Christian Church" and includes such topical sermons as "Evolution Compatible with Faith," "The Voice of God in the Old Testament" and "Inspiration," as well as more directly exegetical sermons that Driver hoped "show more particularly how 'the specific lessons of the Old Testament' may be enforced, and its 'providential purpose' recognized, without interpreting its words in a sense alien to their original meaning or context, or otherwise deviating from a strict application of critical and exegetical canons" (Driver 1892, vi).

This collection of sermons as well as *The Ideals of the Prophets: Sermons by the Late S. R. Driver* (1915) function as a useful companion to Driver's more theoretical discussions about how modern criticism is compatible with belief in the continuing value, inspiration and religious authority of the Old Testament. In addition they show how Driver's close attention to the language and style of the original text at times spawns fresh and insightful readings, some of which continue to be relevant. For example, Driver's close reading of the Hebrew text of Genesis 2 leads him to an interpretation of the creation of woman that anticipates some feminist readings of Genesis 2 from the late twentieth century. Driver states:

> They [the animals and birds] pass before him in order, but amongst them all there is found no help "meet for him"—i.e. no help, corresponding, or adapted to him—in a single word, no consort. Only an origin most closely associated with himself can provide man with the social and intellectual complement which his nature lacks: he recognizes woman's equality with himself, and the work of creation is complete. (Driver 1892, "Evolution Compatible with Faith," 2)

Driver's commentaries were written for different series and vary accordingly in length, emphases and intended audience. However, they all aimed to make the best and most up-to-date scholarship available to a wide readership. His commentaries are generally commended for their careful elucidation of the literary and historical-critical issues from the perspective that became identified with liberal Protestant theology. In addition, because of Driver's knowledge of Hebrew syntax and vocabulary and text criticism as well as his ability to read the text closely with special attention to its literary style, many of his commentaries have remained standard reference works throughout the twentieth century (notably his commentaries on Genesis, Exodus, Deuteronomy, Daniel, Joel and Amos).

Questions about the theological and religious value of the various Old Testament books were always of interest to Driver, though some commentaries are more helpful than others in terms of providing the reader with rich theological insights into the meaning of biblical texts (notably *The Book of Genesis*, 1904). However, because Driver often found the religious meaning or lesson in a text through moralizing or psychologizing, he has been criticized for passing over other important dimensions of the text's religious meaning.

For example, commenting on Driver's commentary on the book of Daniel, in which he presents the critical position on the dating and authorship of Daniel, Brevard *Childs laments: "Yet Driver's interpretation has flattened out the message of the book to make it a political tract for the Maccabean age from which the modern reader can extract, at most, a few lessons in piety. Theology has been transformed into anthropology" (Childs, 80). Driver's commentaries nonetheless contain a mature, scholarly, reverent and influential presentation of the critical and theological issues that were on the cutting edge of Old Testament scholarship during the late nineteenth and early twentieth centuries.

Although Driver's *Notes on the Hebrew Text of the Books of Samuel* (1890) has many features in common with a commentary, it deserves note since it was written for specialists and has remained an important resource. In the introduction Driver discusses Hebrew paleography and the ancient versions of the books of Samuel. He then provides notes on the text, making "judicial and responsible use" of earlier German critical works, especially Wellhausen's (McHardy, 166-67). Although Driver's *Notes* are dated, especially in light of issues and problems raised by the discovery of the Dead Sea Scrolls, they continue to be useful to scholars working on the books of Samuel.

A few other efforts of Driver deserve mention. From 1891 to 1905 Driver collaborated with Francis Brown and Charles Augustus *Briggs in the preparation of the *Hebrew and English Lexicon of the Old Testament*, which continues to be used as a standard lexicon by students of biblical Hebrew. He also helped revise and write comments for the margins of the Revised Version. He contributed extensively to J. Hastings's *Dictionary of the Bible*, the *Encyclopaedia Britannica*, and other reference works. Moreover, Driver's Schweich Lectures, published as *Modern Research as*

Illustrating the Bible (1909), attest to his interest in archaeology, which is also evident in his commentaries.

Methods of Biblical Interpretation. Driver began his academic career as a Hebraist, and all of his later work as a critical scholar builds on this foundation. He insisted that his students should have a similarly solid foundation of language study before they began the critical enterprise. Cooke, who thought that Driver's basic approach to scholarship was perhaps "the chief moral" of his life work, described Driver's approach as follows: "Accurate scholarship must be the starting point of all else; a great deal of patient drudgery with grammar, lexicon, and concordance must go to the making of a sound interpreter of the higher sense of the sacred texts" (Cooke 1916, 251). Cooke also suggests that Driver's mental habit as a grammarian determined his method as a critic:

> He proceeds cautiously on inductive lines after a close observation of facts. He sets out the critical process in detail, tabulates the distinctive features of style and usage, and, where no certain conclusion appears to be possible, he is careful to indicate the degrees of probability; with a natural leaning towards a conservative position, he prefers to suspend rather than announce his judgment. (Cooke 1916, 251)

Undoubtedly Driver's work has been so enduring because it was grounded upon a careful analysis of the text itself rather than on secondhand analyses and interpretations of it.

Driver's basic approach to the study of the Old Testament can be characterized as "reverent critical." He was concerned about the implications that the critical study of the Bible had for Christian theology and doctrine and for the "weak brethren," for whom changes in the understanding of the nature of the Scriptures were devastating. Accordingly many of his more popular writings were didactic and apologetic in nature and included illustrations of the types of problems that historical and

literary criticism attempted to account for as well as assurances that the Old Testament texts could still be regarded as inspired and revelatory and as containing a spiritual and moral message. In one of his earliest presentations of the critical position on Deuteronomy, Driver states:

> Reluctantly the present writer makes the admission which the facts extort from him: he does not see how the Mosaic authorship of Deuteronomy can be maintained. But Deuteronomy is not, on this account, to be set down as a "forgery". . . . The laws which he incorporated were, for the most part, ancient, and recognized by the Israelites: the author, instinct with prophetic inspiration, merely threw them into a new framework, emphasized the motives by which their observance should be dictated, and accommodated the whole to the position of the legislator, Moses. (Driver 1895, 5)

Driver then defends the critical view of the formation of the Pentateuch against the criticism it was "framed in the interests of unbelief, or has its foundation in the premises of a negative theology" (Driver 1895, 7). Accordingly Driver argues that the critical position itself rests on theologically "neutral" grounds and "consists simply of the application to a particular case of the canons and principles by which evidence is estimated and history judged" (Driver 1895, 7). Thus he undertakes the critical enterprise with great confidence in the objectivity and neutrality of the methods used by historical critics to evaluate data and with a concomitant commitment to follow where the facts lead.

In this same piece Driver sketched the parameters within which a Christian critic should work. First, while a Christian critic was bound to accept the authority of the Old Testament, to view it as a "Divine preparation for the revelation of Jesus Christ made in the Gospels," the critic was under no obligation to hold to a specific theory of either its literary structure or its narration of the course of history (Driver 1895, 7).

Second, because Driver believes that criticism affects the form but not the fact of revelation, he states: "The Christian critic does not question the fact of a revelation being embodied in the Old Testament Scriptures; he assumes *that*, and proceeds to inquire under what conditions it was developed historically, in what order its different parts took shape, and how they are mutually connected together" (Driver 1895, 8). Where the critics' results differed from views sanctioned by tradition, Driver suggests that the results have to be "accommodated to the main body of Christian truth" (Driver 1895, 8).

Accordingly Driver thought that one of his tasks as a Christian critic was to demonstrate that the teaching of the Old Testament continues to have value, although that value may be different than that assumed by tradition (i.e., the Old Testament's ideas are more important than dates; Driver 1895, 8-9). For example, in his critical notes on Genesis 1 (1887), Driver introduces the idea of the P source and focuses his attention on the ideas communicated by the writer(s). He uses comparative ancient Near Eastern creation stories as a foil for Genesis 1 and suggests that an inspired Hebrew historian breathed into and unified and transformed ancient theories about the beginnings of life and adapted them to teach through "representative pictures" religious, as opposed to scientific, truth (Driver 1887, 10). Similarly Driver suggests that the "J writer" may have reworked an ancient Near Eastern story into "a profound and impressive allegory" of the creation and fall that must be penetrated and interpreted "by the light of the Bible as a whole" in order to find, for example, "the deep ethical and social significance which underlies the difference between the sexes" (Driver 1887, 14-16). By pointing to the abiding spiritual and moral worth of the Old Testament texts, Driver sought to justify the historical-critical approach to a Christian audience.

Driver also felt that the Christian critic could maintain a view of the inspiration of the Old Testament. He explained it as "an influence which gave to those who received it a unique and extraordinary *spiritual insight,* enabling them thereby, without superseding or suppressing the human faculties, but rather using them as its instruments, to declare in different degrees, and in accordance with the needs or circumstances of particular ages or particular occasions, the mind and purpose of God" (Driver 1892, "Inspiration," 146-47). Moreover, Driver held that "it was the function of inspiration to guide the individual writer in the choice and disposition of his material, and in his use of it for the inculcation of special lessons" (Driver 1891, xix). This open and fluid understanding of inspiration allowed Driver to bridge the gap between criticism and faith. Thus with great conviction he declared:

Criticism in the hands of Christian scholars does not banish or destroy the inspiration of the Old Testament; it *presupposes* it; it seeks only to determine the conditions under which it operates, and the literary forms through which it manifests itself; and it thus helps us to frame truer conceptions of the methods which it has pleased God to employ in revealing Himself to His ancient people of Israel, and in preparing the way for the fuller manifestation of Himself in Christ Jesus. (Driver 1891, xxii)

Further, Driver believed that the adoption of critical conclusions implied "no change in respect to the Divine attributes revealed in the Old Testament; no change in the lessons of human duty to be derived from it; [and] no change as to the general position (apart from the interpretation of particular passages) that the Old Testament points forward prophetically to Christ" (Driver 1891, xviii). His conservative opponents, like William Henry Green of Princeton, criticized him vehemently for attempting "to revolutionize the doctrine of the entire Christian Church from the beginning respecting the inspiration of the Scriptures and the person of Christ" (Green, 344).

Driver was interested in modern scientific, historical and archaeological discoveries and sought to explore their implications for the study of the Old Testament. His attempts to reconcile the findings and theories of nineteenth-century science with faith stand as evidence of his great confidence in science and historical criticism and of his willingness to move away from what he regarded as traditional and "misleading" interpretations of texts (Cooke 1916, 253). In a sermon entitled "Evolution Compatible with Faith," delivered at St. Mary's, Oxford, before the university community in 1883, Driver argued that biblical criticism demonstrated how the Christian faith was compatible with Darwin's theory of the progressive development of humans from their anthropoid ancestors:

Science warns us that we have been wrong in insisting upon a strictly literal interpretation [of the creation narratives]; historical criticism comes forward and shows us how, without prejudice to theology, we may abandon it . . . what was once treated as historical, may be regarded as symbolical; and how, as thus understood, the theological teaching of Genesis accords with what a progressive revelation might be expected, from analogy, to contain. (Driver 1892, 25)

Similarly Driver often brought the findings of modern historians and archaeologists to bear on his understanding of the Old Testament texts (for example, his attempt to synchronize the history of Genesis with ancient Near Eastern history and his discussion of archaeology in Driver 1904, xxxviii-xxxiv, xlviii-liii).

Significance. Driver's contribution lies in several areas. Most significant was his work as a popularizer of historical criticism. Because of his ability and acknowledged learning, his high ecclesiastical and academic position, his well-known personal integrity and cautious temperament, he was able to convince many that the higher-critical approach to the study of the Old Testament was compatible with Christian faith.

Moreover, his contributions to the study of the Hebrew language, its vocabulary, grammar and syntax, have been enduring. Finally, Driver's contributions to the exegesis of Scripture through his numerous commentaries, which have remained standard resources for students and pastors throughout the English-speaking world, deserve mention.

BIBLIOGRAPHY

Works. S. R. Driver, *The Book of Daniel: With Introduction and Notes* (Cambridge: Cambridge University Press, 1900); idem, *The Book of Exodus* (Cambridge: Cambridge University Press, 1911); idem, *The Book of Genesis* (London: Methuen, 1887); idem, *The Book of Job in the Revised Version: Edited with Introductions and Brief Annotations* (Oxford: Clarendon, 1906); idem, *The Book of the Prophet Jeremiah: A Revised Translation, with Introductions and Short Explanations* (London: Hodder & Stoughton, 1906); idem, ed., *The Books of Joel and Amos* (Cambridge: Cambridge University Press, 1897); idem, *A Critical and Exegetical Commentary on Deuteronomy* (ICC; Edinburgh: T & T Clark, 1895); idem, *An Introduction to the Literature of the Old Testament* (New York: Charles Scribner, 1891); idem, *Isaiah: His Life and Times and the Writings Which Bear His Name* (New York: Fleming H. Revell, 1888); idem, ed., *The Minor Prophets: Nahum, Habakkuk, Zephaniah, Haggai, Zechariah, Malachi: introduction, Revised Version with notes, index and map* (New York: Henry Frowde, 1906); idem, *Modern Research as Illustrating the Bible* (London: H. Frowde, 1909); idem, *Notes on the Hebrew Text of the Books of Samuel* (2d ed., rev. and enl.; Oxford: Clarendon, 1913 [1890]); idem, *Sermons on Subjects Connected With the Old Testament* (London: Methuen, 1892); idem, *Studies in the Psalms,* ed. C.F. Burney (London: Hodder & Stoughton, 1915); idem, *A Treatise on the Use of the Tenses in Hebrew* (Oxford: Clarendon, 1874); idem and G. B. Gray, *A Critical and Exegetical Commentary on the Book of Job* (ICC; Edinburgh: T & T Clark, 1921); G. A. Cooke, ed., *The Ideals of the Prophets: Sermons by the Late S. R. Driver* (Edinburgh: T & T Clark, 1915), including a bibliography of Driver's published writings compiled by his son G. R. Driver in Appendix A.

Studies. F. Brown, "Samuel Rolles Driver," *BW* 43 (1914) 291-94; T. K. Cheyne, *Founders of Old Testament Criticism* (New York: Charles Scribner's Sons, 1893) 248-372; B. S. Childs, *Old Testament Books for Pastor and Teacher* (Philadelphia: Westminster, 1977); G. A. Cooke, "Driver, Samuel Rolles," *DNB* 1912-1921 (1929) 162-63; idem, "Driver and Wellhausen," *HTR* 9 (1916) 249-57; W. Glover, *Evangelical Nonconformists and Higher Criticism in the Nineteenth Century* (London: Independent Press, 1954) 36; G. B. Gray, "Samuel Rolles Driver, The Character and Influence of his Work," *CR* (April 1914) 484-90; W. H. Green, "Review of *An Introduction to the Literature of the Old Testament,* by S. R. Driver," *PRR* 3 (1892) 344; W. D. McHardy, "S. R. Driver. Notes on the Hebrew Text of the Books of Samuel," *ET* 90 (1979) 164-67; "Review of *An Introduction of the Literature of the Old Testament,* by S. R. Driver," *MR* 74 (1892) 327; J. W. Rogerson, "Driver, Samuel Rolles (1846-1914)" (*TRE* 9, ed. G. Krause; Berlin: Walter de Gruyter, 1982) 190-92; idem, *Old Testament Criticism in the Nineteenth Century: England and Germany* (London: SPCK, 1984); W. Sanday, *The Life-Work of Samuel Rolles Driver* (Oxford: Clarendon, 1914).   M. A. Taylor

Edwards, Jonathan (1703-1758)

Scion of the Puritans and student of the "new learning" propounded by the leaders of the British Enlightenment, Jonathan Edwards stood on the cusp of modern American biblical criticism. After earning his bachelor's (1720) and master's (1723) degrees at Yale College and serving brief stints at churches in New York City and Bolton, Connecticut, Edwards spent the bulk of his career as pastor of the First Church of Christ in Northampton, Massachusetts (1726-1750). After his ejection from the Northampton pulpit for his changing views on church membership and the Lord's Supper, he moved to Stockbridge, Massachusetts, and worked as a missionary to a Native American group comprised primarily of Mahicans and Mohawks, also serving as the pastor of the English church at this frontier missionary outpost. The author of numerous published sermons and major theological treatises such as *A Treatise Concerning Religious Affections* (1746), *Free-*

dom of the Will (1754) and *The Nature of True Virtue* (published posthumously), by the 1740s Edwards enjoyed a reputation as one of the American colonies' leading Calvinist divines and as the most famous theologian of New England's Great Awakening. Consequently in 1757 he was offered the presidency of the College of New Jersey (later Princeton) and in January of 1758 assumed the leadership of that institution. Soon after settling in, he provided a courageous example for frightened Princetonians by receiving an inoculation for smallpox in response to an outbreak of the disease. Unfortunately, however, he contracted a "secondary fever" from the inoculation and died soon after his move to Princeton.

Context. Though Edwards died more than a century before the rise of higher biblical criticism in America, he was not unaware of the intellectual currents that eventually yielded its scholarly methods. Indeed, he spent the lion's share of his academic life defending traditional Calvinist orthodoxy against the inroads made by liberalism in British religion and morality. By the 1750s especially, most of his major theological treatises were devoted to combatting theological liberalism in its Arminian and deist forms. His private notebooks, moreover, are filled with information and criticism concerning the rise of "infidelity" in the modern West (one recent estimate suggests that more than 25 percent of Edwards's "Miscellanies," the most famous of his private theological and philosophical notebooks, treated either deism itself or the issues raised by deists).

As a pastor Edwards's work grew out of a deep knowledge and love of the Bible, and almost everything he wrote is full of biblical exegesis. His nearly twelve hundred extant sermons (the vast majority of which survive in manuscript) reveal a man with the highest regard for the authority of Holy Scripture. Following the Puritan pattern of structuring sermons by means of text, doctrine and application, Edwards used these sermons to provide his people with a full-orbed biblical theology. Always beginning his sermons with an exposition of the biblical text at hand, he then extracted a doctrine or teaching from the contents of that text. After developing his doctrinal theme and arguing for its significance, Edwards applied this biblical teaching to the lives of his parishioners.

In his sermon preparation Edwards relied quite heavily on his private notebooks, a series of exegetical, theological and philosophical manuscripts containing thousands of pages of his most serious reflections. One such notebook, or notebook series, is known as Edwards's "Notes on Scripture," a four-book manuscript collection of miscellaneous exegetical writings. Another workbook that contains an even greater amount of Edwards's exegesis is usually referred to by those who know it as Edwards's Blank Bible (though its formal title is "Miscellaneous Observations on the Holy Scriptures"). The Blank Bible is a manuscript volume given to Edwards by his brother-in-law, Benjamin Pierpont, into which someone had sewn the leaves of a King James Bible. To the side of every leaf Edwards wrote a manuscript page of commentary, covering the entire biblical canon from the book of Genesis to Revelation. When used in tandem with the "Notes on Scripture," the Blank Bible provides the student with a vivid understanding of Edwards's exegetical skills. When compared with Edwards's sermons on particular texts and topics (along with the other, lesser manuscripts in which Edwards discusses the Bible), his biblical interpretation itself springs to life.

Biblical Interpretation. Not only Edwards's sermons and manuscript notebooks but his major treatises as well reveal his lifelong preoccupation with the Bible. In most of his treatises, for example, he makes his case with lengthy arguments from both the things we can know from reason and the things revealed in Scripture. Even in the context of his most public rational discourse, then, the Bible provides Edwards with the surest guide to things divine. Edwards's view of the relationship

between reason and revelation perhaps is best illustrated in his dissertation *Concerning the End for Which God Created the World* (1765). He divided this dissertation into two major chapters: one "Wherein Is Considered What Reason Teaches Concerning This Affair"; and the other "Wherein It Is Inquired, What Is to Be Learned from Holy Scriptures Concerning God's Last End in the Creation of the World." As he explained, "the endeavors used to discover what the voice of reason is . . . may serve to prepare the way [for revelation], by obviating cavils insisted on by many; and to satisfy us that what the Word of God says of the matter, is not unreasonable; and thus prepare our minds for a more full acquiescence in the instructions [the Bible] gives" (Edwards, 8:463). For Edwards rational arguments did prepare the mind for divine truth, but it was Scripture that conveyed this truth in the most clear and reliable manner.

The remarkable extent to which Scripture shaped Edwards's vision of reality becomes apparent upon the examination of his two great unfinished projects. The first, a "History of the Work of Redemption," was to build upon a sermon series first preached in the spring and summer of 1739. In it he hoped to provide "a body of divinity in an entire new method, being thrown into the form of a history, considering the affair of Christian theology, as the whole of it, in each part, stands in reference to the great work of redemption by Jesus Christ." He intended to discuss the history of the world (including heaven, earth and hell) "so far as the Scriptures give any light; introducing all parts of divinity in that order which is most scriptural and natural." This history was to be comprehensive, including each epoch and the entire world. But it was to be centered in the redemptive themes of the Christian Bible. Edwards's second unfinished project, his "Harmony of the Old and New Testament," was to be written in three major exegetical parts (the first two of which he fleshed out in the later "Miscellanies"): "the first considering the prophecies of the Messiah" and their fulfillment in the person of Christ; the second "considering the types" of the gospel of Christ in the Hebrew Scriptures; and "the third and great part, considering the harmony of the old and new testament, as to doctrine and precept." Edwards hoped that "in the course of this work . . . there will be occasion for an explanation of a very great part of the holy scripture; which may, in such a view be explained in a method, which to me seems the most entertaining and profitable, best tending to lead the mind to a view of the true spirit, design, life and soul of the scriptures, as well as to their proper use and improvement" (Edwards, 16: forthcoming).

Hermeneutics. Both these projects show that Edwards, even at the height of his intellectual powers, viewed all the world through the sacred lens of Scripture. His insights into the meaning of the entirety of human history came from his reading of redemptive history revealed in the Bible. When it is combined with the rest of his biblical writings, moreover, the sheer mass of this unfinished work suggests that Edwards may be the most prolific exegetical scholar in American history—a possibility vastly underappreciated by most historians of American religion.

Edwards's mention of his method for expositing the soul of the Christian Scriptures also betokens the hermeneutical strategy for which his exegesis is best known. While he maintained a typically Protestant respect for the literal sense of Scripture, and though he appreciated the emergent Enlightenment esteem for modern biblical criticism, Edwards's most significant contribution to the history of exegesis lay in his typological interpretation of the Bible. In Edwards's view the Bible is full of symbolic religious images that point to Christ, to Christian redemption or to the glory of the kingdom of God. These biblical types, which Edwards usually found in the books of the Old Testament, found their fulfillment in various antitypes represented in the New Testament. As in his projected "Har-

mony of the Old and New Testament," so in many of his other works, Edwards viewed the world as replete with what he called "images" or "shadows" of divine things (Edwards, 11). And this intensely theocentric vision of the integrity of the world produced a biblical hermeneutic in which he refracted all of Scripture through the prism of divine redemption. Thus as he read the Hebrew Scriptures, Edwards often focused on their symbols, keeping an eye out for their adumbration of the gospel. He took a special interest in prophecy and believed the essential message of Scripture to be that God is working to redeem the world in Christ.

Edwards was not the first to employ typological exegesis. Nor did he prove the most sophisticated exponent of biblical prophecy in Christian history. But his typological faith in the divine structure of reality provided his thought with a unique and powerful redemptive focus. Moreover, Edwards proved unique in his application of typology, for he refused to limit its scope to the Christian Scriptures. For him all the world was laden with images of the divine, and the gospel was shadowed forth in the workings of nature itself. He believed, for example, that "the extreme fierceness and extraordinary power of the heat of lightning is an intimation of the exceeding power and terribleness of the wrath of God." He thought, further, that the "the silkworm is a remarkable type of Christ, which, when it dies, yields us that of which we make such glorious clothing. Christ became a worm for our sakes, and by his death finished that righteousness with which believers are clothed, and thereby procured that we should be clothed with robes of glory" (Edwards, 11:59).

In short, for Edwards what was most real in the external world and its development was what his Lord was doing to redeem the world from sin. Though he held that natural and social history did subsist outside the mind, it was salvation history that gave the world its purpose and coherence. He knew that this conviction would not win him points in scholarly circles. He expected "by very ridicule and contempt to be called a man of a very fruitful brain and copious fancy." But he persisted nevertheless in his typological vision of reality, proclaiming "I am not ashamed to own that I believe that the whole universe, heaven and earth, air and seas, and the divine constitution and history of the holy Scriptures, be full of images of divine things, as full as a language is of words; and that the multitude of those things that I have mentioned are but a very small part of what is really intended to be signified and typified by these things" (Edwards, 11:152).

Significance. Edwards's commitment to reading the Bible with such a view to its hidden symbols makes him a fascinating example of a modern thinker with premodern sympathies. Though he participated actively in the discourse of the early British Enlightenment, he did not allow its historicism to impoverish his interpretation of Scripture. Rather, while he affirmed the modern concern for careful historical and critical scholarship, he also retained a traditional interest in theological interpretation. He viewed the Bible as a special book, inspired by God and uniquely sacred, and he proved unwilling to interpret its teachings like those of any other book.

Rather, Edwards allowed his metaphysic to shape his reading of the Bible and to guide him into what many of his premodern forebears deemed its higher and nobler senses. He always claimed, however, to derive this theological metaphysic from the sacred pages of holy writ itself. Thus in the end Edwards proved to be a dialectical biblical thinker, or one for whom Scripture yielded a theology that in turn he employed in interpretation. His love affair with Scripture did yield a kind of exegesis insufficiently informed by the critical work of the avant-garde. But it also produced theology that was pregnant with images and shadows of redemption for a lost and needy world.

BIBLIOGRAPHY

Works. J. Edwards, *The Works of Jonathan Ed-*

wards (14 vols. to date; New Haven, CT: Yale University Press, 1957-).

Studies. F. W. Beuttler, "Jonathan Edwards and the Critical Assaults on the Bible" (M.A. thesis, Trinity Evangelical Divinity School, 1988); C. Cherry, "Symbols of Spiritual Truth: Jonathan Edwards as Biblical Interpreter," *Int* 39 (1985) 263-71; J. H. Gerstner, "Jonathan Edwards and the Bible," *Tenth* 9 (1979) 1-71; idem, *The Rational Biblical Theology of Jonathan Edwards* (3 vols.; Powhatan, VA: Berea Publications, 1991-1993); S. T. Logan Jr., "The Hermeneutics of Jonathan Edwards," *WTJ* 43 (1981) 79-96; M. I. Lowance, *The Language of Canaan: Metaphor and Symbol in New England from the Puritans to the Transcendentalists* (Cambridge, MA: Harvard University Press, 1980); K. D. Pfisterer, *The Prism of Scripture: Studies on History and Historicity in the Work of Jonathan Edwards* (Anglo-American Forum 1; Frankfurt: Peter Lang, 1975); S. J. Stein, "The Quest for the Spiritual Sense: The Biblical Hermeneutics of Jonathan Edwards," *HTR* 70 (1977) 99-113; idem, "The Spirit and the Word: Jonathan Edwards and Scriptural Exegesis" in *Jonathan Edwards and the American Experience,* ed. N. O. Hatch and H. S. Stout (New York: Oxford University Press, 1988); R. C. Turnbull, "Jonathan Edwards—Bible Interpreter," *Int* 6 (1952) 422-35.   D. A. Sweeney

Eichhorn, J(ohann) G(ottfried) (1752-1827)

A student of Johann David *Michaelis, Christian Gottlob Heyne and A. L. Schlözer at Göttingen, Johann Gottfried Eichhorn became professor of oriental languages at Jena (1775) and then served as professor of philosophy at Göttingen (1788) until his death.

Work. Eichhorn was a tireless worker who once advised two Harvard students that they need work only twelve hours a day since they were not used to serious study. His output is more readily measured in width than in pages, a tribute to his routine of starting work at four in the morning, wrapped in his overcoat so he would not have to ask the servants to get up to light the fire. Along with multiple-volume works, some in several editions, Eichhorn published two journals, *Repertorium für biblische und morgenländisch Literatur* (1771-86) and *Allgemeine Bibliothek der biblischen Literatur* (1787-1803). Some of his more important work was first published as long articles in these journals. Apart from his achievements in the area of biblical studies, Eichhorn had wide-ranging interests from oriental languages (Arabic, Syriac, Aramaic) to the history of art and literature. For some years at Göttingen he lectured regularly on modern European history and even published two volumes on the French Revolution. Like Michaelis, he was never a member of the theological faculty, but unlike Michaelis, he had little interest (and little talent) in the area of systematic theology. The effect of Eichhorn's work in the area of biblical studies was to sweep away dogmatic presuppositions that interfered with the scholarly investigation of the date, origin and authorship of documents from the biblical period.

Eichhorn found the key to understanding Scripture in Heyne's lectures on the early Greek classics, especially his idea of myth. By applying Heyne's methods to the Bible, Eichhorn escaped from the tacit assumption of the Enlightenment that human reason was much the same anywhere and therefore parts of the Bible that were out of keeping with Enlightenment philosophy and morals were to be seen as the failures of a barbarian people who should have known better. Eichhorn demonstrated that those who wrote the biblical books did not share the same cultural world as did modern people; therefore they have to be understood and appreciated in terms of their own type of thinking that existed before the development of rational thought.

Eichhorn first set this perception out in his "Urgeschichte—ein Versuch," published anonymously (1779) as a long article in his *Repertorium*. He invites his readers to contemplate in Genesis an ancient temple "full of nature and simplicity, only touched here and there by art. A single and narrow path leads to it, a path now wild and over-

grown and without any sign that it was once passable, because since for more than a thousand years now art has gone along other ways." Despite the themes that echo the pleasurable melancholy of early Romanticism, Eichhorn may be appreciated for his attempt to get beyond the deadlock between the orthodox and the enlightened of his day.

It is often asserted that Eichhorn, along with J. P. Gabler, is the founder of the mythical school of biblical interpretation. Two points of difference between them should be borne in mind. First, for Gabler the new method was a way of defending the Bible against the scorn of the cultured despiser; for Eichhorn it was a way to an essentially aesthetic appreciation of Scripture. If Eichhorn had any particular audience in mind when he wrote, it was the orthodox whose possible objections he tries to circumvent by an appeal in the last two pages of the work. This explains why it was Gabler, despairing of Eichhorn's dealing with the problem directly, who put out a new edition of the *Urgeschichte* in book form to make it more available to the public, and in his copious notes it is clear Gabler is presenting the work as a contribution to systematic theology by his discussion of mythology and other problems. It is interesting that in his review of Gabler's edition of his work, Eichhorn does not comment on this apologetic aspect of Gabler's presentation. Second, for whatever reason, Eichhorn in contrast to Gabler remained relatively unwilling to use the term *myth* in talking about the Bible. Eichhorn does use the word, but relatively seldom, though he clearly makes use of the various conceptions behind the term.

In his interpretation of the past, Eichhorn applied the analogy of the growth of the child to the development of civilizations. While this idea has roots in classical antiquity, it attained a certain popularity in the latter part of the eighteenth century, as is shown in its independent use by Gotthold Ephraim Lessing and Johann Gottfried von Herder. Thus for Eichhorn one has to make a special effort to appreciate ancient texts such as the second creation story in Genesis, an effort increasingly more difficult as one goes back in time. For Eichhorn this analogy was more than a useful illustration; it was the principle behind all cultural development. In his *History of Literature* he states specifically that "the same stages of culture and understanding lead to the same sorts of thinking and understanding, to the same morals and customs" so that humanity proceeds by general stages of development and everywhere raises itself up according to the same laws of its nature. This explains resemblances between the Hebrews and other peoples who could have had no contact with them.

The pattern of Hebrew history for Eichhorn was that Moses, having been trained in the enlightened ways of the Egyptians, tried to raise his own people from their condition of cultural childhood. This was not immediately possible, so he trained a priesthood to carry on this work; but they betrayed his trust by keeping their learning as a monopoly. Furthermore the narrowness of Israelite laws kept the people from contact with other nations who might have enriched their lives. Even the Hebrews' doctrine of a single Creator was too exalted for them until after the exile. While all this was not original with Eichhorn, many of these themes—Hebrew religion as primitive religion, Egypt as the source of enlightenment for Moses, the nefarious role of the priesthood in holding back Israel's development, the contrast between the culture of the Hebrews compared with the enlightened Greek—played a part in scholarly discussion about Hebrew religion for more than a hundred years, and even now distant echoes are heard.

Two observations need to be made about this approach. First, despite the idea of step-by-step development, Eichhorn on occasion seems to have a preference either for the greatest antiquities of a culture, when poetry was at its purest, or its productions at its later stage of enlightenment.

This is evident even in his introduction to the books of the Apocrypha, where his highest praise is for the Wisdom of Solomon because it reflects the enlightened attitude of Greek culture in Alexandria. Second, Eichhorn retained the Enlightenment conviction that the obvious goal of human development was the rational eighteenth-century person, that is to say, himself. Earlier stages of human development might well arouse his aesthetic appreciation but not his assent. In his trips to the past Eichhorn remained a tourist rather than a student.

Eichhorn wrote introductions to the Old and New Testaments as well as the Apocrypha. "Introduction" as a type of book had existed in Germany for some time, but Eichhorn put the last piece into place in the modern form of this genre, for he added serious discussions of authorship, dating and sources of books to treatments of language, texts and versions. In particular he raised in a systematic way the problem of documents behind books in both Testaments.

Biblical Interpretation. Eichhorn's introduction to the Old Testament went through various editions after it first appeared in 1780 to 1783 and was one of the more successful academic works of its type. In Genesis he made use of the criterion of the divine names in Genesis suggested by Jean Astruc and taken up by J. F. W. Jerusalem. In his treatment of the prophets he broke free from the question of their prophecy about the Messiah (or otherwise) and saw them as particular figures of their age. Eichhorn also applied documentary criticism to the books of the prophets, distinguishing among different oracles according to their historical circumstances. Most notably Eichhorn was perhaps the first to recognize the later provenance of Isaiah 40, although J. C. Doederlein also has a claim to this discovery. He also treated Jonah as unhistorical and argued for the late date of Daniel.

In his New Testament introduction Eichhorn again applied his interest in recognizing sources to the Synoptic Gospels. He argued that the present form of the Synoptics dates from the latter part of the second century and that they all independently used an early source, a gospel written in Aramaic that did not contain the legendary, miraculous accretions of the canonical Gospels. Eichhorn also recognized the difference between John and the Synoptics but curiously enough attributed its authorship to the apostle. In his discussion of Revelation, considered by J. A. Noesselt to be one of his most important works, Eichhorn treated the book as a symbolic drama drawing on the poetic imagery of the prophets. One has to give him credit for giving the book a historical and literary context for its interpretation that avoided the Scylla and Charybdis of seeing it either as a precis of coming world history or as an incomprehensible puzzle.

In the eighteenth century, matters of biblical interpretation played a larger part in cultured society than they did in later periods, and these links should not be ignored in the study of literature and other subjects. For example, although he never intended to study theology, Michaelis was one of the reasons Johann Wolfgang von Goethe would have liked to have gone to Göttingen. Eichhorn's ideas were of interest outside academic circles, for his introductions to the Bible sold widely and went through several editions. He himself knew Goethe and Herder well while he was at Jena, and Alexander von Humbolt attended Eichhorn's lectures at Göttingen.

Significance. Eichhorn's influence on the English-speaking world, apart from those who could read him in German, was indirect. Only a part of his Old Testament introduction was translated into English in a version printed privately in 1888. However, there is the possibility that his shadow was longer than his presence. E. B. Pusey had been a student under Eichhorn during his time in Germany (not a good student, according to an English contemporary), and the relatively radical results of Eichhorn's researches may well have influenced Pusey's later horror of German scholarship. The figure of Eichhorn may also lie behind some of the passages in George Eliot's *Middlemarch.*

Eichhorn was essentially an investigative scholar with little real interest in the implications of his work for theology. Occasionally he made polite remarks about dampening the criticism of the scornful, but his heart was clearly not in it. For him the idea of the inspiration of Scripture existed only vestigially as a vague reference to providence providing for the preservation of so many biblical texts. Essentially he was not of a combative nature. In his preface to a later edition of his Old Testament introduction, Eichhorn tells how he had prepared rebuttals to his critics but then decided not to print them and simply let his argument stand on its own. His habit of referring to his own writings as the definitive discussion of a problem strikes the modern reader as somewhat ingenuous, though similar, more recent examples can be found.

While much of Eichhorn's work is now only of historical interest, his contribution to the advance of biblical studies in his own day was considerable. It is possible to criticize him for a certain failure to study his sources carefully, for often his enthusiasm outran his accuracy, and he was not given to examining alternatives to his interpretations. His interest appears to have been in extending his knowledge relentlessly without undue concern about either consistency within his own work or its significance on a wider scale. Early in the nineteenth century his reputation declined because of obvious weaknesses in his work.

Yet one area where Eichhorn is still worth reading is in his summing up of the work of other scholars. In particular his long and detailed obituary of Johann Salomo *Semler in the *Repertorium* is a masterpiece of honesty and good taste which even in its account of Semler's unfortunate later years refrains from detracting from the dignity and the achievement of a man Eichhorn had the grace to recognize as greater than himself.

BIBLIOGRAPHY

Works. J. G. Eichhorn, *Commentarius in Apocalypsinn Joannis* (2 vols.; Göttingen: Typis Jo. Christ. Dieterich, 1791); idem, *Einleitung in das Neue Testament* (various editions: Leipzig: Weidmannischen Buchhandlung, 1804-1827); idem, *Einleitung in das Alte Testament* (various editions: 3 vols.; Leipzig: Weidmannischen Buchhandlung, 1780-1783; 5 vols.; 1820-1824); idem, *Einleitung in die apokryphischesen Schriften des alten Testaments* (Leipzig: Weidmannischen Buchhandlung, 1795); idem, *Introduction to the Study of the Old Testament: a fragment translated by George Tilly Gollop, Esq.* (London: Spottiswoode, printed for private circulation 1888); idem, *Urgeschichte, herausgegeben mit Einleitung und Anmerkungen von D. Johann Philipp Gabler* (3 vols.; Altdorf and Nuremberg, 1790-1795); idem, "Urgeschichte ein Versuch," *Repertorium für biblischen und morgenländische Literatur* 4 (1779) 129-256.

Studies. W. Baird, *History of New Testament Research* (Minneapolis, Fortress, 1992); C. Hartlich and W. Sachs, "Die mythische Schule" in *Der Ursprung des Mythosbegriffs in der modernen Bibelwissenschaft* (Tübingen: J. C. B. Mohr, 1952); H. J. Kraus, *Geschichte der historisch-kritischen Erforschung des Alten Testaments* (3d ed.; Neukirchen-Vluyn: Neukirchener Verlag, 1982); J. A. Noesselt, *Anweisung zur Kenntnis der besten allgemeinern Bücher in allen Theilen der Theologie* (4th ed.; Leipzig, 1800); E. Ruprecht, "Die Frage nach den vorliterarischen Überlieferungen in der Genesisforschung des ausgehenden 18.jh," *ZAW* 84 (1972) 293-314; E. Sehmsdorf, *Die Prophetenauslegung bei J. G. Eichhorn* (Göttingen: Vandenhoeck & Ruprecht, 1971); R. Smend, "Johann David Michaelis und Johann Gottfried Eichhorn: Zwei Orientalisten am Rande der Theologie" in *Theologie in Göttingen,* ed. B. Moeller (Göttingen: Vandenhoeck & Ruprecht, 1987) 58-81.

J. Sandys-Wunsch

Ernesti, Johann August
(1707-1781)

Johann August Ernesti studied at Wittenberg and Leipzig, and after being a private tutor he obtained a position at the Thomasschule in Leipzig (co-rector 1731; rector 1734) and then at the University of Leipzig. He became professor of litterarum humaniorum (1742), rhetoric (1754) and finally theology (1759). In 1770 he retired. Apart from his work as a scholar he is best remembered for his jurisdictional dispute with J. S. Bach, which eventually he lost.

Ernesti was one of the dominating figures of his time. Though he never admitted his indebtedness, he was greatly influenced by Christian Wolff (1679-1754), Germany's best-known forgotten philosopher. In the mid-eighteenth century Wolff's influence was denounced violently and somewhat uncritically by both orthodox and Pietist theologians, which may have been a factor in Ernesti's silence on the subject. Wolff meant his philosophy—and he used the term "my philosophy" deliberately—to provide a systematic framework for all knowledge (see Immanuel Kant's fulsome tribute to Wolff in the preface to the second edition of the *Critique of Pure Reason*). Wolff's interests were far-ranging, and Ernesti's hermeneutics shows the influence of Wolff's treatises "Von Uebersetzungen" and "Von dem Gebrauche der demonstrativischen Lehrart in Erklärung der heiligen Schrift" (1731). More significantly Ernsti derived from Wolff a rational view of the universe in which revelation as a distinct source of knowledge apart from reason had a well-defined place. Ernesti, like his contemporary S. J. Baumgarten (1706-1757), introduced a moderate rational approach into theological study and research as part of the second wave of enlightenment in eighteenth-century Germany that succeeded the initial explorations of C. Thomasius (1655-1728), J. F. Buddeus (1667-1729) and C. M. Pfaff (1686-1760).

Ernesti began his university career by teaching classics, and in the course of his life he edited editions of various Latin and Greek authors. He was regarded as one of the best Latinists of his day, and his early textbook on mathematics and physics went through various editions on the strength of its excellent Latin style. His abilities in Greek were not quite so outstanding, and his paucity of references to Hebrew suggests he had no special competence in that area. After his appointment to the theological faculty he continued to lecture in classics and even had Goethe as a student in one of his classes on Cicero.

Interpretation of Scripture. Ernesti was a conservative advocate of the introduction of exact philological principles into the interpretation of Scripture. Orthodox Lutheran interpreters had introduced general dogmatic conclusions as presuppositions, such as the universal presence of Christ's threefold ministry throughout the Bible. But it had been Pietist writers, particularly August Hermann Francke (1663-1727), Joachim Lange (1670-1744) and Johann Jakob Rambach (1693-1735), who devoted a great deal of attention to hermeneutics in the early part of the eighteenth century. While they were not very different from their predecessors, the Pietists had a different emphasis, insisting on the personal effect Scripture had on its interpreter as a part of the hermeneutic process. Furthermore, like the orthodox, they approached Scripture with definite presuppositions. For example, Rambach defined *analogia fidei* as the principle of interpretation derived from seeing Scripture as the work of a single author, namely, the Holy Spirit, who used the different biblical writers as its amanuenses. Rambach emphasized this unity of Scripture by saying that neither the prophets nor Christ taught anything that is not already in the Mosaic writings.

Ernesti represents a mitigated rational approach to hermeneutics. In place of earlier orthodox and Pietistic treatments, he insisted on interpreting the Bible by the same principles used for any other book. Essentially this meant that the literal meaning of the text, interpreted by a reasonable application of philological principles, was the whole meaning of the text. For him the correct method was important; the spiritual condition of the interpreter or the effect of the interpreter's reading in his or her personal life was not a concern. Interpretation was a rational exercise in which nonrational factors had no deciding role. His emphasis on the literal or grammatical sense of language had two consequences. First, there was only one meaning to a text—what it actually said—and one did not have the right to seek out allegorical or mystical meanings. Second, Ernesti rejected a traditional approach that even if a particular doctrine were not explicitly mentioned in a text, nonetheless one had the right to assume that this doctrine was to be found in the text if one only looked a little harder. In "De vanitate philosophantium in interpretatione librorum sacrae scripturae" he illustrated abuses where doctrines were derived illegitimately from inappropriate proof-texts.

Ernesti inched away from the docetic view of inspiration that refused to recognize the human and cultural background of Scripture. In "De difficultatibus novi testamenti recte interpretandi" he insisted on the particularities of New Testament Greek, which came from the background of its writers, who were for the most part not learned men whose linguistic background was the Hebrew Bible. Taking this situation into account thus made them more difficult to interpret, for their vocabulary did not necessary correspond to that of the exegete. Therefore the exegete should be careful not to attribute to these writings ideas their authors did not know. However, this recognition of the humanity of biblical authors did not lead Ernesti into an appreciation of the difference of their culture in the fashion of Johann David *Michaelis, Johann Gottfried von Herder or Johann Gottfried *Eichhorn. For example, in his review of Sigmund Jacob Baumgarten's posthumously published book on hermeneutics, Ernesti could agree that the biblical books were written in such a way that they could easily be understood by the readers of the times in which they were written, but he felt it was going too far to suggest that God left the choice of words and style to the historical authors to save them from an overemphasis of inspiration.

Similarly he had serious reservation about J. G. Toellner's attempt at reconciling the historical nature of biblical books with a more rational concept of their inspiration in *Die Göttliche Eingebung der heiligen Schrift* (1771).

At the same time in "De Necessitate revelationis divinae adversus eos qui eius cognitionem rationi humanae assertum eunt" Ernesti preserved Wolff's insistence on the necessity of a special revelation that would add to the truths that could be known from reason alone. This a priori assumption explains why Ernesti, while rejecting the *analogia fidei* in Rambach's sense of the term, still insisted on the impossibility of self-contradictions within Scripture. This led to his principle, perhaps in some tension with his insistence on the historical nature of the New Testament writings, that contradictions could not exist within Scripture and were to be explained by an appeal to clearer passages or, in the last resort, textual corruption.

Significance. Most of Ernesti's academic work appeared in Latin monographs, few of which were translated into German. His only important scholarly work to appear in German in his lifetime consisted of the two periodicals he edited and to which he contributed most of the book reviews. Here he showed a wide grasp of his times and was scrupulously fair to works he did not agree with, indicating his own position with a graceful irony. He was praised for the fact that so widely circulated were his periodical publications, they were even known in the far-off wildernesses of Scotland. In this respect Ernesti showed an openness of mind not necessarily found in other theologians of his day. His "De Libertate ingenii in causa religionis" (1764), while not mentioning his former student W. A. Teller by name, was apparently designed as a defence of this latter's *Wörterbuch des Neuen Testaments,* which had caused a scandal when it was published in 1762.

In English Ernesti became known in the nineteenth century thanks to two versions

of his *Institutio Interpretes Novi Testamenti,* one by C. H. Terrot and the other by Moses *Stuart. Terrot's version is a translation of Ammon's edition, of which Terrot did not approve, so added to the translation are numerous notes in which Terrot vents his wrath on Ammon's supposedly godless views. Stuart eliminated much of Ammon, abbreviated some of Ernesti, and included material from German scholars since Ernesti, in particular Ernesti's successor at Leipzig, S. F. N. Morus. No doubt it was not only Ernesti's excellent grasp of hermeneutics but also his apparently conservative stance that appealed.

Ernesti's influence was also felt through the quality of his teaching. K. F. Bahrdt, the most idiosyncratic and best-informed theological gossip of the day, paid Ernesti the tribute that he attracted and inspired the best students (adding a pointed aside that the less gifted students tended to gravitate to C. A. Crusius). Bahrdt gave Ernesti credit for taking the trouble to help students by privately giving them important hints about possible researches. Among the notable theologians of the next generation who had been students of Ernesti were J. A. Dathe, W. A. Teller, C. C. Tittmann and C. F. Ammon.

Ernesti nonetheless had certain weaknesses. According to Bahrdt, Ernesti, for all his extraordinary erudition, lacked two qualities that would have made him the greatest of all scholars, namely, philosophy and taste. Ernesti did not alter his philosophical stance, and eventually his unstated adherence to Wolff in the changing times of eighteenth-century philosophy meant an inevitable progress from radical to fossil. In his reviews of newer theological ideas, he remained fair but not open to the possibility of new thought.

Johann Wolfgang von Goethe echoes Bahrdt's judgment about taste. In *Dichtung und Wahrheit* he tells how before he went, somewhat unwillingly, to Leipzig, Ernesti appeared as a shining light, but that he subsequently discovered that while Ernesti's lectures gave him a great deal, it was not what he was looking for, namely, a standard for literary judgment. Ernesti lacked the imagination to recreate the thought world of the Bible, and Goethe describes how Ernesti shied away from the romantically attractive world of the prophets in favor of the Mosaic legislation.

A further weakness that Bahrdt's own slapdash approach to scholarship would not have revealed was Ernesti's failure to appreciate the importance of the textual studies that were carried on in the eighteenth century.

In effect the tension between Ernesti's predefined stance and the direction of his researches meant that while he could hold these two parts together within himself, for his students the system fell apart, and they continued on into more radical viewpoints.

BIBLIOGRAPHY

Works. J. A. Ernesti's principal Latin writings were gathered into two volumes: *Opuscula Philogicaet Critica* (Leiden: Luchtmen, 1764) and *Opuscula Theologica* (Leipzig: C. Fritsch, 1773); idem, *Elements of Interpretation,* trans. M. Stuart (Andover, Mass.: M. Newman, 1842); idem, *Neue Theologische Bibliothek* (10 vols.; Leipzig: Breitkopf, 1760-1769); idem, *Neueste Theologische Bibliothek* (Leipzig: Breitkopf, 1770-1775); idem, *Principles of Biblical Interpretation,* trans. C. H. Terrot (2 vols.; Edinburgh: Clark, 1832).

Studies. C. F. Bahrdt, *Kirchen und Ketzer Almanach aufs Jahr 1781* (slightly changed in 1787 edition); W. Baird, *History of New Testament Research* (Minneapolis: Fortress, 1992) vol. 1; J. H. Ernesti, *Leipziger Universitats-Programmauf den wohlseligen Herrn D. Ernesti,* trans. from Latin to German by G. Küttner (Frankfort and Leipzig, 1782); J. W. von Goethe, *Dichtung und Wahrheit,* Pt. 2, bks. 6, 7; G. Heinrici, "Ernesti, Johann August" in *Hauck's Realenzyklopedia* (ET in the *NSHERK* in a poorly done abbreviated version); E. Hirsch, *Geschichte der neuern evangelischen Theologie* (3d ed.; Bertelsmann: Gütersloh, 1964) vol. 4, chap. 36; W. Phillipp, "Ernesti, Johann August," *RGG³*; B. F. Schmieder, *Ernestiana* (Halle: J. L. Kurt, 1782); J. S. Semler, Zusätze (supplement to Teller's book; Halle: Hemmerde, 1783); W. A. Teller, *Des Herrn Joh. August Ernesti ... Verdienst um die Theologie und der Religion* (Berlin: Mylius, 1783).   J. Sandys-Wunsch

Griesbach, Johann Jakob (1745-1812)

Johann Jakob Griesbach was born on January 4, 1745, at Butzbach, Hessen-Darmstadt. He was the only son of Konrad Kaspar Griesbach, a Lutheran pastor and educator, and Dorothea (Rambach) Griesbach. His mother was the eldest daughter of Johann Jakob Rambach (1693-1735), a distinguished preacher, hymnologist and scholar who taught Bible and dogmatic theology at Jena (1719-1723), Halle (1723-1731) and Giessen (1731-1735).

Griesbach's early education took place in Frankfurt and its immediate environs, where his father served local churches. He attended the University at Tübingen for five semesters; then Halle (1764-1766; 1767-1771) and Leipzig, where he spent a year "reading the ancient sources of Church History" (1766-1767).

In February of 1768 Griesbach's first publication appeared, a historical-theological dissertation that dealt with some of the ideas of Leo I (pope from 440 to 461; Griesbach 1768a). Some months later, on October 22, 1768, Griesbach published his master's thesis and received the degree of master of philosophy from the University at Halle (Griesbach 1768b).

Griesbach then embarked on an international study tour that took him through Germany (six months), the Netherlands, England (September 1769 to June 1770) and France. In addition to studying the teaching styles of professors of theology, Griesbach acquainted himself with the ancient manuscripts of the Bible that were then preserved in the British Museum in London, the Bodleian Library at Oxford, at Cambridge University, the Royal Library in Paris, the library at Saint Germain, and elsewhere. Much of Griesbach's work on this tour laid the foundations for his subsequent and significant contributions to text criticism of the Bible, particularly of the Greek New Testament. From October 1770 through Easter 1771, Griesbach returned home for a visit with his parents before commencing his own teaching career, which began at Halle (1771-1775) and continued at the university in Jena (1775-1812).

While he was at Halle (1764-1775), Griesbach became a student of Johann Salomo *Semler, who had been called to Halle as professor of theology (1752). Semler was a prolific scholar whose work included, among many other types of publications, editing and supplementing the work of such distinguished biblical scholars and text critics as Johann Albrecht *Bengel, Johann Jakob Wettstein (1693-1754) and Johann David *Michaelis. Semler saw Griesbach's promise as a scholar and publicly praised his text-critical work when Griesbach was twenty-five years old (Semler).

Upon completing a critical dissertation on the texts of the four canonical Gospels as preserved by *Origen, Griesbach was made privatdozent at Halle (see Griesbach 1771). In celebration of this event Friedrich Andreas Stroth (1750-1785) congratulated Griesbach with a treatise of his own that dealt with biblical text criticism (Stroth 1771; cf. Delling, 183-84 n. 27). Like Henry Owen (1716-1795; see his work from 1764), Stroth advocated the Griesbach hypothesis in print (1781) before Griesbach himself published anything about it (1783). In an anonymously published article of 1781, Stroth affirmed, "I presuppose that which perhaps no one can deny, that Mark had Matthew in front of him and epitomized him with a drawing in of Luke" (Stroth 1781, 144; trans. D. B. Peabody).

Griesbach explicitly acknowledged scholars who had anticipated the source theory about the Gospels that was eventually identified with his name, but he did not name his precursors, at least not in a context where such an acknowledgment would have been the most appropriate. Toward the beginning of his *Demonstration That Mark Was Written after Matthew and Luke,* Griesbach wrote:

The most ancient writers, starting with Papias, have handed down, almost nanimously, that Mark committed to writing

what he had heard from Peter, whose interpreter they name him. Augustine was, as we know, the first to state that Mark followed Matthew as a sort of abbreviator and close imitator. From that time most scholars have been accustomed to hold both opinions, *viz.* that Mark derived his narrative partly from the Gospel of Matthew and partly from the mouth of Peter. But more recently some have shrewdly observed that the conformity of Mark with Luke is also so great that he [Mark] would seem to have had his [Luke's] Gospel at hand. (Griesbach 1789)

Here Griesbach acknowledges both the tradition of the church since *Augustine that Mark made use of the earlier text of Matthew in composing the later Gospel of Mark and what he believed to be the finding only of more recent scholars, that is, Mark utilized not only Matthew's Gospel but that of Luke as well.

Although Griesbach does not name any of those "shrewd observers" who anticipated his source theory, Stroth must have been one of them. Stroth published work presupposing the Griesbach hypothesis in 1781, two years prior to Griesbach's earliest publication on this subject (Griesbach 1783; cf. 1789-90). And Stroth's piece congratulating Griesbach (1771) proves that they had a professional relationship at least by that date. But Stroth chose to publish his 1781 article, in which he reveals his views about the sources of the Synoptic Gospels "anonymously." This last fact alone could explain the absence of a footnote naming Stroth, and perhaps other precursors of Griesbach's source theory, in Griesbach's *Demonstration* (1789-1790). Even if Griesbach knew by 1789 or 1790 that Stroth wrote the article that was published anonymously in 1781, Griesbach might still have chosen not to name Stroth as a precursor in deference to Stroth's earlier desire not to be publically identified with this article. Stroth had died in 1785.

By 1773 Griesbach had been promoted to Extraordinary Professor at Halle, and in

1774 and 1775 his critical edition of the Greek New Testament first appeared. This edition was distinctive for several reasons.

First, although Griesbach's text did not radically depart from the so-called Textus Receptus (Greeven reports that Griesbach's text departed from the Textus Receptus in 352 places; RGG^3), his edition was the first by a German to print a main text of the Greek New Testament that was different from the Textus Receptus. Most earlier editors of the Greek New Testament throughout Europe had been satisfied to continue to reprint the Textus Receptus as the main text and to call attention to manuscript variants only in some sort of apparatus (footnotes, marginal notes, a separate listing). Griesbach's decision to "correct" the Textus Receptus was still a radical move in his day, and he was criticized for making it (see Metzger, who cites Archbishop R. Laurence and Frederick Nolan as two of Griesbach's critics, 121 n. 1; 270).

Second, in establishing preferred readings for the Greek New Testament, Griesbach utilized a number of canons of criticism, some of which he adopted and refined from text critics before him. One of Griesbach's refinements of the earlier work of Bengel and Semler was the theory of families or recensions of manuscripts. On the basis of his thorough study of quotations from the New Testament in works by early church fathers, Griesbach divided manuscripts known to him into three families: the Alexandrian, the Western and the Byzantine or Constantinopolitan. He then applied a method by which manuscript evidence from two different families would weigh more heavily in coming to a text-critical decision than would manuscript evidence confined to a single family.

Third, in this first edition of the Greek New Testament, Griesbach printed the entire texts of the Gospels of Matthew, Mark and Luke in parallel columns. This synoptic presentation was prepared partly as an aid for text critics seeking to study harmonistic and other types of variant readings. But this arrangement also allowed Griesbach to see

those details of the relationships among the Gospels of Matthew, Luke and Mark that led him to advocate and later defend his source theory about the Gospels (Luke made use of Matthew; Mark made use of both Matthew and Luke). All multicolumned synopses of the Gospels derive their basic form from Griesbach's synopsis, and the very terms *synopsis* and *Synoptic Gospels* also go back to Griesbach (see Griesbach 1776).

Prior to Griesbach many attempts had been made to write harmonies of the Gospels, that is, attempts to explain all of the dissimilarities, even contradictions, among the four canonical Gospels. Griesbach's purpose in making his synoptic arrangement of the Gospels differed from that of the earlier harmonists. Since Griesbach eliminated most of John's Gospel from his synoptic arrangements, he did not even try to harmonize most of John with the other three canonical Gospels. The name "Synoptic Gospels" therefore came to be applied only to the Gospels of Matthew, Mark and Luke. And Griesbach even gave up on the attempt to harmonize the Synoptic Gospels. Instead he arranged the Gospels of Matthew, Mark and Luke so that comparative analysis, not necessarily harmonization, would be facilitated (see Greeven 1978).

During his years in Halle (1764-1775) Griesbach became friends with a student of the Greek and Latin classics, Christian Gottfried Schütz (1747-1832), and his sister, Frederike. After a long engagement, Griesbach married Frederike on April 16, 1775. That same year Griesbach received a call to the university at Jena and was installed as professor in December.

During his earlier years at Jena (1775-1791) Griesbach typically taught four lecture courses a semester in the general areas of New Testament, church history and theological dogmatics. In exegesis he was an advocate of the historico-grammatical method that had been popularized by Johann August *Ernesti. Compared to his teacher Semler, or to his one-time colleague at Jena, Heinrich Eberhard Gottlob Paulus (1761-1851), Griesbach was theologically conservative. Nevertheless, given what he knew about the history of the text of the Bible, Griesbach could not accept the doctrine of verbal inspiration as that doctrine was generally understood by conservative theologians of the day (see, for instance, Griesbach's Whitsun Programmes for 1784-1788, all of which addressed *Stricturae in locum de theopneustia librorum sacrorum*).

In 1776 Griesbach's synoptic arrangement of the Gospels was first published as a separate volume. A year later Griesbach was named doctor of theology and began to contribute articles to the *Repertorium for Biblical and Oriental Literature* that was published in Leipzig from 1777 through 1786 with Johann Gottfried *Eichhorn as its editor.

While he was at Jena, Griesbach also published a number of programs that he first presented, under the sponsorship of the university, in celebration of important days in the Christian calendar. One such program dealt with the sources from which the several canonical Evangelists drew their narratives of the resurrection of the Lord (see Griesbach 1783). This work was fittingly presented as the Easter program in 1783. Within this piece Griesbach first published his views on the interrelationships among the Gospels. In conformity with long-standing tradition of the church, Griesbach affirmed that the Gospels of Matthew and John were the products of the apostles by those names. He explained the differences among the reports of the resurrection on the basis of differing sources. Griesbach claimed that John's narrative was based in part on the testimony of Mary Magdalene, while that of Matthew appealed to the testimony of Mary, the mother of James. Luke drew his report partly from the Gospel of Matthew and partly from traditions attributed to Joanna. Mark simply conflated the narratives of Matthew and Luke.

For the Whitsun programs of 1789 and 1790 Griesbach went further than he had for the Easter program of 1783 and demonstrated that the whole of the Gospel of Mark was derived from the earlier Gospels of Matthew and Luke. These two programs were later combined into a single, expanded *Commentary* that included not only Griesbach's original arguments for his source theory but also responses to objections that had been raised against his hypothesis by 1794 *(Commentatio qua Marci Evangelium)*. In its most developed form, the *Commentary* began with a brief history of the discussion of the sources of the Gospels and a summary of Griesbach's hypothesis in fifteen points. Next Griesbach provided three arguments for his hypothesis. First, with the aid of a synoptic chart, Griesbach demonstrated Mark's alternating agreement in pericope order, now with Matthew and now with Luke. Second, Griesbach claimed that Mark was composed entirely of pericopes from Matthew or Luke with the exception of twenty-four verses. And even some of these twenty-four verses, in Griesbach's opinion, had been suggested to Mark by materials in Matthew. Third, Griesbach demonstrated that the order of words within individual pericopes in Mark, like the order of pericopes in Mark, was characterized by alternating agreement with Matthew and Luke. Section 3 of the *Commentary* included a collection of Griesbach's responses to no fewer than eight categories of objections to his hypothesis and concludes with a summary of his arguments in thirteen points.

Following the publication of this *Commentary* the Griesbach hypothesis became the most popular hypothesis about the sources of the Synoptic Gospels for at least the next forty or fifty years (for a list of scholars who advocated the Griesbach hypothesis into the first decades of the twentieth century see Neirynck and Van Segbroek). Only in the second half of the nineteenth century was the Griesbach hypothesis eclipsed by the theory of Markan priority (see Farmer).

With his Whitsun program of 1801

Griesbach joined the ranks of many scholars who had been debating the authenticity of selected chapters and verses of Matthew and Luke since John Williams (1727-1798), a nonconformist English divine, opened these debates in 1771 (Griesbach, "ἐπίμετρον *ad Commentarium Criticum in Matthaei Textum*" [Halle, 1801]; see Griesbach 1798/1811, 2:45-64; cf. J. Williams, *A Free Enquiry into the Authenticity of The First and Second Chapters of St. Matthew's Gospel* [London, 1771; 2d ed., 1789]). Stroth's article of 1781 was a contribution to this debate, and Stroth took the side of Williams against the authenticity of Matthew 1—2. In addition Stroth argued that many more verses in Matthew and Luke 1—2 were also interpolations into the original texts of Matthew and Luke.

A second edition of Williams's argument was published in 1789, and Griesbach made explicit reference to this second edition in his response of 1801. Griesbach organized his argument against Williams into ten sections. In section 10, as part of his defense of the authenticity of Luke 1—2, Griesbach called attention to several linguistic characteristics within those first two chapters of Luke and then demonstrated that these same characteristics were present in the balance of Luke and the Acts of the Apostles. With the aid of this evidence, Griesbach concluded that the same author responsible for Luke 1—2 was also responsible for the balance of that Gospel. Within this same section 10, Griesbach utilized the dream motif found in Matthew 27:19 and in several places in Matthew 1—2 to argue in a similar way for the integrity of authorship of Matthew.

In 1802 Christoph Gotthelf Gersdorf (d. 1834), then a rural pastor at Tautendorf (Saxony-Altenburg), read Griesbach's 1801 contribution to these debates and was prompted to draw together the results of his own investigations into the linguistic characteristics of all of the New Testament authors. Gersdorf then corresponded with Griesbach about his work and made an appointment to see him in the fall of 1803, while Griesbach was still suffering from an illness that may have plagued him for as long as five years (for further evidence of Griesbach's illness, consult the data, mostly excerpts from letters, collected by Delling, 185 n. 54). After this face-to-face discussion with Gersdorf and after reviewing the linguistic characteristics of New Testament authors that Gersdorf had collected by that time, Griesbach wrote the following letter to Gersdorf on October 22, 1803:

I feel obliged to thank you very much for kindly sharing some examples of your "Characteristics of the Authors of the New Testament" with me. The results of your sharp mind and exceptional diligence really do offer very important advantages in the fundamental study of the New Testament which results are to be valued all the more highly since, up until now, this aspect of the matter has been kept in view much too little. To be sure, in individual cases, critics and commentators have drawn conclusions from an analysis of the language of the individual authors of the Bible in the course of their investigations and a few years ago a couple of dissertations appeared in Holland—which I suppose have come into a few hands—in which "a similar way," so to speak, has been adopted in an investigation of the Johannine writings. But no one else has yet recognized the methodology which has been employed by you to its full extent so successfully and used it in its multifaceted applicability. Your work, therefore, is to be commended as much for its originality as for its usefulness and I, therefore, look forward to its swift completion and publication.

Surely there is still a publisher who does not simply provide reading libraries with recent publications, but who also prefers to do something for the promotion of basic studies, especially since, in my opinion, virtually nothing is to be risked by publishing this work of yours. Although such a work doesn't sell as fast as a novel, by contrast, it has an even longer lasting value.

For everyone who is interested in an exact knowledge and a basic judgment of the New Testament writings, your work will be welcome as an important aid:

1) for judging the authenticity or inauthenticity of whole books and individual parts of them;

2) for deciding such debated questions about the origin and the original character of our gospels because, by this means, many a flimsy, although highly-praised, hypothesis may be more clearly demonstrated to be unacceptable;

3) for correcting the text in individual places;

4) for determining the value of the ancient manuscripts which have been judged to vary so;

5) for correcting or confirming the generally accepted meaning of many passages in the New Testament. (Gersdorf, v of foreword, trans. D. B. Peabody)

With such encouragement from Griesbach, Gersdorf did publish his work on the linguistic characteristics of the New Testament authors (1816), and he published this letter from Griesbach in its preface because he thought it gave a brief and pertinent overview of the results of Gersdorf's research. Griesbach died in Jena on March 24, 1812, so he did not live to see this publication by Gersdorf. But when D. David Schulz (1779-1854) published a third edition of Griesbach's Greek text of the four canonical Gospels in 1827, he annotated many of his preferred readings with notes quoted from Gersdorf (see Schulz).

Two hundred years after the separate publication of Griesbach's synopsis (1776), an international and ecumenical colloquium convened at Münster (Westphalia; July 26-31, 1976) to recognize Griesbach's past and present contributions to New Testament study, especially in the areas of text criticism, synopsis making and Synoptic source criticism. The volume of essays that came out of that conference, *J. J. Griesbach: Synoptic and Text-Critical Studies 1776-1976*, is not only a fitting tribute to Griesbach but also indispensable reading for those who would know more about this major biblical interpreter (see Orchard and Longstaff).

BIBLIOGRAPHY

Works. J. J. Griesbach, "Auszüge aus einer der ältesten handscriften der LXX. Dollmetscher Uebersetzung," *RBML* 1 (1777) 83-141; idem, *D. Io. Iac. Griesbachii, Commentarius Criticus in Textum Graecum Novi Testamenti* (2 vols.; Jena: J. C. G. Goepfedt, 1798 [vol. 1], 1811 [vol. 2]); idem, *Dissertatio critica de Codicibus Quattuor Evangeliorum Origenianis Pars Prima* (Halle: University at Halle, 1771); idem, *De Fide Historica ex Ipsa Rerum Quae Narrantur Natura Iudicanda* (Halle: University at Halle, 1768b); idem, *Dissertatio Historico-Theologica Locos Theologicos Collectos ex Leone Magno Pontifice Romano Sistens* (Halle, February 24, 1768a); idem, *Epistolae Apostolorum cum Apocalypsi. Textum ad Fidem* . . . (Halle: Io. Iac. Curtii, 1775); idem, "Fortgesetzte Auszüge aus einer der altesten Handschriften der LXX. Dollmetscher Uebersetzung," *RBML* 2 (1778) 194-240; idem, *Inquiritur in Fontes, Unde Evangelistae Suas de Resurrectione Domini Narratione Hauserint* (Jena: Strankmannio-Fickelscherria, 1783); idem, *Io. Iac. Griesbachii Theol. D. et Prof Primar in Academia Jenensi Commentatio Qua Marci Evangelium Totum e Matthaei et Lucae Commentariis Decerptum Esse Monstratur, Scripta Nomine Academiae Jenensis (1789. 1790) jam Recognita Multisque Augmentis Locupletata* in *J. J. Griesbach: Synoptic and Text-Critical Studies 1776-1976*, ed. B. Orchard and T. R. W. Longstaff (SNTSMS 34; Cambridge: Cambridge University Press, 1978) 68-102; idem, *Libri Historici Novi Testamenti Graece. Pars Prior, Sistens Synopsin Versionum et Patrum Emendavit et Lectionis Varietatem Adiecit Io. Iac. Griesbach* (Halle: Io. Iac. Curtii, 1774); idem, *Novum Testamentum Graece. II. [counting Libri Historici 1-2 as 1.1-2]*; idem, *Pars Posterior, Sistens Evangelium Ioannis et Acta Apostolorum. Textum* . . . (Halle: Io. Iac. Curtii, 1775); idem, *Synopsis Evangeliorum Matthaei, Marci et Lucae. Textum Graecum ad Fidem Codicum, Versionum et Patrum Emendavit et Lectionis Varietatem adiecit Io. Iac. Griesbach, Theologiae Prof. Publ.* (Halle: Io. Iac. Curtii, 1776); idem, "Ueber die verschiedenen Arten deutscher Bibelübersetzungen," *RBML* 6 (1780) 262-300.

Studies. G. Delling, "Johann Jakob Griesbach: seine Zeit, sein Leben, sein Werk," *TZ* 33

(1977) 81-99; translated in *J. J. Griesbach: Synoptic and Text-Critical Studies 1776-1976*, ed. B. Orchard and T. R. W. Longstaff (SNTSMS 34; Cambridge: Cambridge University Press, 1978) 5-21 (includes bibliography and works on Griesbach); W. R. Farmer, *The Synoptic Problem: A Critical Analysis* (New York: Macmillan, 1964); C. G. Gersdorf, *Beiträge zur Sprach-Charakteristik der Schriftsteller des Neuen Testaments, eine Sammlung meist neuer Bemerkungen. Erster Theil* (Leipzig: Weidmann, 1816); H. Greeven, "The Gospel Synopsis From 1776 to the Present Day" in *J. J. Griesbach: Synoptic and Text-Critical Studies 1776-1976*, ed. B. Orchard and T. R. W. Longstaff (SNTSMS 34; Cambridge: Cambridge University Press, 1978) 22-49; idem, "Griesbach, Johann Jakob," *RGG³*; J. J. Kiwiet, ed., *A History and Critique of the Origin of the Marcan Hypothesis 1835-1866 A Contemporary Report Rediscovered. A Translation with Introduction and notes of* Geschiedenis en critiek der Marcushypothese [History and Critique of the Marcan Hypothesis] by Hajo Uden Meijboom at the University of Groningen, 1866 (New Gospel Studies 8; Macon, GA: Mercer University Press, 1993); B. M. Metzger, *The Text of the New Testament: Its Transmission, Corruption and Restoration* (2d ed.; New York and Oxford: Oxford University Press, 1968); F. Neirynck and F. Van Segbroeck, comps., "The Griesbach Hypothesis: A Bibliography" in *J. J. Griesbach: Synoptic and Text-Critical Studies 1776-1976*, ed. B. Orchard and T. R. W. Longstaff (SNTSMS 34; Cambridge: Cambridge University Press, 1978) 176-81; B. Orchard and T. R. W. Longstaff, eds., *J. J. Griesbach: Synoptic and Text-Critical Studies 1776-1976* (SNTSMS 34; Cambridge: Cambridge University Press, 1978); H. Owen, *Observations on the Four gospels: Tending Chiefly to Ascertain the Times of the Publication, and to Illustrate the Form and Manner of Their Composition* (London: T. Payne, 1764); D. B. Peabody, "Chapters in the History of the Linguistic Argument for Solving the Synoptic Problem. The Nineteenth Century in Context" in *Jesus, the Gospels and the Church: Essays in Honor of William R. Farmer*, ed. E. P. Sanders (Macon, GA: Mercer University Press, 1987) 47-68; D. D. Schulz, *Novum Testamentum Graece. Textum ad Fidem Codicum, Versionum et Patrum Recensuit et Lectionis Varietatem Adjecit D. Jo. Jac. Griesbach. Vol. I, IV Evangelia Complectens. Editionem Tertiam Emendatam et Auctam Curavit D. David Schulz* (Berlin: Friedrich Laue, 1827); Semleri, I. S., *Epistola ad Clarissimum Ioannem Iacobum Griesbachium de emendandis Graecis V. T. Interpretibus cum appendice ad Programma Ienense* (Halle and Magdeburg: Io. Christ. Hendel, 1770); F. A. Stroth, *Commentatiunculam de Codice Alexandrino Scripsit* (Halle, September 28, 1771); idem, "Von Interpolationen im Evangelium Matthaei" in *Repertorium für biblische und morgenlandische Litteratur* 9 (1781) 99-156.

D. B. Peabody

Hodge, Charles *(1797-1878)*

An American conservative Presbyterian theologian, Charles Hodge is well known in the United States (and to a lesser extent Canada, Northern Ireland and Scotland) as a proponent of both traditional Calvinist theology and the plenary inspiration of Scripture. During his lifetime his influence grew from the more than three thousand students he taught at Princeton Theological Seminary and from a river of writing that poured into journals, polemical tracts and full-scale books. Especially important for establishing Hodge's reputation as one of the nineteenth century's most able polemical theologians was *The Biblical Repertory and Princeton Review*, which he edited from 1824 until 1871. Since his death, most of Hodge's books have remained in print, especially the three-volume *Systematic Theology*, published (1872-1973) as a summation of his work as a theological professor.

Context. Though Hodge is remembered most as a didactic theologian, he began his career as a teacher of Scripture. Archibald Alexander, Princeton's first professor, invited Hodge to join the faculty in order to supervise instruction in the biblical languages, a service that he performed from 1822 to 1840. Hodge gained a solid grounding in Greek at the College of New Jersey in Princeton, from which he graduated in 1815, and during his study under Alexander at the seminary (graduated 1819). Before he began his teaching, he studied Hebrew privately in Philadelphia.

Hodge's devotion to the Bible—expressed through a lifetime of preparing exegetical sermons and meditations, an on-going engagement with the doctrines of revelation, considerable labor on exegetical commentaries, and a great deal of lecturing on biblical subjects—was marked by the same set of general commitments that also shaped his theology. Against what Hodge himself claimed—about merely upholding a consensual Reformed theology—and what some modern students have claimed—that Hodge let principles of naive biblicism or Scottish commonsense philosophy overwhelm his thought (e.g., Ahlstrom)—his convictions were anything but simple. Hodge did uphold Reformed theology, especially as defined in Swiss and English traditions (more from François Turretin's seventeenth-century than John *Calvin's sixteenth-century Geneva; more the Westminster Confession than Scottish Presbyterianism or New England Puritanism). But he also regularly gave full place to a full-orbed piety (though more in popular works like *The Way of Life* [1841] than in formal academic treatises like the introduction on method to his *Systematic Theology*). In addition, he did exploit popular American understandings of Scottish realist philosophy, but much more in writing about theological method than in defining the capacities of the natural moral sense.

Finally, Hodge's theology was also always marked by a desire to harmonize the academic world's best scientific learning with historical Protestant commitments. The range, depth and sometimes inconsistency of these convictions made Hodge's writing on Scripture, as well as his theology more generally, passionate, erudite, quasi-scientific, pious and not always predictable.

Controversies. Early in his publishing life, which would extend for nearly sixty years, Hodge donned the mantle of a conservator. In an era that witnessed not only the passing of various forms of Calvinism as the United States's dominant intellectual influence but also an incredible national expansion—denominational, philosophical, intellectual, as well as geographical—Hodge made his most convincing defense

of historic Calvinism through polemics directed at some of the era's most prominent theological alternatives. So it was that, mostly in the pages of the *Princeton Review,* Hodge chastised Nathaniel Taylor and the New Haven theology for departing from the theocentricity of Jonathan *Edwards. While remaining nervous about revivalism more generally, Hodge also attacked specifically the revivalism of Charles Finney as Pelagian. He called to account the Mercersburg theologians, John W. Nevin and Philip Schaff, for wandering into mysticism. In a particularly momentous exchange of learned essays with Edwards Amasa Park of Andover Seminary in 1850 and 1851 (themselves occasioned by Horace Bushnell's notable "Dissertation on Language" of 1849), Hodge defended the capacity of language to communicate theology propositionally. Late in his life he wrote a sturdy critique of Darwinism, not so much for misinterpreting the Bible or even for promoting evolution but for Darwin's claim that biological change happened randomly, without purposeful design.

The kind of theological defense to which Hodge committed himself more generally also provided the framework for his work on Scripture. In his first years as a seminary teacher, Hodge lectured on, among many other subjects, several Old Testament books as well as "biblical criticism," hermeneutics, and "sacred criticism." His first publication, a pamphlet designed to advertise his credentials for a regular appointment at Princeton, appeared in 1822 with the title *A Dissertation on the Importance of Biblical Literature.* It combined an apology for biblical infallibility and an exhortation to read the Bible more deeply, with an appeal for full exposure to a burgeoning literature concerning the ancient world, Semitic history, biblical languages, and similar specialized subjects. When Hodge took a study tour in Europe from 1826 to 1828, he spent as much time working up fields related to biblical interpretation as in pursuing theology directly.

In Paris he studied Hebrew and Arabic; in Halle he worked on Semitic languages with Wilhelm Gesenius before being drawn more toward theology by the pietistic confessionalist Friedrich August Gottreu *Tholuck; and in Berlin he continued to pursue studies in the biblical and cognate languages even as he came under the theological influence of Ernst Hengstenberg and Johann Neander. When Hodge returned to Princeton (1828), he expanded the seminary's offerings in Old Testament subjects. M. A. Taylor, the best student of Hodge's Old Testament scholarship, concludes that "the students who learned Hebrew from Hodge from 1828-1833 studied with one of the most qualified Hebrew teachers in early nineteenth-century America" (Taylor, 85).

Hodge moved to the New Testament from the Old when Joseph Addison Alexander, his friend and the son of his theological mentor, began to exercise his remarkable philological gifts in service to the seminary, and because the first major polemical debate of Hodge's career centered on the meaning of the book of Romans. Hodge had lectured on the Pauline epistles from 1822, his first year at the seminary, and would continue to do so annually until 1878, the year of his death (after J. A. Alexander came to the seminary, he and Hodge developed a plan to write a commentary series for the whole Bible; it was one of the few writing projects that Hodge did not finish).

Hodge's serious publication on the New Testament began with his reaction to one of the first truly significant biblical publications by an American, the commentary on Romans by Moses *Stuart of Andover Seminary that appeared in 1832. Stuart was the nation's leading Hebraist of the time but also a moderate proponent of Congregationalist Calvinism. Stuart's brand of theology retained much from the Puritan past but also felt the influence of American ideology concerning self-sufficiency as well as commonsense understandings of morality. Such modern

principles made it particularly difficult for Stuart to believe that biblical writers could have taught that the moral results of one person's action could be transferred to others.

Hodge's lengthy essay "Stuart on the Romans," which appeared in the *Princeton Review* in 1833, was a foretaste of his own full commentary published in 1835. Hodge was particularly disturbed by Stuart's treatment of traditional Reformed themes like the imputation of the guilt of Adam's sin to the whole human race, the imputation of Christ's righteousness to the redeemed and the substitutionary character of the atonement. His sharply critical review of Stuart in 1833, with its concentration on the theological meaning of Paul's arguments, set the tone for his own commentary.

Before that commentary appeared, however, Hodge had taken a second opportunity to attack what he considered faulty understanding of the Pauline epistle. Albert *Barnes, a New School Presbyterian who went even further than Stuart in revising older Reformed doctrines of imputation, solidarity with Adam and union with Christ, published his book on Romans in 1834. When Hodge's commentary appeared the next year, his brief preliminary discussion of the book's provenance, authorship and historical context bore the marks of his specialized study in Europe. But his main concern was to uphold the traditional Reformed doctrines that he thought Stuart, Barnes and the more revivalistic wings of American Calvinism were leaving behind. So it was that theological discussion made up the high points of Hodge's own work.

Hodge's theological interest is illustrated best by his extensive discussion of the critical passage Romans 5:12-21, which begins with Paul's assertion that "as by one man sin entered into the world, and death by sin; and so death passed upon all men, for that all have sinned," and includes the critical analogy in Romans 5:18—"Therefore as by the offence of one judgment came upon all men to condemnation; even so by the righteousness of one the free gift came upon all men unto justification of life." In his commentaries Hodge regularly expended considerable energy in working out the meaning of Greek phrases, but like almost all of his contemporaries, he used the Authorized Version as his basic English text.

Hodge's extensive exegetical discussion of the passage was followed by an even longer consideration of its doctrine. His style in treating the Greek text, as well as his concern for synthetic theological conclusions, is well illustrated in his discussion of Romans 5:18: "The words Ἄρα οὖν (therefore) are the inferential particles so often used in Paul's epistles, at the beginning of a sentence, contrary to ordinary classical usage—vii. 3, 25; viii. 12; ix. 16, etc. They frequently serve to introduce a summation of what had previously been said. . . . It followed, for all the apostle had said of the method of justification through Jesus Christ, that there is a striking analogy between our fall in Adam and our restoration in Christ. The carrying out of this comparison was interrupted, in the first place, to limit and explain the analogy asserted to exist between Christ and Adam, at the close of ver. 14. This is done in vers. 15-17. Having thus fortified and explained his meaning, the apostle now states the case in full. The word *therefore*, at the beginning of ver. 12, marks an inference from the whole doctrine of the epistle; the corresponding words here are also strictly inferential. It had been proved that we are justified by the righteousness of one man, and it had also been proved that we are under condemnation for the offense of one. *Therefore*, as we are condemned, even so are we justified" (Hodge 1864, 169).

Hodge's discussion of the doctrines of this passage included lengthy quotations from Stuart and Barnes with refutations of their positions. These quotations were cut back considerably in the thorough revision he published in 1864, but the burden of his argument remained the same. Thus Hodge

was at pains to insist that "the doctrine of imputation is clearly taught in this passage." Characteristically he was also at pains to say what he thought was not being taught:

It does not teach that his offence was personally or properly the sin of all men, or that his act was, in any mysterious sense, the act of his posterity. Neither does it imply, in reference to the righteousness of Christ, that his righteousness becomes personally and inherently ours, or that his moral excellence is in any way transferred from him to believers. (Hodge 1864)

But also characteristically Hodge was at pains to make sure that his point was not obscured:

This doctrine merely teaches, that in virtue of the union, representative and natural, between Adam and his posterity, his sin is the ground of their condemnation, that is, of their subjection to penal evils; and that in virtue of the union between Christ and his people, his righteousness is the ground of their justification. This doctrine is taught almost in so many words in verses 12, 15-19. It is so clearly stated, so often repeated or assumed, and so formally proved, that very few commentators of any class fail to acknowledge, in one form or another, that it is the doctrine of the apostles. (Hodge 1864, 178)

On that note Hodge launched into what was also characteristic of his exegesis at its most intense: a catena of quotations from historical figures (usually ancient, Reformation or seventeenth-century Puritan and European Reformed) whose opinions coincided with his own.

In the fullest treatment of the Hodge-Stuart debate over the meaning of Romans 5, historian S. J. Stein has noted that Hodge's penchant for drawing up such quotations into battle array was the weakest point of his exegesis:

Hodge was markedly inconsistent in his appeal to authority. Sometimes he cited only orthodox Reformed theologians, thus implying the orthodoxy of his position. In other instances he quoted 'neologists' who concurred with his interpretation, seemingly to add the weight of scientific philology. At times he canvassed a wide spectrum of authorities, seeking a consensus. Apparently he was willing to cite manifold references as long as they agreed with him. (Stein, 350)

The qualities that marked Hodge's commentary on Romans were the qualities that marked most of his further work on Scripture. He was keen on philological matters, although the freshness of his scholarship faded as the decades rolled by. He was eager to show where his own exegetical conclusions lined up with main Christian traditions, although his use of history could be more adventitious than contextual. He exegeted with an intent to explain the main theological emphases of a passage, an author or the entirety of Scripture, even if such procedures did not always handle convincingly every detail of the passage at hand. And theological conclusions remained the most important thing in his exegesis.

Hodge's three later commentaries—Ephesians in 1856, 1 Corinthians in 1857 and 2 Corinthians in 1859—followed this same pattern, though none of these works displayed quite the energy or depth found in both editions of his commentary on Romans. But even these somewhat slighter commentaries continued to benefit from Hodge's acquaintance with classical Protestant authors as well as with some of the more recent German work in philology, Semitics and ancient Near Eastern history. Hodge's conclusions in these commentaries, about introductory matters as well as theology, are conservative, but his writing is also disarmingly clear so that, for almost all debatable issues or passages, readers can follow exactly the steps that led Hodge to his conclusions.

In the latter parts of his career, Hodge's concern for Scripture was more theological and methodological than exegetical. Major essays on the doctrine of the Bible continued to come from his pen, like a watershed article on "Inspiration" for the *Princeton Review* (1857), which in its concerns for negative effects of modern criticism anticipated the fuller statement of a conservative view from Hodge's son, Archibald Alexander Hodge, and B. B. Warfield under the same title for the *Presbyterian Review* (April 1881).

In addition Hodge continued to develop early Princeton notions on the harmony of human learning and scriptural study by emphasizing the ways it is appropriate for interpretations of Scripture to be revised by well-attested scientific conclusions (documented in Hodge 1994). Such doctrinal and interpretive statements were never divorced from questions of exegesis, even if those questions received less and less direct attention.

An unusually helpful assessment of Hodge as a teacher of exegesis was left by B. B. Warfield, who later succeeded to Hodge's chair of theology at Princeton. Warfield observed Hodge as a student at the seminary in the early 1870s and recorded his observations shortly after Hodge's death. The balance of his conclusions nicely summarize the strengths and weaknesses of Charles Hodge as a biblical interpreter:

I thought then, and I think now, that Dr. Hodge's sense of the general meaning of a passage was unsurpassed. . . . Nothing could surpass the clearness with which he set forth the general argument and the main connections of thought. Neither could anything surpass the analytical subtlety with which he extracted the doctrinal contents of passages. . . . He seemed to look through a passage, catch its main drift and all its theological bearings, and state the result in crisp sentences, which would have been worthy of Bacon; all at a single movement of mind. He had, however, no taste for the technicalities of Exegesis. . . . On such points he was seldom wholly satisfactory. . . . He made no claim, again, to critical acumen; and in questions of textual criticism he constantly went astray. . . . Even here he was the clear, analytical thinker, rather than a patient collector and weigher of detailed evidence. He was great here, but not at his greatest. Theology was his first love. (Warfield, 589-90)

BIBLIOGRAPHY

Works. C. Hodge, *Romans* (London: Banner of Truth, 1975 [2d ed. 1864); idem, *Essays and Reviews* (New York: Garland, 1987 [1857]), which contains his essay on Moses Stuart's commentary on Romans from the 1833 *Princeton Review;* idem, *1 and 2 Corinthians* (London: Banner of Truth, 1978 [1857, 1859]); idem, *Ephesians* (London: Banner of Truth, 1991 [1856]); idem, *Systematic Theology* (3 vols.; Grand Rapids: Eerdmans, 1949 [1872-1873]); idem, *What Is Darwinism?* ed. M. A. Noll and D. N. Livingstone (Grand Rapids: Baker, 1994 [1874]), which includes a few of Hodge's other short writings on the Bible and science.

Studies. S. E. Ahlstrom, *Theology in America: The Major Protestant Voices from Puritanism to Neo-Orthodoxy* (Indianapolis: Bobbs-Merrill, 1967) 47-58, 251-92; A. A. Hodge, *The Life of Charles Hodge* (New York: Charles Scribner's Sons, 1880); M. A. Noll, "Charles Hodge" *ANB;* T. H. Olbricht, "Charles Hodge as an American New Testament Interpreter," *JPH* 57 (summer 1979) 117-33; S. J. Stein, "Stuart and Hodge on Romans 5:12-21: An Exegetical Controversy about Original Sin," *JPH* 47 (December 1969) 340-58; J. W. Stewart, "The Tethered Theology: Biblical Criticism, Common Sense Philosophy and the Princeton Theologians, 1812-1860" (Ph.D. diss., University of Michigan, 1990); M. A. Taylor, *The Old Testament in the Old Princeton School [1812-1929]* (Lewiston, NY: Edwin Mellen, 1992); B. B. Warfield, "Dr. Hodge as a Teacher of Exegesis" in A. A. Hodge, *The Life of Charles Hodge* (New York: Charles Scribner's Sons, 1880) 588-91.

M. A. Noll

Kierkegaard, Søren Aabe (1813-1855)

The Bible was the most important piece of literature in Søren Kierkegaard's life. Victor Eremita, one of Kierkegaard's pseudonyms, observed, "The Bible is always on my table and is the book I read most" (Kierkegaard 1988, 218). Surely this is true of Eremita's creator. More than fifteen hundred references to Scripture are indexed in his major works, with numerous other references in his *Journals and Papers* (Pedersen, 2:27). There is little doubt that Kierkegaard spent much time each day reading and reflecting on the Bible's contents. As P. S. Minear and P. S. Morimoto have observed, "We can be absolutely sure of one fact: his adult life was characterized by frequent, regular, thorough and thoughtful listening to the Bible" (Minear and Morimoto, 3). Yet Kierkegaard confessed his impatience with the church's seeming inability to hear the Bible on its own terms. In an 1854 *Journal* entry he proposed: "Let us collect all the New Testaments there are and bring them out to an open place or up on a mountain and then, while we all kneel, let someone talk to God in this manner: Take this book back again. We human beings, such as we are, are not fit to involve ourselves with such a thing, it only makes us unhappy" (Kierkegaard 1967-1978, 1:87, no. 216).

Approach to the Bible. Kierkegaard's major criticism of Lutheran orthodoxy was the faulty logic with which it approached the Bible as a textbook from which to draw doctrinal confessions rather than spiritual guidance (Kierkegaard 1941, 24-25). This necessitates an objective study of the Bible that raised all the historical and critical questions about the Bible. To the believer these things are a "temptation for the spirit," while the unbeliever does not wish the Bible to emerge as "inspired" (Kierkegaard 1941, 27). Therefore, asked Kierkegaard, "Who then really has interest in the whole inquiry?" (Kierkegaard 1941, 28).

The objective study of the Bible is a mistake from beginning to end, Kierkegaard maintains, for faith does not need the promise of proof. Just as a historical accident cannot be the basis for an eternal happiness, neither can the Bible, objectively considered, be the basis of such a happiness. The emergence of the higher-critical method of studying the Bible was equally fallacious. Kierkegaard saw only two opposite options open with this approach: either a more scientific and less dogmatic defense of the biblical tradition, or a more scientific rejection of the biblical faith on grounds beyond simple denial. In an 1850 entry in the *Journals* Kierkegaard drew an analogy between the imperfections of the natural world and the imperfections of the Bible and declared that difficulties in the Bible were there precisely because "God wants the Holy Scripture to be the object of faith and an offense to any other point of view" (Kierkegaard 1967-1978, 3:275, no. 2877).

Kierkegaard did not oppose critical scholarship per se. He frequently utilized insights on the background and context of a biblical passage in his own Bible study. However, Kierkegaard recognized that historical study could provide only an "approximate" understanding of the Bible (Kierkegaard 1941, 26). He warned that "the great mass of interpreters damage the understanding of the New Testament more than they benefit" and compared numerous commentaries to "spectators and spotlights" that prevent the enjoyment of a play at the theater (Kierkegaard 1967-1978, 1:83, no. 202). He suggested reading the New Testament "without a commentary" and asked rhetorically, "Would it ever occur to a lover to read a letter from his beloved with a commentary?" (Kierkegaard 1967-1978, 1:85, no. 210).

Kierkegaard never wrote an extended treatise on exegesis or hermeneutics, however his own hermeneutic is a principle of imitation through imaginative identification. He argued for an active appropriation of Scripture by personal examination in the light of the biblical witness. The Kierkegaardian position is one of a "radical revaluation" which in the "personal and direct obedience of faith has the Bible appear as the bearer of the unconditioned and its messenger" (Pedersen, 2:41-42). As one reads about the heroes of faith in the Bible,

one should not "doubt our likeness, however remote, to these men of God," for, observed Kierkegaard, "The deep sorrow, the terrible battles within our attitudes, must not allow us to doubt completely our strength to bear what is our lot to bear. Inasmuch as such instances remind us of the dark and bright hours in our own experience, we shall not lose equilibrium, we shall not imagine that everything is accomplished in one stroke, and we shall not despair when we see that this cannot be done" (Kierkegaard 1967-1978, 1:83-84, no. 205).

Kierkegaard lamented that his generation had forgotten "that this letter [the Bible] is from God and entirely forgotten that it is to the single individual" (Kierkegaard 1967-1978, 1:86, no. 213).

Personal appropriation, then, is the standard by which Kierkegaard judged methods of studying the Bible as having value or not having value. Kierkegaard saw simply learning the Bible by heart as an example of childishness. A mature person learns only "by appropriation" (Kierkegaard 1941, 38). Kierkegaard's concern was not that one should exegete Scripture in a certain way but rather that Scripture should be allowed to exegete life.

Kierkegaard assumed the existential truth of and worked from the biblical material. There is no formal or elaborate theory of biblical revelation in his works. He utilized the Bible as philosopher, sage, prophet and poet. The various approaches to the Scriptures of both the early pseudonymous aesthetic and philosophical works and the later "second literature" display a diversity of models for "appropriation," depending on the specific purpose and concerns of a given work. Kierkegaard's existential philosophy and religious concerns interacted in a creative and dynamic way in his use of the Scriptures. An examination of Kierkegaard's biography indicates that religious concerns were part of his life from his earliest days. His intellectual interest in and ultimate repudiation of speculative philosophy grew out of his larger religious interests. It is therefore impossible fully to distinguish Kierkegaard's Christian concerns from his philosophical concerns. His understanding of the purpose of his various writings was that these contained the religious element from the beginning.

The Bible as a Literary Work. As is obvious from even a cursory reading of the Kierkegaard corpus, he had an intimate familiarity with and appreciation for the Bible as a literary work. The numerous passing allusions, aphoristic quotes, utilization of biblical characters and events, and other passing references of his earliest works illustrate this. He also had a deeper concern with regard to the Bible. Kierkegaard vigorously sought to reintroduce the radical demands of New Testament Christianity into Christendom. The vocabulary of faith was, for Kierkegaard, discovered, defined and clarified through the revelation of God contained in the Scriptures. Regardless of the final verdict that one may reach concerning the accuracy of his biblical exposition and the validity of his theological position, there can be little doubt that his religious pilgrimage involved a deep and profound struggle with appropriating the message of the Bible. The numerous references to the Bible and its creative application in the Kierkegaard corpus are ample evidence that "Kierkegaard persisted in seeking the truth in Scripture through imaginative and total immersion in its content" (Fishburn, 229).

The pseudonyms of Kierkegaard's early works employed the Bible in a variety of ways. The pseudonyms represent various aspects of the aesthetic, ethical and religious existence spheres. Each of these "caricatures" has a slightly different approach to the Scripture. In general the hermeneutical pattern of each corresponds roughly to the existence sphere it represents. The aesthetic pseudonyms had a preference for Old Testament characters and illustrations. In the later works there was an obvious preference for the Synoptic Gospels, for Kierkegaard built his understanding of the life of Jesus

upon traditional conflations of these accounts. He also made frequent use of the Gospel of John. The book of James, because of its practical concerns with faith and practice, was also a favorite source in Kierkegaard's "second literature."

The hermeneutic of the aesthete is characterized by an attitude of indifference to the Scripture. Allusions to Scripture in the first volume of *Either/Or* and the aesthetic potion of *Stages* are of a general nature. The Bible is used as a literary device. Theological concerns are not directly evident. Therefore, the Scriptures are not cited as authoritative or as proofs in the development of an argument. A reader's knowledge of the Bible may make some of the allusions more meaningful in terms of irony, humor or their general illustrative value. Indeed, Kierkegaard appears to have assumed a general biblical literacy for his audience or he would not have used so many remote references to the Bible. However, in most cases other nonbiblical references could be used without a significant change in the meaning of his text.

The hermeneutic of the ethical, as exemplified by Judge William in volume 2 of *Either/Or*, the relevant passages of *Stages* and discussion of the ethical in the other philosophical works appeals to the Bible as a source for corroboration of universal law. This approach was also consistent with the immanental religion of what Kierkegaard later condemned as Christendom. Although the concern is with duty in relation to an external standard, even here the Bible is not the foundation for the ethical point of view; it simply offers support. Dissatisfaction with an appeal to the ethical universal characterized the use of the Scriptures in *Fear and Trembling*. This work and *The Concept of Anxiety* stand on the transitional ground to the hermeneutic of paradox.

Paradox and Polemic. The hermeneutic of paradox characterized Kierkegaard's polemical approach to Christendom. This approach was evident in both the transitional philosophical works, *Philosophical Fragments* and *Concluding Unscientific*

Postscript, as well as the later, more directly polemical *Training in Christianity* and *Attack Upon "Christendom."* In the earlier works, references to the Scripture with regard to the paradox are infrequent. There are enough allusions to indicate the importance of biblical sources for Kierkegaard's conception of the Incarnation. There is, however, not the direct appeal to the New Testament characteristic of both *Training in Christianity* and the *Attack Upon "Christendom."*

Kierkegaard's emphasis upon and understanding of the paradox of the God-man is not substantially different in *Training* and *Attack* from the conception in the earlier works. The major difference is that the lines of demarcation between Christendom and New Testament Christianity are more sharply drawn. However, the paradox was consistently the key to Kierkegaard's deepest religious understanding of the Scripture. The major difference between the earlier and later utilization of Scripture with regard to the paradox is twofold. In the early works Kierkegaard himself is engaged in "indirect communication." In the later, more polemical works, Kierkegaard communicated directly. However, the paradox itself and hence the message of the Bible, remained an "indirect communication."

Kierkegaard, especially in the later works, claimed that the Scriptures are fully authoritative. However, he appeared to favor different parts of the Bible for different purposes. As noted, he used the Old Testament more than the New Testament in the numerous allusions of the aesthetic pseudonyms. Moreover, the Bible was not cited for its authority in this context. The Old Testament characters of Abraham and Job were utilized as important pointers beyond themselves to the absolute paradox. Kierkegaard's analysis of sin in *The Concept of Anxiety* takes both the Old Testament account of the fall and its New Testament interpretation seriously.

The Christian demands of the New Testament are also significant for Kierkegaard.

Repeatedly he contrasted these to the easy faith of Christendom. Although he had a personal preference for the Synoptics and the book of James, there is no indication that these were any more authoritative for him than any other portion of the Scripture. He cited the Gospels as providing a complete picture of the offense of the paradox and the demands of the teaching of Jesus. James was important to Kierkegaard because of its emphasis on the relationship of faith to works. Both 1 Corinthians 13 and relevant passages from 1 John provided the biblical data for his discussion of love. Paradox is the key category for Kierkegaard. It is the prism through which he viewed the whole of the Scripture. His interpretation of the Bible was, in keeping with the Reformed tradition, intentionally christocentric. In his journals Kierkegaard said that "the Holy Scriptures are the highway signs: Christ is the way" (Kierkegaard 1967-1978, 1:84, no. 208).

The paradox is the divine confrontation with and transformation of the human. Kierkegaard was not concerned with the what of Christianity but with how one becomes a Christian in Christendom. Thus it is the existentially compelling force of the gospel message, addressed to the individual who would allow himself or herself to hear, that comprises its authority. Christianity is not a doctrine; it is the communication of personal truth. The Bible is intrinsically authoritative as it confronts the human heart. The nature of the God-man as a communication of the divine and the response of the human heart in either faith or offense are indications of the Bible's authority. Human freedom guarantees the opportunity of either response, but these are the only options available. There is no middle ground of accommodation. Thus the message of the Bible and its existential fit are the only proofs of its authority. No external proofs can otherwise substantiate its authority or message.

Kierkegaard used frequent allusions to the Bible to illustrate a variety of points. Theologically he took the biblical account of the fall, the Incarnation, the passion and resurrection of Christ all at face value. These were events that happened. But the paradox is more than mere history. It is a divine communication.

Kierkegaard carefully cited biblical evidence for his understanding of "religion B," the religion of transcendence. The Bible is utilized to demonstrate the essential otherness of God, the offense of the paradox, becoming contemporaneous with Christ, and the true nature of faith. Also, the demands of the Christian life, the Christian ethic of love and related issues are developed along biblical lines. When he was defining key concepts, Kierkegaard was generally a careful exegete of the text.

However, when Kierkegaard used the Bible along the way to the religion of transcendence, such as the account of Abraham's sacrifice of Isaac in *Fear and Trembling,* he was not nearly as careful, nor was he even concerned with the larger contextual problems surrounding the historical meaning of a passage. He warned that exegesis and the science of biblical interpretation had become diversions from hearing and appropriating the message of the Bible.

Kierkegaard rejected any appeal to the proofs, either from history or reason, to substantiate the claims of Christianity. Such proofs could at best only render Christianity plausible. They also open the door for scientific skepticism. Indeed, appeals to the historical accuracy of the biblical record, the subsequent history and influence of Christianity, and philosophical proofs for the existence of God are in Kierkegaard's analysis a betrayal of faith.

The paradox of God coming as a suffering servant is absurd. It is fundamentally an offense to human reason. The realization of one's own sin and finitude is the catharsis that opens the door to transcendence. The leap of faith and a life of repentance toward God cannot be mediated in any other way. The radical demands of the Christian life are in Kierkegaard's view compromised with any attempt to settle for less.

Significance. There are a number of positive contributions to be noted in Kierkegaard's utilization of Scripture. First, there can be little doubt about the centrality of the Scripture in Kierkegaard's thought. He sought, for better or worse, to hear and appropriate the biblical word. It should be evident that Kierkegaard did not secularize the vocabulary of the gospel via his psychological and existential interests. As a Christian believer he sought to be a faithful expositor of the biblical message.

Second, Kierkegaard was surely correct regarding the limits of apologetic proofs. These can lead only to an approximation and reduce the Christian message to the status of probability. This remained a strong and persistent theme throughout his works. A convinced mind is not a convicted heart. The absurdity and offense of the paradox is in the affirmation that "God was in Christ." Kierkegaard had no doubts about the facts of the gospel. He had serious reservations about their significance as only facts. The crucial issue for Kierkegaard was both the type of apologetic offered and what one hoped to accomplish with it. He warned that the real propensity of traditional apologetics lay not in making a case for Christianity but in opening the door to skepticism. Yet his analysis of the gospel's remedy for the human condition is an apologetic of sorts.

Nor can Kierkegaard be fairly accused of being an irrationalist or believing in absurdity for absurdity's sake. He was simply describing what he saw in both the human condition and the divine response to this condition in the gospel. He contended that an individual is not a fully constituted self apart from God. This realization is for Kierkegaard the only preparation available for appropriation of the gospel. Kierkegaard was consistent in his appeals to Scripture on this point and, in this writer's view, is absolved of culpability with regard to a lack of apologetic approach.

Third, the various hermeneutical models in Kierkegaard's work serve as a reminder that there are indeed a variety of possible readings of the Bible. His is an early reader-response approach. One's life view includes basic presuppositions that will influence the reading and appropriation of the Scripture. In many respects the various approaches to the Bible exhibited by the various Kierkegaardian pseudonyms are ways of appropriating Scripture. However, the majority of these are ultimately unsatisfactory. The Christian way of appropriation is for Kierkegaard realized through a passionate concern or inwardness that allows the message of the gospel to confront the human heart.

Finally, Kierkegaard's approach to Scripture offers a possible alternative to the polarities of the current revisiting of the modernist-fundamentalist controversy in evangelical circles. Kierkegaard rightly repudiated the kind of rationalism that sought to go beyond simple faith. The critical study of the Bible asked the wrong kinds of questions and in the wrong way, for Kierkegaard. These issues were, he warned, a diversion from hearing the biblical word.

However, he also condemned the rigid dogmatism of orthodoxy. He warned that Christian truth could not be reduced to propositional affirmations about God. Christianity was for Kierkegaard not a doctrine but a person—the God-man, the Lord Jesus Christ. In many ways both the extreme right and left have succumbed to the seduction of the modern scientific mindset, as Kierkegaard warned.

Kierkegaard's ties to existential philosophy and neo-orthodox theology have been the basis for a general closed-mindedness to his thought by many in the United States conservative evangelical community. Vernon C. Grounds and Edward J. Carnell were notable exceptions to this trend (cf. V. C. Grounds, "Take Another Look at S. K.," a review of Carnell's "The Burden of Søren Kierkegaard," *CT* [February 18, 1966, 33]). Recently, however, his work has become the focus of a new appreciation among evangelicals. Calling Kierkegaard "an intellectual's intellectual," C. Steven Evans has observed: "Kierkegaard, more

than anyone I know, can help remind evangelicals that Christianity is a manner of being, a way of existing, not merely an affirmation of doctrine. But he can remind us of this in a way that will not precipitate a slide back into the contempt for reason and the life of the mind that has sometimes infected evangelicalism and fundamentalism" (C. S. Evans, "A Misunderstood Reformer," *CT* [September 21, 1984], 29).

As Carnell said of the Danish gadfly, "it is easy to follow the very one who wanted no followers" (Carnell, *Christian Commitment* [New York: Macmillan, 1957] 73).

BIBLIOGRAPHY

Works. S. A. Kierkegaard, *Attack Upon "Christendom," 1854-55* (Princeton, NJ: Princeton University Press, 1968); idem, *Christian Discourses* (London: Oxford University Press, 1949); idem, *The Concept of Anxiety: A Simple Psychologically Orienting Deliberation on the Dogmatic Issue of Hereditary Sin* (Princeton, NJ: Princeton University Press, 1980); idem, *Concluding Unscientific Postscript* (Princeton, NJ: Princeton University Press, 1941); idem, *Thoughts on Crucial Situations* (Minneapolis: Augsburg, 1941); idem, *Either/Or*, ed. and trans. H. V. Hong & E. H. Hong (2 vols.; Princeton, NJ: Princeton University Press, 1987); idem, *Fear and Trembling*, ed. H. Hong and E. Hong (Princeton, NJ: Princeton University Press, 1969); idem, *The Journals of Søren Kierkegaard, A Selection*, ed. A. Dru (London: Oxford University Press, 1938); idem, *On Authority and Revelation: The Book of Adler, or, a Cycle of Ethico-Religious Essays* (Princeton, NJ: Princeton University Press, 1955); idem, *Parables of Kierkegaard*, ed. T. C. Oden (Princeton, NJ: Princeton University Press, 1978); idem, *Prayers of Kierkegaard*, ed. P. LeFevere (Chicago: University of Chicago Press, 1956); idem, *Purity of Heart* (2d ed.; New York: Harper & Row, 1948); idem, *The Sickness Unto Death: A Christian Psychological Exposition for Upbuilding and Awakening* (Princeton, NJ: Princeton University Press, 1980); idem, *Søren Kierkegaard's Journals and Papers*, ed. H. Hong and E. Hong (7 vols.; Bloomington, IN: Indiana University Press, 1967-1978); idem, *Søren Kierkegaard's Papirer*, ed. P. A. Heiberg, V. Kuhr and E. Torsting (20 vols.; Copenhagen: Gyldendalske Boghandel Nordisk Forlag, 1909); idem, *Stages on Life's*

Way, ed. and trans. H. V. Hong & E. H. Hong (Princeton, NJ: Princeton University Press, 1988); idem, *Training in Christianity* (Princeton, NJ: Princeton University Press, 1967); idem, *Works of Love* (New York: Harper & Row, 1962).

Studies. P. Bigelow, "Kierkegaard and the Hermeneutical Circle," *M&W* 15 (1982) 67-82; S. Cavell, "Kierkegaard's On Authority and Revelation" in *Kierkegaard: A Collection of Critical Essays*, ed. J. Thompson (New York: Doubleday, 1972); J. L. Dunstan, "The Bible in Either/Or," *Int* 6 (1952) 310-20; F. A. Early, "The Problem of Religious Knowledge in the Writings of Søren Kierkegaard" (unpublished Ph.D. dissertation, Southern Baptist Theological Seminary, 1944); J. F. Fishburn, "Søren Kierkegaard, Exegete," *Int* 39 (1985) 229-45; J. R. Jones, "Some Remarks on Authority and Revelation in Kierkegaard," *JR* (July 1977) 232-51; E. Kallas, "Kierkegaard's Understanding of the Bible With Respect to His 'Age'," *Dial.* 26 (1987) 30-34; P. S. Minear and P. S. Morimoto, *Kierkegaard and the Bible—An Index* (Princeton, NJ: Princeton Pamphlets, 1953); D. A. Pailin, "Abraham and Isaac: A Hermeneutical Problem Before Kierkegaard" in *Kierkegaard's Fear and Trembling: Critical Appraisals*, ed. R. L. Perkins (Birmingham, AL: University of Alabama Press, 1981); J. Pedersen, "Kierkegaard's View of Scripture" in *Bibliotheca Kierkegaardiana*, ed. N. Thulstrup and M. M. Thulstrup (Copenhagen: C. A. Reitzels Forlag, 1978) vol. 2; E. Perry, "Was Kierkegaard a Biblical Existentialist?" *JR* 36 (1956) 17-23; L. J. Rosas III, "The Function of Scripture in the Thought of Søren Kierkegaard" (Ph.D. dissertation, Southern Baptist Theological Seminary, 1988); idem, *Scripture in the Thought of Søren Kierkegaard* (Nashville: Broadman & Holman, 1994).

L. J. Rosas III

Lightfoot, J(oseph) B(arber) (1828-1889)

Joseph Barber Lightfoot was born in Liverpool on April 13, 1828. His father was an accountant from Yorkshire, and his mother's family had come from Newcastle. After his father's death in 1843 his family moved to Birmingham, where he went to King Edward's school, which Brooke Foss *Westcott, his successor as bishop fifty

years later, had just left. Lightfoot followed Westcott to Trinity College, Cambridge, in 1847, the beginning of a dazzling academic career. He was top of the classical tripos (1851), elected fellow of Trinity College (1852), Hulsean Professor of Divinity (1861) and Lady Margaret's Professor (1875). Four years later, after much heart searching, he accepted appointment as Bishop of Durham (1879), a position he held for a further ten years before his untimely death on December 21, 1889.

Though Lightfoot was preeminently a scholar, it is important to note that his scholarly work was part of a larger whole. This is particularly evident during the last ten years of his life. He was, for example, a pioneer in advocating and promoting lay ministry, giving laypeople a new and effective voice in the church's councils and calling into existence a trained body of lay readers, lay preachers and lay evangelists. In 1885 he was calling for a general representative assembly in the Church of England.

Lightfoot's study of Romans 16 led him to commend female deacons as warmly as male deacons. Indeed, he gave Phoebe the deacon (Rom 16:1) a place in the window of Trinity Chapel, Cambridge, a century before the college itself was ready to admit women. On the theme of priesthood he maintained the controversial view, but on the basis of his typically careful scrutiny of the New Testament and the early Fathers, that priestly ministry is competent as such only insofar as it is representative of the priestly people (Lightfoot 1868, "Christian Ministry"). Further, as bishop he saw through the creation of the Newcastle diocese and in ten years oversaw the building of no fewer than forty-five churches and mission halls.

Historical Critic. Lightfoot, however, is principally to be remembered as the almost ideal model of the responsible historical critic. It was here that Lightfoot's greatest strength as a scholar was most fully displayed. Lightfoot's commitment to historical inquiry, his expertise in historical texts and the measured quality of his findings mark him out as probably the finest commentator on early Christian texts that Great Britain has ever produced.

First, Lightfoot's whole scholarly career was built on the assumption of the primacy of the original source. That is easily stated as a principle. What made it so effective in Lightfoot's case was his mastery of these sources—not just Christian texts but also classical texts and Jewish texts, and not just texts but inscriptional evidence that was just then being gathered and published. Where modern students often seem most concerned to cite present-day secondary sources for and against an interpretation of the text, Lightfoot went directly to the original sources of the time. Such was his knowledge of these texts that he was able to write freely, citing the appropriate texts from memory, with only occasional indications in the margin that a quotation should be checked for accuracy. On any significant point or expression his exegesis or interpretation is typically so fully documented with such references, and the references so thoroughly and convincingly marshaled, that the reader is usually ready to concede the case well before the display of evidence has been completed.

Second, Lightfoot well demonstrates the importance of setting the language of a text in the context of the usage of the time if its meaning is to be understood. He would have found it exceedingly puzzling if any in his own day had claimed that texts like the New Testament epistles could be thought to have legitimate meaning independent of what the words used in these texts meant at the time they were written. For the language of these texts is Greek, and not modern Greek but ancient Greek. Consequently the meaning of the words individually and in their given syntactical combinations cannot be independent of the way these words were understood and used at that time. To presume to read meaning from these texts without reference to ancient usage would be irresponsible.

Some of Lightfoot's most effective observations in this vein are directed against the anonymous author of the book *Supernatural Religion,* whom he accused, in effect, of such bad scholarship. To understand an ancient text, he insisted, one must know "how men in actual life do speak and write now, and might be expected to speak and write sixteen or seventeen centuries ago" (Lighfoot 1889, 91). Lightfoot's resulting word studies are a model for all such analysis and are often still valuable in themselves, despite the passage of time and the accumulation of further data (see particularly his *Colossians).* His paraphrastic translations at the beginning of sections of his commentaries are still effective in filling out the meaning of the following paragraph of text in the light of the more detailed commentary.

Third, it was equally important for Lightfoot that a text as a whole cannot be properly understood unless it is set within and related to its particular context in history. The fact that Paul could speak in one tone and language to one audience and very differently to another, a problem of inconsistency for some scholars today, was for Lightfoot no problem whatsoever so long as the context in each case was taken into account. Martin* Luther, he notes, was able to bid the timid and gentle Philipp *Melanchthon to "sin and sin boldly"; but Luther would have sooner cut off his right hand than pen such words to the antinomian rioters of Münster (Lightfoot 1865, 349-50). So with Paul, Lightfoot set a new trend in writing commentaries by taking care to gather as much information as possible on the destinations to which Paul wrote. He fully recognized that the particular terms in which Paul wrote his individual letters could well have been shaped or determined in greater or less degree by the situations addressed in these letters.

So too with Ignatius, writing some fifty years later than Paul, whose intensity of passion for suffering and martyrdom is unnerving for many a modern reader. Lightfoot properly points out that such sentiment cannot be fairly appreciated without some awareness of the atmosphere of persecution and martyrdom that the repressive policies of the emperors Domitian and Trajan engendered in the years preceding Ignatius's arrest (Lightfoot 1885, 2-30). Or again, when the author of *Supernatural Religion* found it incredible that Ignatius was able to receive visitors and write letters while under close arrest on the way to Rome, Lightfoot was able to provide a complete answer by referring to what was already well enough known of Roman remand and arrest at that time (Lightfoot 1889, 74-78; Lightfoot 1885, 342-47). The problem posed by a text read out of historical context was immediately resolved by setting it back in its historical context.

Finally, it is worth noting the care with which Lightfoot sought to avoid speculation that went beyond the available evidence. To the author of *Supernatural Religion* he points out: "In the land of the unverifiable there are no efficient critical police" (Lightfoot 1889, 36). When a writer's thesis was constructed by building hypothesis upon hypothesis, he was beyond the reach of refutation. Where questions outran information, the scholar should not be afraid to say, "We do not know." Where the page was blank, it would be an idle and unprofitable exercise to fill it with mere conjecture. In these and other such matters the fineness of Lightfoot's judgment was never less than impressive. As one Scottish visitor to Auckland Castle observed: "He always speaks with a pair of balances in his hands, like Justice, only he is not blindfolded like her" (Eden and Macdonald, 35-36). Or in the words of the compliment paid him by the great German scholar, Adolf von Harnack, Lightfoot "never defended a tradition for the tradition's sake" (Eden and Macdonald 133).

In all this Lightfoot clearly demonstrates the importance of reading a historical text within its historical context, so that the meaning of a text does not arise out of the text alone but out of the text read in context, and so that the original context

and intention of the author is a determinative and controlling factor in what may be read from such a text. It is important in turn to remember the historical context of Lightfoot's own work. In particular he was primarily concerned with historical questions and not with how such texts might be properly appropriated by the church of later generations. Again, all the texts on which he commented were letters, addressed by known individuals to known communities or persons, whose content is inevitably much more context-specific and context-dependent than wisdom literature or even the Gospels. Nevertheless Lightfoot would have approved a referential theory of meaning: that to which the language of a text refers exercises a crucial determinant and control on the meaning of that text. And in his own terms and time Lightfoot can be justly hailed as a classic exponent of the skill and art of the historical critic in finest measure.

Lightfoot and Baur. In the course of Lightfoot's scholarly and episcopal career the major test for his historical-critical method was undoubtedly his running controversy with the Tübingen school and with its major exponent, Ferdinand Christian *Baur. Baur had developed a theory of Christian origins from quite proper exegetical observations on Paul's letters to the Corinthians and Galatians. The indications that Paul had withstood Peter to his face at Antioch, on the question of Christian Jews eating with Christian Gentiles, and that there were Paul and Peter parties in the church at Corinth, encouraged Baur to draw the conclusion that these episodes were symptomatic of earliest Christianity's condition as a whole, evidence of a much more extensive split between these two parties running throughout the earliest Christian movement. This insight and hypothesis Baur then made into an organizing principle or critical *Tendenz* around which the development of the whole of Christianity during the first two centuries could be reconstructed.

At this point exegesis began to do service to an overarching philosophical schema: that the thesis of Petrine or Jewish Christianity and the antithesis of Pauline or Gentile Christianity reached their resolution and synthesis in the old catholic church of the late second century. This schema provided the Tübingen school with the vital clues as to when the New Testament and early Christian documents should be dated. The key was to ask where each document best fit into the process just described. If a document gave evidence that the controversy between the Pauline and Petrine parties was still vigorous, then that document was to be dated early. If the document reflected a situation in which there was no controversy or that it had petered out, then that must mean it was late. So, Paul was obviously early, but documents like Acts, John and Ignatius had to be dated well through the second century.

Lightfoot replied to all this by pointing out that historical criticism must provide not simply the starting point for such reconstructions of earliest Christian history but must be determinative throughout. Writing with Baur in mind he summarized the difference between true criticism and false criticism thus:

Ingenuity often wears the mask of criticism, but is not infrequently the caricature of criticism. Ingenuity is not necessarily divination; it is not wholesome self-restraint, is not the sober weighing of probabilities, is not the careful consideration of evidence. Criticism is all these, which are wanting to its spurious counterfeit. (Lightfoot 1875)

In demonstration of such (true) criticism, Lightfoot subjected to analysis key documents in the Tübingen viewpoint—the letters of Ignatius in particular—and succeeded in showing with abundant clarity just how forced and improbable were the interpretations of the apostolic fathers in the Tübingen reconstructions.

This is not to say that Lightfoot rejected totally Baur's analysis of the situation confronting Paul. On the contrary, he recognized clearly enough the tensions that

called forth a letter like Galatians—more clearly than did many of his successors in rebuking the Tübingen school. But by use of criticism rightly so-called, he effectively undermined the ingenuity that wove an elaborate hypothesis round basic data, which had been passed off as criticism and which had captivated two generations of scholarship—a classic example of how the historical-critical method works, of how setting a text in its historical context can prove an effective check on more speculative theories.

Scholarship and Faith. In all this, Lightfoot showed how faith and critical scholarship can be important allies. As he had observed much earlier, in unpublished notes of lectures delivered in the Lent term of 1855:

The timidity, which shrinks from the application of modern science or criticism to the interpretation of Holy Scripture evinces a very unworthy view of its character. If the Scriptures are indeed true, they must be in accordance with every true principle of whatever kind. It is against the wrong application of such principles, and against the presumption which pushes them too far that we must protest. It is not much knowledge, but little knowledge that is the dangerous thing, here as elsewhere. From the full light of science and criticism we have nothing to fear. (Kaye, 219)

This is the model of responsible criticism of which Lightfoot himself is the exemplar. He was not an unblemished exemplar. He never really tackled the historical problems posed by the Gospels; and he was much stronger on questions historical than questions theological. But in terms of his own time, he was a scholar far in advance of his time. He was the pioneer of a new generation of commentaries, which more than one hundred years after they were written still shed illuminating light on these texts so crucial for Christian self-understanding. And he was the model of scrupulously judicious critical scholarship in the service of truth.

BIBLIOGRAPHY

Works. J. B. Lightfoot, *The Apostolic Fathers. Part 1, S. Clement of Rome* (2d ed.; London: Macmillan, 1890 [1869]); idem, *The Apostolic Fathers. Part 2, S. Ignatius, S. Polycarp* (London: Macmillan, 1885); idem, *Biblical Essays* (London: Macmillan, 1893); idem, *Epistle to the Colossians* (London: Macmillan, 1875); idem, *Essays on the Work Entitled Supernatural Religion* (London: Macmillan, 1889); idem, *Notes on the Epistles of St. Paul* (London: Macmillan, 1895); idem, *Saint Paul's Epistle to the Galatians* (London: Macmillan, 1865); idem, *Saint Paul's Epistle to the Philippians* (London: Macmillan, 1868).

Studies. C. K. Barrett, "Joseph Barber Lightfoot," *DUJ* 64 (1972) 193-204; idem, *"Quomodo historia scribenda sit,"* *NTS* 28 (1982) 303-20; F. C. Baur, *Paul, the Apostle of Jesus Christ* (London: Williams & Norgate, 1873 [1845]); J. D. G. Dunn, ed., "The Lightfoot Centenary Lectures" (lectures by D. M. Thompson, M. Hengel, C. K. Barrett and J. D. G. Dunn) *DUJ* (special number, 1992); G. R. Eden and F. C. Macdonald, *Lightfoot of Durham: Memorials and Appreciations* (Cambridge: Cambridge University Press, 1932); B. N. Kaye, "Lightfoot and Baur on Early Christianity," *NT* 26 (1984) 193-224; J. A. T. Robinson, *Joseph Barber Lightfoot* (Durham Cathedral Lecture, 1981); G. R. Treloar, "J. B. Lightfoot and St. Paul, 1854-65: A Study of Intentions and Methods," *Luc* 7 (1989) 5-34; G. R. Treloar and B. N. Kaye, "J. B. Lightfoot on Strauss and Christian Origins: An Unpublished Manuscript," *DUJ* 79 (1987) 165-200.   J. D. G. Dunn

Meyer, Heinrich August Wilhelm *(1800-1873)*

This exegete was born on January 10, 1800, in Gotha, Thuringia. His father was a shoemaker for the duke. Meyer's educational preparation and study at a classic German gymnasium in Gotha included an in-depth exposure to Latin. He finished this preparation in 1818 with remarks about his exams that indicated his teachers hoped for great promise in his future pursuits. He then went to university at Jena, where he studied theology, history, philosophy and philology, including such languages as Arabic. The university had a reputation for rationalism, an ethos common to the time.

Meyer was able to remain at the university for only five semesters because of financial demands from his family. Nonetheless he was able to pass both his major theology exams with commendation (1821-1822). He then became a teacher at a boarding school under the direction of Pastor Oppermann in Grone near Göttingen. He married the pastor's daughter, Elise, in 1823, shortly after the call to his first pastorate in Osthausen, Thuringia, in December 1822.

The key move of Meyer's life came with a call in 1830 to serve as pastor in the Hanoverian state church in Harste near Göttingen. This allowed Meyer to live near a major university town and to have access to its library resources. It also put him close to the publishing house of Vandenhoeck und Ruprecht in Göttingen.

Meyer had a reputation as a tireless worker. He rose at about 4 a.m. to do his "scientific" New Testament study before fulfilling the duties of his parish later in the morning. An hour's predawn walk was also a daily custom. His discipline led to a particularly fruitful period: Meyer issued a text-critical Greek edition of the New Testament with a modern German translation (1829). With it came some study notes on the four Gospels, part of an unfulfilled plan to cover the entire New Testament. But this work eventually laid important groundwork for the commentary series known by his name (the Meyer series, also known as the Kritisch-exegetischer Kommentar zum Neuen Testament, designated today by the abbreviation KEK). In 1830 he issued a Latin version of the Symbolical Books of the Lutheran church.

Volumes of Meyer's commentary were issued in quick succession, including frequently updated versions. The Synoptics were published in 1832, reaching a sixth edition by 1876. Matthew became its own volume in a second edition in 1844, with Mark and Luke following in 1846 and reaching a fifth edition by 1867. John was initially published in 1834 (5th ed., 1869). Acts was released in 1835 (4th ed., 1870); Romans followed in 1836 (5th ed., 1872). Next came 1 Corinthians and 2 Corinthians in 1839 and 1840 (both had a 5th ed. by 1870). Galatians was issued in 1841 (5th ed., 1870) and then Ephesians in 1843 (4th ed., 1867).

During this period Meyer had moved to Hoya (1837) as superintendant of a school, and then he came onto a church council (1841), serving as superintendant and pastor at the Neustadter Court and Castle Church in Hanover. Here he had pastoral responsibility for a parish with five thousand members. Eventually the combination of responsibilities wore him down, and he fell seriously ill in February 1846. In 1848 he stepped down from his pastoral duties. Yet the commentaries continued: Philippians appeared in 1847, while Philemon and Colossians were published with a reissued volume on Philippians in 1848 (4th ed., 1874 with a commemorative short biography written by his son Gustav). The commentaries to the rest of the New Testament were completed by younger scholars, with the entire New Testament exposition being published in 1859 (sixteen volumes). This massive undertaking was so successful that all of Meyer's volumes were translated into English through a publisher in Edinburgh, a project that took from 1873 to 1885 to complete.

During this time Meyer continued to serve on the Hanoverian church council and took up a leader's role in 1861. He was also engaged as an examiner of theological students during the time and served as a professor at Giessen from 1841. He was awarded an honorary doctorate from Göttingen on March 24, 1845. He retired in 1865, though he continued to serve as an examiner of theological students for the church. He died on June 21, 1873, in Hanover.

Reputation and Legacy. Meyer had a reputation as a man of integrity, piety and humility. He was known for his exceptional discipline and philological rigor. He wanted a commentary that explained the meaning of the Bible in the sense it was originally understood to have possessed. His preaching was said to be similar in force, paying careful attention to the meaning of the text while aiming for the heart. Theologically he was said to be a moderate, and as he aged he became less rationalistic and more open to the supernatural. He reacted against a rising conservative German Pietism that often feared technical study of Scripture while fiercely opposing the more liberal views of David Friedrich *Strauss and the emerging liberal Tübingen school under Ferdinand Christian *Baur. Meyer's passion was said to be the message of the text wherever it led.

The series that bears Meyer's name has had a long life, with a series of editors and contributors who are well-known in German New Testament circles. It was one of the first series on the entire New Testament to argue strictly for the historical-grammatical sense of the text. The theological range of the commentaries today has broadened significantly; for example, O. Michel's work on Romans is a careful, theologically sensitive treatment of this book, which has never been translated into English, while Rudolf *Bultmann on John and E. Haenchen on Acts press the limits of critical examination of the text.

Work. A sense of Meyer's approach can be gained by considering a sample from his work on Acts. In a forward to Acts, Meyer notes the work of Baur and speaks of a need to avoid a faith that is uncritical while avoiding a criticism that is unbelievable. He held to the famous saying of Martin *Luther: that he sought "what pursued the figure of Christ" *(was Christum treibt);* with the courage of the Reformer he also sought to examine what the text meant (Meyer 1870, vi).

Meyer's work in Acts begins with an introduction to the work's historical background along with careful attention to the testimony of the church fathers to the work, including clear notation of specific citations. The exegesis begins with text-critical discussion that interacts with the great text-critical works of his day (e.g., Tischendorf). Having established the wording of the Greek text, Meyer then proceeds through the text a verse at a time. The first generation of editors (e.g., Henrici on 1 Corinthians) of his work often supplied a short outline to the basic units in the chapter before beginning comment on the verses.

Most of the exposition is a careful exercise in historical-philological definition. A term is noted; then its other New Testament uses are mentioned along with a contextual consideration of the specific meaning of the term. All of this is done in a prose style, not in reflective notes. Along the way contrary views are noted and secondary literature is cited briefly with specific page numbers of the discussions given, so readers using the commentary could follow the debate if they wished. References to historical background include citations to the Old Testament, Josephus and Philo as well as the Jewish rabbinic writings through the scholarly resources that point to them. For example, in Acts 2:1 the discussion of Pentecost ranges from references in Deuteronomy 16:9-10 to Tobit 1:1 to Leviticus 23:15-25 to explain how the first Pentecost was celebrated on a Sunday. All of this is related to the Passover chronology in the Gospels and the debate over its timing at Jesus' death, a debate that continues today. The entire discussion is covered in a page full of detail.

Another side of Meyer emerges when the coming of the Spirit in Acts 2:2 is compared to a "rush of a violent wind." Here he refuses to rationalize the text as simply a reference to a windstorm, as Johann Gottfried *Eichhorn did, noting that the text is clearly a comparison rather than a description. Imagery like that from classical authors is also noted in this discussion.

Discussing tongues in Acts 2:7, Meyer notes that the believers are speaking in foreign languages, a view that goes back to the church fathers, but also argues that an unjustified expansion occurs when it is suggested that the gift includes the ability to speak in all foreign languages. He then notes that Paul's portrait in 1 Corinthians 12:10, 12, 14 indicates a prayer speech that is to lead to exposition and not a speaking in a foreign language. He also discusses that the tongues (Acts 2:7) appear to be a symbolic reversal of Genesis 11 and the tower of Babel, as it was expected in the messianic times that there would again be one people of the Lord and one language. He notes all of this with an allusion to the *Testament to the Twelve Patriarchs* to show the historical background of the remark.

When he comes to Peter's speech in Acts 2, Meyer, proceeding phrase by phrase, notes carefully how the citation of Joel is like and unlike the passage in the Hebrew and Greek Old Testaments. The discussion of Joel explains how the citation prepares for Acts 2:36 and concludes that it is "a first fruit of the pouring out of the Spirit!"

Significance. A reading of Meyer discloses an interpreter working carefully with the text, noting and defining terms with a sense of the context and the New Testament usage. He is aware of the historical background available in his day, and possesses a knowledge of the discussion about the passage in question extending back to the church fathers. Here is a careful exegete who reflects the strengths of his century while avoiding many of its weaknesses.

BIBLIOGRAPHY
Works. H. A. W. Meyer, *Kritisch-exegetischer Kommentar über das Neue Testament* (16 vols.; Göttingen: Vandenhoeck & Ruprecht, 1832-1859); idem, *Critical and Exegetical Hand-book to the Gospel of Matthew* (New York: Funk & Wagnalls, 1884); idem, *Critical and Exegetical Hand-book to the Gospels of Mark and Luke* (New York: Funk & Wagnalls, 1884); idem, *Critical and Exegetical Hand-book to the Gospel of John* (New York: Funk & Wagnalls, 1884); idem, *Critical and Exegetical Hand-book to the Acts of the Apostles* (New York: Funk & Wagnalls, 1883); idem, *Critical and Exegetical Hand-book to the Epistle to the Romans* (New York: Funk & Wagnalls, 1884); idem, *Critical and Exegetical Hand-book to the Epistles to the Corinthians* (New

York: Funk & Wagnalls, 1884); idem, *Critical and Exegetical Hand-book to the Epistle to the Galatians* (New York: Funk & Wagnalls, 1884); idem, *Critical and Exegetical Hand-book to the Epistle to the Ephesians* (New York: Funk & Wagnalls, 1884); idem, *Critical and Exegetical Hand-book to the Epistles to the Philippians and Colossians, and to Philemon* (New York: Funk & Wagnalls, 1885).

Studies. F. Dusterdieck, "Meyer, Heinrich August Wilhelm," *RPTK* (3rd ed., 1903), 13:39-42; W. G. Kümmel, *The New Testament: The History of the Investigation of Its Problems* (Nashville: Abingdon, 1972); M. Winter, "Meyer, Heinrich August Wilhelm" in *Biographisch-Bibliographisches Kirchenlexikon*, ed. F. W. Bautz and T. Bautz (1993) cols. 1419-27.

D. L. Bock

Michaelis, Johann David (1717-1791)

Johann David Michaelis was born on February 27, 1717, in Halle an der Saale, into a family that was deeply committed both to Pietism and to the importance of studying oriental languages as part of the church's mission. It was thus natural that his early education, including that at the University of Halle, was devoted to languages, including classical and talmudic Hebrew, Aramaic, Arabic and Ethiopic.

After completing his doctorate in 1739 (his dissertation defended the antiquity of the Hebrew vowel points) he traveled to England and Holland in 1741 and 1742. In England his contact with deism led him to abandon the Pietism in which he had been brought up in favor of a rationally-based orthodoxy. His visit to Leiden brought him under the influence of one of the founders of comparative Semitic philology, Albert Schultens.

In 1745 Michaelis became an assistant professor of oriental languages at the recently established University of Göttingen, and in 1750 he was promoted to a full professorship. Honors in the form of prestigious positions quickly came his way. In 1751 he became secretary of the Göttingen Academy of Sciences, and from 1761 he

was its director. From 1771 to 1785 he edited the *Orientalische und Exegetische Bibliothek* and from 1786 to 1791 a new series of that important journal. He was appointed a privy counselor and enjoyed vast influence in university and church matters in the state of Hanover. He died in Göttingen on August 22, 1791.

Work. Michaelis was an eighteenth-century polymath for whom any piece of information about any subject from any part of the world had relevance for the study of the Bible. Thus when he wrote about the institution of levirate marriage in the Old Testament (e.g., Deut 25:5-10), he drew upon analogies from Mongolia, or when he discussed the right of the Hebrew ancestors such as Abraham to claim possession of ancient Palestine, he cited the example of Canadian Indians.

One of Michaelis's most important achievements was to persuade King Frederick V of Denmark to sponsor a scientific expedition to Arabia in 1761, whose task was to investigate the botany, geography, customs and architecture of that region. The survivor and hero of that expedition, the Danish surveyor Carsten Niebuhr, brought back copies of cuneiform inscriptions that he had made at Persepolis, and these were the basis for the earliest attempts to decipher cuneiform.

Michaelis justified his attempts to elucidate the Bible with the help of extrabiblical, especially Arabian, materials, in his *Beurteilung der Mittel welche man anwendet, die ausgestorbene Hebräische Sprache zu verstehen* (1757). He pointed out that, in the Hebrew Bible, we possessed only a small part of what had once been ancient Hebrew, and he ruled out later, postbiblical Hebrew as a resource for understanding the Bible. It was Arabic, especially spoken Arabic, that providentially offered the greatest help for understanding biblical Hebrew. In the time of Moses, Arabic and Hebrew had been like two spoken dialects of the same language, and Michaelis appealed to the story of Ishmael in Genesis as evidence that part of the Israelite family spoke Arabic, assuming that Ishmael was the father of the Arabs. Thus for Michaelis, Arabic dialects, customs and social organization preserved features of the life of ancient Israelites that had been lost within Jewish communities and which could be used to elucidate the Bible.

Michaelis worked out this theory in many papers on the language and customs of ancient Israel; but the most important expression of this side of his work was his *Mosaisches Recht* (6 vols., 1770- 75), which was translated into English by Alexander Smith under the title *Commentaries on the Laws of Moses* (4 vols., 1814).

In this work Michaelis was trying to emulate Montesquieu's celebrated *De l'esprit des lois;* but he was also engaging in a controversy that had raged particularly in England. With its Puritan background, English theology took a positive view of the continuing binding force of the Mosaic law in moral and civil matters. However, the deists had attacked this law on the grounds that it had no doctrine of rewards and punishments in an afterlife and that it had enriched the priests and Levites at the expense of the poor. Another criticism was that Moses' command to exterminate the Canaanites (e.g., Deut 20:16-19) was immoral. Writers such as Moses Lowman and William Warburton defended the Mosaic legislation. This English discussion was observed in Germany through the translation into German of the principal works concerned. In entering the fray, Michaelis followed his own path, criticizing both sides of the English debate when necessary.

Michaelis's main point was that the Mosaic legislation had no binding force on present-day believers, a viewpoint less strange to Lutheran Germany than it was to Anglican and Puritan England. The Mosaic laws were suitable to the times and circumstances of the ancient Israelites, and they were outstanding examples of ancient legislation that could be profitably studied as such. Michaelis's task was to set the background to the laws, in terms of the geography and climate of ancient Israel,

and then to treat the laws thematically. The discussions are wide-ranging and draw analogies not only from Arabia but also from the Far East and North America, as well as from ancient Greece and Rome and from European history.

Among other things, Michaelis argued that there was no doctrine of rewards and punishments in an afterlife in the Mosaic laws. In this he agreed with the deists, but he turned his position to the defense of Moses against the deists, arguing that only an irresponsible legislator would delay to an afterlife the punishments that were justly deserved here and now for offenses committed. Again, his defense of the Israelite occupation of Canaan and of the extermination of the Canaanites was peculiarly his own. He rejected the standard apologetic that the Canaanites were so wicked that they deserved to be wiped out. Instead, he maintained that the Hebrew ancestors, beginning with Abraham, had established a title to the land and that the Canaanites had migrated to the land from the Red Sea area. In attacking the Canaanites, the Israelites were reclaiming their land from intruders.

Throughout *Mosaisches Recht* Michaelis did not waver from belief in Mosaic authorship. He maintained that while he was in Egypt, Moses was inspired by God to legislate for the Hebrews. This explained parallels with Egyptian practices but also why there were inconsistencies in the laws. Moses had had to change his mind about certain laws since they had to operate in Israel, not Egypt. Thus Michaelis acknowledged that there were inconsistencies without this in any way undermining his belief that God had inspired Moses the lawgiver.

Another fruit of Michaelis's concern to study the Old Testament in the light of other Semitic languages, especially Arabic, and customs and beliefs from Arabia and the ancient world was his *Deutsche Übersetzung des Alten Testaments mit Anmerkung für Ungelehrte*. This new translation with explanatory notes appeared in thirteen volumes (1769-1783) and was followed by six volumes on the New Testament (1790-1792). However, the translation was judged to be a failure in comparison with the German of the Luther Bible.

Michaelis's other major work to be considered here was his *Einleitung in die göttliche Schriften des neuen Bundes* (1750), which was the first modern introduction to the New Testament and which was translated into English by Herbert Marsh. In this work Michaelis expressed unusual opinions on the inspiration, authority and canonicity of the New Testament. He rejected the view that acceptance of the inspiration of the New Testament was a matter of faith, assisted by the internal testimony of the Holy Spirit. By making similar claims Muslims could maintain that the Quran was inspired. Michaelis linked inspiration and thus canonicity to authenticity; that is, a New Testament book was inspired and canonical only if it could be proved to have been written by an apostle. This meant that the Gospels of Matthew and John were inspired but that those of Mark and Luke were not. It could even be said that the original Gospel of Matthew composed in Aramaic or Hebrew was inspired, while its Greek version was not. At the same time, the noninspired Mark and Luke were not valueless; they contained authentic historical material. In his wish to provide a rational defense of orthodoxy Michaelis thus made belief in the inspiration and authority of the Bible a matter for the historical investigation of each book. He accepted the truth of Christianity because he accepted the testimony of the New Testament writers that miracles had occurred. When Gotthold Ephraim Lessing published Hermann Samuel *Reimarus's attack on the resurrection, Michaelis replied (1783 and 1785) with a defense of the biblical accounts.

Significance. During his lifetime Michaelis enjoyed a great national and international reputation, but by the time of this death he was already an outdated scholar within the German scene. He was essentially a compiler and observer,

whereas from the 1770s German biblical scholarship concentrated upon the close study of the text, looking for sources or fragments that underlay the final form. An older documentary hypothesis established itself in the work of Johann Gottfried *Eichhorn (who would later succeed Michaelis in Göttingen), while New Testament scholars such as Johann Jakob *Griesbach were laying the foundations for the synoptic criticism of the first three Gospels. Thus less than two decades after his death, Michaelis's work was playing no part in critical German scholarship.

It was otherwise in Britain, where the new, critical German scholarship was resisted until the 1860s. In Britain Michaelis was valued because he championed the Mosaic authorship of the Pentateuch, and he could be held up as an example of a great German scholar who had not embraced the new criticism. The translator of *Mosaisches Recht,* writing in 1814, could praise the worth of Michaelis's New Testament introduction and commend his defense of the "foundations of revealed religion" by observing that while "disdaining to employ those weak and untenable arguments, to which *some* authors have resorted for this purpose, Michaelis uniformly takes possession of ground impregnably strong, from which, while he challenges the enemy to attack him, and concedes to him every imaginable advantage, he still defies him to effect his dislodgment" (Alexander Smith in preface to vol. 1 of Michaelis's *Commentaries on the Laws of Moses,* 1814, xiv-xv).

Another instance of Michaelis's importance in Britain at the beginning of the nineteenth century is the Oxford edition (1830) of Michaelis's version of Robert Lowth's lectures on Hebrew poetry. These lectures, originally delivered in Oxford beginning in 1741 (Michaelis was present to hear the second of the thirty-four lectures) and published in Latin in 1753, laid the groundwork for the modern study of biblical Hebrew poetry. Michaelis published a Latin edition in Göttingen in 1758 with many additional notes, and this version issued from the Oxford University Press in 1830. The fact that both Lowth and Michaelis had traditional orthodox opinions about the authorship of the books of the Old Testament is an indication of the vast gulf that existed between Germany and Britain in matters of biblical criticism in the early nineteenth century.

There is, however, one respect in which Michaelis's work endured. Throughout the nineteenth century and well into the twentieth century it was accepted that the Arabic language and Arabic customs could be used to shed light on the Old Testament. Julius *Wellhausen and William Robertson *Smith at the end of the nineteenth century and Godfrey Rolles Driver in the present century are examples of scholars who mined Arabic sources in order to propose new meanings for obscure Hebrew words (Driver), to discover the original purpose of Semitic sacrifice (Robertson Smith) or to reconstruct ancient heathenism (Wellhausen). Arabic sources now receive much less attention than do the ancient Near Eastern texts that are contemporary with the Old Testament. Had the latter been available to Michaelis there is no doubt that he would have used them extensively.

BIBLIOGRAPHY

Works. J. D. Michaelis, *Beurteilung der Mittel welche man anwendet, die ausgestorbene Hebräische Sprache zu verstehen* (Göttingen: Vandenhoeck, 1757); idem, *The Burial and Resurrection of Jesus Christ: According to the Four Evangelists* (London: J. Hatchard, 1827); idem, *Einleitung in die göttliche Schriften des neuen Bundes* (London: F. C. and J. Rivington, 1750; ET *Introductory Lectures to the Sacred Books of the New Testament* [London: J. & R. Tonson, 1761]); idem, *Mosaisches Recht* (6 vols.; Frankfurt am Main: J. G. Garbe, 1770-75; ET *Commentaries on the Laws of Moses* [4 vols.; (Göttingen: Vandenhoeck, 1814]).

Studies. E. Hirsch, *Geschichte der neuern evangelischen Theologie* (Gütersloh: Gerd Mohn, 1964) vol. 4; W. G. Kümmel, *The New Testament: The History of the Investigation of Its Problems* (London: SCM, 1973); A-R. Löwenbrück, "Johann David Michaelis' Verdienst um die philologisch-historische Bibelkritik" in *Historische*

Kritik und biblischer Kanon in der deutschen Aufklärung, ed. H. G. Reventlow et al. (Wolfenbüttler Forschungen 41; Wiesbaden: Otto Harrassowitz, 1988) 157-70; J. W. Rogerson, *Anthropology and the Old Testament* (Sheffield: Sheffield Academic Press, 1984 [1978]); R. Smend, "Aufgeklärte Bemühung um das Gesetz. Johann David Michaelis' 'Mosaisches Recht' " in *Epochen der Bibelkritik* (Gesammelte Studien Band 3, Beiträge zur evangelischen Theologie 109; Munich: Christian Kaiser Verlag, 1991) 63-73; idem, "Johann David Michaelis 1717-1791" in *Deutsche Alttestamentler in drei Jahrhunderten* (Göttingen: Vandenhoeck & Ruprecht, 1989) 13-24.

J. W. Rogerson

Reimarus, Hermann Samuel (1694-1768)

Hermann Samuel Reimarus came from an old clergy family. He taught briefly on the philosophy faculty at Wittenberg and as a schoolmaster in Wismar. Between these two posts he spent some time in Holland and England (1720-1721), where he became acquainted with the literature of deism. He spent his last forty years as a teacher of oriental languages at the Gymnasium Johanneum in his native Hamburg, where his home became a center of intellectual life. The titles of his numerous publications breathe the spirit of the German Enlightenment. His works range from his early dissertation on Hebrew (1717) through various historical, scientific and philosophical studies such as *Abhandlungen von den vornehmsten Wahrheiten der natürlichen Religion* (*The Principal Truths of Natural Religion* [1754; ET 1766]), *Betrachtungen über die Kunsttriebe der Thiere* (*General Observations on the Behavior of Animals* [1760]) and *Die Vernunftlehre* (*The Doctrine of Reason* [1766]). Though they are rationalistic, such works give little hint of Reimarus's views on the Bible and Christian origins, which were reserved for an unpublished manuscript on which his posthumous fame rests. Reimarus's *Apologie oder Schutzschrift für die vernünftigen Verehrer Gottes* (*Apology or Defence of the Ra-*

tional Worshippers of God), which was known only to an intimate circle of family and friends, was a compendious attack on the historical foundations of Christian orthodoxy and a defense of deism.

The Wolfenbüttel Fragments. Two factors stood in the way of publishing the *Apology*, which was published in its entirety only in 1972. One was its inordinate size and wide-ranging argument. The other was its controversial character, which in an age of censorship would readily invite vilification and prosecution. However, within a decade of the author's death seven anonymous excerpts were published by the dramatist and man of letters Gotthold Ephraim Lessing. Subsequently they were reprinted in the various editions of Lessing's collected works.

Lessing had gotten to know the Reimarus family during his stay in Hamburg as literary critic of the short-lived National Theater. He was a patient of Reimarus's son, Dr. Johann Albrecht Heinrich Reimarus, whom he also knew as a friend together with his sister, Elise. Lessing obtained a copy of the manuscript, which he took with him on his appointment as librarian to the Duke of Brunswick's library at Wolfenbüttel. Between 1774 and 1778 Lessing published seven excerpts in a series of works "On History and Literature" ostensibly found among the treasures in the ducal library at Wolfenbüttel. Lessing called these excerpts *Fragmente eines Ungenannten* (*Fragments of an Unnamed Person*), and they are commonly known as *The Wolfenbüttel Fragments.* Lessing had the foresight to obtain exemption from censorship for his series, which included a variety of other works. But the ensuing controversy led to forfeiture of this privilege and confiscation of Lessing's manuscript, which has disappeared from history. Correct guesses as to the true identity of the author were made at the time. However, the question continued to remain in doubt until Johann Reimarus made the disclosure in 1813-1814, when he donated copies of different drafts to libraries in Göttingen

and Hamburg. In the meantime Lessing suggested the name of J. L. Schmidt as a possible author in order to throw heresy hunters off the scent. Schmidt was a well-known deist who had spent his latter days in Wolfenbüttel.

The first fragment, *Von der Duldung der Deisten* (*On the Toleration of the Deists* [1774]), presented Jesus as a teacher of rational, practical religion whose message had been distorted by the Jewish messianic ideas of the apostles. The Christian church had replaced the simplicity of Jesus by a religion full of mysteries. The author pleaded for the same toleration to be accorded to the deists that Jews and pagans enjoyed. In 1777 five further fragments were published. *Von der Verschreyung der Vernunft auf den Kanzeln* (*The Decrying of Reason in the Pulpits*) and *Unmöglichkeit einer Offenbarung, die alle Menschen auf eine gegründete Art glauben Könnten* (*The Impossibility of Believing in a Revelation that All Human Beings Could Believe to Be Established*) continued the deistic argument. The next two fragments, *Durchgang der Israeliten durchs Rothe Meer* (*The Passage of the Israelites Through the Red Sea*) and *Dass die Bücher des A.T. nicht geschrieben wurden, eine Religion zu offenbaren* (*That the Books of the Old Testament Were Not Written to Reveal a Religion*), bitterly attacked the credibility and use of the Old Testament. The sixth fragment, *Ueber die Auferstehungsgeschichte* (*On the Resurrection Story*), detected inconsistencies in the Gospel narratives and concluded that, since the Evangelists disagreed about the circumstances, they were also mistaken about the fact of the resurrection of Jesus.

Whereas the earlier fragments had assaulted the outer walls of the Christian edifice, the seventh and final fragment, *Von dem Zwecke Jesu und seiner Jünger* (*On the Intention of Jesus and His Disciples* [1778]), attempted to storm the inner citadel. In a manner evocative of the English deists whom he had studied, Reimarus insisted that there were no "mysteries" in the teaching of Jesus. Jesus himself remained a Jew and intended that his followers should also remain Jews. The notions of a triune God never entered Jesus' head but were the inventions of later ages. Even when the expression "Son of God" is found on Jesus' lips, it is not a designation of personal divinity. It means what it meant in the Old Testament: "God's Beloved." At most it indicates that Jesus identified himself as the Messiah and believed that he had a special role in God's purposes.

Reimarus contended that Jesus sought neither to found a new religion nor to introduce any new ceremonies. His call to repent and believe the kingdom of God (Mk 1:15) was a call to personal purity and moral elevation in preparation for the Messiah and his imminent kingdom. Baptism was the revival of the Jewish practice of proselyte baptism. The Last Supper was essentially a Passover meal. The first major turning point in Jesus' career came when he allowed himself to be sidetracked into embracing political messianism. The second came when he decided to force through his program at all costs, even if it meant his own martyrdom. Unfortunately Jesus had miscalculated popular support. He had alienated the Pharisees with his criticism of their legalism and his refusal to prove himself by performing a miracle. The disturbance that Jesus created in the temple confirmed the authorities in their decision to have him liquidated. At the crucial moment he was deserted by his disciples, and he died a broken man. His cry "My God, my God, why have you forsaken me?" (Mk 15:34) expresses his disillusionment with the God who had failed him.

Christianity might well have ended then but for the duplicity of the disciples. Once they realized that there was to be no mass persecution, they transformed the situation by two master strokes, both of which were equally fraudulent. The first was the claim that Jesus had been raised from the dead. The second was that he would return to establish his messianic kingdom. As time went on, the church kept postponing the date of Christ's return, and since then few

people have realized that the time of the promised imminent return has long passed and that this item of Christian belief is patently false. Nor may the tottering edifice of traditional belief be saved by appeal to the traditional twin pillars of Christian apologetics: miracles and fulfilled prophecy.

In a fashion typical of the deists and David Hume, Reimarus impugned the credibility of the Gospel miracles. He argued that the New Testament writers themselves admit that Jesus performed no miracles before the more educated sections of society, and when the latter asked for proof they were answered with abuse. The Gospels were written thirty to sixty years after the alleged events, when no one could question their veracity. In any case, different religions appeal to the miraculous and thus cancel each other out. With regard to prophecy, Reimarus claimed that events were either contrived to make them fit or the prophecies had to be interpreted in an allegorical way in order to give them a Christian application.

The Fragments Controversy. The *Fragments* produced a major pamphlet war that is reviewed in the works listed in the bibliography. Of the many replies the most substantial was that of Johann Salomo *Semler of the University of Halle, who was the leading exegete of his day and is credited with being the founder of liberal theology. Semler's *Beantwortung der Fragmente eines Ungenannten insbesondere vom Zweck Jesu und seiner Jünger (Answer to the Fragments of an Unnamed Author, Especially "On the Intentions of Jesus and his Disciples"* [1779]) took the form of a line-by-line refutation. Semler exploited the numerous self-contradictions that he found in the fragments, challenged the antisupernaturalism of their author and argued that the traditional interpretation of Jesus and the Gospels fitted the Judaism of Jesus' day.

The controversy provided Lessing with a platform from which to air his views. He adopted the stance of one who did not necessarily approve of everything that the "Fragmentist" had written. Nevertheless he ought to be heard. In true Enlightenment fashion Lessing distinguished between accidental historical truths that cannot be proved and the necessary truths of reason. Seeking to undercut the appeal to history in support of Christian beliefs, Lessing proclaimed that "accidental truths of history can never become the proof of necessary truths of religion" (*Ueber den Beweis des Geistes und der Kraft* [*On the Proof of the Spirit and of Power*]). The truth of religion does not lie in its historicity but in its spiritual and moral values. Such values may take on different forms in the history of religion, whose goal is the spiritual and moral education of the human race. In that history Jesus has a place as the first reliable practical teacher of the immortality of the soul. Lessing went on to preach his version of religious tolerance in his play *Nathan der Weise* (*Nathan the Wise* [1779]). The villains in the play were modeled on various protagonists in the controversy, and the hero was modeled on the leading figure of the Jewish Enlightenment, Moses Mendelssohn, who was a friend of both Lessing and the Reimarus family.

Significance. A. Schweitzer credited Reimarus with initiating the quest of the historical Jesus and saw Reimarus without precursors or successors. Indeed, his was "perhaps the most splendid achievement in the whole course of the historical investigation of the life of Jesus, for he was the first to grasp the fact that the world of thought in which Jesus moved was essentially eschatological" (Schweitzer, 23).

Though Schweitzer's assessment has been widely accepted, critical examination does not support Schweitzer, except on the point that Reimarus had no successors. Few have been prepared to believe that the emergence of the church together with Christian belief in the resurrection of Jesus was the fraudulent invention of the first disciples. Moreover, recent scholarship has shown that Reimarus was heavily indebted to the English deists, whom he freely quoted in his manuscript and whose ideas were already well known in Germany by the time that the fragments were published. It would be more accurate to say that the question of the historical Jesus was initiated by the English deists in the late seventeenth and early eighteenth centuries but that the publication of the fragments forced onto German theological scholarship the need to address the questions that they posed. While current work on Jesus and the Gospels seeks a better understanding of Jesus in the context of Second Temple Judaism, it has called in question the eschatological interpretation of Reimarus, Weiss and Schweitzer and the constructions that these authors placed on it.

BIBLIOGRAPHY

Works. H. S. Reimarus, *Apologie oder Schutzschrift für die vernünftigen Verehrer Gottes,* ed. G. Alexander (2 vols.; Frankfurt: Suhrkamp Verlag, 1972); idem, *The Goal of Jesus and His Disciples,* ed. G. W. Buchanan (Leiden: E. J. Brill, 1970); H. Chadwick, ed., *Lessing's Theological Writings* (London: A & C Black, 1956); C. H. Talbert, ed., *Reimarus Fragments* (Philadelphia; Fortress; London: SCM, 1971).

Studies. A. Altmann, *Moses Mendelssohn: A Biographical Study* (London: Routledge, 1973); W. Baird, *History of New Testament Research,* 1: *From Deism to Tübingen* (Minneapolis: Fortress, 1992); C. Brown, *Jesus in European Protestant Thought, 1778-1860* (Grand Rapids: Baker, 1992 [1985]) 1-56; idem, *Miracles and the Critical Mind* (Grand Rapids: Eerdmans, 1984); W. G. Kümmel, *The New Testament: The History of the Investigation of Its Problems* (Nashville: Abingdon, 1972); H. G. Reventlow, *The Authority of the Bible and the Rise of the Modern World* (Philadelphia: Fortress, 1985); A. Schweitzer, *The Quest of the Historical Jesus: A Critical Study of Its Progress from Reimarus to Wrede* (New York: Macmillan, 1968 [1910]) 13-26; W. Walter et. al., *Hermann Samuel Reimarus (1694-1768): Ein "bekannter Unbekannter" der Aufklärung in Hamburg* (Göttingen: Vandenhoeck & Ruprecht, 1973).   C. Brown

Schleiermacher, Friedrich Daniel Ernst *(1768-1834)*

A German theologian, philosopher, preacher and philologist, Friedrich Daniel Ernst Schleiermacher was born into a family of clergymen. His father was a chaplain in the Prussian army, and both grandfathers had been Reformed pastors. He was educated first at the Moravian school in Niesky (1783-1785) and later at the seminary of the Brethren in Barby and the University of Halle. After his ordination he served as a private tutor to the family of the Count zu Dohna in Schlobitten (1790-1793), Reformed chaplain of the Charité hospital in Berlin (1796-1801) and pastor of a small Reformed congregation in Pomerania (1802-1804). In 1804 he accepted an appointment as professor of theology in the University of Halle, but he was forced to abandon this post when Napoleon's troops occupied the university in 1806. In 1807 Schleiermacher returned to Berlin and remained there for the rest of his life. He was one of the founders of the new University of Berlin, and he served as Reformed pastor of Trinity Church, where he preached almost every week from 1809 until his death in 1834.

Work. Schleiermacher is often called the father of modern theology or the father of liberal theology, and he is best remembered for his pioneering systematic theology, *The Christian Faith* (1st ed. 1821-1822; 2d ed. 1830-1831). Less well known, particularly among those whose only access to the Schleiermacher corpus is through translations, is that he made significant contributions—ground-breaking in their own time—to critical biblical studies. From the beginning of his teaching career in 1804, he lectured almost continuously in New Testament studies. At Halle he offered courses on Galatians, Thessalonians, Corinthians, Romans, Ephesians, Philippians, Colossians, Philemon, Timothy, Titus and Hebrews. At the University of Berlin, from 1810 to 1834, he lectured at least once each academic year (except in

1827) on some theme in New Testament studies. He offered eleven semester-long courses on the Gospels, six on Acts, nineteen on the Pauline, Pastoral and Catholic epistles and Hebrews, four on the life of Jesus and two on introduction to the New Testament. While the texts for his lectures on the introduction and the life of Jesus were published posthumously in Schleiermacher's collected works, the notes for his lectures on individual New Testament books are presently available only in unpublished manuscripts.

In addition to his critical work on the New Testament, Schleiermacher was a pioneer in the field of hermeneutics. During his teaching career at Halle and Berlin he lectured nine times on hermeneutics and criticism, and his lecture notes were published in several editions after his death. The influence of Schleiermacher's work in hermeneutics extends well into the twentieth century; his views on the art of understanding provided the fertile soil for debate between philosophers such as Wilhelm Dilthey, Martin Heidegger and Hans-Georg Gadamer. He is rightly called the founder of modern hermeneutics.

Biblical Interpretation and the Theological Encyclopedia. To appreciate the contributions he made to biblical interpretation, it will be useful to look first at Schleiermacher's understanding of the organization of theological disciplines, laid out in his *Brief Outline on the Study of Theology* (1811; 2d ed. 1830). The whole of the theological curriculum is directed toward church leadership. It encompasses the scientific (i.e., theoretical) and practical knowledge without which successful leadership of the church would not be possible. The curriculum is divided into three main branches: philosophical theology, historical theology and practical theology.

The task of philosophical theology is to establish the idea or essence of Christianity, and it is carried out in two subdisciplines: apologetics and polemics. Historical theology unfolds the content of Christian faith in three divisions, corresponding to three periods in the history of the church: exegetical theology, which examines primitive Christianity; church history, which studies the unfolding career of Christianity; and dogmatics and statistics, which state the content of Christian faith in a particular church in the present time. Practical theology has to do with the technological rules or art of church leadership, and it is divided into two main branches: church service and church government. In spite of this complex and extensive ordering of the theological disciplines, however, Schleiermacher argues that historical theology is the heart of the theological curriculum since it is the foundation of practical theology and the verification of philosophical theology.

The Role of Exegetical Theology. The overall task of exegetical theology is to arrive at the correct understanding of the normative (canonical) representation of Christianity. This task is divided into two subdisciplines: higher criticism, whose purpose is to establish the canon, and lower criticism, whose purpose is to arrive at an accurate original reading of a particular text.

Schleiermacher argued that the task of determining the canon was especially important to Protestant theology. The need for such an effort arises from the fact that no certain boundary can be established between the canon and the writings of postcanonical authors such as the apostolic fathers; moreover, the judgment that distinguishes between canonical and apocryphal writings is open to constant criticism and revision. Finally, Schleiermacher thought it at least possible that materials would emerge in the process of archaeological discovery that were of equal importance to already established canonical writings. The process of establishing canonicity proceeds by external and internal evidence. The scholar must ask first whether the piece of literature in question belongs to the time of the apostolic fathers; second, whether the content of the piece corresponds to already established canonical materials.

Schleiermacher argued that the Old Testament did not have the same normative status as the New, since it was first and foremost the Scripture of Judaism, and he understood Christianity not as a development of Judaism but as a genuinely new faith. The Old Testament therefore could not provide the scriptural basis for peculiarly Christian doctrines, though it could be a help to understanding them. Moreover, he thought that treating Jewish Scripture as an authoritative source for Christian doctrines necessarily required dishonesty on the part of the interpreter, who would try to read Christian themes into pre-Christian texts and thus obscure their genuine historical and linguistic sense. Nonetheless, Schleiermacher argued that the Old Testament should still find its place in Christian Bibles, perhaps as an appendix rather than as the first part of the Scripture. And he maintained that candidates for the Protestant ministry needed to learn Hebrew and Aramaic, since the New Testament authors articulated their faith in Christ in language and themes borrowed from the Hebrew Scripture.

The Theory of Interpretation: Schleiermacher's Lectures on Hermeneutics. Schleiermacher's hermeneutics provided the theoretical background to his criticism of individual New Testament books. Though they were never published during his lifetime, his lectures on hermeneutics were made available four years after his death (1838) by his friend and former student Friedrich Lücke, and they have been the subject of much discussion ever since. Lücke's edition was based mainly on a set of Schleiermacher's handwritten notes from 1819, amplified with additions taken from several student notebooks. Subsequent scholarship has established that Lücke's edition presents a seriously one-sided view of Schleiermacher's theory of interpretation, and the following summary of his views is based on the fuller edition of Heinz Kimmerle (1959).

Hermeneutics, or the art of understanding, is Schleiermacher's technical theory of interpretation. He learned about it, he tells us, from ordinary conversation. There he discovered a universal element, the shared language of speaker and hearer, and a particular element, the personal message to be transmitted in the speech. Correspondingly, hermeneutics has two parts: the universal, or grammatical, and the particular, or psychological. The grammatical interpretation of language involves the discovery of meaning in the words and grammar that form the discourse a particular communication presents. The psychological side involves understanding the intention and meaning of the author of the text—what he or she tried to communicate in writing. Although these two sides of the art of interpretation can be distinguished for the purposes of discussion, in practice they form a continuous, circular and self-correcting process. In addition Schleiermacher spoke of two complementary methods of reading a text: the divinatory and the comparative. In the latter the language and style of a text or author are compared with other similar texts or authors to determine the meaning appropriate to the kind of text or communication. The good interpreter, however, will also have the ability to divine or to intuit how language as a living and dynamic entity has uniquely shaped the thought processes and patterns of expression of the particular text and author.

Schleiermacher thought that New Testament hermeneutics was only a specialized version of general hermeneutics, warranted by and developed from the general theory of interpretation. What justifies the development of any specialized hermeneutics is a distinctive language or content, something that sets the work or group of works apart. The New Testament writings are distinguished by their common presentation of a novel idea: the redemption accomplished in Jesus of Nazareth. Although the authors of the New Testament writings were conditioned by their own historical circumstances in producing language to communicate this idea, they also creatively reshaped and transformed their inherited language, thereby producing a unique literature. Hence it is a failure in interpretation to reduce the biblical texts to their historical roots without appreciating the genuinely novel elements of the texts.

The purpose of New Testament hermeneutics is to aid biblical exegesis. To this end Schleiermacher discussed questions such as the use of parallel passages, the difference between literal and figurative meanings, and the appropriateness of stressing or discounting certain terms within a particular discourse. He was careful to criticize dogmatic maxims that have crept over into the field of biblical interpretation without proper scrutiny, and he shared the Enlightenment view that the Bible must be read as any other book insofar as it asserts that dogmatic appeals to divine authorship can never ultimately settle questions of meaning.

The Epistles of Paul. Schleiermacher's first published venture into the field of exegesis, *On the So-Called First Letter of Paul to Timothy: A Critical Open Letter to J. C. Gass* (1807) made history in the scientific study of Scripture with its argument for the pseudonymity of the epistle. The method he followed in this work was not so much to apply new historical-philological materials to the biblical texts but rather to put new questions to the text and see what kind of answers would emerge. What clinched the case for pseudonymity, according to Schleiermacher, were the many turns of phrase and argument that were uncharacteristic of the authentic Paul and the remarkable comparisons he found with the second letter to Timothy and and the letter to Titus. He took 1 Timothy for a first-century compilation from the latter epistles, created among other reasons to strengthen the diaconal office. This application of internal critical evidence to the text of the New Testament was innovative at the time, even though the biblical critical work of the neologists and Schleiermacher's and Schlegel's work on Plato gave portents of this turn in biblical studies.

Schleiermacher took Romans and Galatians as the theological benchmarks of the Pauline corpus in their argument for the universality of Christianity, and he took 1 Thessalonians and 1 Corinthians and 2 Corinthians as the epistles that agreed most closely with what we know from other sources (Acts) about the life of the apostle. Questions of authenticity had to be settled with reference to these epistles.

Many of the details of Schleiermacher's work on the Pauline epistles have not stood the test of time. Few scholars today would trust the chronology of Acts or its presentation of Pauline theology as a measure for determining the authenticity of individual letters. And what Schleiermacher took to be an unwarranted and radical view regarding the authorship of the Pastoral Epistles, that all three were pseudonymous, has won wide support. But his free application of methods used in establishing the authenticity of other ancient texts to the corpus of the New Testament has become a commonplace of modern biblical scholarship.

The Gospels. Schleiermacher is most often remembered as the champion of the Gospel of John. He believed that, unlike the other three Gospels, it was penned by an apostle and that because of its mature theological view and its carefully constructed presentation of the life of Jesus it deserved the place of honor among the four Gospels, especially for the purposes of dogmatic theology. Nonetheless he worked carefully at the Synoptic problem as well, and in 1817 he published his *Luke: A Critical Study.* Schleiermacher rejected the view of Johann Gottfried *Eichhorn that all three Synoptic authors were relying on an original gospel. He thought that each Gospel contained some fairly reliable material from eyewitnesses but that each was put together according to the point of view of the particular author. After the testimony of John, Schleiermacher took Luke as the most valuable source for historical details about the life of Jesus that were of principal importance for the church's faith. He thought the author of Luke tended to in-

sert documents without altering them much, even at the risk of interrupting the narrative unity of his Gospel. Thus Luke could be used to supplement the account of John. Matthew he considered less reliable and Mark the least reliable of all in terms of providing historical details.

Once again many of the details of Schleiermacher's Gospel criticism seem not to have survived the test of time, while his methods, with some further development, seem to have become commonplaces. In particular his emphasis on understanding the point of view of the author or editor of a text leads directly to redaction criticism.

Quest for the Historical Jesus. As in so many other fields, Schleiermacher was also a pioneer in what has been called the quest of the historical Jesus, since he was the first person to deliver a course of academic lectures on the life of Jesus (in 1819), a series he repeated four times afterward. Isolating and explicating the authentic teaching of Jesus was of prime importance for Christian faith, according to Schleiermacher, because through this means Christ communicated his perfect God-consciousness both to the original disciples and to all subsequent generations of Christians. The period of time that is of most interest to the biographer of Jesus who shares this theological position is the time of Jesus' public ministry: after his baptism and before his arrest. For this reason many of the miracles recorded in the New Testament—especially those regarding the person of Christ himself, including his conception and birth and his resurrection after three days—can be subjected to relentless criticism with equanimity. Schleiermacher considered unhistorical the accounts of Jesus' birth, and he speculated that Jesus may not have really died on the cross and hence may not have really risen from the dead. What chiefly interested him was the person of Jesus communicated through what he taught his disciples and how he established thereby the beginnings of the church.

Schleiermacher's lectures on the life of Jesus were published only after his death, but they caused great furor nonetheless. For orthodox critics they went too far in arguing away cherished details of the biblical narrative. But for more radical critics, such as David Friedrich *Strauss, Schleiermacher's historical reconstruction was purely the product of his pious Moravian imagination—a Jesus seen to be one way rather than another because of the needs of a pietistic Christian faith. The details of Schleiermacher's scholarship on Jesus may stand up somewhat better over time, if only because this area of research is still so hotly contested that mutually exclusive positions can be found on almost any question.

Role of the Bible in Dogmatics. Many first-time readers of Schleiermacher's dogmatics may find his theology far removed from the colorful metaphors and persuasive rhetoric of the biblical text. He spent enormous effort to understand the New Testament, and he argued for the primary importance of exegetical theology in the theological encyclopedia. Every discipline has its proper place, however, and the proper place for one's exegesis, according to Schleiermacher, was prior to and alongside one's dogmatics, not within it. The language of Scripture itself, because it comes from a foreign time and place, is bound to be misleading if it is introduced uncritically into contemporary dogmatic discussions. Schleiermacher argued that there are three types of religious language—poetic, rhetorical and descriptively didactic—and that only one of these types of language is appropriate for dogmatics, namely, the descriptively didactic. Scripture contains little didactic language (language intended to teach concepts correctly). On the contrary, most of what we find there is poetic (the direct utterance of religious experience) or rhetorical (language spoken to move or persuade others). Thus scriptural language must be transformed into language that is more precise and scientific, but only for the sake of sound presentations of the Scriptures from the pulpit. Hence this must be done in such a way as to preserve the essential content of the scriptural witness.

Throughout *The Christian Faith,* Schleiermacher referred to the biblical texts that pertain to the discussions in the various propositions. But his exegetical work is not given directly in the footnotes or in the exposition of the propositions. In order to learn his views, one must consult his lectures on introduction to the New Testament and other exegetical works. The witness of the primitive Christian community remains normative, and all later representations of Christian faith, even old and revered dogmas, must be measured by it.

The Bible in the Church. Schleiermacher was almost universally hailed in his own day as a great preacher. He filled the pulpit weekly for most of his life, and perhaps there we learn most about his view of the Bible—that it is a book that still speaks. As a historical critic and philologist, Schleiermacher could be very skeptical. As a dogmatician, he stayed away from what he perceived to be the imprecision of biblical language. But as a preacher, he lived in the text in much the same way as the great Reformation exegetes and theologians had. Biblical allusions saturate his sermons, texts interpret other texts, and that fusion of horizons occurs that allows an ancient book to become a living voice.

It would be difficult to characterize Schleiermacher's sermonic exegesis in a few words. He preached two different kinds of sermons: topical and expository. In the topical sermon, he sought to unfold a topic that he took to be the main point of a particular text in such a way as to connect the experience of faith witnessed in the text and the believer's experience of faith in the present. In his expository preaching, he worked his way slowly through entire books of the New Testament, commenting on each passage verse by verse, both for its meaning and for its application. In all his preaching his aim was to present Christ in a way that could be apprehended by the eyes of faith. This often involved an interpretation that minimized the distance between the past and the present. In this arena

his biblical interpretation remains close to
the style of the evangelicals in the Reformation era, and he may well deserve Alexander
Schweizer's epithet "the reviver of the Reformed consciousness in the modern period." What is perhaps most remarkable
about Schleiermacher in retrospect is how
well he was able to combine in one person
such a diverse set of attitudes and approaches to the Biblical text: relentless historical criticism, dogmatic abstraction,
philological precision, pious reverence, enthusiastic conviction. He models an integration that has become difficult in the
increasingly specialized world of the twentieth century.

BIBLIOGRAPHY

Works. F. D. E. Schleiermacher, *Brief Outline on
the Study of Theology* (Lewiston, NY: Edwin Mel-
len, 1989 [1811, 1830]); idem, *The Christian
Faith* (Philadelphia: Fortress, 1976); idem, *A
Critical Essay on the Gospel of Luke* (Schleier-
macher Studies and Translations 13; Lewiston,
NY: Edwin Mellen, 1993); idem, *Einleitung ins
neue Testament* in *Friedrich Schleiermacher's
Sämmtliche Werke*, ed. G. Wolde (31 vols. in
three divisions: Theology, Sermons, Philosophy;
Berlin: Reimer, 1834-64) div. 1, vol. 8; idem,
Hermeneutics: The Handwritten Manuscripts, ed.
H. Kimmerle (AAR Texts and Translations Series
1; Missoula, MT: Scholars Press, 1977); idem,
The Life of Jesus, ed. J. C. Verheyden (Philadelphia: Fortress, 1975); idem, *Selected Sermons of
Schleiermacher* (London: Hodder & Stoughton,
1890); idem, *Servant of the Word: Selected Sermons of Friedrich Schleiermacher*, with introduction by D. DeVries (Philadelphia: Fortress,
1987); idem, "Über Kolosser 1,15-20," *TSK* 5
(1832) 497-537; idem, *Über den sogenannten
ersten Brief Paulos an den Timotheos: Ein kritisches
Sendschreiben an J. C. Gass* (Berlin: In der Real-
schulbuchhandlung, 1807); idem, "Über die
Zeugnisse des Papias von unsern beiden ersten
Evangelien," *TSK* 5 (1832) 735-68; T. N. Tice,
*Schleiermacher Bibliography: With Brief Introduc-
tions, Annotations and Index* (Princeton, NJ:
Princeton University Press, 1966; updated in
1985); Tice has updated his bibliography twice
in the journal *New Athenaeum/Neues Athe-
naeum*, and he intends to publish regular updates
there. Particularly worth consulting are the following entries in Tice's bibliography: 309a, 318,

411a, 558, 611a, 617, 618, 708a, 755, 902,
1374, 1569, 1737, 1738a, 1778, 1783a, 2094,
2173, 2428, 2554, 2570, 2585.
    Studies. D. DeVries, *Jesus Christ in the
Preaching of Calvin and Schleiermacher* (Louisville, KY: Westminster John Knox, 1996); B. A.
Gerrish, "Friedrich Schleiermacher" in *Nineteenth-Century Religious Thought in the West*, ed.
N. Smart et al. (3 vols.; Cambridge: Cambridge
University Press, 1985) 1:123-53; idem, *A
Prince of the Church: Schleiermacher and the Beginnings of Modern Theology* (Philadelphia: Fortress, 1984); R. A. Harrisville and W. Sundberg,
*The Bible in Modern Culture: Theology and His-
torical-Critical Method from Spinoza to Käsemann* (Grand Rapids: Eerdmans, 1995); R. R.
Niebuhr, *Schleiermacher on Christ and Religion:
A New Introduction* (New York: Scribner's,
1964); H. Patsch, "Die Angst vor dem Deu-
teropaulinismus: Die Rezeption des 'kritischen
Sendschreiben' Friedrich Schleiermachers über
den 1 Timotheusbrief im ersten Jahrfünft," *ZTK*
88 (1991) 451-77; H. D. Preuss, "Vom Verlust
des Alten Testaments und seinen Folgen
(dargestellt anhand der Theologie und Predigt F.
D. Schleiermacher)" in *Lebendiger Umgang mit
Schrift und Bekenntnis: Theologische Beiträge zur
Beziehung von Schrift und Bekenntnis und zu
ihrer Bedeutung für das Leben der Kirche*, ed. J.
Track (Stuttgart: Calwer Verlag, 1980) 127-60;
M. Redeker, *Friedrich Schleiermacher: Life and
Thought* (Philadelphia: Fortress, 1973); M.
Stiewe, "Das Alte Testament im theologischen
Denken Schleiermachers" in *Altes Testament For-
schung und Wirkung: Festschrift für Henning
Graf Reventlow*, ed. P. Mommer and W. Thiel
(Frankfurt: Peter Lang, 1994) 329-36.

D. DeVries

Semler, Johann Salomo (1725-1791)

Johann Salomo Semler was born on December 18, 1725, at Saalfeld, Thuringia,
into the family of a Lutheran pastor. The
precocious youth and avid reader conformed only reluctantly to the religious
expectations of local Pietist circles that his
father served as a minister and that received
the support of the regional nobility. This
climate of enforced religious compliance
had consequences for Semler's life in that
it established early a disdain for the relig-

ious world of German Pietism, with which he would cross swords throughout his life. His exposure to Halle Pietism as a student from 1743 on did not result in more positive relations. Instead he became the protégé of S. J. Baumgarten, an Enlightenment theologian and biblical scholar, under whom he also wrote his master's thesis on an issue in textual criticism.

The thesis of 1750 was ostensibly directed against the work of the English textual critic William Whiston, and signals the international scope of Semler's academic work. Throughout his life he encouraged by review, translation and introduction especially the work of English and Dutch Enlightenment theologians in Germany. After completing his master's degree, Semler was briefly employed in Koburg as a newspaper editor and teacher in the local high school. In 1751 he accepted a position as professor of history and Latin poetry in the university of Altdorf, but already one year later, upon the recommendation of Baumgarten, he became a full professor at Halle, where he worked side by side with his old teacher and later became the most renowned theologian in the university.

The scope of Semler's teaching and research was vast, even by eighteenth-century standards, and ranged from textual criticism to the study of insects, but his main contributions were in the areas of biblical criticism, church history and theology. Though Semler has been identified as one of the major representatives of the Enlightenment and is often placed into the company of the neologians, he was by no means uncritical toward contemporary deism, as is demonstrated by his intellectual disputes with the work of Hermann Samuel *Reimarus, as published by Gotthold Ephraim Lessing and Karl Friedrich Bahrdt. His opposition to deism and naturalism had political consequences as well, in that he opposed the employment of deists in the university and supported in 1788 the religiously conservative edict regarding religion by the Prussian minister J. C. Wöllner. He was able to do this consistently because of

the distinction he drew between private and public religion, the latter of which permitted the state to determine the boundaries of ecclesiastical teachings. While he devoted himself in later years also to natural science, he did not abandon theology and church, which consumed his last energies and interests. He died on March 14, 1791, in Halle.

Work. While the list of Semler's published works numbers 218, the work on which his abiding fame was based remains the four-volume *Abhandlung von freier Untersuchung des Canons (Study of the Free Investigation of the Canon)*, published in Halle (1771-1775). His biblical research had convinced Semler that any study of the Bible had to start with the biblical text and its tradition. In doing so he concluded that the biblical books were written by human authors with the language and in the idiom of their specific culture. Although he retained a belief in the "real inspiration" of Scripture, he came to reject the verbal inspiration and dictation theories of Lutheran orthodoxy. Likewise the canon of Scripture, which in the view of Lutheran orthodox theologians was a direct, verbally inspired and unchanging result of divine action, he considered the result of a lengthy historical and human process in response to practical considerations. He saw in the classic proof-text for the inspiration of Scripture (2 Tim 3:16) at most a reference to the Old Testament canon.

And Semler noted particularly that the Bible remained rather silent about the mode of its inspiration. He said, "We have the basic principles of Christianity from God's revelation and inspiration to the apostles. They did not consider it necessary to describe especially the kind and manner of this action upon the soul" (Semler, *Johann Kiddel's Abhandlung von Eingebung der heiligen Schrift* [1783], cited in Hornig, 69). Notably Semler rejected the dictation theory as a likely mode of inspiration because for him it lacked any textual verification. Semler felt that verbal inspiration and dictation were notions based not on Scripture but upon a fundamental religious need: to insure a greater certainty for Christianity's supreme religious authority. Such certainty would vanish, however, once one studied the history and tradition of the text. In any case the exegete has no access to the products of such assumed supernatural dictation—the apostolic autographs themselves—but only later manuscripts and versions characterized by multiple textual variations.

The absence of a universally agreed upon canon during much of the patristic period was also to Semler an indication that the formation of the canon did not have the direct divine causation Lutheran orthodoxy claimed for it. He considered himself on classical Protestant turf in considering the canon a changing entity produced by the church and not verbally inspired and immutable. The biblicism of Lutheran orthodoxy which assumed otherwise was, according to Semler, contradicted by historical-critical research and could be sustained only by an intellectual sacrifice. Such wholesale divine production also seemed to level the theological distinctions between the Old and the New Testaments as well as those among the individual writings. A human canon and the absence of verbal inspiration did not mean for Semler, however, the abandonment of biblical religion and authority. Instead it demanded theological judgments as to what truly represents the central message of the Bible: the salvific truths of Christ's redemptive death and resurrection. While, according to Semler, much in the Bible was adjusted to the state of mind of its earliest readers and writers, it nevertheless contained all that was necessary for salvation.

Throughout his writings Semler used the Enlightenment notion of accommodation, according to which the religious truths in the Bible were adjusted to the mental capacities and thought world of a given period and culture. Lessing and the Enlightenment "Lives of Jesus" avail themselves of a similar explanatory principle. The task of the biblical theologian is thus the separation of the local and temporal husk from the abiding and universal truths. Rather like Martin *Luther, who did not merely espouse a formal principle of *sola Scriptura* but considered Scripture at its best where it "put forth Christ," Semler distinguished a christological and salvific center in biblical religion from the culturally specific representation of those central truths. Semler took recourse to existing Lutheran schemata, especially the notion of law and gospel, when separating the kernel from the husk in biblical religion. This also led him also to reject the Protestant principle of the multiple uses of the Old Testament and espouse instead a christologically oriented New Testament Christianity. The ready use of the accommodation principle, however, exposed Semler and his contemporaries to the very danger they sought to avoid: the modernization of the biblical text. For such is possible not merely by projection but also by elimination. This becomes obvious where Semler relegates apocalyptic eschatology as an accommodation to the apostles' contemporary Jewish thinking and not a crucial dimension of Jesus' proclamation and the faith of early Christianity. By doing so, Semler violated his own canon of interpreting the Bible within the historical context and the original intention of its authors.

Semler rejected both the formalism and leveling of the Bible by Lutheran orthodoxy and what he considered to be the excessively subjective hermeneutic of Pietism. Semler's own position sought to avoid biblical literalism as well as a flight into subjective meanings and allegory. However, he did invoke a pneumatic certainty in the believer as an internal verification principle. This inner testimony of the Spirit does not operate, however, independently of the Word. Semler hoped to help contemporaries who had given up faith in Lutheran traditionalism and Pietistic introspection and thus exhibited pastoral considerations as well as constructive religious options in his writings. The historical-critical procedure was ultimately designed to establish the universal moral truths of Scripture. By "moral" Semler meant not merely the ethical but also, as the studies of G. Hornig have shown, the theological and especially the salvific elements of Christianity.

For Semler a necessary precondition for separating the temporal from the eternal was historical interpretation: the discernment of the authorial intent of a historical writing. Hermeneutics was thus raised to a pivotal discipline that not only was to formulate the general rules of exegesis but also became an instrument for determining the particular character of the biblical text and its meaning. Hermeneutics was to use for the accomplishment of its tasks grammar, rhetoric and logic, but also text and tradition criticism. Semler formulated a hermeneutical principle that would govern much of the subsequent exegetical work: that the interpreter ought to seek in a passage exclusively the "understanding of the author and writer" based upon "the language [of the biblical text] and its demonstrable use." He stated that "the sacred authors alone must be the lords and masters of what they have truly meant" (in Hornig, 79). He warned his readers to be vigilant and never project into the text the exegete's own thought and conscience. Such objectivism laid the groundwork for the historical-critical method of the nineteenth and twentieth centuries, with its ideal of recreating the original intentions of the authors, a procedure that has only in the twentieth century become seriously questioned by hermeneutical theory and postmodern exegesis.

One consequence of this critical procedure was the separation of Scripture and the Word of God, which Lutheran orthodoxy had considered to be identical. Already the biblical valuation of the New Testament over the Old Testament called, according to Semler, for a distinction among the biblical writings. This was heightened by the fact that the proclaimed Word of God had priority in early Christianity over any other Scripture. Further, the christological center of Scripture demanded a differential valuation of the biblical writings and not a homogeneous identification of the total Bible with the Word of God. At times Semler accentuated the contrast of law and gospel to such an extent that the Old and New Testaments are in danger of representing irreconcilable differences. A Marcionite separation is prevented, however, by relating divine revelation to concrete historical individuals in the Old Testament also, even though such divine self-disclosure does not extend to the Bible as a whole and keeps intact the personality of the biblical writers.

It would be wrong, however, to accuse Semler of having dispensed with revelation altogether. For Semler biblical religion retains both historical and supernatural elements. It is centered in the divinity of Christ and his redemptive death. That message finds manifold expression in the New Testament and should not be pressed, said Semler, into a dogmatic straightjacket. The New Testament doctrine of salvation is primarily the object of personal and practical appropriation, since through it God continues to act in the church. The Christian faith finds its most poignant articulation in the Gospel of John and the major Pauline writings. Here Semler reproduced for modern people a soteriological judgment of biblical writings already seen in Luther's work. To that extent, the enemy of Lutheran orthodoxy became an eloquent spokesperson for Luther's theological emphases on strictly biblical grounds.

Semler has often been accused of being a rationalist and has been grouped with the deists, who base their religion on universal reason instead of Scripture. The careful work of Hornig has, however, shown that such a view cannot be maintained. Not only is Semler's public criticism of deism an indicator of his critical stance toward a religion of reason but also he asserted "precisely the notion of a supernatural revelation of God, which through the incarnation of Jesus Christ became a historical reality" (Hornig, 125). Semler did not affirm an autonomous, rational source of religious truth but made Christian theology dependent upon Scripture and the historically discernable events contained in it.

Though Semler's main contributions to biblical studies are of a foundational nature for the establishment of the historical-critical method in theology, his more specialized historical and exegetical work is legion. Of abiding significance were his contributions to textual criticism. Following Johann Albrecht *Bengel's distinction between textual families, Semler divided the New Testament text into "Eastern" and "Western, Egyptian, Palestinian, Origenian" recensions. According to W. G. Kümmel, he "thereby reveals the first inkling of the difference between the large mass of later manuscripts (which he called the "Eastern" recension) and the smaller group of more valuable witness (Kümmel, 66). He also pointed out the importance of patristic biblical quotes for the establishment of a critical text. And methodologically he sought to formulate firm principles for the evaluation of individual biblical manuscripts.

Significance. Semler's significance for the history of biblical scholarship is, with the exception of his work in textual criticism and New Testament introduction, based not so much on specific exegetical results but on fundamental hermeneutical principles and methodological convictions and their consequences for theology. Semler has been judged by friend and foe as one of the seminal figures in the history of modern theology. He signals a radical break with the biblical formalism and doctrine of inspiration held by the Lutheran orthodoxy and champions rigorously a historical-critical method in biblical studies and theology. What Semler objected to particularly was the normativity of the orthodox Lutheran dogmatic presuppositions brought to the Bible as well as its authoritarian claims. And yet Semler did not remain unaffected by the intellectual world of his day. In fact, the accommodation hypothesis of the Enlightenment enabled him to preserve a religious supernaturalism and christological orienta-tion amid historical-critical and exegetical work that otherwise permitted no compromises.

BIBLIOGRAPHY

Works. J. S. Semler, *Abhandlung von freier Untersuchung des Canons* (4 vols.; Halle: C. H. Hemmerde, 1771-1776); idem, *D. Joh. Salomo Semlers Lebensbeschreibung von ihm selbst abgefasst* (2 vols.; Halle: C. H. Hemmerde, 1781-1782); idem, *Hermeneutische Vorbereitung* (2 vols.; Halle: C. H. Hemmerde, 1765-1769); idem, *Vorbereitung zur theologischen Hermeneutik* (2 vols.; Halle: C. H. Hemmerde, 1760-1761).

Studies. W. Baird, *History of New Testament Research* 1: *From Deism to Tübingen* (Minneapolis: Fortress, 1992) 116-1727; P. Gastrow, *Joh. Salomo Semler in seiner Bedeutung für die Theologie mit besonderer Berücksichtigung seines Streites mit G. E. Lessing* (Giessen: Alfred Töpelmann, 1905); E. Hirsch, *Geschichte der neuern evangelischen Teologie* (5 vols.; Gütersloh: Gütersloher Verlagshaus Gerd Mohn, 1975 [1951]) 4:3-89; G. Hornig, *Die Anfänge der historisch-kritischen Theologie: Johann Salomo Semlers Schriftverständnis und seine Stellung zu Luther* (Göttingen: Vandenhoeck & Ruprecht, 1961); W. G. Kümmel, *The New Testament: The History of the Investigation of Its Problems* (Nashville and New York: Abingdon, 1973) 62-69.   H. Rollmann

Smith, William Robertson (1846-1894)

The oldest son of a pastor in the Free Church of Scotland, Smith was educated at home, entered Aberdeen University at age fifteen and graduated with highest honors. He enrolled at Edinburgh for a theological degree and came under the influence of A. B. Davidson, the well-known professor of Hebrew and Old Testament studies. During the summers of 1867 and 1869 Smith traveled in Europe and attended lectures by a number of professors representing new forms of theological method (e.g., Albrecht Ritschl). Davidson described him as "by far the most distinguished student I have ever had in my department" (Black and Crystal 1912b, 119). In spring 1870, at age twenty-three,

Smith was elected professor of Hebrew and Old Testament exegesis in the Free College of Aberdeen University.

Smith was invited to write several entries in the ninth edition of the *Encyclopaedia Britannica,* eventually becoming its editor. His entry on "Bible," published in 1876, was the cause of concern among some in the Free Church, and the ensuing controversy in church courts over his views in this and other writings continued for five years. Smith was neither convicted of heresy nor suspended from the church, but he was removed from his professorship in 1881 by decision of the church's general assembly. He continued with public lectures on biblical criticism that were attended by thousands, and he accepted additional duties with the *Encyclopedia Britannica.* During the controversies Smith twice turned down a professorship at Harvard University. Subsequently he was named university librarian at Cambridge and eventually (1889) was appointed to a chair in Arabic studies. He died of tuberculosis at age forty-seven.

Smith was an able writer and editor who maintained contacts with a variety of scholars through travel in Europe and the Middle East and through correspondence. His memory, the breadth of his knowledge and his debating skills were legendary. Although he was bitter over the outcome of his church trials, Smith never repudiated his Christian faith; he consistently maintained that he was an evangelical Protestant and that his detractors were unable to see that his employment of higher-critical methods of biblical interpretation were not in essential conflict with the Westminster Confession of Faith, the doctrinal standard of his church.

Smith played a major role in introducing critical analysis of the Bible in Great Britain. But his historical and cultural analysis of Semitic religion earned him recognition as a founder of the science of comparative religion and that of anthropological study (Beidelman). His emphases on the primacy of ritual over myth, the communion element of sacrifice in ancient religion and the importance of group identity for cultural analysis were influential on such figures as Émile Durkheim and Sigmund Freud.

Biblical Inspiration, Authority and Revelation. Smith claimed allegiance to the Protestant principle that the Bible is the Word of God, arguing that his position was closer to that of the great Reformers, particularly Martin *Luther and John *Calvin, and less like that of the post-Reformation scholastics who viewed the Bible more as a deposit of doctrine. The clue to biblical authority comes in rightly apprehending the function of the Bible as an indispensable medium of God's self-revelation culminating in Christ. Smith relied heavily on the claim that an assurance of biblical authority, like the appropriation of the gospel message itself, came from the inner testimony of the Holy Spirit:

> It is the testimony of the Holy Spirit to which our Protestant theology ultimately refers the authority of Scripture. And what can this mean but that Scripture is the medium through which we come face to face with the divine revelation in Christ, and being thus brought under the living influence of the Person are by the Holy Spirit enabled rightly to apprehend Him as so presented to us, and so of course to recognise the medium whereby alone we can approach the historical Christ as really divine? (Black and Crystal 1912b, 133)

Smith's most often-quoted statement derives from his published reply to the libel formulated against him in the church's court:

> If I am asked why I receive the Scripture as the Word of God, and as the only perfect rule of faith and practice, I answer with all the fathers of the Protestant church, 'Because the Bible is the only record of the redeeming love of God, because in the Bible alone I find God drawing near to man in Christ Jesus, and declaring to us, in Him, His will for our salvation. And this record I know to be true by the witness of His Spirit in my heart, whereby I am assured

that none other than God Himself is able to speak such words to my soul.' (Smith 1978, 21) Smith used the phrase "means of grace" to describe both the function of the Christian sacraments and that of Scripture in its role of conveying the God of grace to a believer. Although he did not develop the analogy between sacraments and Bible in any detail, the comparison fits his overall understanding of divine revelation. Just as the risen Christ is "spiritually present" in the partaking of the eucharistic elements, so God's self-revelation comes through the words of Scripture. Thus Smith accepted the phrase "the Bible is the Word of God" as long as the function of the text was made clear: "Scripture is, essentially, what it is its business to convey" (Smith 1978, 26).

One might be inclined to hear this explanation as affirming that Scripture only conveys God's word in such a fashion that the latter somehow must be extracted from it. Smith would not agree; the means by which God communicates divine grace is not superfluous because form and function cannot be rigidly separated: "Scripture contains the Word of God, the pure Word of God, as the mould contains the silver seven times tried. The pure silver takes the shape of the mould, it may be an imperfect shape, but it is pure silver, and the man is enriched thereby at once without any further act" (Free Church of Scotland, 61).

Smith's ecclesiastical opponents were unable to demonstrate that Smith was unfaithful to the confessional standards of the church. What they sought to demonstrate was fatal theological inconsistency in his method: that he attempted the union of German rationalistic interpretation with Scottish Reformed piety. This is a complicated judgment to make, for it not only professes to understand Smith's theology better than he himself understood it but also concludes that historical judgments about date and authorship of biblical texts can be a mortal threat to a doctrine of divine revelation.

Historical Interpretation of Scripture.

Smith supported the claim of higher criticism that the Bible, like any other book, should be interpreted historically. He did not believe such an approach was injurious to the Christian faith; on the contrary, he maintained not only that it was a help to faith but also that consistency with Reformation doctrine required it:

It is our duty as Protestants to interpret Scripture historically. The Bible itself has a history. It was not written at one time, or by a single pen. . . . It is our business to separate these elements [in the Bible] from one another, to examine them one by one, and to comprehend each piece in the sense which it had for the first writer, and in its relation to the needs of God's people at the time when it was written. In proportion as we succeed in this task, the mind of the Revealer in each of His many communications with mankind will become clear to us. We shall be able to follow his gracious converse with His people of old from point to point. Instead of appropriating at random so much of the Word as is at once perspicuous, or guessing darkly at the sense of things obscure, we shall learn to understand God's teaching in its natural connection. For of this we may be assured, that there was nothing arbitrary in God's plan of revelation. . . . There was variety in the method of His revelation; and each individual oracle, taken by itself, was partial and incomplete. But none of these things was without its reason. The method of revelation was a method of education. (Smith 1881, 14)

This is a remarkable statement for the ways in which it portrays Smith's approach to Scripture. It is assumed that God's dealings with people partake completely of the broader historical process, which is completely open to human inquiry and potentially explicable in human terms. The composition and transmission of the Bible have histories to them like that of all other documents, and biblical interpreters should proceed in their examination by using the canons of accepted critical analysis. Nevertheless, by faith a person recognizes that the historical processes in Scripture are teleological. In light of God's supreme revelation in Christ, the historical particulars of Scripture are part of God's educational design for the needs of that day.

Smith emphatically affirmed a supernatural element to God's self-revelation in the historical process. At the same time he held to an understanding of history and social relations that he described as "organic," a type of evolutionary development in which all processes are linked by cause and effect:

The fundamental principle of the higher criticism lies in the conception of the organic unity of all history. . . . A tradition that violates the continuity of historical evolution and stands in no necessary relations to the conditions of the preceding and following age must be untrue . . . just as the name of Providence may be used to express the most diverse theories of God's working in the world, the word *organic,* applied to the providential development of history, may cover the widest differences of thought; for to one thinker the organic development of history will mean the unbroken sweep of natural law without one breath of the creative Spirit from on high, while to a higher school of thought the one purpose of history is the purpose of everlasting love, worked out, in, and through human personality, by a personal redeeming God. Now, the sphere in which all differences on this point appear in clearest relief is that part of history of which the Bible is the most authentic monument. For the problems of Israel's history are essentially religious problems. Rightly to conceive the progress of religious faith, thought, and life in the people of Israel, until the theocratic development received its absolute conclusion in the life of Him who gathered all the rays of splendour that flash through the Old Testament into the effulgent focus of His transcendent

personality, and in the course of this task to inweave the Bible record with the history of which it is itself a part—such is the critical problem of the theocratic history. (Black and Crystal 1912a, 164-66)

Although he adopted the language common to historical criticism in the late nineteenth century, Smith's view of an unfolding of revelation in history appears closer to that of Calvin, who proposed a model of "divine accommodation" whereby God adopts a mode of approach suited to the limitations of the audience. Smith's adherence to a developmental model of biblical truth should not be confused either with a simple evolutionary progression, as if one could dispense with the earlier forms of revelation once Christ had come. Old Testament piety, rightly interpreted, remained instructive for Christian faith.

Significance of Biblical Prophecy. Smith became convinced that the Pentateuch was produced over a long period of time, reaching its final form in the postexilic period. He did not deny Moses a significant place in Israelite religion, but he was unable to believe that Moses wrote the Pentateuch. This conclusion placed the early, preexilic prophets (e.g., Elijah, Amos, Hosea) in the role of major spokespersons during times of national crisis in Israel; and the analysis of the prophetic books were parade examples for Smith of the value of historical analysis for both critical analysis and piety. Much of his own understanding of a teleological plan in history culminating in the eternal kingdom of God, the requirement that true religion have a moral base, and the necessity of personal communion with God were drawn from the prophetic corpus. For him the characteristics of prophetic religion form a basis for the abiding significance of the Bible as a whole:

The ideal of the Old Testament is a dispensation in which all are prophets . . . the essential grace of the prophet is a heart purged of sin, and entering with boldness into the inner circle of fellowship with Jehovah. . . . The knowledge and fear of Jehovah is the sum of all prophetic wisdom, but also of all religion; and the Old Testament spirit of prophecy is the forerunner of the New Testament spirit of sanctification. (Smith 1881, 291) Some elements of Smith's own professional life bore resemblance to his portrait of the prophetic personality. During the years of official inquiry into his theological views, Smith's writings show him to be passionate in debate and zealous for his cause. When he was removed from his chair (1881), he refused to lead a secessionist movement in the church, although such a course was urged upon him. In later years, after international acclaim for his scholarly work, he maintained his evangelical convictions in intellectual circles where it was not always acceptable. Perhaps the best indication of his theological temperament comes in a letter (1887) to his younger brother, Herbert, who was close to death.

I hope that you also in spite of your pain are able to think of the rest that remaineth to the people of God. None of us can enter that rest without passing through pain and trial, even as He passed Who is our great Forerunner. You have had a sore share of trials, and yet perhaps one easier to bear than a long life of prosperity and worldly cares which make it very hard to keep near to God. At all events we know that He who orders all things wisely has dealt with you and with us all according to His will, which is the same as His purpose of love; and He will not forsake you, even in the valley of the shadow of death, if you lean on Him. Do not look inwards and vex yourself with self-questionings about faith and assurance and such like things. God gives a joyous assurance to some of His servants, but He gives peace to all who simply throw themselves on Him, humbly accepting His will, looking to Him as children to a father, and beseeching Him to be with them and carry all their burdens. (Black and Crystal 1912b, 493)

These poignant lines echo a number of scriptural texts (e.g., Ps 23; Hebrews) and show the pastoral sense of the renowned scholar, a sensitivity also seen in his sermons on individual texts. The same disease would claim him seven years later.

BIBLIOGRAPHY

Works. W. Robertson Smith, *Answer to the Form of Libel Now Before the Free Church Presbytery of Aberdeen* (Edinburgh: D. Douglas, 1978); idem, *Additional Answer to the Libel, with Some Account of the Evidence That Parts of the Pentateuchal Law Are Later Than the Time of Moses* (Edinburgh: D. Douglas, 1978); idem, *Kinship and Marriage in Early Arabia* (Cambridge: Cambridge University Press, 1885); idem, *Lectures on the Religion of the Semites: First Series, The Fundamental Institutions* (Edinburgh: A & C Black, 1889; 2d ed., 1894); idem, *The Old Testament in the Jewish Church: Twelve Lectures on Biblical Criticism* (Edinburgh: A & C Black, 1881; 2d ed., 1892); idem, *The Prophets of Israel and Their Place in History to the Close of the Eighth Century B.C.* (Edinburgh: A & C Black, 1882; 2d ed., 1897); J. S. Black and G. Crystal, eds., *Lectures and Essays of William Robertson Smith* (London: A & C Black, 1912a); J. Day, ed., *Lectures on the Religion of the Semites (Second and Third Series) by William Robertson Smith* (JSOTSup 183; Sheffield: Sheffield Academic Press, 1995).

Studies. T. O. Beidelman, *William Robertson Smith and the Sociological Study of Religion* (Chicago: University of Chicago Press, 1974); J. S. Black and G. Crystal, *The Life of William Robertson Smith* (London: A & C Black, 1912b); N. G. de S. Cameron, *Biblical Higher Criticism and the Defense of Infallibilism in Nineteenth-Century Britain* (Lewiston, NY: Edwin Mellen, 1987); Free Church of Scotland, *The Libel Against Professor William Robertson Smith: Report of Proceedings into the Free Church Presbytery of Aberdeen, Feb. 14, to March 14, 1878, with Form of Libel* (Aberdeen: Murray, 1878); W. Johnstone, ed., *William Robertson Smith: Essays in Reassessment* (JSOTSup 189; Sheffield: Sheffield Academic Press, 1995); R. Riesen, *Criticism and Faith in Late Victorian Scotland* (New York: University Press of America, 1985); J. Rogerson, *The Bible and Criticism in Victorian Britain: Profiles of F. D. Maurice and William Robertson Smith* (JSOTSup 201; Sheffield: Sheffield Academic Press, 1995).

J. A. Dearman

Strauss, David Friedrich
(1808-1874)

David Friedrich Strauss's *Life of Jesus Critically Examined* marks an epoch in the history of both biblical scholarship and christology. The interest of posterity in this book and its reception, however, misses both the spiritual pilgrimage of its author and his wider ambitions as a cultural critic. The political and intellectual context in which a handful of early nineteenth-century philosophers and theologians thought they could appropriate Christian truth in a form that would establish a new, bourgeois Christian culture for the modern world is long dead, their elevation to a state of identification with the divine Spirit by the redemptive power of Hegelian philosophy long buried, but historians owe it to Strauss to recall that his Gospel criticism was intended as the negative preliminary to a more constructive project.

Strauss was born in Ludwigsburg near Stuttgart and educated in the junior seminary at Blaubeuren and the *Stift*, or Protestant seminary for Württemberg theologians, at the University of Tübingen. After a short curacy and further study in Berlin he returned to the *Stift* as a *Repetent* (instructor) in 1832, taught philosophy with great success and wrote his *Life of Jesus*. Its first volume was published in June 1835, and despite some support from colleagues, the minister and students, he was transferred to a teaching post in classics.

His former teacher Ferdinand Christian *Baur argued, like Strauss himself, that his mythical interpretation of the Gospel miracles and other tales of the supernatural had merely developed a theological opinion that was current in Protestant theology. But the devastating effect of the book could not be confined to academic debate, and Strauss was in effect dismissed, not for his Hegelian metaphysics but for challenging the historical foundation of the gospel. The verbal inspiration of Scripture and the traditional belief in miracles and dogma had long been abandoned by the educated elite,

but Strauss's *succès de scandale* compelled a wider readership to reckon with the notion of the largely unhistorical character of the Gospels and the weakness of a theology built upon the assumption of their historicity. His elegant but cold and ruthless exposure of contradictions and implausibilities in each section of the Gospels sharply discounted centuries of harmonizing and forced Protestant theology to confront the issues at hand.

The reasons for rejecting supernaturalist interpretations of these narratives were bluntly stated. Knowing the laws of nature "we" no longer believe in miracles, angels and demons or a heavenly world hovering over our own. This had led to the natural explanations by which rationalist theologians like Heinrich Eberhard Gottlob Paulus sought to preserve a historical kernel in each story while excising their supernatural elements. But Strauss was able to show that going against the grain of the narratives in this way involved implausible and sometimes laughable constructions. The failure of both interpretative strategies opened the door for his own solution, that these incredible stories were "myth," that is, "the representation of an event or of an idea in a form which is historical, but at the same time characterized by the rich pictorial and imaginative mode of thought and expression of the primitive ages" (Strauss 1972, 53).

This "mythical interpretation" had already been applied to many Old Testament narratives and to the beginning and end of the Gospel story, but Strauss applied it step by step to the whole, making a devastating impression of the Gospels' generally unhistorical character. He discounted his predecessors' attempts to preserve some historical foundations by distinguishing between historical, philosophical and poetic myths, and he emphasized the part played . by Old Testament narratives, especially the Elijah and Elisha cycles, in these unconscious formations of the Christian communities during the period of oral tradition. Like the later form critics whom in some respects he anticipated, he admitted some historical data and saw the difficulty of drawing the boundary between the historical and the unhistorical (Strauss 1972, 90-91), but he was not very interested. For him the truth of Christianity was contained in the idea of the God-man. The Gospels communicate this through pictorial "representations," unhistorical stories that grew up around the historical man from Nazareth. Modern theologians could see the truth of the idea in these narratives and so translate them for themselves while speaking the traditional language from the pulpit.

The cultural significance of the book lay in weakening established authorities, its theological significance in confronting christology with modern critical study of history. But Strauss himself cared as little for the Jesus of the church as for the Jesus of history. His second volume appeared in November 1835 and concluded its critical analysis with a dissertation "On the dogmatic importance of the life of Jesus," aiming "to re-establish dogmatically that which has been destroyed critically" (Strauss 1972, 757). After a brief survey of ancient and modern christologies, Strauss unveils his own development of G. W. F. Hegel's philosophy. He cannot conceive of the unity of the divine and human natures in an individual person but only in the human race as a whole.

Nineteenth-century Protestantism was not tempted by this intellectual proposal, and radical Hegelianism found its future not in idealist theology but in a materialist philosophy (Ludwig Feuerbach) and in social theory. The young Karl Marx appreciated Strauss's negative achievement and thought that "the criticism of religion is the presupposition of all criticism"—but also the beginning of the end for religion. The theologian's radical revision of the Christian tradition thus interested neither the revolutionary social philosophers nor the liberal theologians seeking to develop their Protestantism without losing its center. In his isolation Strauss briefly retreated. After

trenchantly answering some of his critics in three polemical writings (*Streitschriften*), the third edition of his *Life of Jesus* (1838-1839) tempered his criticism of the Fourth Gospel. When he was appointed to a chair of dogmatics at Zurich (1839) he tried to be conciliatory. But that offer was withdrawn following controversy, and Strauss reaffirmed his earlier, more critical views in the definitive fourth edition (1840).

Preparing lectures on dogmatics for Zurich reactivated Strauss's plan to show that "the history of doctrine is at the same time its criticism." He described Christian doctrine "in its historical development and in the struggle with modern knowledge" in a two-volume sequel to the *Life of Jesus, Die christliche Glaubenslehre* (1840-1841). Each doctrine is analyzed historically from its biblical origins to the dissolution of its classical expressions by modern rationalism before being reinterpreted by Strauss in terms of his speculative philosophy. Again brilliantly written and containing sharp insights, its negativity was predictable, and the book aroused less interest than it deserved.

Strauss now abandoned theology, made a disastrous marriage (1842), entered the Stuttgart parliament (1840-1848) and wrote mainly on politics, music and literature. Working on a two-volume biography of Martin *Luther's supporter, the humanist poet Ulrich von Hutten (1857; ET 1874), and translating his *Gesprache* (1860) turned Strauss back to religious issues. In 1860 he reviewed an account of Gotthold Ephraim Lessing's dispute with Johann Melchior Goeze and the following year published his own account of Hermann Samuel *Reimarus and his *Apologie* or defense of deists, fragments of which Lessing had made public (1774-1778). Then in 1864 (ET 1865) his new *Life of Jesus* appeared, intended "for the German people," that is, the wider educated readership that Ernst Renan's *Vie de Jésus* had captivated in France.

This second monument of New Testament scholarship neither charmed the educated laity nor enraged the clergy, but still deserves some attention. Baur's Gospel criticism of the 1840s had confirmed Strauss's earlier option for the Synoptic record against Friedrich Daniel Ernst *Schleiermacher's preference for John, and an introduction of monograph length now summarized the state of research as brilliantly, savagely and one-sidedly as did his later admirer's *Quest of the Historical Jesus*, only without Albert *Schweitzer's humor. The priority of Mark was still a minority view, and Strauss remained true to the Tübingen preference for Matthew, again (like Schweitzer) without attaching much importance to this question. Influenced by Baur, Strauss now credited more to the redactional intentions of the Evangelists and slightly less to the creativity of the earliest communities.

The 1835 *Life* had consisted mainly in critical analysis. Strauss now summarized his conclusions synthetically, and so with Renan (1863) initiated the liberal "lives of Jesus." Book 1 sifts the Gospels for the authentic teaching of Jesus and establishes the outlines of his ministry and passion and the emergence of resurrection faith. His sensitive account of Jesus' self-consciousness is freed from Schleiermacher's dependence on the Johannine discourses, and a chapter (39) on Jesus' eschatology confronts the problems honestly and more intelligently than did much subsequent theology. Book 2 provides a much longer "mythical history of Jesus." This further discussion of Gospel material understands it all as the developing product of early Christian reflection. The unhistorical Johannine miracle stories are discussed, but it is striking that the equally unhistorical Johannine discourses, excluded from the historical book 1, are omitted from book 2, where they belong. Strauss is not interested in restating Christianity by interpreting the Evangelists' christologies. He is seeking to detach faith from history and attach it to a Kantian moral exemplar. That finds no support in these discourses.

In his earlier *Life* Strauss had proposed a drastic reinterpretation of the Christian tradition. Here he remains closer to Christian faith by attending to the biblical Christ, however distorted by sifting out the history from the kerygma and mutilated by excision of the christologically most powerful material and branded as unreal. Strauss has abandoned the reference of his Hegelian idea to humanity, but his ideal Christ as moral exemplar of humanity is still distinct from Jesus of Nazareth. Jesus himself is admired only for his contribution to this ideal, which is symbolized by the biblical Christ. There he "stands at all events in the first class" (Strauss 1977, 2:437), making patience, gentleness and charity predominant features of that image, however little his first followers grasped of this and despite the defects in his own historical achievement.

Strauss's distinction between the man tentatively unearthed by historical research and the symbolic expressions of postresurrection faith in him found in Paul, the Gospels and subsequent Christianity remains fundamental to historical study of the Gospels. The theological question of how this insight of modern historians is reflected in the attempts by christology to make intelligible the Christian confession of God and salvation in Jesus of Nazareth, the crucified and risen Lord of faith, remains inescapable. The failure of Strauss's answer to satisfy most Christians is best clarified by his disagreement with Schleiermacher, which reached as far back as his student days in Berlin. This erupted when the master's *Lectures on the Life of Jesus* (1864; ET 1975) were published thirty years after his death. Strauss knew that his own earlier work had rendered Schleiermacher's historical evaluation of the Gospels obsolete, and he rejected Schleiermacher's attempt to hold together what historical science had put asunder.

The title of Strauss's critique, *The Christ of Faith and the Jesus of History* (1865; ET 1977), specifies what history must not confuse and theology (he thought) can no longer fuse. Schleiermacher's presentation of a faith portrait of Jesus in the guise of historical reconstruction depended on an indefensible use of John's Gospel as history, but Strauss did not consider whether that aim might not nevertheless be achieved through a more critical use of the Gospels. Subsequent scholarship would ask whether Strauss's own historical conclusions might not be combined with other relevant data in a more satisfactory theological portrait of Jesus. If, as Strauss agreed, the religious value of the Gospels is only very partially and indirectly contained in their historical data, a theological interpretation of Jesus may be compatible with a historian's tentative and partial reconstruction without corresponding to it. Schleiermacher's particular portrait was destroyed by Strauss's historical criticism, but his aim of integrating whatever historical data is judged reliable in a theological portrait of Jesus need not fail unless the continuity between Jesus and Christian faith has to be stretched beyond breaking point.

Strauss did not explore this christological possibility of setting the grains of historical memory in a broader account of Jesus' religious significance for Christians because he still shared the Enlightenment's depreciation of history. Even the historical particularity of Jesus was still ultimately unimportant to him.

The mild unorthodoxy of Strauss's middle age had replaced the daring innovation of his Hegelian youth, but finally this yielded to the disavowals of his last book. His attempts at mediation had failed, and in *The Old Faith and the New* (1872; ET 1873) he repudiated the name *Christian*. His worldview was materialist, and while he remained religious, he thought modern culture better served by Goethe and Schiller, Bach, Handel, Haydn, Mozart and Beethoven than by a deluded fanatic. The book was a best seller but criticized on all sides, most famously by Friedrich Nietzsche in the first of his *Untimely Meditations*(1873; ET 1909; rev. 1983). Strauss was already dying. He stipulated in his will that no clergyman should speak at his fu-

neral. A generation later Schweitzer made him the hero of *The Quest of the Historical Jesus,* and his first book remains the best between Reimarus and William *Wrede or beyond, and the decisive stimulus in New Testament scholarship. Rudolf *Bultmann wanted to dedicate *The History of the Synoptic Tradition* in memory of Strauss, and even Karl *Barth, who was more than aware of Strauss's theological deficiencies, can sparkle when writing of him in *Protestant Thought in the Nineteenth Century* (ET 1972). He credits Strauss, however, only with seeing through a bad solution to the problem of theology, failing to improve on it and abandoning the subject matter of theology. New Testament scholars will continue to judge him more kindly than will systematicians.

BIBLIOGRAPHY

Works. D. F. Strauss, *Die christliche Glaubenslehre in ihrergeschichtlichen Entwicklung und im Kampf mit der modernen Wissenschaft dargestellt* (2 vols.; Darmstadt: Wissenschaftliche Buchgesellschaft, 1973 [1840-41]); idem, *Der Christus des Glaubens und der Jesus der Geschichte. Eine Kritik des Schleiermacherschen Lebens Jesu* (Berlin: Franz Duncker, 1865; ET *The Christ of Faith and the Jesus of History,* ed. L. E. Keck [Philadelphia: Fortress, 1977]); idem, *Das Leben Jesu, kritisch bearbeitet* (2 vols.; Tübingen: Osiander, 1835; *The Life of Jesus Critically Examined,* ed. P. C. Hodgson [Philadelphia: Fortress, 1972]); idem, *Das Leben Jesu für das deutsche Volk bearbeitet* (Leipzig: Brockhaus,1865); idem, *Streitschrften* (Tübingen: Osiander, 1837).

Studies. C. Brown, *Jesus in European Protestant Thought, 1778-1860* (Durham, NC: Labyrinth, 1985); R. S. Cromwell, *David Friedrich Strauss and His Place in Modern Thought* (Fair Lawn, NJ: R. E. Burdick, 1974); H. Frei, *The Eclipse of Biblical Narrative* (New Haven, CT: Yale University Press, 1974); F. Graf, *Kritik und Pseudo-Spekulation* (Munich: Kaiser, 1982); H. Harris, *David Friedrich Strauss and His Theology* (Cambridge: Cambridge University Press, 1973); V. A. Harvey, "D. F. Strauss's *Life of Jesus* Revisited," *CH* 30 (1961); D. Lange, *Historischer Jesus oder mythischer Christus* (Gütersloh: Gütersloher Verlagshaus, 1975); E. G. Lawler, *David Friedrich Strauss and His Critics* (Bern:

Lang, 1986); M. E. Massey, *Christ Unmasked: The Meaning of "The Life of Jesus" in German Politics* (Chapel Hill: University of North Carolina Press, 1983); J. F. Sandberger, *David Friedrich Strauss als theologischer Hegelianer* (Göttingen: Vandenhoeck & Ruprecht, 1972); D. F. Strauss, *The Christ of Faith and the Jesus of History*, ed. L. E. Keck (Philadelphia: Fortress, 1977), see the introduction; idem, *The Life of Jesus Critically Examined*, ed. P. C. Hodgson (Philadelphia: Fortress, 1972), see the introduction; J. E. Toews, *Hegelianism* (Cambridge: Cambridge University Press, 1980).

R. Morgan

Stuart, Moses *(1780-1852)*

Moses Stuart pioneered critical study of the Bible in North America. As professor of sacred literature at Andover Theological Seminary in northeastern Massachusetts for nearly four decades (1809-1848), he set a high standard of academic inquiry. At the same time he maintained fidelity to creedal and evangelical Christianity in the face of burgeoning Unitarianism in his native New England and other challenges to trinitarian Christianity from the Continent.

Work. Stuart was born in Wilton, Connecticut, and grew up amid the rigors of New England farm life. He graduated from Yale College. There he was influenced by Timothy Dwight (1752-1817), grandson of Jonathan *Edwards. As Yale's president from 1795 until his death, Dwight championed religious revival. A third of Yale's students converted under his preaching in 1802. Dwight called for the training and sending out of highly literate and theologically savvy ministers, stating this concern forcefully at the opening of Andover Seminary (1808), the first full-fledged theological education institution in North America. Beginning shortly thereafter, Stuart's life work as a professor at Andover would directly address these concerns.

Following college, where he graduated head of his class in 1799, Stuart tried teaching school for two years. But he decided to pursue law instead and was admitted to the bar in 1802. In that same year, as he both

tutored at Yale College and pursued further legal studies, Stuart was gripped by Dwight's revival preaching. His legal career proved to be stillborn, for in January 1803 Stuart reentered Yale College to devote himself to such divinity studies as were available.

By early 1805 Stuart had married Abigail Clark and become assistant pastor at Center Congregational Church in New Haven. He assumed the office of pastor there in 1806. His energetic Calvinist preaching was warmly received, and the congregation grew. His success marked him as a promising future leader in New England Congregationalism. It was natural for the Andover Seminary trustees to turn to him in 1809 when the chair of sacred literature fell open. At the age of twenty-nine he convened his first seminary class. At Andover for the next forty years he would see seven of his nine children survive childhood and hundreds of seminary graduates enter vocational ministry or scholarly careers like his own. He would also pen the thousands of pages that are his chief legacy, an enduring tribute to the first stages of biblical scholarship on the North American continent.

Writings. Numerous Stuart manuscripts remain unpublished, though it is unlikely that any contributes materially to knowledge of his thought as expressed in published works. Stuart published six books on Hebrew and one on Greek grammar and syntax. Some of these enjoyed various reprintings and new editions. He wrote commentaries on six books of the Bible: Proverbs, Ecclesiastes, Daniel, Romans, Hebrews and Revelation. Seven other volumes treat themes as various as Cicero's view of the soul's immortality, the biblical doctrine of future punishment, and the history of the Old Testament canon. He translated at least five other works from Latin or German, bringing the total number of books published to more than two dozen. An additional two dozen items appeared under Stuart's name in the form of tracts, pamphlets and printed sermons.

In a day when scholarly theological journals were not numerous and learned discussion of biblical topics relatively rare in North America, Stuart published continuously in such organs as *American Biblical Repository* and *Bibliotheca Sacra*. Biographer J. H. Giltner concurs in the judgment that his periodical writings alone would fill two thousand octavo pages. These cover a remarkably wide range of topics, among them hermeneutics, extrabiblical writings like the book of Enoch and the Samaritan Pentateuch, Old and New Testament exegesis, Hebrew and Greek lexicography, and various historical-theological matters.

In this last-named category one finds titles hinting at the breadth of Stuart's interests and learning: "Creed of Arminius with a Sketch of His Life and Times"; "Sacred and Classical Studies"; "German Theological Writers"; "On the Manuscripts and Editions of the Greek New Testament"; and most ponderously, "On the Discrepancy Between the Sabellian and Athanasian Methods of Representing the Doctrine of the Trinity, by Friedrich Schleiermacher, Translated with Notes." Stuart's expertise extended far beyond technical mastery of the Bible's contents and original languages. Yet it was on account of these that he is primarily remembered, for it was to biblical interpretation that he devoted his life's primary energies.

Biblical Interpretation. The historian continually confronts the question of whether persons make history or vice versa. Both are true; but in Stuart's case, the times seem to have been far more determinative for him than he was for his times. Stuart was a capable thinker possessing enormous energy, an admirable work ethic and winsome doctrinal poise. But three priorities arising during the decades of his scholarly career, each somewhat interlocking with the other, exerted strong influence on the objects and shape of his biblical scholarship.

The first priority was pedagogical. There was pressing need for theological education, especially in biblical languages. Stuart fell heir to a theological heritage that in the

eighteenth century excelled in apologetics and doctrinal system-building, not biblical philology and theology. And this was in relatively well-educated New England; biblical learning was in a far more chaotic state, where it existed at all, in the vast reaches of the young republic where populist religious forms of the Second Great Awakening were rapidly gathering strength. Stuart himself lacked knowledge of Hebrew upon assumption of his professorial chair. He remedied this by assiduous personal study. There followed thirty-five years of intense labor in the search, largely successful, for effective means of grounding seminarians in the language of more than three-fourths of the Christian canon.

In addition to personal study Stuart drew on the first editions of Wilhelm Gesenius's (1786-1842) celebrated Hebrew and Aramaic grammar. He strove to develop a less pedantic approach that would involve students in inductive learning from the start rather than demand of them endless rote learning before exposing them to the more rewarding work of biblical translation and exposition. He devoted similar efforts to Greek pedagogy, drawing on such German authorities as Buttmann, Matthiae and Winer but attempting to improve on European systems of information delivery that he felt were ineffective.

A second priority was apologetic in nature. Stuart witnessed not only the Yale revival but also, at some distance, the Second Great Awakening, with its widespread contempt for the type of learned clergy that Andover sought to produce. He also witnessed the continuing spread of post-Enlightenment variations of Christian doctrine and practice, typified by the Unitarian views boldly proclaimed in 1819 by William Ellery Channing (1780-1842) in a celebrated sermon. While Channing later cast stones at the Transcendentalists for their radical break with Christian theism, Stuart recognized that Channing's own rejection of the Trinity, Christ's divinity and human depravity left him living in a glass house. Stuart crafted lengthy, gracious and exhaustive public letters in response. A modern biographer's complaint that Stuart failed to engage Channing on the fundamental hermeneutical issues is beside the point; Channing based his claims on biblical exegesis, and it was on these grounds that Stuart properly responded.

Apologetic response was called for by assaults from a third quarter, as well: European, especially German, rationalism. From as early as 1812 Stuart gained firsthand acquaintance with critical theories and methods emanating from the Continent. As he had taught himself Hebrew, he mastered German. Much of his life's work contains, at least between the lines, implicit correction of German critical excesses. But he refused to anathematize European learning, since he found so much of high value even in works with which he profoundly disagreed.

In sum, while it would be wrong to call Stuart a polemicist, he was ready to ply the sword "when the attempt is made to take our citadel by sword" (Stuart 1849a, 2).

A third and chief priority was biblical exposition. As befit his Protestant heritage, all Stuart did was meant to further the propagation of the gospel. Language learning and teaching were foundational; apologetics were unavoidable; but biblical interpretation was the heart and soul of the minister's calling—and therefore of the equipper of ministers, as well. His half-dozen commentaries explicitly serve this end. In them he exhibits a wealth of classical learning, mastery of Old Testament and intertestamental background, careful attention to philological and syntactical detail, and awareness of historical theology. In addition he displays a depth of familiarity with other commentators that is surprising given his heavy teaching load and the scarcity of good theological books to which his letters occasionally attest.

Weaknesses, however, are also evident in Stuart's biblical analysis. One is numbing prolixity. Another is a certain philological positivism, as if meaning could always be certifiably generated out of proper scientific methods applied to words. Today it sounds naive, even simpering, when Stuart writes, "The simple stone and sling of historical criticism are all that I assay to use," or when he affects to take leave "even of theology itself. . . . [I] aim to act merely the part of a historical inquirer, who applies to the appropriate sources of information, and endeavours in this way to find out what he ought to believe" (Stuart 1849a, 3, 22). Historical interpretation has proven to be a more subjective and self-reflecting enterprise than Stuart could envision. Another weakness is a certain incaution and impulsiveness in rendering judgments, especially in the classroom. This tendency left its traces in his many writings.

Still, the rapidly changing times called for expositional resources that would help students, pastors and scholars understand and appropriate the venerable charter documents of the Christian faith. From Stuart's confessional standpoint, theology was imperiled from a number of directions. Prolixity, hermeneutical naiveté and rash judgments were common in the writings of Stuart's contemporaries too. It is to be regretted that Stuart's commentaries (e.g., on Romans) have fallen into disuse. The interpreter with the requisite linguistic training will often find Stuart's discussions well worth consulting. Suspicion that he lacks the critical independence from Christian belief required of modern scholarship begs the question of whether that independence and the suspicion that sometimes spawns it are not themselves impediments to understanding. That Stuart could exercise surprising freedom of judgment—he broke with the Westminster tradition on the question of imputed guilt through Adam—suggests that his exegesis was not always bound to travel along rails already laid by others.

Significance. Stuart deserves recognition for being among the first biblical scholars in North America to assimilate the findings of German historical criticism. As a fledgling academician he cut his professional teeth on the imposing three-volume

Old Testament introduction of Johann Gottfried *Eichhorn, decrying its eccentric rationalism but recognizing its deep learning and historic importance. Later he published a hundred dense pages of interaction with German New Testament scholarship stretching back at times to Martin *Luther (Stuart 1836, 677-777). Many of his critical judgments (e.g., that 1 Peter was written from Babylon, not Rome; all words attributed to Jesus in the Gospels were actually spoken by him) are rejected today. But to his credit he realized that "higher criticism judiciously applied could be as useful to defend as to destroy" (Giltner, 31).

Rather than ignore biblical difficulties or cavil at those who pointed them out, he called for informed response: "We must show our readiness and our ability to meet the objector to the sacred scriptures, on grounds which are capable of fair examination, and which are common to all ancient writings." He added, "Such ground being admitted, we have no reason to fear the result" (unpublished lecture, cited in Giltner, 36). In time it became clear that there was more to fear from unsympathetic scholars of Christian origins than Stuart foresaw, but his openness to alternate views and insistence on courteous, informed handling of opponents are commendable ideals. He claimed that it was his grasp of critical questions first posed in Germany that enabled him to respond with such assurance and vigor to rejection of the Trinity and other central doctrines in disputes with Channing and others.

More positively, Stuart helped establish a historical and philological approach to questions of biblical interpretation. In his own time he was hailed as the father of biblical philology on North American shores. Then as in every age, popular currents of left and right spawned ideologies that imposed themselves on the biblical data. Unitarianism and various anticreedalisms of the Second Great Awakening serve as examples. Stuart effectively championed a rigorous *ad fontes* approach

to the problem, as George Ernest *Wright recognized in an essay appearing in 1970. That Stuart did not always transcend his own ideologies does not detract from his achievement in progressing in the right direction. Original language research, not orthodox doctrinal tradition or post-Christian religious philosophy alone, must be determinative in establishing the message, if any, of biblical texts.

In an age of hyperspecialization among many biblical scholars, Stuart is a reminder of the importance of breadth of learning and not merely depth. He is calm in debate with Andrews Norton's *Evidence of the Genuineness of the Gospels* because, he says, he is familiar with the same arguments put forth by Porphyry and Celsus sixteen centuries before (Stuart 1849a, 11). He chalks up many a misreading of Revelation to lack of understanding of the Hebrew prophets, a subject in which he excelled. In his zeal for philological precision he understands the importance of cultural background, attention to "whatever belongs to the circle of Hebrew archaeology; which comprises civil History, Geography, Chronology, natural History, agriculture, cult and manufactures, Religion, Literature, Philosophy, and manners and customs both religious and civil" (unpublished lecture, cited in Giltner, 53). He cast no less wide a net as a Greek philologist.

Stuart's exegesis is expansive rather than atomistic because his eyes are open not merely to current critical discussion but also to a balanced range of evidence from ancient and medieval sources. And modern too: in explaining how Moses' writings were reduced in number under Manasseh's half-century of idolatries and persecutions to the single copy found by Hilkiah in Josiah's reign, he points out how completely Bibles were removed from Paris, where they had abounded in the thousands, during the reign of terror (Stuart 1849a, 77). Such argumentation, while obviously not conclusive in itself, has something to say for it when compared with the bloodless narrations offered in many a more recent technical history of Israel or early New Testament literature.

Stuart was a journeyman, not a super-star. He was a custodian of truths, as he saw them, rather than a master of innovation. But worse things can be said of a scholar than that he was competent, productive and appropriately reverent toward the data of his discipline. Western societies are witnessing the bankruptcy of institutional iconoclasm toward Christian tradition, whether they realize it or not, and in their lucid moments wonder whether they will survive the social disintegration abounding on every hand. The clock cannot be returned to Stuart's times, but it would mark progress if more scholars returned to his civil tone and informed level of debate, his truly humanistic educational ideals, and his well-placed trust in the redeeming value of biblical subject matter approached in learned humility.

BIBLIOGRAPHY

Works. M. Stuart, *A Commentary on the Epistle to the Romans,* ed. and rev. R. D. C. Robbins (4th ed.; Andover, MA: Warren F. Draper, 1865); idem, *Critical History and Defence of the Old Testament Canon* (New York: M. W. Dodd, 1849a); idem, *Exegetical Essays on Several Words Relating to Future Punishment* (Philadelphia: Presbyterian Publication Committee, 1867 [1830]); idem, *A Grammar of the New Testament Dialect* (Andover: Gould & Newman, 1834); idem, *Hug's Introduction to the New Testament,* trans. from 3d German ed. by D. Fosdick Jr. with notes by M. Stuart (Andover, MA: Gould & Newman, 1836); idem, *Letters on the Divinity of Christ Addressed to the Rev. W. E. Channing, in Answer to His Sermon "On the Doctrines of Christianity"* in *The Christian Treasury; A Selection of Standard Treatises on Subjects of Doctrinal and Practical Christianity,* ed. T. S. Memes (London: Henry G. Bohn, 1849b [1819]).

Studies. J. H. Giltner, *Moses Stuart: The Father of Biblical Science in America* (Atlanta: Scholars Press, 1988); N. Hatch, *The Democratization of American Christianity* (New Haven, CT, and London: Yale University Press, 1989); L. Woods, *History of the Andover Theological Seminary* (Boston: J. R. Osgood, 1885); C. Wright, *The Beginnings of Unitarianism in*

America (Hamden, CT: Archon, 1976 [1966]); G. E. Wright, "Historical Knowledge and Revelation" in *Translating and Understanding the Old Testament,* ed. H. T. Frank and W. L. Reed (Nashville and New York: Abingdon, 1970) 279-303.   R. W. Yarbrough

Tholuck, Friedrich August Gottreu *(1799-1877)*

Friedrich August Gottreu Tholuck was a noted nineteenth-century German theologian, commentator and preacher. Born at Breslau, March 30, 1799, Tholuck studied at the gymnasium and university there, then focused on Near Eastern languages at the University of Jena under Johann Gottfried Ludwig Kosegarten. Beginning in 1817 he studied theology at the University of Berlin, where he was influenced by Johann Neander, Friedrich Daniel Ernst *Schleiermacher and G. W. F. Hegel. He experienced a Pietistic conversion as the result of personal conversations with Baron Ernst von Kottwitz, a Moravian. The conversion in turn influenced his lifelong theological perspective. In an address in 1870 in conjunction with a celebration of his fifty years of teaching, he commented:

> Nothing fills me more with adoring wonder than to think how this spirit of fire has ever been given to me since the hour when I received the baptism of fire from above. From the age of seventeen I have always asked myself, "What is the chief end of man's life?" I could never persuade myself that the acquisition of knowledge was this end. Just then God brought me into contact with a venerable saint who lived in fellowship with Christ, and from that time I have had but one passion, and that is Christ, and Christ alone.

In 1821 Tholuck commenced lecturing as a privatdozent at the University of Berlin, and in 1824 he was appointed extraordinary professor of oriental literature. In 1825 he traveled to Holland and England at the expense of the Prussian government. He aspired to a professorship in the school founded by August Hermann Francke at Halle and gratefully accepted a position there in 1826 as ordinary professor of theology, a position he held until his death. When Tholuck arrived, the school was permeated by German rationalism, as represented by Wilhelm Gesenius and Julius August Ludwig Wegscheider, but after a decade, and with support from Prussian officials, he was influential in effecting a change. One of his later works, unfinished, was a *Geschichte des Rationalismus* (1865). In 1870 his friends celebrated the fiftieth anniversary of his teaching career, and his former students in Europe and America founded a seminary adjacent to his home.

Tholuck was especially interested in students, inviting them to accompany him on daily two-hour walks. Because of his facility in English and a compatible theological outlook, he was able to befriend and influence several English and American students, including E. B. Pusey, Samuel Davidson, Edward Robinson, Charles *Hodge, Joseph Addison Alexander, James Waddel Alexander, Robert Patton, Henry Preserved Smith, John W. Nevin, Edwards Amasa Park, Philip Schaff and George Lewis Prentiss. Though Tholuck was married, he had no children of his own.

The first American to study under Tholuck was Edward Robinson, later professor at Union Theological Seminary. Robinson became recognized internationally for his topographical explorations of Palestine. In 1826 Robinson traveled to Europe, and before the year was over he arrived at Halle. Robinson described Tholuck:

In person, Professor Tholuck is slender and feeble; his conversation is uncommonly engaging and full of thought; and although not yet 32 years old, he possesses a greater personal influence and reputation than any other theologian of Germany. To an American Christian, who travels on this part of the continent, Tholuck is undoubtedly the most interesting person whose acquaintance he will make. (Robinson, 29)

When Charles Hodge of Princeton proposed to make the same journey, Robinson encouraged him to forget about the rest of Europe and make his way to Halle. Robinson regarded Halle as "the great theological school of Germany." In 1830 Halle had twice the number of theological students as the University of Berlin. On January 29, 1827, Hodge wrote to Archibald Alexander at Princeton, from Paris:

I have made up my mind to go to Halle instead of Göttingen. Mr. Robinson informs me that more attention is paid to Biblical literature at Halle than at any other university. It has also the great advantage of having Tholuck within its walls, who is as much distinguished for piety as for his learning. (A. A. Hodge, *The Life of Charles Hodge* [New York: Charles Scribner's Sons, 1880], 114).

Tholuck confirmed Hodge, as well as many other conservative Americans, in the conviction that viable biblical studies may proceed upon traditional Reformation grounds. Tholuck also convinced Hodge that Hebrew was the most important language for perceiving New Testament backgrounds. On Thursday, March 15, 1827, Hodge wrote in his journal,

Tholuck called at eleven for me to walk with him. He said he thought the Rabbinical dialect more important for the illustration of the New Testament than any other whatever, and therefore, more useful to the Biblical student than either Arabic or Syriac. Arabic was of little use except to make use of the "helps" in reading the Old Testament. He said he had been very much struck with the coincidence between the manner of expression and argument in the Rabbinical writers and those of the New Testament. (A. A. Hodge, *The Life of Charles Hodge,* 123)

Most of all Hodge was impressed by the theological posture of Tholuck. He especially relished Tholuck's attacks on the neologians who questioned the authenticity of a number of biblical books. Although he respected Tholuck's opposition to neology, Hodge, true child of Scottish realism, was annoyed by Tholuck's idealism. He wrote:

> Even the Biblical Theologians of Germany are so led away by the speculative spirit, so characteristic of its inhabitants, that is seems impossible they should be restrained with the bounds of sober and important truth, except by the influence of religion on their hearts. Tholuck, himself, who was much of this philosophizing spirit, considers matter as only a different modification of spirit, the essence of both being the same. (A. A. Hodge, *The Life of Charles Hodge*, 119)

To Hodge, committed to Baconianism as he was, Tholuck seemed far too speculative. The Germans in contrast perceived him as lacking in constructive innovation as well as philosophical rigor.

Work. Tholuck eschewed creeds and dogmatic theology along with censure of minor defections from orthodoxy. He opposed both rationalism and idealism. He grounded his theology in what he perceived to be the biblical message but also incorporated the human will and feeling. He specifically focused on the doctrine of sin and reconciliation. Much like Ernst Hengstenberg he defended the accuracy and apologetics value of the messianic prophecies. He was positioned as a theologian of the German Revival by Karl *Barth, who wrote that "the one man, Tholuck, was and remained a pure theologian of the Revival, and there was no one beside him" (Barth, 509).

The manifestation of the German Revival in America is sometimes designated mediating theology. Should theological descendants of Tholuck be identified, the right wing was mostly in America and Great Britain. The left wing was represented by Martin Kähler and Wilhelm Herrmann, both of whom served as assistants to Tholuck in Halle. But the theology of Tholuck was not so distinct as to warrant the delineation of a school. He set forth his early quarrel with Enlightenment, rationalistic thought in *Guido and Julius* (1823), a response to Wilhelm Martin Leberecht *de Wette's *Theodore*.

Along with his numerous works on theology and church history, Tholuck published commentaries on Romans; John, which was more popular in approach; the Sermon on the Mount, his most scholarly commentary; as well as commentaries on Hebrews and Psalms. He also published a response to David Friedrich *Strauss's writings on the Gospels, *Die Glaubwürdigkeit der evangelischen Geschichte* (1837), as well as *Die Propheten und ihre Weissagungen* (1861). According to W. Baird, "in terms of the developments of New Testament criticism, Tholuck's most important work" is *Die Glaubwürdigkeit* (Baird, 284). His commentaries were widely circulated in the United States, impressing Moses *Stuart and his numerous students. In this manner Tholuck uniquely influenced those who laid the groundwork for American biblical studies in the latter half of the nineteenth century.

In *Die Glaubwürdigkeit* Tholuck argued against Strauss that proofs are possible for the miracle stories of the Gospels. Each miracle account must be taken up in turn. Their reliability was enhanced, since in Tholuck's view, the Gospels are authentic and written by the author to whom they are ascribed. He held Luke, for example, to be more reliable than Josephus. He held the Gospel writers to be independent witnesses to the story of Jesus and therefore eschewed attempts in Synoptic studies to show dependency of one writer on another. His views were emulated by Andrews Norton of Harvard in his *The Evidences of the Genuineness of the Gospels* (1837-1844). He dismissed the *Griesbach hypothesis, which was accepted by Strauss on the grounds that Mark did not abbreviate Matthew and Luke but made use of the authentic traditions of Simon Peter. He held the Gospel of John to be an independent witness and therefore different. John was able to narrate the story of Christ from memory, assisted by the Holy Spirit and perhaps notes taken down in respect to the discourses. He held that the background of the Logos was Jewish, not Philonic or Hellenistic. He concluded that Jesus was involved in two cleansings of the temple.

Though Tholuck was especially influential upon American and British biblical scholarship, he pioneered no major innovations. W. G. Kümmel, in *The New Testament: The History of the Investigation of Its Problems* (Nashville: Abingdon, 1972), includes only a bibliographical reference. Baird concluded: "When all is said and done, Tholuck's Pietism has added an element of vitality to his understanding of the NT, but, in the main, the spirit is captive to an apologetic biblicism" (Baird, 286).

Tholuck was a master of many languages, having studied nineteen of them before he was 17. He spoke English, French, Italian, Greek, Arabic and other languages fluently. He brought works in all these languages to bear on his exegesis, especially his insights into Near Eastern literature, both Jewish and Islamic. It is in philology that his expertise may sometimes still be drawn upon (for example, J. Smit Sibinga, "Exploring the Composition of Matth. 5-7" *FN* 7 [1994] 175-96). As an exegete Tholuck was most thorough in philological observations. In commenting on Romans 1:17, for example, he cited similar constructions in Heliodorus, Theophylact and *Clement of Alexandria. He then reviewed the philological conclusions of *Origen, *Theodoret, *Augustine, Zegerus, Philipp *Melanchthon, Theodore *Beza, Abraham Calovius, Jean Clericus, Salomon Glassius and Henry Hammond.

In 1832 Moses *Stuart published his commentary on Romans. The commentary featured discussion with German commentators, especially Tholuck. Stuart wrote:

Most of all am I indebted to the excellent book of Tholuck on this epistle. In particular, I have often relied on him in my statements with respect to the opinions of other commentators, whom I had not at hand, or whom I did not think it important to consult myself,

because I confided in his account of their views. . . . Prof. Tholuck will easily perceive, also, if the following sheets should pass under his eye, that I am indebted to him for various classical quotations and allusions, and also for not a few valuable philological remarks, as well as views of the reasoning and argumentation of the apostle. (Moses Stuart, *Commentary on the Epistle to the Romans* vi)

In his exposition on John, Tholuck utilized the insights of the Reformation fathers, especially Martin *Luther, Martin *Bucer, Johann Crell and Juan Maldonatus, along with Johann Albrecht *Bengel, all of whom he charged were largely neglected. In his commentary on the Psalms, prepared for theological students and laypeople, he followed John *Calvin in focusing upon the religious ideas from the perspective of the Christian faith. He criticized de Wette's work because it gave little attention to religious ideas. In the introduction he wrote:

In writing my Commentary on the Psalms, my object was this: to interpret the Book of Psalms in the spirit of Calvin; and basing it on the helps derived from the newly-gained views of modern times, to adapt the volume to the wants of the people, and also to professional men, who, besides strictly grammatical Commentaries, look for a guide to the spiritual understanding of this portion of Holy Writ. (Tholuck 1858, xi)

Hodge's decision to study under Tholuck adumbrated the course of American biblical studies, especially those at Princeton, for at least a century. Hodge was the first New Testament exegete at Princeton specifically trained for that position. He, along with Stuart, was the first American to publish commentaries of significance. His presuppositions cast a long shadow over Princeton exegetical theology as it unfolded in the nineteenth century, and this in turn influenced biblical scholars to the south and west. When the Society of Biblical Literature was founded in 1880 by thirty-two

American biblical scholars, somewhat more than half were students of Stuart, Robinson, Hodge, James Waddel Alexander and Henry Preserved Smith—all of whom were influenced by Tholuck. Philip Schaff, perhaps the key person in the founding of the society, was a student of Tholuck.

BIBLIOGRAPHY

Works. F. A. G. Tholuck, *Auslegung des Briefes Pauli an die Romer* (Berlin: F. Dummler, 1825; ET: *Exposition of St. Paul's Epistle to the Romans* [Edinburgh: T. Clark, 1834-1836]); idem, *Die Bergpredigt* (4th ed.; Gotha: F. A. Perthes, 1856); ET: *The Sermon on the Mount* (1835, 2 vols.; ET 1834-1837); idem, *Gesammelte Werke* (11 vols.; Gotha: Berthes, 1962-1873); idem, *Geschichte des Rationalismus* (Berlin: Wiegandt & Grieben, 1865); idem, *Die Glaubwürdigkeit der evangelischen Geschichte* (Hamburg: Friedrich Perthes, 1837); idem, *Kommentar zur Briefe an die Hebraer* (Hamburg: Friedrich Perthes, 1836; ET: *A Commentary on the Epistle to the Hebrews* [2 vols.; Edinburgh: T. Clark, 1842]); idem, *Kommentar zum Evangelio Johannis* (Hamburg: Friedrich Perthes, 1827; ET: *Commentary on the Gospel of John* [Philadelphia: Smith, English, 1859]); idem, *Die Propheten und ihre Weissagungen* (Gotha: Berthes, 1860); idem, *Uebersetzung und Auslagung der Psalmen für Geistliche und laien der Christlichen Kirche* (Halle: Eduard Anton, 1843; ET: *A Translation and Commentary of the Book of Psalms* [Philadelphia: William S. & Alfred Martien, 1858]).

Studies. W. Baird, *History of New Testament Research from Deism to Tübingen* (Minneapolis: Fortress, 1992); K. Barth, *Protestant Theology in the Nineteeth Century: Its Background and History* (Valley Forge, PA: Judson, 1973); T. H. Olbricht, "Charles Hodge as an American New Testament Interpreter," *JPH* 57 (1979) 117-33; Kim, Sung-Bong, "Die Lehre von der Sunde und vom Versohner" in *Tholucks theologische Entwicklung in seiner Berliner Zeit* (Europaische Hochschulschriften, Reihe 33; New York: P. Lang, 1992); E. Robinson, "Theological Education in Germany," *BR* 1 (1831) 1-51, 201-26, 409-51, 613-37; K. Toivianen, *August Tholuckin Teologinen antropologia* (Helsinki: Suomalaisen, 1968); L. Witte, *Das Leben D. Friedrich August Gotttreu Tholuck's* (2 vols.; Bielefeld: Velhagen & Klasing, 1884-1886); W. Zilz, *August Tholuck: Professor, Prediger, Seelsorger* (Giessen: Brunnen, 1962).

T. H. Olbricht

Von Hofmann, Johann Christian Konrad (1810-1877)

Pietism of the nineteenth century was driven by the belief that a personal experience of faith lay at the heart of Christianity. To understand revelation as witnessed in Scripture, the exercise of human reason was not enough. One had to be part of the community of faith and share in its experience of rebirth. Without that rebirth whatever knowledge reason gained through investigation of the Scriptures was inadequate. Genuine theology could not be practiced by confining intellectual analysis to the facts of the biblical story. To do so was to miss the inner truth and driving force of the gospel. To this belief the Erlangen theologians gave their allegiance, however reconciled they may have been to the spirit of the modern age. Their stance toward historical criticism of the Bible was open yet wary, a combination of characteristics that appears most clearly in the work of Johann Christian Konrad von Hofmann.

Life. Von Hofmann was born in Nuremberg on December 21, 1810, to parents attracted to the German Awakening and shaped by the Pietism of Bavaria and Swabia. Following secondary school education, he studied at the University of Erlangen, where he came under the influence of advocates of the Awakening. He completed his studies at Berlin, where for a time he came under the spell of the historian Leopold von Ranke (1795-1886). In 1832 von Hofmann was appointed instructor in an Erlangen gymnasium, and from 1835 to 1841 he served as nonsalaried university instructor and associate professor at Erlangen University. After three years as full professor at Rostock, he returned in the same capacity to Erlangen, where he served until his retirement. For three years von Hofmann was representative to the Bavarian state legislature, attacked by contemporaries for his commitment to parliamentary democracy. He died at Erlangen on December 20, 1877.

Biblical Interpretation. Two antithetical forces furnished von Hofmann the occasion for his work. The one was the new science represented by David Friedrich *Strauss; the other was Protestant scholasticism. Hofmann saw in Strauss an enemy of the Christian religion "who maliciously drives nails into its living flesh to kill it, and thus adds the passion of Christianity to that of our Lord" (in Hirsch, 5:424). But it was Protestant scholasticism that evoked the greater reaction. Von Hofmann opposed the legalism he believed to be inherent in its structure, as well as in its doctrine of verbal inspiration—a conception, he contended, that obviated understanding of the Bible's historical character (von Hofmann 1959, 14-16). Von Hofmann asserted that to make the Bible as Word of God dependent upon the belief that it was without error, even regarding data available to natural knowledge, would be to assign it characteristics attributable to God alone. On the other hand von Hofmann rejected the popular definition of the Bible as containing the word of God, labeling it an error that resulted in distancing religious from nonreligious truth in the Bible.

Opposition to the new science as well as to Protestant scholasticism had its consequence in von Hofmann's hermeneutical theory. Over against the new science von Hofmann insisted that the interpretation of Scripture required faith or "spiritual understanding." He wrote:

A complete lack of presuppositions on the part of the interpreter would be unthinkable. It is impossible for the interpreter to be neither Christian nor non-Christian, neither religious nor irreligious, but merely interpreter. He approaches Scripture as a person with a definite character and nature and experience, not as a blank sheet upon which Scripture inscribes itself. (von Hofmann 1841, 1:14)

Over against scholasticism von Hofmann contended that biblical hermeneutics was based upon the general principles of interpretation. These principles, however, required an addition that facilitated their application in harmony with the demands made by the Bible's peculiar subject matter. The Bible's distinctive character, then, and not the principles of its interpretation, created the hermeneutical task (von Hofmann 1841, 1:13, 15).

Von Hofmann located the addition in the fact of the Christian's rebirth, "the most immediate witness of God himself." This witness was mediated through church and Scripture and yet was independent of either, thus with the right to set its content alongside Scripture and church (cited in Steck, 19-20). Far from regarding this fact of experience as self-generated, von Hofmann nevertheless insisted that the church did not arise through doctrinal statements but through the sum of individual experiences of personal relationship to God. This fact, von Hofmann asserted, guaranteed certainty in the face of a skepticism that no adducing of proofs could ever effect.

Task and Method of Theology. According to von Hofmann, theology's task was to explicate the fact of rebirth, to give it scientific expression. And since this experience was mediated through church and Scripture, the decisive scientific test of theology was the spontaneous coming together of the fact of rebirth, of Scripture and of church in a harmonious unity. The movement among these three totalities was thus reciprocal: When interpreted as a unified whole, Bible and church ratified the fact and vice versa. But the fact of rebirth remained the point of departure. To this reciprocal movement corresponded von Hofmann's method, a method he entitled the Two Ways.

The First Way was the experience of the relation to God. The statement for which von Hofmann may be best remembered reads:

Theology is a truly free science, free in God, only when precisely that which makes a Christian to be a Christian, his own independent relation to God, makes the theologian to be a theologian through disciplined self-knowledge and self-expression: when I the Christian am for me the theologian the essential material of my science. (von Hofmann 1959, 10) The Second Way von Hofmann described as the "historical way," setting forth the totality transmitted in the Bible. These Two Ways led to the scientific certainty of those facts without which there could be no theology.

Von Hofmann devoted his life and energy to the elucidation of the Second Way, the way of the *Heilsgeschichte*, or history of God's saving acts. The Bible was the primary object of research for this Way, not merely because it recorded but because it shared in the "miracle" of salvation history. The Reformation, von Hofmann contended, gave legitimation to this Second Way, since it restored the "historical" meaning of Scripture to its proper place (von Hofmann 1959, 9, 28-29, 47-48).

In his first great work, *Weissagung und Erfüllung im Alten und im Neuen Testamente (Prophecy and Fulfillment in the Old and New Testament)*, von Hofmann described the whole sweep of salvation history:

In Act One occurred humanity's creation and thus the possibility of sinning. Act Two was marked by the assurance that the continuance of human life should be a means toward salvation. The Third Act depicted the granting of grace to the righteous, an act leading to the great flood. In Act Four occurred the separation of the single family of Israel. In subsequent acts of the *Heilsgeschichte*, Israel received the law by which it assumed national peculiarity. In midst of this community Jesus appeared. With his birth a new nature was created, and the history of God with humanity came to preliminary conclusion. Sent from the Father, Christ was the object of his love, but having assumed sinful human nature he was also subject to the Father's wrath. Holy by virtue of his origin in God, the Son as incarnate was obliged to be obedient in order to be holy.

Christ as holy had thus assumed an existence for which his divine nature was not suited. But precisely for this reason human nature could become new. (see Hausleiter, 38, 47)

This interpretation of Christ's obedience led to the rejection of traditional views of the atonement. Any conception of the atonement, wrote von Hofmann, must begin from the fact of God's originating love: God loved humanity on the basis of what he intended to do in Christ. The atonement was therefore not something God would have needed had he not willed to need it. It was a "self-satisfaction of his love with its ground only in himself" (von Hofmann 1857, 2:99). At the end of von Hofmann's *heilsgeschichtlich* scheme stood Israel with its new Jerusalem, descending intact from heaven after the one thousand years' reign.

However attracted to the great thinkers of his day, von Hofmann was not a philosopher, and throughout his writings he insisted that the history of what occurred in God was not part of the *Heilsgeschichte*. He had, however, a certain affinity for tracing the *Heilsgeschichte* to a decision made within the Godhead. Von Hofmann wrote: "The Triune God assumed into the relation within the Godhead the contradiction between the living and holy God and a sinful humanity subject to death, in order to resolve that contradiction and redeem humanity from sin and death" (in Hausleiter, 38-39).

But if this Second Way had its presupposition in life within the Godhead, it nevertheless assumed the First Way, or experience of faith. The Second Way thus recapitulated the First. More, it was "authenticated" by it. All "essential events of Holy History" had to be contained within the experience itself.

Human nature as the nature of the eternal Son; the contradiction between God and humanity taken up into the relation within the Godhead; events between the fall and restoration as reflecting the relationship interior to the divine life—this "eternal" presupposition furnishes a clue to von Hofmann's spiritual ancestry, to the influence of Jakob Böhme (1575-1624), the great seventeenth-century mystic and metaphysician, whose system may have given him "the most and the best" (Hirsch, 5:420-21, 426).

Von Hofmann had encountered Böhme through contact with Friedrich Schelling (1775-1854), in whose circle of ideas he had once lived with relish. But however von Hofmann may have encountered Böhme, no modern Protestant theologian before or after von Hofmann so accented corporeality as the historical medium of the life of God. And none before or after Böhme, with the exception of Hegel, had countered the deist separation of heaven and earth with the assertion that God had willed corporeality, the Incarnation, from eternity. More, Böhme had written that if the hidden God had not willed creaturely life and thus differentiation, the single will of God would not have become known to itself. To the question How can all this be known? Böhme had replied: Only one who has put on Christ's God-manhood as his own may know him. This faith was a recapitulation of the Unconditioned's search for conditioned form, a repetition of the suffering of God, the overcoming of the dialectic of the earthly and heavenly in a new birth.

Significance. The ideas originating with or introduced by von Hofmann have continued to influence theology to the present. Following more than a hundred years of theologies of the Old as separated from theologies of the New Testament, scholars have once more taken up the problem of the relation between the two Testaments. In face of the division of the Testaments from Georg Lorenz Bauer (1755-1806) in the eighteenth to Rudolf *Bultmann in the twentieth century, it was von Hofmann who insisted upon a theology of both.

In opposition to the scholastic view, which he believed ignored the difference between the presentations of salvation in Old and New Testaments, von Hofmann wrote that what is recorded in the Old is a history reaching toward realization. Its record was thus to be interpreted teleologically. For this reason there could be no correct "spiritual" understanding of the Old Testament if historical interpretation were omitted. Von Hofmann nonetheless opposed a purely historical approach, according to which Jewish religion served merely as one among many antecedents of Christianity. Every Old Testament detail had to be oriented to the conclusion that in Jesus Christ the history of God with humanity came to preliminary completion. Viewed "teleologically," the Old Testament mirrored the same divine will to love as does the New, a will intent on realizing itself despite all opposition, an intention marking the whole sweep of the *Heilsgeschichte.*

A host of students in the United States were weaned from scholastic orthodoxy through introduction to *Heilsgeschichte.* Otto A. Piper's *God in History* (1939), John Bright's *The Kingdom of God* (1953), George Ernest *Wright's *The Book of the Acts of God* (1957) and Oscar *Cullmann's *Christ and Time* (ET 1962) all belonged to that flood of literature for which von Hofmann furnished stimulus. In his foreword to the translation of von Hofmann's *Interpreting the Bible,* Piper wrote, "He had not only defined the starting point of Protestant exegesis, but also discovered with ingenious certainty what the basic attitude and the guiding perspective are that are consonant with the Christian faith without in any way hampering the legitimate scholarly treatment of the biblical books" (von Hofmann 1959, ix).

From such stimulus as von Hofmann furnished with his rejection of traditional interpretations of Christ's death and his appeal to the Reformation in support derived a new period of research on Martin *Luther, a research begun with the Erlangen edition of Luther's works (1826-1857), continued in the work of Theodosius Harnack (1817-1889), Ernst Troeltsch (1865-1923), and others, and reaching maturity with the Weimar edition

(1883-) and the studies of Karl Holl (1866-1926).

The criticisms of von Hofmann are legion. From one quarter has come the attack upon his wedding of faith and criticism in the Two Ways as inconsistent. From another the reproach for first lifting out from Bible and church what he allegedly derived from experience. From still another the reproach of anthropocentrism, of describing the human without restriction as subject of the entire theological enterprise.

As to the *Heilsgeschichte* itself, von Hofmann has been perennially blamed for lack of clarity regarding its relation to the remainder of human history, although he did make an attempt at synthesis. For example, in the first thesis of his theological dissertation, he wrote that no other difference existed between universal and ecclesiastical history than the difference between Gentiles to be gathered to the church and the church to be extended among the Gentiles (quoted in Steck, 22).

Finally, the assumption that all of history is evident to the eye of faith would lead to an idea that von Hofmann would never have embraced, the idea that the course of history as such is evident, an idea resulting in the notion of the signal role of a single nation within the *Heilsgeschichte*, climaxing in the horrors of the twentieth century. Attention to salvation history as theocentric, which allows that God is free to act, even to reverse what God has begun, furnishes effective reaction to such perversions.

BIBLIOGRAPHY

Works. J. C. K. von Hofmann, *Encylopädie der Theologie,* ed. H. J. Bestmann (Nördlingen: C. H. Beck, 1871); idem, *Interpreting the Bible* (Minneapolis: Augsburg, 1959); idem, *Der Schriftbeweis, Ein Theologischer Versuch* (Nördlingen: C. H. Beck, 1857); idem, *Schutzschriften für eine neue Weise, alte Wahrheit zu Lehren* (4 vols.; Nördlingen: C. H. Beck, 1856-59); idem, *Weissagung und Erfüllung im alten und im neuen Testamente* (2 vols.; Nördlingen: Beck'schen Buchhandlung, 1841); idem, "Die wissenschaftliche Lehre von Christi Versöhnungswerk" in *Grundlinien der Theologie Joh. Christ. K. v. Hofmanns, in seiner eigenen Darstellung,* ed. J. Hausleiter (Leipzig: A. Deichert'sche Verlagsbuchhandlung Nachfolger, 1910) 34. *Studies.* J. Hausleiter, ed., *Grundlinien der Theologie Joh. Christ. K. v. Hofmanns, in seiner eigenen Darstellung* (Leipzig: A. Deichert'sche Verlagsbuchhandlung Nachfolger, 1910); E. Hirsch, *Geschichte der neueren Evanagelischen Theologie* (5 vols.; Gutersloh: C. Bertelsmann, 1954); K. G. Steck, "Hofmann" in *Die Idee der Heilsgeschichte* (Zollikon: Evangelischer Verlag, 1959) 19-35; K. W. Schiebler, ed., *Jacob Bohmes sämmtliche Werke* (Leipzig: Johann Ambrosius Barth, 1847).   R. A. Harrisville

Wellhausen, Julius *(1844-1918)*

Julius Wellhausen was born the son of a Lutheran pastor in Hamelin, Germany, and after completing his schooling he proceeded to Göttingen University (1862) in order to study theology. He became disenchanted with this institution for its conservative outlook and showed interest both in *Germanistik* studies and in the new critical movement, which had reshaped the study of classical (Greek and Roman) history. After reading Heinrich Ewald's *Geschichte des Volkes Israel (History of the People of Israel)* during Easter 1863, he became fired with enthusiasm for the task of presenting such a major critical piece of research. He recognized that several of Ewald's conclusions still remained provisional and that much additional work needed to be undertaken. To achieve this end he devoted himself energetically to the study of Hebrew and Semitic languages in Göttingen, where he became a privatdozent (1870). He was appointed professor in Greifswald for the teaching of Hebrew and Old Testament (1872) but resigned (1882) after strong ecclesiastical objections were raised against his critical views of the biblical history. These had been aroused in response to the publication of his *Geschichte Israels* I (Marburg, 1878; rev. ed., *Prolegomena zur Geschichte Israels* [1883; ET *Prolegomena to the History of Israel,* Edinburgh, 1885]). He then taught Semitic languages for three years in Halle before being appointed as professor in Marburg (1885). In 1892 he returned to Göttingen as professor of Semitic languages in succession to Paul de Lagarde and remained there until his death in January 1918.

Work. Wellhausen's work in the fields of biblical history and interpretation can be divided into three major areas. His early work was devoted to the study of Hebrew philology and textual criticism and more extensively to the subject of the literary structure, source analysis and chronological ordering of the material contained in the first six books of the Bible, the Hexateuch, which had been the subject of scholarly research and criticism for approximately half a century. The second area arose directly out of this and concerned a careful historical reconstruction of the rise, growth and eventual decline of the people of ancient Israel. This focused chiefly on the rise of the major institutions but contained much evaluation of the national spirit and piety of the Israelite-Jewish people and the manner in which Jewish religious history prepared for the emergence of Christianity.

After his resignation from Greifswald and his consciousness of strong church opposition to his views, Wellhausen devoted much attention to early Arab history, in particular to the life of Muhammed, the rise of Islam and its background in pre-Islamic Arabia (chiefly in publications after 1882). Though these studies only indirectly related to his biblical researches, Wellhausen displayed in his Arab studies much of the same critical insight and brilliant linguistic ability that had made such an impact in the study of the Old Testament tradition. His goal was to trace the rise of a major new religious movement against the background of a period of confusion and religious decline.

In a third and final phase of research after the turn of the century, Wellhausen devoted his attention to examining the early Christian tradition and the historical Jesus, beginning with the Gospel of Mark (1903). In these researches the same inci-

sive critical spirit and freshness were evident as in his Old Testament work, with a strong awareness of the importance of the elaboration of ideas as a criterion for establishing chronology of development. Becoming deeply skeptical about the preservation of any reliable historical tradition in the primary Christian documents, Wellhausen continued to provoke strong orthodox criticism and reactions.

After Wellhausen's death, several of the basic questions that he had raised in New Testament research were reformulated and used for fresh attempts to reconstruct details concerning the history that underlies the Gospels. A parallel line, in which Wellhausen had participated strongly, focused on the Aramaic background of the Synoptic Gospels and Acts of the Apostles. In Old Testament research his source analysis of the Hexateuch was increasingly supplemented by form-critical and tradition-historical methods in which the smaller units, rather than the larger supposed documents, were examined, especially by Hermann Gunkel and Hugo Gressmann. More directly historical issues became refocused around the developing science of archaeology of the biblical lands. Nevertheless the influence of the work of Wellhausen as a pioneer biblical historian has remained considerable.

Sources of the Hexateuch. To a significant degree the primary problem for the reconstruction of the historical development of Israelite religion during the nineteenth century lay in the unraveling of the complex literary structure of the first six books of the Old Testament, which were regarded as constituting a Hexateuch. By the first quarter of that century critical research had established that a careful evaluation of the date and historical reliability of its constituent source documents was a primary necessity. Only after this had been achieved could a history of ancient Israel be attempted comparable to what was being envisaged for the study of the ancient Greek and Roman empires.

Biblical scholars recognized a sharp disparity between the picture of an advanced and complex religion with elaborate cultus, portrayed in the books of Exodus, Leviticus, Numbers and 1 and 2 Chronicles, and the much simpler religion, with widespread disunity, portrayed in Judges and 1 and 2 Samuel. Wilhelm Martin Leberecht *de Wette had established a historical link between the book of Deuteronomy and Josiah's reform in 622 B.C., and he used this as a hinge point to establish a major rise in the power and prestige of the Jerusalem temple and its worship.

That there were different literary sources present in the remaining (non-Deuteronomic) material was accepted among critical scholars, but opinions varied between recognizing two or three primary narrative sources or a multiplicity of small units that had been added to a central core text. These came to be described as the documentary hypothesis and the fragment hypothesis, with increasing adherence to the former.

A major stimulus toward the acceptance of the documentary hypothesis came with the rather speculative reconstruction of Israel's religious development by Wilhelm Vatke (1835). This received a measure of support from the more radical Dutch scholar Abraham Kuenen, who sought to trace a consistent evolutionary pattern of development. Nevertheless a really convincing picture of the analysis and structure of the Hexateuchal text eluded scholars. It was to this problem that Wellhausen directed his attention in the years from 1870, publishing a masterly series of essays on the subject that were subsequently combined into book form as *The Composition of the Hexateuch and the Historical Books of the Old Testament (Die Composition des Hexateuchs und der historischen Bücher des Alten Testaments;* most originally published in journal articles in 1876-77).

Wellhausen had been anticipated in his major reassessment of the literary growth of the Hexateuch by the French scholar Eduard Reuss and Reuss's German pupil Karl Heinrich Graf. Yet neither scholar had

published extensively. The major innovation of these scholars, which Wellhausen now advanced and set out with great skill and clarity, was a recognition that the source that had been labeled the First Elohist and that scholars had, with few exceptions, regarded as of early origin was in fact a late composition. This source is now universally called the Priestly (or P) source, although Wellhausen called it Q (for *Quattuor,* since it was the fourth major source and portrayed Israel's history around four major covenants). It was recognized by Wellhausen as of postexilic origin and contained most of the Mosaic ritual law code. Accordingly this religion of a Book of Law was regarded as later than the time of the great prophets and representative of a legalistic-Judaistic type of faith.

Thus Wellhausen arrived at what came to be termed a four-document hypothesis for an explanation of the literary origin and growth of the Hexateuch. Virtually the entire Hexateuch was included in such major documentary source analysis, and Wellhausen's original studies extended further to cover the books of Samuel and Kings. These source documents had been skillfully combined by scribes whose own contribution was minimal and almost exclusively editorial. Within a twenty-year period after its publication, Wellhausen's hypothesis became widely adopted in Europe and America as the most plausible literary explanation for Hexateuchal origins. It could then be used, as Wellhausen had intended, as a basis for reconstructing the historical course of Israel's religious development.

History of Israelite-Jewish Religion. Wellhausen's primary goal in his research into the literary formation of the Hexateuch had been to reconstruct the actual historical course of Israel's national and religious development. To this task he devoted great skills as an oriental linguist and text critic, publishing in addition to the works mentioned important studies on the books of 1 and 2 Samuel and the Twelve Prophets, where major text-critical problems were present.

However, it was as a historian in the German tradition of B. G. Niebuhr and T. Mommsen that Wellhausen wished to work. He recognized especially that accounts of religious beginnings, known almost exclusively from sources composed within that religion and therefore promoting its claims, may appear very different when they are seen from outside and in a more neutral critical light. The commendatory and apologetic purpose of primary religious documents will hide the more complex tensions and conflicts of the situations in which they were written. So it may be almost impossible to trace more than an outline sketch of the work of such religious founders as Moses, Jesus and Muhammed or account for the rise of such great monotheistic religions. Throughout his research Wellhausen remained profoundly convinced of the immense importance to humankind of the rise of a practical, ethically responsible monotheism. He viewed the break between Christianity and Pharisaic Judaism as a major turning point in which the historical Jesus, himself a Jew, had become embroiled.

The great impact of Wellhausen's research into textual and literary questions of the Bible first began to be seriously felt after the publication of his *Geschichte Israels* I (1878). This was, as its later title *Prolegomena* implies, a detailed reconstruction of the major religious and political institutions of ancient Israel. It traced the nation's development through these institutions, especially those of kingship, priesthood, the sacred ark and tent of meeting, and all their attendant rituals. The reconstruction used the evidence of the recently established documentary analysis of the Hexateuch, the problems of which had absorbed so much scholarly attention for three-quarters of a century. In substantial measure it was the combination of a fresh literary analysis with a clear presentation of results that made Wellhausen's work so attractive. It appealed to ideas of historical consistency and natural evolutionary development tracing a process whereby simple forms of religion became increasingly elaborate and complex.

Wellhausen went on to publish a short summary sketch of his reconstructed picture of Israel's religious life in a long article "Israel" in *Encyclopaedia Britannica* (1880; the privately printed German original was reprinted in 1965) and, in a more extensive form, in a volume entitled *Israelite-Jewish History (Israelitische-Jüdische Geschichte*, 1894). Both publications served to familiarize an international body of scholars with Wellhausen's views, making the *Prolegomena* easily the best known, if not the most widely read, work of Old Testament historical criticism. It won widespread support but also drew much opposition, particularly from Jewish scholars who found its tendency to denigrate later Jewish religious developments as offensive. Orthodox and conservative Christian scholars also reacted against Wellhausen's views, sensing that they sought only a secular, nonrevelatory model of Israel's history.

Origins of Christianity. Wellhausen was deeply and genuinely interested in the origins of the world's great monotheistic religions and saw their rise as important intellectual and cultural developments. His reconstruction of Israelite-Jewish history had led him to regard the postexilic, law-centered religion of Judaism as a decline from the higher prophetic insights of the earlier period. As early as 1874 he had published a short study on early Judaism entitled *The Pharisees and the Sadducees (Die Pharisäer und die Sadducäer)*. He believed that Jesus and the early church had recaptured the old prophetic spirit, reacting sharply against the narrow and enmeshed legalism of Pharisaic Judaism. He embarked on a series of studies to examine the Semitic Aramaic background of the New Testament tradition (1895, 1896, 1899) and then turned to provide a critique of "The Gospel Behind the Gospels." These began with the Gospel of Mark (1903); Matthew and Luke (1904) and *An Introduction to the First Three Gospels (Einleitung in die drei ersten Evangelien*, 1905). He continued with studies of the Apocalypse (1907) and the Gospel of John (1908). He finally published *A Critical Analysis of the Acts of the Apostles* (*Kritische Analyse der Apostelgeschichte*, 1914).

Wellhausen was convinced that it was essential to reconsider the traditions that underlie the written Gospels, of which Mark was the earliest. Then next in date and importance came *The Sayings of Jesus* source (usually Q = *Quelle*). This has clearly been used by both Matthew and Luke in different ways, with Luke being the later composition. The Gospel of John represented a parallel tradition, with only a brief historical kernel. Much of the original gospel has undergone extensive expansion. Both Mark and the Sayings source contained strong evidence of Aramaisms, though this can only be used with care as a criterion for establishing the authenticity of a saying or narrative report. The early Christians too were a Judean, Aramaic-speaking community that was broken up after the martyrdom of James. Wellhausen believed that Mark was a Greek translation of an Aramaic original, built up chiefly around two sources. Neither contained much in the way of reliable historical information.

In the first decade of the twentieth century New Testament studies were passing through a transitional stage, with careful examination of the Semitic (Judean) background of the Gospels and Acts beginning to emerge and the full impact of the nineteenth-century attempts to unravel the so-called Synoptic Problem being assimilated and furthered. Wellhausen's research into the Old Testament tradition had encouraged his perception of a sharp contrast between the old, nation-oriented outlook of the prophets and the later hardened legalism of emergent Judaism in the postexilic period. It is not surprising therefore that he saw the rise of the early Christian church as a revival of these tensions that had arisen in the Old Testament period. It is significant that Wellhausen followed Ewald's perspective in regarding the New Testament and the Christian church as the true fulfill-

ment and goal of the entire biblical tradition (Wellhausen's *Israelite-Jewish History* had concluded with a chapter on Jesus).

However, when they are examined critically, the Gospels were held to be highly tendentious documents, written to promote the separation of the church from its Jewish cradle and containing little by way of reliable historical information from which a reconstruction of the life of Jesus could be attempted. The post-Easter resurrection faith of the early apostles has been projected back into even the earliest strata of the traditions from which the Gospels have been composed. That Jesus was a Jew was an unquestioned fact and that he had reacted sharply against the currently authorized Jewish tradition of his day could be discerned within those aspects of his teaching that remained trustworthy. He had not proclaimed himself to be a messiah in the conventional, expected sense but had aroused the anger of the central authorities, who had agitated for his crucifixion. Only toward the latter part of the first century had antagonism between the Roman government and the church arisen, by which time the separation of the church from Judaism had become an accomplished fact.

Significance. As a historian Wellhausen had little in common with the history of religions movement that the early Rudolf *Bultmann and Wilhelm Bousset espoused, yet he also differed sharply from the theories of a consistent eschatological-apocalyptic Jesus as seen by Albert Schweitzer. Much of the brilliance of his work lay in his careful analysis of sources and the skill with which he traced a sequence of ideological developments demonstrating how the progress of ideas could be interpreted. Overall his study of the history of Israel remained the most influential aspect of his work, not least because of the skill with which he handled a complex series of literary-analytical questions. Behind this, however, lay important historiographic principles that can be seen to have been rooted in the German Enlightenment. Wellhausen rejected any rigid philosophical schema for interpreting history, even religious history, seeking to work from close analysis of the primary documents that were attainable.

BIBLIOGRAPHY

Works. J. Wellhausen, *The Book of Psalms* (New York: Dodd, Mead, 1898); idem, *Die Composition des Hexateuchs und der historischen Bücher des Alten Testaments* (2d ed.; Berlin: Georg Reimer, 1889); idem, *Einleitung in die drei ersten Evangelien* (Berlin: Reimer, 1905); idem, *Das Evangelium Johannis* (Berlin: Reimer, 1908); idem, *Das Evangelium Lucae* (Berlin: Reimer, 1904); Idem, *Das Evangelium Marci* (Berlin: Reimer, 1903); idem, *Das Evangelium Matthaei* (Berlin: Reimer, 1904); idem, *Geschichte Israels* (Berlin: G. Reimer, 1878); idem, *Israelitsche und jüdische Geschichte* (Berlin: Reimer, 1894 [1880]); idem, *Kritische Analyse der Apostelgeschichte* (Berlin: Weidmann, 1914); idem, *Prolegomena zur ätesten Geschichte des Islams* (Berlin: Reimer, 1899); idem, *Prolegomena to the History of Israel* (Atlanta: Scholars Press, 1994); idem, *Der Text der Bücher Samuelis* (Göttingen: Vandenhoeck & Ruprecht, 1871).
    Studies. J. Blenkinsopp, *The Pentateuch: An Introduction to the First Five Books of the Bible* (New York: Doubleday, 1992); F. Boschwitz, *Julius Wellhausen: Motive und Masstabe seiner Geschichtsschreibung* (Darmstadt, 1968 [1938]), a critical review of Wellhausen's historiographic method; R. E. Clements, *A Hundred Years of Old Testament Study* (Philadelphia: Westminster, 1976). *Julius Wellhausen and His Prolegomena to the History of Israel* (*Semeia* 25, 1982), for the main outlines of Wellhausen's works and valuable background studies. K. Marti, ed., *Studien zur semitischen Philologie und Religionsgeschichte: Julius Wellhausen zum siebzigsten Geburtstag* (BZAW 27; Giessen: Töpelmann, 1914) 351-68, a bibliography of Wellhausen's writings, compiled by A. Rahlfs.   R. E. Clements

Wesley, John *(1703-1791)*

John Wesley, a fellow of Lincoln College, Oxford, and a priest of the Church of England, was one of the leaders of the evangelical revival in Great Britain during the eighteenth century. It was his intention "to reform the nation, particularly the Church; and to spread scriptural holiness over the land." Despite his efforts to avoid schism, his Methodist societies evolved into a number of Methodist, Wesleyan and holiness churches around the world.

Context. In the first third of the eighteenth century English Christianity was at a low point. The latitudinarian movement, which had sought to heal the wounds of the civil war and incorporate the new science into the culture, had moved toward a shallow moralism. The church failed to take steps to respond to population shifts to the cities. Theologically the challenge of deism was the focus of some of its best minds. The evangelical revival sought to battle nominal Christianity and to find a way for believers to experience God's grace in their hearts.

Wesley was the fifteenth child of Samuel Wesley, rector of Epworth, and his wife, Susanna Annesley Wesley. Both Samuel and Susanna were children of men who were ejected from their livings by the Act of Uniformity (1662). Yet Wesley's parents had both turned to High-Church Anglicanism, and the Wesley children were reared in a devoutly Christian home with strong tendencies toward the Tory side of the Church of England. Susanna was well-educated, and she was a significant influence on John throughout her life.

Influences. A number of influences helped shape Wesley's theology and approach to Scripture. His parents had been reared in the Puritan tradition. He was exposed to the religious societies and Anglican thought at home. In 1725 he committed himself to the priesthood and started a serious study of the holy living tradition, reading the works of William Law, Thomas á Kempis and Jeremy Taylor. He became a fellow of Lincoln College, and during his years in Oxford he was exposed to the Non-jurors and those who stressed the importance of the early church. The formation of a group of students, sometimes called the "Holy Club," to study and care for the poor led to the name *methodist* being applied to Wesley's efforts.

In 1735 Wesley, his brother Charles (1707-1788), and two other members of the Oxford Holy Club went to Georgia. There John served as pastor of the church in Savannah and made attempts to convert native Americans. During the journey to Georgia, he encountered a group of Moravians. He was deeply impressed with their faithful behavior during a storm and inquired about their religious experience. In his discussions with them, he was driven back to the sixteenth-century homilies protected in the Thirty-Nine Articles of the Church of England and thereby rediscovered his own doctrinal roots.

During 1738 and 1739 Wesley's theology was solidified. In the process, however, he came to doubt his own salvation. Under Moravian tutelage he felt his heart "strangely warmed" at a meeting in Aldersgate Street on May 24, 1738. In this experience he said, "I felt I did trust in Christ, Christ alone for salvation: And an assurance was given me, that he had taken away my sins, even mine, and saved me from the law of sin and death." Wesley came to believe that this experience of the assurance of salvation was an important privilege all believers should have.

Wesley broke with the Moravians and then stumbled upon several techniques for spreading the revival. In 1739 he started preaching out of doors to large crowds. He formed Methodist societies wherever he preached and soon developed the idea of class meetings where persons watched over each other and helped them progress toward full salvation. Despite his initial objections, he soon allowed lay preachers to serve as his assistants in the preaching ministry. In spite of strong objection and some mob violence, Methodism grew as a reform movement within the Church of England. In 1784 Wesley made provision for a separate Methodist Episcopal Church in America by ordaining two men for the ministry and by setting apart Thomas Coke to the office of general superintendent, later called bishop. He also provided that year for the continuation of the Methodist societies in Great Britain after his death.

Major Writings. Wesley's major theo-logical work was published in his *Sermons on Several Occasions, Explanatory Notes Upon the New Testament* and several treatises. The first four volumes of sermons, the notes and the minutes of his annual conferences of Methodist preachers became the doctrinal standards for his movement.

Wesley sought to expound "plain truth for plain people," avoiding unnecessary "philosophical speculations." Most of his writings were occasional, directed to a particular audience with a particular purpose in mind. He published hymnals, devotional tracts and a magazine for the use of common persons.

Wesley's theological method was to insist on the authority of Scripture. His often quoted phrase "let me be *homo unius libri*" ("a man of one book") emphasized the importance the Bible should play in one's life and thought. However, the phrase does not mean one should ignore other sources of religious knowledge. Wesley used classical Latin and Greek quotations in addition to Christian theologians in all of his writings. Rather, Wesley insisted frequently that the Bible, as the oracles of God, should be the ultimate standard for Christian faith and practice. In his mind, however, all sources of truth were unified. Wesley understood that four other authorities formed a unified locus of authority along with Scripture. Scripture rightly interpreted is always reasonable; it is best interpreted by the early church; it was most fully expressed in his time by the doctrine of the Church of England; and it will be realized in the experience of believers. Thus this fivefold locus of Scripture, reason, the early church, the Church of England and Christian experience all work together to determine the truth. While Scripture alone is the authority, it is never alone.

Wesley's understanding of these authorities points to a distinctive understanding of the way of salvation. The various aspects of this doctrine, seen as covering the whole of the Christian life, form the main subject matter of his publications. Wesley insisted that salvation is a process consisting of several parts: creation in the image of God, original sin, repentance, justification and sanctification. Every step we take in this process depends on the grace of God and the faith with which we respond. Within justification, he stressed the doctrines of the new birth and assurance of faith, which he called "the witness of the Spirit" (based on Rom 8:16). His doctrine of sanctification was controversial in the eighteenth century because he stressed the possibility of entire sanctification by grace in this life. While Wesley denied advocating "sinless" perfection, he did suggest that God's grace through our faith could enable human beings to live in such a way that all of their conscious motivations were controlled by the love of God and love of neighbor. While it is not clear whether such a gift of entire sanctification usually comes instantaneously or gradually, Wesley clearly allowed for both.

In addition Wesley dealt with practical issues appropriate to the leadership of an ongoing revival within a larger church. He discussed sacramental issues under the topic "The Means of Grace" and talked about the practices of class meetings, societies and annual conferences and the issues of avoiding schism within the church.

Hermeneutics. Wesley understood the purpose of biblical interpretation to be the salvation of souls. God has revealed the way to heaven in Scripture, and that one book will enable us to get there. We are saved by the grace of God, and Wesley conceived of studying Scripture as one of the means of grace mandated by Christ. He interpreted John 5:39, "Search the Scriptures" (AV), as a commandment to find Christ in the Bible.

Wesley's rules for interpreting Scripture are best summarized as follows: (1) One should "speak as the oracles of God." In quoting this phrase from 1 Peter 4:11 (AV), Wesley seeks "always to express Scripture sense in Scripture phrase." Thus his sermons are filled with scriptural quotations used in a free-flowing manner as well as more sustained arguments from particular texts. In many respects Wesley argued for a minimal amount of interpretation, preferring to let the text speak for itself wherever possible.

(2) "Use the literal sense unless it leads to a contradiction with another Scripture or implies an absurdity." Along with most Protestant interpreters of the eighteenth century, Wesley insisted on the priority of the literal sense over allegorical or spiritual senses. However, he acknowledged places where an absurdity requires an alternate reading to preserve the unity of the Scripture's teaching.

(3) "Interpret the text with regard to its literary context." Wesley sought to consider the proper literary context to avoid misinterpretation. In one such example, he argued that Exodus 14:13, "Stand still and see the salvation of God," cannot be used to avoid the means of grace. Rather, "standing still" means marching forward with all one's might when the text is read in the context of the whole book of Exodus. Thus even this verse should reinforce the practice of prayer, holy communion and the study of Scripture.

(4) "Scripture interprets Scripture, according to the analogy of faith and by parallel passages." In his application of this rule Wesley stood in the mainstream of Protestant interpreters of his time. No external authority provides a corrective to Scripture—the Bible must be self-interpreting. One does this by appealing to the general tenor of the whole text. Wesley followed others by calling this general tenor "the analogy of faith." This is a technical term that appears in the writings of a number of Protestant interpreters of the sixteenth and seventeenth centuries. Like them, Wesley based it on Romans 12:6, which says that prophecy should be according to the "analogy" of one's faith. While the English translations of his day use the term *proportion,* Wesley preserved the older understanding in order to talk about the wholeness of Scripture. In one notable sermon, "Free Grace," Wesley argued that any particular passage that appears to teach pre-

destination cannot possibly mean that a loving God condemned some of his creatures to eternal punishment unconditionally. Such an interpretation violates the general tenor of the whole Bible, which says that God is love and that God desires the salvation of all.

(5) "Commandments are covered promises." Wesley understood the unity of law and gospel in both Testaments to be such that every time God gives a commandment, it is at the same time a hidden promise that God will enable the persons to do what God had commanded. In a similar way, all promises are also covered commandments. The power of grace is such that God would help anyone who accepted God's grace by faith to accomplish God's will. Thus Matthew 5:48 is best understood as both commandment and promise. Wesley translated it, "Therefore ye shall be perfect," in place of the Authorized Version's imperative form, "Be ye therefore perfect." He thereby preserved the ambiguity between the imperative and future indicative that exists in the Greek text.

(6) "Interpret literary devices appropriately." Wesley paid attention to the literary styles and devices the biblical authors used. At various points he called attention to metaphors, synecdoche, gradation and the use of different voices by the same author.

(7) "Seek the most original text and the best translation." Wesley followed closely the work of Johann Albrecht *Bengel (1687-1752), one of the foremost text critics of that time. Wesley knew that the Greek text could be improved and that a better English translation was important. His *Explanatory Notes Upon the New Testament* included a new translation of the text with many improvements, some of which have found their way into the most recent English translations. Most notably, he translated *makarioi* in Matthew 5:1-12 as "happy." He printed the text without making each verse a separate paragraph.

Two significant contributions of Wesley's should be noted. First, he focused the interpretation of Scripture on the life of the ordinary believer. Wesley had few thoughts that were completely original. Most of his theology and interpretation of Scripture can be traced to other sources. However, his focus on the lives of poor men and women in his time led to a distinctive understanding of the meaning of classical Christian teaching in the eighteenth century.

Wesley, along with other evangelicals of his time, provided an alternative path into modernity. He resisted the criticisms of the deists and insisted that modern categories of individual experience and reason could be related to the Scripture in new ways. His focus on the gospel's fulfillment in the experience of the individual and the formation of new forms of Christian community helped create an expression of Christianity appropriate to the modern world.

Second, in his understanding of the wholeness of Scripture Wesley provided an important reading of the whole text. He claimed that the main theme of the Bible is the doctrine of salvation understood as the process from creation through sin to entire sanctification. Wesley's work offers a reminder to modern interpreters on two counts. First, it insists on the wholeness of Scripture as a primary hermeneutic tool. Second, it claims that the general tenor of Scripture is the saving activity of God and God's way of salvation that has been opened for all humankind.

BIBLIOGRAPHY

Works. J. Wesley, *Explanatory Notes Upon the New Testament* (2 vols.; Peabody, MA: Hendrickson, 1986 [1955]); idem, *The Works of John Wesley*, ed. F. Baker and R. P. Heitzenrater (15 vols.; Clarendon: Oxford University Press; Nashville: Abingdon, 1984-).

Studies. W. S. Gunter, S. J. Jones, T. A. Campbell, R. L. Miles and R. L. Maddox, *Wesley and the Quadrilateral: Renewing the Conversation* (Nashville: Abingdon, 1997); S. J. Jones, *John Wesley's Conception and Use of Scripture* (Nashville: Abingdon, 1995); D. A. D. Thorson, *The Wesleyan Quadrilateral: Scripture, Tradition, Reason and Experience as a Model of Evangelical Theology* (Grand Rapids: Zondervan, 1990).   S. J. Jones

Westcott, B(rooke) F(oss) (1825-1901), and F(enton) J(ohn) A(nthony) Hort (1828-1892)

Brooke Foss Westcott and Fenton John Anthony Hort are best known for their contributions to New Testament textual criticism, overthrowing the Textus Receptus as the basis for translation and commentary and replacing it with a reconstructed text based on more ancient readings. Hort is also remembered for his work on the English Revised Version (1881). With their colleague Joseph Barber *Lightfoot, Westcott and Hort planned a historical-critical commentary on the entire New Testament as their answer to Ferdinand Christian *Baur's Tübingen school. Lightfoot was originally to write on the Pauline epistles and Hebrews; Westcott, on the Johannine writings; and Hort, on the Synoptics, James, the Petrine epistles and Jude. Westcott eventually published commentaries on the Gospel of John, the Johannine epistles and Hebrews. Hort published no commentaries, though after his death students published fragments of his work on James (Jas 1:1—4:7), 1 Peter (1 Pet 1:1—2:17) and Revelation (Rev 1—3). By demonstrating that historical-critical tools could be applied without the radical assumptions of their Continental counterparts, the Cambridge Trio popularized the historical-critical method in Britain.

Context. The Victorian period (1837-1901) felt seismic change as the ideas of Charles Darwin (*The Origin of Species by Natural Selection,* 1859; *The Descent of Man,* 1871) and Karl Marx (*Communist Manifesto,* 1847; *Das Kapital* 1867-1894) reverberated throughout the West, redefining disciplines. Nineteenth-century biblical scholarship was not insulated from such foundation-shaking realignment. These shocks were, however, first felt as eighteenth-century scholars pioneered textual and historical criticism.

In 1720 R. Bentley, Westcott's and Hort's predecessor at Trinity College,

Cambridge, proposed a critical edition of the Greek New Testament that would abandon the Textus Receptus and reconstruct the text as it stood in the fourth century. Unfortunately his death ended the project. In 1725 Johann Albrecht *Bengel laid down critical principles for evaluating the variant readings and pioneered classification of manuscripts into large groups according to text type. Johann Salomo Semler added to textual criticism by expanding Bengel's manuscript groups to three: the Alexandrian, the Eastern and the Western text types. Westcott and Hort took over these groupings, adding a fourth, their so-called neutral text. Semler's student, Johann Jakob *Griesbach, furthered textual criticism with fifteen principles for evaluating variant readings. Griesbach was the first German scholar to abandon the Textus Receptus at many places for a critically reconstructed text (Metzger, 109-10, 112, 115, 120-21).

In the early nineteenth century, K. Lachmann (1793-1851) resurrected Bentley's project of reconstructing the fourth-century text. Hort wrote of Lachmann's first critical edition: "A new period began in 1831, when for the first time a text was constructed directly from the ancient documents without the intervention of any printed edition, and when the first systematic attempt was made to substitute scientific method for arbitrary choice in the discrimination of various readings" (Westcott and Hort, 13).

Constantin von Tischendorf (1815-1874) combed the libraries of Europe and the Middle East, uncovering ancient manuscripts and collecting variant readings. In 1862 he published the text of Codex Sinaiticus, a fourth-century Greek manuscript of the entire New Testament that he had discovered at the St. Catherine monastery in the Sinai. The Sinaiticus manuscript (א) and Codex Vaticanus (B) were to form the basis for Westcott's and Hort's neutral text. Samuel Prideaux Tregelles (1813-1875) examined most of the then-known early and important manuscripts, adding to the growing bank of variant readings (Metzger, 126-28).

Works by Semler and Johann David *Michaelis handled the origins of various New Testament writings and of the canon in a nondogmatic, consciously historical manner. In 1787 J. P. Gabler called for separating biblical theology from systematics, arguing that biblical writings be interpreted in their historical contexts and that the real differences in the writings be acknowledged (Black and Dockery, 50-52).

Drawing on Hegel's dialectic, Baur and his Tübingen school reconstructed early Christian origins. Baur's *Kirchengeschichte der 3 ersten Jahrhunderte* (1853) reveals a narrow-minded, Jewish Christian thesis (best represented by Revelation) that confronted its antithesis, Paul's law-free, universalistic gospel (best represented by Galatians, Corinthians and Romans). A synthesis was sought in the developing catholicism of the second century. The Synoptics, the Acts and most other New Testament works represented the mediating tendency of this stage. An irenic synthesis was achieved only late in the second century with John's Gospel. To answer the Tübingen challenge, the Cambridge Trio planned "an equally comprehensive survey, on basically the same critical principles, but far more soberly . . . realistically, with far greater attention to accuracy, and with far fewer presuppositions" (Neill, 34).

In Britain, Darwin's *Origin of Species by Natural Selection* (1859) cast doubts on the doctrine of special creation and a supernatural worldview. In *Essays and Reviews* (1860) seven liberal Anglicans wrote in defense of free inquiry in biblical and theological studies. Benjamin Jowett (1817-1893), master of Balliol College, Oxford, wrote on "The Interpretation of Scripture." Jowett's self-assigned task was to interpret the Bible "like any other book." He wrote that "any true doctrine of inspiration must conform to all well-ascertained facts of history or of science." Considering the varied contents of Scripture, the only tolerable principle was that of "progressive

revelation." Earlier stages of revelation were thus imperfect. The essays were condemned by a group of bishops (1861) and by synod (1864). Westcott and Hort attempted to chart a via media between the essayists and the conservative backlash (Barrett, 10).

Hort's Career. While he was at Rugby (1841-1846), Hort began a half-century friendship with classmate J. B. Mayor, later professor of classics and then of moral philosophy at King's College, London. The classicist Mayor was to publish major commentaries on James, Jude and 2 Peter, books assigned to Hort, by Macmillan, the Cambridge Trio's publisher.

At Trinity College, Cambridge (1846-1850), Hort, the most broadly educated of the Cambridge Three, studied the new triposes in both moral and natural sciences, taking the moral philosophy prize. Hort maintained a lifetime interest in the sciences, especially botany, and had both the technical background and open-minded disposition to enter the dialogue between faith and science that raged in the second half of the nineteenth century. Regrettably Hort wrote nothing on the subject. Upon graduation, Hort served as a fellow of Trinity College, Cambridge, until his marriage.

From 1857 to 1863 Hort labored as a parish priest, suffering from frequent poor health. During 1859 and 1860 the Cambridge Trio outlined the commentary plan. Hort was assigned the "historico-Judaic" writings (i.e., the Synoptics, James, Peter and Jude). In the heat of the controversy surrounding the publication of *Essays and Reviews* (1860), Westcott expressed second thoughts about assigning the Synoptics to Hort, who was in greater sympathy with the essayists' call for free inquiry in biblical studies. Hort, however, convinced Westcott and Lightfoot of his faith in the providential ordering of the human elements in Scripture, and the collaboration continued.

In 1870 Hort began work as member of the New Testament revision company, a commitment that continued until May 17, 1881, when the work was published. From

1872 to 1878 Hort served as a lecturer at Emmanuel College, Cambridge. Hort's lecture topics included Ephesians, 1 Corinthians, James and Revelation 1—3, as well as patristics. He received the B.D. and D.D. degrees in 1875. Between 1878 and 1887 Hort served as Hulsean Professor, Cambridge. His lecture topics included James, Revelation 1—3, 1 Peter, Romans and "Judaistic Christianity in the Apostolic and Following Ages."

On May 12, 1881, Hort and Westcott published *The New Testament in the Original Greek, with Introduction and Appendix.* The extensive introduction was Hort's work.

From 1887 until his death in 1892, Hort served as Lady Margaret Professor, Cambridge. Following his death, his students published his fragments on 1 Peter (1898), Judaistic Christianity (1904), James (1909) and Revelation (1908).

Westcott's Career. Schooled at Trinity College, Cambridge (1842-1848), Westcott was graduated first class classical tripos (1848). He continued at Cambridge as a fellow of the college from 1849 to 1852. After marrying, Westcott labored as assistant master and housemaster at Harrow (1852-1869). While he was at Harrow, he began his collaboration with Hort on a critical edition of the Greek New Testament (c. 1853-1881), published his *History of the New Testament Canon* (1855) and accepted the Johannine writings—his portion of the Macmillan commentary project (1859-1860). From 1870 to 1890 Westcott was Regius Professor of Divinity at Cambridge. Those years saw the publication of *The New Testament in the Original Greek* (1881), as well as commentaries on John's Gospel (1882), the Johannine epistles (1883) and Hebrews (1889). Westcott was made an honorary fellow of King's College, Cambridge, in 1892.

Westcott, like Lightfoot, rose in the ecclesiastical ranks, serving as canon of Peterborough (1869-1883) and of Westminster (1883-1890) and finally succeeding Lightfoot as Bishop of Durham (1890-1901). As bishop, Westcott was deeply concerned about the plight of workers and mediated the coal miners' strike of 1892.

Approaches and Methods. The "altogether new type" of commentaries produced by Lightfoot, Westcott and Hort inaugurated "a new era for biblical exegesis in England" that "fully accepted the demands of the new historical criticism, and yet at the same time recognized that the New Testament is made up of documents written 'from faith to faith'" (Patrick, 68). Though each member of the Cambridge Trio had his own strengths and weaknesses, all shared a common, fivefold approach to biblical interpretation (Neill, 87-88).

A Text-Critical Approach. The Cambridge Trio and contemporaries such as Henry Alford broke with tradition, basing their commentaries not on the Received Text but on a "scientifically" reconstructed text. Resting on thirty years of collaborative effort by Westcott and Hort on *The New Testament in the Original Greek,* "the textual work in the commentaries is what one would expect it to be" (Barrett, 16).

In their Greek Testament, Westcott and Hort "refined the critical methodology developed by Griesbach, Lachmann, and others, and applied it rigorously, but with discrimination, to the witnesses of the text of the New Testament" (Metzger, 129). In evaluating variants, they considered several types of evidence: the "Internal Evidence of Readings," subdivided into "Intrinsic Probability" (i.e., "what an author is likely to have written") and "Transcriptional Probability" (i.e., "what copyists are likely to have made [an author] seem to write"); the "Internal Evidence of Documents" (i.e., whether a given manuscript is generally credible); the genealogical relationship among witnesses, which calls for rejection of conflated readings; and the "Internal Evidence of Groups" (i.e., whether a given text type is generally credible; Westcott and Hort, 19-20, 31, 40, 60). In attempting to reconstruct "The New Testament in the Original Greek," Westcott and Hort gave the greatest weight to the witness of their so-called neutral text, represented by ℵ and B (225). Their critical edition was "truly epoch-breaking. They presented what is doubtless the oldest and purest form of text that could be attained with the means of information available in their day" (Metzger, 137).

A Linguistic Approach. The Cambridge Trio's exegesis entailed careful investigation of the biblical writers' language, combining attention to historical and comparative linguistics and to matters of syntax.

Westcott's and Hort's numerous word studies—some full New Testament studies, some restricted to a given book—were important precursors to those in G. Kittel's *Theologisches Wörterbuch.* All attempted to locate the New Testament writers' Greek within its proper historical place. These studies frequently included cross-references to classical writers; the Old Testament, in both Greek and Hebrew; the intertestamental Jewish literature then available; Greek writers such as Epictetus, Dio Chrysostom and Lucian, who were roughly contemporary with the New Testament writers and who shared "an affinity, in objective and tone . . . which can scarcely be found" between the New Testament writers and the census papers of Egypt (Barrett, 20); the Greek fathers, particularly to cap an argument; and Latin and Syriac translations, where they cast light on the Greek text. Hort described what such a method would necessarily entail for James: "minute study of the LXX, of Proverbs, and the kindred books of the Old Testament and perhaps still more Wisdom and Ecclesiasticus" (A. Hort, 1:470).

Such an exhaustive methodology was criticized even in the nineteenth century. Jowett complained that such "minuteness of study" had "a tendency to introduce into the text associations which are not really found there . . . making words mean too much," drawing fine shades of meaning "perhaps contained in their etymology, which are lost in common use" (*Essays and Reviews,* 391).

Westcott described his concern for syntax in the prefix to his *Hebrews* (Westcott 1889, vi):

Some perhaps will think that in the interpretation of the text undue stress is laid upon details of expression; that it is unreasonable to insist upon points of order, upon variations of tenses and words, upon subtleties of composition, upon indications of meaning conveyed by minute variations of language in books written for popular use in a dialect largely affected by foreign elements. The work of forty years has brought me to the surest conviction . . . that we do not commonly attend with sufficient care to their exact meanings.

A Historical Approach. Lightfoot and Hort saw Scripture as more than a timeless repository of monochrome dogmatic texts. For them, Scripture rather consisted of a variegated collection of books, each best understood within the historical contexts that gave rise to it. Hort, for example, wrote that James's "very unlikeness to other books is of the greatest value to us, as showing through Apostolic example the many-sidedness of Christian truth" (Hort 1909, ix). According to Hort's historical reconstruction, James addressed Christian Jews living in Antioch and Syria in about A.D. 60. He wrote to correct the lukewarm formality into which the community had fallen, to revive their faith in the face of persecution and to correct a misunderstanding of Paul's teaching (Hort 1909, ix). In contrast Westcott was more of a theologian by temperament and has been accused of neglecting the historical setting of Hebrews and John. S. Neill, however, concedes that John's "theological content can be treated without direct reference to time and circumstances" (Neill, 93).

An Exegetical Approach. Westcott's and Hort's primary task was historical rather than hortatory, to make plain to readers what the words meant to the first writer and readers rather than what the words demand today. Hort is generally credited with the greater historical interest; Westcott, with the greater theological interest. C. K. Barrett praised Westcott's fine sense for the construction of a Greek sentence and "his ability to convey this sense to his reader" (Barrett, 16).

A Believing Approach. "The Cambridge Three were convinced and practicing Christians . . . [who] believed themselves to share the faith of the early Christians among whom and for whom the New Testament was written" (Neill, 88). As such, their exegesis reflected "a very real theological and devotional concern" (Patrick, 68). Barrett ranked Westcott's "conviction that in handling the Bible he was handling the Word of God, and his readiness, or rather his determination, to hear, faithfully and obediently, whatever should be spoken through the written word" as his "first and greatest" qualification for the interpretation of Scripture (Barrett, 2-3).

Significance. Westcott's and Hort's lasting contributions include the overthrow of the Textus Receptus and the substitution of critical texts as the basis for commentaries and contemporary translations; the popularization of historical-critical methodology among English-speaking scholars; and an understanding of Scripture that acknowledges both its divine and human elements.

According to B. M. Metzger, "one of the chief contributions made by Westcott and Hort was their clear demonstration that the Syrian (or Byzantine) text is later than the other types of text" (Metzger, 135). Westcott and Hort marshaled three types of evidence: "the Syrian text contains combined or conflated readings . . . clearly composed of elements current in earlier forms of the text"; distinctively Byzantine readings are not quoted by ante-Nicene fathers; and Byzantine readings, on comparison with rival readings, appear to be improbable originals. With the exception of the New King James Version, which follows the Received Text, modern English translations are based on critical texts substantially identical with that published by Westcott and Hort in 1881. Even among evangelicals, the New International Version

now outsells the King James Version.

At that critical point when British scholarship was in transition between a complacent, precritical stance to a guarded acceptance of critical methodology, if not conclusions, Lightfoot, Westcott and Hort took the Tübingen challenge seriously. By careful use of historical-critical methods in their commentaries and other works, they showed that more conservative answers could be given to the questions Baur had raised. Lightfoot's unique contribution was his work in patristics; Westcott's, his *History of the Canon of the New Testament;* Hort's, his *Judaistic Christianity.*

Barrett has characterized Westcott as "in danger of an Apollinarian doctrine of Scripture," uncovering "a divine significance in every mood, tense, and case" (Barrett, 24). He concluded that "theology, exegesis, and history, are all of them better served when we see in Scripture a divine force, a divine authority, wrestling with human memory, human integrity, and human language, all of them subject to limitations, just as when we are speaking of Christology we must recognize our Lord's own human nature was subject to human limitations" (Barrett, 24-25). This Hort did, charting a realistic via media between fundamentalism's inerrancy of Scripture with its rejection of the human element and naturalism's irrelevancy of Scripture with its rejection of the supernatural element.

In the wake of the *Essays and Reviews* controversy, Hort responded to Westcott's and Lightfoot's concern that Hort, who had been assigned the Synoptics, was too open to the essayists' naturalism and rationalism. Hort's colleagues had decided a priori that "the results of criticism could not prove errors in Scripture; if they seemed so, this was due simply to our imperfect knowledge and inadequate criticism" (Barrett, 7). Hort could not assume such orthodox results in advance:

I shall rejoice on fuller investigation to find that imperfect knowledge is sufficient explanation of all apparent errors, but I do not expect to be so fortunate.

If I am ultimately driven to admit occasional errors, I shall be sorry; but it will not shake my conviction of the providential ordering of human elements in the Bible. (A. Hort 1:422)
Since Hort's realistic view of Scripture acknowledged "human agency as the instrumentality by which the Spirit of God works," he might be "driven to admit occasional errors." Hort's balanced view, however, also affirmed a "strong sense of the Divine purpose" or "special Providence" controlling the formation of the canonical books (A. Hort 1:420, 422). The New Testament epistles were thus the result of the apostles use of their own "best endeavours" together with "the help of the Holy Spirit within them" (Hort, *Village Sermons*, 250).

BIBLIOGRAPHY
Works. F. J. A. Hort, *The Epistle of St. James: The Greek Text with Introduction and Commentary as Far as chap. iv, verse 7, and Additional Notes* (London: Macmillan, 1909); idem, *The First Epistle of St. Peter i,1—ii,17: The Greek Text, with Introductory Lecture, Commentary and . . . Notes* (London: Macmillan, 1898); idem, *Judaistic Christianity* (London: Macmillan, 1904); idem, *Revelation i—iii* (London: Macmillan, 1908); idem, *Village Sermons* (London: Macmillan); B. F. Westcott and F. J. A. Hort, *The New Testament in the Original Greek, with Introduction·and Appendix* (London: Macmillan, 1881); B. F. Westcott, *The Epistles of St. John: The Greek Text with Notes and Essays* (London: Macmillan, 1883); idem, *The Epistle to the Hebrews: The Greek Text with Notes and Essays* (London: Macmillan, 1889); idem, *The Gospel According to St. John: The Authorized Version, with Introduction and Notes* (London: Macmillan, 1882).
Studies. C. K. Barrett, *Westcott as Commentator* (Cambridge: Cambridge University Press, 1959); D. Black and D. S. Dockery, eds., *New Testament Criticism and Interpretation* (Grand Rapids: Zondervan, 1991); note: *Essays and Reviews* has no "author," *Essays and Reviews* (London, 1860); A. Hort, ed., *Published Life and Letters of Fenton John Anthony Hort* (2 vols.; London: Macmillan, 1896); W. G. Kümmel, *The New Testament: The History of the Investigation of Its Problems* (Nashville: Abingdon, 1972); B. M. Metzger, *The Text of the New Testament: Its*

Transmission, Corruption and Restoration (New York and Oxford: Oxford University Press, 1968); S. Neill, *The Interpretation of the New Testament: 1861-1961* (Oxford: Oxford University Press, 1964); F. Olafsson, *Christus Redemptor et Consummator: A Study in the Theology of B. F. Westcott* (Uppsala: Uppsala University Press, 1979); G. A. F. Patrick, *F. J. A. Hort—Eminent Victorian* (Sheffield: Almond, 1988); J. K. Riches, *A Century of New Testament Study* (Valley Forge, PA: Trinity Press International, 1993); E. G. Rupp, *Hort and the Cambridge Tradition* (Cambridge: Cambridge University Press, 1970); A. Westcott, ed., *Life and Letters of Brooke Foss Westcott, Sometime Bishop of Durham* (London: Macmillan, 1903).   C. L. Church

Wrede, William *(1859-1906)*

Friedrich Georg Eduard William Wrede was born on May 10, 1859, at Bücken in Hanover into the family of a Lutheran pastor of conservative theological leanings. After thorough training in the humanities at the Gymnasium Ernestinum in Celle, a high school with a long humanist tradition, where his classics teacher was an ardent defender of the liberal theologian Albrecht Ritschl, he began theological studies at Leipzig. The latter was often preferred over Göttingen by the theologically conservative pastors who did not wish to expose their children to the theology of Ritschl, wishing to send them instead to more confessionally oriented theology teachers. But Wrede, disappointed academically by the confessional Lutheran theologians Karl Friedrich August Kahnis, Christoph Ernst Luthardt and Franz Delitzsch, turned quickly to Adolf von *Harnack, then a youthful lecturer at the beginning of his academic career, and to the circle of students who venerated this approachable and gifted teacher (1878-1879).

In Leipzig Wrede was first introduced to Ritschl's theology in a reading circle that gathered around Harnack, and in which the students read the liberal theologian's high school textbook, *Instruction in the Christian Religion*. After this, Wrede went to Göttingen to become a personal student of

Ritschl. Here he also took courses with his future father-in-law, Hermann Schultz, as well as with the Old Testament scholar Bernhard Duhm. Duhm's experiential concept of religion would prove influential for the so-called *Religionsgeschichtliche Schule*, the Göttingen-based history of religions school, of which Wrede became a prominent member.

After teaching at a private school (1881), as was customary among Lutheran theological candidates, Wrede became a student in the elite theological Lutheran seminary at Locum, at that time presided over by Abbott Friedrich Uhlhorn, who encouraged much independence and teamwork among his seminarians. In an autobiographical sketch Wrede attributed the thorough study of *Clement of Alexandria with having significantly shaped his own theological method.

At the end of his Locum stay, Wrede won a scholarship that enabled him to travel throughout Germany and Switzerland to gain first-hand knowledge of Protestant charitable and social institutions. His academic talents at Göttingen and Locum helped him later also gain a tutor's post at the Göttingen Theological College, a dorm and preparatory school for theological students. While he was at Göttingen (1884-1886), he met and developed a close friendship with Albert Eichhorn, the future head of the history of religions school, among whose members were Wilhelm Bousset, Ernst Troeltsch, Johannes Weiss and Hermann *Gunkel. Eichhorn was a severe critic of Ritschl's church- and culture-oriented liberal theology and espoused a strict historical-critical method in academic matters. It was Eichhorn who also taught Wrede to see religious traditions in their religiohistorical context and study only the decisive developments rather than the entire range of doctrinal concepts in biblical theology.

From 1886 to 1889 Wrede became a successful pastor in the country parish of Langenholzen-Hörsum. His practical-theological interests and association with the Ritschlian pastors in the region also resulted in a much lauded study of modern desiderata for preaching, which in turn would recommend him later to several German theological faculties.

After the death of his parents and consultations with friends and his former teacher Harnack, Wrede decided to enter into a university career. He received his licentiate in theology from Göttingen (1891) with a dissertation on *1 Clement* that studied the apostolic father strictly in his own right as an opponent of charismatic religion at Corinth and as being void of any firsthand information about the Corinthian circumstances. This dissertation showed the same experiential foci that were contemporaneously developed by other members of the history of religions school, especially Gunkel and Weiss. In his licentiate thesis he understood *1 Clement's* religion as that of an accommodated second-generation "Bible Christianity" whose distance to early Christianity is measured by the latter's use of the Old Testament and its lack of a living pneumatology and eschatology.

Wrede continued as a private lecturer at Göttingen until 1892, when he received an appointment as associate professor *(Extraordinarius)* in the University of Breslau, the Lutheran provincial theological institution for Silesia. Upon receiving this appointment, Wrede married Elisabeth Schultz, the daughter of his former Göttingen Old Testament professor.

Wrede's activities in Breslau from 1892 until his death, first as *Extraordinarius* and later as *Ordinarius* (from 1895), saw the publication of three influential theological works: his critique of New Testament theology (*Über Aufgabe und Methode der sogenannten Neutestamentlichen Theologie* [1897]); his methodologically innovative study on *The Messianic Secret in the Gospels* (*Das Messiasgeheimnis in den Evangelien* [1901]); and his reassessment of Paul (*Paulus* [1904]). Wrede's uncompromising exegesis and radical historical-critical conclusions led to considerable tensions within the theological faculty and the conservative Silesian church. But they earned him among friend and foe a lasting place in biblical scholarship.

Wrede was an able teacher, and his major works, while they are written with academic rigor, can be understood by nontheologians as well. He was also an accomplished musician who actively participated in the music life of Breslau and for several years presided over the Institute of Church Music at Breslau University. He died on November 23, 1906, of heart disease.

Context. Wrede was a key figure in the group of young biblical scholars and theologians at Göttingen during the 1890s who became known as the *Religionsgeschichtliche Schule.* This school had no unified approach but shared methodological procedures and foci. Notably they were imbued with the nineteenth-century ethos for "presuppositionless" historical-critical research and sought to exclude from theology any philosophical and theological guiding interests not directly found within the sources. In doing so, they never seriously took into account the subjectivity of the critical historian and interpreter or contemporary thinkers' constructive dialogue with history. Their major methodological contribution consisted of understanding the Bible as the product of living faith communities, which they studied with categories of a psychological or sociological kind. In the view of the history of religions school, some of the key driving forces of Judaism and early Christianity were eschatology, pneumatology and cultic religiosity. Some members of the school, such as Troeltsch, Bousset and Gunkel, expected a revivification of Protestantism from such a vitalist understanding of biblical religion.

Work and Significance. In his Gospel research as well as in his other writings, Wrede followed Eichhorn's lead in focusing attention on the tradition history of theological motifs and ideas, which were viewed as living responses to the existential and social needs of religious communities. Paradigmatic for such work is Wrede's *The*

Messianic Secret in the Gospels (1901), which in Albert *Schweitzer's judgment, as well as that of many other biblical scholars, marked a new era in Gospel studies. This methodology sought to avoid purposefully psychological and developmental conjectures, which in Wrede's view had rendered the liberal lives of Jesus very subjective.

Wrede considered much of the Gospel of Mark as consisting of theological traditions that could be understood only from the historical needs of early Christianity but not from the life of Jesus. While such a procedure had already been implemented to a degree, Wrede's skepticism toward any doctrinal or literary features as being historical was new, as was his rigorous exclusion of any supernatural features in the narrative as comprehensible from the life of Jesus. Wrede rejected the assumption of a historical nucleus in theologically suspect traditions but considered these traditions as valuable evidence for the quality of the author's or the source's religious thought and experience. Consequently the messianic secret—especially the prohibitions to silence about Jesus' true nature but also the incomprehension of the disciples and the esoteric teaching in the parables as well as the recognition of the demons of who Jesus was—were understood by Wrede not as historical facts of the life of Jesus but as components of a theological construct that attempted to reconcile a nonmessianic life of Jesus with a faith in his adoption as Messiah after Easter. In so doing, Wrede destroyed the liberal confidence in the historical reliability of Mark, which among the liberal exegetes was one of the pillars for reconstructing the life of Jesus.

If Mark could no longer be trusted historically as providing a reliable outline of Jesus' ministry, the confidence of reconstructing Jesus' life from Mark and his teaching from a sayings source was severely shaken. Many modern biblical interpreters have followed Wrede's method but have assigned vastly different reasons for the prominence of the messianic secret in Mark's Gospel. Wrede understood his book on the messianic secret as the first in a series of studies, no other of which was ever completed, designed to answer the question of whether Jesus ever considered and proclaimed himself to be the Messiah. Shortly before his death, as documented in a letter to his old teacher and benefactor, Harnack, Wrede changed his mind about the messianic consciousness of Jesus, which he now considered much more likely, though he saw no reason to abandon his tradition-historical approach. This approach, while being much more skeptical of ever being able to separate tradition and redaction in the Gospel narratives, helped prepare subsequent methodologies such as form and redaction criticism.

Even prior to his book on the messianic secret, Wrede had subjected another field to rigorous criticism: biblical and New Testament theology as practiced by his contemporaries Bernhard Weiss and Heinrich Julius Holtzmann. In his criticism Wrede was motivated by the same historical-critical agenda that characterized his study of the Gospels. He thus sought to remove any practical and contemporary theological concerns from the discipline and change New Testament theology into a religious history of early Christianity. Because of the thoroughly historical orientation of such a discipline, he also rejected the canon of the Old and New Testaments as a valid demarcation for the study of biblical religion. Instead, concerned with the religion and theology of early Christianity, the exegete was to place New Testament religion in the appropriate religiohistorical contexts without respect as to whether that context could be found inside or outside the canon. Within such a tradition-historical framework, topics of special interest for Wrede were the critically reconstructed proclamation of Jesus as well as the faith of the early church in its varying geographical and intellectual settings, with special attention devoted to the theologies of Paul and of John as well as their effective trajectories. Wrede felt that much of early Christianity did not lend itself to the minute articulation

of individual doctrinal viewpoints, the so-called doctrinal concepts, as expressed in the major biblical theologies of his day. He argued that such micrology prevented the recognition of what was important for an author and lumped together the significant with the insignificant in early Christian thought. Here can be seen an influence of Eichhorn, who had strenuously argued for the study of what was decisive in the thought of early Christian writers. The thrust was also strengthened by Wrede's assumption that much in New Testament literature represented a shared deposit of religious thought and experience.

Wrede was equally innovative and set the scholarly agenda for years to come in several other writings that influenced modern biblical scholarship. He considered the Gospel of John as originating in an anti-Jewish setting. He thus anticipated the modern scholarly tradition that understands the theology of John as being shaped theologically by the process of separation from the Jewish synagogue. In addition Wrede considered elements of the Gospel comprehensible only in a gnostic religiohistorical context. In this he followed his mentor Eichhorn, who had seen Mandean influences in the Fourth Gospel, a notion later also expressed in more detail by Rudolf *Bultmann and his school.

In his popular study of Paul, Wrede furnished historical-critical reasons for an older tradition in German thought and scholarship that saw a great gulf between the proclamation of Jesus and the theology of Paul. Two issues Wrede brought into the forefront of subsequent discussions were the question of the savior myth—Christ's supernatural origin and salvific intentions, alleged to have been transferred by Paul from an existing religious context to Christianity in order to understand the work of Christ—and the polemical significance of the doctrine of justification within Paul's theology. This latter point put him at odds with traditional Lutheran theology but had earlier been championed by Wrede in his dissertation defense. Similar thoughts on

Paul were also expressed by a variety of thinkers such as the philosophers Friedrich Schelling and Friedrich Nietzsche and the theological contemporaries Ernst Renan and Paul de Lagarde. Wrede also contributed to biblical studies through monographs on 1 Thessalonians and Hebrews as well as through several smaller works.

BIBLIOGRAPHY

Works. W. Wrede, *Charakter und Tendenz des Johannesevangeliums* (Sammlung gemeinverständlicher Vorträge 37; Tübingen: J. C. B. Mohr, 1903); idem, *Die Echtheit des zweiten Thessalonicherbriefes* (TU n.s. 9, 2; Leipzig: Hinrichs, 1903); idem, *Die Entstehung der Schriften des Neuen Testaments* (Tübingen: J. C. B. Mohr, 1907; ET *The Origin of the New Testament* [Harper Library of Living Thought; New York: Harper, 1909]); idem, *Das literarische Rätsel des Hebräerbriefes: Mit einem Anhang über den literarischen Charakter des Barnabasbriefes* (FRLANT 8; Göttingen: Vandenhoeck & Ruprecht, 1906); idem, *Das Messiasgeheimnis in den Evangelien: Zugleich ein Beitrag zum Verständnis des Markusevangeliums* (Göttingen: Vandenhoeck & Ruprecht, 1901; ET *The Messianic Secret* [Cambridge: Clarke, 1971]); idem, *Paulus* (Religionsgeschichtliche Volksbücher 1, 5-6; Tübingen: J. C. B. Mohr, 1904; ET *Paul* [London: Philip Green, 1907; Boston: American Unitarian Association, 1908]); idem, "Der Prediger und sein Zuhörer," *ZPT* 14 (1892) 50; idem, *Über Aufgabe und Methode der sogenannten Neutestamentlichen Theologie* (Göttingen: Vandenhoeck & Ruprecht, 1897; ET "The Task and Methods of 'New Testament Theology'" in R. Morgan, *The Nature of New Testament Theology: The Contribution of William Wrede and Adolf Schlatter* [SBT 2d series 25; London: SCM, 1973] 68-116, 182-93); idem, *Untersuchungen zum Ersten Klemensbriefe* (Göttingen: Vandenhoeck & Ruprecht, 1891); idem, *Vorträge und Studien* (Tübingen: J. C. B. Mohr, 1907). *Studies.* L. Blevins, *The Messianic Secret in Markan Research: 1901-1976* (Washington, DC: University Press of America, 1981); G. Lüdemann and M. Schröder, *Die Religionsgeschichtliche Schule in Göttingen: Eine Dokumentation* (Göttingen: Vandenhoeck & Ruprecht, 1987); F. Regner, " 'Paulus und Jesus' im 19 Jahrhundert: Beiträge zur Geschichte des Themas 'Paulus und Jesus' in der neutestamentliichen Theologie" (Studien zur Theologie und Geistes- geschichte des Neunzehnten Jahrhunderts 30; Göttingen: Vandenhoeck & Ruprecht, 1977); H. Rollmann, "Paulus alienus: William Wrede on Comparing Jesus and Paul" in *From Jesus to Paul: Studies in Honor of Francis Wright Beare,* ed. P. Richardson and J. C. Hurd (Waterloo, ON: Wilfrid Laurier University Press, 1984) 23-45; idem, "William Wrede, Albert Eichhorn and the 'Old Quest' of the Historical Jesus" in *Self-Definition and Self-Discovery in Early Christianity,* ed. D. J. Hawkin and T. Robinson (SBEC 26; Lewiston, NY: Edwin Mellen, 1990) 79-99; A. Schweitzer, *The Quest of the Historical Jesus: A Critical Study of Its Progress from Reimarus to Wrede* (2d ed.; London: A & C Black, 1911); G. Strecker, ed., "William Wrede: Zur hundertsten Wiederkehr seines Geburtstages," *ZTK* 57 (1960) 67-91.

H. Rollmann

Zahn, Theodor (1838-1933)

A German Protestant theologian and a New Testament and patristics scholar, Theodor Zahn is known as an original and erudite scholar, a prolific author, a conservative historical critic and an orthodox Lutheran believer.

Zahn was born at Mörs and was educated at home and at his father's preparatory institute; later he attended the universities of Basel, Erlangen and Berlin (1854-1858). After a three-year interruption due to illness, he continued his education while teaching in the advanced high school at Neustrelitz (1861-1865) and as student-lecturer *(Repetent)* at the University of Göttingen (1865-1868). His announced goal, from which he never wavered throughout his career, was to come to a historical understanding of the beginning of Christianity grounded on an original investigation of the sources *("ein auf selbständige Quellenforschung gegründetes geschichtliches Verständnis der Anfänge des Christentums,"* Zahn 1925, 233).

Zahn continued at Göttingen as privatdozent (1868-1871) and as associate professor (1871-1877). During his twelve-year stay at Göttingen, Zahn published several of his "original investigations" in early church literature: *Marcellus von Ancyra*

(1867), *Hermas* (1868), *Ignatius* (1873) and his contributions to *Patrum Apostolicorum Opera* (1875-1888), which he published jointly with Adolf von *Harnack and O. von Gebhardt. In spite of such productivity, he failed to win appointment to several professorial posts (see his account, Zahn 1925, 235-37), no doubt because of his viewpoints on early Christianity sources were not congruent with the contemporary critical positions.

Finally Zahn was appointed as professor at the University of Kiel (1877) and then at the University of Erlangen (1878) as the successor to Johann Christian Konrad *von Hofmann, who had especially influenced Zahn during his student days at Erlangen. He was professor at Erlangen until his retirement (1909), except for a four-year stint at the University of Leipzig (1888-1892). Though he was retired, Zahn continued publishing, including commentaries on four New Testament books.

Context. Zahn was the virtual leader of the conservative wing of New Testament criticism. In Germany the heyday of rationalistic criticism of the Bible extended from the late eighteenth century through the nineteenth century and formed the foil for Zahn's work. For example, under the influence of Friedrich Daniel Ernst *Schleiermacher and G. W. F. Hegel, New Testament critics wrote rationalistic "lives of Jesus" (see the *Leben Jesu* of David Freidrich *Strauss [1835]) in which Jesus became little more than a Jewish wise man. Also under Hegel's influence, Ferdinand Christian *Bauer argued that of the thirteen epistles ascribed to Paul in the New Testament, only four (Galatians, 1 Corinthians, 2 Corinthians and Romans) were authentically Pauline. In the context of this kind of radical criticism, Zahn pursued his studies. Although Zahn was committed to a "historical understanding" of Christian beginnings, he did not accept the rationalistic premises of the liberals. For this reason and because of his vast erudition, thoroughness and original research he became the leader of the conservative wing of New

Testament criticism.

Zahn's relationship with Harnack typifies some important aspects of Zahn's historical context. Both men were outstanding scholars and both pursued similar fields of study. At the beginning (1873-1882) they collaborated on a project (a work on the apostolic fathers) and enjoyed a relationship of mutual respect and friendship. Though some differences surfaced even in this early period (see Hauck 1952), their disputes soon became more open and bitter. Part of the conflict sprang from their different approaches to the sources. On problematic issues Zahn tended to prefer the ecclesiastical tradition over critical solutions; Harnack more frequently resorted to brilliant hypotheses in order to solve the problems.

Part of the conflict centered in different personal faith commitments that came to expression over the meaning and role of the Apostles' Creed. Harnack viewed the creed as a kind of husk that obscured for many people what he considered to be the kernel of the gospel, namely, the fatherhood of God and the eternal value of the human soul. He argued that the use of the creed in the worship service should be optional. Zahn defended in the main the contents of the creed and felt obliged to hold to the creed as a part of what it meant to be a confessing Christian.

Other issues became divisive (e.g., on the formation of the New Testament canon), so that their friendship ruptured and their mutual respect declined. Like ships passing in the night, each continued his work alongside the other. Harnack was a leader in radical biblical criticism and liberal theology; Zahn the leader of conservative biblical criticism and orthodox theology. In their twilight years the two became personally reconciled, in spite of their differences.

Publications. Zahn published extensively in four areas: the literature of the early church fathers, the history of the New Testament canon, New Testament introduction, and the interpretation of New

Testament books. The fourth and last (also chronologically) was the intended goal and capstone of all of his work. He was given a long and productive life so that he could see most of the work brought to completion.

Zahn's investigations into early church literature covered the period from the apostolic fathers to about A.D. 450. Some of his earlier investigations are mentioned above; several of his later ones were included in the successive fascicles of his *Forschungen zur Geschichte der neutestamentlichen Kanons* (10 parts, 1881-1929).

In addition to the *Forschungen,* Zahn wrote his *Geschichte des neutestamentlichen Kanons* (2 vols. in 4 parts, 1888-1892). As a kind of supplement to his *Introduction,* he wrote the compact but readable *Grundriss der Geschicte des neutestamentlichen Kanons* (1901; the improved edition of 1904 is recommended).

Zahn wrote his *Einleitung in das Neue Testament* in 2 volumes (1897-1899), which went through several editions. The third edition was translated into English as *Introduction to the New Testament* (3 vols., Edinburgh, 1909; reprinted later).

As the acme of his work, Zahn edited the *Kommentar zum Neuen Testament* (1903-). He himself was responsible for writing commentaries on seven New Testament books: Matthew (1903), Galatians (1905), the Gospel of John (1907), Romans (1910), Luke (1913), Acts (2 vols., 1919-1921) and Revelation (2 vols., 1924-1926). For the other books Zahn chose scholars who shared with him and with one another the same basic approach to the historical criticism of the New Testament and the same high religious evaluation on its content.

Central Concerns. Several central concerns can be recognized through Zahn's works.

Zahn held that the regular reading of a book in the worship service was the essential mark (*"das wesentliche Merkmal,"* Zahn 1904, 12) for a book to be considered as Holy Scripture. His original investigations of the church fathers included concern for how they described the books read in the worship services. Zahn's approach to the history of the canon involved describing part of that history backwards. In his *Grundriss* he began with the period of 170-220, where the sources were abundant for establishing which books were read and thus considered as Holy Scripture. He moved backwards to the epoch of 140-170 and from there back to "the earliest traces" of the canon prior to 140. Then he jumped ahead and traced the history of the New Testament canon from the time of *Origen to about 450.

The divergent views of Zahn and Harnack on the formation of the New Testament canon sparked a sharp controversy between them. Harnack held that the catholic church established the canon over against the truncated canon of Marcion. Zahn argued that it was the regular reading of a book in the worship service that functioned as the canonical mark of a book. Harnack argued versus Zahn (correctly in my opinion) that one cannot equate the total sum of books read in the worship services with *the* New Testament; Zahn argued (correctly in my opinion) that one cannot give such determinative importance to the role of Marcion, since the sources indicate that Marcion formulated his canon over against that of the church. The question can therefore be raised whether seeking to establish canonical marks is appropriate at all, be that mark the reading in the service or the opposition to heresy. The truth is that many sources indicate that the early church was aware of "receiving" the books of the New Testament and thus "confessing" them to be canonical.

In his *Introduction* Zahn defended the authenticity of all of the New Testament books. This position is related to taking the testimony of the early church with utmost seriousness. When in doubt, Zahn always went with the tradition. This tendency has in some instances stood the test of time, at least within the bounds of conservative New Testament criticism. For example, what Zahn has to say about the authenticity of the Pastoral Epistles is still worth reading (Zahn 1909, 1:1-133). This statement is typical of his starting point: "The confident denial of the genuineness of these letters—which has been made now for several generations more positively than in the case of any other Pauline Epistle—has no support from tradition" (Zahn 1909, 1:85).

This loyalty to tradition also yielded positions that are highly dubious. Being loyal to the statement of Papias about the origin of the Gospels of Matthew and Mark, Zahn argued that Matthew wrote his Gospel originally in Aramaic in Palestine (A.D. 62); Mark, writing in Rome (A.D. 64), used the preaching of Peter and the Aramaic Matthew; later (c. A.D. 85) the Greek Matthew appeared, the author of which used our Mark as he made his translation of the Aramaic Matthew. Not many critics today would hold that Matthew was originally composed in Aramaic (or Hebrew), and only a few would hold that it was written prior to Mark.

Another not widely held position is Zahn's account of the dating of and the relationship between 1 Peter and 2 Peter and Jude, all three of which he regards as authentic. He argues that 2 Peter was the earliest (A.D. 62), written by Peter to a Jewish Christian audience, thus to a different audience than the later 1 Peter (A.D. 64), helping to account for their admitted differences. He affirmed that Jude (c. A.D. 75) was dependent upon 2 Peter—a possible position, but not widely held. To affirm that 2 Peter was written as early as 62 involves among other things affirming the unlikely conclusion that the phrase "the other Scriptures" (2 Pet 3:16), which had become a technical phrase meaning "a collection of sacred writings," was here used in a nontechnical sense (Zahn 1909, 2:276-78). Nor is it likely that 2 Peter was written directly by Peter.

Zahn brought to New Testament exegesis, along with considerable expertise in textual criticism, an enormous wealth of data from the early church materials. These materials, being close in time to the New Testament, were a reliable source for interpreting the New Testament—a truth often overlooked in much current New Testament interpretation. Zahn's commentaries do not excel, however, in presenting the parallels from either the Jewish or profane Greek literature.

Along with this historical understanding, Zahn's commentaries reveal a high estimate of the religious value and spiritual content of the New Testament. F. W. Grosheide, an admirer and friendly critic of Zahn, concluded that the spiritual content of the New Testament comes through forcefully in Zahn's earlier commentaries (e.g., on Matthew, John and Romans) while the historical understanding so predominates in the later commentaries (e.g., on Acts and Revelation) that justice is not done to the spiritual message of these books (Grosheide, 423-24). This judgment seems to be true, but that does not mean that concern for the spiritual is absent from the later commentaries. In his commentary on Revelation, for example, Zahn argued for the futurist rather than the contemporary-historical interpretation (see also Zahn 1909, 3:436-49). The latter interpretation was widely promoted by radical biblical critics who on rationalistic grounds had no room for biblical prophecy. But Zahn promoted the futurist interpretation—rooted, to be sure, in the contemporary historical situation of the author—thus allowing the spiritual message of biblical prophecy to be heard.

Significance. Zahn has left behind many books and articles (more than two hundred items in the 1918 bibliography). Unfortunately for many English speakers, most of them are in German. His works are still worth studying, in large measure because of his mastery of the sources in early church literature. Zahn said of himself that he never had his own system and never attempted to construct one (Zahn 1925, 238). Though this is true in comparison with many other New Testament scholars, it is also true that he had his own approach to his academic work which has become part of his legacy. Two things stand out. First, his resolve to do original research in the sources has been an inspiration to all who have become familiar with his writings. Second, the combination of his Christian faith commitment with his pursuit of careful historical investigation has been an encouragement to many, especially those in the more conservative wing of New Testament criticism.

BIBLIOGRAPHY

Works. T. Zahn, *Altes und Neues* (3 vols.; Leipzig: A. Deichert, 1927-30); idem, *The Apostles' Creed: A Sketch of Its History and an Examination of Its Contents* (London: Hodder & Stoughton, 1899); idem, *Einige Bemerkungen zu Adolf Harnack's Prüfung der Geschichte des neutestamentlichen Kanons* (Erlangen: Deichert, 1889); idem, *Einleitung in das Neue Testament* (2 vols.; Leipzig: Deichert, 1897-1899; ET: *Introduction to the New Testament* [3 vols.; Edinburgh: T & T Clark, 1909]); idem, *Grundriss der Geschichte des Apostolischen Zeitalters* (Leipzig: Deichert, 1929); idem, *Grundriss der Geschichte des Lebens Jesu* (Leipzig: Deichert, 1928); Idem, *Grundriss der Geschichte des neutestamentlichen Kanons* (2d ed.; Leipzig: Deichert, 1904); idem, *Die Religionswissenschaft in Selbstdarstelungen*, ed. E. Stange (Leipzig: Meiner, 1925) 230-48; idem, *Skizzen aus dem Leben der Alten Kirche* (3d. ed.; Leipzig: Deichert 1908); Autobiography with updated bibliography; *Zahn-Bibliographie*, ed. friends and colleagues (Leipzig: A. Deichert, 1918) for his eightieth birthday.

Studies. W. Elert, "Theodor Zahn," *LU* 49 (1938) 289-99; F. W. Grosheide, "Theodor Zahn," *ST* 22 (January-June 1933) 413-24; F. Hauck, "Briefe Adolf Harnacks an Theodor Zahn," *TL* 77 (1952) 498-502; idem, "Briefe Theodor Zahns aus seinem ersten Studiejahr in Basel, 1854/55," *ThZ* 6 (1950) 261-70; A. Meyer, *RGG* (2d ed., 1931) 5 cols. 2070-71; H.-O. Metzger, *RGG*, (3d ed., 1962) 6 col. 1865; *NSHERK* 12 (1912) 496; 5 cols. 2181-82; *ODCC* (1st ed., 1957) 1487; (2d ed., 1974) 1510; H. Preuss, "Zahn, Theodor von" in *Lebensläufe aus Franken*, ed. A. Chroust (Munich: Dunker & Humblot), 5:523-30; J. Schmid, *LTK* (2d ed., 1965) 10 col. 1306; W. C. Van Unnik, *CE* (2d ed., 1961) 6:664; H. Windish, *RGG* (1st ed., 1913).   A. J. Bandstra

PART FIVE

Biblical Interpretation in Europe in the 20th Century

THIS OVERVIEW IS DIVIDED INTO TWO MAIN PARTS. THE FIRST PART HIGH-lights some key twentieth-century events and ideas constitutive of a late modern form of knowing, especially pertaining to the interpretation of literature generally; after this signs of emergent "postmodern" alternatives from the 1960s to the present. Its primary concern is the climate of perception, the dominant forms of knowing literature, so that relatively little attention is given to Scripture. The second part of this overview discusses late modern biblical interpretation in Europe and then offers observations on the current postmodern debate among biblical scholars. This cursory treatment of persons, events and ideas can give only a glimpse of a period replete with significant publications that represent great diversities in language, history, culture and literature.

The Modern Form of Knowing in Europe

The twentieth century opened in the shadow of the fathers of suspicion: Sigmund Freud (1856-1939), Friedrich Nietzsche (1844-1900) and Karl Marx (1818-1883). Nietzsche died in 1900, before the century could find its footing; but he left behind *Thus Spoke Zarathustra* (1883-1892) written almost as a scripture for the modern age. His idea of "the Superman" would be used decades later to buttress a genetic theory of racial superiority by a German dictator not compromised by Nietzsche's own nihilistic bent. From an entirely different angle, the revolutions throughout Europe in 1848 had given credence to Marx's "dialectical materialism," now applied as a positive theory for revolutions in Russia (1917) and later in China. Moreover, Freud argued that patients might gain "transcendence" over repressed desires that had produced symptoms of psychotic behavior.

These three pioneers of late modern thought shared a discontent with naive, or premodern, interpretations of surface phenomena. Each looked beyond overt human choices to expose real, universal yet esoteric determinants that have beguiled us by masquerading as moral virtues, capitalistic philanthropy and confessions of sin. At a minimum, their great contribution was to demystify sentimental and pious language. They also proved that powerful forces were at work on deeper levels of our lives than we might ordinarily assume. Their contributions to late-nineteenth- and early-twentieth-century thought coincided with a general sense in Europe that new "foundations" had been found buried beneath the older modern ones detected since Immanuel Kant's (1724-1804) contribution at the end of the eighteenth century. In this sense we may think of Freud, Nietzsche and Marx as introducing a major adjustment to the mechanism of modernity, after almost a century of its triumph as the dominant form of knowing in most of Europe.

Reflecting this enthusiasm of late modernity, the first published use of the English word *pre-critical* occurred in 1881, in the *Encyclopedia Britannica* (23:847/2), to describe theories prior to "the period of Kant's development" and his *Critique of Pure Reason* (1781). In England during the seventeenth century, John Dryden (1631-1700) and his colleagues had not hesitated to describe as a "criticism" Aristotle's discussion of criteria that make literature pleasurable to a reader. What Dryden and his colleagues had once granted Aristotle and others, the nineteenth-century partisans of late modernity now denied. While one might point to a few prophetlike sentences in the ancient classics or to Baruch Spinoza and John Locke in the seventeenth century for surprising anticipations of modern analysis, Kant alone had opened the door to the possibility of a genuinely modern "criticism," in opposition to the alternatives of dogmatism and skepticism.

The word *modern* derives from late Latin of the sixth century, with cognates in French *(moderne)*, Spanish, Portuguese, Italian, German and other European languages. In English the simple adjective has occurred frequently since the sixteenth century (e.g., "modern English"). At the beginning of the twentieth century, however, the adjective *modern* began to signify more than simply something contemporary or new. In England a "modern school" (or "modern side") in the mid-nineteenth century indicated public education on "modern" subjects without a requirement of Greek or Latin; "modern faced type," developed in France in the early nineteenth century, came into vogue among printers in England; and by the mid-nineteenth century "modern art" could refer to a radical departure from all earlier artistic styles and values. By the third decade of the twentieth century, "modern first edition" became a technical term for a book published around 1900 or later.

By the beginning of the twentieth century, "the Modern Age" came to denote an entirely fresh era without precedent in ages past. In literary studies at the turn of the century, serious modern realism declined in influence in deference to social-scientific descriptions of the causes of social decay and the promise of reform. Freud, Nietzsche and Marx excited entirely new programs for literary criticism, so the aesthetic features of a text often became less interesting to critics than the text's implied relation to the social, psychological or economic determinants of power. From another angle, new historical criticisms of the classics sought to recover the oldest parts of a text which might refer most accurately to original events in the past.

In the public response to the sciences, many new "advances" such as the invention of the airplane in the first decade and the first public radio broadcast in 1920 signaled the triumph of all things "modern" in the twentieth century. Consequently, at the beginning of the twentieth century the Modern Age seemed to be potentially a positive end of the ages. If in the last decades of the nineteenth century, anything pre-Kantian might have been called "pre-critical," now *pre-modern* and *pre-critical* began to be used as synonyms.

In England, a robust effort to push the modern perspective into a new key may be seen in the pragmatic analysis of language by Ludwig Wittgenstein (1889-1951). Wittgenstein himself points to the great impact of William James's *Principles of Psychology* (1890). In his *Varieties of Religious Experience* (1902), James used anecdotal accounts of human experience to argue that the sense of presence associated with metaphysical and religious ideas might actually take precedence over any conclusions that might be reached by a Kantian rationalism of pure reason. James declared, "Our impulsive belief is here always what sets up the original body of truth, and our articulately verbalized philosophy is but its showy translation into formulas" (James 1902, 73). Wittgenstein made similar direct observations of the sociopragmatic use of "public" and "private" (technical, specialized) language, on analogy to how "games" are played according to an implicit agreement on the rules and the range of effects. His posthumously published *Philosophical Investigations* (1953) shows his rejection of interpretations of language that are either primarily referential, as if words were signs pointing to external objects and events, or expressive, as if words essentially conveyed deep feelings only minimally regulated by public rules of discourse. Wittgenstein clearly could agree with Kant that we apply unconscious principles to the structure of human experience, but unlike Kant he recognized that these principles vary according to different cultures, genders, economic situations, languages and epochs in the form of knowing. Therefore, none of the "rules" regulating the pubic perception of reality and the use of language are fixed, universal, absolute or timeless. In this respect, Wittgenstein in his later life became a critic of modern perspectives generally and may be viewed as a forerunner of postmodern anxiety.

A later contribution to modern pragmatism is the "speech-act" theory developed by J. L. Austin (1911-1960) in his *How to Do Things with Words* (1962, 2d ed. 1975). Austin argued that words, rather than passively communicating ideas, seek to change the reader in some way. He distinguished between overtly "performative" uses of words and "constative" uses by philosophers when they seem to name facts in the world but actually construct a reality with words. Referential or expressive *dimensions* of language remain indeterminate until we know what someone is trying to do by using words. Then their significance becomes self-evident and consonant with the sociopragmatic circumstances in which language is used.

Austin's observations also pertain to written texts and are integral to their proper interpretation, despite an easier illustration of them in oral discourse. Obviously, biblical language of confession or absolution enacts a reality in its usage. A strictly referential or expressive interpretation of these words could not do justice to the form and function of such language in the Bible. Such positive pragmatic approaches to language and literature gained more attention in England and in the United States than in most other places in Europe.

Many Continental philosophers tried to develop further a phenomenology after Kant, encouraged by Edmund Husserl's (1859-1938) *Logical Investigations* (1900) and closely followed by the almost mystical contemplations of Being by Martin Heidegger (1889-1976). Many scholars, like Heidegger, tried to identify certain pervasive human values ("existentials") that accompany the concreteness of human existence, instead of arguing for "a priori" ideas as Kant had suggested. Later came a tremendous variety of "existentialist" proposals, with such brilliant champions as Jean-Paul Sartre (1905-1980). The idea that human existence precedes and delimits what is the essence of being human in the world became a common cliché for describing that movement.

Other influential antimetaphysical and "sociological" approaches developed with strong ties to the earlier work by Marx and Freud. Some such approaches have been called "critical theory," in association with scholars of "the Frankfurt School" and the Institute for Social Research. Max Horkheimer (1895-1973) guided the school and set the group's direction in his inaugural lecture of 1931. It thrived in Germany before and after World War II. In the 1930s many Jewish intellectuals, among others, helped to found the New School for Social Research in New York City. In the aftermath of the war, Theodor W. Adorno (1903-1969) returned to Germany and became identified with the radical politics of students in the 1960s. Adorno anticipated many of the postmodern arguments against modern philosophy that aspired to make totalizing, rational descriptions of society. Adorno defended the illuminating power of social-scientific investigations restricted in each case to a limited cluster of specific phenomena. One of his students, Jürgen Habermas (b. 1929), remains skeptical of almost all postmodern proposals. Habermas sees modernity as an unfinished project and argues for sophisticated points of consensus in communication within a diverse group of participants in order to avoid the biases associated with older liberal modern social theory. He strongly criticizes both Hans-Georg Gadamer (b. 1900) and linguistic pragmatists in England for condoning conservative politics by failing to take into account persistent sociopolitical elements intrinsic to the life world of texts.

Gadamer concedes to pragmatic-linguistic approaches that hermeneutics should derive from an examination of the concreteness of textual interpretations rather than start from theoretical principles. Gadamer wants hermeneutical generalizations to arise from critical reflections both on the activity of interpreting texts and from assessments of the "effective history" *(Wirkungsgeschichte)*, or the results and consequences of interpretation over time. In his *Truth and Method* (1960; ET 1975) Gadamer accepts the limits imposed by Kant's conception of pure reason and agrees that a philosopher, unlike a prophet, must fully recognize the limits of a phenomenal description. He wants to describe "the universal hermeneutics" which "has nothing to do with any metaphysical conclusions" (Gadamer, xxiv-xxv). A particularly attractive aspect of Gadamer's thought has been his concern to describe the merging of two historical horizons, that of the text and of the reader. Many other philosophers and theologians have tried to define that same relationship with greater specificity. Gadamer's concept of "effective history" requires an account of the history of interpretation, a topic often neglected in older modern hermeneutical theory.

Obviously, many philosophers in the twentieth century abandoned the classical philosophical pursuit of metaphysics for social-scientific descriptions of forces behind social change and the politics of discourse, whether oral or written. This direction found support from new proposals in the social sciences, from Émile Durkheim's (1858-1917) *Rules of Sociological Method* (1895) to Max Weber's (1864-1920) *The Protestant Ethic and the Development of Capitalism* (1905) and later his *Economy and Society* (1922). Ferdinand de Saussure's (1857-1913) *Cours de linguistique generale* (1915) paved the way for a variety of later structuralist and semiotic efforts to describe functions of language as written and spoken "signs." In England, Bertrand Russell (1872-1970) and Alfred North Whitehead's (1861-1947) *Principia Mathematica* (1910-1913) and Whitehead's later *Process and Reality* (1929) used mathematical arguments to illustrate the relativity of systems of measurable reality analogous to poststructuralist efforts to negotiate levels of significations. These efforts encouraged a late modern view of language and texts as symbolic expressions at the end of a complex process driven by subtle sociological and psychological forces.

For those living in North America, the effect of two world wars (1914-1918 and 1939-1945) was measured mainly by their human toll, in contrast to the greater devastation suffered in Europe—the reduction of historic homes, churches, universities and villages to rubble; the wanton destruction of civilian lives; systematic murder of people who identified with certain sociopolitical groups (Jews, communists and homosexuals); and in many countries in Eastern Europe, the injustices of living under the thumb of a foreign power. Whole cities had to be rebuilt by survivors who had few doubts about the inhumanity of their neighbors.

The roles that had been played by intellectuals such as Heidegger, who gave tentative support to the Nazi forces, forever threw into doubt any inherent superiority that philosophers' practical reasoning might have been assumed to possess. The churches' record of response was equally clouded, with some notable exceptions such as the Barmen Declaration, which rejected the Nazification of the German Lutheran Church, and Dietrich Bonhoeffer's (1906-1945) valiant effort in the underground resistance. Bonhoeffer's despair over defining a Christian ethics under such circumstances inadvertently gave support to later proposals of the God-is-dead theologies and even movements of "Christian" atheistic ethics in the 1960s.

A surge of nationalism after the two great wars reignited heated patriotic loyalties and provided a catalyst for nations to establish distinctive schools of thought. In many Eastern European countries under communist control, churches became key diplomatic centers in the struggle for freedom against totalitarianism. Many of the most gifted scholars in these countries, who might have become theologians, majored in comparative literature. In literary studies they could aggressively engage religious themes relevant to texts they interpreted, often with a conviction more than merely academic. In seminaries, professors could discuss "biblical theology," forged in the eighteenth and nineteenth centuries, as detached descriptions of beliefs stemming from ancient Israel or the Mediterranean world, without being accused of preaching. To non-Christians, modern criticisms raised serious doubts about the accuracy of the Bible and its reliability as a testimony to truth. Nonetheless, many biblical scholars found other ways to link the results, no matter how historically iconoclastic, to convictions of Christian faith.

Significant doubts about the certainty of scientific evidence also developed in the first half of the twentieth century due to questions raised in scientific theory about the foundations of Cartesian-Newtonian theories of physics. In the eighteenth century Kant had attributed to science the strongest warrants of pure reason and access to the possibility of absolutes. Atoms had been thought to be composed of small, solid particles of matter; time and space had been reliable constants within a perceived equilibrium of phenomenal presences of things and events. Clashing with this idea of certain fixed dimensions to our physical reality, Max Planck (1858-1947) proposed his quantum physics starting around 1900, and Albert Einstein's (1879-1955) essays on special relativity in 1905, followed by his general theory of relativity in 1916, cast doubt on the older modern confidence in the existence of constants in physics. Werner Karl Heisenberg's

(1901-1976) "uncertainty principle" in physics in 1927 contributed to a new understanding of light as indeterminately either a wave or a particle and of the Brownian Movement as random activity. Atoms were found to contain more space than matter and to be composed of strange subatomic particles that defy older modern laws of physics. Time and mass vary according to velocity, and space curves around planets. Galileo's view that the earth moved had shocked the Reformers, and now Planck, Einstein, Heisenberg and others confirmed that everything moves and all our observations are relative to indeterminate factors.

A greater awareness of the anthropocentric nature of all our scientific observations raised further questions about whether we even have the capacity to know the external world apart from our own very limited, imagined reconstructions. In other words, theories of the subatomic ironically undermined the very foundation of a physical reality which earlier generations assumed they knew and upon which they thought they could stand in order to look optimistically into the future. Moreover, Thomas S. Kuhn (b. 1922) and Karl R. Popper (1902-1994) questioned the objectivity of dominant scientific paradigms and the power of experimentation to disconfirm them. Scientific theory, almost like church doctrines, proved to have vested interests in certain beliefs about reality, such that these beliefs are much less open to change than might be apparent on the surface. How one actually conducts and interprets the results of an experiment betrays its own complicity with one set of possibilities over others.

While the physical and natural sciences in late modernity began to lose their privileged position as interpreters of reality according to pure reason, the results of new scientific inventions became more threatening in both intentional and unintentional ways. The same nuclear fusion that delivered electrical energy produced a dangerous byproduct with a half-life of millennia of years. The unparalleled destruction by an atomic bomb might help win a war and concurrently make imaginable the elimination of human beings on the entire planet. A neutron bomb might sound even more horrendous because it can kill every living creature in an area without doing great harm to buildings or other inanimate objects. Furthermore, unexpected negative consequences of technology—pollution, the greenhouse effect, imbalanced exploitation of resources—could be as destructive over time as the use of thermonuclear weapons.

While belief in the effectiveness of science escalated, its deadly side effects created serious concerns over its ethical, political and environmental implications. In brief, by the end of the first half of the twentieth century, science has ceased to be regarded as a benign contributor to progress with only minor, unforeseen penalties.

Transitions Toward the Postmodern

With admitted overstatement, we may argue that most of the major hermeneutical issues in the modern debate had already gained expression by the end of the nineteenth century, so that twentieth-century modernists represent the indefatigable efforts of new generations to tackle, in successive waves of fresh imagination, the same old problems often in the same old terms and at times reduplicating or rediscovering problems already fully recognized in the nineteenth century. The major questions as framed by twentieth-century scholars often appear unchanged, yet the solutions began to push the boundaries of what seemed possible before.

The need for an entirely fresh paradigm seemed justified by evidence of diminishing returns in the results of modern criticisms just when crises in the world demanded immediate humanitarian and practical responses—the imperialism of corporate interests, physically and sexually abused children, racism, male chauvinism, violent attacks on sexual minorities. In the fifties and sixties, scholars began to doubt the capacity of modern social theory either to diagnose these problems or to offer a liberal prescription for reform. The injustices of the day could no longer be expressed adequately by modern historical narrative but required subjective sensitivities to an array of very different signs of inhumanity. Without narratives of oppression, no metanarrative of general hermeneutics could interpret them or account adequately for the reality to which they belonged.

With differing degrees of disillusionment, a few artists, poets and architects in the 1940s and 1950s began to employ the term *postmodern* to indicate a rejection of modern conventions. To them, "modern" ideas or artistic efforts no longer meant something positive and contemporary. For example, the Surrealists, epitomized by Salvador Dali (1904-1989), dismissed the idea that the Modern Age was a step forward in the ascent of human knowledge, much less an important stage in the history of progressive revelation. Modern perceptions were judged as distorted as the melted clocks Dali painted on the limbs of a tree. Later the word *postmodern* was used to name a new age, only by stating its relation in time to another epoch (analogous to "the Middle Ages") without volunteering any of its content. One of its most significant effects was a description of the Modern Age itself as only one of many various epochs of altered human perceptions of reality. If modern interpretation focused on historical narrative, unified fields, universal truths and general hermeneutics, the postmodern era gave preference to a widespread perception of unrelated difference, without an innocent eye from which to view it.

The earliest and most prolific postmodern theory comes from France. After World War II, France underwent rapid change from a largely agricultural economy to the pursuit of modern innovations and achievement of spectacular renewal on almost all fronts. Postmodern options became vibrant alternatives in a poststructuralist movement spawned partly by the reorganizing of universities in the aftermath of the student revolts in 1968. French scholars' interest in Nietzsche and Heidegger over the constructive liberal views of the Frankfurt School often put them in direct conflict with Habermas and other German theorists.

French existentialism in the 1950s had put priority on the concrete conditions of human existence as the only real source for defining values and humane social transformation. Poststructuralist approaches questioned the capacity of modern methods to make sense of the present existential situation. Michel Foucault (1926-1984), one of the most influential historians of the epochs of human consciousness, offered a descriptive approach that can appear to lack a clear moral stance and may be accused of lending support by default to conservative political theory. Yet Foucault's preoccupation with the nodes and shifts in the avenues of power from one epoch to another clearly aims at a better understanding of the provisional mechanisms of social change, reform and revolution. Other scholars in this vein include Jean Baudrillard (b. 1929), Gilles Deleuze (b. 1925), Jacques Derrida (b. 1930) and Jean-François Lyotard (b. 1924).

In brief, French postmodern theorists have argued that words as signifiers are multivalent, so that interpretation requires a centering of these possibilities in some arbitrarily chosen sense of presence. The danger is that any centered set of words and images might seduce us into accepting its claim to order reality. With computer technology, the images of an alternative vision of the world might be experienced as hyperreal, more attuned to our limited human receptors of the real than the ordinary interactive stimulations of life itself. Conversely, every textual configuration of meaning can be decentered or shown to depend on prior biases or leaps of faith.

While allowing for trivial communication, postmodern theory focuses on a variety of problems attendant to the higher ideals of confronting reality itself. A characteristic of postmodern criticism is to vivify "difference" without seeking premature agreements, closure or harmonizing of differences diachronically into a historical narrative. Postmodern theory questions any objectively secured foundations, universals, metaphysics or analytical dualism (Hegelian or otherwise). Marxist theory, for example, needs to be reformulated with an awareness of the differences it represses within its own totalizing theory of socioeconomic reality. Postmodern critics feel free to attack the failures of modern humanism, liberalism and even revolutionary social systems without offering a positive alternative.

Steven Best and Douglas Kellner conclude their impressive study *Postmodern Theory* with the comment "In our view, no postmodern theorist has formulated an adequate political response to the degraded contemporary conditions they describe" (Best and Kellner, 285). Postmodern theory seems to suggest that there can be no "general hermeneutics" drawn from the arts and human sciences, as Friedrich D. E. *Schleiermacher (1768-1834) sought to find, but only regional, provincial or period-piece hermeneutics that do justice to specific sets of differences. The right of one regional hermeneutics to exercise dominance instead of another, or all other, regional hermeneutics would require a metaphysical, moral,

political or aesthetic conviction outside the bounds of most postmodern hermeneutical theory. A promising possibility may be that people identified by certain
differences might form temporary hegemonies with others for the sake of
accomplishing smaller projects. So feminists might side with ecologists, marginalized ethnic groups (e.g., Gypsies in Europe) might strike an alliance with
churches that have a strong stake in liberal social democracy, and so forth.

The postmodern debate has forced every interpreter to reconsider the ABCs
of literary interpretation. The title of an essay by Foucault asks, "What is an
author?" After the collapse of modern foundationalism, we need to reopen these
elementary questions in order to affirm, as a play on postmodern terminology,
life after difference. Even the structure of this essay on "European" interpretation,
distinct from other regions of the world, has raised as many problems in the
treatment of hermeneutics as it has attempted to solve. In the final analysis, the
postmodern movement itself may be only a transitional fad, which by calling the
bluff on every modern quest for the innocence of reason pushes us inadvertently
to face metaphysical issues that have never lost their grip on us, even if we have
lost our intellectual grip on them.

Biblical Interpretation in Twentieth-Century Europe

The focus of this overview now turns to the ongoing search for "the literal
sense" of Scripture as a classical and essential requirement of biblical interpretation in service to Christian theological understanding. The essay on eighteenth and nineteenth-century European interpretation discussed key elements
of the literal sense and the problem of recapitulating it in later epochs.
Certainly, twentieth-century biblical interpretation continued the modern
pursuit of historical origins of biblical texts and propensity to read biblical
texts as *sources* that refer, accurately or not, to ancient events, ideas, places,
religious rituals and/or "the [historical] author's intent." Alongside this
historicist and social-scientific preference, modern hermeneutics since the late
eighteenth century can be characterized by its pursuit of a "general hermeneutics."

As modern science interpreted complex material events by reducing them to
smaller interactions explainable by physics and its governing laws, so modern
literary theory drew on the latest insights of the arts and human sciences to
understand the foundational, general or universal elements of literary interpretation itself and what principles should therefore govern it. This conception finds
an incentive in Kant's linking of the sciences with pure reason and universal truths.
In the essay on eighteenth- and nineteenth-century European biblical interpretation and in the first part of this essay, we see some of the debate and options
for a "general hermeneutics." The classic Christian conception of the literal sense
of Scripture had to be related somehow to this modern perspective. The literal

sense of Scripture might be treated as simply identical with the best of modern literary theory (e.g., we read the Bible like any other book), or as a modification due to concerns peculiar to Scripture (e.g., we look for the Gospel that we already know as a preunderstanding before we read the Bible), or as an approach independent or alien to modern theory (e.g., the Holy Spirit directs our reading so we need few if any secular rules for interpretation).

In the formulation of a modern "general hermeneutics" and its relation to Bible and theology, the pioneer European scholar was Friedrich Schleiermacher. At the beginning of his *Brief Outline on the Study of Theology* (1810), Schleiermacher stated, "Theology is a positive science whose parts join into a cohesive whole only through this common relation to a particular mode of faith, i.e., a particular way of being conscious of God" (Schleiermacher 1965, 19). Schleiermacher distinguished his position from that of "rational theologians," who tried to locate theology within the sciences, and from speculative science, which relies on hypotheses based on empirical evidence. Theology may be called a "positive science" because it depends on scientific data assembled for "a practical task." Although he presupposed human consciousness of God as a historical universal, he saw no possibility of a Christian theology on that basis alone and, more radically in *The Christian Faith* (1821-1822), disclaimed "the task of establishing on a foundation of general principles a Doctrine of God" (Schleiermacher 1928, 3). He insisted on the necessity of historical "revelation" for Christian faith, while requiring the use of modern sciences to better understand it. Schleiermacher proposed a "general hermeneutics" for interpreting all literature, including the Bible; he then made allowance for the peculiarities of "inspiration" and "revelation" in biblical interpretation by suggesting, "Specialized hermeneutics and not general hermeneutics must deal with these questions" (Schleiermacher [1819] in Mueller-Vollmer, 83).

Schleiermacher's "specialized (or 'special') hermeneutics," designed to handle issues unique to the Bible and beyond the scope of his "general hermeneutics," remained remarkably undeveloped in his own work. Most later interpreters of Schleiermacher have simply ignored it. Yet biblical scholars and theologians often made implicit room for what might belong to a "special hermeneutics" when they interpreted the Bible. Many Roman Catholic scholars, for example, began to speak of a "sensus plenior" ("a full sense") either belonging somehow to the literal sense or beyond it. The sensus plenior of Scripture could account for the Christian interpretation of prophetic or theological ideas in a text even though these ideas might not have been historically in the mind of its human author. Sometimes Protestant theological interpretation advocated implicitly a "special hermeneutics," as in the cases of "demythologizing" proposed by Rudolf Bultmann (1884-1976) and "actualization" as used by Gerhard von Rad (1901-1971). For von Rad and many others, "actualization" described a way of reinterpreting traditions, even changing them significantly, in order to allow them to have a present effect in continuity with their original, liberating purpose. This theory helped rationalize dramatic changes in past traditions as they were transmitted over time before they became part of a Scripture (Groves, *Actualization*, 7-62). Likewise, von Rad tried to redefine the premodern idea of "typology" according to a modern evidence of an unfolding historical pattern of God's activity in "salvation history." Bultmann's efforts to speak of an inner "kerygmatic" essence to biblical tradition found its counterpart in Old Testament description of the "theology" of various prophets or traditions, for example, the theology of the deuteronomistic history or historians. The neutrality of method was occasionally questioned, as in Bultmann's brilliant essay on the question "Is Exegesis with Presuppositions Possible?" (Mueller-Vollmer, eds., *The Hermeneutics Reader*, 242-48). Especially in New Testament theology, the "new hermeneutic" of Gerhard Ebeling (b. 1912) and Ernst Fuchs (b. 1903) tried to find in Heidegger's theories of Being a way to interpret the language of faith, beyond Bultmannian demythologizing. Despite these exceptions most biblical scholars assumed general hermeneutics provided the essential foundations for a pretheological exegesis of Scripture prior to a subsequent theological interpretation of the same. The premodern idea of "the literal sense" might correspond to one or more of these levels of interpretation. At a pretheological level, historical criticisms provided the methods of choice for most biblical scholars at least in the first half of the twentieth century.

By the end of the nineteenth century, biblical scholars more often than not interpreted the Bible as an ancient source, among other ancient manuscripts, of imperfect *references* to ancient events, persons and beliefs. Julius *Wellhausen (1844-1918) had published his famous *Geschichte Israels* in 1878. In Leipzig, Rudolf Kittel (1853-1929) and later Albrecht Alt (1883-1956) contributed impressive historical studies of ancient Israelite religion, for example, concerning "the god of the fathers" in Genesis and the origins of ancient laws. This work responded to spectacular archaeological discoveries. The translation and publication in the 1870s of newly discovered materials from ancient Babylon and Assyria had begun to influence other areas of Old Testament studies. In 1895 Hermann *Gunkel's (1862-1932) *Schopfung und Chaos in Urzeit und Endzeit* (1895) demonstrated brilliantly how these materials illuminated the use of *Rahab*, *Leviathan* and other terms in Old Testament traditions. From ancient Arabic texts, the British scholar William Robertson *Smith (1846-1894) drew on promising anthropological parallels to ancient Israel in his *Lectures on the Religion of the Semites* (1885). William O. E. Oesterley (1866-1950) and Theodore H. Robinson (1881-1964) employed comparative anthropology to describe features of a "primitive" culture and psychology in ancient Israel. At an extreme in Germany, Friedrich Delitzsch (1850-1922) contended in lectures published as

Babel und Bibel in 1902-1903 that most Old Testament ideas derive from Babylonian culture and that the Israelite prophets malign their Babylonian mentors with false charges.

Among the most enduring contributions were Gunkel's efforts to use comparative ancient Near Eastern materials, complemented by his remarkable sensitivity to the aesthetic conventions that govern oral traditions. Drawing on recent studies of folklore, he could argue for the existence of unconscious rules of poetic beauty that governed the articulation and structure of outstanding oral literature. By holding together an "aesthetic criticism" of the *form* with a social-scientific sense for how oral units of tradition *function* in ancient rituals, Gunkel undermined Wellhausen's preoccupation with written "sources" as the earliest evidence of historical value. In his Genesis commentary and his studies of hymnic materials in the Psalms and elsewhere in the Bible, and by comparison with ancient Mesopotamian hymnology, Gunkel defended the antiquity of many traditions in the Old Testament against a trend among source critics to date the bulk of the Old Testament in the postexilic period.

New Testament scholar Martin Dibelius (1883-1947) identified Gunkel's approach as "form criticism," which he and others applied to parables, hymns and other types of literature in the New Testament. In New Testament studies, for example, if Q were a written source shared by Matthew and Luke, then its independent units would imply an oral prehistory and historical significance prior to Q. Gunkel himself tried to find in the typical elements retained in ancient oral tradition unconscious and trustworthy historical references to religious ideas in the ancient past. His goal, like that of many scholars in New Testament studies, was to write a history of literature, followed by a history of religion, that could be a resource for dogmatic theologians. The significance of the term "biblical *literature*" had shifted with Gunkel from written to oral, from lengthy redactional compositions (J, E, D, P or Q) to the smallest "units," yet the goal of interpretation remained the "religion" or "faith" of those who wrote and used these ancient texts in ancient times.

One trend in European scholarship between and after the wars has been for nations or groups of nations to develop distinctive "schools." Thus Spanish scholars often chose to work intensively on Targumic and Septuagintal studies. In England, Samuel H. Hooke's (1874-1968) *Myth and Ritual* (1935) helped establish the so- called myth and ritual school, which partly built on the studies of a Norwegian scholar, Sigmund *Mowinckel (1884-1965), a student of Gunkel. Other Scandinavian scholars, like Aage Bentzen (1894-1953) and Ivan Engnell (1906-1964), similarly defended the antiquity of many prophetic traditions on the basis of their continuous use in cultic rituals. Instead of a complex series of redactional layers in biblical texts, many Scandinavian scholars proposed a long oral transmission history with its own rules for preserving and changing these traditions. While such evidence supported the antiquity of oral tradition and provided a corrective to the negative view of "late" written texts, its relation to the theological interpretation of the Bible was less well developed.

From an entirely different perspective, a group of French scholars, including René Bloch and A. Robert, pioneered extensive studies in "anthological midrash," an ancient and learned technique of reusing phrases from prior normative traditions to create new texts. Arguably their best evidence could be found in so-called intertestamental texts such as Sirach and Baruch (Sheppard 1990, 111-14). They thought this style of rewriting traditions could be found in many places in both Old and New Testaments—for example, in Proverbs, Song of Songs and in many New Testament stories about Jesus. This evidence could seem to confirm rabbinic claims that later midrashic interpretation derives its rules from within the Jewish Scripture itself. A recent, exhaustive study by Jewish scholar Michael Fishbane describes this evidence as overdrawn and argues for at most a "trajectory" from "inner-biblical" interpretations to the later "rules" of rabbinic midrash (Fishbane, 525-30). How a Jewish midrashic approach, though treating Jewish tradition with greater appreciation, relates to the Christian search for the "literal sense" of both Old and New Testaments deserves much more careful research.

In the Netherlands, a debate arose among Calvinists, roughly between those who advocated "exemplary" preaching about figures in the Bible and those who preferred salvation-historical approaches (Greidanus). Does the presentation of a person in the Bible invite an interpretation of him or her as a model of righteous or sinful behavior? Or are biblical figures simply historical persons who testify to God's revelation in history or to "salvation history," in which case the depiction of the lives of the prophets is incidental and not testimony? Here a premodern literal sense assumption, maintained by *Calvin, that the Bible *in all its literary forms,* including its depiction of persons, can be read as a witness to revelation clashes with an equally "evangelical" but more peculiarly modern position that persons mentioned in the Bible were at most witnesses to historical events in which God's revelation occurred. In this latter case, prophets could explicitly bear witness to revelation within certain historical events, but most of the narratives about prophets merely provide us with supportive historical details about the witnesses. This strategy primarily uses the Bible as a resource that refers to a salvation history we can reconstruct outside of the Bible. The relation of the Bible itself to its literal sense and revelation becomes a new problem.

Another Dutch movement of biblical scholars, "the Amsterdam school," developed in full force after World War II, though its legacy goes back to the inaugural lecture by Juda Palache at the University of Amsterdam in 1925. These scholars were strongly influenced by comparative Near Eastern studies, Jewish theories of revelation and translation of the Hebrew Bible by Martin Buber

(1878-1965) and Franz Rosenzweig (1886-1929), and the Christian theological need to take the Bible's own context and intertext more seriously than scholarly speculation about the historical "origins" of biblical tradition. Just as Buber and Rosenzweig produced a translation that might help German Jewish readers understand midrashic interpretation, including its intertextual plays on similar words, so M. A. Beek and F. H. Breukelman strongly criticized the translation of the Bible in 1951 by the Dutch Bible Society because it failed to show the synchronic features of the biblical text integral to understanding both the New Testament use of the Old Testament and literal sense interpretations of Scripture prior to the modern period. While the Dutch Bible Society claimed to use "dynamic equivalence" to put into the "target" language what they regarded as the "kernel meaning" of each biblical text, the Amsterdam school advocated a translation that is "idiolectic," a term they prefer instead of "concordant." In other words, they called attention to the importance for theological interpretation of the surface structure of the text and its resonances with similar features of other texts in the Bible, in contrast to a consistent trend in the United Bible Societies to locate meaning only in a deep structure which made the surface structure expendable or only a provisional vehicle of a text's "message." Karel A. Deurloo in the Old Testament chair at the University of Amsterdam has been among the most prolific and profound scholars in this approach, which gives fresh emphasis to a classic principle of the literal sense: Scripture interprets Scripture (Kessler, *Voices From Amsterdam*, 37-51, 95-112).

In Germany many biblical scholars have recently employed comparative social scientific and anthropological analysis to find political insights, such as in the impressive work of the New Testament scholar Gerd Theissen, in Heidelberg. Beyond the uses of older modern criticisms, Ulrich Luz, a New Testament scholar in Tübingen, has built significantly on Gadamer's stress on the "effective history" of texts and has reopened important questions about the role of the history of interpretation and its methodological implications for biblical scholars. Finally, as an outstanding example of postmodern changes, special mention may be made of Rolf Rendtorff, who, as an Old Testament professor in Heidelberg and protégé of von Rad, has possibly done more than any other German scholar to create a fresh conversation with international Jewish scholars. Furthermore, Rendtorff stands out as one of the few German scholars who has critically challenged giving theological priority to theories of tradition history rather than to Jewish and Christian Scripture itself. His prolific contributions are "postmodern" in that he refuses to interpret as "biblical" the texts reconstructed by modern scholars who harmonize away differences in fragments of the Bible in order to rediscover homogeneous, historically more reliable "sources" or "original" pristine "forms." Instead, he has focused more on the "composition" of whole biblical books that derive from prebiblical traditions. Rendtorff stresses the importance of editorially self-conscious "cross-references" that create resonating religious themes across once independent prebiblical traditions. He suggests the need for a radically new type of biblical theology, one that presupposes the independent value of Jewish Scripture apart from Christian Scripture, as well as the need for a Christian reassessment of the Old Testament in the context of a Christian Bible.

This overview cannot do justice to the massive biblical theology debate among Old and New Testament scholars from the 1930s to the 1960s. Its history and issues have been well rehearsed in many accessible surveys. (See Sheppard 1991, 437-59, for details about the emergence and demise of both late modern neo-orthodoxy and the biblical theology movement in the 1960s.) In Europe, as elsewhere, the effort to define an independent theological contribution by biblical scholars through "biblical theology" often participates in a modern fallacy of dividing disciplines into territories of specialized discourse without any clear relationship to each other.

In 1951 Gerhard Ebeling examined clearly the problems facing any "biblical theology" when it sought to find an "inner unity of manifold testimony of the Bible" (Ebeling, 96). From a modern perspective one may ask what the word *testimony* means in this sentence. If it employs a premodern term now as though it signified modern "reference" to historical events, then biblical theology is not really reading the Bible but a history to which the human words of the Bible point. If, as Ebeling is aware, it is used in the premodern sense of a witness to revelation, whose subject matter is not history but the Torah and the Gospel which itself defines the nature of human history, then we must ask about the role of a "general hermeneutics" in such a peculiarly theological interpretation.

From a postmodern perspective, the problem with Ebeling's definition of "biblical theology" is also its modern preoccupation with "inner unity," as if to say that "inner difference" need be less helpful as a testimony to God's revelation of reality, which must remain to some extent a mystery in the best of our imagination. Arguably inner unity is something Christians can attribute only by faith to the subject matter of revelation to which the testimony of the Bible points and from which—certainly not from history alone—it finds whatever validity it may claim to have. It lives only from its subject matter without denying for an instant the full embeddedness in history of the human testimony itself. For these reasons a postmodern definition of "biblical theology" requires a reformulation of a pre-Gabler (*see* Biblical Interpretation in the 18th & 19th Centuries) definition to allow for the arbitrary specializations of contemporary biblical scholars without compromising their attempt, shared with theologians, to find the literal sense of Scripture, which is inherently both "biblical" and "theology."

A very common modern error in "biblical theology" has been to label as "biblical" almost any reconstruction of tradition found partially preserved in the

Bible. In most cases the reconstruction is technically "prebiblical," as is Q in Gospel studies, for example. If biblical theology depends in fact on prebiblical traditions for making normative theological statements, then it fails to understand the particular nature of a scripture, Jewish or Christian. It fails to recognize the possibility that a tradition will become scriptural in no predictable relationship to a modern historian's estimate of its original historical value as a prebiblical tradition. A hymn to the sun god might become part of a biblical Torah psalm (Psalm 19), while an ancient normative document (perhaps an early edition of Q) may in itself attain no scriptural status at all.

European biblical scholarship has felt the impact of liberation theology and responded in a great variety of ways. In terms of the present debate over the literal sense of Scripture, liberation theology makes explicit an element it rightly assumes to be within the *regula fidei:* God's special response to the laments of the poor and the oppressed. Likewise, liberation theology lends support to a European postmodern exercise in practical theology by its insistence on the social and cultural location of the interpreter as a factor that informs his or her perception of priorities and what are the more important generalizations for theological discourse between conflicting groups. Finally, wisdom literature in the Old and New Testaments accepts an informed experiential knowledge of differences as a crucial factor in an interpreter's capacity to ask profound questions both of a text and of its subject matter. Many European biblical scholars regularly engage these issues and bring profound sociopolitical sensitivity to their work in dialogue with liberation theologians.

In Europe, as elsewhere, the older modern historical criticisms remain dominant, though they are no longer the only reasonable methods of textual interpretation. The variety of other approaches may be driven less by a fresh theological understanding of the literal sense of Scripture than by innovations in other university disciplines applicable to biblical texts. The postmodern debate in literary criticism must continue to influence the future of biblical studies. Biblical scholars today confront a situation that forces an admission that more things can be done with texts, including biblical texts, than might have ever been imagined.

Surely there are some intellectual benefits in disciplined investigations of almost any kind. We might readily admit that most biblical scholars today lack the sophistication in rhetorical theory requisite of their counterparts in the sixteenth and seventeenth century, long before the emergence of modern referential interpretations of the Bible that gave preference to various historical criticisms. Most certainly the choices are not simply between synchronic and diachronic interpretation. If more and more things can be done with texts, then biblical scholars may be forced to declare more self-consciously why they want to do anything with biblical texts at all. Surely one reason historical criticism won the day was an implicit theological agreement that the Bible claims something about God's revelation *within history*. While modern Marxist and sociological studies attempted to describe dimensions of political significance in literature, the prevailing modern historicism of biblical studies could be wedded to a radical hopefulness for democratic socialism, if not a revolutionary liberation. Therefore esoteric historical interpretations of biblical texts met the appetites of a wide-ranging modern elite, whether it shared a theological agenda or none at all. This climate of opinion has been altered remarkably since the 1960s.

In considering a postmodern future to biblical studies in Europe, I would like to recall Karl *Barth's reflections on Schleiermacher's theory. In his Göttingen lectures of 1923-1924, Barth tentatively considered the proposal of a special hermeneutics for Scripture if one took into account its subject matter as the Word of God: "What if special New Testament hermeneutics, whether gratefully employing Schleiermacher's method or any other general method, were to consist quite simply of taking these texts more seriously in this specific sense?" (Barth 1982, 157). Later, in his *Church Dogmatics,* Barth took a more negative position and tried to turn the whole proposal of Schleiermacher on its head by declaring,

It is from the word of man in the Bible that we must learn what is to be learned concerning the word of man in general. . . . There is no such thing as a special biblical hermeneutics. But we have to learn that hermeneutics which is alone and generally valid by means of the Bible as the witness to revelation. (Barth 1956, 466).

From a postmodern perspective we might agree with Barth that there is no hermeneutic "in general" that can be derived objectively through the arts and human sciences. The historical dimensions of a biblical text remain indeterminate until the text is read in a specific way. Certainly a biblical scholar can measure differences in the historical lines of continuity and discontinuity from prebiblical texts to the other roles they play as biblical traditions. The most important historical dimension for interpreting Christian Scripture scripturally may not be the origin of isolated traditions so much as the role of retentions from their prehistory and, just as significant, how the context of Scripture has *rehistoricized* prebiblical texts when they became incorporated in a scripture.

If biblical interpretation is to remain neutral theologically and politically, is there any reason why one method ought to have priority over another? If, however, biblical interpretation belongs to a particular theological and/or political vision of reality, then priorities in methodology ought to follow logically and consistently. In other words, Barth is right to ground all literary interpretation in an exercise of faith when one seeks to interpret a Scripture scripturally. The Christian preference for the literal sense of Scripture in no way precludes the value of other priorities, especially not Jewish midrashic exegesis. Nor does it deny God's revelation through nature and through human wisdom found everywhere in the world. What it does admit is a human decision to live by faith according to an unseen, though perhaps strongly sensed, presence whose full revelation of the Gospel can be heard only through the sufficient historical testimony of Jewish and Christian Scripture. We confront today a need to reconfigure in a postmodern mode the premodern terms of the literal sense of Scripture—including our hearing the biblical text as human testimony; the logic of revelation; proper uses of the resources of the arts, humanities and sciences; the nature of the rule of faith; how Scripture interprets Scripture; the role of a limited use of typology as phenomenal prophecy; critical discernment of interpretation within the community of faith; and a fresh sense of what the gospel of Jesus Christ requires and grants to us politically, personally and socially. A promising postmodern response cannot be postmodern by circumventing modern criticisms but must move back into premodern criticisms and armed with the insights of modernity push past it in order to frame in a new way the old persistent questions raised by Scripture, history and revelation.

BIBLIOGRAPHY

J. L. Austin, *How to Do Things with Words* (2d ed.; Cambridge, MA: Harvard University Press, 1975 [1962]); K. Barth, *Church Dogmatics* (1/2; Edinburgh: T & T Clark, 1956); idem, *Theology of Schleiermacher: Lectures at Göttingen, Winter Semester of 1923-24* (Grand Rapids: Eerdmans, 1982); S. Best and D. Kellner, *Postmodern Theory: Critical Interrogations* (New York: Guilford, 1991); B. S. Childs, *Biblical Theology in Crisis* (Philadelphia: Westminster Press, 1970); idem, *Biblical Theology of the Old and New Testaments* (Minneapolis: Fortress, 1993); R. E. Clements, *One Hundred Years of Old Testament Interpretation* (Philadelphia: Westminster Press, 1976); R. J. Coggins and J. L. Houlden, eds., *A Dictionary of Biblical Interpretation* (London: SCM Press; Philadelphia: Trinity Press, 1990); G. Ebeling, "The Meaning of 'Biblical Theology' " in *Word and Faith* (Philadelphia: Fortress, 1963) 79-97; E. J. Epp and G. W. MacRae, eds., *The New Testament and Its Modern Interpreters* (Philadelphia: Fortress, 1989); M. Fishbane, *Biblical Interpretation in Ancient Israel* (Oxford: Clarendon, 1985); M. Foucault, "What Is an Author?" in *The Foucault Reader*, ed. P. Rabinow (New York: Pantheon, 1984) 101-20; H.-G. Gadamer, *Truth and Method* (2d ed.; New York City: Seabury, 1975 [1965]); S. Greidanus, *Sola Scriptura: Problems and Principles in Preaching Historic Texts* (Toronto: Wedge, 1970); J. W. Groves, *Actualization and Interpretation in the Old Testament* (SBLDS 86; Atlanta: Scholars Press); H. F. Hahn, *The Old Testament in Modern Research* (Philadelphia: Muhlenberg, 1954); M. Kessler, *Voices from Amsterdam: A Modern Tradition of Reading Biblical Narrative* (Atlanta: Scholars Press, 1994); D. E. Klemm, ed., *Hermeneutical Inquiry, 1: The Interpretation of Texts; 2: The Interpretation of Existence* (Atlanta: Scholars Press, 1986); D. A. Knight and G. M. Tucker, eds., *The Hebrew Bible and Its Modern Interpreters* (Chico, CA: Scholars Press, 1985); H.-J. Kraus, *Die Biblische Theologie: Ihre Geschichte und Problematik* (Neukirchen-Vluyn: Neukirchener, 1970); W. G. Kümmel, *The New Testament: The History of the Investigation of Its Problems* (Nashville: Abingdon, 1972); F. Lentricchia, *After the New Criticism* (Chicago: University of Chicago Press, 1980); G. Maier, *Biblical Hermeneutics* (Wheaton, IL: Crossway, 1994 [1993]); O. Merk, *Biblische Theologie des Neuen Testaments in ihrer Anfangszeit* (Marburg: Elwert, 1972); S. Neill and T. Wright, *The Interpretation of the New Testament, 1861-1986* (2d ed.; New York: Oxford University Press, 1988); B. Ollenburger, E. A. Martens and G. F. Hasel, eds., *The Flowering of Old Testament Theology: A Reader in Twentieth-Century Old Testament Theology, 1930-1990* (Winona Lake, IN: Eisenbrauns, 1992); R. E. Palmer, *Hermeneutics: Interpretation Theory in Schleiermacher, Dilthey, Heidegger and Gadamer* (Evanston, IL: Northwestern University Press, 1969); R. Rendtorff, *The Old Testament: An Introduction* (Minneapolis: Fortress, 1985 [1983]); idem, *The Problem of the Process of Transmission in the Pentateuch* (Sheffield, U.K.: JSOT Press, 1990 [1977]); H. G. Reventlow, *Problems of Biblical Theology in the Twentieth Century* (Philadelphia:

Fortress, 1986 [1983]); J. K. Riches, *A Century of New Testament Study* (Valley Forge, PA: Trinity Press, 1993); J. Rogers and D. K. McKim, *The Authority and Interpretation of the Bible* (San Francisco: Harper & Row, 1979); J. Rogerson, C. Rowland and B. Lindars, *The Study and Use of the Bible* (Grand Rapids: Eerdmans, 1988); F. Schleiermacher, *Brief Outline on the Study of Theology*, trans. T. N. Tice (Richmond, VA: John Knox Press, 1965 [2d ed. 1830]); idem, *Christian Faith* (Edinburgh: T & T Clark, 1928 [2d ed. 1830]); idem, "General Hermeneutics" in *The Hermeneutics Reader*, ed. K. Mueller-Vollmer (New York: Continuum, 1992) 73-86; G. T. Sheppard, "Biblical Interpretation After Gadamer" *Pneuma* 16, no. 1 (1994) 121-41; idem, "How Do Neoorthodox and Post-neoorthodox Theologians Approach the 'Doing of Theology' Today?" in *Doing Theology in Today's World: Essays in Honor of Kenneth S. Kantzer*, ed. J. Woodbridge and R. E. McComiskey (Grand Rapids: Zondervan, 1991) 437-59; idem, *Wisdom as a Hermeneutical Construct: A Study in the Sapientializing of the Old Testament* (Berlin: Walter de Gruyter, 1990); R. Tarnas, *The Passion of the Western Mind: Understanding Ideas That Have Shaped Our World View* (New York: Ballantine, 1991); A. Thiselton, *New Horizons in Hermeneutics: The Theory and Practice of Transforming Biblical Reading* (Grand Rapids: Zondervan, 1992); R. Wiggershaus, *The Frankfurt School: Its History, Theories and Political Significance* (Cambridge, MA: MIT Press, 1994).

G. T. SHEPPARD

Barr, James *(b. 1924)*

James Barr was born in Glasgow, was raised in the Church of Scotland and received a classical British education. He attended the University of Edinburgh and became a minister in his church, serving briefly in Tiberias, Israel. He has taught at various institutions both in the British Isles and in North America. These include the Presbyterian College in Montreal (1943-1955); the University of Edinburgh (1955-1961); Princeton Theological Seminary (1961-1965); the University of Manchester (1965-1976); and the University of Oxford (1976-1989). He became Distinguished Professor of Hebrew Bible at Vanderbilt University in 1989. Barr has received numerous awards, honorary degrees, fellowships and guest lectureships throughout his career.

Context. Barr defends the modernist tradition in the field of biblical criticism. He stands at the convergence of three competing philosophies, each having emerged since the Enlightenment. The biblical scholars of the Enlightenment sought objectivity through critical dissection of the ancient text, treating it as if it were any other human artifact. In opposition Romanticism eschewed logic and objectivity, insisting that interpretation be passionate and imaginative. Fundamentalism tries to preserve biblical authority by seeking a return to a precritical understanding of the ancient biblical text. Modernism is the Enlightenment's defense against Romanticism and fundamentalism. Barr, the quintessential modernist, has spent his professional lifetime combating these two tendencies. With prosecutorial zeal, much of Barr's work examines one or the other of these movements as they intersect with biblical scholarship.

In the Enlightenment there begins a whole new way of approaching theology and biblical study. Rationality and logic would now hold sway, and both scientists and critics strived toward objectivity, a complete, disinterested noninvolvement with the subject that enabled one to see things "as they truly are" *(wie es eigentlicht gewesen)*. This movement culminates in the three undergirding theories of the modern world: the theory of evolution as a means to understand the natural world (Darwin), the notion of the unconscious as the key to understanding the individual soul (Freud) and class struggle as the key to understanding the structures of society (Marx).

Romanticism reacts strongly against this intrusion of science and scientific method upon humanistic studies. Its impact upon the wider intellectual culture came through literature. Major literary figures such as William Blake, Henry David Thoreau and William Wordsworth felt that the intellect presented the greatest hindrance to the development of the soul and that one might discover true human value only by unleashing the passion of the body and the intuition. This new movement, called Romanticism, influenced theology and biblical criticism significantly. In the years following World War II the biblical theology movement claimed that only a Hebraic (that is, intuitive, emotional) reading of the biblical text could be in any way faithful. The biblical theology movement was at heart a Romantic reaction to the cold rationality of historical criticism, which was the Enlightenment's contribution to biblical interpretation. Barr found unconvincing the arguments that evidence for a Hebrew mindset might be found in the Bible.

Fundamentalists found historical criticism of the Bible unfaithful because it appeared to undermine the authority of the biblical text. They sought to develop a hermeneutic that would return them to a pristine past where God's authority was applied more clearly and without ambiguity. When Barr faced the fundamentalists, he strongly questioned whether it was possible to gain access to such a past through the Scriptures. In contrast to the fundamentalists, Barr projects the model of a scholar for whom one's religious commitment would have no impact upon one's interpretation of the biblical text.

Barr rejects any effort to remove the examination of the Bible from scrutiny by human reason. He describes himself (albeit facetiously) as heir to the "Scottish tradition of Common Sense philosophy" (Barr 1968, ["Common Sense,"] 385). This puts him at odds with those in the biblical theology movement, such as George Ernest *Wright, John Bright, William Foxwell *Albright and Thorlief Boman, who claimed that the western European intellectual tradition (based on Plato or Aristotle) is alien to Hebraic thinking. Hebraic thinking, this wild, primitive sensibility of ancient man, proceeded from the seat of the passions and opposed rationality. The Greek tradition of dispassionate reason as the source of reality could never truly understand the inner dynamics of the Bible.

The members of the biblical theology movement wanted to recover the transcendent, which they regarded as proceeding from the nonrational faculties. The nonrational is then associated with God. The Enlightenment had severely questioned the transcendent claims of the Bible. Wright and others believed that if they could preserve some corner of Scripture from rational scrutiny, they could claim for that piece divine origin and divine authority. So, for instance, Wright believed that the Bible witnessed to "the God who acts," found not in rational propositions or words on a page but rather in God's mighty acts intervening in the fortunes of the nation of Israel, as in the exodus. When we read the accounts of these mighty acts, the events re-actualize themselves in the experience of the reader. The reader encounters the God who acted so in the past. In this manner, as

Jews celebrate the Passover Seder or Christians the Eucharist, the exodus event and the passion of Christ are experienced anew.

Barr applied himself to those claims in *The Semantics of Biblical Language* (1961) and *Old and New in Interpretation* (1966) and tested them against three sources of evidence: the actual text of the Bible; the artifactual remains left in ancient Israel (archaeology); and the modern field of linguistics. Barr thereby found the transcendent claims of the biblical theology movement wanting. According to Barr, they lacked methodological precision and thus their conclusions were questionable.

Because Barr takes on popular and powerful adversaries, he is something of a loner, aligning himself with no particular group or school but rather speaking forcefully against those who identify with various schools or movements within the biblical academy.

Major Writings. Barr has produced a prodigious quantity of detailed, quality scholarship in diverse areas. His mastery of many languages and cultures and his capability to include entire fields within his critical horizon (such as linguistics, analytical philosophy, European history) have been a great asset in his work. A few representative works from his lengthy bibliography embody some major trends in his writings.

Barr wrote his first major work, *The Semantics of Biblical Language,* in 1961. In this book he declared independence from his teachers, and the work reflects the concerns that have continued to occupy Barr over the length of his career. Here Barr analyzed the linguistic assertions of the biblical theology movement, responding to their claims that the Hebrew language in its very structure reflects the particular mode of thinking characterized as the Hebraic mindset. Barr never addressed whether there might have been a Hebraic mindset or whether it might be different from a western European one. Rather, he pointed out that the claims of a unique Hebraic way of thinking were insufficiently supported by the evidence. He applied the rigors of scholarly methodology (in this case, in the field of linguistics) to the linguistic claims of Boman (*Hebrew Thought Compared with Greek* [Norwegian; German, 1954; English 1960]) and others. Barr found many examples in which Hebrew used abstract concepts, specific time references and such—concepts characteristic of so-called Greek thought and not Hebraic. Barr's book was widely acknowledged as having effectively undercut the claims of the biblical theology movement. Nevertheless, biblical theology's claims have continued to crop up in scholarly writings and in the teaching of the Bible in graduate schools, and this has been a source of great exasperation to Barr.

Almost a decade after the publication of *Semantics*, Brevard *Childs, teaching at Yale, published *Biblical Theology in Crisis* (1970), which examined the same territory Barr had already covered. When Barr wrote *Semantics*, the biblical theology movement was enjoying its heyday; when Childs published his work, the movement was facing near-terminal decline. But Childs, unlike Barr, offered his own proposal (canonical criticism) to replace the biblical theology movement. Childs wanted to preserve the possibility that the Bible still might maintain its transcendent value in some other fashion.

Barr treated Childs's project in *Canon, Scripture and Authority* (1983). In it he exposed Childs to the same blistering critique he had brought against the biblical theology movement, arguing that Childs was repeating the mistakes of those he was seeking to displace. The biblical theology movement claimed that within the biblical acts of God one encounters a witness to divine presence. Childs simply deferred that divine presence to the period of canonical development, when the Bible took its final form. Childs asserted that the final form of the text and the history of its interpretation by faithful Christian communities become witnesses to divine presence. For Barr, however, it does not matter

whether one makes a totalizing, transcendental claim (God's presence) for an ancient historical event (the biblical theology movement) or for a putative textual process (canonical criticism). The claim is still unsupported. Barr accused the biblical theology movement of seeking to dominate the interpretation of the Bible through false intellectual claims. When interpreters claim for a particular part of the literary process (whatever part they might choose) the divine presence, they thereby claim that their interpretation cannot be questioned and must necessarily displace all other possible interpretations. It is the true, the "inner" interpretation. As such it is an act of power.

Another target of Barr's scrutiny was the conservative Protestant intellectual tradition. Barr came out of a tradition not dissimilar to that of the fundamentalists. If Barr's books regarding the biblical theology movement and Childs represent his reaction against the Romantic assumptions of his teachers and colleagues, then in his two books on fundamentalism (*Fundamentalism* [1977] and *Beyond Fundamentalism* [1984]) he reacts against the religious training of his youth and early adulthood. Barr saw Protestant evangelical apologetics as a smokescreen for irrational metaphysical claims.

Fundamentalism and evangelicalism, as intellectual movements within Christianity, begin with the Reformation tradition found in the English, Scottish and Dutch branches of Calvinism. Writers within these traditions worked hard to establish intellectual credibility for their Christian claims. They did so through three related assertions: that all intellectual systems are based on presuppositions, and these presuppositions are by definition unsupported by any evidence; that the Christian presupposition is that God has reliably communicated God's will through the Scriptures; and that a respectful, consistent application of hermeneutical techniques will uncover the original intent of the writers. This original intent is identified with the content of God's communication. The different presuppositions of modernism naturally result (by this explanation) in different conclusions regarding the nature of the Bible or the understanding of the God who wrote the Bible. The modernist conclusions would not therefore threaten a fundamentalist worldview.

Barr responds to this on two levels. First, he attacks the inconsistencies between what the fundamentalists claim and what they do. For instance, with regard to the fundamentalists' claim to base their methodology on the Scripture understood in its original context, Barr demonstrates that many of their claims are based on nonbiblical philosophical systems rather than the Bible. These other systems might have their validity, but they do not reflect the Scriptures. By the fundamentalists' own assertions, to demonstrate a mixed foundationalism (the Scripture plus something else) constitutes the invalidation of their entire system.

Further, Barr points out how this apologetic tradition functions for the nonprofessionals within the fundamentalist or evangelical community. He notes that for most, to know that someone from their group has read one of the giants of theological modernism (Karl *Barth, Reinhold Niebuhr, Hermann Gunkel, Julius *Wellhausen, Martin Heidigger or Jean Paul Sartre, for instance) is sufficient. They are thereby relieved from the responsibility of interacting with these major figures themselves: "Because B. B. Warfield had read Wellhausen, I don't have to. Because Francis Schaeffer had read Sartre and Camus, and has told me that their systems are barren, I don't have to even consider them." Barr argued that the quest for reliable hermeneutical principles that seek to honor the authority of the sacred text protects the fundamentalist or evangelical from having to think about painful and threatening challenges to their extrabiblical theological systems.

In 1992 Barr published *The Garden of Eden and the Hope of Immortality*. For those who have complained that Barr only tears down the work of others, offering no

constructive theological reflection of his own, this book creatively and skillfully approaches an old problem with a sensitive hand. Barr's constructions are provocative and thoughtful. One will find in this book his continued preoccupation with the "errors" of the biblical theology movement. In this case he is concerned with the popular notion that the ancient Israelites did not believe that the soul was immortal. That was (they said) a Greek concept.

But here, through an examination of the early stories of Genesis (the Garden of Eden and the flood in particular), he suggests that notions of immortality were not as unusual in the Hebrew conception as is widely thought. We find here an important observation regarding Barr's work. Even in his primary examinations of ancient texts he works on a secondary level, a metacriticism. He examines the way others have interpreted various biblical passages and questions their objectivity. He seeks to uncover the hidden assumptions and ideological biases that inform their work. Such biases, Barr argues, reflect their own cultural and political location, not an objective approach that honors the integrity of the text, as they claim. His concern is to uncover the ideological concerns that have dominated the interpretation of the Bible when it strays from the path of the Enlightenment.

Major Themes. We return to an earlier comment, that Barr owes an intellectual debt to "the Scottish tradition of Common Sense philosophy." More than anything else, this is the theme that Barr revisits again and again. He challenges colleagues within his field of biblical criticism to be honest about their assumptions and presuppositions and to apply their methodology consistently. He implores them to look at the evidence and not claim expertise in fields that are unfamiliar, not to avoid the obvious or to follow slavishly the obscure or fashionable.

Further, Barr shows a distinct aversion to metaphysical claims or at least to metaphysical claims that masquerade as scholarly observations. Barr's academic writings assume a division between scholarship (intellectual activity) and devotion (existential, liturgical activity). One could frame his perspective by imagining an impenetrable wall between the two modes of thinking or being. According to Barr, one might have a personal faith, but it must not intrude upon scholarly activity or pollute its goal of objectivity.

Significance. Barr's primary contribution to the field of biblical criticism has been a negative one. By this is not meant that he has hurt the field of biblical criticism. Rather, he has served the field by exposing the weaknesses of other systems. He has not offered to his colleagues an alternative system that others might subscribe to in order to reach the putatively correct interpretation of biblical texts. Barr would be suspicious of all such systems. Rather, he offers a skepticism of the claims of others, and thus he promotes a kind of care and intellectual rigor that does the craft of biblical interpretation good.

Long before deconstruction became part of the critical jargon, Barr was exposing the power relationships that remain at the heart of all interpretive endeavors. When biblical interpreters seek to control the way the Bible is read, such efforts at hegemony cannot but affect both the methodology and the results of any serious hermeneutical effort.

BIBLIOGRAPHY
Works. J. Barr, *Beyond Fundamentalism* (Philadelphia: Westminster, 1984); idem, *Biblical Words for Time* (London: SCM, 1962); idem, "Common Sense and Biblical Language," *Bib* 49 (1968) 377-87; idem, *Fundamentalism* (Philadelphia: Westminster, 1977); idem, *The Garden of Eden and the Hope of Immortality* (Minneapolis: Fortress, 1992); idem, *Holy Scripture, Canon, and Authority* (Philadelphia: Westminster, 1983); idem, *Old and New in Interpretation* (London: SCM, 1966); idem, *The Semantics of Biblical Language* (London: Oxford University Press, 1961). **Studies.** T. Boman, *Hebrew Thought Compared with Greek* (The Library of History and Doctrine; London: SCM; Philadelphia: West-

minster, 1960); D. Penchansky, *The Politics of Biblical Theology* (Macon, GA: Mercer University Press, 1995); G. E. Wright, *The God Who Acts: Biblical Theology as Recital* (Studies in Biblical Theology 8; London: SCM, 1952).

D. Penchansky

Barrett, C(harles) K(ingsley) (b. 1917)

C. K. Barrett is the outstanding British New Testament scholar of the second half of the twentieth century. He was born on May 4, 1917, the son of a Methodist minister. His name, Charles Kingsley, reveals a family admiration for the nineteenth-century Anglican clergyman, Christian socialist, writer, scholar and supporter of the views of Charles Darwin.

Barrett was educated at Shebbear College, Pembroke College and Wesley House in Cambridge, where he first studied mathematics and then theology. He was awarded the B.D. (1947) and D.D. (1956). In recognition of his contribution to New Testament scholarship, other honorary doctoral degrees have followed. He was elected a fellow of the British Academy (1961), awarded the Burkitt medal for biblical scholarship (1972) and elected president of *Studiorum Novi Testamenti Societas* (1973). Recognition of the quality of his scholarship has also taken the form of the award of prestigious lectureships in the United States, Canada, Europe and Australia.

After serving as a Methodist minister at Darlington, Barrett became lecturer in theology at Durham University (1945) and professor of divinity (1958). Throughout his teaching career he was identified with Durham, where he was dedicated to teaching, especially in the honors school and the graduate program. He supervised a large number of graduate students, attracting many researchers from the United States and elsewhere. Something of his contribution can be measured by the placement of many of his graduate students in teaching positions in universities around the world.

Yet these students do not constitute a discrete school like those generated by some scholars in Europe and the United States. Rather they show an indebtedness to a tradition of a historical reading of the New Testament, an eclectic reading of the text in the context of whatever historical evidence is relevant and making use of whatever methods are appropriate to the task. Thus there is also an eclecticism when it comes to methods. Methods themselves are contingent and influenced by the nature of the task at hand. Barrett has always referred to himself as a historian, a historian of early Christianity, of the New Testament. But he also recognized that these texts are profoundly theological in content, and the historical interpreter is inevitably involved in theology.

Context. To understand his work as a New Testament scholar, it is necessary to take into account Barrett's commitment to the church. He was brought up in the Methodist church, in which he became a minister, and throughout his academic career he maintained a regular ministry in the churches around Durham. A commitment to Methodism has marked his career but not in a narrow sense, as can be seen in his support for such ecumenical agencies as the Bible Society. Nevertheless the traditions of Methodism run deeply in his life. Evidence of this is in his publications relating the New Testament to church issues of the time, such as Anglican-Methodist relations, the nature of ministerial authority, church, ministry and sacraments, and what Methodists should believe about righteousness and justification. Reformation motifs lie close to the surface here.

The most important influence on Barrett's theological development came through the work of Sir Edwyn Hoskyns and F. Noel Davey. While it may be that Hoskyns was the primary contributor in this partnership, the significance of Davey's contribution has often been overlooked. But it has not been ignored by Barrett, whose continuing friendship with Davey was significant. This is seen in his publishing relationship with SPCK, where Davey was editor. In addition to inspiring him to a life of New Testament scholarship, Hoskyns, who was one of the early English readers of Karl *Barth and the translator of his *Romans* into English, probably introduced the young Barrett to Barth. It is thus no accident that in his own commentary on Romans, Barrett should refer to Barth and his influence, not only on the commentary on Romans but also in relation to his continuing life as a Christian. References to Barth are also in his commentaries on Paul's letters to the Corinthians. These draw attention to the Reformation, to John *Calvin and Martin *Luther and through them to a tradition of the interpretation of Paul.

Barrett's reading of Barth is also indicative of his early relationship with German theology and New Testament scholarship; he read Rudolf *Bultmann's *New Testament Theology* in German as it came out in parts. In these early postwar years Barrett was one of the few English New Testament scholars who maintained a positive relationship to German New Testament scholarship. The Marburg connection with Bultmann is evident in his reviews of Bultmann's works and his articles dealing with the overall significance of Bultmann as well as various specific aspects of his work.

Further, there has been an ongoing connection with Tübingen, for more than forty years with Ernst *Käsemann, one of Bultmann's students, and later with Martin Hengel. While a positive relationship to German New Testament scholarship is now not so uncommon, in the decades immediately following World War II this was not true of English New Testament scholarship generally. Barrett was one of the few scholars in England making positive and yet critical use of the work of Bultmann. Even at the end of the twentieth century, English New Testament scholars are not generally sympathetic to the work of Bultmann, and his work is not well understood even in areas in which conclusions he reached have been widely accepted.

Barrett's positive and critical use of Bultmann was possible because he also drew on another important tradition of New Testament scholarship. This tradition is linked with both Cambridge and Durham in the person of Joseph Barber *Lightfoot, Bishop of Durham (1879-1889). Barrett has lectured and written on Lightfoot and Brooke Foss *Westcott on a number of occasions. Lightfoot himself entered into critical dialogue with Ferdinand Christian *Baur, the great Tübingen New Testament scholar of Lightfoot's day. The focus of Lightfoot's work on the New Testament was the epistles of Paul, which was also a major focus for Baur. In terms of volume, concentration over a number of years, and Barrett's own evaluation of the relative importance of Paul, there can be no doubt that in his own estimation his work on Paul is his most important.

Work. Using other criteria it might be argued that Barrett's commentary on John and other associated publications constitute Barrett's most significant work. Not only has the commentary on John seen two major English-language editions (1955, 1978), but also in 1990 there was a new edition of the commentary in German in the Meyer series, where it stands alongside the commentary by Bultmann. The comparative strengths of these two commentators become apparent. Bultmann, with his development of a daring and complex hypothesis, offered a solution to a whole range of critical problems. Barrett, however, has shown a reluctance to adopt hypotheses that move far from justifying evidence. It is not enough to show that the hypothesis has the power to resolve intractable problems. Barrett's work grows out the careful linguistic and historical analysis of the text, in the tradition of earlier great British New Testament scholarship but in full appreciation of the history of religions tradition that finds abundant expression in the work of Bultmann.

Running against the stream of much contemporary Johannine scholarship, which accepts a distinctive hypothetical source as the basis of the Gospel (Bultmann's "signs source"), Barrett championed John's dependence on known sources: the Synoptic Gospels, primarily Mark; to a lesser extent and perhaps less certainly, Luke. On this basis the distinctive contribution of the Fourth Evangelist becomes quite apparent. Barrett argues that the Evangelist came to an understanding of the gospel, which was rooted in Judaism but which in an interaction with Hellenism found expression in universal terms. Thus, although the approach of the historian is dominant in his work, the attention to theology is also important, even if it is not as obvious as it is in Bultmann's commentary.

One of the distinctive marks of Barrett's treatment arises from an acceptance of the basic unity of the Gospel, apart from John 21, which he allows was probably a later addition by another author. The Evangelist has prepared a unified interpretation of Jesus on the basis of his understanding of the Synoptics. That being so, perceived tensions in the Gospel need to be understood in ways compatible with a single author, an author who exhibited carefulness and skill. Thus Barrett stresses the paradoxical nature of Johannine thought because he thinks that the paradox lies in the Evangelist's understanding of God himself. God is hidden and God is revealed. Inasmuch as God is hidden, Jesus affirms "the Father is greater than"; but because God is also revealed, Jesus can say "I and the Father are one." This foundational paradox has consequences in other places in which the necessity of the determining drawing of the Father is asserted alongside the call to come and believe in Jesus, and in which the eschatological fulfillment is affirmed in the present alongside the expectation of future fulfillment.

In addition to the commentary on John, *Essays on John* collects a number of important pieces. There is also Barrett's *The Gospel of John and Judaism* and a later essay "Johannine Christianity," both of which appeared first in German. Together these (there are other individual essays on John) constitute a significant contribution to Johannine scholarship. Yet this is only one aspect of Barrett's contribution to New Testament scholarship.

From the beginning of his published work Barrett has shown an interest in the formation of the Gospel tradition. A major concern was to discern which elements in the Synoptic tradition can be traced back to Jesus and to ascertain their earliest form. The earliest work of this sort was *The Holy Spirit and the Gospel Tradition* (1947), which was followed twenty years later by *History and Faith: The Study of the Passion* (1967) and *Jesus and the Gospel Tradition* (1967). While this area has not been given the same detailed treatment as Paul, John and Acts, it was foundational and necessary as a basis for understanding the significance of the contributions they were to make.

Evidence of the concentration on Paul appeared in 1957 in the form of the first of four commentaries on the Pauline corpus. Barrett's *Epistle to the Romans* appeared in the Black series with its set format (a second edition appeared in 1991). Modest in size, the commenatry was nevertheless succinct, clear, well-balanced and persuasive as an interpretation of Romans, thus embodying features characteristic of Barrett as a commentator. The commentary was restricted in scope because of the series it was in and the existence of the Sanday and Headlam commentary, which meant that English readers were already well served. *From First Adam to Last* (1962), an incisive essay investigating Pauline anthropology and christology, arose from the study of Romans and prepared the way for the study of 1 Corinthians.

Next to appear, however, was a small commentary on the Pastoral Epistles (1963) in the Clarendon series, which imposed strict limits on the commentator. This was to prepare the way for Barrett's interpretation of the fate of Paul following his death. His reading of the Pastorals took them to be a defense of Paul in an age unsympathetic to and lacking under-

standing of Paul. In some ways these epistles are to be seen as an updating of Paul, to make him relevant to the issues of a later situation. His essay "Pauline Controversies in the Post-Pauline Period" contributes further to his position. A similar line was later developed in relation to the presentation of Paul in Acts, which Barrett describes as "the legendary Paul" though he views it as not devoid of historical value.

Throughout the 1960s Barrett was publishing essays relevant to the Corinthian correspondence and leading to his second commentary in the Black series, *1 Corinthians* (1968; 2d ed., 1986) and *2 Corinthians* (1973). His contribution to specific Pauline epistles also includes a systematic set of essays, *Freedom and Obligation: A Study of the Epistle to the Galatians* (1985), which deals with history, theology and ethics. Many of the preparatory essays are collected in his *Essays on Paul* (1982). All of this is drawn together in *Paul: An Introduction to His Thought* (1994). Only someone who had spent many years in detailed work on the major epistles and on Acts could write such a book. It is deceptively concise, precisely because the author has elsewhere worked his way in detail through all the difficult problems and knows what he wishes to say.

This study proceeds on the basis of a brief outline of Paul's career in which certain lines of interpretation become clear. Barrett asserts, contrary to some recent views, that Paul was a convert to the early Christian movement, and this was the basis of his vocation to his mission to the Gentiles. In this way too it is made clear from the beginning that Paul was not a systematic theologian operating from his study but a missionary pastor pitted in the struggle for the souls of the men and women of his day. In keeping with contemporary recognition of Paul's situational theology, Barrett has concentrated his work on specific epistles, noting their occasional nature. Paul's theology was worked out in a series of controversies, and Barrett concludes that controversy is an essential element of theology. The theologian must be willing to engage in controversy because of commitment to truth. To make this clear Barrett notes those epistles that are almost universally regarded as genuine and sets his interpretation of each of them in its controversial context. Nevertheless Barrett is convinced that Paul did not work out random answers to the various controversies in which he engaged. Rather, a coherent position is discernible in the midst of his responses to the various controversies. Here Barrett somewhat sidesteps the debate about whether there is a central Pauline motif in the midst of the variety of concrete letters. He does not claim to identify a central motif. Rather his conclusion that in Romans we have Paul's most complete and systematic expression of his theology grows out of the conviction that Paul's theology is coherent and not arbitrary.

The presentation of Paul's theology is based on the more or less undisputed letters, drawing heavily on Romans because of its more comprehensive presentation. An outline of Paul's theology is given under a number of heads: the reign of evil; law and covenant; grace and righteousness; Christ crucified; the church; the Holy Spirit and ethics. This order does not follow any one of the epistles, not even Romans. It is a persuasively logical ordering of Paul's thought. Throughout this treatment Barrett incisively gives expression to Paul's thought. The cosmic expression of evil (the demonic) is set alongside the existential (anthropological), raising the question of whether one might not be the interpretation of the other. The nature of the law as good and yet flawed as a means for people to find their way to God—flawed not in itself but because of human sinfulness—is worked out in detail. Surely Paul knew the law and the way it was used, and he asserts that he had sought to build up credit with God by his observance of the law. In this way Barrett defends Pauline theology against the frequently made charge that the Pauline construct of Jewish legalism is a

fiction corresponding to no Jewish reality. At least Paul places his analysis of his former life in this category.

No doubt there is already evidence in the first volume of the commentary on Acts (ICC) for arguing that Barrett's work on Acts is his finest contribution. Although the full introduction is reserved for the second volume, in the preliminary introduction and commentary on the first fourteen chapters there is a good indication of the direction of this work. There are also earlier articles dealing with some aspects to be covered in the second volume. Special features emerging concern the history of the text of Acts and lead in the direction of accepting that the work circulated in different versions, with the possibility that the one known as the Western text was first widely accepted. Attitude to the history of the text obviously has important implications for interpretation. For a work like Acts there is also the crucial question of sources. Barrett argues that Luke made use of written and oral traditions from Caesarea, Antioch, possibly from a companion of Paul on some of his journeys, and traditions gathered from inquiries to churches of the Pauline mission. By reference to traditions rather than sources oral or written, Barrett questions whether these traditions came to Luke extensively arranged or in piecemeal fashion and whether the wording was precisely fixed rather than fluid. His conclusion emphasizes the limitations imposed by the nature and availability of the traditions used by Luke.

Here as elsewhere in his work Barrett affirms that he approaches New Testament theology through New Testament history. Consequently come the questions of what Luke might have known on the basis of sources. The character and reliability of those sources are crucial for his interpretation. There remains the question of Luke's purpose in writing Acts and the determination of the overall plan of the work. In general terms it is accepted that Luke sets out the expanding mission from Jerusalem to take in the Gentiles, a plan restricted by available sources. Because Luke obscures the conflict over the mission to the Gentiles that is apparent in the letters of Paul, it is unlikely that he made use of them. Nevertheless, while Luke's aim was to provide a picture of the life and preaching of the early church as a basis of inspiration and instruction for his contemporaries, most of all he aimed to show how the gospel came to be accepted in the Gentile world, thus affirming the Gentile mission and the role of Paul as the hero of this story in the context of the plan expressed in Acts 1:8.

Because only Luke undertook a history of the continuation of the Jesus movement, a history of the beginning of Christianity, from at least the late second century Acts has had an unparalleled influence on the understanding of Christian origins. Barrett's commentary provides an illuminating approach to the history of the text, careful attention to the language, a reserved and constructive attitude to sources, and an interpretation of Luke's understanding of history and theology that takes account of the limitations of Luke's knowledge. The second volume of the commentary on Acts will undoubtedly confirm that Barrett is the most distinguished British New Testament scholar of our time. The breadth and depth of his work sets it alongside the work of the outstanding interpreters down through the ages.

BIBLIOGRAPHY

Works. For a complete bibliography to 1982 see *Paul and Paulinism: Essays in Honor of C. K. Barrett,* ed. M. Hooker and S. G. Wilson (London: SPCK, 1982). The following is a select bibliography. C. K. Barrett, *The Acts of the Apostles* (2 vols.; Edinburgh: T & T Clark, 1994-) vol. 1; idem, "The Centre of the New Testament and the Canon" in *Die Mitte des Neuen Testaments: Festschrift für Eduard Schweizer,* ed. U. Luz and H. Weder (Göttingen: Vandenhoeck & Ruprecht, 1983) 5-21; idem, *The Epistle to the Romans* (2d ed.; London: A & C Black; New York: Harper, 1991 [1957]); idem, *Essays on John* (London: SPCK, 1982); idem, *Essays on Paul* (London: SPCK, 1982); idem, *The First Epistle*

to the Corinthians (2d ed.; London: A & C Black; New York: Harper & Row, 1971 [1968]); idem, *Freedom and Obligation: Study of the Epistle to the Galatians* (London: SPCK, 1985); idem, *From First Adam to Last: A Study in Pauline Theology* (London: A & C Black, 1962); idem, *The Gospel According to St. John* (2d ed.; London: SPCK, 1978 [1955]); idem, *The Gospel of John and Judaism* (London: SPCK, 1975 [from German ed., 1970]); idem, *History and Faith: The Study of the Passion* (London: BBC Publications, 1967); idem, *The Holy Spirit and the Gospel Tradition* (London: SPCK, 1947); idem, *Jesus and the Gospel Tradition* (London: SPCK, 1967; Philadelphia: Fortress, 1968); idem, "Jesus and the Word" in *Rudolf Bultmann: Werk und Wirkung,* ed. B. Jaspert (Darmstadt: Wissenschaftliche Buchgessellschaft, 1984) 81-91; idem, *Jesus and the Word and Other Essays* (Pittsburgh: Pickwick, 1996); idem, "John" in *Peake's Commentary on the Bible,* ed. M. Black and H. H. Rowley (London: Nelson, 1962) 844-69; idem, "Johannine Christianity" in *Christian Beginnings,* ed. J. Becker (Louisville, KY: Westminster John Knox, 1993 [from German ed., 1987]) 330-58; idem, "Joseph Barber Lightfoot," *DUJ* 44 (33) 193-204; idem, "J. B. Lightfoot as Biblical Commentator" in *The Lightfoot Centenary Lectures,* ed. J. D. G. Dunn (Durham: Durham University Journal, special edition, 1992) 53-70; idem, *New Testament Essays* (London: SPCK, 1972); idem, *Paul: An Introduction to His Thought* (London: Geoffrey Chapman; Louisville, KY: Westminster John Knox, 1994); idem, "Pauline Controversies in the Post-Pauline Period," *NTS* 20 (April 1974) 229-45; idem, *The Pastoral Epistles in the New English Bible* (Oxford: Clarendon, 1963); idem, *The Second Epistle to the Corinthians* (London: A & C Black, 1973); idem, *The Signs of an Apostle* (London: Epworth, 1970); idem, "St John: Social Historian," *PIBA* 10 (1986) 26-39; idem, "The Third Gospel as a Preface to Acts? Some Reflections" in *The Four Gospels 1992: Festschrift for Frans Neirynck,* ed. F. Van Segbroek, C. M. Tuckett, G. van Belle and J. Verkeyden (Louvain: Peeters, 1992) 1451-66; idem, "Vincent Taylor," *ER* 14 (1987) 29-36; idem, *Westcott as Commentator* (Cambridge: Cambridge University Press, 1959); idem, "What Is New Testament Theology? Some Reflections" in *Intergerini Parietis Septum (Eph. 2:14): Essays Presented to Markus Barth on His Sixty-Fifth Birthday,* ed. D. Y. Hadidian (Pittsburgh: Pickwick, 1980) 1-22.

J. Painter

Barth, Karl *(1886-1968)*

Born in Basel, Switzerland, in 1886, Karl Barth was the son and grandson of Swiss Calvinist ministers. As a student at Berne, Berlin, Tübingen and Marburg, Barth was privileged to study with some of the best theological teachers of his day, including Adolph von *Harnack and Wilhelm Herrmann. From 1909 until 1911 he served as an apprentice pastor in Geneva before becoming pastor of the Reformed church in Safenwil in north-central Switzerland in 1911. In 1922, after the publication of his first book, *The Epistle to the Romans* (1919; 2d ed., 1922), he was appointed to a chair in Reformed theology at the University of Göttingen.

From 1925 to 1930 Barth was professor of dogmatics and New Testament exegesis at the University of Münster in Westphalia. He became professor of systematic theology at the University of Bonn in 1930, where he remained until his refusal to swear allegiance to Adolph Hitler led to his dismissal in 1935. In 1934 Barth had been the principal author of the Theological Declaration of Barmen, a document that opposed the encroachments of Hitler's National Socialism upon the churches in Germany and called for obedience to Christ alone as the church's only *Führer.* Immediately upon being deported from Germany to Switzerland, Barth was appointed professor at the University of Basel, a post he held until his retirement in 1962. Barth died in 1968.

Barth's engagement with the Christian Scriptures marked a watershed in twentieth-century theology. Laying aside all appeals to a faultless biblical text (as in Protestant scholasticism), or to an irrefutable teaching office to interpret those texts (as in Roman Catholicism), Barth embraced the inescapable fallibility of all human language about God. Even the biblical texts themselves, he believed, were not immune from fallibility. The Bible's validity rests not upon its presumed lack of error but squarely upon the authority of God alone. There is no other Lord, no other authority, than God—the God revealed in Jesus Christ by the power of the Holy Spirit, the God attested to in canonical Scripture. This complex understanding of an authority that resides not in the biblical texts themselves but in God lies at the heart of Barth's theological project.

Barth's doctrine of Scripture was first forged during his years in the Safenwil pastorate, when he was confronted with the burden of preaching the Word of God to his congregation week after week. Barth discovered that the liberal theology he had so readily embraced during his student days, with its largely anthropocentric focus, left him ill-prepared to preach and interpret God's Word for a world staggered by the nightmare of world war. Thus he found it necessary to counter anthropocentric liberalism with a theocentric concentration on the "deity of God." So great is God, declared Barth, that one cannot say "God" by saying "human being" in a loud voice. Neither, he might have added, can one say God by saying "Scripture" in a loud voice.

Regarding Scripture, Barth's strategy was to move in the opposite direction of the many anxious attempts in the modern era to set biblical authority upon a secure and indisputable foundation. By drawing an analogy to the doctrine of justification— the doctrine that we are saved not by merit but by grace alone—Barth argued that authority does not reside in the "merits" of the texts themselves but on the gracious divine reality to which the texts are pointing. Hence Barth shifted the focus away from belief in a perfect text toward belief in the perfect obedience embodied in Jesus Christ. The doctrine of *sola Scriptura* (Scripture alone) must yield to the doctrine of *solus Christus* (Christ alone).

This intentional focus on the centrality of Jesus Christ and his obedience unto death characterized Barth's magnum opus, the *Church Dogmatics,* which lumbered off the press from 1936 to 1967. A thoroughgoing reinterpretation of the Christian gospel, the *Church Dogmatics* is a declaration of God's gracious decision in Jesus Christ to be "for" and "with" human beings as their Creator, Reconciler and Redeemer.

Triune God and Biblical Revelation. To grasp Barth's innovative approach to Scripture, one must understand his dynamic, trinitarian view of revelation, a topic he sets forth, along with his doctrine of Scripture itself, in the prolegomena to the *Church Dogmatics,* comprising volumes I/1 and I/2. Unlike the nineteenth-century theologian Friedrich Daniel Ernst *Schleiermacher, who relegated God's triunity to the status of an appendix, Barth made it the organizing framework for his entire theology. Triunity forms the implicit grammar that should guide all our ways of speaking of God.

One cannot speak intelligibly of God at all, that is to say, apart from a divine self-disclosure: "God can be known only through God." God is not just any god we might dream up but the God revealed in Jesus Christ by the power of the Holy Spirit and attested in Scripture.

What we learn through Christ is not just information about God; the Christ event is God's very self-disclosure. In Christ God's own being, or perhaps we might say God's character, is enacted in human history as an unfolding story. This drama is not presented as a "datum" or "deposit" of cognitive truths, but it is the giving of God's own self in gracious and transformative encounter. Thus for Barth receiving revelation is synonymous with receiving God.

If it is true that revelation is self-identical with the being of God, then we discover something vital about the peculiar way God enacts God's being in the world. Barth formulates this discovery according to an if-then style of reasoning. If the eternal and ever-living God, who as mystery exceeds our every thought, has been truly revealed in Jesus Christ, then this same God must live according to an unusual mode of being. God must be able to reduplicate God's being, Barth reasoned, in the mode of a historical act. As E. Jüngel has paraphrased Barth, in Christ we see that God enacts

God's being in "becoming." By actually becoming human in Jesus of Nazareth, God replicated God's own character for the world. God became "other" than God in a human form yet without ceasing to be God.

Since revelation is divine self-disclosure, it is never a given to be possessed but a giving, an event *(Ereignis)* that has a beginning, a middle and an end toward which it is still moving. Barth capsulized this threefold movement in the declaration that God is our Creator, Reconciler and Redeemer. This is the concrete specification, drawn from Scripture, of the tripartite way God acts in the economy of salvation. Creation, reconciliation and redemption constitute the one, biblically attested work of the living God—a singular activity that assumes a triune shape (*CD* I/1, §8-12).

First, as Creator, God the Father is the primary subject or actor in revelation. This divine action has its beginnings in the primordial decision of election. According to Barth, biblical election is not in the first instance an election of specific individuals to salvation but primarily God's own self-election. It is an election to be God in a particular way in Jesus Christ by the efficacy of the Spirit. Through election the Creator God has determined to be for us (*CD* I/1, §10; II/2, §§32-35).

Second, as Reconciler, God has determined not only to be for human beings but in Jesus Christ to be with us as well (*CD* I/1, §11). The dramatic history of God is centered in the person of Jesus Christ, who is "Son of God." In Jesus Christ, God accomplishes the fulfillment of all of time. God can do this because, unlike human reality, the reality of God is pre-, supra- and posttemporal. God goes before, accompanies and follows after all temporal events.

This view of time and incarnation has implications for how one views Scripture. The time of Jesus Christ naturally has a time that precedes and succeeds it. The time that precedes the Christ event is the time of anticipation, that is, the time of Israel as recorded in the Old Testament. The time that succeeds Christ is the time of recollection, the time of the church as recorded in the New Testament (*CD* I/2, §14).

Third, as Redeemer, God the "Spirit" is the author of new life for those who are becoming the children of God. If God the Creator is for us and God the Reconciler is with us, God the Redeemer is at work in and among us (*CD* I/1, §12). Whereas redemption was traditionally conceived as a "second article" term pertaining to the Son, Barth's reading of the New Testament (e.g., Lk 21:18; Rom 8:23; Eph 4:30; Heb 11:35) led him to reconceive it as a "third article" term focused on the eschatological work of the Spirit.

To sum up, the God revealed in Scripture is one who enacts a three-part, dramatic story of salvation as the Revealer, Revelation and the very act of Revealing itself. God is simultaneously the Who, the What and the How of revelation. In this threefold manner God speaks God's life-giving Word.

Word of God. The Word of God is not simply a cognitive message for Barth but a dynamic event. Transcending Scripture even as it calls Scripture into existence, this event finds its focus in the person of Jesus Christ and is made efficacious by the power of the Holy Spirit.

The Word of God is first of all the speech of God. As utterance it is a spiritual event in which one person addresses another. God's Word is not just idle talk, but it aims toward the redemption of the person whom it addresses (*CD* I/1, §5.2).

The Word is also the act of God. The term *act* in Barth's vocabulary connotes the actualization in history of God's eternal election to be for and with humanity in Jesus Christ. Thus, in distinction from an event that occurs only once and is then finished, the "act" of God continues to confront human beings with a "contingent contemporaneity." God's act is contemporaneous not only with the time of Jesus of Nazareth but also with the time of the first witnesses to Jesus and with the time of the church throughout the ages (*CD* I/1, §5.3).

The Word is thirdly the mystery of God. By "mystery" Barth is not referring merely to a negative limit that arises within our own horizon of knowledge; mystery has also the positive significance of being the mystery of God. To be sure, there is a negative side to God's mystery in that we cannot know God unless God chooses to be revealed in God's Word. But God is mystery positively in that God has become revealed by means of the humanity of Jesus of Nazareth (*CD* I/1, §5.4).

The Word of God is unfolding in history according to another threefold structure: the Word is preached, written and revealed (*CD* I/1, §4). The Word is not only the Word that God speaks as the acting subject of revelation; this same Word is also embodied in human words that through grace bear genuine witness to their object.

In the first place, there is the Word of God preached, which is the Word made known in the church's ongoing proclamation. The Word simultaneously commissions proclamation, is the theme of proclamation and judges the authenticity of proclamation. Not every word uttered in the church is proclamation, but only those utterances that truly intend to speak about God. Just as God is not a human possession, proclamation is never a given. It must ever and again "become" proclamation. In thus committing God's own cause to the frailty of the church's own human proclamation, God assumes a remarkable risk: entrusting the unimpeachable Word to the care of witnesses who are themselves impeachable (*CD* I/2, §22.1).

Second, there is the Word of God written. In the providence of God, the original witnesses to revelation have recorded their proclamation in written form. The written word sets forth proclamation, is itself proclamation and has the Word of proclamation as its criterion. This written record, embodied in the Scriptures of the two Testaments, can make no claim to being the Word of God in itself, since for Barth nothing exists properly in itself. All things, including human life and the life-giving witness of Scripture, find their existence only in God. Therefore the Scriptures can only "become" the Word of God in the concrete working out of the event of revelation. Just as God has God's own being in becoming, so also the Bible is the Word of God only as it has "its being in this becoming" (*CD* I/1, 110).

Third, there is the Word of God revealed, the incarnate Word, Jesus Christ, the one who himself proclaims, is proclaimed and verifies proclamation. The time of Jesus is the fulfilled time, which confronts us as a promise to be seized and enacted (*CD* I/2, §14.1). Thus, the Word of God as revelation is never present to human beings as a simple fact. It is with us in the mode of a "coming presence" (*CD* I/2, 95). To this dynamic event Scripture bears witness.

Scripture as Witness. According to Barth, the canonical Scriptures of the Old and New Testaments mediate the Word of God to the church (*CD* I/2, §§19, 20). This does not mean that God's Word is restricted to the church; but it does mean that the church itself is restricted to the biblically attested Word. In this way Barth embraced the principle of the sixteenth-century Protestant Reformers, that all Scripture is inspired by God and that all other ecclesial authorities must subordinate themselves to the authority of Scripture. Nevertheless, in contrast to the form it took in seventeenth-century orthodoxy, Barth transformed the Scripture principle in significant ways.

First, Barth made a more radical link than did orthodoxy between biblical inspiration and Incarnation and Pentecost. The Bible speaks only as part of the dynamic event in which the Word became flesh and in which human beings by the Spirit's inspiration continue to hear the Word and to obey. A crucial corollary, as mentioned earlier, is that Scriptures are not in and of themselves the Word of God, but they bear witness to the Word that always lies on a horizon beyond themselves. In other words, the Scriptures are "signs" that point

to and are subject to God's grace (*CD* I/2, 457). Therefore, even though Scripture is a *norm normans*, a norm that is normative for all other norms, it also remains a *norm normanda*, a fallible norm that must itself continually be normed by the Word of God in revelation.

Second, the Scriptures can only point to God's grace in their limited and fallible capacity as human witnesses. From one viewpoint the Scriptures are but a time-bound set of writings reflecting the cultural biases of the numerous contexts in which they were composed. Said Barth, the New Testament is at one level a collection of documents about "a Hellenistic spiritual movement" (*CD* I/2, 72). As such, its fallibility lies not only at the level of incidental facts, such as dates and places, but also at the level of material content. Much of the Bible's content is subjoined with mythologies and worldviews that prevailed in the ancient world but are no longer credible. With this in mind we must treat the texts as testimonies and not "sources" of an archival sort (*CD* I/2, 64). Besides, our access to the texts is problematic, since we are not even certain which variants in the manuscripts are authentic.

Thus for Barth biblical authority does not reside in any inherent property the texts supposedly possess (e.g., inerrancy or infallibility) but in the unique function they perform in the life of the church. Still, this functional authority is more than the authority of historical precedence; rather, it is a living authority born of the one revelation of God, which is Jesus Christ, and of the one revelatory deed, which is the internal testimony of the Holy Spirit. That Scripture performs this divine function through time-bound human media echoes the Chalcedonian doctrine of two natures, according to which Jesus is fully human and fully divine.

Third, if the texts themselves are fallible, then at what level of meaning does biblical authority lie? Here too Barth differs from the Reformers. Biblical authority lies neither at the level of the text nor at the level of the supposed historical facts to which the texts refer. The Bible is authoritative only to the extent that its theological content *(Sache)* bears a faithful witness to the identity of God as revealed in Jesus Christ.

Fourth, the Word of God as mediated in Scripture is radically free and must be heard and obeyed continually afresh. God always remains free to speak in a different way to a different context. Although Barth, like John *Calvin, was unwilling to discard a single biblical text and refused to embrace the notion of a "canon within the canon," nevertheless he did hold that the biblical canon remains open to revision, at least in principle. It is open because all human media are contingent, fallible and to that extent subject to correction under the freedom of the Word. Yet any such revision of the canon would require the serious and momentous decision of the whole church and not the capricious suggestions of a few.

Fifth, Barth stretched the Reformers' traditional doctrine of inspiration to cover not only the initial divine act of bringing the texts into being but also the continual act of receiving, hearing and obeying them. The older orthodoxy called this ongoing process of interpretation "illumination." Barth's point was that the church's ongoing interpretation should be vitally connected to the original event of inspiration itself.

Interpretation. Biblical interpretation, Barth believed, should not claim special insight unavailable to hermeneutics in general. The hermeneutics of biblical texts are no different in principle from the hermeneutics of any other text.

Early critics such as Adolf Jülicher and Harnack accused Barth of rejecting historical-critical methodologies. However, Barth wished not to reject such methodologies but to push beyond them. He complained that too many historical-critical commentaries were only a "prelude" to a commentary. The point of interpretation is not simply to parrot the text. Rather than limiting one's focus to what the prophets and

apostles said, Barth was concerned to know what we must say on the basis of the prophets and apostles *(CD* I/1, 16). Again, the biblical witness is never static but engenders ongoing proclamation.

Neither historical nor hermeneutical skill alone can produce understanding of God's Word. No one is able to reproduce the text "as it is" or to recover what it "really" says. The point of interpretation, biblical or otherwise, is not to uncover the secret intention of the human authors but to recapture that to which the author's words are pointing.

The inherent ambiguity in interpretation places the interpreter in an awkward position. The theological content of Scripture matters most, but since this content is never simply present in the text, it must continually be reconstructed under the pressures of a forever changing situation. Or, to put it another way, the biblical narrative must always be renarrated by the community. The theological content must be extracted from a diversity of texts and then rendered anew, as, for example, Barth's own narrative presentation of Jesus as the "Royal Man" *(CD* IV/2). Contrary to some commentators, it was Barth himself and not the biblical text per se that was doing the narrating in the *Church Dogmatics.*

This complex task of interpretation proceeds through three movements. It starts with explication of the biblical content *(explicatio)*, moves to critical and constructive reflection *(meditatio)* and culminates in practical application *(applicatio; CD* I/2, 722-40). Interpretation must proceed through the threefold discipline of biblical, dogmatic and practical theology. From the standpoint of practical theology, the Word is always speaking afresh to the circumstances of each new situation. As such, the Word of God is also the command of God. To hear the Word means to obey. Theology therefore always culminates in ethics *(CD* II/2; III/4; IV/4). But this ethical dimension of the Word must remain open-ended and somewhat ambiguous, since to define with precision what the Word is commanding would infringe upon God's sovereignty.

Some examples of Barth's own unique interpretive approach are worth mentioning. Barth treated the Old Testament stories of Genesis, for instance, not as straightforward history but as "sagas" pointing beyond themselves to the identity of God. Turning to the New Testament, Barth interpreted the virgin birth as but a "sign" of God's miracle of incarnation and not as embodying the miracle itself. The stories of the virgin birth gesture toward something profoundly true, that humanity is the recipient and not the initiator of grace.

Many of Barth's most significant theological moves depended on novel interpretations of Scripture. For example, Barth relied on Ephesians 1:4 ("just as he chose us in Christ before the foundation of the world") to recast fundamentally the traditional doctrine of election. For Barth all people are elect "in Christ" (*CD* II/2). This does not entail a strict universalism, however, because apparently not all people realize their vocation to be Christian (Barth 1936, 67, IV/3.2). Another of Barth's favorite passages was Colossians 3:3 ("for you have died and your life is hidden with Christ in God"). Because the Christian life remains hidden, no one can claim to be Christian in a straightforward sense, for one is always in the process of still becoming one.

One of the most famous examples of Barth's creative exegesis was his christological interpretation of the prodigal son (*CD* IV). It is Jesus Christ himself, insisted Barth, who, like the prodigal, has left the Father to be humiliated in the "far country" of human sinfulness. Thus he is the "Lord" who encounters us as "Servant" (*CD* IV/1). Like the prodigal, Jesus Christ has returned to the Father and is also the "Servant" who is exalted as "Lord" (*CD* IV/2). Once dead to the "Father" but now alive like the prodigal, Jesus as the resurrected one is both God and human, "True Witness" (*CD* IV/3).

These examples do not mean that Barth thought interpretation should be idiosyncratic; instead, it must always occur within the context of the community of faith. In order to place oneself in a position to hear and to obey, the reader and the community must prescind from the various cultural presuppositions they bring to the text. They must let the text itself speak, treating it as though it means what it says. Yet paradoxically these cultural presuppositions provide the preconditions by which understanding occurs. Indeed, just such cultural presuppositions are infused throughout the various worldviews of the biblical texts. The goal of interpretation, then, is for all merely contingent worldviews, whether they are those of the contemporary interpreter or of the biblical writers themselves, to yield themselves to the substance *(Sache)* of Scripture—the gracious and triune character of God, revealed in Christ by the efficaciousness of the Spirit.

BIBLIOGRAPHY

Works. K. Barth, *Church Dogmatics*, ed. G. W. Bromiley and T. F. Torrance (Edinburgh: T & T Clark, 1936-1967) I/1—IV/4; see esp. I/1 and I/2; idem, *Epistle to the Romans* (Oxford: Oxford University Press, 1975); idem, *Evangelical Theology: An Introduction* (Grand Rapids: Eerdmans, 1963); idem, "The Strange New World Within the Bible" in Karl Barth, *The Word of God and the Word of Man* (London: Hodder & Stoughton, 1928) 28-50.

Studies. G. Eichholz, "Der Ansatz Karl Barths in der Hermeneutik" in *Antwort: Karl Barth zum siebzigsten Geburtstag am 10. Mai 1956*, ed. E. Wolf, C. von Kirschbaum and R. Frey (Zollikon-Zürich: Evangelischer Verlag, 1956) 52-68 [repr. in G. Eichholz, *Tradition und Interpretation: Studien zum Neuen Testament und zur Hermeneutik* (Munich: Kaiser, 1965) 190-209]; H. Frei, "Karl Barth: Theologian," "Barth and Schleiermacher: Divergence and Convergence" in *Theology and Narrative: Selected Essays*, ed. G. Hunsinger and W. C. Placher (New York and Oxford: Oxford University Press, 1993) 167-76, 177-99; A. von Harnack, "Fifteen Questions to Those among the Theologians Who Are Contemptuous of the Scientific Theology," "An Open Letter to Professor Karl Barth" and "Postscript to My Open Letter to Professor Karl Barth" in *The Beginning of Dialectical Theology*, ed. J. M. Robinson (Richmond, VA: John Knox, 1968) 165-66, 171-74, 186-87; G. Hunsinger, *How to Read Karl Barth: The Shape of His Theology* (New York and Oxford: Oxford University Press, 1991); W. G. Jeanrond, "Karl Barth's Hermeneutics" in *Reckoning with Barth: Essays in Commemoration of the Centenary of Karl Barth's Birth*, ed. N. Biggar (London and Oxford: Mowbray, 1988) 80-97; W. S. Johnson, *The Mystery of God: Karl Barth and the Postmodern Foundations of Theology* (Louisville: Westminster John Knox, 1997); A. Jülicher, "A Modern Interpreter of Paul" in *The Beginning of Dialectical Theology*, ed. J. M. Robinson (Richmond, VA: John Knox, 1968) 72-81; E. Jüngel, *Karl Barth: A Theological Legacy* (Philadelphia: Westminster, 1986); D. H. Kelsey, *The Uses of Scripture in Recent Theology* (Philadelphia: Fortress, 1975); G. Lindbeck, *The Nature of Doctrine: Religion and Theology in a Postliberal Age* (Philadelphia: Westminster, 1984); B. L. McCormack, "Historical Criticism and Dogmatic Interest in Karl Barth's Theological Exegesis the New Testament" in *Biblical Hermeneutics in Historical Perspective, Studies in Honor of Karlfried Froehlich on His Sixtieth Birthday*, ed. M. S. Burrows and P. Rorem (Grand Rapids: Eerdmans, 1991); idem, *Karl Barth's Critically Realistic Dialectical Theology: Its Genesis and Development 1909-1936* (Oxford: Clarendon, 1995); P. McGlasson, *Jesus and Judas: Biblical Exegesis in Barth* (AAR Academy Series 72; Atlanta: Scholars Press, 1990); T. E. Provence, "The Sovereign Subject Matter: Hermeneutics in the *Church Dogmatics*" in *A Guide to Contemporary Hermeneutics: Major Trends in Biblical Interpretation*, ed. D. K. McKim (Grand Rapids: Eerdmans, 1986) 241-62; K. Runia, *Karl Barth's Doctrine of Holy Scripture* (Grand Rapids: Eerdmans, 1962); R. Smend, "Nachkritische Schriftauslegung" in *Parrhesia: Karl Barth zum achtzigsten Geburtstag am 10 Mai 1966*, ed. E. Busch, J. Fangmeier and M. Geiger (Zurich: EVZ, 1966); 215-37; M. I. Wallace, *The Second Naivete: Barth, Ricoeur and the New Yale Theology* (SABH 6; Macon, GA: Mercer University Press, 1990); G. Ward, *Barth, Derrida and the Language of Theology* (Cambridge: Cambridge University Press, 1995); S. H. Webb, *Re-Figuring Theology: The Rhetoric of Karl Barth* (Albany, NY: State University of New York Press, 1991); J. A. Wharton, "Karl Barth as Exegete and His Influence on Biblical Interpretation" *USQR* 28 (1972) 5-13.   W. S. Johnson

Bornkamm, Günther (1905-1990)

Günther Bornkamm was born on February 6, 1905, at Görlitz, east of Dresden, and studied at Marburg, Tübingen, Berlin and Breslau. As one of Rudolf *Bultmann's early pupils he completed his Marburg licentiate (Ph.D.) in 1930. His thesis, *Mythos und Legende in den apokryphen Thomas-Akten* (1933), is a contribution to the history of Gnosticism and the prehistory of Manicheanism, major concerns of Bultmann's at that time. In 1934 Bornkamm qualified as a university teacher at Königsberg with a work on *Homologia* (confession) and wrote the first of many distinguished articles on Paul, later collected and translated into English as *Early Christian Experience* (1969).

Bornkamm's academic career was disturbed but not destroyed by the years of Germany's disaster. His lectureship was terminated (1936) on account of his activities in the confessing church. Banned from teaching in a state university, he was appointed to the church faculty at Bethel in Bielefeld (1937), but this institution was closed by the Gestapo in 1939. After three years in a parish he was drafted as a soldier, returning to Bethel in 1945. In 1946 he moved to Göttingen and in 1949 to Heidelberg, as Martin Dibelius's successor. There he became what Bultmann had been: doctoral supervisor to many of the next generation's ablest professors. Writings and recognition followed; only his anticipated synthesis, a commentary on Matthew for the Lietzmann *Handbuch* series that he edited, was incomplete when he died on February 18, 1990, in Heidelberg.

Context. Several of Bornkamm's wide-ranging publications are word studies and encyclopedia articles on early Christian literature, but most of them have the strong theological orientation characteristic of German Protestant New Testament scholarship in the mid-twentieth century. Many of them, centered on the word *confession*, bear the marks of the German church struggle. The kerygmatic focus of this theology is reflected in his coediting and contributing to the *Göttinger Predigtmeditationen*, which mediated biblical scholarship for the church. Above all Bornkamm was a product of the 1920s dialectical theology, the seedbed of twentieth-century theology in which the biblical scholars' form criticism was combined with neo-Reformation and existentialist emphases and further fueled by the Luther renaissance to produce a new synthesis in New Testament theology. Bultmann's philosophical and hermeneutical sophistication was maintained by pupils equally loyal to church and university and equally determined to remove the false stumbling blocks of an outmoded worldview by translating the New Testament into a more appropriate theological conceptuality. In 1963 Bornkamm reported at length on the recent discussion of Bultmann's theology, especially the demythologizing debate (*ThR* NF 29 [1963] 33-141; repr. in *Geschichte und Glaube* [1968]), and contributed to a similar American symposium (ed. C. W. Kegley, *The Theology of Rudolf Bultmann* [New York: Harper & Row, 1966]). Since 1951 he had published several articles on the subject.

As the leading member of the Bultmannian right, together with Ernst *Käsemann, Bornkamm tilted Bultmann's synthesis in a more traditional direction by placing more weight on the centrality of christology while remaining true to the critical principles of the history of religions school and form criticism and to a markedly Lutheran theology. Bornkamm shared some of Käsemann's more polemically expressed reservations about Bultmann's theology but was always more cautious and balanced and less passionate than was his younger contemporary. Bornkamm rejected several of Käsemann's more daring exegetical proposals, his scholarly style reflecting a personal modesty and self-effacement that was perhaps aggravated by his slight verbal impedi-

ment. Like Bultmann's, his strong theological commitment was reined in to allow the biblical scholar's historical judgment its necessary freedom. Comparison with both his more famous teacher and with his more colorful contemporary helps sharpen the contours of his major contributions to New Testament scholarship.

The twin towers of Bultmann's classic New Testament theology are his existential interpretation of Paul and John. He draws these authors out of their history of religions milieu and interprets their talk of God for a new cultural context. His demythologizing program (1941; in ET *The New Testament and Mythology and Other Basic Writings*) gave public and controversial expression to some forty years' work as a liberal Protestant deeply etched by the patterns and passions of dialectical theology to communicate the gospel through critical theological interpretation of the New Testament. His monumental work on the Synoptic tradition appeared at the watershed of his own theological development (1921; ET *History of the Synoptic Tradition*) and contained seeds that could hardly prosper in the antihistorical ground of the time. It yielded rich but damaged fruit in his brilliant book on Jesus (1926; ET *Jesus and the Word*), and despite its suggestive pages on the composition of the Synoptic Gospels (ET, 337-67) these three Evangelists suffer comparative neglect in his later New Testament theology.

Historical Jesus. Bornkamm both continued the Bultmannian tradition and helped remedy its defects. His major articles on Paul were synthesized in a compact yet profound popular presentation of the apostle's life and thought (*Paulus* [1969; ET 1971]), and years of theological engagement with Matthew resulted in his pioneering a new method of Gospel criticism, redaction criticism (*Überlieferung und Auslegung im Matthäusevangelium* [1960]; ET *Tradition and Interpretation in Matthew* [1963]), and in creating a new interest and lasting achievement in the historical study of Jesus (*Jesus von Nazareth*

[1956]; ET *Jesus of Nazareth* [1960]). These three main areas of his work all stand firmly within the rubrics of New Testament theology, and that is equally true of his important essays on John and Hebrews and on particular theological themes such as creation, law, confession, faith and history, eschatology and New Testament ethics. In none of these areas can Bornkamm's quality contributions be called revolutionary, and most of his Pauline studies contain more consolidation than innovation, but all his work represents a certain style of New Testament theological exegesis and interpretation at its best.

Of the three areas highlighted, it was in the third that Bornkamm found the greatest resonance, both inside and outside professional New Testament scholarship. This is explained by its intrinsic importance for Christian theology and practice. What J. M. Robinson labeled "The New Quest of the Historical Jesus," that is, within the Bultmann school, began with Käsemann's lecture to the "alte Marburger" in 1953 (or more strictly with Nils Dahl's article in the same year), but Bornkamm's *Jesus of Nazareth* (1956) was and remains its flagship and the classic "Jesus book" of a whole generation. Within twenty years it was translated into ten languages and is with good reason still widely read. Bultmann's *Jesus* (1926; ET 1934) had been content to mediate a "dialogue with history" and to assist others to encounter the reality of God through a presentation of the earliest postresurrection traditions of the Palestinian community. It was not the historical figure, much less his personality, that mattered but the message that Jesus brought, a message that placed him theologically as well as historically within Judaism, not Christianity, even though Jesus' call to decision implied a christology. Bornkamm, like Dahl and Käsemann, was clear that the historical person does matter to Christian faith and theology and that however little the historian can say about him, Jesus' message was significantly different from that of John the Baptist and illuminates Christianity.

The shape and content of Bornkamm's portrayal of the history or story *(Geschichte)* of Jesus overlaps largely with Bultmann's account of the message. They share the assumptions of classical form criticism and in tracing the history of the synoptic tradition come to broadly similar conclusions. Both, for different reasons, include secondary material in their pastiches of Jesus' teaching. Like Bultmann (following William *Wrede), Bornkamm doubts that Jesus believed himself to be the Messiah and thinks that by the title "son of man" he referred to a heavenly figure other than himself coming to exercise world judgment. Whereas Bultmann followed his own teacher Johannes Weiss in stressing the future orientation of Jesus' proclamation of the kingdom of God, Bornkamm makes the present decisive, despite generally talking about the coming kingdom. What was the eleventh hour for the Baptist was now the twelfth hour for Jesus: the kingdom was dawning.

Nearly half of Bornkamm's book consists in its two central chapters on Jesus' teaching: "The Dawn of the Kingdom of God" and "the Will of God." This shows that for Bornkamm too "the Word of Jesus" remains the heart of the matter. But the person is not reduced to "the bearer of the word," as in Bultmann's presentation, where the corresponding account of Jesus' proclamation constitutes almost 90 percent of the whole. Both books contain important theological introductions and sketches of the historical context, but Bornkamm also prefaces the central chapters with ten fascinating pages on "the rough outlines of Jesus' person and history," speaking of his "authority" though hardly his personality. He also adds short chapters on discipleship, the passion, "the messianic question" and the resurrection faith of the early church. This last hints at how the words of Jesus and the gospel about Jesus Christ have become a unity and is one of several indications that in this book more is being attempted than an historian's reconstruction. A strong element of theological interpretation is present, for example, in Bornkamm's claim that "the essential mystery of Jesus" is "to make the reality of God present" (Bornkam 1956, ET 1960, 62). This goes beyond the modern historian's categories insofar as the writer silently associates himself and his Christian readers with the presumed judgments of Jesus and the Evangelists. Even the many negative critical judgments about the historicity of the Gospels are made in such a way as not to offend religious sensibilities more than necessary. The Gospels "do not permit us to paint a biographical picture of the life of Jesus" (Bornkamm 1956, ET 1960, 53), but even an unhistorical story may be "a historical document in a higher sense" (Bornkamm 1956, ET 1960 162).

Bornkamm has been criticized both by other theologians such as Leander E. Keck and by historians such as E. P. Sanders for confusing historical and theological perspectives. He writes as a Christian theologian, and the precise relationship of historical reality, history writing and Christian faith is arguable. He considers the historical reality of Jesus theologically important and uses the best available historical methods to help him understand it. How far persons can or should detach themselves from their Christian convictions when trying to understand a historical phenomenon is open to debate. But Bornkamm's independent yet fundamentally sympathetic attitude to his sources allows Jesus to emerge as a religious figure, unlike more hostile interpretations, and at no point is his presentation incompatible with the historical probabilities. It is surely right that some material that in its present form may be judged inauthentic may well throw light on the historical figure and that any search for a critically assured minimum of reliable information must be balanced by a consideration of all the possibly reliable data too.

Bornkamm's presentation gains much of its cogency from the sheer quantity of Synoptic material drawn upon, much of it secondary in its present form. In the hands of a sensitive critic the criterion of coher-

ence allows some enlargement of the picture. Bornkamm writes that "it is not apparent why a word or a story which was first formulated by the Church should not have preserved *in der Sache* historical genuineness" (Bornkamm 1956, 9; ET 1960, 11). Bornkamm's program "to seek the history *in* the Kerygma of the Gospels, and in this history to seek the Kerygma" (1956; ET 1960, 21) is enlightening, and notions such as "immediacy" catch something of the historical reality. More empirically minded scholars will prefer their history less coordinated with personal standpoints, and any historical presentation of the story of Jesus will say less than orthodox Christians believe. This one intends to be open to Christian belief (Bornkamm 1956; ET 1960, 10). Unless modern historical study is necessarily a weapon of anti-Christian argument, that is in principle legitimate.

A more serious criticism was that the book continued in a mild form the unjust Christian tendency to contrast Jesus with his environment in ways that caricature the Judaisms of his day. Bornkamm acknowledged this fault and in the tenth edition (1975) introduced major revisions that have unfortunately not been incorporated into the English translation. Even so, it remains arguable that the pervasive Lutheran dialectic of law and gospel distorts the historical analysis. The work benefits less than do some of its successors from the advances made in the study of early Judaism during the twentieth century. However, those which rightly build on these advances differ among themselves more than ever. Historical reconstructions of Jesus remain tentative interpretations, and Bornkamm's continues to challenge and attract new readers.

Redaction Criticism. Renewed interest in the historical Jesus within the Bultmann school coincided with a movement in the other direction. Form criticism had concentrated on the pre-Markan oral period of the history of the Synoptic tradition. Bultmann's final pages of *The History of the Synoptic Tradition* on "The editing of the narrative material and the composition of the gospels" (1921; ET 1976, 337-67) had identified an area for further study, and after the Second War *redaktionsgeschichte* (and *Kompositionsgeschichte*) were born— or reborn, since Wrede's *Messianic Secret* had already pointed history of traditions research in this direction. Bornkamm's short essay on "The Stilling of the Storm in Matthew" was the harbinger of a new period in Synoptic research. It was reprinted in *Tradition and Interpretation in Matthew* (1960; ET 1963) together with two of his pupils' doctoral theses that used the same method and his own long essay on "End-expectation and church in Matthew," which had first appeared in 1954 and 1956. Bornkamm was later persuaded by the majority view that the Matthean church had already broken with the synagogue, but the main lines of his Matthean interpretation have proved broadly persuasive. The theological conceptuality used here to interpret this Gospel shows how redaction criticism, as developed in Germany, was originally intended to contribute to New Testament theology. Its literary and historical analysis of the latest stages of the Synoptic tradition still reflected the alliance of history of traditions research with kerygmatic theology. This was less religiously fruitful outside German Protestantism and has been overtaken in the English-speaking world by a stronger emphasis on social history and more secular literary approaches to the Gospels.

Paul. The gains of redaction criticism are now widely taken for granted. By contrast, Bornkamm's tradition of Lutheran Pauline interpretation is on the defensive. Here a better understanding of Judaism has changed perceptions of the apostle in a way that challenges the Bultmannian model of Paul's theology more radically than Käsemann's attempted reorientation had done in the 1960s. Bornkamm rejected Käsemann's appeal to the importance of apocalyptic but stood somewhere between the rebel and his teacher in allowing more weight to christology, to the future and to the community and social emphases in

Paul. His popular synthesis followed a long encyclopedia article (*RGG* 3, 5:166-90). Their account of the apostle's life and work stands firmly in the tradition of Ferdinand Christian *Baur's skepticism, maintained by Bultmann, about the historical reliability of Acts.

Equally firmly they maintain the Lutheran and existentialist distillate found in Bultmann's *New Testament Theology*. This interpretation depends above all on a reading of Romans and is justified by an earlier chapter of *Paul*, which repeats Bornkamm's much discussed thesis that Romans is Paul's testament. It also continues the tradition of reading Romans doctrinally and with the anthropological orientation found in Philipp *Melanchthon's *Loci Communes* of 1521. This is defensible because Paul is the one New Testament writer to provide in effect an anthropology, and this is most visible in Romans. Bornkamm rightly sets it in the context of a theology of the cross and gives it some of his own characteristic emphases, notably Paul's insistence on the value of human reason. A final chapter echoes his 1930s battles against the German Christian hostility to Paul's Jewishness and concludes that "Paul's gospel of justification by faith alone matches Jesus' turning to the godless and lost" (Bornkamm 1969; ET 1971, 237).

Many scholars doubt whether dialectical theology's continuation of the Augustinian, medieval and Reformation doctrine of justification interprets this first-century Jewish Christian correctly. The central issue is whether what Paul says about "the law" in Romans is rightly applied to all human moral achievement or whether it is not more narrowly conditioned by his defense of the law-free Gentile mission. Perhaps the phrase "works of the law" refers specifically to the ritual system. Bornkamm gives "the law" even greater prominence than does Bultmann, placing it at the head of his discussion of Paul's anthropology. This whole systematic presentation says much that is surely right about Paul's understanding of the gospel and says it as economically and precisely and penetratingly as anyone could wish. Anthropology, the saving event, present salvation, the life of grace, eschatology and ethics are brilliantly sketched. But both the historical accuracy of the whole and its theological adequacy depend on the Lutheran dialectic of law and gospel. This is based on what Paul wrote and is historically and theologically far more true to the apostle than Marcion was. It may nevertheless achieve its theological goal by giving undue weight to a contingent historical argument. If so, Bornkamm's profound book, backed up by some powerful exegetical argument, belongs as much to the history of the reception of Paul's theology as to its historical elucidation. Here as in his work on the Gospel and Jesus, the exegete who restates his own tradition is above all a Christian theologian.

BIBLIOGRAPHY

Works. G. Bornkamm, "Authority to 'Bind' and 'Loose' in the Church in Matthew's Gospel" in *Jesus and Man's Hope* (Pittsburgh: Pittsburgh Theological Seminary, 1970) vol. 1; idem, "A Discussion of *The Testament of Jesus* by Ernst Käsemann" (1968) in *The Interpretation of John,* ed. J. Ashton (Philadelphia: Fortress, 1986) 79-96; idem, *Das Ende der Gesetzes: Paulusstudien* (Munich: Kaiser, 1952); idem, *Geschichte und Glaube* (Munich: Kaiser, 1968) vol. 2; idem, "The Heresy of Colossians" (1948) in *Conflict at Colossae,* ed. F. O. Francis and W. A. Meeks (Missoula, MT: Scholars Press, 1973) 123-45; idem, "The History of the Origin of the So-Called Second Letter to the Corinthians" *NTS* 8 (1961-62) 258-64; idem, *Jesus of Nazareth* (New York: Harper & Row, 1960 [1956]); idem, "The Risen Lord and the Earthly Jesus: Matthew 28:16-20" (1964) in *The Future of Our Religious Past,* ed. J. M. Robinson (New York: Harper & Row, 1971); idem, "The Significance of the Historical Jesus for Faith" (1962) in *What Can We Know About Jesus?* trans. G. Foley (Philadelphia: Fortress, 1969) 69-86; idem, *Studien zu Antike und Urchristentum* (Munich: Kaiser, 1959); idem, G. Barth and H. J. Held, *Tradition and Interpretation in Matthew* (London: SCM, 1963 [1960]).

Studies. R. S. Barbour, "Ernst Käsemann and Günther Bornkamm," *ET* 76 (1965) 379-83; J. D. Dobbin, "Günther Bornkamm and the New Quest of the Historical Jesus" (unpublished Ph.D. dissertation, Rome, 1970); L. E. Keck, "Bornkamm's Jesus of Nazareth Revisited," *JR* 49 (1969) 1-17; D. Lührmann, "Bornkamm's Response to Keck Revisited" in *The Future of Christology,* ed. A. J. Malherbe and W. A. Meeks (Minneapolis: Fortress, 1993) 66-78; R. Morgan, "Günther Bornkamm in England" in *Kirche: Festschrift für Günther Bornkamm zum 75 Geburtstag,* eds. D. Lührmann and G. Strecker (Tübingen: J. C. B. Mohr, 1980) 491-506; G. Theissen, "Theologie und Exegese in den neutestamentlichen Arbeiten von Günther Bornkamm," *EvTheol* 51 (1991) 308-32.

R. Morgan

Bruce, F(rederick) F(yvie) (1910-1991)

An evangelical biblical scholar, F. F. Bruce was born in Elgin, Scotland, on October 12, 1910, and was educated at Elgin Academy (1921-1928), the universities of Aberdeen (M.A., 1928-1932), Cambridge (B.A., M.A., 1932-1934) and Vienna (research student in Indo-European philology, 1934-1935), where he won numerous prizes (gold medalist in Greek and Latin, Fullerton Scholar in classics, Croom Robertson Fellow at Aberdeen; Scholar of Gonville and Caius College and Sandys Studentship at Cambridge; Ferguson Scholar in Classics and Crombie Scholar in Biblical Criticism from the Scottish universities). His early studies were in Greek and Latin, following in the tradition of Sir William M. Ramsay and Alexander Souter, his teacher at Aberdeen. He graduated at the top of his class at Cambridge. He also obtained the M.A. in Hebrew language and literature from Manchester University (1963).

When Aberdeen University awarded him an honorary D.D. (1957) the comment was made that Bruce had brought more honor to his alma mater than had any other Aberdeen student who had pursued an academic career in the preceding fifty years, even though he was only midway in his professional life and had published only a half dozen books at the time. Bruce was to go on to publish more than fifty volumes, not counting the numerous editions and translations of his most influential works or the many series of commentaries and other biblical studies he edited. Though he received honorary doctorates from Aberdeen and Sheffield universities, he never completed an earned doctorate.

Academic Career. Bruce began his academic career as an assistant lecturer in Greek at Edinburgh University (1935-1938) and then was lecturer at Leeds University (1938-1947), from which he was called to develop a new department of biblical history and literature at Sheffield University (as head, 1947-1959; professor, 1955-1959), in spite of—tradition has it, because of—the fact that he had never studied theology or biblical studies in a formal sense. In 1959 he was called to the John Rylands Chair of Biblical Criticism and Exegesis at Manchester University, where he supervised more Ph.D. dissertations in biblical studies than any other scholar of his generation (1959-1978). Research students came from around the globe to work under his supervision and then to take their places as teachers in theological schools, colleges and universities in Europe, North and South America, Asia, New Zealand, Australia and Africa.

From his childhood Bruce possessed a love of the Bible and languages that would go with him throughout his life. While other children were playing games, he was home (according to his sister) charting the chronology of the kings of ancient Israel and Judah and studying Latin and Greek. Those charts were to appear ultimately in his *Israel and the Nations* (1963). His father, Peter Fyvie Bruce, was an itinerant evangelist among the Christian Brethren and exerted a strong influence in his personal life. Though he had left school at twelve, he was a natural lifelong learner. Bruce once commented that he had a sense of his father's looking over his shoulder when he wrote, especially early on; and in

his autobiography, he said, "I have never had to unlearn anything I learned from him."

Bruce's love of languages and the Bible shaped the course of his life. He read all the ancient languages appropriate for the study of the Bible and the classics, the modern European languages in which material of scholarly significance or general Christian interest was published, and the Celtic languages of his ethnic heritage. For twelve years he edited *Yorkshire Celtic Studies* (1945-1957). He was a voracious reader, building a huge personal library that was eventually to be willed to the John Rylands University Library of Manchester. He was elected to the presidencies of many academic societies, including both the Society for Old Testament Study (1965) and the Society for New Testament Study (1975); he was only one of two individuals to serve as president of both.

In his early years as a scholar, Bruce tended to limit his travels to the United Kingdom and the European Continent, generally to give lectures, preach or attend the meetings of learned societies. He had edited the *Palestine Exploration Quarterly* for many years (1957-1971) before he ever took time out to visit the Holy Land—his first visit to Israel was with a group of colleagues in 1969.

However, from the late 1950s Bruce began to travel widely to give lectures in the United States, Canada, Australia, New Zealand and East Africa (where his daughter and her family lived [1965-1974]) as well as in Europe. He drew unusually large crowds to his scholarly lectures, probably due to the wide readership of his books. Most of his audience were thrilled at the opportunity to hear the man whose writings they had enjoyed, but some laypeople were heard to wonder how someone who was such an interesting writer could be such a dull speaker. This was when he was reading from a manuscript, which was his usual style. But whenever he spoke extemporaneously, especially when answering questions from the audience, he was spellbinding. A selection of the succinct answers to questions about the Bible and contemporary church life sent in by readers of *The Harvester*, to which he contributed a regular column for many years (1952-1972), were published in *Answers to Questions* (1972). They are a model of effective communication, a gift all too rare among scholars.

Theology. Bruce was above all a biblical theologian. Though he edited *The Evangelical Quarterly*, described as a journal "for the defense of the Reformed faith," for more than thirty years (1949-1980), he was by no means Reformed in a sectarian or an ideological sense. When people asked him about a particular theological position, he tended to inquire of them what particular passage of Scripture they had in mind. Then he would offer an interpretation of that text for their edification. He was well-known as an evangelical—he was an enthusiastic supporter of the Inter-Varsity Fellowship (now Universities and Colleges Christian Fellowship) and all of its ministries and was also a contributing editor of *Christianity Today* (1956-1978).

But even here he was by no means partisan. When he was asked on one occasion whether he would describe himself as a conservative evangelical, he replied that he preferred to be "an unhyphenated evangelical," one who is wholeheartedly committed to the message of good news about Jesus Christ but who did not wish to narrow this message in a manner that would separate him from either the whole counsel of God or the broader community of believers (Bruce 1972, 204). Like his hero, Paul, he was the Lord's free man. Some of his views, he said, might be described as liberal; others as conservative. He chose to believe them, however, because he thought them to be true, not because they fit in with a particular mindset or theological tradition. His sympathies were made clear by the choice he made in the title of the British edition of his magnum opus on Paul: *Paul, Apostle of the Free Spirit* (1977), published in North America as *Paul, Apostle of the Heart Set Free.*

Bruce's knowledge of the Bible was prodigious. Those who knew him well believed that he had the whole Bible, both in the original languages and in several translations, committed to memory. When he was asked a question about the Bible, he did not have to look up the text. He would sometimes take off his glasses, close his eyes as if he were scrolling the text in his mind, and then comment in such an exact manner that one knew that he was referring to the Hebrew or Greek text, which he either translated or paraphrased in his answer. If he were in an academic context, the reference might be directly to the original language; in speaking to students who were not necessarily theologians, he would normally use a contemporary translation; in church he would use the appropriate translation familiar to the majority of his hearers, whether the Revised Standard Version, the New International Version, the New English Bible, the King James Version or, in conservative Brethren circles, the New Translation by John Nelson Darby, again normally quoting exactly from memory. He also seemed to know all the hymns of the classical and evangelical Christian traditions by heart as well as a large body of secular poetry—English, Scottish, Greek and Latin.

Bruce had a simple filing system to keep the information he needed to write his books and essays. During the war, when he did not have much money, he began to use discarded cereal boxes to store the notes he had made in his reading. They were arranged simply according to the order of the Bible, from Genesis 1:1 to Revelation 22:21. For Bruce this was the natural way to think of everything in reference to the general flow of Scripture. He did not think topically but according to chapter and verse. His mind was fundamentally exegetical. In due course he transferred the materials into more traditional office files.

Writings. Bruce's first major work was a commentary on the Greek text of the Acts of the Apostles (1951; 3d ed., 1990), the publication of which heralded the resurgence of evangelical biblical scholarship associated originally with the work of the Tyndale Fellowship for Biblical Research, in whose founding he had been a driving influence and to which he gave important leadership for more than four decades. The commentary was highly technical; the emphasis was historical and linguistic rather than theological. The learning displayed was immense, and the care with which he wrote was a model of lucid brevity. He published a second commentary on Acts in the New London/New International Commentary series (1954; 2d ed., 1988) that was much more expositional and theological, intended for pastors rather than scholars. Together these two works set the pattern for the burgeoning commentary series that were to be produced in English by an increasing number of evangelical Bible scholars during the next half century, many of them written by former students or people whom he had encouraged in their academic careers.

Bruce went on to write commentaries on every one of the Pauline writings and nearly all the books of the New Testament. In addition to Acts, his major commentaries were on Hebrews (NICNT 1964), Colossians (NICNT 1957, to which Ephesians and Philemon were added in 1984), and Galatians (NIGTC, 1982). Other smaller but also influential commentaries by Bruce include Romans (TNTC 1963) and 1 Corinthians and 2 Corinthians (NCB 1971). In 1965 he published *An Expanded Paraphrase of the Epistles of Paul,* in which he translated the letters in the order he believed them to have been written and set them in their historical context. Bruce wrote numerous other smaller commentaries on both New Testament and Old Testament books as well as hundreds of essays and articles devoted largely to biblical exegesis.

Rarely did Bruce decide on his own to write a book or an essay. The normal pattern was to be invited to write a book or an article or to give a lecture on a particular subject. His commentaries on the Greek texts of Acts and Galatians were exceptions (though the latter was co-opted for the NIGTC series). Since he wrote out his lectures carefully in manuscript form, it was an easy matter to publish them. His earliest book, *The New Testament Documents: Are They Reliable?* (1943; revised many times), a volume that has been translated into many languages and has been reprinted regularly for more than a half century, grew out the talks he was invited to give to university student groups associated with the British Inter-Varsity Fellowship when he was still a lecturer in Greek. His history of the early church, published first in three small volumes but then as *The Spreading Flame* (1953) and *The Books and the Parchments* (1950), grew out of the lectures he had to give when he went to Sheffield and which two good friends in the publishing business asked for permission to publish. His classic textbook *New Testament History* (1969) was the first volume in a new series of theological texts and remains in print after all other volumes in the series have been long out of print. Each of these books, along with the majority of his other textbooks, general introductions and commentaries, remained in print and were revised regularly throughout his life. Nearly everything he gave in lectures, he published. And, to the disappointment of some of his students, much of what he published he subsequently read verbatim to his students, some of whom were known to follow along in the text as he read.

Guiding Principles. Bruce was at home at the highest levels of academe, as when he was presiding over the Manson Society meetings at Manchester or giving a lecture to the British Academy or some other learned society. But he was also at home among ordinary lay believers, as well as seekers, whether they were undergraduate students, educated or uneducated church members or the vast array of people who came to here his lectures in the United Kingdom or on his trips to Canada, the U.S., Australia, New Zealand and Uganda. During the fall and winter months of most years, he conducted a regular lay Bible school in his home church in Stockport, England.

Scholars who did not know him and who had not read his writings carefully sometimes regarded him as a fundamentalist; however, no one who knew him would have thought of him in these terms. Evangelical, yes, but an evangelical who focused on the centrality of Christ and the heart of the evangel (good news) rather than the doctrines or customs of a section of the Christian community. He believed that there was no incompatibility between the confession of historic Christianity and modern biblical criticism (see his essay on "Biblical Criticism" in NBD [1st and 2d ed.]; and "Criticism and Faith," *Christianity Today* 5 [1960-61] 34-35), an assumption that underlies all his writings. Studying the Bible critically was simply an attempt to use one's God-given mind and all the tools provided by contemporary historical and literary scholarship so as to understand the Bible accurately. He was aware that some of his colleagues came to the study of Scripture with different presuppositions than he did—some of them assuming a rather hostile stance toward traditional Christian understandings, others adopting a rather hostile attitude toward what they view as liberal Christianity—but he refused to lay any stress on these differences. Rather, he sought to embrace the whole community of biblical scholars, those of every faith (including Jewish) and those of little or no faith (including humanists), joining hands with them wherever possible in an attempt both to interpret and to commend Scriptures.

If Bruce had a hobbyhorse that he was occasionally tempted to ride, it was the principle of liberty, which he regarded as at the heart of the Pauline gospel. "I find it hard to understand," he commented to the writer on one occasion, "that some people simply do not wish to be free. They are afraid of liberty. They are afraid of having too much liberty themselves; and they're certainly afraid of letting other people . . .

have too much liberty. . . . It seems much better to move in predestinate grooves" (from unpublished notes, Gasque). He took his cue from Paul, "who had an exceptional insight into the mind of Christ and realized that in Christ and nowhere else is true freedom to be found. Among all the followers of Christ, I suppose there has never been a more emancipated soul than the soul of Paul" (Gasque, unpublished notes). Near the conclusion of his celebrated book on Paul, Bruce selected four central themes in Paul's teaching: "(a) True religion is not a matter of rules and regulations. . . . (b) In Christ men and women have come of age, as the new humanity brought into being through his death and resurrection-life. . . . (c) People matter more than things, more than principles, more than causes. The highest of principles and the best of causes exist for the sake of people; to sacrifice people to them is a perversion of the true order. (d) Unfair discrimination on the grounds of race, religion, class or sex is an offence against God and humanity alike" (Bruce 1977, 463).

The last principle led him, over against the majority in his religious tradition, to become a champion of women in ministry and biblical egalitarianism (see his comments in his commentaries on Gal 3:26-28; 1 Cor 11:2-16; 14:33-35; Eph 5:21-33; 1 Tim 2:8-15). To make a distinction of principle in church service between men and women was in his view unacceptable. "If, as evangelical Christians generally believe, Christian priesthood is a privilege in which all believers share, there can be no reason that a Christian woman should not exercise her priesthood on the same terms as a Christian man" (W. W. Gasque and L. Gasque, "An Interview with F. F. Bruce," *SMR* 139 [spring 1989] 8).

Significance. For fifty years Bruce towered over British biblical scholarship. He commended the viability of a moderate, intelligent and contemporary evangelicalism to his academic colleagues; and he set an example of scholarship, balance, integrity, humility and ecumenicity for his evangelical brothers and sisters to follow. Hundreds of younger scholars flocked from around the world to study with him, many of whom are teaching in colleges, universities and theological schools today; and thousands of other teachers, pastors and laypeople were influenced by his writings. Among contemporary evangelical academics who teach biblical or theological studies, no single person has been more influential; and it is likely that his influence will continue for another generation.

However, Bruce's significance as a biblical interpreter transcends the evangelical tradition. He demonstrated for all the importance of studying the New Testament within the context of the Greco-Roman world, using all the resources of classical and Hellenistic literature, archaeology, geography and the results of more than a century of revolutionary historical research to illuminate the text of the New Testament and of the Old Testament. He also enriched the biblical literacy of the serious but nonacademic students of the Bible and equipped numerous pastors to expound the Scriptures more accurately to their congregations.

BIBLIOGRAPHY

Works. F. F. Bruce, *The Acts of the Apostles: The Greek Text with Introduction and Commentary* (3d rev. and enlarged ed.; Grand Rapids: Eerdmans, 1990 [1953]); idem, *Answers to Questions* (Grand Rapids: Zondervan, 1972); idem, *The Canon of Scripture* (Downers Grove, IL: InterVarsity Press, 1988); idem, *Commentary on Galatians* (NIGTC; Grand Rapids: Eerdmans, 1982); idem, *Commentary on the Book of the Acts* (rev. ed.; NICNT; Grand Rapids: Eerdmans, 1988); idem, *1 & 2 Corinthians* (NCB; London: Oliphants, 1971); idem, *The Epistle to the Hebrews* (rev. ed.; NICNT; Grand Rapids: Eerdmans, [1964] 1990); idem, *The Epistles to the Colossians, to Philemon, and to the Ephesians* (NICNT; Grand Rapids: Eerdmans, 1984); idem, *The Epistle of Paul to the Romans* (TNTC; Grand Rapids: Eerdmans, 1969); idem, *The Hard Sayings of Jesus* (Downers Grove, IL: InterVarsity Press, 1983); idem, *In Retrospect: Remembrance of Things Past* (Grand Rapids: Eerdmans, 1980); idem, *Israel and the Nations* (Grand Rapids: Eerdmans, 1963); idem, *A Mind for What Matters* (Grand Rapids: Eerdmans, 1990); idem, *The New Testament Development of Old Testament Themes* (Grand Rapids: Eerdmans, 1968); idem, *New Testament History* (Garden City, NY: Doubleday, 1969); idem, *Paul, Apostle of the Heart Set Free* (Grand Rapids: Eerdmans, 1977); idem, *Philippians* (GNC; San Francisco: Harper & Row, 1983); idem, *1 & 2 Thessalonians* (WBC; Waco, TX: Word, 1982). **Studies.** Three collections of essays have been published in honor of Bruce: *Apostolic History and the Gospel*, ed. W. W. Gasque and R. P. Martin (Grand Rapids: Eerdmans, 1970); *Pauline Studies*, ed. D. A. Hagner and M. J. Harris (Grand Rapids: Eerdmans, 1980); "Studies in Honor of F. F. Bruce," *JSS* 23, 2 (autumn 1978). *Apostolic History and Pauline Studies* contain extensive bibliographies of his writings; a supplemental bibliography of Bruce's writings was published in *JCBRF* 22 (November 1971) 21-47, which also contains essays on his influence as a scholar, church leader, teacher, writer and friend.

W. W. Gasque

Bultmann, Rudolf *(1884-1976)*

Rudolf Bultmann was one of the leading theologians and New Testament scholars of the twentieth century. The son of a Lutheran pastor, he was born near Oldenburg in the north of Germany. He studied in the universities of Tübingen, Berlin and Marburg, where his teachers included many of the leading biblical scholars and theologians at the turn of the century: Adolf von *Harnack, Hermann *Gunkel, Julius W. M. Kaftan, Johannes *Weiss and Wilhelm Herrmann. Bultmann's academic career followed a typical German pattern, and from 1921 until his retirement (1951) he held a chair in Marburg. He continued to live there until his death. A street was named after him in 1984 on the centenary of his birth.

Bultmann's various writings are marked by his break with liberal theology and biblical scholarship, his commitment to dialectical theology, the influence of Martin Heidegger's philosophy, his existential interpretation of Pauline and Johannine theology, and his (in)famous demythologizing program of the 1940s and 1950s. His writings nonetheless display an impressive unity and consistency over a period of more than forty years.

Theological Influences. Bultmann's training was as a New Testament scholar in the history of religions school. In 1910 he completed his qualifying dissertation begun under Weiss. This dissertation compared the style of the Pauline sermon with the Cynic-Stoical diatribe. His work as a historian of the New Testament alerted him to the difficulties that were being identified by the turn of the century with the dominant theology of liberalism.

The work of the history of religions school *(religionsgeschichtliche Schule)* attempted to understand the origin of the Christian religion within its first-century religious and cultural context. This cast doubt upon liberalism's elevation of Jesus as the supreme moral and spiritual exemplar. Did the texts provide us with reliable access to the historical Jesus? Could the message of Jesus be detached from its Jewish apocalyptic-eschatological setting? By 1920 Bultmann was pointing out that the Jesus presented by W. Heitmüller and others was little more than a cultural ideal retrojected upon the figure of Jesus.

If these historical conclusions tended toward skepticism, this was counteracted by the influence of Herrmann. Herrmann claimed that the province of religion was unique and *sui generis.* It could not be assimilated to either science, philosophy or history. For the Christian, faith is formed through the power of the personality of Jesus working upon one's inner life. The notion of faith as trust *(fiducia)* is central to Herrmann's thought. Faith is not to be viewed as the assent of the mind to dogmatic propositions or even to the words of Scripture. It is not to be construed as the intellectual acceptance of a Christian worldview *(Weltanschauung).* Faith is to be understood as personal trust in the power of Jesus. Any attempt to prove the validity of faith by either philosophy or science can only resemble a desire to be justified by

works rather than by faith alone. Herrmann regards this as a legitimate extension of the doctrine of justification into the realm of epistemology.

While Bultmann follows Herrmann in much of this, the historical difficulties that were raised regarding the latter's understanding of our access to Jesus led to significant differences. Martin Kähler and Ernst Troeltsch argued that the sources do not yield the kind of information about Jesus that Herrmann's theology requires. The earliest Christians were not so much interested in the development of Jesus' personality as in proclaiming the gospel of his death and resurrection. The inner life of Jesus, so central to Herrmann's christology, is not a dominant theme of the New Testament.

The clarification of Bultmann's own position emerged in the early 1920s under the influence of Karl *Barth's dialectical theology. The second edition of Barth's *Römerbrief* (1922) launched an assault upon the most cherished assumptions of liberal theology concerning God, human nature, the kingdom and the church. According to Barth, the Bible witnesses to the "infinite qualitative distinction" (Søren *Kierkegaard) between God and the world. The term *dialectical* refers to the sharp contrast between Creator and creation. The central axiom of Paul's epistle is that the gospel of God does not arise from the world of human experience and possibility. It is a message that comes from above and beyond, bringing judgment on human endeavor while also offering a gracious release. The mode of knowledge in which this message is heard and received is that of faith. The word of God is not to be found through the "objectivizing" investigations of a historical scholar or through the insights of the ethicist. Even religion as a work of the human spirit is distinguished sharply from the gift of faith, which depends entirely upon the uncontrollable action of God.

Bultmann was the first major New Testament scholar to receive Barth's *Romans* commentary sympathetically. He perceived it as a timely warning against attempts to locate God through psychological analysis of religious experience or through the historical study of the Bible. To be a Christian involved hearing and receiving the message of the cross through faith, rather than communing with the religious personality of Jesus (Herrmann) or enrolling as a member of an ethical kingdom of God (Albrecht Ritschl and Harnack). Although his alliance with Barth proved to be only temporary, Bultmann may be considered to have remained a dialectical theologian for the rest of his life. His stress upon the Word of God, the cross of Christ and the nature of faith as gift, together with his hostility to religious metaphysics and theologies of religious experience, position him as a thoroughly dialectical theologian. The principal distinction between Barth and Bultmann concerned the very different ways in which they sought to elucidate the content of the Word of God. For Bultmann the theologian had to describe the act of faith as an existential event in the life of the believer. For Barth this entailed a relapse into liberalism. The theological task could be executed only through considering the object of faith, and this involved the revitalization of Christian dogmatics. For Bultmann the task was to describe the character of faith, for which Heidegger's existentialism was to provide a useful tool.

Hermeneutical Strategy. Bultmann's interpretive strategy covering both historical and theological issues is set out in his 1950 essay on "The Problem of Hermeneutics" (reprinted in *New Testament and Mythology and Other Basic Writings).* Different types of interpretation are determined by different objectives. The ancient historian, the art critic and psychoanalyst will each approach a text with questions that shape the subsequent interpretation. There is also the possibility of an "existential interpretation," which reads a text in terms of its expression of the most fundamental possibilities of human life. Since the ultimate questions of existence are posed for both text and interpreter there is a

shared horizon of meaning.

Other, more technical facets of Bultmann's hermeneutics are the concepts of preunderstanding *(Vorverständnis),* the distinction between *Historie* and *Geschichte,* and content criticism *(Sachkritik).* Every interpreter has some preunderstanding of the questions and concerns of the subject matter of the text. In the case of existential interpretation this involves the basic questions of existence. To this extent, philosophy has a significant though subordinate role to play in the theological interpretation of the Bible through framing these basic questions. Interpretation can proceed only where there is some prior understanding of the subject matter, though this can be radically altered in the act of interpretation. The possibility of existential interpretation is captured by the distinction between *Historie* and *Geschichte,* a distinction almost impossible to render in English synonyms. *Historie* refers to the activity of scientific history as it reconstructs the past. It is concerned typically with dates, places, documents, battles, personalities and social and economic forces. *Geschichte* refers to that dimension of the same history that challenges and transforms human existence. In Bultmann's writings the paradigmatic example of this is the crucifixion of Jesus. As a datable event in the time of Pontius Pilate it is a *historisch* event that is accessible to scientific study. Yet it is also a *geschichtlich* event in which human existence before God is reoriented.

Only in the light of some conception of the central meaning of the text can the individual parts be understood. This phenomenon is referred to as *Sachkritik,* sometimes translated as "content criticism." It denotes the way in which an interpretation is controlled by an overall understanding of what the text is saying. As such, it is a manifestation of the hermeneutical circle by which the parts of a text are interpreted in the light of the whole and the whole in light of the parts. The concept of *Sachkritik* enables Bultmann to distinguish what is essential to a writer's intention from what is peripheral. Thus, for example, it is possible to read some portions of Paul's letters as inessential and even inappropriate to his main intention in other passages. This strategy underlies Bultmann's demythologizing program.

The influence of Martin Heidegger (1889-1976) must be understood not in terms of a capitulation to the most fashionable philosophy of the age but as providing Bultmann with the tool that his hermeneutical program required. Bultmann and Heidegger collaborated closely during their time together in Marburg (1922-1928). Heidegger's *Being and Time* (1927) was the most persistent philosophical influence upon Bultmann's theology, though the former's subsequent enthusiasm for National Socialism led to a cooling of their personal friendship. Heidegger's description of the historicity of human being *(Dasein)* shapes the categories in which Bultmann interprets the New Testament. The human being lives in time and is confronted with fundamental choices about how to live and how to face the future. There are two basic possibilities of human existence—authentic *(eigentlich)* and inauthentic *(uneigentlich)*. These categories enable Bultmann to view human life in terms of two theological possibilities; existence prior to faith and existence under faith. This emerges clearly in his reading of the Pauline distinction between justification by works and justification by faith. Thus while Heidegger's terminology enables Bultmann to describe the most fundamental issues of human existence, it enables him also to propose distinctively Christian answers, inaccessible to philosophical analysis. At most, philosophy can speak of the possibility of authentic existence. Where and how this is actualized is known only through hearing the Word of God in faith.

New Testament Interpretation. Bultmann's approach to New Testament interpretation is most prominently found in his works on the Synoptic Gospels, the theology of Paul and the Fourth Gospel.

Synoptic Gospels. Bultmann is widely regarded as a scholar who was deeply skeptical about our knowledge of the historical Jesus. At most this is a half truth. Bultmann judged (against liberalism) that while the Gospels do not furnish us with a biography of the life of Jesus or a description of his personality, they nonetheless provide us with reliable information about what he said and did. Theologically this restriction is to be regarded positively. The quest of the historical Jesus is not essential, for it is the church's task only to proclaim him as Savior through his death and resurrection.

In the *History of the Synoptic Tradition* (1921) Bultmann established himself as a pioneer form critic of the New Testament. Following the work of William *Wrede and Julius *Wellhausen, he assumed that Mark's Gospel (the earliest) did not furnish us with an outline of the progress of Jesus' ministry. Mark himself had used a source comprised of a series of disconnected units (pericopae) that recounted incidents or sayings in the life of Jesus. Bultmann classifies the different forms into four categories.

Apothegms present an incident or saying of Jesus in order to show its character as significant for the early Christian community. Its life setting *(Sitz im Leben)* is that of the early church rather than the Christian community. An example of this is the calling of the disciples in Mark 1:16-20 and Mark 2:14. The point of these stories is to show how Jesus summons men and women from the everyday affairs of life.

Dominical sayings can be subdivided into wisdom utterances, legal sayings and apocalyptic and eschatological utterances. Some of the wisdom utterances have direct parallels in rabbinic literature and may have been put into the mouth of Jesus by a Christian scribe. Many of the legal sayings, however, probably derive from Jesus, as it is unlikely that they were derived from Judaism or invented by the early church. Bultmann refers here to much of Jesus' teaching in Matthew 5:21-48. The apocalyptic and eschatological passages reflect the concerns of the early church, such as the delayed parousia, although it is highly probable that Jesus himself appeared as an eschatological prophet proclaiming God's' judgment and grace and the imminence of the kingdom.

The miracle stories conform to a pattern familiar in Hellenistic literature and probably grew up around the memory of Jesus in a way similar to tales of heroes and leaders in the ancient world.

Historical stories and legends are narratives, the main intent of which is religious rather than historical. Bultmann classifies some of the key stories in the Synoptic Gospels as largely legendary in character: the baptism of Jesus; Peter's confession at Caesarea Philippi; the entry into Jerusalem; the Last Supper; and the resurrection narratives.

The effect of this classification is to render impossible any attempt to produce a biographical account of Jesus' ministry. However, we should not allow this to obscure Bultmann's belief that it is possible to draw a consistent picture of the message of Jesus. This is set out in his 1926 study *Jesus* (ET *Jesus and the Word*). Jesus appeared as an eschatological prophet proclaiming the nearness of God's kingdom and as a teacher of the law. Under the radical demand of God all human life is sinful. One's only hope is to throw oneself upon the divine grace and forgiveness. God is not apprehended in general truths or religious dogmas but only through an encounter with the Word of God, which calls forth decision and commitment. In subsequent Christian preaching, Jesus' message about the kingdom is displaced by the message of Jesus crucified and risen. In this respect Jesus displaces his own message in the kerygma of the church.

Theology of Paul. According to Bultmann, theology and anthropology are closely connected in Paul's writings. His thought can be organized under two headings, "existence prior to the revelation of faith" and "existence under faith" (Bultmann 1951, 1). Paul asserts the fallenness of all people in virtue of a universal disre-

gard for the claims of God. This is the force of the expression "according to the flesh" *(kata sarka)* when it is used as a modifier of verbs: "The sinful self-delusion that one lives out of the created world can manifest itself both in unthinking recklessness (this especially among the Gentiles) and in considered busy-ness (this especially among Jews)—both in the ignoring or transgressing of ethical demands and in excessive zeal to fulfil them" (Bultmann 1951, 1:239).

Prior to faith in Christ there is no genuine fulfillment of the law (Rom 3:9). Yet it is not even intended by God that human beings should be justified in this way. Bultmann's understanding of the Old Testament here is dominated by his conception of the relationship between law and gospel. The law exposes the situation of the sinner who hears the gospel of Christ. In their presentation of the moral demands of God, the Hebrew Scriptures thus form an indispensable place in the canon of the Christian church (see Bultmann 1963).

The immediate background to Paul's understanding of justification by faith, according to Bultmann, is the legalism of first-century rabbinic Judaism. Justification is a forensic term that denotes the acknowledgement of a person as righteous. This justification is attained through faith in Christ rather than works of the law. It is an eschatological declaration that has already been announced. It is made effective and known through the proclamation of Christ crucified. The death of Jesus is to be understood not in terms of a theory of the atonement (this would be to seek the false security that Herrmann so vigorously opposed) but existentially. It is as a new possibility of existence arises through the word of the cross that one can understand its significance. For Bultmann, Paul's theology is essentially a distinction between possible forms of self-understanding. Authentic existence is made possible by faith in the crucified Christ as God's Word.

The Fourth Gospel. Bultmann's commentary, *The Gospel of John* (1941 [ET 1972]), has often been regarded as his masterpiece. It blends the historical, theological and devotional themes that dominated his work (many of the ideas are also present in Bultmann 1955, 2). Bultmann believed that the Evangelist had drawn heavily upon Gnostic ideas and imagery. The symbolic dualism of the Gnostics is employed: light and darkness, truth and falsehood, above and below, freedom and bondage—but always to depict the significance of Jesus. The two possibilities of existence presented by the appearance of Jesus correspond to the Pauline distinction between two forms of righteousness.

The Fourth Gospel contains a reworking of traditional eschatological themes. Those few vestiges of futurist eschatology are judged controversially to be the work of a redactor. The eschaton has already occurred in the coming of Christ. To have faith in him is already to know eternal life. To reject him is to live in darkness: "The earlier naive eschatology of Jewish Christianity and Gnosticism has been abandoned . . . in favour of a radical understanding of Jesus' appearance as the eschatological event" (Bultmann 1972, 155).

In interpreting the discourses of Jesus, Bultmann argues that they point to the bare fact that Jesus is the revealer. There is no attempt to buttress this claim with metaphysical or historical proof. The sayings merely witness to the simple truth that Jesus is the one in whom God is revealed. This feature of the Fourth Gospel is thus particularly appropriate to Bultmann's own (Herrmannian) concern to reject objectivizing patterns of thought in theology: "Jesus as the Revealer of God *reveals nothing but that he is the Revealer.* . . . [John] presents only the fact *(das Dass)* of the Revelation without describing its content *(ihr Was)*" (Bultmann 1955, 2:66).

From the 1940s Bultmann's name was associated with the demythologizing controversy. The original 1941 essay was presented at a conference of the German Confessing Church and argued against a narrow orthodoxy (the key texts can be found in *The New Testament and Mythology*

and Other Basic Writings). Its conclusions are entirely consistent with Bultmann's theology and exegesis prior to that time. The purpose of demythologizing was to strip away from the essential message of the New Testament both the outmoded worldview of the first century and the tendency toward a false objectivizing of truths that can be grasped only existentially. Thus the "myths" of the New Testament include not only the three-story cosmos, Jewish eschatology and theories of demon possession but also theological dogmas of the virgin birth, incarnation, atonement, resurrection and ascension.

The task of demythologizing is not simply to eliminate myth but to interpret it. Christian faith does not require intellectual assent to a worldview or a dogmatic system. It involves personal response to God's address in Jesus Christ. Bultmann appeals once more to the understanding of human existence outside faith and the understanding of human existence under faith as the categories into which New Testament myth is to be translated. The transition to a new mode of existence is made possible by believing that the cross of Christ is the event in which God addresses me and determines my life: "As the salvation occurrence, then, the cross of Christ is not a mythical event but a historical occurrence *(ein geschichtliches Geschehen)* that has its origin in the historical event of the crucifixion of Jesus of Nazareth *(dem historischen Ereignis)"* (Bultmann 1984, 35). Despite the apparent reductionism of Bultmann's demythologizing project and its subsequent notoriety, it is an attempt to present a strong kerygmatic theology.

Significance. Bultmann's theology and New Testament interpretation constitute an impressive weaving together of various themes. He combines existential interpretation, Lutheran doctrine and radical biblical criticism in a way that distinguishes him as one of the leading figures in twentieth-century theology. Nonetheless his conclusions have been challenged on several fronts, and at the end of the century his influence has waned.

Bultmann's skepticism as to our knowledge of Jesus' life ministry has not prevented other scholars from continuing to pursue the quest of the historical Jesus. Several of Bultmann's leading pupils—Ernst *Käsemann, Günther *Bornkamm and Gerhard Ebeling—reopened the quest in the postwar period, while more recent times have seen a further proliferation of lives of Jesus. Dissatisfaction with Bultmann's position has much to do with a perceived theological weakness. His exclusive concentration on the bare fact of the crucifixion has proved an unstable position. Commitment to Jesus makes sense only on the basis of information about his life prior to his crucifixion. In this respect the story of his life is held to be indispensable for the elucidation of Christian faith.

Bultmann's tendency to reduce New Testament theology to its presentation of two anthropological possibilities has also provoked criticism. This tendency may reflect the influence of Herrmann and Heidegger upon his work. Yet Paul's theology, it may be argued, contains more than mere theological anthropology. It contains an account of salvation history, of the person of Christ, his atoning death and his resurrection from the dead. It is not clear that these can be eliminated in favor of a bare existential interpretation without doing violence to the text. In this respect Bultmann's *Sachkritik* may be regarded as yielding a Procrustean treatment of Paul. Also problematic for Bultmann's reading of Paul has been the recent criticism of E. P. Sanders and others that he misreads rabbinic Judaism as a thoroughly legalistic religion. In doing so, Bultmann's reading of Paul overstresses the controlling function of anthropology.

Similar problems attend Bultmann's existential reading of the Fourth Gospel. It is not clear that passages containing a futurist eschatology can easily be assigned to the hand of a redactor or that the hypothesis of the Gnostic source can be sustained. As with Paul, it is questionable whether everything can be reduced to the presentation of two fundamental possibilities of existence. The Evangelist, like the subsequent theological traditions of the church, attempts to present the significance of Jesus in terms of an understanding of his identity as the Son of God and the incarnate Logos. Rather than viewing it as the adaptation of uncongenial source material, we might see the Fourth Gospel as an attempt to expound the cosmological and metaphysical significance of the Jesus whose story is essential to Christian faith.

The individualism of existential interpretation has also occasioned much criticism in an age that is conscious of the political dimensions of anthropology and theology. An early example of this line of criticism is found in Jürgen Moltmann's *Theology of Hope* (1967). Bultmann, it is alleged, abstracts the human being from his or her relationships to other people and the world. His discrimination between authentic self-understanding and belief in a worldview separates the individual from the historical and social world. Similarly the reduction of the resurrection to the rise of faith in the first Christians detaches the risenness of Jesus from its biblical context in hopes about the destiny of creation, the resurrection of the dead and the future of humanity.

While Bultmann's writings represent one of the most significant attempts to resolve many of the problems inherited from liberal theology and biblical criticism, his specific conclusions have ceased to command widespread consent.

BIBLIOGRAPHY

Works. R. Bultmann, *Existence and Faith: Shorter Writings of Rudolf Bultmann* (New York: Meridian Books, 1960); idem, *Faith and Understanding,* ed. R. W. Funk (New York: Harper & Row, 1969 [1958-1965]); idem, *The Gospel of John* (Philadelphia: Westminster, 1972 [1941]); idem, *History of the Synoptic Tradition* (rev. ed.; New York: Harper & Row, 1976 [1921]); idem, *Jesus and the Word* (New York: Scribner's, 1962 [1926]); idem, *Jesus Christ and Mythology* (London: SCM, 1958); idem, *The Johannine Epistles*

(Herm; Philadelphia: Fortress, 1973 [1967]); idem, *New Testament and Mythology and Other Basic Writings,* ed. S. Ogden (Philadelphia: Fortress, 1984); idem, "The Significance of the Old Testament for Christian Faith" in *The Old Testament and Christian Faith,* ed. B. W. Anderson (New York: Harper & Row, 1963) 8-35; idem, *The Second Letter to the Corinthians* (Herm; Minneapolis: Augsburg, 1985 [1976]); idem, *Theology of the New Testament* (2 vols.; New York: Scribner's, 1951, 1955 [1948-1953]).

Studies. D. Fergusson, *Bultmann* (Collegeville, MN: Liturgical Press, 1992); R. A. Harrisville and W. Sundberg, *The Bible in Modern Culture: Theology and Historical-Critical Method from Spinoza to Käsemann* (Grand Rapids: Eerdmans, 1995); J. Kay, *Christus Praesens: A Reconsideration of Rudolf Bultman's Christology* (Grand Rapids: Eerdmans, 1994); R. Morgan, "Rudolf Bultmann" in *The Modern Theologians,* ed. D. Ford (2 vols.; Oxford: Blackwell, 1989) 1:109-33; S. Ogden, *Christ Without Myth* (New York: Harper, 1961); W. Schmithals, *An Introduction to the Theology of Rudolf Bultmann* (London: SCM, 1968).   D. Fergusson

Caird, G(eorge) B(radford) (1917-1984)

George Bradford Caird, a distinguished British biblical scholar, was born in London in 1917. A Dundee Scot, he received his early education in Birmingham, England, where his father worked as a construction engineer. Later he was able to attend Peterhouse, Cambridge, on a major scholarship in classics, receiving the B.A. (1939; first class honors in both parts of the classical tripos, with distinction in Greek and Latin verse). Moving to study theology at Mansfield College, Oxford, Caird gained the Oxford M.A., first class honors (1943). A year later he submitted "The New Testament Conception of *Doxa* (Glory)" to the theology faculty at Oxford, for which he was awarded the D.Phil. degree. After a challenging three-year wartime pastorate in the much-bombed London district of Highgate, Caird and his young bride, Viola Mary (Mollie), moved to Canada (1946), where they were to spend the next thirteen

years. While in Canada Caird served as professor of Old Testament at St. Stephen's College, Edmonton, Alberta, and later as professor of New Testament at McGill University and principal of the United Theological College of Montreal.

In 1959 Caird returned to Mansfield College, Oxford, serving first as senior tutor under John Marsh and later as principal (1970-1977). Caird's reputation as a biblical scholar of judiciousness and insight grew steadily. His vast knowledge of both Testaments (he remains one of the few major modern interpreters to have been a professor of both Old and New Testaments), his fastidiousness with words and his poetic imagination brought him numerous international distinctions, including four honorary doctorates (climaxed by the Oxford D.D.), election to the British Academy and the awarding of its coveted Burkitt Medal for Biblical Studies, appointment to be Dean Ireland's Professor of the Exegesis of Holy Scripture at Oxford, and the winning of the Collins Religious Book Award (for *The Language and Imagery of the Bible,* 1980). Caird's later years were taken up with biblical translation as a member of the translation panel of the Revised English Bible (following his previous experience as a translator of the New English Bible's Apocrypha) and editorial work (coeditor of *The Journal of Theological Studies,* 1977-1984). The author of approximately sixty articles, more than a hundred book reviews and six major volumes, Caird was hard at work on his seventh substantive work, *New Testament Theology,* when he died of a heart attack. A memorial volume, *The Glory of Christ in the New Testament: Studies in Christology in Memory of George Bradford Caird,* was published in his honor (1987). There an extensive bibliography of his works may be found.

Context. Some of Caird's most formative educational years were carried on in turbulent international times (1939-1944) and equally turbulent theological times. The influence of Karl *Barth and Albert *Schweitzer had by 1939 made deep inroads in mainstream theological circles. The old liberalism of the nineteenth century was now out, as was the fundamentalism of the early twentieth. Caird, in some ways influenced by the neo-orthodox insights of Barth and Emil Brunner, was affected more deeply by his teachers at Mansfield College, particularly Nathaniel Micklem and C. H. *Dodd (who, like Barth, stressed heavily the importance of history within theology and the essential trustworthiness of the apostolic witness but without the rigidity of fundamentalism). But now there was a new presence on the British scene. Rudolf *Bultmann and the form critics were beginning to be taken seriously in Britain, and Caird, like Dodd, took up a vigorous stand against the incursions of German historical skepticism while at the same time employing the historical-critical method in ways that were new, positive and challenging.

As is the case with most profoundly influential thinkers, it would be impossible to trace all of the influences that helped to make Caird the scholar he was to become. It may be said, however, that he can never be understood apart from the history and significance of Mansfield College, Oxford, for much of the twentieth century a rich source of theological and intellectual ferment. There many notable scholars had lectured, including Schweitzer, P. N. Harrison, T. W. Manson, C. J. Cadoux, A. S. Peake, J. S. Whale, John Marsh, A. M. Hunter and Dodd. The stronghold of dissenting (non-Anglican) religious education in Oxford, the theological milieu on Mansfield Road enhanced in the young classics scholar from Cambridge what was already a fiercely independent and creative temperament. Many of the themes that were to prevail in his lifelong work can in some ways be seen as a microcosm of the larger contribution that Mansfield College has made to the theological milieu of the twentieth century—the stands on the importance of the laity, the obligation of scholarship to serve the church, the centrality of the gospel in daily life, the need for vigilance in the

face of the constant corruption of political and religious authority, the equality of the sexes within the Christian community—such emphases are typically dissenting, Congregationalist, Mansfield themes. What made Caird's presentation of them unique was the erudition and authority with which they were expressed, together with the way in which they were combined with his crisp and elegant writing style, subtle humor and a knack of placing familiar questions against the larger picture in new and revealing ways. As N. T. Wright has said, "His literary ability was outstanding . . . his clear, crisp sentences say more in a few words than some scholars manage in several pages. A slim volume from Caird, easily mistaken for a slight or negligible work, is likely to be an explosive charge, packed with pithy wisdom" (Wright in Caird 1997, xv).

Work. Caird's first published book, *The Truth of the Gospel* (1950), is a careful and comprehensive defense of the Christian faith; its simple yet profound questioning of common objections to Christianity make it the peer of C. S. Lewis's more famous *Mere Christianity.* In 1954 Caird produced his first sustained work of exegetical scholarship, the introduction to and exegesis of 1 Samuel and 2 Samuel in *The Interpreter's Bible.* His second book, *The Apostolic Age* (1955), is a brilliant and succinct historical study of the life, institutions and thought of the early church to the end of the first century. *Principalities and Powers* (1956), while ostensibly a discussion of one aspect of Paul's theology, is a compendium of that theology on a wide range of topics.

Caird's first full-length commentary, *The Gospel of St. Luke,* was, like his previous work on 1 Samuel and 2 Samuel, brimming over with historical confidence: despite some qualifications, the biblical writers can be trusted to provide good and accurate history. The same may be said of his small but important study *Jesus and the Jewish Nation.* His second commentary, *The Revelation of St. John the Divine,* was a landmark work and was in no small measure responsible for Caird's being awarded the Oxford D.D. The volume *Our Dialogue with Rome: The Second Vatican Council and After*, continues to be influential in ecumenical dialogue; it resulted from Caird's experience of serving as a Protestant observer at the Second Vatican Council. Caird's third and last biblical commentary, *Paul's Letters from Prison*, is a succinct analysis of Colossians, Ephesians, Philippians and Philemon. As always, Caird's clarity and incisive historical-critical acumen are used to produce what were for many readers surprisingly conservative results: Paul, author of Colossians and Ephesians, is a writer whose insights, properly interpreted, are not that difficult to translate into twentieth-century experience; they will be ignored by modern society at its own peril. Caird's *The Language and Imagery of the Bible* (1980) is a treasure trove of linguistic and literary insights into the methods and meanings of the biblical authors.

In addition to these major works Caird produced numerous influential shorter studies on a variety of topics: Septuagintal lexicography ("Towards a Lexicon of the Septuagint," 1969), the Christian's attitude to war (*War and the Christian*, 1979; Caird was a lifelong but undemonstrating pacifist) and apartheid (*South Africa: Reflections on a Visit*, 1976). Toward the end of his career he was commissioned to write a number of important books, including the New International Critical Commentary on Hebrews and the volume on Paul in Oxford University Press's Past Masters series. But these were to take a back seat to his *New Testament Theology*, intended to be the ultimate statement of his thinking on the New Testament, on which he had been working for some years. He was not to live to see its completion, though it was published posthumously by the Oxford University Press (1994).

Significance. Caird's unique combination of methods (he abominated the word *methodology*, which for him "was often an excuse for not getting on with the job") and themes make him difficult to catego-

rize in terms of his significance. It may be best, therefore, to consider his primary contributions to twentieth-century scholarship under eight major headings.

Linguist and lexicographer. Two of Caird's clearly distinguishable but related concerns were the intricate ways in which language works and the meaning of words. These concerns were early seen in his Grinfield Lectures on the Septuagint at Oxford (1961-1965), followed by his various published studies on Septuagintal lexicography; his analysis of what Paul meant by *Principalities and Powers* (1956); and his brilliant, sustained study of *The Language and Imagery of the Bible* (1980).

Of related importance to these concerns was his repeated claim that the meanings of what the ancient authors wrote must remain primary in biblical study. Caird saw modern structuralist approaches as "Gadderene precipitations into the Dark Ages" (Caird 1994, 423). "If the hearer takes words in a sense not intended by the speaker, that is not an enlargement of meaning but a breakdown of communication" (Caird 1994, 423). Caird insisted that the biblical writers must be allowed to speak with their own voices and that the easiest way to distort those voices is to allow modern fashions, presuppositions and dogmatic regimentation to get in the way. As H. Chadwick notes, Caird "believed in the perspicuity of the substance of Holy Scripture, a principle which the medieval schoolmen and the Reformation inherited from St. Augustine, but which the disciples of Rudolf Bultmann have found it notoriously hard to share" (Chadwick, xx). Caird was constantly sparring with German theology in general and Bultmann in particular. Unlike many of his Mansfield contemporaries, he had never studied in Germany, and he remained puzzled as to why German scholarly fads were so popular in England and North America; for him they got in the way of the interpreter's task of discerning the clear meanings of the biblical writers (exempt from this antipathy was the work of Bo Reicke, Martin Hengel and, most particularly, Joachim *Jeremias, for whom Caird often expressed a great admiration). While it is clear that the current hermeneutical flow continues largely in the opposite direction, Caird's warnings to modern scholarship are being heard by many.

New Testament theology. Much of the last twenty years of Caird's life was spent planning his definitive, full-dress treatment of *New Testament Theology*. His approach was characteristically original. Presiding over "an apostolic conference on faith and order" (cf. Acts 15, Gal 2), he attempted to allow the New Testament writers "to speak for themsleves" on a host of subjects (predestination, sin, salvation, the life of the church, eschatology, christology) rather than to use artificial force to bludgeon their views into the arbitrary dictates of a system. The resulting unison of Caird's New Testament colloquium was therefore akin to that of a choir, sung not in total harmony but with appropriate counter-melodies. For him the issue was "not whether these books all say the same things, but whether they all bear witness to the same Jesus and through him to the many spendoured wisdom of the one God" (Caird 1994, 24). Thus Caird allowed them a forum in which they could place their own questions on the agenda in a way which might permit their resulting emphases to rest where they wish them to rest, rather than where a tradition of systematic theology might try to force them to rest.

As elsewhere in his writings, Caird's approach was essentially directed to the meanings and intentions of the ancient writers, without those meanings and intentions being distorted by passing theological fads. Although he knew the problems of twentieth-century hermeneutics extremely well, his conception of New Testament theology had little time for them; abstract and philosophical concerns are almost entirely absent. For him they had produced results which are far too often negative and colored by modern concerns; after all, "New Testament theology is a historical discipline . . . its purpose is descriptive" (Caird 1994, 1).

Consequently the discipline, if it is to remain pure, will have nothing to do with systematics or apologetics; its job is to understand the meanings of the ancient writers, with modern theologians and apologists deciding what significance those meanings may have for today, or whether or not they may be ultimately true (Caird 1994, 3). Here, and elsewhere, Caird probably came as close to a being a "pure exegete" as will be found among mainstream modern biblical interpreters, and for this reason he was always attracted to the most purely exegetical of the New Testament writers: Luke, Paul, and the authors of Hebrews and the Apocalypse. His understanding of Hebrews in particular went against the grain of other interpreters by claiming that one of the author's primary concerns was to inquire after *the original meaning* of his Old Testament texts (Caird 1994, 63-64; "The Exegetical Method of the Epistle to the Hebrews") rather than impose upon them forced, arbitrary and allegorical meanings. Consequently Caird saw the author as a person who was, in some ways, rather like himself.

Yet another integral feature of Caird's *New Testament Theology* was his inclusion as the final chapter of a treatment of the theology of Jesus, which is not the presupposition (as it was for *Bultmann) but "the starting point and goal of New Testament theology" (Caird 1994, 25-26, 346). Stressing the essential trustworthiness of the Gospels, Caird concentrated on the corporate, national context of much of Jesus' teaching—which, according to him, meant that Jesus was concerned not only with the salvation of individual souls in the hereafter but with the renewal of Israel as the people of God. Caird's decision to place Jesus' teaching last in his *New Testament Theology* once again demonstrates his robustly independent temperament.

New Testament eschatology. One of the questions that had dominated Mansfield theology from Schweitzer to Dodd was how the talk in the New Testament about the end of the world can be understood today. Caird's solution to the problem remains one of his lasting and most original gifts to biblical scholarship. For years he was fond of beginning his lectures on a personal note, claiming that when he began the study of theology he felt that he had learned at least three things: that the earliest Christians unanimously expected that Jesus would return in their lifetime; that they had the authority of Jesus for this belief; and that it did not happen. "Now, after forty years of study," he then would add, "I remain firmly convinced *only of the third.*" The other two he spent much of his later career challenging.

It is still widely held that Jewish apocalyptic had abandoned all hope for this world and looked only to an imminent, final, divine intervention in history. Caird saw this as a dangerous caricature. The apocalyptic writers were like the prophets in that they never gave up on their belief in divine action within history. Instead, by the use of a device known as prophetic camera technique, they employed metaphorical language that telescoped events within history and the final climactic victory of God at the end of time. Thus the flow went both ways: this-worldly events were used to enhance and understand the end, while the end was used to view historical events in a new perspective. In the same way Jesus looked forward to a searching test, both for himself and his followers, within his own generation (the near lens). This included persecution, martyrdom and the eventual loss of the holy city, Jerusalem. But he also saw in these events the last judgment and God's final victory over evil (the distant lens). For him the future is constantly interpenetrating the present.

The same may be said of the writers of the four Gospels, Paul and the author of the book of Revelation. Caird's *The Revelation of St. John the Divine* remains one of the most persuasive examples of the preterest interpretation of the Apocalypse. For Caird "that which must swiftly come to pass" is not the end in the usual sense; it is the end that was swiftly facing the first-century

church—its persecution and possible annihilation. The opening of the seven seals, the pouring out of the divine wrath in the bowls and the trumpets, the scarlet woman and the dragon, and so forth are metaphors of this first-century ordeal. The final end will eventually come, and that is something that John sees with amazing foresight, once one properly appreciates the nature of his metaphorical language; but that is not the end that concerns John. "He no more expects the end of the world than any of the other prophets before him," said Caird. In these views Caird was in some ways indebted to Dodd's realized eschatology. But, through the use of modern linguistic theory and the power of his imagination, he went far beyond Dodd in establishing his views. It may be added that because of Caird, Dodd's understanding of eschatology is now undergoing a renewed study and appreciation.

Integration of theology and politics. Long before it became fashionable, Caird saw the importance of politics in theological discussion. He had no use for piety in the sense that word is often used, as a description of the temperament that tends to concentrate entirely on spiritual things and has no use for the corporate affairs of life in this world. This is seen first in his seminal study of Paul's *Principalities and Powers,* which, he repeatedly insisted, represent for Paul the political, social, economic and religious power structures of this world. They were once God's powers, but they had fallen with the rest of creation. Nevertheless they were created in Christ, and their destiny is to be reconciled to him. The political, ecological and religious implications of Caird's views are being widely appreciated and will probably grow in importance as concern for the environment grows. As is true of many of his distinctive themes, he was one of the first to see their significance.

The same may be said for Caird's emphasis on the importance of politics in an overall appreciation of Jesus' teaching, so provocatively expressed in his commentary on Luke's Gospel, as well as in his shorter studies *Jesus and the Jewish Nation* and "Eschatology and Politics: Some Misconceptions." For him the integration of theological and political concerns was hardly limited to the past; it is also seen in his interest in such varied topics as the modern Christian attitude to war, the status of women in society, and apartheid. His courageous addresses to the South African Reformed churches (during his tenure in 1975-1976 as worldwide moderator of the United Reformed Church), later published as *South Africa: Reflections on a Visit,* helped to create the climate of tolerance that eventually brought peace to that embattled land. For Caird "the truth of the gospel" is deeply religious but not strictly religious, for it reaches into every area of personal and corporate human life.

The renewed quest of the historical Jesus. One of Caird's lifelong preoccupations was the historical Jesus, and it is being recognized that *Jesus and the Jewish Nation* was one of the earliest studies by a scholar that helped to launch a new phase in the study of the subject (called by N. T. Wright "the Third Quest of Jesus"). Caird's comments were little short of a clarion call. Like many New Testament scholars who were first trained as classicists, Caird could not understand the skepticism that theologians often feel about the worth of their historical sources. Consequently his work tends to lack negative presuppositions, and more recent scholars such as E. P. Sanders, M. J. Borg and N. T. Wright, to mention several, have seen in Caird's work a pointer forward to new levels of understanding. But to say that Caird was in favor of a new quest would be incorrect: he had never given up on the old quest. What permeates his work is the claim that, using proper historical and critical tools, the life and teaching of Jesus shine through the Gospels not only with remarkable uniformity but also with a high degree of historical credibility if seen in the context of first-century Jewish politics. For Caird one of the central questions posed by Jesus' teaching was, What does it mean for Israel,

in the year A.D. 30, to be God's holy people in a world overrun by pagans? This intermixing of political concerns and the study of the Gospels clearly helped to set the stage for a fresh appraisal of the Gospels that allows more room for history than was available in the first two quests.

Scholarship as service to the church. Caird was never a pure academic; he had little use for the dialogue carried on behind privileged walls by a small preserve of scholars and clerics, with no ability of laypeople to participate in or benefit from the exchange. Consequently it is sometimes difficult to distinguish in his writings between Caird the scholar and Caird the preacher. His life was so integrated that, as D. A. Sykes has put it, "To know [Caird] you had to hear him preach, for here became apparent one of the great strengths of his life. It was clearly the same man who conducted advanced seminars and helped graduate students to see through the complexities of their work. Many of those who went to his lectures remarked not only on the vigorous academic discipline they were invited to share, but on the direct relationship they were encouraged to see between honest probing and the preaching of the Gospel" (Hurst and Wright, vii). Adds Chadwick: "He understood the task of the exegete to be not only the discernment of the author's original intention but also the elucidation and proclamation of the Gospel of God. Just as he could hardly endure sermons without intellectual content, so his lectures were truly evangelical" (Chadwick, xxi).

Understandings of Paul. In addition to *Principalities and Powers, Paul's Letters from Prison* and comments dispersed throughout *The Language and Imagery of the Bible* and *New Testament Theology,* Caird wrote a number of articles that made clear his ungrudging admiration for Paul (e.g., Caird 1972). This sometimes earned him the criticism of other scholars, but Caird, as usual, did not care. His admiration of Paul, however, could never approach anything like hero worship. "If he had ever seen St. Paul approaching in the

High Street, he wouldn't have treated him with exaggerated deference, nor would he have crossed the street to avoid him. He would probably have invited him to read a paper to his Postgraduate Seminar, and would have felt no embarrassment at taking him into the Senior Common Room for tea beforehand" (Barr, 509).

Church unity. For those who have read it, *Our Dialogue with Rome: The Second Vatican Council and After* remains one of the most creative attempts by a Protestant scholar to penetrate the dense wood of Protestant-Roman Catholic dialogue. To describe its contents would be difficult, since Caird apparently designed it to be something of a Columbus's Egg: it could be fully appreciated only after it had been put into practice. It remains widely appreciated by ecumenists.

On a scholarly level it may be said of Caird that "despite his independence, [he] belonged to and typified a marked tradition within British scholarship. Points of similarity with C. H. Dodd, less often with T. W. Manson, are frequent. What Caird displayed in a highly illuminating way is the manner in which theological conviction, literary values, and historical reasoning worked together in that current of learning . . . in this respect the rethinking of Caird's thoughts can be, and is, a contribution to the whole intellectual history of an era" (Barr, 520-21). On a personal level those who knew him will never forget that tall figure who seemed to walk faster than anyone else, black Oxford gown trailing him in the breeze, who never spoke in public with a note, and who—perhaps as a fitting symbol of his life—always seemed to be out of the lecture hall before his listeners had written down his last word or had had the opportunity to consider the meaning of what they had just heard.

BIBLIOGRAPHY

Works. G. B. Caird, *The Apostolic Age* (Essex and London: Duckworth, 1955); idem, "Eschatology and Politics: Some Misconceptions"in *Biblical Studies: Essays in Honor of William Barclay,* ed. J. R. McKay and J. F. Miller (London: Collins, 1976) 72-86, 202-3; idem, "The Exegetical Method of the Epistle to the Hebrews," *CJT* 5 (1959), 44-51; idem, *The Gospel of St. Luke* (Pelican Gospel Commentaries; Harmondsworth: Penguin, 1963); idem, "Introduction, and Exegesis to I and II Samuel," *The Interpreter's Bible,* ed. G. A. Buttrick et al. (4 vols.; Nashville: Abingdon, 1954), 2:855-1175; idem, *Jesus and the Jewish Nation* (London: University of London, Athlone Press, 1965); idem, *The Language and Imagery of the Bible.* Foreword by N. T. Wright (Grand Rapids: Eerdmans, 1997 [1980]); idem, *New Testament Theology,* completed and ed. L. D. Hurst (Oxford: Clarendon, 1994); idem, *Our Dialogue With Rome: The Second Vatican Council and After* (Oxford: Oxford University Press, 1967); idem, "Paul and Women's Liberty," *BJRL* 54 (1972) 268-81; idem, *Paul's Letters from Prison* (NClB; Oxford: Oxford University Press, 1976); idem, *Principalities and Powers* (Oxford: Clarendon, 1956); idem, *The Revelation of St John the Divine* (2d ed.; London: A & C Black, 1985 [1966]); idem, with J. Johansen-Berg, *South Africa: Reflections on a Visit* (London: The United Reformed Church in England and Wales, 1976); idem, *The Truth of the Gospel* (London: Oxford University Press, 1950); idem, *War and the Christian* (Surrey: The Fellowship of Reconciliation, 1979).

Studies. J. Barr, "George Bradford Caird," *PBA* 71 (1985) 493-521; H. Chadwick, "George Bradford Caird, 1917-1984: A Memoir" in *The Glory of Christ in the New Testament: Studies in Christology in Memory of George Bradford Caird,* ed. L. D. Hurst and N. T. Wright (Oxford: Clarendon, 1987); L. D. Hurst and N. T. Wright, "Foreword" in *The Glory of Christ in the New Testament: Studies in Christology in Memory of George Bradford Caird,* ed. L. D. Hurst and N. T. Wright (Oxford: Clarendon, 1987) v-viii. E. Kaye, *Mansfield College, Oxford: Its History and Significance* (Oxford: Clarendon, 1995); J. Muddiman, "The Scholarly Achievement of George Caird," *Mansfield College, Oxford, Magazine* (1994-1995) 45; idem, *Jesus and the Victory of God* (Minneapolis: Fortress, 1996).

L. D. Hurst

Conzelmann, Hans Georg (b. 1915)

Hans Conzelmann was born in Tailfingen,

Germany, on October 27, 1915, and studied at the universities of Tübingen and Marburg (1934-1938). In World War II he was wounded during military service. After the war he took his doctorate at Tübingen (1951). His teaching career included stints at Tübingen, Heidelberg, Zurich and Göttingen. A member of the evangelical church, he was involved in the international Lutheran-Roman Catholic dialogue.

Work. Conzelmann's work was done in the context of the post-Bultmannian movement in Germany after World War II. His approach to the New Testament can be understood only when it is seen in relation to that of Rudolf *Bultmann and certain of his post-Bultmannian peers. Two aspects of Bultmann's work are particularly important for reading Conzelmann aright: Jesus research and the theology of the New Testament.

Jesus research. Bultmann's research on Jesus involved a historical and theological critique of late nineteenth-century lives of Jesus. These lives aimed to present a Jesus freed from dogma who would be intelligible to that time. Since the work of David Friedrich *Strauss (1835), the Fourth Gospel had been given up as a historical source. By the 1860s the two-source theory had become the dominant explanation of the Synoptic problem. The priority of Mark, for late nineteenth-century scholars, had two corollaries: Mark was considered objective history, the type that nineteenth-century historians aspired to write, and Mark was believed to contain developmental information about Jesus. The picture of Jesus that resulted from this aim and this view of the sources was a developmental biography in which the inner and outer development of Jesus' life and career was traced. The inner development was traced in terms of Jesus' developing messianic consciousness. The outer development was characterized by initial success and popularity followed by gradual desertion and ultimate isolation, with Jesus being forsaken by all. The drive to discern development grew out of the cultural assumption

that the way to understand anything (nature, society, being, the individual self) is in terms of development. The religious relevance of such a life was that it presented Jesus as a moral paradigm that was self-evidently superior to any other so that he compelled assent.

For Bultmann the nineteenth-century quest was historically impossible and theologically illegitimate. It was historically impossible because a proper view of the sources prohibited it. Bultmann assumed the two-source theory. He also assumed William *Wrede's work on Mark (1901), which contended that Mark's messianic secret was a reflection not of Jesus' history but of Mark's theology. If so, the first corollary of the nineteenth-century view of Markan priority was destroyed. Mark is not objective history. Bultmann also assumed the work of K. L. Schmidt (1919), which concluded that the Markan narrative framework came from Mark, not the history of Jesus. If so, then the second corollary of the priority of Mark for nineteenth-century scholars was undermined. Mark does not provide developmental information about Jesus. If Mark is not objective history and does not give us developmental information about Jesus, then the late nineteenth-century attempt to trace the inner and outer development of Jesus' life and career is historically impossible. The sources do not provide that type of information.

Moreover, Bultmann regarded the late nineteenth-century quest as theologically illegitimate because Christian faith is produced by the Easter kerygma rather than the historical Jesus and a Jesus produced by human effort who is self-evidently authoritative violates the Pauline strictures against works righteousness and empties faith of its meaning. With Bultmann the nineteenth-century quest had come to an end.

It was possible, however, Bultmann thought, to say something about Jesus' message. As a form critic, he believed that once the Markan narrative framework was recognized as redactional, what was left to work with were the individual bricks of oral tradition. In order to determine which bricks of oral tradition come from Jesus a criterion of discontinuity was used. Early traditions that showed signs of discontinuity with the interests of the church could be regarded as probably coming from Jesus. From such self-contained units of oral tradition, one could reconstruct the message of Jesus. From this message one could infer a picture of Jesus as the eschatological bearer of the Word of God's judgment and forgiveness.

Conzelmann's efforts in relation to the Jesus research of Bultmann were twofold. He took Bultmann's model of the Jesus tradition's development that had formerly been used to go behind the Gospels to Jesus and reversed it so that it became a tool for working with the final form of a Gospel text in a quest for the theology of the Evangelists, in particular, Luke-Acts. If the narrative framework is redactional, he contended, it could serve as a means of interpreting the theological vision of the redactor. Further, by noting Luke's changes of his Markan source one gained yet another clue to the mind of the Evangelist. Contending that the Lukan tendency was to eliminate from his Markan source references to an imminent end and observing that only the Lukan framework included a history of the early church (Acts), Conzelmann argued that the theological tendency of Luke-Acts was the elimination of an imminent eschatology and its replacement by a history of salvation. The occasion for this redactional effort was, he believed, the delay of the Parousia (following Bultmann and Albert *Schweitzer before him). This interpretation of the theology of Luke-Acts Conzelmann set forth in his doctoral dissertation, *Die Mitte der Zeit* (1954), and in its popularization under the English title *The Theology of St. Luke* (1960). The method he had developed, redaction criticism, was to become the rage among New Testament scholars for more than a generation.

Conzelmann also employed the Bultmannian methodology as a part of the new quest of the historical Jesus. In 1953, at a meeting of old Marburgers, Ernst *Käsemann presented a paper in which he called for a new quest of the historical Jesus. It would be based on the Bultmannian view of the sources and so would not repeat the errors of late nineteenth-century developmental lives of Jesus in trying to trace Jesus' inner and outer development. It would operate within the Bultmannian theological framework and neither promote works righteousness nor undermine faith. This new quest was motivated by the need to show the continuity, not identity, between the historical Jesus and the kerygma. It was made possible by a new view of the self associated with the existentialist historiography of the period just after the war. In this historiography the self was not understood in terms of its development but in terms of its acts of intention, decisions made in crisis situations that revealed who the person really was. Such a view of the self and how it was to be understood fit perfectly with the nature of the material. The Gospels do not offer a motion picture of Jesus' career. They do, however, offer a series of snapshots in which Jesus' intentionality may be seen in the decisions he makes in crisis situations. This new quest produced only two full-scale treatments of Jesus: one by Günther *Bornkamm, the other by Conzelmann.

Conzelmann built on Bultmann's positions. He did not regard the Gospel of John as a source for historical material about Jesus's teachings. He also employed a criterion of discontinuity. His criterion, however, went further than Bultmann's. Whereas Bultmann said the earliest Jesus tradition should show signs of discontinuity with the church that passed it on, Conzelmann (in agreement with Käsemann) argued that only what fits neither into Jewish thought of Jesus' time nor into the views of the early church can be regarded as authentic. There must be discontinuity not only with the church that passed the material on but also with the Judaism out of which it came.

Using this criterion, Conzelmann produced a major article for *Die Religion in Geschichte und Gegenwart* (1959) that was later translated into English and published as *Jesus* (1973). Certain of its positions deserve comment.

Like Bultmann, Conzelmann believed Jesus held to an imminent eschatology. The difference between Jesus and John the Baptist in their eschatology was that Jesus emphasized the salvation dimension instead of the judgment aspect of eschatology. In this Conzelmann differed from Bornkamm, who argued that Jesus held to an inaugurated eschatology in contrast to the Baptist's imminent eschatology.

Like Bultmann and Bornkamm, Conzelmann denied Jesus' use of any christological titles for himself. Rather Jesus's self-understanding was that of himself as the one who made the final appeal, confronting people directly with God through himself. Unlike Bultmann and Bornkamm, Conzelmann denied the authenticity of even the future Son of man sayings that seemed to distinguish between Jesus and the future Son of man (Mk 8:38; Q = Lk 12:8-9 par. Mt 10:32-33).

Like Bultmann, Conzelmann regarded Jesus himself as the historical presupposition of faith. One comes to faith through preaching of the risen Lord. The historians' Jesus is neither an alternate route to faith (as with J. M. Robinson) nor the criterion of Christian proclamation (as with Käsemann).

Like Käsemann and Bornkamm, Conzelmann holds that the purpose of the new quest is to keep us from losing sight of the historicity of the revelation. The impact of the new quest was short-lived in the English-speaking part of the world. Moreover, Conzelmann's *Jesus* was overshadowed by the more comprehensive book, *Jesus of Nazareth*, by Bornkamm.

In any case Conzelmann used Bultmann's model of the history of the development of the Jesus tradition to work in both directions: both as a control for interpreting the theology of the Evangelists and

as a means of going behind the Gospels to what can be known about Jesus with modern critical tools.

Theology of the New Testament. Bultmann understood New Testament theology as the explication of believing self-understanding. This task, he thought, should be done not topically but in connection with a description of the development of early Christianity. Bultmann followed the outline of early Christianity's development already set forth by W. Bousset. So Bultmann's *Theology of the New Testament* unfolds: a reconstruction of the message of the historians' Jesus, the kerygma of the church apart from Paul, Paul, John, developments toward the ancient church. He regarded the pre-Easter Jesus as the historical presupposition of Christianity. Jesus belonged to Judaism, not to Christianity. He held to the normative status of Paul and John. He relegated the rest of the New Testament to the development toward early catholicism (e.g., Luke-Acts, the Pastorals, 2 Peter), that is, a fall away from the normative kerygmatic center of the New Testament. These judgments he made on the basis of a content criticism whose norm was authentic self-understanding.

Conzelmann's *An Outline of the Theology of the New Testament* (ET, 1969, based on the second German edition of 1968) is the post-Bultmannian theology of the New Testament. Unlike Bultmann, Conzelmann regards theology as the exegesis of the original texts of the faith, the oldest formulations of the creed (following H. Schlier). This affects his understanding of content criticism. The norm to be used in content criticism is not authentic existence but the creed. Like Bultmann, Conzelmann thinks the historical Jesus is not a theme of New Testament theology. So New Testament theology does not begin with the reconstructed teaching of Jesus. It rather starts with the kerygma of the primitive community and the Hellenistic community. There were, in early Christianity, moreover, two very different kinds of theological development of the kerygma. On the one hand there was historical narration; on the other there was conceptual exposition (in agreement with U. Wilckens). Within the development of the kerygma by historical narration fall the Synoptics and the Fourth Gospel. Mark, for example, is understood as a commentary on the kerygma. Within the conceptual exposition of the kerygma are found Paul and the developments after Paul (e.g., Acts, the Pastorals, Hebrews). All that matters to Paul about Jesus is his saving work, the cross and resurrection. In Conzelmann's outline the developments after Paul are treated before the Fourth Gospel is taken up. Conzelmann does this to avoid Bultmann's negative judgment on the period. Unlike Bultmann, Conzelmann will not allow the term "early catholic" to be used for any of these New Testament writings. Each in its own way is a reliable if not perfect expositor of the kerygma.

Significance. Conzelmann's main contribution to New Testament study has been his pioneering work in redaction criticism. He refocused research on the final form of the Gospel text and offered an objective method to be followed in such study. The flowering of redaction-critical studies of the Synoptics in the generation after *Die Mitte der Zeit* is ample testimony to his influence. Synoptic studies today have tended to move away from his historical and diachronic paradigm in favor of a literary and synchronic paradigm that employs various types of literary methodologies to the final form of the Gospel text. This has involved both gain and loss. There has been the gain of being able to study Mark and John with the same method as that used for Matthew and Luke, since the former's sources are unknown and cannot be used for comparison. There has been, with the implementation of newer literary methodologies, a loss of interest in the theological and religious dimensions of the final form of the Gospel text.

Conzelmann's impact on research on the historical Jesus has been minimal. The influence of the new quest has been felt mainly through Bornkamm's *Jesus of Naz-*

areth. The criterion of discontinuity Conzelmann shared with other new questers has been criticized as producing a Jesus wholly abstracted from his culture and hence unreal. The eschatological Jesus that Bultmann, Conzelmann and the latter's post-Bultmannian peers saw in the oldest tradition has been challenged by the Jesus Seminar, although it is upheld by E. P. Sanders and others like D. C. Allison. In the English-speaking world, at least, except for E. P. Sanders, N. T. Wright and J. P. Meier, Jesus research has been left mainly to the eccentric left.

The lasting legacy of Conzelmann's redaction-critical and form-critical work on the Synoptics has been the vision that New Testament research on the Synoptic Gospels must encompass both a quest of the historical Jesus and a quest of the theology of the Evangelists.

Conzelmann's *Outline of the Theology of the New Testament* has borne no fruit to date. Recognition of the multiple kerygmata in earliest Christianity has undermined his use of the early creed and kerygma as the unifying element in New Testament theology. No satisfactory substitute has been found to replace it and to give theological unity to the New Testament's acknowledged diversity. For the most part current New Testament study is obsessed with method and poetics and is devoid of serious theological interest. The replacement of a historical paradigm with a literary one in New Testament study has been accompanied by general unconcern about any synthetic reconstruction of the history of early Christianity. As a result there is no comprehensive vision, either theological or historical, of early Christianity's development.

Conzelmann's legacy in this area is to hold out the vision that New Testament research must operate with a comprehensive historical and theological vision, tentative though both may be.

BIBLIOGRAPHY
Works. H. Conzelmann, *Acts of the Apostles*

(Herm; Philadelphia: Fortress, 1987); idem, *1 Corinthians* (Herm; Philadelphia: Fortress, 1975); idem, *History of Early Christianity* (Nashville: Abingdon, 1973); idem, *Jesus* (Philadelphia: Fortress, 1973); idem, *Outline of the Theology of the New Testament* (New York: Harper & Row, 1969); idem and M. Dibelius, *The Pastoral Epistles* (Herm; Philadelphia: Fortress, 1972); idem, *Theology of St. Luke* (New York: Harper & Brothers, 1960); idem and A. Lindemann, *Interpreting the New Testament* (Peabody, MA: Hendrickson, 1988).

C. H. Talbert

Cullmann, Oscar *(b. 1902)*

Oscar Cullmann is the sole surviving representative of a hermeneutical revolution that began in the late nineteenth century and later found diverse expressions in the works of theologians such as Karl *Barth, Rudolf *Bultmann and Cullmann himself. Though he was initially sympathetic with certain hermeneutical aims of the dialectical theology represented by Barth and Bultmann in the 1920s, Cullmann later forged his own approach to biblical interpretation. His emphasis on the role of God's history of salvation *(Heilsgeschichte)* in both the formation and the understanding of the biblical canon influenced what became known as the biblical theology movement on both sides of the Atlantic (Childs, 13).

Early Development. Cullmann was born and reared in Strasbourg during a period when the city was under German rule. His early education included the study of theology, which he pursued out of academic rather than religious interests. His professors at the gymnasium were advocates of German liberal theology, which left the young Cullmann strongly opposed to all forms of orthodox Christianity. He subsequently enrolled at the University of Strasbourg following the First World War, after the city had reverted to France.

At the university Cullmann's exposure to the ideas of Albert *Schweitzer, Barth and Bultmann (among others) caused him to abandon the liberal theology he had

heretofore embraced. Schweitzer's *The Quest for the Historical Jesus* convinced Cullmann that efforts by nineteenth-century German liberal scholars to reconstruct a nonsupernatural historical Jesus reflected the prevailing culture of German philosophical idealism and naturalism rather than the witness of the New Testament. From that point on, his lifelong concern was to discover "what is new in New Testament theology" as over against other religions and philosophies, whether ancient or modern (Cullmann 1966, 683).

In his opposition to theological liberalism Cullmann found himself in company with Barth and Bultmann. These two, like Cullmann after them, concluded that the German theological enterprise had become captive to contemporary culture, thereby equating the word of God with German culture. Barth, for example, was forced to rethink his initial commitment to liberalism after a number of his former professors signed a statement in 1914 endorsing the German kaiser's wartime policies.

What Cullmann shared with Barth and Bultmann was a rejection of liberal theology's concept of Christianity, a concept that went back to the early nineteenth-century German theologian Friedrich Daniel Ernst *Schleiermacher. Specifically, Schleiermacher sought to make peace with the Enlightenment prejudice against miracles by denying that Christianity had anything to do with committing oneself to the historical and doctrinal claims of the Bible, which includes numerous accounts of miracles. Instead Schleiermacher defined Christianity in terms of the inward religious consciousness of the biblical writers and of Jesus himself. Christian faith for Schleiermacher and the liberal tradition was thus defined as subjective, inward feeling, "the consciousness of being absolutely dependent . . . of being in relation with God" (Schleiermacher, sec. 4). This in turn meant that for Schleiermacher biblical interpretation had as its subject matter the inward psychology of Jesus and the biblical writers. If by reading the Bible one could come to an understanding of the religious feelings of Jesus and the disciples, that person would gain further insight into his or her own religious experience.

Barth rebelled against this notion that the Bible is a book about the writers' subjective religious experiences. For Barth the Bible is a book about God, not about the history of people's feelings about God. At the same time Barth accepted the results of liberal historical-critical scholarship, which viewed the Bible as a book filled with historical inaccuracies. Yet for Barth, and for Bultmann as well, this was not important. Both viewed the subject matter of Scripture not as historical events or the interpretations of those events by the biblical writers but rather as the suprahistorical Spirit of God who dwells outside the bounds of history and human contingencies. This emphasis on the fundamental discontinuity between God and humanity (as opposed to liberalism's view of humanity's basic harmony with God at the level of inward religious feeling) became the basis for what was later termed dialectical theology.

Cullmann found much to endorse in Barth's complaint that liberal theology was merely anthropology in theological garb. In addition Cullmann followed Bultmann and other advocates of form criticism *(Formgeschichte)* in their attempts to go behind the biblical documents to recover the oral tradition that forms the basis for the New Testament. In his first scholarly essay (1925), Cullmann insisted that form-critical analysis confirms that the earliest Christians did not merely seek to follow the teachings of Jesus or to emulate Jesus's religious experience. Rather, the earliest layers of that tradition depict Jesus both as fully human and as the one who was worshiped by those who knew him. To put it in the language of later dogmatic formulas, the first Christians saw Christ as having both a divine nature and a human nature. The goal of the form-critical enterprise is therefore neither to discover a nonsupernatural Jesus of history nor to psychoanalyze Jesus and the disciples. It is instead to acquaint us with what the earliest Christians believed about Christ.

In 1928 Cullmann defined his own exegetical method over against that of Barth (Cullmann 1928). He endorsed Barth's notion that the "Spirit of Christ" and not a so-called historical Jesus of modern scholarship is the subject matter of the New Testament. At the same time Cullmann believed that Barth's methodology left too little room for historical control. Barth saw biblical exegesis as merely a "preliminary" step to the more important task of "theological interpretation," that is, reflecting upon one's encounter with the object of faith: the risen Christ. Cullmann, however, believed that the Christian exegete's theological interpretations not only must be elicited by the text of Scripture but also must be controlled by the text.

The reason Barth would not subject his "theological exegesis" to historical control, noted Cullmann, was that he was operating with a neo-Kantian dualism that places divine revelation completely outside of the bounds of history. Barth, along with Bultmann and other advocates of dialectical theology, had reacted against the naturalistic historicism of liberal hermeneutics by defining revelation in ahistorical, noncognitive terms. That is, they refused to define revelation either as divinely bestowed information or as God's activity within the flow of history. Instead, dialectical theologians viewed revelation as a personal encounter between the Spirit of Christ and humankind. Barth stressed the giver of revelation (God), while Bultmann spoke of revelation from the standpoint of the individual who is addressed by God (an emphasis that led Bultmann to focus on the faith experience of the individual, much as Schleiermacher had done).

Cullmann's view of revelation attempted to stress both the giver of revelation (Christ) and the receivers (the church). In addition Cullmann saw cognitive knowledge of God as possible because divine revelation, while coming to us from outside of ourselves, has entered into the framework of history. Thus Cullmann saw historical exegesis as being able to exercise a positive role in the theological task.

Hermeneutics of Heilsgeschichte. In 1930 Cullmann was nominated as a professor of New Testament at his hometown university. Surrounded by French colleagues who were more interested in the history of early Christianity than in the various forms of German dialectical theology, Cullmann gradually moved away from his earlier endorsement of Barth's notion that the suprahistorical "Spirit of Christ" was the subject matter of the New Testament and that the New Testament exegete must have a prior "encounter" with the risen Christ before historical investigation can begin. Instead Cullmann adopted what he later called a "purely scientific" approach (Cullmann 1966, 685) that viewed the subject matter of the New Testament not as suprahistorical but as the events and interpretations surrounding the life, death and resurrection of Jesus as experienced by the earliest Christians. This meant that the subject matter of the New Testament must be understood only in light of the text of the New Testament, rather than the text being understood in light of a previously understood subject matter.

Between 1931 and 1938 Cullmann also perceived the New Testament as speaking of the Christ event within the context of God's entire plan of redemptive history. Biblical eschatology thus became the focus of several articles Cullmann wrote during his tenure at Strasbourg. By his own account, the most important insight he gained at Strasbourg was that the New Testament writers viewed the kingdom of God neither as totally future (as per Schweitzer's thoroughgoing eschatology) nor as already fully present (C. H. *Dodd's realized eschatology). Instead, "It was now clear to me that it was not one or the other, but both: already realized but yet still future. With Christ, the event which accomplishes my salvation has occurred, but the completion of it has yet to occur. *Already and not yet.* This 'tension' determines the

situation in which we, along with the New Testament, find ourselves" (Schlaudraff, xvi).

Cullmann continued to emphasize this tension that exists between the first and second advents of Christ after he left Strasbourg in 1938 to accept the chair of New Testament and patristic studies at the University of Basel in Switzerland. During the Second World War he continued to publish articles that elaborated on the "already and not yet" nature of New Testament eschatology. The year after the war ended Cullmann's first major book, *Christ and Time,* set forth his thesis that God's revelation in Jesus Christ can be understood only in light of God's entire history of salvation *(Heilsgeschichte),* which began with the call of Abraham, finds its central event in the resurrection of Jesus, continues to find expression in the work of the Spirit in Christ's church and will culminate with the return of Christ.

Christology and Heilsgeschichte. The fact that the already-not yet tension of God's *Heilsgeschichte* has been created by the Christ event in turn makes christology central to Cullmann's interpretation of the New Testament. It also gives Cullmann's christology a somewhat nontraditional focus. This became apparent a decade after *Christ and Time* first appeared, when Cullmann published his *Christology of the New Testament.*

For Cullmann "all Christology is *Heilsgeschichte,* and all *Heilsgeschichte* is Christology" (Cullmann 1963, 326). This means that Jesus Christ must be understood within the context of the entire history of salvation as opposed to being understood merely by means of a suprahistorical encounter with the Spirit of Christ (as per dialectical theology). It also means that salvation history can be understood only in light of the Christ event. This being the case, the New Testament witness to Jesus Christ must be interpreted by intellectual categories that are derived from the history of salvation itself and not from prior philosophical constructs.

Such a hermeneutics of *Heilsgeschichte* leads Cullmann to present a christology very different from the traditional dogmatic formulas of Nicea and Chalcedon. Whereas these postapostolic creeds focused on the divine and human natures of the person of Christ, Cullmann notes that the New Testament focuses not on who Christ was but on what Christ did. New Testament christology is therefore functional christology, centering itself on the work of Christ as opposed to his nature or being. Thus, for example, the New Testament's central christological confession ("Jesus is Lord") refers not so much to Christ's divinity as it does his role as the One designated by God to rule over the history of salvation, both now (by means of his Spirit through the church) and in the age to come (following his return).

To those who object that such a functional christology ignores the great ecumenical christological formulas, Cullmann's reply is twofold. First, he does not wish to imply that those postapostolic formulas are inappropriate expressions of faith because their focus is different from that of the New Testament; to the contrary, he views them as consistent with the New Testament portrayal of Christ (Cullmann 1963, 41). Second, Cullmann nevertheless insists that part of his task as a New Testament exegete is "to forget the manner in which the problem presented itself at the time of the councils." That is, rather than reading the New Testament in light of later church tradition, he said, "I deliberately abstain from *subjecting the texts of the New Testament to questions raised by the later dogmas.*" Failure to follow this procedure, Cullmann believes, will "always risk placing the accents elsewhere than do the authors of the New Testament" (Cullmann 1963, 42).

New Testament Canon and Heilsgeschichte. Cullmann's desire to keep New Testament exegesis apart from later dogmatic reflection is not so much a result of Protestantism's principal of *sola Scriptura* as it is of Cullmann's view of the relationship of the New Testament canon to the rest of redemptive history. The New Testament belongs to that period of *Heilsgeschichte* wherein the Spirit-inspired interpreters of the Christ event were eyewitnesses to the events they recorded and interpreted or were close associates of such apostolic eyewitnesses. In other words, the New Testament differs from postapostolic interpretations by virtue of its eyewitness quality and thus belongs with Christ himself at what Cullmann calls the midpoint of salvation history.

This midpoint of God's *Heilsgeschichte* is what Cullmann refers to as the *Offenbarungsgeschichte,* or "history of revelation," since it serves as the norm for all previous and subsequent events and interpretations of salvation history. The Holy Spirit does continue to reveal himself in the postapostolic church, but whether or not it is the Spirit who speaks in any instance must be determined in light of the literary deposit of the *Offenbarungsgeschichte:* the New Testament canon. This qualitative differentiation between apostolic and postapostolic church tradition separates Cullmann from his Roman Catholic counterparts, who stress the work of the Holy Spirit in the formation of the entire Christian tradition while generally deemphasizing the uniqueness of the New Testament as eyewitness tradition (see Cullmann 1953).

Significance. Cullmann's emphasis on the positive relationship between revelation and history gives his method of biblical interpretation a common ground with historical inquiry that is lacking in the hermeneutical tradition of Barth and Bultmann, which emphasized the necessity of the biblical interpreter's prior encounter with a suprahistorical subject matter ("the Spirit of Christ"). In this respect Cullmann, despite his rejection of nineteenth-century liberal theology, continues to stand in the liberal tradition in seeing Christianity as a historical phenomenon subject to historical investigation.

At the same time, Cullmann's analysis of the New Testament leads him to reject

Schleiermacher's claim that the subject matter of Christianity is the religious experience of the first Christians. In this respect Cullmann joins Barth over against Schleiermacher and Bultmann in affirming that the subject matter of the New Testament is not "the experience of faith" but rather something that has occurred apart from one's faith experience (Cullmann 1966, 687). Unlike Barth, however, Cullmann defines God's self-revelation in Christ—the subject matter of the New Testament—in terms of historical event and apostolic interpretation as opposed to placing his main emphasis on the suprahistorical "Spirit of Christ." In this way Cullmann seeks to avoid what he views as docetic tendencies in the thought of both Barth and Bultmann.

The fact that Cullmann views the Scripture not merely as a witness to God's revelation in Christ but as a part of that revelation (the *Offenbarungsgeschichte*) leads him to interpret the subject matter of the New Testament in light of the text rather than the other way around. For Cullmann there is no "canon outside of the canon" as is the case both in liberalism (the so-called historical Jesus) and dialectical theology (the suprahistorical "Spirit of Christ"). Nor will Cullmann tolerate a "canon within the canon," wherein a particular theological motif (e.g., Paul's emphasis on justification by faith) becomes the grid through which all other New Testament statements are forced to pass. In this way Cullmann stakes out a position that enables him to stand over against all forms of confessional orthodoxy as well as liberalism as he seeks to practice and inculcate in his readers an "obedient listening to the strangeness of the Bible" (Cullmann 1966, 687).

This was precisely the aim of the biblical theology movement that Cullmann so deeply influenced. To the degree that Cullmann has inspired many of his contemporaries to take with utmost seriousness the foundational documents of Christianity, he has made a major positive contribution over against those who seek to begin the theological enterprise elsewhere. Whether or not biblical theology can in turn become the basis for significant confessional consensus among Christians of different persuasions is a major challenge facing the church at the end of the twentieth century.

BIBLIOGRAPHY

Works. O. Cullmann, "Autobiographische Skizze" in *Vorträge und Aufsätze*, ed. K. Froelich (Tübingen: J. C. B. Mohr [Paul Siebeck], 1966); idem, *Baptism in the New Testament* (London: SCM Press, 1958); idem, *Christ and Time* (3d ed.; Philadelphia: Westminster, 1964); idem, *The Christology of the New Testament* (2d ed.; Philadelphia: Westminster, 1963); idem, *Immortality of the Soul; or, Resurrection of the Dead?: The Witness of the New Testament* (London : Epworth, 1958); idem, "Les problemes posés par la méthode exégétique de l'ecole de Karl Barth," *RHPR* 8 (1928) 70-83; idem, "Les récentes études sur la formation de la tradition evangelique," *RHPR* 5 (1925) 459-77, 564-79; idem, *Peter; Disciple, Apostle, Martyr : A Historical and Theological Essay* (2d ed.; New York: Meridian Books, 1961 [1960, 1952]); idem, *Salvation in History* (New York: Harper & Row, 1967 [1965]); idem, "The Tradition: The Exegetical, Historical, and Theological Problem" in *The Early Church* (Philadelphia: Westminster, 1953).

Studies. B. S. Childs, *Biblical Theology in Crisis* (Philadelphia: Westminster, 1970); T. M. Dorman, *The Hermeneutics of Oscar Cullmann* (San Francisco: Mellen Research University Press, 1991); K-H. Schlaudraff, *"Heil als Geschichte"? Die Frage nach dem heilsgeschichtlichen Denken, dargestellt anhand der Konzeption Oscar Cullmanns* (Tübingen: J. C. B. Mohr [Paul Siebeck], 1988); F. D. E. Schleiermacher, *The Christian Faith,* ed. H. R. Mackintosh and J. S. Stewart (Edinburgh: T & T Clark, 1928); D. K. Wallace, "Oscar Cullmann" in *Creative Minds in Contemporary Theology,* ed. P. E. Hughes (2d ed.; Grand Rapids: Eerdmans, 1969).

T. M. Dorman

Davies, W(illiam) D(avid) (b. 1911)

William David Davies was born December 9, 1911, in the Welsh-speaking village of Glanaman, Dyfed, South Wales, not far from Swansea. After graduating with honors in classical Greek and Semitic languages at the University of Wales in Cardiff (1934), he went on to get his ministerial degree (B.D.; 1938) at the Memorial College, Brecon, Wales, where he won distinction in New Testament. Davies then pursued graduate studies at the University of Cambridge, where he completed the master's degree (1942).

During this period Davies was ordained in the Congregational church and began serving a pastoral charge at Fowlmere and Thriplow, not far from Cambridge. His academic career began simultaneously when he became assistant tutor at Cheshunt College in Cambridge (1941-1942). At this time Davies was deeply involved in the study of the letters of Paul, an area of research in which he was soon to make one of his greatest contributions. In 1946 he left the parish to become professor of New Testament at Yorkshire United College, Bradford, Yorkshire. Four years later he moved to the United States, where he was to remain for the rest of his career, serving with distinction in three institutions: Duke University (1950-1955; 1966-1981), Princeton University (1955-1959) and Union Theological Seminary in New York (1959-1966).

During his long career Davies received honors too numerous to list here, including many distinguished lectureships and the presidency of the prestigious international organization of New Testament scholars, the Studiorum Novi Testamenti Societas. His sixty-fifth year was honored by the presentation of a festschrift, a congratulatory volume of essays by colleagues and former students, *Jews, Greeks and Christians: Religious Cultures in Late Antiquity.* A complete bibliography of his work up to 1976 is found in this volume (Hamerton-Kelly and Scroggs, 1-10). In 1989 Davies was elected honorary fellow of Fitzwilliam College, Cambridge.

Pauline Studies. Davies's stature in New Testament scholarship was established immediately upon the publication of his first book, *Paul and Rabbinic Judaism: Some Elements In Pauline Theology* (1948). In the preface the author pays tribute to the two scholars who supervised his research: Charles Harold *Dodd and David Daube. This was by no means a superficial nod of appreciation. Throughout his career Davies has demonstrated that he learned much from the careful, nonspeculative scholarship of Dodd, the dean of British New Testament scholarship. Similarly he listened intently to Jewish scholars of the New Testament such as Daube, with whom he has had a lasting friendship.

The book was warmly praised in reviews by prominent scholars, but it was perhaps only in retrospect that its importance was fully perceived. E. P. Sanders, a former student, declared in 1977 that Davies's study "marks a watershed in the history of scholarship on Paul and Judaism" (Sanders, 7). T. Wright a decade later called it "one of the few epoch-making books in modern Pauline studies" (Neill and Wright, 412).

Scholars had always acknowledged that there were Jewish elements in Paul's thought, but adherents of the history of religions school, intent on explaining the sharp contrast between Paul and Judaism, presupposed that this divergence was due to the fact that Paul incorporated elements of Hellenistic religions. Accordingly, it was commonly argued that Paul transformed Christianity into a mystery religion, worshiping a dying and rising god just as in the mysteries of Attis, Osiris and Dionysus. The sacraments of baptism and the Lord's Supper were formulated by Paul on the basis of comparable pagan rituals. Rudolf *Bultmann, the most imposing New Testament scholar of the twentieth century, insisted that Paul's theology is incomprehensible unless one assumes that significant changes occurred when the Christian message was taken out of the sphere of Palestinian Judaism and planted in Hellenistic communities that were more open to non-Jewish influences. It was to this Hellenistically oriented Christianity that Paul was converted in Damascus (Bultmann, 1:63). Although

Davies was by no means the first to protest against this view of Paul, his book is now regarded as the point when the tide began to turn.

Davies's intention was modest. He did not set out to present "an exhaustive account of Pauline theology" but rather to demonstrate that "certain pivotal aspects of Paul's life and thought" could be better assessed "against the background of the contemporary Rabbinic Judaism" (Davies 1948, preface). Toward this end he first established that the reigning assumption of a profound divergence between Palestinian and Diaspora Judaism was simplistic and misleading. For centuries Palestinian Judaism had been influenced by Hellenistic thought. Moreover, contact between Diaspora Jews and Jerusalem was constant, because of the temple tax and the annual flood of pilgrims. While there were differences, they should not be exaggerated. As a Pharisee, Paul was a product of mainstream Judaism.

Davies examined elements of Paul's thought that had been claimed as evidence of Hellenistic influence. The Pauline contrast of flesh and Spirit, for example, is not representative of Hellenistic philosophical dualism but is based on the Old Testament contrast between humanity and God as developed in rabbinic thought. In particular the rabbinic idea of "the evil impulse" provides a better basis for understanding Paul's thought about sin as a power than does anything in Hellenistic thought. It is significant that Davies laid out this argument before further supporting evidence was provided by the Dead Sea Scrolls (see his 1957 article "Paul and the Dead Sea Scrolls: Flesh and Spirit," reprinted in Davies 1962).

In response to the history of religions thesis that Paul's concept of dying and rising with Christ in baptism (Rom 6) derives from the mystery religions, Davies argued that whatever similarities there are must be regarded as superficial. Paul's thinking takes its departure from Jewish ideas about the solidarity of the pious with the Messiah.

One of Davies's most original contributions was his claim that significant features of Paul's christology derive from rabbinic thinking about the Torah. Christ had taken the place of Torah for Paul as the focus of divine revelation; Christ, in his life and teaching, is the new Torah. It was natural, therefore, that the apostle should apply to Christ some of the features associated with Torah in rabbinic thought. Among these is the identification of Torah with divine Wisdom. Accordingly, Paul attributed not only preexistence to Christ but also a cosmological role in the creation of the universe.

One of the most controversial claims made in the book is that justification by faith is not the center of Paul's theology. Here Davies was taking over and developing a proposal of Albert *Schweitzer (Schweitzer, 205-6). It is only in polemical contexts in Galatians and Romans, where he is defending the Christian faith against judaizing opponents, that Paul resorts to this language. The apostle had no intention of opposing faith to obedience. Far more central to Paul's thought, as Schweitzer also maintained, is the concept of being "in Christ." Whereas justification by faith concerns the individual only, "in Christ" is a corporate concept that links the individual with the new humanity created in the Messiah, the second Adam. It is thus the key to Paul's understanding of salvation, the church, the sacraments and the Spirit-directed life. Davies argued that the traditional Protestant reading of Paul in terms of a stark contrast between gospel and law was erroneous and misleading for two reasons: it ignores the importance in Paul's thought of "the law of Christ," and it exalts Paul's uniqueness at the cost of deprecating Judaism as a sterile religion of legal righteousness. For Paul Christianity was not the antithesis of Judaism but its fulfillment.

Here is expressed a concern that has dominated Davies's entire career. Perhaps partly in response to the Holocaust, partly in outrage at injustice, Davies has devoted his energies to repudiating the caricature of Judaism presented in much Christian writing. By placing such emphasis on the Jewish inheritance of Paul, he has reminded his readers that first-century Judaism was by no means an arid wasteland of unspiritual legalism. Paul did not turn his back on the synagogue because its worship and theology were woefully inadequate but rather because its adherents refused to accept Jesus as Messiah, Savior and Lord.

It was not surprising, therefore, that Davies chose for his presidential address to the Studiorum Novi Testamenti Societas in 1976 the topic "Paul and the People of Israel." Paul's critique of the role of Torah in Judaism, he urged, was not an attack on legalism but issued from the fact that the Messiah had come and must henceforth be the central principle of religious thinking and behaving: "Faith in the Messiah, rather than the observance of the traditional norms or the Law becomes the essential mark of belonging to the people of God" (Davies 1977, 5). Nevertheless, Paul did not consign the religion of the synagogue to the ash heap. In Romans 11:26 Paul declares that "all Israel will be saved." This does not mean that Jews will give up their religion. Paul implies that the Deliverer mentioned in the same verse will be Jesus, the Messiah, and that the consummation he anticipates will be not the end of Judaism but its fulfillment.

Against critics who accuse Paul of inconsistently adhering to the ethnic superiority of the Jews despite his universalism (Gal 3:28), Davies insisted that Paul's hope for Israel is based on its peculiar role in God's plan in the past. He concludes: "Paul at least provides a basis for the mutual respect and mutual recognition of Christians and Jews as they co-exist in history" (Davies, "Paul and the People of Israel," 35).

Matthean Studies. Because of Davies's continuing interest in the Jewish background of early Christianity, it was not at all surprising that his next major publication focused on the Gospel of Matthew, which he had referred to in his first book as "the Gospel of Christian Rabbinism" (Davies 1948, 137, 149). *The Setting of the*

Sermon on the Mount (1964; abbreviated for the general reader in *The Sermon on the Mount,* 1966) makes no pretense of interpreting Matthew 5—7. The intention is rather to examine the sermon's context in Matthew, Jewish messianic expectation, contemporary Judaism, the early church and the ministry of Jesus. Hailed by one scholar as "one of the most valuable contributions to the study of the gospels that has appeared in some years," this volume immediately established its author as a Matthean scholar to be reckoned with.

Intrigued by the possibility that Matthew presents the sermon as the new Torah of the new Moses delivered on a new Sinai, Davies carefully examines Pentateuchal motifs in the First Gospel. He concludes that Mosaic allusions are present but transcended, because Matthew understands the relationship of believers to Jesus as being very different from that of Torah-observant Jews to Moses. Although Matthew makes no use of Paul's "in Christ" formula, his understanding of the relationship is the same: "The Sermon is that of the Messiah, the Son of Man and the community addressed is incorporated in him" (Davies 1964, 99). In conformity with the dominant opinion in Judaism, Matthew conceives of the Messiah not as bringing a new Torah but rather as providing the definitive, God-authorized interpretation of how the immutable Torah is to be observed.

Davies devotes almost fifty pages to an examination of evidence linking the First Gospel with the religious perspective of the Dead Sea Scrolls. He concludes that there are allusions to matters of concern at Qumran, indicating that Jesus himself intentionally reacted to the Essene movement. Matthew, however, has transposed these allusions so that they relate to the debate between his community and the Pharisaism of his day.

One of Davies's distinctive contributions in this study is the thesis that rabbinic Judaism as it developed in Jamnia (Yavneh) after the destruction of the temple was aware of and reacted to Jewish Christianity.

Although the evidence he adduces is by no means free of ambiguity, the thesis itself is a reasonable one and has been taken seriously by subsequent scholarship, both Jewish and Christian. Less controversial is his insistence that Matthew is at a number of points reacting to Jamnia. After an extended examination of the relevant evidence, Davies concludes: "It is our suggestion that one fruitful way of dealing with the Sermon on the Mount is to regard it as the Christian answer to Jamnia" (Davies 1964, 315).

In all his major works, as well as in a number of articles in encyclopedias and periodicals, Davies has shown a special interest in New Testament ethics. In *The Setting of the Sermon on the Mount* he studies the relationship between the radical demands of Jesus and the ethical regulation of life in Matthew's community. Davies argues that Matthew should not be seen as subordinating gospel to law; for this Evangelist the gospel of the Messiah includes revelatory teaching about how to live in accordance with God's will. As in *Paul and Rabbinic Judaism*, Davies opposes a common Protestant perception that Matthew and Paul are opposed rather than complementary.

More recently Davies's interest in Matthew has issued in a mammoth three-volume commentary in the new International Critical Commentary, in collaboration with D. C. Allison Jr., totaling more than twenty-three hundred pages. This commentary will remain an indispensable resource for Matthean studies for years to come.

The Land of Israel. A third area in which Davies has made a particularly significant contribution concerns the territorial dimension of Judaism. *The Gospel and the Land* (1974) examines the theological significance of the land in the Old Testament and postcanonical Jewish sources. As would be expected, Davies found that there was no unified dogma concerning the land. While many statements emphasized the close relationship uniting God, Israel and the land, others insisted on the authenticity of Jewish life and worship in the Diaspora.

The writings of the New Testament, however, even though they were written primarily by Jews, show little interest in this territorial dimension. Here the land is significant primarily because it was the historical scene of the life, death and resurrection of Jesus: "In sum, for the holiness of place, Christianity has fundamentally, though not consistently, substituted the holiness of the Person: it has Christified holy space" (Davies 1974, 368). A subsequent volume, *The Territorial Dimension of Judaism,* pursues the theme further, focusing this time not on the Christian response but on the significance of the land in modern Judaism.

Other Contributions. During his long career Davies has published numerous significant articles. Many of these have been reprinted in two collections, *Christian Origins and Judaism* (1962) and *Jewish and Pauline Studies* (1984). In 1963 he delivered a series of lectures on television that were subsequently published as *Invitation to the New Testament.* Here and in *The New Creation: University Sermons,* Davies displays his gift as a communicator to a general audience.

Finally it should be noted that Davies, in collaboration with L. Finkelstein, edited a series of volumes for *The Cambridge History of Judaism.* The first two volumes, *The Persian Period* and *The Hellenistic Age,* appeared in 1984 and 1989 respectively. A third volume is forthcoming

BIBLIOGRAPHY.

Works. W. D. Davies, *Christian Origins and Judaism; A Collection of New Testament Studies* (London: Darton Longman & Todd; Philadelphia: Westminster, 1962); idem, *The Gospel and the Land: Early Christianity and Jewish Territorial Doctrine* (Berkeley: University of California Press, 1974); idem, *Invitation to the New Testament: A Guide to Its Main Witnesses* (New York: Doubleday, 1966a); idem, *Jewish and Pauline Studies* (Philadelphia: Fortress, 1984); idem, *The New Creation: University Sermons* (Philadelphia: Fortress, 1971); idem, *Paul and Rabbinic Judaism, Some Rabbinic Elements in Pauline Theology* (London: SPCK, 1948; rev. ed. with additional notes, 1955; Harper Torchbook ed. with new introduction: New York: Harper & Row, 1967; 4th ed. with an additional essay and a fourth appendix, Philadelphia: Fortress, 1980); idem, "Paul and the People of Israel" *NTS* 24 (1977) 4-39; reprinted in *Jewish and Pauline Studies* (Philadelphia: Fortress, 1983); idem, *The Sermon on the Mount* (Cambridge: Cambridge University Press, 1966b); idem, *The Setting of the Sermon on the Mount* (Cambridge: Cambridge University Press, 1964); idem, *The Territorial Dimension of Judaism* (Berkeley: University of California Press, 1982; rev. ed. with symposium and further reflections: Minneapolis: Fortress, 1991); W. D. Davies with D. C. Allison Jr., *The Gospel According to Saint Matthew* (ICC; 3 vols.; Edinburgh: T & T Clark, 1988, 1991, 1997); W. D. Davies, with L. Finkelstein, *The Cambridge History of Judaism* (2 vols.; Cambridge: Cambridge University Press, 1984, 1989).

Studies. R. Bultmann, *Theology of the New Testament* (2 vols.; New York: Scribner's, 1951); R. Hamerton-Kelly and R. Scroggs, eds., *Jews, Greeks and Christians: Essays in Honor of William David Davies* (Leiden: E. J. Brill, 1976); S. Neill and T. Wright, *The Interpretation of the New Testament 1861-1986* (2d ed.; Oxford: Oxford University Press, 1988); E. P. Sanders, *Paul and Palestinian Judaism: A Comparison of Patterns of Religion* (Philadelphia: Fortress, 1977); A. Schweitzer, *The Mysticism of Paul the Apostle* (New York: H. Holt & Company, 1931).

D. R. A. Hare

Dodd, C(harles) H(arold) (1884-1973)

C. H. Dodd is probably to be reckoned as the leading British New Testament scholar of the mid-twentieth century. He was born in Wrexham, a market town in North Wales, into an English-speaking family of nonconformists who worshiped in a Congregationalist chapel named Pen-y-bryn. His father was a self-educated schoolmaster who was also a deacon and Bible-class teacher in the chapel.

Dodd matriculated at University College, Oxford (1902), where he demonstrated his exceptional abilities by achieving a double first, one in classics and one in greats (i.e., Greek and Roman history, philosophy). After some temporary teaching in the classics department at Leeds University, Dodd studied Roman numismatics in Berlin (1907), where he also attended Adolf von *Harnack's lectures. Upon his return to Britain he was awarded a four-year fellowship at Magdalen College, Oxford. During this period he studied theology at Mansfield College, the nonconformist college at the university, where his teacher in Greek New Testament was Alexander Souter, without, however, ever taking a theology degree.

After ordination to the Congregationalist ministry (1912), Dodd served as the minister of the Brook Street Congregational Church in Warwick until 1915, when the opportunity came to succeed James Moffatt, who had succeeded Souter, in the post of New Testament lecturer at Mansfield College. He remained in this position until 1930, when he received the call to become the Rylands Professor of Biblical Criticism and Exegesis at the University of Manchester, as the successor to A. S. Peake. After five years at Manchester, Dodd was called to succeed F. C. Burkitt as the Norris-Hulse Professor of Divinity at Cambridge. From the time of the Restoration in 1660, all divinity professorships in Oxford and Cambridge had been limited to members, usually clergy, of the Church of England. Dodd's appointment was notable in that this rule was now broken in favor of a Congregationalist minister. Dodd remained at Cambridge and retired from his chair at the compulsory age of sixty-five (1949).

After his retirement Dodd moved back to Oxford and engaged himself for the next twenty-five years in producing the books for which he is most famous—his books on the Fourth Gospel—and with the responsibilities of chief editor of the translation of the Bible that would become known as the New English Bible. His last book, *The Founder of Christianity* (1970), was published when he was eighty-six.

Dodd was the recipient of many honors. In addition to his numerous special lectureships, he was granted many honorary doctorates, including one from each of Britain's ancient universities, and upon the presentation of the New Testament of the New English Bible (1963), he was invested by the Queen as Companion of Honour (which enabled him to put C. H. not only before his name but also after it, as some of his friends joked).

Writings. Dodd's first book was *The Meaning of Paul for Today,* published in 1920 but reissued in 1958 and enjoying several printings in the 1960s. This book indicated Dodd's lifelong concern to bridge between the past and the present. Paul had to be studied exegetically and historically but then also had to be clarified for contemporary Christians. Dodd said he found in Paul "a religious philosophy oriented throughout to the idea of a society or commonwealth of God" (Dodd 1958, 11). This was the community of the church with the oneness and the fellowship of its members, potentially comprehending the whole of humanity. Paul's vision was of "a world made one and free" (Dodd 1958, 176).

The next book Dodd published was a nontechnical exposition of *The Gospel in the New Testament* (1926) and was dedicated to his beloved wife, whom he had married a year earlier. It was written for Sunday school teachers and published by the National Sunday School Union. It is notable for treating the most basic questions with superb clarity, and it serves as evidence of Dodd's commitment to and concern for the church.

In 1928 Dodd published *The Authority of the Bible,* in which he discusses the authority of individual inspiration, of corporate experience, of the Incarnation and of history. In the preface he indicates that his purpose is to deal with the subject inductively, to emphasize "the life which lies behind the word," the meaning of which is determined by "the fact of Christ," all in a way that will make the authority of the Bible "tenable in the face of rational criticism." A notice on the cover of the Fontana reissue of the book says: "This convincing

book demonstrates that the modern approach to the Bible, using all the resources of the historical method, is both positive and constructive in its results." That can be said to be typical for a book by Dodd. Dodd's biographer, F. W. Dillistone, regards this book as "the most systematic, the most theological and the most definitive of his own personal convictions" (Dillistone, 130). Nevertheless the view of the Bible's authority reflected here is rather more liberal and subjective in tone than that expressed in *The Bible Today* (1946). There Dodd could speak more objectively of the Bible as a revelation of God (e.g., Dodd 1946a, 12, 98; Frederick Fyvie *Bruce also makes this observation).

Passing over Dodd's 1929 commentary on Ephesians, Colossians and Philemon in the *Abingdon Commentary,* we come to the short, popular *The Bible and Its Background* (1931), which was originally a series of talks given on the BBC, devoted to how the books of the Bible came to be written and how the canon was formed. Here Dodd answers the question What is the Bible? with these words: "the Bible is a unity of diverse writings which together are set forth by the Church as a revelation of God in history" (Dodd 1931, 14, cf. 98). He further writes that "the biblical history is controlled by a factor which belongs to the realm beyond history. . . . This 'supernatural' factor cannot be explained away without re-writing the Bible and falsifying the witness of its writers" (Dodd 1931, 100).

In 1932 Dodd published his commentary on Romans in the Moffatt Commentary series. The cover of the paperback reissue refers to the commentary as one "of surpassing beauty and clarity. His scholarship is impeccable, but so is his English." In the same year Dodd published his only nontheological book, *There and Back Again,* consisting of stories written for children. The "there" consisted of the unusual, the unfamiliar, the unseen, often the world of the religious or the magical; "back again" was a reference to the familiar, the seen and the known. Dillistone finds these stories as typifying Dodd's own life: there and back again was "a controlling pattern of his life from start to finish . . . he constantly went out to explore. . . . Regularly he returned to base and shared the results of his explorations with others" (Dillistone, 216). In Dodd's words: "The ideal interpreter would be one who has entered into that strange first-century world, has felt its whole strangeness, has sojourned in it until he has lived himself into it, thinking and feeling as one of those to whom the Gospel first came, and who will then return into our world, and give to the truth he has discerned a body out of the stuff of our own thought" (from "The Present Task of New Testament Studies," Dodd's inaugural lecture at the University of Cambridge; cited by Robinson, 102).

Two important books were published in 1935: *The Bible and the Greeks* and *Parables of the Kingdom*. The former is described by Dodd as studies "from the notebooks of a student of the New Testament"; the material consisted of the Grinfield Lectures on the Septuagint given at the University of Oxford (1927-1931). In part one of this book, Dodd studies the vocabulary of the Septuagint: the names of God; the law; righteousness, mercy and truth; sin; and atonement. Part two studies the Hermetic corpus for traces of Jewish influence, after which the conclusion is drawn that "Judaism has a larger part than is, perhaps, always recognized, in shaping the higher thought of paganism" (Dodd 1935, 247).

The Parables of the Kingdom provided an exposition of realized eschatology, for which Dodd was to become especially well known. Dodd stressed the reality of the coming of the kingdom of God in the ministry of Jesus. He accepted A. Jülicher's argument that each parable contained one single, main point and that allegorization of the parables was improper. But rather than seeking the main point in some ethical truth, Dodd rightly insisted upon the importance of understanding the parable in its original historical setting. Joachim *Jeremias, in the foreword to his own book on

the parables, paid tribute to Dodd's work: "How much the work is indebted for stimulus and instruction to C. H. Dodd's fundamentally important book . . . is indicated at many points. Professor Dodd's book has opened a new era in the study of the parables; although differences of opinion with regard to some details may exist, yet it is unthinkable that there should ever be any retreat from the essential lines laid down by Dodd for the interpretation of the parables of Jesus" (Jeremias, 8).

In 1936 Dodd published *The Apostolic Preaching and Its Developments*, which consisted of lectures given the preceding year at King's College, University of London. Here Dodd studies the recorded sermons in the book of Acts to determine the common elements of the early church's kerygma. Then he looks for traces of the kerygma elsewhere in the New Testament, finding that Mark's Gospel is based on the kerygma, indeed as a kind of commentary on it, as it is found for example in the sermons of Acts 10 and Acts 13. Paul's letters and the Gospel of John also reveal that the original kerygma remains fundamentally important. The book included a large foldout sheet displaying the parallel elements of the kerygma in the sermons in Acts and in several of Paul's letters. At the conclusion of the book, Dodd notes that the question facing the New Testament student is "whether the fundamental affirmations of the apostolic Preaching are true and relevant . . . but without answering this question, we cannot confidently claim the name of Christian for that which we preach" (Dodd 1936a, 186-87).

In 1938 Dodd traveled to the United States to give the Hewett Lectures at the Episcopal Theological School in Cambridge, Massachusetts, as well as at Union Theological Seminary in New York and at Andover-Newton Theological School. These lectures were published in the same year under the title *History and the Gospel*, in which Dodd discusses Christianity as a historical religion, historical tradition in the New Testament, the historical criticism of the Gospels, the gospel story and the church in history. Dodd defends the importance of historical events for Christianity and the integrity of the historical tradition about Jesus as it is reflected in the early church. He describes Gospel criticism as pointing to both fact and interpretation in the tradition, as well as to the inescapably eschatological character of the Gospels.

Dodd made his second contribution to the Moffatt Commentary with the publication of *The Johannine Epistles* (1946). On the basis of linguistic and theological differences, Dodd denied that the Johannine letters were written by the same author as that of the Fourth Gospel.

As we have noted, it was after his retirement that Dodd published his greatest books. We begin with the 1952 publication of *According to the Scriptures,* which bears the subtitle *The Substructure of New Testament Theology.* This volume consists of lectures given at Princeton Theological Seminary two years earlier. Dodd explores how the early church used Old Testament texts to elucidate the kerygma. Rather than depending on isolated proof-texts, the early Christians made use of extended portions of the Old Testament considered as wholes, especially of Isaiah, Jeremiah, certain minor prophets and the Psalms. These passages were interpreted using "intelligible and consistent principles" and were regarded as finding their fulfillment in the gospel. The pattern and manner of usage are common to the main writers of the New Testament, and this usage serves as the substructure of New Testament theology in that it "contains already its chief regulative ideas" (Dodd 1952a, 127).

The Interpretation of the Fourth Gospel, arguably Dodd's greatest book, was published in 1953. In this volume, which he dedicated to his wife, Dodd provides "general principles and lines of direction" for interpreting this Gospel (Dodd 1953, vii). He first discusses the setting of the Gospel in early Christianity and then the various backgrounds against which it may be interpreted, namely, the Hermetic literature,

Philo, rabbinic Judaism, Gnosticism and Mandaism. The middle section of the book is devoted to the leading ideas of the Gospel and the third part of the book to the argument and structure of the Gospel. According to a note on the back cover of the paperback edition of the book "the reader is asked to work very hard; the reward will be commensurate." The brilliance of the book and its importance for the study of the Gospel has often been noted.

Ten years later (1963) Dodd published his second great book on the Fourth Gospel, *Historical Tradition in the Fourth Gospel.* This book is a sequel to the first but more precisely an expansion of the appendix of that volume, which was devoted to "Some considerations upon the historical aspect of the Fourth Gospel." Dodd studies in succession the passion narrative, the ministry of Jesus, and John the Baptist and the first disciples before turning in the final section of the book to the sayings material. Painstaking analysis leads Dodd to the conclusion that an ancient and often trustworthy historical tradition underlies the Gospel and that this tradition is independent of the Synoptic Gospels. The book concludes with a description of the precanonical Johannine tradition together with a comparison with the Synoptic tradition.

Dodd's last book was on Jesus, *The Founder of Christianity.* This work can be regarded as the fulfillment of the conviction expressed at the end of *Historical Tradition in the Fourth Gospel:* "The enterprise of working towards a clear and well-based conception of the historical facts upon which our religion is founded is a promising one, and the mood of defeatism which for some time prevailed is rightly beginning to give way to a more hopeful resumption of the 'quest of the historical Jesus'" (Dodd 1963, 432). The documents upon which our knowledge of Jesus depends are described by Dodd as presenting remembered and interpreted facts, written from the standpoint of faith but facts nonetheless. Dodd portrays Jesus as accepting the designation Messiah, but as modified by the simultaneous understanding of his mission as that of the Suffering Servant of Isaiah. In his depiction of the ministry of Jesus, Dodd evinces an openness to the possibility of the genuinely miraculous. Of the resurrection of Jesus, Dodd writes: "It is not a belief that grew up within the church; it is the belief around which the church itself grew up, and the 'given' upon which its faith was based" (Dodd 1970, 163). As for the event itself, while Dodd finds himself disposed to conclude that the belief depends on the "genuine memory" of an empty tomb, as a historian he suspends judgment (Dodd 1970, 167).

Mention must be made of the project that occupied much of Dodd's later years, the translation of The New English Bible (New Testament first published in 1961; the Old Testament and Apocrypha in 1970). In the preface to the New Testament Dodd indicates the purpose of the translation was different from that of the earlier translations in that it was to enjoy a freedom from literal representation to a conveying of the Greek by the equivalent, natural idioms of contemporary English. Dodd's gifts made him the natural leader of this project. In leading sessions of the New Testament panel members, Dodd regularly began with a prayer in Latin that contained a line that in fact well described his own abilities: "Give us keenness of understanding, subtlety of interpretation, and grace of expression" (Dillistone, 205, 247-48).

Significance. Dodd's great contribution to the study of the New Testament lies in his work as a historian of the New Testament era. His particular strength in historical study was in the Hellenistic world. His writings consistently placed the Greek New Testament and the Septuagint within their Hellenistic context and demonstrated the great usefulness of this approach to the understanding of their contents. Yet Dodd resisted the conclusion that Hellenism explained the origin of the New Testament faith. Thus, for example, he can write: "The two evangelical sacraments are directly based upon biblical foundations, whatever importance Hellenistic ideas may have had in elucidating and extending their significance" (Dodd 1952a, 137).

Most characteristic in Dodd's analysis of New Testament Christianity is his emphasis on realized eschatology. The present dimension in the eschatology of Jesus and the writers of the New Testament cannot be missed. To an extent Dodd was justified in his emphasis on the reality of present eschatology in the New Testament. He pushed that dimension, however, as far as it could be pushed—in the opinion of most New Testament scholars, farther than he should have. Without question Dodd had a distaste for apocalyptic and future eschatology, which he regarded as a falling away from the teaching of Jesus. He did not like the Revelation of John (Dodd 1926, 59-63).

Dodd thus would not talk about a future eschatology yet to be experienced within history. Nevertheless he could and did talk about the end of history. History would not go on indefinitely but would one day reach its *telos*. The life of the human race on earth will one day end (Dodd 1951a, 24; cf. Dodd 1938, 171). But the last frontier post, as Dodd liked to call it, was beyond history, and one was most likely to encounter it at death, when "one steps into the presence of the Eternal" (Dodd 1951a, 26). For all the importance of realized eschatology in the New Testament, "there remains a residue of eschatology which is not exhausted in the 'realized eschatology' of the Gospel, namely, the element of sheer finality" (Dodd 1936a, 231).

Scholarship for Dodd was to be pursued not for its own sake but for the sake of the church. His life was marked by commitment to the gospel of Jesus Christ, but that commitment, rather than dulling his scholarship, sharpened it. He devoted his life to the study of the Bible because in his view the Bible was unique, irreplaceable and indispensable. He was often recruited by the BBC to speak concerning the Bible and the Christian faith. This he was happy to do, for he wanted above all to be a bridge between the world of the scholar and the world of the ordinary person. His presentations were always positive and constructive and often found their way into print (e.g., Dodd 1950, 1951a).

What strikes one about Dodd is the sane and balanced character of his scholarship. This fact is surely due to his respect and love for the truth of the biblical texts he studied. He was the first to admit that our knowledge could take us only so far: "True wisdom for man is to acknowledge his limitations" (Dodd 1951a, 25). Yet what Dodd put his hand to produced consistently edifying results. His book *The Founder of Christianity* puts to shame more recent efforts of the so-called third quest of the historical Jesus. Not without reason did the *Methodist Times* write, "It is a wise thing to read everything that Mr. Dodd writes" (from the paperback edition of Dodd 1960).

A limerick much enjoyed by Dodd and his family was composed by a close friend and was eventually inscribed on a glass tumbler:

I think it extremely odd
That a little professor named Dodd
Should spell, if you please,
his name with three D's
When one is sufficient for God.

Dodd, with his fine sense of humor, greatly enjoyed this limerick precisely because he knew himself to be a diminutive professor in the service of the great God who had revealed himself in the Bible. To that literature, so loved by Dodd, he eagerly devoted himself with such rich results.

BIBLIOGRAPHY

Works. C. H. Dodd, *About the Gospels* (Cambridge: Cambridge University Press, 1950); idem, *According to the Scriptures* (London: Nisbet, 1952a); idem, *The Apostolic Preaching and Its Developments* (London: Hodder & Stoughton, 1936a); idem, *The Authority of the Bible* (London: Collins Fontana Series, 1960 [1928]); idem, *The Bible and Its Background* (London: Unwin, 1931); idem, *The Bible and the Greeks* (London: Hodder & Stoughton, 1935); idem, *The Bible Today* (Cambridge: Cambridge University Press, 1946a); idem, *The Coming of Christ* (Cambridge: Cambridge University Press, 1951a); idem, "Ephesians, Colossians and Philemon" in *The Abingdon Commentary*, eds. E. L. Eiselen and D. G. Downey (Nashville: Abingdon, 1929); idem, *The Epistle to the Romans* (London: Collins Fontana Series, 1959 [1932]); idem, *The Founder of Christianity* (New York: Macmillan, 1970); idem, *Gospel and Law* (Cambridge: Cambridge University Press, 1951b); idem, *The Gospel in the New Testament* (London: National Sunday School Union, 1926); idem, *Historical Tradition in the Fourth Gospel* (Cambridge: Cambridge University Press, 1963); idem, *History and the Gospel* (London: Nisbet, 1938); idem, *The Interpretation of the Fourth Gospel* (Cambridge: Cambridge University Press, 1953); idem, "Introduction" to *The New English Bible: New Testament* (Oxford: Oxford University Press; and Cambridge: Cambridge University Press, 1961a); idem, *The Johannine Epistles* (MNTC; London: Hodder & Stoughton, 1946b); idem, *The Meaning of Paul for Today* (London: Collins Fontana Series, 1958 [1920]); idem, *More New Testament Studies* (Manchester: University of Manchester Press, 1968); idem, *New Testament Studies* (Manchester: University of Manchester Press, 1952b); idem, *The Parables of the Kingdom* (rev. ed.; London: Collins Fontana series, 1961b [1935]); idem, *The Present Task in New Testament Studies* (Cambridge: Cambridge University Press, 1936b); idem, *There and Back Again* (London: Hodder & Stoughton, 1932).

Studies. F. F. Bruce, "C. H. Dodd" in *Creative Minds in Contemporary Theology*, ed. P. E. Hughes (2d ed.; Grand Rapids: Eerdmans, 1969) 239-69; W. D. Davies and D. Daube, *The Background of the New Testament and Its Eschatology: In Honor of C. H. Dodd* (Cambridge: Cambridge University Press, 1954); F. W. Dillistone, *C. H. Dodd: Interpreter of the New Testament* (Grand Rapids: Eerdmans, 1977); R. W. Graham, *Charles Harold Dodd 1884-1973: A Bibliography of His Published Writings* (Lexington Theological Seminary Library Occasional Studies; Lexington, KY: Lexington Theological Seminary Library, 1974); J. Jeremias, *The Parables of Jesus* (2d ed.; New York: Scribner's, 1972); J. A. T. Robinson, "Theologians of Our Time: XII. C. H. Dodd" *ET* 75 (1963-1964) 100-102; J. T. Williams, *Aspects of the Life and Works of C. H. Dodd* (Honourable Society of Cymmrodorion, 1974).

D. A. Hagner

Eichrodt, Walther *(1890-1978)*

Walther Eichrodt was born on August 1, 1890, in Gernsbach, Germany. He was educated at the universities of Greifswald, Heidelberg and Erlangen and studied under Otto Procksch at the University of Erlangen (1915-1922). In 1921 Eichrodt began teaching at the University of Basel, where he succeeded Albrecht Alt as professor of history of religions and Old Testament (1922). He taught there for forty-five years (until 1966) and died in 1978. Eichrodt's three volumes in Old Testament theology (two in English translation), in which he synthesized Old Testament material around a central concept, have cast a long shadow across the twentieth century. Those volumes (1933-1939) have been evaluated as "incomparably the greatest work ever to appear in the field of Old Testament theology, in terms both of sheer magnitude and of depth of insight" (Dentan, 66). Eichrodt set biblical studies onto a new path in which the Bible's message rather than its religious history was most important.

Shift in Biblical Interpretation. Eichrodt began his scholarly career toward the end of World War I. The mood generally was one of disillusionment. The massive destruction in the war raised large questions about the decades-long mood of optimism, an optimism fueled by the belief in the inevitability of progress. In biblical scholarship too, evolution had been a basic assumption: ideas and institutions evolved from the primitive to the more advanced. Julius *Wellhausen had crystalized a theory (1878), long in emerging, that the prophets preceded in time the complex legislation in the Pentateuch. The Pentateuch itself was a product, so the Graf-Wellhausen theory held, of an evolutionary process in Israel and contained material from both early and late time periods: J (c. 850 B.C.), E (c. 750 B.C.), D (c. 650 B.C.) and P (c. 450 B.C.).

Apart from research into literary sources, scholars had been alerted at the end of the nineteenth century, through archaeological excavations, to Babylonian creation myths such as the *Enuma Elish.* There was now great interest in religious comparative studies. How was Israel's religion similar to that of its neighbors? How was it different? What conclusions could be drawn about Israel's religious development? Biblical scholars were enamored with the history of religions approach. A. B. Davidson, a British scholar, wrote: "We do not find a *theology* in the Old Testament; we find a *religion*" (Davidson, 11). The net result of such an exclusive approach was to ignore the message of the Old Testament.

Life and Work. But Eichrodt was to focus on the message. In 1919 Karl *Barth had published his commentary on Romans. Barth moved away from the hyperconcentration on religion as a human endeavor and in his theology, now known as neo-orthodoxy, turned attention away from the human dimensions to an emphasis on God as the "wholly other." Eichrodt was in Barth's league in the sense that he was part of the shift away from a historicist approach in biblical studies to an approach more theological.

That shift was not so easily made. Otto Eissfeldt held that while the study of the history of religion was a scientific discipline, the study of Old Testament theology was not. In Eissfeldt's view, the confessional or dogmatic (denominational) glasses that the interpreter wore precluded an objective description of the Bible's message. The theologian, though not able to contribute to knowledge, could contribute nonscientifically to the Old Testament's faith statement. Eichrodt disagreed. The scientific approach to history, Eichrodt said, was not as objective and detached a discipline as Eissfeldt imagined—a position now almost universally accepted but not so obvious then. Eichrodt maintained further that one could use the historical-critical methods to get at the essence of the Old Testament religion—to study it not only for its history but also for its message. The two position essays by Eissfeldt (1926) and Eichrodt (1929) represent important benchmarks in biblical interpretation (see Eichrodt's essay in Ollenburger, Martens, Hasel, 20-39).

Interpretation at the Macro Level. One way to study the Bible is to exegete it passage by passage, a micro approach. Another way is to reach for its overall framework or message, a macro approach. The two methods are complementary. Eichrodt gave his energies to both approaches but is best known for his macro system.

Having laid the groundwork for such an endeavor in his essay (1929), the next step was to set out a synthesis of the Old Testament. The first of several volumes appeared in 1933, the same year Adolf Hitler became chancellor of Germany. Eichrodt did not disparage the then-current interest in the development of Israelite religion; but more significant for him and for the church was determining "the constant basic tendency and character" of Israel's religion, (Eichrodt 1961, 1:11). What was the unifying structure that lay at the base of the diverse developments that could be chronicled? Working more cross-sectionally than developmentally, Eichrodt concluded that the constant was the intersection of an Almighty God with man *(Mensch)* for the purpose of establishing a close relationship (the German *Mensch* includes both genders). Dip into the Old Testament at any point, he would contend, and one is met by a God who desires a relational engagement with humankind.

Eichrodt employed a kind of shorthand and used the word *covenant* to symbolize this reality of divinely initiated divine-human engagement. He broke new ground by positing that the message of the Old Testament could be captured in a central theme or construct, namely, covenant. By covenant Eichrodt understood not a particularistic covenantal action by God with an individual or a people (where the Hebrew word *berit* ["covenant"] might be used) but the broader overall engagement by God with humans.

Eichrodt's three volumes developed the three dimensions of this engagement in turn: God and Israel, God and World, God and Man. The first volume, leaning heavily on the Sinai covenant, lays bare the thesis that God has set himself in a posture of engagement with a people, Israel. Several chapters develop the theme of the nature of the covenant God. Other topics of the first volume are the covenant statutes, the instruments of covenant (priests and the king), covenant breaking and the consummation of the covenant.

Parts two and three (vol. 2 in English) are devoted to "God and World" and "God and Man." In part two the subject is again God, but now the themes are God's self-manifestation, the Spirit of God, the Word of God, cosmology, creation, the celestial world and the underworld. While the interactive nature of God with humankind is in view throughout, only one chapter is solely devoted to humanity ("The Place of Man in the Creation").

In part three the interaction of God with humanity is viewed from the anthropological perspective, with chapters on "The Individual and the Community," "Fundamental Forms of Man's Personal Relationship with God," "The Effect of Piety on Conduct" and "Sin and Forgiveness." Eichrodt returns to his overall theme in the final chapter, "The Indestructability of the Individual's Relationship with God."

For this threefold division of his theological material Eichrodt was indebted to his teacher, Otto Procksch. But it was only after the appearance of Eichrodt's work that Procksch himself published, with the result that for the larger world it was Eichrodt who was the spokesperson in what was to be a renaissance of biblical theology.

Eichrodt gave his critics pause. Those who felt that a theology could not be scientifically respectable were now faced with a two-pronged research methodology. Eichrodt clarifies his approach in the opening pages. He sees his task and his method to be "how to understand the realm of Old Testament belief in its structural unity and how, by examining on the one hand its religious environment and on the other its essential coherence with the New Testament, to illuminate its profoundest meaning" (Eichrodt 1961, 1:31). He looks about to examine how the topic or text was treated in religions adjacent to Israel. He looks forward to see the end result in the New Testament. So, for example, in commenting about the Word of God he first discusses the comparative significance of "word" in Babylonian material and then moves to the thought of the New Testament on the subject (Eichrodt 1967, 2:69-71, 79-80). An Old Testament text is to be interpreted contextually, both culturally and biblically.

Analysts have observed that Eichrodt's method is twofold in still another sense: developmentally and synthetically. His exposition of covenant includes a history of the concept (Eichrodt 1961, 1:45-69). The topic is treated by discussing its origin and its development up to the postexilic period. In other instances, however, he elaborates on a subject not diachronically but synthetically. It is as though he takes a vertical cut through the Bible, gathering material under predetermined classifications. For example, in discussing the fundamental forms of humanity's personal relationship with God, Eichrodt opts for the second method by using categories such as "fear of God," "faith in God" and "love for God." The operative method is synoptic. Yet Eichrodt concludes the section in the diachronic vein under the heading "The personal relationship with God in the post-exilic period" (Eichrodt 1967, 2:268-315). So in this discussion both the horizontal (longitudinal) and the vertical (synthetic) methods are employed to delineate a system of belief at the macro level.

Interpretation at the Micro Level. Eichrodt distinguished himself also as an exegete at the micro level with commentaries on Isaiah 1—39 and on Ezekiel. For the most part his exegetical methods were the methods of the day. The historical location of a book was important, and source research was regarded as critical. Eichrodt

had researched the composition of Genesis in a dissertation in 1908. Attention was also given to form criticism (though not extensively) and to textual criticism.

As for historical criticism, to use the commentary on Ezekiel as an example, Eichrodt distanced himself from earlier interpreters who held that Ezekiel's ministry was in two places, Palestine and Babylon (A. Bertholet) or who advocated that the book was a pseudograph written in the third century (C. C. Torrey). Eichrodt granted a historical setting to the book according to the book's claims. As for source criticism, in which he was well-versed, his position was not as extreme as that of some interpreters. Still, he gave what seems in retrospect too much room to largely speculative emendations. He was quite self-confident in identifying displaced passages (e.g., Ezek 3:24-26; 4:7-8; Eichrodt 1970, 21). He detected editorial activity, citing additions made by Ezekiel's disciples, who sometimes amplified Ezekiel's message but sometimes recast it with a bias of their own (see examples in Ezek 16; Eichrodt 1970, 21, 202, 214-20). Certain few passages, such as the well-composed poem on Tyre and its worldwide trade (Ezek 27:9b-25a) were extraneous compositions that were inserted by a redactor (Eichrodt 1970, 41, 386-88). As a form critic Eichrodt was sensitive to formulae and to genre (e.g., sacral law, Ezek 14:1-11; 18; and symbolic action in Ezekiel), but he did not give these major attention.

As for textual criticism, in Ezekiel Eichrodt preferred the terser Septuagint, which was based, he thought, on an earlier Hebrew recension to the currently used Masoretic Hebrew text; the latter had too many amplifications (Eichrodt 1970, 12). So, for example, he omitted Ezekiel 1:23b-25 from his translation (Eichrodt 1970, 49, 51). Overall he regarded "the text achieved by critical research . . . as being in the main that committed to writing by Ezekiel himself" (Eichrodt 1970, 13). He was adept at single-word research, as demonstrated in his discussion of the term *bereshit* (Gen

1:1; Eichrodt 1962). But Eichrodt did not get lost in details. He characteristically assessed the direction of the biblical argument, determined what agenda (often unmentioned in the text) was addressed and specifically noted the theological dimensions.

While his contemporaries would have readily endorsed the technical aspect of these methods, not all shared Eichrodt's view on "typology" (cf. Irwin, 5). For Eichrodt, typology, which was envisioned to play only an ancillary part in exegesis but which was a method in line with ancient use, was premised on *Heilsgeschichte,* a distinctive way of looking at history. Eichrodt held that it was the "intercourse of God with his people [which] represented, warranted, and actualized by them, that validates them [types]" (Eichrodt 1964, 226-27). Persons, institutions and events of the Old Testament become "divinely established models or prerepresentations of corresponding realities in the New Testament salvation history (Eichrodt 1964, 225). For example, there is a parallel, a "typological correspondence," between Moses and Jesus in both their service *(diakonia)* and their glory *(doxa;* Eichrodt 1964, 225). Along with other mid-twentieth-century interpreters, such as Gerhard *von Rad, Eichrodt insisted on typology having a role in modern exegesis.

Significance. Eichrodt's significance as a biblical interpreter is linked to his view on typology. The essay on typology, as well as his intention in his theology of the Old Testament to connect with the New Testament, make it clear that the relationship between the Old and New Testament was one of Eichrodt's major themes. "That which binds together indivisibly the two realms of the Old and New Testaments . . . is the irruption of the Kingship of God into this world and its establishment here," he wrote (Eichrodt 1961, 1:26). In following this interest in the entire Scripure, Eichrodt was more than an Old Testament scholar. He was a biblical scholar.

Another theme, not strange to one who took the whole Bible within his sweep, was God's gracious initiative in involving himself with humanity and there establishing his kingdom. For Eichrodt the word *covenant* was the integrating category that captured this reality. Moreover, that the covenant God consistently moves into engagement with the world makes Israel's religion *sui generis* (Eichrodt 1961, 1:517). For Eichrodt, Israel's thought is dominated by a God who "is free, transcendent, an ordering will . . . whose aim is the creation of a community responsive to him" (Gottwald, 31). The effect of such a repeated emphasis on God in the divine-human equation is to give more weight to the theological (God-talk) than to the anthropological (talk about humans). In reading his work one breathes within an environment of transcendence. Eichrodt was a theologian; his subject was God. The translator of his work is correct: "The focus of these volumes is not any one concept but only God." (Eichrodt 1967, 2:10).

In emphasizing a central concept, such as covenant, as capturing the structural unity of the Old Testament, Eichrodt did not ignore the diversity others saw in the Old Testament. However, he started with the notion of a theological unity. Other scholars since Eichrodt have been more enamored with theological diversity in the Old Testament. The issue of whether the Old Testament has a center has been much debated. J. Goldingay goes so far as to say that this assumption about the unity of the Old Testament "seems implausible in an age aware of the diversity of faith" (Goldingay, 154). One can agree, however with Goldingay, "In terms of content, works such as Eichrodt's will long remain of very great value for enabling us to appreciate themes of Old Testament faith" (Goldingay, 156).

Given the direction he took, Eichrodt became a hinge in the history of interpretation. Prior to Eichrodt the emphasis in biblical interpretation had been on the historical facets. Eichrodt asked fresh questions. He asked for the message, specifically for the core, the "self-contained entity" of the Old Testament (Eichrodt 1961, 1:11). Whereas there had been a dearth of theologies of the Old Testament in the seventy years prior to Eichrodt, in the seventy years since Eichrodt there has been a steady stream of works dealing with Old Testament theology. Eichrodt, clearly a pivotal figure, helped set the agenda for subsequent generations. His *Theology of the Old Testament* is "a magnificent cathedral among Old Testament studies" (Spriggs, 99), and stands alongside Gerhard von Rad's *Old Testament Theology* as a classic.

Eichrodt became somewhat a pivotal figure, along with Barth, in the larger religious ethos of the 1930s and beyond. By means of his expositional and theological works, Eichrodt gave a biblical foundation to the neo-orthodox movement, of which Barth was the most notable exponent. With the emphasis on the transcendent God, he delivered a poignant critique to a humanism and a secularism that had come, following the cues of the Enlightenment, to view human resources as the solution for human ills. Eichrodt had a significant hand in redirecting the theological discussion away from the anthropological to the more purely theological.

To biblical interpretation Eichrodt brought a refreshing wind. His style, especially as it figures in English translation, may be ponderous, but the substance is judicious and balanced. From a distance of seventy years one could fault him for an undue preoccupation with questions of composition and sources (disciples, redactors). But the ways in which his commentaries on biblical texts as well as his essays moved out from the immediate textual statements into the larger frame of a theology represent a holistic, nuanced method of interpreting the Bible. The genius of Eichrodt's work is the way in which he proceeds in balanced fashion to draw on the historical findings so much in vogue earlier and also the exegetical and theological insights in interpreting the Bible. It is easy to agree with one analyst: "It is in the en-

deavor to unite exegetical/historical craftsmanship and theological reflection that Eichrodt makes his greatest contribution" (Gottwald, 25).

BIBLIOGRAPHY

Works. W. Eichrodt, *Ezekiel: A Commentary* (OTL; Philadelphia: Westminister, 1970 [1959-1966]); idem, "Does Old Testament Theology Still have Independent Significance within Old Testament Scholarship?" [1929] in *The Flowering of Old Testament Theology,* ed. B. C. Ollenburger, E. A. Martens and G. F. Hasel (Winona Lake, IN: Eisenbrauns, 1992) 30-39; idem, *Der Heilige in Israel: Jesaja 1—12* (Die Botschaft des Alten Tesaments 17.1; Stuttgart: Calwer, 1960); idem, *Der Herr der Geschichte: Jesaja 13—23 und 28—39* (Die Botschaft des Alten Testaments 17.2; Stuttgart: Calwer, 1967); idem, "The Holy One in Your Midst: The Theology of Hosea," *Int* 15 (1961) 259-73; idem, "In the Beginning" in *Israel's Prophetic Heritage,* ed. B. W. Anderson and W. Harrelson (New York: Harper, 1962); idem, "Is Typological Exegesis an Appropriate Method?" in *Essays on Old Testament Hermeneutics,* ed. J. L. Mays (2d ed.; Richmond, VA: John Knox, 1964) 224-45; idem, *Man in the Old Testament* (London: SCM, 1951 [1947]); idem, *Religionsgeschichte Israels* (Bern: Francke, 1969); idem, *Theology of the Old Testament* (2 vols.; Philadelphia: Westminister, 1961, 1967 [1933-1939]).

Studies. R. E. Clements, "They Set Us in New Paths, Pt. 4: The Old Testament: Fresh Questions, New Gateways," *ET* 100 (January 1989) 124-27; A. B. Davidson, *The Theology of the Old Testament* (New York: Scribner's, 1910); R. C. Dentan, *Preface to Old Testament Theology* (rev. ed.; New York: Seabury, 1963); J. Goldingay, "Diversity and Unity in Old Testament Theology" *VT* 34, 2 (1984) 151-68; N. Gottwald, "W. Eichrodt: *Theology of the Old Testament*" in *Contemporary Old Testament Theologians,* ed. R. B. Laurin (Valley Forge, PA: Judson, 1970) 23-62; W. J. Harrington, *The Path of Biblical Theology* (Dublin: Gill & Macmillan, 1973); G. F. Hasel, *Old Testament Theology: Basic Issues in the Current Debate* (4th ed.; Grand Rapids: Eerdmans, 1991 [1972]); W. A. Irwin, "A Still Small Voice . . . Said, What Are You Doing Here?" *JBL* 78 (March 1959) 1-12; B. C. Ollenburger, E. A. Martens and G. F. Hasel, eds., *The Flowering of Old Testament Theology* (Winona Lake, IN: Eisenbrauns, 1992); M. Saebø, "Eichrodt, Walther," *TRE* 9:371-73; W. H. Schmidt, "Theologie des Alten Testaments 'vor und nach von Rad,'" *Verkündigung und Forschung* 17 (1972) 1-25; D. G. Spriggs, *Two Old Testament Theologies: A Comparative Evaluation of the Contributions of Eichrodt and von Rad to Our Understanding of the Nature of Old Testament Theology* (SBT 2, 30; Naperville, IL: Alec R. Allenson, 1974); H. J. Stoebe, J. J. Stamm and E. Jenni, eds., *Wort, Gebot, Glaube: Beiträge zur Theologie des Alten Testaments: Walther Eichrodt zum 80. Geburtstag* (ATANT 59; Zurich: Zwingli, 1970).

E. A. Martens

Gunkel, Hermann (1862-1932)

Hermann Gunkel began his work in New Testament studies when he was appointed in 1888 at Göttingen as a licentiate in theology on the basis of a study of early Christian views of the Holy Spirit. In Göttingen Gunkel was a member of a religio-historical circle, the orientation of which is shown by the fact that its name ties together the words *religion* and *history*. It opposed both a dry-as-dust historical criticism that neglects the spiritual character of its subject matter (religion) and a view of religion that does not see it as thoroughly involved in the historical process.

Gunkel, however, was not popular at Göttingen. In part that was due to the fact that the religio-historical circle was understandably not well liked by those whose programs it opposed. Perhaps more importantly, Gunkel struck others as being too sharp in his oral criticisms (in writing he was much more gentle). Thus the Prussian authority that oversaw academic appointments told Gunkel to move to Halle and to pursue Hebrew Bible studies there.

In large part since he was new to the field of Hebrew Bible, Gunkel forged a fresh path in it. He decided to relate his work to comparable endeavors in ancient Near Eastern studies, classics and Germanics. He thus made personal contact with colleagues in these different fields.

In Halle Gunkel wrote his second major work, *Schöpfung und Chaos in Urzeit und*

Endzeit (1895), which dealt with "Creation and Chaos in Original and End Time" as a complex of themes running from Babylonia to the Hebrew Bible and the New Testament. After this effort at integration—then and now considered speculative by many scholars—Gunkel suffered a nervous breakdown, which led to a two months' stay in a sanitorium.

Just before then, however, in 1895, he had moved to Berlin, although only as a poorly paid extraordinary (not regular, full) professor. There, at the center of German learning, he made contact with Ulrich von Wilamowitz-Moellendorff, a towering authority on ancient Greece; with Adolf Erman, a leader in Egyptology; and others. He treated as a fatherly guide the philosopher Adolf Lasson. In short, Gunkel knew how to build bridges.

Gunkel not only learned from persons outside his field of specialization but also reached out to them. He expressed the hope that general historians and literary scholars would benefit from his work. He lectured and wrote quite extensively for nonspecialist audiences, in part (although not only) because this activity gave him some needed extra income.

In 1907, relatively late in life, Gunkel obtained a full professorship in a small university, Giessen. In 1920 he moved to the larger Halle, where he retired in 1927. Gunkel's academic career was marginal, and he often expressed a sense of isolation. It should be noted, however, that he received some crucial behind-the-scenes support from important scholars such as Julius *Wellhausen, without his knowledge. Posterity has showered praise on him as perhaps the most important biblical scholar of the century, although his deep assumptions are not necessarily accepted.

In order to survey his contributions, it is best to focus on one topical area at a time and to observe in each the procedural and substantive angles Gunkel pursued.

New Testament Work. Gunkel's first work, on the Holy Spirit (1888; ET *The Influence of the Holy Spirit*), was subtitled "a biblical-theological study" to underscore the fact that it presented meaning, not just external description. More specifically it reflected a deep belief that religion is something that lives and is not just something one thinks about or observes detachedly. It is something that happens and is experienced. The work further reflected a populist sense that religious life takes place in ordinary people. Thus its full title reads: "The workings of the Holy Spirit according to popular opinion in the apostolic period and according to the apostle Paul." In Paul's view as portrayed by Gunkel, the working of the Spirit is a power that is "received" (Gunkel 1979, 73).

There is some reason to think that Gunkel himself had ecstatic experiences. To judge from the preface to the second edition of his work in 1899, they were enhanced by this study. In an 1898 article he expressed interest in the "religious awakening" in Wales, which came to be an important beginning point for twentieth-century Pentecostalism. The not-just-rational character of his life was reflected in the fact that he published poetry over the years. All of his writings have a high emotional tone.

Gunkel's second major work *Schöpfung und Chaos in Urzeit und Endzeit* (1895) treated symbolism of creation and chaos in the Bible (especially Revelation 12) in relation to similar symbols in Babylonia. A central point of this line of investigation was that the symbolism did not relate primarily to specific events that occurred at the time of writing (such as in the Roman Empire) but expressed long-standing religious themes. An immediate implication of such continuity is that biblical texts highlight a faith that transcends a specific time in its significance (this may be a conservative conception) and, furthermore, that it transcends the limits of one particular religious tradition (this can be considered a liberal point).

Genesis. Within the Hebrew Bible Gunkel gave close attention to the book of Genesis. A major aspect of his endeavor was to reconstruct the oral background of the book. Often such an effort has been understood as a part of historical criticism. Gunkel, however, believed that historical criticism is valid only to a limited extent, for he considered criticism to be an attempt to determine the external circumstances (time and place) of a text. In his mind, to do so is possible in only rough terms. Gunkel did, however, favor what he called historical study, by which he meant a recognition of the relations of texts to human life. His attention to the oral background of Genesis thus had as its aim not the pursuit of chronological "facts" but an understanding of the human existence that entered into the texts.

Gunkel saw Genesis as a somewhat reflective literary version of popular oral traditions. The aesthetic and theological aspect of the written version was noted by him along with the reconstructed background.

To guess at a background is, however, a speculative endeavor even apart from uncertainty about specific times and places. The very nature of the oral material is in question. In fact Gunkel's reconstructions differed in the three editions of his commentary on Genesis and would have differed again considerably, he said, in a prospective fourth one. In the first edition of *Genesis übersetzt und erklärt* (1901) Gunkel hypothesized that many of the stories of Genesis had as their starting point "aetiologies," that is, accounts that were designed to explain phenomena by telling how they came about. At that time he expressed caution about assuming that all narratives began that way. A year later, in the second edition, his doubt about the role of aetiologies was stated more strongly. In the third edition (1910), the doubt was stronger still.

The change in Gunkel's perspective was related to a concurrent development in folklore studies. Investigators of the histories of folklore found that an aetiological twist is often added to a story secondarily and does not furnish the kernel from which the rest grows. For somewhat different reasons, W. Wundt set forth a developmental scheme according to which nonmythological folktales are older than myths (among which aetiologies were classed), rather than vice versa, as some previous theorists had thought. (A third option, that both are equally old, was also proposed and was more widely accepted later.) Gunkel accepted Wundt's theory and came to hold that folktales rather than aetiologies lie behind many biblical accounts.

The German word used for such folktales is *Märchen*. This word is especially well-known as a term that designates more or less magical stories told to children (in English, fairy tales). In 1917 Gunkel adopted this term as a way to describe motifs present in Genesis and in other parts of the Hebrew Bible (*Das Märchen im Alten Testament*). Because of its association with children's stories, the word is in some ways jarring. Yet it fits well with Gunkel's populist orientation and with his often childlike delight in dealing with biblical literature. How his new perspective would have worked itself out in a fourth edition of his commentary of Genesis cannot be said.

Psalms. On the heels of the first and second editions of his commentary on Genesis, Gunkel began a series of studies on the Psalms. It is typical of his way of writing that his first descriptions of Psalms were directed to a broad audience; in fact a number of them appeared first in English (1903). Eventually he produced a commentary, *Die Psalmen übersetzt und erklärt*, that examined carefully every one of the 150 psalms (1926) and a detailed survey of psalm types, *Einleitung in die Psalmen: Die Gattungen der religiösen Lyrik Israels*, which was completed after his death by his student J. Begrich (1927-33).

Gunkel's analysis of psalm types has made a profound impact. What made his analysis of psalms new was not the typology itself, which was for the most part standard by then, but the fact that he used the typology as a way to get into the psalms as representing forms of faith. If the psalms are thought of primarily as particular texts directed to a specific historical situation, their relevance to another time is not immediately apparent. The types, however, as Gunkel underscored, lasted over a long time. The major ones could be shown to be both preexilic and postexilic and to have prebiblical antecedents. Furthermore, each of the types has a special character. For each it is not hard to see, with Gunkel's help, the inner logic in which a kind of context peculiar to it (e.g., trouble) is related to a certain content and emotion (such as lament) and to certain forms of expression, which are largely conventional but not in an entirely arbitrary way.

One of the controversial aspects of Gunkel's analysis of psalm forms is that he regarded some of them as having been borrowed from other literary realms, such as prophecy and wisdom. This belief was based on the assumption that literary types were originally pure (i.e., separate) and that combinations or overlaps are secondary. That assumption runs counter to what has long been known to be the case outside of biblical literature. Gunkel's awareness of other fields thus fell short in this regard.

Prophecy. From quite early on Gunkel also focused on prophecy, though not in as much detail as on psalms. Gunkel believed that prophecy was based on secret experiences. Undoubtedly his own ecstatic inclinations contributed to this conception, but it was well-based in comparative religious studies. Quite questionably, however, he believed that the basic expressions of ecstatic experiences were very brief (similarly, he thought that the oldest forms of Genesis stories were short, contra what can be observed in oral cultures).

According to Gunkel's analysis (*Die Propheten* [1917]), the prophecies that appear in the Bible not only use forms that are strictly prophetic but also adapt a variety of other forms. For instance, a prophet can speak like someone who recites a dirge as a way of announcing what will or may happen in the future. Social criticism was thought by Gunkel to be secondary relative to predictions in time, though not in importance. That is, he imagined that the prophet first received an intimation about the future and then looked for reasons that would justify the intimation. The prophet's reflection can, in Gunkel's opinion, be theologically profound. In this case as in others, Gunkel valued thoughtful reflection in addition to ecstasy.

Other Texts. Gunkel produced a brief but comprehensive overview of Israelite literature (1906) for a multivolume survey of world literature. He was, further, coeditor of *Die Religion in Geschichte und Gegenwart*, the most important German encyclopedia on religion, to which he contributed quite a few articles (the encyclopedia began to appear in 1909; his involvement with it presumably gave him some needed income). Thus Gunkel covered many topics, including methodological ones. These many contributions are too varied to be covered here, but one must mention that he furnished a fine description of the literary character of the Elisha stories, *Elias, Jahve und Baal,* in a series designed for a general readership (1922).

Significance. Gunkel's greatest contribution probably was that he made the Bible interesting to people by showing structures of life that appear in it (Karl *Barth, for instance, reported that among his teachers in Hebrew Bible, Gunkel was the one who showed that the material is important). In all his work he maintained a delicate balance between seeing the particularity of a text and the generality of structures in it extending worldwide. He never got lost in facts, although he observed what was in front of him.

A major factor in this contribution lay in the process whereby Gunkel drew together different aspects of biblical literature. He made it a point to see connections among the life situation, the content (including the emotion) and the verbal form of texts. This interweaving is the scholarly angle of his work that has the most lasting significance.

Gunkel's primary intellectual mistake was in assuming that oral culture is rigid. This assumption did only a limited amount of damage to his work, for he focused largely on the text at hand, in which the rigidity had been loosened, as he thought, and he was rightly vague about the precise nature and circumstances of the background that he reconstructed. A major aspect of his emphasis on tradition and genres was that the date of a text does not indicate with any degree of certainty the antiquity of the material contained in it. A number of his students, however, tried harder than he to reconstruct an oral history and made many doubtful proposals (they included Martin Dibelius, Rudolf *Bultmann, Joachim Begrich, Sigmund *Mowinckel and even more so scholars in subsequent generations, including Albrecht Alt, Gerhard *von Rad and Martin *Noth).

In treating Gunkel's project as though it were an exercise in historical criticism, these researchers dropped both his worldwide vision and his aesthetic interest. Since it was in these respects that Gunkel had differed most from his German colleagues, they thus continued the scholarly tradition that had largely shut out Gunkel during his lifetime. For many, however—not specifically his students—the sensitive human quality of his writing has been attractive, even when they differ from him theologically or in scholarly assumptions.

BIBLIOGRAPHY

Works. H. Gunkel, *Ausgewählte Psalmen* (Göttingen: Vandenhoeck & Ruprecht, 1904); idem, *Einleitung in die Psalmen: Die Gattungen der religiösen Lyrik Israels,* completed by J. Begrich (Göttingen: Vandenhoeck & Ruprecht, 1933); idem, *Elias, Jahve und Baal* (Tübingen: J. C. B. Mohr, 1906); idem, *Genesis übersetzt und erklärt* (Göttingen: Vandenhoeck & Ruprecht, 1901; ET *Genesis* (Macon, GA: Mercer University Press, 1997 [3d ed., 1910]); idem, "The 'Historical Movement' in the Study of Religion," *ET* 38 (1926-1927) 532-36; idem, "The History of Religion and Old Testament Criticism" in *Proceedings and Papers of the Fifth International Congress of Free Christianity and Religious Progress,* ed. C. Wendte (1911) 114-25; idem, *Israel* *and Babylon* (Philadelphia: J. J. McVey, 1904); idem, *Das Märchen im Alten Testament* (4th ed.; Tübingen: J. C. B. Mohr, 1921; ET *The Folktale in the Old Testament* [Sheffield: Almond, 1987]); idem, "The Poetry of the Psalms: Its Literary History and Its Application to the Dating of the Psalms" in *Old Testament Essays*, ed. D. C. Simpson (London: Griffin, 1927) 118-42; idem, *Die Psalmen übersetzt und erklärt* (Göttingen: Vandenhoeck & Ruprecht, 1926); idem, *The Psalms: A Form-Critical Introduction* (Philadelphia: Fortress, 1967, translation of articles on the Psalms in *RGG*¹ and *RGG*²); idem, *Reden und Aufsätze* (Göttingen: Vandenhoeck & Ruprecht, 1913); idem, *Die Sagen der Genesis* (1901; ET *The Legends of Genesis* [Chicago: Open Court, 1901], which is a separate printing of the introduction to *Genesis* (1901); its English translation is superseded in important ways by his later work, *The Stories of Genesis* [Berkeley, CA: BIBAL, 1994] which translates the introduction to the third edition of *Genesis* [1910]); idem, *Schöpfung und Chaos in Urzeit und Endzeit* (Göttingen: Vandenhoeck & Ruprecht, 1895); idem, *Der Prophet Esra (IV.Esra)* (Tübingen: J. C. B. Mohr, 1900); idem, "The Religio-Historical Understanding of the New Testament," *Mon* 13 (1903) 398-455; idem, *What Remains of the Old Testament and Other Essays* (1928); idem, *Die Wirkungen des heiligen Geistes* (1888; ET *The Influence of the Holy Spirit* [Philadelphia: Fortress, 1979]); idem, essays on psalms in *Biblical World* 21 (1903) 28-31, 120-23, 206-9, 281-83, 366-70, 433-39; *Biblical World* 22 (1903) 209-15, 290-93, 363-66; **Studies.** W. Klatt, *Hermann Gunkel* (FRLANT 100; Göttingen: Vandenhoeck & Ruprecht, 1969); additional information, especially concerning Gunkel's background, is discussed by M. J. Buss, *Biblical Form Criticism in its Context* (forthcoming); *Eucharisterion: Studien zur Religion und Literatur des Alten und Neuen Testaments (Fest. Hermann Gunkel)*, ed., H. Schmidt (2 vols.; FRLANT 36; Göttingen: Vandenhoeck & Ruprecht, 1923); vol. 2 includes a bibliography of Gunkel's writings up to 1922; Klatt's study brings it up to date.

M. J. Buss

Harnack, Adolf von *(1851-1930)*

Karl Gustav Adolf von Harnack was born on May 7, 1851, at Dorpat (now Tartu), Estonia, and died June 10, 1930, at Heidelberg. Harnack is more widely known as a historian of church and theology than as an interpreter of Scripture. Summing up his work, he once said that his was the life of a German professor who changed his places of work but not his occupation; whatever new tasks came his way, he integrated them into the broadly conceived task of church history, which was the only one in his life. It is as a historian that he contributed to the study and interpretation of Scripture.

Work. The son of a professor of church history and homiletics deeply rooted in a personal faith and in the Lutheran church, Harnack became one of the most representative figures of European Protestantism at the end of the nineteenth and the beginning of the twentieth century. Still, the Protestant church of Germany opposed him for nearly all his public life. Suggesting that his was an "unbelieving theology," the church did not allow him to be part of the commissions of accreditation for clergy. At issue was Harnack's view on the canon of the New Testament, Christ's resurrection and the sacramental nature of baptism. The Roman Catholic press attacked him for "his anti-Christian teachings."

Harnack found his life in the university, especially in scholarly methodology. An academic from age twenty-four until his retirement at seventy, he taught at the universities of Leipzig, Giessen, Marburg and Berlin. He was cofounder and for almost thirty years editor of *Theologische Literaturzeitung*. His students founded and edited the weekly *Christliche Welt*, "an evangelical Lutheran congregational paper for the educated members of the Protestant churches," as it called itself on the masthead. Next to his teaching duties as church historian in Berlin, Harnack was executive director of the Royal Library in Berlin for sixteen years, president of the German Royal Society of Sciences (from 1911 until his death) and president (1903-1911) of the Evangelisch-Soziale Kongress, a society for the promotion of Christian values in society. On his seventy-fifth birthday President Hindenburg awarded him a citation of honor: "To the

Bearer of German Culture."

Harnack's hermeneutical home is the Enlightenment. It had called into question the certainty about Scripture that was grounded in the doctrine of the verbal inspiration of Scripture, a doctrine that was a response to the objective and subjective unassuredness of human beings before the biblical text and its contents. The Enlightenment repudiated every form of and claim to supernatural certainty. Whatever happens in history is relative, it declared; reason alone determines what is of validity, including in Scripture. Biblical hermeneutics has to establish what is rational; critical biblical study has to sort out all that is less than rational, less than human, less than divine.

Accordingly biblical criticism is literary and substance criticism. As this form of biblical criticism developed, a critique of the purely rationalistic emerged within the Enlightenment: it was recognized that next to the human faculty of reason, there was also that of feeling, the sensibility for the good, true and beautiful. The nineteenth century and the generation that influenced Harnack directly spoke of a sensitiveness for what is religious, the reflection or imprint of revelation in certain unique or uniquely perceptive individuals. In relation to Scripture the interpreter needs to have religious openness (referred to as the principle of congeniality) and the sense for how religion itself changes historically (the principle of development).

However essential to the work of interpretation, such openness or sensitivity is not amenable to scholarly methods. But the practice of exegesis is. Harnack held that the Bible is literature and therefore subject to every rule of critical literary and historical study. He was profoundly influenced by the historical *Geisteswissenschaften*, the scholarly historical disciplines, of the nineteenth century, especially those of oriental and classical antiquity. In 1891 Harnack cofounded the Commission on the Church Fathers, whose purpose was to publish the Greco-Christian literature up to the year 325. By 1924 forty-five of the planned fifty volumes had appeared, most of them edited by Harnack.

The work of biblical exegesis had to be free from dogmatic and confessional strictures. But—and this was crucial for Harnack—biblical criticism and personal faith had to be mediated. Faith and history, faith and human culture, scholarly methods and religious sensitivity had to be related. In all his work Harnack sought to create and then to maintain the unity of the gospel and what Germans call *Bildung,* all which gives formation to or makes for the cultivation of mature, educated persons. The public correspondence of 1923 between Harnack and Karl *Barth is testimony of Harnack's lifelong struggle to demonstrate that the Christian religion, represented in an unsurpassably pure manner in the person of Jesus and in the gospel he taught, protects human culture and civilization from secularization, barbarism and atheism.

For Harnack culture was the fullest development of individuality and consequently of freedom from mere natural or material reality and freedom for self-transcendence into the higher realm of the spiritual. Culture is a "naiveté regained." The gospel, as he interpreted it, was none other than the original, the naive. It is, as he was to say in his 1900 lectures on "The Essence of Christianity," eternal life in the midst of time in the power and before the face of God. The meaning and power of the gospel that Jesus taught is to give people freedom and responsibility in the higher things of life and to maintain them. It is the imperative of the Christian religion to inform and shape all aspects of life so that life may achieve the religious significance that is both its foundation and destiny.

Major Works. In his major works Harnack sought to show how historically the Christian religion progressed from its early stages in the Hebrew Scriptures to the New Testament, how it declined from that expression on account of its combination with Greek metaphysics and finally how it developed anew from the dissolution of dogma by Martin *Luther into a renewed progress toward a new community of nobleness of heart, mind and spirit.

This is the focus particularly of his *History of Dogma* (3 vols., 1886-1889; ET 1896-1899) and *Outlines of the History of Dogma* (1889; ET 1893). Detailed and multifaceted exposition of the early church's history is found in *Mission and Expansion of Christianity in the First Three Centuries* (1902; ET 1904-1905). Harnack's doctoral dissertation (Leipzig, 1873) on "Source Criticism and the History of Gnosticism" and his *Habilitationsschrift* (Leipzig, 1874) on *De appelis Gnosis monarchica* (it had to be written in Latin) focused on the subject that was to occupy him again in his last major monograph, written at the age of seventy and revised again three years later: Gnosticism and Marcion (the title of this late work is *Marcion: Das Evangelium vom fremden Gott* [1921], *Marcion: The Gospel of the Alien God*, thus far untranslated into English). In these studies, as elsewhere, Harnack demonstrated his superb text-critical skills and knowledge of detail. One also encounters his firm belief that the heart of theology is to be found in the history of the ancient church. "All our crucial problems in Church History," he once wrote, "are in the field of ancient history. I am sure that the future of the church, as far as university-faculties and teachers are concerned, will be decided by how Church History is advanced." The tools of his scholarly study, of *Wissenschaft,* were to serve Christian spirituality and the church within which that spirituality is to find its public expression.

Harnack's most widely read publication is *What Is Christianity?* The book is a stenographic reproduction of the sixteen lectures on the essence of Christianity that Harnack presented—without a prepared manuscript—to about six hundred listeners during the fall of 1899 and the spring of 1900. These lectures were published in 1900 (ET the same year) and translated into fourteen languages.

Seeking to do without the demands of the scholarly apparatus, Harnack wanted to speak as simply as possible about what was at the heart of Christian faith. The true substance of the gospel is to be grasped on the basis of its transmitted sources. Biblical interpretation is therefore paramount. But the decisive matter for exegesis is that Jesus was not about self-revelation, that he did not proclaim certain mysteries. Jesus' teachings are what matter: the fatherhood of God, the brotherhood and sisterhood of all and the infinite value of the human soul. Harnack staunchly maintained that it is not the Son but the Father alone who belongs in the gospel. This book speaks most plainly the language and approach of theological liberalism.

Harnack's critical studies of early Christianity have turned out to be pathbreaking for the history of women in that period. Some interpreters of New Testament Christianity, for example, L. Schottroff, discern the influence of Harnack's only sister Anna, two years his senior, who throughout all her adult life was deeply engaged in the work for and with women. In 1900 Harnack published two studies that have remained seminal in their argumentation. The first is *"Probabilia über die Adresse und den Verfasser des Hebraerbriefs"* ("Who might have written the Epistle to the Hebrews and to whom might it have been addressed?"). The second is *"Über die beiden Recensionen der Geschichte der Prisca und des Aquila in Acta Apostolorum 18:1-7"* ("Concerning the two recensions of the story of Priscilla and Aquila in Acts 18:1-7"). In the former, Harnack shows his grasp of New Testament and early Christian literature in arguing that the author of the epistle is Priscilla and to a lesser extent her husband, Aquila, and that subsequent generations, if not even their contemporaries, suppressed that information since the work of women in the church, especially in positions of teachers and preachers, came under heavy attack. The latter article shows how the two versions of Acts 18:1-27 reflect this attack on the leadership position of women in the early church. The earlier version (identified as alpha = Greek Majuscule Text as opposed the later version, beta = Syro-Latin Text and codex D) had given unstinting recognition to the position of Priscilla and her ability as a teacher and colleague of Paul, whereas the later version suppresses this, thereby not only reducing Priscilla's work personally but also subjugating the tradition of women and their place in the life and expansion of Christianity.

Biblical Interpretation. Harnack's historical work continues to yield solid factual materials to this day; his judgment testifies to the times of his work and the Europe he represented. In relation specifically to his biblical interpretation, two aspects require critical attention on the part of today's readers.

Harnack was anti-Judaistic in his interpretation of the Old Testament: for him it was an anachronistic work. There is a disconcerting assertion of his Marcion study: "The rejection of the Old Testament in the second century was a mistake which the Great Church rightly refused to make; the retention of it in the sixteenth century was due to a fatal legacy which the Reformation was not able to overcome; but for Protestantism since the nineteenth century to continue to treasure it as a canonical document is the result of a religious and ecclesiastical paralysis" (Harnack 1921, 248-49).

Living in what he regarded to be an age of science, Harnack set out to provide a scholarly, scientific foundation for Christianity. The means and gifts of the sciences can and should serve faith and piety; that was his conviction. When he rejected the supranatural foundations for faith of the older orthodoxy of Protestantism and of Pietism, he did not reject the notion that human tools and methods could provide foundations for God's truth and human faith. His methodological response to human unassuredness before the substance and meaning of God's word in Scripture is, from a certain perspective, the opposite side of the supranatural response embedded in the doctrine of verbal inspiration. Both are a human construct; both escape from the inevitable human condition of not having disposition over God's word.

Harnack's biblical work, as much as his historical work, reflects the conviction that once source-critical work, carried out in tandem with the principle of congeniality, has been done correctly, we know not only what a text says but also what it means: revelation has been discerned. Harnack's work is still under what H. Frei called "the eclipse of biblical narrative." For him the Scriptures were external forms of specific internal religious essence or truth. Because of these two aspects, Harnack is used more profitably for the historical background to scriptural interpretation than for his exegesis of the biblical text.

BIBLIOGRAPHY

Works. A. von Harnack, *The Acts of the Apostles* (New York: G. P. Putnam's Sons, 1909); idem, *Bible Reading in the Early Church* (New York: Putnam's, 1912); idem, *The Constitution and Law of the Church in the First Two Centuries* (New York: Putnam's, 1910); idem, *Geschichte der altchristlichen Literatur bis Eusebius* (4 vols.; Leipzig: J. C. Hinrichs, 1958 [1893-1904]); idem, *History of Dogma* (3 vols.; London: Williams & Norgate, 1896-1899); idem, *Marcion. Das Evangelium vom fremden Gott. Eine Monographie zur Geschichte der Grundlegung der katholischen Kirche* (rev. ed.; Leipzig: J. C. Heinrichs, 1924 [1921]); idem, *The Mission and Expansion of Christianity in the First Three Centuries* (New York: Putnam's, 1904-1905); idem, *New Testament Studies* (6 vols.; New York: Putnam's Sons, 1908-1925); idem, *Outlines of the History of Dogma* (London: Hodder & Stoughton, 1893); idem, *Reden und Aufsätze* (7 vols.; Giessen: Ricker [collected addresses and essays published in German between 1911 and 1930]); idem, *What Is Christianity?* (New York: Putnam's, 1923). Harnack's bibliography, published in 1931, lists more than sixteen hundred titles.

Studies. A. E. Garvie, *The Ritschlian Theology* (Edinburgh: T & T Clark, 1899); G. W. Glick, *The Reality of Christianity: A Study of Adolf von Harnack as Historian and Theologian* (New York: Harper & Row, 1967); W. Pauck, *Harnack and Troeltsch: Two Historical Theologians* (New York: Oxford University Press, 1968); H. M. Rumscheidt, *Revelation and Theology: An Analy-*

sis of the Barth-Harnack Correspondence of 1923 (Cambridge: Cambridge University Press, 1972); idem, ed., *Adolf von Harnack: Liberal Theology at Its Height* (Minneapolis: Augsburg Fortress, 1989); A. von Zahn-Harnack (Harnack's daughter), *Adolf von Harnack* (2d ed.; Berlin: Walter de Gruyter, 1951).

H. M. Rumscheidt

Jeremias, Joachim *(1900-1979)*

Joachim Jeremias, one of the most influential and respected New Testament scholars of the twentieth century, was born in Dresden, Germany, in 1900. As a youth he spent five years in Jerusalem (1910-1915) while his father, Dr. Friedrich Jeremias, served as provost of the Deutsche Gemeinde there. Jeremias studied theology and oriental languages and received his Ph.D. from the University of Leipzig in 1922. Following a five-year term as professor at the University of Greifswald (1929-1934), Jeremias had a long and distinguished career in the New Testament chair at the University of Göttingen (1935-1968). He received honorary doctorates from Leipzig, Oxford, St. Andrews and Uppsala. When Jeremias died in 1979 he had written more than 250 scholarly articles (including several key studies in G. Kittel's *TDNT*) and more than 30 books, many of which went into several editions and were translated widely (for a complete bibliography through 1970 see his festschrift, *Der Ruf Jesu und die Antwort der Gemeinde*).

Context. The decades in which Jeremias was active (1920-1970) were turbulent ones for biblical scholarship, especially in Germany. The hermeneutical assumptions of old German liberalism were challenged by the dialectical theology of Karl *Barth and the existential interpretations of Rudolf *Bultmann. Gospel research relied heavily upon methods called form criticism (following World War I) and redaction criticism (following World War II), both of which were often used to stress the origin and evolution of Jesus' message within the Christian community.

The early part of Jeremias's era was marked by little interest in the historical Jesus. Bultmann, in fact, had called the quest both impossible and illegitimate. A new quest for the historical Jesus did emerge in the early 1950s, employing a method commonly called the criterion of dissimilarity to evaluate the authenticity of the teachings of Jesus. Because this method validated as historical the material about Jesus that is dissimilar to teachings commonly found in first-century Palestine, it tended to dissociate Jesus from his Jewish environment. Jeremias is a product of this era methodologically, though he does have his own distinctive approaches.

What sets Jeremias apart from the scholarly status quo are two themes that influence almost everything he wrote: Jesus and the New Testament must be interpreted within the linguistic and historical setting of first-century Judaism, and it is both possible and important for the Christian faith to find the teachings of the historical Jesus.

Work. The volume of Jeremias's publications makes a comprehensive review impossible, but analysis of certain key works gives an accurate overview. An important early and still-used volume is Jeremias's *Jerusalem in the Time of Jesus* (1923; based upon his dissertation; ET 1969), an investigation of life in Jerusalem and Palestine as it serves as a background for the interpretation of Jesus. Its four main divisions are "Economic Conditions in the City of Jerusalem," "Economic Status," "Social Status" (i.e., clergy, lay nobility, scribes, Pharisees) and "The Maintenance of Racial Purity." Jeremias based his account on archaeological material, ancient histories and especially rabbinic sources. His use of the rabbinic materials is rather uncritical; rabbinic writings from various periods and origins are assumed to be historically accurate, a surprising approach for one who so painstakingly weighs the historical value of materials in the Gospels (for a criticism of Jeremias concerning his interpretations of Jewish material, see Sanders). Nevertheless this vast collection of material about first-century Jewish thought continues to be a helpful reference tool, and it indicates an early interest in what would be a ongoing theme in Jeremias's thought. Numerous other articles on the history and archaeology of Palestine appear in this early part of his career.

In 1935 Jeremias published his source-critical tour de force, *The Eucharistic Words of Jesus* (ET 1955; significantly revised in later editions). His purpose in this volume is essentially threefold: to show that the Last Supper was a Passover meal, to illustrate the liturgical evolution of the eucharistic material now found in the Gospels and Paul, and to recover the eucharistic words used by the historical Jesus in order to understand what he meant by them.

Jeremias's hallmark optimism about hearing the voice of the historical Jesus (the *ipsissima vox Jesu*) is based upon his assumption that historical remembrance has been preserved, sometimes inadvertently, in the midst of later traditions found in the Gospels. This earlier layer of material can be detected by comparing Gospel accounts to understand what sources were used, by finding references to the Eucharist as a Passover meal (something the early church did not always recognize), and, perhaps most characteristic of Jeremias's approach, by noting words that are translations of Aramaic, the language Jesus spoke. Of the three strands of tradition about the Lord's Supper (Mark/Matthew, Paul/Luke, John), Mark, because of its many Semitisms, is judged to contain the oldest tradition, although Jeremias admits that even Mark is based on an *Urform* that is no longer retrievable. Nevertheless Jeremias was confident that his method of evaluating the various forms of the eucharistic account does yield a reliable understanding of what Jesus said and did. Jeremias reconstructed the Last Supper as a traditional four-part Passover meal in which Jesus interprets the liturgy in terms of his own mission. Based upon the Lukan account (and rabbinic and early Christian information about fasting), Jeremias offered the rather unusual inter-

pretation that Jesus himself fasted during the meal as a sign of the nearness of the end and as an indication of his intercession for his enemies.

Jeremias's understanding of Jesus' purpose in the Last Supper is traditional. Jesus expands his prayers over the bread and the third Passover cup into similes in which he speaks of his own atoning sacrifice. He is the Passover lamb, the Suffering Servant who has come to die for the many. Jesus' command that all of this be done "in remembrance of me" is interpreted by Jeremias to be a command to pray that God may remember Jesus' actions and hence usher in the kingdom, an interpretation that many scholars have questioned. Though not all agree with the details of Jeremias's reconstruction and interpretation, it cannot be denied that this erudite analysis of the Last Supper not only secures Jeremias's place as a world-class exegete but also clearly delineates the scholarly concerns of his later career, especially his search for the *ipsissima vox Jesu* on the basis of the Semitisms found in the Gospels.

The volume for which Jeremias is most well known is *The Parables of Jesus* (1947; ET 1954; a popularized version of the book was published under the title *Rediscovering the Parables*). Like *Eucharistic Words*, it is an attempt to find the *ipsissima vox Jesu*, now in terms of his most common form of speech, the parable. Jeremias consciously moved beyond the work of parables scholars A. Jülicher and Charles Harold *Dodd; the parables must be interpreted within the specific context of Jesus' ministry and seen as explanations of his central message, the kingdom of God in process of realization. The author clearly states the importance of grasping the words and situation of the historical Jesus. As Jeremias says in his foreword and repeats elsewhere, "Only the Son of Man and his word can invest our message with full authority."

The problem, according to Jeremias, is that the parables now found in the Gospels have been altered and embellished in the early church. He spends the entire first section of the book discussing the nature of these changes and how we might return to the words of Jesus. An inevitable change in meaning occurred when the parables were translated into Greek from the original Aramaic. Just as significant is the movement from a Palestinian setting to a Hellenistic one in the early church and how this affected the telling of the parables. As the church increasingly applied the parables to its own situation, allegorization was used to deemphasize the polemical and eschatological nature of Jesus' parables and to emphasize current concerns, especially missionary activity and the delay of the second coming (parousia). When the parables were put into the larger narratives found in the Gospels, they were given a new literary context that influenced or generalized their meaning. Jeremias's task is to work his way back from the current form of the parables, noting Semitisms, hints of a primitive Palestinian setting, and embellishments and allegorizations of the church, reconstructing the parables in their original setting.

In the last section of his book Jeremias revealed his findings, distilled into what he sees as the basic themes in Jesus' parabolic message. When they are reconstructed, the parables present a clear picture of Jesus' eschatological proclamation, with themes such as the imminence of the catastrophe, the call to discipleship and decision, the necessity of the suffering of the Son of man and the great consummation of the kingdom. As is typical in Jeremias, Jesus is described as being fully aware of his special role in the coming of the kingdom and his atoning task. This section of *The Parables of Jesus*, filled with characteristic references to Palestinian life and rabbinic literature, encapsulates Jeremias's christology.

Jeremias's volume on the parables has been immensely popular and is still required reading fifty years after its publication. *The Parables of Jesus* established Jeremias as one of the founders of modern parable study and also as one who rekindled the quest for the historical Jesus. As is often noted, Jeremias does not have a sophisti-

cated understanding of the metaphorical nature of the parables. His interests are more strictly textual and historical (see Perrin, 106). Yet in what he does, especially in seeing the parables in light of Jesus' social and linguistic environment in Palestine, this study is seminal.

Of the many important word studies Jeremias produced for Kittel's *Theological Dictionary of the New Testament (TDNT;* i.e., ἄνθρωπος, γέεννα, λίθος, Μωυσῆς, παράδεισος, πάσχα, πολλοί), his article on the servant of God (Παῖς Θεοῦ, 1952; written with W. Zimmerli and later published as a monograph) is one of the most significant because it clarifies a central theme in Jeremias's work, the nature of Jesus' atoning task. Jeremias asserts that the early Palestinian church applied to Jesus the Deutero-Isaiah passages that speak of the Messiah as the Suffering Servant of God, even using it as a title for Jesus (Mt 12:18; Acts 3:13, 26; 4:27, 30).

This interpretation of the Messiah was considered inappropriate by the Gentile church, and already in the New Testament we see instances where the older "servant of God" is interpreted as "child of God" (Mk 1:11) or "lamb of God" (Jn 1:29, 36). The Palestinian church's understanding of Jesus as Suffering Servant grows out of Jesus' own teachings about his death, according to Jeremias. Several of the Gospels' statements about Jesus' death are either translations from Aramaic or would not have been produced by the later church (i.e., the prediction of Jesus' death tied to a description of Peter as Satan; Mk 8:31-33) and thus must go back to the historical Jesus. Jeremias's theological conclusion is that "because [Jesus] goes to his death innocently, voluntarily, patiently and in accordance with the will of God (Isa 53), his dying has boundless atoning virtue" (Jeremias 1952; ET 1957, 104). This article is characteristic of the last two decades of Jeremias's work in that there is more of a theological or christological focus.

Typical too is *Jesus' Promise to the Nations* (1956; ET 1958), in which Jeremias wrestles with the concept of Christian mission as it is portrayed in the Gospels. The author deals with the apparent contradiction between Jesus' mission to the Jews and his promise of salvation to the Gentiles through an interpretation of Matthew 8:11 and an emphasis upon salvation history and God's prerogative in mission.

The Central Message of the New Testament (1965) is one of Jeremias's clearest statements of christology. According to Jeremias, four theological tenets lie at the heart of the Christian message as it is presented in the New Testament: Jesus' relationship with God as Father as expressed in his use of the word *Abba,* the sacrificial death of Jesus, justification by faith, and the revealing word or Jesus Christ as *Logos* (based upon a study of the prologue in the Gospel of John).

This theological focus is continued in his last major work, *New Testament Theology: The Proclamation of Jesus* (1970; ET 1971). What is unusual about this book in comparison with New Testament theologies being produced at the time is that the entire volume deals with the teaching of Jesus rather than that of the individual Gospel writers, a clear indication of where Jeremias's concern lies.

Jeremias begins with a particularly helpful statement about method. While the criterion of dissimilarity is legitimate, it is also a source of error because it may too quickly dismiss material that shows continuity between Jesus and Judaism. Jeremias's corrective, as he states here, is the examination of language and style. Material must be evaluated on the basis of possible Aramaic roots, ways of speaking preferred by Jesus (i.e., the divine passive as a circumlocution for God, antithetic parallelism, certain kinds of rhythm, etc.) and characteristics of his *ipsissima vox* (his use of parables, reference to the kingdom of God and his rather unusual employment of *Amen* and *Abba).*

Jeremias is not nearly as pessimistic about finding the teachings of the historical Jesus as were many of his contemporaries. His general principle is that "the inauthen-

ticity, and not the authenticity, of the sayings of Jesus must be demonstrated" (Jeremias 1971 [ET], 37). The final chapters of his *New Testament Theology* give an overview of the teaching and mission of the historical Jesus. Jesus accepts his mission in his temptation (chap. 2) and sees himself as one who initiates the new kingdom in his proclamation to the poor (chap. 3). Jesus taught the suddenness of the coming consummation and not its delay (chap. 4); he has a radical sense of discipleship and what that means in the life of the believer (chap. 5). Jeremias pictures Jesus as one who has a clear sense of his mission to die as the Suffering Servant of God (chap. 6). The author concludes with a discussion of Easter, noting especially the uniqueness of such an event in Jewish thought and how the disciples must certainly have seen it as the dawn of the eschaton. This volume is not so much a theology about Jesus as a theology of Jesus; the historical Jesus himself is the starting point for all theological reflection for Jeremias.

Significance. Innovative scholars such as Jeremias are often difficult to classify methodologically. Writing in his early career—during the flowering of form criticism—Jeremias is typically identified with this approach. But even though he used some of the tools of form criticism, he did so to discover the source of the New Testament writings in the historical Jesus, not the early Christian community, nor was he particularly concerned with the oral forms and their classification. Jeremias was not a redaction critic, because his purpose was rarely to discover the theology of an individual Gospel writer. The detailed comparative analysis he does in the Gospels more closely resembles the work of older source critics.

Jeremias's most significant contribution methodologically is his interpretation of the criterion of dissimilarity. While he consistently applied the latter half of this formula (when a saying or teaching could not have been produced in the church, it may have its origin in Jesus), he challenged a thoroughgoing application of the first half of the formula, asserting that Jesus is in many cases a product of his Jewish environment. Thus when Jeremias sees evidence of Palestinian life or the Aramaic language in a passage, he attempted to link that evidence with the historical Jesus. The result is a more Jewish Jesus, one who may at times be unique in comparison to Jewish thought but one who cannot be separated from his linguistic and social roots.

Jeremias's contribution to New Testament scholarship is hard to overestimate. His steady insistence that the recovery of the historical Jesus is both possible and important for the Christian faith, coming as it did in the midst of a period dominated by Bultmann's more pessimistic assessment, was surely in part responsible (with the work of Ernst *Käsemann and Günter *Bornkamm) for the so-called new quest. It was especially Jeremias's work that reminded two generations of New Testament scholars of the importance of study in the Semitic languages and the necessity of grasping the historical setting of first-century Palestine.

Jeremias's work also had the effect of validating what conservative Christians often called higher criticism. He showed that working with the modern critical methodologies need not lead to a refutation of traditional teachings of the church (e.g., the nature of Jesus' atoning task). Finally one might argue that Jeremias's greatest contribution lies in the details of his exegetical work, that wonderfully minute and erudite analysis that is still yielding insight for modern scholars.

Of all the issues raised by Jeremias's writings, the most important for the contemporary church is the relationship between the historical Jesus and the writings now found in the New Testament. Jeremias was right in rejecting the kind of docetism that denies the significance of the historical Jesus, a view common among New Testament scholars of his day. But is it correct to say that we must seek the words of Jesus as our primary authority? Is not the later tradition about Jesus now found in the New Testament also inspired and authoritative? Does not Jeremias's approach raise the possibility of a scholarly gnosticism, where only the educated have the ability to find and interpret the authoritative biblical words, the words of Jesus himself? In a real sense modern scholarship has spoken to these issues in its use of redaction criticism, narrative criticism and canonical criticism; it is necessary to move beyond an atomistic, historical approach to one that appreciates the whole of a book or narrative. Yet the recent revival of interest in recovering the words of the historical Jesus (e.g., the Jesus Seminar) suggests that this issue will be an ongoing one. In this continued discussion, the work of Jeremias provides a significant model for assessing the value of the historical Jesus for the Christian faith.

BIBLIOGRPAHY

Works. J. Jeremias, *Die Abendmahlsworte Jesu* (Göttingen: Vandenhoeck & Ruprecht, 1935; ET *The Eucharistic Words of Jesus* [Oxford: Blackwell, 1955]); idem, *Die Bergpredigt* (Stuttgart: Calwer Verlag, 1959; ET *The Sermon on the Mount* [London: Athlone Press, 1961]); idem and H. Strathmann, *Die Briefe an Timotheus und Titus; Der Brief an die Hebraer* (Gottingen: Vandenhoeck & Ruprecht, 1953); idem, *The Central Message of the New Testament* (London: SCM, 1965); idem, *Die Gleichnisse Jesu* (Zurich: Zwingli-Verlag, 1947; ET *The Parables of Jesus* [London: SCM, 1954]); idem, *Jerusalem sur Zeit Jesu. Kulturgeschichtliche Untersuchung zur neutestamentlichen Zeitgeschichte* (Ph.D. diss., Leipzig, 1923; ET *Jerusalem in the Time of Jesus: An Investigation into Economic and Social Conditions during the New Testament Period* [London: SCM, 1969]); idem, *Jesu Verheissung fur die Volker* (Stuttgart: W. Kohlhammer Verlag, 1956; ET *Jesus' Promise to the Nations* [London: SCM, 1958]); idem, *Die Kindertaufe in den ersten vier Jahrhunderten* (Göttingen: Vandenhoeck & Ruprecht, 1958; ET *Infant Baptism in the First Four Centuries* [London: SCM, 1960]); idem, *Neutestamentliche Theologie. Erster Teil. Die Verkundigung Jesu* (Gutersloh: Gutersloher Verlaghaus, 1970; ET *New Testament Theology: Part 1: The Proclamation of Jesus* (London: SCM, 1971]); idem, "The Present Position in the Con-

troversy Concerning the Problem of the Histori-
cal Jesus," *ET* 69 (1957) 333-39; idem, "Παῖς
Θεοῦ," *TDNT* 5:677-717, with W. Zimmerli,
The Servant of God (London: SCM, 1957); idem,
*Die Sprache des Lukasevangeliums: Redaktion
und Tradition im Nicht-Markusstoff des dritten
Evangeliums* (Gottingen: Vandenhoeck & Ru-
precht, 1980); idem, *Unbekannte Jesusworte*
(Zurich: Zwingli-Verlag, 1948; ET *Unknown
Sayings of Jesus* [London: SPCK, 1957]); idem,
Das Vater-Unser im Lichte der neuren Forschung
(Stuttgart: Calwer Verlag, 1960; ET *The Lord's
Prayer* [Philadelphia: Fortress, 1964]).

    Studies. M. Black, "Theologians of Our
Time. Joachim Jeremias," *ET* 74 (1962-63)
115-19; E. Lohse, "Joachim Jeremias im Memo-
riam," *ZNW* 70 (1979) 139-40; idem, ed., *Der
Ruf Jesu und die Antwort der Gemeinde. Exegetis-
che Untersuchungen Joachim Jeremias sum 70.
Geburtstag gewidmet von seinen Schulern* (Göt-
tingen: Vandenhoeck & Ruprecht, 1970); B. F.
Meyer, "A Caricature of Joachim Jeremias and
His Scholarly Work," *JBL* 110 (1991) 451-62;
N. Perrin, "Joachim Jeremias and the Historical
Interpretation of the Parables of Jesus" in *Jesus
and the Language of the Kingdom* (Philadelphia:
Fortress, 1976) 91-107; E. P. Sanders, "Defend-
ing the Indefensible," *JBL* 110 (1991) 463-77;
J. W. Sider, "Rediscovering the Parables: The
Logic of the Jeremias Tradition," *JBL* 102
(1983) 61-83.   L. D. Vander Broek

Käsemann, Ernst *(1906-1998)*

Born in the Dahlhausen region of Bochum,
Westphalia, Germany, on July 12, 1906,
Ernst Käsemann pursued theological studies and held academic posts in his native
land. He studied at Bonn, Tübingen and
Marburg, presenting a dissertation in 1931
under Rudolf *Bultmann's direction that
was published in 1933 as *Leib und Leib
Christi: Eine Untersuchung zur paulinischen Begrifflichkeit (Body and Christ's Body:
A Study of Pauline Conceptuality).* He
served as pastor in Gelsenkirchen in the
Ruhr.

    Käsemann served in World War II. In his
later publications he took on the role of
ambivalent critic, both opposing the German Christian wing of the state church and
yet resigning from the Westphalian confess-

ing church on the grounds of its cooperation with the German state church. He
entered academic life. Yet his radical resistance to National Socialism in the Hitler
years is seen in his arrest by the Gestapo in
1937 for the use he made of Isaiah 26:13
("O LORD our God, other lords besides
thee have ruled over us, but thy name alone
we acknowledge"). In his imprisonment
he drafted the first version of a study of the
letter to the Hebrews, as he explains in the
preface to *Das wandernde Gottesvolk* (1939;
2d ed. 1957; ET *The Wandering People of
God,* 1984). This theme of the Christian
church as a pilgrim people, tied to no
earthly fatherland, became the setting for
his criticism of the tenets of the Nazi ideology and introduced the idea of conflict that
belongs to the destiny of the church on
earth.

    At this time (1941-1942) Käsemann
was engaged in churchly debates on the
role of women's ministries, mainly to do
with preaching, which was forbidden by a
conservative Lutheran group on the basis
of the injunction to silence in 1 Corinthians
14:34. Käsemann appealed to the role of
women prophets at Corinth to espouse a
more flexible position.

    Käsemann's transit from pastoral to aca-
demic life holds a clue to his subsequent
development, as D. V. Way, following B.
Ehler, notes when he writes: "For him the
task of interpreting scripture is closely related to the ministry of preaching." This
contribution to church life as the academy
impinged on congregational affairs shows
Käsemann's enduring interest in theological issues in a churchly setting. This engaged his concern as he moved through a
succession of teaching posts at Mainz
(1946-1951), Göttingen (1951-1959) and
Tübingen (1959-1971).

    It is with the last-named place that his
influence is associated and where that influence persisted mainly through some illustrious students who in turn, if not always
uncritically, have carried on his work. Käsemann's provocative style and penetrating
questioning of both liberal and Bultman-

nian assumptions, mixed with an acerbic denunciation of all forms of ecclesiastical and doctrinal triumphalism, gave him an important place in the European New Testament and theological scene, with his academic interests reaching a wider public through his preaching and speaking to the audiences at *Kirchentag* (i.e., Bible study conferences for laypeople) occasions.

From 1960 to 1980 Käsemann's social activism as an expression of his exegetical-theological work was seen in his limited support of German student protest. This was galvanized by the tragic death of his daughter Elisabeth on May 24, 1977. She had been working in Argentina and was killed in an Argentinian jail at thirty years of age. He espoused the claims of left-wing students at Tübingen and on the political front opposed nuclear weapons in Europe. His broadened interest in world mission was illustrated by his participation in the World Conference for Mission and Evangelization in Melbourne, Australia, in 1980, as earlier (1977) he had left his Lutheran fold to become a Methodist in response to student unrest in Tübingen.

Influences. No theologian works in a vacuum. To appreciate anyone's contribution requires that we attempt to set that person's work in the cultural context and have regard to antecedents and discussion partners. In the case of Käsemann this exercise is of the first importance. It is possible to detect a bevy of theological movements and personalities that both shaped his thinking and provided the targets of his polemics.

Modern German theologians are in constant indebtedness to and conversation with their heritage derived from Martin *Luther. Käsemann is no exception, and from Luther he learned the primacy of God's grace seen in the justification of sinners by faith—a teaching that was hotly debated in Germany in the 1920s. The twist that Käsemann gave to this heritage was to interpret justification in some novel ways, namely, as cosmic rather than severely individualistic; as having the character of

both gift and power; and as providing him with the larger, overarching rubric of the lordship of Christ, which may rightly be taken to be Käsemann's central theological axiom and statement. To draw out the implications of this will come later; here we simply note it as the ground plan of his thought going back to Luther.

Twentieth-century European interpreters of the New Testament stand equally under the shadow of Ferdinand Christian *Baur. In summary, Baur's chief contributions were to set Paul's theology as the key to Christian theology in general and yet to view Paul in his Hellenistic background as part of the interest in the history of religions interpretation. This attempted to place early Christianity in a wider setting than the Old Testament-Judaic worldview and to trace its genius to its drawing on concepts and ideas of a syncretism that came to be known as Gnosticism. Käsemann never abandoned his commitment to the centrality of Paul as the New Testament interpreter par excellence, though in his earlier writings (on baptism, the spirit, the body of Christ, and his interpretation of the letter to the Hebrews) he used the categories of Hellenism-Gnosticism, which later on he rejected in favor of the Jewish framework of apocalyptic.

The trio of Karl *Barth, Adolf *Schlatter and Bultmann may be grouped together as providing those who were Käsemann's teachers and dialogue partners. Barth's *Romans* (1919; rev. ed., 1922) posed an issue that left an indelible mark on Käsemann's subsequent development: in general it focused on Paul's epistle to the Romans as the center of Pauline and New Testament theology (again going back to Luther), leading him to confess about Romans, "No literary document has been more important for me."

Hence Käsemann's later commentary on Romans (4th ed., 1980) is the place where his distinctive contributions to Pauline theology are most evidently to be seen. Yet it is the more particular issue of how to interpret the Bible that Barth addressed and set the agenda item for Käsemann to pick up. This turns on the question of the true subject matter *(die Sache)* of the scriptural text and what is the criterion by which the modern reader is to measure it. The issue is one of hermeneutics, as we ask how to relate the answers of the text to the questions that underlie it and are provoked by it. As stated by Bultmann, the definition of *Sachkritik* ("theological criticism" is one translation; literally it is "content criticism") is fundamental; "it distinguishes between what is said and what is meant, and measures what is said by what is meant." True, Bultmann's use of this technique is turned against Barth, since Bultmann taxed Barth with ignoring historical criticism and neglecting the history of religions input to the text. Yet Käsemann was to learn from this debate that the issue of hermeneutics, as stated in theological exegesis *(Sachexegese)*, is the way forward.

Käsemann's agreement with his teacher Bultmann on this point should be noted. Their point of dissension seems to have arisen from Bultmann's adherence to the justification doctrine as overly individualistic and anthropological (i.e., human-centered; here Luther's influence is strong). Käsemann resisted this move, which he regarded as a capitulation to existentialist understanding; it ignored the primacy of God's sovereignty over the world, and it failed to give to righteousness its distinctive character of the eschatological triumph that is seen in Christ's kingly rule now and will harbinger the divine lordship at the end time: "God coming to his right on this earth" (Käsemann's lecture on Romans and letter of 1949, cited in Way, 123 n. 12). This note of theological primacy is what Käsemann learned from Schlatter, whom he praised for reasserting God's lordship as central and as interpreted through the prism of the kerygma of Christ crucified, which has genetic links with the Jesus of history. Käsemann's thinking, beginning with his address on October 20, 1953, at Marburg, took on a new turn as he re-opened the new quest for the historical

Jesus. But the germ of interrelation between the Jesus of the Gospels and the Christ of faith was already present in his indebtedness to Schlatter.

In summary, Käsemann's pilgrimage led, by way of reaction to the triumphalism of idealistic liberalism and the soon-to-be-overthrown dominance of the history-of-religions school and in interaction with the triumvirate of Barth, Schlatter and Bultmann, to a coherent view that gave centrality to God's grace in justification, to Paul's theological preeminence in New Testament canon, and to the cruciality of the cross. These are themes that can well (with Way) be subsumed under the caption the lordship of Christ, or in a more nuanced designation, "the lordship of the Crucified" (Ehler's title, drawn from Käsemann's commentary on Rom 8:3-4 [ET, 219]).

Themes. In a writer whose interests have ranged widely across the terrain of New Testament and theological curricula, it is not easy to sum up Käsemann's chief contribution(s). Using the perceptive insight of Way that Käsemann's academic interest shifted from the period up to 1960 to what followed in the 1960s, we may list the distinctive features in this transition.

His earlier espousal of the history of religions backgrounds in Hellenism and Gnosticism gave way to a more positive appreciation of Jewish apocalyptic, which he came to regard as "the mother of early Christianity."

The first period contained studies of Pauline concepts, mainly ecclesiological and soteriological (e.g., union with Christ, body of Christ). After the 1961 essay on "God's Righteousness," he came to attach more importance to this key term, which led to his exposition of Romans with this as its leitmotif. This involved him in debate with and an eventual break from Bultmann, whose existentialist understanding of justification made it a self-referencing concept to be seen as part of Paul's soteriological and highly personal anthropology. Käsemann argued that righteousness has both the character of gift (with Bultmann) but more especially power that creates salvation (*heilschaffende Macht*) and embraces the cosmos in its scope. Thus the world is placed under a new lordship.

Whereas in the earlier time of his career Käsemann was devoted to the theological value of certain historical questions, the concern to see some central doctrinal issues as paramount came to occupy his mind. Among the latter, in the post-1960 period the following stand out: his giving priority to justification or righteousness as a clue to Paul's theology and his reopening of interest in the Jesus of history question. Also in the post-1960 period he returned to ecclesiological questions, partly in revision of his earlier view of Paul's Gnostic background to the body of Christ idea, partly driven by political and social events in Europe and beyond, mirrored in *Jesus Means Freedom* (appearing in 1968 as *Der Ruf der Freiheit*), and partly out of a concern to address questions of the rule of faith and the canon for the church's guidance. These three matters can be treated seriatim.

Taking his starting point from the Pauline phrase "the righteousness of God" as a traditional formula borrowed from the Old Testament (Deut 33:21) and Jewish literature, Käsemann maintains that the phrase means not only that God is the author of a righteousness bestowed on humans but also that it has the power to achieve what it promised and enters the world as a force to overcome the old eon and call into being a new order (based on Rom 4:17) in which "the godhead of God" (i.e., his sovereignty) is proclaimed and acknowledged. The apocalyptic backdrop of this view should be noted and its distinction from the individualized notion of righteousness by faith in traditional Lutheran circles observed. Critics have resisted this extension of meaning, arguing that God's lordship is more suitably expressed by kingdom language than righteousness (Wright, though Käsemann regards the two terms as interchangeable, *Romans*, 29), that God's saving action is directed not to the cosmos as such but to

sinners (K. Kertelge), that the atonement-sacrifice wrought at the cross is not prominent in his exposition (Käsemann regards such idioms as Jewish traditional, not Pauline) and that Paul's target audience in Romans cannot be modern pietism or religious persons but Jewish compatriots (K. Stendahl). The last-named objection reveals Käsemann's interest in having Paul speak to the modern scene, as the twin foes of legalism and enthusiasm are obviously in Käsemann's sights.

As we note one further aspect of Käsemann's construct of Paul's thought, it will serve as a bridge to the next section. He regards Paul's justification teaching as one with Jesus' earthly ministry in which he called sinners in preference to the pious and entered into fellowship with them (Lk 15:1-2; Mk 2:17). This intermeshing of Paul and Jesus lies at the heart of Käsemann's reopening of the quest of the historical Jesus, to which we now turn.

It is well known that one facet of Bultmann's characterization of Jesus' life came in for acute criticism. He was prepared apparently to make the personality of the human Jesus dispensable and to deny any saving significance to our knowledge of how Jesus acted in Galilee and Jerusalem. It was sufficient to know that he lived; our concern with the how and what was misdirected on the twin grounds that form criticism has placed a serious question mark over the veracity of the Gospels' accounts and in any case faith cannot suspend its activity while historians debate the issue, Did it happen? Faith resides in the proclaimed word that Jesus Christ is God's salvation.

Käsemann raised a telling voice against such negativism, chiefly on the score that the logical outcome of Bultmann's denials is docetism; that is, the human Jesus becomes a cipher, a mathematical point that has punctiliar fixity but no content or character. What Käsemann attempted was to forge a bridge between the earthly Jesus and the post-Easter kerygma, and to find certain characteristics in the mission of the earthly Jesus (his unrivaled authority, his attitude to the law, his role as bearer of the spirit in power, his awareness of standing at the turning point of the ages with John the Baptist as the messenger of his coming, his announcement of the imminent kingdom of God where God is creator-parent, and above all, his offer of forgiveness in grace to the ungodly and outcasts) that betokened the presence of the lordship of God that, as we saw, formed the *esse* of Paul's teaching.

Käsemann's theology of the cross *(theologia crucis)* lies at the heart of his unpacking of the New Testament kerygma. He cites approvingly from M. Kähler: "without the cross no christology, and in christology no single feature which cannot find its justification in the cross." This hyphenated christology-of-the-cross lays the basis for his ecclesiology, which remains subservient always to the *theologia crucis.* Against earlier views that gave a realistic presence to the church as the body of Christ, Käsemann's final understanding came to rest in the picture of the church as the servant-instrument of the crucified Lord. Here Käsemann's position marks it out in opposition to catholicizing tendencies he found in the deutero-Pauline epistles and later New Testament books (Luke-Acts, 2 Peter) and in defense of the primacy of the spirit over the letter. Moreover, officeholders in the early church, notably Paul's opponents in 2 Corinthians 10—13, were a constant threat to the true kerygma (hence Paul's severe warnings in 2 Cor 11:13-15; 13:1-4) and the charismatic ministries are valid only as they truly represent and embody the grace *(charis)* of salvation. Apostolic existence is always to be lived under the sign of the cross, against forces of pietism and authoritarianism (he avers) that would destroy it.

Canonical authority too stands under the same delimiting criterion. Here Käsemann distinguishes between the "formal principle" of the canon as a bulwark against the Gnostic heresy and in opposition to freewheeling charismatic groups and the "material (i.e., salvation-centered) principle," which he located in justification by faith. In such books as 2 Peter, Käsemann judged that the essential gospel had been overlaid and corrupted. The contribution it makes to the New Testament canon is a negative one, which is what happens when the material principle is lost or replaced (more discussion and critique of this is in R. P. Martin, "Early Catholicism," *DPL,* 223-25 and *DLNTD,* 310-13; A. Chester and R. P. Martin, *The Letters of James, Peter and Jude* [Cambridge: Cambridge University Press, 1994], 148-51).

Significance. While it is fairly straightforward to list the contributions made by Käsemann over five decades of his career, it is less easy to assess their enduring worth. One assessment, while sympathetic and supportive of many of his ideas, doubts whether his influence will last, given the shift in climate and concern in the theological world since the mid-1970s and given too that there has been no loyal school formed to perpetuate the influence of the teacher.

In retrospect, the following are the seminal ways that Käsemann played such a visible role in New Testament theological scholarship in the decades of 1950 to 1970.

He reasserted, in breach with his teacher Bultmann, the theological business of the New Testament interpreter. It is not enough to stay with Bultmann's anthropology; the theologian must be true to the name and make God, creator and justifier of the ungodly, the theme of discourse.

Against Bultmann's interest in how people come to faith and gain salvation, Käsemann focused on christology as the leading theme to explain the apostle's thought and the church's raison d'être. Moreover, this christology is wedded to Christ crucified, who is the benchmark to test both genuine faith and valid ecclesiology and ministry.

As far as Pauline thought is concerned, God's saving action is expressed in a universalistic way, with righteousness assuming the character of gift-in-power that transforms the world and leads believers to a new obedience, as the basis for Christian ethics.

The overarching rubric is rightly seen to be Christ's lordship over the world and the church. This is both the conclusion of Käsemann's earlier exegetical work (e.g., on Phil 2:5-11 [see Morgan]; Col 1:15-20), and paradoxically (or as he would say, dialectically) it became the defining theme for all of Käsemann's interests. What Käsemann wrote of E. Lohmeyer, one of the earlier scholars on whose shoulders he stood, may justifiably be credited to him: His works "mark a turning-point insofar as they lift us out of the old ruts, and therefore have forced the 'exegetical fraternity' and their usual readers to face new and suggestive questions."

BIBLIOGRAPHY

Works. E. Käsemann, *Commentary on Romans* (Grand Rapids: Eerdmans, 1982 [trans. of 4th German ed. 1980; 1st German ed., 1973]); idem, *Essays on New Testament Themes* (Naperville, IL : Allenson, 1964); idem, *Exegetische Versuche und Besinnungen* (2 vols.; Göttingen: Vandenhoeck & Ruprecht, 1960, 1964); idem, *Jesus Means Freedom* (Philadelphia: Fortress, 1970 [1969]); idem, *Kirchliche Konflikte* (Göttingen: Vandenhoeck & Ruprecht, 1982); idem, *Das Neue Testament als Kanon* (Göttingen: Vandenhoeck & Ruprecht, 1970); idem, *Perspectives on Paul* (Philadelphia: Fortress, 1971 [1969]); idem, *The Testament of Jesus: A Study of the Gospel of John in the Light of Chapter 17* (Philadelphia: Fortress, 1978 [1968]); *The Wandering People of God: An Investigation of the Letter to the Hebrews* (Minneapolis: Augsburg, 1984 [1939, 1957]). *Studies.* B. Ehler, *Die Herrschaft des Gekreuzigten* (Berlin and New York: Walter de Gruyter, 1986); P. Gisel, *Vérité et historie: La théologie dans la modernité: Ernst Käsemann* (Paris: Beauchesne, 1977); R. A. Harrisville and W. Sundberg, *The Bible in Modern Culture: Theology and Historical-Critical Method from Spinoza to Käsemann* (Grand Rapids: Eerdmans, 1995); R. Morgan, "Incarnation, Myth, and Theology: Ernst Käsemann's Interpretation of Philippians 2:5-11" in *Where Christology Began: Essays on Philippians 2*, ed. R. P. Martin and B. J. Dodd (Louisville, KY: Westminster John Knox Press, 1998) 43-73; D. V. Way, *The Lordship of Christ,*

Ernst Käsemann's Interpretation of Paul's Theology (Oxford: Clarendon, 1991), includes full bibliography; N. T. Wright, "A New Tübingen School? Ernst Käsemann and His Commentary on Romans," *Them* 7 (1982) 6-16; J. Friedrich, W. Pöhlmann and P. Stuhlmacher ed., *Rechtfertigung: Festschrift für Ernst Käsemann zum 70. Geburtstag* (Tübingen: J. C. B. Mohr, 1976; Göttingen: Vandenhoeck & Ruprecht, 1976).

R. P. Martin

Mowinckel, Sigmund (1884-1965)

Sigmund Mowinckel, the son of a Lutheran pastor, was born at Kjerringøy in northern Norway. He studied at the University of Kristiania (renamed Oslo in 1924), and after enrolling as a theological student, he completed the theological examinations in 1915 but was not ordained until 1940. After commencing his theological studies he decided to work in the field of Old Testament and enrolled for a doctorate. He then spent years abroad (1911-1913) before returning to Kristiania to become a student assistant (1915) and docent at his university (1917). His doctorate had been awarded for a dissertation entitled *Stadholderen Nehemia* (1916). Mowinckel was elected a professor (1922), becoming the professor of Old Testament (1933) in succession to S. Michelet. He retired from this post (1954) but remained active in writing and teaching.

During his period of study abroad in Denmark and Germany, Mowinckel came under the influence of Hermann *Gunkel in Giessen in the field of biblical poetry and literature and of W. Grønbech in Copenhagen on the subject of anthropology and history of religion. The impact these two scholars had on the youthful Mowinckel was to prove profound and shaped the direction of his future research. He also studied Assyriology with P. Jensen in Marburg since it was vital for his interests to recognize the close links between the world of the ancient Near East and that of the Bible. His scholarship as an oriental linguist, as an astute literary critic of poetic form and meter, and of comparative method in the study of religion were all to bear fruit in his subsequent work. Together with his former teacher, Michelet, and his later pupil A. S. Kapelrud, Mowinckel made a major contribution to the translation of the Old Testament into Norwegian (4 vols., 1929-63). The most lasting impact of his work was to arise from his linking the new directions of religious and anthropological research initiated by Grønbech with contemporary biblical research, especially into the Psalter.

Old Testament Prophecy. The initial influence of the work of Gunkel on Mowinckel was to bear almost immediate effect in the first of his major publications, which was devoted to the sources of the prophetic book of Jeremiah. In a study published in 1914, Mowinckel examined closely the differing forms of material preserved in the book of Jeremiah, taking particular issue with the current criticism advocated by B. Duhm. Where Duhm had taken poetic form as indicative of closeness to the original prophet's words, regarding prose as highly suspect and inauthentic, Mowinckel maintained that the differing strata in the book consisting of poetry, prose narrative and elevated prose homilies merely indicated different sources, or streams, of preservation. The work has retained lasting interest on account of its drawing attention to the prose homilies contained in Jeremiah 1—25, which Mowinckel labeled Source C. Where Duhm had classed these as inauthentic to the prophet and of very late origin, Mowinckel insisted that the distinctive form of the material did not justify such a conclusion.

The question of the various style-forms employed in prophecy and its oral preservation and transmission before being committed to writing was to remain a continuing interest. It led in particular to a stimulating and provocative study entitled *Isaiah's Disciples (Jesaja disiplene* [1926]) and a more comprehensive treatment of Jeremiah, and of the nature of the prophetic literature in *Prophecy and Tradition*

(1946). Mowinckel remained convinced that oral and written preservation of oracular and instructional sayings went side by side. Prophets drew to themselves disciples who remembered the master's sayings. However, in the course of time the necessity to fix their preservation in written form became paramount and led to the formation of specific scrolls, or books. In the case of the study of the complex book of Isaiah Mowinckel went much further, being particularly struck by the close psalm-style of parts of the book, as well as noting the presence of prophetic speech-forms in the Psalms and also in the Decalogue of Exodus 20 (see Mowinckel *Le Décalogue* [1927]). In trying to find a comprehensive explanation for these features, Mowinckel posited that a group of Isaiah's disciples had maintained a long period of active work in Jerusalem, preserving prophecies from the great eighth-century figure but also writing psalms and establishing a basis for the later Deuteronomic movement. This was essentially an early essay in the field of what has come to be termed tradition history, in which the historical development of particular themes and motifs in literary works is traced.

It is noteworthy that this particular thesis was one that Mowinckel did not directly follow up and revise in his later writings, though the question of the formation of the prophetic writings from their original oral form to the written text remained a central interest. Similarly questions of poetic form and metrical structure were to continue to occupy his attention through his work as translator and literary historian.

The Psalms. In his period of study with Gunkel, Mowinckel had become aware of the importance of classification of type and formal structure for the understanding of the biblical Psalter. Gunkel saw this as a primary task still awaiting attention. Mowinckel's studies under Grønbech had provided the basis for a fresh approach to the whole subject. The most important aspect here was appreciation of the importance of religious cultus to ancient societies and of the way in which ritual served to unify and shape both the formal political structure of society and its piety. Accordingly cult was not a late, stereotyped and formalized growth out of an older and simpler folk piety. It was an ancient and comprehensive drama in which an entire community symbolized and enacted the annual renewal of its life.

Mowinckel saw this as a "cultic actualization" and recognized that Hebrew psalmody testified to the one-time existence in ancient Israel of this cult drama. Initially he published (in Norwegian) a first essay in this field with a study of the evidence that the Psalms offered of the status of the Israelite king (*Kongesalmerne i det Gamle Testamente* [1916]). In this Mowinckel argued that the king had played a central role in the temple cultus, embodying the divine life and persona, making him a form of divine incarnation. He followed this by a long essay in Norwegian (*Norsk Teologisk Tijdskrift* 18 [1917] 13-79) on the role played by the Israelite king in the fall festival.

This essay was followed by no fewer than six studies (*Psalmenstudien* 1-6 [1921-24]) in which further aspects of the Israelite psalm tradition were explored. Chief among these was a detailed study of the Israelite fall festival, titled "The Enthronement Festival" since he ascribed to it the groups of psalms (Ps 47, 95—100) that Gunkel had classed as enthronement psalms. These celebrated the role of God as king. However, a great many other psalms also owed their origin to this festival, the most important event of the Israelite calendar. Other studies examined the relationship between cultus and magic, in which Mowinckel argued that the distinctions are nowhere near as sharp as are usually supposed and that many psalms were composed as counterspells. A special feature of Mowinckel's interpretation was the claim that the enemies from whose power the psalmists sought deliverance were often believed to be persons wielding magical power. Another important study (*Psalmen-*

studien 3) was devoted to a study of the relationship between psalms and prophecy, noting many connections and positing the existence of cultic prophets in ancient Israel.

Surprisingly these studies gave little additional attention to the role of the Israelite king, without retracting any of the earlier claims. By the time of the publication of his later, extensively reworked interpretation of the Hebrew Psalms (*Offersang og Sangoffer* [1951]; ET *The Psalms in Israel's Worship* [1964]) Mowinckel came to reemphasize the role of the king, extending the number of psalms in which the cultic activity of the king was presupposed. He accepted that many psalms that complained of personal or national enemies presupposed that the king was the intended speaker.

Overall, the work on Hebrew psalmody has proved the most lasting area of Mowinckel's influence, particularly in its reconstruction of a rich and elaborate form of ritual and cultus for which the various classes of psalm had originally been composed. It recognized that formal public worship shaped the development of private piety and prayer and that nurtured patterns of oracular and prophetic utterance.

The Forms of Biblical Literature. Mowinckel's doctoral dissertation (1916) had been on the governorship of Nehemiah and had focused attention on the first-person form of the major source of the present book of Nehemiah as Nehemiah's memoir. He traced this form to types of royal *apologia* to which a number of ancient inscriptions bore testimony. Once again the role of the king assumed great significance. This was followed almost simultaneously by a study of Ezra the scribe (1916). Both studies were revised and republished with only relatively minor changes in 1964 and 1965.

These studies are important on two fronts. First they show the importance that Mowinckel attached to the task of the biblical scholar as historian and the necessity of making a close examination of primary source material for reconstructing historical developments. Both Nehemiah and Ezra had left accounts of their activities, couched in first-person memoir form, which were of prime value to the historian of postexilic Jewish development.

Second, this reconstruction period of Jewish history bore a primary relationship to the emergence of the written Mosaic law so that the latter needed to be understood in light of the activities of these men. Since the emergence of this written law in the postexilic period had been a major issue for nineteenth-century criticism, Mowinckel discerned the importance of anchoring religious and literary developments in a known history for understanding such a formative development of the biblical tradition.

In these early studies Mowinckel reveals his high regard for the historical task and in particular his respect and admiration for the work of Julius *Wellhausen. Form criticism, as advocated by Gunkel, could be a valuable tool for the historian, and in this respect Mowinckel was closer to the historical aims of Wellhausen than to the contemporary history of religions movement with which Gunkel was identified.

The study of the Decalogue (published in French [1927]) represented a further extension of Mowinckel's attention to the forms of prophetic psalmody, since its primary focus was on the divine use of the first-person speech form in the Ten Commandments. Such a usage must have had its origin in the cultus, so that Mowinckel drew sharply away from the earlier attempts to interpret these commandments against a background of legal, or didactic, forms.

Although he was a pioneering Scandinavian scholar who had challenged decisively many of the main currents of German literary criticism, Mowinckel did not follow the more radical attempts that emerged in Sweden in the 1930s to abandon the Graf-Wellhausen literary-critical explanation for the origin of the Hexateuch. Mowinckel accepted much of the major, four-document hypothesis with the proviso that oral and literary preservation of texts could continue

side by side. Accordingly he rejected the notion of an E (Elohist) documentary source, seeing this as a revised and supplemented form of the earlier J document in which additional oral material had been incorporated (J variatus; see Mowinckel, *Erwägungen zur Pentateuch Quellenfrage* [1964]).

With the publication in 1943 of Martin *Noth's major revision of the older literary source analysis of the six books of the Former Prophets, Mowinckel addressed several aspects of such a new hypothesis with enthusiasm (*Tetrateuch-Pentateuch-Hexateuch* [1964]). He saw great value in the more comprehensive and constructive approach that Noth's concept of a Deuteronomistic history brought. Nevertheless he also recognized that it overthrew too readily many of the reasons and insights that had led the nineteenth-century literary critics to think of a Hexateuch rather than a Pentateuch. He saw that Noth had not sufficiently addressed the questions relating to the way in which the later material contained in Joshua 13—19 related to the postexilic period and in particular to the Priestly document (P). Even more seriously, he felt that the formation of the Pentateuch, and with that much of the insights gained by the scholars of the Wellhausen era, required closer attention. If the idea of a Deuteronomistic history were to be upheld, it was essential to consider fully how and why this had been broken apart to join Deuteronomy to Joshua-Numbers.

In a similar regard Mowinckel was unwilling to approve of the more radical attempts on the part of the Uppsala school, which emerged in the 1950s, to speak only of a Tetrateuch and to deny the links between the book of Joshua and the traditions contained in Genesis-Numbers.

In recognizing the complex patterns of development of ancient religious literature, Mowinckel consistently argued that oral and literary composition were complementary, not radical alternatives. The two modes of creating and preserving documents were governed by varying needs and differing functions in society, so that the one naturally fed into the other. This led him to a general acceptance of the established methods and conclusions of the literary-critical school, which had been so strongly led by Wellhausen, but with a reasoned skepticism about many of its details. In particular he recognized that written source documents frequently contained far older traditions and laws, so that establishing the date of a documentary source did not fix with any certainty the date of its contents.

Kingship and the Messianic Hope. We have already noted the 1916 study in which Mowinckel argued for the major role played by the Israelite king in the worship of ancient Israel, especially regarding the king as symbolically enacting the role of God in an annual enthronement festival. Much of the evidence in support of this claim Mowinckel found in ancient Mesopotamian, especially Babylonian, culture, for which an increasing number of texts were becoming available. In Egypt too, the king was the "son of God." In the Babylonian festival, which heralded the beginning of a new year, the king fulfilled a divine role by bearing away the shortcomings of the year that had passed and renewing the divine gift of life. Mowinckel believed that this pattern of cultic renewal took place in Israel too, with the king playing a major role. The emergence of a radical future hope in Israel (eschatology) Mowinckel regarded as an outgrowth of this cultic pattern of renewal, projected into a more distant time.

Mowinckel had clearly leaned too heavily upon comparative evidence from non-biblical cultures in postulating this divine role for the Israelite king, and he set forth a much revised and distinctive interpretation in *Han Som Kommer* [1951]; ET *He That Cometh* [1956]). In this volume he recognized that each national culture carries distinctive features, so that the use of comparative evidence must be undertaken with caution. The Israelite king could cer-

tainly be seen from the evidence of the Psalter to have played a prominent role in ancient Israel's cultus but was certainly not thought of as a divine incarnation. Nevertheless high titles were ascribed to the king as God's representative on earth, and these eventually acquired new meaning and significance in giving birth to Israel's messianic hope.

This arose in the postexilic age, when the hopes of restoring a Jewish kingdom became progressively postponed and took on an increasingly radical form. It carried forward many of the older royal titles but filled them with new meaning. In this period too the original royal dimension of many psalms became obscured or deliberately expunged as the use of the Psalter in a political context where Jews lacked any native king became the norm. It has proved a major contribution from Mowinckel to have shown that the Israelite king, and more directly Israel's elevated religious interpretation of monarchy, displayed a remarkable uniqueness, even where they were rooted in the complex cultic life of the ancient Near East.

Significance. In Mowinckel's intellectual development, his early years show how strongly the history of religions movement influenced him. Yet he came to sense that it tended to reduce all religious achievement to antecedent impulses and prior levels, with little regard for uniqueness and creative individuality. Mowinckel's own spiritual commitment was deeply affected in 1934 by the Oxford Movement led by F. Buchman, which led him to look more attentively to the unique theological features of the Old Testament. The initial outcome of this more traditional and orthodox approach was a recognition of the limitations of a purely genetic-historical approach to the study of religion. His response is to be seen in *Det Gamle Testament som Guds ord* (1938; ET *The Old Testament as Word of God* [1960]), in which the uniqueness of the biblical revelation is stressed. One of its chapters is entitled "Away with Relativism!"

BIBLIOGRAPHY

Works. ScanJT 2 (1988) 95-168, for a full bibliography of Mowinckel's writings; S. Mowinckel, *Der achtundsechzigste Psalm* (Oslo: J.Dybwad, 1953); idem, *Le Décalogue* (Paris: Felix Alcan, 1927); idem, *Erwägungen zur Pentateuch Quellenfrage* (Oslo: Universitetsforlaget, 1964); idem, *Zur Frage nach dokumentarischen Quellen in Josua 13-19* (Oslo: J. Dybwad, 1946); idem, *He that Cometh* (New York: Abingdon, 1954 [1951]); idem, *Zum israelitischen Neujahr und zur Deutung der Thronbesteigungspsalmen; zwei Aufsätze* (Oslo: J. Dybwad, 1952); idem, *Jesaja-Disiplene: Profetien frå Jesaja til Jeremia* (Oslo: Aschehoug, 1926); idem, *Der Knecht Jahwäs* (Giessen: A. Töpelmann, 1921); idem, *Zur Komposition des Buches Jeremia* (Oslo: J. Dybwad, 1914); idem, *The Old Testament as Word of God* (New York: Abingdon, 1959 [1938]); idem, *Prophecy and Tradition* (Oslo: J. Dybwad, 1946); idem, *The Psalms in Israel's Worship* (New York: Abingdon, 1962 [1951]); idem, *Psalmstudien* (6 vols.; Oslo: Kristiania, 1921-24); idem, *Real and Apparent Tricola in Hebrew Psalm Poetry* (Oslo: Aschehoug, 1957); idem, *Studien zu dem Buche Ezra-Nehemia* (Oslo: Universitetsforlaget, 1964); idem, *Tetrateuch, Pentateuch, Hexateuch: die Berichte über die Landnahme in den drei altisraelitischen Geschichtswerken* (Berlin: A. Topelmann, 1964); idem, *The Two Sources of the Predeuteronomic Primeval History (JE) in Gen. 1-11* (Oslo: J. Dybwad, 1937).

Studies. D. R. Ap-Thomas, "An Appreciation of Sigmund Mowinckel's Contribution to Biblical Studies," *JBL* 85 (1966) 315-25; J. de Fraine, *Dictionaire de la Bible, Supplément* 5 (Paris: Letouzey et Ané, 1957) col. 1387-90; A. S. Kapelrud, "Sigmund Mowinckel and Old Testament Study," *ASTI* 5 (1967) 4-29; M. Saebø, "Sigmund Mowinckel," *TRE* 23, (1994) 384-88; idem, "Sigmund Mowinckel and His Relation to the Literary Critical School," *StT* 40 (1986) 81-93; D. Kvale and D. Rian, *Sigmund Mowinckel's Life and Works* (Oslo, 1984).

R. E. Clements

Noth, Martin *(1902-1968)*

One of the most provocative and influential Old Testament scholars of the twentieth century, Martin Noth was born in Dresden, Germany. He studied at the universities of Erlangen and Rostock and finally at Leipzig under Albrecht Alt and Rudolf Kittel. After teaching at Greifswald and Leipzig he was appointed to a professorship at Königsberg in 1930. In 1945 Noth accepted the position of professor of Old Testament theology at the University of Bonn, where he remained until 1965. Following his retirement he maintained his scholarly activity and served as the director of the German Evangelical Institute for the Study of the Holy Land *(Deutschen Evangelischen Institut für Alterwissenschaft des Heiligen Landes)* in Jerusalem. He died of a heart attack on May 30, 1968, while inspecting the ruins of Shivta (Subeita) in the Negeb desert.

Context. Noth's academic career spanned the years between World War I and World War II as well as the postwar era. His independent character and personal integrity are attested by the fact that he vigorously pursued his research interests during a period of time when Old Testament studies in Germany were exceedingly unpopular.

Noth's early work focused on the origins of ancient Israelite traditions contained in the Hexateuch. At twenty-six he published his study on the significance of Israelite personal names, *Die Israelitischen Personennamen im Rahmen der gemeinsemitischen Namengebung* (1928), which was followed by his analysis of the tribal structure of premonarchial Israel, *Das System der zwölf Stämme Israels* (1930). Both works reflect the influence of his mentor Albrecht Alt and represent a careful elaboration of his ideas (e.g., A. Alt, *Der Gott der Väter* [1929]).

The influence of Julius *Wellhausen is also apparent in Noth's scholarship. While he accepted Wellhausen's basic premise that the Pentateuch is comprised of four major documents or sources (J, E, D and P), Noth went on to conclude that a fifth, underlying tradition was detectable in the Tetrateuch. Noth's G, or *Grundlage*, source was proposed to explain the common elements in J and E in much the same way that Q has come to be viewed as a source used by the authors of the New Testament Gospels of Matthew and Luke. Noth went on to challenge the prevailing notion that the Pentateuchal sources continued on into the book of Joshua.

Unlike Wellhausen, who emphasized the literary formation of Israelite traditions from the time of the monarchy to the postexilic period, Noth was particularly interested in the preliterary origins of the biblical traditions. At this point one can see the influence Hermann *Gunkel had upon Noth's thought. He shared Gunkel's notion that J, E and P were collectors of traditions rather than authors and that the traditions they assembled could be traced back to their original, preliterary state as early as the time of the patriarchs and in some cases even earlier. Noth served as a bridge between Wellhausen and Gunkel in the sense that he viewed J, for example, as an imaginative editor-cum-author who forged the traditions he collected into a literary work that bore the unmistakable signature of his own creative historical and theological perspective. Whereas Gunkel tended to focus on the earliest, oral manifestations of biblical traditions and Wellhausen on the latest, written sources, Noth's attention was primarily on the intermediate period, that is, the period of the tribal confederacy when the preliterate traditions started coming together.

Although he was an accomplished literary critic, Noth, like Wellhausen, was essentially a historian. He viewed his detailed literary analysis not as an end in itself but rather as an instrument to be used in the service of the attempt to reconstruct an objective history of ancient Israel. Similarly Noth employed the results of geographical and archaeological studies in his analysis of biblical traditions. Unlike members of the Albright school (e.g., John Bright, George Ernest *Wright, Frank Moore Cross and William Foxwell *Albright himself), Noth often questioned the historical accuracy of the biblical traditions and the ability of archaeology to verify the historical veracity of the biblical accounts (Noth 1960). Nev-

ertheless Noth demonstrated his interest in and appreciation of the potential contributions of archaeological research by participating on several excavations and directing the German Archaeological Institute in Jerusalem near the end of his life. The accusation that Noth failed to take seriously the external evidence produced by archaeological investigations has been overstated and ignores his extensive familiarity with and use of archaeological information in his publications. He was more cautious in his interpretation of the archaeological data and viewed its implications as being much more ambiguous than did Albright and his students.

Major Themes. The major themes and issues to which Noth devoted most of his time and energy and for which he is best known can be summarized as follows: (1) the significance of the prestate, Israelite, tribal confederacy, or amphictyony; (2) The delineation of the form and content of the Deuteronomistic historical work; (3) the analysis of pentateuchal sources or documents and their preliterate, oral origins; (4) the origins and development of pentateuchal themes or traditions; and (5) the reconstruction of a comprehensive history of ancient Israel.

Like Alt, Noth's interests in biblical studies were exceedingly broad. Building on Alt's ideas regarding the early history of Israel, Noth's first major publication dealing with Israelite personal names (1928) and the nature of the tribal confederacy (1930) presented the conclusion that the Israelite confederacy was similar to early Greek amphictyonies. He also argued that the Canaanite origin of certain names suggested that the Israelite tribal amphictyony did not arise until after settlement or occupation of Canaan had occurred and consisted of originally independent, unrelated clan and tribal groups.

Brought together by their common worship of a single deity (Yahweh/Jahveh) at a central sanctuary (originally Shechem; Josh 24:1-27) housing the ark of the covenant, the various tribal traditions became intertwined and ultimately artificially connected by means of genealogies. The twelve-tribe structure of the amphictyony was maintained by the necessity of having representatives of each tribe perform priestly services at the central sanctuary for one month each year. During this prestate and premonarchial period, according to Noth, the prehistoric religious traditions (e.g., the worship of patriarchal deities and the El cult as articulated by Alt in *Der Gott der Väter)* came to be identified with Yahweh. It was also during this time that the patriarchal stories were united so that once-independent tribal traditions now formed a family history that fostered unity among the various components of the confederacy.

Noth's commentary on the book of Joshua, *Das Buch Josua* (1938), and his analysis of the historical works in the Old Testament, *Überlieferungsgeschichtliche Studien: Die sammelnden und bearbeitendes Geschichtswerke im Alten Testament* (1943) led him to dispute the dominant view that the pentateuchal sources J, E, D and P continued into the book of Joshua and beyond. Failing to find evidence of these traditions outside the Pentateuch, Noth concluded that the final Priestly redactor of the Pentateuch eliminated the conquest stories from J and E, since they were not contained in the P source. Noth further proposed that the books of Joshua, Judges, 1 Samuel and 2 Samuel, and 1 Kings and 2 Kings were produced by a single author whom he designated as the Deuteronomistic historian (Dtr.).

The Deuteronomistic historian, according to Noth, compiled his history of Israel from the time of the conquest to the Babylonian exile by utilizing existing historical sources and religious traditions (e.g., most of the book of Deuteronomy, the court history and succession narrative of 2 Samuel 9—20; 1 Kings 1—2 and numerous annals alluded to in the books of 1 Kings and 2 Kings). Writing during the time of the exile, the historian sought to explain the reasons for the destruction of the kingdoms of Israel and Judah. Noth came to similar conclusions in his analysis of the Chronicler's history (Chr.), arguing that 1 Chronicles, 2 Chronicles, Ezra and Nehemiah were produced by a single author during the third century B.C.

With minor modifications Noth's view of the Deuteronomistic historian, the Chronicler and the pentateuchal sources J, E, D and P has been adopted by many modern biblical scholars. Because of his work with the Former Prophets and the historical sections of the Bible, Noth is often referred to as the father of Deuteronomistic studies.

In *Überlieferungsgeschichtliche des Pentateuch* (1948; ET *A History of Pentateuchal Traditions* [1972]) Noth was concerned to go beyond the source criticism of Wellhausen and the form-critical analysis of Gunkel in order to explain the final structure and organization of material in the Pentateuch. Noth concluded, in agreement with Gerhard *von Rad *(Das formgeschichtliche Problem des Hexateuch* [1938]), that the cultic, confessional statements (e.g., Deut 26:5-9; 6:20-24; Josh 24:2-13), from the period of the confederacy, were the seeds from which the Pentateuch grew, defining both its form and content. He was confident not only that careful traditio-historical analysis could identify and isolate the basic themes of the ancient creeds and their elaboration in the Pentateuch but also that it was possible to determine their relative significance and age. Noth (1972, 46) wrote:

These confessional statements had as their content certain *basic themes* derived from Israel's own history which God had directed in a special way. These themes were not added to one another all at once in order to form the basis for the further expansion of the Pentateuchal tradition, but rather were joined together step by step in a definite sequence which can be determined in general. We can therefore put these themes in a definite order according to their traditio-historical priority.

Noth identified five major themes found in

both the early creeds (with the exception of the Sinai theme) and the Pentateuch. His listing of these themes in accordance with their importance also reflects his interpretation of the order in which they became incorporated into the religious tradition of Israel. The themes are guidance out of Egypt; guidance into the arable land; promise to the patriarchs; guidance in the wilderness; revelation at Sinai.

The absence of references to Sinai in the early creeds was taken as evidence that this was an originally independent tradition that was the last to be added to the matrix of Pentateuchal themes. Noth further argued that each of these themes originated in different, unrelated clan or tribal groups. As various groups joined the amphictyony their family traditions were combined with those of other members of the confederacy until on the eve of the monarchy these themes had become a coherent, all-Israelite religious history.

Noth's *A History of Pentateuchal Traditions* is among his most important publications. The influence of von Rad's *Das formgeschichtliche Problem des Hexateuch*, published ten years earlier, is apparent in Noth's analysis, although the conclusions reached by the two scholars are not identical. Largely because of these two publications von Rad and Noth became known as the fathers of the traditiohistorical approach to biblical studies.

In the English-speaking world Noth is best known for his *Geschichte Israels*, first published in 1950 (ET *History of Israel* [1960]). Widely used as a textbook throughout Europe and to a lesser extent in the United States, this publication draws together the previous twenty years of Noth's scholarship. In this work he expanded on Alt's original suggestion that apart from a few isolated, regional conflicts, the Hebrew occupation of Canaan was essentially the result of a series of peaceful migrations at the end of the Late Bronze Age rather than a violent military campaign as is presented by the Deuteronomistic historian in Joshua 1—12. Although Noth

relied heavily upon geographical and archaeological research, his treatment stands in stark contrast to John Bright's *A History of Israel* (1959) and has drawn frequent criticism from members of the Albright school.

Significance. Noth consistently refused to accept uncritically the methodology or conclusions of his predecessors or contemporaries. However, he was quick to recognize the value of different methodologies and employed them readily in his own research. Because of his eclectic approach and his creative genius, it is difficult to categorize Noth as a member of a particular school of thought, although he is sometimes referred to as an Altian. Although he was greatly influenced by Alt, as well as Julius Wellhausen, Hermann Gunkel and Gerhard von Rad, Noth's scholarship bears his own unique stamp. Despite his sometimes controversial assumptions and conclusions, Noth's scholarship is generally more rigorous and sound than is that of his detractors.

Along with his professor, Alt, and his contemporary, von Rad, Noth is universally recognized as one of the leading German Old Testament scholars of the twentieth century. His innovative scholarship has left an indelible mark on biblical studies and continues to influence the direction of Old Testament research.

BIBLIOGRAPHY

Works. M. Noth, "Der Beitrag der Archäologie zur Geschichte Israels" in *Congress Volume: Oxford, 1959* (VTSup 7; Leiden: E. J. Brill, 1960) 262-82; idem, *Das Buch Josua* (HAT 1.7; Tübingen: J. C. B. Mohr, 2d ed.; 1953 [1938]); idem, *Das dritte Buch Mose, Leviticus, übersetzt und erklärt* (2d ed.; ATD 6; Göttingen: Vandenhoeck & Ruprecht, 1966; ET *Leviticus: A Commentary* [Philadelphia: Westminster, 1965]); idem, *Gesammelte Studien zum Alten Testament* (Munich: Kaiser, 1957; ET in *The Laws in the Pentateuch and Other Studies* [2d ed.; Edinburgh and London: Oliver & Boyd, 1966]); idem, *Geschichte Israels* (2d ed.; Göttingen: Vandenhoeck & Ruprecht, 1954 [1950]; ET *The History of Israel* [rev. ed.; New York: Harper & Row, 1960]);

idem, "Hat die Bibel doch Recht?" in *Festschrift für Günther Dehn zum 75. Geburtstag* (Neukirchen-Vluyn: Neukirchener Verlag, 1957) 7-22; idem, *Die Israelitischen Personennamen im Rahmen der gemeinsemitischen Namengebung* (BWANT 3.10; Stuttgart: W. Kohlhammer, 1966 [1928]); idem, *Das System der zwölf Stämme Israels* (BWANT 4.1; Stuttgart: W. Kohlhammer, 1930); idem, *Überlieferungsgeschichtliche des Pentateuch* (Stuttgart: W. Kohlhammer, 1948; ET *A History of Pentateuchal Traditions* [Englewood Cliffs, NJ: Prentice-Hall, 1972]; idem, *Überlieferungsgeschichtliche Studien: Die sammelnden und bearbeitendes Geschichtswerke im Alten Testament* (Tübingen: Max Niemeyer, 1967 [1943]); idem, *Das vierte Buch Mose, Numeri, übersetzt und erklärt* (ATD 7; Göttingen: Vandenhoeck & Ruprecht, 1966; ET *Numbers: A Commentary* [Philadelphia: Westminster, 1968]); idem, *Die Welt des Alten Testaments: Einführung in die Grenzbegiete der alttestamentlichen Wissenschaft* (4th ed.; Berlin: Alfred Töpelmann, 1964; ET *The Old Testament World* [Philadelphia: Fortress, 1966]); idem, *Das zweite Buch Mose, Exodus, übersetzt und erklärt* (4th ed.; ATD 5; Göttingen: Vandenhoeck & Ruprecht, 1968 [1959]; ET *Exodus: A Commentary* [Philadelphia: Westminster, 1962).

Studies. S. L. McKenzie and P. M. Graham, eds., *The History of Israel's Traditions: The Heritage of Martin Noth* (JSOTSup 182; Sheffield: Sheffield Academic Press, 1994).

D. W. McCreery

Robinson, Henry Wheeler (1872-1945)

Henry Wheeler Robinson, an English Baptist theologian, is known principally as an Old Testament scholar and distinguished former principal of Regent's Park College, Oxford. He was born on February 7, 1872, and died on May 12, 1945.

Life. Variously described by his students and contemporaries as outstanding, a commanding presence, indefatigable and self-disciplined, Robinson was awe-producing. Others considered him as hypnotic in his authority, austere, possessed of great willpower and fearlessly honest in his thinking. Recognizing Robinson's limitations or darker aspects, one friend remembered him as "a Victorian . . . dressed soberly making little concession to changing seasons . . . addicted to tobacco . . . not naturally gracious whose friendliness seemed an act of will . . . shy, happiest when in the seclusion of his study . . . a lover of poetry and classical music . . . no interest in games or sport . . . chief hobby was walking." Robinson is described as he grew older as having become more genial and approachable: "his pipe, the love of a good story well told, and the fondness for detective fiction" mark the "human characteristics" that had always been present (*Baptist Quarterly* 24, 6 [April 1972]).

Robinson studied successively at Regent's Park College, London; the University of Edinburgh; Mansfield College, Oxford; and Marburg and Strasbourg universities (1890-1900). He became a Baptist minister (1900) and served two congregations (1900-1906) prior to his appointment as tutor at Rawdon Baptist College. Robinson established himself as a formidable teacher, scholar and churchman. He received various honors and was elected to many professional and ecclesiastical offices. He was awarded every major prize in his field at Oxford (e.g., prizes in Septuagint studies, Syriac, and Hebrew language). He was named president of the Yorkshire Baptist Association (1918), and in addition to his memberships in learned societies such as the London Society for the Study of Religion, the Baptist Historical Society, the Oxford Society of Historical Theology and the British Society for Old Testament Study, Robinson served the latter three as president. He was principal of Regent's Park College (1920-1942) and was instrumental in moving the college from London to Oxford in October 1927.

Work. Robinson's bibliography shows a remarkable scholarly productivity spanning more than thirty-seven years. Several strands of his concern became hallmarks of his biblical interpretation and revealed his religious commitments.

Robinson was given to historical interpretations of Scripture bearing on the articulation of Baptist principles and church government ("Interpretation of Congregationalism in the Sub-Apostolic Period" [1906] and "Baptist Principles before the Rise of Baptist Churches" [1911]). He also demonstrated a practical concern for the ever-significant task of proclamation of the gospel ("The Emphasis of Preaching," 1908).

Linguistic and grammatical observations on the biblical languages, as well as a wealth of information about Jewish religion and practices are found in his Century Bible contributions on Deuteronomy and Joshua (1907). As Robinson continued his career he wrote articles and/or volumes on every part of the Old Testament and included significant commentary on New Testament passages as well. Both skill and appreciation mark Robinson's contributions on Canticles, Hosea and Habakkuk for the eleventh edition of *Encyclopaedia Britannica*. Hebrew psychology became one of Robinson's later special contributions to biblical interpretation, with his first articulation of the issue coming as early as 1909 in "Hebrew Psychology in Relation to Pauline Anthropology."

Knowledge of several disciplines and fields of study is evident in Robinson's early writings. He discussed the relation of Old and New Testaments without sacrificing the integrity of either, and demonstrated a knowledge of patristics, Reformation and Post-Reformation history, science and currents of contemporary thought of human personality, as well as societal and moral issues. Substantial discussion of all these is present in *The Christian Doctrine of Man* (1911).

In his *Religious Ideas of the Old Testament* (1913, 1923, 1926) Robinson demonstrated the intellectual skills of clarity, distillation and logic as well as a literary acumen. The volume brought together what might well have been the beginning of a genre of biblical studies, a thematic approach to the Old Testament unlike those Old Testament theologies that had followed the outlines of dogmatic theol-

ogy. Later, in *Inspiration and Revelation in the Old Testament*, Robinson's first volume of a projected two-volume work, he made a form/content distinction for his Old Testament theology. The first volume was the form. It was properly prolegomenon demonstrating the action of God in nature, humanity, history and responses to God as found through the prophets, priests, psalmists and sages. Thus theology and history were wedded. Since his death prevented completion of the second volume, scholars will never know precisely whether the content of his Old Testament theology would have been articulated in propositions, topically, chronologically or in some other arrangement.

This listing from the first seven years is not the end of observations of Robinson's scope. His grasp of philosophical issues related to Christian theology is shown by *The Christian Experience of the Holy Spirit* (1928). His developing sense of Old Testament history and some of the insights of the nascent archaeological discipline were drawn together into *The History of Israel* (1938). Robinson recognized the need for solid and well-written introductory materials for both teachers and students. The latter concern is seen in *The Old Testament: Its Making and Meaning* (1937). Here is an introduction not given to the detailed critical analysis of which Robinson was capable. Instead he wrote for a more popular audience of the literary, historical and religious appreciation of Old Testament content. Robinson explained that he wrote for the beginning professional student as well as for "the ordinary reader of general education . . . to orientate him and to make the Old Testament more interesting as literature and more inspiring for religion" (Robinson 1937, preface).

The foregoing demonstrates that for sheer volume and variety as well as discipline and depth, one could scarcely find a finer exemplar of biblical and theological education than is set forth in the writings of Robinson.

Themes. The following themes are representative of Robinson's work, though the list is hardly exhaustive: the concept of suffering; corporate personality; the work of the Holy Spirit; time and history; attention to creation within wisdom literature; methodology and style of biblical and theological interpretation.

Robinson's *Suffering, Divine and Human* (1939) demonstrated a sophisticated understanding of both the theology involved and the condition of suffering humanity. Rather than referring to the problem of suffering, he chose to address God's suffering, anticipating or being current in a profound way with such conceptions as A. Heschel's divine pathos. Robinson quoted Patrick Fairbairn: "Theology has no falser idea than that of the impassibility of God." Three things came together for Robinson: the recognition of redemption by divine suffering, the suffering of the Lord Jesus Christ, and each person's fellowship with human sufferers. Robinson thought that such ideas were not solely theologically foundational but also should serve as significant pastoral aids.

Robinson's articulation of the Hebrew concept of corporate personality and its theological consequences has been a powerful antidote to the excessive individualism of many persons influenced by Western culture and theology. The conception recognized the social solidarity of the ancient Hebrew people in their relation to God, emphasizing the singular identity of individual, family, clan and nation. Corporate personality means that in community the individual has meaning only as one related to the group.

The theological consequences of corporate personality extended to such matters as the fluidity in identifying oneself with the group as the prophet did and interpreting the psalms of obviously individual experience as the experience of all. This makes sense of the psalmist's frequent transition between singular and plural because of the ready identification of one with the whole (i.e., the identity of the "I" of the psalms). Robinson suggested the concept as the key to unlock the mystery of the identity of the Servant of Yahweh in deutero-Isaiah. He also employed the concept to help explain New Testament ideas of atonement, the relationship of Jesus Christ to the church and the Pauline doctrine of human connection with Adam.

Robinson's view was not without its later critics, most telling of which is J. Rogerson. Nevertheless corporate personality was one of Robinson's most distinctive contributions to Old Testament study.

Robinson's *The Christian Experience of the Holy Spirit* (1928) considered issues such as the relation of the Holy Spirit to the church, the nature of the kingdom of God and the developments of trinitarian formulations, including challenges to them. The work extended to the problems for philosophical thought raised by the work of the Spirit and characteristically closed with the "practical value of the doctrine as restated" to individual Christians and congregations.

In Robinson's *Inspiration and Revelation in the Old Testament,* the section on "Time and Eternity" deals with the Hebrew vocabulary for time and the notion that "time and eternity are the ultimate constituents of history." With regard to history, Robinson coined the term *actuality* and its corresponding abstract noun, "actualization." Robinson wrote that history is properly "the continuous methodical record of events." We need a word to describe the quality or status of the event as that which has taken place once for all. We can hardly find a better term than "actuality." Since we know only interpreted and not bare events, Robinson also applied "actuality" to an interpreted event and speaks of such as becoming vital factors in history and thus able to be recognized as revelation of what God was doing in Israel's history.

The last half of the twentieth century has seen a plethora of studies in Wisdom Literature. Robinson's part six of *Inspiration and Revelation,* entitled "Revelation in Wisdom," shows he was one of the pioneers in such studies. While his explanation is short of W. Zimmerli's articulation of "wisdom theology as creation theology," Robinson saw them operating in the same intellectual territory. In the first section of the same work Robinson discusses the Hebrew conception of nature, creation and what we would call ecological theology, all by means of much attention to passages in wisdom books.

Three brief observations explore Robinson's methodology and style of biblical interpretation.

Trained in the classical style, knowing Greek and Latin early on, Robinson excelled in Hebrew and cognate languages during the course of his studies. Here was a scholar of extraordinary erudition who quoted quite naturally from the world's great literature of philosophy and poetry. He knew as well the work of his contemporaries, with the exclusion of the Scandinavian school of biblical scholars, whose work Robinson eschewed.

Despite the demanding tasks of administration Robinson was given to a continuous growth in learning. He used a burgeoning body of data coming from several quarters, including the budding archaeological finds of antiquity, textual studies and fresh critical observations. He has been said not easily to have changed his theological opinion, a matter that is demonstrated by comparison of early writing with the posthumous work, *Inspiration and Revelation.*

While Robinson used the biblical criticism of his day, it was always in combination with a special regard for the meaning of the texts and for how their teachings were of benefit to the church and Christian theology. By some standards Robinson must have seemed to share rather liberal views on matters of source criticism of the Pentateuch, the date of Daniel and other such litmus tests of orthodoxy, but clearly his biblical scholarship was always directed toward the ends of clearer understanding, practical application and deepening of personal faith.

Significance. O. Eissfeldt dedicated his *Einleitung des Alten Testaments* to three generations of British Old Testament scholars. Eissfeldt was aware of the immense contribution Robinson had made, and his way of acknowledgment was to dedicate his magnum opus of Old Testament learning in order to Robinson, H. H. Rowley and A. R. Johnson. Robinson was rightly considered the dean of Old Testament scholars.

Robinson also played an important role in the Society for Old Testament Study. Not only did he serve as president of the organization, but also he edited its systematic study of the Old Testament to which many distinguished scholars from Britain and the Continent were contributors (e.g., *Record and Revelation: Essays on the Old Testament,* 1938).

Finally, a case could be made for the thesis that Robinson spearheaded, quite without personal awareness of his doing so, a direction in biblical studies that came to be known as the biblical theology movement. Many of the elements of the new trends in biblical theology were present in his work. For example, consider his apparent commitment to historicogrammatical exegesis, the emphasis on Hebrew psychology, insistence on relating the Old and New Testaments through the exploration of quotations and by a limited typological exegesis, constancy in maintaining the value and practical application of his studies for growth in personal faith, recognition of the radical nature of sin, and stress on the revelational character of historical data. All these items of biblical and theological interest found their way into the biblical studies of the 1950s and early 1960s. Though the rise of the movement is attributed to the influence of others, Robinson would have applauded many of the directions taken in its study of the Bible. That scholars have come to an impasse with that approach should not reflect anything adverse toward Robinson.

Robinson was held in great esteem by colleagues and students and honored by generations of biblical scholars. One special, lasting tribute is found inscribed on a tablet at the entrance to the Regent's Park College Chapel: "He was a good man, and full of the Holy Spirit and of faith."

BIBLIOGRAPHY.
Works. H. W. Robinson, "Baptist Principles before the Rise of Baptist Churches" in *The Baptists of Yorkshire* (London: Kingsgate, 1911); idem, "Canticles," *Encyclopaedia Britannica* (11th ed.; 1911); idem, *The Christian Doctrine of Man* (Edinburgh: T & T Clark, 1911); idem, *The Christian Experience of the Holy Spirit* (Library of Constructive Theology series; ed. W. R. Matthews and H. W. Robinson; London: Nisbet, 1928); idem, *Deuteronomy* (NCB; Edinburgh: T C and E C Jack, 1907); idem, "The Emphasis of Preaching," *MCM* 6 (1908) 69-80; idem, "Habbakkuk," *Encyclopaedia Britannica* (11th ed.; 1911); idem, "The Hebrew Conception of Corporate Personality" in *Werden und Wesen des Alten Testaments,* ed. J. Hempel (BZAW 66; Berlin: Topelmann, 1936); idem, "Hebrew Psychology" in *The People and the Book,* ed. A. S. Peake (Oxford: Clarendon, 1925); idem, "Hebrew Psychology in Relation to Pauline Anthropology" in *Mansfield College Essays* (London: Hodder & Stoughton, 1909); idem, *The History of Israel: Its Facts and Factors* (The Studies in Theology Series; ed. N. Micklem; London: Duckworth, 1938); idem, "Hosea," *Encyclopaedia Britannica* (11th ed.; 1911); idem, *Inspiration and Revelation in the Old Testament,* ed. L. H. Brockington and E. A. Payne (Oxford: Clarendon, 1946); idem, "Interpretation of Congregationalism in the Sub-Apostolic Period" in *The Communion of Saints,* ed. J. H. Shakespeare (London: Baptist Union Publication Department, 1906); idem, *Joshua* (NCB; Edinburgh: T C and E C Jack, 1907); idem, *The Old Testament: Its Making and Meaning* (London Theological Library; ed. E. S. Waterhouse; London: University of London Press, 1937); idem, ed., *Record and Revelation: Essays on the Old Testament* (Oxford: Oxford University Press, 1938); idem, *Religious Ideas of the Old Testament* (Studies in Theology Series; ed. N. Micklem; London: Duckworth, 1913; eds. 1923, 1926); idem, *Suffering, Divine and Human* (Great Issues of Life Series; ed. R. Jones; New York: Macmillan, 1939). *Studies.* M. E. Polley, "Bibliography of H. Wheeler Robinson's Writings," *BQ* 24, 6 (April 1972) 296-322; J. Rogerson, "The Hebrew Concept of Corporate Personality: A Re-examination," *JTS* 21 (April 1970) 1-16.

R. A. Coughenour

Schlatter, Adolf *(1852-1938)*

Adolf Schlatter contributed more than four hundred publications to various fields of learning, including New Testament exegesis and theology, ancient Judaism, ethics, dogmatics, church history and philosophy, especially during forty years of academic and church involvement in the famous German university town of Tübingen.

Life and Work. Schlatter was born in St. Gallen, Switzerland, the seventh of nine children, and his early life was shaped by his parents' fervent Christian example. His father had left the Swiss state church to join a baptistic group years before Schlatter's birth. His mother could not bring herself to follow suit. Yet their marriage was free of religious rancor "because their faith was grounded in Jesus, not in the church" (Neuer 1995, 32), as Schlatter later observed. His lifelong ecumenical openness may be traced in part to his parents' example of unity in diversity.

Educated in Basel and Tübingen, Schlatter served in several pastorates (1875-1880). Theological conservatives in the Swiss church, aware of the intellectual gifts he had shown in his student years and concerned about the rise of theological liberalism in the Swiss theological faculties where pastors were trained, then persuaded him to try for a post as university lecturer in Bern. Against great odds Schlatter succeeded, serving with a dedication and pedagogical effectiveness that earned the respect of theological liberal and conservative alike.

Schlatter remained at Bern (1881-1888), lecturing in New Testament, historical theology and philosophy. Thereafter he served as professor of New Testament alongside H. Cremer in the northeastern Germany city of Greifswald (1888-1893). His work there was fruitful, but he yielded to a call to the prestigious University of

Berlin (1893), where as professor of systematic theology he counterbalanced the liberalism of his colleague Adolf von *Harnack. Yet the two men enjoyed a cordial, even warm, personal relationship.

Schlatter's Berlin years (1893-1898) ended when he assumed his longest and most productive post as professor of New Testament in Tübingen (1898-1922). He was also permitted to lecture in systematics. In Tübingen Schlatter weathered major personal blows in the form of his wife's sudden death (1907) and then later the loss of his youngest son, a promising history student, to battlefield injuries (October 1914). Schlatter never remarried. Two of his daughters remained single, caring for their father until his death and conducting ministries of their own, while a third daughter married a pastor and a second son entered the pastorate. The Schlatter heritage is still alive today among German and Swiss Pietists.

Following official retirement (1922), Schlatter continued to offer lectures and seminars for eight years. During this time his students included Ernst *Käsemann and E. Fuchs, who decided on a career in theology rather than law after hearing Schlatter lecture. After one hundred semesters of teaching, Schlatter devoted the strength of his final years to voluminous correspondence (his archives include more than eight thousand letters), various practical ministries and publication of nine critical commentaries, among other works. He died May 19, 1938, in Tübingen.

Schlatter's career spanned a complex era that began with neo-Kantianism's meteoric rise to prominence in Germany theology (Willey), extended through the heyday of dialectical theology in the 1920s and witnessed the tumult of Hitler's seizure of power in 1933. His writings offer solid scientific insight and creative Christian witness across a wide range of subjects.

Major Writings. Much of Schlatter's literary output was devoted to intertestamental and New Testament philology, exegesis and theology. Characteristic is his *Der Glaube im Neuen Testament (Faith in the New Testament),* first published in 1885. With a careful eye to Old Testament, rabbinic, and other relevant background data (e.g., the works of Polybius, Philo and Josephus), Schlatter produced an exhaustive examination of this key biblical word. The book is a model of diachronic word study. It was fitting that G. Kittel would later devote the first volume of the famous "Kittel" (*Theological Dictionary of the New Testament,* ten volumes) to his teacher Schlatter.

For some scholars, academic biblical research restricts or even eliminates association with Bible-believing churchgoers and their practical concerns. This was never the case with Schlatter. Over a twenty-three-year period (1887-1910) he produced a set of commentaries (*Erläuterungen zum Neuen Testament [Expositions of the New Testament]*) treating every New Testament book at an advanced lay level. Dozens of other books, articles and published sermons reflect a similar concern and gift for making the fruits of technical academic research available for the nurture and guidance of the church.

In his more technical exegetical publications Schlatter gained notoriety for refusing to take part in the scholasticism of his scholarly peers. Schlatter saw scholasticism at work "when the thinker no longer arrives at the object [of study] but deals only with the ideas of his predecessors" (*Die philosophische Arbeit seit Cartesius [History of Philosophy since Descartes],* 182). Schlatter claimed that when faced with the choice of mastering the ancient sources or modern secondary literature, he chose the former. As a result his exegesis is not dominated by quotes from other scholars or extended interaction with their writings. This gave rise to the occasional charge of "unscientific" from some of his peers.

Such charges, always somewhat gratuitous, were decisively refuted when in his last decade of life Schlatter published the fruit of years of thought and research in the form of nine critical commentaries. The

New Testament books covered and original dates of publication are Matthew (1929), John (1930), Luke (1931), James (1932), 1 Corinthians and 2 Corinthians (1934), Mark (1935), Romans (1935), 1 Timothy and 2 Timothy and Titus (1936) and 1 Peter (1937). All retain value and remain available in reprint editions.

Schlatter synthesized his New Testament interpretation in a two-volume New Testament theology, *Die Theologie des Neuen Testaments* (1909, 1910; 2d ed., 1920, 1922). Whereas Rudolf *Bultmann would later be done with Jesus in the first thirty-five pages of his New Testament theology, Schlatter's whole first volume of more than five hundred pages *(Die Geschichte des Christus [The History of the Christ])* deals with Christ's life and ministry. In recent times Tübingen *Neutestamentler* P. Stuhlmacher, who continues to champion aspects of Schlatter's hermeneutical and theological method, described Schlatter's difference from Bultmann as follows: "Schlatter saw in Jesus the Messianic Son of God. Therefore for Schlatter Jesus is the most important content of New Testament theology. . . . This is what furnished the basis for Schlatter's exegesis" (personal communication from P. Stuhlmacher, November 2, 1994). No less important were the methodological remarks that explained his rationale. His short treatise on New Testament theology is in some ways the most important of his few works yet translated into English (Schlatter 1973).

Schlatter's interests and competence extended beyond the areas of New Testament interpretation proper. He produced a systematic theology, *Das christliche Dogma (Christian Dogmatics),* in 1911 (2d ed., 1923) that is notable both for its unabashed confessional outlook and its strategically modern sophistication. Schlatter begins, for example, with anthropology, despite a high view of Scripture that might lead one to expect the Bible, Jesus Christ or God to occupy the book's opening sections. His approach, however, reflects his commitment to history as the medium of human life and human existence as the starting point of human observation and reflection; it does not signal complicity in the post-Enlightenment faith in the primacy of reason over revelation shared by most of his contemporaries. A measure of the intellectual depth undergirding his dogmatics is the metaphysical treatise that he composed (1915) at the urging of a Hungarian Lutheran correspondent, to relate his theological outlook to classic philosophical discussion. Long unpublished, *Metaphysik: Eine Skizze (Metaphysics: A Sketch)* finally appeared in 1987.

Two other important studies illustrate the volume (more than four thousand published pages between 1908 and 1915 alone), range and profundity of Schlatter's output. One is *Die christliche Ethik (Christian Ethics),* which appeared in 1914. It is surprisingly comprehensive in coverage and richly biblical in orientation. Praised in a German medical publication fifty years later for its "contemporary" and "timelessly valid" insights (Neuer 1995, 123), it was reprinted for the fifth time in 1986.

A second notable work is *Die philosophische Arbeit seit Cartesius* (3d ed., 1923; last reprinted 1981). With a familiar ease and philosophical acumen rarely found in biblical exegetes, Schlatter characterized the nature of modern thought as it first crystalized in Descartes. Passing on to Spinoza and Leibniz, he then deals extensively with Kant. Finally he turns to a selection of Kant's heirs: Fichte, Schelling, von Baader, Hegel, *Schleiermacher, Herbart, Schopenhauer and Nietzsche. He concludes with reflections clarifying the effect of philosophy on "the inner condition of Christentum" and defending the necessity of rigorous intellectual work by and within the church. This penetrating and suggestive volume is a condensation of lectures given first in Bern in the early 1880s and then later in Tübingen (1905-1906 and again in 1908). Decades later H. Thielicke praised it as a work of genius. Even when first published it received critical acclaim both from theologians and professional philosophers.

Biblical Interpreter. Studied assessment of Schlatter's biblical interpretation *per se* has barely begun in the English-speaking world. S. Dintaman's *Creative Grace*, appearing fifty-six years after Schlatter's death (1994), is the first and so far only English-language monograph seeking to characterize Schlatter's method and its underlying rationale (H. R. Dymale's University of Iowa dissertation [1966] was never published). In some ways Dintaman's findings echo those of W. Neuer). Dintaman rightly notes that in Schlatter's view persons receive "the form and content of their life from history and from the community that bears that history" (Dintaman, 53). Again, "A relationship to the resurrected One can arise in no other way than through a knowledge of his earthly work" (Dintaman, 64 n. 37).

Both of these characterizations of Schlatter's thought point to the importance of the Bible and of history in general, ancient and modern, for theological thought—not just as a concession to tradition (whether "Christian" or "critical") but as the marrow of sound theological reflection and construction. A primary contribution of Schlatter to biblical scholarship, then, is his highly sophisticated and multifaceted defense of Scripture (not "pure" reason, religious feeling or autonomous will) as primary source and arbiter for redemptive relatedness to the God who took on flesh in Jesus. As Dintaman notes, "Schlatter saw his mission as one of restoring to biblical scholarship the ability to see the presence and work of God within history" (Dintaman, 158), especially as that presence and work are attested by the biblical writings.

Amidst theology's and society's fragmentation and disarray, we can look for Schlatter's use of the Bible to draw increasing attention, since upon careful scrutiny "Schlatter does not look as naive at the end of the twentieth century as he did at the beginning of it" (Dintaman, 160).

Contribution and Significance. Schlatter's biographer, W. Neuer, underscores the following six aspects of Schlatter's abiding importance (Neuer 1994).

First is Schlattter's careful attention both to historical-philological exegesis and to theological-spiritual interpretation. He avoids each of two possible and common interpretive miscues: excessive focus on empirical detail to the distortion or exclusion of the theological verities that gripped the biblical writer; excessive devotion to a dogmatic system that forces itself onto the biblical material instead of letting the biblical material present its message in its own idiom and framework. Stuhlmacher (1978) has not been alone in noting that Schlatter deserves some of the credit usually accorded to Karl *Barth (who as a student heard Schlatter lecture) for insisting on a theological dimension to biblical interpretation in response to liberalism's tendency to ban it from consideration.

Second, Schlatter thoroughly investigated Hebrew, Jewish and rabbinic backgrounds as a more plausible historical and literary setting for understanding New Testament theology than the often exclusively Hellenistic sources that were in vogue at the time. To this end Schlatter produced a number of studies on Josephus, Jewish history from Alexander to Hadrian and rabbinic theology. Like other major New Testament scholars of his era, he wanted "to interpret from a history of religions point of view; but he wished to do so more effectively than those who counted themselves as members of the 'school' of this name" (Althaus, 96). For example, Schlatter intelligently advocated the Palestinian provenance of the Fourth Gospel at a time when the critical consensus sought its roots in Plato or Philo. The Dead Sea Scrolls have since vindicated his position decisively.

Third, he made a concrete ethical application of the New Testament in the light of his theologically positive (though not naive) view of nature as God's creation. Not only traditional concerns like marriage, family and the state come into view; elements of an ecological ethic are visible long before late-twentieth-century ecological awareness arose. Schlatter deftly links a creation ethic (in which he endorses the idea of natural law) with a discipleship ethic; the ultimate norm for the latter is the love of God revealed in Jesus Christ.

Fourth, Schlatter insisted that despite the necessity of the Reformation, it is time to transcend old impasses and for Christendom as a whole to reform yet further. Schlatter's special penchant for the epistle of James, devalued by Martin *Luther and much of Protestantism ever since, constitutes an ecumenical bridge toward gospel-minded Roman Catholics. While he was not critical of Reformation and Protestant scholastic dogmatics in their place, he was critical of their ultimate shortcomings. One of these was too little attention to practical service, flowing from the divine presence among God's people as expressed in active love. The ultimate goal of grace is not right doctrine alone, purely intellectual didactic abstraction, but active interpersonal and social activity—love manifested through the gospel's power in the church—as the necessary embodiment of doctrine.

Fifth, he worked out a coherent critical realism as a historian and philosopher. In today's postmodern climate and attendant epistemological relativism, Schlatter remains a wise and literate guide: "In his systematic works but most of all in his *Metaphysik* he developed an epistemology which grounded the knowability of reality and therefore the possibility of objective truth. He also unfolded an understanding of reality that sought to avoid every form of ontological reduction and to do full justice to the fullness of what is real" (Neuer 1994). Schlatter's work challenges the post-Kantian hegemony of contentless faith; at the same time it faults traditional conservatism for refusing to engage in the hard work of thinking, as the last words of *Die philosophische Arbeit* (241) suggest: "In order to teach, [the church] must think; for without thinking there is no knowing. This necessity, that [Christians] must think, stands as one of the bedrock results of the course and outcome of the history of phi-

losophy we have surveyed."

Sixth, Schlatter understood biblical and theological scholarship as a means of service to other Christians, to the church and to as yet unchurched society. Hardly less striking than Schlatter's prodigious scholarly output is his consistent involvement in innumerable pastors' conferences, retreats for students and professionals from various fields, women's Bible study circles, mission weekends, and the like. He spoke and wrote for both trained and lay readers. From 1888 until 1936 he opened his home each Monday evening to students of any major. Schlatter, cigar box under his arm, would enter the room, shake hands with each visitor and then field whatever questions might be posed. One student recalled, "Schlatter was always great, because he breathed the air of eternity" (Neuer 1995, 137). Another summarized his academic effectiveness with the words: "He gave himself!"

BIBLIOGRAPHY

Works. A. Schlatter, *Der Brief des Jakobus* (Stuttgart: Calwer, 1956 [1932]); idem, *Das christliche Dogma* (Stuttgart: Calwer, 1977 [1911, 1923]); idem, *Die christliche Ethik* (Stuttgart: Calwer, 1961 [1914]); idem, *The Church in the New Testament Period* (London: SPCK, 1955); idem, *Erläuterungen zum Neuen Testament* (10 vols.; Stuttgart: Calwer, 1961-1965 [1887-1910]); idem, *Der Evangelist Johannes: Ein Kommentar zum vierten Evangelium* (Stuttgart: Calwer, 1930); idem, *Der Evangelist Matthaus* (Stuttgart: Calwer, 1948); idem, *Das Evangelium des Lukas* (Stuttgart: Calwer, 1929); idem, *Der Glaube im Neuen Testament* (Stuttgart: Calwer, 1963 [1885]); idem, *Die Kirche der Griechen im Urteil des Paulus: Eine Auslegung seiner Briefe an Timotheus und Titus* (Stuttgart: Calwer, 1958 [1936]); idem, *Markus: Der Evangelist für die Griechen* (Stuttgart: Calwer, 1935); idem, *Metaphysik* (Tübingen: J.C.B. Mohr, 1987); idem, *Paulus, der Bote Jesus: Eine Deutung seiner Briefe an die Korinther* (4th ed.; Stuttgart: Calwer, 1969 [1934]); idem, *Petrus und Paulus nach dem ersten Petrusbrief* (Stuttgart: Calwer, 1937); idem, *Die philosophische Arbeit seit Cartesius nach ihrem ethischen und religiösen Ertrag* (Stuttgart: Calwer, 1959

[1906]); idem, *Romans: The Righteousness of God* (Peabody, MA: Hendrickson, 1995 [1935]); idem, *Die Theologie des Neuen Testaments* (2 vols.; Stuttgart: Verlag der Vereinsbuchhandlung, 1909, 1910; ET Vol. 1 [2d ed., 1923]: *The History of the Christ: The Foundation for New Testament Theology* [Grand Rapids: Baker, 1997]); idem, "The Theology of the New Testament and Dogmatics" in R. Morgan, *The Nature of New Testament Theology* [SBT 2d series 25; London: SCM, 1973]).

Studies. P. Althaus, "Adolf Schlatters Wort an die heutige Theologie," *ZST* 21 (1950) 95-109; S. Dintaman, *Creative Grace: Faith and History in the Theology of Adolf Schlatter* (New York: Peter Lang, 1994); W. Neuer, *Adolf Schlatter,* trans. R. Yarbrough (Grand Rapids: Baker, 1995); idem, *Adolf Schlatter: Ein Leben für Theologie und Kirche* (Stuttgart: Calwer, 1996); idem, "Schlatter, Adolf (1852-1938)" in *ELTG* 3, ed. H. Burkhardt with O. Betz (Wuppertal: Brockhaus, 1994); P. Stuhlmacher, "Adolf Schlatter's Interpretation of Scripture," *NTS* 24 (1978) 433-446; idem, "Jesus of Nazareth as Christ of Faith" in *Jesus of Nazareth—Christ of Faith* (Peabody, MA: Hendrickson, 1993) 1-38; T. Willey, *Back to Kant: The Revival of Kantianism in German Social and Historical Thought, 1860-1914* (Detroit: Wayne State University Press, 1978). R. W. Yarbrough, "Adolf Schlatter's 'The Significance of Method for Theological Work': Translation and Commentary." *SBJT* ½ (Summer 1997) 64-76.   R. W. Yarbrough

Schweitzer, Albert *(1875-1965)*

Albert Schweitzer was one of the truly incredible and wide-ranging minds of the twentieth century. His written productivity is impressive in quantity, range and quality. He published more than thirty major works on philosophy, theology, biblical studies and music. Approximately one-third are on important issues in biblical and theological studies. This remarkable man has attracted much attention from both academics and the general public. A 1981 comprehensive bibliography (Griffith and Person) lists more than five thousand items.

Born the son of a Lutheran pastor on January 14, 1875, in Kaysersberg, Upper Alsace, Germany, Schweitzer studied philosophy, theology and music theory at the University of Strasbourg. Following a brief stint in the military, he returned to Strasbourg and received a doctorate in philosophy and one year later a doctorate in theology. In 1913 he acquired a medical doctorate, and beginning that year he spent much of his life as a medical missionary in Lambaréné, in the Gabon province of French Equatorial Africa, building a hospital and leper colony. It was primarily his work as jungle doctor that endeared him to the public. He was an accomplished organist and a devout humanitarian, winning the Nobel Peace Prize in 1952 for his efforts on behalf of "the brotherhood of nations." He died September 4, 1965, as one of the most famous men in the world.

Work. The general direction of Schweitzer's analysis of Jesus and the early Christian writings is due in large part to the influence of his religion teachers at the University of Strasbourg, most of whom were German. Many of these professors became his friends, and he grew to have the highest regard for their contributions to an understanding of Jesus and the early church. Schweitzer's principal New Testament teacher, who was also the foremost German New Testament scholar at the time, was H. J. Holtzmann. By Schweitzer's era the Gospels, in terms of their historical value, were viewed with suspicion by the vast majority of prominent Protestant biblical scholars in Germany.

Schweitzer's contribution to New Testament studies is found in four main books, the first of which he published in 1901, when he was twenty-six years old. *Das Abendmahl im Zusammenhang mit dem Leben Jesu und der Geschichte des Urchristentums* (1901; ET of second part: *The Mystery of the Kingdom of God* [1914]), his clearest presentation of his views on the subject, was not widely or well received. His second work, the one for which he is most famous in the field of biblical studies, was *Von Reimarus zu Wrede: Eine Geschichte der Leben-Jesu Forschung* (1906), published under the English title of *The Quest of the*

Historical Jesus (1910). A significantly expanded second edition appeared in 1913. Because it addressed the whole life of Jesus and was so well-written, it reached a wider public than do most scholarly books.

This landmark title in retrospect can be viewed as the epitaph to the nineteenth-century liberal quest for the historical Jesus. In his masterfully thorough and penetrating review of all (mostly German) significant prior attempts to write a life of Christ, Schweitzer showed that the enterprise was hopeless because the materials do not exist for writing a modern biography. The nineteenth-century, mostly liberal, lives of Jesus were in essence projections of the authors who were reading their own contemporary and relevant image of Jesus into the ancient sources. In this liberal framework, the kingdom of God has to do with the fatherhood of God, the brotherhood of humanity and the attempt to establish the kingdom through love and good will. It was fifty years before there was another significant German attempt to write the life of Christ.

Having dispensed with the "liberal Jesus" and having set forth his own view of Jesus as a mistaken apocalyptic preacher firmly rooted in his own time, Schweitzer turned to Paul to explain how Christianity developed into an organized religion. In *Geschichte der paulinischen Forschung von der Reformation bis auf die Gegenwart* (1911; ET *Paul and His Interpreters* [1911]) Schweitzer surveyed the history of Pauline criticism. In *Die Mystik des Apostels Paulus* (1930; ET *The Mysticism of Paul the Apostle* [1931]) he interpreted the apostle in light of Jewish apocalyptic and in ways consistent with Schweitzer's understanding of Jesus. Paul's mysticism is an eschatological mysticism, which Schweitzer distinguished from the pantheistic mysticism of Hinduism, for example.

It is Schweitzer's interpretation of Jesus and his teaching, especially regarding the kingdom of God, that has had the most influence on subsequent New Testament studies. In this regard Schweitzer developed and popularized the views first presented by Johannes *Weiss, who argued that the kingdom as proclaimed by Jesus was an entirely future cataclysmic act of God. Weiss limited his study to Jesus' teaching; Schweitzer extended Weiss's finding to the entire life of Jesus, championing what he called a "thoroughgoing eschatology" *(konsequente Eschatologie)*. Further, according to Schweitzer, Jesus was convinced he was the one chosen by God to bring about the end time. The kingdom of God in Jesus' teaching, in Schweitzer's view, was firmly set in the context of first-century Jewish apocalyptic. Schweitzer's view, apparently, in large measure was derived early in his studies as a result of his reflections on the mission of the Twelve (Mt 10), which Schweitzer saw as a literal account of Jesus sending out the disciples. Schweitzer has been criticized for basing too much of his subsequent work on his reading of this text.

Schweitzer said that the central feature of Jesus' life and teaching was his expectation of the coming eschatological kingdom of God in the immediate future, specifically at harvest time of the year in which he spoke the words of Matthew 10. For Jesus the appropriate ethical response to this apocalyptic proclamation is repentance and moral renewal in preparation for the coming kingdom. The ethic is, in a term coined by Schweitzer, an interim ethic *(Interimsethik)* because it will be in force only during the short period between the proclamation of the coming kingdom and its actual coming.

Jesus was convinced he was the hoped-for Jewish Messiah sent by God, the instrument for bringing in the end time. He sent his disciples out with the message of the coming kingdom of God in order to hasten the process. In apocalyptic thinking, things must get worse before they get better. The disciples will encounter the final woes and the end will arrive: "See, I am sending you out like sheep into the midst of wolves . . . they will hand you over to councils and flog you. . . . You will be dragged before governors and kings. . . . I have not come to bring peace, but a sword" (Mt 10:16-18, 34). Jesus did not expect the disciples to return: "You will not have gone through all the towns of Israel before the Son of Man comes" (Mt 10:23). The turning point in Jesus' life came when the disciples did return and with no kingdom in sight. Jesus decided he must personally suffer death in order to force in the kingdom of God. About A.D. 30 Jesus entered Jerusalem, disrupting the temple and challenging those in authority. As Jesus expected, he was arrested and condemned to the cross. He died in despair and disillusionment because there was no sign the kingdom of God was coming.

Since Jesus' program failed, a deeschatologizing of Jesus' preaching about the kingdom of God developed, which brings us to Paul as a key figure in the process. In Schweitzer's day, Paul was increasingly being read against a Hellenistic Jewish background. As with his interpretation of Jesus, Schweitzer viewed Paul primarily in light of Jewish apocalyptic. Paul's theology of mystical redemption through being "in Christ" (Greek *en Christ*) overshadows his view of salvation through faith. According to Schweitzer, in an internalization of the coming kingdom, Paul saw Jesus being resurrected into the life of the early believers.

Prior to Schweitzer's *Quest of the Historical Jesus* (1906), William *Wrede had published *Das Messiasgeheimnis in den Evangelien* (1901; ET *The Messianic Secret in the Gospels* [1971]). Along with Schweitzer's book, Wrede's work successfully challenged the old liberal quest. Wrede, however, offered an alternative solution to Schweitzer. Wrede interpreted the secrecy motif in the Gospels as a creation of the disciples to explain why Jesus had not been recognized as the Messiah during his lifetime. The larger significance of Wrede's work is in seeing the Gospels as theological rather than historical, a framework later thoroughly developed by redaction criticism. Whereas Wrede saw the Gospel writers as "theologians," Schweitzer saw Jesus as such.

Significance. The thoroughgoing eschatological interpretation of Jesus was negatively received in Schweitzer's day. It became, however, a dominant scholarly interpretation of Jesus and framed much of the subsequent discussion. The program of Weiss and Schweitzer raised the possibility of a tension between the historical Jesus' proclamation of the kingdom of God and its continuing relevance. It has generally been accepted by scholars that the kingdom of God in Jesus is an apocalyptic concept. Its futuristic orientation, however, has been interpreted in a variety of ways. Some interpreters followed Schweitzer in viewing the kingdom as future in Jesus' teaching, some saw it as present, and others saw it as both future and present. Still others reframed the issues (e.g., Rudolf *Bultmann's existentialist interpretation and Charles Harold *Dodd's realized eschatology) or denied the apocalyptic interpretation altogether (e.g., W. Rauschenbusch).

Schweitzer's personal humanitarian commitment, given his scholarly belief in a Jesus who was a "stranger," that is, one who held to an antiquated and mistaken worldview, has intrigued and puzzled many people. In Schweitzer's analysis the historical Jesus is indeed irrelevant to theology and to the modern world. It is Jesus' heroic spirit, which lives on in the hearts of people, that moved Schweitzer to a life of serving humanity in Africa. Schweitzer's ethical reflections, such as his "reverence for life" as a foundation for rebuilding culture, are not, however, to be understood only in reference to his scholarly analysis of Jesus. Schweitzer developed his ethic in conversation with various philosophical systems, apart from his biblical works. This is not to deny that in some paradoxical and mysterious way, Schweitzer was moved by the spirit of Jesus. Along this line, the concluding paragraph in *Von Reimarus zu Wrede* sums up his scholarly and personal understanding of Jesus. The paragraph, perhaps the most famous he ever penned, bears repeating:

He comes to us as One unknown, without a name, as of old, by the lake-side, He came to those men who knew Him not. He speaks to us the same word: 'Follow thou me!' and sets us to the tasks which He has to fulfill for our time. He commands. And to those who obey Him, whether they be wise or simple, He will reveal Himself in the toils, the conflicts, the sufferings which they shall pass through in His fellowship, and, as an ineffable mystery, they shall learn in their own experience Who He is. (Schweitzer 1910, 403)

BIBLIOGRAPHY

Works. A. Schweitzer, *Das Abendmahl im Zusammenhang mit dem Leben Jesu and der Geschichte des Urchristentums* (1901), ET of second part as *The Mystery of the Kingdom of God: The Secret of Jesus' Messiahship and Passion* (New York: Dodd Mead, 1914); idem, *Geschichte der paulinischen Forschung von der Reformation bis auf die Gegenwart* (Tübingen: J. C. B. Mohr, 1911; ET *Paul and His Interpreters: A Critical History* [New York: Macmillan, 1912]); idem, *Die Mystik des Apostels Paulus* (Tübingen: J. C. B. Mohr, 1930; ET *The Mysticism of Paul the Apostle* [New York: Henry Holt, 1931; 2d ed., 1953]); idem, *Die Psychiatrische Beurteilung Jesu: Darstellung und Kritik* (Tübingen: J. C. B. Mohr, 1913; ET *The Psychiatric Study of Jesus: Exposition and Criticism* [Boston: Beacon, 1948]); idem, *Reich Gottes und Christentum* (Tübingen: J. C. B. Mohr, 1967; ET *The Kingdom of God and Primitive Christianity* [New York: Seabury, 1968]); idem, *Von Reimarus zu Wrede: Eine Geschichte der Leben-Jesu Forschung* (Tübingen: J. C. B. Mohr, 1906; ET *The Quest of the Historical Jesus: A Critical Study of Its Progress from Reimarus to Wrede* [2d ed.; New York: Macmillan, 1911 (1910)]).

Studies. C. K. Barrett, "Albert Schweitzer and the New Testament," *ET* 87, 1 (October 1975) 4-10; J. Brabazon, *Albert Schweitzer: A Comprehensive Biography* (London: Victor Gollancz, 1976); N. S. Griffith and L. Person, *Albert Schweitzer: An International Bibliography* (Boston: G. K. Hall, 1981); J. L. Ice, *Schweitzer: Prophet of Radical Theology* (Philadelphia: Westminster, 1971); J. M. Murry, *The Challenge of Schweitzer* (London: Jason, 1948); W. Picht, *The Life and Thought of Albert Schweitzer* (New York: Harper & Row, 1964); G. Seaver, *Albert Schweitzer: Christian Revolutionary* (New York: Harper, 1944); idem, *Albert Schweitzer: The Man and His Mind* (New York: Harper, 1947).

C. R. Mercer

Von Rad, Gerhard *(1901-1971)*

At the turn of the twentieth century Old Testament scholarship had become increasingly atomistic, with ever-new layers being detected in the Pentateuch and late glosses being located in prophetic and narrative texts. The form-critical approach championed by Hermann *Gunkel and carried through with such effectiveness in a commentary on Genesis and to some extent in Psalms depended on the isolation of the smallest oral units underlying longer written texts. The older source criticism, applied with increasing exactitude to the Pentateuch, also focused on brief phrases or single words and tended to ignore the final form of a given text.

At the same time, various approaches to interpretation added to a sense of atomization, resulting in something of a stalemate. Historians of religion emphasized the phenomena of Israel's religious practice. Biblical theologians insisted on a pneumatic (spiritual) interpretation of the faith described in the Bible. Conservatives and skeptics, enthusiasts and the uncommitted vied for dominance in journals and monographs.

Born on October 21, 1901, into a patrician medical family of Nuremberg, Gerhard von Rad felt the power of these competing approaches to the Bible but resisted them as well. Like historians of religion, he recognized the importance of history to religious belief, but he refused to equate the two. Like the pneumatics, he viewed the history of Israel as the result of the Spirit leading ever onward toward the New Testament, but his typology included both promise and fulfillment in each Testament. He adopted a skeptical stance toward the facts of history, but his unique approach exalted ancient Israel's confessions of the saving acts of its God.

Life. After studying at Erlangen and Tübingen, von Rad entered the pastorate in the Bavarian national church in 1925. He soon returned to academic pursuits, completing a dissertation at Erlangen under the direction of Otto Procksch (*The People of God in Deuteronomy,* 1929). Here he taught briefly, writing *The Chronicler's View of History* (*Das Geschichtsbild des chronistischen Werkes* [1930]) and studying Semitics with Albrecht Alt at Leipzig. In 1930 he was invited to teach at Leipzig, where he prepared himself to work in archaeology and wrote important studies on the tent and the ark, false prophecy, the concept of rest and the priestly writing in the Hexateuch. In 1934 he moved to Jena, where he taught few students but was active in the underground resistance of the church against National Socialism. He addressed this issue directly in *The Old Testament: God's Word for the Germans* (*Das Alte Testament—Gottes Wort für die Deutschen!*) A brief book on Moses (*Mose* [1940]) signaled a skepticism bathed in evangelical fervor.

With the publication of *The Form-Critical Problem of the Hexateuch* (*Das formgeschichtliche Problem des Hexateuch* [1938]) von Rad moved into the front ranks of Old Testament scholars. Other important publications followed: "Notes on the Royal Psalms," "The Beginnings of Historical Writing in Ancient Israel," "The Promised Land and Yahweh's Land in the Hexateuch" and "The Basic Problems of a Biblical Theology of the Old Testament."

From the summer of 1944 until June of 1945 von Rad knew the rigors of military service; from mid-March of 1945 to June he was a prisoner of war at Bad Kreusnach. After teaching briefly at Bethel, Bonn and Erlangen, he moved to Göttingen, where he taught until 1949. Here he wrote *Studies in Deuteronomy* (1948) and the first fascicle of *Genesis.* A move to Heidelberg occurred in 1949, where he taught until retiring in to Göttingen in 1967. At Heidelberg he wrote his most influential works, especially *Old Testament Theology*

(1957-1960), *Holy War in Ancient Israel* (1951), *Genesis* (1956), *Deuteronomy* (1964), *Wisdom in Israel* (1970), *The Sacrifice of Abraham* (*Das Opfer des Abraham* [1971]), and more. Here also he lectured and preached to huge audiences.

Von Rad's stature in the discipline led to membership in the Heidelberg Academy of Sciences and the *Order pour le merite* for Science and Art. He was awarded five honorary degrees (Leipzig, Glasgow, Lund, Wales, Utrecht), accorded honorary membership in the Society of Biblical Literature and the British Society for the Study of the Old Testament, and was the recipient of two festschriften plus a memorial volume.

On being inducted into the Heidelberg Academy of Sciences, von Rad commented on his own career, noting the good and the bad. The positive influences were his birth in the patrician class, which taught him respect for tradition, and the influence of Alt. The negative, which he openly opposed, was the atomization of Old Testament scholarship and excessive systematization. Von Rad insisted that the Old Testament itself should dictate the form of a theology, specifically confessional historical statements. On yet another occasion he observed that he read to learn and read to teach. In his view a radical gulf existed between the ancient world and the modern. He emphasized the final form of a text, the whole unit, and viewed the ever-new interpretation in the light of God's action in history. Von Rad also mentioned his struggle against National Socialism.

In an obituary K. Rahner observed that von Rad treasured the silence of God and was rewarded with this mystic silence. His death occurred on October 31, 1971. Besides leaving a legacy of scholarly interpretation and influencing numerous students, von Rad also left examples of his preaching and meditation. His next to last sermon at St. Peter's Church was on Joshua 5:13-15. To a campus divided by Marxists and Social Democrats he identified the falsest of questions, "Are you for us or against us?"

Interpretative Stance. Von Rad's primary interest, a history of tradition, is best illustrated in his book on holy war. Conjecture prevails, for he assumes that a huge mountain of traditions associated with a (hypothetical) Solomonic enlightenment obscured early from late material. He begins by constructing a model from texts dealing with holy war that he takes to be early; then he tests the construct by applying it to other texts. The whole process is circular, and the picture is an idealized one. Assuming that Israelite religion before Solomon was pansacral, von Rad insisted that a new humanism arose in the Solomonic court, the cultivation of the individual. Prior to the monarchy, holy war was voluntary and defensive. Kings altered the nature of war, mobilizing a professional army and going on the offense to enlarge their territory and fill their treasury. Von Rad thinks of four decisive stages: ancient holy war, post-Solomonic "historical" accounts, prophecy and Deuteronomy. Isaiah revitalized and internalized the idea of holy war and the demand for faith. Deuteronomy actualized it, with catastrophic consequences. After that debacle, the concept was entirely spiritualized.

In an article on the traditions of the ark and the tent, written twenty years earlier, von Rad had used a method that began at the final stage of a tradition and worked backward. He understood the ark as a symbol of divine presence, an enthronement of an invisible deity. The tradition of the tent was associated with the God who comes in a theophany. Two competing traditions thus referred to divine accompaniment and meeting, immanence and transcendence. Above all, von Rad argued, Yahweh was a God of history. In *The Form-Critical Problem of the Hexateuch* he developed the theory that a brief confessional statement, a historical credo, gave rise to the entire Hexateuch, Genesis through Joshua. This credo (Deut 26:5-9; 6:20-24; Josh 24:2-13) underwent free adaptation in cult lyrics (1 Sam 12:8; Ps 136; Exod 15; Ps 105; 78; 135) and was eventually embellished with elements of the Sinai tradition (Neh 9:6-37; Ps 106). The core tradition testifies to divine activity in settling Israel within the promised land, whereas the Sinai tradition of covenant making and theophany deals with divine justice. In von Rad's view creation played a subordinate role in Yahwism, the Canaanite threat of fertility religion being overcome by Deutero-Isaiah's transformation of themes from the exodus to fit the myth of creation, specifically the battle against chaos. One additional tradition complex caught von Rad's eye, that of David and Zion, representing Yahweh's anointed and his holy city. In peeling off layer after layer of tradition von Rad emphasized the centrality of the cult as the locus of each tradition. For him Deuteronomy functioned as a compass; he returned to it twice in publications after his dissertation. He understood it as levitical preaching of the law, a theology of the name, and situated its final form in a late era when a chastened people faced a choice similar to that confronting Moses' companions.

With publication of "Some Aspects of the Old Testament World View" and *Wisdom in Israel* von Rad moved away from exclusive tracing of Yahweh's redemptive history to warn against excessive emphasis on history. He also gave up his tradition-historical approach when wisdom literature resisted such interpretation. His last three publications (*Wisdom in Israel*, "Doxology of Judgment" and *The Sacrifice of Abraham*) wrestle in one way or another with divine silence perceived at times as abandonment.

Who were the transmitters of Israel's traditions? Von Rad identified the following: the Yahwist, Elohist, Deuteronomist, Priestly writer, Chronicler, prophets and sages. Refusing to believe that the Yahwist was merely a collector, von Rad praised the author's literary craft and theological subtlety. Rejecting Martin *Noth's theory of a Tetrateuch and the traditional linking of the first five books into a Pentateuch, von Rad claimed that the theme of promise and fulfillment runs from Genesis to Joshua. The Yahwist collected four cycles of tradition about Abraham, Isaac, Jacob and Joseph, then derived his outline from the settlement tradition (the historical credo). To this he added the story of beginnings, which placed Israel in the context of the world. The Yahwist postulates hidden grace alongside a widening gulf between God and humankind. Von Rad also accepted the oft-challenged theory of an Elohist, seeing his skillful hand best in Genesis 20 and Genesis 22.

The Deuteronomist best exemplified for von Rad the powerful tradition of levitical preaching originating in the northern kingdom. Its polemical nature combined with lofty rhetoric to convey a theology of the divine name present in the central sanctuary. That message was further elaborated by a great doxology of judgment, the Deuteronomistic history in Joshua, Judges, Samuel and Kings, albeit with a hopeful ending. The Priestly tradition, in von Rad's view, concentrated on a history of the cult, and the Chronicler exalted Yahweh's anointed, David, emphasized messianic themes, and by citing earlier texts as authoritative suggests a loss of spontaneity.

Von Rad examined Israel's prophetic traditions under categories such as election and creation, with special attention to Davidic messianism and to myths about the holy and inviolable city. On turning to traditions championed by the sages, he shifted his method to problem history, particularly in dealing with the books of Job, Ecclesiastes and Sirach. Von Rad accepted the hypothesis of court wisdom, argued for the existence of schools as the surest explanation for the high literary quality of Israel's wisdom, and claimed that this literature was essentially a variant form of Yahwism. Wisdom, in his view, served royal purposes and was self-consciously religious.

How did these transmitters convey their favorite traditions to the people in general? They used verbal pictures, painting historical portraits illustrative of cherished insights. Von Rad describes five of these in great detail: Moses, Abraham, Joseph, David and Jeremiah. Each one illustrates a particular relationship with God—the servant Moses who points to Christ; the faithful Abraham who walked the lonely road of divine abandonment; the brother Joseph whose trials were orchestrated by a providential God intent on educating him; the anointed king, God's sinner whose heart was right even when his behavior left much to be desired; and the lonely prophet whose mission took him along a *via dolorosa*.

These historical portraits were not intended for moral examples but for witnesses to divine faithfulness in leading Israelites toward the goal envisioned for them. Von Rad acknowledged the fictional character of the descriptions, for the most part, together with their theological pedagogy. A walk through this picture gallery enabled Israelites to experience in their leaders the agony and ecstasy of the centuries. In the same spirit Ben Sira described the interrelationship between Yahweh and great men of repute, adopting the literary form of a eulogy, and the later author of Hebrews alludes to a host of heavenly witnesses.

This reference to a New Testament author raises the question of von Rad's view of the relationship between the Testaments. He believed that the Old Testament laid the foundation for the New Testament by providing a religious language—that of confessional saving deeds—and by attesting to the encounter with a deity who always retreats into the dark unknown.

Significance. How much of von Rad's interpretation of the Old Testament has stood the test of time? In a sense his approach has suffered because of its connection with neo-orthodoxy and the biblical theology movement that declined even before von Rad's death. Postmodernists have found it increasingly problematic to speak of mighty acts of God, and Jewish thinkers have chafed under what they understand as von Rad's denigration of Second Temple Judaism. Systematic theologians have bristled at his imprecise categories, especially his use of history in both senses, factual and mythic.

Many specifics of von Rad's overarching

assumptions have succumbed to a barrage of criticism. The little historical credo has been turned on its head, for the evidence indicates that it came at the end of the compositional process rather than at the beginning. The isolation of the Sinai tradition from the exodus experience has not won acceptance. The Solomonic enlightenment has been shown to have been an illusion, as has Noth's theory, which von Rad endorsed, that early Israel banded in an amphictyony. The identification of Job 38 with onomastica, a "discovery" that von Rad mentions with pride, has no adequate basis in fact. His view of the Hexateuch has suffered from the general malaise of criticism on the Pentateuch. The Wellhausenian consensus, such that it was, has undergone enormous change, with some critics challenging the preexilic dating of the literary strata, especially the Yahwist.

Von Rad's understanding of wisdom literature has been called into question at many points. His basic assumption that the texts were composed in a school associated with the royal court fails to take into account the overwhelming evidence for the popular origin of Proverbs in small villages. His claim that apocalyptic originated in wisdom circles gives undue weight to mantic wisdom in Daniel; his emphasis on idolatry as a sapiential polemic rests on flimsy data; his belief that the sages emphasized a science of the times lacks cogency. The baptism of wisdom, von Rad's insistence that wisdom was a branch of Yahwism, reduced the unique phenomenon to something entirely foreign to it. His preoccupation with the cult resulted in an overlooking of ethics.

An irony of his work in Jena was the publication of a book that gave voice to national consciousness (*The Old Testament: God's Word to the Germans*). In one sense von Rad retained this attitude, refusing to enter into dialogue with other scholars, particularly those outside Germany. The persuasive power of his rhetoric and his popularity reinforced this insularity of scholarship.

To some degree von Rad's star has faded because of two powerful directions taken by Old Testament scholarship. The shift away from form and tradition history, particularly outside Germany, has been so substantial that some interpreters envision a shift in paradigm from historical criticism to literary analysis, from diachronic to synchronic studies. Similarly sociological theory, often using ethno-anthropological models, has emerged as another mode of reading ancient texts. This change has also witnessed the emergence of secular approaches, championed by faculty in religious studies, and increasing aversion to anything theological. Much of this recent scholarship has come from North America and to a lesser extent Great Britain, Scandinavian countries, Israel and Italy. The emergence of Roman Catholic scholarship during this short era has also reinforced synchronic analysis.

That von Rad's contribution to Old Testament studies has survived at all attests to his genius. He championed the Old Testament at a time when the church could have fallen into the Marcionite heresy. His approach to the text emphasized the vitality of competing traditions, the continual actualization of Yahweh's word for each new generation. Moreover, he recognized the role of the cult in shaping religious belief and in transmitting that faith by means of confessional statements. Von Rad thus garnered a theological maximum from a historical minimum. His sensitive reading of the Old Testament enabled many others to span the vast chasm separating them from the ancient text. The sheer beauty of his prose captivated minds, and the passion with which he explored such topics as knowledge and its limits, trust and attack, and divine abandonment came through with enormous force.

The charge that his theology of the Old Testament never moved outside the realm of a history of Israelite religion seems accurate, for he described ancient confessional statements instead of using them to construct a systematic theology. His disdain for systematics partly explains his failure to move a step further, but another reason surely exercised more power on him—a propensity for poetics. His appreciation for aesthetics gave him a sense of the rich ambiguity of the biblical text. That background inherent to the sacred text yielded to his patient probe, opening up insights for those willing to hear.

BIBLIOGRAPHY

Works. G. von Rad, *Biblical Interpretation in Preaching* (Nashville: Abingdon, 1977); idem, *Deuteronomy* (Philadelphia: Westminster, 1966 [1964]); idem, *Genesis* (Philadelphia: Westminster, 1976 [1956]); idem, *Das Geschichtsbild des chronistischen Werkes* (Stuttgart: Kohlhammer, 1930); idem, *Holy War in Ancient Israel* (Grand Rapids: Eerdmans, 1991 [1951, 1958]); idem, *The Message of the Prophets* (New York: Harper & Row, 1967 [1967]); idem, *Moses* (London: Lutterworth, 1960 [1940]); idem, *Old Testament Theology* (2 vols.; New York: Harper, 1962, 1965 [1957, 1960]); idem, *Das Opfer des Abraham* (Munich: Chr. Kaiser, 1971); idem, *The Problem of the Hexateuch and Other Essays* (New York: McGraw-Hill, 1966 [1938 et al.]); idem, *Studies in Deuteronomy* (London: SCM, 1953); idem, "Typological Interpretation of the Old Testament" in *Essays in Old Testament Hermeneutics,* ed. C. Westermann (Richmond, VA: John Knox, 1969) 17-39; idem, *Wisdom in Israel* (Nashville: Abingdon, 1973 [1970]).

Studies. M. E. Andrew, "Gerhard von Rad—A Personal Memoir," *ET* 83 (1972) 296-300; J. L. Crenshaw, *Gerhard von Rad* (Peabody, MA: Hendrickson, 1991 [1978]); idem, "Wisdom in Israel, by Gerhard von Rad," *RSR* 22 (1976) 6-12; G. H. Davies, "Gerhard von Rad, 'Old Testament Theology'" in *Contemporary Old Testament Theologians,* ed. R. B. Laurin (Valley Forge, PA: Judson, 1970) 63-89; K. Koch, "Gerhard von Rad" in *Tendenzen der Theologie in 20 Jahrhundert: Eine Geschichte in Porträts,* ed. H. J. Schultz (Stuttgart and Berlin: Kreuz, 1966) 483-87; K. Rahner, "Gerhard von Rad," *Das Parlament* 35 (August 26, 1972) 10; D. G. Spriggs, *Two Old Testament Theologies* (SBT 2d series 30; Naperville, IL: Alec R. Allenson, 1974).   J. L. Crenshaw

Weiss, Johannes *(1863-1914)*

Johannes Weiss was the son of the noted New Testament scholar Bernhard Weiss. He was educated at the universities of Marburg, Berlin, Göttingen and Breslau. Weiss began his teaching career at Göttingen in 1888, where he married the daughter of his teacher, the leading liberal systematic theologian of the day, Albrecht Ritschl (1822-1889). In 1885 Weiss became a full professor at Marburg. He moved to Heidelberg in 1908, where he remained until his premature death at age fifty-one.

Weiss established his scholarly reputation with a brief study of 67 pages on *Die Predigt Jesu vom Reiche Gottes* (*Jesus' Proclamation of the Kingdom of God* [1892]), which in a second edition (1902; ET 1971) he enlarged to 251 pages in order to respond to critics. In 1892 he published *Die Evangelien des Markus und Lukas,* a commentary on Mark and Luke. In 1895 he published *Die Nachfolge Christi und die Predigt der Gegenwart* (*The Imitation of Christ and Contemporary Preaching*) and in 1897 *Beiträge zur paulinischen Rhetorik* (*Contributions to the Study of Pauline Rhetoric*) and *Ueber die Absicht und den literarischen Charakter der Apostelgeschichte* (*The Purpose and Literary Character of the Book of Acts*). In 1901 *Die Idee des Reiches Gottes in der Theologie* (*The Idea of the Kingdom of God in Theology*) defended his earlier position and assessed its relevance. Other major works were a study of Mark entitled *Das älteste Evangelium* (*The Oldest Gospel* [1903]) and *Die Offenbarung des Johannes* (*The Revelation of John* [1904]). Weiss was the author of numerous technical articles and pioneered form criticism in "Literaturgeschichte des NT" ("The Literary History of the New Testament") in the first edition of *Die Religion in Geschichte und Gegenwart* 3 (1912): 2175-215. He served as general editor of the popular commentary *Die Schriften des Neuen Testaments* (*The Writings of the New Testament* [1906]), for which he wrote an introduction and sections on the Synoptic Gospels and Revelation.

Following the move to Heidelberg, Weiss dealt with Christian origins in a series of popular works: *Die Aufgaben der neutes-tamentlichen Wissenschaft in der Gegenwart* (*The Task of New Testament Science at the Present Day* [1908]), *Christus: Die An-fänge des Dogmas* (*Christ: The Beginnings of Dogma* [1909]), *Paulus und Jesus* (*Paul and Jesus* [1909]), *Jesus im Glauben des Urchristentums* (*Jesus in the Faith of Primitive Christianity* [1910]), *Jesus von Naz-areth: Mythus oder Geschichte?* (*Jesus of Nazareth: Myth or History?* [1910]). In entering the "Christ myth" controversy he countered the contention of A. Drews and others that the figure of Christ was no more than a myth. On a more technical level Weiss set out his position in "Das Problem der Entstehung des Christentums" ("The Problem of the Rise of Christianity") in the *Archiv für Religionswissenschaft* 16 (1913) 423-515, which together with his commentary on 1 Corinthians, *Der erste Kor-intherbrief* (1910) laid the foundation for what was to be his greatest work, *Das Urchristentum* (ET *Earliest Christianity: A History of the Period* A.D. *30-150* [1937]). The first volume appeared in 1914, but the second volume was unfinished at the time of his death. It was completed by his friend Rudolf Knopf, who added the three final chapters. Weiss ranged widely over the whole field of New Testament studies. The following discussion will focus on those areas where he made the most lasting impact.

The Kingdom of God and Eschatology.

Weiss had written *Jesus' Proclamation of the Kingdom of God* some years before its publication in 1892. The fact that Weiss delayed publication while his father-in-law was still alive is not without significance. A central theme of Ritschl's theology was the kingdom of God, understood as the moral transformation of the individual believer and of society. Christ's vocation was to be the bearer of God's ethical lordship in the world. Weiss had long concluded that this ethical interpretation of the kingdom, which appealed to the liberal and Kantian ethical traditions, was utterly at variance with the outlook of primitive Christianity

and of Jesus himself. The kingdom that Jesus proclaimed was not an ethical relationship of love for God and humankind but a religious, eschatological-apocalyptic event that would introduce a new world order.

Weiss identified a number of characteristics in the teaching of Jesus (Weiss 1971, 129-31). Jesus was governed by the unwavering feeling that the messianic time was imminent. Occasionally he felt that the opposing kingdom of Satan was already broken and that the kingdom of God had dawned (Mt 10:7; 12:28; Lk 10:9, 11, 20). At other times Jesus encouraged his disciples to pray for its coming (Mt 6:10; Lk 11:2), knowing that human beings could do nothing to establish it. Jesus' messianic consciousness consisted in the certainty that when God established the kingdom, judgment and rule would be transferred to him (Jn 3:11; 5:27; Acts 2:36).

Though Jesus initially hoped to live to see the establishment of the kingdom, he became convinced that he must die as a condition of its coming. After that he would return on the clouds of heaven at the establishment of the kingdom and would do so within the lifetime of the generation that had rejected him. With the arrival of the kingdom, God would destroy the present evil world and create a new world in which human beings would be like angels. This event would be accompanied by the judgment of Jews and Gentiles, living and dead. The land of Israel would arise in new, glorious splendor to form the center of the new kingdom. Aliens would no longer rule over it but would acknowledge God as Lord. Sadness and sin would be abolished, and Jesus and his faithful ones would rule over this newborn people of the twelve tribes, which would include the Gentiles. The rule of God would not be suspended by the rule of the Messiah but would be actualized by it, either in the form of reigning side by side or Jesus reigning under the higher sovereignty of God.

Although Weiss frankly recognized that his understanding of the kingdom contradicted that of Ritschl, he remained a Ritschlian at heart. While he believed that he had recovered the teaching of Jesus, he could not accept Jesus' eschatological program. The kingdom had not materialized in the form that Jesus envisaged, and thus this notion of the kingdom was no longer viable. He concluded:

> Under these circumstances, one will perhaps judge the connection of the modern dogmatic idea [i.e., the rule of God as the highest religious good and supreme ethical ideal] with the words of Jesus to be a purely external one. This is, in fact, the case. That which is universally valid in Jesus' preaching, which should form the kernel of our systematic theology is not his idea of the Kingdom of God, but that of the religious and ethical fellowship of the children of God. This is not to say that one ought no longer to use the concept of 'Kingdom of God' in the current manner. On the contrary, it seems to me, as a matter of fact, that it should be the proper watchword of modern theology. Only the admission must be demanded that we use it in a different sense from Jesus'. (Weiss 1971, 135)

Christian Origins. Weiss believed that all historical events are conditioned by previous events and by their environment. Primitive Christianity was no exception, and to that extent Weiss shared the convictions and methods of the history of religions school. The beliefs of the early church concerning eschatology were conditioned by Jewish apocalyptic. But the early church's eschatological expectation could not have been so widely embraced if that expectation did not derive ultimately from Jesus himself. The messianic consciousness of Jesus was the ultimate basis for the messianic faith of the disciples. In Jewish thought the Messiah was an abstract concept, but for the disciples the heavenly Messiah bore the personal features of Jesus. Weiss wrote: "Precisely because after his death they could not get away from him, and in spite of his apparent defeat were still

convinced in their very souls that he had been divinely ordained to rule, the Easter-experience had a determinative influence upon their whole future" (Weiss 1959, 1:30).

The experience of following Jesus as disciples was transformed into the worship of Christ. Belief in the parousia, which would bring with it the overwhelming confirmation of the Lord, was an inheritance from Jewish apocalyptic messianism. But as the church expanded into the Gentile world, especially through the missionary work of the apostle Paul, its beliefs were shaped increasingly by concepts drawn from the Hellenistic world. Among them was the concept of rebirth or dying and rising again with Christ. In Paul are to be found the spiritual currents of Old Testament prophetic piety and rabbinic Judaism; Hellenistic Jewish enlightenment and Stoic ethics; syncretistic Hellenistic mysticism and dualistic, ascetical Gnosticism (Weiss 1959, 2:650). In addition there was the high ethics of Jesus, the eschatological emphasis of John the Baptist and above all the victorious conviction that the salvation of the final age has come. But to identify the historical, cultural elements in which Christian faith was expressed was not to deny its supernatural origin. It is rather to seek to understand the forms of the activity of "the divine Spirit" (Weiss 1959, 1:43).

Significance. Albert *Schweitzer contended that after Hermann Samuel *Reimarus "the whole movement of theology, down to Johannes Weiss, appears retrograde" in view of its neglect of eschatology and its failure to see it as the key to understanding Jesus (Schweitzer, 23). Indeed, it was Weiss's understanding of eschatology that provided Schweitzer with the tools with which to construct what he considered to be a coherent account of the historical Jesus as an alternative to the skepticism of William *Wrede (Schweitzer, 238-41, 330-97). Wrede had contended that the messianic secret (Jesus' refusal to allow his messiahship to be publicized) was the creation of Mark, for Jesus did not even think of himself as the Messiah. As an alternative, Schweitzer contended that an eschatological program such as that proposed by Weiss enabled one to make a coherent picture of Jesus' beliefs and activities and that Jesus deliberately refrained from making messianic claims until he judged that the time was ripe. Schweitzer termed his own position "consistent" or "thoroughgoing eschatology." Whereas Weiss believed that Jesus taught eschatology but believed that the kingdom would come in God's good time, Schweitzer saw the eschatological kingdom as the key not only to Jesus' teaching but also to his actions, which were designed to bring about the kingdom. Jesus finally realized that it could be done only by going to Jerusalem in order to die. Like Reimarus, Schweitzer concluded that this aspect of Jesus' activity ended in failure, for the kingdom never materialized.

Both Schweitzer and Weiss saw eschatology as the key to understanding the historical Jesus in contrast with the liberal portraits of Jesus and the contention of the skeptics that the historical Jesus could not be recovered. However, neither of them thought that such eschatology was any longer tenable and valued Jesus for other reasons. Weiss's most famous student, Rudolf *Bultmann, was convinced that Weiss's account of New Testament eschatology was essentially correct (see his foreword to Weiss 1971, xi-xii). His own solution to the problem was to grant that the thought world of the New Testament was shaped by Jewish apocalyptic eschatology and Gnosticism but to insist that it needed to be demythologized.

The teaching of Weiss and Schweitzer on the nature of the kingdom initiated debate that shows no signs of abating. Most recently their interpretation has been seriously challenged by scholars like N. T. Wright, M. J. Borg and B. Chilton, who contend that for Jesus the kingdom did not mean the end of the world but God's presence in power. If this is so, a radically different understanding of Jesus' aims and teaching is called for.

BIBLIOGRAPHY

Works. J. Weiss, *Das älteste Evangelium* (Göttingen: Vandenhoeck & Ruprecht, 1903); idem, *Die Aufgaben der neutestamentlichen Wissenschaft in der Gegenwart* Göttingen: Vandenhoeck & Ruprecht, 1908); idem, *Beiträge zur paulinischen Rhetorik* (Göttingen: Vandenhoeck & Ruprecht, 1897); idem, *Christ: The Beginnings of Dogma* (Boston : American Unitarian Association, 1911 [1909]); idem, *Der erste Korintherbrief* (Göttingen: Vandenhoeck & Ruprecht, 1910); idem, *Die Evangelien des Markus und Lukas* (Göttingen: Vandenhoeck & Ruprecht, 1892); idem, *Die Idee des Reiches Gottes in der Theologie* (Giessen: J. Ricker, 1901); idem, *Earliest Christianity: A History of the Period A.D. 30-150*, ed. F. C. Grant (2 vols.; New York: Harper, 1959 [1937]); idem, *Jesus im Glauben des Urchristentums* (Tübingen: J. C. B. Mohr, 1910); idem, *Jesus' Proclamation of the Kingdom of God*, ed. R. H. Hiers and D. L. Holland (Philadelphia: Fortress, 1971 [1902]), with extensive introduction and bibliography of Weiss's major writings in German; idem, *Jesus von Nazareth: Mythus oder Geschichte?* (Tübingen: J. C. B. Mohr, 1910); idem, *Die Nachfolge Christi und die Predigt der Gegenwart* (Göttingen: Vandenhoeck & Ruprecht, 1895); idem, *Die Offenbarung des Johannes* (Göttingen: Vandenhoeck & Ruprecht, 1904); idem, *Paul and Jesus* (New York: Harper, 1909); idem, ed., *Die Schriften des Neuen Testaments* (Göttingen: Vandenhoeck & Ruprecht (1906; 2d ed., 1913; 3d ed., 1917-20); idem, *Ueber die Absicht und den literarischen Charakter der Apostelgeschichte* (Göttingen: Vandenhoeck & Ruprecht, 1897).

Studies. M. J. Borg, "Jesus and Eschatology: A Reassessment" in *Images of Jesus Today*, ed. J. H. Charlesworth and W. P. Weaver (Valley Forge, PA: Trinity Press International, 1994) 42-67; idem, *Jesus in Contemporary Scholarship* (Valley Forge, PA: Trinity Press International, 1994) 47-68; F. C. Burkitt, "Johannes Weiss: In Memoriam," *HTR* 8 (1915) 291-97; B. Chilton, "The Kingdom of God in Recent Discussion" in *Studying the Historical Jesus: Evaluations of the State of Current Research*, ed. B. Chilton and C. A. Evans (New Testament Tools and Studies 19; Leiden: E. J. Brill, 1994) 255-80; D. L. Holland, "History, Theology and the Kingdom of God: A Contribution of Johannes Weiss to Twentieth Century Theology," *Biblical Research* 13 (1968) 54-66; W. G. Kümmel, *The New Testament: The History of the Investigation of Its Problems* (Nashville: Abingdon, 1972), 226-30,

238-40 and passim; B. Lannert, *Die Wieder-entdeckung der neutestament lichen Eschatologie durch Johannes Weiss* (Tübingen: Francke, 1989); G. Lundström, *The Kingdom of God in the Teaching of Jesus: A History of Interpretation from the Last Decades of the Nineteenth Century to the Present Day* (Edinburgh and London: Oliver & Boyd, 1963) 3-9, 27-34; N. Perrin, *The Kingdom of God in the Teaching of Jesus* (London: SCM; Philadelphia: Westminster, 1963) 16-23; M. Saucy, *The Kingdom of God in the Teaching of Jesus in Twentieth-Century Theology* (Dallas: Word, 1997) passim; A. Schweitzer, *The Quest of the Historical Jesus: A Critical Study of Its Progress from Reimarus to Wrede* (New York: Macmillan, 1968 [1910]) 238-41, 330-97; W. Willis, "The Discovery of the Eschatological Kingdom: Joahnnes Weiss and Albert Schweitzer" in *The Kingdom of God in Twentieth-Century Interpretation*, ed. W. Willis (Peabody, MA: Hendrickson, 1987) 1-14; N. T. Wright, *The New Testament and the People of God* (Minneapolis: Fortress, 1992) 280-338.   C. Brown

Westermann, Claus *(b. 1909)*

Claus Westermann, one of the most influential interpreters of the Bible in the twentieth century, was born in Berlin on October 7, 1909, to Katharina and Diedrich Westermann. His father had been a missionary in Africa and later became a professor of African languages and ethnology in Berlin. Westermann studied theology and philosophy at the universities in Tübingen, Marburg (where one of his teachers was Rudolf *Bultmann) and Berlin. He worked as a pastor in Berlin-Dahlem and was drafted and served in the German army from 1940 to 1945.

In 1949 Westermann received his doctorate in theology from Zurich, writing his dissertation, "The Praise of God in the Psalms," under Walter Zimmerli. From 1949 to 1952 he was pastor at the Kaiser Wilhelm Memorial Church in Berlin and taught Old Testament at the church seminary *(Kirchliche Hochschule)* there; from 1953 to 1958 he taught full-time at the *Kirchliche Hochschule*. In 1958 Westermann was called to join the Old Testament

faculty at Heidelberg and remained there until his retirement in 1978. Since his retirement he has continued his work of teaching, preaching and writing. He and his wife, Anna (d. 1991), are the parents of one daughter.

Context. Westermann's theological writing arose from the context of the time of National Socialism in Germany and the struggles of the church during that period. He finished his first theological examinations in 1933, the year that the National Socialists seized power in Germany. The church sent him to the practical seminary *(Predigerseminar)* in Frankfurt/Oder to continue his education leading toward becoming a pastor. When students there were urged to join the pro-Nazi German Christians *(Deutsche Christen)*, Westermann was among a group of thirteen who left the seminary to continue their studies in Berlin under Martin Niemoeller, a leading pastor in the confessing church *(Bekennende Kirche)*, and then in Naumburg under Dr. Gloege. Westermann recalls this period:

> I remember one study group on the Psalms where we discussed whether or not we could recognize the Psalter as a part of our Christian Bible. That was the issue in dispute between the two parties: the German Christians rejected the Old Testament as part of the Christian Bible. . . . The church was being oppressed by the Nazi government, and there were already plans to eliminate it altogether. The Old Testament, which was of special interest to me, was hated as a Jewish book that should be silenced at all costs. But this hopeless situation could not change the fact that my questions and investigations, focused on the Bible, never let up. (Westermann 1992, 338-39)

Then came World War II. Westermann reflects on those wartime years:

> In one respect, the war was my teacher, even if a hard one. I had with me only the New Testament with the Psalms, which I retained even in Russian POW camp. The Bible was no longer merely

an uplifting book, as it had been in my childhood and my parental home. Life had gotten too hard for that. The only thing in the Bible with enduring value was that which spoke directly to my present existence. First and foremost, that was the psalms. (Westermann 1992, 340)

While he was in prison in Russia, Westermann began what was to become his dissertation on the psalms. He recalls:

After the German defeat, I became a prisoner of the Russians. I need not mention that this was even a harder school; I still don't know how I emerged from it alive. . . . I thought about the psalms and tried to relate my own wartime thoughts to the Psalter. In doing so, I sat on a block of wood and wrote on a board held on my knees. Sometimes I traded bread for paper. This was the origin of my later book, *The Praise of God in the Psalms,* with no Hebrew text; in fact, with no books at all. The war made me encounter the psalms in a totally unacademic and unscientific way, and it became very important for me to see that the people who gave rise to the Psalter were simple and ordinary; they were not what we would call highly intellectual or cultivated, but folks who had rather simple ideas, who earned their living with their hands, and who, as a result, were close to the earth, the stars, and all creatures—as the psalms make clear. My thinking about those things was the same as that of the women and men in the Psalter, and that has remained with me until this day. (Westermann 1992, 340-41)

Work. In 1978, the year that Westermann retired from teaching at the University of Heidelberg, his *Theologie des Alten Testaments in Grundzügen* (*Elements of Old Testament Theology* [1982]) appeared. The divisions of that book provide a convenient framework for summarizing his writings on the Old Testament.

What does the Old Testament say about God? The answer to this question, says

Westermann, must be based on a consideration of the Old Testament as a whole; no single concept, such as covenant, election or salvation, can be taken as the center. "The Old Testament tells a story," Gerhard *von Rad had said, and this statement can be the starting point. The canonical division of the OT—Torah, Prophets and Writings—provides the clue for understanding the story as a whole: "The theology of the Old Testament is thus determined by the shape of a story entrusted to us, which includes the word of God entering into the story and the response of those experiencing this story" (Westermann 1978, 7, Limburg translation). The story is a unity because it tells of the one God and God's relationship to creation and to human beings.

The delivering God and history. The major shapes of God's activity, says Westermann, are the actions of delivering or rescuing *(Rettung)* and of blessing *(Segen):*

From the beginning to the end of the story told in the Bible, these two ways in which God deals with humanity—deliverance and blessing—are found alongside one another. *They cannot be reduced to a single concept.* This is so because these two ways in which human beings experience the actions of God are experienced differently: delivering and the deliverance of God are experienced as an event, corresponding to an "intervention" of God. Blessing is a continuous action of God that is either present or not present; it cannot be experienced in an event any more than can growth, maturing, or the declining of strength. (Westermann 1968, 11-12, Limburg translation)

The primary biblical examples of God's delivering activity are the exodus in the Old Testament and the cross and resurrection in the New. The Lord may rescue an individual (Ps 30; Jn 9), a whole nation (the exodus) or all of humankind (Is 25:6-10; Christ's death and resurrection).

The blessing God and creation. The Lord's actions with humans cannot be limited to the mighty acts of God. Alongside God's acts of rescuing either the nation or an individual, the Bible also speaks of the ongoing, sustaining, blessing activity of God:

> It is a quiet, continuous, flowing and unnoticed working of God which cannot be captured in moments or dates. Blessing is realized in a gradual process, as in the process of growing, maturing, and fading. It is not as if the Old Testament is reporting only a series of events which consists of the great acts of God; the intervals are also part of it; in them God gives growth and prosperity unnoticed in a quiet working, in which he lets children be born and grow up, in which he gives success in work. (Westermann 1979b, 44)

God's judgment and God's mercy. "The word of God entering into the story" is also a part of the story of God and people. In this way prophecy is linked to the story theme. The prophet is God's messenger, typically introducing a message with the messenger formula "Thus says the Lord." Westermann's analysis of prophecy of judgment is found in *Basic Forms of Prophetic Speech,* while salvation prophecy is considered in *Prophetic Oracles of Salvation in the Old Testament.* Prophecy is also dealt with in *What Does the Old Testament Say About God?, Elements of Old Testament Theology, A Thousand Years and a Day* and *Isaiah 40—66.*

The response. The Old Testament also records "the response of those who experience this story." "The response in words" is found in the psalms, with their contrasting themes of praise and lament. In considering "the response in action," Westermann discusses commandments, law and worship in the Old Testament.

In a final section Westermann deals with "the response in thinking or reflection." The Psalter is not only a hymnbook but also a devotional book. Psalms such as Psalm 119 and Psalm 139 are the result of considerable reflection; Pslams 39, 49 and 90 offer reflections on death. This sort of theo-logical reflection resulted in the great historical works of the Yahwist, the Deuteronomist and the Priestly writer. These works show with particular clarity what theology is in the Old Testament . . . God is never abstracted to a conception of God. . . . One can only speak about God as the one who speaks and acts. Everything one can say about God remains in the context of a reciprocal occurrence between God and world, God and his people, God and a single individual. (Westermann 1982, 215)

Some of Westermann's most recent writing has been in this response category. A 1994 study of the historical books in the Old Testament counters Martin *Noth's notion of a Deuteronomic historical work, contending rather that each of the books from Deuteronomy through 2 Kings ought to be heard on its own (Westermann 1994). *Roots of Wisdom* (1990; ET 1995) investigates proverbs and wisdom sayings in the Bible, including the words of Jesus. *Das Buch der Sprüche* (1996) indicates the relevance of Proverbs for our time.

The Old Testament and Jesus Christ. Westermann deals with this topic in a book with this title as well as in *What Does the Old Testament Say About God?* and *Elements of Old Testament Theology.* Consistent with his concern to deal with the Old Testament as a whole, each of the three parts of the canon is discussed in its relationship to Christ. The theme of deliverance or rescue reappears: "The beginning of the O.T. tells the story of a rescue in the book of Exodus. The beginning of the New Testament tells the story of a rescue in the Gospels" (Westermann 1979b, 81; cf. Westermann 1982, 217).

Biblical Interpretation. Throughout the half-century of his scholarly work, Westermann has consistently employed the form-critical method. His doctoral thesis on the psalms worked out from Hermann *Gunkel's form-critical approach; books and articles on the psalms, as well as studies like *Basic Forms of Prophetic Speech, Prophetic Oracles of Salvation in the Old Testa-*

ment and *Roots of Wisdom* all provide examples of form criticism in action. Westermann's discussion of the nature of narrative and storytelling in *Genesis 12—36* (Westermann 1985, 44-50) is helpful for understanding all biblical narratives.

Fundamental in Westermann's approach to biblical interpretation is his conviction that the Bible is not only of historical interest but also communicates God's word to people of today. His study of the Joseph story is a model for linking exegesis to practical application (Westermann 1996). In an early piece that originated as part of a radio series in Germany, Westermann said:

> The basic prerequisite for a personal approach to the Bible rests in the fact that everyone who opens its pages should question it in terms of his [or her] own life. Only thus can there be an encounter between the reader, the Bible, and what the Bible really attempts to be—the living word of God. . . . If we listen to the Bible and out of our own human experience direct questions to it, unexpected access to the Bible will be opened to us. We will then notice that the persons who speak and act in the Bible are much like us in that they, too, usually are not models of piety at all and by no means always immediately believe everything God says. We will discover that the great acts of God reported in the Bible do not always encounter the appropriate human counterpart, but encounter failure, indecision, and egoism, too. It will then become clear to us that the Bible also shares in the brokenness of human existence and in this way bears witness to the fact that God has accepted us just as we are. (Westermann 1969, 116)

Biblical Themes. Westermann's work ranges through the central themes of the Bible. His study of creation is found in his commentaries on Genesis but is also present in other works, including *A Thousand Years and a Day, Creation, Elements of Old Testament Theology* and a number of shorter

books and articles. In a theological context that has spoken much about the mighty acts of God, Westermann has called attention to the less dramatic but equally significant blessing activity of God and the significance of that activity for the life of the church (Westermann 1978, 1982;throughout his works). His piece on the historical books (Westermann 1994a) counters one of the accepted hypotheses of contemporary Old Testament scholarship. His investigations of prophetic speech and the psalms are models of the form-critical method and have become standards in Old Testament study. His essay on "The Formation of the Psalter" was first published in German in 1962 and anticipates the current emphasis on the canonical form and formation of biblical books (Westermann 1981, 250-58). Most recently his work on wisdom calls for a fresh assessment of that literature in the Old Testament as well as its importance for understanding the New Testament. Westermann's study of the book of Lamentations exemplifies how a little-known book of the Bible can be shown to have an important message for the contemporary scene.

Westermann has also written on New Testament themes. His popular *Abriss der Bibelkunde,* an introduction to the Bible (the English *Handbooks* are out of print) continues to be updated and reprinted in Germany; a 14th edition revised by F. Ahuis will appear in 1998. *The Parables of Jesus in the Light of the Old Testament* (1990) translates a comprehensive study of biblical comparative devices, *Vergleiche und Gleichnisse im Alten und Neuen Testament* (1984). *The Gospel of John in the Light of the Old Testament* (1998) translates a German work published in 1994.

A collection of essays, *Das mündliche Wort: Erkundungen im Alten Testament* includes pieces on the significance of the Old Testament for practical theology and on preaching (Westermann 1996). These and other essays give evidence of Westermann's concern for promoting interchange between the Old Testament and other theological disciplines.

Significance. What can be said about the significance of Westermann's work and its contribution to scholarship and the life of the church?

Because Westermann's books are remarkably clear, with an absence of jargon and technical vocabulary, they are accessible to laypersons as well as to professional theologians. In German or in translation, these works have had an immeasurable impact on students, lay study groups and pastors.

The three-volume commentary on Genesis will long remain a standard work on that biblical book. The insights on creation, earth care, blessing and the nature of biblical narrative, as well as Westermann's comments on the application of each text investigated, mark this commentary as indispensable for study of the first book of the Bible. His conclusion that there was never an E document will continue to be debated among scholars.

One comes away from reading any of Westermann's biblical studies with fresh insights into familiar texts. The commentary on Isaiah 40—66 and the studies of the book of Lamentations, on Job, on selected psalms or the Gospel of John are all marked by thorough analysis, always coupled with thoughtful and imaginative application.

In conclusion, consider a comment from one of Westermann's earliest works, a small book on Luke, written near the end of World War II in 1945 and addressed to Westermann's five-year-old daughter, looking toward her confirmation a decade later:

> It is almost five years now that I have been away from you and your mother. And who knows what tomorrow will bring? What will the world look like, when you are grown up and this war and all its suffering belongs to the distant past? . . . For now, I am going to give you today a small present. I hope that you will find the same clear and indestructible joy in the Bible that your parents have found. . . . This I wish for you

with my entire heart. (1960, 5; Limburg translation)

Throughout the hundreds of pages of technical essays and biblical expositions, in lectures, Bible studies and sermons, one finds this "clear and indestructible joy" communicated through Westermann's writings on the Bible.

BIBLIOGRAPHY

Works. C. Westermann, *Basic Forms of Prophetic Speech* (Philadelphia: Westminster, 1991a [1960, 1967]; idem, "The Bible and the Life of Faith: A Personal Reflection," *W&W* 13 (1993) 337-44, abridged from "Ein Rückblick," *TB* 23 (1992) 223-32; idem, *Blessing in the Bible and the Life of the Church* (Philadelphia: Fortress, 1978 [1968]); idem, *Creation* (Philadelphia: Fortress, 1974 [1971]); idem, *Elements of Old Testament Theology* (Atlanta: John Knox, 1982 [1978]); idem, "Experience in the Church and the Work of Theology: A Perspective on Theology for Christian Ministry," *W & W* 10 (1990) 7-13; idem, *Genesis 1—11* (Minneapolis: Augsburg, 1984 [1974]); idem, *Genesis 12—36* (Minneapolis: Augsburg, 1985 [1981]); idem, *Genesis 37—50* (Minneapolis: Augsburg, 1986 [1982]); idem, *Genesis: A Practical Commentary* (Grand Rapids: Eerdmans, 1987 [1986]); idem, *Die Geschichtsbücher des Alten Testaments* (Gütersloh: Chr. Kaiser, 1994a); idem, *God's Angels Need No Wings* (Philadelphia: Fortress, 1979a [1957]); idem, *Handbook to the New Testament* (Minneapolis: Augsburg, 1969a); idem, *Handbook to the Old Testament* (Minneapolis: Augsburg, 1967. Both *Handbooks* are translations derived from *Abriss der Bibelkunde* [Stuttgart: Calwer Verlag, 1962; 13th updated and expanded edition 1981]); idem, *Isaiah 40—66, A Commentary* (Philadelphia: Westminster, 1969b [1966]); idem, *Das Johannesevangelium aus der Sicht des Alten Testaments* (Stuttgart: Calwer Verlag, 1994b); idem, *Lamentations: Issues and Interpretations* (Minneapolis: Fortress, 1993 [1990]); idem, *The Living Psalms* (Grand Rapids: Eerdmans, 1989 [1984]); idem, *Our Controversial Bible* (Minneapolis: Augsburg, 1969 [1960 2d ed.]); idem, *The Parables of Jesus in the Light of the Old Testament* (Minneapolis: Fortress, 1990 [1984]); idem, *Praise and Lament in the Psalms* (Atlanta: John Knox, 1981 [1961, 1977]); idem, *Prophetic Oracles of Salvation in the Old Testament* (Louisville, KY: Westminster John Knox, 1991b [1987]); idem, *Roots of Wisdom: The Old-*

est Proverbs of Israel and Other Peoples (Louisville, KY: Westminster John Knox Press, 1995 [1990]); idem, "Sechzig Jahre mit dem Alten Testament" in *Das mündliche Wort* (Stuttgart: Calwer Verlag, 1996); idem, *So Sagt es Lukas* (Berlin: Ev. Verlaganstalt, 1960); idem, *The Structure of the Book of Job* (Philadelphia: Fortress, 1981 [1956]); idem, *A Thousand Years and a Day* (Philadelphia: Muhlenberg, 1962 [1957]); Idem, *What does the Old Testament Say About God?* (Atlanta: John Knox, 1979b).

Studies: J. Limburg, "Old Testament Theology for Ministry," *W & W* 1 (1981) 169-78. A detailed bibliography of Westermann's works through 1979 is in *Werden und Wirken des Alten Testaments* (Festschrift for his 70th birthday), ed. R. Albertz et al. (Göttingen: Vandenhoeck & Ruprecht, 1980). Another Festschrift was presented to Westermann for his eightieth birthday, *Schöpfung und Befreiung,* ed. R. Albertz, F. W. Golka, J. Kegler (Stuttgart: Calwer Verlag, 1989).   J. Limburg

PART SIX

Biblical Interpretation in North America in the 20th Century

As THE NINETEENTH CENTURY WOUND DOWN, MOST OF THE ACADEMIC BIBLI-cal interpreters in North America were committed to an approach hammered out earlier in that century by Moses *Stuart (1780-1852) but honed by his students and their successors. The emphasis was upon philological and historical aspects of the text. Both liberal and conservative scholars accepted the hegemony of philological investigation. They both too were committed to historical analysis. Influenced by the developing German history-of-religions school, the liberals were beginning to move away from the historical trajectories as found in the Scriptures themselves. Earlier reconstructions, such as those by Ferdinand Christian *Baur (1792-1860) in regard to the early church and by Wilhelm Vatke (1806-1882) of the history of Israel, employed Hegelian dialectic. Conservative Americans accepted the need to examine historical backgrounds, but they were committed to the import of the narratives which they believed implicit in the Scriptures, a case in point being William Henry Green (1825-1900) of Princeton Theological Seminary. As Hans Frei wrote of *Augustine, they "envisioned the real world as formed by the sequence told by the biblical stories."

In the 1890s biblical scholars in major North American seminaries (especially on the eastern seaboard) who were more advanced in critical studies embraced higher criticism. This engaged them in such controversial issues as documentary hypotheses of the composition of the Pentateuch, the multiple authorship and dating of Isaiah, Zechariah and Daniel, the Synoptic problem and the disputed authorship of various epistles.

The interpretation of the Scriptures in North America in the twentieth century may be divided into four periods. (1) The Germanic period (1900-1915), which emphasized new perspectives on grammaticohistorical criticism obtained by North Americans studying in Germany. (2) The British period (1916-1945), which entailed North Americans training in the United Kingdom and North American seminaries and universities employing British professors. Scholars in this period emphasized scientific, social and cultural history, as well as biblical archaeology. Some scholars still studied in Germany, but not nearly as many as did in the previous period. (3) The Continental period (1945-1980) which featured North Americans studying in European universities, especially German, Italian, Swiss and Scandinavian, and the professorial employment in North America of Continental scholars emphasizing biblical theology and form criticism as well as redaction, tradition and canonical criticism. (4) The North American period (1981-) in which scholars in North America, utilizing previous approaches but adding social, sociological, anthropological, feminist, rhetorical, narrativist and imaginist criticism, seem well on the way to the status of being leaders among international biblical scholars.

The Germanic Period (1900-1915)

Training in biblical criticism in North America at the opening of the twentieth century was in service of the church and its ministers. Even major biblical scholars such as Charles Augustus *Briggs (1841-1913) positioned biblical scholarship as a science that enabled the church to appreciate its heritage and provide a clearer view of its mission. William Rainey Harper (1856-1906) hoped to bring technical biblical studies to the masses through correspondence courses in Hebrew, Chautauqua lectures and study guides written by University of Chicago scholars and published by the University of Chicago Press. The presuppositions of these scholars retained Reformation consensus positions in regard to the authority of the Scriptures, trinitarianism, Chalcedonian christology, Reformation soteriology and ecclesiology. Briggs was dismayed in the 1910s when younger colleagues openly denigrated the virgin birth of Jesus.

At the turn of the century North American scholars in some quarters began to diverge from the consensus. A significant influence was the great influx of North Americans studying in German universities. In the 1890s more than four hundred Americans studied in German theological faculties during most years. Not all of these students received German degrees, but several did. Some were professors who spent a year or more in Germany under the supposition that in order to keep abreast of biblical scholarship, a stint in Germany was imperative. Benjamin W. Bacon (1860-1932) attended lectures in several German universities in the 1890s. James Frederick McCurdy (1847-1935) of the University of Toronto studied at Göttingen and Leipzig in the early 1880s. Also studying in Germany were Jewish professors Louis Ginzberg (1873-1953) at Strasbourg and

Heidelberg, and Julian Morgenstern (1881-1976) at Berlin and Heidelberg. Roman Catholic scholars studied in Paris, among them Joseph Bruneau (1866-1933) of St. John's Seminary, Brighton, Massachusetts, and Henry Poels (1868-1948) at Louvain. Poels taught for a time at the Catholic University of America. Even persons of conservative commitments went to Germany: John Gresham *Machen (1881-1937) of Princeton Theological Seminary studied at Marburg and Göttingen in 1905 and 1906.

At first the new higher-critical positions that attained consensus status in Germany met with considerable resistance in North America. Church bodies evicted resolute scholars; for example, the Presbyterians ousted Briggs, and the Southern Baptists, Crawford Howell Toy (1836-1919). Toy later accepted an appointment at Harvard. By 1910 several biblical critics in the older seminaries had embraced critical German positions. Princeton was one of the few exceptions and remained so until 1929, when it was reorganized to bring about a more inclusive theological spectrum. These critical perspectives regarding reconstructed history, the documentary hypothesis of the Pentateuch and the rejection of the traditional authorship of several Old Testament books as well as some New Testament books (e.g., the Pastoral Epistles) were not widely disseminated in the churches.

At this time most of the seminaries were denominational and remained in the service of the churches. The result was a developing rift in mainstream Christian and Jewish seminaries that extended into the churches and synagogues. Those on the left openly embraced modernism, while those on the right frequently congealed as fundamentalistic movements (the famous set of twelve volumes on the Protestant "fundamentals," published between 1910 and 1915 being a case in point).

Benjamin W. Bacon, a professor at Yale (1896-1928), may serve as an example of a professor who openly embraced the newer perspectives. Bacon was in part educated in Europe: two years in a gymnasium in Coburg, Germany, and three years in the Collège de Genève, Switzerland (1872-1877). After earning a bachelor of divinity degree from Yale, he served as a pastor in Connecticut and New York until 1896, when he was appointed to the Yale Divinity School faculty. In 1897 he spent a long summer visiting the premier biblical scholars in Germany. Through the influence of Harper, Bacon became interested in Pentateuchal criticism. He published several articles in Harper's journal, *Hebraica,* from 1888 to 1891. In 1893 he published *The Genesis of Genesis* and in 1894 *The Triple Tradition of the Exodus.* In these publications Bacon clearly embraced the consensus Graf-Wellhausen documentary hypothesis. His appointment at Yale, however, was in New Testament, so he spent the rest of his career focusing on the Gospels.

Bacon worked under the thesis that just as the history of Israel should be reconstructed, so also should the life of Jesus. He focused on the background and motives of each of the Gospels and their sources, employing a methodology along the lines of what later came to called *redactionsgeschichte* (redaction criticism). But unlike his European counterparts, he was interested in the text in its present form rather than its sources and their composition. He did, however, accept the existence of Q, as well other source materials, especially connected with Luke-Acts. His literary mentor was Ferdinand Christian Baur, with whom he shared the hegemony of ideas as propounded by Hegel.

Bacon's unique reconstruction of early Christianity featured the significance of a Petrine thread of influence. He believed that Mark was influenced by Peter and that Matthew drew upon the Petrine trajectory as the result of its authoritative character. The Fourth Gospel likewise was indebted to an interpreter of Peter for the depiction of the beloved disciple. Bacon perceived Paul's letters as a combination of Petrine and lyric wisdom traditions. In this manner he gave considerable historical probability to the historical Jesus. But his reconstructions of the details were far from conventional, and this fact provoked his critics to oppose several wild reconstructions. Machen was particularly exercised by Bacon's "tendency-criticism" and charged that from any conventional perspective he was mistaken. In this regard Machen, likewise trained in and influenced by German biblical scholarship, nevertheless opposed what he considered modernizing reconstructions.

Many other scholars of the time studied in Germany, including George Foot Moore (1851-1931), who taught at Andover Theological Seminary and Harvard University and Divinity School. Moore was in Germany in 1895 and again in 1909 to 1910, when he was an exchange professor. In 1895 he published the International Critical Commentary on Judges. Late in his career he published a highly regarded study in three volumes, *Judaism in the First Centuries of the Christian Era*. Moore proceeded methodologically according to the dictates of the history of religions. Like Bacon, he was interested in the development of religious ideas, arguing that second-century Judaism was a continuation of many of the concepts endemic in the prophetic movement.

A new North American school of biblical criticism influenced by German predecessors was the empirical, sociological perspective propounded at the University of Chicago. The Chicago approach was centered upon a so-called scientific methodology, that is, that the Scriptures are to be scrutinized from a philological, exegetical, historical and developing sociological perspective. It took on, however, a North American empirical and pragmatic cast. In contrast with the consensus *sola Scriptura,* this school also held that the weight of experience is equal with and (later) more important than the witness of the Scriptures. Apart from Harper, who in 1892 became president of the university, four persons were chief engineers of the school: Ernest DeWitt Burton (1856-1925), Shailer

Mathews (1863-1941), Edgar Johnson *Goodspeed (1871-1962) and Shirley Jackson Case (1872-1947). All four spent time in Germany: Burton at Leipzig in 1887, Mathews at Berlin in 1890, Case at Marburg 1910 and Goodspeed at Berlin from 1898 to 1900, though he traveled also to Great Britain, the Near East and Egypt.

The views of Mathews were typical of the school. He published several books on the New Testament with Burton and even more books by himself. In *The Social Teaching of Jesus* Mathews set out Jesus' perspectives on humanity, society, the family, the state, wealth, social life, forces of human progress and the process of social regeneration. This approach is now designated biblical anthropology. Mathews pointed out that while the Gospels contain various corruptions and editorial additions, these may be easily ascertained through criticism, leaving a sizable body of authentic Jesus material. He argued that "divine sonship and consequent human brotherliness" comprised the core of Jesus' social doctrine.

In *The Faith of Modernism* Mathews criticized early Protestantism because it "detached the Bible from history and declared it to be the sole and divinely given basis of revealed truth." He declared that a modernist is one who "implicitly trusts the historical method." He further argued that the Bible as understood by grammaticohistorical criticism is "a trustworthy record of human experience of God." He rejected the inerrancy of the Scriptures and accepted standard critical positions but affirmed inspiration of the Bible in regard to those persons (rather than words) who had experienced the Spirit of God.

By World War I a number of major North American biblical scholars had accepted the consensus thesis that a reconstruction of the biblical narratives was imperative because of both literary and historical considerations. As the result of anti-German sentiments that grew from the beginnings of the World War I in 1914, the stream of North American scholars making their way to Germany came to a halt. Even Bacon took a strong anti-Wilhelmian stand during the war and badgered pacifists.

The British Period (1916-1945)

As the result of World War I, North Americans going abroad now were more likely to go to the British Isles, especially Oxford or Cambridge. While not many German scholars were brought to the United States to teach prior to the war (e.g., Paul Haupt [1858-1926] at Johns Hopkins University in 1883), various British scholars were now offered posts in the United States, including Kirsopp Lake (1872-1946), who was educated at Oxford and who in 1914 took up a position at Harvard; Frederick John Foakes-Jackson (1855-1941), who studied at Cambridge and came to the Union Theological Seminary in 1916; James Moffatt (1870-1944), who was educated at Glasgow, taught at Oxford and United Free Church College in Glasgow and came to Union Theological

Seminary in 1927; and A. D. Nock (1902-1963), who took a Cambridge M.A. and came to Harvard in 1930. Throughout this period several professors from the British Isles were employed in Canadian seminaries. Among these were two scholars who later came to Union Theological Seminary in New York: E. F. Scott (1868-1941) and James D. Smart (1908-1982).

Several North Americans studied in the United Kingdom, including Erwin Ramsdell Goodenough (1893-1965), who took a doctorate at Oxford in 1923 and commenced teaching at Yale University; Amos Niven Wilder (1895-1991), who studied at the University of Brussels (1920-1921) and Oxford (1921-1923) and who ended his teaching career at Harvard; and H. L. Ginsberg (1903-1990), who taught at Jewish Theological Seminary from 1936 and, though he was born in Montreal, received his Ph.D. in Semitics from the University of London.

In this period the emphasis moved away from religious concepts, a trend reflecting a general shift from Hegelian idealism to empiricism. The move was widespread but perhaps was more pronounced in Great Britain than on the Continent, though the British universities were not without Platonistic and Hegelian periods. Nevertheless the biblical critics especially tended to remain consistently dedicated to British empiricism. Biblical scholars emphasized scientific philology and history, social and cultural history, and biblical archaeology. Robert M. Grant (b. 1917) argued that American biblical studies accented common sense, archaeology and paleography, and eschewed philosophies or philosophical theologies (1968). He especially bemoaned the 1950s assent to biblical theology formulated upon existential foundations.

The ascendancy of the Albright school of Old Testament studies in this period serves as an appropriate example of North American scholarship. Although William Foxwell *Albright (1891-1971) was not trained in Britain, his presuppositions reflect the outlooks of an Americanized British empiricism. He had contacts with the British scholars H. H. Rowley (1890-1969) and D. Winton Thomas (1901-1970), but he considered Albrecht Alt (1883-1956) and Martin *Noth (1902-1968) more his intellectual peers, and they shared his basic empirical outlook. H. F. Hahn appropriately wrote:

> This careful attention to technical detail, with its faith in the value of empirical and statistical method, reflected the pragmatic attitude of American enterprise. First it was American excavators and their institutional sponsors who were chiefly responsible for the introduction of the modern techniques into archaeological exploration. They made archaeology a scientific discipline, operating with concrete data and marshaling evidence with objective care. (Hahn, 188)

In 1918, after World War I, Albright was appointed Thayer Fellow at the American School of Oriental Research in Jerusalem. In 1921 he was made director of the school, a position he held until 1929, when he was appointed W. W. Spence professor of Semitic languages at the Johns Hopkins University. The first major effort to survey the history of religious thought in the Near East from its beginning down to the origin of Christianity was undertaken by Albright in *From the Stone Age to Christianity*. In this book Albright utilized archaeological and historical data, thus formulating the faith of Israel along lines considerably different from previous reconstructions, especially that of Julius *Wellhausen (1844-1918). Albright turned away from the standard history of religion trajectories such as that religions evolve from polytheism to henotheism to monotheism. He argued the case for montheism in the early history of Israel's faith. From his perspective, "Our knowledge of history is governed . . . by the same logical principles, inductive, deductive, and statistical, which control our knowledge in the 'natural' sciences."

The students of Albright set the agenda for American Old Testament studies from after World War II until the present, though other presuppositions started making headway in the 1970s. These students included George Ernest *Wright (1909-1974), George Mendenhall (b. 1916), John Bright (1908-1989), David Noel Freedman (b. 1922), Harry M. Orlinsky (1908-1992), Frank M. Cross (b. 1921) and Roland E. Murphy (b. 1917).

The important work on Acts in five volumes, *The Beginnings of Christianity* (1920-1933), edited by Frederick J. Foakes-Jackson and Kirsopp Lake, provides an example of New Testament studies. These volumes exhibit the empirical studies of which British and American scholars were capable and were among the first major North American works as comprehensive and detailed as German studies.

The first volume provided backgrounds to Acts; the second volume covered the composition, purpose, authorship and the history of Acts criticism; the third volume by James Hardy Ropes (1866-1933) examined the text of Acts; the fourth was a commentary on Acts under the authorship of Lake and Henry Joel Cadbury (1883-1974), though the work was mostly that of Lake; the fifth volume consisted of thirty-seven notes to the commentary. The persons involved in these volumes were the most capable North American New Testament scholars of the era. Some skepticism as to the historicity of Acts appeared in the comments of Lake and Cadbury, Lake being the more skeptical of the two. They argued that the interests of the author of Acts are apparent, that in some cases he was without adequate information, and in a few cases mistaken, but for the most part Acts is reliable history. They, however, did not herald its accuracy in the manner of William M. Ramsay (1851-1939) of Oxford.

In this period between the world wars, North American scholars were busy publishing tools for biblical studies that reflected various German undertakings but that were more often directed toward the use of ministers and seminary students, as well as being more conventional than German counterparts. Some of the works listed here were published earlier in the century: Brown, Driver and

Briggs, *Hebrew and English Lexicon of the Old Testament* (1907), for which Francis Brown did the lion's share of the work; the International Critical Commentary, edited by Charles Augustus Briggs, Samuel Rolles *Driver (1846-1914) and Alfred Plummer (1841-1926), with volumes by several North Americans, including Harper, Briggs, James A. Montgomery (1866-1949), Toy, G. Hinckley Mitchell (1862-1920), Julius A. Bewer (1877-1953), Ernest DeWitt Burton, Marvin R. Vincent (1834-1922), James Moffatt, Ropes, Moore and Henry Preserved Smith (1847-1927), as well as several introductions to both the Old and New Testaments. Goodenough assembled much data in order to answer the question as to why Christianity became so early and quickly Hellenized. Goodspeed collected manuscripts and published numerous textual studies and a widely circulated translation of the New Testament. He notably argued that Ephesians was a cover letter to the earliest assembling of Paul's letters and was written by the collector. Goodspeed published a frequently employed introduction to the New Testament (1937), and Robert H. Pfeiffer (1892-1958) of Harvard produced a comparable introduction to the Old Testament (1941).

The Continental Period (1945-1980)
Accompanying the emergence of the theological movement broadly known as neo-orthodoxy, the theological scene as well as that of biblical studies began to change in Europe through the influence of prominent figures such as Karl *Barth (1886-1968), Emil Brunner (1889-1966) and Paul Tillich (1886-1965). The crises of two world wars in Europe with a major depression in between changed the optimism of the halcyon days at the turn of the century. The confidence that the kingdom of God was breaking in as the result of enlightened human effort was broken. No longer was the hegemony of human experience held in such high regard. Theologians as well as biblical scholars now focused more on a God who reveals himself in history and Scripture and increasingly sought out theological answers to human questions. A new generation of biblical scholars looked beyond philological and historical investigations and took up a growing interest in biblical theology. Smart, in articles published in the *Journal of Religion* (1943), sensed the same change of focus in North America, which in turn resulted in a revived interest in biblical theology. The rise and fall of American biblical theology as a movement has been traced by Brevard *Childs (b. 1923) in *The Crisis in Biblical Theology* (1970).

After World War II an influx of veterans overran North American universities and colleges. Starting with the University of Iowa, state universities began offering courses in biblical studies. The major seminaries enrolled an increasing number of doctoral students. In addition to those studying in North America several prospective biblical scholars enrolled in European universities, among them George MacRae (1928-1985), later a professor at Harvard, and Carl

Holladay (b. 1943) later at Emory, both of whom received Ph.D's from Cambridge; E. Earle Ellis (b. 1926) of Southwestern Baptist Theological Seminary with a Ph.D. from Edinburgh; and James M. Robinson (b. 1924) of Claremont, from Basel. North American professors of Bible on sabbaticals visited European universities, especially Marburg, Tübingen, Heidelberg, Oslo, Uppsala, Cambridge, St. Andrews and the Pontifical Institute in Rome.

Several Europeans were newly employed at major universities and seminaries, including Krister Stendahl (b. 1921), with a Ph.D. from Uppsala, and Helmut Koester (b. 1926) from Marburg, at Harvard; Nils Dahl from Oslo at Yale; Markus Barth (1915-1994) from Basel at the University of Chicago and Pittsburgh Theological Seminary; Hans Dieter Betz (b. 1931) from Mainz at Chicago; Hendrikus Boers (b. 1928), a South African who took his doctorate at Bonn, at Emory; J. Christiaan Beker (b. 1924; B.D., Utrecht; Ph.D., Chicago) at Princeton Theological Seminary; and Ralph P. Martin (b. 1925) from London at Fuller Theological Seminary.

The result of this amalgamation of scholarship was that North America after the 1950s became the melting pot for international biblical scholarship, thereby paving the way for its later emergence as the source for innovative approaches to biblical criticism. Most major North American biblical scholars during these years either studied in Europe or visited scholars there.

Graduate schools of religion and seminaries were rapidly expanding in the United States. Despite the attraction of Europe, the majority of persons receiving doctorates in biblical studies from 1945 to 1980 received them from American schools, especially Union, Yale, Harvard, Chicago, Princeton, Claremont, Vanderbilt, Southern Methodist, Emory, Toronto, Hebrew Union, Weston School of Theology, Pennsylvania, Graduate Theological Union, Berkeley, the Johns Hopkins University, and the Catholic University of America. The seminaries that expanded the most rapidly were evangelical, such as Southwestern Baptist Theological Seminary, Fuller Theological Seminary, Dallas Theological Seminary, Trinity Evangelical Divinity School and Gordon-Conwell Theological Seminary. Evangelicals commenced attending major graduate programs in the early 1940s, with several going to Great Britain to study under such scholars as Frederick Fyvie *Bruce (1910-1991) at Manchester: for example, W. Ward Gasque (b. 1939), dean of Ontario Theological Seminary, and Clark Pinnock (b. 1937) at McMaster Divinity College. The evangelical biblical scholars tended to work in biblical languages and textual studies. Several attended Harvard because of the divinity school's tradition in biblical studies, its reputation and good scholarships; among them were George Eldon *Ladd (1911-1982) who spent his career at Fuller Theological Seminary.

With the increase in schools, students and professors, biblical scholars in North America rapidly became more specialized and began producing comprehensive and in-depth studies, some of which were comparable to those that in the past were chiefly produced in Europe. By 1970 the Society of Biblical Literature (SBL, founded in 1880) had expanded its programming, enabling most scholars interested in presenting papers to do so. By 1981 the society had more than five thousand members and had established Scholars Press (1974). The press was a joint venture with the American Academy of Religion (AAR) and launched a significant effort to make available the work of younger scholars, often based on dissertations, and other studies that were in some cases too technical for commercial publishers. Much credit for the vision of Scholars Press must go to Robert Funk (b. 1926), who from 1968 to 1974 was secretary of SBL and the first director of the press (1974-1980). The aim of the press was to make available to scholars at a reasonable rate materials that otherwise would go unpublished. In addition to the *Journal of Biblical Literature,* in 1974 the society founded *Semeia,* as an experimental journal, and jointly with the American Academy of Religion *Critical Review of Books in Religion* (beginning in 1988). Because of the increasing significance of the English reading market, major German works were rapidly translated into English; two such works were Rudolf *Bultmann's *Theology of the New Testament* (2 vols., 1951, 1955) and Gerhard *von Rad's *Old Testament Theology* (2 vols., 1962, 1965). In the 1980s German presses began publishing monographs in English written by those for whom English was a first language.

Roman Catholic scholars moved into the mainstream of international biblical scholarship in 1965 with the approval of the Constitution on Divine Revelation, *Dei Verbum.* Some of major scholars were Roland E. Murphy, Raymond E. *Brown (b. 1928) and Joseph A. Fitzmyer (b. 1920), all of whom took Ph.D.'s at the Johns Hopkins University but also spent time in Rome. These scholars quickly moved from traditional perspectives to consensus scholarly positions. For example, Fitzmyer now argued for a Paulinist authorship of the Pastorals, and Brown, though he argued in his commentary on John (2 vols., 1966, 1970) for authorship by John, son of Zebedee, later rejected this position. The Catholic Biblical Society was founded in 1937, and the *Catholic Biblical Quarterly* began publication in 1939. By the 1970s the leading Roman Catholic scholars embraced most of the consensus scholarly perspectives.

After World War II North Americans were involved in a number of key enterprises. Only a few of the major contributions that have tended to highlight an understanding of extrabiblical texts, as well as philological, archaeological and background studies, can be mentioned here.

The Nag Hammadi codices were discovered in Egypt in 1945. These documents included several gospels that were known by title but were not available in early manuscripts. The publication of these codices contributed to later revisionism in regard to the history of Jesus. James M. Robinson of Claremont, who earlier had mediated to North America the post-Bultmannian "new quest" of the historical Jesus, supervised the first facsimile edition of the codices (1972) and continued to oversee subsequent editions, the latest being 1984. He also edited with M. Meyer *The Nag Hammadi Library in English* (1977; 3d ed., 1988, with R. Smith).

The Dead Sea Scrolls were discovered in 1947. The earliest publication (1950, 1951) was by Millar Burrows (1889-1980) of Yale. The scrolls made available several early Hebrew texts of the Old Testament, and additional Qumran manuscripts provided new insights for backgrounds of the New Testament. Many North Americans have been involved in the study of these scrolls and their ultimate publication. In 1961 Frank Moore Cross of Harvard published *The Ancient Library of Qumran.* Other contributors have been Joseph A. Fitzmyer in 1966; James H. Charlesworth (b. 1940) in 1981; Lawrence H. Schiffman in 1983; John J. Collins (b. 1946) in 1984; and Joseph A. Callaway (b. 1920) in 1988. The first facsimile version has been published with the assistance of James M. Robinson.

North Americans continued to take the lead in various archaeological digs in Palestine. Earlier in the period, aside from Albright, Wright was the best known of the archaeologists. Since then other archaeologists who moved to the forefront were William G. Dever, James A. Sauer (b. 1945), James F. Strange (b. 1938) and L. E. Toombs (b. 1919). Hershel Shanks (b. 1930) has taken the lead in popularizing biblical archaeology through the founding of the *Biblical Archaeology Review* (1975). Dever has questioned whether there can be such a discipline as biblical archaeology as conceived by Albright. But he has recently somewhat modified his outlook. Various persons have been interested in collecting and reporting upon artifacts that may contribute to the understanding of the New Testament, including Helmut Koester and his students in his *Archaeological Resources for New Testament Study* (1987, 1994).

Whereas for a time the reconstruction of the history of Israel proceeded according to presuppositions of the Albright school, the historical textbook of John Bright (*A History of Israel,* 1959, 1972, 1982) being the major statement, the hegemony of the school has eroded because of the work of other scholars. The Albright school argued that though the patriarchal narratives cannot be acclaimed as actual history, yet they report adequately what can be known about the period when compared with extrabiblical sources. Some of the confidence in patriarchal biblical depictions resulted from Mendenhall's work on the Assyrian and Hittite covenant treaties and the amphictyonic political structures (1954, 1973). Furthermore, methodologically the Albright school agreed upon a consensus position in regard to the dating of the Yahwist, Elohist, Deuteronomic and Priestly documents in the Pentateuch. But more recently the accuracy of the patriarchal narratives and the chronology of the documents have been challenged especially by John Van Seters (b. 1935) in 1975 and 1994 and J. Maxwell Miller (b. 1937) in 1986. While the turn-of-the-century move away from the historical perspectives as provided by biblical insight itself was subsequently restrained by the Albright school, chronological claims today are unsettled.

In North America much effort has gone into understanding the background of the New Testament, especially Greco-Roman backgrounds. Some of the leaders in this field have been Abraham J. Malherbe (b. 1930) and Wayne A. Meeks (b. 1932) at Yale Divinity School. Malherbe has been interested in the social settings for New Testament documents, as seen in his *Social Aspects of Early Christianity* (1983). More of his publications, however, have drawn upon insights provided in Hellenistic texts of ancient forms of literature and philosophy (1987, 1989). Meeks commented on the social backdrop of the early church by interpreting work in Grecian materials, including those from Hellenistic Judaism, in *The First Urban Christians* (1983). Younger scholars who have been trained at Yale include Stanley Stowers (b. 1948), L. Michael White (b. 1949), Ronald Hock (b. 1942), John Fitzgerald (b. 1948) and David Balch (b. 1942). Foremost among the scholars who have employed sociological models have been Bruce Malina (b. 1933) in *New Testament World Insights from Cultural Anthropology* (1993) and Jerome H. Neyrey (b. 1940) in *Paul, in Other Words: A Cultural Reading of His Letters* (1990).

Canonical criticism is an approach chiefly advocated in North America. James A. Sanders (b. 1927) first coined the phrase in *Torah and Canon* (1972). He sought a common hermeneutic running throughout the biblical materials, but he later preferred the term "canonical criticism." Childs early employed the terminology as a method of reflecting on the total shape of books in Scripture, of collections within Scripture (e.g., the Pentateuch) or the Scripture as a whole in his *Introduction to the Old Testament as Scripture* (1979) and more recently in *Old Testament Theology in a Canonical Context* (1985). Within this context, however, he gave attention to standard critical observations in regard to the construction of the text. A common thread that runs through the works of scholars with an interest in canonical criticism is that these larger aspects have been neglected through form-critical analysis.

William R. Farmer (b. 1921) has gathered a group of scholars interested in reviving the *Griesbach Synoptic solution, now labeled the Two-Gospel hypothesis. In this theory Matthew was written first, as opposed to the consensus Two-Source hypothesis that Mark and Q provide the basic beginning point for Matthew and Luke, who utilize these two sources for structure and content. Farmer argues rather that Matthew is the first Gospel, that Luke-Acts was written second, that Mark was written third as a selective combination of Matthew and Luke, and that Q is the figment of scholarly imagination. Farmer's early statement of this position is *The Synoptic Problem* (1964). Other involved North Americans are David L. Dungan (b. 1936), Allan J. McNicol (b. 1939) and David B. Peabody (b. 1946).

North America has not been especially fertile soil for biblical theology in terms of major publications on the subject. After World War II George Ernest *Wright expressed interest in Old Testament theology in *The Old Testament Against Its Environment* (1950) and *God Who Acts* (1952). Wright argued that God revealed himself in history in unique ways and that his actions were the fundamental foci of his revelation. The explanations of these actions within Scripture constituted a secondary and sometimes human component. At about the same time Americans became aware of the theological work of Bultmann and his predilection for Heideggerian existentialism. In the 1950s existentialism and phenomenological analysis made some headway into philosophy and literature departments in North America and into the discussion of biblical scholars with the publication of Bultmann's *Theology of the New Testament* (ET 1951, 1955). In some circles, for example, at Yale, the influence of Bultmann was felt in the early 1950s.

At many seminaries, however, especially among biblical scholars, interest in Bultmann's New Testament theology did not come to the forefront until the late 1950s. Despite the demise of biblical theology as a movement, North American scholars continued to produce monographs in biblical theology. More works have been produced in Old Testament than New. In the Old are Millar Burrows (1889-1980), *An Outline of Biblical Theology* (1946); Otto J. Baab (1896-1956), *The Theology of the Old Testament* (1949); Walter C. Kaiser Jr. (b. 1933), *Toward an Old Testament Theology* (1978); Samuel Terrien (b. 1911), *The Elusive Presence: Toward a New Biblical Theology* (1978). These works are more indebted to Walther *Eichrodt (1890-1978) and *von Rad than to Wright. More recently there have been new offerings by Brevard Childs, *Biblical Theology of the Old and New Testaments: Theological Reflections on the Christian Bible* (1993), and Walter Brueggemann (b. 1933), *Theology of the Old Testament Theology: Testimony, Dispute, Advocacy* (1997).

In New Testament theology are works by George Eldon Ladd, *A Theology of the New Testament* (1974), and John Reumann (b. 1927), *Witness of the Word: A Biblical Theology of the Gospel* (1986) and *The Promise and Practice of Biblical Theology* (1991).

Toward the end of the 1970s more and more biblical critics perceived their work to be in service of international biblical scholarship rather than of the church. Those teaching in state universities especially embraced such a driving force, though the same attitude prevailed among some scholars in seminary settings.

The North American Period (1981-1999)

In the 1980s biblical scholarship came of age in North America. The brightest and best of the biblical scholars no longer went to Europe but took up graduate residencies in North American universities and seminaries. Biblical scholars from Europe, Africa, Asia, Australia and Europe came to North America to study and to learn newly developing approaches. A new mood swept over biblical studies. Specialism diverted biblical studies in various directions, and specialists promoting new approaches tended to be North Americans. Furthermore, it appears that postmodernism has affected North Americans more than it has Europeans. Criticism has arisen from various quarters as to the merits of classical grammaticohistorical studies, though reports of its demise are premature. Even yet, the majority of North American biblical scholars work within the parameters of traditional studies.

Newer approaches have been the Third Quest for the historical Jesus, narrative analysis, rhetorical analysis, literary criticism, ideological criticism, feminist hermeneutics and imaginative reconstructions.

New approaches to the continuing discussion of the Jesus of history, sometimes called the Third Quest, have emerged. Major positions are set forth by Burton L. Mack (b. 1931), who characterizes Jesus as a Hellinist Cynic sage in *A Myth of Innocence* (1988); John Dominic Crossan (b. 1934), as a Jewish Cynic peasant in *The Historical Jesus* (1991); Marcus Borg (b. 1942), as a Jewish visionary in *Meeting Jesus Again for the First Time* (1994); Elisabeth *Schüssler Fiorenza (b. 1938), as an egalitarian child of the divine Sophia in *Jesus: Miriam's Child, Sophia's Prophet* (1994); John P. Meier (b. 1942), as an eschatological prophet, present and future, in *A Marginal Jew* (vol. 1, 1991; 2, 1994); and E. P. Sanders (b. 1937), as a prophet of imminent restoration eschatology in *Jesus and Judaism* (1985).

The Jesus Seminar, founded by Robert W. Funk in 1985 under the auspices of his Westar Institute in Sonoma, California, has been a significant factor in the quest. Dominic Crossan of DePaul University in Chicago has been cochairman. About forty scholars have been involved in the proceedings. The Jesus Seminar began with the assumption that the Gospels are not accurate history and spent its first years on determining the authentic sayings of Jesus. Decisions have been rendered by scholars voting with colored marbles: red signifying "that's Jesus"; pink, "sure sounds like Jesus"; gray, "maybe"; black, "there's been a mistake." In Funk's projection, the work of the seminar has been more to inform the populace of conclusions than making a contribution to scholarship. The major publication of the seminar to date is *The Complete Gospels* (1994), edited by Robert J. Miller (b. 1954), which contains the four canonical Gospels as well as several apocryphal gospels, though they are not treated as apocryphal by the seminar. Though a few major scholars have been involved, the seminar has been widely criticized from some quarters of the scholarly guild, as shown in Luke Timothy Johnson's (b. 1943) *The Real Jesus: The Misguided Quest for the*

Historical Jesus and the Truth of the Traditional Gospels (1996). As to future focus, the seminar intends to discuss the works of Jesus as well as reopen the question of New Testament canon.

Because of certain observations of H. Richard Niebuhr (1894-1962), since the 1940s considerable interest has arisen in the narrative aspects of the Scriptures. Scholars instrumental in formulating two different approaches to the issue have been connected with Yale (Hans Frei [1922-1988], Stanley Hauerwas [b. 1940], David Kelsey [b. 1932]) and Chicago (Paul Ricoeur [b. 1913], David Tracy [b. 1939], Julian Hartt [b. 1911]).

According to Frei, even though the Scriptures have historylike materials, the result of the Enlightenment has been to separate what the story says from what it is about and thereby denying narrative a role in the presentation of theology. He proposed that the biblical narratives should be evaluated on their own terms rather than as to their historicity or universal truths in the manner of philosophy. The theology in these narratives must therefore be presented according to the dictates of biblical narrativity. Old Testament scholars such as Robert Alter (b. 1935), Adele Berlin, Meir Sternberg, David M. Gunn (b. 1942), Danna Nolan Fewell (b. 1958) and Phyllis *Trible (b. 1932) have been especially interested in presenting parts of the Old Testament from the perspective of narrative.

In the 1968 presidential address to the Society of Biblical Literature, James *Muilenburg (1896-1974) proposed that form-critical studies were too focused on discrete units of Scripture. He declared that rhetorical analysis was now mandated so as to move beyond studies to date in order to gain appreciation for larger movements in the text and more specifically in retaining the historical context and in keeping in mind the text's unique features. He generated some interest among Old Testament scholars, but it has been particularly among New Testament scholars, sparked by Hans Dieter Betz's commentary on Galatians (1979), that classical rhetorical analysis has been applied to the epistles of Paul. Others who soon took up this interest and focused on argument and arrangement were Wilhelm Wuellner (b. 1927), James D. Hester (b. 1939) and Robert Jewett (b. 1933). In the meantime George Kennedy (b. 1928), a classics professor at North Carolina, became interested in the rhetorical analysis of the Scripture and published *New Testament Interpretation Through Rhetorical Criticism* (1984). He also trained such younger scholars as Duane Watson (b. 1956), who has pursued classical rhetoric in the investigation of several epistles (see Duane F. Watson and Alan J. Hauser, *Rhetorical Criticism of the Bible: A Comprehensive Bibliography* [1994]).

Rhetorical criticism has had a wider context. In the early part of the century in America, classical rhetoric was studied and employed by teachers of public speaking. In the 1960s professors of English composition developed a renewed interest in rhetoric. Since that time, philosophers, philosophers of science, anthropologists and many other academics have become interested in rhetoric. The neo-classical rhetoric of Chaim Perelman (b. 1912) and Lucie Olbrechts-Tyteca is exemplified in *The New Rhetoric: A Treatise on Argumentation* (1969). The result has been an amalgamation of rhetoric with other forms of literary, sociological, sociobiological or anthropological analysis. At present a group of younger scholars has moved away from classical rhetoric and is attempting to construct a rhetoric that brings together most if not all of the modern studies that focus upon discourse. The work of Vernon Robbins (b. 1939) of Emory is representative as expressed in *Exploring the Texture of Texts: A Guide to Socio-Rhetorical Criticism* (1996). These studies have highlighted multidimensionality, relief (a metaphor borrowed from topography), shape and form. Rhetorical studies have also attracted international scholars, especially in South Africa, Scandinavia and Asia (see Stanley E. Porter and Thomas H. Olbricht, eds., *Rhetoric and the New Testament: Essays from the 1992 Heidelberg Conference* [1993] as well as subsequent volumes to be published from conferences at Pretoria [1994], London [1995], Malibu [1996] and Florence [1998]).

Rhetorical criticism has embraced many different kinds of criticism, including modernism and formalism, exemplified by Cleanth Brooks (b. 1906) and T. S. Eliot (1888-1965); the reader response criticism of Kenneth Burke (1887-1995), Walter J. Ong, S.J. (b. 1912) and Stanley Fish (b. 1938); structuralism and semiotics of Ferdinand de Saussure (1857-1913) and Roland Barthes (1915-1980); the deconstruction of Jacques Derrida (b. 1930) and Paul de Man (1919-1983); psychological and psychoanalytic criticism of Michel Foucault (1926-1984) and Peter Brooks (b. 1938); Marxism and new historicism of Raymond Williams (1921-1988); the feminism of Elaine Showalter (b. 1941) and Hélèn Cixous (b. 1937); the African-American criticism of Henry Louis Gates Jr. (b. 1950); and the ethical and canonical concerns of Northrop Frye (1912-1991) and J. Hillis Miller (b. 1928). These have now extended to ideological criticism, feminist hermeneutics and imaginist perspectives.

Conclusion

Twentieth-century American biblical studies has moved from connoisseurship of premier German criticism to trendsetter for international biblical scholarship. Some persons will view these North American developments with much enthusiasm as a triumphal rise to scholarly hegemony. But on the Continent and in Great Britain, traditional biblical scholars view these developments with alarm and characterize what transpires in North America as avant-garde and ephemeral. And those of a more conventional and conservative bent, both in North America and throughout the world, lament the manner in which North American leadership of this stripe may well bring about the demise of the biblical scholarship and also faith during the new century about to burst upon the horizon.

A new world civilization is in the making, one much more diverse in ethnicity, culture and religion. Since the religious complexion in North America has become increasingly diverse, no one religion prevails. One may therefore have some sympathy with the proposition that each community of faith should be granted the privilege of telling its own story. This makes it imperative to rediscover the narratival and rhetorical features of Scripture while still prioritizing long-standing grammatical, historical, literary criticism. Interest in the story line as found in Scripture has returned, not necessarily because scholars regard it as actual history but because ensconced in it is the account of the faith of Israel and of the church, which has and still motivates oncoming generations into pursuing biblical scholarship.

BIBLIOGRAPHY

R. E. Clements, *One Hundred Years of Old Testament Interpretation* (Philadelphia: Westminster, 1976); R. J. Coggins and R. P. Martin, "American Interpretation" in *A Dictionary of Biblical Interpretation*, ed. R. J. Coggins and J. L. Houlden (London: SCM; Philadelphia: Trinity Press International, 1990) 16-19; A. Y. Collins, ed., *Feminist Perspectives on Biblical Scholarship* ((Atlanta: Scholars Press, 1985); F. Danker, *A Century of Greco-Roman Philology Featuring the American Philological Association and the Society of Biblical Literature* (Atlanta: Scholars Press, 1988); W. G. Doty, *Contemporary New Testament Interpretation* (Englewood Cliffs, NJ: Prentice-Hall, 1972); R. S. Eccles, *Erwin Ramsdell Goodenough: A Personal Pilgrimage* (Atlanta: Scholars Press, 1985); E. J. Epp and G. W. MacRae, eds., *The New Testament and Its Modern Interpreters* (Philadelphia: Fortress, 1989); G. P. Fogarty, S.J., *American Catholic Biblical Scholarship: A History from the Early Republic to Vatican II* (San Francisco: Harper & Row, 1989); H. Frei, *The Eclipse of Biblical Narrative: A Study in Eighteenth- and Nineteenth-Century Hermeneutics* (New Haven, CT: Yale University Press, 1974); R. Grant, "American New Testament Study, 1926-1956," *JBL* 87 (1968) 42-50; H. F. Hahn, *The Old Testament in Modern Research* (Philadelphia: Muhlenberg, 1954); R. A. Harrisville, *Benjamin Wisner Bacon: Pioneer in American Biblical Criticism* (Missoula, MT: Scholars Press, 1976); P. Henry, *New Directions in New Testament Study* (Philadelphia: Westminster, 1979); C. R. Holladay, "Contemporary Methods of Reading the Bible" in *The New Interpreter's Bible,* ed. L. E. Keck (Nashville: Abingdon, 1994) 125-49; W. J. Hynes, *Shirley Jackson Case and the Chicago School* (Chico, CA: Scholars Press, 1981); D. A. Knight and G. M. Tucker, eds., *The Hebrew Bible and Its Modern Interpreters* (Chico, CA: Scholars Press, 1985); J. S. Moir, *A History of Biblical Studies in Canada* (Chico, CA: Scholars Press, 1982); M. A. Noll, *Between Faith and Criticism: Evangelicals, Scholarship and the Bible in America* (San Francisco: Harper & Row, 1986); L. G. Perdue, *The Collapse of History: Reconstructing Old Testament Theology* (Minneapolis: Fortress, 1994); J. K. Riches, *A Century of New Testament Study* (Valley Forge, PA: Trinity Press International, 1993); E. W. Saunders, *Searching the Scriptures: A History of the Society of Biblical Literature, 1880-1980* (Chico, CA: Scholars Press, 1982); J. D. Smart, *The Interpretation of the Scripture* (Philadelphia: Westminster, 1961); S. D. Sperling, ed., *Students of the Covenant: A History of Jewish Biblical Scholarship in North America* (Atlanta: Scholars Press, 1992).

T. H. OLBRICHT

Albright, William Foxwell
(1891-1971)

Called the dean of biblical archaeologists in his last decades, William Foxwell Albright was also to become a well-known biblical interpreter. As the first of six children, four boys and two girls, born to self-supporting Methodist missionary parents in Chile, he benefited by schooling he received mainly from his well-educated mother and preacher father and by tutoring his siblings. He became as fluent in Spanish as in English and also learned French and German in Chile in his first twelve years. The austere life and strict religion of his early years produced a frugal, conservative lifestyle that he never abandoned, which enabled him to accomplish much with little support.

Albright's left hand was crippled when he was five by an accident at his grandmother Foxwell's Iowa farm. This misfortune as well as his myopia early turned him from sports to books—history and theology in his father's library. He devoured R. W. Rogers's two-volume *History of Babylonia and Assyria,* which he ordered with errand money he had earned. By eleven he already knew that he wished to become a biblical archaeologist but feared that by the time he grew up, everything would have been discovered.

While attending Upper Iowa University, Albright taught himself Hebrew from his father's Harper textbook. He also learned Akkadian, besides studying math, science and ancient languages and participating in debating and literary clubs. Since he had to do hard manual labor he became quite adept even with his crippled hand. While he later considered the college to have been culturally narrow, he appreciated the good foundation he had gained in Greek, Latin and mathematics.

A year as a high school principal in Ger-

man-speaking Menno, South Dakota, the year after his 1912 graduation from college, convinced Albright that his talents did not lie at that level of teaching. But in that year, because he could send with his application to Johns Hopkins University a proof of an article he had submitted to a German scholarly publication on an Akkadian word, he was accepted and received a small scholarship.

This started four years of doctoral study under Paul Haupt, a leading biblical scholar who was founder and chair of the Oriental Seminary, today called the Department of Near Eastern Studies. There Albright was trained in a mythical and historical-critical approach to biblical studies, as well as in Semitic languages. His first published articles, before and after his 1916 graduation, reflect Haupt's more liberal views, although a decade later he confessed in a letter to Haupt that he had since reverted to the more conservative viewpoint he had learned in his early years and solidified in college, views that were already full-blown in his mind before he came to Johns Hopkins.

After graduation Albright taught in Haupt's department, supported by further scholarships, until in 1918 he had to endure six painful months of limited service as a clerk in World War I. A letter to his mother during his months in the Army reveals his thinking. He said he was not spreading ideas of higher criticism there—those men needed only to have simple faith in the Nazarene. While the philosophical and scientific investigation of the religious development of humanity was not relevant for the person's soul needs, such research must be undertaken in the future, building on his or similar studies, by those who would be guides in religious thought.

After Albright was able to return to teaching and writing, by the end of 1919 he was finally able to use the Thayer Fellowship he had won for a year of study in Palestine. The decade of the 1920s in Jerusalem, where in August 1921 he married Ruth Norton, a Hopkins Ph.D. in Sanskrit, was an intense time of study of modern Hebrew and modern Arabic, of teaching ministers who came for a few months of study with him in the American School of Oriental Research (now the W. F. Albright Institute of Archaeological Research), where he soon became director, and of his beginning excavations. Three of four sons were born in Jerusalem during that decade.

Work. Albright first dug at Gibeah (King Saul's headquarters at Tell el-Ful) and later at Bethel and Beth-zur. Especially important were his four landmark seasons of excavation at Tell Beit Mirsim, which he identified as biblical Debir, Kiriath-sefer. There he established pottery chronology for western Palestine and refined his theory of dating the biblical exodus of the Hebrews from Egypt to the thirteenth century B.C. He was in touch with other archaeologists, involved in dating their finds to correlate with biblical data and in deciphering the newly discovered Ugaritic tablets (1929-1930) and an Egyptian stele found at Beth-shan. With his conservative religious viewpoint, and as a result of his explorations of the land of the Bible even before beginning to excavate, he came to realize the reality of the Bible's stories grounded there, and he entirely changed the focus of his writings. He began a decades-long effort to counteract the work of Julius *Wellhausen and other scholars who thought that the Bible contained little reliable history.

After Haupt's death, Albright became chairman of the university department. For a few years in the 1930s he divided his time between Baltimore and Palestine, while he began to publish books as well as articles on archaeology. After his decade in Palestine, he became editor (1930-1968) of the *Bulletin of the American Schools of Oriental Research (BASOR)*, which was started by his mentor, J. A. Montgomery, and which

at first contained mainly reports on his explorations and excavations. He tried to write in a popular style to attract a wider audience among laypeople and more financial support for archaeology. In time, however, *BASOR* became more and more technical, so a more popular journal, *Biblical Archaeologist,* was begun in 1938 by one of his outstanding students, George Ernest *Wright, who followed Albright as a leading biblical archaeologist and theologian.

In 1940 Albright published *From the Stone Age to Christianity,* which set forth not only his view of the light thrown by archaeology on the Bible but also his basic philosophy of interpretation of the Bible and religion. In it he traced the development of humankind's idea of God from prehistoric times to the time of Christ. He recognized the historical value of the patriarchal stories and of Moses and monotheism. A review in the Baltimore *Sun* (March 23, 1941) stated: "The Bible was responsible for Dr. Albright's interest in archaeology; . . . and archaeology in turn has stimulated his interest in the Bible, for the foundation of his latest book rests upon archaeological research." Shortly thereafter he published a companion work, *Archaeology and the Religion of Israel,* in which he filled out the outline of the history of Israel's religion provided in *From the Stone Age to Christianity,* especially for the earlier historic period. *From the Stone Age to Christianity* and several other books went through a number of editions and were translated into other languages.

In those years Albright not only was developing a number of outstanding scholars in archaeology and biblical studies but also was working to find posts in American universities for Jewish scholars fleeing Hitler's Germany. After World War II Albright participated in several excavations in the Sinai Peninsula and in South Arabia, but mainly he taught, holding the William Wallace Spence Chair of Semitic Languages as well as chairing the Oriental Seminary. He also published much in *BASOR* and other journals and lectured widely.

Albright was the first scholar in America to hear about and recognize the value of the discovery of the Dead Sea Scrolls toward the end of the 1940s. He conducted weekly seminars on them and on Hebrew poetry until his mandatory retirement in 1958.

In the preface to his *History, Archaeology and Christian Humanism* (1964), Albright stated that the keynote of the book is struck in the first chapter, "Toward a Theistic Humanism." Its contents did not repeat but in many ways supplemented what he had published in *From the Stone Age to Christianity* in 1940. He credited help from friends, one of his four sons, Hugh, and especially his wife, who patiently read to him during the times of his nervous exhaustion and when medication for glaucoma prevented the use of his eyes. One of the subsections of the first chapter (to show his kind of biblical interpretation) concerned "Archaeological Discovery and Literary-Historical Criticism of the Bible"; another section was "Religion in History," with subsections titled "Religion and Civilization," "Higher Culture Prepares for Christianity" and "The Biblical Drama of Salvation." The third chapter was entitled "The Place of the Old Testament in the History of Thought." Albright called the Old Testament "a masterpiece of empirical logic." Chapter five was on "The Ancient Near East and the Religion of Israel." His projected work on the religion of ancient Israel was not completed before his death.

In the "more personal" part four, chapter fourteen of *History, Archaeology and Christian Humanism* he stated in a "background note" on his life: "Beginning with the evangelical Protestantism characteristic of the late 19th century I have attended, for a year or more at a time, Methodist, Baptist, Lutheran, Episcopalian, and Presbyterian churches." He had married "an Anglo-Catholic who joined the Church of Rome a little over a year later. Through my family, my colleagues, and especially through my students, my ties with Catholicism have continued to become closer. At the same time my Jewish associations have also become progressively closer. . . . Until I was twenty-one I had never met anyone whom I knew to be Jewish, but after nearly half a century of friendly association I am in some ways more at home in Jewish circles than anywhere else" (Albright 1964, 288).

Albright wrote that enthusiasm for scientific research of all kinds had dominated his work, and he had always read scientific materials extensively: "Friendship with men of science and study of scientific method have been decisive in fixing the character of my own research, culminating in election to the National Academy of Sciences in 1955." That he considered his greatest honor. In addition he received nearly thirty honorary doctorates from universities in Europe and America, several festschriften (1951, 1961, 1969, 1971) and many other awards.

Albright wrote further in *History, Archaelogy and Christian Humanism* that it was "misleading to insist on any fundamental difference between the nature of historical and scientific knowledge"; "judgments of cause are shared with the social and biological sciences," and "when history is applied for didactic purposes, value judgments are entirely proper." He continued: "In the center of history stands the Bible. The latter has suffered more in many respects from its well-intentioned friends than from its honest foes, but it is now being rediscovered by the labors of archaeologists and philologians. We are rapidly regaining our balance after generations of bitter controversy" (Albright 1964, 291). "The Bible is the heir of the civilizations which had preceded it: Egyptian, Mesopotamian, Syrian, Anatolian, and others. Israel preserved older values, but it also tranfigured them by its own genius into a great spiritual culture which was passed on to Europe and has ever since been the guiding light of Western civilization. Thanks to modern research we now recognize its substantial historicity" (Albright 1964, 293). "There has been a general return to appreciation of the accuracy, both in general sweep and in factual detail, of the religious history of Israel" (Albright 1964, 294). "To sum up, we can now again treat the Bible from beginning to end as an authentic document of religious history" (Albright 1964, 295).

In 1966 Albright's Whidden Lectures for 1961 were published in *New Horizons in Biblical Research* (Oxford University Press), with chapters titled "Archaeology and Israelite Tradition," "The Ancient Israelite Mind in Its Environmental Context" and "New Testament Research after the Discovery of the Dead Sea Scrolls."

In the late 1950s Albright and one of his former students, David Noel Freedman, the scholar who became Albright's editorial associate, cofounded the Anchor Bible series, which is still in process of publication by Doubleday. In the mid-1960s, with the help of research assistants Leona Glidden Running and especially C. Stephen Mann, Albright took over the Anchor Bible volume on Acts, the author of which, Johannes Munck, had died before completing work on his manuscript. After that Albright and Mann took on the assignment of the Anchor Bible volume on Matthew, the latter scholar doing the main writing. In both books Albright contributed not only to the content of the commentary but also with valuable introductory articles. Albright could not be barred from New Testament studies any more than he could be kept out of Egyptological studies (e.g., *The Vocalization of the Egyptian Syllabic Orthography,* 1934). There are about eleven hundred items in his lifetime bibliography, published after his death by Freedman.

Albright considered himself an orientalist. One time, answering a question as to what are the Bible lands, he specified the region from the Indus River in India to the Pillars of Hercules (Gibraltar) and from Ethiopia to the southern part of Russia, with special emphasis on the Fertile Crescent. Of all the lands within that territory, Albright knew the history, archaeology, languages, dialects, art, and artifacts.

Two months after his eightieth birthday

celebration (May 24, 1971), Albright suffered severe strokes. On September 22, friends and colleagues came from near and far for his funeral, mourning the loss of this scholar.

Since he was always on the cutting edge of his disciplines, Albright was always willing to change his opinion when further information became available. It is thus inevitable that later scholars, including his own students, are modifying and sometimes even recasting his published views. His enduring legacy lies in his voluminous publications and in the scholars who are continuing the development of his various fields.

BIBLIOGRAPHY

Works. W. F. Albright, *Archaeology and the Religion of Israel* (Baltimore: Johns Hopkins University Press, 1942); idem, *The Archaeology of Palestine* (rev. ed.; Harmondsworth, England: Penguin, 1954 [1949]); idem, *The Archaeology of Palestine and the Bible* (New York: Fleming H. Revell, 1932); idem, *The Biblical Period from Abraham to Ezra* (Oxford: Blackwell, 1952); idem, *The Excavation of Tell Beit Mirsim* (AASOR 12, 13, 17, 21-22; New Haven, CT: American Schools of Oriental Research, 1932, 1933, 1938, 1943); idem, *From the Stone Age to Christianity: Monotheism and the Historical Process* (Baltimore: Johns Hopkins University Press, 1940); idem, *History, Archaeology and Christian Humanism* (New York: McGraw-Hill, 1964); idem, with C. S. Mann, *Matthew* (AB; Garden City, NY: Doubleday, 1971); idem, *The Proto-Sinaitic Inscriptions and Their Decipherment* (Cambridge, MA: Harvard University Press, 1969 [1966]); idem, *Samuel and the Beginnings of the Prophetic Movement* (Cincinnati: Hebrew Union College Press, 1961); idem, *The Vocalization of the Egyptian Syllabic Orthography* (New Haven, CT: American Oriental Society, 1934); idem, *Yahweh and the Gods of Canaan: A Historical Analysis of Two Contrasting Faiths* (Garden City, NY: Doubleday, 1968). Festschriften include H. Goedicke, ed., *Near Eastern Studies in Honor of William Foxwell Albright* (Baltimore: Johns Hopkins University Press, 1971); A. Malamat, ed., *Eretz Israel* (W. F. Albright volume) 9 (1969); E. A. Speiser, ed., *Bulletin of the American Schools of Oriental Research* 122 (April 1951); G. E. Wright, ed., *The Bible and the Ancient Near*

East: Essays in Honor of William Foxwell Albright (Garden City, NY: Doubleday, 1961).

Studies. E. Hardwick, "Change and Constancy in William Foxwell Albright's Treatment of Early Old Testament History and Religion, 1918-1958" (Ph.D. diss., New York University, 1966); D. N. Freedman, ed., *The Published Works of William Foxwell Albright: A Comprehensive Bibliography* (Cambridge, MA: American Schools of Oriental Research, 1975); L. G. Running and D. N. Freedman, *William Foxwell Albright: A Twentieth-Century Genius* (centennial ed.; Berrien Springs, MI: Andrews University Press, 1991 [1975]); B. O. Long, *Planting and Reaping Albright: Politics, Ideology, and Interpreting the Bible* (University Park, PA: Pennsylvania State University Press, 1997); G. Van Beek, ed., *The Scholarship of William Foxwell Albright: An Appraisal* (Atlanta: Scholars Press, 1989 [1984]).   L. G. Running

Brown, Raymond E. *(1928-1998)*

Father Raymond Edward Brown, S.S., was Auburn Distinguished Professor Emeritus of Biblical Studies at Union Theological Seminary (New York), where he taught for some twenty years until his retirement in June 1990. Initially he served a joint professorship between the Jesuit seminary, Woodstock, and Union in New York (1971-1974). Earlier Brown taught Scripture studies at St. Mary's Seminary in Baltimore (1959-1971); previously he taught classics at St. Charles College, Catonsville, Maryland (1953-1954). Brown was adjunct professor of religion at Columbia University, New York (1979-1990); visiting professor of New Testament at the Pontifical Biblical Institute in Rome (1973, 1988); annual professor at the Albright School of Archaeology in Jerusalem (1978), where he was also a Jordan Fellow (1958-1959) and a trustee (1962-1963, 1974-1975); he was several times scholar in residence at the North American College in Rome.

Brown was born in New York City on May 22, 1928, and moved with his family to Florida in 1944. He did preparatory studies for the Roman Catholic priesthood at St. Charles College, Catonsville, Mary-

land (1945-1946); the Catholic University of America in Washington, D.C. (B.A., 1948; M.A., 1949); Gregorian University, Rome (1949-1950); and St. Mary's Seminary in Baltimore (S.T.B., 1951; S.T.L., 1953). Brown was a member of Phi Beta Kappa. He was ordained in 1953 as a priest of the Florida (St. Augustine) Diocese. He was a member of the Society of St. Sulpice (S.S.), which is not a religious order but a fellowship of diocesan priests who are permanently released by their bishops for the exclusive work of teaching in seminaries. He became a candidate for the society in 1951 and was admitted in 1955. Brown received the S.T.D. from St. Mary's Seminary and University (Baltimore, 1955). He studied Semitic languages at the Johns Hopkins University, where he received his Ph.D. (1958). He held the S.S.B. (1959) and the S.S.L. from the Pontifical Biblical Commission in Rome (1963).

Work. In addition to delivering numerous lectures in North America, Brown lectured in Asia, Australia, Europe and South America. His lectureships were nearly ninety by 1998. He was a fellow of the American Academy of Arts and Sciences and a corresponding fellow of the British Academy. He was the first person to have served as president of all three of these societies: the Catholic Biblical Association of America (1971-1972), the Society of Biblical Literature (1976-1977) and Studiorum Novi Testamenti Societas (the international Society of New Testament Studies; 1986-1987).

In 1963 Brown attended the first session of the Vatican II council as advisor to Archbishop Hurley of St. Augustine, Florida. He was the first Roman Catholic ever to address the Faith and Order Conference of the World Council of Churches in Montreal, Canada (1963). Brown was a member of the national commission for theological discussions between the Lutheran churches of the United States and the Roman Catholic Church (1965-1974). He was the only American Catholic of the Joint Theological Commission established by the World

Council of Churches and the Roman Catholic Church to discuss "Apostolicity and Catholicity" (1967-1968). Pope Paul VI named Brown as a consultor for the Vatican Secretariat for Christian Unity (1968-1973); and by agreement between the Vatican and the World Council of Churches, he served as the only American Catholic member of the Faith and Order Commission (1968-1993). Brown was the only American member of the Roman Pontifical Biblical Commission, by papal appointment (1972-1978), an appointment that Pope Paul VI accorded to twenty scholars he deemed to be "outstanding for their learning, prudence, and Catholic regard for the Magisterium of the Church." Brown was granted this award after the pope consulted with the National Conference of Catholic Bishops.

Time referred to Brown as "probably the premier Catholic Scripture scholar in the U.S." In 1971 the Catholic Theological Society of America chose him as "the outstanding American Catholic theologian of the year." Brown held thirty-one honorary doctorates. In addition to degrees from Roman Catholic institutions in the United States, such as Boston College (Litt.D.), DePaul (L.H.D.), Fordham (Litt.D.) and Villanova (Litt.D.), Brown was awarded honorary degrees from Presbyterian, Lutheran, Catholic, Episcopal and unaffiliated universities in Europe and North America: the universities of Edinburgh (D.D.) and Glasgow (D.D.), Uppsala (Th.D.), Louvain (Th.D.) and Episcopal Theological Seminary (D.D.) and Northwestern University (S.T.D.) in the U.S.

Brown was the author of twenty-five major books on the Bible and fifteen briefer books concerned with the study of Scripture. His writings have been honored with at least a dozen book awards. He contributed articles to a range of scholarly journals and served on the editorial boards of *Catholic Biblical Quarterly, Journal of Biblical Literature, New Testament Studies, Anchor Bible, Theological Studies,* and *Louvain Theological and Pastoral Monographs.*

Exposition. One may view the majority of Brown's books in five classifications that complement one another in a fashion that becomes clear in books that form a sixth grouping.

1. Brown's work was devoted in a significant way to exegetical treatment of books or key portions of books of the Bible. Of chief significance in this category one may look to these volumes. First is the collection *New Testament Essays* (1965), which brought together fourteen previously published articles that summarized then-current biblical studies and their cross-confessional implications, as well as making a series of significant probes into the Gospels, especially John. Many scholars still cite these essays as models of exegetical precision done from a historical-critical point of view with a concern for the theological dimensions of the biblical texts.

In 1966 the first of Brown's two-volume treatment of *The Gospel According to John* appeared; the second volume came out in 1970. Together these books formed a milestone in North American English-language commentary writing. Brown expanded the format of the Anchor Bible by providing not only a fresh translation of the biblical text with brief notes and comments but also provided a seemingly exhaustive analysis of the textual, historical and philological problems associated with the text with extensive and incisive theologically oriented commentary on John's Gospel. Along the way he touched on nearly every facet of past scholarship related to the Fourth Gospel, both integrating from and reacting against previous studies to form his own synthesis, so that the work was neither idiosyncratic (John is pious fiction) nor superfluous (John is bald history). Insights in the first volume concerning the historical situation faced by the author gained sharpened focus in the second volume and would find subsequent development in later years in relation to other Johannine literature. In general, Brown joined those who advocated reading the Fourth Gospel against the background of Hellenistic Judaism rather than in relation to non-Jewish Hellenism; and in particular for the first time he demonstrated the correctness of this interpretation in relation to the entire Gospel rather than in relation to key segments of the text.

Brown's next major exegetical endeavor produced the first edition of *The Birth of the Messiah* (1977), a work that is now updated and expanded in a second edition that forms part of the Anchor Bible Reference Library (ABRL; Doubleday, 1993). In this study Brown examined the birth, infancy and childhood stories of the Gospels according the Matthew and Luke. He worked in a manner similar to that adopted for his Anchor Bible commentary on John, offering translations, notes on technical matters of interpretation and comments on the meaning or significance of each of the scenes in the narratives. Matthew's and Luke's accounts were treated independently, avoiding artificial harmonization of the stories and relating the materials in the canonical birth narratives to the respective Gospels in which the stories are told. Brown was concerned with the similarities and dissimilarities between the two accounts. Both in the course of the comments and in a series of free-standing appendices, Brown discussed key issues (e.g., levirate marriage, Jesus' Davidic descent, the birth at Bethlehem, virginal conception, the census under Quirinius) that have vexed interpreters and generated extensive scholarly debates.

Still another massive exegetical contribution came in Brown's commentary on *The Epistles of John* (1982). Brown offered an extensive introduction to the Johannine epistles and to their study, and then he examined the documents by providing a translation, extensive notes on technical matters and comments on meaning and significance—a format he had developed with precision in earlier works. In the commentary Brown read the epistles in relation to the historical hypothesis that the conflict between the author of the epistles and his opponents, to whom the author made regular reference, was a struggle between members of the Johannine community concerning two different interpretations of their tradition, especially the meaning of the Fourth Gospel, and deeply christological in nature.

Brown's last major exegetical contribution was his two-volume work *The Death of the Messiah* (ABRL; 1994). This study is a detailed analysis of the portions of the four canonical Gospels that focus on Jesus' passion and death from the time in Gethsemane to the grave. At appropriate points and in specific appendices Brown brought pertinent materials from noncanonical early Christian writings into his analysis of the passion narrative(s). In distinction from the manner in which Brown worked earlier in *The Birth of the Messiah,* here he worked "horizontally," studying parallel episodes in each of the Gospels simultaneously. Nevertheless he was not interested in harmonization of the accounts; rather, he sought throughout the study to keep in view what was peculiar or distinctive in each of the particular Gospels for each scene in the narrative. Materials that would have appeared in notes in Brown's earlier exegetical works are either integrated into the comments on the various scenes or are committed to footnotes. While issues of history and historicity are discussed continuously in the study and in specific appendices in volume two, Brown was more concerned with the dramatic effect of the scenes and their theological intent or significance than with their mere facticity. As in all of Brown's major exegetical studies, the bibliographies for the distinct sections of this work seem as nearly complete as is possible.

Along with these works, Brown produced a steady stream of more concise exegetical studies. In general these works are meant to be more accessible to nonspecialists than are the detailed analyses in the full-blown critical studies, although the presentation in these briefer treatments is not merely haute vulgarization. Brown's shorter exegetical books represent something of the breadth of the range of his interests in biblical studies: *Gospel and Epistles of John* (3 eds., 1960, 1965, 1982); *Daniel* (1962); *The Parables of the Gospels* (1963); *Deuteronomy* (1965); *The Semitic Background of the Term "Mystery" in the New Testament* (1968); and *The Gospel and Epistles of John: A Concise Commentary* (1988).

2. During his career as a scholar and teacher Brown produced a procession of focused works that examine topics that may be viewed in the realm of New Testament theology. Four books received widespread attention.

In 1967 Brown led off such work with *Jesus, God and Man*. By applying the tools of exegesis to relevant texts, Brown identified what the New Testament said about both the early Christian application of the designation *God* to Jesus and the canonical understanding of the boundaries of Jesus' human knowledge. Brown was not seeking to study the issue of the divinity of Jesus; rather, in the two main parts of this work he sought to demonstrate that while the New Testament at times specifically refers to Jesus as "God," the same New Testament materials recall that Jesus' knowledge of the future and his self-understanding had real limits. Thus Brown argued that the New Testament indicates that clear consciousness rather than precise knowledge characterized the mind of Jesus on particular, crucial theological issues.

In *Priest and Bishop: Biblical Reflections* (1970) Brown made a concise study of the biblical background of priesthood, particularly in the Roman Catholic tradition. Brown made a vigorous case for the biblical basis of the traditional ideas of priesthood without equating biblical thought about priests and bishops to the developed forms of those offices that have emerged in the life of the church; thus he examined the biblical basis of two church offices without suggesting there is a biblical prescription or description of these forms of ministry.

The Virginal Conception and Bodily Resurrection of Jesus (1973) was a focused study of the biblical evidence related to the two topics named in the title of the book. While the work was highly exegetical, Brown was concerned to establish the precise nature of the biblical perspective on Jesus' virginal conception and bodily resurrection in order to relate the findings of biblical scholarship to the discussion of the developed doctrines of the church. Roman Catholic in focus, the study was ecumenical in scope; it was widely discussed in Protestant as well as Roman Catholic theological settings.

In 1994 Brown published *An Introduction to New Testament Christology*. As always, the study was highly exegetical; but at the same time this work summarized and critiqued the modern scholarly discussion of christology. Brown explained the variety of ways in which christological reflection is usually done, asked about the identity of Jesus as discernible from his teaching and actions, treated the variety and unity in New Testament appreciations of Jesus, summarized a set of key items in the development of christological reflection, and offered an evaluative list of selected books on New Testament christology. His own position was that the classic christological discussions of the fourth and fifth centuries were not abstract conversations but vital questions of the reality of God and Christianity; Brown argued that concern with christology should be the same today.

In a series of more popular works Brown dealt with the principal texts that guide the Roman Catholic church's reflection during the key seasons of the liturgical year. The works are informed by the best of exegetical scholarship, focused in relation to theological concerns and addressed to pastoral issues. They are *An Adult Christ at Christmas* (1978); *A Crucified Christ in Holy Week* (1986); *A Coming Christ in Advent* (1988); *A Risen Christ in Eastertime* (1991); and *A Once and Coming Spirit at Pentecost* (1994). The title of each of the books recognizes that the liturgical season is a theological look forward that finds meaning in life by recalling the past actions of God with humanity in history.

3. A third category of Brown's writings may be described as creative, summary works in critical biblical studies, and these works take a variety of forms.   ·

Brown's first doctoral dissertation was entitled *The 'Sensus Plenior' of Sacred Scripture* (1955), a study devoted to assessing and clarifying an idea long important in (primarily) Roman Catholic interpretation of Scripture. Brown argued that the recognition of two traditional senses of Scripture—the "literal" that is expressed by the text and clearly understood by both God and the human writer and the "typical" that the Holy Spirit uses to signify things other than the literal words of the text—are valid but inadequate classifications of the senses of Scripture. Thus interpreters recognize a *sensus plenior,* a deeper sense of Scripture not perceived precisely by the human author but intended by God. Brown's concern with the sensus plenior was a move to reduce the distance between more traditional forms of Roman Catholic interpretation and historical-critical study of Scripture that simultaneously recognized the limited compass of the literal sense of Scripture and still appreciated a later, even biblical, development in the application of the original text.

Along with J. A. Fitzmyer and R. E. Murphy, Brown edited (making major contributions to the writing) both *The Jerome Biblical Commentary* (1968) and *The New Jerome Biblical Commentary* (1990); the latter work is a completely redone edition of the original one-volume commentary. These volumes provide precise, scholarly commentary on the books of the Bible (the Roman Catholic canon) by offering a brief introduction to the particular biblical book and then discussing the contents and problems of interpretation associated with the Scriptures in a paragraph-by-paragraph format. Along with the commentary on the biblical materials, there are many articles on scholarly topics of importance (e.g., the Penteteuch, prophetic literature, Old Testament apocalypticism and eschatology, deutero- and trito-Isaiah, wisdom litera-

ture, the Synoptic problem, epistolary literature, inspiration, canonicity, the Dead Sea Scrolls, texts and versions, modern biblical criticism, hermeneutics, church pronouncements, geography, archaeology, Israel's life and thought, Old Testament theology, Jesus, Paul, early church, New Testament theology, Pauline theology, Johannine theology) and suggestions for further study. The work is a testimony to the range and depth of involvement of Roman Catholic scholars in contemporary biblical studies. The work is frequently recommended in Protestant seminaries and schools of theology as the best one-volume commentary on the Bible.

In other works Brown sought to advance the understanding, the impact and the appreciation of critical biblical studies on issues in the life of the church; the titles of the works are descriptive and self-evident: *Biblical Reflections on Crises Facing the Church* (1975), related to theology, christology, ecumenism and change; *The Critical Meaning of the Bible* (1981), which affirmed that the biblical texts are the inspired word of God and that every word of the Bible comes from humans and is conditioned by their limitations, yet insisted that a critical scholarly reading of the Bible challenges all Christians and the church; and *Recent Discoveries and the Biblical World* (1983), which discussed approximately twenty-five recent archaeological and documentary discoveries and elucidated the way in which they aid our comprehension of the biblical world, thereby bringing the Bible to life for life.

4. Some contributions manifest Brown's commitment to and involvement with ecumenical biblical studies.

In an early, brief work, *Biblical Tendencies Today: An Introduction to the Post-Bultmannians* (1969), Brown and P. J. Cahill sketched the course of biblical studies from the time and work of Rudolf *Bultmann to the time that they wrote, delineating the accomplishments of a crucial decade of New Testament research and analyzing the challenges that seemed to lie ahead in the future. Of special focus was the study of the life of Jesus.

Two works—*Peter in the New Testament* (1973) and *Mary in the New Testament* (1978)—came from a collaborative assessment of the respective topics by Protestant and Roman Catholic scholars that was sponsored by the United States Lutheran-Roman Catholic Dialogue and conducted by a task force of New Testament scholars from these denominations. The studies were published in English in North America and Great Britain, and in German, French, Spanish, Dutch and Japanese. Both discussions focused on the exact nature of the biblical presentation of Peter and Mary, two key figures that distinguish Roman Catholic and Protestant thinking, and recognized that agreement on what texts "meant" is not a guarantee of agreement regarding what texts "mean."

5. Brown's work often focused on the reconstruction of early Christian history.

In *The Community of the Beloved Disciple* (1979) Brown studied "the life, loves, and hates of an individual church in New Testament times." The book moved like a detective story to treat the life of the Johannine community from the time before the Gospel according to John, through the subsequent times of the writings of the Gospel and the Johannine epistles, to the time after the writing of the epistles. While the work was historical reconstruction, the nature of the community and the literature it produced gave a pronounced theological overtone to the reflection on the past life of the Johannine community. Brown's study recognized but did not elaborate upon the life of a congregation that was much like the life of the church(es) in the modern world.

In a complementary study, *Antioch and Rome* (1983), coauthored with J. P. Meier, Brown worked to reconstruct the life of another significant Christian community, the church in Rome. From New Testament and other early Christian writings, both Brown and Meier identified Christian communities associated with Peter that were slightly more conservative than Pauline

congregations regarding Jewish heritage for Christians. These two centers of Christianity were both crucial in the emergence of classical catholic Christianity.

Brown's concern with the life of early Christianity found still further, broader expression in *The Churches the Apostles Left Behind* (1984). This work focused on seven different churches from the period of the New Testament and the time following the death of the apostles. Brown considers three churches of the Pauline heritage illustrated by the Pastoral Epistles, Colossians and Ephesians and Luke-Acts; one of the Petrine heritage (1 Peter); two of the heritage of the Beloved Disciple (the Johannine epistles); and one from the heritage of the Gospel according to Matthew. Brown reflected on the subapostolic period (the last third of the first century) in general and then recognized the great variety in early Christian thought and life by asking what the Christians of this era were being told that would enable their churches to survive the deaths of the authoritative figures of the apostolic period. Brown found that ecclesiologies and theological emphases differed but that taken together the pictures preserved in New Testament writings reveal the unity and diversity of early Christian community life.

6. A further category of contributions is somewhat artificial. These items could be located in the foregoing classifications. Yet four of Brown's books illustrate how all his work pursued the aims of advancing biblical studies, relating biblical studies to the life of the church and educating clergy and laity alike in biblical studies and theological reflection.

In *Biblical Exegesis and Church Doctrine* (1985) Brown pointed out the significance of historical-critical exegesis for sophisticated appreciation of church doctrine. Faulting both overly liberal and ultraconservative readings of Scripture for failing to see lines of development between the biblical period and the subsequent times of doctrinal formulation, Brown argued that the church under the guidance of the Spirit articulates insights into the divine revelation to which the Scriptures themselves bear witness. In the heart of the book Brown made his case by focusing on the biblical and doctrinal materials related to Mary, the Spirit, the local church and the preaching in Acts and early Christian beliefs.

Responses to 101 Questions on the Bible (1990) brought together a series of questions and answers that had remained prominent in discussions throughout the course of Brown's teaching and lecturing. Brown noticed in addresses to more than one hundred different audiences that the same questions recurred regularly. Using memory and imagination, he stated the questions he had encountered and recast the answers he had given. Although he addressed many topics in this work, Brown created clusters of questions in which one question naturally followed the answer to another, as was the case in real discussions. This book was such a success that Paulist Press created a series of "101 Questions" books related to crucial areas of theological studies (e.g., the Dead Sea Scrolls, feminism, Jesus, the Psalms and other writings).

In handbook form *The New Jerome Bible Handbook* (1992), of which Brown was again coeditor, makes the insights of recent biblical scholarship available in briefer form for laypersons (students, individual adults and church study groups) without significant theological training. The work functions nearly as an introductory text to biblical studies.

An Introduction to the New Testament (1997) is a magisterial survey of the books of the New Testament, the critical issues of interpretation related to each of those writings, the results of scholarly study of the New Testament and the key theological concerns of the various New Testament books. The book includes massive bibliographies and major discussions of Jesus, Paul, the world of New Testament times and ancient literature related or pertinent to the study of the New Testament.

Significance. Brown himself wrote and spoke often about three movements in Roman Catholic biblical studies in the twenti-

eth century. From approximately 1900 to 1940 there was a vigorous rejection of modern biblical criticism. This attitude grew out of the Roman Catholic church's confrontation with the modernist heresy, and during this time certain Roman Catholic scholars who worked using the modern methods of critical scholarship were censured by the church, so that they were strictly limited in the manner and areas in which they could work if they were to remain part of the church.

From 1940 to 1970 there was a gradual introduction of critical biblical studies into Roman Catholic scholarship. This new movement came by order of Pope Pius XII in *Divino Afflante Spiritu* (1943), which directed Roman Catholic exegetes to be principally concerned with the literal sense of the Scripture in order to set forth the theology (belief and morals) of the individual books of the Bible. Through such concerns exegetes were to articulate the spiritual sense of the texts. Historical foundations and historical problems became crucial elements for the recognition of and reflection on the theological dimensions of biblical writings.

From 1970 through the 1990s the Roman Catholic church and Roman Catholic scholars were engaged in the arduous task of assimilating the insights and implications of critical biblical studies into the life of the church, its doctrine, theology and practice.

Brown was trained and began his career as a scholar and teacher during the second period of twentieth-century Roman Catholic biblical studies. He emerged in that period as one of the major international figures in biblical studies, Roman Catholic and Protestant. As such he was at the forefront of both biblical studies and the Roman Catholic church's development (in the second period) and growth in the third period of the twentieth century. Brown's fame is related to the quality of his scholarship and the crucial role he played in bringing Roman Catholicism into the ecumenical work of biblical studies. Today, in every facet of biblical studies, Roman

Catholic scholars stand in the lead or among those in the lead of contemporary scholarship. This achievement would have been impossible without the work of many of those who taught Brown and others during early part of the second period of the twentieth century and without the work that Brown and other did during the latter half of that period and throughout the third period.

Brown's early concern with the sensus plenior grew into his mature work as a historical-critical exegete with pronounced concerns for theology and church life. His scholarly activity was an exploration, even a celebration, of the depth and complexity of the canon of the Scriptures. Repeatedly he illustrated the complex nature of Christian thought and life during the biblical period itself. His work pointed to the variety of beliefs and practices in earliest Christianity, recognizing that real boundaries existed in such complexity but perceiving and suggesting that modern varieties of Christian religious sensibilities are not so much cause for confrontation as they are illustrations of the complementarity that characterized even earliest Christianity. Commitment to the importance of history for critical biblical studies, recognition of the validity of developments from biblical foundations to subsequent doctrinal formulations, dedication to open and honest pursuit of truth, and faithfulness to his religious heritage were the hallmarks of the life and work of Brown.

Brown lived and worked in retirement at St. Patrick's Seminary, Menlo Park, California, until his death on August 8, 1998. A few days before his untimely death, Brown's penultimate book, *A Retreat with John the Evangelist: That You May Have Life* was published by St. Anthony's Messenger Press. Still in press and awaiting publication is *Christ in the Gospel of the Ordinary Sunday* (Liturgical Press).

BIBLIOGRAPHY

Works. R. E. Brown, *An Adult Christ at Christmas* (Collegeville, MN: Liturgical Press, 1978); idem, *Biblical Exegesis and Church Doctrine* (New York: Paulist, 1985); idem, *Biblical Tendencies Today: An Introduction to the Post-Bultmannians* (Martinez, CA: Corpus, 1969); idem, *The Birth of the Messiah* (Garden City, NY: Doubleday, 1977); idem, *The Churches the Apostles Left Behind* (New York: Paulist, 1984); idem, *A Coming Christ in Advent* (Collegeville, MN: Liturgical Press, 1988); idem, *The Community of the Beloved Disciple* (New York: Paulist, 1979); idem, *The Critical Meaning of the Bible* (New York: Paulist, 1981); idem, *A Crucified Christ in Holy Week* (Collegeville, MN: Liturgical Press, 1986); idem, *Daniel* (Paulist Pamphlet Bible; New York: Paulist, 1962); idem, *The Death of the Messiah* (ABRL; Garden City, NY: Doubleday, 1994); idem, *Deuteronomy* (Old Testament Reading Guide 10; Collegeville, MN: Liturgical Press, 1965); idem, *The Epistles of John* (AB 30; Garden City, NY: Doubleday, 1982); idem, *The Gospel According to John* (AB 29, 29A; Garden City, NY: Doubleday, 1966, 1970); idem, *Gospel and Epistles of John* (New Testament Reading Guides 13; Collegeville, MN: Liturgical Press, 1960, 1965, 1982 [3 eds.]); idem, *The Gospel and Epistles of John: A Concise Commentary* (Collegeville, MN: Liturgical Press, 1988); idem, *An Introduction to New Testament Christology* (New York: Paulist, 1994); idem, *An Introduction to the New Testament* (ABRL; Garden City, NY: Doubleday, 1997); idem, *Jesus, God and Man* (New York: Macmillan, 1972 [1967]); idem, *Mary in the New Testament* (Philadelphia: Fortress; New York: Paulist, 1978); idem, *New Testament Essays* (New York: Paulist, 1982 [1965]); idem, *A Once and Coming Spirit at Pentecost* (Collegeville, MN: Liturgical Press, 1994); idem, *The Parables of the Gospels* (New York: Paulist, 1963); idem, *Peter in the New Testament* (Minneapolis: Augsburg; New York: Paulist, 1973); idem, *Priest and Bishop: Biblical Reflections* (New York: Paulist, 1970); idem, *Recent Discoveries and the Biblical World* (Wilmington, DE: Michael Glazier, 1983); idem, *Responses to 101 Questions on the Bible* (New York: Paulist, 1990); idem, *A Risen Christ in Eastertime* (Collegeville, MN: Liturgical Press, 1991); idem, *The Semitic Background of the Term "Mystery" in the New Testament* (Facet Books/Biblical Series 21; Philadelphia: Fortress, 1968); idem, *The "Sensus Plenior" of Sacred Scripture* (Baltimore: St. Mary's University Press, 1955); idem, *The Virginal Conception and Bodily Resurrection of Jesus* (New York: Paulist, 1973); idem, and P. J. Cahill, *Biblical Reflections on Crises Facing the Church*

(New York: Paulist, 1975); idem, J. A. Fitzmyer, R. E. Murphy, eds., *The Jerome Biblical Commentary* (New York: Prentice-Hall, 1968); idem with J. A. Fitzmyer and R. E. Murphy, eds., *The New Jerome Bible Handbook* (Collegeville, MN: Liturgical Press, 1992); idem, J. A. Fitzmyer, R. E. Murphy, eds., *The New Jerome Biblical Commentary* (New York: Prentice-Hall, 1990); idem, and J. P. Meier, *Antioch and Rome* (New York: Paulist, 1983).   M. L. Soards

Brueggemann, Walter *(b. 1932)*

Since 1986 Walter Brueggemann has been professor of Old Testament at Columbia Theological Seminary in Decatur, Georgia. There he was named William Marcellus McPheeder Professor of Old Testament (1992).

Born in Tilden, Nebraska, Brueggemann was educated at Elmhurst College (A.B., sociology, 1955). He is a graduate of Eden Theological Seminary (B.D., Old Testament, 1958), Union Theological Seminary in New York (Th.D., Old Testament, 1961) and St. Louis University (Ph.D., education, 1974). From 1961 to 1986 he was professor of Old Testament at Eden Theological Seminary, and from 1967 to 1981 he served as dean. Brueggemann and his wife, Mary Bonner Miller, are ordained ministers in the United Church of Christ.

Beyond classroom and church Brueggemann has served in editorial capacities for Fortress Press, the *Journal of Biblical Literature, Interpretation, Theology Today, Sojourners* and *Journal for Preachers*. Among his many distinguished lectureships are the Beecher Lectures at Yale Divinity School, the Cole Lectures at Vanderbilt Divinity School and the Sprunt Lectures at Union Theological Seminary (Virginia). In 1990 he served as president of the Society of Biblical Literature. A prolific writer, he has published more than a dozen books and scores of articles.

Context. Brueggemann's professional career has coincided with periods of much unrest and searching in both the sociopolitical and academic worlds. His tenure as dean of Eden spanned the tumultuous years of the civil rights movement and the student restlessness of the Vietnam era. Matters were in transition in the world of biblical scholarship as well. In the 1960s the so-called biblical theology movement that had been so influential in American biblical studies began to be seriously questioned by scholars like James *Barr, Langdon Gilkey and Brevard *Childs. In the same decade scholars also began to voice dissatisfaction with the historical-critical methods of biblical exegesis as they had been practiced. The 1968 presidential address by one of Brueggemann's Union professors, James *Muilenburg ("Form Criticism and Beyond"), was pivotal in shifting methods of biblical study from dominantly historical to more literarily oriented approaches.

The 1970s to the 1990s saw the proliferation of various forms of literary criticism (e.g., the new literary criticism; structuralism; rhetorical criticism) and differently nuanced sociological analyses (e.g., Marxist sociology; cultural anthropology) into the world of biblical studies. As modernist philosophical underpinnings of scientifically objective methodology and textual determinacy began to crumble, various combinations of literary and sociological insights gave rise to ideological readings (e.g., deconstructionism; reader response; liberationist readings [feminist, African-American, womanist]). During decades of change, Brueggemann's work has been informed by these shifts, and he has sought to bring some order to the scene especially by forming an alliance between literary and sociological modes of reading the Bible.

It is revealing that in the midst of this social and methodological upheaval Brueggemann conducted his work at theological seminaries instead of a university-based graduate department of religion. One is not surprised, then, when he begins a study of prophecy with the line: "The time may be ripe in the church for serious consideration of prophecy as a crucial element in ministry" (Brueggemann 1978b, 9). Nor does it seem odd to read near the opening of his commentary on Genesis: "The primary task of this commentary has been to bring the text and its claims closer to the faith and ministry of the church" (Brueggemann 1982b, vii). The religious communities that gave birth to and that were subsequently guided by the biblical texts never seem far from this scholar and churchman's mind.

Work. Brueggemann is both an exegete and a theologian. To be sure, the two tasks are intricately connected, and this is especially so for him. However, it is helpful to distinguish between the two in order to appreciate the breadth of his work.

Brueggemann's exegetical work has resulted in significant commentaries on Genesis (1982b), Exodus (1994), 1 Samuel and 2 Samuel (1990) and Jeremiah (Brueggemann 1988b; 1991c). Although it is not a commentary in the strict sense of the word, if his influential volume on the Psalms, subtitled "A Theological Commentary" (Brueggemann 1984), may be mentioned here, he has written commentaries on portions of the three major divisions of the Hebrew Bible: Torah, Prophets and Writings.

Brueggemann's work of commentary, especially on the Prophets and the Writings, is buttressed by a spate of monographs and articles on specific portions of the Hebrew Bible. Titles like *David's Truth In Israel's Imagination and Memory* (1985), *Power, Providence and Personality* (1990), *1 Kings and 2 Kings* (1982c), *The Prophetic Imagination* (1978) and *Hopeful Imagination* (1986) reflect his interest in the prophetic corpus. Monographs on the Writings are represented by *In Man We Trust: The Neglected Side of Biblical Faith* (1972), *Israel's Praise* (1988) and *Abiding Astonishment* (1991). Many of Brueggemann's articles on the prophets have been gathered and edited by P. D. Miller under the title *A Social Reading of the Old Testament: Prophetic Approaches to Israel's Communal Life* (Brueggemann 1994). Miller has also arranged representative articles on the Psalms

into the volume *The Psalms and the Life of Faith* (Brueggemann 1995).

The force of this selective review of titles by Brueggemann demonstrates that his exegetical interest and activity range over major portions of the Hebrew Bible. He is a specialist who astutely refuses to overspecialize.

Brueggemann's theological work that takes up themes and trajectories in the Hebrew Bible is extensive.

First, his work as an editor for the Fortress Press series Overtures to Biblical Theology can be noted. Conceived in 1973 during conversations between biblical scholars and Fortress Press representatives, the series represented an effort to move theological reflection beyond the heavily historical and descriptive work that had characterized many theological efforts of the century (Brueggemann 1977, ix-xiii). It sought to speak both to biblical scholars and, without resorting to dogmatic categories, to faith communities seeking guidance from biblical texts. Realizing that the state of biblical studies was too unsettled for grand syntheses, the series editors believed it was time for the "pursuit of fresh hints, for exploration of new intuitions which may reach beyond old conclusions, set categories, and conventional methods" (Brueggemann 1977, xi). The series was launched with Brueggemann's own volume, *The Land* (1977). The book traces Israel's relationship to the land through both Testaments and concludes with a discussion on how this complex relationship is suggestive for contemporary hermeneutics.

Many of Brueggemann's monographs have arisen as a result of lectureships and presentations. Religious education (Brueggemann 1982a), preaching (Brueggemann 1989), evangelism (Brueggemann 1993) and urban renewal (Brueggemann 1993d) are themes he has addressed theologically, drawing on the resources of Scripture. Two things are apparent. First, each theme is of significance to the ongoing life of religious communities, and while the theme is not divorced from it, it is not pursued exclusively for the academy. This interaction between confessing communities and the academic world is one of Brueggemann's trademarks. Second, these themes are as wide-ranging as Brueggemann's work of commentary and demonstrate his concern to bring theological insights to bear on many aspects of life.

At the same time Brueggemann has tackled the technical and thorny issues of theological method. Noteworthy are two articles that appeared in 1985 in *Catholic Biblical Quarterly* 47, "A Shape for Old Testament Theology, I: Structure Legitimation" and "A Shape for Old Testament Theology, II: Embrace of Pain." These along with thirteen other articles appear together in the volume edited by Miller, *Old Testament Theology: Essays on Structure, Theme and Text* (Brueggemann 1992).

Brueggemann's monograph-length Old Testament theology was published in 1997. In this work he takes up two fundamental questions: What does Israel say about God? and What else does Israel say when speaking about God? By focusing intentionally upon Israel's speech about God, Brueggemann seeks to sail between the scylla and charybdis of historical event and confession about the event. He is clearly concerned with Israel's confession. To sort out Israel's witness about God, he proposes a dialectic between what he describes as core testimony and countertestimony and uses the metaphor of a courtroom trial to interrogate the competing voices. Among the former are Israel's most characteristic utterances about God, while countertestimonies challenge and qualify the core claims. However, Israel does not speak about God abstractly and so must also comment upon God's conversation partners: creation, humans and the nations. With these partners God mediates via the social and religious institutions of Torah, kingship, prophecy, cult and wisdom (Brueggemann 1996, letter to author).

Analysis. Brueggemann's exegetical and theological work rests on three methodological pillars. He has a preference for literary modes of reading biblical literature; he is intensely concerned about the social function of biblical texts; he is fiercely dialectical.

Literary Modes. Brueggemann is fully aware of the strengths and weaknesses of the historical-critical approach to studying the Bible. For example, his indebtedness to the tradition-historical approach is evident in *The Land* (Brueggemann 1977) and especially in his essay on "The Kerygma of the Priestly Writers" (Brueggemann 1975). However, his interpretive eye is typically drawn to the literary dimensions of biblical texts. For this mode of study he has been much influenced and well trained by his teacher James Muilenburg, whose work refocused scholarly attention upon the artistic dimensions of the Bible.

In addition one might judge from the many references in Brueggemann's writings that the canonical approach of Brevard Childs has exercised considerable influence upon him. While Childs has insisted that his approach is not to be confused with newer literary criticism (Barton, 153), the emphasis both place on the final form of the text suggests obvious connections. Though not content with Childs to claim that the final form of the text is the only legitimate perspective from which to read Scripture (Brueggemann 1982a, 4-7), Brueggemann clearly senses and exploits the interpretive possibilities presented by the shape of the canon. This is plainly evident, for example, in his study on the shape of the book of Psalms (Brueggemann 1995, 189-213), as well as his proposal for a shape for Old Testament theology that depends upon sensing the tensions that stand together in biblical literature (Brueggemann 1992, 1-44).

A related though slightly different tack is taken in Brueggemann's commentary on the books of Samuel. Again, he tips his hat to Childs's focus upon the whole story (Brueggemann 1990a, 6), but his plan for reading is more aligned with narrative analysis.

Social Function. Brueggemann's work reveals an intense concern for the social function of biblical texts in both their ancient and modern contexts. His sociological analysis is informed especially by the sociology of knowledge as mediated by Karl Mannheim, Peter Berger and Thomas Luckmann. Depending on who wields authoritative texts and traditions, they are either a part of the prevailing culture's process of constructing, legitimating and maintaining social worlds, or they are countercultural in their effort to construct alternative social worlds. The same text can sometimes function in both ways, as his shrewd analysis of Psalm 37 demonstrates (Brueggemann 1995, 235-57). Brueggemann's social reading is also influenced by the work of Norman Gottwald (*The Tribes of Yahweh*, 1979) and Paul Hanson (*The Dawn of Apocalyptic*, rev. ed. 1979). In particular, Gottwald's description of Israel's emergence as an intentional social alternative to the Canaanite city-state power structures—a daring social experiment that disintegrates with the emergence of monarchy in Israel—attracts Brueggemann. It is Hanson's discussion of the exilic and postexilic tensions between the ideologically minded pragmatic program of (largely) priestly circles and the utopian, visionary agenda of (largely) prophetic circles as the seedbed of apocalyptic that Brueggemann finds suggestive. Additionally, part of Hanson's analysis draws on Mannheim's distinctions between ideology and utopia, another formal link with Brueggemann's use of sociology of knowledge.

The upshot of this approach is that Brueggemann is able to distinguish between two competing groups in Israel whose voices emerge throughout the biblical literature. One group is aligned with the dominant and central power structures of Israelite society and appeals to a distinct set of theological traditions to legitimate and maintain its social control. The other group is normally marginalized and alienated from the central power structures and appeals to a competing set of theological traditions to present its program for an alternative social reality.

Dialectical Approach. Much influenced by the theological tradition of Reinhold Niebuhr, Brueggemann's dialectical approach also arises from his literary and social reading of the text. The canonical approach allows him to see linkages and trajectories among texts that are chronologically distant and theologically at odds with one another. For example, in "Prayer as a Daring Act of Dance" he discerns a "theological sequence . . . [i]n terms of posture and attitude" among prayers by David, Hezekiah, Jacob and Moses—in that order. As one prayer is read over against the others, dialectical tensions emerge that chart a trajectory, in this case from formal plea to impassioned address to God (Brueggemann 1995, 147).

Brueggemann's dialectic is most clearly focused in his discussions of the social functions of texts. At the heart of this dialectic is the tension that exists between the covenant traditions of Sinai and Zion. The former are associated with Moses and the exodus, the latter with David and the monarchy. This tension appears in his writing under many names: "the land as gift and grasp" (Brueggemann 1977); "the king of majesty and mercy"; "songs from above" and "songs from below" (Brueggemannn 1988a); "accessibility and freedom, assurance and precariousness" (Brueggemann 1992); "a movement of protest" and "a movement of consolidation" (Brueggemann 1994b); "hurt and hope" (Brueggemann 1992); "orientation, disorientation, new orientation" (Brueggemann 1984). Under whatever set of names, at the heart of this dialectic is the tendency of the Davidic covenant tradition to legitimate oppressive social structures and to guard the status quo and the countertendency of the Mosaic covenant to protest the social arrangements made by royal power and to negotiate an alternative, egalitarian social world.

Significance. Among Brueggemann's

many contributions to the field of biblical interpretation, the following may be mentioned.

First, probably more than any other Old Testament scholar active today he has shown the convergences and relationships among many disciplines. This article has mentioned only his wedding of literary and social-world approaches in order to read biblical literature. But his writing constantly interacts with the insights of systematic, liberation and practical theologians, historians, psychologists and novelists. One can argue that sometimes the finely nuanced points of the original arguments are blunted when Brueggemann exploits them. However, in a time when the explosion of knowledge has driven scholars more and more toward narrow specialization, his synthesis of so many diverse modes of thought is nothing short of remarkable.

As an Old Testament theologian, Brueggemann has demonstrated the gains of viewing the task of Old Testament theology as theological and not purely historical or descriptive. Further, he has advanced the way of approaching that task by moving beyond the elusive search for a *Mitte* (center) and has argued persuasively for a bipolar approach.

Brueggemann has also brought the professional inquiry of the Bible into the lives of confessing communities as much as has any scholar alive. He was the first lecturer in November 1995 at an effort sponsored jointly by the Endowment for Biblical Research, the American Academy of Religion, the American Schools of Oriental Research and the Society of Biblical Literature to convey the findings of biblical studies to the general public. His lecture was titled "Texts That Linger: Words That Explode." He has sensed well that faithful theological work has one foot in the church and the other in the academy. Or, to borrow his own words, Brueggemann has worked out his creative insights both in the fray and above the fray (Brueggemann 1992, 3).

BIBLIOGRAPHY

Works. W. Brueggemann, *Abiding Astonishment: Psalms, Modernity and the Making of History* (Literary Currents in Biblical Interpretation; Louisville, KY: Westminster John Knox, 1991a); idem, *Biblical Perspectives on Evangelism* (Nashville: Abingdon, 1993a); idem, *The Creative Word: Canon as a Model for Biblical Education* (Philadelphia: Fortress, 1982a); idem, *David's Truth in Israel's Imagination and Memory* (Philadelphia: Fortress, 1985); idem, *Exodus* (The New Interpreter's Bible; Nashville: Abingdon, 1994a); idem, *Finally Comes the Poet: Daring Speech for Proclamation* (Minneapolis: Fortress, 1989); idem, *Genesis* (Interp; Atlanta : John Knox, 1982b); idem, *First and Second Samuel* (Int.; Louisville, KY: Westminster John Knox, 1990a); idem, *Hopeful Imagination: Prophetic Voices in Exile* (Philadelphia: Fortress, 1986); idem, *In Man We Trust: The Neglected Side of Biblical Faith* (Atlanta: John Knox, 1972); idem, *Interpretation and Obedience: From Faithful Reading to Faithful Living* (Minneapolis: Augsburg, 1991b); idem, *Israel's Praise: Doxology Against Idolatry and Ideology* (Philadelphia: Fortress, 1988a); idem, "The Kerygma of the Priestly Writers" in *The Vitality of Old Testament Traditions,* ed. W. Brueggemann and H. W. Wolff (Atlanta: John Knox, 1975); idem, *1 Kings; 2 Kings* (Knox Preaching Guides; Atlanta: John Knox, 1982c); idem, *The Land* (Overtures to Biblical Theology; Philadelphia: Fortress, 1977); idem, letter to author (March 20, 1996); idem, *The Message of the Psalms: A Theological Commentary* (Augsburg Old Testament Studies; Minneapolis: Augsburg, 1984); idem, *Old Testament Theology: Essays on Structure, Theme and Text,* ed. P. D. Miller (Minneapolis: Fortress, 1992); idem, *The Psalms and the Life of Faith,* ed. P. D. Miller (Minneapolis: Fortress, 1995);idem, *Power, Providence and Personality: Biblical Insight into Life and Ministry* (Louisville, KY: Westminster John Knox, 1990b); idem, *The Prophetic Imagination* (Philadelphia: Fortress, 1978b); idem, *A Social Reading of the Old Testament: Prophetic Approaches to Israel's Communal Life,* ed. P. D. Miller (Minneapolis: Fortress, 1994b); idem, *Texts Under Negotiation: The Bible and Postmodern Imagination* (Minneapolis: Fortress, 1993c); idem, *Theology of the Old Testament: Testimony, Dispute, Advocacy* (Minneapolis: Fortress, 1997); idem, *To Build and to Plant: A Commentary on Jeremiah 26—52* (Grand Rapids: Eerdmans, 1991c); idem, *To Pluck Up, To Tear Down: A Commentary on Jeremiah 1—25* (Grand Rapids: Eerdmans, 1988b); idem, *Using God's Resources Wisely: Isaiah and Urban Possibility* (Louisville, KY: Westminster John Knox, 1993d).

Studies. J. Barton, *Reading the Old Testament: Method in Biblical Study* (Philadelphia: Westminster, 1984); J. R. Middleton, "Is Creation Theology Inherently Conservative? A Dialogue with Walter Brueggemann," *HTR* 87, 3 (1994) 257-77; P. D. Miller, "Introduction" in *The Psalms and the Life of Faith*, ed. P. D. Miller (Minneapolis: Fortress, 1995); idem, "Introduction" in *A Social Reading of the Old Testament* (Minneapolis: Fortress, 1994); idem, "Introduction" in *Old Testament Theology: Essays on Structure, Theme and Text* (Minneapolis: Fortress, 1992); J. Muilenburg, "Form Criticism and Beyond," *JBL* 88 (1969) 1-18.

V. S. Parrish

Childs, Brevard *(b. 1923)*

Brevard S. Childs's contributions to biblical interpretation, though they are rooted in the study of the Old Testament and Jewish Scripture, bridge a wide range of disciplines, including the history of Jewish and Christian biblical interpretation, an *Introduction to the New Testament* independent from his *Introduction to the Old Testament as Scripture*, traditiohistorical studies of ancient Israelite traditions, and Christian theology. Any assessment of his work requires some understanding of what is at stake for him in each of these fields.

Adding to this complexity, Childs has shown an ability to change his mind on issues and approaches over time. Ambiguities or lacunae at later stages in his work cannot be uncritically clarified by appeal to earlier positions. Yet what persists from his earlier work may remain presupposed by later formulations. He may be considered one of the most important biblical scholars of the twentieth century, because he has not only kept track of changes in disciplines related to his field but also made original contributions to them.

For these reasons Childs's work mirrors major shifts in biblical hermeneutics after World War II, the subsequent demise of the modern age signified by the intellectual tumult of the 1960s, and the radical reformulation in academic disciplines currently associated with the postmodern debate in the decades that have followed. He embodies deep convictions of Christian faith conjoined with indebtedness and empathy for Jewish faith, alongside an effort to see the strengths and weaknesses of methodologies uncompromised by any appeal to piety.

Childs became arguably the first able pioneer in biblical studies of a postmodern effort to reopen the most elementary questions about the nature of Jewish and Christian Scripture with an approach that was tentatively labeled "canonical criticism" (following the suggestion of James Sanders), then intentionally altered to "a canonical approach" and various other labels. Regarding these efforts he states, "Whether one calls a new approach 'canonical,' 'kerygmatic,' or 'post-critical' is largely irrelevant. I would only reject the categories of mediating theology *(Vermittlungstheologie)* which seek simply to fuse elements of orthodoxy and liberalism without doing justice to either." Childs's approach contributes less to the invention of a new methodology and more to the rediscovery of a new perspective on Scripture while trying to take into account "the complexity of all human knowledge and the serious challenge of modernity to any claims of divine revelation" (Childs 1992, 99).

Work. Childs (b. September 2, 1923) grew up in Southern Presbyterian churches and studied at the University of Michigan (A.B. and M.A.). After serving in the army in Europe during World War II, he earned his B.D. at Princeton Theological Seminary before pursuing a doctorate at the University of Basel, Switzerland. At Basel Childs studied Old Testament with Walther *Eichrodt, among others. In addition to his studies in Basel, he took advantage of Near Eastern scholarship at Heidelberg University (Childs 1992, xv).

In Basel Childs met his wife, Ann, who had attended some of Karl *Barth's lectures with him. This was an exciting period for theological study. Besides the vigorous table talk among the visiting and local students, inexpensively published journals of essays and debates between theologians, biblical scholars and historians further stimulated the intellectual atmosphere.

At the University of Basel Childs completed his dissertation on the problem of myth in the opening chapters of Genesis just at the time when Walter Baumgartner replaced Eichrodt as the senior Old Testament scholar. Creating consternation at the time, Baumgartner informally refused to accept the methodology of Child's dissertation, so Childs had to change his plans in order to undertake a full revision, now informed by a new grasp of form-critical analysis. That obligation helps explain why Childs became one of the leading tradition historians in North America. The revised dissertation, *Der Mythos als theologische Problem im Alten Testament* (1953), was never published, though Childs circulated major portions of it under the title *A Study of Myth in Genesis 1—11* (1955) among his wide network of English-speaking scholarly friends.

In 1954 Childs began teaching Old Testament at Mission House Seminary and in 1958 accepted a teaching position at Yale Divinity School. In that same year he published his first essays in standard scholarly journals: "Jonah: A Study in Old Testament Hermeneutics" in the *Scottish Journal of Theology* and "Prophecy and Fulfillment: A Study of Contemporary Hermeneutics" in *Interpretation*.

From the outset he had an interest in hermeneutics as a mediating language in response to enormous gaps that began to appear between disciplines and even within the subdisciplines of Old Testament studies. We see his early effort to hold together his traditiohistorical criticism and the best of contemporary biblical theology, which sought to let the biblical traditions inform the basis for Jewish and Christian faith.

His first book, *Myth and Reality in the Old Testament* (1960), reflects further hermeneutical refinements of his dissertation. In it he argued for a persistent tendency in

the tradition history of the Bible for myths to become historicized. In these examinations of biblical texts and traditions, Childs's understanding of form criticism goes well beyond a loose literary appeal to genre and includes a social-scientific concern for both form and content.

In line with Hermann *Gunkel he understood that the meaning of a unit of oral tradition belongs to its role in a specific cultural deployment. Its value as a window into ancient history could be located in its mirroring of incidental or typical conceptions of the period rather than by overt references it might seem to make to historical events or to an author's intent.

Childs shows interest in how the editors of Jewish Scripture incorporate older oral and written traditions in a manner quite different from the originary significance of these same traditions. The significance of these changes cannot be ascertained by a modern reconstruction of the "authorship" of their oldest parts or by appeal to the "intent" of a final redactor. Instead, scholars may more profitably begin by describing how the later form and function of Jewish Scripture implies its own criteria regulating its own peculiar social, historical and theological import. An empathetic description of Scripture can therefore be impious in its use of historical criticisms, minimalist in its appeal to theological categories, expressed in conversation with a broad horizon of interrelated disciplines, and forthright about its investments in matters of faith while rejecting a false modern choice between subjectivity and objectivity.

Childs's acceptance and use of liberal modern historical criticisms have always played an integral role in his work, so that his growing criticisms of older modern methods, particularly since the 1960s, must be seen in that light. By presupposing the triumph of these methods within the modern debate of the late nineteenth and twentieth centuries, he felt little need to reassert his indebtedness to them when he turned to examine in a fresh way the form and function of Jewish and Christian Scripture.

His grounding in traditiohistorical studies, which never disappears from his work, can be illustrated by publications such as *Memory and Tradition in Israel* (1962); "The Enemy from the North and the Chaos Tradition" (*JBL* 78 [1959]); "A Study of the Formula, 'Until that Day' " (*JBL* 82 [1963]); "The Birth of Moses" (*JBL* 84 [1965]); "Psalm Titles and Midrashic Exegesis" (*JSS* 16 [1971]); a monograph, *Isaiah and the Assyrian Crisis* (1967); in the relevant sections of his commentary on *The Book of Exodus* (1974); and again in what he calls the "usefulness of recovering a depth dimension within the canonical form of the biblical text" in two large sections (95-322) of his most recent work, *Biblical Theology of the Old and New Testaments* (1992; 104).

In the 1960s Childs lived through and documented the collapse of the so-called biblical theology movement. Subsequently he experimented with a variety of options, sometimes breaking entirely from his own earlier proposals, in pursuit of a different relationship between biblical criticisms and the interpretation of the Bible, Jewish and Christian. *Memory and Tradition in Israel* (1962) and *Isaiah and the Assyrian Crisis* reflect his efforts to refine how we might best access the value and limitations of biblical traditions from a modern historical perspective.

In these books and essays in the late 1950s into the 1960s, we hear the language of dialectical interpretation, of the key relation between myth and history, and of salvation history as a constructive category in spite of its many problems. However, in *Biblical Theology in Crisis* (1970), Childs writes an epitaph for the modern biblical theology movement, which had become so vigorous in the United States after the war. The primary demolition of late modern biblical theology and neo-orthodoxy came less from biblical scholars than theologians, especially the essays by Langdon Gilkey, J. A. T. Robinson's *Honest to God* (1963) and Harvey Cox's *The Secular City* (1965). Childs observes that "the breakdown of the

theological consensus that had been held together within the amorphous category of 'neo-orthodoxy' came more quickly than anyone could have expected" (Childs 1970, 78). Childs felt that it had been built by an ad hoc coalition of diverse positions in reaction to the liberalism of the 1930s. Once the common enemy ceased to be seen as a real threat and no longer required a united response in opposition to it, the participants were left in disarray.

In the concluding chapters, "Seeking a Future" and "Recovering an Exegetical Tradition," Childs experimented with what he called a new biblical theology. Here he pointed out a major flaw in older modern criticism in its tendency to label all pre-nineteenth-century biblical interpretation as precritical. Whatever a new biblical theology might be, it could no longer afford the luxury of dismissing centuries of interpretation as irrelevant or a waste of time. He also knew that any promising alternative needed to be far more than a reaction to the failures of the modern biblical theology movement. No longer could we say as glibly as did Frederic Farrar in the late nineteenth century: "We shall see that past methods of interpretation were erroneous" (F. Farrar, *History of Interpretations* [Grand Rapids: Baker, 1961 repr., 9). While Farrar was certainly correct in his judgment that premodern interpretation did not usually meet his own modern standards that defined the meaning of a text in terms of reconstructing an ancient author's original intent, these basic assumptions about how a scriptural text has meaning needed to be debated.

Hence Childs's questioning of how historical critics had made a "sharp break with the church's exegetical tradition" forced him to launch an even more formidable project than he had fully recognized before, namely, the need to reinterpret the entire history of premodern interpretation (Childs 1970, 138). This task belonged as much to the biblical scholar as it belonged to a church historian or theologian.

At the same time Childs regarded himself as a text-oriented scholar who wanted to define anew the task of scriptural interpretation in such a way that it could invoke its own different criticisms of earlier efforts in the history of interpretation. For that reason he tentatively proposed in *Biblical Theology in Crisis* that a point of departure might be the New Testament use of the Old Testament.

In four examples he illustrates in detail some exegetical implications: on Psalm 8, Exodus 2:11-22, Proverbs 8 and biblical texts relating to Israel and the church. For the first time we hear Childs use the term *canon* as a technical term to describe the boundaries and interplay within Scripture. He tries to circumscribe how a text can serve as a normative arena to hold in dialectical tension a text, its prehistory, its history of interpretation and the present effort to hear it afresh. This text is understood scripturally as a testimony in human words that points to God's own revelation to us. In Christian theological terms it is "the rule that delineates the area in which the church hears the Word of God" (Childs 1970, 99). As "testimony" Scripture "does not exist as a book of truth in itself," though the reality to which it points cannot simply be separated from it: "The text of Scripture points faithfully to the divine reality of Christ, while, at the same time, our understanding of Jesus Christ leads us back to the Scripture, rather than from it" (Childs 1970, 103).

Childs's description of Scripture began to have some specific dimensions, without denying that the same text could be envisioned and interpreted in possibly an infinite number of other ways and that there can be great value in any of these interpretations for how one tries differently to interpret Jewish or Christian Scripture scripturally.

Canonical Context. For the practical activity of interpreting a biblical text as Scripture, what becomes important is the Bible's own "canonical context." This context informs readers regarding both how to read the originally prebiblical traditions

within a biblical book and how to hear books as commentaries on each other. This mode of interpreting—often anachronistic from an older modern historical-critical perspective—is warranted by the canonical context and belongs integrally to how Jews and Christians have read their respective Scriptures scripturally. Contemporary interpretation of Scripture must conjoin this classic mode of reading Scripture on its own critical terms, while drawing new lines of continuity and discontinuity with past practices of interpretation.

Therefore Childs's proposal in no way suggests that we try to return to premodern or precritical interpretation. It takes seriously in a scriptural reading the historically particular nature of the biblical texts themselves. We may say that Childs's proposal thrives on a modern awareness of the differences and unharmonized dimensions within the canonical context. So Childs can argue, "The witness of the Song of Songs corrects and opposes the tendency in Proverbs to view the positive value of sex chiefly in its function as an antidote to sexual incontinence" (Childs 1970, 194). Likewise, Childs wants to interpret Proverbs and Song of Songs in light of a Jewish conception of the Torah with its framework of a revealed covenant and laws, concerned with both morality and nonmoral issues of holiness as a sign of a divinely chosen people with their own special purpose in the world. When he comes to his section on "the New Testament context," Childs shows how the New Testament's use of Old Testament texts confirms and expands on these same issues. In some cases the New Testament presupposes material in the Old Testament without making much comment. In other cases it may reformulate these issues in the idiosyncratic language of the Gospel, but in many cases Childs allows for a deficiency of the New Testament if it is read by itself. In his treatment of Proverbs and sexuality, for instance, he argues, "The Pauline discussion of the role of sex and marriage is a good illustration of the need of the theologian to understand the New

Testament in the light of the Old" (Childs 1970, 199).

Canonical Shape. In 1972 Childs delivered the Sprunt Lectures at Union Theological Seminary in Richmond, Virginia. He focused on larger textual territories: Second Isaiah, the crossing of the sea and the books of Psalms and Daniel. He began to speak of the canonical shape of biblical books or larger expanses of tradition. In an essay published that same year, "The Old Testament as Scripture of the Church," he laid out a strategy of trying "to describe the actual characteristics of the canonical shape" and an effort "to determine the theological significance of this shape" (*CTM* 43 [1972] 715).

Childs examines specifically the beginnings and endings of the five books of the Torah. These features confirm that the late editors marked the divisions of the Torah to give a specific context to the diverse and often unharmonized traditions contained within them. These features make sense specifically to the community of faith that brings a commitment to the Scripture, seeking to hear it as the bread of life. Canon and community are necessarily reciprocal of each other.

Interpretive Approaches. Childs's commentary on *The Book of Exodus* (1974) pulls together as many dimensions as possible on a grand scale. Each unit of biblical text is introduced by a new translation with text-critical notes aiming at "not only the best text but . . . seeking to understand how the text was heard and interpreted by later communities." Next we find a thorough reworking of source analysis, traditiohistorical issues and the redactional evidence in the formation of the scriptural text. Then comes "the Old Testament Context" which is for Childs the "first major section," "form[ing] the heart of the commentary." He stresses his focus on "its final form" and "its canonical shape" (Childs 1974, xiv). Finally he offers two other sections: one on how the New Testament treats the Old and another on the history of biblical exegesis, Jewish and Christian. This impressive commentary, with a novel structure, cannot be fairly described here, but at a minimum it confirms that Childs's conception of biblical commentary has not reduced the intellectual challenge to a few minor adjustments to modern criticism but opens up a broad horizon of interaction between disciplines, each reformulated in a new way.

In a later essay on "The *Sensus Literalis* of Scripture: An Ancient and Modern Problem" (1976), Childs began to call specifically for "a search to recover a new understanding of the *sensus literalis* of Scripture" (In *Beiträge zur Alttestamentlichen Theologie: Festschrift für Walther Zimmerli zum 70 Geburtstag,* ed. H. Donner [Göttingen: Vandenhoeck & Ruprecht, 1976] 22). He takes seriously the centuries of Christian debate over the nature of the literal or the plain sense of Scripture that since the time of *Irenaeus became the normative basis for arguments about doctrine from Scripture. While midrash rather than peshat (plain, historical, literal sense) became the norm for rabbinic exegesis, Christians had their own rules to govern their privileging of this literal sense. Childs's survey of the Christian debate over the centuries leads to his criticism of modern methodologies that confused this particular conception of the literal sense with the earliest, original historical, grammatical or even the best possible sense of a text. Instead, the literal sense of Scripture could be found only when the human witness of the text and its subject matter of revelation could be heard together and only "in the closest connection with the community of faith." Hence the subject matter of faith, the text of Scripture and the community of faith cannot be separated.

Childs also reopens the premodern debate over the rule of faith as a summary of the essentials of the revealed gospel that traditionally accompanies a reader of Scripture. Irenaeus himself had first cited it as a proto-creedal consensus of faith familiar from baptismal confessions that seeks understanding by means of Scripture and corresponds to a pattern found in Scripture itself. Childs agrees that "the church's *regula fidei* encompasses both text and tradition in an integral unity as the living Word of God."

Most significantly, he argues that the canonical context of Scripture has already begun to presuppose elements within the rule of faith. Furthermore, this same canonical context of Scripture provides warrants for a Christian assumption that "the literal and the figurative [typological] sense of a text are not in stark tension." Instead of inviting us to base faith on an esoteric spiritual sense, the Holy Spirit helps us find "the proper actualization of the biblical text in terms of its subject matter for every succeeding generation of the church" ("The *Sensus Literalis,*" 93). Hence Childs's discovery of what he calls the canonical context, forged in conversation with modern historical criticisms and in response to their results, helps us understand how we can read as Scripture the originally prebiblical traditions we now find in the Bible. Still, as a literal or public sense, subject to the discernment of the community of faith, it remains not merely the property of academics and priests.

At the level of major book projects that further develop what Childs calls a canonical approach, he next published his *Introduction to the Old Testament as Scripture* (1979) and, a few years later and even more boldly for an Old Testament scholar, *The New Testament as Canon: An Introduction* (1984). In his Old Testament introduction, he offers for each book a section on "Historical Critical Problems," then moves to "The Canonical Shape" of each book and finally to "Theological and Hermeneutical Implications." A weakness of this book as an introduction is that it does not teach a beginning student the rudiments of modern historical criticisms, yet each treatment of a biblical book begins with a vigorous debate among a vast number of modern critics at a mature and demanding level. The last two sections more simply describe the canonical context and implications for how we are invited to understand as Scrip-

ture the underlying traditions each book includes. The stress on individual books does have the liability of allowing for only a limited sense of how these individual books interact with each other. However, the whole conception of the canonical shape is Childs's own postmodern formulation, and it can be argued that he proves its efficacy in a detailed examination of every book in the Old Testament.

At various places in this volume Childs also took the liberty to answer some criticisms, such as the charge that his terminology of "the final form" of a scriptural text sounded too flat historically and might suggest modern historical criticism is irrelevant to it. Childs acknowledged that the earliest canonical texts of Scripture have been transmitted to us carefully but "contained within a post-canonical tradition," so that "There is no extant canonical text" (Childs 1979, 100). Moreover, because the Scripture is not determined by a singular ecclesial decision in time and space, "It is still semantically useful to speak of an 'open canon.' "

Childs likewise cautions against "limiting the term [canon] only to the final stages of a long and complex process which had already started in the pre-exilic period" (Childs 1979, 58). However, he explicitly rejects canonical criticism as advocated by Sanders, which tries to find evidence of a consistent "canonical hermeneutic" in the tradition history of Scripture. While Childs has himself repeatedly argued for the importance of the late editing of biblical books for defining the canonical shape of a book, he now warns, "It is not the (redactional) process which is normative for the later community, but the scriptures which reflect the process" (Childs 1979, 429). In other words, Childs admits that the canonical text is not a simple object existing in time and space, but each generation must reenvision what is the canonical text that it receives from the past according to own capacity to recognize the form and function as Scripture.

Conversely, any contemporary effort to

rewrite the canon of Scripture or to harmonize away a new perception of differences within it would not make it a better Scripture: So we are wise to consider other factors, including the long tradition of text criticism and, in the case of the Old Testament, the relationship it establishes between Christians and Jews. Just because a text variant is earlier in time does not necessarily make it more canonical. Childs became fully aware that most texts that we can reconstruct from the prehistory of scriptural texts prove according to modern criticism to be originally prebiblical traditions and not biblical traditions at all. It is a modern fallacy to read uncritically all these prebiblical traditions as though they constituted parts of a Scripture or to try to construct a biblical theology from them as was commonly done in the older modern period. Such a pious reading of prebiblical traditions as well as any ad hoc pious interpretation of reconstructed events in ancient Israel misses entirely the thrust of Childs's proposal.

Childs's introduction to the New Testament has not received the attention it deserves, and we can give it only passing mention. One problem is that his unique contributions intermingle with his effort to mediate major conflicting positions among New Testament critics, wheras in the Old Testament introduction the engagement with older modern positions precedes his own effort to describe the shape of each biblical book. Consequently he can sound as if he is playing the ends off against a less exciting middle position.

For example, it may be easy to miss the import of his claim that John 21 is not best understood as an appendix or epilogue but as "a layer of tradition" that had "the entire Gospel already in mind" (Childs 1984, 141-42). What remains understated is what role this tradition plays in transforming this book from a prebiblical statement into a book of Scripture, since only here do we find its writer designated and its content identified as a witness or testimony to these things, using technical language analogous

to how we hear of Moses' own testimony about the revelation of the Torah at the end of Deuteronomy. Similarly, only in the Gospel of John do we see the testimony of Jesus compared with that of Moses (cf. Jn 5:30-47; 3:1-21). The place of John as the last of four Gospels could also be more explicitly highlighted.

One of the most remarkable parts of this introduction is his treatment of the problem of a "harmony of the Gospels." There he shows how a different set of differences emerge from one epoch to another regarding this problem and attempts to resolve it. As the form of knowing changes, so does the capacity to see a problem and what might prove satisfying in response.

This volume also forewarns Christians scholars of the Old Testament that they must engage the critical issues raised by the New Testament if we want to understand how Jewish Scripture belongs to the Christian Bible at all. A discipline of Old Testament studies cannot exist without New Testament studies, any more than Jewish Scripture can be understood adequately apart from some engagement with the rabbinic exegetical tradition and oral Torah.

Childs again sought to refine and modify his proposals in two later books, *Old Testament Theology in a Canonical Context* (1985) and *Biblical Theology of the Old and New Testaments* (1992). In *Old Testament Theology* Childs specifically endeavors "to outline a canonical approach to the Old Testament" that seeks to grasp its "witness in its own right in regard to its coherence, variety, and unresolved issues" (Childs 1985, 17).

Childs knows well that the term "biblical theology" was first used in the seventeenth century and became divided into Old Testament and New Testament theologies only in the nineteenth century. His goal is to redefine it into a new discipline in the wake of the collapse in the 1960s of the biblical theology movement. Recognition of the different canons and accompanying traditions between Jews and Christians confirms for Childs why Old Testament theology must be considered an intrinsically Christian discipline, something Jewish scholars have refused to conjoin for good reasons. While Jewish interpretation often proves invaluable, we ought not to presume that the opposite will be equally true. At a minimum the Old Testament can be seen by Christians "as a completed entity which is set at some distance in some sort of dialectical relationship with the New Testament and the ongoing life of the church." Even when it is "unexpressed" an Old Testament theology presupposes "a relation of some sort . . . between the life and history of Israel and that of Jesus Christ" (Childs 1985, 7). At the same time Childs emphasizes the sufficiency of the Old Testament on many issues of Christian theology, so the New Testament may sometimes add almost nothing and at other times we need to read the New Testament in the light of the Old Testament rather than only the other way around.

Childs sees his approach as offering an alternative to "the stalemate" and "present impasse" attained by the older modern efforts at biblical theology. One of the newer issues he addresses concerns how to adjudicate references within the Bible beyond itself to past persons or events. While accepting many of the insights of his colleague Hans Frei, Childs is leery of reducing the Bible to its crucial narratives, read as nonreferential though realistic and historylike depictions of reality. Childs contends, "because the biblical text continually bears witness to events and reactions in the life of Israel, the literature cannot be isolated from its ostensive reference" (Childs 1985, 6).

Childs chooses to let the canonical context itself define when and where we find the Bible's own "theological use of historical referentiality rather than to construct a contrast between *Geschichte* [historylike story] and *Historie* [a modern history] at the outset" (Childs 1985, 16). In the core of the book he discusses an anthology of key theological themes and issues. Childs puts emphasis on how Christian readers properly "construe" the biblical text, fully aware that a person's "stance to the text affects its meaning" though without wanting to move in the direction of reader-response criticism (Childs 1985, 12).

Finally we need to convey something of what is perhaps Childs's most ambitious project, his *Biblical Theology of the Old and New Testaments*. Among the most original parts of this book are the first two sections: "Prolegomena" and "A Search for a New Approach." Here he explicitly judges his earlier proposal in *Biblical Theology in Crisis* of starting from the New Testament use of the Old Testament as "an inadequate handling of the problem." He emphatically rejects two common modern historical theories, that of Rudolf *Bultmann and others who overstated the discontinuity by viewing the Old Testament primarily as a testimony to the failure of Jews to obey the law prior to the gospel, and that of many recent scholars, like Helmut Gese, who see the two Testaments as linked by "a unified traditio-historical trajectory" (Childs 1985, 76).

Here we confront a recurring factor in Childs's work as a tradition historian, namely, his acceptance of radical differences discovered in the prehistory of both Jewish and Christian Scripture. What makes Childs's proposals postmodern is his consistent acceptance of results of liberal modern historical criticisms wedded to his equally consistent refusal to find in a modern general hermeneutic a resolution to the differences they clarify.

At the outset Childs presents this latest work as a response to a seminal presentation of problems in G. Ebeling's essay on "The Meaning of Biblical Theology" (ET in *Word and Faith* [London and Philadelphia: Fortress, 1963]). Ebeling laid out the two common types of biblical theology as either a description of theological views found within biblical traditions or a theological construction corresponding closely to the primary traditions of Scripture itself. Childs finds in Ebeling's own proposal allowance for premodern efforts to join theology to history, a concern for the "inner-unity" of

Testaments to which Childs brings his conception of the canonical context, and a recognition that the Scripture is a testimony beyond the reduction of it to modern historical or philosophical categories. Also, Childs supports Ebeling's stress on the need for "an essential descriptive component" that respects "each testament's own voice" and allows for the full historical diversity of the Scripture.

However, Childs also sees Ebeling's proposal needs "an important post-Enlightenment correction," because biblical theology must necessarily move according to an inner logic of faith beyond any basis that can be found for it in the delimited objectivity of historical and social scientific evidence. What is entirely unnecessary from a strict historical point of view may be, from the perspective of faith, a matter of life and death. While theological interpretation trades upon these other descriptive efforts, it ought never be confused with them, especially when biblical theology pursues what Ebeling called "the inner unity of the manifold testimony of the Bible" (Childs 1985, 6-8).

Childs further refines his understanding of the literal sense of Scripture in dialogue with the classical debates about the canon, the "scope" (earlier "shape") of biblical books and the regula fidei. Likewise he argues that "the Christian understanding of canon functions theologically in a very different way from Judaism" (Childs 1985, 64). In considering the church's criteria for a biblical book and the history of the so-called apocrypha, Childs concludes, "Perhaps the basic theological issue at stake can be best formulated in terms of the church's ongoing *search* for the Christian Bible" (Childs 1985, 67). We are reminded that these issues require theological rather than merely historical assumptions.

Among Childs's constructive proposals in this book, one of the most ingenious and simple formulations is the sharp distinction he draws between hearing the Bible as a testimony to revelation and hearing it as a resource for recovering independent traditions, history, beliefs or other dimensions of the ancient social world.

The core of this volume (95-322) is a sweeping overview of the "trajectory" of the biblical witness, as distinguished from a general history of the development of ancient traditions or religion. What should be obvious is that Childs does not use the term *trajectory* in the social-scientific sense of a typical pattern of predictable movement by an object (e.g., an arrow) or community over time. The word is used only to describe how one might track the traces of the biblical witness from its origins in the prehistory of the Bible through to the Bible itself. It reminds us of the "depth dimension" that requires a theologian to consider the biblical witness from more than merely a synchronic point of view. In this sense Childs endorses a kerygmatic understanding that looks back into the prebiblical tradition to find those historically unpredictable lines of continuity between older events and the later biblical testimony itself. The stance of faith therefore must look back to history because its claims are not biblicistic or symbolic statements but claims about the presence and revelation of God within the real history of the world.

The last sections of Childs's biblical theology engage various crucial texts and key themes of Christian theology to illustrate the full implications of his approach. Their significance lies beyond the scope of this article. At a minimum we may say that the prehistory of the biblical text remains important. It provides a necessary lexicon for scholars when or if they want to hear the Bible as a scriptural testimony to revelation but must be employed in other ways when scholars want to use biblical texts as a resource for reconstructing even more ancient texts or any of the accompanying historical events along the path of an ancient and serendipitous tradition history. As Childs sees it, "This shaping activity functioned much like a *regula fidei*. It was a negative criterion which set certain parameters within which the material functioned, but largely left to exegesis the positive role of interpretation within the larger construal" (Childs 1985, 71).

Significance. Childs's discovery of the canonical context of Scripture, using the tools of historical criticism and relativizing some of its own assumptions, may be his most important contribution, though his work has also pursued its implications on a scale unrivaled by almost any other contemporary biblical scholar. While the canonical context does not offer a satisfying statement about revelation, it does stake out a boundary, arena or area in which one seeks to hear together the biblical text as witness and its subject matter of revelation. Otherwise, even when the words and grammar of a verse of Scripture are unequivocal, its literal sense has eluded us.

BIBLIOGRAPHY

Works. B. Childs, *Biblical Theology in Crisis* (Philadelphia: Westminster, 1970); idem, *Biblical Theology of the Old and New Testaments: Theological Reflections on the Christian Bible* (London: SCM, 1992); idem, *The Book of Exodus: A Critical, Theological Commentary* (OTL; Philadelphia: Westminster, 1974); idem, *Introduction to the Old Testament as Scripture* (Philadelphia: Fortress, 1979); idem, *The New Testament as Canon: An Introduction* (Philadelphia: Fortress, 1984); idem, *Old Testament Theology in a Canonical Context* (Philadelphia: Fortress, 1985); idem, "The *Sensus Literalis* of Scripture: An Ancient and Modern Problem" in *Beiträge zur Alttestamentlichen Theologie: Festschrift für Walther Zimmerli zum 70. Geburtstag,* ed. H. Donner (Göttingen: Vandenhoeck & Ruprecht, 1976). **Studies.** M. G. Brett, *Biblical Criticism in Crisis? The Impact of the Canonical Approach on Old Testament Studies* (Cambridge: Cambridge University Press, 1991); G. T. Sheppard, "Canon," *MER* 3:62-69; idem, "Canon[ical] Criticism," *ABD* 1:861-66; idem, "Canon[ical] Criticism: The Proposal of Brevard Childs and an Assessment for Evangelical Hermeneutics," *Studia Biblica et Theologica* 4, 2 (1974) 3-17.

G. T. Sheppard

Goodspeed, Edgar Johnson (1871-1962)

In their last interview together, William Rainey Harper, first president of the University of Chicago, said prophetically to Edgar Goodspeed: "Universities are made for fellows like you." Born in Quincy, Illinois, on October 23, 1871, Goodspeed began the study of Latin at ten and his formal training in Greek before he was thirteen. An A.B. degree from Denison University, Ohio (1890), was followed by graduate studies at Yale University in Hebrew, Arabic and Old Testament legal literature.

A year later Goodspeed returned home to pursue an advanced degree at the new University of Chicago. While learning Assyrian, Syriac and Ethiopic, he taught beginning Latin and Greek. During his third graduate year at Chicago he transferred to the New Testament field, and it was in that discipline that he earned the doctor of philosophy degree (1898). Soon after, Harper offered him an associate position in the New Testament department, provided he would first go abroad to visit the German universities. A semester at Berlin, attending Adolf von *Harnack's lectures and working on Greek papyri under Fritz Krebs, was followed by a tour of the major universities and libraries of Europe and visits to Egypt and the Holy Land. In 1902 Goodspeed became an instructor at the University of Chicago and in thirteen years had advanced to the rank of full professor.

From the outset of his career Goodspeed embraced the scholar's responsibility to publish. Beginning with such technical publications as *Greek Papyri from the Cairo Museum* (1902) and *Index Patristicus* (1907), a steady stream of books and articles flowed from his pen, now independently, now in collaboration with other scholars. In 1923 he became chair of the New Testament department and in 1933 was designated the university's Ernest DeWitt Burton Distinguished Service Professor. Officially retired in 1937, Goodspeed moved to California and established a fruitful academic relationship with the University of California at Los Angeles. He continued to publish, issuing *Matthew,*

Apologist and Evangelist just three years before his death on January 13, 1962.

Context. Goodspeed's career spanned the first half of the twentieth century, an eventful period for New Testament studies. Scholars were determined to do competent, historical investigation with the help of geography and archaeology. The work of W. F. Petrie, B. P. Grenfell, A. S. Hunt and Adolf Deissmann on papyri established decisively that the Greek of the New Testament was not a peculiar language but rather the common dialect of the Mediterranean world. The discovery of Codex Washingtonensis and the Chester Beatty Biblical Papyri enriched manuscript materials available to establish the text of the New Testament. The expanding knowledge of its grammar and lexicography was reflected in widely read modern speech translations prepared by individual scholars as well as in the Revised Standard Version.

The study of Gospel origins led to vigorous discussion and debate in response to advocates of Aramaic originals, form criticism and the four-document hypothesis. Fourth Gospel research moved toward A.D. 100 as the Gospel's most likely date, a disciple of the apostle as the probable author of its final form and Judaism rather than Hellenism as its primary background. Pauline studies in this period focused on such issues as the authenticity of Ephesians and the Pastorals, the identity of the recipients of Galatians, the provenance of the Prison Epistles, Paul's relation to Hellenism, and the recovery of the *centrum paulinum*.

Meanwhile, the optimistic, activistic social gospel movement, which operated with an inadequate doctrine of sin and a weak christology, went aground on the reality of two world wars and the Great Depression. While the investigations into New Testament eschatology conducted by Johannes *Weiss and Albert *Schweitzer convinced many that the simple, human Jesus of nineteenth-century liberalism never existed, the skepticism of the form critics made scholars increasingly hesitant to attempt to set down the life of Jesus. During these same decades the contributions of Karl *Barth, Gerhard Kittel and Oscar *Cullmann brought about a revival of biblical theology.

The theological dimensions of this scholarly ferment had little discernable impact on Goodspeed, perhaps because he tended to speak of the New Testament's religious values rather than its traditional doctrines. Accordingly, he wrote New Testament studies, not commentaries; a New Testament introduction, not a New Testament theology. Of major interest to him were the challenge of translation, the origin of Ephesians and the formation of the New Testament, and the debate over whether the Gospels were originally written in Greek or Aramaic.

Work. For most people Goodspeed's name remains most readily associated with Bible translation. *The New Testament: An American Translation* was three years in preparation and appeared in 1923. His reasons for undertaking this task were clear and compelling: the continuing progress in establishing the text and vocabulary of the New Testament; the conviction that the Koine Greek of the New Testament could be properly represented only by translation into vernacular English; the fact that a version in a definitely American idiom was long overdue; and the need for a dynamic equivalence translation that would maintain the exciting readability that the Gospels and Acts had for the Christians of the second century. In both binding and format Goodspeed's New Testament also sought the commonplace in appearance.

Goodspeed's recollection of the storm of criticism and protest that greeted his translation constitutes one of the liveliest chapters in his autobiography *As I Remember* (1953, 155-90). Peering through this storm, he discerned the shape of two formidable opponents. One was the appalling ignorance of the history of the English Bible and of progress in biblical science displayed by the public press. The other was the massive resistance to change made by the zealous adherents of the King James

Version. Much bewildered and a little angry, Goodspeed rose to do battle with both. Taking advantage of the notoriety created by his bad press, he launched a counterattack from lecture platforms from coast to coast. The form and content of his lectures soon became clear and fixed: a brief presentation of the case for translating the New Testament, spiced with a generous sampling of choice editorials and letters, and reinforced by a platform display of copies of the seven famous predecessors of the King James Version. More than one hundred such lectures were given during the first year of the translation's appearance.

In 1925 Goodspeed published *The Making of the English New Testament,* and in 1945 *Problems of New Testament Translation,* a book that introduced the reader into the translator's workshop to see how translations, commentaries, lexicons, concordances, papyri, inscriptions, monographs and articles served the primary goal: to determine precisely what each of the New Testament writers meant each sentence to convey. Although twenty-two years separated this book from the American translation, the two were companion volumes.

Shortly after Goodspeed had collaborated with J. M. Powis Smith to produce *The Bible: An American Translation* (1931), he was persuaded that no one can have the complete Bible, as source book for the cultural study of art, literature, history and religion, without the Apocrypha. His response was to publish *The Apocrypha, An American Translation* (1938) and *The Story of the Apocrypha* (1939).

In the more specialized areas of New Testament study, Goodspeed became intensely involved in two issues. The first was the origin of Ephesians and the formation of the New Testament. The germ of his hypothesis first appeared as a passing allusion in *The Formation of the New Testament:* "Ephesians was written in the latter part of the first century, not to any single church but as a general letter. It shows the influence of Colossians and must have been written in connection with the movement to collect Paul's letters, probably as an introduction to them" (Goodspeed 1926, 28). The following year the allusion became a chapter, and with *The Meaning of Ephesians* (1933), it reached book-length proportions.

The Goodspeed reconstruction presupposes a well-defined historical setting. The time is A.D. 80-90. Paul has passed from the scene and in the year since his death has been all but forgotten. His letters, often composed swiftly in the daily press of mission labors and intended to meet a specific need in the time and place of the recipients, lie dusty in the church chests of his scattered flocks. The Gospels of Mark and Matthew have been written but betray no knowledge of Paul's letters. More significantly still, the author of Luke-Acts, with his obvious interest in Paul, appears equally ignorant of this rich primary source.

The theory now posits a Christian, probably an Asian, who is in close relationship to the church at Colossae. In his possession is a copy of Paul's letter to that congregation, a letter he has read and reread until he almost knows it by heart. Perhaps he is also familiar with the letter to Philemon. These two documents are sufficient to make this man a Paulinist through and through. One day there comes into his hands a copy of the recently published Acts. As the drama of the mission journeys unfolds before his mind's eye, a whole new dimension is added to his devotion to the man he had previously known only as a writer. It occurs to him that just as Paul wrote to the Colossians, so also he might have written letters to the congregations mentioned in Acts. What a magnificent thing it would be if some of these letters had survived and could be assembled. It would be like Paul returning to the center of the Christian scene once more. The churches of Acts are hopefully contacted, and with impressive results. Five different churches proved to have letters from Paul: Rome, Corinth, Philippi, Thessalonica and Galatia. His efforts have been richly rewarded, for he is the first man ever to read the collected letters of Paul! Having been stirred by Colossians alone, the spiritual heights and depths of the collection overwhelm him with the force of a revelation.

Naturally this treasure must be shared. The time is ripe, for Acts has awakened the church at large to its massive indebtedness to Paul. But would Christians everywhere trouble to perceive the permanent riches so thoroughly intertwined with the apostolic word for specific situations long since past? What better guarantee could be devised than to preface the collection with a letter of introduction? Thus it was that this unknown Christian, fired by the inspiration of his master, unconsciously leaning most upon Colossians but drawing upon the riches of the entire corpus, weaving through his work the call to Christian unity needful for his day, composed the untitled covering letter of commendation destined to be misnamed in future years the letter to the Ephesians. Naturally he put Paul's name at the head of it, for it was his intention that what he wrote should be Paul speaking through him. He was therefore the first Christian pseudepigrapher. In later statements of the hypothesis, Goodspeed yielded to the temptation to identify this unknown collector-author. He drew attention to the reflection of John Knox that Paul's young protege and the bishop of Ephesus in Ignatius's day (A.D. 110-117) bore the name Onesimus. By assuming that these two are in fact the same person, Onesimus becomes both the collector of the Pauline corpus and the author of Ephesians. While conceding that this identification was in the realm of conjecture, Goodspeed claimed for it no small degree of probability.

If the implications of Goodspeed's Ephesian contribution reached backward to the Pauline corpus, they also reached forward to the subsequent Christian literature. The key, as expressed in *An Introduction to the New Testament,* was his conviction that the collection of Paul's letters "has as much importance as the writing of almost any book in the New Testament" (Goodspeed 1937, vii-viii). Indeed, he saw this collection as the dominating influence in Christian literature from A.D. 90 to 110. Revelation, argued Goodspeed, was the first document to reflect that influence, as may be seen in the remarkable but overlooked fact that this Christian apocalypse begins with a corpus of letters to churches. Moreover, the letter to the Hebrews, 1 Peter, the letters of John, and other early Christian literature were further evidence that the use of letters for Christian instruction had suddenly become general.

The second issue that engaged Goodspeed was the learned controversy concerning the original language of much of the New Testament. The Semitic or Aramaic hypothesis, championed especially by Charles Cutler Torrey, held that the distinct and continuous Semitic tinge of the Greek of the Gospels, Acts 1—15 and the Apocalypse indicates that they are translations of Aramaic originals. Understandably, Goodspeed has been regarded as the leader of Torrey's critics, for his published opposition spanned more than twenty years and challenged the Aramaic hypothesis at every point.

With the authority provided by his three solid years of specialization in pure Semitics, Goodspeed maintained that the original language of the Gospels was the vernacular Greek of the papyri, as pointed out by Deissmann and discovered afresh by Grenfell and Hunt at Oxyrhynchus and Tebtunis. If the linguistic evidence indicated that the New Testament books in question were not written in Aramaic, the literary-historical situation decreed that they could not and would not have been so written. Moreover, the disagreement among the Semitists themselves over the identification of Semitisms and mistranslations became, in Goodspeed's hands, an effective weapon against their position.

Significance. By any standard of measurement Goodspeed made a sizeable contribution to biblical studies. As a teacher, he helped shape the careers of such New

Testament scholars as E. C. Colwell, F. W. Gingrich, John Knox, S. V. McCasland, D. W. Riddle, A. P. Wikgren and H. R. Willoughby. As an author he published more than fifty books and two hundred articles in periodicals ranging from the *Journal of Biblical Literature* to *Look* magazine. As a communicator he took seriously the responsibility to mediate the results of biblical research to the educated public through a number of popular Bible study books.

If Goodspeed did not create a school, the reason may be that he was more New Testament technician than theologian. At collating and deciphering manuscripts, wrestling with the problems of translation, and formulating literary hypotheses regarding the provenance of primitive Christian documents, he was at his best. The only serious attempt made at exegesis or hermeneutics is found in the first part of *The Meaning of Ephesians,* and this is not so much a commentary as an effort to demonstrate the validity of a hypothesis.

This is not to say, however, that Goodspeed's impact, especially among Americans, was slight or momentary. His obituary notice in *Publishers' Weekly* bore eloquent witness to his literary impact. At the time of his death in 1962, his American translation of the New Testament had sold 220,000 copies and his New Testament introduction 27,000 copies. In 1995 the University of Chicago Press reported that sales of his popular *The Story of the New Testament* (1916) and *The Story of the Old Testament* (1934) totaled 97,900 and 48,500 respectively.

Enjoying a modest but successful reputation as a magazine essayist, Goodspeed prided himself on his ability to write the familiar, spoken English of his day. He exercised this talent both in his translation of Scripture and in his translation of the advances of biblical studies into the language of the reading public. In many ways he was that most useful and practical of persons—an articulate scholar.

BIBLIOGRAPHY
Works. E. J. Goodspeed, *The Apocrypha: An American Translation* (Chicago: University of Chicago Press, 1938); idem, *The Apostolic Fathers: An American Translation* (New York: Harper & Bros., 1950); idem, *As I Remember* (New York: Harper, 1953); idem, *The Formation of the New Testament* (Chicago: University of Chicago Press, 1926); idem, *A History of Early Christian Literature* (Chicago: University of Chicago Press, 1942); idem, *Index Patristicus* (Leipzig: J. C. Henrichs, 1907); idem, *An Introduction to the New Testament* (Chicago: University of Chicago Press, 1937); idem, *The Making of the English New Testament* (Chicago: University of Chicago Press, 1925); idem, *Matthew, Apologist and Evangelist* (Philadelphia: Winston, 1959); idem, *The Meaning of Ephesians* (Chicago: University of Chicago Press, 1933); idem, *The New Testament: An American Translation* (Chicago: University of Chicago Press, 1923); idem, *Problems of New Testament Translation* (Chicago: University of Chicago Press, 1945); idem, *The Story of the Apocrypha* (Chicago: University of Chicago Press, 1939); idem, *The Story of the New Testament* (Chicago: University of Chicago Press, 1916); idem, *The Story of the Old Testament* (Chicago: University of Chicago Press, 1934); **Studies.** J. H. Cobb and L. B. Jennings, *A Biography and Bibliography of Edgar Johnson Goodspeed* (Chicago: University of Chicago Press, 1948); J. I. Cook, *Edgar Johnson Goodspeed: Articulate Scholar* (Chico, CA: Scholars Press, 1981).   J. I. Cook

Ladd, George Eldon (1911-1982)

George Eldon Ladd was born in Alberta, Canada. Soon after, his family moved to the United States, where his father served as a physician in a rural community in New Hampshire. His conversion to Jesus Christ came in 1929 while he was living in Maine and attending a Methodist church. Later that year he enrolled as a student at Gordon College in Massachusetts and served as a student pastor in a small Baptist church in Gilford, New Hampshire. Following his graduation in 1933 he married Winifred (Winnie) Webber, was ordained as a Northern Baptist minister (now American Baptist) and began his bachelor of divinity degree at Gordon Divinity School (now Gordon-Conwell Theological Seminary). After graduation (1936), he moved to Montpelier, Vermont, where he pastored a small Baptist church. In 1942 he and his wife returned to Boston to pastor the Blaney Memorial Church while Ladd enrolled in the classics department of Boston University.

A year later Ladd transferred to Harvard University, where he began and completed the Ph.D. degree in classics (1949). His primary mentor was H. J. Cadbury, who insisted on proficiency in linguistics (Greek, Latin and Hebrew) and an awareness of the contributions of historical and literary criticism to the interpretation of the Bible. He also gained further appreciation for careful historical critical inquiry during his studies in Heidelberg, where he became friends with Günther *Bornkamm, Eric Dinkler and other critical New Testament scholars. In these contexts Ladd gained a greater appreciation for studying the Christian faith and Christian origins in their historical setting and also realized the importance of making his traditional evangelical faith more credible in the scholarly world. Before coming to Fuller Theological Seminary in 1950, Ladd taught Greek at Gordon College and New Testament classes at the Gordon Divinity School.

Work. Ladd's interest in the mission of the church, impacted by his earlier ministry as a pastor, lasted throughout his career. His primary aim was to prepare persons for Christian ministry in churches as well as for academic pursuits that would advance the Christian cause. Most of his colleagues and students also knew that he had little patience for trivia in theological pursuits. His own interests demanded he pursue the critical questions that faced the church rather than retreat into the obscure issues that had been characteristic of many evangelical scholars who had preceded him. Ladd's primary contributions to biblical scholarship came during his thirty-year tenure as professor of New Testament exegesis

and theology at Fuller Theological Seminary in Pasadena, California. He was known as a gifted communicator both in the pulpit and in the classroom. He influenced not only a generation of evangelical scholars but also numerous preachers who welcomed his insights into biblical eschatology and biblical criticism. From a survey taken in the 1980s, Ladd has been acknowledged as the most influential evangelical scholar in North America (Noll, 209-14).

Among his fourteen books and some sixty-five articles, Ladd's most significant and enduring theological contributions include *Jesus and the Kingdom* (1964; republished as *The Presence of the Future* [1974]), *The New Testament and Criticism* (1967) and *A Theology of the New Testament* (1974). Several of his other works also received widespread acceptance in evangelical schools as well as in major universities in Europe and the United States.

In the classroom, Ladd had an imposing presence. Being large in stature, he could be intimidating, especially to those students who had not prepared well for classes. But he also challenged those of a more fundamentalist perspective who refused to engage in a critical examination of their faith. He was not fond of lecturing but instead preferred to use class time to raise questions that would enable students to come to grips with the critical issues involved in careful biblical inquiry and to think critically about their faith. He was committed to the exegesis of the biblical text using all the historical and literary disciplines available to enable him to understand what the text meant before he brought to the pulpit what it means. He urged his students to pursue advanced degrees in major universities in the United States and in Europe and encouraged them to study carefully the current trends of biblical scholarship.

Major Themes. Several major themes emerge in Ladd's work.

History and historical criticism. At the center of Ladd's contributions to biblical interpretation was his belief in the activity of God in creation, in the history of Israel, especially in Jesus of Nazareth whom he raised from the dead, and also in the history that is yet to be, eschatology. Better than most of his evangelical contemporaries, he understood the nature and practice of historical explanation and the history of its development in the Christian community (see Ladd 1964b, 1967). He believed that God has acted in remarkable ways in human history, but he also knew that he could not ask the historian as a historian to demonstrate that activity historically. He recognized that biblical criticism, because of its close ties to a positivistic approach to history, could not adequately inquire into such activity. Nevertheless he maintained that historical criticism need not be an enemy of the evangelical faith. If properly understood, it could support and even clarify the conservative conclusions.

Though Ladd acknowledged that a critical historian could not prove the supernatural activity of God in history, such activity nevertheless was consistent with the historical evidences that are discernible by the historian (Ladd 1967, 189). In regard to the resurrection of Jesus, these evidences include "the death and burial of Jesus; the discouragement and disillusionment of the disciples; their sudden transformation to be witnesses to Jesus' resurrection; the empty tomb; the rise of the Christian church; and the conversion of Saul" (Ladd 1974b, 13). He conceded that if the historian could come up with an adequate historical or natural explanation for these facts, then his own "confidence in the integrity of the New Testament witness to the resurrection would be deeply undermined, if not completely shattered" (Ladd 1974b, 27). Since Christian faith is a historical religion in every sense of the term in that it speaks of God's activity in Jesus of Nazareth and its origins can be tracked in the historical continuum, then Christian faith must be capable of being understood and explained historically (Ladd 1974b, 16-27).

However, the historical methodology that developed since the Enlightenment was essentially negative in its conclusions about the biblical understanding of the activity of God in the causal nexus of human history. Ladd held that this bias in historical inquiry left it incapable of making final judgments on the unique activity of God since the positivistic approach to history that developed out of the nineteenth century eliminated in principle the existence and activity of God and relegated to myth all such talk of divine interventions in history. Though many scholars retreated from the notion that God had intervened in human affairs in objectifiable ways—that is, in ways that suspended the laws of nature—Ladd believed that such abandonment of the claims of traditional Christianity was unwarranted. He was aware of the limitations of historical explanation because of its positivistic assumptions of a closed causal nexus, that historical events must have historical analogy, and that historians must evaluate their sources based on laws of probability and their own experience.

Ladd, however, knew that this critical-historical methodology was hardly capable of adequately explaining the phenomenon of Christian faith. He therefore called for a historical-theological approach that could do justice both to the historical context of early Christianity and to its claims of God's activity in creation and redemption. This theological methodology included the acceptance of the truthfulness of the Bible in matters that could not be established by the historian (Ladd 1967, 16-18). Ladd's approach was largely dependent upon the *Heilsgeschichte* ("salvation history") perspective of Oscar *Cullmann and Leonhard Goppelt, who contended that New Testament history must be interpreted theologically as well as historically. Ladd concluded that "the Bible can be rightly understood only by those who accept its basic message, and this requires the response of faith as well as a historical scientific methodology" (Ladd 1967, 51).

Eschatology. One of Ladd's most enduring interests was biblical eschatology. Seven of his fourteen books and thirty-one of his sixty-five articles and essays were on this subject. His focus on the presentness of the kingdom is where he departed from his earlier dispensational background that had placed the kingdom of God completely in the future. He continued to maintain his belief that Jesus would return to earth to establish the kingdom of God but stressed that aspects of the rule of God were present not only in the ministry, death and resurrection of Jesus but also in the life of the church through the presence and power of the Holy Spirit. This belief, he argued, was at the core of the message of the New Testament, and he stressed that Jesus claimed that the kingdom—that is, the reign or rule of God rather than the realm of God—was present in Jesus' own life and ministry even though its fullness was yet future (Ladd 1974d, 62-67).

Ladd based this view in part on the time when Jesus read the messianic prophecy of Isaiah 61:1-2 and claimed that this promise had come true in his ministry (Lk 4:16-21; cf. Mt 11:2-6) but especially on Jesus' reference to the kingdom being present in his own ministry (Mt 12:28; Lk 17:20). In the resurrection of Jesus especially, the age to come had broken into the present age and overlapped with it (Ladd 1974d, 66-67). Ladd maintained, however, that the future aspects of the kingdom of God were yet to be fulfilled and that this eschatological hope lies at the heart of the New Testament's eschatological message. The consummation of the kingdom is yet future and is inseparably linked to the person and mission of Jesus (Ladd 1968, 303-24).

Unlike the dispensationalists, Ladd also contended that the church is the true Israel that is made up of Jews and Gentiles alike and that the new covenant for the church is the same for the Jews and the Gentiles. He taught that the destinies and prophecies of the Old Testament must be interpreted in light of their fulfillment in the person and mission of Jesus in the New Testament (Ladd 1978, 9-18). He acknowledged the confusion even among Jesus' disciples over how Jesus, the lowly Suffering Servant of God, could also be the ruling and reigning messiah-king of the Old Testament prophets. This matter was resolved, he claimed, when the early church taught two comings of the messiah: the first one, following the example of the Suffering Servant of Isaiah 53, when Jesus came to offer his life as a sacrifice for sins and the second when he will come as the ruling and reigning messiah-king (Ladd 1978, 11-13).

Easter. The resurrection of Jesus also occupied a considerable amount of Ladd's interest. He concluded that Jesus' career would have ended in a lie if he had remained in the grave, and redemptive history would have also ended in a Palestinian grave (Ladd 1974b, 144). He stressed that the hope of the kingdom of God, which is central to the teaching of Jesus, was lost and a delusion if Jesus is dead (Ladd 1974b, 145). Eschatology and Easter are therefore inseparably bound together, and in the resurrection of Jesus God has preeminently become involved in human affairs. Without the Easter event, Ladd contended, there could be no Christian faith.

He further stressed that the resurrection of Jesus is the only adequate explanation to account for the resurrection faith and the admitted historical facts surrounding the event (discouragement of disciples, the empty tomb, resurgence of faith), even though he denied that a historian could prove the resurrection of Jesus (Ladd 1974b, 24-27).

Unity and disunity in the Bible. The problem of the similarities and the differences in the New Testament writers was a special concern for Ladd. He argued that the unity of Scripture was to be found in its record of God's activity in human history and not in forced harmonizations. He rejected the popular notion of biblical inerrancy that led to the conclusion that an error in any part of the Bible would effectively destroy the validity of all of its message. Such beliefs, he claimed, prevented the fundamentalists from examining the biblical data honestly and carefully as well as engaged the church in the hopeless battle of defending every apparent contradiction in Scripture. While affirming the full inspiration and authority of the Scriptures, Ladd spoke of different levels of theology in the New Testament (Ladd 1969), and he abandoned the notion of biblical inerrancy.

Biblical theology. Ladd saw the importance of studying the New Testament theologically, keeping separate the distinctives of its various writers and not blurring their message through forced harmonizations. *A Theology of the New Testament,* which has become the most popular volume on biblical theology among evangelical students, was his most significant attempt at producing a book that would do justice to the individual contributions of each writer of the New Testament. This culmination of his thinking became an evangelical forerunner to redaction criticism, especially in terms of how he approached the Gospels. He wanted the message and intent of each writer to be considered carefully without forcing them all to say the same thing. While the editor of the revised edition saw the need to include a theology of the individual Synoptic Gospels (Ladd 1993 [rev ed. of 1974d], 212-45), the point is still valid. The weakness of Ladd's work at this point lies in its title. It does not represent so much "a theology of the New Testament" as it does the theologies of the New Testament. Little is done to draw all of the strands of theology together or to trace those common elements of New Testament theology. Although in several respects this work is now dated, there is still little in the evangelical community to take the place of Ladd's *Theology.*

Significance. Ladd was essentially a product of the fundamentalist-modernist controversy of the 1920s and 1930s in the United States in which conservative Christianity generally retreated from engaging in a critical study of the Scriptures and abandoned the mainline seminaries where, it was believed, the traditional teachings of the church had been abandoned. The liberalism of that era taught that the Christi-

anity of the future must adapt itself to the recent critical findings of biblical investigation and to the naturalistic presuppositions that gave rise to these finds. It is generally conceded that fundamentalism suffered a serious setback as a result of retreating from honest and forthright engagement with the critical issues of its day. The modernists of that era had adopted the critical historical methodologies of the day and were generally skeptical of the biblical stories of miracles and all such talk of God's activity in history. The conservatives who rejected these conclusions on theological grounds rather than on the basis of historical-critical evidence were not infrequently considered to be uncritical in their worldview, a view that was no longer viable in the modern age.

The general withdrawal of the fundamentalists from the mainline denominations, seminaries and major universities was followed by their forming new denominations and schools and seminaries for the training of their ministers. The founding of Fuller Theological Seminary was one example of this attempt to provide a theological education for those entering ministry without giving up on what was believed to be the essential biblical teachings. Many such schools rejected any critical study of the Bible as being foreign to its content and inspiration. Some of the scholars who served in these institutions, however, saw that a withdrawal from biblical criticism effectively marginalized the evangelical impact upon the church as a whole. Ladd, along with a few other New Testament scholars (Ned B. Stonehouse, Bruce M. Metzger and Everett Harrison) accepted the responsibility of redirecting the conservative students back to a serious study of the Bible that involved them in the critical disciplines that developed concurrently with the post-Enlightenment understanding of history.

Ladd was convinced that the Scriptures were the Word of God and that they were an essential part of the ministry of both the pulpit and the lectern. He struggled with many personal matters in life that were at times overwhelming to him. Most of these stemmed from his dealing with his fundamentalist past. He saw that he was sometimes caught between two fierce opponents: the fundamentalists on the right, who were literalists in their interpretation of the Bible and suspicious of critical scholarship, and the liberal scholars, who distrusted any evangelical or conservative contributions to biblical scholarship. Fundamentalist leaders were suspicious of Ladd because he was willing to engage in dialogue with critical scholars as well as use the methodologies and conclusions of biblical criticism, which many of them believed were opposed to the God of the Bible and Christian faith itself. Ladd was also criticized by the reductionist scholars of his day, who relegated his beliefs in miracles, including the resurrection of Jesus from the dead and most traditional Christian dogma, to a preenlightened and mythical worldview that was no longer tenable to modern individuals who use the light bulb and the radio.

Ladd interacted with the historical issues raised by Rudolf *Bultmann's existentialist hermeneutics (Ladd 1964b, 1964a). But he also sought to encourage conservative students to study the Bible critically and to understand the perspectives of critical biblical scholarship (Ladd 1967).

In terms of liberal criticism, the most significant negative review of Ladd's widely read book *Jesus and the Kingdom* came from Norman *Perrin (Perrin, 1965), who accused Ladd of not understanding the scholarly works that he had read (especially those of Martin Kähler and Bultmann) and using them only to the extent that they appeared to support his conclusions while ignoring their major contributions and interpretations. Perrin also criticized Ladd for failing to do adequate exegesis of many of the primary texts that dealt with the subject matter of his book (the kingdom of God). In the same review Perrin claimed that Ladd had a primitive understanding of history and a tendency for uncritically accepting the historical perspective of the Bible. Though there was

some justification in Perrin's review, it does illustrate the difficulty evangelical scholars had in establishing their credibility and scholarship in the 1960s. In 1976, just prior to his death, Perrin moderated some of his criticisms, but not before they had taken their toll on Ladd.

To some extent the review had a positive impact on Ladd, which can be seen in his meticulous referencing of critical scholars, making certain that he was not misquoting them or ignoring their other contributions to issues that he was investigating. He also made a more substantial case for his views on the kingdom of God and for his understanding of history when he revised his book on *Jesus and the Kingdom* and republished it as *The Presence of the Future* (1974). Criticisms from both the conservatives and the liberals were quite painful to him and took an emotional toll. But they did not dissuade him from pursuing his primary goal of investigating the Scriptures in their original setting and interacting with critical biblical scholarship. He continued his dialogue with the current trends of critical scholarship and defended the traditional teachings of the church.

Ladd's publications and classroom contributions were significant in bringing evangelicalism back into the mainstream of Christianity in the United States. It is no longer unusual to find evangelical scholars doing significant work in biblical exegesis and producing responsible commentaries. The generation of evangelicals following Ladd has advanced considerably in this regard and has rejoined the mainstream of biblical scholarship without abandoning their traditional beliefs. This was one of Ladd's stated objectives in his *New Testament and Criticism* when he urged students to employ biblical criticism within the context of their evangelical faith to make important contributions to the study of Scripture (Ladd 1967, 53).

BIBLIOGRAPHY

Works. G. E. Ladd, *The Blessed Hope* (Grand Rapids: Eerdmans, 1956); idem, *Commentary on the Book of Revelation* (Grand Rapids: Eerdmans, 1974a); idem, *Crucial Questions About the Kingdom of God* (Grand Rapids: Eerdmans, 1952); idem, *The Gospel of the Kingdom* (Grand Rapids: Eerdmans, 1959); idem, *I Believe in the Resurrection* (London: Hodder & Stoughton; Grand Rapids: Eerdmans, 1974b); idem, *Jesus and the Kingdom* (Waco, TX: Word, 1968 [1964]); idem, *Jesus Christ and History* (Chicago: Inter-Varsity Press, 1964a); idem, *The Last Things: An Eschatology for Laymen* (Grand Rapids: Eerdmans, 1978); idem, *The New Testament and Criticism* (Grand Rapids: Eerdmans, 1967); idem, *The Pattern of New Testament Truth* (Grand Rapids: Eerdmans, 1969); idem, *The Presence of the Future* (Grand Rapids: Eerdmans, 1974c; revision of *Jesus and the Kingdom);* idem, *Rudolf Bultmann* (Chicago: InterVarsity Press, 1964b); idem, "The Search for Perspective," *Int* 25 (1971) 41-62; idem, *A Theology of the New Testament* (Grand Rapids: Eerdmans; London: Lutterworth, 1974d; rev. ed., ed. D. A. Hagner [Grand Rapids: Eerdmans, 1993]); idem, *The Young Church* (London: Lutterworth; New York: Abingdon, 1964c).

Studies. R. A. Guelich, ed., *Unity and Diversity in New Testament Theology* (Grand Rapids: Eerdmans, 1978); M. A. Noll, *Between Faith and Criticism: Evangelicals, Scholarship and the Bible in America* (San Francisco: Harper & Row, 1986) 91-121; N. Perrin, "Review of Jesus and the Kingdom," *Int* 19 (1965) 228-31.

L. M. McDonald

Machen, J(ohn) Gresham (1881-1937)

Better known for his opposition to liberal Protestantism in the Northern Presbyterian Church (PCUSA) during the fundamentalist-modernist controversy, J. Gresham Machen was foremost a professor of New Testament, a well-respected member of the guild of professional biblical scholars and throughout his career produced solid work from a conservative perspective. After studying Greek classical literature as an undergraduate (B.A., 1901) and a year of graduate work at Johns Hopkins University in his hometown, Baltimore, Machen went on to Princeton Seminary, where he completed the bachelor of divinity degree (1905) along with a master of arts in philosophy at Princeton University (1904).

While he was a seminarian Machen honed his interest in ancient languages and literature to focus on the study of the New Testament's history and texts. To that end he went to Germany for a year, studying for a semester at both Marburg and Göttingen. Though he was uncertain about ordination, Machen returned to the United States to become lecturer in Greek and New Testament at Princeton Seminary (1906). Upon ordination to the ministry (1914), Princeton's directors promoted him to assistant professor of New Testament, a position he held until 1929, when he left Princeton to found Westminster Theological Seminary in Philadelphia. There he was professor of New Testament until his death.

Context. Machen labored at a time when traditional Protestant interpretations of the Bible were coming in for serious revision. Though many biblical scholars continued to be ministers and so oriented to ecclesiastical concerns, professional biblical scholarship during the late nineteenth and early twentieth centuries became increasingly a specialized discipline within the new academic environment of the research university. In this context, biblical scholars emulated the scientific methods that dominated research in the natural and social sciences.

The effects of this process were twofold, both with serious consequences for believers who looked to the Bible as the norm for matters of faith and practice. The first was to move the study of Scripture away from the theological categories of the churches and to put Bible on a par with other texts from antiquity, whether sacred or not. Scholars increasingly ignored the Bible's divine character and attended instead to its human qualities.

The second consequence of professionalization, which fed the first, was the triumph of naturalistic perspectives in the study of Scripture. As definitions of science narrowed to restrict legitimate knowledge to only what was observable, biblical scholars increasingly overlooked or explained away the miraculous events and accounts of divine intervention into human history narrated in the biblical writings.

These changes in the study of Scripture were important for the antagonism between fundamentalists and liberal Protestants. While the latter still attached great religious significance to the Bible, especially as it contained the life and teachings of Jesus Christ, liberals did make large concessions to the new scholarship. Their hope was to retain the Bible's uniqueness and authority but to place that uniqueness and authority in those aspects of Scripture uncontaminated by the supernatural or miraculous, those things that to the modern scientific mind seemed incredible. Fundamentalists saw such concessions as gross infidelity and stressed the Bible's divine origin and scientific truthfulness. Thus the Protestant community polarized between those who opposed and those who embraced the new learning of the research university.

Despite Machen's reputation as one of the leading and certainly the most scholarly of fundamentalists, his own work on the New Testament fell into neither of the competing camps within Protestantism but mediated elements on both sides of the modernist-fundamentalist divide. With fundamentalists he affirmed the historical truthfulness of the biblical narratives and defended the necessity of the supernatural to scriptural teaching. Yet Machen eschewed dispensationalism, the method of interpretation that dominated fundamentalist circles throughout much of the twentieth century, calling it by the end of his life a menace to Presbyterian orthodoxy.

As much as Machen underscored the supernatural and miraculous in the biblical text, he nevertheless shared with liberal Protestants a genuine interest in the human aspects of Scripture and strove to use the variety of scholarly methods to understand the Bible better. In this regard he leaned heavily not just on the theological tradition at Princeton Seminary but also upon his training as a classicist at Johns Hopkins University.

Yet, despite his appreciation for academic approaches to the study of ancient texts, Machen did not hesitate to repudiate the naturalistic assumptions that often accompanied professional studies. Thus with fundamentalists Machen affirmed the divine and supernatural aspects of the Bible, and with liberal Protestants he recognized the importance of exploring the human dimensions of Scripture.

Although it is commonly identified with naive and simplistic readings of the Bible, Princeton Seminary's doctrine of Scripture provided Machen with a stable foundation for his scholarship. While Princeton notables such as Charles *Hodge and B. B. Warfield did articulate a doctrine of biblical inerrancy that claimed that the original autographs of Scripture were entirely free from error, the Princeton doctrine of inerrancy was also rooted in the broader Reformed understanding of special revelation. Rather than restricting critical study, Princeton's teaching on the nature of biblical writings generated close reading and rigorous study of Scripture.

What was crucial to the Princeton's doctrine of the word were Reformed notions about *concursus* and providence. Princetonians readily confessed that God intervened in human history to reveal himself and save his people, hence their affirmation of the supernatural aspects and miraculous content of the Bible. But they also believed that God ordinarily worked through secondary causes. In the case of Scripture this meant that God used human or natural developments to produce the text, and to understand the Bible, scholars could not be content with explanations that focused on the Bible's divine origin. They also needed to attend to the human qualities of the text. At both levels, then, the divine and the human aspects of the Bible, God was the sovereign author. But Princetonians recognized that God used human vessels to reveal himself, thus making critical research into questions of authorship, date, linguistics and history necessary. The Princeton doctrine of inerrancy was not a defensive tactic but a remarkably supple device for incorporating many of the advances in biblical scholarship.

Major Works. In addition to many articles, both popular and scholarly, and instructional material written for Christian education, Machen wrote two books. Both stemmed from endowed lectureships at southern Presbyterian seminaries. The first, *The Origin of Paul's Religion* (1921), originated as the Sprunt Lectures for 1921 at Union Seminary (Richmond). The second, *The Virgin Birth of Christ* (1930), was originally delivered as the Thomas Smyth Lectures for 1927 at Columbia Theological Seminary (South Carolina). Both books display Machen's commitment to conservative Protestant theology and careful scholarship.

In the first Machen addressed the critical question of Christianity's historical origins. The question could be answered in two ways, either through a study of the Gospels or through the Pauline epistles. The early date and genuineness of the apostle's writings, Machen argued, made the epistles the best evidence for understanding the character and history of early Christianity. As a contemporary of Jesus and a member of the disciples only a few years after Jesus' death, Paul had an extensive knowledge of the church both before and after his conversion and therefore abundant opportunity to acquaint himself with the facts of Jesus' life and death. Unlike German scholars and, increasingly, American students of the New Testament, Machen argued that Paul was not a second founder of Christianity who had departed from and added to the teaching of Jesus. Rather he concluded that Paul's religion was essentially the same as that of the other apostles and the early church.

Moreover, the substance of the early church's religion was "perfectly plain": Jesus Christ was a heavenly being who came to earth, died on the cross for the sins of believers, rose again from the dead, and was present with the church through his spirit. Along the way, Machen marshaled extensive linguistic, historical and exegetical evidence to refute the arguments of liberal and radical scholars who tried to explain away Christianity's uniqueness and supernaturalism as either the product of Greek mystery religions or the outcome of tendencies within Jewish apocalypticism. Machen believed that in the end the conclusions of the most radical scholars vindicated the teaching of historic Christianity while discrediting liberal Protestantism by making supernaturalism essential to the gospel.

In *The Virgin Birth of Christ* Machen employed a similar argument in trying to account for the early church's belief in the miraculous conception of Jesus. Again he interacted extensively with the available scholarship on the birth narratives. He also demonstrated a keen understanding of the literary and historical dimensions of the debate. But in the end, Machen's erudition served the conventional belief that Christ's birth was no mere natural phenomenon but involved the intervention of God into human history. Naturalistic explanations, he argued, were finally unsatisfactory; the historical evidence pointed to the conclusion that the early church believed exactly what the narratives in Matthew's and Luke's Gospels declared, namely, that Christ was conceived by the power of the Holy Spirit in the womb of the virgin Mary and was born of her yet without sin.

In both of these books Machen added to his defense of traditional interpretations of the Bible a poignant criticism of liberal Protestantism, a stricture that he developed at length in *Christianity and Liberalism* (1923), his most popular and polemical book. He believed that the most recent scholarship, that of the so-called history of religions school, demonstrated the folly of liberal attempts to separate the ethical instruction of the Bible, especially Christ's teaching, from the book's supernatural elements. Machen was convinced that ultimately the church would have to choose between the Christ of the Bible, complete with his miraculous birth and resurrection, or an altogether different religion. The supernatural and the natural were so closely interwoven as to make all efforts at separation impossible.

Machen, Commonsense Realism and Fundamentalism. Scholars have long attributed Machen's biblical studies to the early modern scientific outlook commonly associated with fundamentalism. By stressing the factual, historical, scientifically true character of the New Testament, some argue, Machen exhibited the fundamentalist habit of reading Scripture in a wooden and rationalistic manner. Unlike liberal Protestants, who were open to developmental models of truth (that truth was relative to time and place), fundamentalists held on to older Enlightenment conceptions of science and stressed that scientific truths, including the historical facts narrated in Scripture, were static and enduring. Because Machen appealed to the facts of Christ's life and ministry and argued that historical truths cannot with the passing of time be denied, historians have often equated his defense of the New Testament narratives with fundamentalists' defense of the first chapters of Genesis.

Machen, who refused to testify at the Scopes trial and avoided the controversy over creation and evolution, used methods in the study of the New Testament that he had learned not just at Princeton Seminary but also at Johns Hopkins University. Reviews of his books indicate that Machen's methods were standard fare in the academy of his day, even if the conservative theological conclusions to emerge from those methods were not. Indeed, the dominant interpretation of the fundamentalist controversy as one between rival conceptions of truth (static versus progressive) and also rival ways of reading the Bible (literal versus figurative) misses the degree to which students of ancient writings employed similar techniques to figure out the authorship, date and even meaning of a given text. On this score Machen's methods differed little from those of historians, philologists and

related scholars in the humanities who also conceived of ancient texts as having a fixed meaning that changed only in the light of new discoveries.

Where Machen differed from other biblical scholars was not in deciphering the meaning of a given passage but rather with what to do with that meaning in the modern context. Machen argued that the original meaning of the Bible was binding upon twentieth-century believers, while liberals often resorted to the symbolic or spiritual meaning of the Bible in order to free the modern church from difficult, if not incredible, teachings. What Machen did in arguing that the teachings in Scripture were binding upon Christians throughout all times and places was no different from the expectation of philosophers that modern-day Platonists conform to Plato's original teachings.

Significance. Estimates of Machen's abilities and importance as a New Testament scholar run the gamut of theological opinions and historical perspectives. For fundamentalists who clung to inerrancy severed from the confessional Presbyterianism of the Princeton theology, Machen was an important source who showed the holes in the so-called science of professional biblical scholarship. For conservative Presbyterians who supported and studied at Westminster Seminary, founded in 1929 by Machen and others to carry on the ideals of Old Princeton, he was a model of rigorous scholarship always informed by theological reflection. And for mainline Protestants, whether liberal or moderate, Machen and his efforts to oppose theological liberalism in the Presbyterian church were examples of where a commitment to inerrancy logically led.

Convenient though it may be to pigeonhole Machen on the far theological right with the rest of the fundamentalists, the estimate of F. V. Filson, professor of biblical theology at McCormick Theological Seminary, bears some consideration. Writing at the height of the influence of neo-orthodoxy upon mainstream American Protestantism, Filson declared that Machen's argument that traditional Christian theology was the necessary outcome of faithfulness to the message of the New Testament looked "far truer" than much of the "shallow theology" that characterized liberal Protestantism and the social gospel (Filson, 60).

Indeed, good reasons exist for connecting Machen's defense of the theology of the New Testament in the 1920s with the return in the 1940s to biblical theology among mainline Protestants. Despite different conceptions of the doctrine of the Word of God, both recognized that Scripture is more than morality, that it primarily narrates dramatic events in the unfolding of redemptive history. In turn, both criticized liberal Protestantism for reducing Christianity to little more than ethics and religious experience. And both Machen and the biblical theology movement strove to preserve the Bible as the church's book, as the norm for God's people, as opposed to liberal Protestantism, which too often took its cues from the academy and had trouble arguing that the Bible was different from other religious writings of the ancient Near East.

But where Machen veered significantly from the later biblical theology movement was in this matter of the church and its claims upon the Bible. Unlike biblical theologians and neo-orthodox leaders who criticized the witness of mainline Protestantism but continued to work under its auspices, Machen took his case against liberal Protestantism directly to the assemblies of the church, challenging whether a theology that compromised the witness of Scripture had a rightful place in a body that claimed Scripture as its norm and guide. It is Machen's attempt at consistency—between what he taught in the classroom and what he preached in the church—that is responsible for the various assessments of his significance. Nevertheless his scholarship stands as a testimony to the impossibility of separating the study of Scripture from theological conviction or ecclesiastical witness.

BIBLIOGRAPHY

Works. J. G. Machen, *The Christian Faith in the Modern World* (New York: Macmillan, 1936); idem, *The Christian View of Man* (New York: Macmillan, 1937); idem, *Christianity and Liberalism* (New York: Macmillan, 1923); idem, "Forty Years of New Testament Research," *USR* 40 (1928) 1-11; idem, *God Transcendent, and Other Sermons,* ed. N. B. Stonehouse (Grand Rapids: Eerdmans, 1949); idem, "Karl Barth and 'The Theology of Crisis,'" *WTJ* 53 (1991) 197-207; idem, *The New Testament: An Introduction to Its Literature and History,* ed. W. J. Cook (Edinburgh: Banner of Truth Trust, 1976 [1914-1915]); idem, *New Testament Greek for Beginners* (New York: Macmillan, 1923); idem, *The Origin of Paul's Religion* (New York: Macmillan, 1921); idem, "The Relation of Religion to Science and Philosophy," *PTR* 24 (1926) 38-66; idem, *The Virgin Birth of Christ* (New York: Harper & Bros., 1930); idem, *What Is Christianity?* ed. N. B. Stonehouse (Grand Rapids: Eerdmans, 1951); idem, *What Is Faith?* (New York: Macmillan, 1925).

Studies. F. V. Filson, "The Study of the New Testament" in *Protestant Thought in the Twentieth Century: Whence and Where?* ed. A. S. Nash (New York: Macmillan, 1951) 47-69; D. G. Hart, *Defending the Faith: J. Gresham Machen and the Crisis of Conservative Protestantism in Modern America* (Baltimore: Johns Hopkins University Press, 1994); B. J. Longfield, *The Presbyterian Controversy: Fundamentalists, Modernists and Moderates* (New York: Oxford University Press, 1991); G. M. Marsden, *Fundamentalism and American Culture: The Shaping of Twentieth-Century Evangelicalism, 1870-1925* (New York: Oxford University Press, 1980); idem, "J. Gresham Machen, History and Truth," *WTJ* 42 (1979) 157-75; M. A. Noll, *Between Faith and Criticism: Evangelical, Scholarship and the Bible in America* (San Francisco: Harper & Row, 1986); J. B. Rogers and D. K. McKim, *The Authority and Interpretation of the Bible: An Historical Approach* (San Francisco: Harper & Row, 1979); E. R. Sandeen, *The Roots of Fundamentalism: British and American Millenarianism, 1800-1930* (Chicago: University of Chicago Press, 1970); N. B. Stonehouse, *J. Gresham Machen: A Biographical Memoir* (Grand Rapids: Eerdmans, 1954).   D. G. Hart

Muilenburg, James
(1896-1974)

James Muilenburg was born on June 1, 1896, in Orange City, Iowa, and died at his home in Claremont, California, on May 10, 1974. He graduated magna cum laude from Hope College in Holland, Michigan (1920), and served as a teaching instructor in English composition at the University of Nebraska from 1920 to 1923 while studying for a master of arts degree, which he received in the latter year. In 1921 he married Mary (Mayme) Kloote, with whom he had three children. The Muilenburgs went on to Yale University, from which he received a Ph.D. in 1926 with a dissertation on the *Epistle of Barnabas* and the *Didache*. He was assistant and later associate professor of history and literature of religion at Mt. Holyoke College from 1926 to 1932 and was granted a sabbatical for the academic year 1929-1930, which he spent at the University of Marburg. He went originally to study under Karl Budde, but as was the custom he traveled to other German universities as well; at Halle he studied under Hermann *Gunkel. Gunkel's influence may be said to have determined the course of Muilenburg's career.

After several more years at Mt. Holyoke, Muilenburg served as dean of the College of Arts and Sciences at the University of Maine from 1932 to 1936. He received his first appointment in his chosen field, Billings Professor of Old Testament Literature and Semitic Languages at the Pacific School of Religion, where he stayed from 1936 until his call to be Davenport Professor of Hebrew and the Cognate Languages at Union Theological Seminary in New York in 1945. During his nineteen years at Union his reputation as a great teacher was built. After his retirement in 1963 he returned to California as Gray Professor of Hebrew Exegesis and Old Testament at San Francisco Theological Seminary in San Anselmo until 1969 and as scholar in residence at the Graduate Theological Union until 1972.

Muilenburg was one of the original thirty-two scholars who collaborated on the Revised Standard Version of the Bible, first published in 1952. He served as resident director of the American Schools of Oriental Research in Jerusalem (1953-1954) while working at the site of Khirbet el Mefjir, which he identified with biblical Gilgal. He was elected an honorary member of the British Society of Old Testament Studies. He was given honorary doctoral degrees by, among others, Hope College, the University of Maine, the Pacific School of Religion and the Church Divinity School of the Pacific. Two festschriften were dedicated to him, with articles by distinguished international colleagues and students. The crown of his career was his presidential address to the Society of Biblical Literature in November of 1968, published in the March 1969 issue of the *Journal of Biblical Literature* as "Form Criticism and Beyond."

Work. Muilenburg began his career at the height of the historical-critical view of the Bible. The influence of German literary critical study of the Old Testament was considerable. Julius *Wellhausen's classical statement of the results of higher criticism and his reconstruction of Israel's religion and literature had been translated and published in 1885 *(Prolegomena to the History of Ancient Israel)*, and Muilenburg's own heavily annotated copy of William Robertson *Smith's *Lectures on the Religion of the Semites* (3d ed.) is dated 1927 (Muilenburg contributed a prolegomenon to the reissue of this work by Ktav Press in 1969). Harry Emerson Fosdick's lectures on *The Modern Use of the Bible* (Macmillan, 1924) were widely influential in the United States and served to introduce a popular version of the current scholarly consensus to a wider public. Muilenburg himself never abandoned the documentary theory of the composition of the Pentateuch; generations of his students had to prepare a "Pentateuch paper" on the Abraham or Jacob cycles, indicating the alleged problems or inconsistencies in the text that had led to the hypothesis.

But Muilenburg was not captivated by the theory or primarily interested in the stages of the Bible's construction. His whole effort in the introductory course for seminarians was directed to bringing the text alive. To this end he would take on the persona of Adam in the Garden, would become David pleading for the life of his bastard son. The graduate students who worked as his teaching assistants cringed with embarrassment in the back of the lecture hall as Muilenburg seemed to make a fool of himself. Pearls before swine, we thought. The seminarians knew better and returned in upper-class years to experience his teaching again. He was far more than a showman; his insight into the theological intention of the author(s) pressed beyond dissection of the sources to the core of the text itself to reveal its inner meaning.

While he was still at the University of Nebraska, Muilenburg showed his interest in "the main literary types that are found in the Bible" with his first book, *Specimens of Biblical Literature* (1923). It was a textbook designed to serve the new high school and college courses in the Bible as literature. In it he gave examples from the American Standard Edition of the Revised Bible (1901), classified as narrative (history, short story, parable, fable), poetry (lyric, dramatic), reflection (Proverbs), essay (Ecclesiastes, James), prophecy (rhapsody, invective, emblem prophecy, satire, lament, dramatic prose), gospel, oratory (Joshua 23, Amos 3, sermons in Acts) and letters. His encounter with Gunkel heightened and refined his search for the biblical literary types, this time in terms of the Hebrew text. Gunkel's commentary on Genesis had sought to recover the different kinds of orally transmitted stories that underlay the written sources of that book, concentrating on the shortest examples as presumably the oldest and assigning them a typology following the nomenclature of Germanic literature (e.g. saga, legend, folktale, fable). But as Muilenburg showed in his commentary on Isaiah 40—66, it is not always wise to divide the text into brief

snippets, and Germanic forms may not provide suitable parallels to ancient Semitic literature. Throughout his work Muilenburg sought first to establish the limits of each unit, noting that mistakes in the beginning or ending (e.g., Is 6:1 *through* 13:22; Is 52:12-15 *as well as* Is 53) can be as fatal as misidentification of the type (Gen 1 is not a scientific treatise).

Muilenburg's method of interpretation of the Bible developed over the years; he never remained static or completely satisfied with any one approach. To the end he maintained his allegiance to the liberal school, by which he understood the rediscovery of the historical dimension of Israel's faith, its rootedness in the experience of God in human history. Yet his interest was not primarily in the attempt to relate passages of the Bible to datable human events, let alone to prove that the Bible was true (i.e., that its accounts were historically accurate). To him its truth was far more profound. Although he appreciated the contributions of archaeology, he was never tempted to overestimate their importance for the interpretation of Scripture. He used to challenge students that to ask "what actually happened" *(Was eigentlich geschehen ist)* at the Red Sea "is a third-rate question," deflecting attention from the God of the exodus to modern human concerns. At the same time he insisted on the actuality of the human experience reflected in the Bible, especially in the prophets. Under his hand the struggles of Jeremiah became intensely personal, so that the listener entered into the interior life of the prophet.

From Gunkel, Muilenburg gained an appreciation of the text's *Sitz im Leben* or situation in the common life of Israel's people. But whereas Gunkel believed it possible to rediscover the actual social situation that had given rise to particular texts, Muilenburg drew attention to the many ways in which the biblical writers had appropriated conventional oral forms of speech and transformed them for their own purposes. That is what he meant by his title to his presidential address: form criticism or *Gattungsforschung* is essential and must be utilized in the study of biblical texts, but the unique quality of each text needs to be heard. Whereas the complaints in Jeremiah's confessions have much in common with the psalms of lament and should be compared with them, they exhibit singular features peculiar to the prophet that must not be obscured in the assignment of a passage to a common *gattung* or genre. Each text's uniqueness can be recovered only by careful attention to its literary features (i.e., its rhetoric). Muilenburg devoted great care to the discovery of those features, such as repetition, inclusion, chiasm, parallelism, climax, assonance and alliteration, in order to reveal the structure and movement within each literary unit. Only by such attentive *listening* (for Muilenburg stressed the importance of hearing the Word once addressed to Israel) to the text is it possible to discern the thrust of the message, since form and content cannot be separated. Hence his dictum, "a proper articulation of form yields a proper articulation of meaning."

In Muilenburg's hands the approach that he came to call rhetorical criticism never became a rigid method of interpretation to be applied after other methods, let alone instead of them. Rather it was a more careful attention to the inner and outer structure of each unit that shared much in common with the method of close reading of the text. He was sometimes accused of an essentially trivial interest in aesthetics, in mere stylistics. On the contrary, Muilenburg's concern was to unlock the theological thrust and intention of the text, to which end a careful investigation of the text's rhetoric was only a means.

The bibliography of Muilenburg's scholarly writings is not long. Perhaps this is not surprising for one who had such a concern with the choice and sequence of words. He worked over what he wrote with great care, concerned to express himself not only clearly but also persuasively. This attention to the form of his presentations extended even to his lectures. One summer when he was away from Union Seminary he asked this writer to look up his opening lecture on Jeremiah. The desk drawer revealed sixteen successive outlines. Each year he had begun anew, eager to find just the right way to present Jeremiah to his class. Similarly he made his literary executors promise not to publish any unfinished works, lest the world be offered anything less than his best. Consequently his commentary on Jeremiah, the fruit of his mature years, lies unpublished in the Princeton Theological Seminary library.

Muilenburg's articles published in leading technical journals, dictionaries, commentary series and festschriften reveal the breadth as well as the depth of his scholarship. He was interested in all aspects of his chosen field, from archaeology to philology, from the history of Israel to the nuance of usage of a Hebrew particle. Through his writings and through his wide correspondence he kept in touch with all the leading Old Testament scholars worldwide. This acquaintance with so many others enriched his classes, for he was able to share with students not only what another scholar really thought but also what members of a previous generation had said. Many of his own students have become distinguished scholars, including Bernhard Anderson, Walter Harrelson, Walter *Brueggemann and Phyllis *Trible—all later presidents of the Society of Biblical Literature. Yet Muilenburg never intended to found a school or succession of like-minded scholars. Demanding on his graduate students he certainly was, but his fiercest wrath was reserved for the brash follower who would presume to repeat or even accept his teaching uncritically.

The world of biblical scholarship associates Muilenburg's name with rhetorical criticism, but those students who saw him in action and heard his words were indelibly impressed by his presence. Muilenburg was a big man; his powerful shoulders were surmounted by a large and commanding head. In action, his nose almost seemed to meet his prominent chin as he shuffled forward, his body bent as if into a strong wind. As he spoke his fingers carved the air as God made the first human of clay or reformed the vessel at the potter's house for Jeremiah. Always a twinkle lurked in his eyes, for he was ever conscious of the faintly absurd in the human condition. Muilenburg expected much of his graduate students and could be devastating in his critique of work not up to his standards, but the gentleness and respect often leading to affection for them was genuine. To this day he is referred to as "the master."

BIBLIOGRAPHY

Works. J. Muilenburg, "Form Criticism and Beyond," *JBL* 88 (1969) 1-18; idem, "Isaiah chs. 40—66 Introduction and Exegesis," *IB* 5:381-773; idem, *Specimens of Biblical Literature* (New York: Thomas Y. Crowell, 1923); idem, *The Way of Israel* (New York: Harper, 1961). *Studies.* B. W. Anderson, "The New Frontier of Rhetorical Criticism: A Tribute to James Muilenburg" in *Rhetorical Criticism: Essays in Honor of James Muilenburg*, ed. J. J. Jackson and M. Kessler (Pittsburgh Theological Monograph series 1; Pittsburgh: Pickwick, 1974) ix-xviii; B. W. Anderson and W. Harrelson, "Preface" in *Israel's Prophetic Heritage: Essays in Honor of James Muilenburg*, ed. B. W. Anderson and W. Harrelson (New York: Harper & Bros., 1962) xi-xiv; I. J. Ball Jr., "Additions to a Bibliography of James Muilenburg's Writings" in *Rhetorical Criticism: Essays in Honor of James Muilenburg*, ed. J. J. Jackson and M. Kessler (Pittsburgh Theological Monograph series 1; Pittsburgh: Pickwick, 1974) 285-87; T. F. Best, ed., *Hearing and Speaking the Word: Selections from the Works of James Muilenburg* (Chico, CA: Scholars Press, 1984), esp. his "Additions to the Bibliography of James Muilenburg's Writings," 448; R. L. Hicks, "A Bibliography of James Muilenburg's Writings" in *Israel's Prophetic Heritage: Essays in Honor of James Muilenburg*, ed. B. W. Anderson and W. Harrelson (New York: Harper & Bros., 1962) 233-42; P. Trible, *Rhetorical Criticism: Context, Method and the Book of Jonah* (Minneapolis: Fortress, 1994) 25-32.

J. J. Jackson

Perrin, Norman *(1920-1976)*

At his untimely death in 1976 Norman Perrin was one of the most influential and creative New Testament scholars in the United States. During a productive seventeen-year career, he had the drive and flexibility to work at the constantly changing cutting edge of New Testament scholarship and to make important contributions to a number of critical questions. His career is paradigmatic of major contours in modern Synoptic Gospel research.

Life. Born in England in 1920, Perrin attended Manchester University as an undergraduate, where he came under the influence of T. W. Manson. During his years at London University, where he received two advanced degrees, he acquired some of the more technical knowledge necessary for a specialty in New Testament studies. Although he was ordained to the ministry of the Baptist Union of Great Britain and Northern Ireland and served two churches during his graduate years at London, he became less interested in the institutional church as he increasingly immersed himself in biblical studies.

Perrin discerned that a close knowledge of German scholarship was crucial for anyone aspiring to make a name for himself in biblical studies. He took his doctor of theology degree at the University of Göttingen under Joachim *Jeremias.

Through contacts with American scholars at Göttingen, Perrin received an invitation to teach at Emory University's Candler School of Theology, where he served for five years. In 1964 he was appointed to a New Testament post at the University of Chicago Divinity School. He reveled in the increased opportunity to do research and direct doctoral students.

Form Criticism. Until roughly the last half of the twentieth century, critical New Testament scholarship was primarily in the service of a historical paradigm. When Perrin was being introduced to biblical scholarship, the reigning method for studying the Synoptic Gospels was form criticism, a method of tracing the oral prehistory of the text and addressing the situation in the life of the early church that led to the emergence, preservation and development of the Jesus material. For many critics, especially the more conservative ones like Manson and Jeremias, a goal of Gospel form criticism was to arrive at knowledge of the historical Jesus. The theological assumption (not always made explicit) driving the quest was that the historical Jesus is important for Christian faith.

Early in his career Perrin concerned himself with strands of the Synoptic tradition, especially teaching material (e.g., kingdom of God, parables, Son of man sayings), which were generally thought to have the potential to yield knowledge of the historical Jesus. Perrin's first two books, *The Kingdom of God in the Teaching of Jesus* and *Rediscovering the Teaching of Jesus,* reflect this early, form-critical phase of his career.

The second book, *Rediscovering the Teaching of Jesus,* for which he is perhaps best known, is an excellent example of the application of form criticism to Jesus' teaching. By the time Perrin wrote this book, he had departed from the conservatism of his two early teachers, Manson and Jeremias, who had high respect for the historicity of the Synoptic tradition. *Rediscovering the Teaching of Jesus* reflects full acceptance of a more skeptical, Bultmannian stance. Like Rudolf *Bultmann, Perrin concluded that much of the Synoptic material reflected the creativity of the early church, and he was therefore extremely skeptical regarding the possibility of learning much about the historical Jesus.

In form criticism Perrin's most significant contribution was the sharpening of criteria utilized to determine if Jesus' sayings are authentic, that is, uttered by the historical Jesus rather than arising out of the early church's experience of what it perceived to be the risen Lord. The fundamental criterion was what Perrin called dissimilarity. A saying is judged as authentic if it is dissimilar to characteristic emphases of both ancient Judaism and the early church. Although he rightly credited both Jeremias and Bultmann with utilizing such a criterion, it was Perrin who most clearly distinguished it and demonstrated its utility by systematically applying it to significant strands of the Jesus material.

Other criteria allowed sayings that are consistent with sayings allowed under dissimilarity (coherence) and sayings that can be discerned behind all or most of the Synoptic sources (multiple attestation).

Perrin was not the first to use any of the three criteria. His contribution was in sharpening the criteria, using terminology that became generally accepted, weaving the three into a program, and rigorously applying them to the Synoptic tradition.

Redaction Criticism. In the 1960s Perrin became increasingly aware of a new method—redaction criticism. Redaction criticism is a method of studying an author's work to determine how and why that author chose and modified available oral and/or written material. The Synoptic redaction critic is concerned with the theological motivations that were at work in the evangelist's mind as he redacted (edited) the Jesus material he had received.

Beginning in 1966, in a series of articles Perrin celebrated the rise of this method and utilized it to unlock the theological message of the Evangelists. Perrin's most significant contributions in this regard were on the Gospel of Mark. He was scheduled to write the commentary on Mark in the Hermeneia series, and although his death prevented this, we can glimpse some of the essential features of that commentary by examining a series of articles he wrote on Mark and the Synoptic Son of man sayings. Many of these articles are contained in a collection entitled *A Modern Pilgrimage in New Testament Christology.*

Perrin's interpretation of Mark was closely related to and fundamentally based on his work on the Son of man sayings, for which he is well known. Scholarly discussion about this title has generally centered around the origin of the concept and the authenticity of the Synoptic sayings.

Perrin challenged the prevailing scholarly opinion that in pre-Christian Judaism there was the uniform concept of a transcendent Son of man who would rescue the righteous and punish the wicked. This apocalyptic concept was thought to form the basis for the Son of man sayings in the New Testament. Arguing against the notion of a uniform Son of man concept in Jewish apocalyptic texts, Perrin showed how the imagery of Daniel 7:13 was used freely and creatively by later Jewish and Christian writers and especially by the author of Mark.

There are three general categories of these sayings: suffering Son of man sayings (e.g., Mk 8:31; 9:31; 10:33-34; Mt 17:12; 20:18-19), sayings about the present activity of the Son of man (e.g., Mk 2:10, 27-28; Lk 19:10) and apocalyptic sayings referring to the coming Son of man on the clouds in power (e.g., Mk 8:38; 13:26; Lk 17:22). A wide variety of opinions existed with regard to the authenticity of these categories.

Contrary to most scholars, Perrin offered strong arguments that none of the sayings is authentic. In a redaction-critical exegesis of Mark 8:27—10:52, he sought to demonstrate how Mark played the crucial role in developing the early Christian Son of man tradition. Perrin identified three cycles in the text (in Mk 8, 9, 10) and demonstrated how each one followed a threefold pattern of prediction of suffering of the Son of man (Mk 8:31; 9:31; 10:33-34), misunderstanding by the disciples (Mk 8:32-33; 9:32; 10:35-37) and teaching about discipleship (Mk 8:34-38; 9:33-37; 10:38-44).

These repetitions were Mark's way of combating a false view of Christ that stressed only his power and glory. Mark used the term "Son of man" to present to his readers a Jesus who was also a suffering Messiah and to press the point that true discipleship involved willing and necessary suffering.

Literary Criticism. The extensive post-World War II expansion of biblical studies beyond theological schools to religious studies departments in secular colleges and universities has seen biblical studies enriched by the application of insights from various disciplines. A good example of this trend is Perrin's last major scholarly book, *Jesus and the Language of the Kingdom.* In it his interest in the kingdom of God and parables is addressed from the perspective of a literary-critical approach informed by the American new critical movement.

American new criticism, associated with Robert Penn Warren, Allen Tate, John Crowe Ransom and Cleanth Brooks, has a disdain for the genetic fallacy of focusing on the historical, political and social factors that bring a text into being. The new critic is concerned with the precious object of literature itself. The meaning of a poem, for example, is found not in authorial intent but rather in the poem itself as a self-sufficient, organic whole. The poem's meaning can be revealed by a close reading emphasizing irony, paradox, structure, metaphor and other such literary techniques—form rather than content, *how* a text means rather than *what* it means.

Perrin contributed to a wave of Gospel studies influenced by new criticism that began in the 1960s with Amos Wilder and eventually included Robert W. Funk, Dan O. Via, John Dominic Crossan and others. Most biblical critics using literary principles have gravitated to Jesus' parables, which easily lend themselves to this approach. Perrin was the first critic to apply literary insights to the kingdom of God. Utilizing terms distinguished by Philip Wheelwright, Perrin suggested that the kingdom of God is fundamentally a tensive symbol, which has a multitude of possible referents, rather than a steno-symbol, which can refer to one thing only. He used these distinctions to interpret the varying ways "kingdom of God" was used in ancient Judaism, in the teaching of Jesus and by selected interpreters in the history of the church.

Hermeneutical Process. Perrin, however, never abandoned his earlier concerns for history. For him literary criticism was one step in a hermeneutical process designed to serve the dynamic interaction between text and interpreter. Historical criticism, which included form- and redaction-critical analyses, were appropriate steps in the process.

Although Perrin worked on a number of the controversial issues in Gospel research (e.g., kingdom of God, Son of man, parables, Gospel of Mark), the central theme energizing all his work was method: how properly to exegete the New Testament. Over the course of his career his methodological shifts were in the direction of viewing history as less and less important. Form criticism was concerned at least in part with reconstructing the teaching of the historical Jesus. With redaction criticism, interpretation moved away from a concern for history—at least the history of Jesus—and toward a greater appreciation for the author of the Gospel text. Finally, with literary criticism the focus is on the text itself rather than the historical and authorial background of the text.

Toward the end of his career Perrin was in the process of formulating a general theory of interpretation, potentially a synthesis of historical and literary approaches, of the best of contemporary European and American thought. Rather than another step along the history-text continuum, this next shift would have been an attempt to bend the continuum into a circle, incorporating a concern for history (form criticism), theology (redaction criticism) and literature (literary criticism).

Additionally, in his concern with hermeneutics proper, the final step in the interpretative process that for Perrin involved the dynamic interplay between text and interpreter, he addressed the role of the reader and the act of reading, major concerns of reader-oriented methods. Although he did not live to develop this "hermeneutical moment" (Perrin 1976, 12) fully, it is clear he was influenced by Bultmann's existentialism in the characterization of this final step.

Perrin intended to write a theology of the New Testament that would have pulled all these strands together. The strength of such a theology would have been his expertise in the Synoptics and his methodological flexibility; its weakness would have been his lack of depth in Pauline and Johannine studies.

Perrin's scholarly pilgrimage, in which he worked to construct a hermeneutic that does justice to various interpretative approaches, was paradigmatic of much twentieth-century biblical scholarship. It was also likely prophetic in foreshadowing a new era in which biblical interpretation moves beyond reductionism relying on unitary frames of reference and toward more integrated, eclectic approaches.

BIBLIOGRAPHY

Works. N. Perrin, *Jesus and the Language of the Kingdom: Symbol and Metaphor in New Testament Interpretation* (Philadelphia: Fortress, 1976); idem, *The Kingdom of God in the Teaching of Jesus* (NTL; London: SCM; Philadelphia: Westminster, 1963); idem, *A Modern Pilgrimage in New Testament Christology* (Philadelphia: Fortress, 1974); idem, *The New Testament: An Introduction—Proclamation and Parenesis, Myth and History* (New York: Harcourt Brace Jovanovich, 1974; rev. ed., N. Perrin and D. Duling, *The New Testament: An Introduction—Proclamation and Parenesis, Myth and History* [Fort Worth, TX: Harcourt Brace College Publishers, 1994]; idem, *The Promise of Bultmann: The Promise of Theology,* ed. M. E. Marty (Philadelphia: Fortress, 1979 [1968]); idem, *Rediscovering the Teaching of Jesus* (New Testament Library; London: SCM; New York: Harper & Row, 1967; paperback ed. with new preface, New York: Harper & Row, 1976); idem, *The Resurrection According to Matthew, Mark and Luke* (Philadelphia: Fortress, 1977; U.K. ed., *The Resurrection Narrative: A New Approach* [London: SCM, 1977]); idem, *What Is Redaction Criticism?* (Guides to Biblical Scholarship, ed. D. O. Via Jr.; Philadelphia: Fortress, 1969); idem, *Was lehrte Jesus wirklich? Rekonstruktion und Deutung* (Göttingen: Vandenhoeck & Ruprecht, 1972).

Studies. D. Duling, "Norman Perrin and the Kingdom of God: Review and Response," *JR* 64 (October 1984) 468-83; V. P. Furnish, "Notes on a Pilgrimage: Norman Perrin and New Testament Christology" in *Christology and a Modern Pilgrimage: A Discussion with Norman Perrin*, ed. H. D. Betz (Claremont, CA: Scholars Press, 1971) 92-112; E. Grässer, "Norman Perrin's Contribution to the Question of the Historical Jesus," *JR* 64 (October 1984) 484-500; W. H. Kelber, "The Work of Norman Perrin: An Intellectual Pilgrimage," *JR* 64 (October 1984) 452-67; H. Koester, "The Historical Jesus: Some Comments and Thoughts on Norman Perrin's *Rediscovering the Teaching of Jesus,*" in *Christology and a Modern Pilgrimage: A Discussion with Norman Perrin*, ed. H. D. Betz (Claremont, CA: Scholars Press, 1971) 123-36; "A Memorial Tribute to Norman Perrin: 1920-1976," *Criterion* 16 (winter 1977); C. R. Mercer, *Norman Perrin's Interpretation of the New Testament: From 'Exegetical Method' to 'Hermeneutical Process'* (Studies in American Biblical Hermeneutics 2; Macon, GA: Mercer University Press, 1986); idem, "Norman Perrin's Pilgrimage: Releasing the Bible to the Public," *CC* 103 (May 14, 1986) 483-86; W. O. Seal Jr., "Norman Perrin and His 'School,' Retracing a Pilgrimage," *JSOT* 20 (1984) 87-107; idem, "The Parousia in Mark: A Debate with Norman Perrin and His School" (unpublished Ph.D. dissertation, Union Theological Seminary, New York, 1982).

C. R. Mercer

Schüssler Fiorenza, Elisabeth
(b. 1938)

Elisabeth Schüssler Fiorenza is the primary theorist of a critical feminist biblical interpretation for liberation who is calling for a major paradigm shift in critical study of the Bible. The old paradigm directed scholars to be objective, value-neutral examiners of Scripture who sought the historical setting and meaning of the biblical texts. But such objectivity is unattainable and also, Schüssler Fiorenza claims, undesirable. She insists that scholars abandon their objectivist stance in favor of decrying the Bible's oppressiveness and discovering its logic of liberation so that it empowers women and other marginalized people ("nonpersons") in their struggles for freedom, justice and well-being.

Life. In the Roman Catholic part of Germany where she grew up, Schüssler

Fiorenza became involved in ministry at age thirteen as a leader of a parish girl scout group and has been involved in ministry to women ever since. From an early age she had trouble fitting herself into the traditional role for a Roman Catholic woman—married with many children. With encouragement from her pastor to find her own way, she discovered theology studies to be liberating in ways the catechism, which encouraged traditional roles, had never been. Consequently, though only 5 percent of Roman Catholic, rural or working-class people or women in Germany (she was all of these) went to university, she went and in 1961 became the first woman in Würzburg to enroll for the full course of theology prescribed for ordination into the priesthood.

But obstacles to her theological study materialized. Her decision to pursue a master of divinity was judged theologically illegitimate. As a woman in the Roman Catholic church, Schüssler Fiorenza was a layperson who had no business studying theology to work within the church. She had to clarify her call and justify her desire to become a professional theologian. Since no German university would hire her when she completed her doctorate, she came to the United States in 1970 to teach at Notre Dame. But in the early 1980s, following frequent furor over her feminist publications, she left Notre Dame for Episcopal Divinity School and, later, Harvard.

In the United States she began to participate in the Society of Biblical Literature just as the feminist and ecumenical ferment got underway in the early 1970s. Having had little contact with different church groups in Germany, she found the encounter with women from other faiths to be new, invigorating and challenging. But the experience also broadened her awareness of women's oppression as she heard the stories and challenges of Jewish and African-American women and women of the two-thirds world. Her own experience and hearing these women's stories confirmed the vastness of the problems women face worldwide and strengthened her commitment to her vision of Christian life, responsibility and genuine (just) community that she has pursued through her biblical scholarship.

"Kyriarchy" and the Bible. A key to Schüssler Fiorenza's biblical interpretation is her analysis of the suffering in the world as the result of kyriarchal oppression and her assessment of the role she believes the Bible has played in sustaining such oppression. Historically, as churches and governments in the Western world have abandoned elitist notions of leadership for democratic ideals, the elites (wealthy, educated, propertied males) have found the means to maintain power, so Schüssler Fiorenza explains, in the ideology of natural or God-given differences between "us" and "them." These elites were thus able to define white women along with subordinated classes, races and peoples as the "others" so as to colonize and exploit them. The result is the creation of multiplicative structures of oppression that form a complex social pyramid of graduated dominations and subordinations (sexism, racism, class exploitation, heterosexism and colonialism). Thus Schüssler Fiorenza replaces the word *patriarchy* as the usual descriptive term for this pyramid with her new word, "kyriarchy" (the rule of the master, lord, father or emperor), so that she communicates oppression's complexity: not all men dominate and exploit all women without difference; rather, elite Euro-American men have benefitted from exploiting women and other nonpersons.

Feminist scholars often note that while the Bible has been a source of liberation for women, it has also served to justify this kyriarchal oppression. Schüssler Fiorenza articulates three intertwining causes of the Bible's oppressiveness: the "kyriarchalness" of the biblical texts; a theological view of the Bible as the set-in-stone Word of God; and "malestream" interpretations of texts.

All biblical texts are written in the grammatically masculine language that was embedded in first-century kyriarchal culture, religion and society. This language functions as it has in our own time (i.e., in an inclusive, generic way). It is inclusive of women but does not mention them explicitly unless the women were exceptional or their actions problematic. Furthermore, some scholars consider the final versions of Acts and the Gospels to have been completed while the move to hierarchical leadership in the church and the corresponding exclusion of women and slaves from these positions was underway. Since New Testament writers were not interested in extolling womens' or slaves' contributions to the church, they doubtlessly record a fraction of the possibly rich traditions of women's participation in the early Christian movement. The results of the masculine language and the writers' circumstances are a diminishment of women's contributions, an intensifying of androcentrism in the New Testament and creation of a potential source for the justification of kyriarchy.

The potential source of kyriarchy becomes an actual source when the androcentrism of the biblical texts is given authoritative status among Christians. This happens when the Bible is viewed as tablets of stone on which the unchanging word of God is engraved for all time. To see the Bible as such, says Schüssler Fiorenza, is to see it as a "mythical archetype" that takes historically limited texts and posits them as universals that are authoritative and normative for all times. When it is treated as a mythical archetype, the Bible makes patriarchy and androcentrism universally valid since it is formulated in androcentric language and reflects patriarchal cultures. By maintaining such an approach to the Bible, the church allows proclamation of God as a God of oppression, since patriarchy and androcentrism are key tools in promoting women's unimportance and sustaining women's powerlessness.

Though scholarly interpretations of biblical texts have modified the mythical archetype view of the Bible over the twentieth century by uncovering the specificity of its historical and cultural contexts, this work has done little to counter the proclamation of a God who affirms kyriarchy. This failure is the result of scholars' having understood their work to be objective, value-neutral and disengaged from current circumstances in the world. "Truly scientific exegetes" step out of their own time and study a historical text on its own terms, unencumbered by contemporary concerns. Disinterested and dispassionate scholarship is thought to enable biblical scholars to enter the minds and worlds of historical people in order to understand objectively what happened and how the text addressed its particular historical situation. Any concern for what the text might mean today is left to theologians and preachers. Thus biblical scholars' concern to understand the Bible only in its historical context and their objective detachment from contemporary situations results in biblical scholarship having had almost nothing to say about the life of the contemporary church.

Scholars in many disciplines now admit, however, that objective, value-neutral scholarship is impossible. Biblical scholars bring the perspectives and biases of their historical-social locations as well as their hermeneutical, theoretical, political and theological presuppositions to their work. Thus the question scholars face is not, Are particular interests being served by my work? but, Whose interests are being served by my work? In Schüssler Fiorenza's estimation biblical scholars' work has served the kyriarchal status quo through their academic institutions and the academy of scholars in the interest of gaining promotion, tenure and power.

Thus the Bible has served as yet another source of oppression for women through its justification of kyriarchy. Schüssler Fiorenza, however, has theorized and articulated a different possibility for it.

A Feminist Critical Interpretation for Liberation. Schüssler Fiorenza argues for retrieving the Bible as an aid in women's struggles for a more just church and world. Though Scripture has been a source of oppression, it has also served to inspire women to struggle against the injustices of kyriarchy. Beyond this inspiration, however, is the impact of the Bible in Western society. Since the Bible is not going to be discarded or forgotten in the West any time soon, Schüssler Fiorenza contends that women must either transform its impact into a new source for liberation or continue to be subject to its kyriarchal tyranny.

An important step in this transformation, according to Schüssler Fiorenza, is to alter our metaphor of the Bible from unchanging tablets of stone to bread that nurtures, sustains and energizes people on their journeys toward God and wholeness. Rather than a mythical archetype, the Bible should be viewed as a "historical prototype" that informs the vision of Christian salvation and liberation. From this perspective, the biblical traditions lay the foundation for a living heritage that understands revelation as ongoing "for the sake of our salvation" in the present.

We interpret the Bible as bread that nourishes liberation by placing at the center of study Everywoman's struggles to transform kyriarchal structures into the discipleship of equals. This interpretive move begins with the basic insight of liberation theology that all theological interpretation and scholarship are engaged, knowingly or not, for or against oppressed people. Intellectual neutrality is not possible in a world of exploitation and oppression. Liberationists choose the side of the oppressed because of their experiences of God's presence with them in their suffering and also because of the Bible itself. They see liberation in Israel's exodus from slavery, the prophets' calls to "let justice roll down like the waters" and New Testament descriptions of God in ever-new images of love, compassion, mercy, peace and community. Among liberationists, feminists intentionally choose to identify with and interpret the Bible on behalf of women, who are always pushed to the bottom of the kyriarchal pyramid.

Some people might assume that interpretation from this new perspective cannot use the same critical tools that so-called objective scholars have used in the past. Schüssler Fiorenza insists, however, that women must not relinquish critical intellectual inquiry. Since knowledge is power, women cannot afford to be uninvolved in the production and distribution of knowledge. Furthermore, historical-critical methods of study have proven to be liberating for Schüssler Fiorenza personally and helpful in her feminist critical interpretation. The way the methods have been practiced needs to be transformed, which is the paradigm shift in biblical scholarship for which she calls.

The shift begins when the critical methods are practiced from an advocacy, or rhetorical, perspective rather than a disengaged one. By "rhetorical" Schüssler Fiorenza means communication practices that link knowledge with action and passion. All persons who read the Bible do so from a particular position within history. Therefore biblical students must become conscious of their presuppositions, prejudices and commitments and also the interests (e.g., political, institutional, clerical or academic) they serve. Furthermore, they must take responsibility for the interpretations of biblical texts that they promote: do their interpretations encourage liberation and salvation for all, or do they support the maintenance of the status quo? Feminists intentionally engage in biblical study as advocates of wholeness, well-being and genuine community for women.

Schüssler Fiorenza sees the need for a new hermeneutical strategy to guide the use of critical methods if biblical scholars are to practice their advocacy of justice for women. She has proposed a four-part critical-feminist rhetorical interpretation for liberation that allows for reading the Bible in emancipatory ways.

First is a hermeneutics of suspicion. "Suspicion" does not denote paranoia but is aroused by the insight that all biblical texts are articulated in grammatically masculine language. On the premise that this

language renders women invisible unless they create problems or are exceptional, and since the texts were written at a time when the male authors wished to hide rather than highlight the contributions of women and slaves to the church, feminists suspect that the New Testament does not tell the whole story of women in the early church.

Second is a hermeneutics of remembrance and reconstruction. Suspicion leads to efforts to recover more of the untold story of women through a hermeneutics of remembrance and reconstruction. Liberationists have signaled that the oppression of any group is total when it has no memory of its history. Therefore feminist biblical scholars seek to reconstruct their foresisters' contributions to the early Christian movement. Drawing on the remnants of the stories that have survived, feminists seek to create a memory and a heritage of what women have done and can do to bring about God's reign of justice. Such a reconstruction requires feminists to read against the grain of androcentric texts. Three examples of such reading would be focusing on forgotten stories of women; intentionally reading all grammatically masculine designations as inclusive of women unless the text requires gender specificity (the grammatically masculine "brothers" is read as inclusive of women; why not also such grammatically masculine words as disciples, apostles, prophets, or teachers?); and understanding injunctions against women's leadership in the early church as prescriptive rather than descriptive (insisting that women be silent and not teach in church suggests that women were not being silent). Schüssler Fiorenza argues that this reconstructing and remembering of women's history allows women today to claim early Christian theology and history as their own history and theology.

A third step is a hermeneutics of liberative vision and imagination. Since much of the history of women is irretrievably lost, Schüssler Fiorenza argues that feminist biblical scholars must also engage in a hermeneutics of liberative vision and imagination. In this process feminists use many forms of artistic media—storytelling, poetry, music, dance, liturgy—to retell biblical stories from a feminist perspective, to reformulate biblical visions and injunctions in the perspective of the discipleship of equals and to create narrative amplifications of the feminist remnants that have survived in patriarchal texts. Through their religious imaginations women enter the biblical texts, enable the silences surrounding women in the early church to speak and enhance their memory of women's contributions to the Christian movement.

The fourth step is a hermeneutics of proclamation that insists that biblical texts that validate kyriarchal relations of domination and exploitation must not be affirmed and appropriated. Instead those texts that transcend their kyriarchal contexts and articulate a liberating vision of human freedom and wholeness should be proclaimed as Word of God. Determining which texts serve as Word of God or bread of life in different circumstances requires discernment. The call to "deny self and take up the cross" issues a powerful invitation to middle- and upper-class persons in the United States to accept the risks of actively opposing injustice as Jesus did. But the same words used to encourage a battered woman to accept her suffering in order to save her marriage become for her a source of oppression. A hermeneutics of proclamation insists that biblical scholars be careful and responsible about what they announce as Word of God in a world of exploitation and suffering.

Thus Schüssler Fiorenza defines her approach to Scripture as a critical feminist-rhetorical interpretation for liberation that is indebted to historical-critical, critical-political and liberation-theological analyses and that is rooted in her own experience and engagement as a Roman Catholic Christian woman. She utilizes biblical criticism and theological hermeneutics as intellectual tools in emancipatory struggles against all forms of oppression. In solidarity

with "the least of these" who struggle for survival and justice, the majority of whom are women and their dependent children, she seeks to examine the ministry of Jesus and the earliest Jesus movements to show the gospel to be God's vision of an alternative community and world distinguished by wholeness and inclusiveness.

BIBLIOGRAPHY
Works. E. Schüssler Fiorenza, *Bread Not Stone: The Challenge of Biblical Interpretation* (Boston: Beacon, 1984); idem, *But She Said: Feminist Practices of Biblical Interpretation* (Boston: Beacon, 1992); idem, *Discipleship of Equals: A Critical Feminist Ekklesia-logy of Liberation* (New York: Crossroad, 1993); idem, "The Ethics of Biblical Interpretation: Decentering Biblical Scholarship," *JBL* 107 (1988) 3-17; idem, "Feminist Theology and New Testament Interpretation," *JSOT* 22 (1982) 32-46; idem, *In Memory of Her: A Feminist Theological Reconstruction of Christian Origins* (New York: Crossroad, 1983); idem, ed., *Searching the Scriptures: A Feminist Introduction,* vol. 1; *Searching the Scriptures: A Feminist Commentary,* vol. 2 (New York: Crossroad, 1993, 1994).

                                             M. L. Minor

Scofield, C(yrus) I. *(1845-1921)*

C. I. Scofield was born on August 19, 1845, and died on July 24, 1921. He was a dispensational Bible teacher, pastor, missions executive, educator, author and editor of the *Scofield Reference Bible*.

Context. Challenged by higher criticism, Darwinism and the prevailing cultural optimism of modernist and liberal theologies, dispensational premillennialists rallied believers to biblical fidelity and world evangelization, impelled by the shadow of prophetic signs.

Scofield was ordained Congregational (1883) and transferred his credentials (1910) to the Presbyterian Church in the U.S. (South), though he ministered primarily in nondenominational institutions. He was prominent in the influential Bible and prophecy conferences, in which Keswick spirituality and dispensational premillennialism predominated. Although he contributed to *The Fundamentals* (the article on "The Grace of God"), he was not a prominent controversialist.

Writings. Scofield's first publication was *Rightly Dividing the Word of Truth* (1888). The book originated as introductory studies for his church. Ten chapters "indicate the more important Divisions of the Word of Truth" (Scofield 1965, 9), though "this could not be fully done short of a complete analysis of the Bible" (Scofield 1965, 9–10). Study that ignores these "right Divisions" "must be in large measure profitless and confusing" (Scofield 1965, 9).

Scofield's characteristic division distinguishes "The Jew, the Gentile, and the Church of God" by their character, motivations, blessings and destinies. Chapter two defines "dispensation," distinguishing seven dispensations. Chapter three, "Two Advents," defends the visible, bodily return of Christ. The "two resurrections" (chap. 4) distinguishes the premillennial resurrection of the righteous from the postmillennial resurrection of the wicked.

The "five judgments" (cf. the traditional general judgment) include the judgment of believers' works at the "judgment seat of Christ," the living nations judged at the end of the seven-year tribulation, and the resurrected dead judged at the close of the millennium (cf. the reference Bible's seven, Rev 20:12, n. 1).

Scofield indicated that "the most obvious and striking division of the Word of Truth is that between Law and Grace" (Scofield 1965, 42). Chapter 7 distinguishes two "natures" in the believer: "one, received by natural birth . . . wholly and hopelessly bad, and a new nature, received through the new birth, which is the nature of God Himself, and therefore wholly good" (Scofiled 1965, 53). The "old, or Adam, nature" (Scofield 1965, 54), "unchanged and unchangeable" (Scofield 1965, 55), is overcome by the indwelling Spirit of God, not "by force of will, or by good resolutions" (Scofield 1965, 58).

Chapter 8, "The Believer's Standing and State," distinguishes the "position" (the legal standing of justification by Christ's imputed righteousness) from the "walk" (actual character and conduct; Scofield 1965, 59). Salvation is distinguished from rewards (chap. 9). The first is "a present possession," equal for all believers, the second "a future attainment" relative to life and service. Salvation is a "free gift" at conversion (Scofield 1965, 66), but "rewards are earned by works" (Scofield 1965, 67). Finally, Scofield distinguishes "true believers" from "mere professors" (Scofield 1965, 70), "the mass of formalists, hypocrites, and the deceived legalists . . . working *for* their own salvation" (Scofield 1965, 70–71).

The *Scofield Bible Correspondence Course* (begun in 1890; rev. 1907), originated in his church, developing the introductory *Rightly Dividing the Word of Truth* and anticipating his *Reference Bible*. Its seven sections, eventually forming three volumes (Old Testament, New Testament and Synthesis of Bible Truth) are "The Scriptures," "The Study of the Scriptures," "The Great Words of Scripture," "God—Father, Son, and Holy Spirit," "The Saints," "The Service of Saints" and "The Future."

Scofield's enormous influence comes primarily from the *Scofield Reference Bible* (1909; 2d ed., 1917). The Bible's clarity and accessibility attracted many readers to its system of dispensationalism.

The "connected topical lines of reference end in analytic summaries of the whole teaching of Scripture on that subject" (Scofield 1909, iii). The "great words of Scripture" are defined in "simple, nontechnical terms." Each book is introduced and outlined; the entire Bible is paragraphed with headings (Scofield 1909, iii) and indexed. In 1917 chronological references were supplied, following Bishop James Ussher's chronology, which placed the creation of Adam 4,004 years prior to the birth of Jesus Christ (Scofield 1909, iv).

More distinctively dispensational features incorporate "the remarkable results of the modern study of the Prophets" (probably premillennialism and the prophecy conferences), previously "closed to the average reader by fanciful and allegorical schemes of interpretation" (Scofield 1909, iii).

Scofield added "A Panoramic View of the Bible" (1917):

The Bible . . . at once provokes and baffles study. . . . No particular portion of Scripture is to be intelligently comprehended apart from some conception of its place in the whole. . . . It is, therefore, indispensable to any interesting and fruitful study of the Bible that a general knowledge of it be gained. (Scofield 1909, v)

Christ is "the central theme" of the Bible's "one continuous story" of "one redemption."

The reference Bible advocates the "gap theory," the earth's catastrophic judgment in the angelic fall, with an unspecified time gap between Genesis 1:1 and Genesis 1:2. This "gives scope for all the geologic ages" (Gen 1:1, n. 2).

Scofield published more than a dozen additional works on Scripture, Christian living and prophecy, mostly from sermons and addresses.

Biblical Interpretation. Concise statements of Scofield's approach are found in *Rightly Dividing the Word of Truth,* the *Scofield Bible Corresponndence Course* and the *Reference Bible.*

The reference Bible's "new system of connected topical references" traces "all the greater truths of the divine revelation" from first mention to last so that "the reader may for himself follow the gradual unfolding of these . . . to their culmination in Jesus Christ and the New Testament Scriptures" (Scofield 1909, iii). This is the Bible reading method, "a string of related texts or passages briefly commented upon" (Sandeen, 137). As E. Sandeen notes, "the Scriptures were God's word . . . and were their own best interpreter. The real need of every man was to listen to God's word, and

the first requirement for every preacher was that he not substitute his own thoughts for God's word. The method of exegesis which resulted from this line of reasoning was the Bible reading" (Sandeen, 137).

Popularized by Plymouth Brethrenism and characteristic of the Bible and prophecy conferences, including Scofield's writings (each chapter of *Rightly Dividing the Word of Truth* is "a brief Bible-reading" [Scofield 1965, 70]), this method is christological and typological.

Literal interpretation of prophecy is Scofield's most well-known hermeneutical contribution. Like other early dispensationalists, however, he required strictly literal interpretation only for prophetic literature. Types "must never be used to teach a doctrine, but only to illustrate a doctrine elsewhere explicitly taught" (Scofield 1943, 1:45). To this traditional restriction on typology and allegory Scofield adds, "It cannot be positively affirmed that anything is a type which is not somewhere in Scripture treated as such."

The historical Scriptures are "(1) literally true. The events recorded occurred. And yet (2) they have [perhaps more often than we suspect] an *allegorical* or *spiritual* significance. . . . It is permitted—while holding firmly the historical verity—reverently to *spiritualize* the historical Scriptures" (Scofield 1934, 1:45; punctuation original). Of prophecy Scofield states, "Here we reach the ground of absolute literalness. Figures are often found in the prophecies, but the figure invariably has a literal fulfillment. Not one instance exists of a 'spiritual' or figurative fulfillment of prophecy. . . . *Histories* may be reverently spiritualized. *Prophecies* may never be spiritualized, but are always literal" (Scofield 1934, 1:46; emphasis original), though "prophetic utterances often have a latent and deeper meaning than at first appears" (Scofield 1909, Mt 2:15, n. 3).

Major Themes. Scofield developed several major themes.

The first theme was the two peoples of God. The anthropological distinction of

Jew, Gentile and the church of God, involving a heavenly (church) and earthly (Jew) dichotomy of their character and destiny, characterizes Scofield's thought, echoing J. N. Darby. Israel is God's national people, but in the church the distinction between Jew and Gentile is "lost" (Scofield 1965, 12) or "disappears" (Scofield 1965, 14). For Scofield "Israel stands connected with earthly and temporal things" but the church "with spiritual and heavenly things" (Scofield 1965, 12). He wrote that "it may safely be said that the Judaizing of the Church has done more to hinder her progress, pervert her mission, and destroy her spirituality, than all other causes combined" (Scofield 1965, 18).

Though Scripture is the word of one God who redeems the world through one Savior only through faith, there is more than one aspect of God's plan. Distinct aspects pertain to distinct peoples of God. The diversity of God's plans for these peoples "divides" Scripture. This distinction is more basic and significant than the better-known dispensational distinctions, which derive from it.

A second theme is law and grace. For Scofield "the most obvious and striking division of the Word of Truth is that between Law and Grace" (Scofield 1965, 42). Though there is grace before the law and during the law, and law before the fall, "it is of the most vital moment to observe that Scripture never, in *any* dispensation, mingles these two principles" (Scofield 1965, 42-43). Law and grace are "contrasting principles": "everywhere the Scriptures present law and grace in sharply contrasted spheres" (Scofield 1965, 43). For

> law always has a place and work distinct and wholly diverse from that of grace. Law is God prohibiting and requiring; grace is God beseeching and bestowing. Law is a ministry of condemnation; grace, of forgiveness. Law curses; grace redeems from the curse. Law kills; grace makes alive. . . . Law says, Do and live; grace, Believe and live. . . . Law is a system of probation; grace, of favor.

(Scofield 1965, 43; see Scofield 1909, Jn 1:17, n. 1)

Every occurrence of "law" in the New Testament (except Rom 7:23) refers to the law of Moses (Scofield 1965, 43). Conversely, the positive references to the law in the psalms, "inexplicable if understood only of the 'ministration of death written and engraven in stones,'" are clarified "when seen to refer also to the types—those lovely pictures of grace" (Scofield 1965, 44). Apparent praise of law must be typological of grace.

Scofield rejects three errors: "Antinomianism" (Scofield 1965, 44); ceremonialism, requiring levitical observation or making Christian ordinances "essential to salvation" (Scofield 1965, 44); and Galatianism, mingling law and grace, "the teaching that justification is partly by grace, partly by law, or, that grace is given to enable an otherwise helpless sinner to keep the law" (Scofield 1965, 45).

The believer's rule of life is found in Jesus' teachings (or commandments) and the work of the Spirit in the heart of the believer (Scofield 1965, 48-49). Antithetical to Mosaic law, these are not "the ministration of death." Scofield condemns "modern nomolators" advocating the Mosaic law as the rule of Christian life (Scofield 1965, 50).

The third theme is dispensations. The dispensations are Innocency, Conscience, Human Government, Promise, Law, Grace and Kingdom (Scofield 1909, Gen 1:28, n. 5). For Scofield "these periods are marked off in Scripture by some change in God's method of dealing with mankind, or a portion of mankind, in respect of the two questions of sin and man's responsibility. Each of the Dispensations may be regarded as a new test of the natural man, and each ends in judgment—marking his utter failure" (Scofield 1965, 19). More concisely, dispensations are "a period of time during which man is tested in respect of obedience to some *specific* revelation of the will of God" (Scofield 1909, Gen 1:28, n. 4).

In the first dispensation "man was created in innocency, placed in a perfect environment, subjected to an absolutely simple test, and warned of the consequence of disobedience" (Scofield 1909, Gen 1:28, n. 5). After the fall "man was responsible to do all known good, to abstain from all known evil, and to approach God through sacrifice" (Scofield 1909, Gen 3:23, n. 2). Then "man is responsible to govern the world for God" (Scofield 1909, Gen 8:21, n. 1) in the third dispensation. "The Dispensation of Promise extends from Gen. 12:1 to Ex. 19:8, and was exclusively Israelitish" (Scofield 1909, Gen 12:1, n. 1).

At Mt. Sinai God "proposed to [Israel] the Covenant of Law. Instead of humbly pleading for a continued relation of grace, they presumptuously answered: 'All that the Lord hath spoken we will do'" (Scofield 1965, 21). Israel "rashly accepted the Law" and "exchanged grace for law" (Scofield 1909, 20 n. 1).

Christ's death and resurrection introduced the "dispensation of pure grace" ("undeserved favor, or God *giving* righteousness, instead of God *requiring* righteousness"); "salvation, perfect and eternal, is now freely offered . . . upon the one condition of faith" (Scofield 1965, 21). Scofield wrote that "the point of testing is no longer legal obedience as the condition of salvation, but acceptance or rejection of Christ, with good works as a fruit of salvation" (Scofield 1909, Jn 1:17, n. 1).

Such statements, implying law keeping as another condition, occasion charges of multiple ways of salvation. This overlooks parallels with federal theology's covenant of works, conditioning eternal life on perfect obedience but insisting that only Jesus, representing sinful humanity, has met those conditions. Finally the millennial reign of Christ is "identical with the kingdom covenanted to David" (Scofield 1909, Eph 1:18, n. 3).

Additional themes are prophecy, the Holy Spirit and Christian living. Scofield consistently highlights prophecy. The eschatological significance of the divisions between Jew, Gentile and the church is manifest in the two advents of Christ, once coming for his saints (the rapture) before the seven-year tribulation and later coming with his saints at its end, inaugurating his thousand-year reign, culminating in the new heaven and earth. The significance is also evident in their distinct heavenly and earthly destinies and distinct future judgments.

Scofield also emphasized the Holy Spirit's distinctive post-Pentecost ministries in believers, especially "filling" (Scofield 1899).

Significance. Scofield so effectively distilled American dispensationalism that it was often called Scofieldism. His reference Bible is "perhaps the most influential single publication in millenarian and Fundamentalist historiography" (Sandeen, 222). Because of the incongruity of championing the "individual interpreter" with a self-interpreting Bible who "then pores over Scofield's notes in order to discover what the text really means" (Weber, 114), Scofield's influence should nuance claims of Scripture's self-interpretation, illustrating tradition's contribution. Scofield's greatest legacy is a host of Bible students, whether Scofieldians or not.

BIBLIOGRAPHY

Works. C. I. Scofield, *Plain Papers on the Doctrine of the Holy Spirit* (New York: Revell, 1899); idem, *Rightly Dividing the Word of Truth: Ten Outline Studies of the More Important Divisions of Scripture* (Grand Rapids: Zondervan, 1965 [1888; at least two textual traditions and numerous reprints]); idem, *Scofield Bible Correspondence Course* (3 vols.; rev. ed.; Chicago: Moody Bible Institute, 1934 [1907]); idem, *Scofield Reference Bible* (rev. ed.; New York: Oxford University Press, 1967 [1909; 2d ed. 1917]).

Studies. W. A. Be Vier, "A Biographical Sketch of C. I. Scofield" (M.A. thesis, Southern Methodist University, 1960); L. V. Crutchfield, "C. I. Scofield" in *Twentieth-Century Shapers of American Popular Religion,* ed. C. H. Lippy (New York: Greenwood, 1989), includes bibliography; A. C. Gaebelein, *The History of the Scofield Bible* (New York: Our Hope Publications/Loizeaux Brothers, 1943); J. D. Hannah, "C. I. Scofield" in *Premillennial Dictionary of*

Theology, ed. M. Couch (Grand Rapids: Kregel, 1997); C. N. Kraus, *Dispensationalism in America* (Richmond, VA: John Knox, 1958); E. Sandeen, *The Roots of Fundamentalism: British and American Millenarianism, 1800–1930* (Chicago: University of Chicago Press, 1970; repr. Grand Rapids: Baker, 1978); C. G. Trumbull, *The Life Story of C. I. Scofield* (New York: Oxford University Press, 1920); T. P. Weber, "The Two-Edged Sword: The Fundamentalist Use of the Bible" in *The Bible in America: Essays in Cultural History,* ed. N. O. Hatch and M. A. Noll (New York: Oxford University Press, 1982).

S. R. Spencer

Trible, Phyllis *(b. 1932)*

Phyllis Trible is one of the leading practitioners of rhetorical criticism of the Hebrew Scriptures. Baldwin Professor of Sacred Literature at Union Theological Seminary in New York since 1981, she was elected president of the Society for Biblical Literature in 1994. Earlier she taught at Wake Forest University and Andover Newton Theological School. Among scholars of the Hebrew Bible/Old Testament, Trible is known for her detailed literary analysis of biblical stories, forays into biblical theology, feminist critique of biblical interpretation and virtuosity as lecturer, teacher and writer.

Work. Trible received her B.A. from Meredith College and her Ph.D. from Columbia University and Union Theological Seminary, where she studied with James *Muilenburg. As a form critic Muilenburg paved the way for literary methods of biblical study by observing the artistry and particularity of scriptural texts, studying their compositional structures and describing their fusions of traditional form and unique formulation. He later named this methodology "rhetorical criticism" (Muilenburg). Its guiding rubric holds that "proper articulation of form-content yields proper articulation of meaning." Trible has appropriated this definition in a variety of ways.

While Trible's work has developed rhetorical criticism, it has also pioneered in feminist biblical interpretation. Early influences on her articulation of feminism included Mary Daly, an outspoken critic of patriarchalism and of traditional religion. While Daly found it imperative that women reject the Bible as irretrievably patriarchal, Trible disagreed with that assessment. For Trible two things were certain: respect for the Bible as the central text of Christian faith and commitment to the equality of women in society. Beginning in her earliest work, Trible sought a means to reinterpret biblical texts pertaining to gender that had previously been used to support male dominance.

In her early programmatic article, "Depatriarchalizing in Biblical Interpretation," Trible argues that some biblical texts are much less patriarchal than either traditional or feminist readers have recognized. Often it is the interpreter who has mistakenly introduced cultural biases. Admitting the patriarchy of the majority tradition of the Bible, she nevertheless maintains that "the intentionality of biblical faith . . . is neither to create nor to perpetuate patriarchy but rather to function as salvation for both women and men" (Trible 1973, 31). She highlights biblical themes that implicitly disavowed sexism and displayed "a depatriarchalizing principle" at work in the Hebrew Bible itself. They include the understanding of YHWH as beyond sexuality, though the deity is described with both feminine and masculine metaphors, and the presentation of women's defiance against oppression, as in Exodus 1.

To demonstrate the recovery of gender-inclusive interpretation, Trible offers readings of two texts that exhibit this depatriarchalizing principle: Genesis 2—3 and the Song of Songs. In them she discovers neglected themes reinforcing the mutuality of men and women. Distorted by disobedience in Genesis 3, this mutuality is retrieved and redeemed in the poetry of the Song.

In her first book, *God and the Rhetoric of Sexuality,* Trible expands upon these insights, using rhetorical methods to uncover language about gender. She notes the various reworkings within the Scripture of the divine attributes in Exodus 34:6-7 as evidence of recontextualization and reinterpretation among biblical authors themselves and draws parallels between that practice of ancient innovation and the interpretations that result when the Bible meets contemporary concerns. She outlines rhetorical criticism as her methodology of choice, one enabling her to explore Scripture's vitality through intrinsic reading of particular texts with attention to the organic unity of form and content, and to the character of texts as both typical and unique, both traditional and transformative.

Trible's starting point is the Bible's first discussion of sexuality (Gen 1:27), which describes humankind's creation in God's image. Drawing attention to the chiastic structure of the verse's first two lines and its showcasing of "in his image," Trible notes that this phrase is placed in synonymous parallel with "male and female." Structurally the short poem attests that "to describe male and female is to perceive the image of God" (Trible 1978, 21).

To elucidate the biblical witness Trible traces the use of the Hebrew root *rahamim,* which means both "compassion" and "wombs." Not only does God control the childbearing of biblical women and mold human life from the mother's womb, but also God's own character is described as *rahum* ("compassionate") and God is compared, as in Isaiah 49:15, to a mother most compassionate toward the child of her womb. Other female imagery for God includes the trembling of God's womb for Ephraim (Jer 31:20), the correlation in Genesis 49:25 of the divine name El Shaddai with the blessings of the breasts *(shadayim),* the description in Deuteronomy 32:18 (cf. Is 42:14) of God's having "writhed in labor pains" with Israel, and the description in Job 38:28-29 of God begetting the dew and giving birth to the hoarfrost.

Trible's most celebrated chapters are the final three, in which she offers fuller discussions of Genesis 2—3 (a "love story gone

awry") and Song of Songs ("love's lyrics redeemed"), as well as a reading of the book of Ruth (a "human comedy" in the Shakespearean sense).

Trible describes the dominant Christian interpretation of the Eden story as one that "proclaims male superiority and female inferiority as the will of God" (Trible 1978, 73). She lists eleven specific interpretations that have reinforced this view, demonstrating that such interpretations are unsupported by the story itself. For instance, Trible shows that the word used to describe the woman, *ezer,* traditionally translated "helpmate" or "helper," connotes no sense of subordination. In fact, the same word is used to describe God's help of humans. Throughout the story the emphasis is not on woman's inferiority but on the mutuality of the first couple—the woman is created as a companion corresponding to the man, a companion whom he calls "bone of my bones and flesh of my flesh." The man's later domination of the woman, far from constituting a divine right, reflects the breakdown of God's purpose, a breakdown resulting from the couple's shared disobedience.

Song of Songs, however, celebrates sexual love and mutuality, redeeming all that was lost in Eden. The woman's voice predominates. Motifs and images from the Genesis story reappear (garden, animals, eating, water, work, childbearing and death). This poetry proclaims not the woman's unrequited desire for her mate but his delightful desire for her (Song 7:10).

Ruth's story describes the struggles of daily life between the tragedy of Eden and the ecstasy of the Song's gardens. In this story "the brave and bold decisions of women embody and bring to pass the blessings of God" (Trible 1978, 195), bringing into harmony the interests of male and female, the survival of a dead man's heritage and a living woman's well-being through the birth of a male child to a daughter-in-law who is worth more than seven sons.

Throughout this book, with careful elucidation of words, motifs and repetitions, Trible highlights subtle textual clues that reveal a depatriarchalizing principle in certain descriptions of human relationships. Though some scholars have differed with points in Trible's readings, her discussion of Genesis 2—3 especially stands as one regularly referenced by subsequent scholars, and her retrieval of liberating texts has inspired a generation of feminist biblical interpreters.

As Trible herself points out, the depatriarchalizing principle represents a minor theme in biblical literature, where male-centered visions more often prevail. In her second book, *Texts of Terror: Literary-Feminist Readings of Biblical Narratives,* Trible examines stories of a very different kind. Like her first book, the second employs feminist perspectives and literary methods to explore gender relationships in Scripture. But the passages chosen for this study are not celebrative. Rather, Trible explores four stories of "terror" against women, stories of women who suffer from human sin and violence: Hagar, the slave of Sarai who is banished into the wilderness with her child; David's daughter Tamar, who is raped by her brother; Jephthah's daughter, who is sacrificed because of her father's foolish vow; and the unnamed concubine who is gang raped, murdered and dismembered. Trible retells their stories in memoriam, to offer sympathetic readings of abused women, in the hope that such terrors will cease.

Trible points out four pitfalls of interpretation: dismissing the stories as reflecting a more primitive, violent time than our own; dismissing the God of the Old Testament as a God of wrath who is not also the God of the New Testament; diminishing the suffering of these women by comparing them to that of Jesus; and seeking a happy ending to these stories in the resurrection. Trible suggests instead viewing the Bible as a mirror aiding insight into human nature and inspiring repentance. As a clue to the experience of reading these difficult stories Trible offers the image of Jacob wrestling the mysterious man at the Jabbok river, refusing to let him go until he had blessed him, and receiving the blessing but not on his own terms (Gen 32:24-32).

In her interpretation of these stories Trible once again traces the details of their language, translating the Hebrew as literally as possible. She points out the ironies surrounding the women, the courage and cowardice, eloquence and muteness, activity and passivity of the various characters. Her careful attention to detail vivifies the women and their surroundings, encouraging readers to reflect on the magnitude of the women's crises.

Whereas her first two books focussed on gender, Trible's third book, *Rhetorical Criticism: Context, Method and the Book of Jonah,* explores the methodology of rhetorical criticism itself. Published in the series Guides to Biblical Scholarship (ed. G. M. Tucker), this new volume offers information and perspectives useful for both students and scholars.

The first half of the book provides a succinct history of literary study of the Bible. Trible's account of the classical roots of rhetoric traces their history from the Sophists (fifth century B.C.) to Cicero and Quintilian (first century A.D.). Her discussion of contemporary literary critical theory distinguishes the various focal points of literary analysis from the time of Aristotle to the present: audience, speaker, text and world. Her description of literary study of the Bible itself similarly begins with Philo and Josephus and proceeds through the Middle Ages to this generation. After describing in depth Muilenburg's work in rhetorical criticism, Trible describes the work of scholars influenced by him. Her survey of other recent studies in secular and biblical literary criticism includes poetics, structuralism, reader-response criticism and deconstruction and explains the effects of these innovations on traditional interpretation. Trible's synopses of the fields of rhetoric, literary study and literary biblical interpretation, while necessarily brief, provide a useful structure and bibliography for further exploration.

The second half of the book teaches rhetorical methodology, using the book of Jonah as an illustration. Trible explains what she means by the maxim "proper articulation of form-content yields proper articulation of meaning," not only spelling out her readings of Jonah's parts but also describing the interpretive and decision-making process by which she arrives at those readings. The payoff is twofold: not only a commentary on the biblical text but also a commentary on the commentary for readers wishing to employ similar methods with other texts.

Trible begins this section by surveying textual, historical, canonical and form-critical findings on Jonah. Then she describes the book's overall structure: the symmetry of the two halves, which is signaled by YHWH's two calls to Jonah to go to Nineveh, and the points where symmetry between these two halves breaks down. In her detailed discussion of the smaller units, Trible walks through both the story and the interpretive process, describing at one point, for instance, four alternative interpretations of the structure of Jonah 1 and explaining why she chose the one she did. Finally Trible includes brief discussions of three anticipated philosophical questions concerning authorial intent, subjectivity and biblical artistry.

Although Trible's preferred methodology is close rhetorical reading within the final form of biblical texts, some of her work employs other methods such as intertextual reading or deconstruction. For instance, her study of Miriam (Trible 1989a) pieces together from fragments in Exodus, Numbers, Micah and other books a tradition of Moses' sister, Miriam, in which she once played a far more significant role than the canonical story acknowledges. Similarly, in a reading of the story of Elijah and Jezebel (Trible 1995), Trible points out the many structural parallels between the two leaders, the one a Sidonian supporter of Baal who killed Israelite prophets and the other an Israelite supporter of YHWH who killed Baal's prophets.

Much sought as a lecturer on college and seminary campuses and in ecclesiastical circles, Trible is widely recognized not only for her intellectual rigor but also for her wit as a wordsmith. Though technological advances have proliferated the written and spoken word, Trible refuses haste and devotes as much attention to the careful composition of her own works as to the careful interpretation of the Bible. It is a sign of unusual durability that, twenty years after publication of her first monograph, all of her books are still in print.

BIBLIOGRAPHY

Works. P. Trible, "Bringing Miriam Out of the Shadows," *BRev* (February 1989a) 14-25, 34; idem, "Depatriarchalizing in Biblical Interpretation," *JAAR* 41 (1973) 30-48; idem, "Exegesis for Storytellers and other Strangers," *JBL* 114, 1 (1995) 3-19; idem, "Five Loaves and Two Fishes: Feminist Hermeneutics and Biblical Theology" *TS* 50 (1989b) 279-95; idem, *God and the Rhetoric of Sexuality* (Philadelphia: Fortress, 1978); idem, *Rhetorical Criticism: Context, Method and the Book of Jonah* (Minneapolis: Fortress, 1994); idem, *Texts of Terror: Literary-Feminist Readings of Biblical Narratives* (Philadelphia: Fortress, 1984).   P. T. Willey

Wright, George Ernest (1909-1974)

George Ernest Wright was born in Zanesville, Ohio, on September 5, 1909. He married Emily DeNyse in 1937, and they had four children. He died of a heart attack at Jaffrey, New Hampshire, on August 29, 1974.

Wright received his B.A. degree from Wooster College (1931), where he was elected to Phi Beta Kappa, and his B.D. degree from McCormick Theological Seminary (1934), where he was granted a graduate fellowship for the years 1934 to 1936. Entering the Oriental Seminary program at Johns Hopkins, Wright received his M.A. (1936) and his Ph.D. (1937). He joined the faculty of the McCormick Theological Seminary, where he taught Old Testament from 1938 to 1958. In 1958 he accepted appointment to Harvard. As Parkman Professor, Wright taught Old Testament at the Harvard Divinity School until his death.

Context. Wright first came into national prominence during the period spanning World War II, roughly 1939 to 1946. For biblical scholarship in the United States, this era was a watershed. During the 1920s and 1930s American biblical studies had been dominated by a liberal theology most clearly illustrated by Harry Emerson Fosdick's popular *Guide to Understanding the Bible* (1938). The biblical liberalism of that period assumed a minimalistic view of Scripture: Jesus was a prophetic teacher, later seen as God's adopted Son; Paul and the early Hellenists were responsible for the christological emphases in the New Testament; and the Old Testament showed how the ancient Hebrews gradually moved from polytheism to monotheism, from the concept of a God of wrath to a God of love. William Oscar Emil Oesterley and Theodore Henry Robinson's *Hebrew Religion* (1930), widely used in Britain and the United States, illustrates this view of progressive revelation. During this period little serious concern was given to the parity of the Testaments or the unity of Scripture. In practice the Old Testament was too often used as a negative contrast to the New.

Also during this period other American scholars, reflecting Continental studies, had been insisting that since Israel had adapted some cultural aspects from other established Near Eastern civilizations, Israel had also depended upon them for its religious ideas. Logically the later must have borrowed from the earlier.

Wright was the most influential of the new generation of scholars who produced a momentous change in the course of American biblical interpretation immediately after World War II. Similar changes were already evident on the Continent, especially in the writings of Walther

*Eichrodt, Rudolf *Bultmann, Karl *Barth and Emil Brunner. But due to wartime conditions these seminal works had been difficult to obtain in the United States.

Wright's studies at McCormick and Johns Hopkins had prepared him well for this position of leadership in the biblical theology movement. At McCormick he was influenced in Old Testament studies by George L. Robinson, who had studied at Berlin and Leipzig and been director of the American Schools of Oriental Research in Jerusalem, and by Ovid Sellers, who had received his Ph.D. at Hopkins and excavated with William Foxwell *Albright in Palestine. In New Testament, Wright studied under Floyd V. Filson, who had done graduate work in Basel.

At Johns Hopkins, Albright's graduate students received thorough grounding in ancient Near Eastern languages, literature and culture and in modern scientific archeological methods. With these came a deep respect for the historical basis of the Old Testament. In a tribute to Sellers, Wright identified the primary importance of the Hopkins training as its insistence upon mastery of Near Eastern literature and languages in order to place the Bible in its proper cultural setting and conceptual world.

Writings. In biblical interpretation, Wright's most influential publications appeared within a span of eight years: *The Challenge of Israel's Faith* (1944), *The Old Testament Against Its Environment* (1950), *God Who Acts* (1952) and "The Faith of Israel" in *The Interpreter's Bible*. Taken together this group had an enormous impact on biblical studies in the United States.

The Challenge of Israel's Faith was a primer of the new biblical theology, setting forth half a dozen themes that long remained major components in Wright's works: his emphasis on revelation through history, on the unity of the Testaments, on the importance of the Old Testament per se for Christians, and on the sovereignty of God.

The principal purpose of *The Old Testa-*

ment Against Its Environment was to challenge the view that Israel's faith was primarily a product of sociological and environmental conditioning—that it developed gradually from primitive to sophisticated ideas. Even in its earliest forms the basic tenets of Israel's religion differ so radically from contemporary pagan culture that they cannot be explained by appeal to evolutionary or environmental categories. The book's major topics—Israel's radical break with its contemporary Near Eastern religions, the unique nature of Yahwistic monotheism, the importance of covenant, the theology of kingship and the meaning of history—show the influence of Albright and Eichrodt. But from the first they were also Wright's own concerns, and he elaborated them in his later writings.

God Who Acts: Biblical Theology As Recital is the most original and influential of Wright's books and formed a foundational block in the biblical theology movement. After defining biblical theology as "the confessional recital of the redemptive acts of God in a particular history, because history is the chief medium of revelation" (Wright 1952, 13), Wright stressed the distinctiveness of the Old Testament, the persistence of promise and fulfillment as major biblical themes, both within the Old Testament and linking the Old with the New, and the importance of confessing God as King and Judge and Christ as Lord. In Christ God has completed the history of Israel; Christ is the climactic event of the God who has acted throughout history in a unique series of saving events (Wright 1952, 57).

Wright's article "The Faith of Israel," if printed separately, would make a book of about 125 pages. Instead of adopting traditional categories from systematic theology, he delineated Israel's faith in its own terms: creation, sin, election, covenant, monotheism, holiness, hope, Messiah, worship and service. He ended with a constructive statement of the indispensable place of Israelite faith in the faith of the Christian church, asserting that it is a fun-

damental affirmation of the church that, as Christ is the key to the central meaning of the Old Testament, the Old Testament is the clue to Christ (*IB* 1:389).

Though Wright's last book in this field, *The Old Testament and Theology* (1969), was the most substantial statement of his mature thinking, it was intentionally practical. Frequently autobiographical, it chronicles his growth as a theologian and explicates his basic beliefs in the light of such issues as existentialism, pacifism, linguistic analysis and God-talk. Wright confesses that his main purpose is to articulate the consequences that follow for theology when a Christian views the Old Testament as vital for his or her own faith. Accordingly it starts by defining the place of Christ in a theology that takes the Old Testament seriously.

In offering his full-grown construction of the interaction among revelation, faith and history, Wright redefines some earlier positions, particularly by a new emphasis on the revelatory character of narrative. There is a notable insistence that narrative also constitutes a proper medium for reporting historical revelation: Wright came to identify an "event-narrative form" along with the "event-confessional" form and even speaks of "the confessional epic."

Wright identifies chapters 3-5 as the center of the book. These expound the themes of God as Creator, Lord and Warrior. The dominant motif is God as "the Cosmic Suzerein." Under this overarching concept Wright deals with such problems as the God of wrath, the patriarchal God and the appropriateness of identifying God as Father. Other chapters discuss the tension between biblical language about God and modern faith and include linguistics, symbolism, hermeneutics, and social and political theory.

The final chapter, on canon, is more practical than theoretical. Partly as a result of this utilitarian approach, Wright posits "a canon within a canon." While acknowledging the authority of Scripture as a whole, he seems reconciled to a selective approach.

Although it is rich and varied, this volume probably should not be read as Wright's magnum opus. When he wrote it, the influence of the biblical theology movement had been waning for years and Wright's own interests were shifting. But the book stands as a testimony to his life-long concern to bring difficult issues in biblical theology into the arena of church debate.

Presuppositions, Methods and Major Themes. Perhaps the most clear and concise presentation of Wright's presuppositions and methods of biblical interpretation is found in an official statement published by the World Council of Churches (WCC) in 1951 for use in addressing social and political questions. Wright attended the first WCC meeting in Amsterdam in 1948 and quickly became a formative member of its working commission on biblical studies. He helped draft this manifesto and followed its principles and techniques in most of his biblical work.

A. Necessary theological presuppositions of biblical interpretation:

1. The Bible is our common starting point;

2. The primary message of the Bible concerns God's gracious and redemptive activity that he might create in Jesus Christ a people for himself;

3. The starting point of the Christian interpreter lies with his community of faith;

4. The center and goal of the whole Bible is Jesus Christ, the fulfillment and the end of the law;

5. The Old Testament must be interpreted in the light of the total revelation in the person of Jesus Christ.

B. Recommended procedures for interpretation:

1. In the interpretation of a specific text one must start with an historical and critical examination of the passage;

2. With an Old Testament text one must examine it in its own period, then turn to the New Testament for possible limitation,

correction, or expansion of its meaning;

3. With a New Testament passage one must examine it in its own setting; turn to the Old Testament to discern its background in God's former revelation; then return to the New Testament and expound the passage in the context of the whole scope of *Heilsgeschichte;*

4. Finally, one must discover the degree to which our own situation is similar to that which the Bible presents and realize that the Bible speaks to the whole world through the Church (Wright 1951, 219-44)

Biblical Interpretation. Wright's *The Biblical Doctrine of Man in Society* (1954) was commissioned by the World Council of Churches and discussed by a committee convened by Wright, but it was written by Wright himself. His emphases on God as active in human history, Jesus Christ as the Messiah and goal of God's creative activity, and the relevance of biblical perspectives for contemporary culture are hallmarks of his theology.

In his later programmatic essay "The Theological Study of the Bible" in *The Interpreter's One-Volume Commentary* (1971), Wright affirmed that event as revelation in human history and the recital of it by the faithful community—that is, history and faith, act and word, revelation and response—these in their interaction are central to "the theological study of the Bible" and thus to our appropriation of Scripture.

Also, Wright's emphasis on the sovereignty of God as ruler, redeemer and judge is not restricted to this theological reading of the Old Testament; it validates its continuity with the New Testament in Jesus' teaching about the kingdom of God. The Christian message opens with the proclamation that the time of preparation and promise has now been fulfilled and the kingdom of God is at hand (Wright 1971, 987).

As examples of Wright's exegetical method with specific books, two may be mentioned. "Deuteronomy: Introduction and Exegesis" (1953) represents his most extensive use of literary critical methods, which were generally conservative, as well as attesting to his concern for the relation between faith and history. Wright of course discusses the book and its composition .in their literary and historical Old Testament contexts. But he also follows the WCC exegetical guidelines, though to a limited extent. At the end he states that the essentials of the Deuteronomic theology "became part of the prophetic eschatology which the writers of the New Testament saw fulfilled in Christ" and that "the inner intention of Deuteronomy reveals to us the will of God even as it did to Israel" (Wright 1953, 329).

In his commentary on Isaiah (1964), Wright delineates its various sections and treats each in reference to its Near Eastern social and historical milieu. For instance, both Isaiah 7:14 and Isaiah 9:2-9 are read in the immediate context of Isaiah 6, and the servant passages following Isaiah 40 are not isolated. All Suffering Servant passages refer to corporate Israel, which bears the sin of the world. But he also notes that in the New Testament, Christ is the Servant who atones for the world's sins. In this faith Christians await the fulfillment of the prophetic promises proclaimed throughout Isaiah.

Major Themes. Among the major themes in Wright's work are the distinctive character of Israelite religion in contrast to other ancient Near Eastern religions; history as a medium of divine revelation and the necessity for a faithful interpreter; recital as a communication and continuation of that relevation; the necessity of the Old Testament for the Christian church; the unity of the Bible; Jesus Christ as the goal and key of the Old Testament; God as warrior and sovereign, as themes also pertinent to the kingdom of God and eschatology; and the interpreter's responsibility to move from hermeneutics to homiletics.

Significance. When Wright died, he was at the crest of a prestigious career as an internationally honored scholar, distinguished by his wide variety of professional achievements and by his personal effectiveness as a leader and teacher. Wright's influence on biblical studies throughout the third quarter of the twentieth century included his leadership in the reshaping of biblical theology, his mastery of Near Eastern studies, his insistence on taking biblical history seriously, and his emphasis on the indisputable value of the Old Testament for its own sake and the church's faith.

Several factors combined to contribute to Wright's significance. First is his timeliness. Much to the benefit of American biblical studies, he appeared on the scene when his views were most needed. Second is his clarity. He combined clarity of perception with clarity of presentation. Third is his persistence. From his earliest writings, Wright articulated his major themes frequently and persistently, though they matured with him. Fourth is his commitment to the church, denomination and parish. Ordained a Presbyterian minister (1934), he always felt responsible for training ministers and by his writings, scholarly as they were, for making the Bible more meaningful for the common parishioner. The publication of his most theologically influential book, *God Who Acts,* had also a practical purpose: Wright wanted to present the historical and theological disciplines in such a way that "the Bible may play its proper role in the revival of evangelical theology" (Wright 1952, 12). Fifth is his popularity. Beyond his immense popularity among his students and among Jewish and Christian communities, he was appreciated by a large company of professionals and scientists who would not normally read the works of a seminary professor but respected him because he possessed authentic credentials as an experienced "dirt archaeologist."

It is a measure of the continued respect for him that, almost twenty years after contributing the major article on the faith of Israel for the initial *Interpreter's Bible,* Wright was chosen to write on the theological study of the Bible for the one-volume edition.

Although Old Testament history and

biblical theology occupied axial positions throughout Wright's professional life, his contributions in the field of archaeology were also remarkable. His pioneering study of Palestinian pottery became the exemplar for future research. His *Biblical Archaeology* (1957; rev. ed., 1962) was widely used, and the *Westminster Historical Atlas to the Bible* (1945; rev. ed., 1956) remained a standard text for decades. During his many seasons at Shechem and Gezer he trained a new generation of archaeologists. For his aggressive leadership of the American Schools of Oriental Research (president, 1966-1974) he was internationally known and respected. In technical competence, number of doctoral students and wealth of publications, Wright can be favorably compared with his mentor, Albright.

But Wright did not work occasionally as an archaeologist, then occasionally as a theologian. Archaeology, history and theology were well-integrated aspects of his total interpretation of the Bible; and the relation of biblical history to personal faith was high among his lifelong personal concerns as a teacher, scholar, exegete and preacher.

BIBLIOGRAPHY

Works. G. E. Wright, *Biblical Archaeology* (Philadelphia: Westminster, 1957; rev. ed., 1962); idem, *The Biblical Doctrine of Man in Society* (London: SCM, 1954); idem, *The Challenge of Israel's Faith* (Chicago: University of Chicago Press, 1944); idem, "Deuteronomy: Introduc-tion and Exegesis," *IB* 2:311-537; idem, "The Faith of Israel," *IB* 1:349-89; idem, "From the Bible to the Modern World" in *Biblical Authority for Today*, ed. A. Richardson and W. Schweitzer (Philadelphia: Westminster, 1951); idem, *God Who Acts: Biblical Theology As Recital* (London: SCM, 1952); idem, *Isaiah* (London: SCM, 1964); idem, *The Old Testament Against Its Environment* (London: SCM, 1950); idem, *The Old Testament and Theology* (New York: Harper & Row, 1969); idem, *The Pottery of Palestine from the Earliest Times to the End of the Early Bronze Age* (New Haven, CT: American Schools of Oriental Research, 1937); idem, "The Theological Study of the Bible" in *The Interpreter's One-Volume Commentary on the Bible* (Nashville: Abingdon, 1971); idem, ed., *The Bible and the Ancient Near East* (Garden City, NY: Doubleday, 1961); idem, and F. V. Filson, eds., *The Westminster Historical Atlas to the Bible* (Philadelphia: Westminster, 1945; rev. ed., 1956).

Studies. B. S. Childs, *Biblical Authority in Crisis* (Philadelphia: Westminster, 1970); G. W. Coats, "The Theology of the Hebrew Bible" in *The Hebrew Bible and Its Modern Interpreters*, ed. D. A. Knight and G. M. Tucker (Chico, CA: Scholars Press, 1985) 239-62; F. M. Cross et al., *Magnalia Dei, The Might Acts of God: Essays on the Bible and Archaeology in Memory of G. Ernest Wright* (Garden City, NY: Doubleday, 1976); W. G. Dever, "Syro-Palestinian and Biblical Archaeology" in *The Hebrew Bible and Its Modern Interpreters*, ed. D. A. Knight and G. M. Tucker (Chico, CA: Scholars Press, 1985) 53-61; R. L. Hicks, "G. Ernest Wright and Old Testament Theology," *ATR* 58 (1976) 158-78; J. A. Wilcoxen, "An Interpretive View of G. Ernest Wright," *Crit* (Summer 1963) 25-31.

R. L. Hicks

Index of Persons

Index of Subjects

saga, 600
salvation history, 1, 89, 267, 290, 293, 311,
   378-80, 414, 416, 455, 467, 469, 470, 485,
   498, 577, 590, 621
Samaritans, 137, 139, 209, 236, 369
sayings of Jesus, 68, 384, 452, 498, 500, 554
scholasticism, 76, 77, 79, 83, 85, 95, 103,
   104, 106, 116-19, 143, 154, 170, 200, 205,
   213-15, 238, 242-44, 247, 249, 293, 296,
   377, 379, 433, 519, 522
scholia, 54, 130, 131, 135, 140, 142, 143, 145
scribes, 187, 238, 292, 382, 452, 495, 507
semantics, 7, 424, 425
Semitic languages, 139, 284, 302, 327, 344,
   380, 381, 472, 499, 546, 558, 559, 562, 599
sensus plenior, 413, 566, 569
Septuagint, 3, 5, 6, 11, 13, 26, 27, 40, 43, 44,
   53, 55, 56, 66, 67, 70, 109, 125, 126, 136,
   137, 144, 147, 149, 209, 210, 251, 415,
   458, 478, 480, 484, 514
Slavonic, 16
social-scientific criticism, 417, 489, 583
socio-rhetorical interpretation, 556
sociology, 154, 155, 272, 274, 363, 396, 406,
   407, 420, 530, 542, 544, 552, 556, 570,
   573, 620
source criticism, 324, 484, 493, 512, 517, 526
spiritual interpretation, 45, 46, 92, 118, 177,
   521
spiritual sense, 6-8, 15, 27, 88, 108, 114, 119,
   128, 139, 189, 194, 207, 312, 568, 580
Stoics, 43, 48, 533
structuralism, 407, 458, 556, 570, 617
symbolism, 38, 165, 168, 488, 620
synagogues, 44, 82, 138, 397, 443, 474, 543
Synoptic problem, 325, 353, 384, 463, 541,
   552, 566
Synoptic tradition, 367, 430, 440-43, 452,
   479, 603
Synoptics, Synoptic criticism, 159, 221, 315,
   333, 340, 345, 389, 390, 393, 429, 466, 605
Syriac, 40, 66, 67, 70, 136, 137, 139, 142,
   146, 149, 282, 302, 313, 373, 392, 514, 584
systematic theology/theologians, 6, 85, 136,
   227, 245, 285, 297, 313, 325, 326, 330,
   350, 430, 433, 459, 519, 520, 529, 530,
   531, 533, 620
Talmud, 76, 208, 209, 211
targums, 125, 126, 136, 137, 139, 144, 145,
   147, 246, 247
textual criticism, 56, 57, 66, 69, 153, 154,
   156, 185-87, 227, 264, 290-92, 330, 356,
   359, 381, 389, 401, 484

textus receptus, 126, 154, 190, 264, 321, 389,
   393
Torah, 1, 2, 6, 42, 263, 418, 419, 473, 474,
   536, 552, 571, 572, 578, 579, 581
tradition history, 358, 396, 417, 506, 530,
   576, 580, 583
Trinity, trinitarianism, 4, 10, 17, 24, 61, 129,
   133, 143, 165, 194, 208, 214, 215, 219,
   223, 225, 254, 280, 302, 312, 336, 350,
   368, 369, 371, 389-91, 394, 434, 516, 549
Tübingen, 226, 228, 285-90, 316, 319, 338,
   339, 341, 349, 359, 364, 366, 367, 376,
   389, 390, 393, 398, 428, 429, 433, 439,
   449, 463, 500, 501, 518-20, 527, 535, 549
two-source hypothesis, 552
typology, 6, 8, 13, 15, 27, 33, 41, 43, 65, 68,
   69, 71, 132, 141, 163, 176, 177, 192, 237,
   246, 254, 265, 311, 312, 414, 421, 485,
   489, 517, 526, 600, 612, 613
Ugaritic, 559
unitarianism, 368, 369, 371, 372, 398
Valentinus, Valentinians, 4, 6, 9, 37, 40, 41,
   53, 61, 62
variant readings, 57, 137, 154, 321, 389, 390
versions, 6, 27, 56, 61, 95, 125, 127, 131,
   136, 137, 139, 140, 144, 147, 205, 209,
   283, 292, 305, 314, 318, 340, 357, 431,
   493, 566, 607
Vulgate, 12, 43, 75, 76, 85, 89, 92, 95, 107,
   109, 112, 114, 120, 124-27, 130, 135-37,
   149, 153, 158, 181-83, 186-88, 205, 253,
   292
Westminster Assembly, 149, 208, 295
Westminster Confession, 197, 282, 295, 326,
   360
wirkungsgeschichte. *See* effective history
wisdom, wisdom literature, 2, 11, 20, 21, 37-
   39, 43, 53, 55, 57, 98, 100, 108, 154, 183,
   194, 227, 237, 245, 263, 314, 338, 363,
   392, 419, 420, 452, 457, 459, 473, 481,
   489, 516, 517, 527-30, 537, 538, 544, 566,
   572
women, 41, 163, 185, 336, 388, 430, 448,
   452, 461, 493, 494, 500, 522, 536, 606-10,
   615-17
word studies, 175, 293, 337, 392, 439, 497,
   519
worship, 48, 93, 168, 184, 195-199, 250,
   382, 399, 400, 461, 474, 475, 507, 509,
   511, 512, 533, 537, 620
Yahwism, 4, 528-30
Yahwist, 528-30, 537, 551
Zwinglians, 223, 250-52, 254

Index of Essays & Articles